THE MOTOROLA MC68332 MICROCONTROLLER

Product Design, Assembly Language Programming, and Interfacing

Thomas L. Harman

School of Natural and Applied Sciences
University of Houston–Clear Lake

Prentice Hall
Englewood Cliffs, New Jersey 07632

Library of Congress Cataloging-in-Publication Data

Harman, Thomas L.
   The Motorola MC68332 microcontroller: product design, assembly
language programming, and interfacing / Thomas L. Harman.
      p. cm.
   Includes bibliographical references and index.
   ISBN 0-13-603127-7
   1. Digital control systems. 2. Motorola 68000 series
microprocessors. I. Title.
TJ223.M53H37 1991   90–25107
621.3916—dc20   CIP

Editorial/production supervision
   and interior design: Laura A. Huber
Cover design: Wanda Lubelska Design
Manufacturing buyers: Kelly Behr/Susan Brunke
Acquisitions Editor: Karen Gettman

 © 1991 by Prentice-Hall, Inc.
A Simon & Schuster Company
Englewood Cliffs, New Jersey 07632

The publisher offers discounts on this book when ordered
in bulk quantities. For more information, write:

   Special Sales/College Marketing
   College Technical and Reference Division
   Prentice Hall
   Englewood Cliffs, New Jersey 07632

Printed in the United States of America
10 9 8 7 6 5 4 3 2 1

ISBN 0-13-603127-7

Prentice-Hall International (UK) Limited, *London*
Prentice-Hall of Australia Pty. Limited, *Sydney*
Prentice-Hall Canada Inc., *Toronto*
Prentice-Hall Hispanoamericana, S.A., *Mexico*
Prentice-Hall of India Private Limited, *New Delhi*
Prentice-Hall of Japan, Inc., *Tokyo*
Simon & Schuster Asia Pte. Ltd., *Singapore*
Editora Prentice-Hall do Brasil, Ltda., *Rio de Janeiro*

Contents

Contents

Contents

Contents   **ix**

Preface

The introduction of the Motorola M68300 family of microcontrollers ushered in a new generation of 32-bit controllers. The MC68332 is the main member of this family. Other family members include the MC68331 and the MC68340. Each is a single-chip microcontroller designed to function as the control unit in a sophisticated system or product. These microcontrollers consist of a Central Processing Unit (CPU) and various modules for specific applications. This book is intended for the student as well as the product designer, programmer or interface designer who wishes to understand the features and applications of the M68300 family controllers.

The aim of the book is to familiarize the readers with the procedures necessary to design and develop hardware and software for applications. One important purpose is to introduce the student, engineer or the practicing computer professional to all of the significant aspects of design using the MC68332. In addition, the book can serve as a reference in which topics are organized according to function and importance for the design of programs, interfaces, or products.

One unique feature of the textbook is the division of the discussions into three distinct categories. Although many applications require considerable overlap, the emphasis is divided as follows:

(a) assembly-language programming,
(b) product design, and
(c) interface-design.

Thus, sections of the book can be studied according to the interests and requirements of readers involved in specific applications. Each section contains examples and exercises to aid the reader's understanding.

This textbook is organized into sixteen chapters. The first two chapters present the M68300 family to the reader. These chapters also describe microcontrollers and their applications. Chapters 3 through 9 explain programming techniques using the CPU32. This CPU is the processing module for the M68300 family controllers. Chapters 10 and 11 describe the capabilities of the CPU32 operating in the supervisor mode.

Chapter 12 describes the Queued Serial Module (QSM) of the MC68332. The QSM module allows asynchronous and synchronous communication with external devices. Chapter 13 explains the Time Processor Unit (TPU). The TPU is a 16-channel microprogrammed timer module which can be programmed to perform counting, timing and pulse generation functions.

Chapter 14 emphasizes hardware design with the MC68332. The chapter covers the System Integration Module (SIM) that controls the MC68332 external bus.

Chapters 15 and 16 combine many of the techniques and details from previous chapters to discuss product design and development. Chapter 15 also presents real-time programming techniques including interrupt timing studies. Chapter 16 describes the available support for MC68332-based hardware and software development.

Answers to selected exercises are included after the final chapter. The appendices summarize pertinent material including the ASCII character set and powers of two and sixteen, a comparison of M68000 family processors, the characteristics of the MC68331 and MC68340, and the complete instruction set of the CPU32. Finally, the book contains both an instruction index and a thorough general index.

CHAPTER DESCRIPTIONS

Chapters 1 and 2 introduce the reader to the Motorola family of products and the MC68332 microcontroller.

(▷) Chapter 1 first presents a number of applications for the MC68332 microcontroller. Then, the M68000 and M6800 families of microprocessors are described. The hardware and software support for these families of integrated circuit devices is also described. Finally, the chapter presents a brief introduction to product design and development.

(▷) Chapter 2 opens with a description of the system organization for typical systems and products using microcontrollers. The MC68332 and its modules are explained. Three views of a product as seen by the product designer, the assembly-language programmer, and the interface designer are given.

Chapters 3 through 9 are devoted primarily to programming techniques using the assembly language for the CPU32. The assembly language for the processor is used to explain the many capabilities of MC68332.

(▷) Chapter 3 explains the internal representation of numbers and characters as used in MC68332-based systems. Binary, Binary Coded Decimal (BCD) and floating-point notations are treated along with details of arithmetic operations. The chapter also describes the ASCII code for alphanumeric characters.

(▷) Chapter 4 begins with a discussion of the characteristics of the MC68332 microcontroller. Then, the programming features of the CPU32 processor are described. The chapter also presents the organization of memory in a typical MC68332-based system.

(▷) Chapter 5 introduces the CPU32 assembly language. The chapter explains the techniques of software development, assembly-language features, and the various addressing modes of the CPU32. The Business Card Computer (BCC) and the 332BUG monitor are described as part of a low-cost development system.

(▷) Chapter 6 presents three important categories of instructions for the CPU32. In particular, the chapter covers instructions for data transfer, program control, and subroutines.

(▷) Chapter 7 contains explanations and program examples showing the arithmetic capability of the CPU32. Binary arithmetic, decimal arithmetic, and conversions between ASCII, binary and BCD are covered. The chapter also describes Input/Output techniques and the table lookup and interpolation instructions of the CPU32.

(▷) Chapter 8 introduces the logical instructions, shift and rotate instructions and bit-manipulation instructions of the CPU32.

(▷) Chapter 9 completes the study of fundamental programming techniques. Methods of creating position-independent code are covered. Program examples are given for the manipulation of data structures, including arrays, queues, and lists. The chapter also presents more advanced subroutine techniques and stack frames.

Chapters 10 and 11 describe the capabilities of the MC68332 that determine the operation of the overall system or product. These chapters are of primary concern to the product designer or programmer who creates supervisor programs.

(▷) Chapter 10 considers the processor's various states and modes of operation. The assembly language instructions to control the system and examples of initialization procedures are presented. The chapter explains the use of the Business Card Computer (BCC) development system as an example of a complete system controlling external devices.

(▷) Chapter 11 covers exception processing and handling by the MC68332. The exceptions include traps, interrupts and various error conditions recognized by the CPU during program execution.

Chapters 12 through 14 present each module of the MC68332 to explain the programming and interfacing techniques for the modules.

(▷) The major topic covered in Chapter 12 is serial communication with the Queued Serial Communication Module (QSM) of the MC68332. The chapter presents many programming and interfacing examples using the QSM.

(▷) Chapter 13 explains the Time Processor Unit (TPU) of the MC68332. Input capture, period measurement, output pulse generation, pulse width modulation and stepper motor control are examples of the topics described. The chapter includes many application examples for the timer module.

($\triangleright$) Chapter 14 describes interface design and the System Integration Module (SIM) of the MC68332. Programming of peripheral chips is also explained. Sections of the chapter cover system expansion using the external bus and other hardware considerations.

Chapters 15 and 16 describe techniques for product design, real-time programming, and product development.

($\triangleright$) Chapter 15 presents the techniques of product design using the MC68332 as the microcontroller unit. The chapter also covers interrupt latency and real-time programming techniques.

($\triangleright$) Chapter 16 treats product development and testing. The discussions cover techniques and support products for software and hardware development. The test modes of the MC68332 modules are also described.

ADDITIONAL REFERENCE MATERIAL AND SUPPORT

The Motorola *User's Manuals* for the MC68332 and its modules provide a more complete treatment of certain characteristics of the microcontroller than is covered in this book. These manuals are available from Motorola.

Since development systems vary considerably, the reader should refer to the *User's Manuals* for the specific system on which programs and hardware applications are being developed. The author's development system is the Motorola MC68332 Evaluation System (EVS) which includes the BCC single-board computer. Also, the reader should refer to the manuals for the specific assembler or compiler and operating system used with the development system.

Motorola provides excellent support for students and instructors through their University Support program. Also, a "Freeware" telephone line for modem access provides the caller with free information and programs for the Motorola microcontroller products. For more information, the reader should contact a Motorola representative.

ACKNOWLEDGEMENTS

The author would like to express his gratitude to all those who contributed to this textbook. The material was developed over several semesters with many helpful suggestions from the students in the Microcontroller Design class at the University of Houston–Clear Lake.

I wish to thank Gary Daniels and Brian Wilkie of Motorola, Inc. for their generous support of the project. Robert Pinteric of Motorola deserves a special measure of gratitude for his time and work in coordinating the effort between Motorola and the author. Chet Freda, Patrick Heath, and Kellye Prosise are to be thanked for their generous supply of chips, development systems and software used for program tests and laboratory experiments.

I also wish to thank the group of reviewers and others at Motorola who contributed to the technical content and readability of the text. The extensive list includes Brad Burgess, John Dunn, James Eifert, Peter Gilmour, Vernon Goler, Stan Groves, Ann Harwood, Patrick Heath, Joe Jelemensky, Robert Pinteric, Craig Shaw, James Sibigtroth, Chris Smallwood, Michael Taborn and John Vaglica. Other support and helpful suggestions came from Tim Ahrens, Jack Davis, Tony Fourcroy, Chad Peckham, and Andy Vaughn. It was a great pleasure working with the courteous and highly competent staff of Motorola during the project.

My sincere appreciation goes to all the people who were involved in the production of the book. Marie Fitzgibbon typed a good deal of the manuscript. Cathy Chilton and Gary Stenerson reviewed many of the chapters. Alan Clapp assisted the author in many of the program tests and preparation of the student laboratory manual. Of course, the staff of Prentice Hall did a fine job of putting the book into production. It was delightful working with Karen Gettman and Laura Huber of Prentice Hall.

I apologize to any other persons who helped in the endeavor but were not cited here. Please send any comments or criticisms to the author in care of the University of Houston–Clear Lake, 2700 Bay Area Boulevard, Houston, Texas 77058.

Typesetting

The camera-ready copy for this book was set with the T$_E$X typesetting system developed by Donald Knuth. The text font is ten point Bitstream Dutch. Macros were developed by Norman Richert of the University of Houston–Clear Lake. The final output device was the 2000 dpi Chelgraph IBX typesetter of Type 2000, Mill Valley, CA. Those interested in T$_E$X should contact the T$_E$X Users Group, P.O. Box 9506, Providence, RI 02940-9506.

1

Introduction to the Motorola Microprocessors and Controllers

1.0 INTRODUCTION

The Motorola MC6800 was introduced in 1974 as an 8-bit microprocessor suitable for personal computers and specialized products that required microcomputer control. As these 8-bit microprocessors reached their limit in performance and capability, Motorola and other manufacturers introduced 16- and 32-bit processors which now serve as central processing units (CPUs) for powerful personal computers and engineering workstations. The emphasis for the latest generation of microprocessors is on high speed of execution for instructions and support of sophisticated operating systems and applications software. A typical system useful for personal or small business applications is shown in Figure 1.1. The CPU requires a number of other integrated circuit chips to allow storage of instructions and data and to perform Input/Output (I/O) operations.

Manufacturers of microprocessors have also created another type of integrated circuit chip called a *microcontroller*. These microcontroller units or MCUs perform the functions of a CPU in a control system or computer-based product and provide additional functions required for real-time control applications. The manufacturer's emphasis for these microcontrollers is to produce an MCU that will respond rapidly to external events such as interrupt requests. The microcontroller typically includes memory, timing circuits, and I/O circuitry on a single chip to reduce the number of integrated circuit chips required in a product. Thus, the purpose of the microcontroller

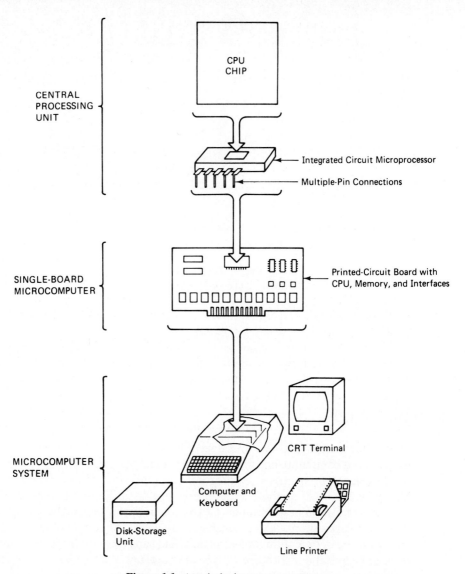

Figure 1.1 A typical microcomputer system.

is to control the operation of a system or product for a particular application. The emulator system shown in Figure 1.2 is an example of such a product using an MC68332 microcontroller to emulate the operation of processors and microcontrollers in the Motorola family of 8-bit devices.

The microcontrollers offered by Motorola have evolved from the 8-bit MC6800 microprocessor, the 16-bit MC68000, and the 32-bit MC68020. Introduced in 1989, the MC68332 is the first microcontroller from Motorola to incorporate many of the features of the 32-bit, MC68020 CPU. In addition, the MC68332 MCU provides serial

Figure 1.2 Emulator system using the MC68332 microprocessor (Courtesy of Motorola, Inc.).

communications, timing functions, on-chip memory and a number of other capabilities in a single-chip microcontroller. This MCU is one of the members of the M68300 family of microcontrollers. In this text, the designation MC68332 with the "MC" prefix refers to a specific chip in the M68300 family.

This introductory chapter presents a number of applications of the MC68332 microcontroller. These products include automotive products, industrial control systems, electronic instruments, and office products as listed in Table 1.1. The Motorola family of microprocessors and microcontrollers is also discussed in this chapter as well as software and development systems used to produce products incorporating the MC68332 MCU. Finally, an introduction to product design and development for microcontroller-based products is presented.

Table 1.1 Applications of the MC68332

Area	Typical Application
Automotive	Antiskid braking, electronic instrument panel, engine control, and ride control
Data Acquisition and Control	Real-time control systems for industrial applications
Instruments	Data acquisition and analysis and front-panel control
Office Products, Peripheral Units and Consumer Products	Printers, copiers, plotters, disk-drive controllers, cameras and appliances

1.1 APPLICATIONS OF THE MC68332

Although the potential applications for a microcontroller such as the MC68332 are only limited by a product designer's imagination, a number of specific applications areas were targeted by the designers of this MCU. A sampling of these applications is presented in this section to indicate the range of products that may be designed based on the MC68332. Those cited are summarized in Table 1.1 which lists the area of application and some specific examples. The role of the microcontroller in these products is discussed in subsequent paragraphs.

1.1.1 Automotive Applications

Microcontroller-based systems dedicated to specific applications are employed extensively in automobiles. These applications require a low-cost microcontroller that is able to withstand the relatively harsh environment of the automobile with respect to temperature extremes and electrical noise. Low power consumption is also mandatory for a microcontroller used in automobile instrumentation and control systems. Self-test and diagnostic programs are required to prevent improper operation of the microcontroller and its peripheral devices as failure of the system could result in inefficient or even unsafe operation of the vehicle.

A typical use of the microcontroller-based system in an automobile is for monitoring and displaying critical engine and vehicle parameters. Sensors are used to allow the MCU to monitor vehicle speed, engine crankshaft rotational speed, oil pressure and other values. These measured values are analyzed by the MCU and displayed on the instrument cluster for the driver in convenient units such as revolutions per minute indicating engine rotational speed. The displays may be given in digital form or as a graphic display according to the dashboard design.

Other uses of microcontrollers in an automobile allow increased fuel economy and reduced emissions of pollution. The air-fuel mixture ratio, for example, can be controlled very accurately to maintain the most efficient engine operation under varying driving conditions. Microcontroller-based electronic systems are also used to prevent skidding by the control of the applied braking force. Dynamic ride-control systems adjust the characteristics of the automobile suspension to provide a comfortable ride with varying road conditions. The MCU in these applications causes various parameters to be monitored and controlled while the vehicle is in motion. As microcontrollers become more powerful, automobile designers can incorporate increasingly sophisticated capabilities such as collision avoidance systems. Obviously, automobile designers are relying to a great extent on microcontroller-based systems to improve the efficiency and comfort afforded by modern automobiles.

1.1.2 Data Acquisition and Control Systems

Most industrial systems for manufacturing employ some form of computer control to enhance the accuracy and quality of the product being produced. Although the complete manufacturing process may be monitored by a central computer facility, many operations can be performed by microcontroller-based systems. The control system receives signals in digital or analog form that monitor the machine or process being controlled. When the data acquisition cycle is complete, the MCU computes the appropriate control action and generates control signals to regulate the operation of the machine being controlled. One specific industrial application of a microcontroller is as the processing unit in a programmable controller. Another application is for the control of robots.

A *programmable controller* is a programmable unit that executes instructions to perform specific functions such as implementing logical equations, sequencing operations, timing, counting, and motor control. In an industrial application, the MCU of a programmable controller performs data acquisition and control functions. The MCU may also direct communication with a central computer. The central computer would store and analyze certain data collected by the programmable controller. This information could then be used for management or technical evaluation of the manufacturing process.

Other important applications of microprocessors and microcontrollers are in the area of *robotics*. The goal in robotics is the development of flexible, automated manufacturing systems that monitor and control a production process in real-time. The machines that actually produce the product are typically called robots if they are programmable and incorporate a certain amount of decision-making capability that was formerly performed by a human being or a centralized computer system. The key features of a microcontroller that directs the action of the robot are its monitoring functions and computational ability. Monitoring of critical manufacturing parameters allows the robot to react and modify its operation based on problems or errors that arise during manufacturing as they occur; i.e., in real-time. The computational capability of the MCU allows a program to calculate precise positioning values that are used to create smooth and efficient motion of the robot.

1.1.3 Instruments

Modern measuring instruments such as oscilloscopes and spectrum analyzers incorporate microprocessors or microcontrollers to provide accuracy and flexibility in measurements. Features such as automatic calibration and range selection are possible with a microcontroller-based instrument. Front panel selections by the operator can be recognized and processed by the MCU through its interface to a front-panel keyboard or a touch-sensitive display. The MCU also controls the display of numerical values or other information for the operator of the instrument.

Although special-purpose circuitry is typically employed in an instrument to actually perform a measurement, the microcontroller serves to sequence the operations required. Another use of the microcontroller within an instrument is to transfer data from the instrument's memory to another computer system. The values are transferred for permanent storage or detailed analysis by programs executed on the computer.

1.1.4 Office Products, Peripheral Units and Consumer Products

Microprocessors and microcontrollers perform the Input/Output and computations for many office products, computer peripheral units and consumer products. The use of microcontrollers to control product operation has led to the development of such products as color copiers, laser printers, inexpensive disk drive units, and appliances with sophisticated features to mention but a few of the many microcontroller-based products for office or home applications. These products typically contain one or more microprocessors or microcontrollers as well as special-purpose circuitry for specific functions.

1.1.5 The Role of the Microcontroller

In many products employing a microcontroller as the controlling device, the user of the product is unaware of the presence of the microcontroller. Such products are said to have an *embedded microcontroller* that cannot be programmed by the user. In fact, the product may function automatically as is the case for an automobile engine control unit. Other products such as appliances may allow the user to select various options to direct the operation of a product. However, knowledge of the particular characteristic of the microcontroller in such products is not necessary for the user. It is the product designer who must understand the features and capabilities of the embedded micro-controller to produce a product with the highest possible performance and reliability at the lowest cost.

   The product designer chooses a microcontroller that can meet the programming and timing requirements of the product. As far as possible, the microcontroller chip should include all of the resources that permit it to serve as the controller of the product. Furthermore, the microcontroller must allow the addition of support chips such as special-purpose peripheral chips to expand the resources of the microcontroller beyond what is available on the chip itself.

   To meet these needs of a product designer, manufacturers of microcontrollers have integrated circuits with various functions in addition to the central processing unit into a single chip. The next section describes the Motorola families of chips and related support for their microprocessors and microcontrollers. The available selection allows a product designer to choose the proper components to meet the requirements necessary to produce a successful product.

1.2 MOTOROLA PROCESSORS AND THE FAMILY CONCEPT

The MC68332 could be chosen as the MCU in the products described in Section 1.1 for a variety of economic and technical reasons. The specific capabilities of the micro-controller are important in the choice, particularly when the finished product exhibits enhanced performance when compared to similar predecessor products employing a less powerful processor. Another vital factor in the choice for most manufacturers of products is the *support* given to the processor line. This support comes from the manufacturer of the microcontroller and a number of other sources. The support consists of hardware, software, development systems, and other items. Such support is provided to enable a product manufacturer to design, build, test and produce the product in the most economical manner. Also, as technological advances allow improvement of performance and lower cost for the product, the manufacturer must modify the product in various ways to remain competitive.

The *family* concept, as applied to microprocessor- and microcontroller-based systems, assures that the processor line is adequately supported and is improved with time. A designer who is familiar with the basic processor has little trouble learning the characteristics of newer processors and various items that constitute other members of the family. For example, the MC68332 microcontroller has a M68000 family CPU as its processing unit. The designation M68000 family includes processors such as the 16-bit MC68000 and the 32-bit MC68020 processors. Programs written for any processor of the M68000 family will execute on the MC68332 with little or no modification. This software compatibility is explored further in Section 4.5 of this textbook.

Table 1.2 summarizes many of the support criteria discussed in Section 1.2. The processor line of integrated circuits contains processors and other circuits to facilitate design of interfaces as well as special devices to improve the performance of a computer system or product. The software support for a family includes operating systems, programs to facilitate software development, and other programs collectively termed *system software*.

Programs are also available for specific applications such as computer-aided design. These programs are usually provided by companies that specialize in software support for a particular processor.

Of course, as part of the support for any processor, a number of documents are required to guide product designers and programmers as they attempt to use the processor in the most efficient way. Such documents include the User's manual for a particular device as well as applications notes, textbooks, and other data relating to the processor and the software.

For those users developing applications software, a number of development systems are available to facilitate software production. In addition to allowing the creation and testing of software, a few development systems aid the integration of the applications software with the prototype hardware of a product being developed by the user. This capability is vital if the final product is a complete system which is the case with most microcontroller-based products.

1.2.1 The Families of Chips from Motorola

Motorola's family of microcontrollers, exemplified by the MC68332, evolved from Motorola's 8-bit microcontroller family and their 16- and 32-bit microprocessor families. The MC68332 combines the traditional capabilities of a microcontroller such as I/O and timing modules with the processing power of a M68000 family CPU on a single chip. This evolution is depicted in Figure 1.3. Several representative microcontrollers and microprocessors are discussed in this section. This section also serves to introduce the M68300 family of microcontrollers and its first member, the MC68332.

Table 1.2 Support for the Microprocessor and
Microcontroller Families

Type	Support
Processors and support chips:	
8-, 16-, and 32-bit microprocessors and microcontrollers	Basic processor and enhanced versions available in various packages and speeds of operation
Peripheral interface circuits	Circuits for interfacing the processor to a wide range of peripheral devices
Special devices and coprocessors	Devices for floating-point mathematics, network control, and other applications
Software:	
Operating systems	Various operating systems for real-time applications, time sharing, or special purposes
Development software	Editors, assemblers, compilers, and debugging programs
Applications software	Special-purpose programs created for a particular product
Documentation	Manuals, application notes, textbooks, and data sheets
Development:	
Development systems	Complete systems for software development and hardware/software integration
Single-board computer modules	Processing units, memory modules, and other complete hardware subsystems

The 8-bit family.   Motorola's family of 8-bit processors was introduced in 1974 with the MC6800 microprocessor. This CPU has eight signal lines for data transfer which classified it as an 8-bit device. Four major families of microcontrollers have evolved from the MC6800 to include the M6801, M6804, M6805 and the M68HC11 families. In these families, the basic MC6800 CPU is augmented with various modules on a single chip to satisfy different requirements in product design. The reader is reminded that the prefix "MC" designates a particular chip within a family of processors. Thus, as shown in Figure 1.3, the M68HC11 family contains the MC68HC11A8, the MC68HC11E2, and the MC68HC11E9. Other members of this family are produced by Motorola but are not shown in the figure.

For example, different versions of the basic microcontroller are offered with Random Access Memory (RAM) or Read Only Memory (ROM) on the chip. Several versions have Analog-to-Digital (A/D) converter circuitry. Most microcontroller chips have timer and counter circuitry in a single integrated-circuit package. The timers may generate interrupts to the CPU, measure external events, or generate output waveforms via the signal lines of the microcontroller. The various microcontrollers in Figure 1.3 have different designations according to their features and the semiconductor fabrication technique used to manufacture them.

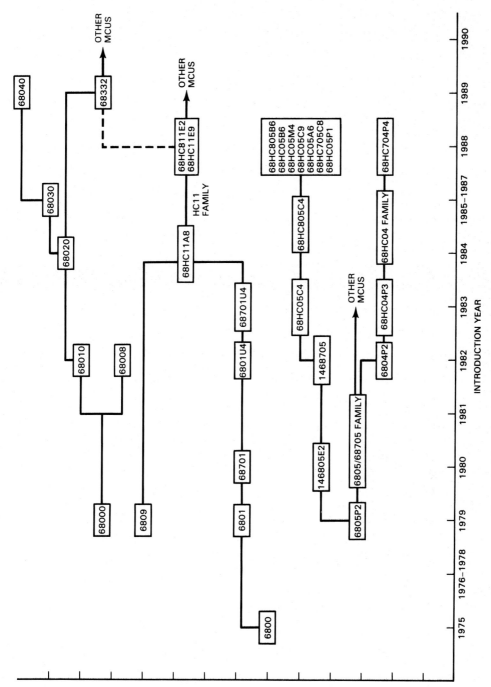

Figure 1.3 Evolution of Motorola microprocessors and microcontrollers.

Example 1.1

The MC68332 microcontroller, as the first member of the M68300 family of microcontrollers, evolved as shown in Figure 1.3. Its features include capabilities of the 32-bit MC68020 CPU and the 8-bit MC68HC11 microcontroller. The M68HC11 family had previously evolved from the M6801 and M6809, 8-bit processor families. The evolution in Figure 1.3 has been possible because of the rapid advance in integrated circuit technology since the MC6800 microprocessor was introduced. The increasing capability of the 8-bit microcontrollers can be shown by describing the evolution of the M6801 and M6805 families.

The MC6801 microcontroller and its derivatives include RAM, timers, parallel I/O, and serial communications capability on the chip. The MC6801 also has 2048 bytes of factory-programmable ROM. The MC68701 has the same features but replaces the ROM with Erasable Programmable ROM (EPROM) so that the product designer can modify programs during the product development cycle. When the program is correct, the program can be sent to Motorola to be incorporated in the ROM of a less-expensive MC6801. This chip would be included in the product when the product is produced in volume. The MC6801U4 has 4096 bytes of ROM but is otherwise practically equivalent to the MC6801.

The parts in the M68HC11 family include most of the features of the M6801 family with the addition of analog inputs to the on-chip A/D converter as well as enhanced timing and communications functions. The fabrication technology is termed the High-speed Complimentary Metal Oxide Silicon process (HCMOS). This process yields lower power consumption compared to that possible in the earlier M6801 microcontrollers. The HCMOS process is indicated by the "HC" in the middle of the part numbers for the devices.

The M6805 family offers a variety of on-chip memory selections and Input/Output functions. These processors and those in the M6804 family are intended for products produced in large volume for which low-cost components are mandatory. The chips do not have many of the powerful capabilities of the MC68HC11 or MC68332 MCUs. In fact, the vertical axis in Figure 1.3 can be regarded as an arbitrary scale indicating the relative performance of the parts specified in the figure. Additional information concerning Motorola's processors and microcontrollers can be found in several of the references in the Further Reading section of this chapter.

The 16-bit family. Motorola responds to the increasing needs of product manufacturers and to technological advances by enhancing the design of a microprocessor such as the MC68000 and producing new versions. The MC68000 was the first CPU from Motorola with 16 data signal-lines. Later versions, such as the MC68010, are distinguished from the basic MC68000 by their numerical designation. These processors are normally compatible with the MC68000 in many ways but offer different features. For example, versions of the MC68000 processor are available with different physical packaging, different operating temperature ranges, and with various speeds of operation. Otherwise, the instruction set and the electrical characteristics of each version are identical to those of the original MC68000. Other processors in the family may show more significant differences, as is the case with several advanced versions of the MC68000. The evolution of the family by year of introduction of each processor is shown in Figure 1.3. Table 1.3 describes the characteristics of the various versions.

The range of operational speeds available for the MC68000 CPU is evident in the Motorola processors designated as MC68000L4, MC68000L6, MC68000L8,

Table 1.3 Motorola's 16- and 32-bit Processors and Coprocessors

Processor	Characteristics of use
16-bit family:	
MC68000L4, MC68000L6 MC68000L8, MC68000L10 MC68000L12	Different speeds of operation indicated by the suffix in millions of clock cycles per second
MC68008	8-bit external data bus
MC68010	Capability to support virtual memory
32-bit family:	
MC68020	32-bit data transfer and addressing capability
MC68030	On-chip memory management
MC68040	On-chip floating point unit
MC68851	Memory management coprocessor
MC68881/MC68882	Floating-point coprocessors

MC68000L10, and MC68000L12. The last numeric designation indicates the maximum number of hardware clock cycles in millions per second (the L12 represents 12.5 million cycles per second). For example, the L12 device will execute the same program 1.25 (12.5/10) times as fast as the L10, 1.56 (12.5/8) times as fast as the L8, and so on. In a given product, the replacement of the CPU by a faster (or slower) processor will change the performance proportionally if the speed of operation is determined by the processor alone.

Motorola has also introduced the MC68008 which is a version of the MC68000 with only eight data signal-lines. This processor retains most of the characteristics of the original MC68000 but is designed for application employing 8-bit data transfers. This reduction in the number of data signal-lines reduces the cost of a system or product and simplifies the interface to certain peripheral units. An important advantage over earlier 8-bit processors in such an application is that the MC68008 executes programs written for the powerful MC68000 CPU.

The MC68010 is an enhanced version of the MC68000 microprocessor designed primarily for virtual-memory systems. In this application, a program is not limited in size by the capacity of the physical memory, since a part of the program may be stored on an external storage device such as a disk unit. Portions of the program stored on disk are transferred to the main memory as they are needed. The processor then has the capability to continue instruction execution after the new program segment is in its main memory. The MC68010 is also available with various speeds of operation, as is the MC68000.

The 32-bit family. Motorola's 32-bit family of processors and coprocessors consists of the MC68020/MC68881/MC68851 chip set, the MC68030/MC68882 chips, and the MC68040 processor. The MC68020 is available with operating speeds of 12.5, 16.67, 20, 25 and 33.3 million operations (clock cycles) per second. The two coprocessors perform floating-point mathematics and memory management, respectively. A MC68020 is compatible with the MC68000 in many ways but embodies a number of enhancements to better support modern operating systems and software or hardware for special-purpose applications. Each member of this family has 32 signal lines for data transfer.

From the programmer's viewpoint, the MC68030 and its MC68882 coprocessor are compatible in many ways with the MC68020 and its coprocessors. The MC68030 has a memory management unit on the chip to speed up address translations required in virtual-memory systems. The MC68882 coprocessor is also designed with more parallelism than the MC68881. For example, concurrent operation of the CPU and the MC68882 mathematics coprocessor is possible with the MC68030.

The MC68040 includes the features of the MC68030 and adds a floating-point arithmetic unit on the chip. Thus, CPU and memory management and floating-point capability are combined on a single chip.

In Motorola literature, the full line of 16- and 32-bit microprocessors and peripheral chips are sometimes designated as the "M68000" family. The 16-bit parts comprise the MC68000 family while the 32-bit components are referred to as the MC68020 family. The reader is referred to Motorola literature for more detailed descriptions of these microprocessors. They are also treated in several of the references in the Further Reading section of this chapter.

Interfacing chips.   Table 1.4 lists a sampling of the numerous types of interfacing devices packaged as integrated circuit "chips" for the Motorola family. Chips for input/output are general-purpose interfacing devices which connect the CPU to a wide range of peripheral units. These chips are programmable to provide a flexible input and output capability under the control of the central processing unit. The other interfacing devices listed in Table 1.4 are also programmable, with each chip responding to coded instructions according to its design and purpose.

Table 1.4 Interfacing Devices for the M68000 Family

Application	Examples of interfacing chips
Parallel and serial input/output	General-purpose interface devices (MC68230, MC68901)
DMA controller	Direct memory access (MC68450)
Communications and local area networks	Controller and conversion devices (MC68605, MC68824, MC68184)
System Control	Interrupt control and bus arbitration (MC68153, MC68452)

Note:
Each interfacing device listed is manufactured as a single-chip integrated circuit. They are called interfacing "chips" in the jargon of the industry.

Motorola as well as other manufacturers, produces interfacing chips for many standard applications, such as the ones listed in Table 1.4. The chips are designed to be compatible with the central processor both electrically and with respect to programming conventions for the M68000 family. Unfortunately, these interfacing chips are difficult to characterize in a simple manner since each has special instructions associated with its specific purpose. Their purpose as discussed here is to simplify the interface between the CPU and other units in a system. The interface designer is thus relieved of the burden of designing and testing the interfacing circuitry when an interfacing chip is available.

The chips listed in Table 1.4 and many of the interfacing chips for Motorola's 8-bit families of processors can be used with the MC68332 microcontroller. This topic is explored further in Chapter 14 of the textbook.

1.2.2 The M68300 family and the MC68332 Microcontroller

The MC68332 is the first member of the M68300 family of microcontrollers from Motorola. A simplified block diagram of the MC68332 microcontroller is shown in Figure 1.4. Integrated on a single chip are a 32-bit CPU and various other modules for parallel and serial Input/Output, timing, motor control and system expansion. The intermodule bus connects these components internally.

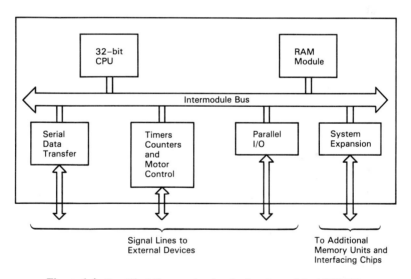

Figure 1.4 Simplified diagram showing the functions of the MC68332.

The CPU is a modified MC68020 processor with an instruction set and other features compatible with Motorola's popular 32-bit CPU. This modular approach to MCU design allows Motorola to produce various versions of the microcontroller with new or modified modules without changing the basic characteristics of the device.

Another advantage deriving from the modular construction of an MCU lies in the capability of the individual modules that can be integrated onto the chip. The MC68332 modules are designed to perform specific functions with a minimum of CPU intervention. Thus, once a module is initialized by the CPU, the CPU program is only interrupted when a module completes a given task rather than at the occurrence of minor events during the activity. For example, the motor controller function is capable of accelerating, driving and halting a stepper motor without CPU intervention once the module is programmed to perform these operations.

When the modules on the chip cannot meet the requirements of an application, additional memory or interfacing chips can be added to expand the capabilities of the system. The chip also has a low-power standby mode of operation useful when a battery backup power supply is needed in a product. All of these features of the MC68332 are treated in Chapter 2 where each module of the MCU is discussed.

M68300 family members. Table 1.5 lists three members of the M68300 microcontroller family. Each family member contains the CPU32 and a System Integration Module (SIM). The MC68331 contains four modules including a General-Purpose Timer (GPT) and a Queued Serial Module (QSM) for serial I/O. The primary member of the family is the MC68332. This MCU has on-chip RAM and a powerful Time Processor Unit (TPU) in addition to the CPU32, QSM, and the SIM. The MC68340 is targeted for products that require high-speed data movement such as Compact Disk (CD) players. Thus, a two-channel Direct Memory Access (DMA) module is included in the MC68340. Appendix III contains a summary of the capabilities of the MC68331 and the MC68340. The reader is referred to Motorola literature for more information about these microcontrollers.

Table 1.5 M68300 Family Microcontrollers

Microcontroller	Features
MC68331	CPU32, GPT, QSM, SIM
MC68332	CPU32, QSM, RAM, SIM, TPU
MC68340	CPU32, DMA, Serial I/O, timers, SIM

1.2.3 Software Support for the MC68332

As the hardware of a microcontroller-based product is constructed, programs must be developed to direct its overall operation. The various programs that are executed by the microcomputer are referred to, generically, as software to distinguish them from the physical equipment (hardware) of the system. For our purposes, it is convenient to discuss three categories or "levels" of software in addition to the hardware level, as shown in Table 1.6.

At the level closest to the hardware, the operating system manages the hardware resources of the system. The operating system is frequently called the executive or supervisor program. At the next level lies the development software used by the programmer to create and debug applications programs. Finally, the applications software is used to tailor the product to perform a specific task. In the M68300 family, many software products are available from both Motorola and from independent software suppliers.

Table 1.6 Software Levels

Level	Examples
Applications software	Programs tailored to solve a specific problem
Development software	Editor, assembler, or compiler to create applications programs
Operating system	Program to control development software, input/output, and disk storage in files of a development system. In the final product, an operating system may control the execution of various applications programs
Hardware level	MCU, interfacing chips, memory and peripheral devices

A product design and development cycle includes both hardware and software development. The software production cycle for the development of programs that require hardware/software integration is shown in simplified form in Figure 1.5. Program coding, debugging and testing are typically performed by a program designer using a software-development system. If the programs execute correctly on the development system, they are then transferred to the memory of the microcontroller-based product for further testing with the actual hardware of the product. This constitutes the hardware/software integration portion of the development cycle. The software discussed in this section includes programs to aid software development as well as operating systems and applications programs that become part of the final product. A complete product development cycle is described in Section 1.3.

Development software. Under the control of an operating system, various programs to aid software development can be executed on a general-purpose computer system. Such programs include a text editor, language translators, and utility programs. A text editor is used to create and edit the program under development before it is translated into machine language statements by the appropriate language translator. The language translator may be an assembler or it may be a compiler to translate a high-level language such as C.

Several special-purpose programs, often called utility programs, supplement the development software for the MC68332. A debug program is a useful tool for isolating programming errors (bugs) that allows a programmer to execute a small portion of a program and test the effects. A linkage editor serves to combine program modules that have been assembled or compiled separately so that a complete program ready for execution by the MC68332 is created.

During program development, the operating system controls program execution as well as input and output operations such as printing the program text or the results. The file management capability allows programs under development to be stored and subsequently loaded into memory for execution using the disk storage unit of the computer. These features of the operating system are required by the development software and may also be used by the applications programs. In the latter case,

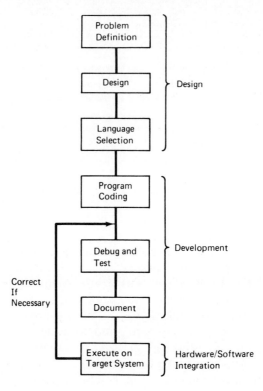

Figure 1.5 Software development and hardware/software integration.

the applications programs are intended to be executed with a particular operating system.

Cross-software for development. In the previous discussion, it has been assumed that the applications programs were developed and targeted for execution on an MC68332-based system. An alternative approach allows applications programs to be created on another computer and translated into executable programs in machine language for the MC68332. This technique, called *cross-development*, is possible for assembly language programs using a cross-assembler. For example, several companies produce cross assemblers for the Digital Equipment Corporation VAX^{TM} minicomputers and the IBM personal computers. Cross-compilers for program development in a high-level language are also available.

When using cross-development software, the programmer creates the program in the chosen language for a product with an MC68332 MCU even though the compiler or assembler executes on another computer called the "host" computer. Thus, a cross-assembler when executed on the host computer assembles MC68332 assembly-language statements and converts those into either executable code or an equivalent machine-readable form that could be executed on an MC68332-based system.

The advantage of the cross-development approach is that a programmer without an MC68332-based development system can use the program development facilities of a host computer. These facilities include a text editor for preparing the program, a disk storage unit to store completed programs, and a printer unit to print the program for correction or documentation.

To execute the cross-assembled program, the machine language instructions can be processed by either a simulator program or an MC68332-based computer system. With a simulator, the operation of the MC68332 is simulated on the cross-development computer. This approach is useful when the MC68332 system hardware is not available, but the programs must be tested. In effect, the simulator provides a software model of the MC68332 processor. However, hardware-dependent aspects such as timing must be tested on the target MC68332-based product. This is accomplished by transferring the cross-assembled program from the development system to the memory of the target system.

Operating systems and applications programs for the product. Product designers may employ operating systems in two different contexts. The first, which was previously discussed, employs an operating system during the software development phase of a project. The other use of an operating system is to direct the overall operation of a product and the execution of applications programs in particular. In this context, the operating system becomes part of the product. Its purpose is to respond to external events such as interrupts, perform Input/Output, and schedule the sequence of execution for programs that perform a specific function. These applications programs are typically organized into independent modules called *tasks*. An operating system used to control the operation of a product in this manner is usually referred to as a *real-time* operating system or a real-time kernel. The capability and features of such operating systems are discussed more fully in Chapter 16.

Motorola and other companies provide real-time operating systems specifically designed to control the MC68332 MCU. In most cases, a product designer will purchase an operating system that is available commercially rather than develop a new one because of the difficulty involved in creating an operating system for a 32-bit CPU. The applications programs or tasks are usually developed by a programmer or programming team as part of the product development effort since the operations performed by the tasks are so specific to a particular product. An interested reader should contact a Motorola representative to determine which operating systems and other software products are available for a particular microcontroller family. Also, several references in the Further Reading section of this chapter list companies that produce software for the MC68332.

1.2.4 Development Systems

When hardware design and development is required to create a product, the overall development effort must include integration of the applications software with the hardware of the product. Integration consists of extensive testing of the software components that control the hardware built for the product. In typical products, such hardware consists of special-purpose interfaces as well as interfacing chips to control standard devices such as an operator's terminal. An example special-purpose interface might consist of circuitry to control the operation of a group of A/D converters used to monitor the values of various measured variables.

The programs that perform computation for the product may be debugged and tested with a software development system. However, the hardware-dependent programs must be tested on the product hardware or a hardware emulator which behaves in a manner similar to the intended hardware of the product. Fundamental concepts of product design and development are introduced in the next section. Chapter 16 is devoted to a discussion of product development and testing including the various development aids that are available.

1.3 INTRODUCTION TO PRODUCT DESIGN AND DEVELOPMENT

Although this textbook is primarily concerned with software and hardware design techniques for products based on the MC68332 MCU, a brief discussion of a complete product creation-cycle is presented in this section. An understanding of the entire cycle influences a designer when making choices with respect to the implementation that employs both software and hardware. Figure 1.6 shows the documents and the stages in a typical product cycle.

At each stage, a designer must keep in mind the intended application which is important to the user as well as the technical and economic factors involved in the production of the product. The first step is to define the *general specifications* for the product. These are typically presented in a document or report that describes the operation and capabilities of the product but does not usually define how the required functions are implemented. The emphasis is on the requirements of the application or market that the product is to serve rather than any considerations of hardware or software.

The specifications of an automobile engine controller for example would include not only the functions to be performed but also any size, weight, or power-consumption constraints imposed by the operating environment. In many products, such constraints may determine the final hardware implementation as much as the operational requirements that the product must meet. For a microcontroller-based product, the required speed of response as control actions are performed is always defined as part of the general specifications.

Depending on the complexity of the product, one or more additional design documents may be written to further specify the *detailed requirements* and the *functional specifications* of the product. It is at this stage that the product designer defines the various functions to be performed in terms of a hardware or a software solution. This is a critical stage when the designer must have a thorough knowledge of the characteristics of the various hardware components that are available as well as an understanding of the software solutions that are possible.

For example, the detailed requirements might specify how often a value being monitored must be sampled. The functional specifications might require a hardware subsystem to acquire and store the values if the required time between samples is very short; perhaps a millisecond or less. The routine for data acquisition in this case might consist of only a few instructions to initialize the subsystem. On the other hand, if the

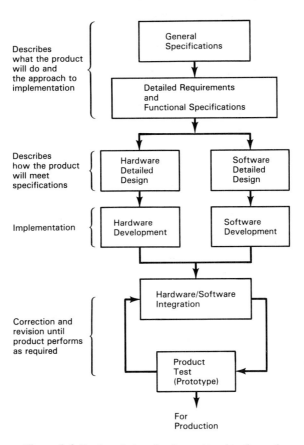

Figure 1.6 Product design, development and testing cycle.

time between samples is relatively long, a design that relies upon simple hardware but more sophisticated programs could be appropriate. The ability to make correct *hardware/software tradeoffs* is one skill possessed by a successful product designer.

Once the functional specifications for a product are written, the design process divides into two paths. A detailed hardware design is created which leads to a prototype unit to be tested independent of the software as far as possible. The hardware design includes the selection of the microcontroller, memory and peripheral chips and the other circuitry needed to complete the prototype of the product. Detailed electrical circuit diagrams indicate how the components connect together to meet the requirements of the specifications. Engineering drawings showing the physical layout of the product are also included in the hardware design document.

The second path leads to the creation of the software modules for the product. These modules are typically combined and tested independently of the hardware under development. The purpose of the separate development and testing of hardware and software is to avoid errors whose cause it may be difficult to determine if untested hardware is controlled by undebugged software. The appropriate test procedures and expected results of independent tests should be specified before the development phase for hardware or software has begun.

The final phase of the development and testing cycle for a product consists of executing the specific applications programs for the product using the prototype hardware. In this integration phase, errors caused by the interaction of the software and hardware are discovered and corrected. As with the independent tests of software and hardware, the procedure and expected results for the integrated tests should be well defined before testing begins. An appropriate development system to aid hardware and software integration is essential to allow the correction of errors that arise during this phase.

This textbook concentrates on software and electrical circuit design using the M68300 family of microcontrollers. To produce an effective design using these microcontrollers, the reader should understand the devices in complete detail. For that purpose, every important characteristic of the MC68332 as an example microcontroller is presented in the text. The last two chapters apply that knowledge of the MCU to the design and development of products using the MC68332.

FURTHER READING

Various products and support for the Motorola families of microprocessors and microcontrollers are announced monthly in many electronics and computer journals such as *Byte, Computer Design, IEEE Computer* and *IEEE Micro*.[1] These publications cover the latest developments in products and components of interest to designers using microcontrollers. Specific recommendations for further reading follow in this section.

The three volume set of manuals from Motorola listed here completely describe the MC68332. These manuals will be referred to collectively as the *MC68332 User's Manuals* in the remainder of this textbook.

Specific information about other Motorola products that support the microcontroller family is available from Motorola, Inc. The reader should contact a Motorola representative for the latest information concerning any specific Motorola component.

The article by Jelemensky and the other designers of the MC68332 gives a detailed discussion of the chip. Ron Wilson's article describes the MC68332 based on the initial announcement of the new chip by Motorola. The article in *The Electronic System Design Magazine (ESD)* presents the MC68332 and lists a number of companies that will supply software and development systems for the microcontroller.

The author's previous textbooks cover the 16- and 32-bit microprocessors offered by Motorola. The books treat assembly language programming, interface design, and system design for the M68000 family of microprocessors and related chips.

Lipovski's textbook treats the Motorola MC68HC11 in detail. Many of the features of the MC68HC11 are employed in the MC68332. Peatman covers product design using two popular 8-bit microcontrollers. He describes the Motorola 68HC11 and the Intel 8096 in a very readable manner.

---

[1] The IEEE publications are available from the Institute of Electrical and Electronics Engineers, Inc.

Motorola Manuals for the MC68332

CPU32 Reference Manual. Motorola, Inc.

MC68332 System Integration Module User's Manual. Motorola, Inc.

M68300 TPU (Time Processor Unit) Reference Manual. Motorola, Inc.

The MC68332

JELEMENSKY, JOE, VERNON GOLER, BRAD BURGESS, JAMES EIFERT and GARY MILLER, "The MC68332 Microcontroller," *IEEE Micro*, **9**, No. 4 (August 1989), 31–50.

WILSON, RON, "Motorola rethinks the fundamentals for one-chip microcontroller," *Computer Design*, **28**, No. 11 (June 1, 1989), 20–23.

"Microcontroller Gets 020 Core," *ESD*, **19**, No. 5 (May 1989), 80.

The M68000 and M68020 Families of Microprocessors

HARMAN, THOMAS L., and BARBARA LAWSON, *The Motorola MC68000.* Englewood Cliffs, N.J.: Prentice Hall, 1985.

HARMAN, THOMAS L., *The Motorola MC68020 and MC68030 Microprocessors.* Englewood Cliffs, N.J.: Prentice Hall, 1989.

Microcontrollers

LIPOVSKI, G.J., *Single-and Multiple-Chip Microcomputer Interfacing.* Englewood Cliffs, N.J.: Prentice Hall, 1988.

PEATMAN, JOHN B., *Design with Microcontrollers.* New York, N.Y.: McGraw-Hill, 1988.

2

Microcontrollers

This chapter introduces the reader to the characteristics of microcontroller-based products and the MC68332 microcontroller in particular. The microcontroller can be characterized in terms of its CPU, memory, I/O circuits, and special modules, all of which are contained on one chip. When the microcontroller is considered functionally without regard to the precise physical structure, the chip may be described in terms of its *organization*. This organizational view focuses on the major modules of the microcontroller and their interconnection on the chip. The product designer or assembly language programmer is concerned with the microcontroller at this level.

A product designer is also concerned with the features of the microcontroller that allow it to be connected to other components that are necessary to complete the product. The expansion capability to allow the addition of memory chips and other peripheral chips in a microcontroller-based product can also be described in terms of the overall organization of the chips in the product. In contrast to the organizational view, more detailed descriptions of the hardware are needed by the interface designer, who must know precise electrical and mechanical details about the product's components. This chapter concentrates on the organization of typical microcontroller-based products. A more thorough discussion of the interfacing capabilities of the MC68332 is presented in Chapter 14.

The first section of Chapter 2 compares the typical organization of systems using microprocessors with that of products employing microcontrollers. The differences are significant when the choice must be made between a microprocessor and a microcontroller as the processing element in a product. The second section introduces the MC68332 and contains descriptions of each of its modules. These modules are treated in more detail in later chapters of the textbook but the basic capabilities of the

MC68332 are presented here.

The final section presents three views of the microcontroller. These views are those of the product designer, the assembly language programmer, and the interface designer. Of course, one person may have the responsibility for the complete product including software and hardware. Alternatively, individuals or even separate teams may be assigned to develop different parts of the product. The three views here apply to different aspects of the complete product development cycle, not particular individuals.

2.1 ORGANIZATION AND BUS STRUCTURE

The elements of a simple microcomputer are shown in Figure 2.1. This block diagram shows the microprocessor (CPU), a memory unit, and I/O circuitry. The CPU communicates with other elements of the system via parallel signal lines which, taken together, constitute the system bus.[1] In Figure 2.1, the bus is shown separated functionally into *address* signal lines, *data* signal lines, and *control* signal lines. These signal lines connect the CPU electrically to external circuits for the purpose of transferring data into and out of the microcomputer.

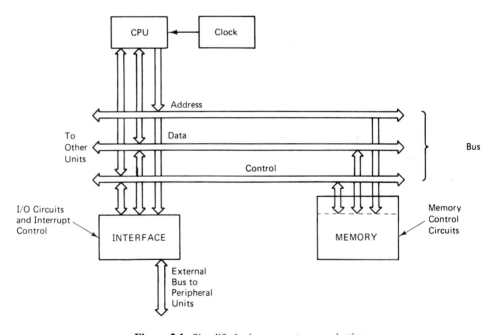

Figure 2.1 Simplified microcomputer organization.

[1] Parallel signal lines indicate that each signal line may be used simultaneously with the others and independently to transfer electrical signals representing information. For example, 32 data signal lines would allow the simultaneous transfer of 32 bits. In contrast, a single serial data line would require 32 transfers of one bit at a time to accomplish the same thing.

The system in Figure 2.1 may be constructed in a number of ways using components of the microprocessor families described in Chapter 1. At the most elementary level, individual integrated-circuit chips for the CPU, memory elements, and I/O circuits can be combined by a hardware designer using knowledge of the electrical characteristics of each element. A higher-level approach, representing board-level design, is implemented by combining a single-board computer with various other circuit boards which contain memory subsystems and I/O subsystems.

The completed hardware system could serve as the basis for a variety of products, from an automatic welding machine to a general-purpose computer. Software would be developed to meet specific requirements. A portion of the software in machine language might be stored in a ROM, so it cannot be altered after the system is complete. Such code is sometimes called *firmware*. Later chapters explore some of the differences between software designed for read/write memories and read-only memories.

In a board-level system, interfaces to special peripheral units may be required. Since the manufacturer of the other modules may not supply the unique interface needed, a custom interface may be developed by an interface designer. The integration of the hardware and the software routines for these special interfaces is a vital part of the system development.

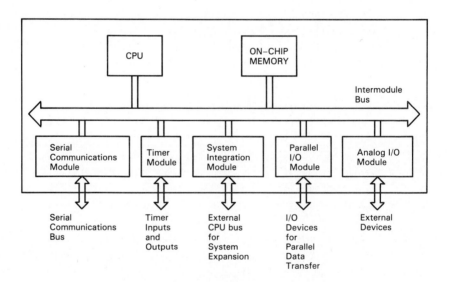

Figure 2.2 Typical microcontroller organization.

Figure 2.2 shows the internal organization of a typical microcontroller chip. As in any computer system, the CPU controls and coordinates all activities of the microcontroller. It executes machine language instructions, fetched from memory, and performs all the arithmetic, logical or other operations required by the instructions. The CPU can *read* data values (operands) from memory or *write* values into memory by sending the appropriate electrical signals (commands) via the intermodule bus.

If the on-chip memory module cannot contain all of the instructions and associated data, the CPU can access external memory units using the external CPU bus. This bus can also be used to connect one or more peripheral units to the microcontroller. In many applications, interfacing circuitry is required to expand the system in this way just as it is required for the microprocessor-based system in Figure 2.1.

An advantage of the microcontroller over the microprocessor, however, is derived from the inclusion of the various modules on the microcontroller chip. These modules can control and interact with external units without CPU intervention. This is normally not the case with microprocessor-based systems. For the microcomputer of Figure 2.1, interrupts are directed to the CPU when a peripheral unit needs attention. With a microcontroller, a request by a peripheral unit to transfer data might be serviced by one of its modules without disturbing the instruction execution of the CPU. The ability to respond rapidly to external events without interrupting CPU program execution is the hallmark of modern microcontrollers such as the MC68332.

Assuming that the microcontroller and its modules are capable of meeting the functional and performance specifications of a product, the use of a microcontroller rather than a microprocessor in the product can lead to lower cost, lower power consumption, smaller overall product size and higher reliability. These benefits arise because a microcontroller-based product generally requires fewer additional chips and hence fewer circuit connections than one based on a single-chip CPU.

In the next section, we introduce the MC68332 as an example member of a new family of microcontrollers derived from the powerful MC68020 CPU. The microcontroller was designed to give product designers the advantage of a 32-bit CPU combined with various on-chip modules to perform parallel and serial Input/Output, timing, and other functions.

EXERCISES

2.1.1. Compare the approach to product design using a microcontroller versus a microprocessor as the processing unit in a product. Consider as many issues as you can think of such as speed of operation, reliability, cost and ease of production. Also, consider the hardware and software tradeoffs required in both types of design.

2.1.2. Create a preliminary design of the system shown in Figure 2.2 but use a CPU and separate components for the modules. Compare the number of chips and other factors that are important when a microprocessor rather than a microcontroller is used to create such a system.

2.2   THE MC68332 MICROCONTROLLER

Figure 2.3 presents a simplified block diagram of the MC68332 that shows each of its major modules. The basic characteristics of these modules are listed in Table 2.1. The primary module is, of course, the central processing unit which is a modified version of the MC68020 CPU. With certain exceptions, the MC68332 executes the same machine-language instructions as programs written for the popular MC68020 microprocessor. Such programs can be held in the on-chip memory or in external memory units. The CPU of the MC68332 is frequently referred to as the *CPU32*. This section introduces each module of the MC68332.

A System Integration Module (SIM) is used for parallel Input/Output, system expansion, and various other functions. The Time Processor Unit (TPU) is used to time events and control motors or other devices independent of the CPU. Various serial communications options are available with the Queued Serial communication Module (QSM). An operator's terminal could be connected to the signal lines of the QSM, for example, to direct the overall operation of a system or product using the MC68332.

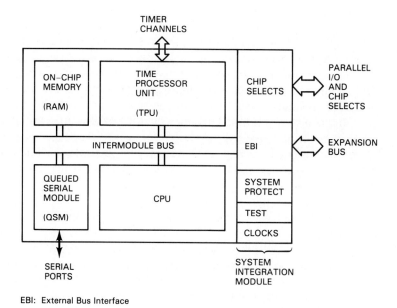

EBI: External Bus Interface

Figure 2.3 Modules of the MC68332.

2.2.1 The Central Processing Unit

Programs written for the CPU direct all of the activities of the MC68332 and any external units. The CPU communicates with the modules of the MC68332 via the intermodule bus depicted in Figure 2.3. External units are addressed and controlled using the external (expansion) bus and other signal lines as explained later.

As far as the operation of the system or product is concerned, the CPU manipulates operands to perform arithmetic, logical, or other operations required by program instructions. The CPU also initializes each module to perform specific functions. Once initialized, the modules operate independently of the CPU for most operations.

Table 2.1 Modules of the MC68332

Module	Characteristic
CPU32	32-bit CPU based on the MC68020
Queued Serial communication Module	Allows asynchronous and synchronous serial communications
System Integration Module	Controls the external bus, I/O functions and system clock. Also provides system protection and test features
Time Processor Unit	16-channel timer and counter unit to control internal or external events
Memory Module	On-chip RAM with stand-by power feature

Several important characteristics of the CPU are useful in determining its capability when incorporated into a product. One measure of the performance of the CPU is its *speed of operation*. This parameter for the CPU32 is considered in more detail in the next section. Two other important characteristics of the CPU are its *word length* for data and its *addressing range*.

The word length usually refers to the number of bits in a data item that may be transferred at one time in parallel between the CPU and other elements of the system. The addressing range defines the number of memory locations addressable by the CPU. As we shall see for the specific case of the MC68332, the intermodule bus and not the CPU limits the word length and the addressing range of the microcontroller.

The CPU itself has the capability to operate on 8-bit (byte), 16-bit (word) or 32-bit (long word) operands. It can also internally store addresses up to 32-bits in length. By these criteria, the MC68332 has a 32-bit CPU. However, the number of data and address signal lines of the intermodule bus and the external bus will be used here to define the word length and the addressing range of the microcontroller.

The intermodule bus of the MC68332. The MC68332 intermodule bus has 16 data signal-lines for the transfer of operands between the CPU and the modules. Thus, an 8-bit or 16-bit operand can be transferred in one read or write cycle. Transfer of a 32-bit operand requires two transfer cycles.

There are 24 address signal-lines on the intermodule bus allowing an addressing range up to 2^{24} locations. Since this represents over *16 million* locations, this addressing range is adequate for most microcontroller applications.

Other signal lines of the intermodule bus are used to control data transfers and similar operations. The exact characteristics of the signal lines of the MC68332 intermodule bus are rarely of interest to the product designer or the interface designer since the external bus is used to connect the circuit chips external to the product. However, the addressing and data transfer capabilities of both the intermodule bus and the external bus are identical.

Memory addressing. In MC68332-based products, the memory may hold both instructions and data to be used by the CPU. Each memory cell in the memory unit contains one bit and the memory cells are organized into groups of m bits as shown in Figure 2.4. Each memory location containing m bits is referenced by a positive number, its *address*, which indicates the position of that location in memory. The CPU can reference an individual memory location via the address signal lines and can control the operation of the memory with selected control lines.

The memory itself is organized into information units, each known as a *word*. The word sizes range from 8 bits, called a *byte* in microcomputers, to 64 bits or more in large computers. For convenience in comparing the information storage capabilities or size of different memories, a word is usually divided into a number of bytes. The MC68332 memory word, for example, is defined as 16 bits or two bytes, as shown in Figure 2.5. The MC68332 CPU can address either one of the two bytes (bits 0–7 or bits 8–15) of a memory word. It can also address word locations, consisting of two bytes, as well as longwords consisting of four bytes.

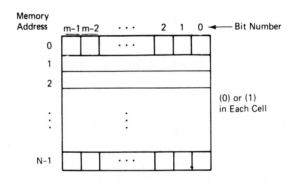

Figure 2.4 Memory organization for an m-bit memory consisting of N locations.

The *contents* of any memory location can be obtained from memory on the data signal lines (CPU read) or the value on the data signal lines can be stored into the addressed location (CPU write). Actual operation of the memory unit is directed by memory control circuits not shown in Figures 2.4 and 2.5. The memory length, given as N locations in Figure 2.4, is typically a power of 2, such as 1024 or 4096. In general, the number of locations is $2^k = N$, where k is an integer.

The MC68332 uses 24 bits to represent an address in on-chip or external memory. Thus, the MC68332 CPU can address 2^{24} different memory locations, each containing a byte of information. Its word address capability is therefore 2^{23}, 16-bit words. Memory length is often given as a multiple of 1024 bytes, which is termed 1 KB (kilobyte) or of 1,048,576 bytes called 1 MB (megabyte).[2]

The number of bits that can be transferred at the same time (in parallel) is determined by the number of data signal lines connecting the memory and the CPU.

---

[2] Strictly speaking, the prefixes kilo-, mega-, and giga- mean 10^3, 10^6, and 10^9 respectively. When referring to memory capacity, these are frequently taken to mean 2^{10}, 2^{20}, and 2^{30}, respectively.

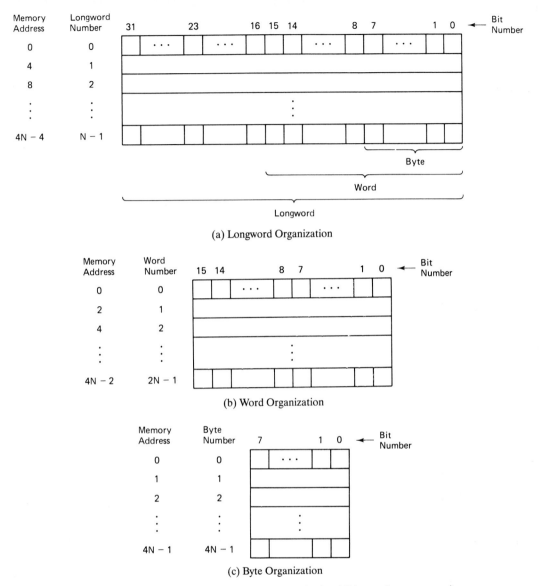

(a) Longword Organization

(b) Word Organization

(c) Byte Organization

Figure 2.5 Organization of memory in a system having $4N$ bytes of storage capacity.

A typical 8-bit microcomputer has eight data lines and the memory is organized in bytes. The MC68332 has a 16-bit-wide data path which allows either a byte transfer on eight lines or a two-byte transfer (16 bits) on the 16 signal lines. In contrast, the 32-bit MC68020 transfers either 8, 16, or 32 bits at one time.

One feature of MC68332-based computers is their ability to operate on byte, word, or longword operands according to program instructions. As shown in Figure 2.5, a byte address may be an odd or even address, a word address is any even address, and a longword address is an even address that is a multiple of 4. The programmer specifies the length of the operand as byte, word, or longword in any CPU32 instruction that references an operand. Memory addressing with the MC68332 is explained further in Section 4.6.

This organizational view of memory just presented applies to both on-chip memory and external memory for an MC68332-based product. The programmer selects between the two memory areas by their address. The addresses of different memory areas are selected by the product designer during the product design. In hardware, the address of external memory is determined by the interface to the memory chips according to the specifications in the product design or hardware design.

The complete system. Figure 2.6 illustrates the possible organization of a microcontroller-based product with respect to the MCU and external circuits. The operating system and the applications programs are assumed to be stored in a ROM for this example. The read/write memory holds values that are likely to be changed during the course of operation of the product. Such memory is typically called Random Access Memory or RAM to distinguish it from the Read Only Memory of the computer. An alternative approach used in most general-purpose systems is to store the bulk of the programs on an external disk unit and load the memory with appropriate programs as needed. The operating system controls the use of the disk in this case.

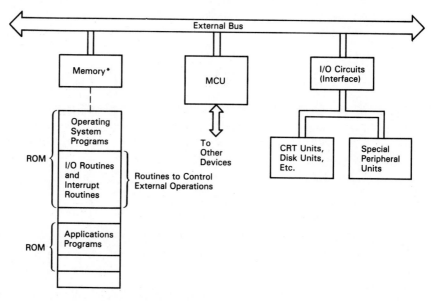

*Memory areas not designated ROM are Read/Write areas.

Figure 2.6 Hardware and software organization for a microcontroller-based product.

Notice that the operating system and its routines to handle I/O and interrupts are separated from the applications programs and their memory area. If an application program requires data transfer to external units, the transfer is typically controlled by the operating system to ensure orderly operation of the system. This type of organization including a disk unit is typical of a product that serves as a computer system, i.e. a product in which the processor is programmable by the user. In a product dedicated to a specific purpose without such programming capability, neither a disk unit nor an operating system may be required. This would be the case, for example, for an automobile engine control system or an appliance.

The MCU is connected to the external bus via the System Integration Module of the MC68332. Its internal organization was shown in Figure 2.3. In the M68300 family, the on-chip modules, external memory and external I/O circuits are addressed by the CPU in the same manner as for any memory location. This is called a *memory-mapped I/O* scheme since the CPU selects different components of the system based on their address only. Chapter 4 introduces specific programming details for the MC68332.

2.2.2 The Modules for I/O, Timing and On-Chip Memory

Each module of the MC68332 has special features to serve the designer of a product. In general, these features were included to increase the performance of a product and to reduce the number of external components needed. The modules also have capabilities to aid the debugging and testing during product development. In this section, the queued serial communication module, the time processor module and the on-chip memory module are considered. The chip's capability for parallel I/O is treated also.

Queued Serial communications Module (QSM).   The Queued Serial communications Module (QSM) provides the MCU with two serial communications interfaces as shown in Figure 2.7. These interfaces, called serial *ports*, are two independent ports to allow bit-by-bit or serial communication between the MCU and other microcontrollers, peripheral chips and peripheral units that have serial communications capability. The submodules of the QSM controlling these ports are designated as the Queued Serial Peripheral Interface (QSPI) and the Serial Communications Interface (SCI).

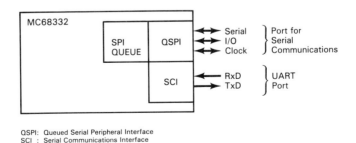

QSPI: Queued Serial Peripheral Interface
SCI : Serial Communications Interface

Figure 2.7   The Queued Serial Module (QSM) and its two serial communications ports.

The QSPI controls a synchronous I/O serial port to allow I/O expansion of the system using serial communications. Transfer baud rate is set by an external or internal clock. The data stream length for each message can be programmed up to 256 consecutive bits. Many other parameters that determine the timing and protocol of the serial transfers are also under program control to allow great flexibility. In Figure 2.7, the two QSPI I/O signals and the clock signal line are shown as bidirectional signals because the QSPI can operate in either the master or slave mode. An initialization program must define the mode of operation and set the direction of the signal lines as explained in Chapter 12.

The QSPI contains a memory area organized as a queue. The *queue* is a storage area on the chip for commands and data associated with SPI serial transfers of data. The QSPI can be programmed to perform up to 16 transfers without CPU intervention after the QSPI is initialized by the CPU. Once the transfers are complete, the sequence can be repeated continually if the QSPI is programmed to scan automatically.

The Serial Communications Interface (SCI) port is for asynchronous, serial, data transmission between the MCU and an operator's terminal or similar unit. It is referred to as a Universal Asynchronous Receiver Transmitter (UART) port that essentially converts bytes of data into a serial data stream and vice versa. The rate of data transmission or baud rate is under program control for the SCI port as are a number of other parameters that define the transmission protocol.

Readers familiar with the Motorola MC68HC11 chip will recognize the serial communications capability of the MC68332. The SCI and QSPI of the MC68332 are greatly enhanced versions of the similar submodules available with the 8-bit microcontroller. Complete details concerning the programming and operation of the MC68332 Queued Serial communication Module are presented in Chapter 12 of the textbook.

The Time Processor Unit (TPU). The Time Processor Unit or TPU is the most powerful module of the MC68332 after the CPU32 itself. It can be programmed to operate independently of the CPU as it performs a wide variety of timing, pulse generation or motor control functions. The block diagram of Figure 2.8 shows the TPU with its 16 channels and an input for an external clock signal.[3] Each channel is associated with an external signal-line of the MCU. The TPU can recognize or generate voltage changes on these signal lines.

In fact, the TPU is a microcomputer itself containing a number of fixed programs to perform its various functions. The CPU program selects the proper TPU program and supplies any parameters required to define the desired function. Once initialized in this way, the TPU completes the programmed function before the CPU needs to be interrupted to select the next TPU function. Chapter 13 discusses programming techniques and explains the complete list of TPU options.

For simplicity, the TPU can be considered as a very powerful *programmable timer*. As such, it is capable of accurately measuring the time interval between events. Each timer channel can recognize an external event, indicated by a voltage change on

---

[3] The clock is a circuit that generates a periodic sequence of pulses that synchronizes all changes in the state of the TPU and its external signal lines. The TPU can be synchronized with the system clock generated internally on the MCU chip or with an external clock circuit.

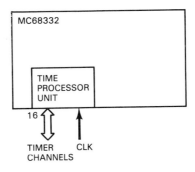

Figure 2.8 The Time Processor Unit (TPU).

its input signal line, to begin or end its timing function. Similarly, each channel can be programmed to cause an external event by changing the voltage on its output signal line at precise time intervals.

The two possible voltage levels for the TPU signal lines are typically 0 volts and 5 volts corresponding to the standard TTL (Transistor-Transistor Logic) voltage levels. As an example, a TPU channel can be programmed to output a pulse of fixed length in time. The output voltage would change from 0 volts to 5 volts at the leading edge of the pulse until the time elapsed. Then the voltage would return to 0 volts at the trailing edge. The 5.0 volt state is also called the *HIGH* or logic {1} state. At 0 volts the signal line is said to be in the *LOW* or logic {0} state.

Another feature of the TPU is its ability to make a measurement of the period of a single pulse or of a train of pulses. The period is the time between the beginning and the end of the pulse or pulse train. The measurement of the period of a pulse train is shown in Figure 2.9. As the flywheel rotates, the number of transitions on a timer input channel are counted until N pulses have been detected. The number of pulses corresponds to the elapsed time. The value of N stored within the TPU can be transferred to the CPU for processing when required by the CPU program. This is only one of the many options available for period measurement.

A TPU channel can also be used to generate a pulse train with an exact time period between pulses. As a variation of this called *pulse width modulation*, a TPU channel can output a train of pulses with a given duty cycle. The duty cycle is defined as the ratio of the time the output is at 5 volts to the period of a complete pulse as shown in Figure 2.10 for duty cycles of 50 and 25 percent. The duty cycle of the output channel can be varied from 0% with constant output of 0 volts to 100% with constant output of 5 volts.

Several TPU channels can be programmed together to control a *stepper motor* . These motors convert electrical pulses into discrete mechanical rotational movement. The TPU channels will generate the proper sequence of pulses to control such a motor. This control requires no CPU intervention once the TPU channels are initialized for the purpose.

Example 2.1

Figure 2.11 shows a much simplified diagram of an engine control unit controlled by the

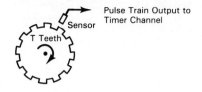

(a) Measurement of mechanical rotation

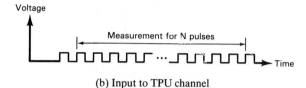

(b) Input to TPU channel

Figure 2.9 Measurement of the period of a pulse train.

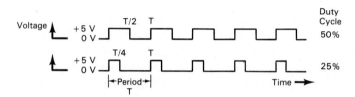

Figure 2.10 Pulse Width Modulation.

TPU. Information about engine rotation is obtained from the camshaft and the flywheel crankshaft which have reference points that generate pulse trains to the TPU. These reference points determine the timing for the ignition firing points and fuel injection pulses that are output by other channels of the TPU.

The TPU is programmed to detect the engine position via its input channels and to output the control pulses at precisely defined times during engine rotation. Speed measured in revolutions per minute can be calculated based on the information acquired by the input channels.

Memory module. Although other members of the M68300 microcontroller family can have different types of on-chip memory, the MC68332 has 2048 bytes of RAM with a standby power feature. The entire MCU including the on-chip memory is powered by the system power supply during normal operation. This power supply may be powered itself by an Alternating-Current (ac) source and rectify the ac voltage to provide the direct-current voltage, typically 5.0 volts, needed by the MCU. Alternatively, the entire system or product may be battery powered for portable use.

In any case, if the primary power supply fails, information to initialize or restart the system when power returns will be lost unless it is held in a non-volatile memory unit. A ROM could retain initial values for a system but not any values generated while the system or product operated. The RAM module of the MC68332 can be used to store critical values if a standby power supply is provided for the product.

Microcontrollers   Chap. 2

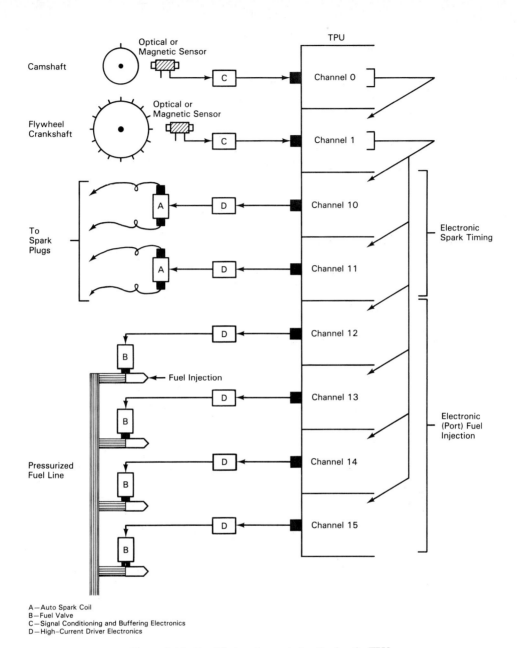

Camshaft

Optical or
Magnetic Sensor

Flywheel
Crankshaft

Optical or
Magnetic Sensor

To
Spark
Plugs

Pressurized
Fuel Line

Fuel Injection

TPU

Channel 0

Channel 1

Channel 10

Channel 11

Channel 12

Channel 13

Channel 14

Channel 15

Electronic
Spark Timing

Electronic
(Port) Fuel
Injection

A—Auto Spark Coil
B—Fuel Valve
C—Signal Conditioning and Buffering Electronics
D—High–Current Driver Electronics

Figure 2.11 Simplified engine control unit using the TPU.

Information saved in the RAM will also be retained if the product is turned off as long as the backup supply is available.

When the system power supply is turned off or fails, the MC68332 automatically switches to the standby power supply connected to the standby signal pin of the

MC68332 shown in Figure 2.12. This standby supply is normally battery operated. The RAM module is designed to require very little power when the chip is in the standby mode.

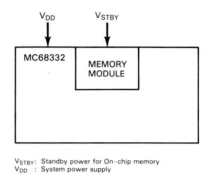

Figure 2.12 Memory module showing stand-by power pin.

Use of the RAM module in normal operation is discussed in Chapter 12. During normal operation of a product, the purpose and use of the RAM module is determined by the executing program. Chapter 15 considers the use of the standby capability in products.

Parallel ports and discrete I/O. The MC68332 is designed to allow many of its signal lines to be used for more than one function. Under program control, such signal lines when not used for their primary purpose can serve as general-purpose I/O signal lines. Figure 2.13 shows the MC68332 configured to have three 8-bit I/O ports designated ports D, E, and F. These ports each have eight signal lines that can be used to perform parallel transfers or discrete I/O operations. Port C can have its seven signal lines programmed as output signals. The sixteen channels of the TPU can also be used as I/O signal lines.

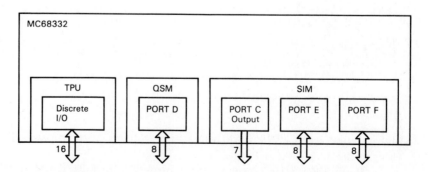

Figure 2.13 Parallel ports and discrete I/O with the MC68332.

The *bidirectional* signal lines of ports D, E and F in Figure 2.13 can be programmed to output a HIGH (5.0 volts) or LOW value (0 volts) or serve as input signal lines. As an input, a HIGH value is registered as a logical {1} and a low value as a logical {0} in the bit of an internal register corresponding to the specific signal line. Ports C, E and F are associated with the System Integration Module and Port D uses 8 signal lines of the QSM. Of course, if the signal lines of the QSM are used for general-purpose I/O, they are not available to perform serial I/O.

Each individual signal line of each port except Port C can be programmed to perform separate I/O operations called *discrete* I/O. The signal lines of the TPU used in this manner can also be programmed to detect transitions or cause a transition in the voltage on any of the TPU channels. Ports D, E, F can also be used as parallel I/O ports in which their eight signal lines operate together to input or output 8-bit values simultaneously. Port C is an output port only when used for general-purpose I/O. These and other capabilities of the MC68332 to allow discrete I/O or parallel I/O are discussed when the individual modules are introduced beginning in Chapter 12.

2.2.3 System expansion and product development

Three important criteria used to select a microcontroller for a product design are its expansion capability, its system protection features, and its features to allow debugging and testing of the prototype product. The MC68332 provides system expansion and protection via the System Integration Module. The CPU32 also has a "background" debugging mode to allow efficient software development or hardware and software integration. Finally, the MC68332 has a number of "test" modes that are employed to test each module of the MCU and assure correct operation.

The System Integration Module (SIM). Various submodules of the SIM are shown in Figure 2.14. Each serves a specific purpose to allow the MC68332 to be incorporated into a product that operates correctly and reliably. The important submodules to consider during the initial product design are the clock synthesizer, chip select, external bus interface and the system protection submodule. Use of the SIM during the product debugging and testing cycle will be discussed later.

The clock synthesizer generates the system clock signal using an external crystal-controlled oscillator or an external clock circuit.[4] This synthesizer is also used to generate other clock signals for "watchdog" timers and a separate periodic interrupt timer on the chip. The periodic interrupt timer can be used to create a *real-time clock* that generates interrupts to the CPU at fixed time intervals.

Chip selects and the external bus are used by a hardware designer to expand the system by adding circuits external to the MCU. A chip select signal selects and enables a particular peripheral unit or a memory unit for data transfer under program control. The interface circuitry is much simpler in this case than if the address signal lines of the external bus are used to select the unit. There are 12 chip select signal

---

[4] For example, a 32.768 KHz watch crystal circuit can be used to generate a system clock of frequency up to 16.78 MHz. The frequency of the system clock, defined as the reciprocal of the period of one clock pulse, can be changed under program control.

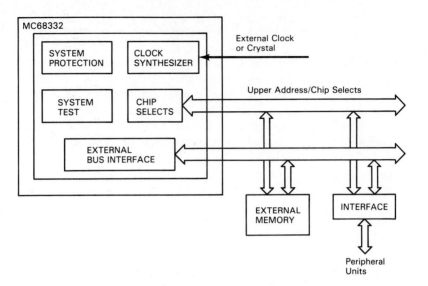

Figure 2.14 The System Integration Module.

lines available with the MC68332. Five of these can be assigned as address signal lines on the external bus if these signals are not used as chip select signals in a product.

The external bus provides a 16-bit data path and up to 24 address signal lines to external units. It also contains the control signal lines for data transfers, interrupt requests, and other functions. This bus essentially connects the CPU to external units when needed.

Thus, the SIM signal lines are controlled by an executing program. Various signals can act as chip selects, an external bus or as I/O ports as previously discussed. Chapter 12 explains the System Integration Module. Chapter 14 considers the hardware details of the external bus and the chip select signals.

System protection. The system protection submodule of the SIM allows activity on the intermodule bus or the external bus to be monitored electrically. If an operation does not finish within a prespecified allotted time, an error is indicated to the CPU32. This hardware watchdog timer feature can monitor data transfers, interrupt acknowledgement cycles, and other types of bus activity.

A software watchdog timer is also available to prevent a program from being trapped in a loop or otherwise exceeding the maximum time allotted to the program by the product or software designer. If the program does not complete its execution in the predetermined time, the MC68332 is reset. Chapter 14 describes the use of the System Integration Module for system protection in this manner.

Example 2.2

A typical use of the hardware error detection capability of the MC68332 is to determine when an external device fails to respond to an I/O transfer request. Once the request is made, a timing circuit in the system could monitor the elapsed time until the device acknowledges the request via the I/O transfer control lines. If no acknowledgement occurs within a specified time (usually several microseconds), an error signal from the "watchdog" timing circuits would be placed on one of the system control signal-lines to the processor.

The processor's error-handling routine would then determine the next action. If the failure is critical, the processor could retry the I/O transfer or indicate a system failure on another system control line.

Product debugging and testing. For an MCU as powerful as the MC68332, techniques of debugging and testing a prototype product require special consideration. One obvious problem is that individual modules within the MCU are not directly accessible for testing using standard software or hardware development systems. Motorola's designers considered this and included several debugging and testing modes of operation to facilitate product development.

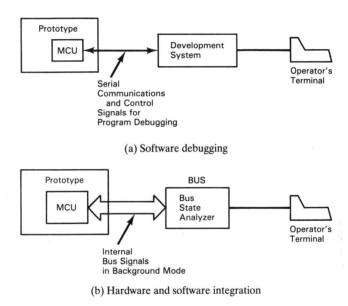

(a) Software debugging

(b) Hardware and software integration

Figure 2.15 Debugging and testing of an MC68332-based product.

The MC68332 has a special debugging mode call the *background* mode to simplify software development or software and hardware integration. This background mode causes normal instruction execution to be suspended to allow debugging operations. As shown in Figure 2.15(a), a development system can be connected to the MCU while it is part of a prototype product. Debugging operations allow the display of register values, reading or writing memory locations, instruction execution and similar functions. Thus, a simple *monitor* program to allow a programmer to perform these basic operations for debugging purposes is included in the MCU.

For hardware and software integration, the internal bus signals are made available to a hardware analyzer as shown in Figure 2.15(b). The internal bus cycles are termed *show cycles* when they appear on the external bus. These show cycles are requested by the development system when the CPU is operating the background mode. Chapter 16 covers both software and hardware development techniques for the MC68332.

A test submodule is part of the SIM as shown in Figure 2.14. This feature allows factory or user testing of the MCU to determine if it is operating properly. Chapter 16 describes the special considerations for the test submodule.

EXERCISES

2.2.1. Consider an earlier generation of 8-bit microcontrollers, using as an example the Motorola MC68HC11 or the Intel 8048. Compare its features to that of the MC68332.

2.2.2. With reference to articles in computer journals determine the most important applications for microcontrollers with 8-bit, 16-bit and 32-bit CPUs.

2.2.3. The MC68332 CPU can address byte (8 bits), word (16 bits), or longword (32 bits) operands. For each operand length, draw a diagram showing the logical organization of an eight-byte buffer in memory starting at location 1000. Label the bit positions and addresses. A buffer is an area of memory that holds data temporarily during I/O transfers. How would the physical organization differ?

2.2.4. How many bits (address lines) are necessary to address a memory with:
(a) 4096 locations;
(b) 65,536 locations;
(c) 16,777,216 locations?

2.2.5. What is the largest program (in bytes) for a microcontroller with:
(a) 16 address lines;
(b) 20 address lines;
(c) 24 address lines;
(d) 32 address lines?

2.2.6. What is the addressing range in hexadecimal and the number of address signal lines needed to address 1 megabyte of memory?

2.2.7. If you have access to an *MC68HC11 User's Manual*, describe the serial communications capability of the Motorola MC68HC11. Distinguish between the synchronous transfers of the SPI and the asynchronous transfer method of the SCI.

2.2.8. Consider a programmable timer that can determine when a leading or a trailing edge of a pulse occurs and subsequently interrupts the CPU. Describe the CPU and timer operations if it is desired to determine the total time interval for N pulses. Compare the operation of the MC68332 using the Time Processor Unit (TPU) to determine the same thing. How often is the CPU interrupted in each case if each pulse has a period of 100 microseconds with a duty cycle of 50%?

2.2.9. Describe an application for the pulse width modulation capability of the TPU of the MC68332. One possible use is to generate a wave train with a specified average direct-current output.

2.2.10. Consider a product that performs some operation at precise times of the day that can be selected by the user. What information should be held in the product's RAM which has a battery backup if the main power supply fails temporarily? What other information must be kept current when the primary power is interrupted?

2.2.11. Compare the advantages and disadvantages of using the parallel I/O ports of the MC68332 for data transfer versus its serial communication capability.

2.2.12. Suppose a product has been fully tested and is operating properly. What is the purpose of software and hardware watchdog timers in a finished product? What are the possible actions by the CPU program if an error is indicated by one of the watchdog timers?

2.3 THREE VIEWS OF THE MICROCONTROLLER

Modern microcontrollers such as the MC68332 are incorporated into products to control the overall operation. The controllers are capable of directing product activity by executing programs and performing the necessary input/output functions. Furthermore, the modern MCUs separate the processing into *supervisor* and *user* modes, allow memory management and protection, and detect various types of errors.

Programming features of the 32-bit CPU in the MC68332 include a general and powerful instruction set as well as a number of different ways to reference an operand in memory (addressing modes). This processor also provides the capability for support of special programming techniques and debugging aids. A number of such features of the MC68332 CPU (CPU32) are introduced in this section.

Interaction of the MCU and the other hardware elements of the system is via the external bus, where transfers of control signals, addresses, and data occur. Both the capability and the flexibility of the microcontroller in this regard are determined by the functions of its signal lines. For example, sophisticated I/O and interrupt capabilities alleviate the need to include a great deal of special hardware in a complex system.[5] The 32-bit CPU provides the state of the processor and other relevant information to external circuits as the processor operates. This is a feature that simplifies the hardware design as discussed in Chapter 14.

The features of 32-bit MCUs that help meet system, programming, and interfacing requirements of complex products are presented briefly in this section. Although the material is somewhat general, it forms the basis for understanding many of the characteristics of the MC68332. Figures 2.16 through 2.18 summarize three different views of a microcontroller. The product designer, assembly language programmer, and the interface designer each focus on different aspects of the MCU, so these views

---

[5] In our discussions, an interrupt is taken to be a signal originating external to the microcontroller which causes a transfer of control from an executing program to a service routine designed to perform the processing required to respond to the interrupt. After completion of the interrupt routine, control returns to the program that was interrupted.

may coincide or even conflict in some instances. Obviously, the assembly language programmer and the interface designer have the same goals in debugging a prototype product, but their approach to producing a correct product may differ considerably.

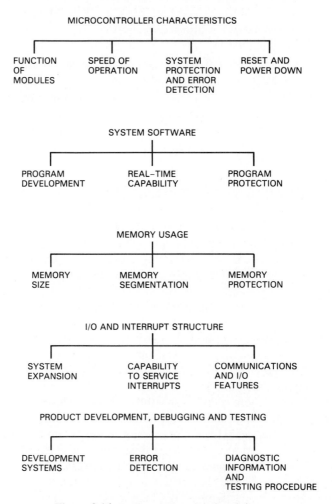

Figure 2.16 Product designer's point of view.

2.3.1 Product Design

The product designer is concerned with the overall operation of the product, including its performance and reliability. Selection of a MCU for the product begins with a careful study of the characteristics of suitable microcontrollers. Once a microcontroller is selected, the system software that is needed must be designed and developed or purchased commercially. The designer also defines the memory usage and how memory areas are to be protected from improper access caused by program errors.

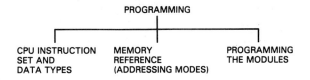

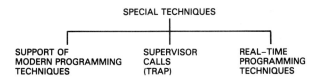

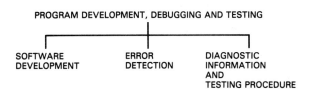

Figure 2.17 Assembly language programmer's point of view.

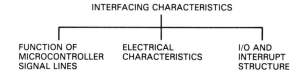

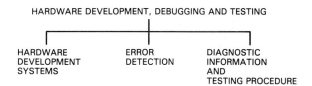

Figure 2.18 Interface designer's point of view.

When many peripheral units are attached to the system, the design of the I/O and interrupt structure is critical to assure proper coordination between programs and hardware during data transfers. A product designer must also consider the features of a microcontroller that allow efficient product development including debugging and testing of the prototype. Table 2.2 summarizes the aspects of product design covered in this section.

Table 2.2 Product Design Considerations

Characteristic	Purpose
Microcontroller	Determines the product performance and reliability to a great extent
System Software	Determines the capability and reliability of the operating system and system programs
Memory Usage	Determines the maximum program size and protection afforded to programs or data
I/O and Interrupt Structure	Determines the number and type of peripheral units to be connected and their priorities
Product Development, Debugging and Testing	Determines the ease with which a successful product can be developed

Microcontroller Characteristics.   To assure that a microcontroller will meet the specifications for a product, the *functions* performed by each module must be understood in detail. If the MCU does not have a needed capability, that function must be added to the system with external circuits. For example, the MC68332 does not have an A/D converter on the chip but it does have the I/O signals to control an A/D converter chip. Therefore, a simple A/D converter could be added without the need for additional circuitry to control the converter. In fact, an inexpensive A/D converter with serial output is easily controlled by the Queued Serial Module as will be described in Chapter 12. The major functions performed by the MC68332 modules were discussed previously in Section 2.2.

One important criterion to measure the performance of a microcontroller is its *speed of operation* while executing a given program. A key element, although not the only one, in determining the speed of operation is the maximum number of clock cycles per second at which the CPU executes. The MC68332 CPU, for example, can execute 16.78 million clock cycles per second. These relative speeds are useful in comparing the performance of different systems based on different versions of the microcontroller. However, the number of clock cycles per second of the CPU is not always easily related to the number of instructions per second that can be executed, sometimes measured in "MIPS" or millions of instructions per second. This is because different instructions may require different numbers of clock cycles to execute.

Predicting the time taken by a microcontroller to perform a specific function is further complicated by the fact that the module involved may operate independently of the CPU. Indeed, independent operation of the modules is a desirable feature of an MCU used by the product designer to increase the performance of a product. The product designer must also consider the response time to interrupts and other events that occur while the product operates. Chapter 15 presents specific timing estimates for MC68332 programs.

Modern microcontroller-based products require features for *system protection and error detection* to assure reliable operation. The MC68332 has a number of mechanisms to prevent certain program or hardware failures or errors from causing un-predictable operation of a product. The watchdog timers on the MC68332 chip have already been discussed in Section 2.2.3. Other features of the CPU to provide protection and error detection are presented here.

To prevent errors in applications programs from affecting the overall operation of the system (or each other), the CPU32 provides two modes of processor execution: the *supervisor* mode and the *user* mode. Programs executing in the supervisor mode have full control of the processor and system functions. As expected, critical routines of the operating system execute in the supervisor mode. This includes all of its routines to handle I/O and interrupts.[6] Typically, applications programs execute in the user mode. In this mode, certain processor instructions and perhaps certain memory areas are inaccessible to the applications program. The selection of the mode for various programs is determined by the product designer or the systems programmer and the transitions between the two modes are carefully controlled.

Figure 2.19 shows an example of CPU operation versus time in which control is passed to a user program and returned to the operating system. The return to the supervisor mode may be caused by program completion, an error detected by the CPU, or an interrupt.

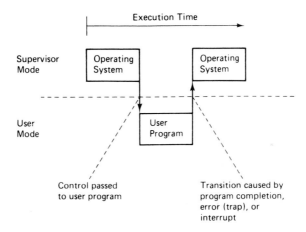

Figure 2.19 Processor modes.

Processors such as the MC68332 CPU allow certain errors occurring during program execution in either mode to be detected and trapped. The trap mechanism passes control of the processor from the program causing the trap to a routine of the system software that processes the error. The execution of an illegal instruction is an example of an operation that causes a trap.[7] In the CPU32, an attempt to divide by zero in an arithmetic operation will also cause a trap.

---

[6] A routine is usually a short program segment intended to accomplish one specific operation (e.g., transferring a data value or similar operation).

[7] An illegal instruction is a machine-language instruction with a bit pattern not recognized by the CPU.

Certain hardware errors can be detected by using the interrupt mechanism. The system could be designed to process an interrupt caused by power failure as an example. The interrupt routine would typically cause the CPU to save information which allows a program to be restarted where it was interrupted after power returns. As described in Section 2.2.3, the MC68332 allows battery backup of its on-chip RAM to facilitate restarting.

Interrupts may occur at any time, asynchronous with program execution. Traps, on the other hand, occur only as a result of execution of program instruction. Each type of trap and the interrupt capability of the MC68332 are described in detail in Chapter 11.

An important consideration in product design is the *reset and power down* sequences. The manner in which a microcontroller is reset or restarted may be critical to the safe operation of a product such as an automobile control system. The MC68332 has a number of features to allow it to be reset to a known initial state. This is necessary when power is applied to the product or it may be necessary if a critical error is detected during operation. The behavior of the MC68332 when power is turned off to the product can also be precisely controlled. Chapter 15 explores these aspects of the MC68332.

System software. A number of programs collectively called system software are sometimes needed to direct the overall operation of the applications software and the hardware of a product. These programs may be only used to sequence execution of the applications programs and perform certain I/O operations in a product that requires little sophisticated software to control the product. In other cases, a complete operating system may be included in the final product. During product development, an operating system and other types of development software are needed to create the applications programs and specific system programs as previously discussed in Chapter 1.

Part of the *program development* effort may include the creation of systems programs for a product. Typically, an operating system is chosen that allows the programmer to add software modules for specific purposes. The routines that handle I/O transfers and interrupts for a special-purpose peripheral device, for example, must be designed and tested based on the specific characteristics of the device. Collectively, these routines are called the *device driver* or *I/O driver* for the peripheral device. There are a number of operating systems that aid such program development for the MC68332. Also, many of the operating systems can be used in the final product, perhaps with the addition of device drivers and other system programs created specifically for the product.[8]

If an operating system is required in a product, the MC68332 has features to support its use. A *multitasking* operating system, for example, allows independent programs to execute concurrently. Each complete program unit is sometimes called a "task." To an observer, the tasks appear to be processed as if their execution overlaps

---

[8] Many products do not require an operating system. This is usually true if there is little interaction between various program modules and the sequence (in time) of operation is well defined. However, if the CPU must switch between programs in response to external events, a multitasking or real-time operating system may be needed for scheduling program execution and switching between programs.

in time. In these systems, several programs or tasks may be in various stages of execution at any given time. One task may preempt another and take control of the CPU according to the priorities of the tasks as set by the operating system. In a "real-time" application, this could occur in response to an interrupt for example. In such cases, all pertinent information for the preempted task must be saved in memory so that it may continue execution when control is returned to it.

The concept of task switching is similar to the processor state transition shown in Figure 2.19, although the tasks usually are executed in the user mode of CPU32. The saving of the information and passing of control to the new task is called *context switching* . The CPU32 facilitates this context switching in several ways, as discussed in Chapter 15.

For our present purpose, the characteristics of various types of operating systems are not of primary importance. The point is that the MC68332 provides the product designer great flexibility when designing or selecting an operating system. The separation of the user mode and supervisor mode and the context switching capability are important features of the microcontroller to the programmer creating system software. Further, selected areas of memory being used by a supervisor task can be protected from access by a user task, as discussed in the next paragraph.

Memory Usage.   Since the CPU32 can address 2^{24} byte locations, very few products would be limited by memory *size*. In most systems, both the operating system and the applications programs can be held in memory without conflict. The product designer or systems programmer determines the allocation of memory by specifying the required number of locations for each program. Particularly in those systems used for program development, a method must be available which prevents an executing program from accessing (reading from or writing into) any memory locations not assigned to that program. This protection is usually provided to the operating system's memory space to prevent access by programs executing in the user mode.

In MC68332-based systems, the memory can be protected in this way by memory management circuits. The MC68332 indicates the type of access as supervisor or user via three of its control signal lines. Simultaneously, external memory management circuits compare the memory location being addressed to the valid range for the mode assigned to the program. A violation is indicated to the CPU by the memory management circuitry. Thus, if the CPU provides the mode and address for each memory access as the CPU32 does, the protection of memory areas is easily accomplished. None of the earlier microcontrollers of the 8-bit class provided this feature. The segmentation and protection of memory for the MC68332 are treated in Chapter 14.

I/O and interrupt structure.   The product designer specifies the number and type of peripheral devices necessary to satisfy the requirements of an application. This capability for *system expansion* is an important feature of microcontrollers. However, design of the product becomes complicated when many devices are attached because different units have different time requirements to complete data transfers.

For example, a line printer is much slower in printing characters than a disk unit is in storing them. Due to these timing variations, the product is typically designed so that each device can issue an interrupt request via the control signal lines from the interface to the MCU. A request is issued when the device is ready to receive or transmit data or when an error condition is detected. From the point of view of an executing program, the interrupt causes a break in execution until the interrupt routine completes the data transfer or other processing. Such routines execute in the supervisor mode in an MC68332-based product.

The *interrupt* mechanism is a primary determinant of the I/O capability of a system when a number of peripheral devices are attached to the microcomputer. In the MC68332, multilevel interrupt circuitry is part of the CPU. Physically, this means that several (seven for the MC68332) control lines are dedicated to interrupt requests from external devices. The seven possible interrupt requests are arranged in priority so that a higher-priority interrupt will interrupt a routine executing due to a lower-level interrupt request. In theory, seven interrupt routines could be in various states of execution at the same time in an MC68332-based system.

At each interrupt level, a number of devices could be given the same priority. Circuitry external to the CPU is required, in this case, to resolve conflicts if two or more devices interrupt on the same level at the same time, or if several interrupts are pending (waiting for the interrupt routine at this level to complete). The MC68332 CPU is capable of handling up to 192 devices distributed according to the product requirements across its seven interrupt levels. However, such a configuration would require extensive hardware design to control the devices that could interrupt at the same CPU interrupt level. The interrupt structure is explained in more detail in Chapters 11 and 14.

The various *communications and I/O* features of the MC68332 have been described in Section 2.2. This capability of the MCU to allow parallel and serial I/O is vital to the product designer since it eliminates or reduces the need for additional peripheral chips in the product.

The MC68332 can be used in products in which several CPUs or other devices using direct-memory access (DMA) for data transfer share the external bus. In this scheme, one unit designated the bus "master" is chosen to utilize the bus at any given time. The MC68332 simplifies the design of the bus arbitration circuitry because it has the control signal lines to relinquish use of the bus or take control of the bus, as necessary. As part of the support for the M68300 family, Motorola produces a "bus arbitration module," which is an integrated circuit to perform the function of bus arbitration. The MC68452 chip listed in Table 1.4 could serve this purpose.

Certain instructions of the CPU32 such as TAS (Test and Set Operand) allow more than one processor to share a common memory area in a multiprocessor application without danger of simultaneous access to the same memory location. If one of the CPUs in the system executes this instruction, no other component of the system can take control of the bus until the instruction has completed its operation of reading the contents of a memory location, testing or modifying the operand, and subsequently writing the result back into memory. The TAS instruction is described in Section 8.3. Chapter 14 discusses other features of the MC68332 that support a computer system with multiple processors or DMA devices.

Product development, debugging and testing.   A product designer must also consider the ease with which a product can be developed including debugging and testing. The MC68332 has many features to aid a designer using a product *development system*. As previously described in Section 2.3, the internal bus cycles can be monitored on the external bus of the MCU. During development and when the product is complete, the MC68332 has extensive *error detection* features. This includes detection of both program errors and hardware errors as discussed previously. Also, *diagnostic information* is saved when certain types of errors occur to aid in the determination of the cause of the error. The types of software errors and the diagnostic information saved is presented in Chapter 11. Chapter 14 describes hardware errors that are detected by the MCU.

2.3.2 Assembly-Language Programming

The ease with which a program may be created, debugged, and tested to satisfy a specific application depends largely on the characteristics of the processor of an MCU, rather than on the development software, if the program is written in assembly language. Editors, assemblers, and other development aids vary in quality and efficiency, but a good development system cannot make up for an inadequate processor. Processors of the CPU32 class are adequate for most applications due to their powerful instruction sets, numerous addressing modes and other special features not typically found in the earlier microcontrollers.

   Table 2.3 summarizes several of the characteristics of a microcontroller which are used to determine the capability of the processor in satisfying the programming requirements of sophisticated software.[9] The general characteristics of the CPU are the same whether systems programs or applications programs are being created. However, other considerations for systems programming were discussed previously in Section 2.3.1. The assembly language programmer as treated here has the responsibility for the design, coding and debugging of programs. We concentrate on assembly language programming because it highlights the basic capabilities of the CPU. In practice, a good part of the product's software may be coded in C or another high-level language.

Programming.   Programming considerations for the MC68332 CPU include the CPU instruction set, data types and addressing modes as well as the programming techniques for the modules. The CPU programming characteristics are discussed briefly here. Programming techniques for the MC68332 modules are introduced in Chapter 12.

   The *instruction set* of a processor is the collection of all the machine-language instructions available to the programmer. Each instruction can be described by its operation or function and the number and type of operands it manipulates. For example,

---

   [9] The term *computer architecture* is sometimes used to refer to the complete set of characteristics of a computer system that are important to the programmer. A description of the architecture would include a definition of the overall organization of the system as well as a complete discussion of the programming characteristics of the CPU. The processor's instruction set and addressing modes constitute two of the most important characteristics of the CPU for this description.

Table 2.3 Programming Considerations

Characteristic	Purpose
Programming	Determines the ease and efficiency of creating sophisticated programs
Special Techniques	Allows efficient control of programs or data structures
Program Development, Debugging and Testing	Determines the correctness and reliability of the software

the binary addition instruction of the CPU32 adds two signed integers. The CPU32 also allows subtraction, multiplication, and division of two integers. In addition, instructions to add and subtract decimal numbers are provided.[10]

In contrast, earlier 8-bit microcontrollers had a more restricted set of instructions for arithmetic operations. Divide and multiply instructions were not available, for example. Routines based on the operations of addition and subtraction were created to accomplish the tasks, such as performing multiplication by repeated addition. In most cases, the equivalent instructions of the 32-bit processors as compared to those in the 8-bit or 16-bit class are more powerful and efficient. This simplifies programming and increases the speed of execution of equivalent programs.

One such example was given in Section 2.1 when data word length was discussed. The CPU32 can perform arithmetic operations on operands considered either 8, 16, or 32 bits in length. When 8-bit processors had equivalent instructions, the operand length was typically only 8 bits.

Both binary and decimal integer operations are available in the instruction set. The CPU32 also has a set of bit-manipulation instructions which allow operations on individual bits within an 8- or 32-bit operand. The bit selected can be tested, set (to {1}), or cleared (to {0}) by the bit instructions. Such operations are important when the status of a device is indicated or set as a binary value (i.e., representing ON or OFF status). The integer and bit operands represent the *data types* that may be directly manipulated by CPU32 instructions. The instruction set of the CPU32 is introduced in Chapter 4 and discussed in detail in subsequent chapters.

The number and type of instructions (including the allowed operands) are examined for their capability and flexibility when comparing processors. If the operands are held in memory, the address of an operand may be specified in an instruction as a 32-bit integer but is limited to a range of 2^{24} for the CPU32 in the MC68332. This method of directly addressing each operand is usually called *absolute addressing*. Other methods of addressing operands are possible and these addressing schemes are called *addressing modes*. The CPU32 for example, has 14 distinct addressing modes.

Instructions for the CPU32 must specify not only the operation to be performed, but also the addressing mode used to refer to each operand addressed by the instruction. The CPU calculates an absolute address, sometimes called the *effective address*

---

[10] Decimal numbers are represented in memory as coded bit sequences in a representation called binary-coded decimal. Chapter 3 discusses the types of operands allowed with CPU32 instructions.

in this context, for each operand as the instruction executes. In terms of the number of addressing modes, the CPU32 is more like a large computer than a microcomputer since previous 8-bit processors usually had restricted addressing capability. For example, a variety of data structures, such as lists and arrays, can easily be created in memory with the addressing modes of the CPU32. These and other data structures are described in Chapter 9.

Special techniques. The CPU32 provides a number of instructions to facilitate the design and programming of operating systems, compilers, and sophisticated applications programs. Some of these instructions allow structured or modular programs to be created. Others are provided to allow user-mode or supervisor-mode programs to control the system operation in various ways.

Modern programming techniques dictate that programs be modular for ease of debugging and testing. Each module performs a concisely defined function, and a complete program is created by linking the modules together.[11] The CPU32 has a number of instructions to support modular programming, including instructions to invoke subroutines. Additionally, the CPU32 allows parameters to be easily transferred between subroutines via its LINK instruction.[12] This instruction combines several operations which normally require a short program segment to accomplish on other processors.

A number of instructions of the CPU32 are useful for controlling system operation using *traps* . For example, when a TRAP instruction is executed in a user-mode program, control is returned to the supervisor mode. This is useful in performing supervisor calls to invoke operating system routines from a user-mode program.

The CPU32 also reserves a set of system-control instructions for programs executing in the supervisor mode. These instructions control the state of the CPU or the external hardware devices. For example, the RESET instruction serves to initialize peripheral chips during the initialization phase of product operation. Such instructions are treated in Chapters 10 and 11.

Many of the instructions of the CPU32 are useful to allow *real-time* programming techniques.These techniques deal with efficient interrupt handling and context switching. Chapter 15 discusses such techniques.

Program development, debugging, and testing. The CPU32 provides several features to aid in the debugging and testing of programs during software development. One mechanism to detect an error is a *trap*. The trap occurs when an instruction causing an error executes. For example, an illegal instruction or an attempt to divide by zero causes a trap. Certain addressing errors and arithmetic conditions can also cause traps. When trapping occurs, control is passed to a specific routine of the operating system which performs any required processing for the type of error detected. Information about the status of the processor and the address of the offending instruction are saved when a trap occurs, to facilitate diagnosis of the problem.

The CPU32 has two "trace" modes of operation. In one mode, the CPU executes

---

[11] In FORTRAN programs, the modules are called *subroutines*. Parameters such as addresses or data values are passed between modules during program execution.

[12] LINK is the assembly-language mnemonic for the instruction, described in Chapter 9.

only one instruction and then enters a trace handling routine that can be programmed to aid debugging. Another trace mode allows the CPU to execute a program until an instruction that changes the sequence of execution is encountered. This second trace function is termed "trace on change of (program) flow." As examples, a change of flow occurs when either a branch instruction is reached or a trap occurs in a program. Using this facility, a programmer can ignore the sequential operation of a program for debugging purposes and concentrate only on decision points in the program. Rather than continuing execution in the new program segment, control is passed to the trace routine associated with this trace mode when the change of flow is detected. Both trace modes use a trap to return control to the debugging routine. The trace feature is activated by the development system software at the request of the programmer. Trace modes are discussed in detail in Chapter 11.

2.3.3 Interface Design

The interface designer is concerned with the implementation of the computer system while designing and debugging interfaces. The functional and electrical characteristics of the MCU signal lines determine the type of the circuitry that connects the processor to external devices. The functional aspects of the signal lines determine their purpose. The electrical characteristics include the timing properties of the signals, the voltage levels, and other details of importance to circuit designers. When interface design is discussed in this section, the emphasis is on the functional approach rather than the electrical details. This subsection considers the interfacing characteristics and hardware debugging features of the MC68332 as listed in Table 2.4. Chapter 14 is devoted to a detailed discussion of the interfacing characteristics of the MC68332.

Table 2.4 Interfacing Considerations

Characteristic	Use
Interface	Determines the number and type of peripheral units that may be connected to the system
Hardware Development, Debugging and Testing Procedure	Determines the correctness and reliability of the hardware components

The *function* and the *electrical characteristics* of the MC68332 signal lines are of primary interest to the interface designer. Figure 2.20 shows the function of the MC68332 signal-lines in simplified form. These signal lines are connected internally to the CPU and the modules by the pins of the integrated circuit package enclosing the MC68332. In Figure 2.20, the number of signal lines of the external bus dedicated to a specific function is designated in parenthesis. Electrical characteristics are covered in detail in Chapter 14 which includes timing diagrams for data transfer and other operations.

Up to twenty-four of the signal lines of the MC68332 can be used to address a memory location. Two of the I/O transfer control lines indicate whether an 8-bit

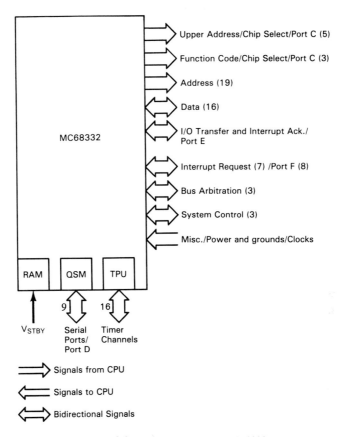

Upper Address/Chip Select/Port C (5)

Function Code/Chip Select/Port C (3)

Address (19)

Data (16)

I/O Transfer and Interrupt Ack./ Port E

Interrupt Request (7) /Port F (8)

Bus Arbitration (3)

System Control (3)

Misc./Power and grounds/Clocks

MC68332

RAM   QSM   TPU

V_{STBY} Serial   Timer
Ports/   Channels
Port D

9

16

Signals from CPU

Signals to CPU

Bidirectional Signals

Figure 2.20 Signal lines of the MC68332.

(one byte) or 16-bit (one word) or 32-bit (longword) location is selected. The 16 data lines transfer data values in either direction, as indicated by the double arrows (bidirectional) in Figure 2.20. Most of the I/O transfer signals initiate processor reads or writes from the addressed location, while two lines allow the external circuitry to acknowledge the processors request. These two lines also indicate the size in bits of the external device's data bus. This is termed *dynamic bus* sizing and occurs for each data transfer operation. A programmer transferring 8, 16, or 32 bits of information to or from a peripheral device need not know the size of the data bus for the device. Thus a four-byte transfer (32 bits) to an 8-bit device would automatically occur in four separate transfers.

The function-code lines indicate the processor mode as either supervisor or user during data transfer. They also differentiate between normal program operation and special operation of the system. For example, these signal-lines can indicate when the CPU is acknowledging an interrupt.

The interrupt-control signal lines consist of seven input signals to determine the priority of the interrupt. When an interrupt is acknowledged, control passes to a routine to handle the interrupt. When more than one device can interrupt at a given level, the CPU or external circuitry must determine which device is recognized and serviced first by the interrupt routine belonging to the device.[13]

The three control lines designated for bus arbitration allow an external circuit to take control of the external bus by issuing a request to the CPU. When the request is acknowledged by the MC68332, the MCU is electrically isolated from the bus. Three other signals for system control are used to detect external errors or to allow the CPU to indicate that it has failed. Other miscellaneous signals include the clock signal and electrical connections for power.

Notice in Figure 2.20 that many of the signal lines serve two or more purposes. For example, the five upper address lines can be used as chip selects or as five of the eight I/O lines of PORT C. The function code lines can be used as the other three I/O lines of this port. The TPU channels and the connections to the QSM are independent of the external bus but they can also be used as I/O ports as previously described in Section 2.2. It is the responsibility of the product designer or the interface designer to determine how the signal lines will be used in a completed product.

The *I/O and interrupt structure* of the MC68332 was designed to allow an interface designer to easily connect peripheral units to an MC68332-based product. Since the MC68332 and similar microcontrollers can be incorporated into complex systems requiring memory protection and a large number of peripheral units, the processor is designed to accommodate such requirements. Figure 2.21 shows a microcomputer system with the signals for memory management, interrupt requests, and error indications separately indicated. As shown, the mode of the processor (supervisor or user) is used by the memory control circuits to address the correct area of memory. If a program in the user mode attempts to read or write in the supervisor area of memory, an error signal would be generated by the memory control circuitry and appropriate action taken by an error routine executed by the CPU.

The bus arbitration control lines are not shown explicitly in Figure 2.21. These three lines determine which device on the system bus will be the master, that is, which will control I/O transfers and similar operations. Such arbitration is required when several processors share the same bus or when any device other than the CPU is capable of initiating I/O transfers on the bus. The direct memory access chips discussed in Chapter 1 are devices of this type.

The interrupt request signals shown in Figure 2.21 are processed by the interrupt circuitry of the MPU. The MPU determines the priority of the interrupt and passes control to the interrupt routine corresponding to the highest-priority peripheral unit that is requesting service. Upon completion of that routine, control passes back to the program that was interrupted.

Hardware development, debugging, and testing.   To aid a hardware designer during *hardware development*, various error signals can be generated by the interface circuitry in Figure 2.21 or perhaps even by the CPU itself. For example, the

---

[13] Up to 192 separate devices can share the seven priority levels; but only one device can be recognized at one time at a given level. Once a device is recognized, it indicates to the CPU which of the 192 possible exception routines it will use, as explained further in Chapter 11 and Chapter 14.

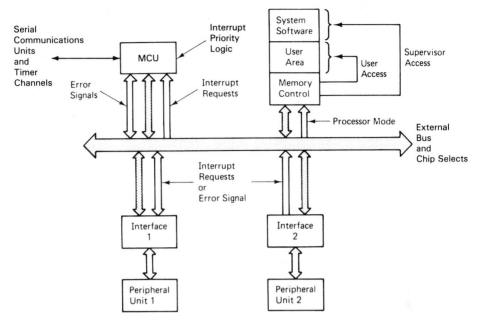

Figure 2.21 Example microcontroller system bus structure.

MC68332 can issue an error signal when it detects that the system cannot continue to operate correctly due to a critical external failure or to a CPU failure. This feature can be vital in a multiprocessor system where one faulty processor must be isolated when other processors in the system detect an error that could have a system-wide effect. Upon detecting failure, the CPU indicates the problem on one of the system control signal-lines. It then ceases to process instructions and another device or CPU must take control of the system.

   If a hardware error is indicated, the CPU saves information in memory about the condition of the system when the error occurred. The information defines the status of the processor, the type of operation in progress, and similar data at the time the error occurred. This information can be used in certain cases to allow the operating system to attempt to recover from a hardware error during operation. Of course, such information is also valuable to the interface designer in debugging the hardware.

   Various other features of the MC68332 to aid hardware development were discussed in Section 2.2.3. A more detailed treatment of the techniques for debugging and testing a prototype product is presented in Chapter 14.

EXERCISES

2.3.1. List the specific characteristics of a microcontroller that might be important for a product designer who desires to create a portable instrument. Include both the capability of the CPU and the on-chip modules that are important.

2.3.2. Based on the discussions in this chapter, list the features of the MC68332 to detect program and hardware errors. Describe how the detected errors would be handled in the following cases.

(**a**) Consider the development phase of a product cycle and determine the program actions that might be taken when the various errors occur.

(**b**) Once the product is on the market, what program actions might be taken if the various errors occur during the operation of the product?

2.3.3. List the characteristics of the peripheral devices and units and the operating system (if one is needed) for the following MC68332-based products.

(**a**) A software development system.

(**b**) An automobile engine controller.

(**c**) A camera with auto-focusing and other sophisticated features.

(**d**) A data acquisition and control system for a chemical process.

Also, describe the role of the microcontroller in each of the products listed.

2.3.4. Draw a diagram or flowchart showing the sequence of program execution in the following cases.

(**a**) An MCU repeatedly executes a program made up of independent routines that execute in a fixed sequence.

(**b**) An instrument responds to requests to make measurements by the user via its keyboard. Each type of measurement is independent of the others but the user can interrupt the instrument to stop a measurement or to start another type of measurement.

(**c**) A continuously operating closed-loop control system must respond to operator requests for display of data as well as various "alarm" conditions. The response to an alarm results in the display of any variable whose measured value is outside of a preset range.

In each case, consider the initialization and power-down sequence. Also, define the timing constraints on each product, i.e. what events determine the required response time of the product?

2.3.5. What are the general advantages and disadvantages of including a real-time operating system in a product? Consider such factors as performance, flexibility and cost.

2.3.6. Assume that three interrupt routines require the following execution times:

$$R_1 = 20 \text{ microseconds}$$
$$R_2 = 30 \text{ microseconds}$$
$$R_3 = 20 \text{ microseconds}$$

The priority levels are such that R_3 has the highest priority and R_1 has the lowest. What is the possible range of time for each routine to be executed when the corresponding interrupt occurs? Let the interrupt response time be 2.6 microseconds if the interrupt is recognized and its routine begins execution.

2.3.7. Discuss the differences between a trap and an interrupt. Include both hardware and software considerations.

2.3.8. What are the possible consequences of allowing the CPU to execute illegal instructions?

2.3.9. Explain the use of the supervisor and user modes. State which programs execute in each mode, and why. What are some of the instructions that might be restricted from user-mode programs?

2.3.10. Discuss the trace modes of the CPU32. What is the purpose of these aids to debugging?

FURTHER READING

A number of articles about the M68300 microcontroller family have been published in computer journals. The reader should refer to the latest issues of the journals to keep abreast of the rapidly changing microcontroller technology. The journal *Embedded Systems Programming* contains articles of interest to programmers and product designers. The two articles by John Dunn and Ann Harwood treat the MC68332 in some detail. The article by Vaglica describes the features of the MC68332. Other such references were cited in Chapter 1. References with specific details about the features of the MC68332 will be cited in later chapters as various topics are introduced. The article by Vaglica and Gilmour defines the choices that must be considered by a product designer when choosing a microcontroller.

DUNN, JOHN, and ANN HARWOOD, "Inside the 68332," *Embedded Systems Programming*, **2**, No. 9 (October 1989), 50–67.

DUNN, JOHN, and ANN HARWOOD, "Programming the 68332," *Embedded Systems Programming*, **2**, No. 10 (November 1989), 38–47.

VAGLICA, JOHN, "Controller Gains Clout with 32-bit Processor," *ESD*, **19**, No. 8 (August 1989), 61–66.

VAGLICA, JOHN, and PETER S. GILMOUR, "How to select a microcontroller," *IEEE Spectrum*, **27**, No. 11 (November 1990), 106–109.

3

Representation of Numbers and Characters

The digital computer has the capability of storing and processing information of interest to the programmer. The information is stored in memory as sequences of binary digits which are processed by the CPU. For example, the machine-language instructions discussed in Chapter 2 represent information that controls the operation of the computer system. *Programs*, consisting of these instructions, operate on other binary sequences of *data* which represent information that has been stored for processing. This chapter explores the storage methods commonly used to represent numbers and characters for MC68332-based computer systems.

Numbers that are interpreted as positive or negative integers or fractions may be represented in memory in many ways. The most common number system used to represent numbers in microcomputers is the *two's-complement* system, which represents signed numbers as binary (base 2) values. The MC68332 provides instructions for addition, subtraction, multiplication, and division of these binary numbers. These two's-complement numbers form a fundamental *data type* for the MC68332 CPU (CPU32).

Decimal numbers can also be added and subtracted with instructions of the CPU32 if the decimal values are coded into binary by a scheme called *binary-coded decimal* (BCD). The *ten's-complement* system is used to incorporate both positive and negative numbers.

Many engineering and scientific applications require a large range for numbers which are represented in a *floating-point* format. This binary equivalent of scientific notation, which uses a mantissa and an exponent to represent a number, is employed and sometimes required in MC68332-based systems. No CPU32 instructions are available to manipulate these numbers directly. However, the floating-point format used in Motorola systems is discussed in this chapter for completeness.

Text is stored in memory by assigning a specific bit pattern to each character in the alphabet. The *ASCII code* is the most popular code used to represent characters in microcomputer systems. As with floating-point numbers, any processing of the ASCII-coded characters is via software routines since the CPU32 has no instructions that operate specifically on characters.

The basic characteristics of the data types commonly used in MC68332-based systems are discussed in this chapter. Machine instructions to manipulate the data types and various other programming considerations are discussed in later chapters. In particular, arithmetic operations using integers are treated in detail in Chapter 7.

3.1 NUMBER REPRESENTATION

This section describes the representation of positive and negative integers and fractions. A general formulation with the base or radix r for each number representation is presented and then applied to the discussion of binary values with $r = 2$ and other bases as appropriate. The generalized presentation is useful for conversion of numbers from one base to another and techniques of numerical analysis. Representation of binary numbers in the sign-magnitude , one's-complement, and two's-complement systems are presented. Decimal representations for the nine's complement and ten's complement systems are also presented.

3.1.1 Nonnegative Integers

A nonnegative integer in base r is written in positional notation as

$$N_r = (d_{m-1}d_{m-2}\cdots d_0)_r \tag{3.1}$$

where each digit d_i has one of the distinct values $[0, 1, 2, \ldots, r-1]$ and m represents the base 10 or decimal number of digits in the integer. Thus the number 324 would have $d_0 = 4$, $d_1 = 2$, and $d_2 = 3$ in Equation 3.1 and could be written as

$$N_{10} = 324_{10}.$$

For numbers in base 10, the subscript is omitted if no confusion could result from its omission. The form specified by Equation 3.1 is generally referred to as *positional notation*. The position of the digit starting from the rightmost digit represents a power of the base r; that is, 324 represents 4 ones (4×10^0), 2 tens (2×10^1), and 3 hundreds (3×10^2). Mathematically, the value of the number is calculated as

$$
\begin{aligned}
N_r &= d_{m-1}r^{m-1} + d_{m-2}r^{m-2} + \cdots + d_1 r + d_0 \\
&= \sum_{i=0}^{m-1} d_i r^i
\end{aligned} \tag{3.2}
$$

in which the digits are restricted in value such that $0 \le d_i \le r - 1$. Thus, the number 324 can be calculated as

$$324 = 3 \times 10^2 + 2 \times 10^1 + 4 \times 1.$$

The arithmetic operations in Equation 3.2 could be carried out in any number base and this equation is frequently used to determine the decimal equivalent of a number in another base.

Table 3.1 Digits in Various Number Systems

Number system	Base r	Digits
Hexadecimal	16	0, 1, 2, 3, 4, 5, 6, 7, 8, 9, A, B, C, D, E, F
Decimal	10	0, 1, 2, 3, 4, 5, 6, 7, 8, 9
Octal	8	0, 1, 2, 3, 4, 5, 6, 7
Binary	2	0, 1

Table 3.1 lists the range of possible values in the digits in the hexadecimal, decimal, octal, and binary number systems. The decimal system is, of course, used primarily for ordinary arithmetic by human beings, and the binary system is used for computer arithmetic. Octal and hexadecimal representations are convenient for writing long binary numbers. For example,

$$01011010_2 = 5A_{16} = 132_8.$$

The decimal value of the number represented in these bases is obtained from Equation 3.2 by converting the base r digits to decimal equivalents such that

$$N = 5 \times 16^1 + 10 \times 1$$
$$= 1 \times 8^2 + 3 \times 8^1 + 2 \times 1$$
$$= 90_{10}.$$

The hexadecimal digits [A, B,...., F] represent the decimal numbers [10, 11,...., 15] in the conversion from hexadecimal to decimal.

Example 3.1

Consider the largest m-digit positive integer in positional notation,

$$N_r = ((r-1)(r-1)\cdots(r-1)),$$

as in $(1111\ldots1111)_2$ or $(9999\ldots9999)_{10}$ with m digits each. The sum of Equation 3.2 indicates that the decimal value is

$$N = (r-1)\sum_{i=0}^{m-1} r^i$$

which is an easily summed geometric series. The result is $r^m - 1$. For example, an 8-bit binary number has a maximum value of $2^8 - 1$, or 255.

Positive fractional values. The positional notation defined by Equation 3.1 is valid for integers only. If a fraction is to be represented, a radix point in the base r is used to separate the integer from the fractional part of the number. The radix point is called the *binary point* in base 2 and the *decimal point* in base 10. Thus, 324.14 has the value

$$3 \times 10^2 + 2 \times 10^1 + 4 \times 1 + 1 \times 10^{-1} + 4 \times 10^{-2}.$$

In general, a k-digit positive fraction is written with a leading radix point as

$$0.(d_{-1}d_{-2}\cdots d_{-k}) \tag{3.3}$$

with the value

$$0.n_r = d_{-1}r^{-1} + d_{-2}r^{-2} + \cdots + d_{-k}r^{-k} \tag{3.4}$$

where the negative subscript for the digits indicates the appropriate negative power of r.

Internally, the processor performs arithmetic on integers without taking into account the position of the radix point . It is then possible to interpret the internal value of a fraction by writing $0.n_r$ in the form

$$0.n_r = r^{-k} \times (d_{-1}d_{-2}\cdots d_{-k})_r \tag{3.5}$$

with the value in parentheses treated as an integer value. For example, the number 0.1000_2 (0.5_{10}) can be written as

$$2^{-4} \times (1000.)_2 = 2^{-4} \times 8$$

both of which have the value 0.5, as expected. The scaling factor r^{-k} has the effect of shifting the radix point k positions to the left. Thus, $0.n_r r^k$ may be used internally as an integer operand and the final result scaled by r^{-k}. For example, the addition of the binary values 0.1000 (0.5_{10}) and 0.0100 (0.25_{10}) can be accomplished as

$$
\begin{array}{rl}
1000. & \times\, 2^{-4} \\
+0100. & \times\, 2^{-4} \\
\hline
1100. & \times\, 2^{-4}
\end{array}
$$

The machine addition results in 1100_2 or 12 decimal, and the programmer must apply the scale factor to obtain the correct arithmetic result:

$$12 \times 2^{-4} = 0.75.$$

In addition and subtraction, each scaled value must have the same scaling factor. The choice of the scaling factor may cause the radix point to be at the right of the number (integer), at the left (fraction), or anywhere within the number. Thus, the value 0.5 in four-digit binary could be written as a fraction

$$.1000_2$$

as an integer with scaling 2^{-4} as

$$(1000.)_2 \times 2^{-4}$$

or as a mixed quantity scaled arbitrarily: for example,

$$(10.00)_2 \times 2^{-2}.$$

When the radix point is fixed for a particular problem and the programmer must take the scaling into account, the system is called a *fixed-point* representation. All integer operations with the CPU32, such as addition or subtraction, assume that the scaling factor is 2^0. Therefore, the binary point is on the right. The importance of Equation 3.5 is that both for analysis and for machine operations, a fractional value may be treated as an integer during all the intermediate steps of a computation. The appropriate scale factor can be applied as the last step when the actual numerical value is desired.

Example 3.2

The first example showed that the largest m-digit integer for unsigned integers has the value $r^m - 1$. Thus, the largest 16-bit (binary) integer

$$1111\ 1111\ 1111\ 1111_2$$

has the value

$$2^{16} - 1 = 65,535$$

in decimal representation. The largest 16-bit fraction

$$0.1111\ 1111\ 1111\ 1111_2$$

has the decimal value

$$2^{-16} \times 65,535 = 0.99998474.$$

This is obtained by scaling the 16-bit fraction as

$$2^{-16} \times (2^{16} - 1) = 1 - 2^{-16}$$

and performing the arithmetic on a calculator with a sufficient number of decimal places.

EXERCISES

3.1.1.1. Convert the binary number

$$0100.0110_2$$

to decimal.

3.1.1.2. What is the decimal value of

$$1111\ 1111\ .\ 1111\ 1111\ 1111\ 1111_2$$

to five decimal places in the fraction?

3.1.1.3. Compute the decimal value of the following numbers:
   (a) 130_9;
   (b) 120_5;
   (c) 0.7632_8;
   (d) $F00A_{16}$.

3.1.1.4. If the base x number

$$111_x = 31_{10}$$

what is the base x?

3.1.1.5. Compute the largest integer representable in a 32-bit computer word. Give the answer as a decimal value.

3.1.2 Representation of Signed Numbers

The positive integers, including zero, can be conveniently represented as shown in Section 3.1.1. However, to represent the complete set of integers, which includes positive integers, zero, and negative integers, a notation for negative values is necessary. In ordinary arithmetic, a negative number is represented by prefixing the magnitude (or absolute value) of the number with a minus sign. Thus -5 is a negative integer with magnitude of 5. For hand calculations, the use of separate symbols to indicate positive $(+)$ and negative $(-)$ numbers is convenient.

Computer arithmetic circuits to manipulate positive and negative integers are also simplified if one of the digits in the positional notation of a number is used to indicate the sign of the integer. Two such possible representations of signed integers are *sign-magnitude* notation and *complement* notation. In both notations, the most significant digit on the left in the positional form of the number indicates the sign. Negative fractions can also be represented in either of these systems. For fractions, the sign digit is written to the left of the radix point.

The binary arithmetic instructions of the CPU32 operate directly on integers in two's-complement notation. Integers in other binary notations or fractions must be manipulated by programs designed for that purpose. The treatment of decimal numbers by the CPU is discussed in Section 3.2 although the mathematical representation of decimal numbers is first introduced in this section.

Sign-magnitude representation. The sign-magnitude representation of a number in positional notation has the form

$$N_r = (d_{m-1}d_{m-2}\cdots d_1 d_0)_r,$$ (3.6)

where the sign of the number is indicated by the most significant (leftmost) digit:

$$d_{m-1} = \begin{cases} 0 & \text{if } N_r \geq 0 \\ r-1 & \text{if } N_r < 0 \end{cases}$$ (3.7)

Thus, using the sign-magnitude representation, 1011_2 and 9003 are four-digit negative numbers in the binary and decimal systems, respectively. The magnitude of the number, written $|N_r|$, is

$$|N_r| = \sum_{i=0}^{m-2} d_i r^i$$ (3.8)

where only the first $m-1$ digits from the right are considered. The representation of a positive number differs from that of the corresponding negative number only in the sign digit. The digits $(d_{m-2}d_{m-3}\cdots d_1 d_0)$ indicate the magnitude. According to the definitions and equation 3.8, the four-digit number 0011_2 represents $+3$, and 1011_2 represents -3.

The number of digits, including the sign digit, in the representation must be specified or confusion could result. For example, 1011_2 in an eight-digit representation is assumed to be 00001011_2, which has the decimal value 11. For binary values, a negative fraction in sign-magnitude notation has a leading digit of 1 followed by the fractional part. Thus 1.100_2 is the number -0.5.

Example 3.3

The number 16 is written in a 16-bit binary system as

$$0000\ 0000\ 0001\ 0000_2$$

The number -16 has the sign-magnitude representation

$$1000\ 0000\ 0001\ 0000_2$$

Complement representation. Most microcontrollers, including the MC68332, have arithmetic instructions that operate on negative numbers represented in a *complement* number system.[1] In these systems, positive numbers have the same representation as in sign-magnitude notation, but the negative numbers are formed by computing the complement of the number according to the rules of the specific system

---

[1] Complement representations have an advantage over sign and magnitude notation because the sign digit does not have to be treated in a special way during addition and subtraction. This simplifies the arithmetic circuits of the CPU somewhat, as is discussed in several references in the Further Reading section of this chapter.

being used. The two most common complement systems are the *radix-complement* and the *diminished radix-complement* systems. The general theory of these systems will be presented first. Then, the two's and ten's complements of numbers will be discussed as examples of radix-complement numbers. The one's and nine's complements are examples of diminished radix-complement systems for base 2 and base 10, respectively.

In general form, the radix complement of an m-digit number is computed mathematically as

$$N'_r = r^m - N_r \tag{3.9}$$

where N'_r is the radix complement of the base r number N_r. In the machine computation, only m-digit values can be represented. If any operation produces a result that requires more than m digits, the higher-order digit is ignored. This is taken to be an out-of-range condition. A machine error of this type is called *overflow*.

The two radix-complement systems used with the CPU32 instructions are the two's-complement and the ten's complement systems. The two's complement of a number N_2 given by Equation 3.9 using 2 as the base r is

$$N'_2 = 2^m - N_2. \tag{3.10}$$

Thus, the four-digit two's-complement form of -1 is

$$N'_2 = 2^4 - 1 = 1\ 0000 - 0001 = 1111_2$$

If the number and its complement are added:

$$
\begin{array}{rl}
0001 & N \\
+1111 & N' \\
\hline
10000 &
\end{array}
$$

the result is 0 to four digits, as expected. In a two's-complement system, negative values always have a leading digit of 1 and positive values have 0 as the leading digit. Thus $+4 = 0100_2$ and $-4 = 1100_2$. If addition is performed in a four-digit representation on two positive numbers, the result must not be greater than 7 or overflow occurs. This limits the range of the m-bit positive numbers to the decimal value $2^{m-1} - 1$. In the case of 4-bit numbers, the addition of $4 + 5$ in binary yields

$$
\begin{array}{r}
0100 \\
+0101 \\
\hline
1001_2
\end{array}
$$

which is a negative number in two's-complement notation. The magnitude as derived from Equation 3.9 would be

$$N_2 = 2^4 - 1001 = 1\ 0000 - 1001 = 0111_2$$

which is $+7$ in decimal, clearly an error. In the CPU32, an indication is given when such an overflow occurs and the programmer must make provisions in the program for such occurrences.

In the ten's complement system, the ten's complement of a number N is formed as

$$N' = 10^L - N \qquad (3.11)$$

in an L-digit representation. For four digits, -1 is represented as

$$N' = 10^4 - 1 = (10,000 - 1) = 9999.$$

The CPU32 has arithmetic instructions to operate on numbers represented in the ten's-complement system.

The diminished radix complement is computed as

$$\overline{N}_r = r^m - N_r - 1 \qquad (3.12)$$

which is one less than the radix-complement value computed by Equation 3.9. The diminished radix complement, or simply complement as it is usually called, is the one's complement for binary values and the nine's complement for decimal numbers. The four-digit decimal value 0002 has the complement

$$\overline{N}_r = (10^4 - 0002) - 1 = 9999 - 0002 = 9997. \qquad (3.13)$$

From the complement, the radix complement is formed by adding 1, as a comparison of Equations 3.12 and 3.9 shows.

Table 3.2 Complement Systems

Value	One's	Two's	Value	Nine's	Ten's
7	0111	0111	4999	4999	4999
6	0110	0110	4998	4998	4998
5	0101	0101	.	.	.
4	0100	0100	.	.	.
3	0011	0011	.	.	.
2	0010	0010	0002	0002	0002
1	0001	0001	0001	0001	0001
0	0000	0000	0000	0000	0000
−0	1111	—	−0000	9999	—
−1	1110	1111	−0001	9998	9999
−2	1101	1110	−0002	9997	9998
−3	1100	1101	.	.	.
−4	1011	1100	.	.	.
−5	1010	1011	.	.	.
−6	1001	1010	.	.	.
−7	1000	1001	−4999	5000	5001
−8	—	1000	−5000	—	5000

Table 3.2 lists the radix complement for four-digit binary and decimal numbers. The one's- and nine's-complement values are also presented for comparison. Notice that in the nine's- and ten's-complement notation, the negative values have leading

digits in the range 5 through 9. The sign digit is not unique as it is in the case of two's complement negative values.

Example 3.4

The radix complement of a number is easily computed by complementing each digit [subtracting it from $(r-1)$] and adding 1 to the result formed from the complemented digits. Thus, the value -2 is represented as follows in various four-digit systems:

$$2\text{'s complement: } -2 = (1111 - 0010) + 1 = 1110_2$$
$$10\text{'s complement: } -2 = (9999 - 0002) + 1 = 9998$$
$$16\text{'s complement: } -2 = (FFFF - 0002) + 1 = FFFE_{16}$$

Example 3.5

For a fraction of length k digits, the radix complement is computed by complementing each digit and adding r^{-k} (not 1) to the result. Thus, the number

$$0101.01_2 = 5.25$$

has as its complement the value

$$1010.10_2$$

Its radix or two's-complement representation would be

$$1010.10$$
$$+ \quad .01$$
$$\overline{1010.11_2}$$

where the value 2^{-2} is added to the one's complement of the number since $k = 2$. Similarly, the fraction 0.01_2 has complement 1.10_2 and two's complement 1.11_2.

Number range. The range of integers (or fractions) for a given number system is specified by the smallest and largest values that can be represented. For positive integers represented in m digits, for example, there are r^m possible values with a numerical range of 0 to $r^m - 1$. For the 8-bit representation of a positive binary integer, the range is 0 to $2^8 - 1$, or 0 to 255. The range of signed integers in an m-digit representation still allows r^m values, but one-half of these values are negative numbers.

The maximum positive integer in sign-magnitude , one's-complement, or two's-complement representation is

$$(0111 \ldots 111)_2$$

where $(m-1)$ 1's are shown. The maximum decimal value is thus $2^{m-1}-1$, considering the discussion in Example 3.1. In an 8-bit representation, the largest positive number is $2^7 - 1$, or 127. In sign-magnitude notation, the most negative value is

$$(1111 \ldots 111)_2 = (2^{m-1} - 1).$$

The most negative one's-complement number $(100\ldots00)_2$ has this same numerical value. Both of these systems allow a positive and a negative value of zero since the "positive" zero

$$(000\ldots000)_2$$

has negative values of $(1000\ldots000)_2$ and $(1111\ldots111)_2$ in the sign-magnitude and one's-complement notations, respectively. In the two's-complement notation, however, only one value of zero is allowed since the two's complement of the number 0 is the same value to m bits. Since there are a total of 2^m values for each m-bit representation, the two's-complement notation allows one more negative value than the others.

The two's complement of the positive value

$$(011\ldots111)_2$$

is the negative number

$$(100\ldots001)_2 = -(2^{m-1} - 1)$$

for m bits. The integer

$$(100\ldots000)_2$$

must then represent -2^{m-1} with no positive counterpart.

The m-digit ten's complement allows 10^m values in the range

$$-10^m/2 \text{ to } 10^m/2 - 1$$

as from -5000 to $+4999$ in the four-digit representation shown in Table 3.2. The positive values are

$$0, 1, 2, \ldots, 499\ldots99$$

for m digits and the negative values are represented as

$$999\ldots999, 999\ldots998, \ldots, 500\ldots001, 500\ldots000$$

with values $-1, -2\ldots$. The nine's-complement representation of the negative numbers has a negative 0 and consequently one less nonzero negative value than the ten's-complement notation allows, that is, a range from

$$-10^m/2 + 1 \text{ to } 10^m/2 - 1.$$

In this case, the magnitude of the number is restricted so that

$$|N| \leq 10^m/2 - 1$$

which causes the most significant digits of 0, 1, 2, 3, or 4 to indicate a positive number and the digits 5, 6, 7, 8, or 9 to indicate a negative value.

Example 3.6

The largest positive number for an m-digit radix-complement number in base r is

$$(1/2) \times r^m - 1$$

since there are $(1/2) \times r^m$, positive integers, including zero. Thus, the two's-complement maximum value is

$$(1/2) \times 2^m - 1 = 2^{m-1} - 1$$

while the ten's complement number has the maximum value of

$$(1/2) \times 10^m - 1$$

as indicated in the previous discussion. The four-digit binary number allows values up to $+7$ in the two's-complement system, while the four-digit decimal value has a largest positive value of 4999.

Example 3.7

Applying the formulas for the most negative and most positive numbers in m-bit representations gives the following results:

Representation	Most negative	Most positive
Sign-magnitude	$-2^{m-1} + 1$	$2^{m-1} - 1$
One's complement	$-2^{m-1} + 1$	$2^{m-1} - 1$
Two's complement	-2^{m-1}	$2^{m-1} - 1$

For a 16-bit representation, the sign-magnitude and one's-complement numbers range from $-32,767$ to $32,767$, and the two's complement numbers range from $-32,768$ to $32,767$.

If a signed, binary fraction is represented as

$$(b_0 b_{-1} \cdots b_{-(k-1)})_2$$

the range is determined by scaling by $2^{-(k-1)}$. For example, the 8-bit fraction in two's-complement representation has the range -1 to $1 - 2^{-7}$. The binary values in this range are

```
1.000 0000   (−1)
1.000 0001
.
.
.
0.000 0000   (0)
.
.
.
0.111 1110
0.111 1111   (1 − 2⁻⁷)
```

EXERCISES

3.1.2.1. Find the two's-complement representation of the following numbers:
(a) -0647_{16} to 16 bits;
(b) -11_{10} to 16 bits;
(c) -00101.110_2 to 8 bits.

3.1.2.2. The most negative two's complement number is $100\ldots0_2$ for m bits. What value results when the two's complement of the number is taken?

3.1.2.3. In the two's-complement notation, the sign bit has the weight -2^{m-1} for an m-bit integer. Determine the procedure to extend the m-bit number to $2m$ bits for the following:
(a) a positive number;
(b) a negative number.
This is called *sign extension*.

3.1.2.4. Represent the given numbers in the notation specified:
(a) nine's complement of 653.72 with five digits;
(b) -223_{16} in sign-magnitude form with four hexadecimal digits;
(c) $-3/8$ in one's-complement form with 8 bits, including the sign bit.

3.1.2.5. Determine the range of numbers for the sign-magnitude , one's-complement, and two's-complement forms for an m-bit representation if:
(a) $m = 8$;
(b) $m = 16$;
(c) $m = 32$.

3.1.2.6. Suppose the largest positive number is limited to 999 (i.e., three digits) in a four-digit, ten's-complement representation. Determine the corresponding range and representation of the negative numbers. Note that negative numbers always begin with 9 as the sign digit when the magnitude of the numbers is limited in this way.

3.1.3 Conversions between Representations

The number systems of most interest to computer users are the binary, octal, decimal, and hexadecimal systems. Although the internal machine representation in micro-computers is binary, the other representations are important for the convenience of the user. In this regard, the conversions of numbers in other bases to decimal, and vice versa, are frequently required.

Conversion between arbitrary number bases is sometimes necessary, although in computer work, the conversions between binary, octal, and hexadecimal systems are of greatest importance. Fortunately, conversions between these bases are straightfor-ward.

Conversion to decimal for positive numbers. The number N_r in base r can be represented in decimal as

$$N.n = D_{m-1}r^{m-1} + \ldots + D_0 + D_{-1}r^{-1} + \ldots + D_{-k}r^{-k} \qquad (3.14)$$

where the D_i are the equivalent values in the base 10 of the digits in base r. The number is converted by multiplying each digit by the appropriate power of r and adding each result to the sum. The number is designated here as $N.n$ to emphasize the fact that it has an integral as well as a fractional part.

Example 3.8

To convert $11\ 1110_2$ to decimal, the value is computed as a series from Equation 3.2 or 3.14 with the result

$$N = 1 \times 2^5 + 1 \times 2^4 + 1 \times 2^3 + 1 \times 2^2 + 1 \times 2^1 + 0$$
$$= 32 + 16 + 8 + 4 + 2$$
$$= 62.$$

Example 3.9

The value of 0.502_8 in decimal is

$$0.n = 5 \times 8^{-1} + 0 + 2 \times 8^{-3}$$
$$= 0.6250 + 0.003906250$$
$$= 0.62890625_{10}$$

as determined by Equation 3.4 or Equation 3.14.

Conversion from decimal to any number base. To convert a decimal number by hand to a number in another base, it is convenient to work in the decimal system with the series representation of the number. Conversion of a positive integer is accomplished by repeated division by the new radix using successive remainders as digits in the new system. A fraction is converted by repeated multiplication by the radix, with the resulting integer parts of the products taken as digits of the result.

Example 3.10

To convert 3964_{10} to octal, the number is repeatedly divided by 8, as follows:

$$3964/8 = 495 + (4/8)$$
$$495/8 = 61 + (7/8)$$
$$61/8 = 7 + (5/8)$$
$$7/8 = 0 + (7/8).$$

The remainders of each division, represented by the numerators of each fraction, are digits in the resulting answer. The order of these digits is the reverse of the order in which they were obtained. Thus, in the example above,

$$3964_{10} = 7574_8.$$

Example 3.11

The number 0.78125_{10} is converted to a hexadecimal fraction as follows:

$$0.78125 \times 16 = 12.0 + 0.5$$
$$0.5 \times 16 = 8.0 + 0.$$

The result is therefore $0.78125_{10} = 0.C8_{16}$.

To understand the theory of these conversions, write Equation 3.14 in the form

$$N = ((\cdots((d_{m-1}r + d_{m-2})r + d_{m-3})r + \cdots + d_1)r + d_0)$$

for the integer part and set it equal to the decimal value it represents. Then divide N by the base desired. Using 8 as the base in Example 3.10, the first remainder is the octal value d_0. Continuing to divide the whole numbers (quotients) by the base successively yields $d_0, d_1, d_2, \ldots, d_{m-1}$ in that order. Try the fractional part of Equation 3.14 in a similar manner with negative powers of r to see how the value in Example 3.11 was computed.

Conversion of a number from any base to another.   A number written in base r_1 can be converted to a number in base r_2 by performing the arithmetic operations in a base other than decimal. For human computation a more acceptable method is to convert the selected number to decimal from base r_1 and then convert the result from decimal to base r_2.

Example 3.12

Converting 112_3 to base 5 is accomplished by converting 112_3 to decimal:

$$1 \times 3^2 + 1 \times 3^1 + 2 = 9 + 3 + 2 = 14_{10}.$$

Then, the decimal number 14 is converted to base 5 in the form

$$14/5 = 2 + (4/5)$$
$$2/5 = 0 + (2/5)$$

or $14_{10} = 24_5$. Thus $112_3 = 24_5$.

Conversion of positive numbers with bases that are powers of 2.   If the relationship between a number base r_1 and another base r_2 is of the form

$$r_2 = r_1^L$$

where L is a positive or negative integer, conversion between the bases is particularly simple using positional notation. In particular, since the binary, octal, and hexadecimal bases are related as

$$16 = 2^4$$
$$8 = 2^3$$

the conversion from binary to octal or binary to hexadecimal requires only the grouping of the binary digits by threes or fours, respectively. The conversion from octal to binary or hexadecimal to binary requires that each octal or hexadecimal digit be replaced by its binary equivalent.

Conversion between octal and hexadecimal numbers is best accomplished by using the binary representation as an intermediate step since the bases 8 and 16 are not related.

Example 3.13

Conversion of the binary number 1011 0111.0010 1_2 to octal requires grouping the digits by threes, starting with the least significant or rightmost binary digit for the integer portion but starting with the most significant or leftmost digit for the fractional portion. Thus, the conversion proceeds as

$$(010)(110)(111).(001)(010) = 267.12_8$$

where extra binary digits of zero were added at each end to yield legitimate octal digits before conversion.

Conversion of negative numbers from binary to decimal. The conversion of a positive binary number to decimal is easily achieved by the power series method shown previously. The conversion of negative numbers in one's-complement or two's-complement notation can also be achieved in this manner when the sign bit is given the proper decimal value or weight. As an example, consider the following negative numbers in 8-bit two's-complement representation and their decimal equivalents:

$$1111\ 1111_2 = -1$$
$$1111\ 1110_2 = -2$$
$$.$$
$$.$$
$$.$$
$$1000\ 0001_2 = -127$$
$$1000\ 0000_2 = -128.$$

By associating the leading digit with $-2^7(-128)$ and adding the positive positional value of the remaining digits, the proper decimal value results. Thus, the decimal value of an 8-bit negative number in two's-complement notation is

$$-2^7 + d_6 \times 2^6 + d_5 \times 2^5 + \cdots + d_0$$

when the negative number in its positional form is

$$(1d_6d_5d_4 \cdots d_0)_2.$$

By inspecting the positive values, the general case for both positive and negative two's complement numbers may be derived to compute the decimal equivalent as

$$N = -d_{m-1} \times 2^{m-1} + \sum_{i=0}^{m-2} d_i \times 2^i \tag{3.15}$$

with $d_{m-1} = 0$ for a positive value or $d_{m-1} = 1$ when the number is negative. From this equation, the 8-bit number $1000\ 0010_2$ has the decimal value

$$N = -2^7 + 0 + \cdots + 1 \times 2^1 + 0 = -126$$

with sign bit $d_7 = 1$. The number $0000\ 0010_2$ with $d_7 = 0$ has the value

$$-0 \times 2^7 + 0 + \cdots + 1 \times 2^1 + 0 = +2.$$

In essence, Equation 3.15 represents a compact notation for computation of the decimal value of an m-bit number in the two's-complement system. The decimal weights of the leading digit for one's-complement and two's-complement integers and fractions are given in Table 3.3. The magnitude of a sign-magnitude number is simply multiplied by $+1$ or -1 according to its sign.

Table 3.3 Values of the Sign Bit

	Weight in decimal	
Representation	Integer (m bits)	Fraction (k bits with sign)
One's complement	$1 - 2^{m-1}$	$2^{1-m} - 1$
Two's complement	-2^{m-1}	-1

Example 3.14

(a) The integer $1000\ 0011_2$ in sign-magnitude notation has the value

$$(-1)(0 \times 2^6 + \cdots + 1 \times 2^1 + 1 \times 2^0) = -3_{10}$$

since the magnitude is multiplied by -1.

(b) The number $1111\ 1001_2$ in one's-complement notation has the value

$$(1 - 2^7) + (1 \times 2^6 + 1 \times 2^5 + 1 \times 2^4 + 1 \times 2^3 + 1 \times 2^0)$$
$$= -127 + 121 = -6_{10}$$

using the weight for the leading bit shown in Table 3.3.

(c) The two's complement number $1111\ 1001_2$ has the value

$$-2^7 + (1 \times 2^6 + 1 \times 2^5 + 1 \times 2^4 + 1 \times 2^3 + 1)$$
$$= -128 + 121 = -7_{10}.$$

Example 3.15

(a) The fraction $1.001\ 0000_2$ in sign-magnitude notation has the value

$$(-1)(0 \times 2^{-1} + 0 \times 2^{-2} + 1 \times 2^{-3})$$
$$= -0.125_{10}.$$

(b) The fraction $1.100\ 1111_2$ in one's-complement notation has the value

$$(2^{-7} - 1) + 1 \times 2^{-1} + 1 \times 2^{-4} + 1 \times 2^{-5} + 1 \times 2^{-6}$$
$$+ 1 \times 2^{-7}) = -0.375_{10}.$$

EXERCISES

3.1.3.1. Convert the following numbers as indicated:
   (a) 1024_{10} to binary;
   (b) 53000_{10} to hexadecimal;
   (c) $FFFF\ FFFF_{16}$ to decimal;
   (d) 35_{10} to base 5.

3.1.3.2. Convert the repeating octal fraction $(0.333\ldots)_8$ to decimal.

3.1.3.3. Show that adding 1 to the complement form of the positive number N yields the radix-complement representation $r^m - |N|$ for an m-digit number.

3.1.3.4. Convert the fraction $1.111\ 1111_2$ in two's-complement notation to its decimal value.

3.1.3.5. Using two's-complement representation, represent numbers in the range -2, $-1\frac{3}{4}, \ldots, 1\frac{1}{2}, 1\frac{3}{4}$.

3.2 BINARY-CODED DECIMAL

Many microcomputers provide instructions to perform arithmetic operations on data considered as decimal numbers. This is convenient for business processing and in representing data that are inherently decimal in nature. Thumb-wheel switches, for example, may present an output as a decimal digit encoded in binary to represent a selected digit on the switch. Many displays are designed to receive encoded decimal digits and display the result in decimal.

One decimal coding system is the *binary-coded decimal* or BCD system. In the BCD system, the first 10 binary numbers correspond to decimal digits. This is sometimes called the "natural" binary-coded decimal system.

This section discusses the binary-coded decimal system and various conversion operations with BCD numbers. The use of ten's-complement notation is convenient to represent negative BCD values, although other representations are possible. Only ten's complement is discussed here since it is the method assumed by addition and subtraction of signed decimal values performed by the MC68332 processor, as treated in Chapter 7.

3.2.1 BCD Representation of Positive Integers

In many applications, particularly those involving financial transactions, a true representation of decimal numbers in a machine that operates on binary digits is desirable. Since any decimal digit can be represented by four binary digits, it is natural to select a binary code in which four binary digits are used for each decimal digit. Such a code is shown in Table 3.4, which lists the binary-coded decimal (BCD) representation. The possible binary values 1010_2 through 1111_2 are not used since the decimal values 10 through 15 require two BCD digits for their representation.

Each decimal digit has the value

$$D_i = b_{i3} \times 2^3 + b_{i2} \times 2^2 + b_{i1} \times 2^1 + b_{i0} \tag{3.16}$$

Table 3.4 Binary-Coded
Decimal Values

BCD	Binary
0	0000
1	0001
2	0010
3	0011
4	0100
5	0101
6	0110
7	0111
8	1000
9	1001

where b_{ij} is the jth binary digit in the representation of the ith decimal digit. The value of the L-digit BCD number is calculated in decimal as

$$N = D_{L-1} \times 10^{L-1} + D_{L-2} \times 10^{L-2} + \cdots + D_0 \qquad (3.17)$$

where each D_i is formed as shown in Equation 3.16. The decimal value 95, for example, would be coded into binary as

$$1001\ 0101_2$$

and it is stored in this form. Using Equation 3.16, we have

$$D_0 = 1 \times 2^2 + 1 = 5$$

and

$$D_1 = 1 \times 2^3 + 1 = 9.$$

Numbers in BCD can be added or subtracted by CPU32 instructions that perform decimal arithmetic. Therefore, the programmer does not need to be concerned with the internal representation. It is only when conversions between BCD numbers and other representations are required that the internal format must be considered.

Example 3.16

The binary number
$$0001\ 0111\ 0011\ 1001$$

has the BCD value

$$N = 1 \times 10^3 + 7 \times 10^2 + 3 \times 10^1 + 9 = 1739.$$

The 16 binary digits encoded as positive BCD numbers have a range of only $0 \leq N \leq 9999$.

Example 3.17

Microcontrollers that perform arithmetic operations on 8-bit (byte) and longer operands may allow such operations on "packed" BCD integers, as the CPU32 does. In this representation, two BCD digits are contained in each 8-bit value rather than storing each BCD digit in a separate byte (called *unpacked notation*).

The BCD number 3475 may be treated for the purposes of machine calculation as either packed BCD or unpacked as follows:

	Decimal value	Memory (binary)
Packed	34	0011 0100
	75	0111 0101
Unpacked	03	0000 0011
	04	0000 0100
	07	0000 0111
	05	0000 0101

In the unpacked representation, the single digit is shown in a byte location with a leading 0 since the CPU32 and most other processors address memory locations containing 8 bits. The unpacked format is typically used when algorithms to perform multiplication or division of BCD numbers are employed.

EXERCISES

3.2.1.1. Show the internal machine representation (binary) of the following positive numbers in packed BCD format:
   (a) 07;
   (b) 13;
   (c) 99.

3.2.1.2. Determine the decimal values of the following positive numbers coded in BCD format:
   (a) $0001\ 1001\ 0111\ 0000_2$;
   (b) $0001\ 1111_2$.

3.2.1.3. Assuming that the representation is packed BCD, compute the decimal range for the positive BCD representation of numbers using:
   (a) 8 bits;
   (b) 16 bits;
   (c) 32 bits.

3.2.1.4. Describe the test required to assure that an out-of-range condition is detected when two positive BCD integers are added (subtracted). Assume that the maximum length is L decimal digits for each BCD integer. The CPU32 has built-in hardware (condition codes) for detecting these conditions.

3.2.2 Conversion between BCD and Binary

When the machine representations as binary sequences are required, arithmetic in base 2 instead of base 10 is convenient with the CPU32. This allows a program to take advantage of its multiply and divide instructions to perform the binary arithmetic. Thus the conversion of the positive BCD number

$$(D_{L-1} D_{L-2} \cdots D_0)$$

can be accomplished by first writing Equation 3.17 in the form

$$N = (\cdots((D_{L-1}) \times 10 + D_{L-2}) \times 10 + \cdots + D_1) \times 10 + D_0.$$

Converting all the digits to binary yields an equation useful for machine implementation. The binary value of the BCD number is then

$$N_2 = (\cdots((D_{L-1}) \times 1010_2 + D_{L-2}) \times 1010_2 + \cdots + D_1) \times 1010_2 + D_0$$

where 1010_2 is 10 decimal and the digits D_i are used in their 4-bit binary form. First, the most significant digit is multiplied by 1010_2, then the next most significant digit is added and the sum multiplied by 1010_2, and so on, until the last digit D_0 is added. The result is an m-digit binary representation of the BCD number. Programming the conversion equation is simple using the CPU32 instruction set. BCD values are sometimes converted to binary for machine processing since the CPU has an extensive set of instructions that operate on binary numbers but relatively few to manipulate BCD integers.

When it is necessary to convert binary numbers to BCD representation, the conversion is accomplished by repeated division by 10 (binary 1010). Each remainder is a BCD digit starting with the low-order digit. This is frequently done before internal binary numbers are output for display as a decimal value.

Example 3.18

Using base 2 arithmetic, 99 in BCD is converted to binary as

$$N_2 = 1001 \times 1010 + 1001 = 0110\ 0011.$$

Example 3.19

The binary number $0010\ 0100_2$ is converted to the machine representation of BCD equivalent using binary arithmetic for division as follows:

$$\frac{0010\ 0100}{1010} = 0011 + (0110)$$

$$\frac{0011}{1010} = 0 + (0011)$$

Here the remainders in parentheses represent the binary sequence

$$0011\ 0110$$

which is 36 as a decimal equivalent.

EXERCISES

3.2.2.1. Convert 1000 0000$_2$ to BCD by repeatedly dividing by 1010$_2$ in binary.

3.2.2.2. Convert the BCD number 509 to binary using both base 10 and base 2 arithmetic.

3.2.2.3. Consider the multiplication of numbers in BCD representation. Devise an algorithm to multiply a multidigit BCD value by a single-digit multiplier, assuming that only binary multiplication is possible and the digits are in unpacked form. Further assume that a BCD addition instruction is available to sum the partial results.

3.2.3 Negative BCD Integers

The CPU32 has instructions to perform arithmetic on BCD numbers represented in ten's-complement notation. As described in Section 3.1, the ten's complement of a decimal number N is formed by

$$N' = 10^L - N \tag{3.18}$$

when L digits are used to represent the number. For hand calculation, the ten's complement is easily formed by complementing the number digit by digit (nine's-complement) and adding 1 to the result.

Example 3.20

The ten's complement of 1319 in a five-digit representation is

$$N' = 100,000 - 1319 = (99,999 - 1319) + 1 = 98,681.$$

The BCD representation in memory would be

$$1001\ 1000\ 0110\ 1000\ 0001_2.$$

Example 3.21

The ten's complement of a number can also be formed by subtracting it from 0 and ignoring the high-order borrow. Thus, the ten's complement of 98,681 is

$$0 - 98,681 = 01319$$

as shown. The CPU32 instruction NBCD (negate decimal) performs this operation to form the ten's complement of a number.

EXERCISES

3.2.3.1. Determine the machine representation (binary) of the following signed BCD numbers with a word length of 16 bits:
   (a) 124;
   (b) −1;
   (c) −1000;
   (d) 5024.

3.2.3.2. What is the range of a signed BCD number that can be represented by m binary digits for the following:
   (a) $m = 8$;
   (b) $m = 16$;
   (c) $m = 32$;
   when the positive value is restricted to the maximum value of $10^L − 1$ for L decimal digits?

3.2.3.3. Show that the nine's complement of a BCD digit can be formed by adding 6 and then forming the one's complement of the result in binary notation.

3.3 FLOATING-POINT REPRESENTATION

The representation for numbers that we considered previously assumed that the radix point was located in a fixed position, yielding either an integer or a fraction as the interpretation of the internal machine representation. The programmer's responsibility would be to scale numerical operands to fit within a selected word length and then unscale the results to obtain the correct values. Of course, the radix point is not actually stored with the number, but its position must be remembered by the programmer. This method of representation is called *fixed point*.

In practice, the machine value is limited to a finite range which is determined by the number of binary digits used in the representation. For a 32-bit word, the range of signed fixed-point integers is about $+2^{31}$ or $+10^{11}$. Thus, the limited range of fixed-point notation is a drawback for certain applications. Furthermore, arithmetic units operating on fixed-point numbers generally have no capability of rounding results. As discussed in several references in the Further Reading section for this chapter, this limits the usefulness of fixed-point notation in scientific computing.

To overcome many of the limitations of fixed-point notation, a notation that is the counterpart of scientific notation is used for numbers in digital systems. The *floating-point* notation represents a number as a fractional part times a selected base raised to a power. In the machine representation, only the fractional part and the value of the exponent are stored. The decimal equivalent is written as

$$N.n = f \times r^e \tag{3.19}$$

where f is the fraction or *mantissa* and e is a positive or negative integer called the *exponent*. The choice for the base is usually 2, although base 16 is sometimes used.

A number of choices are presented to the designer of a floating-point format. This applies whether the arithmetic operations are carried out by the CPU or its coprocessor directly or by a software package containing routines for floating-point arithmetic. The number of formats is bewildering and only recently has an attempt been made to standardize floating-point arithmetic for computers.

The proposed IEEE standard has been adopted by Motorola for a number of their products. This IEEE standard describes precisely the data formats and other aspects of floating-point arithmetic required to provide consistent operation of a program even when it is executed on different computer systems.

3.3.1 Floating-Point Formats

The typical floating-point format stores the fraction and the exponent together in an m-bit representation. The choice for a fixed-length floating-point format is commonly 32 or 64 bits, referred to as single precision and double precision, respectively. Extended formats with $m \geq 64$ are occasionally used when greater range or precision is required.

Once the length of the floating-point representation is chosen, a number of choices for both the length and the format of the fraction and exponent are possible. Since either or both could be negative as well as positive, a signed fraction and a signed exponent are required. Finally, the interpretation of the bits within the floating-point representation depends on the placement of the fraction and exponent.

Many floating-point formats employ a sign-magnitude representation for the fraction. The most significant bit of the word is reserved for the sign, and this facilitates testing for a positive or negative number. The fraction is generally normalized to yield as many significant digits as possible. Thus, in a base r system, the most significant digit is in the leftmost position in the fraction. For nonzero numbers in the binary system, the leftmost digit will be a 1. As the arithmetic unit or the program shifts the digits in the fraction during arithmetic operations, the exponent is adjusted accordingly. When normalized as a base 2 value, the magnitude of the fraction is

$$0.5 \leq |f| < 1 \tag{3.20}$$

unless the number is zero. The number of digits reserved for the fraction represents a compromise between the precision of the fraction and the range of the exponent. A typical single-precision format (32 bits) might contain an 8-bit exponent and a 23-bit fraction, excluding sign.

An exponent could be represented in two's complement or any other notation that allows signed values. A different alternative, which permits the exponent to be represented internally as a positive number only, is to add an offset value. This value is often called an *excess*. For this format, positive bias or offset is added to all exponents such that the number is read as

$$N.n = fr^{e' - N_b} \tag{3.21}$$

where e' is the actual value of the stored exponent and N_b is the positive offset. For an L-bit exponent in a binary base, the positive number added is usually of the form

$$N_b = 2^{L-1} \tag{3.22}$$

although the IEEE standard format discussed later uses a value of $N_b - 1$.

Example 3.22

One IBM floating-point format has the following representation for a 32-bit word:

(a) sign as the most significant bit (leftmost bit);
(b) next 7 bits as exponent with excess-64 or 40_{16} with radix 16;
(c) next 24 bits as fraction in base 16.

Thus $+1.0$ is represented as

$$(0.1)_{16} \times 16^1$$

for which the stored exponent becomes 41_{16}. The internal representation is

$$4110\ 0000_{16}.$$

Example 3.23

One PDP-11 (Digital Equipment Corporation) floating-point format uses the following conventions in a 32-bit word:

(a) sign as the most significant bit (leftmost bit);
(b) next 8 bits as exponent in excess-128 notation with radix 2;
(c) next 23 bits as fraction. These 23 bits are derived from a 24-bit fraction always normalized (i.e., the leftmost bit will be a 1 in a nonzero number). The most significant bit of the normalized fraction is not stored since it is always 1.

The representation of $+12$ is thus

$$0.11_2 \times 2^{132-128}$$

and is represented internally as

$$0\ 1000\ 0100\ 1000\ 0000\ 0000\ 0000\ 0000\ 000_2.$$

Notice that the leading bit of the fraction is a 1 and it is not stored with the floating-point number. This has been termed a *hidden bit* and would be restored by a floating-point hardware processor when the value is processed.

EXERCISES

3.3.1.1. Discuss the various factors that influence the choice of the exponent length, mantissa length, and choice of radix in a floating-point number. Compute the various ranges for a choice of an L-bit exponent in excess notation, a k-bit fraction, and a total length of m bits.

3.3.1.2. Express $1/32$ in binary floating-point representation using an 8-bit excess-128 exponent and a 24-bit fraction with the leading bit implied. The order in the word from left to right is sign, exponent, and then fraction (PDP-11).

3.3.1.3. Convert the numbers indicated to a 32-bit floating-point representation with the characteristics: the leading bit (bit 31) is the sign of the number; the next

Table 3.5 Internal Format by Bit Number

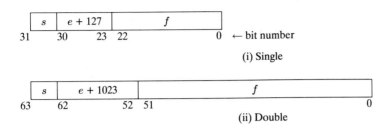

(i) Single

(ii) Double

9 bits are the exponent in excess-256 notation and following bits are 22 bits
of fraction; and a negative number is represented as the integer's two's complement of the positive floating-point number.
(a) $+16.0$;   **(b)** -1.0.

3.3.2 Standard Floating-Point Format

Although the Motorola MC68332 processor does not provide floating-point instructions, many Motorola products support the standard floating-point format proposed
by the IEEE. These products include software routines, routines in read-only memory, and a coprocessor chip to support floating-point arithmetic for the M68000 family
processors.

The basic format allows a floating-point number to be represented in single or
32-bit format as

$$N.n = (-1)^S 2^{e'-127}(1.f) \tag{3.23}$$

where S is the sign bit, e' is the biased exponent, and f is the fraction stored normalized without the leading 1. Internally, the exponent is 8 bits in length and the stored
fraction is 23 bits long. A double-precision format allows a 64-bit representation with
a 11-bit exponent and a 52-bit fraction. Table 3.5 shows the format pictorially.

Various features of these floating-point formats are presented in Table 3.5 and
Table 3.6. Other formats called extended-precision formats are presented in the references in the Further Reading section of this chapter.

Example 3.24

The numbers $+1.0$, $+3.0$, and -1.0 have the following representation in the standard
32-bit format:

(a) Since $1.0 = 1.0 \times 2^0$, the internal value is $3F80\ 0000_{16}$.
(b) Since $3.0 = 1.5 \times 2^1$, the exponent is 128 and the fraction is 1.100_2 without the
    leading 1. Thus, the internal value is $4040\ 0000_{16}$.
(c) Since $-1 = -1.0 \times 2^0$, the result requires the sign bit to be 1 in the representation
    $BF80\ 0000_{16}$.

Table 3.6 IEEE Standard Floating-Point Notation

	Single	Double
Length in bits		
Sign	1	1
Exponent	8	11
Fraction	23 + (1)	52 + (1)
Total	$m = 32 + (1)$	$m = 64 + (1)$
Exponent		
Max e'	255	2047
Min e'	0	0
Bias	127	1023

Note:
Fractions are always normalized and the leading 1 (hidden bit) is not stored.

EXERCISES

3.3.2.1. Write the internal machine representation for the following numbers in the standard floating-point single-precision format:
(a) 0.5;   (b) −0.5;   (c) 2^{-126}.

3.3.2.2. What is the decimal value of the largest positive number that may be represented in single-precision standard format if the biased exponent is limited to a maximum of 254 when a valid number is being represented? (The value 255 is reserved for special operands.)

3.3.2.3. Express the following numbers in the internal representation using standard double-precision floating-point format:
(a) 7.0;   (b) −30.

3.4 ASCII REPRESENTATION OF ALPHANUMERIC CHARACTERS

Since m binary digits can represent 2^m distinct states, it is possible to assign a meaning to each possible combination of the m digits to produce a code that represents alphanumeric, numeric, or other information. One of the major uses of codes is to allow human-readable input or output data to be manipulated internally by the computer. These internal binary representations are seldom desired as output except possibly for debugging purposes. Thus, most computer systems will have routines (or hardware) to convert internal binary codes to readable form, and vice versa.

The code used by Motorola to represent alphanumeric characters is the ASCII (American Standard Code for Information Interchange) code, which is given in Appendix I of this book. The 7-bit codes shown in the appendix are the hexadecimal values of the ASCII characters as the values would be stored in memory. For example, the ASCII value "1" would be stored as 31_{16} or $0011\ 0001_2$.

Numbers, letters and special characters recognized by the assembler and other

Motorola system programs are stored internally in the ASCII code as 8-bit values in which one byte is used to represent one character. On output devices such as CRT terminals or line printers, the ASCII code is transmitted unchanged. If the internal values are in binary or BCD, they must be converted to ASCII format before output for external devices that require ASCII. References in the Further Reading section give a number of examples of such conversions useful to the assembly-language programmer. Programs for this purpose are given in Chapter 7 of this book.

A number of other codes are available for computer applications, each with special characteristics and advantages. Several of the references for this chapter discuss codes in more detail. Mackenzie, in particular, gives a comprehensive discussion of many of the commonly used codes and a complete presentation for the ASCII code.

Example 3.25

The ASCII character string 'INPUT' has the following representation:

$$49 \ 4E \ 50 \ 55 \ 54$$

where each two digits (in hexadecimal) represent one alphabetic character.

EXERCISES

3.4.1. How many bytes of memory are required to store the text of a textbook with 100,000 words if the text is stored in ASCII code? Assume five characters per word. If a MC68332 system memory contains 2^{24} bytes, what percentage of the memory is used by the text?

3.4.2. Convert the following text into ASCII code (internal hexadecimal representation):
"THE MOTOROLA MC68332"

3.4.3. Show the machine representation of the number 255 in the following ways:
(a) binary;
(b) Binary-Coded Decimal;
(c) ASCII.

3.4.4. Define the method and convert the following as directed:
(a) 45 (BCD) to binary;
(b) 45 (BCD) to ASCII;
(c) −45 (BCD in ten's-complement notation) to ASCII assuming a three-digit BCD number with sign.

3.4.5. Can a single binary variable be used to represent the Morse code?

FURTHER READING

The books by Stein and Munro, Hwang, and Sterbenz listed here present a highly mathematical view of number representations. Sterbenz concentrates on floating-point notation. The articles in *IEEE Computer* are recommended for information on the IEEE standard format.

Weller presents a number of conversion techniques between the data types of use to the assembly language programmer. The design of computer hardware and the use of various number representations for arithmetic operations is discussed by Abd-Alla and Meltzer. Mackenzie discusses the details of a large number of codes for representation of characters.

ABD-ALLA, ABD-ELFATTAH M., and ARNOLD C. MELTZER, *Principles of Digital Computer Design*, Vol 1. Englewood Cliffs, N. J.: Prentice Hall, 1976. (Chapter 4 presents a number of codes.)

COONEN, JEROME T., "An Implementation Guide to a Proposal Standard for Floating Point Arithmetic," *IEEE Computer*, **13**, No. 1 (January 1980), 68–79.

HWANG, KAI, *Computer Arithmetic*. New York, NY.: Wiley, 1979.

IEEE Computer, **14**, No. 3 (March 1981). (Several articles in this issue discuss the floating-point standard.) The standard itself is ANSI/IEEE Std 754–1985.

MACKENZIE, CHARLES E., *Coded Character Sets: History and Development*. Reading, Mass.: Addison-Wesley, 1971.

STEIN, MARVIN L., and WILLIAM D. MUNRO, *Introduction to Machine Arithmetic*. Reading, Mass.: Addison-Wesley, 1971.

STERBENZ, PAT H., *Floating-Point Computation*. Englewood Cliffs, N. J.: Prentice Hall, 1974.

WELLER, WALTER J., *Assembly Language Programming for Small Computers*. Lexington, Mass.: Lexington Books, 1975.

4

Introduction to the MC68332

4.0   INTRODUCTION

The characteristics of the MC68332 as a circuit element and as a programmable processor are introduced in this chapter. These characteristics are of interest to the product designer, programmer, and interface designer. For the most part, the terminology used follows that employed by Motorola in its literature. Figure 4.1 is a block diagram of the functional signal groups belonging to the modules of the MC68332. The reader is encouraged to review the description of the MC68332 in Chapter 2 which defines the operation of each module. After introducing the integrated circuit chip in this chapter, we discuss the programming and other features of the CPU. The MC68332 CPU will be frequently designated as the CPU32 for brevity in this textbook.

The instructions that the processor executes are coded in machine-language format in memory. These instructions may be created by a programmer coding these binary sequences directly. More likely, an assembler program translates assembly-language statements written in symbolic notation into machine-language instructions. The assembly language programmer rarely works directly with the machine-language program, but a knowledge of the machine-language formats is necessary for a full understanding of the processor's capability.

This chapter introduces the MC68332 as an integrated circuit. Various sections describe the register set, instruction set, and addressing modes, all of which define the programming model of the processor. The machine language of the CPU32 is also

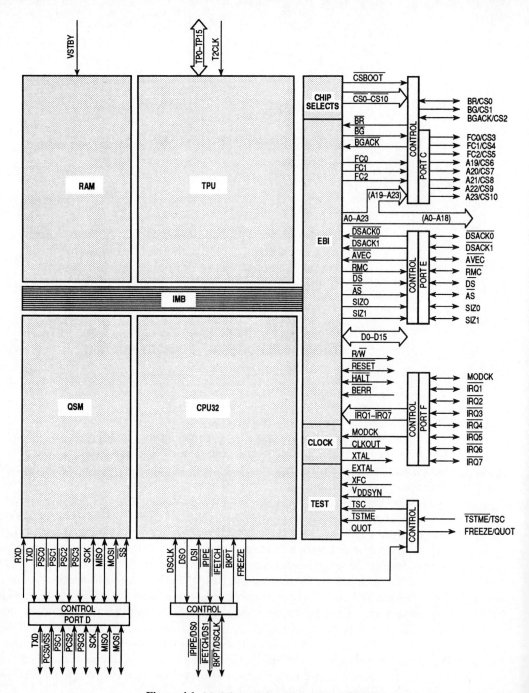

Figure 4.1 Modules and signal lines of the MC68332.

Introduction to the MC68332 Chap. 4

presented, to illustrate the correspondence between the bit patterns of the instructions and the operation of the processor. The chapter concludes with a presentation of the organization of memory in an MC68332-based product or system.

4.1 THE MC68332 AS AN INTEGRATED-CIRCUIT PROCESSOR

The patent for one of the first integrated circuits was filed by Jack Kilby of Texas Instruments in 1959 for a device that was equivalent to several transistors and associated components.[1] According to Motorola, the MC68332 has approximately 422,000 components that are integrated on a piece of silicon smaller than Kilby's device. Improvements in the manufacturing technology of integrated circuits over more than 20 years have resulted in a steady increase in the packing density of a chip as measured by the number of circuit elements per unit area. There has also been an increase in the speed of operation and a lowering of power consumption per element.

Once the chip is produced, it must be packaged in a form suitable for inclusion with other integrated circuits on a printed-circuit board. The MC68332, for example, is sold in a standard package with 132 pins to connect to other components in a product. The function of the signal lines and the total power consumption of the MCU as well as the mechanical attributes of the package influence the electrical and mechanical design of a product.

4.1.1 The MC68332 as an Integrated Circuit

The MC68332 is characterized as a Very Large Scale Integration (VLSI) device since thousands of circuit elements are contained on a single silicon chip. Circuit elements, such as transistors and resistors, are connected to form the control, storage, and interfacing circuitry of the chip itself. Figure 4.2 shows the MC68332 enlarged before it is packaged. The various regions and modules of the chip are designated in the figure. The actual microcontroller when packaged is about 1 inch on each side.

The method of constructing a chip is referred to as the *technology*. The name given to a particular technology broadly indicates the type of transistors (bipolar or field-effect), the fabrication procedure involved, and the characteristics of the finished device. The characteristics of integrated circuits produced by various technologies have different densities of elements per unit area, different speeds of operation, and different power consumptions.[2] Integrated circuits utilizing field-effect transistors, for example, are called metal-oxide-semiconductor (MOS) devices since they are physically constructed with three regions using different materials (metal, an oxide of silicon, and the silicon substrate or bulk region). Several transistors are combined with other circuit elements to form a cell. Each cell might hold 1 bit of information, for example.

The technology for the MC68332 is called high-speed complementary metal-oxide-semiconductor (HCMOS) technology. This technique modifies and scales down

---

[1] Jack Kilby and Robert Noyce are considered co-inventors of the integrated circuit.
[2] Integrated circuits are fabricated using several other technologies. Besides the HCMOS process used for the MC68332, the *bipolar* and the *complementary* MOS (CMOS) technologies are popular.

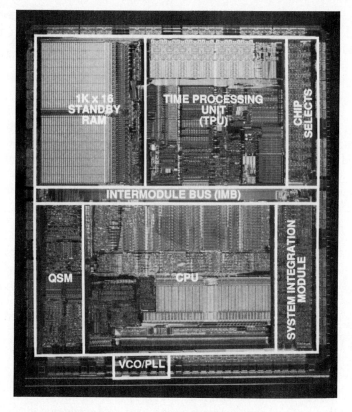

Figure 4.2 Enlarged photograph of the MC68332 chip.

the size of elements compared to the standard MOS process to increase the speed and reduce the power consumption for each transistor in the MCU.

4.1.2 Packaging, Signal Lines, and Power

The microprocessors and other integrated circuits produced by Motorola are available in a number of different physical packages. The MC68332 with 132 signal lines packaged in a plastic leaded chip carrier (PLCC) is shown in Figures 4.4. The packaging method determines the size and mechanical strength of the completed chip. A specific package also influences the amount of heat that can be dissipated from the chip. However, the technology used to fabricate the chip itself determines the power consumption of the finished microcontroller.

Packaging. A final step in the manufacture of an integrated-circuit MCU is packaging the device. The silicon chip, shown enlarged in Figure 4.2, is inserted into a protective case called its *package* so it can be protected from the environment and connected electrically to other elements in a system. The type of package influences the cost, operating temperature range, size, mechanical strength, and similar properties

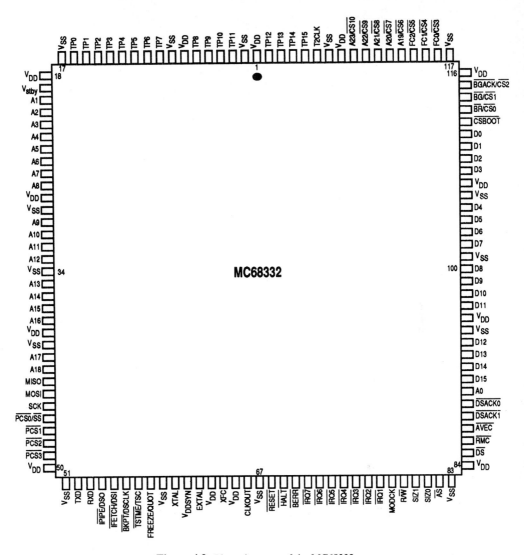

Figure 4.3 Pin assignment of the MC68332.

of the completed product. Figure 4.3 shows the pin assignments for the MC68332. Figure 4.4 is a picture of the MC68332 package ready to be inserted on a printed-circuit board for connection to other components in the product. The PLCC package in Figure 4.4 is approximately 1in. (25mm) on a side.

Signal lines for the MC68332. Figure 4.1 shows a functional diagram of the MC68332 signal lines. The 132 signal lines control the operation of data transfers, interrupt requests, and similar operations. These signal lines originate in the silicon chip and are connected to the pins of the PLCC package. The pins thus form the

Figure 4.4 PLCC package.

electrical connection between the actual silicon chip of the MC68332 and the external system bus of the printed-circuit board on which the package is mounted. Chapter 14 describes the signal lines of the MC68332 in detail.

Power consumption. The PLCC version of the MC68332 has a power consumption of about 0.6 watts. In a computer with hundreds of integrated circuits, the power consumption, and consequently the heat generated, may be excessive. As it is a fact that excessive heating is a major cause of chip failure, forced-air ventilation may be necessary even in a system with a few printed-circuit boards and an apparently low power consumption. Power consumption in MC68332-based products is discussed further in Chapter 15.

4.1.3 Processor Design

As with many microprocessors, the circuit-level operation of the CPU32 is controlled by a *microprogrammed* sequence of instructions stored in ROM sections within the CPU. As machine-language instructions from external memory are fetched and decoded, they, in turn, cause the execution of a microprogram. This microprogram controls all activity on the external signal lines and all the data transfers or operations within the CPU during the execution of that instruction. Since the microprogram cannot be modified except by creating a new chip with different microcode, the user is rarely concerned with the details of the processor operations at this level. However, understanding the microcode is the only way to determine exactly what the processor is doing in response to an instruction.

Figure 4.5(a) represents a simplified block diagram of the major internal sections of the MC68332 CPU. The elements shown constitute a functional view of the CPU rather than a physical representation as was pictured in Figure 4.2. The CPU32 was designed for maximum performance as measured by its rate of instruction execution.

It allows parallel (concurrent) operation of various sections within the CPU. The instruction prefetch and decode section contains a "pipeline" with three stages shown in Figure 4.5(b). All of these elements of the CPU were designed by Motorola engineers to allow the CPU32 to execute the maximum number of instructions per second using techniques frequently employed in the design of modern central processing units.[3]

The instruction prefetch and decode unit of the CPU consists of a three-stage pipeline to validate, interpret, and decode instructions. Three 16-bit instructions or three 16-bit words of a single instruction can be held in the pipeline. As shown in Figure 4.5(b), the pipeline is loaded from main memory by the bus controller. The bus controller can prefetch instructions from the on-chip memory or main memory to keep the pipeline full. At each stage, the instruction is further decoded until the instruction is fully decoded in stage C. It is then ready for execution. Overall processing time for a series of instructions is reduced with the pipeline since processing of a new instruction introduced into the pipeline can begin before the previous ones are fully completed. In effect, portions of different instructions can be processed in parallel.

The CPU32 with its pipeline and highly parallel internal architecture is capable of executing a new instruction every two clock cycles if the instructions reside in on-chip memory. However, the possible overlap in instruction execution times and the prefetch capability make it difficult to predict the processor's operation on a cycle-by-cycle basis for the purpose of making timing estimates for a program. Chapter 15 presents timing considerations for the MC68332.

Example 4.1

According to Motorola designers, the M68000 family processors use microprogrammed CPUs to simplify design, modification, and testing of the product line. In this scheme each machine-language instruction is emulated by a sequence of micro-instructions.

One important benefit of the microprogrammed processors to the manufacturer is that different members of the family can execute the same instruction if the microcode is common to the processors in the family. The CPU32 thus executes the machine-language instructions of the 16-bit MC68000 without modification. Of course, the converse is not true since the CPU32 has instructions that are additional to those of the MC68000.

Finally, microprogrammed instructions are provided in the CPU32 ROM for testing the CPU. These test routines can test logic paths and circuits in the CPU at a level that is inaccessible by machine-language instructions. Such testing is required during production of the CPU to assure that the chip is functioning properly.

The purpose of the pipelined internal architecture of the CPU32 is to allow the processor to execute instructions at a faster rate. In most cases, pipelining increases the number of instructions executed per second as compared to executing instructions with no overlapping in time. However, the system operation must proceed as if a series of program instructions are executed without overlap. Since the typical program is written assuming that one instruction completes before the next is started, the CPU is designed to prevent any conflicts caused by internal overlapping. For all practical purposes, the CPU32 can be viewed as executing a sequence of instructions in sequential

---

[3] The design of a CPU with a pipeline is discussed in several references in the Further Reading section of this Chapter.

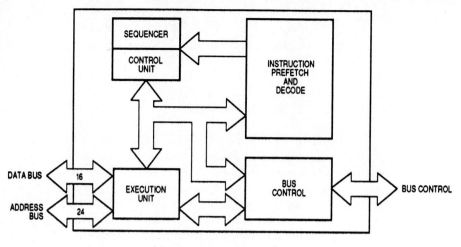

(a) Simplified block diagram

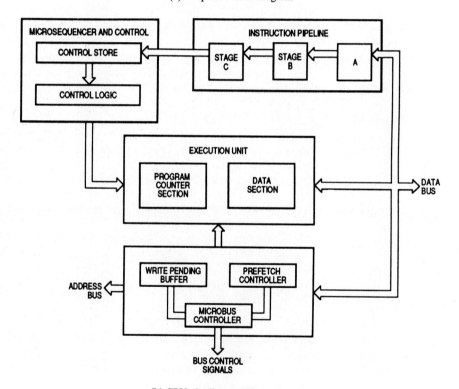

(b) CPU pipeline and internal units

Figure 4.5 MC68332 CPU.

order as expected. Thus, the programmer can view the CPU32 as a sequential machine and ignore the operation of the pipeline.

If hardware is being designed or debugged on a cycle-by-cycle basis, it may be necessary to consider the microprogrammed sequence. For example, because of the prefetch feature of the CPU32, the processor signal lines may be addressing and reading from a new location in main memory before the previous operation is finished. When necessary, the prefetch can be indicated by an external signal to aid hardware debugging of the system as described in Chapter 16.

Example 4.2

One of the specific goals of the MC68332 designers was to design independent modules connected by the intermodule bus. This concept was introduced in Chapter 2 and is shown in Figure 4.2 and Figure 4.6. Since each module is self contained it can be designed and tested independently during production of the MCU.

Figure 4.6 shows different MC68332 chips fabricated with various modules present. The leftmost chip has the RAM, SIM, and QSM but does not have the CPU32 or the TPU. The center chip has all of the MC68332 modules but the CPU32. The rightmost chip in Figure 4.6 is the complete MC68332.

A new type of module such as a ROM can easily be added by replacing the RAM module, for example. Thus, the modular design allows relatively easy production by Motorola of new members of the M68300 family. Any new module must only meet the interfacing requirements of the intermodule bus to work with the CPU and the other modules.

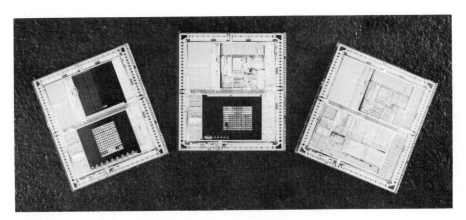

Figure 4.6 Modular design of the MC68332.

EXERCISES

The first three questions can best be answered by reference to several of the articles or textbooks listed in the Further Reading section at the end of this chapter as well as to other references.

4.1.1. The MC68300 family of microcontrollers are microprogrammed. Compare the design of a CPU using microprogrammed control with a design employing custom (hard-wired) logic circuitry. Consider the initial design and testing as well as speed of operation and flexibility when design changes are needed to produce a new family member.

4.1.2. The MC68332 CPU is considered to be a CISC (complex instruction set computer) processor. This implies that the instruction set contains relatively complex instructions. Another approach to CPU design employs RISC (reduced or reusable instruction set computer) principles. Here the instructions are simpler and perhaps more efficient. By reference to appropriate literature compare the two approaches to CPU design.

4.1.3. Discuss the factors that influenced the choice of the pipeline length for the MC68332. A pipeline with more stages should increase execution speed, but consider what happens when an instruction changes the instruction sequence as a branch instruction would.

4.1.4. Determine the percentage decrease in time and the actual improvement in nanoseconds when N instructions in sequence are found in on-chip memory (two clock cycles per access) versus being held in main memory (three clock cycles per access) for the MC68332 with clock rates as follows:
(a) 12.0 MHz;
(b) 16.7 MHz.
This improvement occurs with on-chip memory only for the fetching of the instructions. Each instruction may take a number of clock cycles for execution in addition to the time to fetch the instruction.

4.2 THE MC68332 CPU REGISTER PROGRAMMING MODEL

Just as the memory is used to store instructions and data associated with a program, the CPU32 contains storage elements called *registers*, which hold information needed for the instruction currently being processed. A register consists of one or more storage cells, each containing 1 bit of information. The *length* of the register is defined as the number of bits that may be stored or read simultaneously. A CPU contains a large number of registers, most of them used for specific purposes within the CPU. A few of these registers, called *programmable* registers, are available to the machine-language or assembly-language programmer via the processor's instruction set.

As described in Chapter 2, the CPU32 allows programs to be divided into user-mode programs and supervisor-mode programs.[4] If an operating system is employed in a product, portions of the operating system typically execute in the supervisor mode. The supervisor-mode routines have a higher privilege than those of a user-mode program. For example, these supervisor routines can execute instructions that are forbidden to the user mode. Programs in the user mode are also restricted from modifying the contents of certain processor registers, such as the supervisor stack pointer and the status register of the CPU. A supervisor-mode program can use any processor register when it executes.

This section first describes all of the processor registers that are used for general-

---

[4] In most products, only critical routines of the operating system execute in the supervisor mode. These are usually routines that control the operation of the hardware in some way.

purpose programming. These are the data registers, seven of the nine address registers, the program counter, and the condition code register. Following those descriptions, the system stack pointers and the status register are covered. Programs in both the user mode and the supervisor mode use the same general-purpose registers.

4.2.1 The MC68332 CPU (CPU32) General-Purpose Register Set

The general-purpose registers of a processor hold addresses or data values being manipulated by an instruction. The *program counter* holds the address of the next instruction to be fetched from memory. The *condition code register* contains bits that indicate the results of arithmetic or similar operations. In the MC68332 CPU, the general-purpose registers are divided into eight *data registers* and seven *address registers*. This CPU has a 32-bit program counter and an 8-bit condition code register. However, the CPU program is limited to 24-bit addresses in memory.

Figure 4.7 shows the CPU32 register set and a simplified diagram of the internal and external transfer paths for the processor. The address, data, and control signal lines connect to the intermodule bus as explained in Chapter 2. Internally, the processor contains programmable registers to hold values which are treated as data or addresses. These values can be transferred to the arithmetic and logic unit (ALU) for arithmetic computations. Data values held in the data registers of the processor can be transferred to and from memory or between the CPU and peripheral devices via the data signal lines. Values in the address registers can be placed on the address bus to reference locations in memory. These operations are controlled by machine-language instructions which are fetched from memory via the data signal lines and then decoded by the CPU.

The programmable register set of any processor may be defined in terms of its features useful to a programmer. The number, type, and length (in bits) of the registers and their connection via internal and external data paths determine the basic capability of the processor to execute instructions using these registers. In general, an increased number of available registers will simplify programming at the assembly-language level. Additionally, program execution speed is increased if registers are used to hold operands since operations between registers require less processing time than do operations that reference external devices or memory.

Registers are also used to hold addresses of data items stored externally to the processor. These addresses can easily be changed during program execution by modifying the contents of the registers. Modern programming techniques favor this method of indirect register addressing rather than allowing the program to modify itself by changing an address that is part of an instruction. In any case, this latter method is impossible in a ROM-based program. For most processors, such as the CPU32, the registers holding the address of an operand may be modified by the addition (or subtraction) of the contents of other registers called *index registers*.

The specific register set available to the user programs of an MC68332 CPU is shown in Figure 4.8. In addition to the general-purpose registers just defined, it contains a user stack pointer designated USP or A7 in the figure. The user stack is an area in memory used by the CPU to save return addresses during operations such as subroutine calls. Specific locations in memory for this stack are addressed

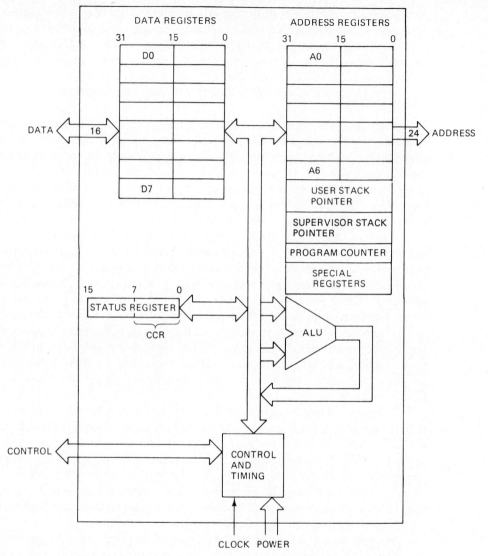

DATA REGISTERS

ADDRESS REGISTERS

Notes:

The low-order byte of the status register is the condition code register (CCR).

Figure 4.7 CPU32 register set and transfer paths.

by the User Stack Pointer. Symbolic notation is used in this text and in an assembly-language program for each register of the CPU as shown in Table 4.1. The assembly-language programmer, for example, would use this notation to designate a register in an assembly-language statement. To refer to the user stack pointer, the notation A7 or SP would be used by a user-mode program. This stack pointer has the same characteristics as the other seven address registers, but it is reserved as a *system stack pointer* when the CPU is in the user mode. The designation SP (stack pointer) is also used for the system stack pointer. The designation USP is reserved for programs executing in the supervisor mode of the CPU, for reasons to be explained later.[5]

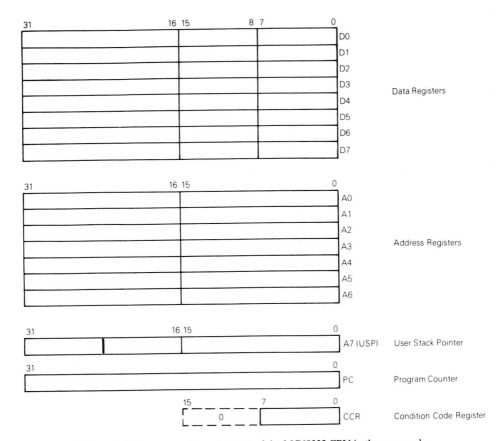

Figure 4.8 Programmable register set of the MC68332 CPU in the user mode.

The contents of a register or memory location are designated here by enclosing the item in parentheses. Thus (D2) means the contents of data register D2. When selected bits of an operand are designated, the bit numbers are enclosed in brackets, with the beginning and ending bit number separated by a colon if consecutive bits are specified. For example, bits 0 through 7 of data register D1 are indicated by (D1)[7:0]. An operand designated by <operand> means that any valid operand, as determined in the discussion, may be substituted into the expression. The designation <Dn>, for

---

[5] An assembly language program in the user mode references the user stack pointer by the mnemonic SP or A7. A supervisor mode program references the user stack pointer with the designation USP in an assembly-language statement. These distinctions are discussed further in Chapter 5.

Table 4.1 Register Usage and Symbolic Notation
(User Mode)

Register	Symbolic notation	Usage
Data	D0	Accumulator
	D1	Buffer register
	.	Index register
	.	Temporary storage
	D7	
Address	A0	Indirect addressing
	A1	Stack pointer
	.	Index register
	.	
	A6	
System stack pointer, User SP	A7 or SP	Subroutine calls in user mode
Program counter	PC	Instruction addressing
Condition code register	CCR	Arithmetic condition codes

example, means that any data register can be specified (i.e., any one of D0, D1, ... , D7).

4.2.2 Data Registers

The CPU32 has eight registers designated as data registers. The registers are referred to symbolically by number as Dn, where $n = 0, 1, ..., 7$. The internal bus structure of the CPU allows a byte operand (Dn)[7:0], a word operand (Dn)[15:0], or a long-word operand (Dn)[31:0] to be manipulated in the data register selected. Since three lengths are possible, the processor instructions that reference a data register must indicate the operand length. Only the corresponding bits of the specified register are modified by that instruction. The portion of the register involved may be used as an accumulator, a storage register, a buffer register, or as an index register.

As accumulators, the data registers hold operands of the specified length and allow arithmetic, logical, and other operations. These registers are also used temporarily to store operands generated by programs of the processor. The data registers act as buffer registers when data values are transferred in or out of the processor via the data signal lines. For the MC68332 with its 16 external data signal-lines, the possible transfers include an 8-bit or 16-bit value in a single transfer or a 32-bit value in two transfers.

A data register can be used as an index register whose contents are added to the value in an address register to form an address of an operand. The power of this addressing capability is such that the index may be modified by any processor instruction that operates on a data register. The index value may be changed in very sophisticated ways during program execution. This usually occurs within a program loop.

Example 4.3

Figure 4.9 shows a data register of the CPU32 with the bits designated from 0 on the right to 31 on the left. The sign bit of a byte-length two's-complement number would be bit 7, as indicated. Any access of the register specifying a byte operand would affect only bits 0 through 7; the remaining bits would be unchanged. Similarly, the sign bit of a word operand is bit 15 and that of a longword operand is bit 31, as shown in the figure.

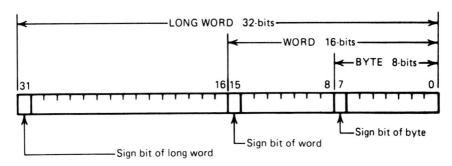

Figure 4.9 Data register format.

4.2.3 Address Registers

The CPU32 has seven general-purpose address registers which accept word or long-word values only. These seven general-purpose address registers, symbolically designated A0, A1, ..., A6, are shared by programs in either the supervisor or the user mode. These seven registers can be used to indirectly address operands in memory or they can be used to address "private" stacks defined by the programmer. The address register designated A7 in an assembly-language program is reserved for use as a system stack pointer as explained later in Subsection 4.2.6.

The primary use of the address registers is to hold the address of an operand in memory. Since an address register is 32 bits in length, an address may range up to

$$2^{32} = 4,294,967,296$$

locations. However, in the MC68332 only the lower 24-bit contents of an address register may be output to its modules or to external circuits since the processor has only 24 address signal-lines.

Private stacks.　In the CPU32, a *stack* consists of a set of contiguous memory locations addressed by a register designated as a *stack pointer*. Items stored on the stack are retrieved in reverse order, reminiscent of a push-down stack of cafeteria plates. The stack is accessed to store or retrieve data from one end only in a last-in-first-out (LIFO) manner.

Functionally, a stack pointer contains a value, designated (SP), that is used as an address to point to the top of the stack. The processor uses the value in the stack pointer to address a location from which the processor reads or to which it writes a data item. Information stored on the stack is said to be *pushed* on the stack by a processor write cycle. The item of information is retrieved by a processor read cycle which is called a *pop* or *pull* of the item.

Each general-purpose address register of the CPU32 may be used as a private stack pointer by a program using one of the addressing modes appropriate for stack operations. In these addressing modes, the value in the address register being used as a stack pointer is automatically changed by the proper amount after each push or pop of a data item. The data values in the stack may be either byte, word, or longword values if any of the registers designated as A0, A1, . . . , A6 are used as stack pointers.

Index registers.   Another use of an address register is as an index register. The index value is added to the contents of another address register to compute an effective address of an operand in memory. The same usage was defined by a data register in the preceding section. Thus, the CPU32 allows both address and data registers to serve as index registers.

Example 4.4

Figure 4.10(a) shows the format of an address register of the CPU32. The address can be either 16 bits or 32 bits in length. However, the corresponding address would be 24 bits in length when output to the address signal lines.

An indirect memory reference is shown in Figure 4.10(b). The address held in A1 in the example points to an operand at hexadecimal location 1000. Thus the effective address of the operand is designated as the contents of A1 or (A1).

Indexed addressing, shown in part (c) of the figure, allows the sum of two values to be used to determine the operand location. The maximum 24-bit hexadecimal address is FF FFFF.

Example 4.5

The *bottom* of the stack is the first item pushed onto the stack and the *top* of the stack is the last added. Removing (popping) an item is done from the top. A private stack may grow from lower addresses to higher memory addresses, or it may grow "down" in memory. These two cases are shown in Figure 4.11(a), where the addressing required is also shown. Our notation ((SP′)) means the contents of the stack (i.e., the contents of the location addressed by the stack pointer). When the stack grows down in memory toward lower addresses, (SP′) points to the last item (top) and must be decremented before a push. After a pop, (SP′) must be incremented to point to the top again. The opposite is true for a stack that grows upward in memory. The increments (or decrements) are 1, 2, or 4 depending on whether the size of each item on the stack is byte, word, or longword. If an instruction specifies the *predecrement* mode of the CPU322, the CPU automatically subtracts k ($k = 1, 2,$ or 4) from (SP′) before the stack pointer value is used as an address. The *postincrement* mode is used to add k to (SP′) after use. These addressing modes are discussed in more detail in Section 4.4.

Figure 4.11(b) shows the stack contents before and after a push of the hexadecimal value 1234 onto a word (16-bit) stack. Before the push, the stack pointer contains the hexadecimal address 1000 in the example and the value ((SP′)) is FFFF. To push the value, the stack pointer is first decremented by 2 and then used as the address of the stack location for the data value. Therefore, the item is pushed to location 0FFE.

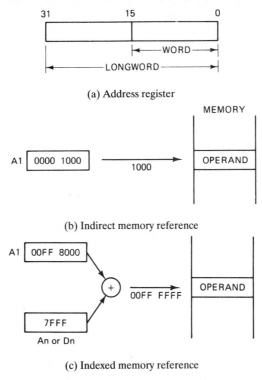

31   15   0

|←——WORD——→|

|←————— LONGWORD ————→|

(a) Address register

(b) Indirect memory reference

(c) Indexed memory reference

Figure 4.10 MC68332 address register usage.

The notation SP′ is used for these private stacks only in this example when referring to the stack pointer. In an assembly-language instruction, one of the address registers A0, A1, . . . , A6 must be designated explicitly as explained in Chapter 5.

4.2.4 Program Counter

In the CPU32, the Program Counter (PC) internally is 32 bits in length. The address signal lines, however, allow an addressing range of over 16 million bytes in memory using a 24-bit address. Since the CPU32 has instructions that vary in length in memory, the program counter is incremented by the proper amount automatically as the current instruction is executed.

    The program counter may be modified by the programmer to change the control sequence in several ways. The normal sequence of execution can be directly altered by a program instruction that causes a jump or branch in the program. In this case, no return address is saved by the CPU since control is not returned to the instruction following the jump or branch instruction. The jump instruction thus loads the program counter with the new address and destroys its previous contents. In contrast, a subroutine call or exception causes the current value of the program counter to be saved on the system stack before its contents are changed to the address of the new

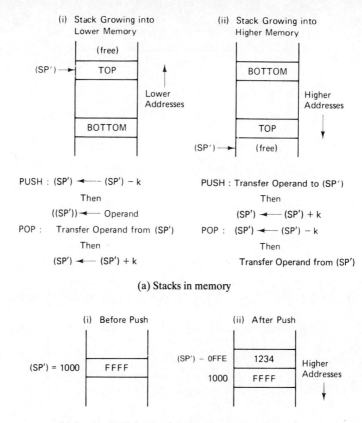

(i) Stack Growing into Lower Memory

(free)

(SP') → TOP

BOTTOM

Lower Addresses

(ii) Stack Growing into Higher Memory

BOTTOM

Higher Addresses

TOP

(SP') → (free)

PUSH : (SP') ←— (SP') − k
Then
((SP')) ←— Operand

POP : Transfer Operand from (SP')
Then
(SP') ←— (SP') + k

PUSH : Transfer Operand to (SP')
Then
(SP') ←— (SP') + k

POP : (SP') ←— (SP') − k
Then
Transfer Operand from (SP')

(a) Stacks in memory

(i) Before Push

(SP') = 1000   FFFF

(ii) After Push

(SP') = 0FFE   1234

1000   FFFF

Higher Addresses

(b) Stack addressing for a push of a word-length operand

Figure 4.11 Stack operation.

routine to be executed. The last instruction in a subroutine must be an instruction (e.g., Return) to restore the contents of the program counter.

4.2.5 Condition Code Register

The condition codes are single-bit variables indicating the results of arithmetic or logical operations. These are set automatically by many of the instructions of the CPU32. For example, if an addition results in a zero sum, the Z bit is set to {1}. The other bits have similar meanings, as shown in Table 4.2.

Example 4.6

The 8-bit operand {1XXXXXXX} would cause N = {1} if tested for a negative value. The setting of the other bits designated by X has no effect on the test. Depending on the program application, the interpretation might be: a negative two's-complement number, an unsigned binary number greater than or equal to 128, or a BCD number greater than or equal to 80.

Table 4.2 Interpretation of Condition Codes

Name	Bit Number	Symbol	Meaning
Extend	4	X	Used in multiple-precision arithmetic operations; in many instructions it is set the same as the C bit.
Negative	3	N	Set to {1} if the most significant bit of the resulting operand is {1}.
Zero	2	Z	Set to {1} if all the bits of the resulting operand are {0}.
Overflow	1	V	Set to {1} if an out-of-range condition occurs in two's complement operations.
Carry	0	C	Set to {1} if a carry is generated out of the most significant bit of the sum in addition. Set to {1} if a borrow is generated in subtraction.

Notes:
1. The other bits [7:5] of the condition code register (CCR) are not used, but the CCR is considered a byte-length register.
2. In the supervisor mode, the CCR is the low-order byte of the status register.

4.2.6 System Stack Pointers

The CPU32 uses stacks to store information when a subroutine call is made by a program or when an *exception* occurs during system operation. These exceptions as defined by Motorola for the CPU32 include traps, interrupts, and several error conditions recognized by the CPU. When any one of these events occurs, the normal flow of control through sequential instructions in memory is altered. Control is passed to the instructions associated with the subroutine, trap, or interrupt until its specific task is completed. Then control is normally returned to the next instruction in the preempted sequence. To allow control to be returned, the CPU stores (saves) the information on the appropriate *system stack*. For a subroutine call, only the contents of the PC need be saved and restored after the subroutine completes. When an exception occurs, the contents of the PC and the status register (SR) are saved as well as other information according to the requirements of the exception. The saving and restoring operations are automatic and require no programmer intervention.

The CPU32 separates the stack location in memory into a user stack area and a supervisor stack area. In the user mode, the system stack is the user stack and the user stack pointer is used to address this stack. The initial location of this user stack, before it is used for saving and restoring information, is assigned by the operating system. When the CPU operates in the supervisor mode, the system stack is a supervisor stack. The supervisor stack pointer (SSP) addresses the supervisor stack areas in memory. A user mode program can alter the user stack pointer, but it cannot access the supervisor stack pointer. Therefore, even if a user-mode program mishandles its stack and causes a serious error, the supervisor stack is not affected. The operating system need only manipulate its own stack properly to assure that the system operates correctly. It should also be noted that the contents of the general-purpose data registers or address registers are not saved on the system stack automatically in response to an exception. Program instructions must be used to save the contents of these registers if necessary.

System stack operations. Any time the CPU32 executes a program, only one system stack is being used. The active stack pointer will be designated SP. In the user mode, SP indicates the user stack pointer. The supervisor stack pointer is explicitly designated as SSP or as SP in a supervisor-mode program. No confusion should result in discussing the stack pointers or in programming since the mode of operation of the CPU determines which SP is being referenced.

When an item is pushed by an instruction onto the system stack, the stack pointer is first decremented by 2 for a word value or by 4 for a 32-bit operand. The system stacks always extend into lower memory addresses as item are pushed. Byte-length values can be pushed onto the system stack but the system stack pointer will be decremented by 2 after the push. This is in contrast to the private stacks defined in Section 4.2.2, which operate according to the design of the programmer. After an item on the stack is retrieved, (SP) is incremented by 2 or 4, as required.

Subroutine calls. Figure 4.12(a) shows the flow of control when a subroutine call is made. The program has executed a JSR (Jump to Subroutine) or BSR (Branch to Subroutine) instruction described in Chapter 6. The CPU saves the 32-bit contents of the program counter on the active system stack and transfers control to the subroutine by loading the starting address in the PC. When the subroutine completes by executing an RTS (Return from Subroutine) instruction, the CPU reloads the PC with the value that was saved on the stack. The value is the address of the instruction following the JSR or BSR instruction. If the subroutine call were made in the user mode, the user stack is employed. In the supervisor mode, the return address is saved on the supervisor stack. Example 4.7 describes the use of both stacks for a subroutine call and an interrupt.

Exception processing. When an exception is recognized by the CPU32, the transition to the exception handling routine is controlled automatically by the CPU, as shown in Figure 4.12(b). Any exception causes the CPU to change to the supervisor mode, regardless of the mode that was current when the exception occurred. When the exception is recognized, the (PC) and (SR), as well as a format word (16 bits), are saved on the supervisor stack. Some exceptions require that even more information be saved. In any case, enough information about the preempted program is available to allow it to resume execution after the exception routine has completed. The last instruction in the exception routine (RTE) causes the information to be restored so that control is returned to the original program.

Example 4.7

Figure 4.13 shows the contents of the stacks used during the execution of a user-mode program. If the program calls a subroutine, the return address is pushed on the stack

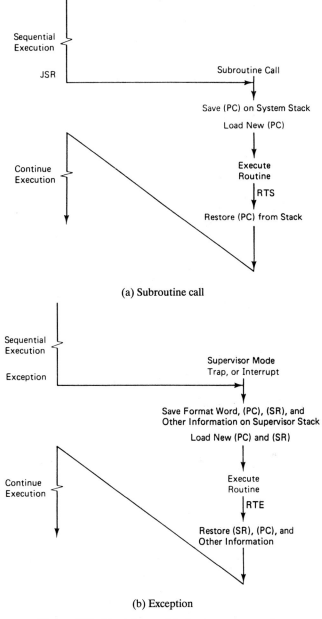

Sequential
Execution

JSR

Subroutine Call

Save (PC) on System Stack

Load New (PC)

Continue
Execution

Execute
Routine

RTS

Restore (PC) from Stack

(a) Subroutine call

Sequential
Execution

Exception

Supervisor Mode
Trap, or Interrupt

Save Format Word, (PC), (SR), and
Other Information on Supervisor Stack

Load New (PC) and (SR)

Continue
Execution

Execute
Routine

RTE

Restore (SR), (PC), and
Other Information

(b) Exception

Figure 4.12 Flow of control during program execution.

using (USP) as the address that is decremented by 4 to accommodate the 32-bit (PC). If an interrupt occurs during subroutine execution, the return address within the interrupted subroutine and the contents of the status register are saved using (SSP). The return from the interrupt processing followed by the eventual return from the subroutine leave (USP) and (SSP) as they were initially.

Sec. 4.2   The MC68332 CPU Register Programming Model   **107**

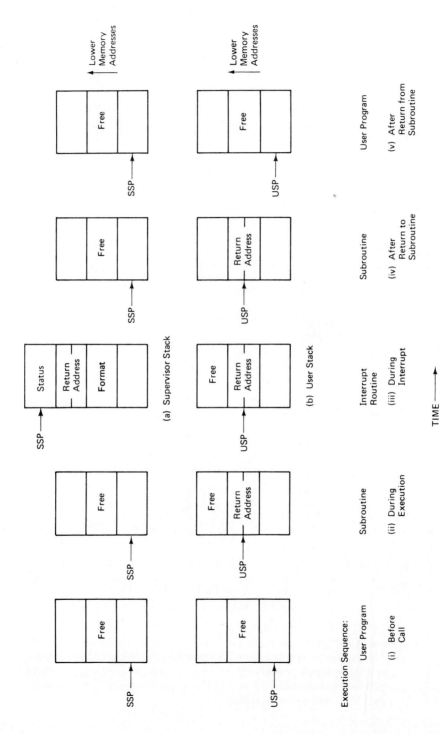

Figure 4.13 Stack usage during subroutine call and interrupt processing.

108

4.2.7 Supervisor versus User Mode

The difference between the supervisor mode and the user mode is one of privilege that concerns control of the CPU itself and perhaps external devices. Programs executing in the user mode are restricted from executing certain instructions and they cannot access the supervisor stack pointer. The user-mode programs may also be restricted from controlling certain elements in the computer system or in the regions of memory they may access for reading or writing operands. These system restrictions must be enforced by external circuitry, not by the CPU. The CPU indicates its mode via several of its control signal lines to allow external circuits to determine the proper action. For example, external circuits can be used to restrict memory access for a user-mode program. If such access is attempted, the memory-management circuits signal the MC68332 CPU and cause an error exception. The supervisor program then determines the appropriate action, such as preventing the offending program from executing further. These system considerations are considered in more detail in Chapters 10, 11, and 14.

Table 4.3 Supervisor Versus User Mode

Use	Supervisor	User
Register usage	D0–D7, A0–A6 PC, SR	D0–D7, A0–A6, PC, CCR
Stack pointer	SSP	USP
Instructions	All	Restricted set
Entered by:	Exception processing	Supervisor program changing mode to user
Special Registers	System control	—

Privilege distinctions and transitions. Table 4.3 indicates some of the differences between the supervisor and user mode. The modes share the same general-purpose register set and the program counter but separate stack pointers are used in the two modes. A user-mode program cannot execute the complete instruction set of the CPU32. In particular, instructions to change the mode or control the system in various ways are not executable by programs operating in the user mode. These are called *privileged instructions*. If an attempt is made to execute a privileged instruction by a user-mode program, a trap occurs and control of the computer is returned to the supervisor program.

The transition between modes is carefully controlled, as indicated in Table 4.3 and Figure 4.14. The user mode is entered only by having the operating system or supervisor-mode program change the processor's mode from supervisor to user. This is accomplished by modifying the status register (a privileged instruction) as explained

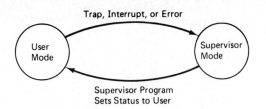

Figure 4.14 Transitions between modes.

in the next subsection. Return to the supervisor mode occurs when an exception is recognized by the CPU. The special register set available only to the supervisor mode includes the entire status register and several other special-purpose registers as defined in Chapter 10.

4.2.8 Status Register

Figure 4.15 shows the 16-bit status register of the CPU32. The low-order 8 bits are called the condition codes and can be read or modified by programs executing in either the supervisor or the user mode. The upper byte is called the *system byte* and can be modified only by a program in the supervisor mode. Each bit of the high-order byte is defined in Table 4.4.

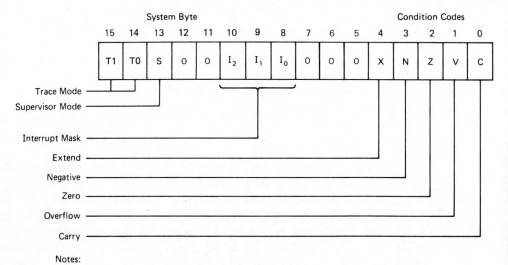

Notes:
(1) Conditions stated are true when the corresponding bit = {1}.
(2) The low-order byte of the status register is referred to as the condition code register (CCR).

Figure 4.15 MC68332 status register.

In the Figure 4.15, each bit of the SR is considered separately except the interrupt mask bits SR[10:8], which are taken together as a 3-bit binary number indicating

Table 4.4 Interpretations of System Status

Name	Symbol	Meaning
Trace	T1	Set to {1} if single-instruction trace is being used
Trace	T0	Set to {1} if trace on change of control flow is being used
Supervisor	S	Set to {1} if the processor program is executing in the supervisor mode
Interrupt	I_0, I_1, I_2	Coded interrupt level. Set to {000} to enable. Set to {111} to disable all interrupt levels but level 7.

the interrupt level. The other bits are considered individual, with a {1} indicating that particular condition is true. Thus (SR)[13] = {1} indicates that a supervisor-mode program is executing, and (SR)[13] = {0} indicates a user-mode program. In practice, the operating system sets (SR)[13] = {0} and modifies other bits as necessary when control is passed to the user-mode program.

If an exception condition then occurs, the CPU operating in the supervisor mode saves information including the current (PC) and (SR) on the system stack. The exception condition automatically changes the S bit to {1} and causes the other bits of the status register to be modified as required. As control is returned to the user program, the previous contents of the status register and program counter are pulled from the system stack and restored. When the previous contents of the program counter are restored, the user program continues execution where it left off. Thus, control of the CPU mode is determined by the setting of the S bit, which provides a simple and efficient means of switching between modes.

To aid program development, the operating system can cause instruction by instruction trace when (SR)[15] is set to {1}. Alternately, when (SR)[14] = {1}, a trace exception is taken when the program flow is changed by an instruction, as discussed in Chapter 2. When the trace exception is taken, execution continues in the appropriate trace-handling routine used as an aid in debugging.

The interrupt system of the CPU32 is controlled by 3 bits in the status register. These bits act as an interrupt mask for the seven-level, priority-interrupt system of the CPU32. Setting these bits with a value from 0 to 6 disables or masks interrupts at the level indicated and those levels below in priority. The level 7 interrupt is referred to as a *nonmaskable interrupt* and cannot be disabled. The decimal value of the interrupt mask is 0 through 7, with priority levels in ascending order. If an interrupt occurs at a given level, the mask bits are automatically set to that level to prevent additional interrupts from that level or a level below it from being received.

Example 4.8

The status register contents 0700_{16} indicates the user mode with all interrupts below level 7 masked (disabled). All the condition codes are {0}. Only a level 7 interrupt will be acknowledged since it is nonmaskable. If such an interrupt occurs, the (SR) will be set to

2700_{16} during interrupt processing, indicating that the processing occurs in the supervisor mode. Upon completion of the interrupt routine, control returns to the user-mode program with $(SR) = 0700_{16}$.

EXERCISES

4.2.1. Determine the status if the CPU32 Status Register contains the following hexadecimal values:
(a) 0400;
(b) 2000;
(c) 0004;
(d) A000;
(e) 6700.

4.2.2. Show the contents of the CPU32 Status Register after a level 4 interrupt is accepted. Assume that the Status Register initially contained 0 for each bit.

4.2.3. What registers must be initialized before the processor can execute a program? Consider first a supervisor-mode program. What registers must the operating system initialize before control is passed to a user-mode program?

4.2.4. Show the contents of the system stack if a program is interrupted by a level 1 interrupt when $(PC) = 101C_{16}$. If the level 1 interrupt routine is itself interrupted by a level 2 interrupt when $(PC) = 200C_{16}$, show the changes to the system stack. Assume that initially $(SR) = 0000_{16}$ and $(SSP) = 8000_{16}$.

4.3 INTRODUCTION TO THE CPU32 INSTRUCTION SET

The instruction set for the CPU32 determines the operations that are available to perform data transfer, arithmetic processing, and control program flow. Each complete CPU32 instruction consists of the following:
(a) an operation code determining the operation to be performed;
(b) a designation of the length of the operand or operands;
(c) specifications of the locations of any operands involved by indicating an addressing mode for each operand.

Figure 4.16 lists the instruction set for the CPU32 in alphabetical order. Each mnemonic represents the operation code. A letter is used to indicate a length of byte (B), word (W), or longword (L) for 8-, 16-, and 32-bit operands, respectively. For example, the symbolic instruction to add two 16-bit operands would be

ADD.W   X, Y

where X and Y designate the locations of the operands.

Instructions for the CPU32 can be classified by type or by the number of operands. The number of operands for an instruction determines whether it is classified as a *single-address* or a *double-address* instruction. Classification by *type* groups the basic

Mnemonic	Description	Mnemonic	Description
ABCD	Add Decimal with Extend	MOVE	Move
ADD	Add	MOVE CCR	Move Condition Code Register
ADDA	Add Address	MOVE SR	Move Status Register
ADDI	Add Immediate	MOVE USP	Move User Stack Pointer
ADDQ	Add Quick	MOVEA	Move Address
ADDX	Add with Extend	MOVEC	Move Control Register
AND	Logical AND	MOVEM	Move Multiple Registers
ANDI	Logical AND Immediate	MOVEP	Move Peripheral
ASL, ASR	Arithmetic Shift Left and Right	MOVEQ	Move Quick
		MOVES	Move Alternate Address Space
Bcc	Branch Conditionally	MULS, MULS.L	Signed Multiply
BCHG	Test Bit and Change	MULU, MULU.L	Unsigned Multiply
BCLR	Test Bit and Clear		
BGND	Background	NBCD	Negate Decimal with Extend
BKPT	Breakpoint	NEG	Negate
BRA	Branch	NEGX	Negate with Extend
BSET	Test Bit and Set	NOP	No Operation
BSR	Branch to Subroutine		
BTST	Test Bit	OR	Logical Inclusive OR
		ORI	Logical Inclusive OR Immediate
CHK	Check Register Against Upper and Lower Bounds	PEA	Push Effective Address
CLR	Clear	RESET	Reset External Devices
CMP	Compare	ROL, ROR	Rotate Left and Right
CMPA	Compare Address	ROXL, ROXR	Rotate with Extend Left and Right
CMPI	Compare Immediate	RTD	Return and Deallocate
CMPM	Compare Memory to Memory	RTE	Return from Exception
CMP2	Compare Register Against Upper and Lower Bounds	RTR	Return and Restore Codes
		RTS	Return from Subroutine
DBcc	Test Condition, Decrement and Branch	SBCD	Subtract Decimal with Extend
		Scc	Set Conditionally
DIVS, DIVSL	Signed Divide	STOP	Stop
DIVU, DIVUL	Unsigned Divide	SUB	Subtract
		SUBA	Subtract Address
EOR	Logical Exclusive OR	SUBI	Subtract Immediate
EORI	Logical Exclusive OR Immediate	SUBQ	Subtract Quick
EXG	Exchange Registers	SUBX	Subtract with Extend
EXT, EXTB	Sign Extend	SWAP	Swap Register Words
ILLEGAL	Take Illegal Instruction Trap	TBLS,TBLSN	Table Lookup and Interpolate (Signed)
JMP	Jump	TBLU, TBLUN	Table Lookup and Interpolate (Unsigned)
JSR	Jump to Subroutine	TAS	Test Operand and Set
LEA	Load Effective Address	TRAP	Trap
LINK	Link and Allocate	TRAPcc	Trap Conditionally
LPSTOP	Low-Power Stop	TRAPV	Trap on Overflow
LSL, LSR	Logical Shift Left and Right	TST	Test Operand
		UNLK	Unlink

Figure 4.16 CPU32 instruction set.

operations allowed by the processor into categories, such as those for data movement or those for arithmetic operations.

A processor instruction set is sometimes separated into types in order to compare it to instruction sets of other processors. After comparison, a processor with an extensive arithmetic set might be chosen over one with less capability to support mathematical programming, for example. The division into types is also convenient for coding instructions since this grouping allows the programmer to select the best instruction to perform an operation of a particular type. The Exchange instruction (EXG), listed in Figure 4.16, for example, exchanges the contents of two CPU32 registers and is more efficient for this purpose than several other data movement instructions that could accomplish the same result.

The basic types of instructions are those for data movement, arithmetic and logical operations, program control, and processor or system control. These categories are expanded in Chapter 5, but for our purposes at present, only a few instructions representing several types will be discussed. For convenience, the instruction set is also presented in the Appendix.

4.3.1 The Clear Instruction

The Clear (CLR) instruction is considered a single-address instruction which has the symbolic form

CLR.X   <EAd>

where X is B, L, or W and the <EAd> is the effective address of the destination. Zeros are transferred to the portion of the destination location specified by the operation, as shown in Table 4.5. If the destination location originally contained all 1's, executing the CLR.X instruction causes the designated portion of the location to be cleared. The operation can be defined as

$$(EAd)[X] \leftarrow 0[X]$$

which is read: "The contents of location EAd of length X is replaced with zeros."

Table 4.5 Operation of the Clear Instruction

Instruction	Contents of the destination after instruction executes
CLR.B <EAd>	FFFF FF00
CLR.W <EAd>	FFFF 0000
CLR.L <EAd>	0000 0000

Note:
The destination contains FFFF FFFF before each instruction executes.

The description of the CLR instruction is shown in Figure 4.17. This summary, taken from the Motorola *CPU32 Reference Manual*, presents the characteristics of the instruction in several ways. The *operation* indicates that the destination location is replaced by 0. The assembler recognizes the CLR mnemonic and converts it and the effective address of the destination location to machine language. The valid destinations, in terms of the possible addressing modes, are listed in the table accompanying the description of the instruction. These modes are discussed in Section 4.4. Other important characteristics, such as the effect on the condition codes and the machine-language format, are also given.

There are a number of ways to specify the location to be cleared by the CLR instruction. The method is chosen from among the nine valid addressing modes shown in the table with Figure 4.17. The length of the operand at the destination location is called its *size* and is specified as byte (8 bits), word (16 bits), or longword (32 bits), with the corresponding symbolic designation B, W, or L, respectively. For example, the assembler recognizes

CLR.B   D1

as the instruction to clear 8 bits of register D1. To describe this operation precisely, our notation will be

$$(D1)[7:0] \leftarrow 0$$

indicating that bits 0 through 7 of register D1 are cleared. The replacement symbol ($\leftarrow$) will mean that the operand on the left is replaced by the value on the right. After the instruction executes, the contents of the destination locations are equal to zero, which is indicated as

$$(D1)[7:0] = 0$$

for this example.

Example 4.9

Several examples of the CLR instruction are given below. The addresses for the destination locations in memory are indicated as decimal values. This conforms with the assembly language notation to be discussed in Chapter 5. A word (16-bit) location in memory consists of two consecutive bytes.

Instruction symbolic form	After execution
CLR.B D1	(D1)[7:0] = 0
CLR.W D1	(D1)[15:0] = 0
CLR.B 1000	(1000) = 0
CLR.W 1000	(1000) = 0
	(1001) = 0

4.3.2 The MOVE Instruction

The fundamental data movement instruction for the CPU32 is the MOVE instruction, which is a double-address instruction written in symbolic form as

MOVE.X   <EAs>, <EAd>

where X = B, W, or L specifies the length or size of the operand. A copy of the source operand of length X in location <EAs> is transferred to the destination location <EAd>, leaving the source location unchanged. Both the source and destination

CLR

Clear an Operand

CLR

Operation: 0 ♦ Destination

**Assembler
Syntax:** CLR ⟨ea⟩

Attributes: Size = (Byte, Word, Long)

Description: Clears the destination operand to zero. The size of the operation may be specified as byte, word, or long.

Condition Codes:

X	N	Z	V	C
—	0	1	0	0

X Not affected.
N Always cleared.
Z Always set.
V Always cleared.
C Always cleared.

Instruction Format:

15	14	13	12	11	10	9	8	7	6	5	4	3	2	1	0
0	1	0	0	0	0	1	0	SIZE		EFFECTIVE ADDRESS MODE			REGISTER		

Instruction Fields:

Size field — Specifies the size of the operation.
   00 — Byte operation
   01 — Word operation
   10 — Long operation

Effective Address field — Specifies the destination location. Only data alterable addressing modes are allowed as shown:

Addressing Mode	Mode	Register		Addressing Mode	Mode	Register
Dn	000	reg. number:Dn		(xxx).W	111	000
An	—	—		(xxx).L	111	001
(An)	010	reg. number:An		#⟨data⟩	—	—
(An)+	011	reg. number:An				
−(An)	100	reg. number:An				
(d$_{16}$,An)	101	reg. number:An		(d$_{16}$,PC)	—	—
(d$_8$,An,Xn)	110	reg. number:An		(d$_8$,PC,Xn)	—	—
(bd,An,Xn)	110	reg. number:An		(bd,PC,Xn)	—	—

Figure 4.17 Description of the CLR instruction.

operands are treated as though they are of length X. The MOVE instruction copies the source operand into bits [7:0], [15:0], or [31:0] for the transfer of a byte, word, or longword, respectively. The effective addresses, <EAs> and <EAd>, are computed by the processor according to the specification of the addressing mode. They may indicate processor registers or memory locations. Figure 4.18 shows the operation of the MOVE instruction for the three operand lengths that were previously defined in Example 4.3. In each case, the destination and source locations contain 32-bit values, but only the specified portion of the operand is copied from the source to the destination location.

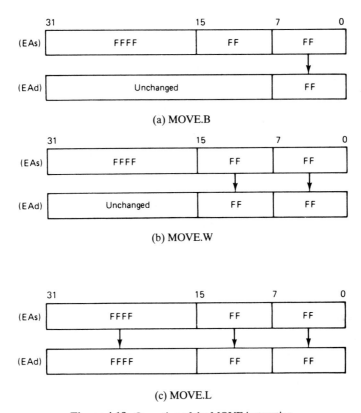

Figure 4.18 Operation of the MOVE instruction.

Example 4.10

A number of examples of the MOVE instruction are shown in the following summary. In each case, the source location is data register D2 and the destination register is D1. The initial contents of the registers are

$$(D2) = \$0FFF\ 0105$$

and

$$(D1) = \$1000\ 0000$$

before each instruction executes.

Instruction	(D1) after execution
MOVE.B D2, D1	1000 0005
MOVE.W D2, D1	1000 0105
MOVE.L D2, D1	0FFF 0105

4.3.3 The ADD Instruction

An important arithmetic instruction is the ADD instruction. It has the form

ADD.X   <EAs>, <EAd>

and performs binary addition between the source operand and the destination operand of length X. In such double-address instructions which compute a result, the result is stored in the destination location according to the replacement

$$(EAd)[X] \leftarrow (EAs)[X] + (EAd)[X]$$

by execution of the instruction. The source operand is not changed by these instructions. The ADD, CLR, and MOVE instructions discussed previously are typical of the CPU32 instructions for arithmetic operations or data transfer. In such instructions, an operand location and length as well as the operation to be performed must be specified.

Example 4.11

Assume that data register D2 contains the hexadecimal value of 0FFF 0105 and D1 contains 1000 0001 before each instruction executes. The results stored in D1 are shown here for addition of operands of the length specified.

Instruction	(D1) after execution
ADD.B D2, D1	1000 0006
ADD.W D2, D1	1000 0106
ADD.L D2, D1	1FFF 0106

4.3.4 Other Instruction Types

Program control instructions may modify the flow of control in a program by changing the value in the program counter and thereby causing a new sequence of instructions to be executed. For example, the Jump instruction

JMP   <EA>

causes program control to be transferred to the instruction contained in the location designated by the effective address <EA>. The Branch Always instruction

BRA   <disp>

adds a displacement value to the contents of the program counter at the time the instruction is executed. This causes program control to be transferred within the range allowed by the value <disp>, which is either a positive or negative integer. Both the BRA and JMP instructions cause unconditional transfer of control. Other branch instructions may or may not cause a branch, depending on conditions set by an arithmetic operation. For example,

BGT   <disp>

causes a branch if the result was greater than zero. The condition is indicated by the setting of the condition code bits in the status registers. These program control instructions are discussed in detail in Chapter 6.

Instructions that control the operation of the processor or the system are generally reserved for programs operating in the supervisor mode. The instruction STOP, for example, causes the processor to discontinue fetching and executing instructions. Such instructions are discussed in more detail in Chapter 10.

EXERCISES

4.3.1. Describe the contents of each byte location affected by the instruction

CLR.L   1000

after the instruction executes.

4.3.2. Before each instruction given executes, assume the following hexadecimal contents of D1, D2, and word location 1000.

$$(D1) = 0601$$
$$(D2) = 0805$$
$$(1000) = 1913$$

Determine the results of execution for each of the following instructions:
(a) MOVE.B   D1, D2
(b) MOVE.B   D1, 1001
(c) CLR.W   1000
(d) ADD.B   D1, D2
(e) ADD.W   1000, D1

4.4   ADDRESSING MODES FOR THE MC68332 CPU (CPU32)

The *addressing modes* of a CPU determine the ways in which a processor can reference an operand held in one of its registers or in memory. For each operand, the addressing mode specifies how the processor is to locate or calculate the actual address of the

Table 4.6 Basic Addressing Modes

Type	Effective Address	Symbolic designation
Direct		
Register	EA = Rn	D0, D1, ... , D7; A0, A1, ... , A7
Absolute	EA = <address>	<decimal address> $<hexadecimal address>
Indirect		
Address register	EA = (An)	(A0), (A1), ... , (A7)
Predecrement	An = An − k EA = (An)	−(An)
Postincrement	EA = (An) An = An + k	(An)+
Relative with displacement	EA = (PC) + <disp>	* + <disp> or (<disp>,PC)
Immediate	None	#<data>

Notes:

1. Rn refers to any register Dn or An.
2. For the predecrement and postincrement modes, k is 1, 2, or 4 for byte, word, or longword operations, respectively.
3. Angle brackets < > imply that the indicated value must be specified.

operand. The actual address is called the *effective address* and is determined when the instruction referencing the operand is executed.[6]

The broad categories of addressing for the CPU32 include direct addressing, indirect addressing, and addressing relative to the program counter. A special immediate mode is also provided. Table 4.6 defines these basic modes for the CPU32. In the table, the category of addressing mode and the effective address that results from instruction execution are listed. The symbolic designation is the reference to the given addressing mode recognized by a Motorola assembler. An absolute address is considered to be a decimal value unless it is preceded by "$" to indicate a hexadecimal value. The symbol "*" in a symbolic instruction references the current value of the program counter and the symbol "#" preceding a number indicates immediate addressing.

Instructions may specify one or two operands in the manner described in Section 4.3. The CLR instruction, for example, may specify the destination by any of the modes indicated in Table 4.6 except relative or immediate. The MOVE or ADD instructions require two operands, and both the source and the destination addressing modes must be specified. A number of examples in this section show how the basic addressing modes are specified symbolically. The discussion presented in this section

---

[6] When the CPU directly addresses the memory, an effective address is the actual or physical hardware address. In many sophisticated systems, special circuitry called *memory-mapping circuitry* is employed. This circuitry then computes the physical address that corresponds to the CPU address. The physical addresses involved depend entirely on the hardware design of the system and are independent of programming references to operands in memory.

is limited to those modes shown in Table 4.6, which represent only 8 of the 14 possible addressing modes for the CPU32. A more detailed study of the CPU32 addressing modes is given in Chapter 5 after assembly-language programming is introduced.

4.4.1 Direct Addressing

The *direct* addressing modes of the CPU32 include register addressing and absolute addressing. In either case, the location or address of an operand is specified directly as part of the instruction, so that no calculation of an effective address by the CPU is necessary. For the register modes, the operand is in one of the address or data registers. In the absolute mode, the operand is in memory at a location designated by a positive integer representing its address.

The basic format for the CLR instruction using register addressing is

    CLR.<X>   <Dn>

where the operand of length X is either B, W, or L to represent a Byte (B), Word (W), or Longword (L), respectively. The register Dn is written specifically as one of D0, D1, ... , D7. Thus, the instruction

    CLR.W   D2

clears the low-order 16 bits of register D2.

The MOVE instruction requires two operands. The form for data register addressing is

    MOVE.<X>   <Dm>,<Dn>

where X is B, W, or L. For example, the instruction

    MOVE.W   D1, D2

copies (D1)[15:0] into (D2)[15:0].

An absolute address may be specified as a decimal or hexadecimal integer in an instruction. For example, the instruction

    MOVE.W   10000, D1

transfers 16 bits from word location 10000 to (D1)[15:0]. According to the conventions of Motorola assemblers, the symbolic form for the same location in hexadecimal would be

    MOVE.W $2710, D1

since the value 2710_{16} corresponds to 10000 and the $ indicates hexadecimal.

Example 4.12

Being the simplest addressing schemes, the direct addressing modes were used in the preceding section to introduce important processor instructions. For example, the instruction

         CLR.W   1000

specifies the absolute address 1000 as the destination. The address is stored with the instruction in memory. The instruction

         MOVE.W   1000, D1

employs absolute addressing for the source location and register direct addressing for the destination. An instruction such as

         MOVE.W   A1, D1

transfers the 16-bit address in A1 to the data register designated D1.

4.4.2 Indirect Addressing

In the CPU32, *indirect* register addressing means the use of the contents of an address register as the address of an operand in memory. The contents are used as a pointer to reference the location. For example, if the instruction

         MOVE.W   (A1), D1

is executed when (A1) = 1000, the 16-bit value in memory word location 1000 would be copied into (D1)[15:0]. To modify the address referenced in memory, the address register may be changed by any instruction that operates on the contents of address registers. This ability to modify the pointer in very flexible ways allows a programmer to address values in sophisticated data structures in memory. A simple example is the stack structure discussed in Section 4.2.3.

Stacks.   In fact, the stack structure is so common in modern programs that the CPU32 has two indirect addressing modes which are used primarily with stacks. Thus, private stacks can be created and used by employing the address register indirect with postincrement or predecrement addressing modes. To add data to a stack that grows from high memory to low memory, for example, the instruction

         MOVE.W   D1, −(A1)

transfers a word from D1 to the stack after the stack pointer (A1) is decremented by two (bytes) to point to the next free memory location. A data item could be retrieved with the instruction

         MOVE.W   (A1)+, D2

which pops the word from the stack addressed by A1 and copies it to (D2)[15:0]. After the transfer, A1 is incremented by 2. The push operation, for the downward-growing stack, employs the predecrement addressing mode using A1 as the stack pointer. The pop requires the postincrement mode for the source addressing mode. Any general-purpose address register of the CPU32 can be used as a private stack pointer. The source location in a push operation or the destination location in a pop operation can be a memory location or any register of the CPU32. If A7 is designated as a stack pointer, the system stack would be referenced.

4.4.3 Relative Addressing

A program counter *relative* address is an address that the CPU calculates by adding a displacement to the value in the program counter. The calculated effective address is then

$$EA = (PC) + <disp>$$

where the displacement value $<disp>$ is specified in the instruction. The displacement is a positive or a negative integer, so the referenced location can be higher or lower in memory relative to the instruction using this addressing mode.

An example of relative addressing is indicated by the instruction

BRA $* + 10$

which, when executed, would cause a branch 10 byte locations ahead of that indicated by the program counter.[7] In the case of the BRA instruction, the value in the program counter is changed to the new address to point to the next instruction six word locations farther up in memory from the location of the BRA instruction. Relative addressing can also be used to address data values in memory.

Since the program counter contents act as a pointer to the instruction currently executing, the displacement value indicates the distance between the operand referenced in the relative mode and the instruction itself. If the program is moved in memory, the relative references in the program are still correct. When the memory references used by a program are relative, the program is said to be *position indepen-dent.* Such programs are discussed in Chapter 9. Programs with absolute references to memory locations within the program cannot be moved unless the absolute addresses are changed to indicate the new locations.

The CPU32 also allows program counter relative addressing with indexing. In this mode, the effective address is calculated as the contents of the PC, plus a dis-placement value, plus the contents of an index register. Such variations on relative addressing are discussed in Chapter 5.

---

[7] When the branch is taken, the value in the PC is the address of the BRA instruction + 2. This BRA instruction requires two word locations in memory. Thus, the BRA instruction shown causes a branch to an instruction six word locations higher in memory than the first word of the BRA instruction itself. An alternate form of the instruction is BRA (10,PC).

4.4.4 Immediate Addressing

The *immediate* addressing mode is used to specify a constant 8, 16, or 32 bits long. The constant is included in the instruction in memory. For example, the instruction

    ADD.W   #5, D1

adds 5 to the value in (D1)[15:0]. The instruction

    MOVE.B   #'A', (A1)

moves the ASCII value 'A' into the byte addressed by A1 in memory. The assembler recognizes the source addressing modes in these two examples as immediate. Of course, the immediate mode is never allowed as a destination mode since the destination location must be alterable (writable).

Example 4.13

The symbolic instruction

        MOVE.L   #'1234', D1

causes the contents of D1 to be replaced with the ASCII equivalent of 1234 or the hexadecimal value 3132 3334. Similarly, the instruction

        MOVE.W   #$F0, D1

has the effect
$$(D1)[15:0] \leftarrow F0_{16}.$$

An instruction with an immediate operand as a destination such as

        MOVE.B   1000, #1000

would be illegal and cannot be assembled.

EXERCISES

4.4.1. Using hexadecimal values for all your answers, determine the operation and locations affected by each of the following instructions:
  (a) MOVE.W   1000, 2000
  (b) MOVE.W $1000, D1
  (c) MOVE.B   1000, D1
  (d) CLR.L $FFFFFC

4.4.2. Define the results from each of the following instructions if (A1) = 1000 and $(1000) = FFE0_{16}$ before each instruction executes:
  (a) MOVE.W   A1, D1
  (b) MOVE.W   (A1), D1

(c) MOVE.W   1000, D1

(d) MOVE.W   #1000, D1

4.4.3. Determine the contents of the destination in hexadecimal after each instruction executes:

(a) MOVE.W   #'AB', D1

(b) MOVE.W   #$C1, D1

(c) MOVE.W   #1000, D1

4.4.4. Using only the instructions and techniques discussed thus far, write the symbolic instructions to store the low-order word of D1 into memory locations 1001 and 1002. Thus, after execution $(1001) = (D1)[15:8]$ and $(1002) = (D1)[7:0]$. Remember that word-length operands must start at even locations in memory and that they occupy two bytes.

Bits 15–12	Operation
0000	Bit Manipulation/MOVEP/Immediate
0001	Move Byte
0010	Move Long
0011	Move Word
0100	Miscellaneous
0101	ADDQ/SUBQ/Scc/DBcc/TRAPcc
0110	Bcc/BSR/BRA
0111	MOVEQ
1000	OR/DIV/SBCD
1001	SUB/SUBX
1010	(Unassigned, Reserved)
1011	CMP/EOR
1100	AND/MUL/ABCD/EXG
1101	ADD/ADDX
1110	Shift/Rotate/Bit Field
1111	Coprocessor Operation

Figure 4.19   Operation codes.

4.5   MACHINE LANGUAGE FOR THE MC68332

The machine language instructions for the CPU32 consist of one or more 16-bit words in memory. The first word is the operation word, which contains the operation code (op code) as well as the size or length and the addressing modes for any operands, if necessary. For most instructions, the op code is contained in bits 12 through 15 of the first word. Various combinations of these four bits yield 16 different op codes.

The meaning of each of these is defined in Figure 4.19. The remaining 12 bits in the operation word are used to define further the operation to be performed. Additional extension words for the machine language instructions may contain immediate data or absolute addresses for source or destination operands. A short absolute address (16 bits) requires one extra word, and a long address (32 bits) requires two. The format of the machine-language instruction is shown in Figure 4.20. The extension words follow the operation code at higher memory addresses.

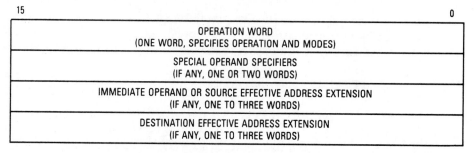

Figure 4.20 Instruction formats.

The formats for single- and double-address instructions are discussed in this section. As in previous sections of this chapter, the CLR, ADD, and MOVE instructions are used for specific examples. Every instruction for the CPU32 is described in the Appendix.

4.5.1 Single-Address Instructions

The operation word for a single-address instruction is shown in Figure 4.21(a). Bits [15:6] define the operation and bits [5:0] designate the addressing mode. The effective address field is itself divided into mode and register subfields of 3 bits each. For an addressing mode employing a register, the register number (0-7) is given in the register subfield. In this case, the mode subfield specifies whether direct or indirect addressing is used and the variations shown in Figure 4.22 apply. Absolute, relative, or immediate addressing modes have a fixed encoding for the entire 6-bit field.

As an example, the instruction

        CLR.B   D1

specifies the destination D1 by direct register addressing. The machine language format is shown in Figure 4.21(b). For data registers, the mode in the effective address field is {000} and the register number for D1 is {001}. The bit pattern in bits [15:8] specifies the CLR instruction. The operand size is a byte in this example and is indicated by {00} in bits [7:6]. Since only register addressing is used, the instruction requires only one word of memory.

A number of other single-address instructions, such as NEG (negate), NOT (one's complement), and NBCD (negate decimal), have the same general format as the CLR instruction. Other instructions with single operands or those with no operands may vary considerably in their machine-language format from that shown for the

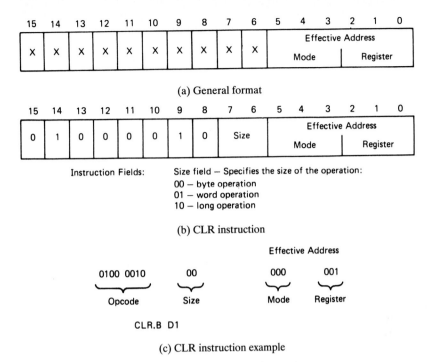

(a) General format

Instruction Fields: Size field — Specifies the size of the operation:
00 — byte operation
01 — word operation
10 — long operation

(b) CLR instruction

(c) CLR instruction example

Figure 4.21   Single-address instructions.

CLR instruction. Instructions to control the processor may have no address specification but use a unique 16-bit operation word with fixed format. For example, the STOP instruction has the single hexadecimal word 4E72 as its op code.

4.5.2 Double-Address Instructions

When an instruction uses two operands, the addressing modes for both the source and destination must be specified in the operation word. If each double-address instruction encoded the addressing modes into 6 bits each, as shown previously, and specified length (byte, word, or longword) for each operand using 2 bits, a total of 14 bits of the 16-bit operation word would be taken; thus only 2 bits would remain for the op code. Since 4 bits are always used for the op code, flexibility in addressing for double-address instructions must be limited further to provide a full set of instructions. A comparison of the MOVE instruction and the ADD instruction shows the approach taken by the designers of the CPU32.

    The MOVE instruction.   The format of the MOVE instruction is shown in Figure 4.23(a) for MOVE.B, MOVE.L, and MOVE.W with bits [13:12] of the op code specifying the length. The source addressing mode is specified as before for single-address instructions. However, the destination addressing mode for MOVE reverses

Address Modes	Mode	Register
Data Register Direct	000	reg. no.
Address Register Direct	001	reg. no.
Address Register Indirect	010	reg. no.
Address Register Indirect with Postincrement	011	reg. no.
Address Register Indirect with Predecrement	100	reg. no.
Address Register Indirect with Displacement	101	reg. no.
Address Register Indirect with Index (8-Bit Displacement)	110	reg. no.
Address Register Indirect with Index (Base Displacement)	110	reg. no.
Absolute Short	111	000
Absolute Long	111	001
Program Counter Indirect with Displacement	111	010
Program Counter Indirect with Index (8-Bit Displacement)	111	011
Program Counter Indirect with Index (Base Displacement)	111	011
Immediate	111	100

Figure 4.22 Effective address encoding.

the mode/register encoding as shown. As an example, the format for the instruction

> MOVE.W   D1, D3

is illustrated in Figure 4.23(b).

The ADD instruction.   The ADD instruction has the general format shown in Figure 4.24(a). It requires the source or destination operand to be held in one of the data registers of the processor. The symbolic form of the ADD instruction is either

> ADD.X   <EAs>, <Dn>

or

> ADD.X   <Dn>, <EAd>

with X = B, W, or L, as before. In the first case, Dn specifies the destination for the result of the addition. The "op mode" bits [8:6] determine the length X and specify the destination as Dn. In the second instruction, the location specified by <EAd> is

MOVE Byte

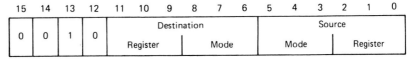

Note Register and Mode location

MOVE Long

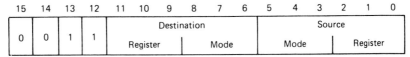

Note Register and Mode location

MOVE Word

15 14 13 12 11 10 9 8 7 6 5 4 3 2 1 0

0	0	1	1	Destination		Source	
				Register	Mode	Mode	Register

Note Register and Mode location

(a) Instruction formats

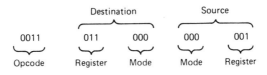

(b) MOVE.W D1,D3

Figure 4.23 MOVE instruction.

the destination and Dn is the source, so the op mode changes. An example is shown in Figure 4.24(b).

Many other double-address instructions restrict the source or destination location to be a processor register. Thus, memory-to-memory operations are not allowed except with the MOVE instruction. The MOVE instruction is therefore the most flexible of the CPU32 instructions with respect to its allowed addressing modes.

Example 4.14

Figure 4.25 shows several examples of the machine language and assembly language forms for the CLR, ADD, and MOVE instructions. The hexadecimal values to the left of the instruction represent the machine language code. Any immediate value or absolute address is held in memory words following the operation word.

15	14	13	12	11	10	9	8	7	6	5	4	3	2	1	0
1	1	0	1	Register			Op-Mode			Effective Address Mode | Register					

Instruction Fields:

Register field — Specifies any of the eight data registers
Op-Mode field —

Byte	Word	Long	Operation
000	001	010	$(<Dn>) + (<ea>) \rightarrow <Dn>$
100	101	110	$(<ea>) + (<Dn>) \rightarrow <ea>$

(a) ADD instruction format

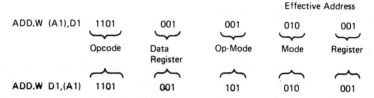

(b) ADD instruction encoding

Figure 4.24 ADD instruction.

```
abs.   LC    obj. code    source line
----   ----  ---------    -----------
  1    0000                    TTL   'FIGURE 4.25'
  2    0000                    LLEN 100
  3    0000               *
  4    8000                    ORG   $8000
  5    0000               *
  6    8000  421D              CLR.B    (A5)+
  7    8002  4258              CLR.W    (A0)+
  8    8004  42B8 0568         CLR.L    $0568
  9    8008  4239 0002         CLR.B    $00020000
       800C  0000
 10    800E              *
 11    800E  D800              ADD.B    D0,D4
 12    8010  D378 308E         ADD.W    D1,$308E
 13    8014  0642 0030         ADD.W    #$30,D2
 14    8018              *
 15    8018  141D              MOVE.B   (A5)+,D2
 16    801A  3401              MOVE.W   D1,D2
 17    801C  33C1 0003         MOVE.W   D1,$300E8
       8020  00E8
 18    8022  1CFC 002D         MOVE.B   #'-',(A6)+
 19    8026  23F9 0002         MOVE.L   $00022000,$14000
       802A  2000 0001
       802E  4000
 20    8030              *
 21    8030                    END
```

Figure 4.25 Program examples of instruction formats for the CPU32.

4.5.3 Compatibility with MC68000 Code

The instructions of the 16-bit MC68000 have the same bit patterns as the corresponding instructions of the CPU32. Thus, the machine-language or object code for a user-mode program written for the MC68000 will execute unaltered on the CPU32. This compatibility also extends to the supervisor mode except for certain operations that manipulate the data contained in the supervisor stack. This slight incompatibility is due to the fact that the stack formats of saved information are not the same for the two processors. However, with few exceptions, software developed for the 16-bit Motorola family will execute correctly on a MC68332-based system. Programs will execute faster since the 32-bit CPU32 has a faster instruction execution time for most instructions. One drawback to executing unmodified MC68000 programs on the CPU32 is that the CPU32 has more efficient instructions for certain operations. Thus, if the programs are not rewritten, they will not take advantage of the enhanced instruction set of the CPU32.

EXERCISES

4.5.1. Write the symbolic statements necessary to add two values in memory together and store the results in a third location.

4.5.2. Assume that (A1) = $1000 and ($1000) = $1000 before the execution of each instruction listed. Determine the resulting action of each instruction:
(a) CLR.B $1000
(b) CLR.W   (A1)
(c) MOVE.W   A1, (A1)
(d) MOVE.W $1000, D1
(e) MOVE.W   #$1000, D1
(f) MOVE.B   (A1), D1
The values are hexadecimal numbers for addresses and contents.

4.5.3. Translate the following machine-language statements, given in hexadecimal, into the assembler-language (symbolic) equivalent:
(a) 4241;
(b) 200B;
(c) 103C 002E.

4.5.4. Write the machine-language instruction for the following symbolic instructions:
(a) CLR.W   D0
(b) MOVE.L   A0, D0
(c) ADD.B   D0, D5

4.5.5. Consider the design of the instruction set of the CPU32. Why must some instructions be limited in their addressing flexibility compared to the MOVE instruction? For example, the ADD instruction requires that one of the operands be held in a data register.

4.5.6. Describe some of the factors that the designers must have considered when selecting the instructions and addressing modes for the CPU32. (This problem is considered in several articles listed in the Further Reading section of this chapter.)

4.5.7. The MC68000 object code for user-mode programs executes on MC68332-based systems. The assembler source code, however, is not necessarily compatible. When is source-code compatibility desirable? When is object-code compatibility advantageous?

4.6 THE MC68332 AND MEMORY ORGANIZATION

A simplified diagram of a MC68332 system is shown in Figure 4.26. The MC68332 is considered a byte addressing processor and each address indicates a byte (8 bits) location in memory or the address of a location associated with an interface. The range of possible addresses is called the *addressing space* of the processor. This space for the 24 address lines of the MC68332 is shown in Figure 4.27.

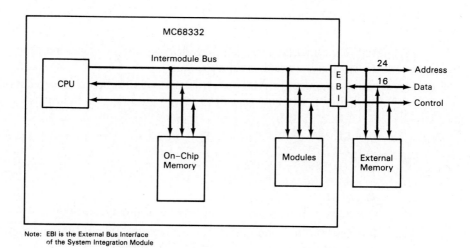

Note: EBI is the External Bus Interface
of the System Integration Module

Figure 4.26 The MC68332 and external memory.

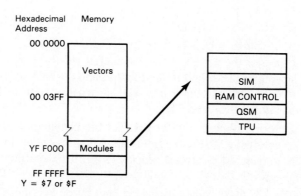

Figure 4.27 MC68332 address space.

The product designer can allocate the addressing space for programs, data, or I/O interfaces as necessary, but certain conventions are required for products that use the MC68332. The lower 1024 locations are reserved by the MC68332 processor for use as exception addresses (called *vectors* by Motorola). These addresses point to routines for servicing interrupts or processing traps. As such, they indicate the starting address of exception handling routines that process exceptions in the supervisor mode. Actually, in MC68332 systems, one or more vector tables can be present.[8]

Since the CPU32 can address byte, word, or longword operands, the physical organization of memory into bytes as shown in Figure 4.27 may be confusing when word or longword operands are addressed. The programmer must be aware of the relationship between the physical organization of memory into bytes and the operand length specified in an instruction. For byte-length operands, the physical address directly identifies the byte addressed. When a word or longword operand is specified in an instruction, the address identifies two or four bytes in memory, respectively.

4.6.1 Memory Organization and Addressing

The physical configuration of MC68332 memory may be logically organized into words as shown in Figure 4.28. This arrangement corresponds to a physical or hardware view of memory. Each byte can be addressed individually. Memory words occupy two bytes and have even addresses. Longwords in memory occupy four bytes and start at addresses that are multiples of four.

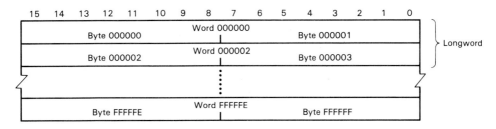

Figure 4.28 Memory organization by address.

Instructions must begin at even addresses. Thus, the instruction

JMP   1001

which attempts to begin the execution of a new program segment at an odd address, is illegal. Instructions are considered to occupy 1 or more words in memory at addresses N, N+2, N+4, ..., where N is an even integer. Organization of data values (operands) in memory is considered in the next subsection.

---

[8] The vector tables can also be relocated in memory. Standard designs reserve the low-memory addresses for a vector table as discussed in Chapter 10. The base address for the modules can be set at $7FF000 or $FFF000.

RAM and module addressing. Figure 4.27 shows the CPU32 addressing range as $000000 to $FFFFFF. The module registers are addressed starting at location $7FF000 or $FFF000. The exact address is set by the initialization program when the product is reset or power is turned on. Each module contains several registers used to program it to perform a specific function. From the programmer's point-of-view, the module registers appear the same as memory locations.

The on-chip RAM of the MC68332 occupies 2KB in memory. Its starting address in the memory space is determined when the MCU is initialized. There is no programming distinction between the on-chip RAM and external memory. Specific program techniques for the modules are introduced in Chapter 10 and discussed in detail beginning in Chapter 12.

4.6.2 Data Organization in Memory

Data values or addresses are stored in memory as shown in Figure 4.29. Within a byte, bit 0 is the rightmost bit and bit 7 is the leftmost bit. For integer data, bit 0 represents the least significant digit in a byte, word, or longword binary operand. In the figure, the word and longword operands are stored at even memory addresses. A longword is stored with the high-order 16 bits in location N and the low-order portion at location N + 2, where N is an even integer. If the value is an address, the address is stored in the same way.

Binary-coded decimal (BCD) values are stored two digits per byte when packed. The two digit unpacked value occupies a word. For BCD values, the least significant digit is always at the highest byte address in the operand.

Example 4.15

Table 4.7 shows a number of items stored in memory at the locations specified. In each case, the address and its contents are hexadecimal. The instructions CLR and MOVE require one word for their operation word. The MOVE instruction also requires an additional word to indicate the short absolute address $1000. The long address $200F6 is stored as shown, with the most significant word appearing first in memory. For example, a return address saved on the system stack would be stored in this manner.

The word location $2000 contains $2001 in the figure, but each individual byte could be addressed. Thus, the byte address $2000 contains $20 and the byte address $2001 contains $01, as shown. The instruction

> MOVE.B $2000, D1

would cause (D1)[7 : 0] = $20. The transfer

> MOVE.W $2000, D1

results in (D1)[15:0]= $2001.

Finally, the location $2008 contains the decimal value 1021 stored as a BCD number. The two low-order digits are stored in byte location $2009 and the two high-order digits are in location $2008. CPU32 instructions that operate on multidigit BCD numbers require this format for BCD data storage.

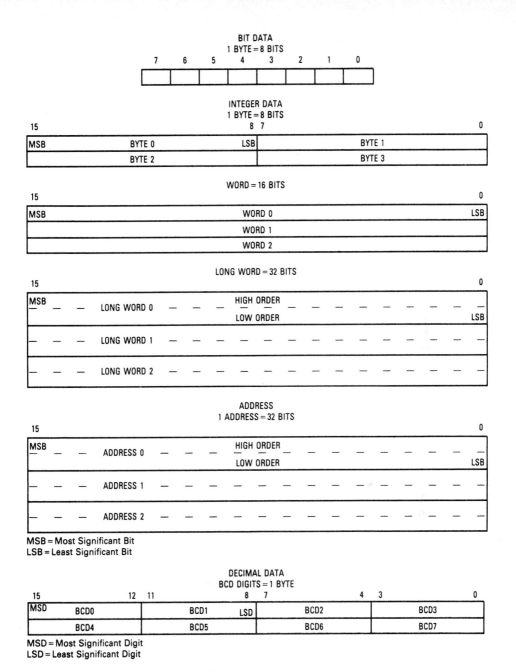

BIT DATA
1 BYTE = 8 BITS

7	6	5	4	3	2	1	0

INTEGER DATA
1 BYTE = 8 BITS

15		8	7		0
MSB	BYTE 0	LSB	BYTE 1		
	BYTE 2		BYTE 3		

WORD = 16 BITS

15		0
MSB	WORD 0	LSB
	WORD 1	
	WORD 2	

LONG WORD = 32 BITS

15		0
MSB — — — LONG WORD 0 — — — HIGH ORDER — — — — — — — — —		
LOW ORDER		LSB
— — — LONG WORD 1 — — — — — — — — — — — — — —		
— — — LONG WORD 2 — — — — — — — — — — — — — — —		

ADDRESS
1 ADDRESS = 32 BITS

15		0
MSB — — ADDRESS 0 — — — HIGH ORDER — — — — — — — — —		
LOW ORDER		LSB
— — — ADDRESS 1 — — — — — — — — — — — — — —		
— — — ADDRESS 2 — — — — — — — — — — — — — — —		

MSB = Most Significant Bit
LSB = Least Significant Bit

DECIMAL DATA
BCD DIGITS = 1 BYTE

15	12	11	8	7	4	3	0
MSD BCD0		BCD1	LSD	BCD2		BCD3	
BCD4		BCD5		BCD6		BCD7	

MSD = Most Significant Digit
LSD = Least Significant Digit

Figure 4.29 Data organization in memory.

Table 4.7 Example of Memory Contents

Memory Address	Contents byte				Meaning
	N	N+1	N+2	N+3	
1000	42	83	X	X	CLR.L D3
1004	11	C0	10	00	MOVE.B D0,$1000
.					
100A	00	02	00	F6	Address $200F6
.					
2000	20	01	X	X	Byte data
.					
2008	10	21	X	X	BCD 1021

Notes:
1. Except for BCD value 1021, all numbers are hexadecimal.
2. X indicates an unknown value.

EXERCISES

4.6.1. Determine the decimal number of bytes, words, or longwords the MC68332 can address.

4.6.2. Show how the following numbers or characters are stored in memory if each starts at hexadecimal location 1000. The data and formats are as follows:
(a) 10,203,040 (BCD);
(b) 0200 00FC (hexadecimal);
(c) 'ABCD' (ASCII).

4.6.3. The program counter contained $02FFF0_{16}$ before it was transferred into memory starting at location 1002_{16}. What are the memory contents in each byte of the memory area where (PC) is stored?

FURTHER READING

The articles and textbooks listed here treat various aspects of the design of modern computer systems and CPU chips. Bowlby's article describes various integrated circuit packages. The articles by Johnson, Kuban, and the Motorola semiconductor group deal specifically with the Motorola family of products. Tredennick's textbook explains the design of microprocessors using the IBM micro/370 and the MC68000 as examples. He was one of the designers of the MC68000 CPU. The textbook by Stone gives a detailed analysis of many of the features of modern microprocessors. The book treats pipelines in some detail.

BOWLBY, REED, "The DIP may take its final bows," *IEEE Spectrum*, **22**, No. 6 (June 1985), 37–42.

JOHNSON, THOMAS L., "The RISC/CISC Melting Pot," *Byte*, **12**, No. 4 (April 1987), 153–160.

KUBAN, JOHN R., and JOHN E. SALICK, *Testing Approaches in the MC68020*, Motorola Publication AR225. Austin, Tex.: Motorola Semiconductor Products Inc.

"MC68000 Microprogrammed Architecture", Motorola Publication AR235. Austin, Tex.: Motorola Semiconductor Group.

STONE, HAROLD S., *High-Performance Computer Architecture*. Reading, Mass.: Addison-Wesley, 1987.

TREDENNICK, NICK, *Microprocessor Logic Design*. Bedford, Mass.:Digital Press, 1987.

5

MC68332 CPU Assembly Language and Basic Instructions

The brief introduction in Chapter 4 to the machine language of the MC68332 CPU (CPU32) should indicate the complexity involved in machine-language programming. An extensive instruction set combined with the variety of addressing modes for many instructions would preclude efficient coding in machine language except for the simplest of programs. In assembly language, instructions and addresses are designated by symbolic names which are eventually translated into the appropriate binary code for execution by the CPU. Motorola has defined a standard assembly language for the CPU32. The rules for the language specify the instruction mnemonics, symbolic addressing references, and the format for each assembly-language statement. These conventions are generally followed by other suppliers of assemblers for the CPU32. However, differences in assemblers must be resolved by reference to the *User's Manual* for a particular assembler.

This chapter begins with a discussion of techniques for software development in Section 5.1. Section 5.2 introduces the assembly-language for the CPU32. The emphasis is on standard features common to all assemblers although the program examples in this chapter were created with Motorola development software. Therefore, techniques may vary if development software for the MC68332 from other manufacturers is employed. Section 5.2 also describes the more sophisticated capabilities available with some assemblers. Section 5.3 describes each addressing mode of the CPU32. Section 5.4 summarizes the addressing modes and their use.

Notation. In this chapter, a hexadecimal number in the text itself is preceded by a $ symbol. Otherwise, numerical values in the text are decimal. However, assembler listings and displayed outputs from monitor sessions use hexadecimal values for addresses of memory locations and their contents, but no preceding symbol is used to indicate hexadecimal notation by these programs. However, the assembly-language statements created by the programmer require the $ preceding a hexadecimal number. As an immediate value, the hexadecimal number $hhhh would be written in a program as #$hhhh.

When an address register is used as the destination location in an instruction, the instruction variations of ADD, MOVE, and SUB become ADDA, MOVEA, and SUBA, respectively. Instruction variations for immediate operands and quick immediate operands (range 1–8) are referenced as ADDI, ADDQ, SUBI, SUBQ, and so on. Most assemblers utilize the most efficient instruction variations even if the programmer does not explicitly define the suffix. The programs used as examples in this chapter explicitly use the variations for clarity. For convenience, the instruction set for the CPU32 is summarized in Appendix IV. Chapter 7 describes the variations of the arithmetic instructions. Chapter 9 presents instruction variations that reference an address register as the destination.

5.1 SOFTWARE DEVELOPMENT

Software development consists of problem analysis, software design, and program coding, followed by debugging and testing. Appropriate documentation should be provided at each stage. The programming activities are shown in simplified form in Figure 5.1, which emphasizes the cyclic or iterative nature of the process. The editor program is used to create an assembly-language *source* program which is translated by the assembler.[1] At this stage in development, the assembler *listing* is used to find errors in the source program. Errors in the source program are indicated on the listing. The listing presents both the assembly-language source program and the machine-language equivalent if no errors are detected by the assembler.

Once the source program is free of assembly errors, an *object module* is produced by the assembler. The object module contains the translated assembly-language statements and other information to allow the program to be loaded into the target machine's memory for execution. Thus, the object module also requires processing by another program before the machine-language code for the CPU is produced. The processed object module is typically called a *load module*. A *binary* load module contains the machine-language program and any data in binary code ready to be loaded at the starting address of the program in memory.[2]

Execution of the code is controlled during debugging by a program called a *debugger*. This program allows the user to control instruction execution and to display

---

[1] The details involved in executing the development software (editor, assembler, debugger) vary with different systems. Also, the source programs are normally stored as disk files on the development system disk. The *User's manual* for a particular system will describe the procedure required to create, store, and execute programs.

[2] In practice, the object program produced by the assembler requires processing by another program before it is loaded into memory for execution. The distinction between assembly, loading, and execution operations is discussed in several of the references contained in the Further Reading section for this chapter.

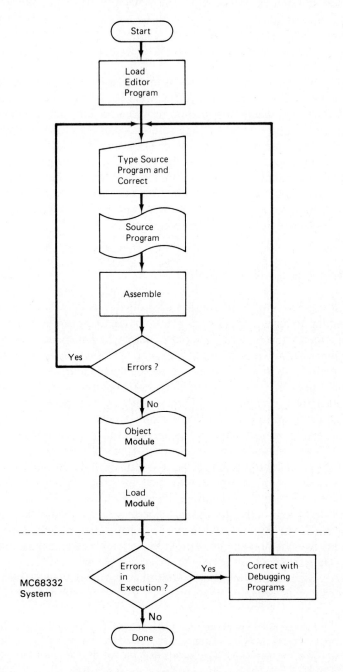

Figure 5.1 Programming a microcomputer.

intermediate results after each instruction completes. Errors in the design of the program may be detected at this stage. To correct the errors, the source program must be re-edited and assembled again.

5.1.1 The Assembler and Listing

As described previously, the assembler translates source statements and checks for errors. Figure 5.2 presents and example listing produced by the assembler. Each statement is either a CPU32 instruction, an assembler directive, or a comment. A symbolic instruction such as

ADD.W   (A1)+,D1

becomes an executable machine-language instruction. The mnemonic ADD, the operand size, and the operand addresses are recognized by the assembler and converted to binary machine code. Assembler directives, on the other hand, are instructions for the assembler, not the CPU.

The origin directive in Figure 5.2, for example, specifies where the program is to be loaded into memory. As an example, the directive

ORG $8000

indicates that the program is to be loaded at the hexadecimal location $8000. This directive specifies an absolute starting address in memory for the program. An object module containing absolute addresses is produced. Thus, the program is not intended to be relocated in memory to another starting address as the program is loaded. In contrast, the program is said to be relocatable in memory if the starting address is assigned after assembly as described in Subsection 5.1.2. For simplicity, the ORG directive is used to specify the absolute load address of the program examples in this chapter.

Comments for the convenience of the programmer may also appear in the source program. These comments are ignored by the assembler and simply printed on the listing.

Example listing.   Figure 5.2 shows a typical CPU32 assembler listing in the same format as example listings to be presented in this chapter. The first column is the decimal line number. The second column is the hexadecimal value of the location counter at each instruction. The location counter keeps track of instruction locations during assembly much as the program counter does during program execution. If the program shown were loaded beginning at location $8000, the program counter of the CPU would change as the program executes just as the location counter in Figure 5.2.

The third column labeled "obj.code" in Figure 5.2 is the machine-language translation of the assembly-language program that is part of the object module. The machine language consists of an operation word for each instruction followed by the value of any extension words required for the instruction as previously discussed in Section 4.5. This is the code that is contained in the object module for the program in this case since absolute addresses are assigned by the ORG directive. Any value to be placed in memory and assigned by an assembler directive, such as the Define Constant (DC) statement shown, also appears in this column.

The machine language is followed to the right by the source program statement that generated it. In our examples, the in-line comments are preceded by an optional semicolon. An entire line is treated as a comment if an asterisk (*) is the first character of the line.

```
abs.    LC   obj. code    source line
----    ----  ---------    -----------
  1    0000                    TTL    'FIGURE 5.2'
  2    0000                    LLEN   100         ;LINE LENGTH
  3    8000                    ORG    $8000       ;ORIGIN IN MEMORY
  4    0000            *
  5    8000            * ADD FOUR 16-BIT NUMBERS STORED IN LOCATIONS $9000
  6    8000            *    THROUGH $9006.  RETURN THE SUM IN D1[15:0].
  7    8000            *
  8    8000 7200    INIT MOVE.L  #0,D1        ;ZERO SUM
  9    8002 227C 0000      MOVEA.L #$9000,A1   ;ADDR OF FIRST NUMBER
       8006 9000
 10    8008 7404            MOVE.L  #4,D2       ;SET COUNTER TO 4
 11    800A            *
 12    800A            * DEFINE LOOP TO ADD VALUES
 13    800A            *
 14    800A D259    LOOP ADD.W   (A1)+,D1     ;SUM NUMBERS
 15    800C 5342            SUB.W   #1,D2       ;DECREMENT COUNTER
 16    800E 66FA            BNE     LOOP        ;TILL (D2)=0
 17    8010            *
 18    8010 4E4F            TRAP    #15         ;RETURN TO MONITOR
 19    8012 0063            DC.W    $0063
 20    8014            END
```

Figure 5.2 Typical assembly listing.

The simple program in Figure 5.2 sums four 16-bit integers in locations $9000, $9002, $9004, and $9006. The result is stored in (D1)[15:0]. The three directives LLEN, ORG, and END define the width of the listing, the origin, and the end of the program, respectively. The TTL (title) directive is optional to identify the program for the convenience of the programmer. INIT and LOOP are labels attached to a particular line in the program so that the line can be referred to symbolically from elsewhere in the program. The labels have values assigned by the location counter.

In the program, INIT indicates the location of the first instruction. LOOP defines the start of a sequence of instructions which is repeated four times during execution to sum the values. This iteration or loop is terminated when the value in D2 reaches zero.

The last instruction, TRAP #15 serves to return control to the monitor program. This is the typical way to transfer control from an applications program to a Motorola operating system or monitor program. A constant that is defined as part of the TRAP instruction by DC.W $0063 (Define Constant) indicates to the monitor that the program has completed execution when the TRAP instruction executes. Various other options are available, as will be described subsequently. The END statement is a directive to the assembler that defines the end of the program being assembled. It must be the last directive in the program.

In Figure 5.2, the numbers (immediate values) that appear in instructions must be preceded by the number symbol (#). However, the numerical values for the assembler directives do not require the designation as immediate values. Such assembler conventions must be determined by reference to the *User's Manual* for the particular assembler being used.

5.1.2 Cross-Assembly and Linking

Figure 5.3 shows the host computer system and software used by the author for program development with cross-assemblers. The IBM PC (Personal Computer) is used for software development. Once the assembly-language program is corrected and ready to be executed, the load module can be transferred to the MC68332-based system for execution and debugging. Alternatively, the execution can be simulated with a simulator program on the host computer. These programs execute under the control of the operating system of the host computer being used. It should be emphasized that the precise steps to create an executable machine-language program depends on the development software being used. Figure 5.3 only shows the steps in program development using the author's development system and software from Motorola.

The first step is to create the source program and translate it with the assembler into an object module. As previously discussed, the object module may contain absolute load addresses if the ORG directive is used in the source program. However, in many applications, several object modules are to be combined into a single load module. These object modules may have been created by separate assemblies or by a compiler as is the case with the C language. With multiple object modules, the object modules generally do not contain absolute addresses but *relocatable* addresses that will be assigned by a development program that is variously called a *linker* or a *linkage editor* or simply a *link editor* program. A linker serves to combine several object modules into a *load module* as shown in Figure 5.3. The link file lists the names and other information for the object modules being linked. All of the programs are stored as disk files on the host computer's disk unit.

The load module in Figure 5.3 is not a binary load module and thus is not ready for loading into the memory of the MC68332 system. In fact, the load module produced by the Motorola linker is a file of ASCII text which must be further processed to produce an executable module. In the author's system, the load module in ASCII form is first converted to the Motorola standard S-record form. The S-record format is used to transfer programs and data between computers. This S-record load module is a file of records (lines of text) in ASCII that is suitable to be transferred to the target MC68332 system. The S-record load module is necessary in the system shown in Figure 5.3 because the host computer and the target MC68332 system use different CPUs.

A standard communications channel can be used to transfer the S-record load module from the host computer to the MC68332 system since the S-record file is ASCII text. In response to the operator's request, the monitor program in the ROM of the MC68332-based development system causes the transfer from the host. This monitor converts the transmitted load module from the form of S-records (ASCII) into machine-language instructions in binary and loads the executable instructions into memory. The host computer need only have the file transfer program to respond

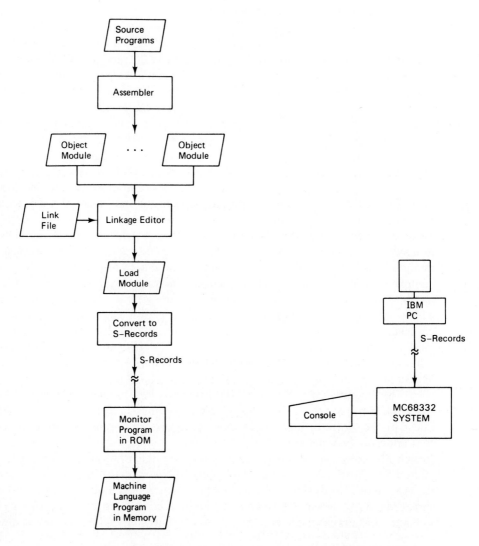

Figure 5.3 Hardware and software involved in program development.

to the monitor's request.[3] Once the machine-language program is in memory, the monitor program is used to execute the program and perform debugging functions as described in Subsection 5.1.3.

Example 5.1

The load module produced by the cross-software is not directly executable on a MC68332-based system. This module is stored as a disk file on the host computer's disk unit. The file actually contains ASCII text in a special format called *S-records* by Motorola. This format was created to allow files to be transmitted between computer systems via serial communication lines. Figure 5.4(a) shows the general format.

A specific example for the assembly-language program of Figure 5.2 is given in Figure 5.4(b). The S0 record indicates the first record of a series of S-records. Each following record (S1), (S2), or (S3) contains the type, the hexadecimal length of the record in bytes, the hexadecimal starting address at which the program segment is to be loaded, and finally, the instructions or data. The length is the number of character pairs following the length specification.

There are 23 ($17) bytes or character pairs in the S1 record of Figure 5.4(b). These values without the checksum characters are to be stored in memory starting at address $8000. The last two characters represent a check sum for verifying the correctness of the record. A termination record (S9) indicates the end of the object module. Notice that the checksum $FC represents the one's complement of the sum of the hexadecimal values ($03) in the S9 record, excluding the type specification itself.

Type	Record Length	Address	Code/Data	Check Sum

Type: S0–S9; 2 characters
Length: hexadecimal value — number of bytes (character pairs) in the record, including the address and the check sum; 2 characters
Address: hexadecimal value — starting address in memory; 4 (S1), 6 (S2) or 8 (S3) characters
Code/Data: data or instructions
Check Sum: the least significant byte of the 1's-complement sum of values in the record excluding the type; 2 characters

(a) Format definition

```
S00C000046303530322E4F424ADD
S11780007200227C000090007404D259534266FA4E4F006330
S9030000FC
```

(b) Sample object module in S-record format

Figure 5.4 S-record format.

---

[3] A number of file transfer programs are available. For example, KERMIT and PROCOMM+ are programs that allow an IBM PC to emulate a terminal and perform file transfers. PROCOMM+ is a program available from Datastorm Technologies, Inc.

Motorola assembler and the BCC.   The particular assembler used in this example is a Motorola cross-assembler designated as MASM (M68000 family structured assembler). The assembler recognizes all of the CPU32 assembly-language statements and converts the assembly program to an object module. A listing is produced in the form shown in Figure 5.2. However, the object module is not ready for execution but must first be processed on the host computer by a linking program. The MASM assembler produces the object module in a format called the Common Object File Format (COFF). The COFF file contains information from the assembly to allow the linker to combine several object modules into a load module. The reader is referred to the *M68000 Family Link Editor User's Guide* available from Motorola for more information about the COFF format.

The Motorola linker program produces a load module that is in ASCII code in the COFF format. When cross-software is used to develop programs, this COFF load module must be further processed by a program called HEX to produce the S-records suitable for loading by the debugger program of the MC68332-based system.

The hardware system used to test most of the program examples in this book is called the Business Card Computer (BCC). This is a single-board computer to be described in more detail in Section 10.3 and Chapter 16. The debugger program is actually part of the monitor program stored in non-volatile memory on the BCC board. The BCC also includes Random Access Memory (RAM) to store programs and data loaded during software development.

When the cross-assembly techniques as described in Section 5.1.2 are employed, the assembler executes on a host computer. The assembled and linked programs must then be loaded into the memory of the target system; the BCC board in this particular case. Subsection 5.1.3 describes the use of the monitor program of the BCC system. The BCC monitor discussed in this textbook is the MC68332 Debug Monitor which is referenced as *332BUG* for abbreviation. Subsection 5.1.4 describes resident assemblers.

5.1.3 Monitor Program

In general, any monitor program will allow the operator to load a program, initialize memory locations and processor registers, and execute the program. The monitor session is carried on interactively via an operator's terminal. At the terminal, values can be changed during execution of the program (at breakpoints) for the purpose of testing. The contents of memory locations and registers can also be displayed. If errors are found, the program is usually modified and then reassembled, linked, and loaded for another debugging session. The 332BUG monitor discussed here is typical of monitor programs for modern computer systems. However, the features of an individual monitor depend completely on the system being used, so that reference to the *User's manual* for a particular monitor is necessary to understand its use.

The Motorola monitor used to execute and debug the examples in this book is designated as 332BUG. One of its primary purposes is to accept commands from the operator. The operator's terminal, consisting of a keyboard and a display unit, can be connected directly to the MC68332-based system. Alternatively, the host computer can serve as a terminal emulator. In either case, the commands allow the operator to control 332BUG and choose functions such as the following:

(a) load programs from a host computer into the memory of the development system;

(b) aid program debugging;

(c) perform diagnostic tests on the hardware components of the system.

The monitor resides in a Read-Only Memory (EPROM). In addition, the monitor requires an additional 12 Kilobytes of memory as its RAM area. This monitor allows loading and execution of programs written for the CPU32. The BCC with its 332BUG monitor is used primarily for program debugging and evaluation. Chapter 16 describes more powerful development systems for hardware and software development.

System features of the 332BUG monitor. After power is first applied to the BCC development system, the monitor program in ROM is the only software available for the system. The 332BUG monitor begins execution automatically and performs several diagnostic tests on the system. If the computer is not faulty, the monitor requests commands from the operator by issuing the prompt

332BUG>

on the operator's display unit. The monitor then awaits operator response in the form of a valid command.

In addition to aiding the operator to perform program loading and debugging, the 332BUG monitor contains routines that allow diagnostic testing of the BCC hardware itself. The operator can select diagnostic tests of the CPU chip, or of the memory. If any of the devices fail the diagnostic tests, a message is displayed on the terminal indicating the type of failure. When a failure is indicated, the operator may take the necessary corrective action. For example, the operator could replace a memory module if the memory failed the diagnostic tests. If no error is indicated during the diagnostic tests, the BCC is ready to use in program development and debugging.

Program development and debugging using 332BUG. Table 5.1 lists a few of the commands for the 332BUG monitor. The monitor prompt on the operator's screen during debugging sessions has the form

332BUG>

to indicate that the monitor is ready to accept commands. The operator enters the one or two letter command followed by any parameters and a carriage return (CR) to invoke a command. In the examples in this chapter, any value displayed by the monitor in response to a command is not preceded by the prompt. Also, all addresses and memory contents are given in hexadecimal unless otherwise indicated. Therefore, hexadecimal values entered by the operator do not use the $ designation which is required by the assembly-language notation. Processor registers are designated by their symbolic names: A0, A1, ..., A7 for address registers and D0, D1, ..., D7 for data registers. The active stack pointer, A7, can be the User Stack Pointer (USP) or the Supervisor Stack Pointer (SSP) depending upon the CPU mode of operation

Table 5.1 332BUG Commands

Command	Meaning
General format:	
332BUG> <operator entered command> (CR)	
Communication with host computer:	
LO;X=<command to host>	Load S-records from host
Initialize register or memory contents:	
MM <address>[;DI]	Memory Modify (sequential)
MS <address> <value>	Memory Set (one location)
RM <register>	Register Modify
Display registers or memory contents:	
MD <start address>[;DI]	Memory Display
RD <registers>	Register Display
Execute and trace:	
BR <address>	Insert a breakpoint
GO	Execute a program
GT <address>	Go till <address>
T	Single-step (trace)
TC	Trace on change of control flow

Notes:
1. <> indicates any valid selection.
2. All values for data and addresses are hexadecimal.
3. Registers are selected by their assembly-language mnemonic.
4. [;DI] indicates an optional value; in this case, assemble or disassemble.

during debugging. The other registers of immediate interest are the PC (program counter) and CCR (condition code register).

Table 5.1 divides the monitor commands into those which allow communication with a host computer and those which are used for program debugging. In the former category, LO (Load) is used to transfer a file from the host to the target computer. The name of the file to be transferred may be part of the command to the host in the LO command. The exact procedure depends on the file transfer program executing on the host computer.

For debugging, the contents of a register or a memory location can be initialized, modified, or displayed by the appropriate command in Table 5.1. A number of other commands control the execution of a program. For example, the T (trace) and TC (trace on change of control flow) commands set trace options for the CPU. In the trace modes, the traced instructions are executed and control is returned to the monitor program. The monitor program displays the contents of the CPU registers and other information after tracing.

The monitor also has a *one-line assembler* which converts a single assembly-language statement into machine language at the address specified. It is an option for the MM (memory modify) command. Such a one-line assembler is of limited use in program development. For example, no labels are allowed to designate program statements.

The reverse process of assembly is termed *disassembly*. When the contents of memory locations containing machine-language instructions are displayed and disassembled, the 332BUG monitor will display the corresponding assembly-language statements in mnemonic form. This can be used to verify the program in memory without translating the machine-language code when the MD (memory display) command is used.

Example 5.2

Figure 5.5(b) shows the use of the 332BUG monitor for program loading, execution, and debugging. An assembly-language listing of the program being tested is included as Figure 5.5(a) for convenience. Its object module is stored on the host computer disk unit as file F0505.OBJ. The file name is indicated in the first S-record when read as ASCII characters. This file of S-records was created using the Motorola cross-assembler and linker programs. Before the object module can be loaded into memory, it is necessary to establish communication with the host computer. This part of the session is not shown in the figure. Once this communication to the host is established, the object module may be loaded by invoking the monitor again with the LO (Load) command.

The host responds to the LO command by transmitting the S-record file. The program is also loaded into memory by the monitor starting at location $8000. The instructions loaded are disassembled when the MD (Memory Display) command is issued with the DI (Disassemble) option. Our simple program adds four 16-bit numbers in memory locations $9000 through $9006 and accumulates the sum in (D1)[15:0].

Before execution, the program counter is initialized to $8000 using the RM (Register Modify) command. The RD (Register Display) command causes the CPU register contents to be displayed to show the initial values. The resulting display shows that the PC is initialized to $8000 as expected and that the Supervisor Stack Pointer points to location $10000. The display SSP* indicates that the SSP is the active stack pointer. The 332BUG monitor initializes the CPU in the supervisor mode with the supervisor stack beginning at $10000.

To test the program, four test values are loaded into memory as shown in Figure 5.5(b) using the MM (memory modify) command. Values of 1, 2, 3, and 4 are used. The last value is followed by a period to indicate to the monitor that no more locations are to be initialized. The MD (Memory Display) command is used to verify that the data are correct.

The selective register display (RD=) command is next issued to cause the monitor to display only register values of interest for the program. This shortens the display by eliminating the display of register values that are not changed by the program.

Then, the GT $8010 command causes execution from the starting location until the instruction at $8010 where the breakpoint is set. The final register display in Figure 5.5(b) shows that the value in D1 is indeed the hexadecimal sum of the values added. The counter value in D2 has been decremented to zero and the address in register A1 was incremented by 2 each time through the loop to point to the next operand in memory. The command GO would cause the TRAP #15 instruction, designated as SYSCALL, to be executed and return control to the monitor.

Debugging could continue by placing different values in memory and setting the PC value to $8000 before execution. More extensive testing would reveal a flaw in the program since the sum in register D1 is not tested to see if it overflows the register length (16 bits) being used. Techniques to test for this situation are discussed in Chapter 6 and Chapter 7.

```
abs. rel.    LC   obj. code    source line
---- ----   ----  ---------    -----------
  1    1    0000                        |        TTL    'FIGURE 5.5(a)'
  2    2    0000                        |        LLEN   100              ;LINE LENGTH
  3    3    8000                        |        ORG    $8000            ;ORIGIN IN MEMORY
  4    4    0000                        |*
  5    5    8000                        |* ADD FOUR 16-BIT NUMBERS STORED IN LOCATIONS $9000
  6    6    8000                        |*    THROUGH $9006.  RETURN THE SUM IN D1[15:0].
  7    7    8000                        |*
  8    8    8000 7200               |INIT     MOVE.L  #0,D1           ;ZERO SUM
  9    9    8002 227C 0000        |         MOVEA.L #$9000,A1        ;ADDR OF FIRST  NUMBER
  9         8006 9000
 10   10    8008 7404               |         MOVE.L  #4,D2           ;SET COUNTER TO 4
 11   11    800A                        |*
 12   12    800A                        |* DEFINE LOOP TO ADD VALUES
 13   13    800A                        |*
 14   14    800A D259               |LOOP     ADD.W   (A1)+,D1        ;SUM NUMBERS
 15   15    800C 5342               |         SUB.W   #1,D2           ;DECREMENT COUNTER
 16   16    800E 66FA               |         BNE     LOOP            ;TILL (D2)=0
 17   17    8010                        |*
 18   18    8010 4E4F               |         TRAP    #15             ;RETURN TO MONITOR
 19   19    8012 0063               |         DC.W    $0063
 20   20    8014                        |         END
```

(a) Assembly listing

```
332Bug>LO                                                  ;LOAD S-RECORDS
S00D00004630353035412E4F424A98
S11780007200227C0000090007404D259534266FA4E4F006330
S9030000FC

332Bug>MD 8000;DI                                          ;DISPLAY MEMORY
00008000 7200                 MOVEQ.L   #$0,D1             ;WITH DISASSEMBLY
00008002 227C0000 9000        MOVEA.L   #$9000,A1
00008008 7404                 MOVEQ.L   #$4,D2
0000800A D259                 ADD.W     (A1)+,D1
0000800C 5342                 SUBQ.W    #$1,D2
0000800E 66FA                 BNE.B     $800A
00008010 4E4F0063             SYSCALL   .RETURN
332Bug>RM PC                                               ;SET (PC)=$8000
PC   =00000000 ? 8000.
332Bug>RD                                                  ;DISPLAY REGISTER
PC   =00008000 SR   =2700=TR:OFF_S_7_.....   VBR  =00000000 ; VALUES
SFC  =5=SD     DFC  =5=SD     USP  =0000FC00 SSP* =00010000
D0   =00000000 D1   =00000000 D2   =00000000 D3   =00000000
D4   =00000000 D5   =00000000 D6   =00000000 D7   =00000000
A0   =00000000 A1   =00000000 A2   =00000000 A3   =00000000
A4   =00000000 A5   =00000000 A6   =00000000 A7   =00010000
00008000 7200                 MOVEQ.L   #$0,D1
332Bug>MM 9000                                             ;MODIFY MEMORY
00009000 FF00? 0001                                        ; INITIALIZE DATA
00009002 00EF? 0002
00009004 FF00? 0003
00009006 00FF? 0004.
332Bug>MD 9000                                             ;DISPLAY MEMORY
00009000 0001  0002  0003  0004    FF10  007F  FF00  08FF
332Bug>RD=PC/D1/D2/A1                                      ;DISPLAY SELECTED
PC   =00008000 D1   =00000000 D2   =00000000 A1   =00000000 ; REGISTERS ONLY
00008000 7200                 MOVEQ.L   #$0,D1
332Bug>GT 8010                                             ;EXECUTE PROGRAM
Effective address: 00008010                                ; AND VERIFY RESULTS
Effective address: 00008000                                ; AT BREAKPOINT
At Breakpoint
PC   =00008010 D1   =0000000A D2   =00000000 A1   =00009008
00008010 4E4F0063             SYSCALL   .RETURN
332Bug>
```

(b) Monitor trace of Figure 5.5(a)

Figure 5.5 A monitor session.

5.1.4 Resident Assembler

The procedure for program development and debugging described previously in Section 1.2 is for the cross-software development. The host computer and the target system used different processors. An assembler that executes on an MC68332-based computer to create programs for the CPU32 is called a *resident assembler* to differentiate it from a cross assembler. To use the resident software, a disk-storage unit with its associated hardware and software must be part of the MC68332-based host computer. The operating system is used to load the program into memory from the disk unit and execute it. The command sequence to accomplish this depends entirely on the characteristics of the operating system being used.

EXERCISES

5.1.1. The single-step and breakpoint features of a debugger are similar. Discuss the use of each technique and compare them.

5.1.2. A number of development systems are available for the MC68332. Select several systems and compare them for both software and hardware development and debugging. Reference to manufacturers' literature is encouraged.

5.1.3. Consider the use and advantages or disadvantages of software development with the following features:
   (a) a monitor program with a one-line assembler and disassembler;
   (b) cross-assembler and simulator executed on a host computer;
   (c) disk-based system with a resident assembler.

5.1.4. Compare the testing and debugging procedure using a high-level language with the techniques available to the assembly-language programmer. Use the simple program shown previously in this section as a specific example.

5.2 ASSEMBLY-LANGUAGE CHARACTERISTICS

The source program statements, as processed by the assembler, consist of strings of ASCII characters combined to form assembly-language statements. These statements are constructed according to the rules of the language. Each statement consists of four *fields*: label, operations, operand(s), and comments. The fields are separated by spaces or other delimiters according to the *format* required. For example, the statement

     INIT   MOVE.L   #0, D1   ;ZERO SUM

consists of label INIT; a mnemonic instruction MOVE, which represents the operation; an operand field (#0,D1); and a comment. In this case, the delimiter between fields is a blank or space character. At least one space is required to separate the fields. However, multiple spaces can be used. This is referred to as a *free-field* format.

Typically, the assembler first scans each source statement to determine that the format and symbol usage are valid. An error results if the format is incorrect or if the operation is not either a processor instruction or an assembler directive.

This section divides the discussion of CPU32 assembly language into three parts. The first deals with the construction of source statements representing executable instructions for the processor. The second covers assembler directives, which control the way the assembler itself operates. Finally, advanced features of the assembler are described.

5.2.1 Statement Formats

The source statements processed by the assembler must follow a precise format defining the order and relationship of the elements in the statement. The CPU32 assemblers recognize source statements composed of the following fields:
(a) label field;
(b) operation code or directive field;
(c) operand(s) field;
(d) comment field.
Each assembly-language statement consists of one or more of these elements separated by spaces.

Table 5.2 shows the format of a general assembly-language statement with optional fields enclosed in brackets. If an asterisk (*) is encountered in the first column of a statement, the entire statement is a comment. If another character is encountered in the first column, the symbol is considered to be a label, which must consist of alphanumeric characters. In most assemblers, the first character of a symbol must be a letter (A–Z), although different assemblers have other conventions. If no label is used, the first column must contain a blank (space) if other fields are present.

The next field encountered is interpreted as an instruction mnemonic or assembler directive. For example, in a statement without a label such as

$$\text{MOVE.W} \qquad \text{D1, D2} \qquad\qquad \text{; COMMENT}$$

the instruction mnemonic must start in column 2 or beyond. A space must precede the operands and the comment. The semicolon is not needed before the comment but is used here to enhance readability.

Labels. The label is optional for most instructions and directives. When one is used, it represents an address. The label is assigned the value of the location counter when the label is encountered. In statements such as

$$\text{HERE} \qquad \text{MOVE.W} \qquad \text{D1, D3}$$

the label HERE defines the location of the instruction in the source program. The label is used to define a location in a program for reference by another program instruction.

Table 5.2 Assembly-Language Format

Label field	Operation code and Directive field	Operand(s) field	Comments
[<LABEL>]	<op code> or <directive>	[<operand1>[,<operand2>]]	[<comment>]

Notes:
1. An asterisk in column 1 indicates a comment line.
2. Angle brackets <> indicate any valid symbol.
3. Square brackets [ ] indicate an optional field.

Example 5.3

Figure 5.6 shows several examples of labels used as addresses. As discussed in Section 5.1, the program adds four values to form a sum. The program starts at location $8000 and initializes the sum to zero when it executes. The symbol INIT is a label associated with the first statement and has the value $8000. Another program (not shown) could use the instruction

        JMP   INIT

to begin execution of this segment. The label LOOP locates the first instruction of a repeated sequence of instructions. The loop is executed four times until the counter value in D2 is decremented to zero. This label is simply for the addition sequence and would not be referenced by instructions other than the BNE instruction in the loop.

```
abs.   LC    obj. code    source line
----   ----  ---------    -----------
  1    0000                       TTL      'FIGURE 5.6'
  2    0000                       LLEN     100          ;LINE LENGTH
  3    8000                       ORG      $8000        ;ORIGIN IN MEMORY
  4    0000               *
  5    8000               * ADD FOUR 16-BIT NUMBERS STORED IN LOCATIONS $9000
  6    8000               *    THROUGH $9006.  RETURN THE SUM IN D1[15:0].
  7    8000               *
  8    8000  7200         INIT    MOVE.L   #0,D1        ;ZERO SUM
  9    8002  227C 0002            MOVEA.L  #$20000,A1   ;ADDR OF FIRST NUMBER
       8006  0000
 10    8008  7404                 MOVE.L   #4,D2        ;SET COUNTER TO 4
 11    800A               *
 12    800A               * DEFINE LOOP TO ADD VALUES
 13    800A               *
 14    800A  D259         LOOP    ADD.W    (A1)+,D1     ;SUM NUMBERS
 15    800C  5342                 SUB.W    #1,D2        ;DECREMENT COUNTER
 16    800E  66FA                 BNE      LOOP         ;TILL (D2)=0
 17    8010               *
 18    8010  4E4F                 TRAP     #15          ;RETURN TO MONITOR
 19    8012  0063                 DC.W     $0063
 20    8014                       END
```

Figure 5.6 Program example of use of labels in a program.

Table 5.3 CPU32 Instruction References

Operand	Format		Typical reference or operand	Instruction examples
None	OPR		External device	RESET
Implied	OPR		PC, SP, or SR	NOP, RTS
Immediate	OPR	#<value>	Processor control or instructions requiring a value	TRAP #15
Single	OPR	<address>	Relative address Instruction address Operand address	BRA LABEL JMP $8000 CLR D1
Double	OPR OPR	#<value>,<destination> <source>,<destination>	Immediate value to destination or double address	ADD #1,D1 MOVE D1,D2

Notes:
1. OPR is any valid operation code.
2. Minor variations from the formats shown are possible.

Operation codes. The second field in the source statement must contain an instruction mnemonic or assembler directive. When the operands require a length to be specified, a length specification is included as part of the instruction field. The length specification, preceded by a period, is appended to the operation code. The choices are B, W, or L to specify byte, word, or longword, respectively. For example, the instruction

> MOVE.W   D1, D2

defines word-length operands.

Operands. Most executable instructions have operands. The general formats for operands are shown in Table 5.3. A few instructions require no operands. Others refer to the processor registers implicitly, and their execution may cause the Program Counter, stack pointer, or Status Register values to be modified. The TRAP and STOP instructions, as examples, require an immediate value in the form of a decimal or hexadecimal number.

Most instructions require operands to be specified by addressing modes. Single-address instructions contain the specification of one operand. Double-address instructions contain two operands which are separated by a comma in the operand field. Processor address registers or data registers are designated symbolically by the letter A or D respectively, followed by the register number. Thus, the instruction

> MOVE.W   A1, D1

designates A1 as the source register and D1 as the destination. Indirect addressing is specified by enclosing the address register symbol in parentheses, as in the instruction

> MOVE.W   (A1), D2

which causes the word in the location pointed to by (A1) to be copied into D2. The addressing modes are described in detail in Section 5.3.

Example 5.4

Figure 5.7 is an assembler listing showing a number of statements to illustrate the specification of operands. The RESET and RTS (Return from Subroutine) instructions require no operands. A TRAP instruction must have the trap number specified as an immediate value. Such instructions have unique requirements for operand specification.

```
abs.   LC   obj. code    source line
----   ----  ---------   -----------
  1    0000                     TTL    'FIGURE 5.7'
  2    0000                     LLEN   100
  3    8000                     ORG    $8000
  4    0000              *
  5    8000              * MISCELLANEOUS INSTRUCTIONS
  6    8000              *
  7    8000 4E70                RESET
  8    8002              *
  9    8002 4E4F                TRAP   #15
 10    8004              *
 11    8004 4E75                RTS
 12    8006              *
 13    8006              * SINGLE ADDRESS
 14    8006              *
 15    8006 4241                CLR.W  D1                 ;DATA REG. DIRECT
 16    8008 4278 1000           CLR.W  $1000              ;ABSOLUTE
 17    800C 4251                CLR.W  (A1)               ;INDIRECT
 18    800E 4261                CLR.W  -(A1)              ;PREDECREMENT
 19    8010 4259                CLR.W  (A1)+              ;POSTINCREMENT
 20    8012 4269 0002           CLR.W  2(A1)              ;INDIR. WITH DISP.
 21    8016 4271 1002           CLR.W  (2,A1,D1.W)        ;INDIR. WITH INDEX
 22    801A 4271 A802           CLR.W  (2,A1,A2.L)
 23    801E              *
 24    801E              * DOUBLE ADDRESS (SOURCE ADDRESS SPECIFIED)
 25    801E              *
 26    801E 3401                MOVE.W D1,D2              ;DATA REG. DIRECT
 27    8020 3409                MOVE.W A1,D2              ;ADDR REG. DIRECT
 28    8022 3438 1000           MOVE.W $1000,D2           ;ABSOLUTE
 29    8026 3411                MOVE.W (A1),D2            ;INDIRECT
 30    8028 3421                MOVE.W -(A1),D2           ;PREDECREMENT
 31    802A 3419                MOVE.W (A1)+,D2           ;POSTINCREMENT
 32    802C 3429 0002           MOVE.W 2(A1),D2           ;INDIR. WITH DISP.
 33    8030 3431 1002           MOVE.W (2,A1,D1.W),D2     ;INDIR. WITH INDEX
 34    8034 343C 0005           MOVE.W #5,D2              ;IMMEDIATE
 35    8038 3439 0000           MOVE.W *+8,D2             ;RELATIVE
       803C 8040
 36    803E              *
 37    803E 4E4F                TRAP   #15                ;RETURN
 38    8040 0063                DC.W   $0063
 39    8042                     END
```

Figure 5.7 Program example of operand specification.

Single-address instructions, such as CLR, require one address in the operand field. The address may be specified by any addressing mode valid for the particular instruction. Several examples are shown for specifying the operand for the CLR instruction.

The double-address MOVE instruction is shown with various addressing modes used to specify the source operand. The destination is a register in each example, although the MOVE instruction does allow other addressing modes for the destination operand.

Expressions as operands. As shown in Table 5.4, the assembler recognizes symbols and expressions in the operand field. A *symbol* may designate an absolute address, an immediate value, or any other valid operand. An *expression* is a combination of symbols, constants, algebraic operators, and parentheses which the assembler evaluates to determine the address or value of the operand.

Table 5.4 Assembler Symbols for Expressions

Symbolic format	Interpretation
$<Number>	Hexadecimal number
<Number>	Decimal number
'<String>'	ASCII string of characters
#<Number>	Immediate operand
#'<String>'	Immediate operand (ASCII)
In expressions:	
+	Add
−	Subtract
*	Multiply
/	Divide
( )	Grouping

To specify a constant value, sometimes called a *literal*, the immediate addressing mode is used. For most assemblers, the constants can represent either numbers or ASCII characters. These constants are the simplest form of expressions and are specified using the definition in Table 5.4. A numerical constant can be any decimal or hexadecimal value that can be represented as an 8-bit, 16-bit, or 32-bit integer. The size specification of the instruction determines the appropriate length. A decimal number is defined by a string of decimal digits, and a hexadecimal number is defined by a dollar sign ($) followed by a string of hexadecimal digits. Thus, the instruction

$$\text{MOVE.W} \qquad \#\$2000, \text{D1}$$

defines the 16-bit hexadecimal value 2000_{16} as the immediate source operand.

ASCII literals consist of up to four ASCII characters enclosed in single quotes. For example, the string 'ABCD' is recognized by the assembler and converted into the hexadecimal code for the ASCII characters as

$$41 \ 42 \ 43 \ 44$$

which occupies four bytes when stored in memory. Longer character strings cannot be used as a literal value in an expression since the size is limited by the 32-bit registers of the CPU32. Appendix I defines the ASCII character set.

The operators for addition, subtraction, multiplication and division can be used in an expression. The result of any arithmetic operation is a 32-bit integer value. The unary minus (−) defines negative numbers. For example, the immediate value −1 in the instruction

$$\text{MOVE.W} \qquad \# - 1, \text{D1}$$

is stored as $FFFF with the instruction. An equivalent specification is

$$\text{MOVE.W} \qquad \#\$FFFF, D1$$

where the value $FFFF is the two's-complement number in 16 bits.

Example 5.5

The short program segment in Figure 5.8 shows various uses of labels and expressions. The labels START and ENDLP serve to define the values of the beginning and end of a group of statements in the example. These values are used in various expressions in the program.

```
abs.   LC    obj. code    source line
----   ----  ---------    -----------
   1   0000                        TTL   'FIGURE 5.8'
   2   0000                        LLEN    100
   3   8000                        ORG     $8000
   4   0000               *
   5   8000               *  USE OF LABELS AND EXPRESSIONS
   6   8000               *
   7   8000
   8   8000  227C 0000    START MOVEA.L #$9000,A1           ;FIRST ADDRESS
       8004 9000
   9   8006 7404                MOVE.L  #4,D2               ;COUNTER
  10   8008               *
  11   8008               *    THE SUM IS ADDED TO THE INITIAL VALUE IN D1
  12   8008               *
  13   8008  D259         LOOP  ADD.W   (A1)+,D1            ;ADD 4 NUMBERS
  14   800A 5382                SUBQ.L  #1,D2
  15   800C 66FA                BNE     LOOP
  16   800E 4E71         ENDLP NOP
  17   8010               *
  18   8010               *  LENGTH OF PROGRAM IN BYTES
  19   8010               *
  20   8010  760E                MOVE.L  #(ENDLP-START),D3   ;(D3)=14
  21   8012               *
  22   8012               *  LENGTH OF PROGRAM IN WORDS
  23   8012               *
  24   8012  7807                MOVE.L  #(ENDLP-START)/2,D4 ;(D4)=7
  25   8014               *
  26   8014               *  CONTENTS OF START (THE INSTRUCTION) TO D5
  27   8014               *
  28   8014  2A39 0000            MOVE.L   START,D5          ;(D5)=227C 0002
       8018 8000
  29   801A               *
  30   801A               *  ADDRESS OF START TO A2
  31   801A               *
  32   801A  247C 0000            MOVEA.L #START,A2          ;(A2)=8000
       801E 8000
  33   8020               *
  34   8020               *  ASCII STRING TO D6
  35   8020               *
  36   8020  2C3C 444F            MOVE.L  #'DONE',D6          ;(D6)=444F 4E45
       8024 4E45
  37   8026               *
  38   8026  4E4F                TRAP    #15
  39   8028  0063                DC.W    $0063
  40   802A                      END
```

Figure 5.8 Program example of use of labels and expressions.

The MOVEA and MOVE instructions initialize the address and counter, respectively, as the program is executed. When the addition is complete, the result is held in D1. The segment length is calculated as 14 bytes (seven words) in D3 by subtracting the values defined by the labels. The length in words is calculated by integer division. The result in D4 is half of the length in bytes. If the machine language instructions were moved in memory without re-assembly, statements referencing START as a source address or operand would be in error. The length calculations, however, would be correct.

The instruction itself at location START is moved into D5 when the source operand in a MOVE instruction specifies the label only. The immediate form #START selects the address.

The final MOVE instruction transfers the ASCII string 'DONE' to D6. Note that the immediate mode must be indicated or the value would be interpreted as an address. A suitable I/O routine (not shown) could be used to print the string to indicate completion of the program.

5.2.2 Assembler Directives

The mnemonic symbols for instruction op codes and those for the various addressing modes are part of an internal *symbol table* used by the assembler to translate the source statements into machine language. The programmer-defined symbols, such as labels, are used to reference instructions or data within the assembly language program. The assembler automatically keeps track of locations and offsets associated with the machine-language program.

The use of symbolic forms as addresses of instructions or as operands is of valuable assistance in writing assembly-language programs. This is one of the principal advantages of assembly language over machine language. However, most assemblers aid the programmer in other ways by providing *assembler directives* which are actually instructions to the assembler rather than for the processor. The action caused by each directive occurs only when the source program is being assembled. The major categories of directives are for assembly control, symbol definition, data definition and storage allocation, and listing control, as shown in Table 5.5.

Assembly control. The location counter of the assembler normally begins with the value $0000 to indicate the location of the first executable instruction unless the ORG directive is used to specify an absolute starting address. This counter is increased by the appropriate amount as each instruction is assembled. If the machine-language program were loaded into memory at location $0000 and executed, the program counter would follow the same sequence as the location counter as each instruction is executed in turn.

Loading programs at location $0000 is not advisable in MC68332 systems since the lowest addressed area in memory is reserved for MC68332 vectors as discussed in Chapter 10. Use of the ORG (origin) directive allows the programmer to define the starting value of the location counter and, consequently, the first address of the program in memory. In the previous examples in this chapter the ORG directive was used to indicate that hexadecimal location $8000 was to be used to store the first machine-language statement in a program.

The format of the ORG directive is

ORG   <expression>

Table 5.5 Assembler Directives

Directive and format	Meaning
Assembly control:	
ORG <expression>	Origin
END	End source program
Symbol definition:	
<label> EQU <expression>	Equate value to <label>
Data definition and storage:	
[<label>] DC.<l> <value(s)>	Define constant(s)[1,2]
[<label>] DS.<l> <number>	Reserve storage
Listing control:	
LLEN <N>	Line length
LIST	List (default)
NOLIST	No listing
SPC <N>	<N> blank lines
PAGE	Next page

Notes:
1. Square brackets indicate an optional field.
2. <l> denotes, B, W, or L.

in which the <expression> has the same meaning as previously defined. When the directive is encountered, the location counter is "loaded" with the value much as a jump (JMP) instruction changes the contents of the PC. The ORG directive can appear anywhere in the source program and can be used, for example, to divide the program into instruction and data sections. This is particularly useful if the instructions are to be held in a read-only memory and data are held in a writable memory at another starting location. Alternatively, the ORG directive could be omitted in the program. In this case, the starting address must be specified for the linkage editor to define the locations in memory corresponding to the assembler's relocatable addresses.

Another assembly control directive is the END directive, which is always the last source statement in a program. It causes the assembler to stop its top-to-bottom scan of the program. Any source statements after the END directive are not processed by the assembler.

Symbol definition.   An EQU directive is used to equate a number to a symbol. The value may represent an address or a constant. The format is

       EQU   <expression>

where <label> is assigned the value of the expression when the statement is assembled. The expression may contain a label if it has been defined previously in the program. Thus, the statement

    TTYOUT EQU $7FFF

assigns the value $7FFF to the symbol TTYOUT. The intent might be to define the starting address of an output buffer area using a mnemonic term. Then, a statement such as

MOVEA.L   #TTYOUT, A1

could be used to transfer the number $7FFF to the address register A1. If the immediate mode is not used for the source, the contents of the location are transferred. The instruction

MOVE.B   D1, TTYOUT

would move a byte from D1 to the location $7FFF, which might be the starting location of an output buffer, for example.

An important advantage of the EQU directive is evident when a value is defined which is referenced several times within a program. If the address TTYOUT needs to be changed in a subsequent assembly, re-assembly with a new EQU set to the correct address would change the value throughout the program. This might be necessary if the program is executed on several systems, each with different buffer locations.

The EQU directive can also be used to give useful names to mathematical constants, as in the statement

ONEK   EQU   1024

which defines ONEK as 1024 decimal. As another example, MAXMEM could be equated to the maximum memory space available for a system. The value could be changed, if necessary, when the program is reassembled on a new system. The only drawback is that the value defined by the EQU directive is known only to the assembler and does not exist in memory. Therefore, it cannot be changed without re-assembly.

Data directives.   The two directives DC (Define Constant) and DS (Define Storage) are available to initialize values in memory and reserve space in memory, respectively. The DC directive is similar to a DATA statement in FORTRAN, in which the variables defined are assigned initial values. The DS directive is similar to the DIMENSION statement, which reserves space for variables but assigns no values to them.

The Define Constant directive causes the assembler to store specified values in the location or locations associated with the location counter value at the time the DC directive is encountered during assembly. When the machine-language program is loaded into memory, the locations involved have the initial values specified. For example, the statement

INITV   DC.W   20

causes the decimal value 20 to occupy a word at location INITV. However, if the program is executed more than once and the value at INITV changes between executions, any program statement depending on the initial value of 20 may not yield the correct results when executed.[4] Thus, the DC directive should never be used to initialize a value that may be modified after the program is loaded into memory if multiple program executions depend on the initial value. A better approach to initialization of values is to reserve space for the values with a DS directive and then initialize the values with executable instructions.

Both the DC and DS directives require a length specification (B, W, or L). The length specification determines whether bytes, words, or longwords are to be reserved. Therefore, the directive

DS.W $10

reserves 16 words in memory. The length of each constant defined by the DC directive is determined by the size specification. For example, the directive

ADDRP1 DC.W   LABEL + 1

will store the address of LABEL plus 1 in the word location at ADDRP1.

Listing control.   The last group of directives in Table 5.5 indicates a few of the options available to format the listing produced by the assembler. The LLEN (line length) directive determines the number of characters in the printed lines. LLEN 72 is typically used for CRT units, but longer lines with more than 72 characters may be used for certain line printers. The SPC directive causes the specified number of blank lines to appear on the printout to enhance readability. Other directives, such as PAGE, are usually offered to format the listing. The PAGE directive causes an advance to the top of a new page each time it is encountered. The page length depends on the printer being used and is generally set as a parameter in the operating system.

Generally, each option for listing has a default value for which the opposite can be specified. The NOLIST directive in Table 5.5, for example, causes the statements following it to be omitted from the listing. Its opposite, the LIST directive, is the default value and need not be specified unless the NOLIST option is to be reversed. Thus, the sequence

LIST

(program segment I)

NOLIST

(program segment II)

---

[4] The contents of the location could change if another program writes a different value into the location. This can occur in systems where the same memory area is shared by programs executing at different times. A time-sharing system is an example in which an area of memory might be shared between users.

                    LIST

(program segment III)

                    END

lists segments I and III of a program but not segment II.

Example 5.6

Figure 5.9 illustrates a program employing a number of assembler directives. The first three directives create a title, set the line length, and set the origin to $8000, respectively. The EQU directives define the constant ONE, the starting address of the program for the second ORG directive, and the constant value ($0063) for the TRAP #15 instruction.

     The first ORG directive defines the area for data storage beginning at location $8000. The executable program begins at location $8100, as specified by the directive

           ORG   PROGRAM

The program clears the data locations between COMMON and the last location used for data.

     The DC directives define a number of constants in the data area. Note that

    INITADD DC.L   INITDT

initializes INITADD with the address of INITDT. The instruction

           MOVE.L   #INITDT, INITADD

would accomplish the same thing, but only as the program executes.

     A total of 55 bytes are reserved by the various DS directives and

           DS.B   55

would accomplish the same results. However, it is assumed that reference to the individual blocks (COMMON, HEXVAL, BYTES) is required in another program segment not shown. The final

           EVEN

directive aligns the next location address on a word (even) boundary.

```
abs.   LC   obj. code    source line
----   ----  ---------   -----------
  1    0000                          TTL    'FIGURE 5.9'
  2    0000                          LLEN   100
  3    8000                          ORG    $8000
  4          0000 0001   ONE         EQU    1                ;A CONSTANT
  5          0000 8100   PROGRAM     EQU    $8100            ;STARTING ADDR
  6          0000 0063   RETURN      EQU    $0063
  7    8000              *
  8    8000              *   DATA AREA
  9    8000              *
 10    8000 0A 05 07 00  INITDT      DC.B   10,5,7,0         ;BYTES-DECIMAL
 11    8004 0000 000A                DC.L   10,5,7           ;LONGWORDS
 11    8008 0000 0005
 11    800C 0000 0007
 12    8010 FF 10 AF 00              DC.B   $FF,$10,$AF,0    ;BYTES HEX
 13    8014 0000 00FF                DC.L   $FF,$20,$AE      ;LONGWORDS
 13    8018 0000 0020
 13    801C 0000 00AE
 14    8020 4142 4344              DC.B   'ABCDEFGH'       ;BYTES ASCII
 14    8024 4546 4748
 15    8028 4100 0000              DC.L   'A','BC'         ;LONGWORDS
 15    802C 4243 0000
 16    8030              *
 17    8030 0000 8000   INITADD     DC.L   INITDT           ;ADDRESS INPUT
 18    8034              COMMON      DS.W   10               ;10 WORDS
 19    8048              HEXVAL      DS.W   $10              ;16 WORDS
 20    8068              BYTES       DS.B   3                ;3 BYTES
 21    806C                          EVEN                    ;EVEN BOUNDARY
 22    806B              *
 23    806C              *   THE LENGTH IS COMPUTED AS THE LAST DATA LOCATION
 24    806C              *   MINUS THE FIRST DATA LOCATION:  (BYTES+3)-COMMON
 25    806C              *
 26          0000 0037   LENGTH      EQU    (BYTES+3-COMMON) ;NUM. OF BYTES
 27    806C              *
 28    8100                          ORG        PROGRAM
 29    8100              *
 30    8100              *   CLEAR COMMON VALUES
 31    8100              *
 32    8100 123C 0037   BEGIN       MOVE.B     #LENGTH,D1   ;COUNTER
 33    8104 227C 0000               MOVEA.L    #COMMON,A1   ;ADDR OF FIRST WORD
       8108 8034
 34    810A              *
 35    810A 12FC 0000   LOOP        MOVE.B     #0,(A1)+     ;CLEAR COMMON AREA
 36    810E 5301                    SUBQ.B     #ONE,D1
 37    8110 66F8                    BNE        LOOP
 38    8112              *
 39    8112 4E4F                    TRAP       #15
 40    8114 0063                    DC.W       RETURN
 41    8116                          END
```

Figure 5.9 Program example of use of assembler directives.

5.2.3 Advanced Features of Assemblers

Most modern assemblers provide a number of features to improve program structure and readability. Most of these features have always been present in assemblers for large computers but were unavailable in assemblers for many microcomputer-based systems until recently. They are introduced only briefly here, to acquaint the reader with these useful techniques. Anyone attempting an extensive development project using assembly language would be well advised to explore these capabilities for the particular computer being used. Most of the features are invoked by including assembler directives in the program. In some cases, the linkage editor is needed to complete the operations.

Table 5.6 Advanced Features of Assemblers

Type	Purpose or definition
Conditional assembly	To allow selective assembly
External references	References to variables or programs in another object module
Library	A collection of object modules taken as a unit
Macro instructions	A group of assembly-language statements referenced by name

Table 5.6 lists a number of capabilities of certain assemblers that go beyond the translation of each assembly-language statement into a machine-language instruction. They are listed in alphabetical order in the table but otherwise have no priority of importance. Their use depends on the application.

The technique of *conditional assembly* allows a programmer to select certain portions of the program to be assembled or not according to certain logical conditions. For example, the conditional-assembly specification (directive)

IFEQ   <expression>

<assembly-language statements>

ENDC

causes the statements between the IFEQ and ENDC directives to be assembled if the value of the <expression> is equal (EQ) to zero. Otherwise, these statements are ignored by the assembler. Other conditions might include a specification of not equal, greater than, or less than zero. The purpose is to allow one program to take care of several variants of the same basic problem. The choice is made only when the program is assembled. Each time a different segment of code is to be assembled, the <expression> must be changed appropriately and the program reassembled.

The ability to reference *external variables* in an assembly-language program is vital when a number of modules are to be linked together to form a load module. With this capability, a program may reference programs or variables by name in another object module without a specification of the exact address of the referenced entity. In one module, for example, the directive

XDEF   Y

defines the variable Y. Another module would include the statement

XREF   Y

to indicate that Y is defined elsewhere. The linkage editor resolves all external references and concatenates separate object modules into one contiguous, relocatable, object module.[5] One or more of these modules can also consist of a "library" of modules.

A *library* in this context is considered to be a group of object modules ready to be linked with the module that references programs or data in the library. For example, a mathematical library is convenient in certain applications. It might consist of routines to perform functions such as calculating the roots of equations and similar functions. An assembly-language program would simply reference the routines by name. The linking program would search the library and add the proper modules to form the complete load module before program loading and execution occurs. A library is created and maintained (modified by having modules added or deleted) by a program that is sometimes called a "librarian." This program works in conjunction with the assembler and linkage editor programs to provide the necessary information to allow the linkage editor to link the appropriate modules together.

Assemblers allow programming to be more modular and convenient by providing a macroassembler to assemble *macro instructions* called *macros* for short. The macro instruction can be viewed as the name of a sequence of assembly-language instructions. In this regard it is similar to a subroutine in a high-level language. An example of a macro structure might be

MAC1   MACRO

<assembly-language statements>

         ENDM

where MAC1 is a label. The statements in the body of the macro instruction are included in the assembly-language program each time the instruction MAC1 is encountered. Values may also be passed into the macro instruction in a manner similar to a subroutine call with various arguments. Section 7.6 presents a program example using macros.

EXERCISES

5.2.1. Write a routine to reserve a 20-word block of memory for storage and then initialize it to the successive values 1 through 20 upon execution.

5.2.2. Find the errors in the following program to add four 16-bit numbers in locations $20000 through $20006.

ORG	$10000
MOVE.L	$20000, A1
MOVE.L	4, D2

---

[5] The exact procedure depends on the system software being used. It differs slightly among computer systems.

```
            ADD.W          (A1)+, D2

            SUB.W          #ONE, D2

            BNE            LOOP

    ONE     DC.W           1
            JMP            RETURN
            END
```

5.2.3. Determine the values (if any) created by the following directives:
(a) DC.B 'N IS'
(b) DC.B 20
(c) HERE EQU *
(d) DS.L 1
(e) DC.L LABEL+2
Assume that the labels HERE and LABEL are defined at fixed addresses in a program.

5.2.4. Assume the EQU directives have been used to assign START the value $10000 and END the value $20000. Find the value computed by the assembler for the following expressions:
(a) START−2;
(b) END−START;
(c) (END−START)/2;
(d) (END−START)/3;
(e) 2 ∗ END.

5.2.5. Discuss how each of the advanced features of the assembler allows programs to be created which are easy to read, debug, and modify (maintain).

5.2.6. Give some applications that show where conditional assembly would be convenient. As a specific example, consider several models of the same basic computer with different memory capacity and disk units with slightly different characteristics. Assume an assembly-language program assigns memory space and determines when memory is full. Other routines handle input/output transfer with the disk unit. Describe the structure of such assembly-language routines. How would they be changed when they are made ready for execution on different models of the computer?

5.2.7. Compare the use of subroutines and macro instructions. Consider memory usage as well as programming convenience and efficiency. A subroutine is sometimes called a *closed* routine, while a macro is called an *open* routine.

5.2.8. Consider a large programming project that involves the development and debugging of a number of assembly-language modules, perhaps written by different programmers. Discuss various problems that might arise if the development software included only a non-relocating assembler with no advanced features. By comparison, how does a relocating assembler with advanced features and a linkage editor facilitate program development?

5.3 ADDRESSING MODES FOR THE CPU32

The different addressing modes of a processor determine the variety of ways that an operand or its address may be referenced by an instruction. Generally speaking, processors employed in sophisticated applications require a large number of addressing modes to be effective and efficient. The CPU32 allows 14 different modes, which classifies it among the most powerful microprocessors in this regard. The basic addressing modes were introduced in Chapter 4, where the operation of the CPU and its machine language were emphasized. In the present sections, all of the modes are discussed using the CPU32 assembly-language notation.

The general classification of addressing modes includes register direct, absolute, indirect, relative, and immediate addressing. In each class, a number of variations is available, as indicated in Table 5.7. For each addressing mode, the processor addressing circuitry computes the effective address of any operand specified in an instruction when that instruction is fetched and decoded. The table defines how the effective address, EA, is calculated or designated for each addressing mode.

The classification of addresses according to mode is convenient for the programmer to determine the ways in which operands can be referenced. Certain addressing modes are allowed and others forbidden to specific instructions. Table 5.8 lists the assembler syntax for each addressing mode and the effective address encoding (mode/register) used as part of the machine-language format. Section 4.5 describes the mode and register fields for various instructions. The symbols in Table 5.8 have the same meaning as those defined in Table 5.7.

Motorola literature further classifies addressing into categories to simplify the discussion of those modes available for an instruction. The addressing categories are *data, memory, control*, and *alterable*, referring to the operand characteristics. The final Subsection 5.3.6 explains these addressing categories and presents the machine-language form of the extension words required by some of the addressing modes.

5.3.1 Register Direct and Absolute Addressing

In both the register direct and absolute addressing modes, the location of an operand is specified explicitly in the instruction. A CPU32 *direct address* must refer to one of the processor data or address registers. The contents of the register is the operand. An *absolute address* is a 16- or 32-bit memory address. In this case the contents of the location is the operand. A 16-bit address is termed *short* and a 32-bit address is considered *long*.

Table 5.7 CPU32 Addressing Modes

Mode	Effective address calculation
Register direct addressing:	
Data register direct	Operand is (Dn)
Address register direct	Operand is (An)
Absolute data addressing:	
Absolute short	EA =(next word following operation word)
Absolute long	EA =(next two words following operation word)
Register indirect addressing:	
Address register indirect	EA = (An)
Indirect with postincrement	EA = (An); (An) ← (An) + N
Indirect with predecrement	(An) ← (An) − N; EA = (An)
Indirect with displacement	EA = (An) + <d_{16}>
Indirect with index (8-bit)	EA = (An) + (Xn) + <d_8>
Indirect with index and base displacement	EA = (An) + (Xn) + <bd>
Relative addressing:	
PC indirect with displacement	EA = (PC) + <d_{16}>
PC indirect with index (8-bit)	EA = (PC) + (Xn) + <d_8>
PC indirect with index and base displacement	EA = (PC) + (Xn) + <bd>
Immediate data addressing:	
Immediate	DATA = next word(s) following operation word
Quick immediate	Inherent data
Implied addressing:	
Implied register	EA = SR, USP, SSP, or PC

Notes:
1. EA   Effective address of operand
   An   Address register
   Dn   Data register
   Xn   Address or data register used as index register
   SR   Status register
   PC   Program counter
   <d_8>   8-bit offset (displacement)
   <d_{16}>   16-bit offset (displacement)
   <bd>   16- or 32-bit value (base displacement)
   ( )   Contents of
   ←   Replaces
2. In the postincrement and predecrement addressing modes, N = 1 for bytes, N = 2 for words, and N = 4 for longwords. If An is the system stack pointer and the operand size is byte, N = 2 to keep the stack pointer on a word boundary.
3. Xn can be scaled by 1, 2, 4, or 8.
4. Both immediate forms are considered as only one mode. Implied addressing is not considered a distinct mode.

Table 5.8 CPU32 Address Encoding and Assembler Syntax

Addressing mode	Mode	Register	Assembler syntax
Data register direct	000	reg. no.	Dn
Address register direct	001	reg. no.	An
Address register indirect	010	reg. no.	(An)
Address register indirect with postincrement	011	reg. no.	(An)+
Address register indirect with predecrement	100	reg. no.	−(An)
Address register indirect with displacement	101	reg. no.	(d_{16}, An)
Address register indirect with index (8-bit displacement)	110	reg. no.	(d_8, An, Xn)
Address register indirect with index and base displacement	110	reg. no.	(bd,An,Xn)
Absolute short	111	000	(xxx).W
Absolute long	111	001	(xxx).L
Program counter indirect with displacement	111	010	(d_{16}, PC)
Program counter indirect with index (8-bit displacement)	111	011	(d_8, PC, Xn)
Program counter indirect with index and base displacement	111	011	(bd,PC,Xn)
Immediate	111	100	#<data>

Register direct addressing. In effect, the processor registers represent a high-speed memory within the CPU and operations between registers require no external memory references. The two modes for register direct addressing are *data register direct* and *address register direct.* The operand for the data register direct mode defined in Table 5.7 is the contents of the specified data register. The address register direct mode specifies the contents of the designated address register as the operand.

The instruction referring to a data register can specify a byte (B), word (W), or longword (L) length for the operand. Thus, the instruction

CLR.<X>   D2

clears register D2 for the length <X> = B or W or L. This is the typical format for a single-address instruction using a data register as the destination. An address register is considered to hold an address 16 or 32 bits long. Instructions are not available for byte operations using address registers. For example, the instruction

MOVE.<X>   A1, D1

will allow a size specification of only <X> = W or <X> = L. In addition to the size restriction, other limitations are placed on the use of an address register as the destination location.

The CPU32 allows manipulation of addresses by a group of instructions which use an address register as the destination. These instructions normally take the suffix A (Address) in assembly-language notation. The instruction

$$\text{MOVEA.L} \qquad \text{A1, A2}$$

transfers the 32-bit contents of A1 to A2, for example. The MOVEA (Move Address) instruction performs the same function as the MOVE instruction, but is designed to treat operands as addresses (i.e., positive numbers), indicating memory locations. Thus, the data registers and address registers of the CPU32 are not considered equivalent for many operations. The differences are presented in detail in Chapter 9, where instructions that operate on addresses are considered.

Absolute short addressing.   The absolute short or 16-bit address for an operand in memory is contained in an extension word to the operation word for an instruction. The address is actually converted to a 32-bit address in the CPU by extending the sign bit (bit 15) of the short address. Figure 5.10(a) shows the calculation. However, due to the 24-bit address bus of the MC68332, only a 24-bit address is presented externally to address memory. The external address is considered to be a positive 24-bit number.

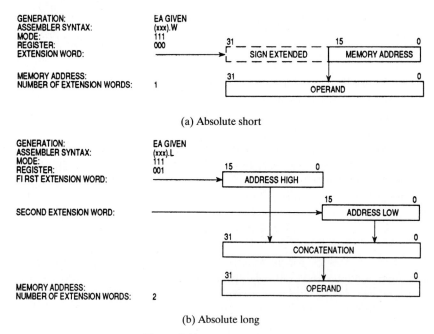

(a) Absolute short

(b) Absolute long

Figure 5.10   Absolute addressing.

Example 5.7

Figure 5.11 shows the effect of using the short addressing mode. If the hexadecimal address is between 0 and $7FFF, the low 32 kilobytes of memory can be addressed. Short addresses $8000 and above are sign-extended internally to 32 bits, resulting in addresses between $FFFF8000 and $FFFFFFFF. The 24-bit addresses in memory would be between $FF8000 and $FFFFFF corresponding to the upper 32 kilobytes of memory addressable by the MC68332. Thus, the designers of the instruction set treated the lower and upper 32 Kilobyte segments of memory in a special way. Normally, the product designer specifies the lowest segment of memory for system parameters. In fact, the MC68332 processor uses the first 1024 bytes for its vectors, which define the starting addresses for trap and interrupt routines. The highest segment is reserved for I/O interfaces in many systems. The absolute short addressing mode allows efficient access to fixed locations in either of these regions.

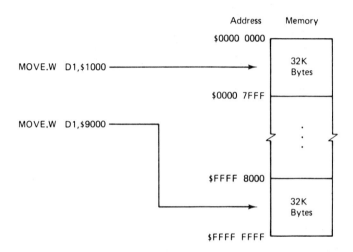

Figure 5.11 Example of absolute short addressing.

Absolute long addressing.   As shown in Figure 5.10(b) a long address is formed from two extension words following the operation word of an instruction. Such an address can span the entire addressing space of the MC68332 memory. The magnitude of the absolute address specified in the assembly-language statement determines whether the short or long absolute addressing mode is used. The instruction

> MOVE.W $12000, D1

requires absolute long addressing for the source operand because the address requires more than 16 bits. An instruction such as

> MOVE.B $3FFF, $12000

specifies both absolute modes. The source address could be given as $0000 3FFF, which would force the assembler to use the long absolute mode. Reference to the assembly-language manual of the particular assembler being used will determine how these addresses are handled and translated into machine language.

Example 5.8

Figure 5.12 shows a few of the addressing modes just discussed as they would be used in instructions. The figure also lists the machine-language statements as they are stored in memory. The instructions specifying register modes are one word in length and are the most efficient for storage and execution. As noted previously, the mnemonic MOVEA is used as the operation code when the destination is an address register.

```
abs.  LC    obj. code   source line
----  ----  ----------  -----------
   1  0000                   TTL   'FIGURE 5.12'
   2  0000              *
   3  0000 2406              MOVE.L    D6,D2        ;(D2)=(D6)
   4  0002 4240              CLR.W     D0           ;(D0)[15:0]=0
   5  0004 2640              MOVEA.L   D0,A3        ;(A3)=(D0)
   6  0006 1038 2001         MOVE.B    $2001,D0     ;(D0)[7:0]=($2001)
   7  000A 21F9 0002         MOVE.L    $214AA,$24   ;($24)=($214AA)
      000E 14AA 0024
   8  0012 21F8 0534         MOVE.L    $0534,$0528  ;($0528)=($0534)
      0016 0528
   9  0018                   END
```

Figure 5.12 Program example of register and absolute addressing.

In the absolute modes, the address is independent of the operand length. The instruction

MOVE.L $0534, $0528

copies the 32-bit value in byte locations $0534 through $0537 into four bytes beginning at address $0528 since longword operands are specified. However, both addresses are short absolute addresses.

5.3.2 Register Indirect Addressing

The CPU32 has several indirect addressing modes to reference an operand that is part of a data structure in memory. All the indirect modes use an address register to hold the basic address, which can then be modified in various ways to compute the effective address of a specific operand. Unlike the absolute addresses that are defined when the program is assembled, the indirect address is computed as the program executes. Address register indirect, register indirect with displacement, and two forms of register indirect with indexing are discussed in this subsection. The postincrement and predecrement indirect modes are discussed in Subsection 5.3.3.

Address register indirect.   Figure 5.13(a) shows the calculation of the operand address for the address register indirect addressing mode. The assembler recognizes indirect addressing when the register designated is enclosed in parenthesis as (An) in an assembly-language program statement.

Any one of the eight address registers of the CPU32 may be used to address indirectly an operand in memory. The effective address of the operand is the contents of the address register An. The effective address (not the operand) is designated in this textbook as

$$EA = (An)$$

when the nth register is designated. The contents of the selected address register is used as the operand address when an instruction using this indirect mode executes. To load the register, an instruction such as

MOVEA.L   #<addr>, A1

transfers the address <addr> to A1. Then, reference to (A1), as in the instruction

MOVE.W   (A1), D1

would move the 16-bit value contained at location <addr> into D1. The specification of the address used as the source in the MOVEA instruction can be by any of the addressing modes, including the immediate mode just shown. For example, the instruction

MOVEA.L $1000, A1

moves the contents of the longword at location $1000 into A1.

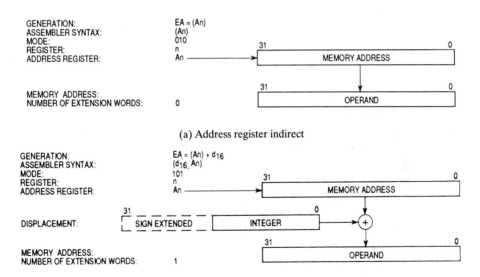

(a) Address register indirect

(b) Address register indirect with 16-bit displacement

Figure 5.13 Register indirect addressing.

Example 5.9

The address held in an address register can be modified in a number of ways during program execution. For example, the instruction Add Address has the format

ADDA.<X>   <EAs>, <An>

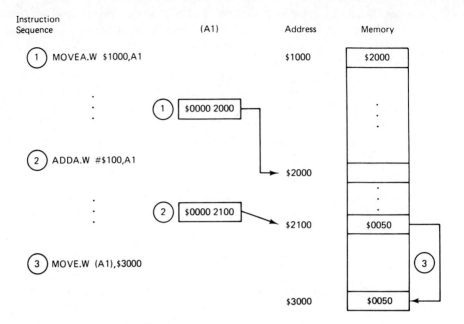

Figure 5.14 Example of indirect addressing using A1.

to add the value in location <EAs> to the value in An. The length specification <X> is restricted to W (16-bit) or L (32-bit) since addresses are either 16 or 32-bit values, respectively. The address

$$<An> \leftarrow <An> + <EAs>$$

is generated when the ADDA instruction is executed. An operand referenced using An in a subsequent instruction would cause the new location to be addressed. Figure 5.14 shows a possible sequence.

The value $2000, representing the contents of location $1000, is first moved into A1. This address $2000 might point to the first word in a data structure in memory. Adding the constant $100 using the ADDA variation of ADD causes A1 to point to location $2100; an offset of $100 locations (hexadecimal) from the beginning of the data structure. Using A1 indirectly in the MOVE instruction transfers the value in the location $2100 to the designated location at $3000.

Another addressing mode called indirect with displacement could be used to eliminate the ADDA instruction in Figure 5.14 and replace the MOVE instruction with the form

MOVE.W   ($100, A1), $3000

which adds a displacement to the value in A1 before the source address is calculated.

Indirect with displacement.   The address register indirect mode just discussed can be used in a variety of ways to address operands in memory. Using the address manipulation instructions of the CPU32 (MOVEA, ADDA, and others), the address in register An can be modified as desired when the program executes. In certain applications, it is not desirable to modify the address in the address register. This could be the case when the register is used to point to a segment of memory, perhaps the first address of an array or table. A selected element in the data structure could be addressed by adding an offset to the value in the address register. The address register thus holds the starting address, and the offset or displacement specifies the relative position of the element within the data structure. When the offset is a fixed value that is known at assembly time, the *indirect with displacement* addressing mode of the CPU32 can be used to reference the operand.

The effective address for this mode is calculated, as shown in Figure 5.13(b), by the equation

$$EA = (An) + <d_{16}>$$

where $<d_{16}>$ is a 16-bit signed integer.[6] The range of this 16-bit offset is $-32,768$ to $+32,767$ bytes in memory. This displacement or offset is stored as an extension word of the machine-language instruction. The assembler uses the indirect with displacement mode in instructions such as

> MOVE.W $<d_{16}>(An), <EAd>$; 16-BIT DISP.

where $<d_{16}>$ is specified as a hexadecimal ($XXXX) or decimal (XXXX) constant. For example,

> MOVE.W $20(A1), D1

transfers 16 bits to register D1 from the location 32 bytes beyond the address in A1. Note that the immediate symbol (#) is not needed since the assembler recognizes $<d_{16}>$ as an offset and not a possible address. The form with the displacement enclosed in parentheses,

> MOVE.W   ($20, A1), D1

is equivalent. However, this assembly-language form allows 8-, 16-, or 32-bit displacements, as described in the next paragraph. It is a form of address register indirect with index addressing but the index register is not specified.

Indirect with indexing, scaling, and base displacement.   When the offset from a base address must be varied during program execution, one of the two register indirect with indexing modes may be used. The effective address is computed as the sum of three components: a value in an address register, plus a value in an index register, plus a displacement. The index register may be any one of the general-purpose address or data registers of the CPU32.

---

[6] In this context the subscript denotes the length of the integer, *not* the number base.

The basic calculation for the effective address is as follows:

$$EA = (An) + (Xi).[S] * SCALE + <displacement>$$

where Xi is the index register designated by any An or Dn. The index value can be designated as either a 16- or 32-bit value in the index register. Hence, the designation Xi.[S] allows a size [S] = W or L for word or longword, respectively. Any 16-bit index value is always sign-extended to 32 bits when used in an address calculation. If the value in the index register is a hexadecimal number from $8000 through $FFFF, the value is considered negative.

The scale value, SCALE, allows scaling by 1 (no scaling), 2, 4, or 8. With a value of SCALE $= n$, the index register effectively indexes by n bytes. Thus, a value of SCALE = 2 indicates word addressing and SCALE = 4 indicates longword addressing. The scaling typically is used to index into a data array with data values of either word, longword, or double longword length to allow incrementing an index register by 1 in a loop that addresses consecutive values.

The index with 8-bit displacement mode is shown in Figure 5.15(a) and defines the calculation of the effective address as

$$EA = (An) + (Xi).[S] * SCALE + <d_8>$$

where $<d_8>$ is an 8-bit signed integer.[7] The assembly-language instruction,

MOVE.W   2(A1, D1.W), D2

moves 16 bits from the address given by

$$EA = (A1) + (D1)[15 : 0] + 2$$

to register (D2)[15:0]. This mode requires one extension word to the instruction in memory.

Figure 5.15(b) shows the effective address calculation for address register indirect addressing with index and base displacement. This differs from the previous mode in that the base displacement is a 16-bit (sign-extended) or 32-bit value. Also, all three of the specified addends are optional. Thus, the instruction

MOVE.L   ($90, A3, D2.W*4), D1

with (A3) = $00020000 and (D2) = $00001000 addresses the hexadecimal location

$20000	base
$4000	index, scaled
$90	base displacement
$24090	

---

[7] The 8-bit displacement is included in the CPU32 instruction set to be compatible with the addressing modes of the MC68000. The 16- or 32-bit base displacement was not allowed by the MC68000.

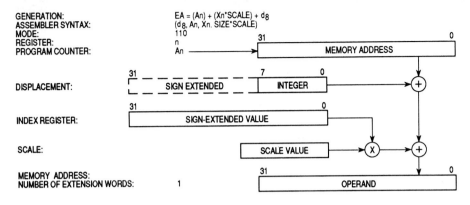

GENERATION: $EA = (An) + (Xn^*SCALE) + d_8$
ASSEMBLER SYNTAX: $(d_8, An, Xn. SIZE^*SCALE)$
MODE: 110
REGISTER: n
PROGRAM COUNTER: An

MEMORY ADDRESS

DISPLACEMENT: SIGN EXTENDED | INTEGER

INDEX REGISTER: SIGN-EXTENDED VALUE

SCALE: SCALE VALUE

MEMORY ADDRESS:
NUMBER OF EXTENSION WORDS: 1

OPERAND

(a) Address register indirect with index (8 bit)

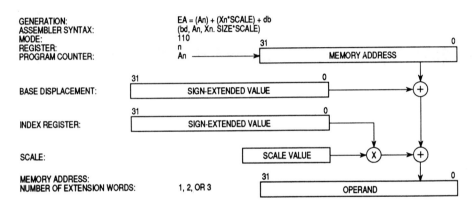

GENERATION: $EA = (An) + (Xn^*SCALE) + db$
ASSEMBLER SYNTAX: $(bd, An, Xn. SIZE^*SCALE)$
MODE: 110
REGISTER: n
PROGRAM COUNTER: An

MEMORY ADDRESS

BASE DISPLACEMENT: SIGN-EXTENDED VALUE

INDEX REGISTER: SIGN-EXTENDED VALUE

SCALE: SCALE VALUE

MEMORY ADDRESS:
NUMBER OF EXTENSION WORDS: 1, 2, OR 3

OPERAND

(b) Address register indirect with index and base displacement

Figure 5.15 Address register indirect with index and base displacement.

and moves 32 bits into D1 from that location. An instruction may require one, two, or three extension words in memory, depending on the length of the base displacement and the options chosen. In the example just given, two extension words are required to specify the form of addressing and the 16-bit base displacement.

Example 5.10

Assume that a list of words is stored in memory starting at location $9000. If the first four 16-bit entries in the list are used to determine the length of the list and similar information, the first data item can be accessed by adding a displacement of eight bytes to the starting address. Consecutive items in the list can be accessed by indexing and scaling. This scheme is shown in Figure 5.16 using A1 as the base address and D1 as an index register. The first execution of the MOVE instruction at label LOOP addresses location $9008.

After the item is transferred by the instruction at label LOOP, the value can be processed as necessary. The processing statements are not shown in Figure 5.16(a). The ADD.W instruction increments the index value in D1 which is scaled (multiplied) by 2 to index word items when the statement at LOOP is executed again. The statement is not shown that causes a branch back to LOOP if the processing is not complete. Chapter 6 presents various branch instructions that would be suitable.

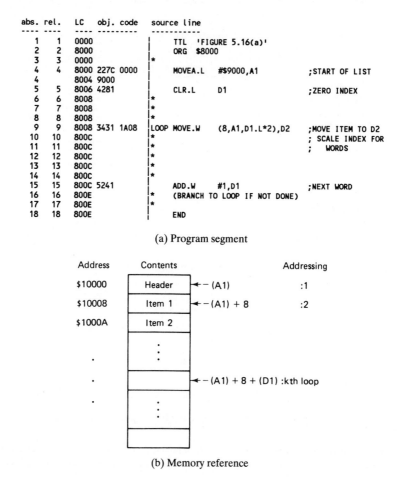

```
abs. rel.   LC   obj. code   source line
---- ----   ---- ----------  -----------
   1    1   0000                    TTL    'FIGURE 5.16(a)'
   2    2   8000                    ORG    $8000
   3    3   0000             *
   4    4   8000 227C 0000          MOVEA.L   #$9000,A1       ;START OF LIST
   4        8004 9000
   5    5   8006 4281              CLR.L    D1                ;ZERO INDEX
   6    6   8008             *
   7    7   8008             *
   8    8   8008             *
   9    9   8008 3431 1A08   LOOP MOVE.W    (8,A1,D1.L*2),D2  ;MOVE ITEM TO D2
  10   10   800C            *                                ; SCALE INDEX FOR
  11   11   800C            *                                ;   WORDS
  12   12   800C            *
  13   13   800C            *
  14   14   800C            *
  15   15   800C 5241              ADD.W    #1,D1             ;NEXT WORD
  16   16   800E            *       (BRANCH TO LOOP IF NOT DONE)
  17   17   800E            *
  18   18   800E                    END
```

(a) Program segment

Address	Contents		Addressing
$10000	Header	◄─ (A1)	:1
$10008	Item 1	◄─ (A1) + 8	:2
$1000A	Item 2		
	:		
	:	◄─ (A1) + 8 + (D1) :kth loop	
	:		

(b) Memory reference

Figure 5.16   Program example of indirect addressing with indexing and scaling.

5.3.3 Predecrement and Postincrement Addressing

In many programming applications, it is necessary to access data stored in consecutive memory locations. If the length of each item is a byte, word, or longword, the indexing can be accomplished using the CPU32 *indirect with predecrement* or *indirect with postincrement* addressing. In these modes, the contents of an address register are changed automatically as the instructions using the modes execute. Thus, no time is wasted increasing index values by program instructions as with the indirect with indexing addressing mode. Perhaps the most important use for these modes is to manipulate operands in a stack in memory as discussed in Chapter 4. However, many other data manipulation operations are simplified through the use of these modes.

The effective address for each mode is calculated as shown in Figure 5.17. In the postincrement mode, the address in a general-purpose address register is used before the address is incremented. The increment is 1, 2, or 4 for byte, word, or longword operands, respectively. The postincrement mode allows a program to address consecutive values stored at increasingly higher addresses in memory. In the predecrement mode, the address is decremented first, then used as a pointer to a memory location.

As previously explained in Section 4.2, the system stack pointer, A7, can only be incremented or decremented by 2 or 4 to keep the system stack pointer on a word boundary in memory. Also, the system stack grows toward decreasing memory addresses as values are pushed on the system stack. A push on the system stack requires the use of the predecrement mode. The corresponding pop of an item requires the postincrement mode in an instruction.

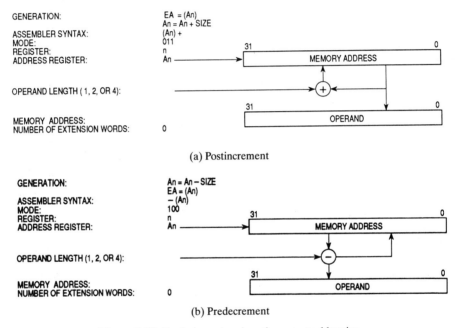

(a) Postincrement

(b) Predecrement

Figure 5.17 Predecrement and postincrement addressing.

The assembler recognizes the predecrement mode as −(An) and the postincrement as (An)+. In the instruction

MOVE.W   −(A1), (A2)+

a word is moved from location (A1)−2 to location (A2). If the instruction is executed again, the source address is one word lower in memory and the destination one word higher than the original values. This is typical usage in program loops in which the autoindexed instruction is repeatedly executed until the condition to quit looping is met.

```
abs.   LC    obj. code    source line
----   ----  ----------   -----------
  1    0000                      TTL       'FIGURE 5.18'
  2    0000
  3    0000                      LLEN      100
  4    8000                      ORG       $8000
  5    0000               *
  6          0000 0063    RETURN  EQU       $0063        ;MONITOR
  7    8000               *
  8    8000               *   MOVE 32 BYTES FROM $6000 TO $7000
  9    8000               *       REVERSING THEIR ORDER
 10    8000               *
 11    8000 123C 0020             MOVE.B    #32,D1       ;SET COUNTER TO 32
 12    8004 227C 0000             MOVEA.L   #$6000,A1    ;SET UP ADDRESSES
       8008 6000
 13    800A 247C 0000             MOVEA.L   #$7020,A2    ;   FOR TRANSFER
       800E 7020
 14    8010               *
 15    8010 1519          LOOP    MOVE.B    (A1)+,-(A2)  ;MOVE NEXT BYTE
 16    8012 5301                  SUBI.B    #1,D1        ;DECREMENT COUNT
 17    8014 66FA                  BNE       LOOP         ;CONTINUE UNTIL
 18    8016               *                              ;   COUNT = 0
 19    8016               *
 20    8016 4E4F                  TRAP      #15          ;RETURN TO MONITOR
 21    8018 0063                  DC.W      RETURN
 22    801A                       END
```

Figure 5.18 Program example of postincrement and predecrement addressing.

These modes are also used to move blocks of data from one memory segment to another when statements such as

$$\text{MOVE.W} \qquad (A1)+, (A2)+$$

are used in a loop. Here (A1) designates the first block and (A2) the second. The addressing in this case is equivalent to using

$$\text{MOVE.W} \qquad (A1), (A2)$$

followed by the instructions

$$\text{ADDA.L} \qquad \#2, A1$$

$$\text{ADDA.L} \qquad \#2, A2$$

where both the source and destination addresses are incremented by 2 after the transfer since the operands are two bytes in length. The ADDA instruction is used here because the destination is an address register.

Example 5.11

The simple program segment in Figure 5.18 moves a 32-byte block of data from location $6000 to location $7000, but in reverse order. The order of the data is reversed by starting the transfer from the first byte of the source block using postincrement addressing to the last byte of the destination block with predecrement addressing. The byte at $6000 is moved to $701F, the byte at $6001 is moved to $701E, and so on. Register D1 is used as a counter for the loop and registers A1 and A2 contain the addresses of the blocks.

5.3.4 Program Counter Relative Addressing

As described in Chapter 4, the PC relative addressing mode is an indirect addressing mode which causes an address in memory to be computed by the general formula

$$\text{effective address} = (PC) + <\text{offset}>$$

where the offset may be an integer displacement or the value in an index register or the sum of both. Thus, the address is specified relative to the current value in the program counter when the instruction using PC relative addressing executes. This value is the location of the next instruction word to be processed in most cases. The offset represents the distance (in bytes) in memory between the address in the PC and the operand being addressed.

The CPU32 has several addressing modes that allow the programmer to describe an address as an offset from the contents of the Program Counter. These modes are identical in form to the corresponding modes using an address register except that (PC) is used rather than (An) as the base address. In some cases, such as with branch instructions, the assembler automatically assigns a PC relative addressing mode. Typically, the destination is a label in the program, the location of which is specified by the assembler. The address is calculated as an offset value from the (PC) when the program executes. This fundamental PC relative addressing mode is termed PC indirect with displacement. The CPU also has two PC with indexing modes.

One important restriction on the use of these modes is that an alterable destination location cannot be addressed by any of the PC relative addressing modes as explained in Subsection 5.3.6. The relative addressing modes are also described further in Chapter 9 when position independent code is introduced.

5.3.5 Immediate and Implied Addressing

The immediate addressing mode for the CPU32 allows byte, word, or longword values to be used as constants in an instruction. The byte or word-length values require one extension word, and the long value adds two words to the instruction in memory. The assembler recognizes the immediate mode in instructions such as

        MOVE.W   #50, D2

by the number symbol (#). The instruction moves 50 (decimal) into the low-order word of D2. As defined previously, hexadecimal values are specified with $ and ASCII characters are enclosed within single quote marks.

Some CPU32 instructions do not require an operand to be specified and other instructions affect processor registers without explicitly referencing them in the instructions. These *implicit* references can be to the Program Counter, the Status Register, or one of the system stack pointers. For example, the instruction

        RTS   ; RETURN FROM SUBROUTINE

which returns from a subroutine to the calling program uses the stack pointer to retrieve the return address from the stack. The instruction does not explicitly reference the stack pointer or the Program Counter, but modifies both during its execution. These types of instructions have an addressing mode which is implied.

5.3.6 Addressing Categories and Extension Word Format

The many addressing modes of the CPU32 may be arranged in categories which determine the type of access that can be made to an operand. These categories further define the restrictions placed on some of the addressing modes. Each unique addressing mode also has a corresponding machine-language format in memory. This format defines the number of extension words, if any, needed by an instruction to address an operand.

Addressing categories.   The individual addressing modes of the CPU32 are further characterized into four groups of *addressing categories.* These categories refer to the characteristics of the operand being addressed. As defined in Table 5.9 the categories are *data, memory, control,* and *alterable.* The *data* category includes every mode but address register direct addressing. This is because the operand in an address register is assumed to be an address, not a data item, in this context. Except for register direct addressing, all the other addressing modes can all refer to an operand in memory and hence are in the memory category.

If an addressed operand can be changed by an instruction, the addressing category is termed *alterable.* The alterable category includes both register direct modes and the other modes shown in Table 5.9.

However, all the memory references are not considered alterable. An immediate value is obviously not alterable. Also, PC relative addressing modes can not refer to an alterable operand. This means that the PC relative modes cannot be used to define destination addresses that are to be written (altered). The CPU designers assumed that the PC is used to address instructions in memory and instructions should not be altered by an executing program. For example, a MOVE instruction requires an alterable destination, which excludes the immediate and PC relative modes to address the destination location according to Table 5.9.

The programmer uses the category information to determine which addressing modes are allowed for particular instructions. In the discussion of the CPU32 instructions in later chapters, the allowed addressing will be described in terms of these categories. For example, according to the description found in the Motorola *CPU32 Reference Manual* or Appendix IV of this text, the CLR instruction allows only data-alterable addressing modes for the destination operand. Thus, any addressing mode used with the CLR instruction to designate an operand must belong to both categories. This excludes address register direct addressing with the CLR instruction because the address register direct mode is in the alterable category but not in the data category according to Table 5.9. Therefore, the instruction

CLR   A1

is not a valid assembly-language instruction.

Table 5.9 Addressing Mode Categories

Address Modes	Data	Memory	Control	Alterable
Data register direct	X	—	—	X
Address register direct	—	—	—	X
Address register indirect	X	X	X	X
Address register indirect with postincrement	X	X	—	X
Address register indirect with predecrement	X	X	—	X
Address register indirect with displacement	X	X	X	X
Address register indirect with index (8-bit displacement)	X	X	X	X
Address register indirect with index (base displacement)	X	X	X	X
Absolute short	X	X	X	X
Absolute long	X	X	X	X
Program counter indirect with displacement	X	X	X	—
Program counter indirect with index (8-bit displacement)	X	X	X	—
Program counter indirect with index (base displacement)	X	X	X	—
Immediate	X	X	—	—

Note:

Effective address modes may be categorized by the ways in which they may be used. The following classifications will be used in the instruction definitions.

Data — If an effective address mode may be used to refer to data operands, it is considered a data addressing effective address mode.

Memory — If an effective address mode may be used to refer to memory operands, it is considered a memory addressing effective address mode.

Control — If an effective address mode may be used to refer to memory operands without an associated size, it is considered a control addressing effective address mode.

Alterable — If an effective address mode may be used to refer to alterable (writable) operands, it is considered an alterable addressing effective address mode.

The PC relative modes are also not allowed with the CLR instruction because these modes are not in the alterable category. The relative addresses as destinations are in the data category but are not alterable according to Table 5.9.

A few observations on the categories in Table 5.9 should be noted:

(a) instructions that require data-alterable addressing cannot use the contents of address registers as operands;

(b) the PC relative addressing modes reference operands that are not alterable by CPU32 instructions;

(c) the address register indirect modes that encompass all four categories are allowed for all instructions that take operands;

(d) the memory category is equivalent to the data category except for data register direct addressing.

Extension word format. The formats for the extension words required by various addressing modes are shown in Figure 5.19. A single-address instruction such as

$$\text{CLR.[l]} \qquad \text{<address>}$$

where [l] = B, W, or L, can have the address specified in any number of ways. With no extensions to the address, the instruction occupies one 16-bit word location in memory. An absolute address requires either one word (16 bits) or two additional words (32 bits) to specify the address. In the modes with indexing and displacement, one or more extension words are required.

Single EA Instruction Format

15	14	13	12	11	10	9	8	7	6	5		0
X	X	X	X	X	X	X	X	X	X	EFFECTIVE ADDRESS		
										MODE		REGISTER

Brief Format Extension Word

15	14		12	11	10	9	8	7			0
D/A	REGISTER			W/L	SCALE		0	DISPLACEMENT			

Full Format Extension Word(s)

15	14		12	11	10	9	8	7	6	5	4	3	2		0
D/A	REGISTER			W/L	SCALE		1	BS	IS	BD SIZE		0	I/IS		
BASE DISPLACEMENT (0, 1, OR 2 WORDS)															

Field	Definition	Field	Definition
Instruction		BS	Base Register Suppress
Register	General Register Number		0 = Base Register Added
Extensions			1 = Base Register Suppressed
Register	Index Register Number	IS	Index Suppress
D/A	Index Register Type		0 = Evaluate and Add Index Operand
	0 = Dn		1 = Suppress Index Operand
	1 = An	BD SIZE	Base Displacement Size
W/L	Word/Long-Word Index Size		00 = Reserved
	0 = Sign-Extended Word		01 = Null Displacement
	1 = Long Word		10 = Word Displacement
Scale	Scale Factor		11 = Long-Word Displacement
	00 = 1	I/IS*	Index/Indirect Selection
	01 = 2		Indirect and Indexing Operand
	10 = 4		Determined in Conjunction with
	11 = 8		Bit 6, Index Suppress

*Memory indirect causes illegal instruction trap; must be 000 if IS = 1.

Figure 5.19 Extension word formats.

Example 5.12

The listing of Figure 5.20 indicates some of the possible extension-word formats for the instructions. The machine-language instructions can be decoded by reference to Figure 5.19.

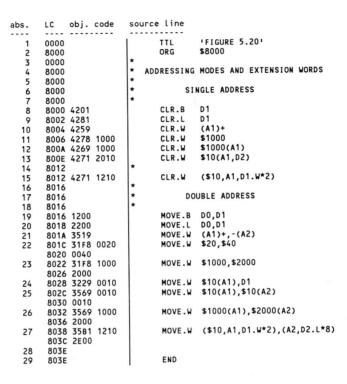

```
abs.    LC   obj. code    source line
----    ----  ---------   -----------
  1    0000                    TTL     'FIGURE 5.20'
  2    8000                    ORG     $8000
  3    0000             *
  4    8000             *  ADDRESSING MODES AND EXTENSION WORDS
  5    8000             *
  6    8000             *        SINGLE ADDRESS
  7    8000             *
  8    8000 4201              CLR.B   D1
  9    8002 4281              CLR.L   D1
 10    8004 4259              CLR.W   (A1)+
 11    8006 4278 1000         CLR.W   $1000
 12    800A 4269 1000         CLR.W   $1000(A1)
 13    800E 4271 2010         CLR.W   $10(A1,D2)
 14    8012             *
 15    8012 4271 1210         CLR.W   ($10,A1,D1.W*2)
 16    8016             *
 17    8016             *        DOUBLE ADDRESS
 18    8016             *
 19    8016 1200              MOVE.B  D0,D1
 20    8018 2200              MOVE.L  D0,D1
 21    801A 3519              MOVE.W  (A1)+,-(A2)
 22    801C 31F8 0020         MOVE.W  $20,$40
       8020 0040
 23    8022 31F8 1000         MOVE.W  $1000,$2000
       8026 2000
 24    8028 3229 0010         MOVE.W  $10(A1),D1
 25    802C 3569 0010         MOVE.W  $10(A1),$10(A2)
       8030 0010
 26    8032 3569 1000         MOVE.W  $1000(A1),$2000(A2)
       8036 2000
 27    8038 35B1 1210         MOVE.W  ($10,A1,D1.W*2),(A2,D2.L*8)
       803C 2E00
 28    803E
 29    803E                   END
```

Figure 5.20 Program example of extension word formats.

EXERCISES

5.3.1. List some reasons why the CPU32 designers restricted the use of PC relative addressing modes. Operands addressed relative to the program counter can be read and manipulated but their locations cannot be written.

5.3.2. The CPU32 does not allow the CLR instruction to specify an address register as a destination. Is the restriction on using CLR with address registers a potential problem? How does a program address location 0?

5.3.3. Discuss the various addressing modes in terms of values to be defined before assembly and those that can be defined or changed during program execution. (Assume that the program will not change its own instructions in memory.)

5.3.4. Discuss the advantages and disadvantages of absolute short addressing compared to absolute long addressing.

5.3.5. If (A1) = $1000, determine the operand address for the following instructions:
(a) CLR.B $FFFF(A1)

(b) MOVE.B   (A1)+, D1

(c) MOVE.W   − (A1), D1

5.3.6. What do these instructions accomplish?

    (a) MOVE.L   4(A0), (A0)

    (b) MOVE.W $9000, D1

    (c) MOVE.B   0(A0, D1), D1

5.3.7. Compare the absolute short addressing mode with the indirect displacement mode when the displacement value is $8000.

5.3.8. Consider the instruction

$$\text{MOVE.L} \qquad (0, A1, D1.W*4), (A2)+$$

in a loop with (D1) incremented during each pass. Initially, (A1) = $00010000 and (D1) = 0.

(a) If (D1) is incremented by 1 during each pass, show the source operand address at each pass through the loop for 1, 2 and N iterations.

(b) If (D1) is incremented by 16 during each pass, what type of data structure is probably being addressed?

5.4   SUMMARY OF ADDRESSING MODES

The CPU32 has a number of addressing modes to reference an operand in a register, in the instruction itself, or in memory. Each instruction of the CPU32 allows certain addressing modes to define the location of operands (if any). With a few restrictions, the addressing modes may be combined with any operation to form a complete instruction. These restrictions will be treated in detail when particular instructions are encountered in subsequent chapters. This section concentrates on the use of various addressing modes and their assembly-language format.

Table 5.10 briefly summarizes the addressing modes and lists possible uses for a particular mode. Examples of the modes are shown in Figure 5.21. In the register direct modes, the operand is held in an address register or a data register. For the immediate mode, also called the "literal" mode, the operand is defined in memory as part of the instruction in machine language. These basic modes are sufficient for many programs in which operands are not part of a data structure in memory, but are treated individually as in mathematical calculations or data transfers. The absolute addressing modes are used to reference fixed addresses in memory: usually hardware related, such as for I/O devices. When the data structure in memory is more complex, an indirect addressing mode is usually more convenient to address an operand. Such data structures are treated in Chapter 9.

Table 5.10 Use of Addressing Modes

Mode	Example use
Register direct	Mathematical or data transfer operations on operands held in registers
Immediate	Increment or initialize values in registers or memory
Absolute	Reference to hardware-related locations
Indirect	Operations on data values in memory
Predecrement or postincrement	Operations on values in arrays, stacks and queues
Indirect with displacement	Reference to an operand in memory from a base address
Indirect with index	Reference to an operand in a table of values in memory
PC relative addressing	Create position-independent references to operands or addresses

```
abs. rel.   LC   obj. code   source line
---- ----   ----  --------- -----------
   1    1   0000                    TTL      'FIGURE 5.21'
   2    2   8000                    ORG      $8000
   3    3   0000             *
   4    4   8000             *      INSTRUCTION                    NAME
   5    5   8000 D481               ADD.L    D1,D2                 REGISTER DIRECT
   6    6   8002 D489               ADD.L    A1,D2
   7    7   8004             *
   8    8   8004 0642 0064          ADD.W    #100,D2               IMMEDIATE
   9    9   8008             *
  10   10   8008 D479 0001          ADD.W    $1F000,D2             ABSOLUTE
  10        800C F000
  11   11   800E D379 0002          ADD.W    D1,$2F000
  11        8012 F000
  12   12   8014             *
  13   13   8014 D451               ADD.W    (A1),D2               INDIRECT
  14   14   8016             *
  15   15   8016 D461               ADD.W    -(A1),D2              PREDRECEMENT
  16   16   8018 D359               ADD.W    D1,(A1)+              POSTINCREMENT
  17   17   801A             *
  18   18   801A D469 1000          ADD.W    $1000(A1),D2          INDIRECT WITH DISPLACEMENT
  19   19   801E D471 0170          ADD.W    ($1F000,A1),D2
  19        8022 0001 F000
  20   20   8026 D479 0001          ADD.W    ($1F000),D2           ;SUPPRESS A1
  20        802A F000
  21   21   802C             *
  22   22   802C D471 1820          ADD.W    $20(A1,D1.L),D2       INDIRECT WITH INDEX
  23   23   8030 D471 1A20          ADD.W    ($20,A1,D1.L*2),D2
  24   24   8034 D471 1B20          ADD.W    ($1F00,A1,D1.L*2),D2
  24        8038 1F00
  25   25   803A D471 1D30          ADD.W    ($1F000,A1,D1.L*4),D2
  25        803E 0001 F000
  26   26   8042 D470 1DB0          ADD.W    ($1F000,D1.L*4),D2    ;SUPPRESS A1
  26        8046 0001 F000
  27   27   804A D470 1990          ADD.W    (D1.L),D2             ;DATA REGISTER INDIRECT
  28   28   804E             *
  29   29   804E                    END
```

Figure 5.21 Program example of register addressing modes.

EXERCISES

5.4.1. For each of the instructions using indirect addressing in Figure 5.21, assume (A1) = $00010000 and (D1) = $00010000 before the instruction executes. What is the indirect address of the source operand?

5.4.2. Let a program have the instruction sequence

$$\text{ADD.W} \quad \text{FIRST(PC), D1}$$

.

.

$$\text{ADD.W} \quad \text{FIRST(PC), D1}$$

.

.

$$\text{END}$$

Assume that FIRST is defined as a label in the program. Is the machine-language code for the two ADD instructions the same? Would the code be the same if (PC) were replaced by (A1)?

FURTHER READING

Barron's short but lucid text describes in detail the operation of an assembler. Many of the textbooks written about the MC68000 and the MC68020 microprocessors are useful for understanding the assembly-language programming techniques for the CPU32. The text by Wakerly is one example. Other such references were cited in Chapter 4.

BARRON, D. W., *Assemblers and Loaders*, 2nd ed. New York: American Elsevier, 1972.

WAKERLY, JOHN F., *Microcomputer Architecture and Programming. The 68000 Family.* New York: Wiley, 1989.

6

Data Transfer, Program Control, and Subroutines

The next several chapters describe the CPU32 assembly-language instruction set. The purpose of these chapters is to analyze each instruction in detail and illustrate its use in assembly-language programs. The instructions and their variations are separated into categories based on the operation performed. As part of the description, the instructions listed in Table 6.1 for *data transfer, program control*, and *subroutine usage* are discussed in this chapter. Subsequent chapters present the instructions for arithmetic, logical, and similar operations.

The MOVE instruction is the primary instruction in the data transfer category. The MOVE instruction does not have many restrictions on the location and length of operands which can be transferred between the CPU and memory. Table 6.1 also lists two variations of this instruction. They are distinguished from the MOVE instruction by adding a letter suffix, Q or M, to form MOVEQ or MOVEM. The MOVEQ "quick" form is a one-word instruction to load a data value into a data register. The MOVEM instruction is a variation that allows the contents of a selected group of registers to be transferred to or from consecutive memory locations. These two variations may be more efficient than the MOVE instruction for some purposes.

Instructions for program control govern the sequence of instruction execution within a program. The BRA and JMP instructions cause unconditional transfer of control. The Bcc and DBcc instructions branch when certain conditions, which are defined by the condition codes, are met. The CMP instruction and its variations, listed in Table 6.1, are discussed in this chapter because these instructions set the condition codes based on the values of the operands compared. Section 4.2 described the bits in the Condition Code Register (CCR).

Table 6.1 Selected Instructions

Instruction	Description
Data transfer	
MOVE	Move
MOVEQ	Move Quick (immediate)
MOVEM	Move Multiple Registers
EXG	Exchange Registers
SWAP	Swap Data Register Halves
Program control	
Unconditional	
BRA	Branch Always
JMP	Jump
Conditional Branch	
and compare	
Bcc	Branch Conditionally
DBcc	Test condition, Decrement and Branch
CMP	Compare
CMPI	Compare Immediate
CMPM	Compare Memory
TST	Test
Subroutine	
BSR	Branch to Subroutine
JSR	Jump to Subroutine
RTR	Return and Restore (CCR)
RTS	Return from Subroutine

Subroutines may be called with the BSR or JSR instructions. The execution of a RTR or RTS instruction in the subroutine returns control to the calling program. The saving and restoring of the return address is handled automatically by the CPU when the call and return instructions are executed in the proper sequence.

This chapter defines the instructions in terms of the assembler syntax, operand length, valid addressing modes, and the effect on the condition codes. Appendix IV presents the entire instruction set.

6.1 DATA TRANSFER

The instructions MOVE, MOVEQ, MOVEM, EXG, and SWAP represent data transfer instructions. The MOVE instruction is the most flexible and, consequently, the most frequently used. The quick variation, MOVEQ, transfers an 8-bit data value to a designated data register. MOVEM has the letter suffix M designating "multiple." The MOVEM instruction is used to save the contents of a selected group of registers in memory or to restore their contents from memory. The EXG and SWAP instructions transfer data between and within registers.

Table 6.2 summarizes the data transfer instructions covered in this section. For each instruction, the listings show the assembler syntax, the allowed addressing modes, and the condition codes affected by the instruction. When a number of modes are possible for the source or destination operand, the addressing modes are defined in terms of the addressing categories introduced in Chapter 5. The data-alterable category excludes address register direct, relative, and immediate addressing. Control-alterable addressing prohibits register direct, postincrement, predecrement, relative, and immediate addressing. The control category does not include the register direct, postincrement, predecrement, or immediate modes. All other addressing modes not excluded in a category can be used to address an operand in an instruction that requires a specific category of addressing.

Table 6.2 Instructions for Data Transfer

Instruction	Syntax	Source	Destination	Condition codes
Move	MOVE.<l> <EAs>,<EAd>	ALL[1]	Data alterable	N,Z V,C ={0}
Move Quick	MOVEQ #<d_8>,<Dn>	Immediate	Dn	
Move Multiple Registers	MOVEM.<l_1> <list>,<EA>	Register list[2]	Control Alterable or predecrement	None
	MOVEM.<l_1> <EA>,<list>	Control or postincrement	Register list[3]	
Exchange Registers	EXG <Rx>,<Ry>	Rx[4]	Ry	None
Swap Register Halves	SWAP <Dn>	(Dn)[31:16] $\leftrightarrow$ (Dn)[15 : 0]		N,Z V,C = {0}

Notes:
1. <l> = B, W, or L; but if the operand size is a byte, <An> cannot be a source.
2. <list> = register list; <EA> = effective address; <l_1> = W, or L;
3. In the MOVEM.W instruction, operands transferred to a register are sign-extended to 32 bits in the destination registers.
4. <Rn> = any Dn or An

6.1.1 The MOVE Instruction

The MOVE instruction transfers data between registers, between registers and memory, or between different memory locations. The format is

$$\text{MOVE.<l>} \qquad \text{<EAs>,<EAd>}$$

in which <l> = B, W, or L, indicating 8-bit, 16-bit, or 32-bit operands, respectively. Only the portion of the destination location specified by <l> is replaced in the operation

$$(EAd)[l] \leftarrow (EAs)[l]$$

where [l] designates the appropriate bits affected. If an address register, An, is specified as a source operand, the length must be a word or longword (W or L) since byte operations on address registers are not allowed. The destination addressing mode must in the data alterable category, which excludes address registers and relative addresses. The instruction variation MOVEA transfers values to address registers.

The value transferred by the MOVE instruction is treated as a signed integer of the specified length. Condition codes N and Z are changed according to the result of the operation and V and C are cleared to {0}. Thus, tests on the operand for negative or zero values are possible immediately following a MOVE instruction. For example, the sequence

$$\text{MOVE.W} \qquad \text{LENGTH, D1}$$

$$\text{BEQ} \qquad \text{DONE}$$

causes a branch to the instruction at DONE if the contents of location LENGTH were zero since BEQ (Branch if Equal Zero) branches when $Z = \{1\}$. Otherwise, program execution continues with the next instruction. This sequence could be used, for example, to manipulate a data table of given length. If the length held in location LENGTH is zero, the instructions to manipulate the data values are skipped and control passes to the instruction labeled DONE.

The instruction

$$\text{MOVE.B} \qquad \#\$FF, D1$$

sets $Z = \{0\}$ since the immediate value is not zero, but also sets $N = \{1\}$ because the 8-bit signed integer is considered negative.

The MOVE instruction is used in most of the example programs in this book, so specific examples of its use are not given here. Instead, variations of the MOVE instruction are presented in the following subsections and the MOVE instruction is compared with each variation.

6.1.2 Move Quick (MOVEQ)

The MOVEQ (Move Quick) instruction is a one-word instruction which has the symbolic form

$$\text{MOVEQ} \qquad \#<d_8>, <Dn>$$

where $<d_8>$ is an 8-bit signed constant. The 8-bit value is sign-extended to 32 bits and transferred to Dn. This instruction is very efficient when loading a data register with a constant in the decimal range -128 to $+127$. It executes in only three machine cycles, which is why it is called "quick." Standard MOVE instructions fetched from main memory require more cycles for all transfers except register-to-register transfers. The condition codes are affected by the MOVEQ instruction exactly as they are for the MOVE instruction, allowing a test for zero or negative.

The instruction to clear a register

$$\text{MOVEQ} \qquad \#0, D1$$

has the same effect as CLR.L D1 since both instructions affect the full 32 bits of the register. There is no basic difference in efficiency or operation between these instructions.

6.1.3 Move Multiple (MOVEM)

The MOVEM (Move Multiple) instruction is another variation of the MOVE instruction. MOVEM transfers data between processor registers and memory locations. The direction of transfer determines the allowed addressing modes to specify memory locations. Table 6.3 summarizes the allowed modes for each direction of transfer. If more than one register is involved, the order of transfer is fixed as defined in Table 6.3 and cannot be changed.

Table 6.3 MOVEM Instruction

Transfer	Transfer Order	Addressing Modes
Register to Memory	D0–D7, A0–A7 into higher address	Control alterable
	A7–A0, D7–D0 into lower addresses	Predecrement
Memory to Register	D0–D7, A0–A7 to registers	Postincrement or control modes

Note:
Register list syntax:
    (a) Selected individual registers are separated by "/"; i.e., the list D1/D3/D4 specifies that the contents of D1, D3 and D4 are to be transferred.
    (b) Consecutive registers are specified by "–" (e.g. D1–D4)

      MOVEM register to memory.   The MOVEM instruction for register to memory transfers has the symbolic form

$$\text{MOVEM.}<l_1> \quad <\text{list}>, <\text{EA}>$$

which copies the contents of the registers in the <list> to memory locations beginning at address <EA>. The low-order word or the whole register contents is moved if $<l_1>$ is W or L, respectively. The syntax for the <list> is defined in the notes to Table 6.3.

      When the destinations of a MOVEM instruction are locations in memory, only control-alterable addressing modes or the predecrement mode are allowed. According to the definitions of addressing categories in Subsection 5.3.6, the control alterable category allows address register indirect and absolute addressing modes to specify the destination locations in memory. This category excludes register direct, postincrement, and program counter relative addressing for the destination <EA>.

In the control alterable modes, the contents of the data registers in the register list are stored in memory at increasing memory addresses beginning with the lowest numbered data register. Then, the address registers in the list are stored in order beginning with the lowest numbered register. The contents are stored in order into memory locations with increasing addresses regardless of the order specified in the register list.

Thus, the instruction

MOVEM.W   D0/D1/A2−A4, $4000

transfers the low-order contents of D0, D1, A2, A3, and A4 to locations $4000, $4002, $4004, $4006, and $4008, respectively. In this case, the absolute short addressing mode is used to address memory.

The predecrement mode is used to store the register contents on a stack growing downward in memory and the order of storage is reversed from that of the control alterable modes. That is, address registers are stored first, followed by data registers. Section 4.2 describes the use of stacks.

MOVEM memory to register.   A transfer from memory to the registers allows only control modes or postincrement addressing for the source operands. The registers are transferred in the order D0, D1, . . . , A0, . . . , A7, regardless of the order in the list. The storage addresses are assumed to increase in memory.

The postincrement addressing is often used to pop the designated register values off a stack that grows down in memory. The register contents are pushed on a stack using decreasing memory addresses when the predecrement addressing mode is used to designate the destination in register to memory transfers.

To transfer the values stored in memory to selected registers, the format is

MOVEM.$<l_1>$ $<EA>, <list>$

where $<l_1>$ and $<list>$ have the same meaning as before. However, if word-length operands are moved to registers (l_1 = W), the operands are sign-extended to 32 bits in the registers.

Example 6.1

The MOVEM instruction is used in several ways in the program shown in Figure 6.1. The first MOVEM saves the 32-bit contents of D4, D3, D2, and D1 on the system stack. The second MOVEM transfers four words from locations $9000, $9002, $9004, and $9006 to registers D1, D2, D3, and D4, respectively. The numbers are added and the sum stored in location $9008. The registers are then restored from the stack in the reverse order from that in which they were stored. There is no test for overflow in the program as a possible result of the 16-bit additions.

```
abs.   LC    obj. code   source line
----   ----  ----------  -----------
   1   0000                        TTL     'FIGURE 6.1'
   2   0000                        LLEN    100
   3   8000                        ORG     $8000
   4   0000              *
   5         0000 0063   RETURN     EQU     $0063              ;MONITOR
   6   8000              *
   7   8000              *   USE OF MOVEM INSTRUCTION
   8   8000              *
   9   8000 48E7 7800              MOVEM.L  D1-D4,-(SP)        ;SAVE REGISTERS
  10   8004              *                                    ; ON STACK
  11   8004 4CB8 001E              MOVEM.W  $9000,D1-D4        ;LOAD DATA
       8008 9000
  12   800A              *
  13   800A D441                   ADD.W    D1,D2             ;ADD THE NUMBERS
  14   800C D642                   ADD.W    D2,D3
  15   800E D843                   ADD.W    D3,D4
  16   8010              *
  17   8010 31C4 9008              MOVE.W   D4,$9008          ;SAVE THE RESULT
  18   8014              *
  19   8014 4CDF 001E              MOVEM.L  (SP)+,D1-D4       ;RESTORE REGISTERS
  20   8018              *
  21   8018 4E4F                   TRAP     #15               ;RETURN TO MONITOR
  22   801A 0063                   DC.W     RETURN
  23   801C              *
  24   801C
  25   801C                        END
```

Figure 6.1 Program example of MOVEM instruction.

6.1.4 Internal Data Transfer (EXG and SWAP)

The instruction EXG exchanges the 32-bit longword in the source register with that in
the destination register. The registers involved can be data registers, address registers,
or an address register and a data register. The instruction format is

$$\text{EXG} \qquad <Rx>, <Ry>$$

where the contents of Rx and Ry are exchanged. Only 32-bit exchanges are allowed
and the condition codes are not affected.

The EXG instruction removes the need for temporary storage of register contents when 32-bit operands in two registers must be interchanged. The use of the
exchange instruction is illustrated in Example 6.2.

Example 6.2

The program shown in Figure 6.2 illustrates two methods of exchanging the contents
of two registers, A0 and D1. In the first method, the value in register D1 is saved in a
temporary location in memory. Then, D1 can be loaded with the value in A0 and, finally,
A0 can be loaded with the original contents of D1 from the temporary memory location.
The second method uses the EXG instruction to accomplish the same operation in one
instruction.

The SWAP instruction exchanges the low-order word with the high-order word
in a single register. The instruction has the form

$$\text{SWAP} \qquad <Dn>$$

in which only a data register can be specified. The condition codes are set according
to the full 32-bit result to allow tests for negative or zero.

Sec. 6.1   Data Transfer

195

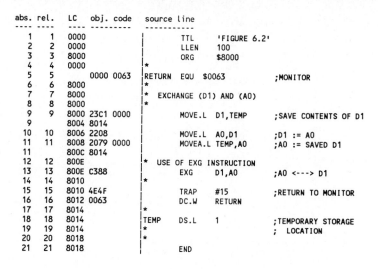

```
abs. rel.   LC    obj. code    source line
---- ----   ----  ---------    -----------
  1    1    0000                      TTL     'FIGURE 6.2'
  2    2    0000                      LLEN    100
  3    3    8000                      ORG     $8000
  4    4    0000             |*
  5    5          0000 0063  |RETURN  EQU     $0063          ;MONITOR
  6    6    8000             |*
  7    7    8000             |*  EXCHANGE (D1) AND (A0)
  8    8    8000             |*
  9    9    8000 23C1 0000   |        MOVE.L  D1,TEMP        ;SAVE CONTENTS OF D1
  9         8004 8014        |
 10   10    8006 2208        |        MOVE.L  A0,D1          ;D1 := A0
 11   11    8008 2079 0000   |        MOVEA.L TEMP,A0        ;A0 := SAVED D1
 11         800C 8014        |
 12   12    800E             |*  USE OF EXG INSTRUCTION
 13   13    800E C388        |        EXG     D1,A0          ;A0 <---> D1
 14   14    8010             |*
 15   15    8010 4E4F        |        TRAP    #15            ;RETURN TO MONITOR
 16   16    8012 0063        |        DC.W    RETURN
 17   17    8014             |*
 18   18    8014             |TEMP    DS.L    1              ;TEMPORARY STORAGE
 19   19    8014             |*                             ;  LOCATION
 20   20    8018             |*
 21   21    8018             |        END
```

Figure 6.2 Program example of EXG instruction.

EXERCISES

6.1.1. Why must the MOVE instruction clear the condition codes C and V?

6.1.2. Write a routine to find the largest value of a set of 16-bit integers stored in consecutive locations in memory. Compare numbers in order and exchange a smaller one for a larger one in a processor register until the register contains the largest one. Try it with and without use of the EXG instruction.

6.1.3. A stack with N words has the first element that was pushed at location BOTTOM. Write the instructions to copy the word values to another stack. Let both stacks grow down in memory.

6.1.4. What advantage does MOVEM have over a series of MOVE instructions to save register contents in memory?

6.1.5. Think of possible uses of the SWAP instruction. Remember that the second most significant byte in a 32-bit register is not directly accessible. What type of instruction is needed to access any particular byte in a 32-bit register?

6.2 PROGRAM CONTROL

Two CPU32 instructions, BRA and JMP, cause *unconditional* transfer of control. For example, the assembly-language instruction

JMP   LABEL

transfers control to the instruction at LABEL unconditionally upon execution. The branch instruction BRA has a similar syntax. Subsection 6.2.1 discusses the CPU32 instructions for unconditional branch and jump.

In every sophisticated program, it is necessary to select which sequence of instructions to execute based on the results of computations. Thus, the flow of control will follow different paths through the program depending on these computations. Such programs require *conditional* transfer of control which is based on the results of an arithmetic or other operation. These operations set the condition codes of the CPU32 Status Register. The conditional branch instructions test these condition codes to determine whether a branch is required.

Subsection 6.2.2 describes the Bcc (Branch Conditionally) instruction which allows one of 14 conditions to be specified. If the selected condition is met, program execution continues at the branch location designated in the instruction. Subsection 6.2.3 discusses conditional branching after the execution of instructions that compare or test operands.

The CPU32 also has a versatile DBcc (Test Condition, Decrement, and Branch) instruction, which is useful for conditional branching in an iterative program structure. The DBcc instruction is described in Subsection 6.2.4.

6.2.1 Unconditional Branch and Jump

Table 6.4 defines the syntax and operation of the unconditional branch and jump instructions. The instructions BRA (Branch Always) and JMP (Jump) cause unconditional transfer of control by changing the value in the program counter when they execute. The JMP instruction differs from the BRA instruction in that the jump address may be specified by different addressing modes, but branch addressing is always relative to the program counter.

Table 6.4 Unconditional Branch and Jump

Syntax	Operation	Addressing modes
BRA <disp>	(PC) = (PC) + <disp>	PC relative
JMP <EA>	(PC) = (EA)	Control modes

Notes:
1. In BRA <disp>, <disp> is a signed 8-bit, 16-bit, or 32-bit integer.
2. (PC) is the BRA instruction location + 2.
3. Condition codes are not affected.

BRA instruction. The symbolic form of the BRA instruction is

$$\text{BRA} \qquad <disp>$$

where <disp> is either an 8-bit, 16-bit, or 32-bit signed displacement. The location to which control is transferred has the effective address

$$\text{effective address} = (PC) + <disp>$$

as previously described in Subsection 5.3.4. Thus, the branch instructions allow only PC relative addressing to determine the branch destination. The *displacement* is an offset (<disp>) added to the PC value which represents the distance in bytes between the current PC value and the destination address in memory when the BRA instruction executes.

For an 8-bit displacement, the branch range is −126 byte locations to +129 byte locations from the BRA instruction location since the value (PC) is the current instruction location plus 2 when the new value is calculated. In the case of a 16-bit displacement, the range is −32, 766 to +32, 769 bytes. A 32-bit displacement allows control to be transferred anywhere within the addressing range of the CPU32 in either a forward or backward direction from the branch instruction. The value of the displacement is determined automatically by the assembler when the displacement is specified as a label in the form

> BRA   <label>

Both the BRA and the JMP instructions accomplish the same thing, but the BRA allows only PC relative addressing.

JMP instruction.   The jump instruction has the form

> JMP   <EA>

where <EA> specifies the location of the next instruction to be executed. Only control addressing modes are allowed, which eliminates the register direct and autoindexing modes. In the absolute mode, the instruction

> JMP $1F000

causes transfer of control to location $1F000. Either a 16-bit or a 32-bit absolute address may be specified. If the address is specified by the assembly-language program or by the linkage editor, the form becomes

> JMP   LABEL

where LABEL is an absolute or relocatable symbol. The absolute form is typically used to transfer control to a routine defined at a fixed address in the system because of hardware considerations.

An effective address in a JMP instruction can also be defined by register indirect or PC indirect addressing. When the jump address is held in an address register, the instruction

> JMP   (A1)

causes transfer of control to the instruction pointed to by (A1). A displacement or index register can be used to modify the base address in the address register, as in the example instruction

> JMP   (0, A1, D1.L ∗ 4)

which jumps to the longword address pointed to by (A1) indexed by (D1). The index value might be used to specify one of several entry points into a routine whose base address is defined in A1. In all these indirect modes, (An) may be replaced by (PC) if PC relative addressing is required.

Example 6.3

The program segment in Figure 6.3 shows how jump tables may be created in memory and utilized. A label JMPTBL defines the entry point for the executable portion of the program. When executed, the MOVEA instruction uses (A0) indexed by (D0) which is scaled (multiplied) by 4 to address a longword offset from (A0). The address is thus transferred to A1. The JMP instruction then uses this address to transfer control.

Two tables are defined in the program. The table defined by TABLE1 holds the starting address of four routines that each occupy $100 bytes of memory. The addresses in TABLE1 are defined by labels using the Equate (EQU) directives in the program beginning at $8010. The second table (TABLE2) defines the absolute addresses of four other routines or entry points within a routine. To select a jump address, the starting address of the selected table must be placed in A0 and the entry number 0, 1, 2, . . . into D0 before execution of the program segment. Each table has the following form:

Entry number	Address	Memory contents
1	(A0)	First address
2	(A0) + 4	Second address
.	.	.
.	.	.
.	.	.
n	(A0) + 4 $*$ (D0)	n^{th} address

In the example, only four entries are defined in each table. The first table begins at location $8010 and the second table begins at location $8020.

The program segment can be executed in several ways. For debugging, the monitor might be used to initialize (A0) and (D0) and then cause transfer of control to location JMPTBL. Of course, executable instructions should be placed in the memory areas defined by the jump tables. When the jump table program segment is part of a larger program module, routines using the jump tables must be linked with the segment in Figure 6.3. The entry point JMPTBL is defined by an XDEF directive which defines the symbol JMPTBL as a "public" or global symbol. Another module referencing JMPTBL must contain the

          XREF   JMPTBL

directive so that the linkage editor can supply the proper address for the load module it creates.

After the jump, the original contents of the PC are lost, so no return is possible in the program as shown. To transfer control and return from a segment addressed by the table, a subroutine call could be used with indirect addressing to specify the beginning location. Subroutines are discussed in Section 6.3.

```
abs. rel.   LC    obj. code   source line
---- ----   ----  ----------  -----------
   1    1   0000                          TTL      'FIGURE 6.3'
   2    2   0000                          LLEN     100
   3    3   8000                          ORG      $8000
   4    4   0000              *
   5    5   8000              * JUMP TABLE EXAMPLE
   6    6   8000              *   INPUT : (D0.W) = ENTRY NUMBER
   7    7   8000              *           (A0.L) = TABLE ADDRESS
   8    8   8000              *
   9    9   8000              *   ENTRY POINT
  10   10   8000              *
  11   11   8000                          XDEF JMPTBL              ;DEFINE GLOBAL SYMBOL
  12   12   8000              *
  13   13   8000              *
  14   14   8000 2270 0C00    JMPTBL  MOVEA.L (A0,D0.L*4),A1       ;DEFINE JUMP ADDRESS
  15   15   8004 4ED1                 JMP     (A1)                 ;TRANSFER CONTROL
  16   16   8006              *
  17   17   8010                      ORG     $8010
  18   18   8006              *
  19   19        0000 4000    SCHED   EQU     $4000                ;SET UP EXAMPLE ENTRY
  20   20        0000 4100    QUEUE   EQU     SCHED+$100           ; POINTS FOR TABLE 1
  21   21        0000 4200    DISP    EQU     QUEUE+$100
  22   22        0000 4300    TIMER   EQU     DISP+$100
  23   23   8010              *
  24   24   8010 0000 4000    TABLE1  DC.L    SCHED                ;JUMP TABLE 1
  25   25   8014 0000 4100            DC.L    QUEUE
  26   26   8018 0000 4200            DC.L    DISP
  27   27   801C 0000 4300            DC.L    TIMER
  28   28   8020              *
  29   29   8020 0000 4500    TABLE2  DC.L    $4500                ;JUMP TABLE 2
  30   30   8024 0000 4520            DC.L    $4520                ;ABSOLUTE ADDRESSES
  31   31   8028 0000 4540            DC.L    $4540
  32   32   802C 0000 4560            DC.L    $4560
  33   33   8030              *
  34   34   8030                      END
```

Figure 6.3 Program example of jump table.

6.2.2 Branch Conditionally

The Bcc instructions allow selection of a control path in a program based on conditions:

      IF (condition "cc" is true)

            THEN (branch to new sequence)

            ELSE (execute next instruction).

The new sequence of instructions may be at either higher or lower memory addresses relative to the branch instruction. When the Bcc instruction executes, the CPU tests its condition codes to determine if the condition is true or not.

Figure 6.4 illustrates the operation of the Bcc instructions. Arithmetic operations as well as a number of other instructions set the condition codes of the CPU32 Status Register based on the result of the particular operation. If the condition is true, the displacement value is added to the value in the program counter. At this time, the PC contains the conditional branch instruction address plus 2.

The assembly-language format for the general conditional branch is

            Bcc   <label>

in which the condition "cc" is defined in the instruction by a mnemonic such as EQ for Equal and <label> is a label defined in the program indicating the instruction that

Instructions:

Arithmetic, MOVE,
CMP, TST, or
others

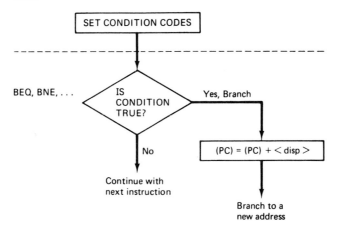

Figure 6.4 Operation of the Bcc instructions.

CC	carry clear	0100	$\overline{C}$
CS	carry set	0101	C
EQ	equal	0111	Z
GE	greater or equal	1100	$N \cdot V + \overline{N} \cdot \overline{V}$
GT	greater than	1110	$N \cdot V \cdot \overline{Z} + \overline{N} \cdot \overline{V} \cdot \overline{Z}$
HI	high	0010	$\overline{C} \cdot \overline{Z}$
LE	less or equal	1111	$Z + N \cdot \overline{V} + \overline{N} \cdot V$

LS	low or same	0011	$C + Z$
LT	less than	1101	$N \cdot \overline{V} + \overline{N} \cdot V$
MI	minus	1011	N
NE	not equal	0110	$\overline{Z}$
PL	plus	1010	$\overline{N}$
VC	overflow clear	1000	$\overline{V}$
VS	overflow set	1001	V

Condition Codes: Not affected.

Instruction Format:

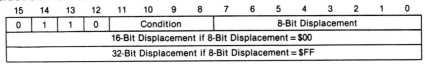

Figure 6.5 Conditional branch instructions.

is the destination if the branch condition is true. The table accompanying Figure 6.5 defines the mnemonics and their meaning based on the condition codes.

The assembler calculates the displacement when the branch destination is a label in the program. The displacement can be either an 8-bit, 16-bit, or 32-bit signed integer as shown in Figure 6.5. Some assemblers accept Bcc.S to force an 8-bit displacement (short) when possible. When a Bcc instruction executes, the appropriate displacement is added to the contents of the program counter to cause branching.

The possible conditions are listed in Figure 6.5 together with the condition code settings that cause a branch. The instruction format indicates how the conditions are coded in machine language. The four bit condition, bits [11:8], in the machine-language instruction and the setting of the condition codes is also defined in Figure 6.5. The condition codes in the CPU32 Status Register have the meaning previously defined in Subsection 4.2.8. For example, the instruction BCC (Branch on carry clear) will cause a branch if the carry condition code C is {0} when the instruction executes. This is described by the designation $\overline{C}$ to mean that the condition CC (Carry Clear) is true when the C bit is {0}. The BCS (Branch on carry set) instruction branches when the carry bit C is {1}. The setting of the condition codes by instructions is discussed further in this chapter and in Chapter 7.

Setting of condition codes for branching. If an arithmetic instruction or a MOVE instruction is executed, the condition codes indicate the arithmetic conditions that apply to the destination operand. For instance, in the addition

$$\text{ADD.}<l> \qquad X, Y$$

the destination value, which can be of length $<l> = $ B, W, or L, is the sum. The contents of the destination, designated (Y), may represent a signed or unsigned integer. In the case of an unsigned integer, the result may have been zero (Z = {1}) or nonzero (Z = {0}). If the sum is too large, it is indicated by a carry (C = {1}). Signed arithmetic could yield an out-of-range condition (V = {1}) or a positive, zero, or negative sum. The possible tests for signed and unsigned integers are listed in Table 6.5.

Table 6.5 Conditional Tests

| Instructions | Conditions for Branch | |
	Unsigned	Signed
ADD.<l> X,Y	(Y) = 0 BEQ	(Y) = 0 BEQ
or	(Y) $\neq$ 0 BNE	(Y) $\neq$ 0 BNE
SUB.<l> X,Y		(Y) $\geq$ 0 BPL
or		(Y) < 0 BMI
MOVE.<l> X		
Out of range for	C = {1} BCS	V = {1} BVS
arithmetic instructions	C = {0} BCC	V = {0} BVC

Note:
For the MOVE instruction with signed integers as operands, BGE, BLT, BGT, and BLE are also valid.

After a MOVE instruction, the condition codes may be examined. No out-of-range condition is possible since the condition codes C and V are cleared so that C = {0} and V = {0} after the transfer. As indicated in Table 6.5, except for the test for zero or nonzero, different conditional tests apply to unsigned versus signed integers. This section introduces the branching conditions required in both cases. Further discussion of the programming techniques for arithmetic operations is presented in Chapter 7.

Branch if zero or nonzero. The conditional instructions BEQ and BNE are logical opposites as shown in Figure 6.5. After an arithmetic instruction executes and sets the condition codes, the instruction

BEQ   <label>

will branch if the result was zero as indicated by the condition code Z being {1}. To branch on a nonzero condition, the program requires the Bcc instruction

BNE   <label>

which causes a branch if Z is {0}. Both instructions are valid for either signed or unsigned arithmetic and represent the only conditional branches that may be used with either.

Looping with Bcc. The Bcc instruction is often used to create loops in a program that perform the iterative parts of an algorithm being implemented. The Branch on Condition instruction is used to exit the loop. For example, the simplest form of iteration occurs when the number of repetitions is known. In several previous programming examples, the termination of a loop relied on a counter value in a register which was initialized with the number of iterations and decremented each time through the loop. A conditional branch instruction tests the condition codes after the register is decremented and terminates the looping when the counter value is zero. The Bcc instruction may be placed before the body of the loop or after all the instructions in the loop.

If the branch instruction is the last statement in the loop, the loop is considered *post-tested* and has the general form

REPEAT
          (body of loop)
UNTIL (count is zero).

These loops execute the instructions in the body of the loop at least once. The program of Figure 5.2, for example, uses the BNE instruction after the counter register D2 is decremented in the loop beginning at label LOOP. When the register value is zero, the loop terminates because the branch is *not* taken.

The FORTRAN loop

DO 10 I = 1, 20
          (body of loop)
10   **CONTINUE**

is a loop of this type. Other types of loop structures are shown in examples elsewhere in this book.

Example 6.4

The program shown in Figure 6.6 adds two one-dimensional arrays or vectors of unsigned 16-bit integers. The program computes $X(I) + Y(I)$ and saves the sum in location $X(I)$ for each element in the arrays. The length of the arrays is input in D0 and the addresses of the arrays must be placed in A0 and A1 before the program is executed. After each

```
abs.    LC    obj. code    source line
----    ----  ----------   -----------
  1    0000                       TTL     'FIGURE 6.6'
  2    0000                       LLEN    100
  3    8000                       ORG     $8000
  4    0000             *
  5    0000 0063    RETURN  EQU     $0063                 ;MONITOR ADDRESS
  6    8000             *
  7    8000             *  COMPUTE SUMS OF UNSIGNED INTEGER ARRAYS
  8    8000             *     INPUT  : (A0.L) = X ARRAY OF 16-BIT NUMBERS
  9    8000             *                (A1.L) = Y ARRAY OF 16-BIT NUMBERS
 10    8000             *                (D0.W) = NUMBER OF ELEMENTS IN ARRAYS
 11    8000             *     OUTPUT : (D0.W) = $FFFF IF ERROR OCCURRED
 12    8000             *
 13    8000 48E7 60C0   SUM     MOVEM.L D1-D2/A0-A1,-(SP) ;SAVE REGISTERS
 14    8004 3200                MOVE.W  D0,D1            ;SET UP COUNTER
 15    8006 6700 0012            BEQ     ERROR            ;IF ZERO, EXIT
 16    800A             *                                 ; WITH ERROR
 17    800A             *
 18    800A 5341        LOOP    SUBQ.W  #1,D1            ;DECREMENT INDEX
 19    800C 6B00 0010            BMI     DONE             ;EXIT WHEN (D1) < 0
 20    8010 3431 1200            MOVE.W  (0,A1,D1.W*2),D2 ;GET Y VALUE
 21    8014 D570 1200            ADD.W   D2,(0,A0,D1.W*2) ;ADD X := X + Y
 22    8018             *
 23    8018 64F0                BCC     LOOP             ;IF NO OVERFLOW, LOOP
 24    801A             *                                 ;    ELSE
 25    801A 303C FFFF   ERROR   MOVE.W  #$FFFF,D0        ;SET STATUS TO ERROR
 26    801E             *
 27    801E 4CDF 0306   DONE    MOVEM.L (SP)+,D1-D2/A0-A1 ;RESTORE REGISTERS
 28    8022 4E4F                TRAP    #15              ; AND RETURN
 29    8024 0063                DC.W    RETURN
 30    8026                      END
```

Figure 6.6 Program to detect overflow for unsigned arithmetic.

addition, the C condition code is checked. If the C bit is {1}, an overflow occurred and the low-order word of D0 will contain the value $FFFF.

In the program, (D1) is used as a counter and also as an index value into the arrays. After D1 is loaded with the word count and tested for zero, the value in D1 is scaled by 2 to yield a word count each time through the loop. In the loop, the counter and index in D1 are decremented by 1 and tested before each addition is performed. The BMI (Branch If Minus) instruction is used so the last addition is performed when (D1) = 0. Address register indirect with index addressing is used to select the values to be added. Notice that the last elements in the arrays are added first since (D1) begins in the loop with the count minus 1 as an index and decrements to zero. If no overflow occurs, the BCC instruction returns control to the first instruction in the loop. Otherwise, an error is indicated.

Branches with unsigned integer arithmetic. Unsigned arithmetic involves the positive integers and zero. For example, addresses should be treated as unsigned numbers. The only condition codes that should be tested after an addition or subtraction of unsigned integers are zero (Z) and carry (C).

The condition code C = {1} indicates that a carry occurred in addition because the sum was too large for the specified length of the operand. In subtraction, a carry bit set to {1} represents a borrow because the subtrahend was larger than the minuend. In either case, the result is not a valid unsigned integer. When arithmetic with unsigned integers is performed, the test for Branch on Carry Set (BCS) or Branch on Carry Clear (BCC) can be used to select between paths in the program.

Branching with signed arithmetic.   If the numerical values being manipulated are two's-complement numbers, the condition codes N, Z, and V are applicable. After arithmetic operations, V = {1} indicates an out-of-range condition. The instruction BVS branches when V = {1} and BVC branches when V = {0}. If the result is valid, the operand may be tested for a zero, nonzero, positive, or negative value. After a MOVE instruction, V = {0} and BGE, BLT, BGT, and BLE also perform valid tests according to the logic equations from Figure 6.5 since $\overline{V}$ is {1} in the equations. When V = {0}, BGE has the same effect as BPL. Chapter 7 discusses the use of condition codes with arithmetic operations in more detail.

6.2.3 Branching after CMP or TST

Table 6.6 lists the CMP (Compare) and TST (Test) instructions which are used to set the condition codes based on operand values. Then, conditional branch instructions can be used to direct the flow of control in a program. The instruction

$$\text{CMP} \qquad \text{X, Y}$$

compares two operands by performing the computation

$$(Y) - (X)$$

to set the condition codes N, Z, V, and C. The instruction

$$\text{TST} \qquad \text{Y}$$

evaluates one operand by performing the computation $(Y) - 0$, which always clears V and C but sets N and Z based on the result. Both of these instructions set the condition codes but do not modify the operands. The CMP instruction has variations Compare Immediate (CMPI) and Compare Memory (CMPM), as listed in Table 6.6.

Table 6.6 Compare and Test Instructions

		Addressing modes		
Instruction	Syntax	Source	Destination	Operation
Compare	CMP.<l> <EA>,<Dn>	All	<Dn>	(Dn) − (EA)
Compare Immediate	CMPI.<l> #<d>,<EA>	d	Data	(EA) − d
Compare Memory	CMPM.<l> (Am)+,(An)+	(Am)+	(An)+	((An)) − ((Am))
Test	TST.<l> <EA>	All	—	(EA) − 0

Notes:
1. <l> denotes B, W, or L.
2. If An is the source for CMP or TST, only word (W) or longword (L) operands are allowed.
3. All condition codes are affected by the compare instructions.
4. The TST instruction affects condition codes N and Z but clears C and V to {0}.

The compare instruction

$$CMP.<l> \qquad <EA>,<Dn>$$

subtracts the source operand from the contents of the specified data register. The computation

$$(Dn) - (EA)$$

is performed without modifying the operand and the length $<l>$ of each operand can be defined as B, W, or L. If the source is an address register, the operand length is restricted to word or longword.

The CMPI (Compare Immediate) instruction compares an immediate value to an operand referenced by a data addressing mode. This excludes the address register direct addressing mode. Byte, word, or longword operands are allowed. For example, the instruction

$$CMPI.B \qquad \#5, \$2000$$

compares the value 5 with the contents of the byte at location \$2000. Unlike the CMP instruction, the CMPI instruction may reference memory locations as the destination.

The CMPM (Compare Memory) instruction is used to compare sequences of bytes, words, or longwords in memory. Only the postincrement addressing mode is allowed for both operands. The instruction

$$CMPM.B \qquad (A1)+, (A2)+$$

compares the bytes addressed by A1 and A2 and then increments the addresses to point to the next bytes.

The TST (Test) instruction has the format

$$TST.<l> \qquad <EA>$$

where $<l>$ can be B, W, or L and $<EA>$ can be specified by all the addressing modes. However, only the word or longword contents of an address register can be tested. The instruction sets the Z and N condition codes based on the value of the operand. However, V and C are always cleared.

Example 6.5

The valid conditional branches after the TST instruction for an unsigned integer operand are BEQ and BNE. These conditions for a zero or nonzero value are also valid for signed integers. Since the TST instruction clears the C and V condition codes, a number of other tests for signed integers are also valid. After the instruction

$$TST \qquad X$$

the conditional branch instructions BGT, BLT or BMI, BGE or BPL, and BLE can be used when the location X contains a signed integer.

When a Bcc instruction follows a CMP instruction in the sequence

CMP   X, Y

Bcc   <label>

the comparison and selection made is
IF (Y) "condition <cc>" (X)
    THEN branch to <label>
    ELSE continue.
For example, the instruction sequence

CMP.W   D1, D2

BGE   DONE

checks if the 16-bit value in D2 is greater than or equal to the 16-bit value in D1. If so, the branch is taken to DONE.

The TST instruction compares an operand with zero in a similar manner. Thus, the sequence

TST.W   D2

BEQ   DONE

has the logic:
IF (D2)[15:0] equals 0
    THEN branch to DONE
    ELSE continue.

Table 6.7 lists the Bcc instructions that would cause a branch if executed after the CMP or TST instruction. The tests for Branch on Less Than (BLT) and Branch on Minus (BMI) as well as BGE and BPL are equivalent after a TST instruction because the overflow bit V is cleared.

Both CMP and TST can be used with either signed or unsigned integer interpretations. However, the processor always performs the computation by using (subtracting) two's-complement arithmetic. Therefore, the valid conditional branch instructions are different for the two interpretations of integers.

Example 6.6

The sample program in Figure 6.7 compares two tables of bytes addressed by A1 and A2. D1 contains the number of bytes in each table and D2 contains a status word or "flag" to indicate if the tables are the same. The flag is initialized to a default value of zero to indicate unequivalent values before the comparison begins. If all corresponding bytes of the two tables are equal, a value of +1 is entered into D2 by the last instruction before returning to the monitor program. If the number of bytes is zero, D2 will be left with the initialized zero value. Such a program is typically used to compare two strings of ASCII characters to see if they are equal.

Table 6.7 Bcc Instructions with CMP and TST

		Branch Condition	
Instruction	Result	Unsigned	Signed
CMP X,Y	$(Y) = (X)$	BEQ (Equal)	BEQ (Equal)
	$(Y) \neq (X)$	BNE (Not Equal)	BNE (Not Equal)
	$(Y) > (X)$	BHI (High)	BGT (Greater Than)
	$(Y) \geq (X)$	BCC (Carry Clear)	BGE (Greater or Equal)
	$(Y) < (X)$	BCS (Carry Set)	BLT (Less Than)
	$(Y) \leq (X)$	BLS (Low or Same)	BLE (Less Than or Equal)
TST X	$(X) = 0$	BEQ	BEQ
	$(X) \neq 0$	BNE	BNE
	$(X) > 0$	BNE	BGT
	$(X) < 0$	—	BLT, BMI
	$(X) \geq 0$	—	BGE, BPL
	$(X) \leq 0$	—	BLE

Notes:

1. In CMP X,Y; the destination is a data register.
2. TST sets C = {0} and V = {0}.
3. BMI (Branch on Minus) is the same as BLT, and BPL (Branch on Plus) is the same as BGE when V = {0}.

```
abs.   LC    obj. code   source line
----   ----  ---------   -----------
  1    0000                          TTL     'FIGURE 6.7'
  2    0000                          LLEN    100
  3    8000                          ORG     $8000
  4    0000              *
  5          0000 0063   RETURN  EQU     $0063          ;MONITOR
  6    8000              *
  7    8000              * COMPARE TWO TABLES OF BYTES
  8    8000              * INPUTS : (A1.L) = ADDRESS OF FIRST TABLE
  9    8000              *          (A2.L) = ADDRESS OF SECOND TABLE
 10    8000              *          (D1.B) = NUMBER OF BYTES IN THE TABLES
 11    8000              *                  (255 MAXIMUM)
 12    8000              *
 13    8000              * OUTPUT : (D2.W) = 0 : NOT EQUAL   ;STATUS
 14    8000              *                   1 : EQUAL
 15    8000              *
 16    8000 48E7 4060    COMPARE MOVEM.L D1/A1-A2,-(SP) ;SAVE REGISTERS
 17    8004 4242                 CLR.W   D2             ;SET FAULT STATUS
 18    8006 4A01                 TST.B   D1             ;IF LENGTH IS ZERO
 19    8008 6700 0010             BEQ     DONE           ; THEN BRANCH TO DONE
 20    800C             *
 21    800C B509        LOOP    CMPM.B  (A1)+,(A2)+    ;ELSE IF TWO BYTES ARE
 22    800E             *                              ;    NOT EQUAL
 23    800E 6600 000A             BNE     DONE           ; THEN BRANCH TO DONE
 24    8012 5301                 SUBQ.B  #1,D1          ;ELSE DECREMENT COUNTER
 25    8014 66F6                 BNE     LOOP           ;    AND TEST NEXT VALUE
 26    8016             *                              ;    UNTIL (D1)=0.
 27    8016             *
 28    8016 343C 0001   EQUAL   MOVE.W  #1,D2          ;THEY ARE IDENTICAL
 29    801A             *                              ;   SET STATUS=1
 30    801A             *
 31    801A 4CDF 0602   DONE    MOVEM.L (SP)+,D1/A1-A2 ;RESTORE REGISTERS
 32    801E 4E4F                 TRAP    #15            ; AND RETURN
 33    8020 0063                 DC.W    RETURN
 34    8022             *
 35    8022                      END
```

Figure 6.7 Program use of CMP and TST instructions.

Before comparison, a TST instruction determines if D1 has a nonzero byte count. Within the loop, the bytes addressed by A1 and A2 are compared and the addresses are automatically incremented. If any two bytes are not equal, the first BNE instruction causes a branch and the test ends. After each successful comparison, the counter value in D1 is decremented. Looping continues until the counter reaches zero. If all the bytes are equal, D2 will be set to 1 by the instruction at label EQUAL. Before the program can be executed, A1, A2, and D1 must all be initialized with the proper input values.

Example 6.7

The program shown in Figure 6.8 compares 16-bit positive integers in a one-dimensional array or table stored in locations NUM1, NUM1 + 2, and so on, and leaves the largest one in D1. Register D3 is used as a counter to determine when all the numbers have been tested. The count of numbers is assumed to be in D3 before the program executes.

Since positive numbers only are considered, BLS (Branch Lower or Same) is used to test if a value in D2 is smaller than the assumed maximum held in D1. If so, the loop is tested for completion. If the new value in D2 is larger than the "maximum" in D1, the register contents are exchanged. In the example, the DS (Define Storage) directive reserves space for forty 16-bit integers. The values must be stored in these locations before the program is executed.

```
abs.   LC    obj. code    source line
----   ----  ---------    -----------
   1   0000                        TTL     'FIGURE 6.8'
   2   0000                        LLEN    100
   3   8000                        ORG     $8000
   4   0000               *
   5         0000 0063    RETURN    EQU     $0063           ;MONITOR
   6   8000               *
   7   8000               *  FIND THE LARGEST 16-BIT POSITIVE INTEGER IN TABLE NUM1
   8   8000               *
   9   8000               *  INPUTS  : (D3.W) = NUMBER OF INTEGERS TO EXAMINE
  10   8000               *                NUM1 = TABLE OF INTEGERS; 40 MAXIMUM
  11   8000               *  OUTPUTS : (D1.W) = MAXIMUM INTEGER FOUND
  12   8000               *
  13   8000 48E7 3040              MOVEM.L D2-D3/A1,-(SP) ;SAVE REGISTERS
  14   8004 227C 0000              MOVE.L  #NUM1,A1        ;LOAD STARTING ADDRESS
       8008 8024
  15   800A 5343                   SUBQ.W  #1,D3           ;NUMBER OF INTEGERS-1
  16   800C 3219                   MOVE.W  (A1)+,D1        ;(D1)= FIRST INTEGER
  17   800E               *
  18   800E 3419          LOOP     MOVE.W  (A1)+,D2        ;GET NEXT INTEGER
  19   8010 B441                   CMP.W   D1,D2           ;COMPARE TO MAXIMUM
  20   8012 6300 0004              BLS     NEXT            ; IF LESS OR SAME
  21   8016               *                               ;    CHECK NEXT ONE
  22   8016 C342                   EXG     D1,D2           ; ELSE:EXCHANGE
  23   8018               *
  24   8018 5343          NEXT     SUBQ.W  #1,D3           ;DECREMENT COUNTER
  25   801A 66F2                   BNE     LOOP            ; LOOP TILL (D3)=0
  26   801C               *
  27   801C 4CDF 020C              MOVEM.L (SP)+,D2-D3/A1 ;RESTORE REGISTERS
  28   8020 4E4F                   TRAP    #15             ;AND RETURN
  29   8022 0063                   DC.W    RETURN
  30   8024               *
  31   8024               NUM1     DS.L    20              ;NUMBERS
  32   8024               *
  33   8074                        END
```

Figure 6.8 Program to compare unsigned integers.

6.2.4 DBcc Instruction

The Test, Decrement, and Branch instruction is a powerful instruction for control of loop structures. The basic assembly-language format is

$$DB<cc> \qquad <Dn>, <label>$$

which designates three parameters: the condition $<cc>$, a data register, and a displacement. The displacement is represented here as a label in an assembly language program. The various conditions and the format for the instruction are shown in Figure 6.9.

CC	carry clear	0100	$\bar{C}$
CS	carry set	0101	C
EQ	equal	0111	Z
F	never true	0001	0
GE	greater or equal	1100	$N{\cdot}V + \bar{N}{\cdot}\bar{V}$
GT	greater than	1110	$N{\cdot}V{\cdot}\bar{Z} + \bar{N}{\cdot}\bar{V}{\cdot}\bar{Z}$
HI	high	0010	$\bar{C}{\cdot}\bar{Z}$
LE	less or equal	1111	$Z + N{\cdot}\bar{V} + \bar{N}{\cdot}V$

LS	low or same	0011	$C+Z$
LT	less than	1101	$N{\cdot}\bar{V} + \bar{N}{\cdot}V$
MI	minus	1011	N
NE	not equal	0110	$\bar{Z}$
PL	plus	1010	$\bar{N}$
T	always true	0000	1
VC	overflow clear	1000	$\bar{V}$
VS	overflow set	1001	V

Condition Codes: Not affected.

Instruction Format:

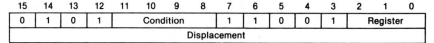

15	14	13	12	11	10	9	8	7	6	5	4	3	2	1	0
0	1	0	1	Condition				1	1	0	0	1	Register		
Displacement															

Figure 6.9 DBcc instruction.

The DBcc instruction can cause a loop to be terminated when either the specified condition, $<cc>$, is TRUE or when the count held in $<Dn>$ is zero when the DBcc instruction executes. Each time the instruction is executed, the value in Dn is decremented by 1. The flowchart for the instruction in Figure 6.10 illustrates the conditions that cause the next instruction in sequence to be executed.

Fourteen of the logical conditions tested by DBcc are the same as those for the Bcc instruction discussed previously. However, the DBcc is sometimes called a "Don't Branch on Condition" instruction. If the condition is TRUE, no branch is taken and program execution continues at the next instruction in line. This is the opposite operation from that of the Bcc instruction.

Example 6.8

A loop structure with the DBcc terminating the loop has the logic:
    REPEAT
      (body of loop)
    UNTIL (condition).
    For example, the sequence of instructions with the structure
    LOOP

        (body of loop)
        TST   X ,   ; TEST FOR ZERO
        DBEQ $<Dn>$, LOOP ; LOOP IF NOT ZERO

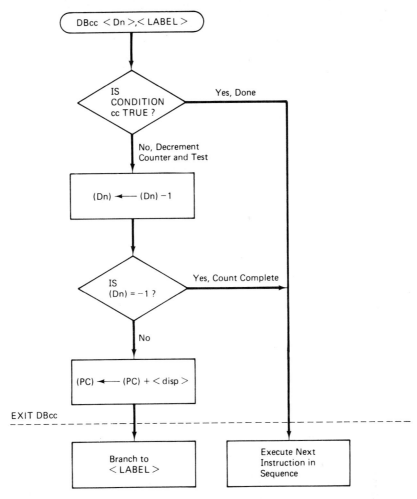

Figure 6.10 Operation of the DBcc instruction.

will continue to loop until the contents of location X are zero or until the count in Dn has been exhausted. The TST instruction sets the condition codes based on the value (X). The DBcc tests the conditions and decrements <Dn> if the condition is false but does not affect the condition codes. When the specified condition is true or when the DBcc instruction decrements <Dn> to −1, the loop is terminated. If the example program above needed to loop (branch) on the X equal 0 condition, the opposite logical condition, DBNE, should be used. Then if X is zero, a branch is taken to LOOP; otherwise, execution continues to the next instruction.

In addition to the 14 testable conditions which are used by both DBcc and Bcc instructions, the DBcc has two other conditions, TRUE(T) and FALSE(F). The DBT instruction never branches. Its logical opposite, the DBF, always branches unless the count is exhausted. For the DBF instruction, no condition is tested. The DBF instruction replaces the "decrement and test for zero" sequence frequently used to terminate a loop.[1] There is one difference, however. The initial value of the counter must be one less than the number of iterations required when the DBcc instruction is used.

The register specified to hold the count contains a 16-bit integer with a decimal value between 0 and 65,535. Assuming that the register initially contained the integer value N and also that the condition $<cc>$ is not true, then in a post-tested loop, the count would be $N, N - 1, N - 2, \ldots, 0$ before the loop is exited; thus $N + 1$ iterations are executed. To loop N times, the counter register should contain the value $N - 1$ initially.

The DBcc instruction is also used to improve program efficiency when it is used in the "loop" mode of the processor. Section 9.5 discusses this application of the instruction.

Example 6.9

The two short program segments shown in Figure 6.11 compare the use of the Bcc and DBcc instructions. Each program tests a table containing $(N + 1)$ word-length operands to locate a nonzero entry. Before execution, address register A1 must contain the first address of the table and D1 contains N. In the first segment, a nonzero entry addressed by (A1) causes a branch to label DONE1. The address of the nonzero entry is (A1)−2 since postincrement addressing is used in the TST instruction. If no nonzero entries are found, (D1) is decremented until it reaches −1, upon which the BPL instruction terminates the loop. Thus, if (D1) = −1 after the program segment is complete, the table contains all zero values.

The instruction to test for a nonzero value and those to decrement and test the loop count in the first program can be replaced with a single DBcc instruction. The second segment in Figure 6.11 shows the instructions to test the $(N + 1)$ locations for a nonzero value as before. When the second loop at LOOP2 is terminated, D1 contains −1 ($FFFF) if no nonzero entries were found.

EXERCISES

6.2.1. Discuss the use of a jump table if the program is in read-only memory but the routines to be executed may have a different starting address in different systems.

6.2.2. Compare the use of indirect addressing in the following instructions:
(a) JMP (A2)
(b) MOVEA (A2),A1
(c) MOVE.W (0, D1.W),D2

6.2.3. If the instruction

$$\text{CMP.W} \qquad \text{I, J}$$

---

[1] Some MC68332 assemblers use the form "DBRA" instead of the mnemonic DBF.

```
abs. rel.   LC    obj. code   source line
---- ----   ----  ----------  -----------
   1    1   0000                        TTL     'FIGURE 6.11'
   2    2   0000                        LLEN    100
   3    3   8000                        ORG     $8000
   4    4   0000              *
   5    5         0000 0063   RETURN    EQU     $0063        ;MONITOR
   6    6   8000              *
   7    7   8000              *    COMPARISON OF DBCC AND BCC OPERATION
   8    8   8000              *       INPUTS  : (D1.W) = LENGTH OF TABLE - 1
   9    9   8000              *                 (A1.L) = ADDRESS OF TABLE
  10   10   8000              *
  11   11   8000              *       OUTPUTS : (A1.L) = ADDRESS OF NONZERO ENTRY
  12   12   8000              *                 (D1.W) = $FFFF : NO NONZERO ENTRIES
  13   13   8000              *
  14   14   8000              *  BCC OPERATION
  15   15   8000              *
  16   16   8000 4A59         LOOP1     TST.W   (A1)+
  17   17   8002 6600 0006              BNE     DONE1        ;DONE IF NONZERO
  18   18   8006              *                              ; ELSE:TEST NEXT VALUE
  19   19   8006 5341                   SUBQ.W  #1,D1
  20   20   8008 6AF6                   BPL     LOOP1        ;TEST TILL COUNTER IS -1
  21   21   800A 5589         DONE1     SUBQ.L  #2,A1        ;ADDRESS OF A NONZERO VALUE
  22   22   800C              *                              ; IF FOUND
  23   23   800C 4E4F                   TRAP    #15
  24   24   800E 0063                   DC.W    RETURN
  25   25   8010              *
  26   26   8020                        ORG     $8020
  27   27   8010              *
  28   28   8020              *  DBCC OPERATION
  29   29   8020              *
  30   30   8020 4A59         LOOP2     TST.W   (A1)+
  31   31   8022 56C9 FFFC              DBNE    D1,LOOP2     ;LOOP IF VALUE IS ZERO
  32   32   8026              *                              ;  OR COUNTER IS >-1
  33   33   8026              *                              ; ELSE:GO TO NEXT INST.
  34   34   8026              *
  35   35   8026 5589         DONE2     SUBQ.L  #2,A1        ;ADDRESS OF FIRST NONZERO
  36   36   8028              *                              ;  VALUE
  37   37   8028              *
  38   38   8028 4E4F                   TRAP    #15          ;RETURN TO MONITOR
  39   39   802A 0063                   DC.W    RETURN
  40   40   802C                        END
```

Figure 6.11 Program comparison of Bcc and DBcc.

has been executed, specify the instruction that will perform the following:
(a) branch to ZERO if I = J;
(b) branch to LESS if I < J;
(c) branch to MORE if I > J,
where ZERO, LESS, and MORE are statement labels.

6.2.4. Rewrite the sequence of instructions

    LOOP...
            (body of loop)
               SUB.W #1, CNT
               BNE   LOOP

to use a DBcc instruction.

6.2.5. Write the assembly-language program to implement the FORTRAN loop

    DO 10 I = 1,20
            (body of loop)
10   CONTINUE

6.2.6. Write the assembly-language program equivalent to the following:

    SUM = 0
    I = MAXVAL
10 SUM = SUM + I
    I = I − 1
    IF (I .NE. 0) **GO TO** 10

Assume that MAXVAL was defined previously. Test the program for the three values MAXVAL = 10, 1, and 0. Modify the program to take into account the case for MAXVAL = 0.

6.2.7. Since the MOVE and TST instructions always set the condition code V = {0}, show that BGE, BLT, BGT, and BLE are valid as branches after a MOVE or TST instruction when signed integers are moved. Also, show that BGE is the same as BPL and that BLT is the same as BMI in this case.

6.2.8. Determine the machine-language codes for each branch instruction:

Address	Label	Instruction	
8000	LOOP1	BRA.B	LOOP2
.			
806E	LOOP2	BRA.W	LOOP3
.			
.			
9000	LOOP3	BRA.L	LOOP4
.			
9600	LOOP4	BRA.L	LOOP1

6.3 SUBROUTINE USAGE WITH THE CPU32

The *subroutine* is a sequence of instructions which is treated as a separate program module within a larger program. The subroutine can be "called", i.e. executed, one or more times as the calling program executes. Generally, the subroutines associated with a program accomplish specific tasks, each of which represents a simpler procedure than that of the entire program. In fact, subroutines are called *procedures* in the Pascal language. Each module or single subroutine should be self-contained; that is, be testable by itself independently of the calling program. When the subroutine is called during execution of a program, control is transferred to the subroutine and its instructions are executed. When the subroutine completes, control is then returned to the calling program. Execution resumes at the next instruction in sequence following the call to the subroutine.

The location of the first instruction of a subroutine is called its *starting address*. This must be defined in each program calling the subroutine. If the subroutine and the calling program are assembled at the same time, the subroutine starting address can be defined by a label at its first instruction. If the subroutine and calling program are not assembled together, the subroutine starting address must be explicitly defined in the call instruction.[2]

The CPU32 instructions to call and return from a subroutine are shown in Table 6.8. The BSR (Branch to Subroutine) and JSR (Jump to Subroutine) instructions perform calls. In each case, execution causes the longword address of the instruction following the call to be pushed onto the system stack. Execution then continues at the subroutine starting address. No other information is saved by the call, so it is the programmer's responsibility to preserve any register contents, including the contents of the condition code register if these are modified by the subroutine. These may be saved before the call and restored after the return, but a well-designed subroutine will save the values and restore them before returning. The latter approach is more reasonable since there are typically multiple calls to a single subroutine.

Also, if subroutines are designed separately, the programmer designing the calling program may not be aware of what registers are modified by the subroutine unless good documentation is available. Therefore, our examples will show subroutines whose execution is *transparent* to the calling program except for modification of registers used to return values calculated by the subroutine.

Table 6.8 Instructions for Subroutine Usage

Instruction	Syntax	Operation
Branch to Subroutine	BSR $<$disp$>$	1. $(SP) \leftarrow (SP) - 4$; $((SP)) \leftarrow (PC)$ 2. $(PC) \leftarrow (PC) + <$disp$>$
Jump to Subroutine	JSR $<$EA$>$	1. $(SP) \leftarrow (SP) - 4$; $((SP)) \leftarrow (PC)$ 2. $(PC) \leftarrow (EA)$
Return and Restore Condition Codes	RTR	1. $(CCR) \leftarrow ((SP))[7:0]$; $(SP) \leftarrow (SP) + 2$ 2. $(PC) \leftarrow ((SP))$; $(SP) \leftarrow (SP) + 4$
Return from Subroutine	RTS	$(PC) \leftarrow ((SP))$; $(SP) \leftarrow (SP) + 4$

Notes:
1. SP denotes the system stack pointer; PC is the program counter.
2. CCR is the condition code register, that is, $(SR)[7:0]$.
3. $<$disp$>$ is an 8-bit, 16-bit, or 32-bit signed integer.
4. $<$EA$>$ must be specified as a control addressing mode.

Two return instructions are available for the CPU32. The RTR (Return and Restore) is used when the condition codes held in the condition code register (CCR) have been saved on the system stack by the subroutine. Otherwise, RTS (Return from Subroutine) is used to simply load the program counter with the return address from the stack.

The instructions for subroutine calling and returning and their use with simple subroutine structures are discussed in this section. A more detailed look at subroutines is given in Chapter 9, where various methods of passing data between calling programs and subroutines is discussed. In the present discussion it is assumed that

---

[2] If a subroutine has several entry points, each address must be defined. Also, when independent programs are assembled separately, the external or "global" references are usually defined when the modules are linked together.

parameters are passed in processor registers. Chapter 4 discussed the use of the system stack during subroutine calls.

6.3.1 Invoking Subroutines

The instructions BSR and JSR cause a transfer of control to the beginning address of a subroutine. In the Branch to Subroutine statement

BSR   <label>

the <label> operand causes the assembler to calculate the displacement between the BSR instruction and the instruction identified by <label>. This displacement is added during execution to the current contents of the Program Counter (the BSR location plus 2) to calculate the starting location of the subroutine. The displacement is stored as an integer in two's-complement notation. The BSR operates in the same manner as the BRA instruction discussed in Section 6.2.1 except that the address of the instruction following the BSR is saved on the system stack.

Similarly, the JSR (Jump to Subroutine) is identical to the JMP instruction except for the saving of the return address. The addressing range of the JSR instruction is 32 bits and any control addressing mode can be used. Thus, the absolute modes, the relative modes, and the indirect addressing modes, except postincrement and predecrement, are allowed to specify the starting address. For example, the instruction

JSR   4(A5)

uses indirect with displacement addressing and transfers control to the instruction four bytes past the address in A5. Control is returned to the instruction following the JSR instruction that called the subroutine if a RTR or RTS instruction is executed in the subroutine.

Example 6.10

Figure 6.12 shows the general structure of the subroutine call. Assume that the system stack pointer is initialized to $4000 before the subroutine is called. The call (JSR) decrements the initial value (SP) = $4000 by 4 and saves (PC) at location $3FFC. In the subroutine, the first MOVE instruction saves the contents of the condition code register on the stack at location $3FFA just below (in memory) the two words containing the return address. The MOVEM.L instruction pushes all 32 bits of each register specified by the list onto the stack using predecrement addressing. Sixty bytes are used.

The instructions in the body of the subroutine are simulated by the No Operation (NOP) instruction in the example. After the instructions in the body of the subroutine are executed, the register values are restored by the last MOVEM instruction before the return. The RTR instruction restores the condition codes to the status register, leaving the upper byte of SR unchanged before returning. If the condition codes had not been saved upon entry into the subroutine, the RTS instruction would be used to return to the calling program. The RTS instruction simply loads the return address from the stack into the program counter.

After return to the main program, other instructions (not shown) would typically be executed. The final TRAP instruction returns control to the monitor program.

```
abs.   LC    obj. code    source line
----   ----  ---------    -----------
  1    0000                        TTL      'FIGURE 6.12'
  2    0000                        LLEN     100
  3    8000                        ORG      $8000
  4    0000              *
  5    8000              *   MAIN PROGRAM
  6    8000              *         ...
  7    8000 4EB9 0000              JSR      SUBR
       8004 800A
  8    8006              *         ...
  9    8006 4E4F                   TRAP     #15            ;RETURN TO MONITOR
 10    8008 0063                   DC.W     $0063          ; WHEN MAIN IS DONE
 11    800A              *
 12    800A              *
 13    800A              *   SUBROUTINE
 14    800A              *
 15    800A 42E7         SUBR      MOVE.W   CCR,-(SP)        ;SAVE CONDITION CODES
 16    800C 48E7 FFFE              MOVEM.L  D0-D7/A0-A6,-(SP) ;SAVE REGISTERS
 17    8010              *         ...
 18    8010 4E71                   NOP
 19    8012              *         ...
 20    8012 4CDF 7FFF              MOVEM.L  (SP)+,D0-D7/A0-A6 ; RESTORE REGISTERS
 21    8016              *
 22    8016              *   RETURN AND RESTORE CONDITION CODES
 23    8016              *
 24    8016 4E77                   RTR
 25    8018                        END
```

Figure 6.12 Program structure of a subroutine module.

Figure 6.13 shows the general form of the stack contents before, during, and after the call to SUBR. The (PC) always occupies two words of the stack. The 8-bit contents of the condition code register are saved in the next (lower) word in memory. Then each register is saved when the MOVEM instruction is executed. The system stack pointer now points to the new TOP of stack, and the stack can be used by interrupt routines or during calls to other subroutines. After the subroutine has completed its processing, the return instruction should leave the stack pointer at its original value.

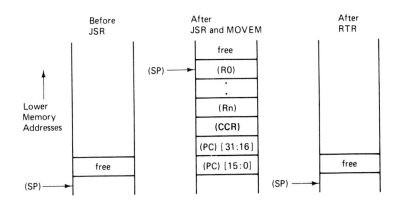

Figure 6.13 System stack usage during a subroutine call.

Sec. 6.3   Subroutine Usage with the CPU32

217

6.3.2 Program Structure

Large programs may be divided into a number of subroutines to accomplish specific tasks. This type of program structuring has the advantage of simplifying program testing and improving maintainability. The execution time is longer than that for a similar program without subroutines, due to the time required by the calling and return sequence for each subroutine. In most cases, the requirement for modularity is more important than minimizing execution time.

Figure 6.14 shows the possible structure of a program to read characters from a keyboard, convert them to BCD, and then process the numerical values. The program begins by initializing values and then calls the first subroutine to read or input the characters as they are typed. After a string of characters is input, each is tested by a second subroutine. This test consists of checking each to see that it is a valid ASCII numeric character. If no error occurs, the routine converts the valid characters to BCD. If an invalid character is detected, an error subroutine is called to display an invalid data message on the CRT screen. If no errors were detected, the BCD data can be processed further by additional subroutines.

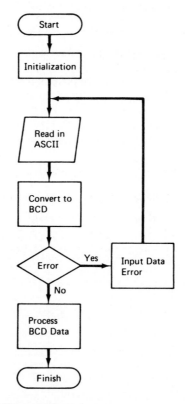

Figure 6.14 Example program structure.

In the next chapter, techniques for binary and BCD arithmetic are covered. The final section of Chapter 7 presents the input/output and conversion routines to allow the programmer to create complete program modules such as the one characterized in Figure 6.14.

EXERCISES

6.3.1. If the instruction

BSR   SUB1

is located at address $3012 and the label SUB1 is at $3022, define the machine-language instruction for

BSR   SUB1

Refer to Appendix IV for the machine-language format.

6.3.2. Draw a diagram of the stack for the program module in Example 6.10 if the initial value of the stack pointer is (SP) = $7FFE.

6.3.3. In the CPU32, what limits the number of subroutines that may be nested? A "nested" subroutine is one called by another subroutine.

6.3.4. Modify the program of Example 6.3 to use subroutine calls (JSR) rather than JMP instructions. Assume that the subroutine ends with an RTS instruction.

FURTHER READING

A number of works discuss assembly-language programming in a manner that is useful to the CPU32 programmer. In particular, the book by Kane et al. listed below gives a number of good examples of programs for the MC68000. These programs will execute on a MC68332-based computer. Many of the textbooks written about the PDP-11 system can be applied to the study of the MC68332 if the differences between the processors are taken into account. For instance, the instruction

CMP   A, B

for the PDP-11 evaluates (A) − (B), which is the reverse of the CPU32. The texts by Eckhouse and Morris and by Lewis explain many of the aspects of assembly-language programming for the PDP-11. Programs for the PDP-11 can be converted to those for CPU32, and vice versa, by a programmer familiar with both machines. The Further Reading section for Chapter 5 lists other references which provide more details about assembly-language programming and the operation of assemblers.

ECKHOUSE, RICHARD H., JR., and L.R. MORRIS, *Minicomputer Systems*, 2nd ed. Englewood Cliffs, N.J.: Prentice Hall, 1979.

KANE, GERALD, DOUG HAWKINS, and LANCE LEVENTHAL, *68000 Assembly Language Programming*. Berkeley, Calif.: Osborne (McGraw-Hill), 1981.

LEWIS, HARRY R., *An Introduction to Computer Programming and Data Structures Using MACRO-11*. Reston, Va.: Reston, 1981.

7

Arithmetic Operations

This chapter is concerned with arithmetic operations on integers. Numerical data may be used as addresses for identification purposes or for representation of quantities such as voltages, temperatures or bank balances. In any case, the fundamental operations of addition, subtraction, multiplication, and division of numbers are essential in algorithms that are designed to process numerical data. Almost all programs incorporate some form of arithmetic operation.

The number system used in microprocessors is binary. The internal use of binary arithmetic and our human interpretation of the results as decimal numbers is possible if suitable conversion routines are available. Decimal values may be first converted to ASCII code for input to the computer system and then be converted further to binary for processing. The reverse conversions may be applied for output. A problem may arise in certain cases, however, due to the finite length of the machine representation. Stated another way, the length in bits of an integer value is a measure of the largest integer representable in a given format. Thus, a 32-bit representation limits the magnitude of a positive integer to $2^{32} - 1$. Certain operations, such as the addition of two 32-bit numbers, carries with it the danger of exceeding the maximum allowable value. The tests for such a condition and the means for extending the precision when necessary are two important aspects of the study of arithmetic operations using computers.

A review of the topics in Chapter 3 is suggested before or during the study of this chapter. Many of the mathematical details of binary and decimal arithmetic presented there are not repeated here. The setting of the condition codes resulting from execution of CPU32 instructions is defined in Appendix IV.

The first three sections of this chapter present the basic arithmetic instructions for the CPU32. These include ADD, SUB, EXT, NEG, MUL, and DIV for operands of length 8-, 16-, or 32-bits treated as binary integers. When the operand or result length exceeds 32 bits, extended-precision schemes are employed, as discussed in Section 7.4. Single- and extended-precision decimal-arithmetic instructions, including ABCD, SBCD, and NBCD, are treated in Section 7.5. Section 7.6 covers the important topic of input/output techniques using a supervisor (monitor) program. The discussion includes the methods of conversion between ASCII characters and binary or decimal values. The final section explains the CPU32 instructions to perform linear interpolation.

7.1 SOME DETAILS OF BINARY ARITHMETIC

In the CPU32, the binary single-precision representation of operands can be 8, 16,or 32 bits in length. Numerically, positive integer values range from 0 to $2^m - 1$, where $m = 8, 16$, or 32. For signed integers, the range is -2^{m-1} to $+2^{m-1} - 1$ in two's-complement notation. In adding or subtracting m-bit integers, various out-of-range conditions can occur. These conditions are indicated by condition code bits of the processor. The out-of-range conditions for unsigned integers are treated differently from those for signed integers since the interpretation of the condition codes changes.

Consider the addition of two unsigned m-digit integers. For example, the 8-bit addition of 125 and 200 using binary addition yields the result:

$$
\begin{array}{r}
0111\ 1101 \\
+\,1100\ 1000 \\
\hline
(1)0100\ 0101
\end{array}
$$

or an incorrect 8-bit result of 69 decimal with a carry. This addition in the CPU32 would cause the carry condition code C to be set to {1} to indicate the carry. Similarly, subtraction with a subtrahend larger than the minuend is indicated by a borrow out of the $(m + 1)^{st}$ place. In the CPU32, the borrow indication is also C = {1}. Thus, whenever the carry bit is {1} after addition or subtraction of unsigned integers, the m-bit result is incorrect and the programmer must decide on the appropriate action.

When integers in two's-complement notation are added or subtracted, the carry bit is ignored and the overflow (V) bit is checked for an out-of-range condition. For an m-bit representation, the positive range is only 0 to $2^{m-1} - 1$, so the addition of two positive numbers must not exceed that value. For example, the binary 8-bit addition of + 125 and + 127 yields:

$$
\begin{array}{r}
0111\ 1101 \\
+0111\ 1111 \\
\hline
1111\ 1100
\end{array}
$$

which is −4! The overflow condition, V = {1}, would be set. The problem which arises is that two positive numbers which were added together produced a negative result. Similarly, if the addition of two negative values produces a positive result, the V condition code is again set to {1}. This mathematical condition is termed *underflow* and means the result is too small (too negative) to be represented. However, the V or overflow bit indicates the error, and reference to out-of-range conditions in the machine is usually called "overflow." If the operands are of opposite sign, no out-of-range condition can occur. When subtraction is performed, the V bit set to {1} again indicates an erroneous result.

In the CPU32, division and BCD arithmetic can also yield out-of-range results. The conditions for these cases are covered in the appropriate sections of this chapter. In summary, the condition codes must be checked after an arithmetic operation to determine if an out-of-range condition occurred. Figure 7.1 indicates the procedure used to check for valid numbers. An error condition indicates that the m-bit representation is not valid. The program should reject the result. An extended-precision representation is required if the single-precision range of integers is not sufficient for an application.

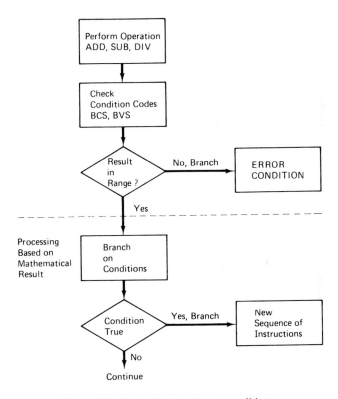

Figure 7.1 Testing for out-of-range conditions.

7.1.1 Conditional Tests

The BCS (Branch if Carry Set) following an arithmetic instruction causes a branch if a carry occurred during addition or a borrow occurred during subtraction of unsigned integers. BVS (Branch if Overflow Set) branches when an out-of-range condition occurs during arithmetic with two's-complement integers. It is recommended that such tests (or the opposite logic of BCC or BVC) be used before other conditional tests are executed.

When conditional branch instructions are executed after arithmetic instructions, the conditional tests as described in Chapter 6 must be used with care. Consider the addition just shown of +125 and +127 for 8-bit signed numbers. The condition codes after the ADD instruction would be

$$Z = \{0\}, N = \{1\}, C = \{0\}, V = \{1\}$$

indicating nonzero, negative, no carry, and overflow, respectively. The result is in error mathematically, but the BMI instruction would cause a branch since it tests only for $N = \{1\}$. Worse yet, BGE would branch but BPL would not. BGE branches whenever N and V condition codes are the same, but BPL branches when $N = \{0\}$ without testing any other condition codes.

If no out-of-range condition is present, the conditional tests operate as shown in Figure 7.2(a). Here BPL and BGE are equivalent for valid signed integers, as are BMI and BLT. Figure 7.2(b) shows the conditions and the tests on the condition code. The "encoding" specifies the condition in the machine language instruction. The instruction sequence in Figure 7.1 is followed in most of the examples in this chapter where the possibility of an out-of-range condition may occur.

EXERCISES

7.1.1. Compare the use of the Bcc instructions after arithmetic operations with their use after the MOVE, CMP, and TST instructions, as discussed in Chapter 6.

7.1.2. Show that BGE and BPL yield opposite results when overflow occurs.

7.1.3. Determine the result of subtracting $-32,768$ from $16,384$ using 16-bit two's-complement arithmetic.

7.1.4. Show that subtraction can be accomplished with binary numbers by adding the two's complement of the subtrahend to the minuend.

7.2 ADDITION AND SUBTRACTION

Binary addition is performed on 8-, 16-, or 32-bit operands with the ADD instruction and its variations, as shown in Table 7.1. Similarly, byte, word, or longword operands can be subtracted with the SUB instruction or its variations. The instructions EXT and EXTB will sign-extend an operand from one length to another. These instructions are useful when mixed-length operands are encountered in an application.

The NEG instruction forms the two's complement (negative) of the operand specified. These instructions and their variations are used to perform basic arithmetic on binary integers. As seen in Table 7.1, each instruction has restrictions on the addressing modes allowed. In the operation of each instruction, which is defined in Table 7.2, the destination operand of specified length is replaced by the result. This is the

Instruction	Branch Condition	Result
UNSIGNED ADD, SUB C = {0}	BEQ BNE	X = 0 X ≠ 0
SIGNED ADD, SUB V = {0}	BEQ BNE BPL, BGE BLE BMI, BLT BGT	X = 0 X ≠ 0 X ≥ 0 X ≤ 0 X < 0 X > 0

(a) Signed and Unsigned Tests

Mnemonic	Condition	Encoding	Test
T	true	0000	1
F	false	0001	0
HI	high	0010	$\overline{C} \cdot \overline{Z}$
LS	low or same	0011	$C + Z$
CC (HS)	carry clear	0100	$\overline{C}$
CS (LO)	carry set	0101	C
NE	not equal	0110	$\overline{Z}$
EQ	equal	0111	Z
VC	overflow clear	1000	$\overline{V}$
VS	overflow set	1001	V
PL	plus	1010	$\overline{N}$
MI	minus	1011	N
GE	greater or equal	1100	$N \cdot V + \overline{N} \cdot \overline{V}$
LT	less than	1101	$N \cdot \overline{V} + \overline{N} \cdot V$
GT	greater than	1110	$N \cdot V \cdot \overline{Z} + \overline{N} \cdot \overline{V} \cdot \overline{Z}$
LE	less or equal	1111	$Z + N \cdot \overline{V} + \overline{N} \cdot V$

(b) Condition Code Tests

Figure 7.2 Conditional branches for valid numbers.

sum for ADD, the difference for SUB, or the negative value when NEG is executed. The condition codes N, Z, V, and C are set according to the result. The X (extend) condition code is also set for use in extended-precision operations.

7.2.1 Addition

The assembly-language format of the ADD instruction is

$$\text{ADD.<l>} \qquad \text{<EA>,<Dn>}$$

when the destination operand is held in a data register. The source is specified as a byte, word, or longword operand (<l> = B, W, or L) unless the source is an address

Table 7.1 Arithmetic Instructions ADD, SUB, EXT, and NEG

	Addressing modes	
Syntax	Source	Destination
Addition or subtraction:		
ADD.<l> <EA>, <Dn> SUB.<l> <EA>, <Dn>	All[1]	Dn
ADD.<l> <Dn>, <EA> SUB.<l> <Dn>, <EA>	Dn	Memory alterable
ADDI.<l> #<d>, <EA> SUBI.<l> #<d>, <EA>	#<d>	Data alterable
ADDQ.<l> #<d$_3$>, <EA> SUBQ.<l> #<d$_3$>, <EA>	#<d$_3$>[2]	Alterable[3]
Sign extend:		
EXT.W <Dn>	(Dn)[7:0]	(Dn)[15:0]
EXT.L <Dn>	(Dn)[15:0]	(Dn)[31:0]
EXTB.L <Dn>	(Dn)[7:0]	(Dn)[31:0]
Negate:		
NEG.<l> <EA>	—	Data alterable

Notes:
1. If the source effective address in the instructions ADD or SUB is an address register, the operand length is word or longword.
2. <d$_3$> is a value between 1 and 8.
3. If An is a destination, only word or longword operations are allowed. In this case, the condition codes are not affected.
4. <l> denotes B, W, or L in all the instructions except as in notes 1 and 3.
5. Except as in note 3, all the condition codes are affected by the arithmetic instructions. EXT and EXTB set N and Z according to the result but clear V and C.

Table 7.2 Arithmetic Instruction Operation

Instruction	Operation
ADD.<l> <EAs>, <EAd>	(EAd)[l] ← (EAs)[l] + (EAd)[l]
SUB.<l> <EAs>, <EAd>	(EAd)[l] ← (EAs)[l] − (EAd)[l]
EXT.W <Dn>	(Dn)[W] ← (Dn)[B]
EXT.L <Dn>	(Dn)[L] ← (Dn)[W]
EXTB.L <Dn>	(Dn)[L] ← (Dn)[B]
NEG.<l> <EA>	(EA)[l] ← 0 − (EA)[l]

Notes:
1. <EAs> and <EAd> are the source and destination effective addresses, respectively.
2. <l> denotes B, W, or L.
3. [l] indicates corresponding bits in the operation.
4. The EXT and EXTB instructions sign-extend the source operand into the same register.

register, in which case the length is restricted to word or longword operands. Thus, the instruction

$$\text{ADD.B} \qquad \text{D1, D5}$$

replaces (D5)[7:0] with the sum

$$(D5)[7:0] + (D1)[7:0].$$

Only the specified length of the destination is affected. As shown in Table 7.1, a data register could hold the source operand when the destination <EA> is defined by a memory alterable addressing mode.

The addition of the value in a data register to an operand in memory is also allowed. For example, the instruction

$$\text{ADD.L} \qquad \text{D1, (A1)}$$

adds the 32-bit contents of D1 to the contents of the location addressed by A1. The destination operand cannot, however, be the contents of an address register or be addressed by program counter relative addressing.

Several variations of the ADD instruction shown in Table 7.1 are ADDI (Add Immediate) and ADDQ (Add Quick). The immediate format can add an 8-, 16-, or 32-bit constant to a data-alterable location. This excludes an address register or a PC relative address for the destination. The ADDI instruction adds a specified constant to a destination location, while the ADD instruction operates only between registers and memory. Thus, the instruction

$$\text{ADDI.B} \qquad \text{\#20, (A1)}$$

is used to add 20 decimal to the byte addressed by A1 as an example.

The ADDQ instruction adds an immediate value between 1 and 8 to the specified destination location. Any alterable destination location is allowed, including an address register. Destinations addressed by the PC relative mode are prohibited. In the cases where An is the destination, the condition codes are not affected, but the whole register (32 bits) is changed. Arithmetic operations with addresses are considered in Chapter 9.

It should be noted that some assemblers select the appropriate variation of an ADD instruction without the programmer specifying it. For instance, the instruction

$$\text{ADD} \qquad \text{\#1, D4}$$

may be interpreted as an ADDI instruction or an ADDQ instruction by certain assemblers. Also, a word-length operation on D4 would probably be chosen as the default length. The practice of letting the assembler choose the variation is not always wise if consistency in program documentation and machine-language instruction length is desired.

7.2.2 Subtraction

The instructions SUB, SUBI, and SUBQ are exact counterparts of the addition instructions. They calculate the difference between the destination operand (minuend) and the source operand (subtrahend). This difference replaces the byte, word, or longword portion of the destination location as specified by the instruction.

If an address register is the destination in a SUBQ instruction, the immediate value can be a word or a longword operand. If the length is word, the immediate value is sign-extended to 32 bits before the subtraction is performed. For example, the instruction

$$\text{SUBQ.W} \qquad \#1, A1$$

has the effect of subtracting 1 from the entire contents of A1. Therefore, both ADDQ and SUBQ affect the 32-bit contents of a destination address register.

All the condition code bits are affected by a subtraction instruction unless the subtraction is made from an address register. The condition $C = \{1\}$ indicates a borrow in unsigned subtraction. In signed arithmetic, N, Z, and V bits set to $\{1\}$ indicate a negative number, zero, and an overflow condition, respectively.

7.2.3 Extension

Each sign-extend instruction extends a signed integer to the specified length. For example, the instruction,

$$\text{EXT.W} \qquad \text{D1}$$

extends or copies bit [7] of the designated data register D1 into bits [15:8]. The three sign-extend instructions serve to extend a byte to a word, a word to a longword, or a byte to a longword. Arithmetic on mixed-length variables is common when different devices generate the signed numbers. For example, an analog-to-digital converter might output its digital values as a 16-bit two's-complement integer. If longword arithmetic is being used to process the values, each 16-bit value must be sign-extended to 32 bits by the EXT.L instruction.

Example 7.1

The subroutine shown in Figure 7.3 adds the elements of a column (vector elements) of 16-bit integers to form either a 16- or a 32-bit sum. Before the subroutine is called, D1 holds the number of integers to be summed and A1 contains the starting address of the column. If the length of the column is zero, D3 contains -1 after the subroutine executes. Otherwise, the low-order word of D3 contains zero if the sum is contained in 16 bits or $+1$ if the sum requires 32 bits. Each time a carry occurs in the addition of a new value to D2, 1 is added to the upper word of D2 to form the proper sum.

The purpose of the program might be to use word (rather than longword) operations in subsequent processing if a 16-bit sum is the result. This would reduce the memory storage needed and be more efficient in time if memory accesses are made.

```
abs.   LC    obj. code     source line
----   ----  ---------     -----------
  1    0000                      TTL      'FIGURE 7.3'
  2    0000                      LLEN     100
  3    8000                      ORG      $8000
  4    0000                *
  5    8000                *  ADD 16-BIT UNSIGNED INTEGERS
  6    8000                *
  7    8000                *  INPUT   :  (D1.W) = NUMBER OF INTEGERS
  8    8000                *             (A1.L) = STARTING ADDRESS OF COLUMN
  9    8000                *                      OF INTEGERS
 10    8000                *
 11    8000                *  OUTPUT : (D3.W) = -1 : NUMBER OF INTEGERS IS ZERO
 12    8000                *                     0 : 16-BIT SUM IN D2 [15:0]
 13    8000                *                     1 : 32-BIT SUM IN D2 [31:0]
 14    8000                *             (D2.L) = SUM
 15    8000                *
 16    8000  48E7 4040     ADDUNS  MOVEM.L D1/A1,-(SP) ;SAVE REGISTERS
 17    8004                *
 18    8004  4282                  CLR.L   D2           ;SUM:=0
 19    8006  363C FFFF             MOVE.W  #-1,D3       ;SET STATUS TO ERROR
 20    800A  5341                  SUBQ.W  #1,D1        ;SET UP LOOP COUNTER
 21    800C  6D00 0016             BLT     DONE
 22    8010  4243                  CLR.W   D3           ;SET STATUS TO 16-BIT
 23    8012                *                            ; SUM
 24    8012  D459          LOOP    ADD.W   (A1)+,D2
 25    8014  6400 000A             BCC     ENDLP        ;IF NO OVERFLOW, THEN SKIP
 26    8018  0682 0001             ADDI.L  #$10000,D2   ; ELSE ADD 1 TO UPPER WORD
       801C  0000
 27    801E  7601                  MOVEQ   #1,D3        ;SET STATUS TO 32-BIT SUM
 28    8020  51C9 FFF0     ENDLP   DBRA    D1,LOOP      ;CONTINUE
 29    8024  4CDF 0202     DONE    MOVEM.L (SP)+,D1/A1  ;RESTORE REGISTERS
 30    8028  4E75                  RTS
 31    802A                        END
```

Figure 7.3 Addition routine for 16- or 32-bit sums.

7.2.4 Negation

The NEG instruction replaces a data-alterable destination location of specified length with the result of the calculation

$$0 - (\text{destination})$$

thus forming the two's-complement value. As an example, if location $1000 contains the value 1, the instruction

> NEG.B $1000

replaces the value with $FF. The only case in which an overflow can occur is when the value negated is -2^{m-1}, since this number has no positive equivalent in two's-complement notation.

Example 7.2

The subroutine shown in Figure 7.4 sums the differences between the elements of two columns or vectors of integers addressed by (A1) and (A2). The length of the columns is initially held in D1. If the length of the columns is zero or an overflow occurs, then

```
abs.   LC    obj. code    source line
----   ----  ---------    -----------
  1    0000                          TTL    'FIGURE 7.4'
  2    0000                          LLEN   100
  3    8000                          ORG    $8000
  4    0000               |*
  5    8000               |* SUM OF DIFFERENCES OF TWO COLUMNS OF 16-BIT
  6    8000               |* INTEGERS
  7    8000               |*
  8    8000               |* INPUT  : (D1.W) = LENGTH OF THE COLUMNS
  9    8000               |*            (A1.L) = ADDRESS OF FIRST COLUMN
 10    8000               |*            (A2.L) = ADDRESS OF SECOND COLUMN
 11    8000               |*
 12    8000               |* OUTPUT : (D3.W) = ABSOLUTE VALUE OF RESULT
 13    8000               |*            (D4.W) = 0 : ERROR OCCURRED
 14    8000               |*                          1 : RESULT IS POSITIVE
 15    8000               |*                         -1 : RESULT IS NEGATIVE
 16    8000               |*
 17    8000 48E7 6060     |SUMDIF MOVEM.L D1/D2/A1/A2,-(SP) ;SAVE REGISTERS
 18    8004 4243          |       CLR.W   D3             ;SUM = 0
 19    8006 4244          |       CLR.W   D4             ;SET STATUS = ERROR
 20    8008 4A41          |       TST.W   D1             ;IF COLUMNS ARE EMPTY
 21    800A 6700 0026     |       BEQ     DONE           ; THEN RETURN ERROR
 22    800E               |*
 23    800E 3419          |LOOP   MOVE.W  (A1)+,D2       ;COMPUTE
 24    8010 945A          |       SUB.W   (A2)+,D2       ;((A1)) - ((A2))
 25    8012 6900 001E     |       BVS     DONE           ;EXIT IF OVERFLOW
 26    8016 D642          |       ADD.W   D2,D3          ;SUM THE DIFFERENCES
 27    8018 6900 0018     |       BVS     DONE           ;ON OVERFLOW,
 28    801C               |*                             ;   EXIT WITH ERROR
 29    801C 5341          |       SUBQ.W  #1,D1          ;DECREMENT COUNT
 30    801E 66EE          |       BNE     LOOP           ;LOOP UNTIL FINISHED
 31    8020               |*
 32    8020 4A43          |       TST     D3             ;IF RESULT IS POSITIVE
 33    8022 6C00 000C     |       BGE     POS            ; THEN PROCESS IT
 34    8026 383C FFFF     |       MOVE.W  #-1,D4         ;   ELSE STATUS =0 NEG
 35    802A 4443          |       NEG.W   D3             ;TAKE ABSOLUTE VALUE
 36    802C 6000 0004     |       BRA     DONE
 37    8030               |*
 38    8030 7801          |POS    MOVEQ   #1,D4          ;STATUS = POSITIVE
 39    8032 4CDF 0606     |DONE   MOVEM.L (SP)+,D1/D2/A1/A2 ;RESTORE REGISTERS
 40    8036 4E75          |       RTS
 41    8038               |       END
```

Figure 7.4 Routine to compute the sum of differences.

(D4)[15:0] is set to 0 to indicate the error. Otherwise, the differences between corresponding entries in the columns are accumulated in the low-order word of D3. Once the summation is complete, the sign of the result is tested for positive or negative.

If the result is negative, the NEG instruction is used to determine the magnitude of the number. A program using this routine must first check the status output in D4 for an error condition. If no error is indicated, the magnitude of the sum of the differences is held in the low-order word of D3. The program might then convert the magnitude to decimal ASCII and prefix the sign to the printed results. If overflow occurs with the 16-bit arithmetic operations in the program, 32-bit arithmetic could be employed.

EXERCISES

7.2.1. Assume that (D1) = $0000 FFFF before each instruction below executes. Determine the results, including the setting of the condition codes after each of the following instructions executes:
(a) ADDI.B #1, D1

(b) ADDQ.L   #1, D1

(c) SUBQ.B   #1, D1

(d) NEG.W   D1

(e) SUB.L   D1, D1

(f) EXT.L   D1

7.2.2. Show that using only one carry bit after an m-bit unsigned addition is sufficient to assure that no information is lost.

7.2.3. For an m-bit subtraction operation $N_3 = N_2 - N_1$, show that the proper result is obtained when N_1 is negative and N_2 is positive, if the sum of the magnitudes of N_1 and N_2 is equal to or less than $2^{m-1} - 1$. Refer to Chapter 3 for the two's-complement formulas.

7.2.4. Write a routine to multiply two unsigned 16-bit integers by using repeated addition.

7.2.5. Modify the program of Example 7.2 to compute the sum of the absolute value of the differences between the two columns of numbers.

7.3   MULTIPLICATION AND DIVISION

The CPU32 provides separate instructions for multiplication and division of unsigned integers and for multiplication and division of two's-complement integers. This section presents these instructions and discusses the operations, numerical ranges, and possible errors involved in their use. Table 7.3 shows the syntax and the operations of the DIV (divide) instruction and the MUL (multiply) instruction.

The suffix "U" for unsigned integers or "S" for signed integers must be specified each time the multiplication or division instructions are used. The multiplicand for the multiplication operation and the divisor for the division operation are specified by a 16-bit or 32-bit source operand. Only address register direct addressing is prohibited for the source. The multiplier and dividend are always held in data registers. The result is a 32-bit value held in a data register.

7.3.1 Unsigned Multiplication

The MULU.W instruction multiplies two unsigned 16-bit operands to yield a 32-bit product. For example, the instruction

$$\text{MULU.W} \qquad \#\$10, D2$$

with $(D2)[15:0] = \$0002$ results in $(D2) = \$0000\ 0020$ or 32 decimal. Since the 16-bit multiplicand and multiplier may each range from 0 to 65,535, the product cannot exceed 4,294,836,225, which is less than $2^{32} - 1$. Therefore, no overflow is possible and the condition code bits C and V are always cleared after the MULU.W instruction. N and Z are set according to the result. In the case of unsigned integers, N = {1} indicates that the product equals or exceeds 2^{31} in magnitude.

A second unsigned multiply instruction (MULU.L) is provided to multiply 32-bit operands together. However, the product is limited by truncation to 32 bits. If the

Table 7.3 Multiply and Divide Instructions

Syntax	Operation
Multiplication:	
MULU.W <EA>,<Dn>	(Dn)[31:0] ← (Dn)[15:0] × (EA)[15:0]
MULS.W	
MULU.L <EA>,<Dn>	(Dn)[31:0] ← (Dn)[31:0] × (EA)[31:0]
MULS.L	
Division:	
DIVU.W <EA>,<Dn>	(Dn)[31:0]/(EA)[15:0]
DIVS.W	(Dn)[15:0] ← quotient
	(Dn)[31:16] ← remainder
DIVU.L <EA>,<Dn>	(Dn)[31:0]/(EA)[31:0]
DIVS.L	(Dn)[31:0] ← quotient

Notes:

1. Only data addressing modes are allowed for the source address <EA> (i.e., An is prohibited).
2. MULU.L and MULS.L cause V = {1} if the product is greater than 32 bits.
3. In division, a zero divisor causes a *trap*; an overflow is indicated by V = {1}.
4. In signed division, a remainder has the sign of the dividend.

product exceeds $2^{32} - 1$ in magnitude, an overflow condition (V = {1}) is set. Therefore, the instruction is of limited use if arithmetic operations create a value requiring more than 32 bits. In this case, extended-precision arithmetic must be employed. The instruction is useful, however, when a product cannot exceed 32 bits, as in the calculation of an index value, for example. In any case, the two single-precision multiplication instructions give the programmer flexibility to choose the length of operands that are appropriate for a specific application.

7.3.2 Signed Multiplication

When signed integers are multiplied, the result is positive or negative depending on the signs of the multiplicand and multiplier. The range of each is -2^{15} to $+2^{15} - 1$, or $-32,768$ to $+32,767$. If the two most negative values are multiplied, the result is 1,073,741,824, or 2^{30}. The largest possible negative result is

$$-2^{15} \times (2^{15} - 1) = -1,073,709,056$$

Therefore, no out-of-range condition can occur for a 32-bit product, and both V and C are always cleared. For MULS.W the N bit indicates a negative product when N = {1}, as expected. If the result is zero, then Z = {1}. The instruction

MULS.W   # − 1, D2

with (D2)[15:0] = $0002 results in the product (D2) = $FFFF FFFE, or -2 in two's-complement notation. The N bit is set to indicate a negative result.

The MULS.L instruction truncates the products of two 32-bit operands to 32 bits, setting V = {1} if an overflow occurs. As with the MULU.L instruction, the V condition code bit should be checked after this instruction executes unless the product cannot exceed 32 bits.

7.3.3 Unsigned Division

The CPU32 instruction DIVU.W performs the division

$$Y/W = Q + R/W$$

where Y is a 32-bit unsigned integer, W is a 16-bit unsigned integer, Q is a 16-bit quotient, and R is a 16-bit remainder. For example, the instruction

DIVU.W   #2, D1

divides the 32-bit operand in D1 by 2. The result, as indicated in Table 7.3, is a quotient in the low-order word of D1 and the remainder, or zero, in the upper word of D1. Thus, if D1 contained $0000 0005 before the instruction executed, the result is

$$(D1) = \$0001\ 0002$$

since $5/2 = 2 + 1/2$.

Two special conditions may arise when any of the division instructions performs a division operation:
(a) division by zero, or
(b) an overflow of the quotient.
Both of these situations are error conditions. Exception processing occurs automatically in the case of division by zero. When a division by zero is recognized by the CPU32, control is passed to an exception handling routine that is part of the supervisor program for the system. The divide-by-zero exception is discussed in Section 11.2.

An overflow can occur because the range of the dividend is 0 to $2^{32} - 1$ but the length of the quotient is only 16 bits. Obviously, dividing an integer greater than $2^{16} - 1$ by 1 would cause an overflow. Or, more generally, if the dividend exceeds the divisor in magnitude by 2^{16} or greater, an overflow will occur. The overflow is indicated by $V = \{1\}$ even though unsigned arithmetic is being performed. If overflow occurs, the operands are not changed.

If the integer quotient can be held in 32 bits, the DIVU.L instruction can be used to perform integer division using 32-bit operands. The instruction, in effect, computes the integer portion of the division to 32 bits. An overflow condition is indicated by $V = \{1\}$. When the divisor is zero, a divide-by-zero trap occurs.

7.3.4 Signed Division

The instruction DIVS.W executes in the same manner as the DIVU.W instruction, but the operands are signed integers. Motorola's convention is that the sign of any remainder is the same as the sign of the dividend. Thus, the instruction

DIVS.W   #3, D1

with (D1) = \$FFFF FFF6 calculates $-10/3$ with the result

$$(D1) = \$FFFF\ FFFD$$

with quotient $Q = -3$ and remainder $R = -1$. The condition code N is set to $\{1\}$ to indicate that the quotient is negative.

In signed division, the quotient can range from -2^{15} to $+2^{15} - 1$. Therefore, overflow will occur unless the magnitude of the 32-bit dividend is less than 2^{15} times that of the divisor. The V bit is set to $\{1\}$ if overflow occurs. A trap occurs if a divisor is zero.

The DIVS.L instruction computes the 32-bit quotient from the division of two 32-bit signed operands. Any remainder is discarded and the V condition code bit is set to $\{1\}$ if an overflow occurs. With this instruction as well as the DIVU.L instruction, the mathematical condition

$$0 < |\text{divisor}| < |\text{dividend}|$$

must be true to obtain a nonzero quotient. If the result is

$$|\text{divisor}| \times |\text{quotient}| = |\text{dividend}|$$

there is no remainder. Here the vertical bars surrounding the operand indicates the absolute value of the number.

Example 7.3

Although the use of a single MULS.W multiply instruction cannot result in an overflow, the use of these instructions in an equation that requires several multiplies could produce a result that exceeds an allowable maximum magnitude. For example, to calculate the sum of squares as

$$\sum_{i=1}^{N} (X(i)^2 + Y(i)^2)$$

the individual products cannot overflow in 32 bits, although the sum of several terms or the entire sum can overflow.

The program in Figure 7.5 computes the sum of squares of N pairs of signed 16-bit integers. The numbers are stored in the order

$$X(1), Y(1), X(2), Y(2), \ldots, X(N), Y(N)$$

as a vector or column of 16-bit words whose first address is given by (A1) when the program is entered. The length N is assumed to be in the low-order 16-bits of D1. The 32-bit result is accumulated in D3 unless an error occurs. After execution, an error is indicated by $(D4)[15:0] = -1$ and any program making use of the result should check the status in D4 before the result is accepted. The address register indirect with displacement mode is used to address the operands, so if an overflow occurs, (A1) points to the current pair of operands. This is also convenient if the program is being traced for debugging. Postincrement addressing with A1 could be used to eliminate the ADD instruction that increments A1 by 4 to point to the next pair of operands. The notation X(i) and Y(i) here indicates the addresses of the values $X(i)$ and $Y(i)$ in memory, respectively.

```
abs.   LC    obj. code    source line
----   ----  ----------   -----------
   1   0000                         TTL     'FIGURE 7.5'
   2   0000                         LLEN    100
   3   8000                         ORG     $8000
   4   0000               *
   5   8000               * SUM OF SQUARES
   6   8000               *
   7   8000               * INPUT :   (D1.W) = LENGTH OF COLUMN
   8   8000               *           (A1.L) = ADDRESS OF COLUMN OF NUMBERS
   9   8000               *                    STORED X1,Y1,X2,Y2,...,XN,YN
  10   8000               *
  11   8000               * OUTPUT:   (D3.L) = RESULT
  12   8000               *           (D4.W) = 0 : SUCCESSFUL
  13   8000               *                   -1 : ERROR
  14   8000               *
  15   8000 48E7 6040     SUMSQ   MOVEM.L D1/D2/A1,-(SP) ;SAVE REGISTERS
  16   8004 4283                  CLR.L   D3            ;SUM := 0
  17   8006 383C FFFF             MOVE.W  #-1,D4        ;SET DEFAULT TO ERROR
  18   800A 5341                  SUBQ.W  #1,D1         ;IF LENGTH IS ZERO
  19   800C 6D00 0024             BLT     DONE          ; THEN EXIT WITH ERROR
  20   8010               *
  21   8010 3411          LOOP    MOVE.W  (0,A1),D2     ;COMPUTE
  22   8012 C5C2                  MULS.W  D2,D2         ;XN**2
  23   8014 D682                  ADD.L   D2,D3         ;ADD TO SUM
  24   8016 6900 001A             BVS     DONE          ;ON ERROR, EXIT
  25   801A 3429 0002             MOVE.W  (2,A1),D2     ;COMPUTE
  26   801E C5C2                  MULS.W  D2,D2         ;YN**2
  27   8020 D682                  ADD.L   D2,D3         ;ADD TO SUM
  28   8022 6900 000E             BVS     DONE          ;ON ERROR, EXIT
  29   8026 D3FC 0000             ADD.L   #4,A1         ;INCREMENT TO NEXT PAIR
       802A 0004
  30   802C 51C9 FFE2             DBRA    D1,LOOP       ;DECREMENT COUNTER AND
  31   8030               *                            ;  CONTINUE UNTIL -1
  32   8030               *
  33   8030 4244                  CLR.W   D4            ;SET STATUS TO SUCCESS
  34   8032 4CDF 0206     DONE    MOVEM.L (SP)+,D1/D2/A1 ;RESTORE REGISTERS
  35   8036 4E75                  RTS
  36   8038                       END
```

Figure 7.5 Routine to calculate sum-of-squares.

7.3.5 Remainder in Division

Consider the unsigned division

$$Y/W = Q + R/W$$

where R/W is the remainder, which must be less than 1. Therefore, R/W has the representation

$$d_{-1} \times 10^{-1} + d_{-2} \times 10^{-2} + \ldots$$

and the number in positional notation can be written

$$Q.d_{-1}d_{-2} + \ldots$$

as long as the division operation did not overflow. If only the fraction is considered, multiplying R/W by 10 yields d_{-1} as the first integer with a remainder of

$$d_{-2} \times 10^{-1} + \ldots$$

Successive multiplications of R by 10 followed by a division by W yields the decimal digits as the quotient for as many places as desired. As an example, 22/7 is 3.142..., which approximates π to three decimal places. The divisions and multiplications yield

$$22/7 = 3 + 1/7$$

$$10/7 = 1 + 3/7$$

$$30/7 = 4 + 2/7$$

$$20/7 = 2 + 6/7$$

and so on until the result 3.142... is computed. Of course, the operations will be done in binary in the computer, but each digit can be converted to binary-coded decimal or ASCII for output if desired. The examples in section 7.6 consider such conversions.

Example 7.4

The subroutine shown in Figure 7.6 computes the average of a series of numbers stored in vector or column form and addressed by A1. If the number of values, which is in D1, is not zero, the 32-bit sum is formed in D3. The sum is then divided by the number of values and the low-order word of D3 contains the quotient and any remainder is in the high-order word. There is no test for overflow in the program.

```
abs.    LC   obj. code    source line
----    ----  --------    -----------
   1    0000                    TTL      'FIGURE 7.6'
   2    0000                    LLEN     100
   3    8000                    ORG      $8000
   4    0000              *
   5    8000              * COMPUTATION OF AVERAGE
   6    8000              *
   7    8000              * INPUT  :  (A1.L) = ADDRESS OF COLUMN OF 16-BIT
   8    8000              *                      NUMBERS
   9    8000              *           (D1.W) = LENGTH OF COLUMN
  10    8000              *
  11    8000              * OUTPUT :  (D3)[15:0] = AVERAGE
  12    8000              *           (D3)[31:16] = REMAINDER OF SUM/LENGTH
  13    8000              *
  14    8000 48E7 6840    AVG  MOVEM.L D1-D2/D4/A1,-(SP) ;SAVE REGISTERS
  15    8004              *
  16    8004 4A41              TST.W   D1              ;IF LENGTH = 0
  17    8006 6700 0014         BEQ     DONE            ; THEN FINISHED
  18    800A              *
  19    800A 4282              CLR.L   D2
  20    800C 4283              CLR.L   D3              ;SUM=0
  21    800E 3801              MOVE.W  D1,D4           ;SET COUNTER
  22    8010 5344              SUBQ    #1,D4           ; TO LENGTH - 1
  23    8012              *
  24    8012 3419         LOOP MOVE.W  (A1)+,D2        ;LOOP TO SUM
  25    8014 D682              ADD.L   D2,D3           ;  NUMBERS
  26    8016 51CC FFFA         DBRA    D4,LOOP
  27    801A              *
  28    801A 87C1              DIVS.W  D1,D3           ;SUM/LENGTH
  29    801C              *
  30    801C 4CDF 0216    DONE MOVEM.L (SP)+,D1-D2/D4/A1 ;RESTORE REGISTERS
  31    8020 4E75              RTS
  32    8022                   END
```

Figure 7.6 Routine for averaging values.

EXERCISES

7.3.1. Determine the quotient, the remainder and the condition code settings that result from the following divisions when the instruction listed is executed using the dividend and divisor as shown:

(a) 10/5; DIVU.W

(b) −10/5; DIVU.W

(c) −10/5; DIVS.W

(d) −5/2; DIVS.W

The negative values should be written in two's-complement notation to perform the divisions.

7.3.2. Suppose two signed integers are multiplied by the MULU instruction. Show that unsigned binary multiplication will cause an error if one or both of the numbers are negative. Test this by multiplying $(-1) \times (-1)$ in two's-complement notation but with unsigned multiplication. How can the result be corrected?

7.3.3. If $N_2 < 2^m \times N_1$ in the unsigned binary division N_2/N_1, prove that overflow cannot occur if the dividend has $2m$ bits and the quotient is m bits.

7.3.4. Write a routine to compute a 32-bit quotient and a 32-bit remainder when overflow occurs with the DIVU.W instruction. The result can be obtained by writing Y/W as

$$(Y2 \times 2^{16} + Y1)/W$$

where $Y2$ is the upper 16 bits of the dividend and $Y1$ represents the lower 16 bits. Compare the results with the DIVU.L instruction presented in the next section.

7.3.5. Determine the results in (D1) and the condition code values for each instruction when (D1) = $FFFF FFFE before each executes:

(a) MULU.L   #2, D1

(b) MULS.L   #2, D1

7.3.6. Find the quotient, remainder (if any) and the condition codes for the following instructions with the dividend and divisor shown:

(a) 3/5; DIVU.L

(b) 21/5; DIVU.L

(c) −3/2; DIVS.L

(d) 10/ − 3; DIVS.W

(e) 3/ − 2; DIVS.L

7.4 EXTENDED-PRECISION INTEGER ARITHMETIC

In scientific measurements, the term *accuracy* refers to the correctness of a measurement; that is, to its freedom from mistake or error. *Precision* refers to the amount of detail used to represent a measurement. For numerical values, the amount of precision is usually expressed by giving the number of significant digits in the numerical value. If a quantity is judged to have insufficient precision for a given application, additional significant digits may be used to produce a more precise result.

Arithmetic units in microprocessors operate on a maximum of m digits when performing arithmetic operations. This maximum length will be called the *single-precision* length. The CPU32 maximum single-precision length is 32 bits, but 8-bit or 16-bit quantities can also be handled. Sequences of greater length cannot be handled as a single arithmetic operand by the processor. Therefore, to extend the precision, several m-digit operands can be considered mathematically as a single value. If k operands were combined, the value would be $k \times m$ digits long. Double-precision values, for example, have $k = 2$. Thus, the CPU32 double-precision length would be 2×32, or 64 bits.

Arithmetic operations with extended-precision operands are performed by using the processor instructions on each m-digit portion of the values, and then combining the results. This procedure yields the correct answer when mathematical details such as carries or borrows between the intermediate results are treated properly.

The CPU32 provides special instructions to facilitate the addition, subtraction, negation, division, and multiplication of double-precision integers. This first section is concerned primarily with the addition or subtraction of two 32-bit values to yield 64-bit double-precision numbers. Subsequent sections cover multiplication and division.

7.4.1 Extended-Precision Addition, Subtraction, and Negation

The extended arithmetic instructions ADDX (Add with Extend), SUBX (Subtract with Extend), and NEGX (Negate with Extend) are defined in Table 7.4. The difference between these extended instructions and the instructions for addition, subtraction, and negation discussed previously is the use of the condition code bits X and Z by the extended operations.

Table 7.4 Extended-precision Arithmetic Instructions

	Addressing modes	
Syntax	Source	Destination
Add or Subtract Extended:		
ADDX.<l> <Dm>, <Dn>	(Dm)	(Dn)
SUBX.<l> <Dm>, <Dn>		
ADDX.<l> − (Am), −(An)	Predecrement	Predecrement
SUBX.<l> − (Am), −(An)		
Negate with Extend:		
NEGX.<l> <EA>	—	Data alterable

Note:
<l> denotes B, W, or L.

As shown in Table 7.5, the extended instructions utilize the X (Extend) bit in their operation. If the X bit was set by a previous operation, the instructions ADDX, SUBX, and NEGX take this setting into account when they are executed. The primary use of the extend bit is to add a carry (ADDX) or subtract a borrow (SUBX) when the upper m bits of a double-precision value are being manipulated. The carry or borrow would have resulted from the single-precision operation on the lower m bits.

For example, the sequence

$$\text{ADD.L} \qquad \text{D1, D3}$$

$$\text{ADDX.L} \qquad \text{D2, D4}$$

adds the double-precision value in D2/D1 to the 64-bit value in D4/D3. The X bit is set to {1} if the addition of the low order portions (D1 and D3) produces a carry. The second instruction adds the carry value to the sum.

Table 7.5 Operation of Extended-precision Instructions

Syntax	Operation
ADDX.\<l\> \<src\>, \<dst\>	(dst)[l] ← (src)[l] + (dst)[l] + X
SUBX.\<l\> \<src\>, \<dst\>	(dst)[l] ← (dst)[l] − (src)[l] − X
NEGX.\<l\> \<EA\>	(EA)[l] ← 0 − (EA)[l] − X

Notes:
1. The addressing modes for the source (\<src\>) operand and the destination (\<dst\> operand are defined in Table 7.4.
2. C, N, and V condition code bits set as for any arithmetic operation.
3. Z is cleared if the result is nonzero; otherwise, it is unchanged.
4. X is set the same as the C bit.
5. \<l\> denotes B, W, or L.
6. [l] indicates corresponding bits in the operation.

In the case of arithmetic instructions, the X bit is set to the same value as the C bit. In general, most CPU32 instructions that are not used for arithmetic operations do not affect the X bit, so the C bit and the X bit should not be considered the same. For example, if D4 in the example just given was tested for zero by the instruction

$$\text{TST.L} \qquad \text{D4}$$

the carry bit would be cleared but the X bit would not be changed.

The zero condition code bit, Z, is also treated in a special way by the extended instructions. The setting of Z, after an extended instruction is executed, is based on both the previous setting of the Z bit and the value of the current operand. Consider the 64-bit integer

$$0000\ 0000\ 0000\ 0001_{16}$$

in which the lower 32-bit value is nonzero. If each 32-bit half is tested for zero separately, Z would be set to {0} for the low-order portion. However, Z would become {1} when the high-order portion is tested. If a conditional test is subsequently made, the results would be based on a zero value!

To obtain the correct results for double-precision conditions, the instructions ADDX, SUBX, and NEGX set the Z bit according to the logical equation:

$$Z = Z_2 \text{ AND } Z_1$$

in which *both* Z_1 and Z_2 must be $\{1\}$ to set $Z = \{1\}$. Here Z_1 was the setting before the extended instruction was executed and Z_2 is the result from the extended operation. This is assumed to involve the high-order portion of a double-precision operand, as in the instruction sequence just given for addition. Thus, if $Z_1 = \{0\}$, then $Z = \{0\}$ regardless of the setting of Z_2. Only if both portions of the double-precision value are zero will Z be set to $\{1\}$. In the example of the 64-bit number, $Z = \{0\}$ indicates that the result is nonzero when the value is computed using the extended instructions.

A double-precision integer can be written in positional notation as

$$(b_{2m-1}b_{2m-2} \cdots b_m b_{m-1} \cdots b_0)$$

where the digits $b_{m-1}b_{m-2} \cdots b_1 b_0$ represent the single-precision length. Two double-precision operands N_1 and N_2 can be written as

$$N_1 = N_{1U} + N_{1L}$$

and

$$N_2 = N_{2U} + N_{2L}$$

where N_{iL} refers to digits 0 through $m - 1$ and N_{iU} refers to the digits m through $2m - 1$, with $i = 1$ or 2. This notation will be used, when it is necessary, to distinguish the lower-precision from the upper-precision portions of a value.

The sequences of instructions to perform double-precision addition or subtraction using the extended-precision instructions require that an ADD instruction be followed by ADDX or SUB be followed by SUBX in the program. For addition, any carry generated from the ADD of the lower portion is indicated by both the C and the X condition code bits. The upper sum is then computed by ADDX, which adds the X bit into the result. A carry generated when the ADDX instruction executes indicates an unsigned result which is too large for the double-precision representation. If signed integers are being represented, an overflow condition is indicated by the condition code bit $V = \{1\}$.

When double-precision integers are subtracted, any borrow required by the low-order subtraction is indicated by the X bit. This is subtracted from the difference of the high-order values. A high-order out-of-range condition is indicated after SUBX executes by $C = \{1\}$ for unsigned integers or $V = \{1\}$ if signed integers were subtracted.

Example 7.5

Examples of extended-precision operations are shown in Figure 7.7. For simplicity the single-precision lengths are eight binary digits. The states of the relevant condition codes are also shown after each portion of the extended-precision operation. In each case, the lower 8 bits of the operands are treated first, and this is followed by the extended instruction operating on the upper 8 bits.

Example 7.6

The subroutine shown in Figure 7.8 adds the elements of two columns or vectors of N unsigned integers element by element. If $X(i)$ represents the address of the ith element in the first vector and $Y(i)$ is the corresponding address of the second, the operation is

$$(Y(i)) \leftarrow (X(i)) + (Y(i))$$

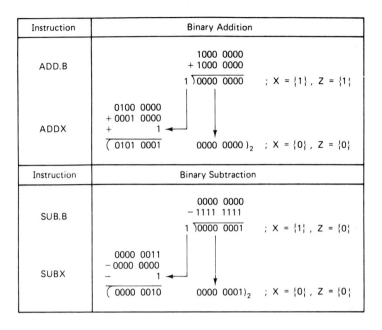

Figure 7.7 Extended-precision operations.

with $i = 1, 2, \ldots, N$. In memory, each 64-bit integer is stored with the least significant 32 bits at the *higher* address of two longword locations. The values are stored with the last element, $X(N)$ or $Y(N)$, at the lowest memory address and each array requires $2N$ longword locations or $8N$ bytes. This storage scheme takes advantage of the predecrement addressing capability of the CPU32 using extended instructions.

When the subroutine is entered, A1 and A2 should point to the next longword location following the first and second vector respectively. Address register A3 must contain the address of the last element in the second vector (i.e., it should point to $Y(N)$).

If no overflow occurs, the additions continue until (A2) = (A3) to indicate the location of the last value to be added. The Compare Address (CMPA) instruction might change the C condition code but leaves X unaffected. When the two addresses are equal, the branch test is FALSE and the loop is terminated. In programs where the state of the X bit must be preserved but the C bit is used for conditional tests, having separate C and X bits is an advantage since the X bit does not have to be saved before the compare operations.

Extended-precision negation.   The sequence

> NEG

> NEGX

performs negation of a double-precision integer when NEG operates on the lower-precision portion and NEGX on the upper-precision portion. An overflow indication ($V = \{1\}$) occurs if the most negative integer is negated.

```
abs.   LC   obj. code    source line
----   ----  ----------   -----------
   1   0000                      TTL      'FIGURE 7.8'
   2   0000                      LLEN     100
   3   8000                      ORG      $8000
   4   0000              *
   5   8000              * ADD TWO VECTORS OF 64-BIT UNSIGNED INTEGERS
   6   8000              *    Y(I) <-- Y(I) + X(I)    FOR I = 1,N
   7   8000              *
   8   8000              * INPUTS :  (A1.L) = LAST ADDRESS OF FIRST VECTOR+4
   9   8000              *           (A2.L) = LAST ADDRESS OF SECOND VECTOR+4
  10   8000              *           (A3.L) = ADDRESS OF LAST ELEMENT IN
  11   8000              *                    SECOND VECTOR (ADDRESS OF Y(N))
  12   8000              *
  13   8000              * OUTPUTS:  (A2.L) = ADDRESS OF SUMS
  14   8000              *           (D1.B) = 0 : ERROR DETECTED
  15   8000              *                    NOT 0 : SUCCESSFUL
  16   8000              *
  17   8000              * NOTES:
  18   8000              *   1.  64-BIT NUMBERS ARE STORED THIS WAY:
  19   8000              *
  20   8000              *       XN [63:32]    LOW MEMORY
  21   8000              *       XN [31:0]      FIRST LONGWORD ADDRESS
  22   8000              *       .
  23   8000              *       .
  24   8000              *       .
  25   8000              *       X1 [63:32]         HIGHER MEMORY
  26   8000              *       X1 [31:0]     LAST LONGWORD ADDRESS
  27   8000              *
  28   8000              *   2.  A1 AND A2 POINT TO X1+4
  29   8000              *       A3 POINTS TO XN [63:32]
  30   8000              *
  31   8000 48E7 8060    SERIES MOVEM.L D0/A1-A2,-(SP) ;SAVE REGISTERS
  32   8004 4201                CLR.B    D1              ;SET STATUS = FAIL
  33   8006 2021         LOOP   MOVE.L   -(A1),D0
  34   8008 D1A2                ADD.L    D0,-(A2)
  35   800A D589                ADDX.L   -(A1),-(A2)
  36   800C 6500 000A           BCS      ERROR           ;OVERFLOW
  37   8010 B7CA                CMPA.L   A2,A3           ;IF NOT LAST NUMBER
  38   8012 65F2                BCS      LOOP            ;THEN CONTINUE
  39   8014              *                               ; ELSE FINISHED
  40   8014 123C 00FF            MOVE.B   #-1,D1          ;SET STATUS = SUCCESS
  41   8018 4CDF 0601    ERROR  MOVEM.L (SP)+,D0/A1-A2 ;RESTORE REGISTERS
  42   801C 4E75                RTS
  43   801E                     END
```

Figure 7.8 Routine for extended-precision addition.

7.4.2 Extended-Precision Multiplication

The instructions MULU.W and MULU.L and their signed counterparts MULS.W and MULS.L yield 32-bit products. MULU.L and MULS.L can cause an overflow if the product of the two 32-bit operands exceeds 32 bits in length. In this case, a product of 64 bits is required and the CPU32 instructions shown in Table 7.6 would be used. For example, the instruction

MULS.L   D0, D6 : D7

multiplies (D0) × (D7) and leaves the 64-bit product in (D6):(D7). According to the syntax in Table 7.6, (D6) holds the high-order results. The source operand, in D0 for this example, can be specified by any addressing mode except address register direct. Thus, the source operand can be held in a 32-bit memory longword addressed by any mode or in a data register. If the source operand is considered the multiplier, the 32-bit multiplicand must be held in the low-order register <Dl> as defined in Table 7.6. The only restriction on the use of registers is that Dh and Dl should not be the same register for 64-bit multiplies. The notation Dl indicates the low-order portion of a value and Dh indicates the high-order portion.

Table 7.6 64-bit Multiplication Instructions

Syntax	Operation
Signed MULS.L <EA>, <Dh>: <Dl>	(Dh)[31:0]:(Dl)[31:0] ← (EA) × (Dl)[31:0]
Unsigned MULU.L <EA>, <Dh>: <Dl>	

Notes:
1. <Dh> and <Dl> are any pair of data registers.
2. <EA> is specified by any data addressing mode.
3. <EA> holds one 32-bit operand and (Dl)[31:0] holds the other. The low-order 32 bits of the product are held in (Dl) and the high-order bits are held in (Dh).

Example 7.7

Figure 7.9 shows the multiplication of two 32-bit integers in hexadecimal to use as a result for testing 64-bit multiplication routines. The partial sums are shown aligned for readability.

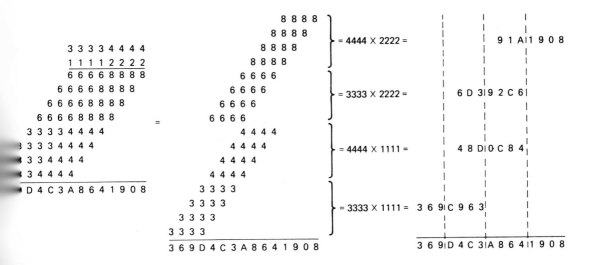

All values are hexadecimal.

Figure 7.9 Sixty-four bit double-precision multiplication example.

Example 7.8

The subroutine of Figure 7.10 multiplies two vectors of 32-bit unsigned numbers, element by element, to form a vector of 64-bit products. In the equation

$$Z(i) = X(i) \times Y(i)$$

$X(i)$ and $Y(i)$ are vectors of N, 32-bit, values. The 64-bit products are held in memory in the array defined as $Z(i)$. The starting addresses of X, Y, and Z are held in A1, A2, and A3, respectively. Data register D3 holds the number of integers N in each vector. The quadword value $Z(i)$ is stored in memory as

$$Z(i)[63\!:\!32], Z(i)[31\!:\!0]; \quad i = 1, 2, \ldots, N.$$

```
abs. rel.   LC   obj. code   source line
---- ----   ----  ---------   -----------
   1    1   0000                  |        TTL      'FIGURE 7.10'
   2    2   0000                  |        LLEN     100
   3    3   8000                  |        ORG      $8000
   4    4   0000                  |*
   5    5   8000                  |*      32 X 32 BIT ELEMENT BY ELEMENT
   6    6   8000                  |*             MULTIPLICATION OF UNSIGNED
   7    7   8000                  |*             INTEGER VECTORS
   8    8   8000                  |*
   9    9   8000                  |*       Z(I) = X(I) * Y(I) ; 64-BIT PRODUCT
  10   10   8000                  |*
  11   11   8000                  |*      INPUT :  (D3.L) = NUMBER OF VALUES
  12   12   8000                  |*               (A1.L) = ADDRESS OF VECTOR X
  13   13   8000                  |*               (A2.L) = ADDRESS OF VECTOR Y
  14   14   8000                  |*               (A3.L) = ADDRESS OF PRODUCTS Z
  15   15   8000                  |*
  16   16   8000                  |*      OUTPUT:  Z(I)
  17   17   8000                  |*               STORED IN MEMORY AS
  18   18   8000                  |*                 Z(I)[63:32]
  19   19   8000                  |*                 Z(I)[31:0]
  20   20   8000                  |*
  21   21   8000       |***********
  22   22   8000 48E7 F070        |        MOVEM.L  D0-D3/A1-A3,-(SP) ;SAVE REGISTERS
  23   23   8004 5343             |        SUBQ     #1,D3             ;N-1 IN D3
  24   24   8006                  |*
  25   25   8006 2019       LOOP  MOVE.L   (A1)+,D0          ;X
  26   26   8008 221A             |        MOVE.L   (A2)+,D1          ;Y
  27   27   800A 4C00 1402        |        MULU.L   D0,D2:D1          ;Z=X*Y
  28   28   800E                  |*
  29   29   800E 26C2             |        MOVE.L   D2,(A3)+          ;Z HIGH
  30   30   8010 26C1             |        MOVE.L   D1,(A3)+          ;Z LOW
  31   31   8012 51CB FFF2        |        DBRA     D3,LOOP           ;MULTIPLY N NUMBERS
  32   32   8016                  |*
  33   33   8016 4CDF 0E0F        |        MOVEM.L  (SP)+,D0-D3/A1-A3 ;RESTORE REGISTERS
  34   34   801A 4E75             |        RTS                       ; AND RETURN
```

Figure 7.10 Routine for double-precision multiplication.

Example 7.9

The CPU32 instructions MULU and MULS form a 32-bit or 64-bit product when two numbers are multiplied. In order to multiply 64-bit operands to yield a 128-bit product, the multiplication instruction can be used repeatedly to form partial products. These partial products are added together to produce the result. For example, consider the multiplication

$$(x + y) \times (w + z) = x \times w + y \times w + x \times z + y \times z$$

which requires four multiplications and three additions. Double-precision multiplication is similar in theory if y and z represent the lower-precision values of the operands and x and w the upper. In machine computation, however, the magnitude ranges of the different partial products is not the same and this must be taken into account. The appropriate calculation can be determined for unsigned numbers by writing the double-precision operand in the form

$$N = N_U \times 2^m + N_L.$$

This is a $2m$-digit number in which N_U and N_L are the m-digit integers formed by the upper and lower portions, respectively. The product of two double-precision integers N_1 and N_2 becomes

$$N_1 \times N_2 = 2^{2m} \times (N_{2U} \times N_{1U}) + 2^m \times (N_{2L} \times N_{1U} + N_{2U} \times N_{1L}) + N_{2L} \times N_{1L}.$$

The total length of the product is $4m$ digits and each partial product has $2m$ digits. The machine algorithm that performs the multiplication operation must align the partial products properly before adding them in the same manner that multiplication by hand is achieved. Any carry from a lower-order result into a higher-order result must be added in properly.

When extended-precision signed integers are multiplied, the scheme just described for unsigned integers fails if one or both of the operands to be multiplied is negative. A mathematical investigation using the two's-complement representation as described in Chapter 3 yields an algorithm that is suitable for this case. Several references in the Further Reading section at the end of this chapter discuss the approach. An alternative approach is to change the sign of (negate) any negative operands and correct the sign after performing unsigned multiplication. The program to accomplish this is left as an exercise.

7.4.3 Extended-Precision Division

The signed and unsigned division instructions of the CPU32 include two forms that allow a 32-bit quotient with a 32-bit remainder to be calculated. As shown in Table 7.7, one form (DIVU.L, DIVS.L) permits a 64-bit dividend to be divided by a 32-bit divisor to yield a 64-bit result. The other instructions (DIVSL.L, DIVUL.L) divide 32-bit operands to compute a 64-bit result. As with any division instruction, a division by zero causes a trap. Also, if the quotient cannot be held in 32 bits, an overflow condition $(V = \{1\})$ is set.

EXERCISES

7.4.1. Determine the range of unsigned integers, fractions, and signed integers for a 64-bit representation. Express the answers as powers of 10.

7.4.2. Diagram the operation necessary to perform a 64-bit $\times$ 64-bit = 128-bit multiplication using the MULU instruction. Write the subroutine and test it.

7.4.3. Show the results of

$$\text{MULU.L} \qquad \#2, D0 : D1$$

Table 7.7 Extended-Precision Division Instructions

Syntax	Operation
DIVS.L <EA>, <Dr>: <Dq>	$(Dq)[31:0]{:}(Dr)[31:0] =$
DIVU.L <EA>, <Dr>: <Dq>	$\dfrac{(Dr)[31:0]{:}(Dq)[31:0]}{(EA)[31:0]}$
DIVUL.L <EA>, <Dr>: <Dq>	$(Dq)[31:0]{:}(Dr)[31:0] =$
DIVSL.L <EA>, <Dr>: <Dq>	$\dfrac{(Dq)[31:0]}{(EA)[31:0]}$

Notes:
1. <Dq> holds the low-order 32 bits of the dividend before division. The 32-bit quotient is placed in this register after division.
2. <Dr> holds the high-order 32 bits of a 64-bit dividend and the 32-bit remainder after division.
3. Overflow occurs if the quotient is larger than a 32-bit integer. Division by zero causes a trap.
4. <EA> may be specified by any addressing mode except address register direct.

if (D1) = $FFFF FFFE initially.

7.4.4. Let (D0) = $FFFF FFFF and (D1) = $FFFF FFFE. State the results if (D0) and (D1) contain these values before each of the following instructions execute:
(a) DIVU.L   #2, D0 : D1
(b) DIVS.L   #2, D0 : D1

7.4.5. Modify the 128-bit multiply routine of Exercise 7.4.2 to multiply two signed integers in two's-complement notation.

7.5 DECIMAL ARITHMETIC

The CPU32 provides instructions for arithmetic operations on decimal values represented in Binary-Coded Decimal (BCD). This code was defined in Chapter 3 and this section applies many of the mathematical principles presented there. The three instructions for BCD arithmetic are defined in Table 7.8. The instructions allow addition, subtraction, and negation of BCD values. For each instruction the operand length is 8 bits, which represents two BCD digits. For example, the Add Decimal with Extend (ABCD) instruction

ABCD   D1, D2

performs decimal addition between byte-length operands. The operation is

$$(D2)[7:0] \leftarrow (D1)[7:0] + (D2)[7:0] + X.$$

Notice that this instruction adds the value of the X condition code bit into the sum to facilitate extended-precision additions. However, the X bit must be cleared before the first ABCD is executed. After the addition operation, X = {1} indicates that a decimal carry occurred because the sum was greater than 99. The Z bit is cleared if the sum is not zero. Otherwise, it is unchanged to allow tests for zero to be performed after extended-precision operations. The Subtract Decimal with Extend (SBCD) operates similarly, but the source operand and the value of the X bit are both subtracted from the destination value.

Table 7.8 Decimal-Arithmetic Instructions

Syntax	Operation
Addition:	
ABCD <Dm>, <Dn>	(Dn)[7:0] ← (Dn)[7:0] + (Dm)[7:0] + X
ABCD − (Am), −(An)	(dst) ← (dst) + (src) + X
Subtraction:	
SBCD <Dm>, <Dn>	(Dn)[7:0] ← (Dn)[7:0] − (Dm)[7:0] − X
SBCD − (Am), −(An)	(dst) ← (dst) − (src) − X
Negation:	
NBCD <EA>	(EA) ← 0 − (EA) − X

Notes:
1. In the predecrement modes of addressing, the destination is (dst) and the source operand is in location (src).
2. All operations perform decimal arithmetic on two BCD digits.
3. N and V condition code bits are undefined.
4. C is set if a decimal carry (or borrow) occurs.
5. Z is cleared if the result is nonzero; otherwise it is unchanged.

The operations of the BCD instructions allow extended-precision arithmetic. However, the BCD instructions do not use the N and V bits. Moreover, the BCD instructions restrict the operand length to 8 bits and the addressing modes to data register direct or predecrement for BCD addition and subtraction. The instruction Negate Decimal with Extend (NBCD) forms the ten's complement of a two-digit operand when X = {0} before the operation. If X = {1}, NBCD forms the nine's complement. The assembly language form is

$$\text{NBCD} \qquad \text{<EA>}$$

which allows any data-alterable addressing mode for the effective address. This excludes an operand in an address register or one addressed relative to the program counter.

Example 7.10

Table 7.9 shows the effect of decimal addition and subtraction for various operands and condition code settings. Addition of the values 65 and 17 yields 82 if the X bit is cleared or 83 if it is set. Adding 42 and 77 yields a result of 19 with an indication of a carry. The proper value of 119 would require an additional BCD digit. The incorrect nonzero indication that results for the addition of 0 and 0 without the Z bit set is also shown.

Subtraction of two BCD digits yields a correct result for unsigned numbers in the range 0 to 99 or signed numbers between −10 and +9. The subtraction of the unsigned numbers 77 minus 32 yields 45 as expected. But 17 minus 65 leaves the ten's-complement result of −48 (52) with a borrow indication. If the X bit is set before the operation, the nine's complement of -48 (51) results when 65 is subtracted from 17. When two equal values are subtracted with the X bit set, the result is 99 or the nine's complement of 0 with a borrow indication.

Table 7.9 Examples of BCD Operations

(a) Addition ABCD (src),(dst)

Before execution				After execution		
(src)	(dst)	X	Z	(dst)	X	Z
65	17	0	1	82	0	0
65	17	1	1	83	0	0
42	77	0	0	19	1	0
0	0	0	0	00	0	0

(b) Subtraction SBCD (src),(dst)

Before execution			After execution	
(src)	(dst)	X	(dst)	X
32	77	0	45	0
65	17	0	52	1
65	17	1	51	1
35	35	1	99	1

Note:
The contents of the source (src) and destination (dst) locations are decimal values.

7.5.1 Extended-Precision Decimal Arithmetic

The ABCD and SBCD instructions can operate only on the low-order byte of a data register. Consequently, operations on BCD numbers with more than two digits are normally performed on operands held in memory rather than in a register. If a decimal string of digits is held in a data register, the rotate instructions to be introduced in Chapter 8 would be needed to shift the digits being manipulated to the low-order byte. Rotation is avoided by performing memory-to-memory operations using predecrement addressing. For example, the instruction

$$\text{ABCD} \qquad -(\text{A1}), -(\text{A2})$$

first decrements (A1) and then (A2) by 1. Then, the two digits in the addressed byte locations plus the X bit value are added into the destination location addressed by A2. To perform operations on numbers with more than two digits, a decimal string is stored in memory with the least significant two digits at the highest byte address. Thus, the decimal number 123456 at location $1000 would be stored as follows:

$$(1000) = 12$$

$$(1001) = 34$$

$$(1002) = 56$$

An addition or subtraction of this value should start with the beginning address initialized at $1003 when the predecrement modes are used.

Example 7.11

The program in Figure 7.11 adds two six-digit BCD integers. Initially, the addresses of the operands as just described are stored in A1 and A2. The sum is left in the location addressed by A2. The X bit must be cleared and the Z bit must be set before the addition begins. If the result is nonzero, the Z bit will be cleared by the addition. If the integers are restricted to positive values, the C bit indicates an overflow condition after the additions.

```
abs.   LC   obj. code   source line
----   ----  ---------   -----------
  1    0000                         TTL     'FIGURE 7.11'
  2    0000                         LLEN    100
  3    8000                         ORG     $8000
  4    0000              *
  5    8000              * BCD ADDITION
  6    8000              *
  7    8000              * INPUTS :  (A1.L) = ADDRESS OF THE BYTE FOLLOWING
  8    8000              *                    FIRST 6-DIGIT BCD NUMBER
  9    8000              *           (A2.L) = ADDRESS OF THE BYTE FOLLOWING
 10    8000              *                    SECOND 6-DIGIT BCD NUMBER
 11    8000              *                    (ADDRESS OF NUMBER + 3)
 12    8000              * OUTPUTS : (A2.L) = ADDRESS OF HIGH ORDER BYTE OF
 13    8000              *                    6-DIGIT BCD RESULT
 14    8000              *
 15    8000              * NOTES:
 16    8000              *   1.  BCD NUMBERS ARE STORED 2 DIGITS/BYTE
 17    8000              *       BCD [6:5]
 18    8000              *       BCD [4:3]
 19    8000              *       BCD [2:1]
 20    8000              *
 21    8000              *   2.  ADDRESS REGISTERS POINT TO BCD [2:1] + 1
 22    8000              *       SO THAT PREDECREMENT ADDRESSING CAN BE
 23    8000              *       USED
 24    8000              *
 25    8000              *   3.  NO TEST FOR OVERFLOW
 26    8000              *
 27    8000
 28    8000 48E7 0060    ADDBCD MOVEM.L A1/A2,-(SP) ;SAVE REGISTERS
 29    8004 44FC 0004           MOVE.W  #4,CCR      ;CLEAR X BIT
 30    8008              *                          ; SET Z BIT
 31    8008 C509                ABCD    -(A1),-(A2) ;ADD THE BCD NUMBERS
 32    800A C509                ABCD    -(A1),-(A2)
 33    800C C509                ABCD    -(A1),-(A2)
 34    800E 4CDF 0600           MOVEM.L (SP)+,A1/A2 ;RESTORE REGISTERS
 35    8012 4E75                RTS                 ; AND RETURN
 36    8014                     END
```

Figure 7.11 Routine for six-digit BCD addition.

Notice that the ABCD instructions were executed in sequence. If the ABCD instruction is used in a loop, the setting of the X bit must be saved before any instructions such as SUBQ for looping are executed because these arithmetic instructions can change the X bit. After testing the appropriate conditions, the program must restore the X bit before ABCD is executed again in the loop. A CMP or CMPA instruction will not change the X bit, as explained in Example 7.6.

Sec. 7.5   Decimal Arithmetic

EXERCISES

7.5.1. Express the following BCD numbers in binary using four digits. Show the machine representation using ten's-complement notation:
(a) +37;
(b) −37;
(c) −1319.

7.5.2. Using the CPU32 formats, perform the following operations on BCD integers:
(a) 1754 − 1319;
(b) 9375 + 3470.
How are the results in part (b) interpreted when only four-digit unsigned integers are allowed?

7.5.3. Perform the addition 127 plus 299 using binary arithmetic but with the values in BCD notation. Adjust the binary result by adding "6" to any digit greater than 9 and add the carry to the next higher digit. (The Motorola CPU32 BCD instructions perform this decimal adjustment automatically.)

7.5.4. Write a subroutine to add or subtract two BCD integers with up to eight digits each. Signed integers are represented in ten's-complement notation. What is the decimal range of the valid integers? What is the decimal range of their sum or difference?

7.5.5. Write a subroutine to multiply two four-digit positive BCD numbers held in memory. The routine might perform multiplication by repeated addition, or an algorithm can be devised to perform decimal multiplication.

7.6 INPUT/OUTPUT AND CONVERSIONS

This section is concerned primarily with techniques that enable a programmer to transfer data between the memory of a computer system and the operator's terminal. Fortunately, many of the details of these transfers are handled by routines that are part of the operating system or monitor. These details are introduced in the first subsection 7.6.1 to follow but are not discussed completely until Chapter 12. After introduction of the physical or hardware aspects of input/output (I/O) transfers, a number of macroinstructions are defined. The macroinstructions call routines in the monitor (via the trap mechanism) to complete the transfers. Finally, conversions between ASCII, binary, and BCD values are presented. For reference, Appendix I presents the ASCII character set.

Figure 7.12 shows the simplified structure of the computer system with emphasis on the I/O transfer hardware and software. This system is similar to that presented in Chapter 2 but with the interface to the terminal shown as a peripheral chip. The chip performs serial-to-parallel conversion for input from the keyboard and parallel-to-serial conversion for output to the display screen. It is programmed for input or output by the I/O chip-control routines that are part of the monitor in this discussion. In an MC68332- based system these I/O transfers could be made by the Serial Communication Interface of the Queued Serial Module as described in Chapter 12.

The I/O macros to be discussed are written to call I/O routines. Conversion routines must be written to perform ASCII-to-binary or BCD conversion for data input. After conversion, the numbers may be manipulated as required by the applications program. Conversely, results from mathematical operations held in memory must be converted to ASCII characters for display at the terminal. An I/O macro library could be created for convenience to hold the I/O and conversion routines. This software module would be linked to the application program when I/O transfers are required.

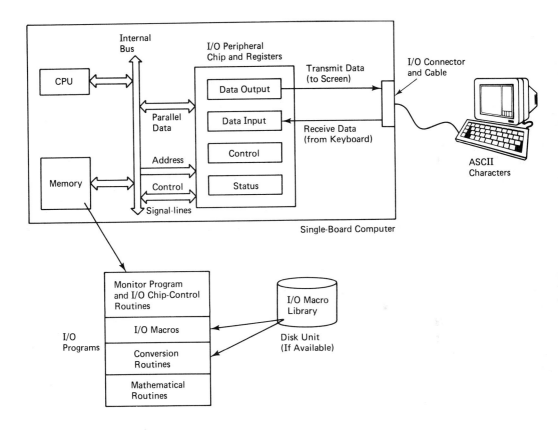

Figure 7.12 Simplified diagram of input/output (I/O) operations.

The BCC single-board computer with a 332BUG monitor is used for the examples in this section. Other details concerning the operation of the monitor were presented in Chapter 5. In that discussion, the monitor served primarily to load and execute programs. Here the capability of the monitor to facilitate I/O transfers is most important.

The BCC board was introduced in Chapters 5. Chapter 16 presents a more complete discussion of its capabilities and hardware configuration.

7.6.1 I/O Transfer

To allow the operator to input a character from the keyboard, the I/O chip in Figure 7.12 must be programmed to accept the character. The simplified procedure for the I/O chip-control routine is as follows:

(a) read the status of the I/O chip from its status register;
(b) if the chip is not busy, program its control register to accept a character. If busy, wait and try again;
(c) once the character is received, transfer the character from the data input register to memory.

This procedure is termed *conditional* I/O transfer because the I/O routine must wait until the chip is ready for transfer. Other types of transfers including those controlled by interrupts are described in Chapter 12.

If the I/O chip is ready for input when the operator strikes a key, the character is received as a serial train of pulses and converted to an 8-bit value for storage in memory. In the present discussion, the 8-bit character is an ASCII character. Similarly, the chip is programmed for output to transmit an ASCII character when the terminal is ready to receive it. The peripheral chip in both cases provides electrical and timing compatibility between the computer and the terminal. In MC68332 systems, the registers of the I/O chip are addressed in the same manner as memory locations.

As the reader will see in Chapter 12, programming the peripheral chip is tedious. It is, in fact, unnecessary when this type of standard I/O transfer is required. Obviously, the monitor must input characters from the keyboard and respond to commands by displaying requested information. To utilize this capability of the 332BUG, it is only necessary to execute the TRAP #15 instruction in a program. Other operating systems and monitors may require a different mechanism to invoke I/O transfers, but all modern computer systems will have an equivalent feature. In most cases, a user-mode program cannot program the I/O chips directly. When an operating system is present, most computer systems require that calls to the operating system be made if a user-mode program requires I/O transfers. The 332BUG monitor in these examples serves as a rudimentary operating system for the BCC single-board computer.

7.6.2 I/O System Calls and Macros

The 332BUG monitor provides various routines that are invoked by the TRAP #15 instruction. These routines are typically used by a programmer to facilitate I/O and other operations. One was encountered in previous examples where the instruction

```
        TRAP            #15


        DC.W            $0063
```

was used to return control to the monitor after a program executed to completion. The use of TRAP #15 in this manner is sometimes termed a *system call*. Table 7.10 lists several of these system calls with their TRAP #15 codes and describes their function. For the input functions (.INCHR, .INLN, .READSTR), the memory or buffer area for the characters must be defined before the call is made. The input character routine (.INCHR) can receive one character at a time. The input line (.INLN) routine can receive a string of characters followed by a carriage return (CR). Output routines (.OUTCHR, .WRITELN, .WRITE) are used to display messages or data to the operator. Several forms in Table 7.10 are available to allow the programmer to format the terminal screen as desired. The .PCRLF routine would cause the cursor of the terminal to return to the beginning of the next line of the screen. The .RETURN call is an example of a useful system call not related directly to I/O transfers. It causes the TRAP #15 operation using code $0063. The 332BUG monitor also has several other calls not shown in Table 7.10.

Table 7.10 332BUG System Calls

Function name	TRAP #15 code	Description
.INCHR	$0000	Read one character
.INLN	$0002	Read a line of characters followed by a (CR)
.READSTR	$0003	Read a string of characters up to 254 characters in length followed by a (CR); maximum string length is defined before call. The character string is echoed to the display unit.
.OUTCHR	$0020	Output a character
.WRITELN	$0024	Output a character string (line) followed by (CR)(LF)
.WRITE	$0032	Output a character string without a (CR)(LF)
.PCRLF	$0026	Output a (CR)(LF)
.RETURN	$0063	Return to monitor

Notes:
1. (CR) = carriage return: ASCII (#0D)
   (LF) = line feed: ASCII (#0A)
2. A *line* is a string of characters followed by (CR) which typically corresponds to one line of characters on a CRT screen. A *string* is limited in length to 254 characters for the 332BUG monitor.

Invoking system calls.   For each system call for I/O except .PCRLF, the programmer must define the locations to be used for input or output. The definitions must conform to the calling conventions defined in Table 7.11. The .INCHR function, for example, returns a single character on the system stack. One word of stack space must be reserved before the call, even though only a byte is input, since the system stack pointer must be kept on a word boundary. Thus, the program segment

SUBQ.L	#2, SP	; SAVE SPACE
TRAP	#15	; CALL .INCHR
DC.W	$0000	

MOVE.B   (SP)+, D0   ; CHARACTER IN D0

allocates space, waits for a character to be input, and finally transfers the character to register D0. The .READSTR function requires that the address of the input area or buffer in memory be placed on the system stack before the call. A maximum number of characters (bytes) must be defined for the string. This length must be placed in the first byte of the input buffer area. Similar conventions are required for each routine as defined exactly by Motorola for use of the system calls. Examples of each call will be given subsequently.

Table 7.11 Calling Conventions for System Calls

Macro system call (SYSCALL)	Calling convention
.INCHR	Reserve one word on stack for character
.INLN	Push address of input buffer
.READSTR	Define maximum string length in input buffer. Push address of input buffer on stack
.OUTCHR	Push character on stack
.WRITELN	Define string length in output buffer. Push address of output buffer on stack
.WRITE	Define string length in output buffer. Push address of output buffer on stack
.PCRLF	None

Notes:
1. The "calling convention" means that the programmer must perform the operations defined here before the system call is issued.
2. The system stack is used with these SYSCALLS.
3. .INLN stores the address of the (CR) following the input string in the input buffer on the system stack after it reads the line from the keyboard.

Macrodirectives for system calls.   One way to simplify the programming of I/O functions and simultaneously improve the readability of a program is to employ macro instructions. The I/O macros considered here simply invoke system calls by name as required in a program. The basic macro structure for this purpose is as follows:

SYSCALL   MACRO

TRAP   #15

DC.W   \1

ENDM

where the \1 indicates a value to be passed to the macro instruction when it is assembled. Each time the instruction SYSCALL is used, the assembly instructions are assembled into the program. Thus, the instruction

SYSCALL   .INCHR

assembles as

TRAP   #15

DC.W $0000

if .INCHR is equated to the value $0000. This is done by the directive

.INCHR EQU $0000

in the calling program.

Example 7.12

The program of Figure 7.13 shows the use of system calls to perform various I/O operations. MACRO directives are used to define the calling structure followed by the parameters for the particular function. When executed, the program first displays the ASCII text at label LINE 1 on the operator's terminal. Before the output of characters defined by LINE 1, LINE 2, LINE 3, LINE 4 and LINE 5 are displayed, each address is pushed onto the system stack at the appropriate place in the program with the PEA (Push Effective Address) instruction.[1]

Figure 7.14 shows the text on the display screen as seen by the operator. After the text corresponding to LINE 2 is displayed, the operator types a character followed by (CR). This character is not displayed on the screen as it is typed but it is stored on the system stack and moved to register D0. It is re-displayed or "echoed" on the screen after the text LINE 3 by the syscall .OUTCHR.

Next a string of characters is received and echoed after the text of LINE 4 is displayed. The maximum string length is defined as 254 characters in the first byte of the input buffer. A 256 byte area is reserved for the input string as INBUF in the data section of the program. The syscall .READSTR reads and echoes the string of characters after the operator types it followed by a carriage return. The call leaves the actual length of the string in the first byte of the buffer INBUF. This buffer also serves as the output buffer for the next system call to .WRITELN to echo the string again.

Calls to .WRITELN display a line or string of characters followed by a (CR) and (LF). In contrast, a syscall to .WRITE would leave the cursor of the CRT unit in a position immediately following the displayed characters unless carriage return and linefeed characters were part of the string as they are in the text of LINE 5. The programmer can thus format the display as desired by transmitting format control characters to the terminal. When the text of LINE 5 is output for example, the (CR) character ($0D) and the (LF) character ($0A) are also sent. By selecting the appropriate format control characters, the programmer can cause such actions as clearing of the screen or tabulating any displayed results. The exact ASCII code for such formatting depends on the format required by the operator's terminal.

[1] The PEA instruction is studied in Chapter 9.

```
abs. rel.    LC    obj. code    source line
---- ----    ----  ----------   -----------
  1   1     0000                            TTL      'FIGURE 7.13'
  2   2     8000                            ORG      $8000
  3   3     0000             *
  4   4     8000             *     I/O SYSCALLS
  5   5     8000             *
  6   6     8000             SYSCALL  MACRO              ;MACRO= SYSCALL
  7   7     8000                      TRAP    #15
  8   8     8000                      DC.W    \1         ;PARAMETER
  9   9     8000                      ENDM
 10  10     8000             *
 11  11     8000             *     I/O SYSCALL PARAMETERS
 12  12     8000             *
 13  13           0000 0000  .INCHR   EQU     $0000      ;INPUT CHARACTER
 14  14           0000 0002  .INLN    EQU     $0002      ;INPUT LINE
 15  15           0000 0003  .READSTR EQU     $0003      ;INPUT STRING
 16  16           0000 0020  .OUTCHR  EQU     $0020      ;OUTPUT CHARACTER
 17  17           0000 0024  .WRITELN EQU     $0024      ;OUTPUT LINE WITH
 18  18     8000             *                           ;  (CR),(LF)
 19  19           0000 0023  .WRITE   EQU     $0023      ;OUTPUT STRING
 20  20           0000 0026  .PCRLF   EQU     $0026      ;(CR),(LF)
 21  21           0000 0063  .RETURN  EQU     $0063      ;RETURN TO MONITOR
 22  22     8000             *
 23  23     8000             *     OUTPUT "TEST OF I/O SYSCALLS"
 24  24     8000             *
 25  25     8000 4879 0000   STARTIO  PEA     LINE1      ;ADDRESS OF MESSAGE-
 25        8004 8076
 26  26     8006             *                           ;  LINE 1
 27  27     8006                      SYSCALL .WRITELN   ;WRITE TO SCREEN
 28  1m     8006 4E4F        +        TRAP    #15
 29  2m     8008 0024        +        DC.W    .WRITELN      ;PARAMETER
 30  28     800A             *
 31  29     800A             *     INPUT AND ECHO A CHARACTER
 32  30     800A             *
 33  31     800A 4879 0000            PEA     LINE2      ;PROMPT FOR CHARACTER
 33        800E 808C
 34  32     8010                      SYSCALL .WRITELN
 35  1m     8010 4E4F        +        TRAP    #15
 36  2m     8012 0024        +        DC.W    .WRITELN      ;PARAMETER
 37  33     8014 9FFC 0000            SUBQ.L  #2,SP      ;SAVE SPACE
 37        8018 0002
 38  34     801A                      SYSCALL .INCHR     ;INPUT
 39  1m     801A 4E4F        +        TRAP    #15
 40  2m     801C 0000        +        DC.W    .INCHR        ;PARAMETER
 41  35     801E 101F                 MOVE.B  (SP)+,D0   ;CHARACTER IN (D0)
 42  36     8020             *
 43  37     8020 4879 0000            PEA     LINE3      ;ECHO
 43        8024 809F
 44  38     8026                      SYSCALL .WRITE
 45  1m     8026 4E4F        +        TRAP    #15
 46  2m     8028 0023        +        DC.W    .WRITE        ;PARAMETER
 47  39     802A 1F00                 MOVE.B  D0,-(SP)
 48  40     802C                      SYSCALL .OUTCHR
 49  1m     802C 4E4F        +        TRAP    #15
 50  2m     802E 0020        +        DC.W    .OUTCHR       ;PARAMETER
 51  41     8030                      SYSCALL .PCRLF     ;NEXT LINE
 52  1m     8030 4E4F        +        TRAP    #15
 53  2m     8032 0026        +        DC.W    .PCRLF        ;PARAMETER
 54  42     8034             *
 55  43     8034             *     INPUT AND ECHO A STRING OF CHARACTERS
 56  44     8034             *
 57  45     8034                      SYSCALL .PCRLF     ;SKIP A LINE
 58  1m     8034 4E4F        +        TRAP    #15
 59  2m     8036 0026        +        DC.W    .PCRLF        ;PARAMETER
 60  46     8038 4879 0000            PEA     LINE4      ;PROMPT FOR STRING
 60        803C 80AF
 61  47     803E                      SYSCALL .WRITELN
```

Figure 7.13 Program examples of I/O system calls.

```
62    1m   803E  4E4F    +         TRAP     #15
63    2m   8040  0024    +         DC.W     .WRITELN       ;PARAMETER
64    48   8042  13FC  00FE        MOVE.B   #254,INBUF ;MAXIMUM LENGTH
64         8046  0000  80CD
65    49   804A  4879  0000        PEA      INBUF          ;ADDRESS OF BUFFER
65         804E  80CD
66    50   8050          |         SYSCALL  .READSTR       ;READ THE STRING
67    1m   8050  4E4F    +         TRAP     #15
68    2m   8052  0003    +         DC.W     .READSTR       ;PARAMETER
69    51   8054          |         SYSCALL  .PCRLF         ; AND ECHO IT
70    1m   8054  4E4F    +         TRAP     #15
71    2m   8056  0026    +         DC.W     .PCRLF         ;PARAMETER
72    52   8058  1039  0000        MOVE.B   INBUF,D0 ;ACTUAL LENGTH
72         805C  80CD
73    53   805E          *
74    54   805E  4879  0000        PEA      LINE5          ;ECHO STRING AGAIN
74         8062  80C0
75    55   8064          |         SYSCALL  .WRITE
76    1m   8064  4E4F    +         TRAP     #15
77    2m   8066  0023    +         DC.W     .WRITE         ;PARAMETER
78    56   8068          *
79    57   8068  4879  0000        PEA      INBUF
79         806C  80CD
80    58   806E          |         SYSCALL  .WRITELN
81    1m   806E  4E4F    +         TRAP     #15
82    2m   8070  0024    +         DC.W     .WRITELN       ;PARAMETER
83    59   8072          *
84    60   8072          |         SYSCALL  .RETURN    ;RETURN
85    1m   8072  4E4F    +         TRAP     #15
86    2m   8074  0063    +         DC.W     .RETURN        ;PARAMETER
87    61   8076          |*
88    62   8076          *    MESSAGES AND DATA
89    63   8076          *
90    64   8076  15      LINE1    DC.B     21,' TEST OF I/O SYSCALLS'
90    64   8077  2054  4553
90    64   807B  5420  4F46
90    64   807F  2049  2F4F
90    64   8083  2053  5953
90    64   8087  4341  4C4C
90    64   808B  53
91    65   808C  12      LINE2    DC.B     18,' INPUT A CHARACTER'
91    65   808D  2049  4E50
91    65   8091  5554  2041
91    65   8095  2043  4841
91    65   8099  5241  4354
91    65   809D  4552
92    66   809F  0F      LINE3    DC.B     15,' CHARACTER IS  '
92    66   80A0  2043  4841
92    66   80A4  5241  4354
92    66   80A8  4552  2049
92    66   80AC  5320  20
93    67   80AF  10      LINE4    DC.B     16,' INPUT A STRING '
93    67   80B0  2049  4E50
93    67   80B4  5554  2041
93    67   80B8  2053  5452
93    67   80BC  494E  4720
94    68   80C0  0C      LINE5    DC.B     12,' STRING IS',$0D,$0A
94    68   80C1  2053  5452
94    68   80C5  494E  4720
94    68   80C9  4953
94    68   80CB  0D
94    68   80CC  0A
95    69   80CD          *
96    70   80CD          |INBUF   DS.B     256            ;INPUT BUFFER
97    71   81CD          |        END
97 lines assembled
```

Figure 7.13 Continued.

```
32Bug>GO 8000
Effective address: 00008000
  TEST OF I/O SYSCALLS
  INPUT A CHARACTER
  CHARACTER IS  5

  INPUT A STRING
TOM HARMAN
  STRING IS
TOM HARMAN
32Bug>
```

Figure 7.14 Trace of program of Figure 7.13.

7.6.3 Data Conversions

The standard data representations for the CPU32 include binary and BCD for integers and ASCII for characters. For input and output, ASCII is generally the code used for data being transferred between the computer system and peripheral devices such as line printers or operator's terminals. Conversions between these representations are therefore frequently required since the arithmetic processing requires binary or BCD values in memory.

Figure 7.15(a) shows the typical steps to convert a decimal number in ASCII to a binary representation. The ASCII characters for the decimal digits are first converted to numbers in the range 0-9. The 4 bits for each digit are also the BCD value in memory. Then, the string of BCD digits is converted to a binary number. This conversion takes into account the positional value of each BCD digit. For example, the ASCII string '123' as an input value is stored in memory as $31, $32, and $33. This is converted to three BCD digits, 1, 2, and 3, and then to the binary value 01111011.

The output of binary values that are to be printed as decimal numbers requires the opposite conversion from binary to BCD and then to ASCII. Of course, the binary value in memory could be printed in binary, hexadecimal, or another code. The binary number in the input example just given has the hexadecimal value 7B. This could be output in ASCII as $37, $42. Figure 7.15(b) shows the ASCII equivalents for decimal and hexadecimal digits.

Example 7.13

Figure 7.16 shows a subroutine to determine the ASCII or BCD value of a hexadecimal digit stored in the low-order 4 bits of D1. If (D2)[7:0] contains a 0 upon entry, the ASCII code is placed in the low-order byte of D2. The value is found by addressing the table ASCTAB and indexing based on the hexadecimal digit in D1. If (D2)[7:0] is 1 upon entry, the BCD digit corresponding to the hexadecimal digit is placed in D2. The value is obtained from the table BCDTAB. This table-lookup scheme is an alternative method for converting values from one form to another.

Example 7.14

If a string of decimal digits is stored as $D_{n-1}D_{n-2} \cdots D_0$ in separate bytes in memory,

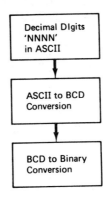

Decimal Digits
'NNNN'
in ASCII

↓

ASCII to BCD
Conversion

↓

BCD to Binary
Conversion

(a) Conversion of Input Data

Meaning	Binary Representation in Memory	To Convert to ASCII	ASCII in Memory
Decimal Digits 0-9 (BCD)	0000 0000 0000 0001 ⋮ 0000 1001	Add 0011 0000$_2$ ($30)	$30-$39
Hexadecimal Digits 0-9	0000 0000 0000 0001 ⋮ 0000 1001	Add $30	$30-$39
Hexadecimal Digits A-F	0000 1010 0000 1011 ⋮ 0000 1111	Add $37	$41-$46

(b) Decimal or Hexadecimal to ASCII for Output

Figure 7.15 Conversion of data values.

the conversion to binary is easily accomplished since the numerical value is

$$(\cdots(D_{n-1} \times 10 + D_{n-2}) \times 10 + \cdots + D_1) \times 10 + D_0$$

as explained in Chapter 3. The binary sum is formed by computing the terms in parentheses using binary arithmetic and adding each term into the total.

Figure 7.17 shows a subroutine to accomplish this conversion for an eight-digit BCD value. On entry, the decimal digits are assumed to be stored right-justified in the byte locations addressed by A1. If no out-of-range condition occurs, the binary value is returned in register D1.

The multiplication by 10 in the program is accomplished by left shifts (multiply by 2) and adding rather than by using the MULU instruction. This code could be replaced by the multiply instruction and a test for overflow for a number greater than 99,999,999.

```
abs.   LC    obj. code     source line
----   ----  ----------    -----------
   1   0000                          TTL   'FIGURE 7.16'
   2   0000                          LLEN  100
   3   8000                          ORG   $8000
   4   8000                          XDEF  CONHAS
   5   8000             |*
   6   8000             |*    HEXADECIMAL TO BCD/ASCII
   7   8000             |*
   8   8000             |*    INPUT  :  (D2.B) = 0      : ASCII REQUESTED
   9   8000             |*                     NOT 0 :  BCD REQUESTED
  10   8000             |*              (D1.W) = HEXADECIMAL DIGIT TO CONVERT
  11   8000             |*                       MUST BE VALID = $0-$F
  12   8000             |*
  13   8000             |*    OUTPUT : (D2.B) = BCD OR ASCII
  14   8000             |*
  15   8000             |*
  16   8000             |*
  17   8000  2F09       |CONHAS MOVE.L  A1,-(SP)      ;SAVE REGISTER
  18   8002  227C 0000  |       MOVE.L  #ASCTAB,A1    ;ASSUME ASCII WAS
       8006  801C       |
  19   8008             |*                            ; REQUESTED
  20   8008  4A02       |       TST.B   D2            ;CHECK REQUEST
  21   800A  6700 0008  |       BEQ     INDEX         ;IF BCD REQUESTED
  22   800E  227C 0000  |       MOVE.L  #BCDTAB,A1    ; THEN CHANGE TO BCD TABLE
       8012  802C       |
  23   8014             |*
  24   8014  1431 1000  |INDEX  MOVE.B  0(A1,D1.W),D2 ;LOOK UP VALUE
  25   8018  225F       |       MOVE.L  (SP)+,A1      ;RESTORE REGISTERS
  26   801A  4E75       |       RTS
  27   801C  3031 3233  |ASCTAB DC.B    '0123456789ABCDEF'
  27   8020  3435 3637  |
  27   8024  3839 4142  |
  27   8028  4344 4546  |
  28   802C  00         |BCDTAB DC.B    0,1,2,3,4,5,6
  28   802D  01         |
  28   802E  02         |
  28   802F  03         |
  28   8030  04         |
  28   8031  05         |
  28   8032  06         |
  29   8033  07         |       DC.B    7,8,9,$10,$11
  29   8034  08         |
  29   8035  09         |
  29   8036  10         |
  29   8037  11         |
  30   8038  12         |       DC.B    $12,$13,$14,$15
  30   8039  13         |
  30   803A  14         |
  30   803B  15         |
  31   803C            |        END
```

Figure 7.16 Routine for table lookup program for hexadecimal and BCD conversions.

An error could occur only if the eight-digit decimal value to be converted is not a valid BCD number. As the program is written, an overflow occurs for a binary number greater than 2^{31} since the BMI instruction is used.

EXERCISES

7.6.1. Write a subroutine to convert an ASCII string of digits to signed binary representation when the range of the input can be up to eight decimal digits plus a sign.

7.6.2. Write a subroutine to convert a string of binary digits to ASCII.

```
abs.   LC    obj. code    source line
----   ----  ----------   -----------
   1   0000                        TTL      'FIGURE 7.17'
   2   0000                        LLEN     100
   3   8000                        ORG      $8000
   4   8000                        XDEF     BCDBN
   5   8000              |*
   6   8000              |*  BCD TO BINARY
   7   8000              |*
   8   8000              |*  INPUTS  : (D2.W) = NUMBER OF DIGITS IN BCD NUMBER
   9   8000              |*            (A1.L) = ADDRESS OF THE MOST SIGNIFICANT
  10   8000              |*                            BCD DIGIT
  11   8000              |*
  12   8000              |*  OUTPUTS : (D1.L) = BINARY VALUE
  13   8000              |*            (D4.W) = 0    :   ERROR DETECTED
  14   8000              |*                     NOT 0 :   SUCCESSFUL
  15   8000              |*
  16   8000              |*  NOTES:
  17   8000              |*  1.  BCD DIGITS ARE STORED ONE/BYTE AND MUST BE
  18   8000              |*          VALID. LIMIT IS 8 DIGITS.
  19   8000              |*  2.  ONLY POSITIVE BCD NUMBERS ARE ALLOWED
  20   8000              |*
  21   8000              |*
  22   8000              |*
  23   8000 48E7 3440    |BCDBN   MOVEM.L  D2/D3/D5/A1,-(SP) ;SAVE REGISTERS
  24   8004 4281                  CLR.L    D1            ;VALUE    := 0
  25   8006 4244                  CLR.W    D4            ;SET DEFAULT TO ERROR
  26   8008 4285                  CLR.L    D5            ;CLEAR ACCUMULATOR
  27   800A 4A42                  TST.W    D2            ;IF LENGTH IS ZERO
  28   800C 6700 002E             BEQ      DONE          ; THEN EXIT WITH ERROR
  29   8010 0C42 0008             CMPI.W   #8,D2         ;IF LENGTH >8
  30   8014 6E00 0026             BGT      DONE          ; THEN EXIT WITH ERROR
  31   8018              |*
  32   8018              |*
  33   8018 1A19         |LOOP    MOVE.B   (A1)+,D5      ;DIGIT IN D5
  34   801A D285                  ADD.L    D5,D1         ;ADD TO SERIES
  35   801C 5342                  SUBQ.W   #1,D2         ;DECREMENT COUNTER
  36   801E 6700 0018             BEQ      SUCCESS       ; IF FINISHED (LAST DIGIT)
  37   8022              |*                              ;       EXIT
  38   8022              |*
  39   8022              |*  MULTIPLY BY 10 AS   10X = (2X)*4+2X
  40   8022              |*
  41   8022 E389                  LSL.L    #1,D1         ;MULTIPLY BY TWO
  42   8024 6B00 0016             BMI      DONE          ; ON OVERFLOW , EXIT
  43   8028              |*
  44   8028 2601                  MOVE.L   D1,D3         ;SAVE THE RESULT OF MULTIPLY
  45   802A E589                  LSL.L    #2,D1         ;MULTIPLY BY FOUR (VALUE*8)
  46   802C 6B00 000E             BMI      DONE          ; ON OVERFLOW , EXIT
  47   8030              |*
  48   8030 D283                  ADD.L    D3,D1         ;VALUE = VALUE * 10
  49   8032 6B00 0008             BMI      DONE          ; ON OVERFLOW , EXIT
  50   8036              |*
  51   8036 60E0                  BRA      LOOP          ;PROCESS NEXT DIGIT
  52   8038 383C 0001   |SUCCESS MOVE.W   #1,D4         ;SET STATUS TO SUCCESS
  53   803C 4CDF 022C   |DONE    MOVEM.L  (SP)+,D2/D3/D5/A1 ;RESTORE REGISTERS
  54   8040 4E75                  RTS
  55   8042                       END
```

Figure 7.17 Routine for BCD-to-binary conversion.

7.6.3. To convert from binary to decimal, it is possible to follow the procedure shown in this section using the decimal expansion for the number to be converted. Repeatedly dividing the number by 10 will yield the decimal digits, as remainders, in ascending order. Write a subroutine to convert a 16-bit unsigned integer to the equivalent BCD value.

7.6.4. Write a routine to convert a string of ASCII digits to BCD when the input string contains a decimal point ($2E). Determine the number of digits and leave the scale factor in a register; that is, determine the number of decimal places and store the BCD number as an integer.

7.6.5. Modify the program of Example 7.14 to convert a string of decimal values in ASCII to binary. Limit the string to positive numbers of up to eight digits in length.

7.7 THE TABLE INSTRUCTIONS AND INTERPOLATION

Interpolation is the process of approximating a number that although not an entry in a table of numbers, lies between two consecutive entries. In the first subsection, linear interpolation of a one-dimensional table of values is discussed. The technique is then generalized in Subsection 7.7.2 to functions of several variables using separate linear interpolation on each of the variables. More advanced techniques and rigorous mathematical treatments of interpolation are presented in several of the references in the Further Reading section of this chapter.

7.7.1 Linear Interpolation Using TABLE (TBLxx) Instructions

Table 7.12 shows the syntax and the operation of the Table Look-up and Interpolate instructions of the CPU32 that interpolate from a table of values in memory. In this subsection, instructions of the general form

TBLxx.<l>   <EA>, Dx

are discussed. The suffix <xx> is one of the possibilities shown in Table 7.12. The address <EA> is the first location of a one-dimensional table of values in memory. The size in bits of the values is designated by <l> as byte (B), word (W), or longword (L). Dx is a data register containing the value of the independent variable X in (Dx)[15:0]. Subsection 7.7.2 treats the TBLxx instructions that can be used for surface interpolation.

Consider a table of entries $F_0, F_1, F_2, \ldots, F_N$ in memory where $F_i = F(X(i))$ is the value of a function representing the dependent variable. Corresponding to the function values are the $N+1$ values, for $i = 0, 1, 2, \ldots, N$, of the independent variable value X_i. A linear interpolation formula determines the value Y as

$$Y = \frac{(F_{(n+1)} - F_n) \times (X - X_n)}{(X_{(n+1)} - X_n)} + F_n \tag{7.1}$$

where $Y = F(X)$ with $X_n \leq X < X_{(n+1)}$. This represents Y as the value at F_n to which is added the linear change in the function value between X_n and X. Figure 7.18(a) shows a graph of a function's values connected by straight line segments. The interpolated value Y will lie on the line connecting F_n with $F_{(n+1)}$.

Several simplifying assumptions are made in Equation 7.1 to yield the interpolation formula used by the TBLxx instructions. First, the independent values X_i are

Table 7.12 Table Look-Up and Interpolate Instructions

Syntax	Operation
Signed values in table:	
TBLS.<l> <EA>, Dx	(Dx) ← interpolated value; rounded
TBLSN.<l> <EA>, Dx	(Dx) ← interpolated value; unrounded
Unsigned values in table:	
TBLU.<l> <EA>, Dx	(Dx) ← interpolated value; rounded
TBLUN.<l> <EA>, Dx	(Dx) ← interpolated value; unrounded

Notes:
1. <l> = B, W or L defines the size of the dependent variable in the table.
2. <EA> is the starting address of the table in memory. Only control addressing modes are allowed.
3. (Dx)[15:0] holds the independent variable before any of the instructions execute. (Dx)[<l>] contains the interpolated value after execution.
4. For the TBLS and TBLU instructions, (Dx)[<l>] contains the interpolated value.
5. For the TBLSN and TBLUN instructions, (Dx)[7:0] holds the fractional part of the result. (Dx)[31:8] holds the sign-extended result for TBLSN or the zero-extended integer result for TBLUN.
6. Condition codes:
   X   –   not affected
   C   –   always cleared
   N,Z –   set according to the result
   V   –   set if the signed integer portion of an unrounded long result is not in the range -2^{23} to $2^{23} - 1$.

assumed to be given at equally spaced intervals. Thus, the values of X_i do not have to be stored if X_0 is specified. The X value corresponding to F_n is

$$X_n = X_0 + h \times n$$

if $h = X_{(n+1)} - X_n$ is a fixed interval. The interval h is computed as

$$h = (X_N - X_0)/N$$

for $N + 1$ points when the range $(X_N - X_0)$ is specified. The second assumption is that the independent variable value X is represented as a 16-bit integer.

The independent variable, held in (Dx)[15:0] before any of the instructions in Table 7.12 are executed, is used as both an index into the table of values in memory and the X value to interpolate. As shown in Figure 7.18 (b), the upper 8 bits, (Dx)[15:8], select one of the possible 257 entries in the table. The lower 8 bits, (Dx)[7:0], represent the value $(X - X_n)$ used for interpolation. This is shown by writing the value X as

$$X = X_n + (X - X_n)$$

to emphasize that X is represented by two quantities. The arithmetic value of X is thus

$$X = (Dx)[15:8] \times 2^8 + (Dx)[7:0]$$

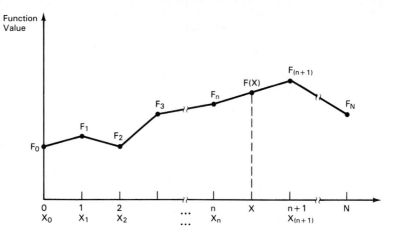

(a) Linear interpolation approximation

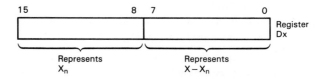

(b) Independent variable as index into a table

Figure 7.18 Interpolation.

as can be seen from Figure 7.18(b). Thus, there are 2^8 (256) interpolation intervals between two values in the table and a maximum of 257 ($2^8 + 1$) entries in the table. The index into the table is related to the X_i values as

$$X_i = 2^8 \times i, \quad i = 0, 1, 2, \dots, 2^8$$

since the X_i values are scaled (shifted) by 2^8 in register Dx. The index X_i and the values in the table have the relationship shown in Table 7.13.

Finally, Equation 7.1 reduces to the following

$$Y = \frac{(F_{(n+1)} - F_n) \times (Dx)[7:0]}{256} + F_n \tag{7.2}$$

which represents the operation performed by the TBLS and TBLU instructions. The range of the dependent variable for TBLS is the signed value

$$-2^{(m-1)} \le Y \le 2^{(m-1)} - 1$$

whereas the unsigned range for TBLU is

$$0 \le Y \le 2^m - 1$$

where $m = 8, 16,$ or 32 for byte, word, or longword table entries, respectively. For these instructions, the condition code bits C and V are cleared to {0}. N and Z are set

Table 7.13 Correspondence
Between X Values and $F(X)$

Index	X value	Function value
0	0	F_0
1	256	F_1
2	512	F_2
3	768	F_3
.	.	.
.	.	.
.	.	.
n	$n \times 2^8$	F_n
.	.	.
.	.	.
.	.	.
255	65280	F_{255}
256	65536	F_{256}

or cleared as for any arithmetic operation. No indication of any error arising from interpolation is given. Therefore, careful analysis of the possible errors is recommended before interpolation is attempted. Equation 7.2 represents the rounded result of linear interpolation. The instructions that leave the results unrounded are discussed shortly.

Example 7.15

One use of the Table Look-up and Interpolate instructions is to compress a table of values so that fewer than $2^{16} + 1$ (65537) points of a function may be stored. This can result in a considerable saving of memory space if the accuracy of the interpolated values is sufficient for an application. To accomplish the compression, the independent variable must be scaled.

As an example, assume that the function

$$y = ax + bx^2$$

for $0 \leq x \leq 16$ represents the decimal voltage value of a variable being measured. For this example, the digital output in binary of a 16-bit A/D converter with the voltage range of 0 to 16 volts is to be converted to engineering units using the function given. Assume that the functional value representing the physical variable being measured can be written in the scaled form

$$Y = 128X + X^2 = F(X)$$

where $0 \leq X < 16$ volts. This function is highly linear over the range of interest. Therefore, it is decided to store only 17 values in the interpolation table. Points in between will be interpolated with the TBLU instruction.

The corresponding A/D converter output is a 16-bit binary value. For convenience, the output is listed here as a hexadecimal integer value in the range $0 \leq \$X \leq FFFF_{16}$. The A/D converter can thus output 65536 (2^{16}) values for an input voltage between 0 and 16 volts. The independent variable for the TBLU instruction is determined directly by the A/D converter reading so that only 17 values of $F(X)$ need be stored. The correspondence is given in Table 7.14. In the table, X ($0 \leq X < 16$) is the decimal voltage being converted by the A/D converter. The corresponding hexadecimal value output by the A/D converter is given as $\$X_i$. For example, an input voltage of 1V results in a converted value of $\$1000$. The functional value is

$$Y = 128 \times 1 + 1^2 = 129\ (\$0081).$$

The value $\$10000$ cannot be output by the A/D converter but it represents one count more than the maximum output of $\$FFFF$ which is necessary to complete the table.

Table 7.14 Scaled Table Entries for $Y = aX + bX^2$

X(volts)	$\$X_i$(Hex)	$F(\$X_i)$
0	$ 0000	$0000
1	$1000	$0081
2	$2000	$0104
3	$3000	$0189
4	$4000	$0210
5	$5000	$0299
6	$6000	$0324
7	$7000	$03B1
8	$8000	$0440
9	$9000	$04D1
10	$A000	$0564
11	$B000	$05F9
12	$C000	$0690
13	$D000	$0729
14	$E000	$07C4
15	$F000	$0861
16	$10000	$0900

In terms of the output of the A/D converter, the value of $F(\$X_i)$ in Table 7.14 is computed as

$$F(\$X_i) = \$80 \times (\$X_i/2^{12}) + (\$X_i/2^{12})^2$$

to form the third column of the table. These values are stored in memory for interpolation. The values actually represents a scaling by 2^4 since only the upper 8 bits of (Dx)[W] are used to determine the points in the table.

An example point is $\$X_i = \$1800$ corresponding to an analog voltage of 1.5V. The A/D output is used to interpolate between F_1 and F_2 in the table since the value of $\$X_i$ for a $2^k + 1$ entry table must be scaled by $2^{-(8-k)}$. The scale factor for $\$X_i$ in this case is 2^{-4}. Thus, the value $\$1800$ is scaled to $\$1800 \times 2^{-4}$ or 180_{16}. The results of the interpolation using TBLU is one of the 256 values between each two entries in the interpolation table.

According to Equation 7.2, the interpolated value with an input of 1.5V becomes

$$F(\$X_i) = \frac{(\$104 - \$81) \times \$80}{\$100} + \$81 = \$C3$$

or a decimal value of 195 ($\$C3$) rounded up to the nearest integer.

```
abs.    LC    obj. code   source line
----    ----  ----------  -----------
   1    0000                        TTL     'FIGURE 7.19'
   2    8000                        ORG     $8000
   3    0000              *
   4    8000              *   INTERPOLATE IN A TABLE OF VALUES
   5    8000              *     THE VALUES ARE UNSIGNED 16-BIT INTEGERS
   6    8000              *
   7    8000              *   INPUTS   :   (A0).L  ADDRESS OF TABLE
   8    8000              *                (D0).W  VALUE OF X
   9    8000              *
  10    8000              *   OUTPUTS  :   (D0).W  INTERPOLATED VALUE
  11    8000              *
  12    8000 E848         INTPLU  LSR.W   #4,D0       ;SCALE INPUT
  13    8002 F810 0140            TBLU.W  (A0),D0     ;INTERPOLATE IN TABLE
  14    8006 4E75                 RTS
  15    8008                      END
```

Figure 7.19 Program example of interpolation.

Figure 7.19 is a subroutine to interpolate the values in Table 7.14. On entry, (A0)[L] contains the starting address of the table. D0[W] contains the independent value X_i used for interpolation. The interpolated value is returned in (D0)[W].

Errors and unrounded results using TBLSN and TBLUN.   The most common method of interpolation uses an *interpolating polynomial* to determine the function values between tabulated values. The interpolating polynomial can be written as

$$P_N(X) = a_0 X^N + a_1 X^{(N-1)} + \cdots + a_N \tag{7.3}$$

with $1 \le i \le N$. At the values of the table entries,

$$P_N(X_i) = F(X_i)$$

where $F(X_i)$ are the table entries for $0 \le i \le N$. Although, the Nth degree polynomial passes through the points in the table, no information is available about the value of $P_N(X)$ between the table entries unless further assumptions are made.

The CPU32 instructions for interpolation use *linear interpolation* as defined in Equation 7.2 for the TBLS and TBLU instructions. Intuitively, the error made by fitting a straight line between the points in the table should not be too great as long as the points are close together even if the actual function $F(X)$ is highly non-linear. The error made by approximating $F(X)$ by a series of straight lines between the table entries is called the *truncation* error because the Nth degree polynomial in Equation 7.3 is replaced or "truncated" to the linear function $P_1(X)$ in each interval between the tabulated values. The maximum error can be calculated if the second derivative of the function being interpolated is known. Exercise 7.7.3 gives an example of this error calculation.

The assumption that only truncation error affects the result implies that the calculation of $P_1(X)$ is made without error, i.e. that no round-off error occurs in intermediate calculations. Another assumption is that the tabulated values $F(X_i)$ are exact. To reduce round-off error when several interpolated values are used to compute a final result, the instructions TBLSN and TBLUN can be used.

Table 7.15 Function of Two Variables

X	$Y = Y_0$	$Y = Y_1$	$\cdots$	$Y = Y_M$
X_0	$F(X_0, Y_0)$	$F(X_0, Y_1)$	$\cdots$	$F(X_0, Y_M)$
X_1	$F(X_1, Y_0)$	$F(X_1, Y_1)$	$\cdots$	$F(X_1, Y_M)$
$\cdot$	$\cdot$	$\cdot$	$\cdot$	$\cdot$
$\cdots$	$\cdot$	$\cdot$	$\cdot$	$\cdot$
$\cdot$	$\cdot$	$\cdot$	$\cdot$	$\cdot$
X_N	$F(X_N, Y_0)$	$F(X_N, Y_1)$	$\cdots$	$F(X_N, Y_M)$

The instructions TBLSN and TBLUN described in Table 7.12 compute the un-rounded value

$$Y = (F_{(n+1)} - F_n) \times (\text{Dx})[7:0] + 256 \times F_n \tag{7.4}$$

which is returned in $(\text{Dx})[31:0]$ for any size operand. Comparing Equation 7.4 with Equation 7.2, the result of the unrounded interpolation contains a fractional part in $(\text{Dx})[7:0]$. An unsigned byte or word result is zero-extended to fill $(\text{Dx})[31:8]$. A signed byte or word result is sign-extended to 32 bits. Notice that when a longword operand is specified, only 24 significant bits are used for the integer part. Thus, an overflow can occur if the integer result of an unrounded, signed operation exceeds 24 bits (-2^{23} to $+2^{23} - 1$ in value). When the interpolations are completed, the result should be shifted right 8 places and rounded if necessary. The reader is referred to the *CPU32 Reference Manual* for more information and examples of use of the TBLSN and TBLSU instructions.

7.7.2 Interpolation in Tables of Two Variables

Consider the function of two variables in the form

$$Z = F(X_i, Y_j), \quad 0 \le i \le N \text{ and } 0 \le j \le M$$

which in tabulated form is a table of $M \times N$ entries. The function could be stored by columns in memory where each column represents the value of $F(X_i, Y_k)$ for a given value of Y_k as shown in Table 7.15. The simplest interpolation method is to interpolate twice using separate one-dimensional interpolation for each of the variables. The two interpolated values are then themselves used to perform a "surface" interpolation.

The CPU32 instructions TBLU, TBLUN, TBLS and TBLSN can be used for two-dimensional interpolation. The formats of these instructions for this purpose are shown in Table 7.16. In their typical application to two-dimensional interpolation it is assumed that the source register <Dym> contains one interpolated value and register <Dyn> contains the other interpolated value from one-dimensional interpolations. Before execution, the register <Dx> contains the fraction for interpolation between the value in the two registers. This is held in $(\text{Dx})[7:0]$. No integer part is necessary since the function values are held in the two source registers. The result in $(\text{Dx})[<1>]$ for TBLS and TBLU is given by Equation 7.2. The unrounded results for TBLSN and TBLUN is defined by Equation 7.4. As with any form of the instructions for unrounded signed operands, a result has a fractional value in $(\text{Dx})[7:0]$ and the sign-extended results in $(\text{Dx})[31:8]$.

Table 7.16 TBLxx Instructions for Functions of Two Variables

Syntax	Operation
Signed values in table:	
TBLS.<l> <Dym> : <Dyn>, Dx	(Dx) ← interpolated value; rounded
TBLSN.<l> <Dym> : <Dyn>, Dx	(Dx) ← interpolated value; unrounded
Unsigned values in table:	
TBLU.<l> <Dym> : <Dyn>, Dx	(Dx) ← interpolated value; rounded
TBLUN.<l> <Dym> : <Dyn>, Dx	(Dx) ← interpolated value; unrounded

Notes:

1. <l> = B, W or L defines the size of the dependent variable in the table.
2. <Dyn> and <Dym> contain the function values used for interpolation.
3. (Dx)[7:0] contains the fractional portion of the independent variable before any instruction is executed.
4. For the TBLS and TBLU instructions, (Dx)[<l>] contains the interpolated value after execution.
5. For the TBLSN and TBLUN instructions, (Dx)[7:0] holds the fractional part of the result after execution. (Dx)[31:8] holds the sign-extended integer result for TBLSN or the zero-extended integer result for TBLUN.
6. Condition codes:

X	–	not affected
C	–	always cleared
N,Z	–	set according to the result
V	–	set if the integer portion of an unrounded long result is not in the range -2^{23} to $2^{23} - 1$.

Example 7.16

Figure 7.20 is a subroutine to perform a two-dimensional interpolation on two tables of values whose entries are word-length. In the case of a function of the form shown in Table 7.15, the contents of A0 and A1 would be the addresses of two consecutive columns (or rows), respectively. The subroutine performs interpolation at the same fractional distance between two entries for both columns (or rows) of a two dimensional table.

Since the table entries are word length, the TBLS instruction should be a long (32-bit) operation to accommodate the 16-bit integer portion and the 8-bit fraction. The result is sign-extended into (D2)[31:0]. Shifting right by 8 places right justifies the integer portion. If the last bit shifted off is a {0}, no rounding is necessary since the fraction is less than 1/2 in value. If this bit were a {1}, the subroutine adds 1 to the integer result to round up to the nearest integer.

EXERCISES

7.7.1. Using linear interpolation, find the sine of 45° from the values sin(30°) and sin(60°) with three decimal place accuracy. Compute the error and the percentage error between the interpolated value and the "correct" value which is taken to be

$$\sin(45°) = 0.707.$$

```
abs.   LC    obj. code    source line
----   ----  ----------   -----------
   1   0000                        TTL      'FIGURE 7.20'
   2   8000                        ORG      $8000
   3   0000              *
   4   8000              *         TWO-DIMENSIONAL INTERPOLATION ROUTINE
   5   8000              *
   6   8000              *         INPUTS : (A0).L = ADDRESS OF FIRST TABLE
   7   8000              *                  (A1).L = ADDRESS OF SECOND TABLE
   8   8000              *                  (D0).W = VALUE FOR EACH LINEAR
   9   8000              *                           INTERPOLATION
  10   8000              *                  (D2).W = 8-BIT FRACTION FOR SURFACE
  11   8000              *                           INTERPOLATION
  12   8000              *
  13   8000              *         OUTPUT : (D2).L = VALUE FOR SURFACE
  14   8000              *                           INTERPOLATION
  15   8000              *
  16   8000 3200         TWODINT MOVE.W    D0,D1      ;ENTRY NUMBER AND FRACTION
  17   8002 F810 0D40            TBLSN.W   (A0),D0    ;LINEAR INTERPOLATION
  18   8006 F811 1D40            TBLSN.W   (A1),D1    ;LINEAR INTERPOLATION
  19   800A F800 2881            TBLS.L    D0:D1,D2   ;SURFACE INTERPOLATION
  20   800E E082               ASR.L     #8,D2      ;FORM AN INTEGER AND
  21   8010 6402               BCC.S     RTN        ; ROUND UP
  22   8012 5242               ADDQ.W    #1,D2
  23   8014 4E75       RTN     RTS
  24   8016                    END
```

Figure 7.20 Routine for two-dimensional interpolation.

7.7.2. Find the value of sin(24°38′) given the following values:

$$sin(24°30') = 0.41469$$

$$sin(24°40') = 0.41734$$

using linear interpolation and rounding all calculations to three decimal places. Compute the error and the percentage error if the correct answer is assumed to be 0.41681.

7.7.3. Henrici's textbook cited in the Further Reading section of this chapter gives the maximum predicted error in linear interpolation as

$$\frac{1}{8}h^2 \times M$$

where M is the maximum of the 2nd derivative of the function being interpolated in the range of interest and h is the distance between the independent variables defining the points used for the interpolation. What are the maximum errors expected in Exercise 7.7.1 and Exercise 7.7.2 using radian values for the independent variables? Notice that the interpolation error dominates in Exercise 7.7.1 but the round off error from the intermediate steps caused a greater error than predicted in Exercise 7.7.2.

7.7.4. Write a subroutine to generate the values in Table 7.14 using the function given in Example 7.15. Then interpolate at the following points:
(a) $1800;
(b) $A00F;
(c) $FFFF.

These values are from the 16-bit A/D converter. Define the resolution and the maximum error for the interpolation.

7.7.5. Write a routine to create a table of 17 byte-length entries for the function

$$Y = 2^4 X, \quad 0 \le X \le 8$$

and

$$Y = 128 - 2^4(X - 8), \quad 8 \le X \le 16$$

for the range of X from 0 to 16. Find the function value in $X = 11.8125$ using the TBLU instruction.

7.7.6. Write a subroutine to generate a table of values for the two-dimensional function

$$F(X_i, Y_j) = 128X_i + 128Y_j$$

where $0 \le i \le 4$ and $0 \le j \le 4$. Using interpolation, find F(1.5,1.5).

FURTHER READING

Knuth's volume on seminumerical algorithms contains a number of useful algorithms and other information for those doing sophisticated mathematical programming. The textbook by Stein and Munro presents the rigorous basis for machine arithmetic.

Interpolation is treated in the textbook by Henrici. He also gives a thorough discussion of the errors involved in polynomial interpolation. Kunz describes both one-dimensional interpolation and interpolation in tables of two or more variables.

HENRICI, PETER, *Elements of Numerical Analysis*. New York, NY.: Wiley, 1964.

KNUTH, DONALD E., *The Art of Computer Programming, Vol. 2: Seminumerical Algorithms*. Reading, Mass.: Addison-Wesley, 1968.

KUNZ, KAISER S., *Numerical Analysis*. New York, NY.: McGraw-Hill, 1957.

STEIN, MARVIN L., and WILLIAM D. MUNRO, *Introduction to Machine Arithmetic*. Reading, Mass.: Addison-Wesley, 1971.

8

Logical and Bit Operations

This chapter introduces three new categories of CPU32 instructions: logical instructions, shift and rotate instructions, and bit-manipulation instructions. The *logical operations* treat an operand as a collection of separate logical variables. This category includes the instructions AND, OR, EOR (Exclusive OR), and NOT. The second category includes the instructions ASL, ASR, LSL, and LSR to *shift* the bits within an operand. Both arithmetic shifts and logical shifts are provided. The instructions ROL, ROR, ROXL, and ROXR rotate the bits of an operand in a cyclic fashion.

Instructions for *bit manipulation* form a separate category of instructions for the CPU32. Separate instructions are provided to test, set to {1}, clear to {0}, and change an individual bit within an operand. In order, they have the mnemonics BTST, BSET, BCLR, and BCHG. Two other instructions show the result of a conditional test by modifying an indicator variable called a flag. They are the Scc (Set According to Condition) and the TAS (Test and Set) instructions.

Logical and bit manipulation instructions are of considerable use when individual bits are to be manipulated. The bits of interest often are part of a larger data structure such as a status word, a string of characters or a bit map. When the data structure is not conveniently divided into byte, word, or longword entities, the instructions presented in this chapter can simplify programming and decrease the execution time of routines that must manipulate logical variables or strings of bits.

Other instructions that might fall in the categories discussed in this chapter have been presented previously. For example, execution of the SWAP instruction described in Subsection 6.1.4 is equivalent to a 16-bit rotation. The TST instruction described in Subsection 6.2.3 tests an operand for zero and changes the conditions code bits according to the result.

Table 8.1 Results of Logical Operations

x	y	NOT x	x AND y	x OR y	x EOR y
0	0	1	0	0	0
0	1	1	0	1	1
1	0	0	0	1	1
1	1	0	1	1	0

Note:
x and y are logical variables. The results for each operation are defined by the "truth" table for the operation. For example, (x OR y) is true or {1} if either x or y or both is {1}.

8.1 LOGICAL OPERATIONS

In some applications, it is convenient to treat each bit in an operand as an individual logical variable. The condition code register, for example, contains five independent bits and the bits may be tested singly.[1] Each logical variable has only two possible states, which are defined variously according to the application as TRUE or FALSE, ON or OFF, {1} or {0}, among other possibilities. Therefore, the m-bit computer word holds m logical variables. In the CPU32, logical instructions may operate on 8, 16, or 32 such variables simultaneously.

If x and y are considered to be logical variables, the truth tables of Table 8.1 define the operations that correspond to CPU32 logical arithmetic. A collection of m logical variables is written in positional notation

$$(x_{m-1}x_{m-2}\cdots x_0)$$

as it would be stored in an m-bit word. This is called an m-tuple of variables. For example, the CPU32 instruction

> NOT.W   X

will complement each bit of an operand containing 16 logical variables, in the memory location addressed by X. The other CPU32 logical instructions perform their operations between the logical variables in the source location and those in the destination. The result is stored in the destination location. Thus, the operation

> AND.W   D1, D2

leaves the results of the operation between 16 variables in D1 and 16 variables in D2 in the low-order word of D2. The operation performed is

$$(D2)[15\!:\!0] \leftarrow (D2)[15\!:\!0] \text{ AND } (D1)[15\!:\!0].$$

---

[1] Condition Code register (CCR) described previously in Section 4.2 refers to the low-order byte of the Status Register, $(SR)[7\!:\!0]$.

The logical instructions are listed in Table 8.2, which shows the assembler syntax and addressing modes for each instruction. The instructions with suffix "I" allow only an immediate value for the source operand. None of the instructions operate on address registers. Also, no memory-to-memory operations are possible with the AND, EOR, and OR instructions. The condition code bits C and V are always cleared after any logical operation and the N and Z bits are set according to the result. The Z bit would be set to {1} if the result is all zeros. The N bit is set to {1} if the most significant bit of the result is a {1}.

Table 8.2 Instructions for Logical Operations

Syntax		Addressing modes	
		Source	Destination
Logical AND			
AND.<l>	<EA>, <Dn>	Data	<Dn>
AND.<l>	<Dn>, <EA>	<Dn>	Memory alterable
ANDI.<l>	#<d>, <EA>	<d>	Data alterable
Logical OR			
OR.<l>	<EA>, <Dn>	Data	<Dn>
OR.<l>	<Dn>, <EA>	<Dn>	Memory alterable
ORI.<l>	#<d>, <EA>	<d>	Data alterable
Exclusive OR			
EOR.<l>	<Dn>, <EA>	<Dn>	Data alterable
EORI.<l>	#<d>, <EA>	<d>	Data alterable
NOT			
NOT.<l>	<EA>	—	Data alterable

Notes:
1. <l> denotes B, W, or L.
2. <d> is an 8-, 16-, or 32-bit logical variable as an immediate value.
3. The condition code bits C and V are always cleared; N and Z are set according to the result.
4. The destination location is modified according to the result.

The AND and OR instructions allow the same addressing modes for their operands. For either instruction, if the destination is a data register, the source operand is addressed by any data mode. This allows all the source addressing modes except address register direct addressing. Alternatively, if Dn contains the source operand, the destination must be addressed by a memory-alterable mode. Thus, only register direct and program counter relative addressing are prohibited for the destination.

The ANDI and ORI instructions use an immediate value as the source operand and any data-alterable location for the destination. For example, the instruction

    ANDI.W   #$000F, D1

clears all but the low-order 4 bits of D1. This instruction might be used to isolate a single BCD digit for subsequent mathematical calculations, for example. If the operand is held in memory, it may be addressed by all the addressing modes except PC relative.

The EOR (Exclusive OR) instruction has slightly different addressing restrictions not conforming to the requirements for AND and OR. It requires a data register for the source location. Also, the destination must be a data-alterable location, as was the case for both ANDI and ORI. The immediate form, EORI, has the same addressing requirements for the destination operand. It is used to perform the Exclusive OR between an immediate value and an operand in either a data register or in memory. Clearly, the regularity in addressing of most CPU32 instructions is missing among its logical instructions to some extent.

The NOT instruction complements each bit of an operand in a data register or in memory using any type of memory addressing except PC relative. The NOT can be interpreted as either forming the logical NOT, if the operand is composed of m logical variables, or the one's complement, if the operand is considered to be a number. The mathematical description of the one's-complement operation was given in Chapter 3.

System control using logical instructions. The immediate forms of the instructions ANDI, EORI, and ORI can reference the Status Register or the condition code register as the destination operand. These forms are usually used for system control as discussed in Chapter 10. The reader is referred to that chapter for a complete discussion.

Example 8.1

Table 8.3 shows several examples of logical instructions operating on various operands. For simplicity, the examples limit the operand length to 8 bits and show only immediate-to-register or register-to-register operations. Before each instruction executes, the low-order byte of D1 contains the value {1101 0001}, which represents eight logical variables. Similarly, (D2)[7:0] = {1101 0101} initially.

Table 8.3 Examples of Logical Operations

Instruction	Operands	Result
ANDI.B #$F0, D1	{1111 0000} {1101 0001}	(D1)[7:0] = {1101 0000}
ORI.B #03, D1	{0000 0011} {1101 0001}	(D1)[7:0] = {1101 0011}
NOT.B D1	{1101 0001}	(D1)[7:0] = {0010 1110}
EOR.B D1, D2	{1101 0001} {1101 0101}	(D2)[7:0] = {0000 0100}

Note:
(D1)[7:0] = {1101 0001} and (D2)[7:0] = {1101 0101} before each instruction executes.

The ANDI instruction, as used in the example, serves to "mask" (clear) the low-order 4 bits of D1. The ORI instruction does the opposite by setting the designated bits (bits 0 and 1) to {1} and leaving the other bits in the destination unchanged. After either of these instructions execute, condition code bit N would be set to {1} in the examples shown.

The NOT instruction inverts the low-order 8 bits of D1. If the original value in D1 is interpreted as the decimal number -46 in 8-bit, one's-complement notation, the inversion produces $+46$, as expected.

The Exclusive OR (EOR) instruction causes a logical variable in the result to be set to $\{1\}$ when the two variables in the corresponding bit positions of the operands are different. For example, if D1 contains the first reading of 8 status bits taken from an external device and D2 contains a second reading taken later, any change in status would be indicated by a nonzero result ($Z = \{0\}$) after the EOR operation. If the readings had been the same, the result would have been all zeros with $Z = \{1\}$. A conditional branch instruction such as BEQ or BNE could be used after the EOR instruction to determine the subsequent program path.

Example 8.2

To illustrate the use of logical instructions with various addressing modes, the example subroutine of Figure 8.1 implements the equations for a "two-line to four-line decoder" using CPU32 instructions. One of four possible output values is determined by the value of two input variables. The input variables are two logical variables, designated as A and B in the example. They are stored in memory in two consecutive bytes with A first and are addressed by A1.

The output is to be four variables designated $Y0$, $Y1$, $Y2$, and $Y3$ stored in four consecutive bytes addressed by A2. All the logical variables are right-justified in their locations. That is, the variable $\{A\}$ has the memory representation $\{0000\ 000A\}$. The truth table and the equations are shown in Table 8.4, which shows that only one output can be $\{0\}$ for each pair of inputs. If A and B together are interpreted as a two-digit binary number, $\{BA\}$, then $Yn = \{0\}$ when the value of the input is n, for $n = 0, 1, 2$, or 3. All the other output variables are $\{1\}$. Hence the output line corresponding to the value of the inputs is selected. In this case, the selected line is considered "TRUE" or "ON" when its value is $\{0\}$.

The subroutine in Figure 8.1 first transfers A and B to the low-order bytes of D0 and D1, respectively. The complement of each input is then formed in the low-order bit of another register. Each equation for Yn is coded in a straightforward way for clarity using the FORTRAN notation for the logical results. The computed result is stored in memory using the appropriate displacement from the base address held in A2.

Table 8.4 Truth Table for Decoder

Input		Output			
B	A	$Y0$	$Y1$	$Y2$	$Y3$
0	0	0	1	1	1
0	1	1	0	1	1
1	0	1	1	0	1
1	1	1	1	1	0

Notes:
$Y0 = $ NOT (NOT A AND NOT B) $= A$ OR B
$Y1 = $ NOT (A AND NOT B) $= $ NOT A OR B
$Y2 = $ NOT (NOT A AND B) $= A$ OR NOT B
$Y3 = $ NOT (A AND B) $= $ NOT A OR NOT B

```
abs.   LC   obj. code    source line
----   ----  ----------    -----------
   1  0000                           TTL     'FIGURE 8.1'
   2  0000                           LLEN    100
   3  8000                           ORG     $8000
   4  0000              *
   5  8000              *  2 TO 4 LINE DECODER
   6  8000              *  INPUT  : (A1.L) = ADDRESS OF 2 BYTES CONTAINING LOGICAL
   7  8000              *                     VARIABLES
   8  8000              *            (A2.L) = ADDRESS OF 4 BYTES FOR DECODED VALUES
   9  8000              *  OUTPUT : 4 BYTES DECODED INTO LOCATION  POINTED TO
  10  8000              *                     BY (A2)
  11  8000              *
  12  8000              *  NOTE :   LOGICAL VARIABLES ARE STORED IN THE LS BIT
  13  8000              *                     OF THE BYTE
  14  8000              *
  15       0000 0000    A       EQU     0
  16       0000 0001    B       EQU     1
  17       0000 0000    Y0      EQU     0
  18       0000 0001    Y1      EQU     1
  19       0000 0002    Y2      EQU     2
  20       0000 0003    Y3      EQU     3
  21  8000              *
  22  8000 48E7 F800    DECODER MOVEM.L D0-D4,-(SP)  ;SAVE REGISTERS
  23  8004              *
  24  8004 1011                 MOVE.B  A(A1),D0      ;GET A
  25  8006 1229 0001            MOVE.B  B(A1),D1      ;GET B
  26  800A              *
  27  800A 1400                 MOVE.B  D0,D2
  28  800C 4602                 NOT.B   D2
  29  800E 0202 0001            ANDI.B  #01,D2        ;COMPLEMENT OF A
  30  8012              *
  31  8012 1601                 MOVE.B  D1,D3
  32  8014 4603                 NOT.B   D3
  33  8016 0203 0001            ANDI.B  #01,D3        ;COMPLEMENT OF B
  34  801A              *
  35  801A 1800                 MOVE.B  D0,D4
  36  801C 8801                 OR.B    D1,D4
  37  801E 1484                 MOVE.B  D4,Y0(A2)     ;A .OR. B
  38  8020              *
  39  8020 1802                 MOVE.B  D2,D4
  40  8022 8801                 OR.B    D1,D4
  41  8024 1544 0001            MOVE.B  D4,Y1(A2)     ;NOT A .OR. B
  42  8028              *
  43  8028 1800                 MOVE.B  D0,D4
  44  802A 8803                 OR.B    D3,D4
  45  802C 1544 0002            MOVE.B  D4,Y2(A2)     ;A .OR. NOT B
  46  8030              *
  47  8030 8602                 OR.B    D2,D3
  48  8032 1543 0003            MOVE.B  D3,Y3(A2)     ;NOT A .OR. NOT B
  49  8036              *
  50  8036 4CDF 001F            MOVEM.L (SP)+,D0-D4  ;RESTORE REGISTERS
  51  803A 4E75                 RTS
  52  803C                      END
```

Figure 8.1 Program for a two-line to four-line decoder.

EXERCISES

8.1.1. Write a simple subroutine to convert ASCII values to the corresponding BCD representation, and vice versa, using logical instructions. The conversion was discussed in Chapter 7.

8.1.2. Improve the decoder program used as an example in this section. Make the program more general to allow four-line to 16-line decoding.

8.1.3. Write a subroutine to exchange the contents of two m-bit words in memory using only the EOR instruction and appropriate data transfer instructions.

8.2 SHIFT AND ROTATE INSTRUCTIONS

The shift and rotate instructions of the CPU32 move the bits in an operand to the right or left a designated number of places. The three different possibilities provided include:
(a) arithmetic shifts;
(b) logical shifts;
(c) rotates.

Arithmetic shifts to the left in effect multiply a signed binary integer by a power of 2. Arithmetic right shifts accomplish division by powers of 2. Of course, the shifted number must be within a valid range or the result is in error. Logical shifts are used to shift an m-tuple of logical variables right or left. The rotate instructions cause bits shifted off one end of the m-tuple to reappear at the other end in a *cyclic* shift.

Instruction	Operand Syntax	Operand Size	Operation
ASL	Dn,Dn #⟨data⟩,Dn ⟨ea⟩	8, 16, 32 8, 16, 32 16	 X/C ← ⟵ ← 0
ASR	Dn,Dn #⟨data⟩,Dn ⟨ea⟩	8, 16, 32 8, 16, 32 16	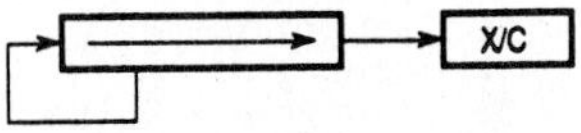 → → X/C
LSL	Dn,Dn #⟨data⟩,Dn ⟨ea⟩	8, 16, 32 8, 16, 32 16	 X/C ← ⟵ ← 0
LSR	Dn,Dn #⟨data⟩,Dn ⟨ea⟩	8, 16, 32 8, 16, 32 16	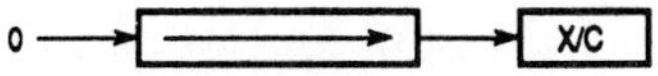 0 → → X/C
ROL	Dn,Dn #⟨data⟩,Dn ⟨ea⟩	8, 16, 32 8, 16, 32 16	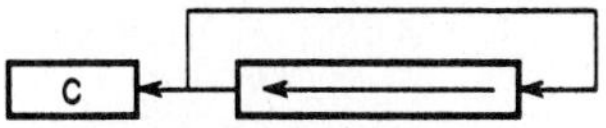 C ← ⟵ ←
ROR	Dn,Dn #⟨data⟩,Dn ⟨ea⟩	8, 16, 32 8, 16, 32 16	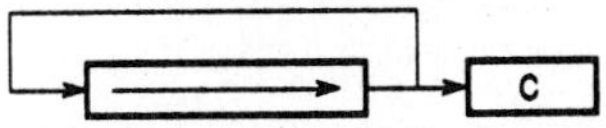 → → C
ROXL	Dn,Dn #⟨data⟩,Dn ⟨ea⟩	8, 16, 32 8, 16, 32 16	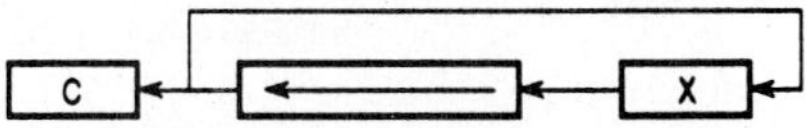 C ← ⟵ ← X ←
ROXR	Dn,Dn #⟨data⟩,Dn ⟨ea⟩	8, 16, 32 8, 16, 32 16	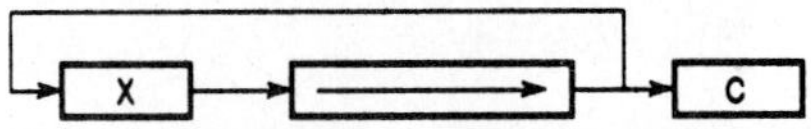 → X → → C
SWAP	Dn	16	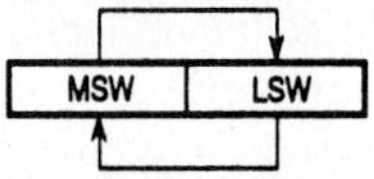 MSW LSW

Figure 8.2 Shift and rotate instructions.

Figure 8.2 shows the operation of the arithmetic shifts (ASL, ASR), the logical shifts (LSL, LSR), and the rotate instructions (ROL, ROR). The rotate instructions

Logical and Bit Operations   Chap. 8

have extended variations for shifting multiple-precision operands. The instructions ROXL and ROXR include the X bit in the cyclic shift. Table 8.5 presents the assembler language syntax for the instructions discussed in this chapter. The SWAP instruction was discussed previously in Subsection 6.1.4.

Table 8.5 Assembly-Language Syntax for Shift and Rotate Instructions

Arithmetic shift left		Arithmetic shift right	
ASL.<l>	<Dm>,<Dn>	ASR.<l>	<Dm>,<Dn>
ASL.<l>	#<d>,<Dn>	ASR.<l>	#<d>,<Dn>
ASL.<l>	<EA>	ASR.<l>	<EA>
Logical shift left		**Logical shift right**	
LSL.<l>	<Dm>,<Dn>	LSR.<l>	<Dm>,<Dn>
LSL.<l>	#<d>,<Dn>	LSR.<l>	#<d>,<Dn>
LSL.<l>	<EA>	LSR.<l>	<EA>
Rotate left		**Rotate right**	
ROL.<l>	<Dm>,<Dn>	ROR.<l>	<Dm>,<Dn>
ROL.<l>	#<d>,<Dn>	ROR.<l>	#<d>,<Dn>
ROL.<l>	<EA>	ROR.<l>	<EA>

Notes:
1. <l> denotes B, W, or L when <Dn> is the destination; <Dm> or #<d> specifies the shift count.
2. When the destination (<EA>) is a memory location, only single shifts or rotates of word-length operands are allowed.
3. Since only memory-alterable addressing modes are allowed for <EA>, register direct and PC relative addresses are excluded.
4. ROXL and ROXR have the same syntax as the rotate instructions.
5. Condition code bits N and Z are set according to the result; V is cleared except by ASL.

Three different formats are available to designate the shift or rotate count and the operand to be shifted. Table 8.6 shows the possibilities. For operands held in a data register, the count can also be held in a register with a range of 0–63 or specified as an immediate value with a range of 1–8. Only a *one-bit* shift or rotate of an word-length operand in memory is allowed.

As an example, the instruction

> LSR.W   D3, D2

shifts the 16-bit operand in the low-order word of D2 to the right by the number of places designated in D3. The number in D3 is treated as modulo 64, so shifts from 0 to 63 places are possible. Of course, after 16 logical shifts left or right in a word-length operand, the value left in the low-order word contains all zero bits. The instruction

> LSL.W   #5, D3

Table 8.6 Operand Formats for Shifts and Rotate

Operand format	Shift count	Destination
<Dm>,<Dn>	(Dm); range 0-63	(Dn)[l]
#<d>,<Dn>	#<d>; range 1-8	(Dn)[l]
<EA>	1	(EA)[15:0]

Notes:
1. the length is B, W, or L for register operands.
2. [l] indicates corresponding bits in the operation.
3. <EA> is a memory-alterable address of a wordlength operand.
4. A shift count of zero in Dm has a special meaning.

performs a left, logical shift of the low-order word of D3 by five places. An immediate shift length can range from 1 to 8.

The third form of specifying operands allows a word-length operand in memory to be shifted or rotated one place at a time. Any operand referenced by a memory-alterable addressing mode may be manipulated. For example, the instruction

ASR.W   (A2)

performs a single-place, right arithmetic shift on the 16-bit operand addressed by A2.

A shift instruction using the shift count held in the data register performs *dynamic shifting* since the shift count may be changed under program control. A shift count of zero will affect only the condition codes, as shown in Appendix IV. For a nonzero shift count, the arithmetic and logical shifts preserve the last bit shifted off in the C and X bits. The rotate instructions affect only the C bit. Rotate with extend operations shift the previous value of the X bit into one end of the operand while saving the latest value rotated out the other end in the C and X bits.

After any shift or rotate operation, the N and Z condition codes are set according to the result, just as they were set for the arithmetic operations. The overflow condition code V is set to {0} after every operation except an arithmetic left shift. The ASL instruction multiplies the operand by 2^r if it is shifted r bits left. If the result exceeds the numerical range of a signed m-bit operand, V set to {1} indicates an out-of-range condition.

If an unsigned number is shifted one bit left to multiply by 2, the carry bit C being set to {1} indicates an overflow after an ASL or LSL instruction shifts the operand.

Example 8.3

Several shift and rotate instructions are shown in Table 8.7. The results shown in the table assume that the low-order byte of D1 contained the binary value {1110 0101} and that the X bit was {0} before each instruction was executed.

In the case of the ASR instruction, the sign bit is extended to the right at each shift. The original number was -27 in two's-complement notation. It becomes -14 and then -7 after successive shifts, thus simulating integer division by 2 each time. Note that -14, however, is not the expected result of the integer division of -27 by 2. Use of the DIVS instructions would result in a quotient of -13 and a remainder of -1. This truncation in the wrong direction will occur whenever an odd, negative integer is shifted to the right.

The LSL instruction, with a shift count of 4, shifts the low-order 4 bits of the byte to the upper 4 bits. The N condition code bit would be set to {0} to indicate that the most significant bit is zero. Rotating a byte four places to the right with the ROR instruction swaps 4 bits and leaves each unchanged. Rotating the original value with X = {0} one place to the right with the ROXR instruction causes a zero to be shifted into the most significant bit. The bit shifted off the right end is saved in both C and X. Notice from Figure 8.2 that if X = {1} before the ROXR executed, the most significant bit of the operand would become {1}.

Table 8.7 Examples of Shift and Rotate Operations

Instruction	Before (D1)[7:0]	After (D1)[7:0]	C	X
ASR.B #2, D1	{1110 0101}	{1111 1001}	0	0
LSL.B #4, D1	{1110 0101}	{0101 0000}	0	0
ROR.B #4, D1	{1110 0101}	{0101 1110}	0	–
ROXR.B #1, D1	{1110 0101}	{0111 0010}	1	1

Note:
X = {0} before each instruction executes.

Example 8.4

The subroutine shown in Figure 8.3 multiplies the 32-bit positive integer in D4 by a positive power of 2. The value specified in data register D1 must be greater than zero. The number is passed to the subroutine in D4 and the 64-bit result is held in registers D5 and D4. If the result causes a carry out of D5, the low-order byte of D2 is set to -1 to indicate the overflow. Otherwise, the error flag in D2 is zero. The loop is an example of dynamic shifting since the power of 2 in D1 is used as a counter and is decremented after each shift.

EXERCISES

8.2.1. Why do the CPU32 instructions allow shifts of up to 63 places when the longest operand is only 32 bits?

8.2.2. State in words and use an equation to define the conditions for an error when a *signed* integer is shifted left or right by the ASL or ASR instructions. Consider both even and odd integers.

8.2.3. Determine the numerical value when the binary number

$$\{1110\ 0101\}$$

is shifted left three places.

```
abs.   LC    obj. code    source line
----   ----  ----------   -----------
   1   0000                         TTL     'FIGURE 8.3'
   2   0000                         LLEN    100
   3   8000                         ORG     $8000
   4   0000               *
   5   8000               *  POWER OF TWO MULTIPLY
   6   8000               *    INPUT  : (D1.B) = POWER OF TWO MULTIPLIER
   7   8000               *                (D4.L) = INTEGER TO BE MULTIPLIED
   8   8000               *                      (MUST BE POSITIVE)
   9   8000               *
  10   8000               *    OUTPUT : (D5/D4)[63:0] = RESULT
  11   8000               *                    (D2.B) = 0  : SUCCESS
  12   8000               *                          -1 : ERROR DETECTED
  13   8000               *
  14   8000  2F01         POWER2  MOVE.L  D1,-(SP)   ;SAVE REGISTER
  15   8002  4285                 CLR.L   D5         ;ZERO RESULT
  16   8004  143C 00FF            MOVE.B  #-1,D2     ;SET DEFAULT TO ERROR
  17   8008               *
  18   8008  E38C         LOOP    LSL.L   #1,D4      ;SHIFT LEFT (MULTIPLY BY 2)
  19   800A  E395                 ROXL.L  #1,D5      ;SHIFT CARRY OUT OF D4 INTO D5
  20   800C  6500 000A            BCS     DONE       ;IF CARRY OUT OF D5,
  21   8010               *                             EXIT WITH ERROR
  22   8010  0401 0001            SUBI.B  #1,D1      ;DECREMENT COUNT
  23   8014  66F2                 BNE     LOOP       ;  UNTIL (D1) = 0
  24   8016               *
  25   8016  4202                 CLR.B   D2         ;SET STATUS TO SUCCESS
  26   8018               *
  27   8018  221F         DONE    MOVE.L  (SP)+,D1   ;RESTORE REGISTER
  28   801A  4E75                 RTS
  29   801C               *
  30   801C                       END
```

Figure 8.3 Program to multiply a number by 2^N, $N > 0$.

8.2.4. Show that the correct rule for doubling a one's-complement number is a left cyclic shift.

8.2.5. Which single instruction will transfer the upper byte in a 32-bit register to the lower byte so that the operand can be used by a CPU32 instruction operating on a byte-length operand?

8.2.6. Write subroutines that pack and unpack 4-bit operands into byte-length values. Assume that the operands are held in memory.

8.2.7. Modify the subroutine shown in Example 8.4 to multiply signed integers by 2^N.

8.2.8. Write a subroutine to multiply a signed integer by 2^r, where r can be positive or negative. If a negative value is truncated by right shifts, correct the result for proper integer division if necessary.

8.2.9. Modify the routine of Example 8.4 to allow a multiplication by 2^0.

8.2.10. Write the instruction sequence to shift a 64-bit operand in D0:D1 left by 3 bits.

8.3 BIT-MANIPULATION AND SCC INSTRUCTIONS

It is convenient in many applications to employ a logical variable to indicate one of two possible results of an operation. A logical variable used in this way is called a *flag*. The flag variable indicates that a condition has occurred and is used to communicate this fact to a routine that must test the flag variable. For example, the flags that indicate the results of arithmetic operations for the CPU32 collectively form the condition code register. In this case, a conditional branch instruction may test one or more condition codes to determine subsequent action.

Another common application of a flag is to indicate the status of a peripheral device. The status would determine if the device is either "busy" or ready to accept data transfers. Usually, a single bit is set by the device when it is ready and this information is used by the processor to begin the transfer of data. In such an application, the logical variable can be termed an *event flag* and it serves to synchronize the operation of the processor with the external device. The CPU32 instructions to change, clear, set to {1}, or test a single bit within an operand are useful for manipulating such flag bits as well as for other operations.

Another important use of logical variables is to communicate information between independent programs or between routines of an operating system or other sophisticated software systems. The conditions for which a flag would be set or cleared can be very complicated and involve a number of conditional tests. The CPU32 provides a Set According to Condition (Scc) instruction which allows a variable to be defined that indicates a TRUE or FALSE result based on the condition code values.

When operating system routines or several processors share an area of memory, a synchronization problem can occur if a routine or processor can access a memory area or location during the time another routine or processor is using this same memory area or location. For example, this can occur in a real-time system where the program execution sequence is controlled in part by external events, signaled to the processor as an interrupt. In a multiprocessor system, the synchronization problem requires a partial hardware solution if the processors act independently. The Test and Set (TAS) instruction is useful for such situations.

8.3.1 Bit-Manipulation Instructions

The CPU32 bit-manipulation instructions operate on a single bit in a data register or in memory. Each instruction tests a specified bit and sets only the Z condition code bit based on the value. As a logical variable, the Z bit indicates the *complement* of the designated bit. The BTST (Bit Test) instruction sets the Z bit according to the state of the bit tested. The instructions BCHG, BCLR, and BSET set the Z bit accordingly and then cause the designated bit to be changed, cleared to {0}, and set to {1}, respectively. The bit-manipulation instructions are shown in Table 8.8.

When the destination operand of a bit manipulation instruction is held in a data register, the operand is a longword operand. The bit number to examine is either contained in a data register or it is specified as an immediate value in the instruction as a modulo-32 bit number with the range 0–31. When the bit number is held in a data register, the bit number can be changed during program execution. This is called "dynamic" specification. For example, if

$$(D1) = \$0000\ 0001$$

and

$$(D2) = \$0000\ 88FF$$

Table 8.8 Bit-Manipulation Instructions

	Syntax	Operation
Bit Change		
	BCHG <Dn>, <EA>	Z = NOT(bn)
	BCHG #<bn>, <EA>	THEN bn ← NOT(bn)
Bit Clear		
	BCLR <Dn>, <EA>	Z = NOT(bn)
	BCLR #<bn>, <EA>	THEN bn ← {0}
Bit Set		
	BSET <Dn>, <EA>	Z = NOT(bn)
	BSET #<bn>, <EA>	THEN bn ← {1}
Bit Test		
	BTST <Dn>, <EA>	Z = NOT(bn)
	BTST #<bn>, <EA>	

Notes:
1. If <EA> refers to a data register, the operand length is 32 bits.
2. If <EA> addresses an operand in memory, the length is one byte.
3. In the immediate mode, <bn> is the bit number of the operand.
4. BTST allows all addressing modes for the destination except address register direct (data modes only).
5. BCHG, BCLR, and BSET allow only data-alterable addressing modes for the destination.

to specify bit 1 of register D2, the instruction

BCHG.L   D1, D2

clears the Z condition code to {0}, the complement of (D2)[1]. The operand in D2 becomes $0000\ 88FD since bit 1 of D2 is complemented by the operation. The value in D1 should be a number between 0 and 31 because the destination is another data register. The instruction using a fixed bit number as an immediate value

BCLR.L   #1, D2

would have the same effect on D2.

When the destination operand is held in memory, only a *byte-length* operand is allowed. Therefore, the bit number defined in a data register or as an immediate value has the range 0–7.

The BCHG, BCLR, and BSET instructions allow only data-alterable addressing modes. Therefore, address register direct and program counter relative addressing modes are prohibited. The BTST instruction, however, allows all addressing modes except address register direct.

Example 8.5

The subroutine shown in Figure 8.4 generates *odd* parity for a single ASCII character held in a location addressed by A1 and leaves the result in the same location. The odd-parity bit (bit 7) is defined to be {0} when the number of {1} bits in the character is odd.

Otherwise, the parity bit is set to {1} so that the number of nonzero bits in the byte is always an odd number.

The routine begins by setting (D0) = $FF indicating that the parity bit should be {1}. In the loop, encountering a {0} bit has no effect and the next bit in sequence is tested. The bits are tested in order 6, 5, 4, 3, 2, 1, and 0. When a {1} bit is found, the value in D0 is complemented. Since (D0) was initialized to indicate that a parity bit was needed, finding 1,3, 5, or 7 bits with value {1} will cause the routine to complement the initial value in D0. Otherwise, if 0, 2, 4, or 6 bits have the value {1}, (D0) will indicate that the parity bit must be set to {1}. The BSET instruction accomplishes this.

```
abs.   LC    obj. code    source line
----   ----  ---------    -----------
   1   0000                      TTL      'FIGURE 8.4'
   2   0000                      LLEN     100
   3   8000                      ORG      $8000
   4   0000               *
   5   8000               * PARITY GENERATOR
   6   8000               * INPUT  : (A1.L) = ADDRESS OF CHARACTER
   7   8000               *
   8   8000               * OUTPUT : PARITY BIT (BIT 7) ADDED
   9   8000               *              TO CHARACTER AT (A1)
  10   8000 48E7 C000     PARITY MOVEM.L  D0/D1,-(SP) ;SAVE REGISTERS
  11   8004 123C 0006            MOVE.B   #6,D1       ;SET UP COUNTER
  12   8008 103C 00FF            MOVE.B   #$FF,D0     ;PARITY INDICATOR= 1'S
  13   800C               *
  14   800C 0311          LOOP   BTST     D1,(A1)     ;CHECK BIT
  15   800E 6700 0004            BEQ      NEXT        ;IF NOT ZERO
  16   8012 4600                 NOT.B    D0          ; THEN COMPLEMENT PARITY
  17   8014               *                                INDICATOR
  18   8014 51C9 FFF6     NEXT   DBRA     D1,LOOP     ;CONTINUE, UNTIL (D1)= -1
  19   8018               *
  20   8018 4A00                 TST.B    D0          ;IF PARITY SHOULD BE 0
  21   801A 6700 0006            BEQ      DONE        ; THEN SKIP (DO NOT CHANGE)
  22   801E 08D1 0007            BSET     #7,(A1)     ; ELSE SET PARITY BIT
  23   8022               *
  24   8022 4CDF 0003     DONE   MOVEM.L  (SP)+,D0/D1 ;RESTORE REGISTERS
  25   8026 4E75                 RTS
  26   8028               *
  27   8028                      END
```

Figure 8.4 Subroutine to generate an odd-parity bit.

8.3.2 Set According to Condition (Scc) Instruction

The instruction Scc sets all 8 bits of a destination location to {1}'s if the condition "cc" is true. Otherwise, the byte is cleared to all {0}'s when the condition is false. The conditions (carry clear, carry set, etc.) are the same as those for the DBcc instruction discussed in Chapter 6. For example, if the Z condition code bit is {1}, the instruction Set if Equal (to zero)

SEQ   D1

writes $FF into the low-order byte of D1, indicating a TRUE condition to any program testing the flag in D1.

The destination <EA> for the instruction must be a data-alterable location. Thus, all addressing modes except address register direct and program counter relative are allowed.

After the operand is set to all {1}'s or all {0}'s, its condition might be tested using the TST.B instruction, which sets $Z = \{1\}$ when the flag has the value {00000000}. In fact, all of the logical instructions operating on a byte-length operand can be used to manipulate the logical variable created by the Scc instruction. For example, if D1 contains the value $FF from the SEQ instruction just shown, the instruction

EORI.B   #$FF, D1

causes $Z = \{1\}$ and reverses the flag.

8.3.3 Test and Set Instruction

The TAS instruction is used to test and modify a byte-length operand held either in a data register or in memory. Its operation is defined in Figure 8.5(a) and the instruction has the symbolic form

TAS   <EA>

where <EA> is specified by any addressing mode except address register direct or PC relative. If the operand is zero, the condition code bit Z is set to {1}. Otherwise, the Z bit is cleared. If bit 7 of the operand is {1}, N is set to {1}. The condition code bits C and V are always cleared to {0}. In terms of the condition code settings, TAS operates much like the TST (Test) instruction operating on a byte value as described previously in Chapter 6.. However, after the operand is examined by the TAS instruction and N and Z are set accordingly, the most significant bit of the operand is set to {1}.

   For example, if the byte used as a flag and addressed by A1 has the initial value of $00, the instruction

TAS   (A1)

causes $Z = \{1\}$ and changes the operand to $80 after the instruction is executed. If the initial zero value indicated that a memory area or other resource was free for use, the Z condition code bit indicates this after the TAS instruction has executed. However, now the flag has been altered. A subsequent test of the flag would indicate that the resource is in use. This subsequent test might be made by another program running concurrently (perhaps activated by an interrupt) or by another processor in a multiprocessor system.

   Notice that if a flag variable set to $80 is tested in a loop such as

LOOP   TAS   (A1)   ; TEST FLAG

        BNE   LOOP   ; LOOP IF NOT ZERO

the next instruction in sequence after the BNE cannot be executed until some other program or processor clears the flag. When the flag is already set as in this example, the TAS instruction does not change it.

If (EA) = 0
   THEN set Z = {1}
   ELSE set Z = {0}

If (EA)[7] = {1}
   THEN set N = {1}
   ELSE set N = {0}

Set (EA)[7] = {1}, C = {0}, V = {0}

Notes:
(1) (EA) is a byte-length operand addressed by data alterable addressing modes.
(2) The read-modify-write cycle is indivisible.

(a) TAS Operation (TAS <EA>)

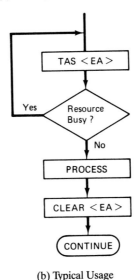

(b) Typical Usage

Figure 8.5 TAS instruction.

As noted in Figure 8.5(a), the operand being tested by TAS cannot be held in an address register or be referenced using program counter relative addressing. Also, the C and V bits are always cleared by the TAS operation. The flowchart in Figure 8.5(b) shows a typical use of the TAS instruction, followed by a conditional test. Here a program is testing to determine if some resource such as a line printer or memory area is available to it. The conditional test is most likely implemented by a conditional branch instruction which causes looping until the flag is clear. With such usage, the processor executing the test is busy executing the loop until either an interrupt occurs which allows the flag to be cleared or until another processor clears it.

If the resource being shared is critical to the continued execution of the program making the test, a wait loop is necessary with the TAS instruction. After the resource is made available, processing can continue utilizing the resource. The flag should be cleared after processing is completed to release the resource for other users. Thus, the TAS instruction may be used as a means to set flags used to communicate between processes, such as real-time routines, or interrupt routines of an operating system. The instruction has another use, however, to *synchronize* accesses to a shared resource when timing is a consideration. It is the synchronization aspect of the TAS instruction that is critically important in many multiprocessor systems in which several processors share resources such as memory areas. Multiprocessor systems are discussed in more detail in several of the references cited in the Further Reading section of this chapter.

Synchronization with the TAS instruction. The TAS instruction is used to prevent access to a shared resource by other programs when one program has control of the resource. This is sometimes termed *lockout*. When hardware access to the shared resource is possible, as in a multiprocessing system, a problem could arise if two processors examine the flag simultaneously and both consider the resource to be available. To prevent this, the TAS instruction has an indivisible, read-modify-write cycle. Once the operand is addressed by the CPU32 executing the TAS instruction, the system bus is not available to any other device, including another processor, until the instruction completes. The first processor executing the TAS instruction controls the shared resource until the flag is cleared. Thus, accesses are synchronized at the hardware level. Details of the hardware operation of the MC68332 are discussed in Chapter 14.

Example 8.6

The subroutine shown in Figure 8.6 illustrates the use of the TAS instruction to allocate and lock a block of memory locations for the calling program. The memory is segmented into eight blocks of 256 bytes with the blocks numbered 0, 1, 2, . . ., 7. The first byte of each block contains a flag or "lock" used by the TAS instruction.

On entry to the subroutine, the label FREEMEM must define the start of the freespace area. Up to eight 256-byte memory blocks are examined to determine whether one is available for use. If a free block is located, its lock byte is set by TAS, its address is returned in A1 and D1[7:0] contains $00 to indicate a free block was found. If no free block is located, D1 is returned with a nonzero value.

EXERCISES

8.3.1. Give the bit test needed to determine the following:
  (a) an integer is even;
  (b) a signed integer m bits long is negative;
  (c) a character is an uppercase or lowercase ASCII alphabetic character.

8.3.2. Compare the following instructions with their equivalent bit manipulation instructions:
  (a) ANDI.W   #$7FFF, D2
  (b) ORI.W   #$8000, D2
  (c) EORI.W   #$8000, D2
  (d) TST.W   D2

```
abs.   LC   obj. code    source line
----   ----  ---------   -----------
  1    0000                       TTL     'FIGURE 8.6'
  2    0000                       LLEN    100
  3    8000                       ORG     $8000
  4    0000              *
  5    8000              *  RESOURCE SHARING USING THE TAS INSTRUCTION
  6    8000              *  INPUT  : FREEMEM = ADDRESS OF FREE SPACE AREA
  7    8000              *
  8    8000              *  OUTPUT : (D1.B) = 0 : FOUND A BLOCK
  9    8000              *                  NOT 0 : NO BLOCK IS FREE
 10    8000              *            (A1.L) = ADDRESS OF THE BLOCK
 11    8000              *
 12         0000 9000    FREEMEM EQU     $9000        ;SET UP FREE AREA
 13    8000 2F03         SHARE   MOVE.L  D3,-(SP)     ;SAVE REGISTER
 14    8002 4201                 CLR.B   D1           ; SET DEFAULT TO FOUND
 15    8004 227C 0000            MOVEA.L #FREEMEM,A1  ;START ADDRESS OF MEMORY
       8008 9000
 16    800A 7607                 MOVEQ   #7,D3        ;SET UP COUNTER
 17    800C             *
 18    800C 4AD1         LOOP    TAS     (A1)         ;IF BLOCK IS FREE
 19    800E 6700 000E            BEQ     FOUND        ; THEN EXIT WITH ADDRESS
 20    8012 D3FC 0000            ADDA.L  #256,A1      ; ELSE GO TO NEXT BLK
       8016 0100
 21    8018             *                             ;    AND CHECK FLAG
 22    8018 51CB FFF2            DBRA    D3,LOOP      ;LOOP UNTIL (D3) = -1
 23    801C             *
 24    801C 1203                 MOVE.B  D3,D1        ;SET STATUS TO NOT FOUND
 25    801E             *
 26    801E 261F         FOUND   MOVE.L  (SP)+,D3     ;RESTORE REGISTER
 27    8020 4E75                 RTS
 28    8022             *
 29    8022                      END
```

Figure 8.6 Routine for memory allocation.

8.3.3. Give the steps needed to generate the arithmetic (or logical) values {1} and {0} from the TRUE and FALSE conditions set by Scc instructions.

8.3.4. Write a subroutine to change a string of alphabetic characters (ASCII) from uppercase to lowercase, or vice versa. Appendix I contains the ASCII character set.

8.3.5. Compare the hardware and software operation of the

TAS   <EA>

instruction with the

BSET   #7, <EA>

instruction. Determine under what conditions a busy-wait loop using the TST and BNE instructions followed by the BSET instruction rather than TAS might not be sufficient to provide a lock of a shared resource. Consider both single- and multiple-processor systems.

8.3.6. Let a "bit map" contain N bits, indicating the availability of N 256-byte blocks of memory. If a bit is {0}, the block is free. Assume that the bit map is held in memory at a fixed location and the first address of the contiguous memory area is known. Write a subroutine to find the first collection of k contiguous blocks. Return the starting address of these blocks and set the proper bits in the bit map to {1} to indicate the memory blocks are in use. If fewer than k blocks are found or if k is not an integer between 1 and N, return an error indication to the calling program.

FURTHER READING

A number of the textbooks referenced in preceding chapters deal with logical and bit operations (Eckhouse and Morris, and Wakerly, for example). The mathematics of shifting is discussed by Stein and Munro, referenced in Chapter 3.

Discussions of the concept of interlocking shared resources are generally found in textbooks dealing with operating systems. The text by Deitel describes in detail some of the concepts introduced in this chapter. Stone's textbook discusses many techniques involved in the design of multiprocessor systems. The Test-and-Set instruction is analyzed, with an emphasis on the potential misapplication of this instruction.

DEITEL, HARVEY M., *An Introduction to Operating Systems.* Reading, Mass.: Addison-Wesley, 1984.

STONE, HAROLD S., *High-Performance Computer Architecture.* Reading Mass.: Addison-Wesley, 1987.

9

Programming Techniques

The preceding chapters introduced the CPU32 instruction set by separating the instructions into categories. The categories contain instructions that are used in programs to move data, perform calculations, or provide simple functions. For the most part, the programs were designed to satisfy a particular application, such as ASCII-to-binary conversion. In contrast, the present chapter explores various programming techniques that are useful in creating more sophisticated programs. The emphasis is on the powerful addressing capability of the CPU32.

Some CPU32 instructions, such as DIVU and MULU, prohibit operations directly on address registers. This restriction is very slight since the contents of address registers and data registers can be easily exchanged. However, the CPU32 provides special instructions to manipulate addresses. The first section introduces these instructions that provide the flexibility necessary for advanced programming techniques.

One special technique involves the creation of *position-independent code*. Program counter relative addressing and base register addressing can be used in programs so that they execute independent of their starting address in memory. Section 9.2 discusses these topics.

Manipulation of typical *data structures* such as arrays, queues and lists involves advanced programming methods. Although Section 9.3 discusses only a few of the many topics concerning the creation and manipulation of data structures, the power and flexibility of the CPU32 instructions are revealed.

Chapter 6 introduced subroutines as a useful technique to aid the programmer in creating modular programs. The linkage between a calling program and a subroutine via the return address on the system stack was discussed there in some detail. Passing data values or addresses between program modules was accomplished using processor registers to hold the values. More sophisticated methods of transferring data values are discussed in Section 9.4. The section also presents techniques to create a stack frame using the LINK and UNLK instructions and to write reentrant subroutines.

Section 9.5 describes the loop mode of the CPU32. The loop mode allows the processor to execute one instruction in a loop controlled by a DBcc instruction without refetching the instruction each time it is executed.

9.1 INSTRUCTIONS THAT MANIPULATE ADDRESSES

Except for values in registers or values specified by the immediate mode of addressing, operands of CPU32 instructions are referenced by their addresses. A distinction is also made between data and addresses because they have separate output signal lines and are held in data registers and address registers, respectively. The address signal lines specify a location in memory (or in the I/O space of the system) and the separate data signal lines are used to transfer values. Internally, both data values and addresses can be manipulated with various processor instructions.

The CPU32 instruction set provides instructions to operate specifically on addresses. The CMPA instruction compares two addresses. Arithmetic operations are performed with the ADDA and SUBA instructions. The MOVEA, LEA, and PEA instructions transfer addresses. Except for the CMPA instruction, these instructions do not alter the condition code register.

Thirty-two bit addresses are calculated internally by the CPU32 for all operations involving addresses. However, the valid address range for the MC68332 is 0 to $FFFFFF as a 24-bit address since there are only 24 address signal-lines.

9.1.1 Arithmetic Address Manipulation

Table 9.1 shows the syntax and operation for the arithmetic instructions that operate specifically on addresses. The instructions Add Address, Subtract Address, and Compare Address operate on a source operand that can be addressed by any mode. However, the destination operand must be held in an address register. These instructions are similar to the ADD, SUB, and CMP operations on data values.

The Add Address (ADDA) instruction adds a value in a register or memory to the value in the destination address register. A common use of the ADDA instruction is to add a constant, which is specified by the immediate addressing mode, to the value in the address register involved. For example, the instruction

        ADDA.L   #20, A1

increments (A1) by 20 when it is executed. In a loop, the instruction allows A1 to address every twentieth element in a data structure. The instructions that operate on addresses provide a much greater flexibility, however, since the source operand can be specified by any addressing mode. For example, an instruction in the form

        ADDA.L   A2, A2

Table 9.1 Operation of ADDA, SUBA, and CMPA

Instruction	Syntax	Operation
Add Address	ADDA.<l> <EA>,<An>	(An) ← (An) + (EA)
Subtract Address	SUBA.<l> <EA>,<An>	(An) ← (An) − (EA)
Compare Address	CMPA.<l> <EA>,<An>	(An) − (EA)

Notes:
1. <l> denotes W or L only.
2. If a word length (W) is specified for the source operand, the address is sign-extended to 32 bits.
3. All addressing modes are allowed for <EA>.
4. ADDA and SUBA do not change the condition codes. CMPA sets the codes according to the result.

doubles the value in A2. The instruction could be used to convert an entry number held in A2 to an index that references a table of 16-bit words. For example, if (A2) = $100 indicates the 256th word in a memory block, then $2 \times \$100$, or $200, is the address of that word as an offset (in bytes) from the starting location of the block.

The Subtract Address (SUBA) instruction forms the difference between a destination address register and the source operand. The instruction

SUBA.L   D1, A1

leaves the 32-bit value of

$$(A1) - (D1)$$

in A1. Like the ADDA instruction, SUBA does not modify the condition codes.

The instruction variations ADDQ (Add Quick) and SUBQ (Subtract Quick) can be used to add and subtract a constant in the range 1 to 8 from the contents of an address register. The source operand is the immediate value of the constant as discussed in Chapter 7. These instructions represent one-word instructions that can be used to increment or decrement an address held in an address register. However, unlike ADDA and SUBA, the quick operations set the condition codes according to the result.

CMPA and TST.   The Compare Address (CMPA) instruction performs a comparison of two addresses and sets the condition codes appropriately. The condition codes are set in the same manner as for the Compare (CMP) instruction discussed in Chapter 6. Addresses should be considered as unsigned integers and tests on the C bit and the Z bit are interpreted as explained in Chapter 6. The conditional branch instructions BHI (higher), BLS (lower or same), BNE (not equal), or BEQ (equal) are also useful to implement tests comparing addresses. For example, the instructions

CMPA.L	A1, A2	; FORM (A2) − (A1)
BHI	LOOP	; BRANCH IF (A2)>(A1)

cause a branch to the instruction at label LOOP if (A2) is greater (higher) than (A1). Otherwise, a branch is not taken. The instruction BHI (Branch if Higher) is used for unsigned integers and the condition tested is "higher" rather than "greater than" which is reserved for signed integers in the instruction BGT.

The CMPA instruction calculates

$$(\text{destination}) - (\text{source})$$

and sets the condition codes based on the result. Table 9.2 summarizes the conditional branch instructions and the true conditions that are valid after a CMPA instruction executes.

Table 9.2 Comparison of Addresses

Instruction	Branch	True condition
CMPA.L A1,A2	BHI (higher)	(A2) > (A1)
	BLS (lower or same)	(A2) ≤ (A1)
	BCC (higher or same)	(A2) ≥ (A1)
	BCS (low)	(A2) < (A1)
	BNE (not equal)	(A2) ≠ (A1)
	BEQ (equal)	(A2) = (A1)

The Test instruction (TST) can be used to determine if the address contained in an address register is zero. Only word or longword operands are allowed when the contents of an address register are tested. Section 6.2.3 describes the TST instruction.

Example 9.1

The subroutine of Figure 9.1 counts the number of negative 8-bit integers in the first byte of contiguous 12-byte tables in memory. The starting address of the block is passed to the subroutine in A0. Address register A1 must contain the address of the end of the last table of bytes upon entry. Each first byte is then tested and the count accumulated in the low-order word of D0.

In each loop, A0 is incremented by 12 each time with the ADDA instruction. The testing terminates when the value in the addressing register A0 becomes larger than the final address in A1.

9.1.2 Transfer of Addresses

Table 9.3 shows the syntax and addressing modes for instructions that transfer addresses. The Move Address instruction loads an address register with an operand that can be held in a register or memory location or be specified as an immediate value. The Load Effective Address instruction computes the effective address of a location in memory and transfers the address value to an address register. The Push Effective Address instruction calculates an effective address and pushes it onto the system stack. LEA and PEA differ from most instructions because the effective address calculated for an operand is transferred rather than the contents of the addressed location.

```
abs. rel.   LC   obj. code    source line
---- ----   ----  ----------   -----------
   1    1   0000                        TTL     'FIGURE 9.1'
   2    2   0000                        LLEN    100
   3    3   8000                        ORG     $8000
   4    4   0000              *
   5    5   8000              * COUNT THE NUMBER OF NEGATIVE FIRST BYTES IN TABLES
   6    6   8000              *
   7    7   8000              * INPUT   : (A0.L) = STARTING ADDRESS OF FIRST TABLE
   8    8   8000              *           (A1.L) = ENDING ADDRESS OF LAST TABLE
   9    9   8000              *
  10   10   8000              * OUTPUT : (D0.W) = NUMBER OF NEGATIVE BYTES
  11   11   8000              *
  12   12   8000 2F08         CNTNEG  MOVE.L  A0,-(SP)     ;SAVE REGISTER
  13   13   8002 4240                  CLR.W   D0          ;CLEAR COUNTER
  14   14   8004              *
  15   15   8004 4A10         LOOP     TST.B   (A0)        ;IF BYTE IS NOT NEGATIVE,
  16   16   8006 6A02                  BPL.S   NEXT        ;    THEN PROCESS NEXT TABLE
  17   17   8008 5240                  ADDQ.W  #1,D0       ; ELSE COUNT IT
  18   18   800A D1FC 0000    NEXT     ADDA.L  #12,A0      ;INCREMENT TO NEXT TABLE
  18        800E 000C
  19   19   8010 B3C8                  CMPA.L  A0,A1       ;IF NOT FINISHED,
  20   20   8012 62F0                  BHI.S   LOOP        ;    THEN CONTINUE
  21   21   8014 205F                  MOVE.L  (SP)+,A0    ;RESTORE REGISTER
  22   22   8016 4E75                  RTS
  23   23   8018                        END
```

Figure 9.1 Program examples of address manipulation.

Table 9.3 Instructions to Transfer Addresses

		Addressing modes	
Instruction	Syntax	Source	Destination
Move Address	MOVEA.<l> <EA>,<An>	All	An
Load Effective Address	LEA <EA>,<An>	Control	An
Push Effective Address	PEA <EA>	Control	−(SP)

Notes:

1. Condition codes are not affected.
2. <l> denotes W or L only. For word-length operands, the source operand is sign-extended to 32 bits, and all 32 bits are loaded into the address register.
3. The operand length for LEA and PEA is 32 bits.

Move address instruction. The MOVEA instruction has the symbolic form

$$\text{MOVEA.<l>}\quad \text{<EA>,<An>}$$

where <l> = W or L and <EA> is designated by any addressing mode. The operation results in the transfer

$$(An)[31:0] \leftarrow (EA)$$

with any 16-bit references being sign-extended to 32-bit quantities before the transfer. When a data register, an address register, or a memory location is the source, the contents of the source is transferred to the specified address register. The instruction

$$\text{MOVEA.L}\qquad \text{TABLE, A1}$$

moves the 32-bit word at location TABLE into A1. The value in this location is considered an address, and TABLE in the discussion might refer to the first address of a table of addresses. Register A1 can then be used to reference the value pointed to by the address at location TABLE. For example, if the MOVEA instruction given above is followed with the instruction

$$\text{MOVE.W} \qquad (A1), D1$$

the 16-bit word referenced by the operand (address) at location TABLE is transferred to the low-order word of D1. The two operations thus perform the transfer

$$(D1)[15:0] \leftarrow ((TABLE)[31:0])[15:0].$$

In contrast, when the immediate mode is used with a label, the address is moved. In the instruction

$$\text{MOVEA.L} \qquad \#TABLE, A1$$

the address of the location TABLE, which is the source operand, is transferred to A1. Thus, the immediate form loads the address of the table itself. Without the immediate symbol, the MOVEA instruction would be used to load the first address within a table of addresses starting at location TABLE into A1.

Load effective address. The LEA instruction calculates an effective address based on the source addressing mode and transfers it to an address register. The symbolic form is

$$\text{LEA} \qquad <EA>, An$$

where $<EA>$ is specified by a control addressing mode. Thus, register direct, postincrement, and predecrement addressing modes are not allowed. The instruction

$$\text{LEA} \qquad TABLE, A1$$

results in the operation

$$(A1)[31:0] \leftarrow TABLE$$

where TABLE is an address in an assembly-language program. This instruction is equivalent to the MOVEA instruction with the immediate form of the source operand address.

When other addressing modes are used for the source operand in the LEA instruction, the instruction performs a function that is not possible with other data transfer instructions. The LEA instruction allows an address to be calculated and transferred to an address register during program execution.

Example 9.2

The LEA instruction can sometimes be used to advantage to reduce the calculation time of effective addresses by the CPU32. In this example, the LEA instruction is used to avoid repeated calculation of an indexed address with displacement. Consider the instruction sequence

	LEA	(2, A1, D1.W), A0	; OPERAND ADDRESS
MULT	MOVE.W	(A0), D2	; PUT VALUE IN D2
	MULU	#5, D2	; 5 x VALUE
	MOVE.W	D2, (A0)	; SAVE IT

which uses LEA to compute an indexed address. This sequence first calculates the address based on the indirect with indexing addressing mode as

$$(A1) + (D1)[15:0] + 2$$

and transfers it into A0. The word-length operand addressed by (A0) is moved into D2, modified, and saved.

The indirect reference (A0) is more efficient in the use of memory than the indirect with indexing reference (2,A1,D1.W), which requires an extension word for the displacement to its instruction. Also, fewer machine cycles are required to calculate the indirect address than to calculate the indirect with index address. Without the LEA instruction, both MOVE instructions would need the indexed addressing to calculate the operand location.

Push effective address. The PEA instruction calculates an effective address and uses the system stack as the destination. The instruction

PEA   <EA>

calculates a 32-bit effective address for an operand specified by one of the control addressing modes. The value calculated is pushed onto the stack by the CPU using the sequence

$$(SP) \leftarrow (SP) - 4$$

$$((SP)) \leftarrow <EA>$$

where the system stack pointer is first decremented by 4 and then used to point to the longword location for <EA>.

Example 9.3

Table 9.4 shows the results of executing the PEA, LEA, and MOVEA instructions. For the PEA instruction, the stack pointer is initialized to $0000 7FFE. The instruction pushes (A0) as shown. Since the system stack is used, the more significant bytes of A0 are stored at lower memory addresses. LEA loads A0 with the source operand itself. To accomplish a similar result, MOVEA with an immediate value could be used. In the next example, if the source operand were specified for MOVEA as an absolute address rather than immediate, the contents of the word location at $8000 would be transferred to A0. As shown, the immediate value $8000 is sign-extended to $FFFF 8000 when the MOVEA instruction executes.

Table 9.4 Address Manipulation Examples

Memory contents (hexadecimal)	Instruction	Results
4850	PEA (A0)	($7FFA) = $00 ($7FFB) = $00 ($7FFC) = $10 ($7FFD) = $20
41F9 0001 2345	LEA $00012345, A0	(A0) = $0001 2345
307C 8000	MOVEA.W #$8000, A0	(A0) = $FFFF 8000

Note:
Initially, (A0) = $0000 1020 and (SP) = $0000 7FFE.

Example 9.4

Figure 9.2 lists the instruction sequences that are equivalent to LEA and PEA. In each case, A0 holds the first address of a table representing blocks of byte-length operands in memory. The low-order word of D0 is an index to select the starting address of a particular block when added to (A0). The OFFSET selects the address of a particular byte when used to calculate the effective address.

EXERCISES

9.1.1. Let (A1) = $0000 1000 before each of the following instructions is executed. Compute the address in A1 after each instruction executes:
(a) ADDA.W #$2000, A1
(b) ADDA.L #$9000, A1
(c) SUBA.W #$2000, A1

9.1.2. Let the hexadecimal values in A0 and A1 be

$$(A0) = \$0000\ 1000$$

$$(A1) = \$0001\ 1F00$$

before the operation

CMPA.W   A0, A1

Which conditional branch statements following the compare instruction will cause a branch?

9.1.3. If the instruction

LEA   (1, A1, D1.W), A2

```
abs.   LC    obj. code     source line
----   ----  ----------    -----------
  1    0000                        TTL      'FIGURE 9.2'
  2    0000                        LLEN     100
  3    8000                        ORG      $8000
  4    0000              *
  5          0000 000A   OFFSET   EQU      10
  6    8000              *
  7    8000              *  COMPARISON OF LEA AND PEA
  8    8000              *
  9    8000              *  INPUT : (A0.L) = ADDRESS OF TABLE
 10    8000              *                  (D0.W) = INDEX INTO TABLE
 11    8000              *                  OFFSET = BYTE WITHIN ELEMENT OF PREDEFINED TABLE
 12    8000              *
 13    8000              *  OUTPUT : (A1.L) = EFFECTIVE ADDRESS (LEA)
 14    8000              *
 15    8000              *  OPERATION OF THE LEA TO LOAD THE ADDRESS OF AN ELEMENT
 16    8000              *
 17    8000 43F0 000A            LEA      (OFFSET,A0,D0.W),A1
 18    8004              *
 19    8004              *  LOAD THE ADDRESS OF AN ELEMENT WITHOUT USING LEA
 20    8004              *
 21    8004 2248                 MOVEA.L  A0,A1
 22    8006 D2C0                 ADDA.W   D0,A1
 23    8008 D2FC 000A            ADDA.W   #OFFSET,A1
 24    800C              *
 25    800C              *  OPERATION OF THE PEA TO SAVE AN ADDRESS
 26    800C              *
 27    800C 4870 000A            PEA      (OFFSET,A0,D0.W)
 28    8010              *
 29    8010              *  SAVE AN ADDRESS WITHOUT USING PEA
 30    8010              *
 31    8010 2248                 MOVEA.L  A0,A1
 32    8012 D2C0                 ADDA.W   D0,A1
 33    8014 D2FC 000A            ADDA.W   #OFFSET,A1
 34    8018 2F09                 MOVE.L   A1,-(SP)
 35    801A              *
 36    801A                      END
```

Figure 9.2 Program comparing LEA and PEA.

is executed with

$$(D1) = \$0000\ 8000$$

$$(A1) = \$0000\ 1FFF$$

what is the address loaded into A2?

9.1.4. How can LEA and PEA be used to debug a program by verifying the addresses from which data are fetched?

9.1.5. The CPU32 allows indirect addressing only using an address register. Suppose that it is desired to hold an indirect address in a given memory location which itself is indirectly addressed. Show how the LEA instruction is used to access the indirect address if the address is at location ADDR1. Then, generalize the concept to allow two levels of indirect addressing with the addresses in memory.

9.2 POSITION-INDEPENDENT CODE AND BASE ADDRESSING

In most of the previous programming examples, the program occupied fixed locations in memory and the starting address was defined by the origin (ORG) directive of the assembler. If these programs were to be moved to another area in memory, reassembly with a new origin would be required. The fact that the programs cannot be moved (relocated) in memory without reassembly is inconvenient in some cases. It is not acceptable at all for ROM-based programs. In these cases, the programs must be able to be relocated after they are assembled.[1] Some operating systems may need to relocate an applications program even after its execution has already started.

A program is said to be *statically position independent* if it can be loaded and executed from any starting address in memory. Most programs in ROM are statically position independent since the starting address of the ROM program is defined by the system designer based on the requirements of the system. A floating-point routine in ROM, for example, may have a starting address of $2000 in one system and start at location $10000 in another. Perhaps the second system requires a much greater contiguous RAM area. Writing *position-independent code* is a technique of coding a routine so that the starting address is arbitrary. A major difference in this type of program is that it does not contain any absolute addresses except those dictated by hardware definitions such as I/O device addresses.

Dynamic position independence defines a program that can be moved after it has begun execution. The situation might arise with a multi-tasking operating system that dynamically swaps tasks in and out of RAM as needed. When the suspended task is reloaded, it may be reloaded into a different memory area.

In MC68332-based systems, the position independence for ROM based programs can be accomplished with PC relative addressing for instruction fetching and reading data. Subsection 9.2.1 discusses PC relative addressing. As described in Subsection 9.2.2, base addressing can be used to achieve position independence for read/write operations on variables. Subsection 9.2.3 summarizes the position independent programming techniques for M68000 family processors.

9.2.1 Position-Independent Code with (PC)

With M68000 family processors, the Program Counter (PC) relative addressing mode can be used to create position-independent code when a location to be read in a program is at a fixed distance from the instruction making the reference. As long as the relative displacement is not changed, the program will execute correctly anywhere in memory. If all memory references use PC relative addressing, the program will be *dynamically* position independent since the effective addresses will be calculated as each instruction executes. Moving the program and restarting it at the point where it was temporarily suspended will not cause a problem as long as the program and data are moved together as a block.

However, CPU32 programs that use only the PC relative addressing mode can-

---

[1] The Further Reading section for this chapter lists several references that discuss relocation using a linkage editor.

not write to destination operands in memory. The technique of base addressing described in Subsection 9.2.2 can be used to access alterable variables.

Table 9.5 shows the type of instructions and memory references which are inherently position independent. Any of the conditional branch instructions or BRA uses program counter with displacement addressing. Immediate values to initialize register are unaffected by moving a program. Relative memory addresses using (PC) to reference variables to be read ensure that the code for read accesses is position independent.

Position independent code can refer to absolute addresses outside of the position independent program. Such addresses might refer to system-defined values which are not changed such as module registers. These values are typically defined in the assembly-language program with the Equate (EQU) directive.

Table 9.5 Position-Independent References

Category	Addressing mode
Branch instructions BRA Bcc DBcc	PC relative with displacement
Immediate instructions Logical (ORI, ANDI, EORI) Arithmetic (ADDI, SUBI, CMPI, ADDQ, SUBQ) Transfers (MOVEQ)	Immediate
Relative memory references	PC relative with displacement, PC relative with index

Table 9.6 lists the instructions that allow PC relative addressing. As shown in that table, most of the CPU32 instructions that specify two operands allow only the source operand to be designated by the PC relative addressing mode. Thus, the instruction

MOVE.W   X, Y

could have only X specified as PC relative. The destination location for BRA, Bcc, DBcc, JMP, or JSR, however, can be specified by a PC relative mode. Basically, the CPU32 does not allow an operand that can be altered to be referenced by PC relative addressing. The CPU32 designers consider a reference using the PC to be a reference to a program instruction, not a data reference.[2] The only exceptions are the Bit Test (BTST) instruction, the Compare Immediate (CMPI) instruction, and the Test (TST) instruction since these instructions do not change the destination operand.

---

[2] This distinction is explained when the function code lines of the MC68332 are discussed later in Chapter 14.

Table 9.6 Relative Addressing
for Instructions

Source	Destination
ADD, ADDA	BRA, Bcc, DBcc
AND	BSR
CHK, CHK2	BTST
CMP, CMPA, CMP2	CMPI
DIV, DIVSL, DIVU, DIVUL	JMP, JSR
LEA	TST
MOVE, MOVEA	
MOVE TO CCR	
MOVE TO SR	
MOVEM	
MULS, MULU	
OR	
PEA	
SUB, SUBA	

Note:
The destination location is not changed by the instructions listed under Destination.

Assembler conventions and position-independent addressing. Assemblers may differ slightly in the manner in which relative addressing is specified by the programmer. As described in Chapter 5, the PC relative addressing mode is invoked for the Motorola assembler with the addressing mode syntax for the source operand

$$(\text{LABEL}, \text{PC})$$

where LABEL is a label in an assembly-language program. The address is generated by adding a displacement (LABEL) to the value in the PC when an instruction using the mode is executed. For example, the instruction

$$\text{MOVE.L} \qquad (\text{DATA}, \text{PC}), \text{D1}$$

moves 32 bits from the location addressed by (PC) + DATA with the result

$$(\text{D1}) = ((\text{PC}) + \text{DATA})$$

where DATA is an 8-, 16-, or 32-bit signed displacement. Thus, "forced" PC relative addressing occurs when the PC is explicitly specified in any addressing mode that is legal for the instruction being coded.

Example 9.5

Figure 9.3 presents two subroutines that compare the use of relocatable and relative addresses. In the first routine, which starts at label ABSMOVE, the starting address of a buffer area in memory of bytes is defined by BUFABS after the registers are saved. The absolute location $0016 would be assigned to the value #BUFABS if the program were loaded at location $0000. However, the assembler marks the label BUFABS relocatable in instructions of the form

$$\text{MOVEA.L} \qquad \text{BUFABS, A1}$$

to indicate that the linkage editor or loader program must supply the correct address before the program is loaded into memory. This is indicated in the assembler's internal symbol table so that the object module contains enough information for the linkage editor to relocate the code. Before the program is loaded at a load address, a relocation value would be added to the offset ($16) in the MOVEA instruction containing the reference to BUFABS. If the routine contained an ORG directive, the label BUFABS would represent an absolute address and the routine could not be relocated.

```
abs.  LC   obj. code    source line
----  ----  ---------    -----------
  1   0000                       TTL    'FIGURE 9.3'
  2   0000                       LLEN   100
  3   0000               *
  4   0000               *  ABSOLUTE VS. RELATIVE ASSEMBLY
  5   0000               *
  6   0000               *  MOVE A BLOCK OF DATA
  7   0000               *
  8   0000               *  INPUT : (D1.W) = NUMBER OF BYTES TO MOVE
  9   0000               *            (A0.L) = ADDRESS OF BLOCK
 10   0000               *
 11   0000               *  OUTPUT : BUFFER IS LOADED WITH BYTES
 12   0000               *
 13   0000               *
 14   0000               *
 15   0000               *     RELOCATABLE SECTION OF CODE
 16   0000               *
 17   0000
 18   0000 48E7 40C0     ABSMOVE MOVEM.L D1/A0-A1,-(SP) ;SAVE REGISTERS
 19   0004 227C 0000             MOVEA.L #BUFABS,A1       ;GET ADDRES OF BUFFER
      0008 0016
 20   000A 12D8          LOOP1   MOVE.B  (A0)+,(A1)+    ;MOVE A BYTE INTO BUFFER
 21   000C 5341                  SUBQ.W  #1,D1          ;DECREMENT COUNTER
 22   000E 66FA                  BNE     LOOP1          ;CONTINUE UNTIL
 23   0010               *                             ;   (D1)=0
 24   0010 4CDF 0302             MOVEM.L (SP)+,D1/A0-A1 ;RESTORE REGISTERS
 25   0014 4E75                  RTS
 26   0016               BUFABS  DS.B    100            ;SET UP BUFFER (ABSOLUTE)
 27   0016               *
 28   007A               *    POSITION INDEPENDENT SECTION OF CODE
 29   007A               *
 30   007A
 31   0000                 SECTION 1
 32   007A               *
 33   0000 48E7 40C0     RELMOVE MOVEM.L D1/A0-A1,-(SP) ;SAVE REGISTERS
 34   0004 43FA 000E             LEA     (BUFREL,PC),A1 ;PC RELATIVE
 35   0008 12D8          LOOP2   MOVE.B  (A0)+,(A1)+    ;MOVE A BYTE; RELATIVE
 36   000A               *                             ; REFERENCE TO DESTINATION
 37   000A 5341                  SUBQ.W  #1,D1          ;DECREMENT COUNTER
 38   000C 66FA                  BNE     LOOP2          ;CONTINUE UNTIL (D1)=0
 39   000E 4CDF 0302             MOVEM.L (SP)+,D1/A0-A1 ;RESTORE REGISTERS
 40   0012 4E75                  RTS
 41   0014               *
 42   0014               BUFREL  DS.B    100            ;SET UP BUFFER (RELATIVE)
 43   0014               *
 44   0078                       END
```

Figure 9.3 Program examples of relocatable and relative assembly.

     The position-independent routine begins at label RELMOVE. Note that a SECTION directive is used to reset the location counter of the assembler to zero. This indicates that this section of the program is independent of the previous instructions. When the program is loaded in memory and executed, the LEA instruction transfers the address (PC) + BUFREL to A1 with the result

$$(A1) = (PC) + BUFREL$$

Here BUFREL = $0E as an offset in the LEA instruction. If the program is loaded at location $8000, for example, the address is

$$\$8006 + \$0E = \$8014$$

since the PC value $8006 points two bytes beyond the LEA instruction when the LEA instruction actually uses (PC) to calculate the address to be transferred to A1. The next MOVE.B instruction transfers a byte from a location pointed to by A0 into the array defined by BUFREL. Thus, the destination address for the MOVE.B instruction is a PC relative address.

The subroutine defined in Section 1 of the program can thus be moved in memory and executed without use of a linkage editor or loader program to assign addresses to BUFREL or LOOP2. In contrast, the relocatable but position dependent instructions in the relocatable section could not be moved in memory and executed unless a linkage editor or loader program assigned an absolute address to label BUFABS. LOOP1 in the relocatable section requires no address assignment since it is defined by the PC relative addressing mode of the BNE instruction.

9.2.2 Base Register Addressing

In the discussion of position-independent code, the program counter was used as a *base address* to which a displacement and possibly an index value was added to locate an operand in memory. The address register indirect addressing modes of the CPU32 can be used to accomplish *base register* addressing using any of the address registers. As the instruction using base register addressing executes, the operand location is calculated by adding an offset to the base address.

For example, the instruction

MOVE.W   (IN, A0), (OUT, A0)

uses base register addressing for the source and destination operands. The displacements IN and OUT are fixed in the program after assembly. However, the program containing the instruction can be moved anywhere in memory and executed if the operating system or another program statement supplies the proper value for A0 before the instruction executes.

In CPU32 programs, the base register addressing is typically used to access data in an array or similar structure or to pass the base address of a data area to a subroutine. This addressing method is particularly useful when the relative position of a data item can be located by a displacement or an index value but the starting address of the structure is not known at the time of assembly.

Example 9.6

Figure 9.4 illustrates the possibility of segmenting memory into blocks using base register addressing. Registers A1, A2, and A3 address different segments. Memory references

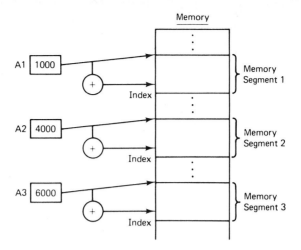

Figure 9.4 Base addressing.

in a program using A1 reference the first segment, and an index value could be added to access a specific location. Similarly, the other address registers could be used to locate data or instructions in other segments. If a segment were moved, the operating system would reload the proper address register with the new starting address.

Of course, only one memory segment may be needed in an application. A ROM based program could access variables in RAM for reading or writing with base register addressing. The base address register must be initialized with the RAM beginning address. This scheme is common in products using microcontrollers.

In many microcontroller applications, the program and various constants are held in ROM and referenced with PC relative addressing. Data variables in read/write memory are addressed using base register addressing with displacements. A specific example is the 332BUG monitor introduced in Chapter 5. The ROM program is position independent and thus can be copied to another area in memory to be executed. The 332BUG RAM area is addressed beginning at location $0000 through $3000.

9.2.3 Position-Independent Code Programming Techniques

If a program contains only immediate values, absolute addresses fixed by the system, and PC relative references for read access to memory operands, the program will be statically position independent. Dynamic position independence is typically achieved by base register addressing for data.

Data values cannot be referenced at absolute addresses within a position independent program. Data values transferred between programs should be defined by base register addressing or be passed in processor registers or on the system stack. Section 9.4 explores data passing techniques when subroutines are discussed.

Table 9.7 summarizes the techniques for statically position-independent code using PC relative addressing for program references or certain data references in a program. Methods for passing data are also listed. These techniques are defined more completely in Section 9.4. In particular, Section 9.3 explains the use of in-line coding and stack frames.

Table 9.7 Position-Independent Programming Techniques

Use	Techniques
Program references	BRA, Bcc, DBcc Explicit PC relative addressing modes or base register addressing
Data references (source)	Immediate values Absolute addresses fixed by system PC relative or base register addressing
Data references (destination)	LEA instruction to transfer PC relative address to an address register; the address register is used to reference the operand Base register addressing
Passing data between programs	Processor registers Transfer on stack Parameter area in memory In-line coding Stack frames

Note:
Chapter 14 explains how the data references cause the CPU to indicate a program space reference if PC relative addressing is used.

EXERCISES

9.2.1. Consider the simple program segment:

```
           ORG        0
START    MOVE.W     FIRST, D1
         ADD.W      SECOND, D1
         MOVE.W     D1, RESULT
         RTS
FIRST    DC.W       1
SECOND DS.W         1
RESULT DS.W         1
         END
```

The program attempts to calculate

$$(RESULT) = (FIRST) + (SECOND)$$

but will not work. Also, the program cannot be moved in memory from location $0000. Correct the program so that it will work anywhere in memory.

9.2.2. Show that the following program segment is statically position independent.

```
STRT    LEA       * + 0, A0           ; GET PC
        ADDA.L    #(DATA – STRT), A0
        MOVE.W    #19, D1            ; COUNTER
LOOP    ADD.W     (A0)+, D2          ; SUM ARRAY
        DBF       D1, LOOP
        RTS
DATA    DS.W      20
        END
```

Show that the pointer to the data array (A0) contains the proper address of DATA after the program is moved. DBRA is also used for DBF in many assemblers.

9.2.3. Suppose that the instructions

```
LEA        Y(PC), A1
ADD.W      X(PC), (A1)
```

are used to create position-independent code. Relative addresses are specified for both the source X and destination Y. After execution of the LEA instruction, A1 contains the address of Y calculated from the (PC) value plus displacement. Show that the program is not dynamically position independent. (*Hint:* Consider the case when the program is moved after the LEA executes but before the ADD instruction executes.)

9.2.4. Compare indexed addressing with base register addressing. For the CPU32, the two addressing modes are identical as far as machine-language code is concerned but have different purposes. Discuss the use of each.

9.2.5. Describe how a program that includes the instruction

```
LEA        (START, PC), A1
```

computes its own load address as it executes. START is a label in the assembly-language program.

9.2.6. Write a position-independent program to sum the values in five locations reserved by a DS directive in the program. Test it by writing another program that moves the program to sum the values and executes it after it is moved.

9.3 DATA STRUCTURES

The fundamental data types for the CPU32 are signed or unsigned integers, BCD integers, and Boolean variables. These data types are considered to be fundamental data types because CPU32 instructions can manipulate them directly. In contrast, character strings must be created and manipulated by algorithms that are devised by the programmer. Thus, character strings represent a data type not available at the assembly language level. The definition of new data types and the logical relationship defining their organization leads to the study of *data structures.*

An *array* is an example of a data structure. Arrays consist of a set of items of a single data type stored in contiguous memory locations. The terms "array" and "table" are usually used synonymously when referring to consecutive storage of values unless it is important to distinguish between applications. Arrays of numbers and tables of addresses have been used in examples of previous chapters. This section generalizes the concepts for both single- and multidimensional arrays.

The address register indirect or PC indirect addressing modes are used to address arrays of operands in memory. When an index register is used to locate an element in an array or table, the CMP2 (Compare Register Against Bounds) instruction presented in this section can be used to ensure that the index value does not exceed certain limits. The CHK and CHK2 (Check Register Against Bounds) instructions perform a similar function. However, these instructions are discussed in Chapter 11 since they cause a trap if the index value exceeds a limit.

A *string* is typically a sequence of ASCII characters treated as a single unit. The CPU32 instruction set allows efficient string manipulation routines to be created. The *queue* is another data structure that is convenient for storing data in certain applications. Programming techniques for string and queue manipulation are introduced in this section.

The *linked list* is another type of data structure useful in many applications. The list structure allows data items to be stored in noncontiguous storage locations using pointers to indicate the location of the next item in the list. The CPU32 with its extensive address manipulation capability, is well suited for programs using linked lists. Review of the CPU32 addressing modes described in Chapter 5 may be helpful to understand the use of the addressing modes in linked list manipulation.

9.3.1 One-Dimensional Arrays

The one-dimensional array is a structure consisting of a collection of items in which each element is identified uniquely by an index value corresponding to its position in the array. Since each item in the array is of the same data type, the structure is homogeneous. In mathematics, a one-dimensional array of numbers is called a *vector*. The position of each element is specified by a subscript. If the first subscript is arbitrarily chosen as 1, the vector elements in mathematical notation are

$$V_1, V_2, \ldots, V_N$$

for an N-element vector. The corresponding N-element array in memory has elements

$$V(1), V(2), \ldots, V(N).$$

Thus, $V(i)$ indicates the address of element V_i where i is the index. Languages such as Pascal or ALGOL allow arbitrary specification of the first index. The FORTRAN convention begins the vector numbering with subscript 1. In assembly language, complete flexibility is available. For the current discussion, V_i will refer to the ith element itself and $V(i)$ will be the address of the ith element.

Address calculation. Sequential storage of the individual elements of a one-dimensional array allows each element to be easily referenced according to its index. If an N-element array X starts at location $X(1)$ and each element occupies C bytes, then the jth element has the address

$$X(j) = X(1) + C \times (j - 1) \qquad 1 \le j \le N$$

where C is a constant.[3] The array length in bytes is

$$\text{length} = (X(N) - X(1)) \times C$$

when $X(N)$ and $X(1)$ represent the last and first addresses of the elements, respectively. Table 9.8 shows the address calculations for various arrays. Figure 9.5 illustrates the general relationship in memory.[4]

Table 9.8 One-Dimensional Array Addressing

Size of element in table	C	j^{th} location	Length of array (bytes)
Byte	1	$X(j) = X(1) + (j - 1)$	N
Word	2	$X(j) = X(1) + 2 \times (j - 1)$	$2N$
Longword	4	$X(j) = X(1) + 4 \times (j - 1)$	$4N$
Strings (fixed length)	k	$X(j) = X(1) + k \times (j - 1)$	$k \times N$

Notes:
1. N is the number of elements each of length C bytes.
2. The index range is $1 \le j \le N$. The first address is $X(1)$, containing the value X_1.

---

[3] If $X(0)$ is the first address, then the jth element in the N element array has a calculated address $X(j) = X(0) + C \times j$ where $0 \le j \le N - 1$.
[4] There is no reason that the array could not have elements with higher indices occupying lower memory addresses and thus have the physical ordering be opposite the logical ordering. In this case, the equations given in this section would require modification.

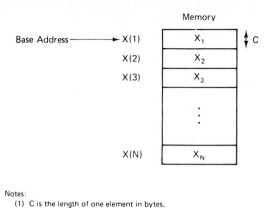

Notes:
  (1) C is the length of one element in bytes.
  (2) X(k) is the address of element X_k.

Figure 9.5 Array storage in memory.

Array addressing with the CPU32.   Addressing elements of an array is accomplished using the indirect or relative addressing modes of the CPU32. If the starting or base address of an array is held in an address register, the indirect modes can be used to locate elements in the array as shown in Table 9.9. When the program counter is used to perform relative addressing, a displacement value or an index plus displacement value is added to the (PC) to reference an element of the array. When relative addressing is specified in an instruction, the fixed displacement is calculated by the assembler. Typically, the array storage is allocated with a Define Storage (DS) directive at a labeled statement.

The postincrement addressing mode can be used to reference array elements in sequence. For byte, word, or longword elements, the postincrement addressing mode allows an element to be examined and manipulated, after which the address register contains the address of the next element in the array. The example instruction

MOVE.W   (A1)+, D1

transfers the 16-bit value addressed by A1 to (D1)[15:0]. Register A1 is then incremented by 2 to point to the next value in the array. For an array whose elements are stored at decreasing memory locations from the base address, the predecrement mode permits the array to be scanned in the reverse order.[5] Without additional programming, only byte, word, or longword elements may be addressed in a sequential fashion with these modes.

The address register indirect with displacement mode can be used to address a specific element in an array. The address register holds the base address of the array and the displacement specifies the relative position of the element as an offset. This mode is often used to compare elements in separate arrays.

---

[5] The predecrement and postincrement modes are useful for manipulating stacks and queues of byte, word, or longword entries. These are *dynamic* arrays since the length varies with program execution. Several of the references in the Further Reading section at the end of this chapter discuss these structures in detail.

Table 9.9 CPU32 Array Addressing

Addressing mode	Typical use
Predecrement	To address byte, word, or longword elements in descending sequence
Postincrement	To address byte, word, or longword elements in ascending sequence
(PC) with displacement or (An) with displacement	To locate an element at an arbitrary position from the base address
(PC) with index or (An) with index	To locate an element at an arbitrary position using an index register
(PC) with scaled index or (An) with scaled index	To locate a byte (SCALE = 1), word (SCALE =2), longword (SCALE = 4), or quadword (SCALE = 8) in an array; the element is located by indexed addressing
(PC) with base displacement and index or (An) with base displacement and index	To locate an element in an array defined by a base displacement and base address held in (PC) or (An)

As an example, consider two arrays with word-length elements. If (A1) points to the first element at location X(1) and (A2) points to Y(1), the instruction sequence

MOVE.W	(4, A1), D1	; (X(3))
MOVE.W	(4, A2), D2	; (Y(3))
CMP.W	D1, D2	; COMPARE (Y(3)) − (X(3))

compares Y_3 and X_3 located at addresses Y(3) and X(3), respectively. Notice that the third element is located by a four-byte offset from the base address.

Address indexing and scaling. The offset in the indirect mode and in the program counter relative with displacement mode cannot be modified after the program is assembled, so these modes do not allow indexing through an array. Indexing is provided by using either the address register indirect with index or PC relative with index addressing mode.

In the indexed modes, the base address consists of a register value (address register or PC) and possibly a sign-extended displacement value. The index into the array may be calculated before it is used by evaluation of an index *expression* of any complexity. For example, in the instruction

MOVE.B   (0, A1, D1.W), D1

the base address is held in A1 and the low-order 16-bit value in D1 contains the index. The value in D1 could be calculated by any mathematical expression before it is used as an index. If the 16-bit index is not sufficient, a long index of 32 bits may be specified according to the discussion of these addressing modes given in Chapter 5.

The address register indirect mode with index and scaling or the PC relative indirect mode with index and scaling is typically used to index into an array with elements of length byte, word, longword, or quadword. As the index register is changed in a loop, the index value is multiplied by 1, 2, 3, 4, or 8 before use, according to the scale factor. Thus, the instruction

$$\text{MOVE.L} \qquad (\text{A1}, \text{D1.W} * 4), \text{D2}$$

with $(\text{D1})[\text{W}] = n$ addresses the source operand at location

$$(\text{A1}) + 4 \times n.$$

This is the nth longword in the array when $n = 0, 1, 2, \ldots$ defines the array index. In terms of the array defined in Figure 9.5, $n = 0$ corresponds to X(1) and $n = N - 1$ corresponds to element X(N) when n is the index value.

The PC and address register indirect with index modes allow a base displacement to be added to the base address in the PC or in An. This is sometimes used to address past a header area in an array which contains information about the array. The instruction

$$\text{MOVE.B} \qquad (4, \text{A1}, \text{D1.W} * 8), \text{D2}$$

would address the first element of the array of source operands at address

$$(\text{A1}) + 4$$

thus skipping four bytes of header information at the beginning of the array whose base address is defined by (A1). Of course, another view is that the example MOVE.B instruction addresses the fifth byte of a quadword element defined whose first byte is addressed as

$$(\text{A1}) + (\text{D1})[\text{W}] \times 8$$

and transfers this byte to D2. Thus, the purpose of the offset depends on the application. Table 9.9 only suggests possible uses for the various addressing modes when addressing data arrays.

Example 9.7

The subroutine ERRMSG in Figure 9.6 calculates the address of a specified element in an array consisting of five elements, each 13 bytes in length. The array of error messages begins at location TABLE and an offset from that address is calculated according to the value in the low-order byte of D0. The address of the element is calculated by multiplying the error number by 13 and adding this value to the base address in A0. The addressing equation in this example would be

$$\text{TABLE}(k) = \text{TABLE} + 13 \times (k)$$

```
abs. rel.   LC    obj. code    source line
---- ----   ----  ----------   -----------
   1    1   0000                          TTL      'FIGURE 9.6'
   2    2   0000                          LLEN     100
   3    3   8000                          ORG      $8000
   4    4   0000            |*
   5    5   8000            |*   ERROR MESSAGES
   6    6   8000            |*
   7    7   8000            |*    INPUT : (D0.B) = ERROR NUMBER BETWEEN 0 AND 4
   8    8   8000            |*
   9    9   8000            |*    OUTPUT : (A0.L) = ADDRESS OF THE CORRESPONDING ERROR MESSAGE
  10   10   8000            |*
  11   11   8000 2F00       |ERRMSG  MOVE.L   D0,-(SP)      ;SAVE REGISTER
  12   12   8002 41F9 0000  |        LEA      TABLE,A0      ;GET ADDRESS OF START OF TABLE
  12        8006 8012       |
  13   13   8008 C0FC 000D  |        MULU.W   #13,D0        ;13 BYTES PER STRING
  14   14   800C D0C0       |        ADDA.W   D0,A0         ;COMPUTE INDEX
  15   15   800E 201F       |        MOVE.L   (SP)+,D0      ;RESTORE REGISTER
  16   16   8010 4E75       |        RTS
  17   17   8012            |*
  18   18   8012            |*   DEFINE TABLE OF ERROR MESSAGES
  19   19   8012            |*
  20   20   8012 4F56 4552  |TABLE   DC.B     'OVERFLOW      '
  20   20   8016 464C 4F57  |
  20   20   801A 2020 2020  |
  20   20   801E 20         |
  21   21   801F 554E 4445  |        DC.B     'UNDERFLOW     '
  21   21   8023 5246 4C4F  |
  21   21   8027 5720 2020  |
  21   21   802B 20         |
  22   22   802C 5355 4253  |        DC.B     'SUBSCRIPT     '
  22   22   8030 4352 4950  |
  22   22   8034 5420 2020  |
  22   22   8038 20         |
  23   23   8039 5A45 524F  |        DC.B     'ZERO DIVIDE   '
  23   23   803D 2044 4956  |
  23   23   8041 4944 4520  |
  23   23   8045 20         |
  24   24   8046 554E 494D  |        DC.B     'UNIMPLEMENTED'
  24   24   804A 504C 454D  |
  24   24   804E 454E 5445  |
  24   24   8052 44         |
  25   25   8053            |*
  26   26   8053            |        END
```

Figure 9.6 Subroutine to address an array element.

where $k = 0, 1, 2, 3,$ or 4 is the error number. If (D0)[B] is not an integer between 0 and 4, the address returned in A0 is not valid.

Example 9.8

The subroutine of Figure 9.7 performs a "bubble" sort on an array of 8-bit integers. When completed, the routine leaves the largest value in the first location with the following values in descending numerical order. The starting address, holding the first value of the array, is supplied in A0. D0 should contain N, the number of elements in the array. The array is sorted by comparing elements starting with the last value in the array for each pass.

This routine uses (D0) to set up two counters in D2 and D3. The inner loop at SORT20 uses the counter in D3 to index into the array and retrieve the elements to sort. The inner loop exchanges elements until the branch condition is true. Then, if any elements were exchanged, it is indicated by the flag in D1 set to $FF. The outer loop is then used to check for elements to exchange again. On the first pass, the array was already sorted if the flag is never set in the inner loop. If values were exchanged, a last pass is necessary after the array is sorted to determine that the algorithm may be terminated. If the operation of the subroutine is not clear from the program comments, more detailed explanations of bubble sorts are given in the references in the Further Reading section for the chapter.

```
abs. rel.  LC   obj. code   source line
---- ----  ---- ---------   -----------
   1    1  0000                 |         TTL      'FIGURE 9.7'
   2    2  0000                 |         LLEN 100
   3    3  8000                 |         ORG $8000
   4    4  0000                 |*
   5    5  8000                 |* SORT A TABLE OF 8-BIT NUMBERS IN DESENDING ORDER
   6    6  8000                 |*
   7    7  8000                 |* INPUT : (A0.L) = ADDRESS OF TABLE TO SORT
   8    8  8000                 |*         (D0.L) = NUMBER OF ENTRIES IN TABLE (N)
   9    9  8000                 |*
  10   10  8000 48E7 F882  SORT     MOVEM.L  D0-D4/A0/A6,-(SP)   ;SAVE REGISTERS
  11   11  8004 5380                SUBQ.L   #1,D0
  12   12  8006 2400                MOVE.L   D0,D2               ;COUNTER 1 = N - 1
  13   13  8008 4201      SORT10    CLR.B    D1                  ;FLAG = 0; ASSUME SORTED
  14   14  800A 2600                MOVE.L   D0,D3               ;COUNTER 2 = N - 1
  15   15  800C                |*
  16   16  800C 4DF0 3800  SORT20    LEA      (0,A0,D3.L),A6      ;START AT BOTTOM OF ARRAY
  17   17  8010 182E FFFF            MOVE.B   (-1,A6),D4          ;GET VALUE (CNT2 + 1)
  18   18  8014 B816                 CMP.B    (0,A6),D4           ;IF VALUE(CNT2+1) >= VALUE(CNT2)
  19   19  8016 6C00 000C            BGE      SORT30              ;   THEN SKIP
  20   20  801A 123C 00FF            MOVE.B   #$FF,D1             ;ELSE SET FLAG AND
  21   21  801E 1D56 FFFF            MOVE.B   (0,A6),(-1,A6)      ; SWAP VALUES
  22   22  8022 1C84                 MOVE.B   D4,(0,A6)
  23   23  8024                |*
  24   24  8024 5383      SORT30    SUBQ.L   #1,D3               ;DECREMENT CNT2
  25   25  8026 66E4                BNE      SORT20              ;   AND LOOP
  26   26  8028                |*
  27   27  8028 4A01                TST.B    D1                  ;IF FLAG = 0, SORTED
  28   28  802A 6700 0006            BEQ      DONE                ; THEN EXIT
  29   29  802E 5382                SUBQ.L   #1,D2               ;ELSE DECREMENT CNT1
  30   30  8030 66D6                BNE      SORT10              ; AND LOOP
  31   31  8032                |*
  32   32  8032 4CDF 411F  DONE     MOVEM.L  (SP)+,D0-D4/A0/A6   ;RESTORE REGISTERS
  33   33  8036 4E75                RTS
  34   34  8038                     END
```

Figure 9.7 Sorting routine.

The CMP2 instruction. The CMP2 (Compare Register Against Bounds) instruction is used to determine if a register value is within a numerical range defined by lower and upper bounds. The instruction checks the register Rn as

$$\text{Lower bound} \leq (Rn) \leq \text{Upper bound}$$

where Rn is any address register or data register. As shown in Table 9.10(a), the bounds are held in memory at the location defined by an effective address. The effective address points to the location holding the lower bound in instructions of the form

$$CMP2.<1> \qquad <EA>, <Rn>$$

in which $<1>$ = B, W, or L and $<EA>$ is defined by any memory addressing mode other than predecrement or postincrement. The upper bound must follow in the next byte, word, or longword location. After the CMP2 instruction executes, the condition

Table 9.10(a) CMP2 Instruction: Instruction Syntax

Syntax	Operation

CMP2.<l> <EA>, <Rn>	*Condition codes:*
	IF Lower bound < (Rn) < Upper bound
	THEN C = {0}, Z = {0}
	ELSE
	  IF (Rn) = Lower bound
	    or (Rn) = Upper bound
	  THEN Z = {1}, C = {0}
	  OTHERWISE OUT-OF-BOUNDS
	    C = {1}, Z = {0}

Notes:
1. <l> = B, W, or L.
2. The source operand <EA> is specified by one of the control modes. The control modes include all memory reference modes except −(An) or (An)+. The destination is any Dn or An.
3. In memory:
   <EA> ← LOWER BOUND
   <EA>+k ← UPPER BOUND
   k = 1 (byte), 2 (word), or 4 (longword).
4. The lower bound must be smaller than or equal algebraically to the upper bound.
5. If <An> is the register to be checked, byte- or word-length operands are sign-extended to 32 bits by CMP2.

Table 9.10(b) Branch Conditions after the CMP2 Instruction

Instruction	Condition codes	Condition
BEQ	Z = {1}	(Rn) equals one of the bounds
BNE	Z = {0}	(Rn) is not equal to one of the bounds
BCC	C = {0}	(Rn) is within bounds
BCS	C = {1}	(Rn) is out of bounds
BHI	C = {0} and Z = {0}	(Rn) is within bounds but not equal to either bound

codes C and Z indicate the result of the comparison. Thus, the CMP2 instruction is typically followed by a Bcc instruction of the form BEQ, BNE, BCC, BCS, or BHI. Table 9.10(b) defines the conditions for a branch.

For signed or unsigned comparisons, the smaller value representing the lower bound must precede the upper bound in memory. The value can be an 8-, 16-, or 32-bit integer whose length is determined by the length specification in the CMP2 instruction. If the register Rn is an address register, a byte or word bound is sign-extended to 32 bits before comparison. The full 32 bits of An are used for comparison. If the register Rn is a data register, only the length specified by <l> is compared. As an example, the instruction

CMP2.L $6000, D2

compares the 32-bit value held in D2 with the longword bounds starting at location $6000. The comparison is

$$(\$6000) \leq (D2)[L] \leq (\$6004)$$

where ($6000) contains the lower bound and ($6004) holds the upper bound. The range of each bound for 32-bit unsigned integers is $0000 0000 to $FFFF FFFF. The range for long signed integers is $8000 0000 to $7FFF FFFF.

The instruction can test the range of an index value or of an effective address that is being calculated during program execution. Thus, the CMP2 instruction can be used to detect indexing errors during program debugging. In other applications, the instruction can indicate an error if a program accesses data outside its designated memory space. However, such control of addressing is entirely up to the applications programmer. When an operating system checks indexing in this way, the CHK and CHK2 instructions are used since they cause a trap exception when a register value is out of bounds. Chapter 11 describes the CHK and CHK2 instructions in detail.

Example 9.9

The subroutine of Figure 9.8 checks the range of the 32-bit contents of register D0. The lower bound and upper bound must be supplied in registers D1 and D2, respectively. These values are written into the locations LOWER and UPPER for the comparison.

The result of the bounds check is defined in D3. If (D3) = 0, the register value in D0 was equal to one of the bounds. If (D3) = 1, the register value is within the bounds. The register value was not within the bounds supplied, if (D3) = −1 when the subroutine returns control to the calling program.

9.3.2 Two-Dimensional Arrays

A generalization of the one-dimensional array is a higher-dimensional array of elements. The elements in a multidimensional array are specified mathematically by more than one subscript. Table 9.11(a) shows the elements for the two-dimensional $M \times N$ array. Table 9.11(b) shows a 3×3 array as a specific example. In the form shown, M is the number of horizontal rows and N is the number of vertical columns. The element in the ith row and j^{th} column is designated X_{ij}, where $1 \leq i \leq M$ and $1 \leq j \leq N$.

An $M \times N$ array has $M \times N$ elements. $X(i, j)$ represents the address in memory of the element X_{ij} in the form X(row, column). The row index has a range of M values and the column index has a range of N values regardless of the starting indices. Questions pertinent to structuring the data in memory concern the method of storage by row and by column as well as the techniques necessary to compute the address of an element.

Array storage. If the $M \times N$ array X is stored sequentially by rows in addresses beginning with X(1,1) as

$$X(1, 1), X(1, 2), \ldots, X(1, N), X(2, 1), \ldots, X(2, N), \ldots, X(M, N)$$

```
abs. rel.   LC    obj. code    source line
---- ----   ----  ---------    -----------
   1    1   0000                 |       TTL      'FIGURE 9.8'
   2    2   0000                 |       LLEN     100
   3    3   8000                 |       ORG      $8000
   4    4   0000                 |*
   5    5   8000                 |*  CHECK (D0) AGAINST LOWER AND UPPER BOUNDS
   6    6   8000                 |*
   7    7   8000                 |*      SUBROUTINE TO DETERMINE IF
   8    8   8000                 |*         LOWER(D1)<=(D0).L<=UPPER(D2)
   9    9   8000                 |*
  10   10   8000                 |*  INPUT :  (D1.L) = LOWER BOUND
  11   11   8000                 |*           (D2.L) = UPPER BOUND
  12   12   8000                 |*
  13   13   8000                 |*  OUTPUT:  (D3.L) = 0 IF (D0) IS EQUAL TO EITHER BOUND
  14   14   8000                 |*                  = 1 IF (D0) IS IN BOUNDS
  15   15   8000                 |*                  =-1 IF (D0) IS OUT-OF-BOUNDS
  16   16   8000                 |*
  17   17   8000                 |*      THE LOWER BOUND MUST BE <= TO THE UPPER BOUND.
  18   18   8000                 |*
  19   19   8000 23C1 0000       |BNDSCHK MOVE.L  D1,LOWER      ;PUT BOUNDS IN MEMORY
  19        8004 8028            |
  20   20   8006 23C2 0000       |        MOVE.L  D2,UPPER
  20        800A 802C            |
  21   21   800C                 |*
  22   22   800C 04F9 0000       |        CMP2.L  LOWER,D0      ;CHECK BOTH BOUNDS
  22        8010 0000 8028       |
  23   23   8014                 |*
  24   24   8014 6700 000A       |        BEQ     EQUAL         ;IF Z={1}, EQUAL
  25   25   8018                 |*
  26   26   8018 6500 000A       |        BCS     OUTBNDS       ;IF C={1}, OUT-OF-BOUNDS
  27   27   801C 7601            |        MOVE.L  #1,D3         ;OTHERWISE, IN BOUNDS
  28   28   801E 4E75            |        RTS
  29   29   8020                 |*
  30   30   8020 7600            |EQUAL   MOVE.L  #0,D3         ;EQUAL TO EITHER BOUND
  31   31   8022 4E75            |        RTS
  32   32   8024                 |*
  33   33   8024 76FF            |OUTBNDS MOVE.L  #-1,D3        ;OUT-OF-BOUNDS
  34   34   8026 4E75            |        RTS
  35   35   8028                 |*
  36   36   8028                 |*      RESERVE LOCATIONS FOR BOUNDS
  37   37   8028                 |*
  38   38   8028                 |LOWER   DS.L    1
  39   39   802C                 |UPPER   DS.L    1
  40   40   8030                 |        END
```

Figure 9.8 Subroutine to check register bounds.

the storage is said to be in *row-major* form. The Motorola C compiler stores a multidimensional array by rows so that the second index changes fastest when accessing consecutive elements.

An alternative scheme is *column-major* form with successive element addresses

$$X(1,1), X(2,1), \ldots, X(M,1), X(1,2), \ldots, X(M,2), \ldots, X(M,N)$$

as shown in Table 9.11(c). The table shows the storage for a 3×3 array of words in the MC68332 memory starting at location $1000. Standard FORTRAN uses this column-major form which will be employed for the examples in this subsection.

Once the storage form is chosen, the indices for a specific element can be computed in several ways. The *address polynomial* for an $M \times N$ array has the form

$$X(i,j) = \text{base address} + C_1 \times (j-1) + C_2 \times (i-1)$$

Table 9.11 Multidimensional Arrays

(a) General form	(b) 3 × 3 Example

$X_{11} \quad X_{12} \quad \ldots \quad X_{1N}$
$X_{21} \quad X_{22} \quad \ldots \quad X_{2N}$

$\quad \cdot \qquad \cdot \qquad\qquad \cdot$

$X_{11} \quad X_{12} \quad X_{13}$

$\quad \cdot \qquad \cdot \qquad\qquad \cdot$

$X_{21} \quad X_{22} \quad X_{23}$

$\quad \cdot \qquad \cdot \qquad\qquad \cdot$

$X_{31} \quad X_{32} \quad X_{33}$

$X_{M1} \quad X_{M2} \quad \ldots \quad X_{MN}$

(c) Column-major storage of a 3 × 3 array starting at location $1000

	Address (hexadecimal)	Array element
X(1,1)	$1000	X_{11}
X(2,1)	$1002	X_{21}
X(3,1)	$1004	X_{31}
X(1,2)	$1006	X_{12}
X(2,2)	$1008	X_{22}
X(3,2)	$100A	X_{32}
X(1,3)	$100C	X_{13}
X(2,3)	$100E	X_{23}
X(3,3)	$1010	X_{33}

for a two-dimensional array with the first address at location X(1,1). When the constants C_1 and C_2 are properly chosen, address calculation is straightforward on a processor with a multiply instruction.[6]

Table 9.12 shows the address polynomials for arrays with elements of length C bytes. The address of X_{ij} in an array stored by column-major form is

$$X(i,j) = B0 + C \times [(i-1) + M \times (j-1)]$$

in which

$$1 \leq i \leq M \text{ and } 1 \leq j \leq N$$

and B0 is the base address. This addressing method is easily implemented with the CPU32 using indirect addressing with indexing if elements in a fixed column (or row) are being selected. If both indices are varied, one address must be calculated separately and added to the value of the effective address computed with indexed addressing.

Example 9.10

When the address of an element in a two-dimensional array is calculated, two indices must be added to the starting or base address. The address register indirect with index

---

[6] In some cases, to save the time required by multiplication or to allow dynamic (during execution) allocation of array storage, special addressing methods are used. These include the use of a "dope vector" describing the array characteristics or addressing by indirection in which the row (or column) addresses are held in a table. Several of the references in the Further Reading section at the end of this chapter describe these techniques in greater detail.

Table 9.12 Multidimensional Array Addressing

Array storage	Address X(i,j)
Column-major storage $X(1,1), X(2,1), \ldots$	$B0 + C \times [(i-1) + M \times (j-1)]$
Row-major storage $X(1,1), X(1,2), \ldots$	$B0 + C \times [(j-1) + N \times (i-1)]$

Notes:
1. B0 is the base address of array $X(i,j)$ with elements C bytes in length.
2. The indices range as follows:

$$\text{rows} : 1 \leq i \leq M$$
$$\text{columns} : 1 \leq j \leq N$$

and the PC relative with index addressing modes of the CPU32 allow two separate offsets and calculate the effective address as

$$<EA> = (R) + (Rn) + <d>$$

The register R here could be either an address register in the indirect mode or the program counter for the relative mode. The index register Rn is either an address register or data register. Figure 9.9 shows the use of this addressing method for an array stored in column-major form. If the number of bytes per element is 1, the address calculation becomes

$$X(i,j) = B0 + [(i-1) + M \times (j-1)]$$

The base address and one index can be stored in registers. The second index can be specified as the offset in the address register indirect with index addressing mode. In the figure, the offset selects the row and remains fixed. The 3×3 array begins at hexadecimal location $1000, which is stored in A1, and the register D1 contains the column index $(j-1) \times M$, which is $0006. The instruction

$$\text{MOVE.B} \qquad (1, A1, D1.L), D2$$

transfers element X_{23} to the low-order byte of D2. To select X_{2j} from another column, (D1) must be changed to indicate the column offset, which is computed as $3 \times (j-1)$ with $j = 1, 2$, or 3.

Example 9.11

The subroutine in Figure 9.10 performs a binary search of a table or array for a word-length bit pattern called a key value. The table is composed of M entries which are each N bytes long. The starting address of the table is supplied in A0 and the key to locate is in (D0)[7:0]. The low-order word of D1 contains the length (N) of each entry and (D2)[15:0] contains the number of entries (M) in the table.

If the search is successful, the address of the key value is returned in A6. Otherwise, A6 contains a zero. Since a binary search is being performed, the data are assumed to be sorted numerically in the table being searched.

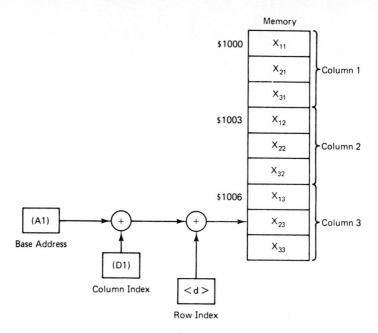

Memory

$1000 X_{11} ⎤
        X_{21} ⎬ Column 1
        X_{31} ⎦

$1003 X_{12} ⎤
        X_{22} ⎬ Column 2
        X_{32} ⎦

$1006 X_{13} ⎤
        X_{23} ⎬ Column 3
        X_{33} ⎦

(A1)
Base Address

(D1)
Column Index

\<d\>
Row Index

Example: Load X_{23} into D2

MOVE.B   (1, A1, D1.L),D2   ;(D2)[7:0] ⟵ ((A1) + (D1) + 1)

(A1) = $0000 1000 (Base)
(D1) = $0000 0006 (Column index = (j − 1)*M)
\<d\> =   1   (Row index = i − 1)

Figure 9.9 Fixed-array addressing.

Example 9.12

Figure 9.11 shows the data structure for a two-dimensional array in memory. The starting address of each column of length M is held in an address table pointed to by A0. The array is defined as

$$X(I, J) \qquad I = 1, 2, \ldots M; J = 1, 2, \ldots N$$

and consists of M rows and N columns of word-length (16-bit) elements. A program could compute the address of element $X(I, J)$ as

$$X(I, J) = ((A0) + 4 \times (J − 1)) + 2(I − 1)$$

where I is the row index and J is the column index. The use of the table of column addresses eliminates the calculation required to compute the column offset to a given column. This is faster during execution but requires a table of N addresses to be stored in memory.

```
abs.   LC    obj. code    source line
----   ----  ----------   -----------
   1   0000                         TTL      'FIGURE 9.10'
   2   0000                         LLEN     100
   3   8000                         ORG      $8000
   4   0000               *
   5   8000               * SEARCH SUBROUTINE DOES A BINARY SEARCH OF A TABLE
   6   8000               *  INPUT : (A0.L) = TABLE TO SEARCH
   7   8000               *          (D0.B) = KEY TO SEARCH FOR IN TABLE
   8   8000               *                   BYTE LENGTH
   9   8000               *          (D1.W) = LENGTH IN BYTES OF EACH ENTRY
  10   8000               *                   IN TABLE
  11   8000               *          (D2.W) = NUMBER OF ENTRIES IN TABLE  (END)
  12   8000               *
  13   8000               * OUTPUT : (A6.L) = ADDRESS OF ITEM IN TABLE WITH VALUE OF
  14   8000               *                   KEY (OR ZERO)
  15   8000               *
  16   8000  48E7 FC00    SEARCH  MOVEM.L  D0-D5,-(SP)   ;SAVE REGISTERS ON STACK
  17   8004  5342                 SUBQ.W   #1,D2         ;INIT :  END (D2)
  18   8006  4283                 CLR.L    D3            ;        BEGIN (D3)
  19   8008  2C43                 MOVEA.L  D3,A6         ;        OUTPUT VALUE
  20   800A               *
  21   800A  B642         SER10   CMP.W    D2,D3         ;IF BEGIN >= END
  22   800C  6E00 0028            BGT      EXIT          ;  THEN EXIT
  23   8010  3803                 MOVE.W   D3,D4         ;  ELSE COMPUTE
  24   8012  D842                 ADD.W    D2,D4         ;       INDEX = (BEGIN
  25   8014  E24C                 LSR.W    #1,D4         ;             + END)/2
  26   8016               *                             ;ENDIF
  27   8016               *
  28   8016  3A04                 MOVE.W   D4,D5         ;COMPUTE ADDRESS
  29   8018  CAC1                 MULU.W   D1,D5         ;INDEX IN TABLE OF KEY
  30   801A               *                             ;TO TEST
  31   801A  B030 5000            CMP.B    (0,A0,D5),D0  ;IF KEY >= ENTRY
  32   801E  6C00 0008            BGE      SER20         ;  THEN BRANCH TO MODIFY
  33   8022               *                             ;       BEGIN
  34   8022  5344                 SUBQ.W   #1,D4         ;  ELSE SET
  35   8024  3404                 MOVE.W   D4,D2         ;       END = INDEX - 1
  36   8026  60E2                 BRA      SER10         ;  TRY AGAIN
  37   8028               *                             ;ENDIF
  38   8028               *
  39   8028  6700 0008    SER20   BEQ      SUCCESS       ;IF KEY = TABLE ENTRY
  40   802C               *                             ;  THEN BRANCH TO UPDATE
  41   802C               *                             ;       OUTPUT
  42   802C  5244                 ADDQ.W   #1,D4         ;  ELSE
  43   802E  3604                 MOVE.W   D4,D3         ;       BEGIN = INDEX + 1
  44   8030  60D8                 BRA      SER10         ;  TRY AGAIN
  45   8032               *                             ;ENDIF
  46   8032               *
  47   8032  4DF0 5000    SUCCESS LEA      (0,A0,D5.W),A6 ;SAVE OUTPUT ADDRESS
  48   8036  4CDF 003F    EXIT    MOVEM.L  (SP)+,D0-D5   ;RESTORE REGISTERS
  49   803A  4E75                 RTS
  50   803C                       END
```

Figure 9.10 Search routine.

9.3.3 Strings

For the examples in this textbook, a *string* is a sequence of ASCII characters considered as a unit. The string is usually stored as an array of bytes. This storage method allows an instruction to use the predecrement or postincrement addressing mode to access to a particular character in a string and leave the pointer at the next character address. The string is defined in memory by its starting address and either its length in bytes or the location of the last byte.

For output, the string can be defined by its starting address and length as in the

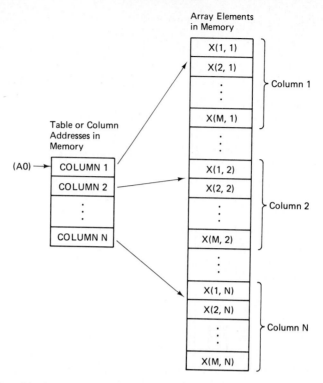

Array Elements
in Memory

X(1, 1)	
X(2, 1)	
.	} Column 1
X(M, 1)	
.	
X(1, 2)	
X(2, 2)	
.	} Column 2
X(M, 2)	
.	
X(1, N)	
X(2, N)	
.	} Column N
X(M, N)	

Table or Column
Addresses in
Memory

(A0) →

COLUMN 1
COLUMN 2
.
COLUMN N

Array is stored in column-major form. Elements are designated
X(row, column) or X(I, J) with I = 1, 2, . . ., M and J = 1, 2, . . ., N.

Figure 9.11 Indirect addressing of multidimensional array.

examples in Section 7.6. This defines a fixed length string. Alternatively, the string can be ended by a special character such as the ASCII NUL character. Section 12.3 presents examples of this method of terminating a string of variable length used for output. For input, a variable length string is usually terminated by a carriage return or other special ASCII character.

Since the CPU32 has no string manipulation instructions, programs must be created to perform string operations. A common operation is the comparison of two strings for equality. The example of Subsection 6.2.3 performs a string comparison. Such string operations can be made more efficient by using the loop mode of the CPU. Section 9.5 describes applications of the loop mode.

9.3.4 Queues

The *queue* is a data structure in which all insertions are made at one end and all deletions are made at the other end. This differs from the stack structure which is accessed at only one end. The queue has an advantage in applications that require items to be accessed in the queue in the same order that they were inserted. In fact, a queue is sometimes called a FIFO (first-in-first-out) although hardware designers usually reserve this term for FIFO memory chips. Also, most software queues are *circular* queues in which the addressing pointer wraps around to the beginning when the last location assigned to the queue is encountered. Otherwise, the size of the queue could grow without limit if more and more items are inserted without the corresponding deletion of items.[7]

Figure 9.12 shows the various operations on a queue. The queue is defined to occupy locations between location New Queue Pointer (NEWQP) and End Queue Pointer (ENDQP).[8] Two other address pointers indicate the active queue locations where data values are to be accessed. QUEOUT points to the first item inserted and hence the next item to be accessed when an instruction uses QUEOUT to point to an item. In other terminology, QUEOUT points to the *head* or the *front* of the queue. QUEIN points to a queue location that is empty. The next item to be inserted into the queue is placed in location QUEIN. The location indicated by QUEIN is often called the *tail* or the *rear* of the queue. As shown in Figure 9.12(a), the queue pointers QUEIN and QUEOUT both point to the head of the queues (NEWQP) when initialized. In fact, any time that the address pointers

$$QUEIN = QUEOUT,$$

the queue is considered empty.

The operation of adding an item to the queue is called an *enqueue* operation or a *put* operation. Figure 9.12(b) shows the queue after item $X(1)$ is added. QUEIN now points to the next empty location. The queue has the form in Figure 9.12(c) after three items are added. After each put operation, QUEIN is incremented by the number of bytes for each item if the queue grows from low to high memory locations. For byte, word or long word operands, the postincrement addressing mode of the CPU32 could be used to put an item on the queue. Of course, the predecrement addressing mode would be used for a put operation if the queue grows from high to low memory.

After an item is accessed as in Figure 9.12(d), QUEOUT points to the next item to be used. The operation of accessing a queue item and changing QUEOUT is called a *dequeue* or a *get* operation. It is clear from Figure 9.12 that if the queue pointers QUEIN and QUEOUT become equal, the queue is empty. An *underflow* condition occurs when a program attempts to get an item from an empty queue. This could mean an error condition or simply that the program has accessed all the items in the queue. The underflow condition in the latter case indicates that all data in the queue have been read and the program should begin processing the data items as required.

Since the queue holds a finite number of data items, the size of the queue and its circular structure must be considered. For example, assume that the queue in Figure 9.12 holds M items. The first $M - 1$ puts will leave the condition

$$QUEIN = ENDQP.$$

---

[7] Knuth's textbook referenced in the Further Reading section of this chapter gives a more thorough discussion of queues.

[8] The notation NEWQP and ENDQP follows that for the queue of the Queued Serial Module discussed in Chapter 12.

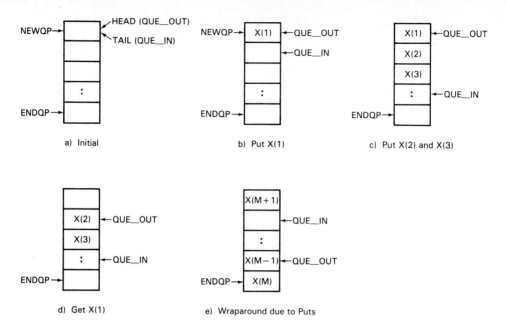

Figure 9.12 Queue structure.

When this occurs, the pointer QUEIN must be re-initialized with the value NEWQP. This condition is shown in Figure 9.12(e) after QUEIN is re-initialized and one more item, $X(M + 1)$, is put on the queue. As long as QUEOUT continues to "chase" QUEIN but does not become equal to it, the queue has space for additional items.

An *overflow* occurs when a put operation is attempted that causes

$$QUEIN = QUEOUT.$$

This equality condition should only occur when the queue is empty and indicates an error at any other time.

In summary, a queue manipulation program should perform the following operations:
(a) initialize QUEIN = QUEOUT to the first location assigned to the queue;
(b) test for overflow before a put operation;
(c) test for underflow before a get operation;
(d) reinitialize QUEIN and QUEOUT if either pointer becomes equal to the address of the last location assigned to the queue.

The queue is an important data structure for I/O programs. In an I/O application, the queue can serve as a buffer area for characters or strings to be transferred. Section 12.3 considers such queue applications as part of I/O driver programs. The Queued Serial Peripheral Interface (QSPI) of the MC683323 contains a 16-element queue to improve the I/O performance of the module. The QSPI queue is discussed in detail in Section 12.4.

9.3.5 Linked Lists

When dealing with arrays, the successor of an item being addressed is located by adding a constant to the address of the present item. For example, the address of a one-dimensional array element $X(i, j)$ is

$$X(j + 1) = X(j) + C$$

where C is the number of bytes occupied by each element. The elements, ordered successively, occupied contiguous blocks of memory, as shown in Figure 9.13.

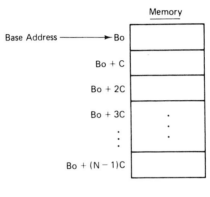

Notes:
(1) Bo is the base address.
(2) Each element is C bytes long.

Figure 9.13 Sequential array storage.

In comparison, the *linked list* is a data structure that does not require contiguous storage of its elements. This subsection discusses the linked list in an introductory manner. Advanced operations on such lists, including management of the memory space occupied by the list and ordering of list elements, are discussed in several of the references in the Further Reading section at the end of the chapter.

Figure 9.14(a) shows a sample linked list of five items. The items are located in memory at addresses A1, A2, ... , A5. Each element in the list contains both a pointer (address) called a *link* to the next element in the list and the data item. The list shown has a *one-way* link since only an item's successor can be found. Also, the sample list is unordered since the data items do not follow one another in numerical order. The pointer to the list is stored at address HEAD. The last element, item 5 in the figure, contains a special symbol. It is designated NULL to indicate the end of the list. A NULL value of zero, for example, could be used in CPU32 programs since no data item would be stored at location $0000. If location HEAD contains the value NULL, the list is empty. Figure 9.14(b) illustrates how the sample list could be stored in memory.

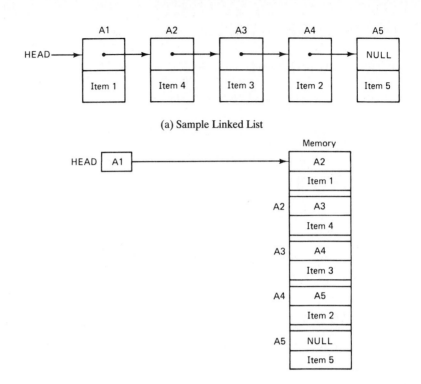

(a) Sample Linked List

Memory

(b) Memory Allocation

Figure 9.14 Allocation for an unordered linked list.

Example 9.13

Figure 9.15 shows a subroutine that creates a linked list in a free area of memory with beginning address AVAIL. The nodes or elements in the list are each eight bytes in length and the list will be initialized to contain 10 entries. The loop starting at label LINK computes the address of the next node in the list and then stores the address as the link to that node. After the loop terminates, the last link that was stored is rewritten with a NULL value.

EXERCISES

9.3.1. Write a subroutine to return the sine of an angle in degrees when an angle from 0 to 360 degrees is specified. Use a lookup table with a 1-degree resolution in angle. Assume that the table with starting address SINE is already provided and contains 16-bit values for the sines of angles from 0 to 89 degrees. If the angle is greater than 90 degrees, compute the sine of the angle using trigonometric identities. [*Note:* The value could be calculated using the Taylor series expansion for $\sin(x)$:

$$\sin(x) = x - (x^3/3!) + (x^5/5!) - \dots$$

```
abs.   LC    obj. code    source line
----   ----  ----------   -----------
   1   0000                         TTL      'FIGURE 9.15'
   2   0000                         LLEN     100
   3   8000                         ORG      $8000
   4   0000               *
   5         0000 0000     NULL      EQU  0       ;SET UP VALUE FOR NULL
   6   8000               *
   7   8000               *  CREATE A LINKED LIST
   8   8000               *
   9   8000               *  INPUT : AVAIL IS THE ADDRESS OF A FREE BLOCK OF MEMORY
  10   8000               *          HEAD IS THE POINTER TO THE TOP OF THE LIST
  11   8000               *
  12   8000               * OUTPUT : LINKS ARE STORED IN THE BLOCK AT AVAIL AND
  13   8000               *          HEAD POINTS TO THE FIRST NODE IN THE LIST
  14   8000               *
  15   8000 48E7 C0C0     LNKLST    MOVEM.L  D0-D1/A0-A1,-(SP)  ;SAVE REGISTERS
  16   8004 41F9 0000     LEA       AVAIL,A0
       8008 802E
  17   800A 23C8 0000               MOVE.L   A0,HEAD        ;SET HEAD TO POINT TO AVAIL
       800E 802A
  18   8010 7008                    MOVE.L   #8,D0          ;SET UP BYTES/NODE
  19   8012 720A                    MOVE.L   #10,D1         ;SET UP NUMBER OF NODES
  20   8014               *
  21   8014 2248          LINK      MOVE.L   A0,A1          ;NODE ADDRESS INTO A1
  22   8016 D1C0                    ADD.L    D0,A0          ;COMPUTE NEXT NODE
  23   8018 2288                    MOVE.L   A0,(A1)        ;STORE LINK TO NEXT NODE
  24   801A 5381                    SUBQ.L   #1,D1          ;DECREMENT NUMBER OF NODES
  25   801C 66F6                    BNE      LINK           ;UNTIL COUNT REACHES ZERO
  26   801E               *
  27   801E 22BC 0000               MOVE.L   #NULL,(A1)     ;REWRITE LAST LINK
       8022 0000
  28   8024               *
  29   8024 4CDF 0303               MOVEM.L  (SP)+,D0-D1/A0-A1 ;RESTORE REGISTERS
  30   8028 4E75                    RTS
  31   802A               *
  32   802A               HEAD      DS.L  1          ;POINTER TO TOP OF LINKED LIST
  33   802E               AVAIL     DS.L  20         ;MEMORY BLOCK FOR LIST
  34   802E               *
  35   807E                         END
```

Figure 9.15 Subroutine to create a linked list.

The series method will yield the sine value to any accuracy but is far slower than the table lookup if the table has sufficient resolution. Create an abbreviated table of sine values and test your routine.]

9.3.2. Write a subroutine to clear a three-dimensional array *without* calculating the three-dimensional address polynomial. Assume that the array in memory is stored in column-major form. The subroutine is passed the starting address, the size of the array ($M \times N \times O$), and the number of bytes in each element.

9.3.3. Write a routine to multiply two 2×2 matrices.

9.3.4. Write the address polynomial for a k-dimensional array if $I_1, I_2, I_3, \ldots, I_k$ are the indices and $L_1, L_2, L_3, \ldots, L_k$ are the lengths.

9.3.5. Write a set of queue manipulation subroutines to perform initialization and the get and put operations. The routines should return an error code if an overflow or underflow condition is detected.

9.3.6. Write a subroutine to remove an entry from the top of the linked list created in Example 9.13. What happens if the list is empty [i.e., (HEAD) = NULL]?

9.3.7. Assume that

$$(D3) = \$ABCD\ FFFC$$
$$(A0) = \$8000$$
$$(\$8000) = \$FFF0$$
$$(\$8002) = \$0040$$

before the instruction

CMP2.W   (A0), D3

executes. What condition codes result after the instruction is executed?

9.3.8. Modify the subroutine of Example 9.9 to be a macrocoded segment to allow Rn and the length of the bounds (B, W, or L) to be specified when the macro is invoked.

9.4 SUBROUTINE USAGE AND ARGUMENT PASSING

The use of *subroutines* or procedures is an important programming technique to create modular programs in which each subroutine performs a specific task within the overall program. The method of transfer of control between the calling program and the subroutine is called *subroutine linkage*. In the CPU32, the call to the subroutine is accomplished by the Branch to Subroutine (BSR) or Jump to Subroutine (JSR) instruction. The JSR instruction syntax is

JSR   <SUBR>

which first pushes the return address within the calling program onto the system stack. Then, control is transferred to the subroutine at address <SUBR>. Thus, transfer of control is accomplished very simply in the CPU32.

In the JSR instruction, the subroutine address may be specified by any of the control addressing modes of the CPU32. This includes all the modes that reference memory except for predecrement and postincrement addressing. The Branch to Subroutine (BSR) instruction uses PC relative addressing. Section 6.3 describes both the JSR and BSR instruction in detail.

When data must be passed between the calling program and the subroutine, a number of methods are available to transfer the information. An important part of the program design is to select the most appropriate transfer method. This section concentrates on the methods to pass values between routines. Subsection 9.4.1 describes argument passing using various methods. Subsection 9.4.2 explains the use of the CPU32 stack frames to pass values on the system stack.

The information needed by the subroutine is defined in terms of *parameters* which allow the subroutine to handle general cases rather than operate on specific values. Each call to the subroutine allows different values, called *arguments*, to be supplied for the parameters. Some typical FORTRAN subroutine references are shown in Figure 9.16. The subroutine is named SUBR and has the parameters A, B, and C.

It may be called with various arguments as long as the arguments are the same data type (integer, floating-point, etc.) as the parameters in the subroutine definition. The names or values of the arguments are arbitrary. The symbolic names for the arguments in the example are actually addresses assigned by the compiler. The specific values 1.0 and 3.0 in the second call can be substituted to take advantage of the flexibility of the FORTRAN language. In assembly language, the distinction between actual values and the addresses of arguments is important.

```
! _ _ _ _ _ _ _ _ _ _ _ _ _ _ _ _ _ _ _ _ _ _ _ _ _ _ _ _ _ _ _ _ _ _ _ _ _ _ _ _
!                                     !                                          !
!  Calling Program                    !  Subroutine                              !
!                                     !                                          !
!- - - - - - - - - - - - - - - - - - -!- - - - - - - - - - - - - - - - - - - - -!
!                                     !                                          !
!                                     !  SUBROUTINE SUBR (A, B, C)               !
!                .                    !      .                                   !
!                .                    !      .                                   !
!                .                    !      .                                   !
!  CALL SUBR (X, Y, Z)                !      .                                   !
!                .                    !      .                                   !
!                .                    !  RETURN                                  !
!                .                    !  END                                     !
!  CALL SUBR (1.0, 3.0, RESULT)       !                                          !
!                .                    !                                          !
!                .                    !                                          !
!                .                    !                                          !
!  CALL SUBR (A(1), W, ANS)           !                                          !
!                .                    !                                          !
!                .                    !                                          !
!                .                    !                                          !
!  END                                !                                          !
!                                     !                                          !
!- - - - - - - - - - - - - - - - - - -!- - - - - - - - - - - - - - - - - - - - -!
```

Figure 9.16 FORTRAN subroutine usage.

The mechanics of defining parameters and transmitting arguments to subroutines are more complex in assembly language. Processor registers, the system stack, or fixed locations in memory may hold arguments. Also, the LINK and UNLK instructions of the CPU32 can be used to create *stack frames* as a subroutine is called. This frame is a block of memory reserved on the stack which holds the return address, arguments, and local variables, if any. Recursive or reentrant subroutines can be implemented using this method of data handling in the subroutine.

9.4.1 Passing Arguments to Subroutines

The parameters, which define the arguments to be transferred between a subroutine and the calling program, can be data values, addresses, or combinations of both. When only a small number of arguments are transferred, they can be passed directly between the programs using processor registers. When many variables are passed or when a data structure such as an array is being referenced, it is more efficient to transfer the starting address of the group of variables or data structure. The distinctions have broad significance in many high-level language programs when the operation of the compiler is considered. In assembly language, the distinction between values and addresses is important because the method of passing the parameters determines how the arguments are accessed.

Table 9.13 lists several techniques used to pass values or addresses between programs. The calling program sets up the calling sequence, including the definition of the arguments to be transferred to the subroutine. The subroutine then accesses the arguments for processing and possibly returns values or addresses to the calling program. The arguments passed to the subroutine are defined as the *input parameters*. The results are values or addresses corresponding to the subroutine's *output parameters*. Of course, a combination of the techniques listed in Table 9.13 could be used when a complicated set of input and output parameters is defined.

Table 9.13 Methods to Pass Arguments

Type	Description	Comments
Register	The calling routine loads predefined registers with values or addresses	Number of parameters is limited
Stack	The calling routine pushes values or addresses on the stack	Subroutine references data using offsets from the stack pointer address
Parameter areas	Parameter areas are defined in memory which contain the values or addresses	The areas can be defined during assembly or using base register addressing
In-line	Values or addresses are stored following the call	The subroutine computes the location of the parameters from the return PC value on the system stack

Register transfer.   The simplest method of passing arguments is using the CPU32 register set. Data values can be passed in any of the eight data registers. Similarly, the address registers can be used to pass addresses that point to data values or to the starting addresses of data structures. The register passing scheme has the advantages of simplicity, small memory requirements, and minimum execution time. The number of arguments that can be passed is limited to the number of registers available: 15 for the CPU32 since the system stack pointer (A7) would not be used for this purpose. The designer of the subroutine and the calling routine must define which registers are used to pass the arguments.

Example 9.14

An example instruction sequence using register transfer of data to subroutine SUBR is

MOVE.W	VALUE, D1	; DATA
MOVEA.L	ADDTAB, A1	; POINTER
LEA	HEAD, A2	; ADDRESS OF HEAD
JSR	SUBR	

which sets up a 16-bit value in D1, the address pointer in location ADDTAB in A1 and the address HEAD in A2. The subroutine SUBR can then access the values in the registers directly to perform its function.

Stack transfer. A private stack or the system stack can be used to pass arguments by having the calling routine push values or addresses on the stack before the call. Section 4.2 describes the difference between private stacks and the system stack.

A private stack, which can be defined in CPU32 programs using address register A0, A1, ..., or A6 to represent the stack pointer, could be used. The values are pushed using the predecrement or postincrement mode of addressing in the calling program. Popping the arguments in the subroutine allows access to the values or addresses. For a private stack, the modification of the stack pointer during execution is handled at the discretion of the programmer and does not affect system operation.

The system stack can also be used to pass data between routines. Section 6.3 describes the form of the system stack for subroutine calls. If the calling routine pushes data on the stack, the stack will contain data and the return address after the call. The subroutine can access the data using an offset from the stack point address. However, the subroutine or the calling program must "remove" the data from the stack by adjusting the stack pointer after the data are processed to avoid leaving extraneous data on the stack.

Example 9.15(a)

Assume A1 is a stack pointer for a private stack growing into *higher* memory locations. The instructions to pass two values to a subroutine SUBR could be

LEA	STACKP, A1	; PRIVATE STACK
MOVE.W	VAL1, (A1)+	; PUSH VALUE
MOVE.W	VAL2, (A1)+	; PUSH VALUE
JSR	SUBR	

where STACKP is the address of the BOTTOM of the stack in memory since the stack increases into higher memory locations. The subroutine accesses the values by the sequence

SUBR	MOVE.W	−(A1), D2	; SECOND VALUE

```
          MOVE.W          −(A1), D1                    ; FIRST VALUE
```

if the object is to load the values into data registers. The stack pointer A1 now contains its original value STACKP. In this example, the argument in register A1 contained the address of a data structure (the stack) in memory.

Example 9.15(b)

The system stack grows into *lower* memory locations when values are pushed on the stack. When the system stack is used to pass arguments, the return address is at the top of the stack when the subroutine begins execution as previously described in Section 4.2. The calling sequence for this method of parameter passing could be

```
          PEA             ADDR                         ; PUSH ADDRESS
          MOVE.W          VAL1, −(SP)                  ; PUSH VALUE
          JSR             SUBR
```

The address ADDR is placed on the stack first, then the value in location VAL1, and finally the return address.

One approach to adjusting the stack pointer after the data are read involves using the stack pointer directly as the pointer to the data. Since (PC) is at the top of the stack, it can be saved and then restored before the return. The sequence to accomplish this might be

```
SUBR      MOVE.L          (SP)+, A1                    ; SAVE (PC)
          MOVE.W          (SP)+, D1                    ; GET DATA
          MOVEA.L         (SP)+, A2                    ; GET ADDRESS
                            .
                            .                          ; PROCESS
                            .
          MOVE.L          A1, −(SP)                    ; RESTORE (PC)
          RTS
```

Since this method is typically used by a program in the user mode, the active stack pointer is the USP. Modifying the stack pointers does not interfere with interrupt processing and similar system operations that use the supervisor stack pointer (SSP). Subsection 9.4.2 describes another approach of data passing using stack frames.

Memory locations for arguments.　　When large numbers of parameters are to be passed, a *parameter area* can be set up in memory. This area contains, in a predetermined sequence, the values or addresses that are accessed by the subroutine after it has been passed the starting address of the area. The same area could be used by several subroutines requiring different parameters as long as the area is large enough to hold the maximum number of arguments.

Another use of this method is common in systems which have subroutines in ROM. The parameter area in RAM (Random Access read/write Memory) memory is defined according to the system requirements and the address is passed to the subroutines to use as a base address in accessing the arguments.[9]

Example 9.16

The calling program could set up a parameter area in the following way: % Add glue to push down

	MOVE.W	VAL1, PRAM	; STORE DATA
	MOVE.W	VAL2, PRAM + 2	; SECOND WORD
		.	
		.	
		.	
	MOVE.W	VAL5, PRAM + 8	; FIFTH WORD
	LEA	PRAM, A1	; PUSH ADDRESS
	JSR	SUBR	
		.	
PRAM	DS.W	5	; PARAMETERS
	END		

in which five words are defined as parameters. The subroutine could access the values using indirect addressing with displacement. For example, the instruction

MOVE.W	(6, A1), D1

transfers the fourth value to D1. Many variations are possible to define the parameter areas in memory.

In-line coding. Another method of passing values to a subroutine is to code the values following the call to the subroutine. This method, called *in-line coding*, defines argument values which are constant and will not change after assembly. These values can be defined by DC directives following the call.

Example 9.17

Consider the instruction sequence

JSR	SUBR	
DC.W	1	; IN-LINE ARGUMENT

which places the constant 1 after the subroutine call. The 32-bits of (PC) are pushed on the system stack by the subroutine call. This address points to the location of the *argument*

---

[9] Another version, used when FORTRAN "common" areas are specified, defines the address of the parameter area to both the calling program and the subroutine during compilation.

in the instruction sequence. The following sequence can be executed by the subroutine to load the argument into the low-order word of D1 and point the return address on the stack to the word beyond the value.

```
        MOVEA.L     (A7), A0          ; GET PC VALUE
        MOVE.W      (A0)+, D1         ; GET ARGUMENT
        MOVE.L      A0, (A7)          ; STORE RETURN PC
                                      ; PROCESS

        RTS
```

The first instruction loads the (PC) into A0 from the stack. Register A0 then addresses the argument and is incremented by 2 after D1 is loaded. After A0 is incremented, it points to the next instruction in the calling program following the in-line argument. The next instruction in the subroutine pushes the correct return address on the stack, overwriting the value saved by the JSR instruction. The RTS instruction is used here to restore (PC) and return control to the calling program. The reference to A7 indicates the system stack pointer: either USP or SSP depending on whether the program mode is user or supervisor, respectively.

9.4.2 Stack Frames

One of the principal issues in the design of subroutines involves the concept of *transparency*. Simply stated, when a subroutine finishes executing, it should have no "visible" effect except as defined by its linkage to the calling program. For example, a subroutine should not change the values in any registers, unless a register is used to return a result. In many example programs in previous chapters, register values not to be changed were saved upon entry to the subroutine if the registers were used by the subroutine. Typically, a MOVEM instruction pushed the contents of the registers on the stack. The values were restored before returning to the calling program. Also, the JSR instruction automatically saved the return address on the system stack and the RTS instruction restored the return address.

The use of the system stack to save and restore the return address and the contents of registers used within the subroutine assured that the details of the subroutine operation were transparent to the calling program. If a subroutine itself made a subroutine call, using the stack for temporary storage of register contents and for each return address by each subroutine allowed nesting of subroutine calls.

The concept of using the stack to store data temporarily during subroutine execution can be extended by defining a stack frame. The *stack frame* is an area on the stack that is used to store return addresses, input data, output data, and local variables. Subroutines can access the data in the stack frame. The input data are passed to the subroutine by the calling program. Output data are returned to the calling program. Local variables are those values used during the subroutine execution that are not transferred back to the calling routine. A loop counter, for example, which changes as the subroutine performs each iteration might be defined as a local variable.

On each call to the subroutine, a new set of parameters, local variables, and return addresses can be accessed by a subroutine using the stack frame technique. If the subroutine is called before it is completely finished, the information in the stack frame will not be destroyed.

CPU32 stack frames. In multiprogramming systems, several independent tasks may use the same subroutine. For example, two CRT terminals may be connected to the system but share the same I/O routine. As the operating system switches control between the terminals, it is possible that the I/O routine of one is interrupted and control passed to the other terminal temporarily. All the data associated with the first terminal used by the I/O routine must be saved so that when the first terminal regains control, the I/O routine begins where it left off. Such usage requires *reentrant* routines in which no data in the program memory area itself changes value during execution. Any values that change are placed on the stack for storage. Thus, the program code is separated completely from the data on which it operates. A special case is the *recursive* routine, which calls itself and so is self-reentrant. The stack frame allows reentrant and recursive routines to be created easily.

The stack frame is created by the calling program and the subroutine using the CPU32 instructions LINK and UNLK. Table 9.14 shows the syntax and operation of these instructions. Access to variables on the stack by the subroutine is accomplished by using offsets (or indexing) from a base register called a *frame pointer*. Although the stack pointer may change value as items are pushed or popped, the frame pointer does not change during the subroutine's execution.

Table 9.14 Operation of LINK and UNLK

Instruction	Syntax	Operation
Link	LINK.<l_1> <An>, #<disp>	1. (SP) ← (SP) − 4; ((SP)) ← (An) 2. (An) ← (SP) 3. (SP) ← (SP) + <disp>
Unlink	UNLK <An>	1. (SP) ← (An) 2. (An) ← ((SP)); (SP) ← (SP) + 4

Notes:
1. <disp> is a 32-bit or 16-bit sign extended integer. A negative displacement is specified to allocate stack area.
2. <l_1> = W or L.

Example 9.18

Figure 9.17 illustrates a possible sequence in the calling program and the operation of the subroutine. Figure 9.18 shows the stack contents for this example. Many variations are possible according to the application. In the case shown, the calling routine first reserves N bytes on the stack for arguments to be returned by the subroutine. Then, an input value and an address are pushed on the stack. The JSR instruction pushes the return address and transfers control to the subroutine. At this point, the stack contains N bytes of space for the result, the 32-bit contents of location ARG, the address X, and the return address.

The subroutine first executes the LINK instruction to create a stack frame and define the frame pointer. This instruction saves the value of <An> on the stack and replaces <An> with the value of the stack pointer using A1 in our example. The frame

```
abs. rel.   LC    obj. code    source line
---- ----   ----  ----------   -----------
   1    1    0000                        TTL      'FIGURE 9.17'
   2    2    0000                        LLEN     100
   3    3    8000                        ORG      $8000
   4    4    0000              *
   5    5    8000              *  CALLING PROGRAM
   6    6    8000              *
   7    7          0000 0008   N          EQU   8 ; 8 BYTES FOR OUTPUTS
   8    8          0000 0008   M          EQU   8 ; 8 BYTES FOR LOCAL VARIABLES
   9    9    8000              *          .
  10   10    8000              *          .
  11   11    8000 DFFC FFFF               ADD.L    #-N,SP         ; OUTPUT AREA
  11         8004 FFF8
  12   12    8006 2F39 0000               MOVE.L   ARG,-(SP)      ; INPUT ARGUMENT FOR SUBROUTINE
  12         800A 801E
  13   13    800C 4879 0000               PEA      X              ; INPUT ADDRESS X
  13         8010 8022
  14   14    8012 4EB9 0000               JSR      SUBR
  14         8016 80EA
  15   15    8018 508F                    ADDQ.L   #8,SP          ; SKIP OVER INPUTS
  16   16    801A 221F                    MOVE.L   (SP)+,D1       ; READ OUTPUTS FROM SUBROUTINE
  17   17    801C 241F                    MOVE.L   (SP)+,D2
  18   18    801E             *           .
  19   19    801E             *  CONTINUE PROCESSING AS REQUIRED
  20   20    801E             *           .
  21   21    801E             *           .
  22   22    801E             *
  23   23    801E             *  (END OF MAIN PROGRAM PROCESSING)
  24   24    801E             *
  25   25    801E 0123 4567   ARG         DC.L     $01234567      ; ARGUMENT TO PASS
  26   26    8022             X           DS.B     200            ; TABLE WHOSE ADDRESS IS PASSED
  27   27    8022             *
  28   28    80EA             *  SUBROUTINE
  29   29    80EA             *
  30   30    80EA 4E51 FFF8   SUBR        LINK     A1,#-M         ; SAVE OLD FP
  31   31    80EE             *           .
  32   32    80EE             *           .
  33   33    80EE 2379 0000               MOVE.L   LOCAL1,(-4,A1) ; SAVE LOCAL VARIABLES
  33         80F2 8112 FFFC
  34   34    80F6 2379 0000               MOVE.L   LOCAL2,(-8,A1)
  34         80FA 8116 FFF8
  35   35    80FE             *           .
  36   36    80FE             *           .
  37   37    80FE 52A9 FFFC               ADD.L    #1,(-4,A1)     ; CHANGE LOCAL VARIABLE
  38   38    8102 2469 0008               MOVEA.L  (8,A1),A2      ; GET X
  39   39    8106             *           .
  40   40    8106             *           .
  41   41    8106 2379 0000               MOVE.L   OUTPUT1,(16,A1) ; PUSH AN OUTPUT
  41         810A 811C 0010
  42   42    810E             *           .
  43   43    810E             *           .
  44   44    810E 4E59                    UNLK     A1             ; RESTORE SP AND RETURN
  45   45    8110 4E75                    RTS
  46   46    8112             *
  47   47    8112 9876 5432   LOCAL1      DC.L     $98765432      ; LOCAL VARIABLES
  48   48    8116 8765 4321   LOCAL2      DC.L     $87654321
  49   49    811C 4142 4344   OUTPUT1     DC.L     'ABCD'         ; OUTPUT VALUE
  50   50    8120                         END
```

Figure 9.17 Program to create a stack frame.

pointer thus points to the *bottom* of the local area for the subroutine. Then the displacement is added to the stack pointer so that (SP) points M bytes farther down in memory. Local variables are stored in this area and accessed by displacements from the value in the frame pointer. Once the input arguments are processed and the outputs are stored on the stack, the UNLK instruction is executed. As defined in Table 9.14, this instruction releases the local area and restores the stack pointer contents so that it points to the return address.

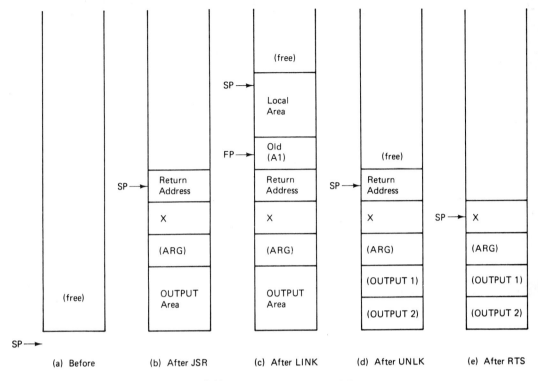

| (a) Before | (b) After JSR | (c) After LINK | (d) After UNLK | (e) After RTS |

Figure 9.18 Stack contents using stack frame.

Specifically, the UNLK instruction first loads (SP) with the value in the frame pointer A1, which points to the old value of A1 saved on the stack by the LINK instruction. Then A1 is restored to its previous value using the autoincrement mode of addressing so that (SP) now points to the return address. The RTS instruction returns control to the calling program, with (SP) indicating the location of the top of the parameter area set up by this program as indicated in Figure 9.18. The calling routine then adds 8 to (SP) by the instruction

    ADDQ.L   #8, SP

which skips over the input parameter area and leaves (SP) pointing to the output arguments. These arguments now represent input values to the calling program. After these are popped, the stack pointer has its original contents.

The Return and Deallocate Parameters (RTD) instruction of the CPU32 could be used instead of RTS to return from the subroutine. In addition to returning control to the calling program, the instruction of the form

    RTD   #<displacement>

adds a 16-bit displacement (sign-extended) to the stack pointer. Problem 9.4.7 requires the use of the RTD instruction.

EXERCISES

9.4.1. Compare the passing of addresses rather than data values as arguments when a subroutine processes an array.

9.4.2. Discuss the advantages and disadvantages of in-line parameter passing.

9.4.3. The dynamic nature of the stack used to hold arguments can result in a considerable savings of memory space when compared to the assignment of individual parameter areas for each subroutine. How does one compute the required maximum size of the stack to hold parameters?

9.4.4. Write a subroutine to compare two multiple-precision integers (64 bits) and place the largest value in a given location. Pass the addresses on the stack with the first integer in location N1, the second in N2, and the result to be placed in location MAX. Be sure to correct the stack pointer value to "collapse" the stack before the subroutine returns control to the calling program.

9.4.5. Compare the instruction sequence

$$\text{LEA} \qquad \$2000, \text{A3}$$
$$\text{LEA} \qquad \$1FF0, \text{SP}$$

with the instruction

$$\text{LINK} \qquad \text{A3}, \# - \$10$$

if (SP) = $2000 when the LINK instruction is executed.

9.4.6. Write a program that produces the sum and the average value of N positive 16-bit integers stored in a fixed area of memory. Use a stack frame to pass all the parameters between the program segments.

9.4.7. Modify the program of Example 9.18 to use the RTD instruction to adjust the stack pointer before the subroutine completes.

9.5 LOOP MODE

The CPU32 enters the *loop mode* when the processor encounters a loop consisting of two instructions using the DBcc instruction to control the looping. In the loop mode, the CPU performs only the data cycles associated with the loop; i.e., no instruction fetches occur until the loop is completed. Thus, the overall execution time in the loop is correspondingly reduced. The instruction in the loop can be any single-word instruction that does not change the program flow.

Example 9.19

The loop mode is particularly suited for operations on strings using either the predecrement or postincrement addressing mode. For example, the loop mode is activated by the instruction sequence

```
LOOP    MOVE.B      (A0)+,(A1)+        ; MOVE CHARACTER
```

DBEQ   D0, LOOP   ; LOOP UNTIL NUL

which moves characters in a string until a NUL ($00) character is encountered or the loop count is exhausted. The registers would be initialized with A0 containing the starting address of the string being copied and A1 containing the starting address of the destination string. The counter register D0 should contain one less than the maximum string length as explained in Subsection 6.2.4. To compare the two strings, the instruction

CMPM.B   (A0)+, (A1)+   ; COMPARE

is used as the loopable instruction.

EXERCISES

9.5.1. Use the loop mode to improve the efficiency of execution for the program in Example 6.5.

FURTHER READING

Most textbooks that treat the PDP-11 or VAX assembly language also discuss position-independent coding. In particular, Tanenbaum explains this technique and also includes discussions of base register addressing and dynamic relocation of programs. Knuth's books gives an excellent discussion of data structures, subroutine usage, and sorting with emphasis on assembly language programming. Data structures as well as the stack frame are discussed in Wakerly's book, which includes MC68000 and MC68020 programming examples.

KNUTH, DONALD E., *The Art of Computer Programming.* Vol. 1: *Fundamental Algorithms.* Reading, Mass.: Addison-Wesley, 1969.

KNUTH, DONALD E., *The Art of Computer Programming.* Vol. 3: *Sorting and Searching.* Reading, Mass.: Addison-Wesley, 1973.

TANENBAUM, ANDREW S., *Structured Computer Organization*, 2nd ed. Englewood Cliffs, N.J.: Prentice Hall, 1984.

WAKERLY, JOHN F., *Microcomputer Architecture and Programming: the 68000 Family.* New York: Wiley, 1989.

10

System Operation

10.0 INTRODUCTION

Chapters 6 through 9 primarily considered the MC68332 CPU (CPU32) applications programs. The emphasis was, therefore, on the instruction set of the CPU32 and programming techniques. The next five chapters, Chapters 10 through 14, discuss the operation of MC68332-based systems and products. These chapters stress the interaction between the various modules of the MC68332 Microcontroller Unit (MCU) and the other components of a system or product. The other components include the operating system or supervisor program, applications programs, memory external to the MC68332, and associated hardware. The term *system* as used here refers to the MCU as well as to the associated software and hardware required to allow the MC68332 to function as the control element in a computer. The products of interest in this textbook employ an MC68332-based computer system to direct their automatic operation.

This chapter presents the general operation of an MC68332-based system without exploring many of the specific details covered in later chapters. Figure 10.1 depicts this general operation. For convenience, the system operation is divided into three distinct categories called initialization, normal processing and the exception state, respectively. Initialization refers to the initialization of the MC68332 and other components of a system. Normal processing and the exception state are states of operation that characterize the CPU32.

The CPU32 operates in the supervisor mode during initialization and while in the exception state. During normal processing, the CPU32 may operate in either the supervisor mode or the user mode. As described in Section 10.1, the supervisor mode is the mode of higher privilege for the CPU.

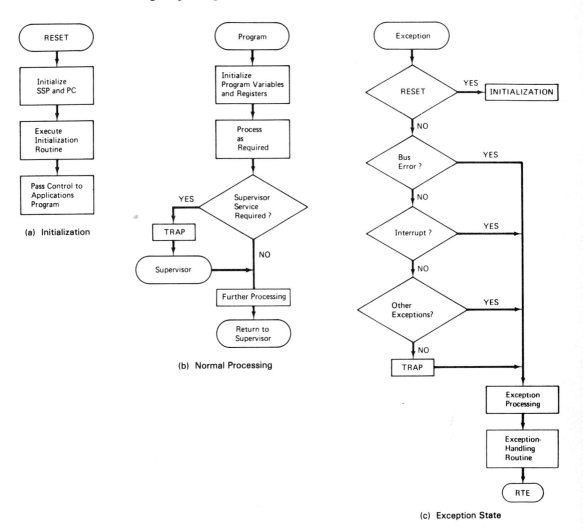

Figure 10.1 System operation for the typical MC68332-based product.

When power is applied to the system, a *reset* initiates the initialization sequence as shown in Figure 10.1(a). The reset can be caused by external circuitry or by other means.[1] After a reset, the required initial values in the CPU registers and module registers as well as other data associated with system operation must be written by an initialization program.

---

[1] A reset can be caused by an external signal line when power is first applied to the product. A reset can also be caused by the System Integration Module as described in Chapter 14.

After initialization, control is typically passed to an applications program that operates as illustrated in Figure 10.1(b). The applications programs direct the operation of a product as it performs its intended function. In most of the discussions in this textbook, it will be assumed that the applications programs execute in the user mode of the CPU. However, the product designer can separate the various programs into supervisor mode and user mode as required to meet the requirements of an application. A supervisor mode program that directs the overall operation of a system including initialization and exception handling will be called the *supervisor*. The term operating system is also frequently used to describe the supervisor program of a computer system.

As shown in Figure 10.1(b), an applications program executes until its task is complete or a supervisor service is required. The applications program may execute a TRAP instruction to return control to the supervisor program to have a system service performed. For example, a supervisor program might be called via a TRAP instruction to perform an I/O transfer. In Figure 10.1(b), a TRAP instruction causes the supervisor to complete the service and return control to the applications program. Once the applications program itself completes, control is passed to the supervisor program or to another applications program.

During the execution of an applications program, a number of *exceptions* can occur which cause control to be passed to a supervisor exception-handling routine. The term *exception* describes a specific event for the CPU32 that causes the CPU to begin exception processing. Figure 10.1(c) shows several possible exceptions. The exception-handling routine consists of the program instructions that perform the required operations to service the exception. For example, a reset is an exception that causes initialization of the system. The bus error and an interrupt represent but two other types of possible exceptions for the CPU.[2] In a typical system, service required by an external device is indicated to the CPU by a bus error signal or an interrupt. The trap exception in Figure 10.1(c) is another exception that is caused by program execution of the TRAP instruction.

When any type of exception is recognized, the CPU first enters the supervisor mode and stores appropriate information on the supervisor stack. Then, control is passed to a specific exception-handling routine. The routine's function depends on the type of exception and the design of the routine.

After exception handling, control may be returned to the program that was executing when the exception occurred. In this case, the RTE (Return from Exception) instruction is executed in the exception-handling routine to restore the stacked information to CPU registers. Then, control returns to the applications program.

Section 10.1 describes all the states and modes of the CPU during program execution and exception handling. Next, the CPU32 system control instructions are described in Section 10.2. A supervisor-mode program typically uses these instructions during initialization and exception handling to control the CPU and other elements of the computer system. Finally, Section 10.3 defines a system initialization sequence. Before reading the present chapter, the reader should be familiar with the organiza-

---

[2] Chapter 11 defines all of the possible exceptions for the MC68332. Chapter 14 describes the external signal lines that are used to cause exceptions.

tion of a MC68332-based system as presented in Chapter 2 as well as register usage for the CPU, including the differences between supervisor and user modes described in Section 4.2.

10.1 PROCESSOR STATES AND MODES

The MC68332 CPU operates in one of four processing states: normal, exception, background mode, or halted. When a program is executing, the processor operation is further characterized by its privilege mode. In normal operation, the privilege mode is either supervisor or user, as determined by the setting of the status bit ("S" bit) in the Status Register. When an exception occurs, the processor is automatically put in the supervisor mode. The Status Register of the CPU32 was introduced in Chapter 4. Section 10.2 describes the use of the Status Register for system control.

10.1.1 Normal, Exception, Background, and Halted States

Table 10.1 summarizes the four states of the processor. The *normal* state is associated with program execution in either the supervisor or the user mode. In this state, the processor is fetching instructions and operands from memory during program execution. The state of the processor will change from the normal state only when an exception occurs or under special conditions as described later.

The *stopped* condition is a special case during CPU operation in the normal state. When stopped, the processor no longer executes instructions but waits for an external event to initiate continued execution. A stopped condition in the normal state occurs when the instruction

$$\text{STOP} \qquad \#<d_{16}>$$

is executed. The 16-bit immediate value $<d_{16}>$ replaces the contents of the Status Register and the (PC) is advanced to point to the next instruction. Until an interrupt or a reset is recognized, the processor stops fetching and executing instructions. The STOP instruction must be executed by a program in the supervisor mode or a privilege violation (exception) will occur. Processor activity resumes when an interrupt is recognized or when a reset is initiated. In practice, the STOP instruction can be considered a "wait for interrupt" instruction used only in special applications and during debugging.[3]

The stopped condition can also be initiated by the Low-Power Stop instruction of the form

$$\text{LPSTOP} \qquad \#<d_{16}>$$

---

[3] A trace exception will occur if the trace condition is set when the STOP instruction is executed. Also, the immediate value that is the operand in the STOP instruction defines the interrupt level in SR[10:8]. An interrupt request that occurs must have a higher priority than the priority set in the SR to cause interrupt processing. Chapter 11 explains the trace and privilege violation exceptions as well as the interrupt priorities.

Table 10.1 Processor States and Modes

State	Condition	CPU activity
Normal	Processing	Supervisor- or user-mode program executing
	Stopped	Waiting for interrupt
Exception	Reset	Initialization
	Interrupt	Interrupt acknowledgement and processing
	Trap	Trap processing
	Trace	Single-instruction trace or trace on change of flow
Background mode	External Control	Used for debugging
Halted	System Error Condition	No activity

Note:
The exceptions listed in Table 10.1 are selected examples. Chapter 11 gives a complete list of the exceptions for the MC68332.

to force the MC68332 into a low-power standby condition. This instruction stops CPU program execution and the clock circuits on the chip to minimize power consumption. Thus, the instruction could be used in a program to discontinue processing in an orderly manner before the MC68332 enters the standby mode. Chapter 15 considers other uses of the LPSTOP instruction.

Exception state. Table 10.1 lists a few of the possible CPU32 exceptions. As previously described briefly in Section 4.2, the *exception* state of the CPU32 is entered when a reset, interrupt, trap, trace, or other exception is recognized. The processor is automatically placed in the supervisor mode and exception processing begins. The purpose of *exception processing* is to save information on the supervisor stack and pass control to an exception-handling routine for the particular exception involved. The address of the exception-handling routine is held in a table in memory called the CPU vector table. The *vector* is the starting address of the exception-handling routine. As described in Section 10.3, the CPU32 has 255 possible vector addresses for exceptions.

Figure 10.2 shows the exception sequence in two parts consisting of exception processing and execution of the exception-handling routine. When an exception is recognized by the CPU32, normal program processing is interrupted and *exception processing* begins. The exception processing for other than a reset exception includes setting the mode of the CPU to supervisor, determining the vector address associated with the exception-handling routine, and saving the contents of the CPU Status Register (SR), Program Counter (PC), and other information on the supervisor stack.[4]

After the required information is pushed onto the system stack, the vector address that points to the exception-handling routine is loaded automatically into the

---

[4] No information is saved on the stack for the reset exception.

PC and control is passed to the routine. The CPU then begins *normal* processing in the supervisor mode until the routine is completed. The distinction between exception processing and normal processing by the CPU during execution of the exception-handling routine is important. Exception processing occurs automatically during transitions between an executing program and the exception-handling routine or after a reset. Certain types of errors that the CPU can detect during exception processing will cause the CPU to halt as described later. The instructions of the exception-handling routine typically execute in the supervisor mode of the CPU, but the CPU is in the normal state unless the RTE (Return from Exception) instruction is executed.

If the routine finally executes the RTE instruction as shown in Figure 10.2, the CPU restores the saved (SR), (PC), and other information stored on the supervisor stack to the appropriate processor registers. The CPU is in the exception state performing exception processing while the RTE instruction executes. Normal program execution resumes when the CPU continues executing the program that was interrupted when the exception occurred.[5]

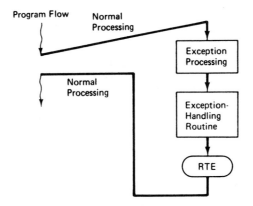

Note: The exception processing is performed automatically by the CPU when an exception is recognized. Control is then passed to the exception-handling routine associated with the particular exception that occurred.

Figure 10.2 Exception sequence.

Background mode. The *background* state of the CPU32 is a special mode of operation used with a development system for hardware or software debugging. During a reset, the background mode must be enabled by an external signal. If the background mode is not enabled, the mode cannot be entered after initialization. This prevents accidental entering of the background mode by a program or hardware error during normal operation of the product.

---

[5] For certain types of errors, the supervisor program may not return control to the program that was executing when the exception occurred. The result depends entirely on the design of the supervisor routine handling the exception.

If the background mode is enabled, it can be entered by several means including execution of the Background (BGND) instruction. Chapter 16 defines the use of the background mode for debugging.

Halted state. The *halted* state provides system protection by causing the CPU to cease all external signaling activity. As explained in Chapter 11, the processor halts if certain types of errors are detected while the CPU is already processing an exception. These error conditions should occur only after a catastrophic hardware failure for which recovery is not possible. A system reset is necessary to restart the halted processor.

In the halted state, the CPU indicates its condition on the system bus via a signal line designed explicitly for this purpose. External circuitry or a human operator must then determine whether to restart the halted processor. If the background mode is enabled when conditions occur that would cause the CPU to halt, the CPU enters the background mode.

The CPU in either the stopped condition or the halted state cannot be restarted by a program since external signal lines control the CPU activity after one of these conditions has occurred. However, a stopped processor is not halted. The stopped condition is initiated by the STOP or LPSTOP instruction as previously described. The halted state is entered when the CPU detects an error during exception processing.

10.1.2 Supervisor and User Modes

Table 10.2 lists the important distinctions between the CPU32 supervisor and user modes. Basically, the supervisor mode represents the level with more privilege. For example, a program in the supervisor mode may execute any CPU32 instruction and may change the Status Register and other special registers. The Supervisor Stack Pointer is the active system stack pointer when the CPU32 operates in the supervisor mode.

As indicated in Table 10.2, the supervisor mode is entered when the CPU recognizes an exception. For example, the processor begins executing the initialization program in the supervisor mode after a reset. A program operating in the supervisor mode can change to the user mode by modifying the status bit, (SR)[13], in the Status Register. Whenever (SR)[13] = {1}, the processor is operating in the supervisor mode and the transition to user mode can be accomplished by setting (SR)[13] = {0}. Subsection 10.3.2 describes the technique to accomplish this transition in an orderly manner.

The User Stack Pointer is the active system stack pointer in the CPU32 user mode. Table 10.2 shows that a user mode program can only access the condition code bits and not the entire Status Register of the CPU. This restriction prevents a user mode program from changing its mode to supervisor or modifying the interrupt mask or trace bits. Also, user mode programs are not allowed to execute certain CPU32 instructions which control the operation of the system. These system control instructions are defined in Section 10.2. Subsection 10.2.1 describes the special-purpose registers listed in Table 10.2.

Table 10.2 Distinctions Between Supervisor and User Modes

	Supervisor mode	User mode
Enter mode by:	Recognition of an exception	Clearing status bit {S}
System stack pointer	Supervisor Stack Pointer	User Stack Pointer
Status bits available	C, V, Z, N, X, I_0–I_2, S, T0, T1	C, V, Z, N, X
Instructions available	All, including system control instructions	All except system control instructions
Special-purpose registers	DFC, SFC, VBR	—

Notes:
1. Address registers A0-A6 can be used as private stack pointers by programs executing in either mode.
2. The special-purpose registers control the function code signal-lines (DFC, SFC), and the location of the vector table (VBR).

Programming model.   Figure 10.3 shows the register programming model of the CPU32. The general-purpose registers D0-D7 and A0-A6, the Program Counter (PC), and the Condition Code Register (CCR) are available to programs in both supervisor and user mode. The programmer is responsible for saving the contents of any general-purpose registers on the system stack when the CPU mode is changed and control is passed to a new program. The new program must restore the values in these registers before the mode is changed back to the previous mode if control is to be returned to the interrupted program.

In either supervisor or user mode, the assembly-language designation A7 or SP refers to the active system stack. However, the designation USP is the assembly-language mnemonic used in a supervisor mode program that must read or change the contents of the User Stack Pointer. Assembly language programmers use the different mnemonics to distinguish between the Supervisor Stack Pointer and the user-mode system stack pointer when writing a program to execute in the supervisor mode.

Figure 10.3(a) displays the general register programming model for the CPU32. Any of those registers can be referenced in either mode by assembly-language statements as described in Chapters 4 through 9. Figure 10.3(b) shows the additional registers available to a supervisor-mode program. The purpose and programming for several of these registers are considered in Section 10.2 and in later chapters of this textbook.

EXERCISES

10.1.1. Draw a diagram or describe in words the possible states of the CPU32 and the transitions between them as presented in Section 10.1.

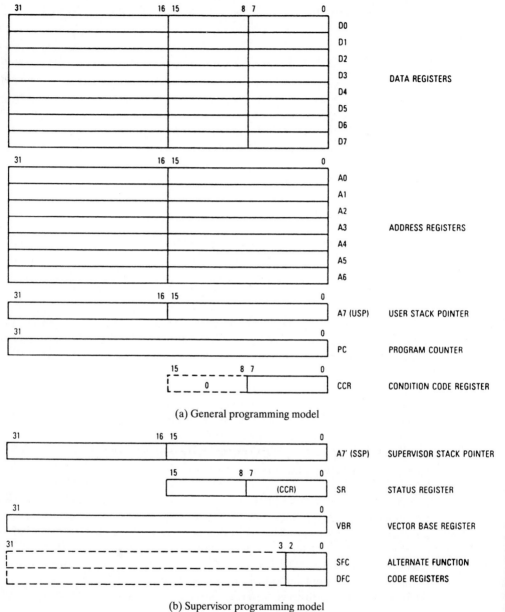

(a) General programming model

(b) Supervisor programming model

Figure 10.3 Programming model.

10.1.2. Compare the stopped condition with the halted state.

10.1.3. Discuss possible applications for the STOP instruction and the stopped condition of the processor.

10.1.4. Discuss the use of the LPSTOP instruction and the information that should be saved in the on-chip RAM in a portable instrument with a display that is temporarily powered down. If standby power is applied to the MC68332 chip during power down, the contents of the on-chip RAM will not be lost. The on-chip RAM has been described previously in Chapter 2.

10.1.5. List the protection mechanisms provided for an MC68332-based system and define the purpose and possible application of each. Include both hardware and software considerations.

10.2   SYSTEM CONTROL INSTRUCTIONS

The CPU32 has a group of instructions termed *system control* instructions. These are privileged instructions that are used to change the operation of the computer system dynamically. Table 10.3 lists the instructions and their operands. A number of these instructions change the contents of the Status Register (SR). Thus, these instructions are considered privileged because they manipulate the contents of the SR. The MOVE instruction can also be used to manipulate the contents of the User Stack Pointer (USP).

The Condition Code Register (CCR) in bits (SR)[7:0] is a valid source or destination register for programs in either the supervisor or the user mode. Thus, instructions that reference only the CCR are not privileged. Subsection 10.2.3 describes how the contents of the CCR can be manipulated by any of the instructions that allow the contents of the Status Register to be designated as an operand.

The RTE (Return from Exception) instruction is used in an exception-handling routine to transfer control to another program. A RESET instruction is typically issued by an initialization routine to cause various peripheral chips to assume their initial state before they are used for Input/Output operations. The MOVEC (Move Control Register) instruction serves to manipulate the contents of the special-purpose registers that are part of the supervisor register set as previously defined in Section 10.1.

This section discusses most of the instructions in Table 10.3 and defines their assembly-language syntax and functional operation. The LPSTOP and STOP instructions were introduced previously in Section 10.1. Chapter 15 describes applications of the LPSTOP instruction in more detail. The MOVES (Move Address Space) instruction is described in Chapter 14.

10.2.1 Status Register Modification

Table 10.4 lists the instructions available to a supervisor mode program that modifies the contents of the Status Register. The logical instructions listed in the table (ANDI, EORI, ORI) operate in the manner described in Chapter 8. When the destination location is the Status Register, these instructions are privileged instructions. Each instruction performs the operation designated by applying the logical operation to the 16-bit immediate value and the contents of the Status Register.

The MOVE instruction can be used to transfer the source operand to the Status

Table 10.3 System Control Instructions

Instruction	Operand syntax	Operand size	Operation (privileged)
ANDI	#<data>, SR	16	Immediate data ∧ SR → SR
EORI	#<data>, SR	16	Immediate data ⊕ SR → SR
MOVE	<EAs>, SR SR, <EAd>	16	Source → SR SR → destination
MOVE	USP, An An, USP	32	USP → An An → USP
MOVEC	Rc, Rn Rn, Rc	32	Rc → Rn Rn → Rc
MOVES	Rn, <EAd> <EAs>, Rn	8,16, 32	Rn → destination using DFC Source using SFC → Rn
ORI	#<data>, SR	16	Immediate data ∨ SR → SR
RESET			Assert $\overline{RESET}$ signal line
RTE		–	((SP)) → SR; (SP)+2 → (SP); ((SP)) → PC; and pop format word; (SP)+6 → (SP); then restore internal register contents according to format word from stack
LPSTOP	#<data>	16	Immediate data → SR; Stop
STOP	#<data>	16	Immediate data → SR; Stop

Notes:
1. ∧ = logical AND.
2. ∨ = logical OR.
3. ⊕ = exclusive OR.
4. Rc is any special-purpose control register or the user stack pointer (DFC, SFC, USP, VBR). Rn is any address register or data register.
5. <EAs> is the source effective address and <EAd> is the destination effective address. The allowed addressing modes for the instructions are defined when each instruction is introduced in the textbook.

Register. The instruction to change the contents of the Status Register is of the form

$$\text{MOVE.W} \qquad <EA>, SR$$

which loads the source operand into SR. The effective address <EA> is specified by any data addressing mode. This addressing mode includes all the CPU32 addressing modes except address register direct. To transfer the contents of the Status Register to a memory location or a data register, the instruction

$$\text{MOVE.W} \qquad SR, <EA>$$

is used.

Example 10.1

Figure 10.4 shows the CPU32 Status Register as it is divided into user byte SR[7:0] and system byte SR[15:8]. The values in the AND and OR column are given in hexadecimal.

Table 10.4 Instructions to Modify the Status Register

Syntax	Operation
ANDI.W #<d_{16}>, SR	(SR) ← (SR) AND <d_{16}>
EORI.W #<d_{16}>, SR	(SR) ← (SR) EOR <d_{16}>
MOVE.W <EA>, SR	(SR) ← (EA)
ORI.W #<d_{16}>, SR	(SR) ← (SR) OR <d_{16}>

Notes:
1. All instructions are privileged.
2. MOVE to SR requires a data addressing mode for the source address <EA>. Thus, all addressing modes but address register direct are allowed for the source operand.
3. The contents of SR are read with a MOVE.W SR,<EA> instruction. The destination address can be defined by any data-alterable addressing mode; therefore address register direct and PC relative addressing are prohibited.

The AND mask clears any bit in the Status Register which corresponds to a {0} in the mask. The OR of (SR) with the bit pattern shown as ENABLE sets the corresponding bit to {1}. Thus, the instruction

ANDI   #$7FFF, SR

sets T1 = {0} to disable the single-instruction trace mode but does not affect the other bits. The instruction

ORI   #$8000, SR

enables the single-instruction trace mode. The use of the other bits is similar. When bit 13 is {0}, for example, the processor is operating in the user mode.

The interrupt-level value {I_2, I_1, I_0} is not treated as a logical variable but as a 3-bit integer. A value of 0, {000}, indicates that all interrupt levels will be accepted with increasing priority from 1 to 7. During interrupt processing, the value indicates the current level as explained in Chapter 11. Except for level 7, interrupts at the current level and below are ignored. The instruction

ANDI   #$F8FF, SR

enables all interrupt levels by setting the interrupt bits to {000}. The interrupt levels are disabled by the instruction

ORI   #$0700, SR

which disables all interrupts below level 7 since a level 7 interrupt cannot be masked (disabled).

Operations on the user byte or CCR are also shown in Figure 10.4. The immediate values listed do not affect the system byte when used with the ANDI or ORI instructions as shown. The instruction

ANDI   #$FF00, SR

would clear the CCR, for example. Thus use of ANDI with the {MASK} value shown clears the corresponding bit to {0} in the CCR. The bit is set to {1} when ORI is used with the immediate value given as {ENABLE} in Figure 10.4.

15	14	13	12	11	10	9	8	7	6	5	4	3	2	1	0	←	Bit Number
T1	T0	S	0	0	I_2	I_1	I_0	0	0	0	X	N	Z	V	C		

←————— System Byte —————→ ←————— User Byte —————→

Condition	Status Bit	AND {MASK}	OR {ENABLE}
Trace Mode (Single)	(SR) [15] = T1	{7FFF}	{8000}
Trace Mode (Change)	(SR) [14] = T0	{BFFF}	{4000}
Supervisor Mode	(SR) [13] = S	{DFFF}	{2000}
Interrupt Level	(SR) [10:8] = level	{F8FF}	{0700}
Extend	(SR) [4] = X	{FFEF}	{0010}
Negative	(SR) [3] = N	{FFF7}	{0008}
Zero	(SR) [2] = Z	{FFFB}	{0004}
Overflow	(SR) [1] = V	{FFFD}	{0002}
Carry	(SR) [0] = C	{FFFE}	{0001}

Notes:

(1) SR [15:8] is System Byte; SR [7:0] is User Byte or CCR.

(2) ((SR) AND {MASK}) sets bit to {0}; ((SR) OR {ENABLE}) sets bit to {1}.

(3) For the interrupt level, the value $\{I_2 I_1 I_0\}$ is interpreted as a 3-bit code.

(4) Either single-instruction trace (T1) or trace on change of flow of control (T0) can be enabled. Enabling both simultaneously results in an undefined operation according to the Motorola *CPU32 Reference Manual*

Figure 10.4 Status Register operation.

10.2.2 User Stack Pointer Manipulation

A program executing in the supervisor mode can save, restore, or change the contents of the User Stack Pointer. The privileged instruction

MOVEA.L   USP, <An>

copies (USP) into address register An. The opposite transfer has the form

MOVE.L   <An>, USP

and is used to initialize or modify (USP). In each case, a 32-bit transfer occurs.

As would be expected, a program operating in the supervisor mode has control of the initial contents of the User Stack Pointer. Therefore, the address of the user stack must be loaded into USP by the supervisor program during initialization. The proper address could be transferred to <An> and then to the User Stack Pointer by the instructions

$$\text{MOVEA.L} \quad \#\text{USERSTK}, <\text{An}>$$

$$\text{MOVE.L} \quad <\text{An}>, \text{USP}$$

where USERSTK is the address of the bottom of the user's stack.[6] A user-mode program refers to the User Stack Pointer when the mnemonic A7 or SP is used in an assembly-language statement, as discussed previously in Section 10.1. If a program intended to execute in the supervisor mode has the mnemonic A7 or SP in an instruction, the supervisor stack will be referenced when the program executes.

10.2.3 Condition Code Register Manipulation

The instructions listed in Table 10.5 are available to both supervisor-mode and user-mode programs. The logical instructions allow the contents of the CCR to be modified using the 8-bit immediate value. For example, the instruction

$$\text{ORI.B} \quad \#\$01, \text{CCR}$$

sets the carry bit $C = \{1\}$ and does not modify any other condition code bits. The entire contents of the CCR can be modified by the instruction

$$\text{MOVE.W} \quad <\text{EA}>, \text{CCR}$$

in which $(<\text{EA}>)[7:0]$ contains the new condition code bits for the CCR. The addressing for <EA> requires a data addressing mode which allows all modes except address register direct. Note that the operation requires a word operand but only the low-order byte is used to update the condition codes.

10.2.4 RTE Instruction

The Return from Exception (RTE) instruction is a privileged instruction used to load the Status Register and the program counter with values stored on the supervisor stack. Figure 10.5 shows the system stack usage by the RTE instruction. The specific operation of the RTE instruction is defined as follows:
(a) load (SR) from system stack

$$(\text{SR})[\text{W}] \leftarrow ((\text{SSP})) \qquad ;\text{POP (SR)}$$
$$(\text{SSP}) \leftarrow (\text{SSP}) + 2 \qquad ;\text{POINT TO (PC)}$$

---

[6] The MOVEC instruction, described in Subsection 10.2.6, can also be used by a supervisor-mode program to move or change the contents of the USP.

Table 10.5 Instructions to Modify the CCR

Syntax	Operation
ANDI.B #<d_8>,CCR	(SR)[7:0] ← (SR)[7:0] AND <d_8>
EORI.B #<d_8>,CCR	(SR)[7:0] ← (SR)[7:0] EOR <d_8>
MOVE.W <EAs>,CCR	(SR)[7:0] ← (EAs)[7:0]
MOVE.W CCR,<EA>	(EA) ← (CCR)
ORI.B #<d_8>,CCR	(SR)[7:0] ← (SR)[7:0] OR <d_8>

Notes:
1. MOVE to CCR requires a data addressing mode for <EAs>; the source address cannot be specified as address register direct.
2. CCR is (SR)[7:0].
3. The destination in the instruction MOVE.W CCR,<EA> must be addressed by a data-alterable addressing mode; address register direct and PC relative addressing are prohibited.

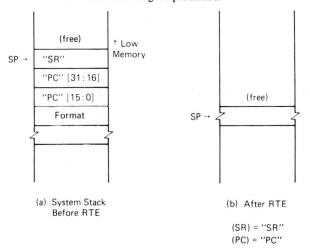

(a) System Stack Before RTE

(b) After RTE

(SR) = "SR"
(PC) = "PC"

Note: "SR" and "PC" are values to replace the current (SR) and (PC), respectively.

Figure 10.5 RTE instruction stack usage.

(b) load (PC) from system stack and read format word

$$(PC)[L] \leftarrow ((SSP)) \qquad ;POP\ (PC)\ AND\ FORMAT\ WORD$$
$$(SSP) \leftarrow (SSP) + 6$$

(c) restore internal register values with information from the stack if necessary.
The notation((SSP)) means the contents of the location designated by the SSP; i.e., the operand stored on the stack. The reference (SSP) means the contents of the Supervisor Stack Pointer register itself.

The RTE is most frequently used as the last instruction in an exception-handling routine. The instruction restores the contents of the PC and SR that were pushed on the supervisor stack when the exception occurred. The RTE instruction is also used to pass control to a user-mode program during the system initialization procedure, as discussed in Section 10.3.

The stack shown in Figure 10.5 represents a four-word stack created by an exception. After recognition of an exception, the CPU saves either 4, 6, or 12 words on the system stack. The 16-bit format word saved with (SR) and (PC) indicates the amount of information to be restored when the RTE instruction executes. This format word and other information on the stack are restored to internal CPU registers that are not part of the CPU programmable register set. Chapter 11 presents the specific stack format for each exception.

10.2.5 RESET Instruction

The RESET instruction is a privileged instruction used to reset external interfaces and devices during system initialization. Its execution asserts a voltage on a signal line that is used as an indication to external circuitry that the processor is requesting initialization of the appropriate interfaces. The exact function of the RESET instruction in terms of system operation is determined by the hardware design of the system. Most of the peripheral chips of the MC68332 family respond to this instruction (via the RESET signal line) by initializing their internal circuitry. This signal line is described further in Chapter 14.

10.2.6 The MOVEC Instruction and Special-Purpose Processor Registers

The CPU32 has a number of special-purpose registers which are part of the supervisor programming model. These registers were shown in Figure 10.3(b) of Section 10.1. The contents of the registers can be manipulated by the privileged MOVEC (Move Control Register) instruction defined in Table 10.6. The MOVEC instruction can transfer values between address or data registers and the special-purpose registers. The instruction can also be used to manipulate the contents of the User Stack Pointer (USP).

Table 10.6 Move Control Register instruction (MOVEC)

Syntax	Operation
MOVEC <Rc>, <Rn>	(<Rn>) ← (<Rc>)
MOVEC <Rn>, <Rc>	(<Rc>) ← (<Rn>)

Notes:
1. <Rn> is any <An> or <Dn>.
2. <Rc> is any one of the special-purpose processor registers or the USP.
3. All operations are 32 bits.

Table 10.7 lists the CPU32 registers designated as special purpose. Operations with these registers are described in appropriate sections of this textbook. For example, function codes are described in Chapter 14. Section 10.3 gives an example showing initialization of the USP. Section 10.3 also defines the Vector Base Register which is used to relocate the vector table of the CPU.

Table 10.7 Special-Purpose Processor Registers

Use and Mnemonic	Definition
Function Codes:	
DFC	Destination Function Code
SFC	Source Function Code
User stack:	
USP	User Stack Pointer
Vector table:	
VBR	Vector Base Register

EXERCISES

10.2.1. Determine the effect of the following instructions:
  (a) MOVE.W   #$0400, SR
  (b) ANDI.W   #$DFFD, SR
  (c) MOVE.W   #$2700, SR
  (d) EORI.W   #$2000, SR
  The instructions are executed by a program in the supervisor mode.

10.2.2. Describe the effect of the following instructions executed by a program in the user mode:
  (a) MOVE.W   #$000C, CCR
  (b) ANDI.B   #$01, CCR
  (c) EORI.W   #$2700, SR

10.2.3. Write the sequence of instructions to initialize (USP) to hexadecimal value $3830. This program must be executed in the supervisor mode.

10.3 SYSTEM INITIALIZATION

The *system initialization* sequence places a product in a known state or condition before any applications program is executed. The sequence is normally initiated by turning on the power of an MC68332-based product. First, a hardware initialization occurs. The hardware sequence is fixed by the MC68332 and the hardware design of the product. Then, an initialization routine is executed to define all constants, addresses, and other data values associated with the product's initial operation.

Figure 10.6 shows a typical memory layout after initialization. The supervisor areas contain CPU32 supervisor mode programs and data. The programs and data for the user mode occupy the user areas. The vector table in most MC68332 systems is lowest in memory and contains the addresses of exception routines. The SSP and USP point to the beginning of the supervisor stack area and the user stack area, respectively. The amount of space reserved for the program and stack areas is determined by the software system design. Enough space must be allocated so that the various stack areas do not overlap the program and data areas during operation. The stacks shown in Figure 10.6 are system stacks and grow toward lower memory locations as return addresses, register contents, and other data are pushed onto the stack. Although Figure 10.6 shows a typical memory layout, any configuration is possible. For example, Table 10.10 in Subsection 10.3.3 defines the memory layout for the author's Business Card Computer (BCC) development system.

The location of the module register set in Figure 10.6 is determined by the initialization value supplied to the System Integration Module (SIM) as explained in Chapter 14. The module register area can begin at $7FF000 or $FFF000. The 2Kbyte RAM can be placed on any 2Kb boundary in memory as long as the RAM does not conflict with the module register set or other memory areas.

Example 10.2

Assume that the software including supervisor and applications programs are stored in ROM in a completed product used for a specific purpose. The starting addresses of all the programs are set and are not intended to be altered unless the product and its software are redesigned. For example, the vector table and the programs in Figure 10.6 would be in ROM. Also, a certain amount of RAM is necessary for the system stacks and to store data that changes dynamically as the product operates. The MC68332 on-chip RAM addressing area can be placed on any 2KB boundary in the memory addressing space as long as it does not overlap other memory areas used in the product. The beginning on-chip RAM location is controlled by the RAM control registers that are part of the memory space reserved for the modules as shown in Figure 10.6.

The initialization routine would be held in read-only memory in the supervisor area. The initialization program executes automatically after a reset. The exact procedure, of course, depends on the hardware configuration and the application of the product.

In contrast to products with ROM-based programs, general-purpose computers incorporating a disk unit typically have a simple initialization routine in ROM to load the operating system (supervisor) software into memory at power-up. The nonvolatile memory holding the loader routine is often called the *bootstrap* ROM. It contains only the routines to read the operating system from the disk unit into the supervisor area of RAM memory of the computer. The operating system in turn loads various application programs in response to operator commands. Having a disk-based operating system allows great flexibility for the programmer. Consequently, software development systems contain an associated disk unit. On the other hand, most of the MC68332-based products such as those described in Chapter 1 have no disk unit and thus their programs are held in ROM.

The remainder of this section describes the basic initialization procedure for a product according to the requirements of the processor and the modules of the MC68332. Chapter 2 introduced the modules and their functional operation.

Once the product is initialized, the supervisor program passes control to an applications program. This section describes the techniques for transfer of control. Before the applications programs are executed however, the supervisor program initializes the values in various control registers associated with the modules. The general approach to module initialization by the supervisor program is also treated in the present section. However, the detailed techniques to initialize and program the modules for specific applications are not discussed until Chapter 12.

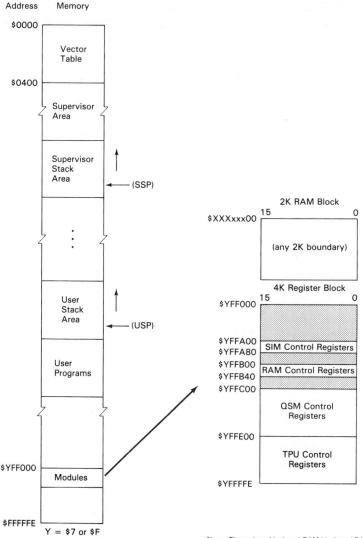

Figure 10.6 Example initial memory layout.

10.3.1 Initialization Procedure

For convenience of discussion, the initialization procedure can be separated into two phases. In the first phase, the MC68332 CPU and the modules are reset. This CPU portion of the initialization is fixed by the processor design and cannot be altered. The CPU then executes the routine at the location indicated by the initial value of the Program Counter. The second phase begins when the initialization routine of the supervisor program executes.

CPU32 reset and initialization.   Initialization begins when a reset is recognized by the MC68332. Figure 10.7 shows the sequence of events for the CPU32. The processor first sets the Status Register contents so that tracing is disabled, the supervisor mode is entered, and all interrupts up to level 7 are masked. The Vector Base Register (VBR) is also initialized to $00000000. Then, in sequence, the CPU reads the Supervisor Stack Pointer and the Program Counter addresses from the first eight bytes in memory. Program execution then begins at the location defined by the Program Counter contents.

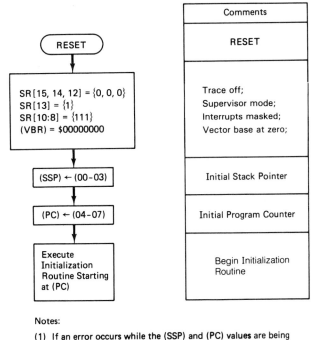

Notes:

(1) If an error occurs while the (SSP) and (PC) values are being fetched, the processor will enter the halted state.

Figure 10.7   Reset operation for the CPU32.

Reset and initialization of MC68332 modules.   After a reset, the Queued Serial Module (QSM), Time Processor Unit (TPU) and the on-chip RAM are disabled. The RAM base address and the initialization of the QSM and TPU are under software control. The module initialization program must define the initial operation of a module by writing bit patterns into appropriate control registers of the module. For example, the QSM signal lines can be initialized for either serial I/O or parallel I/O as previously discussed in Chapter 2 and Chapter 4. This is done by writing the required bit pattern into its pin-control registers to define the use of each signal line.

Once initialized, the operation of the QSM and the other modules must be defined by the applications programs controlling these modules. This section introduces the general principles of initialization for the modules by a supervisor-mode program. Discussion of the specific techniques of initialization and programming the modules begins in detail in Chapter 12.

The initial operation of the System Integration Module (SIM) is determined by both the state of certain MC68332 signal lines during reset and by the initialization program executed by the CPU. Therefore, external circuits as well as software determine the initial state of the SIM after reset and initialization by supervisor-mode software. The SIM, for example, can detect certain types of errors that occur during initialization. The module can even cause another reset sequence to commence if the initialization program is not executing properly. Chapter 14 describes the System Integration Module in detail.

10.3.2 Initialization and the CPU Vector Table

Figure 10.7 shows that immediately after the reset processing only the PC and the System Stack Pointer (SSP) contain valid addresses. The addresses are read from longword location (00-03) for the (SSP) and location (04-07) for the PC value. All of the other registers of the CPU and the modules contain reset "default" values such as all {0} bits. The initialization program, executing in the supervisor mode of the CPU, must write the proper values into the MCU registers and also into areas of RAM that need initial values.

At this stage of initialization, no exceptions such as traps or interrupts should occur if the product is operating properly. However, when control is passed to applications programs after such initialization, various exceptions are expected as the product operates. An exception causes the execution of an *exception-handling* routine. The routine's starting address is called a *vector* which is stored in the CPU exception vector table.

CPU32 exception vector table. The MC68332 exceptions are not discussed in detail until Chapter 11. However, the vector table shown in Table 10.8 lists all the exception vector locations for the CPU. The table in memory contains 256, 32-bit addresses, each of which points to the location of the corresponding exception-handling routine associated with the exception. Only the first two, which give the reset addresses, are mandatory and must be available to the processor upon reset. If the vector table is held in RAM, the other addresses could be filled by an initialization routine according to the requirements defined by the design of the product hardware and software. In many products, the vector table is stored in ROM beginning at address $00000000 as shown in Figure 10.6.[7]

---

[7] In a general-purpose computer, the lower memory locations that hold the vector addresses are typically volatile memory (RAM) locations. Therefore, if power is lost, the contents of such locations should be considered to contain invalid data and instructions until reinitialized. During a system reset, the CPU32 processor reads longword location (00-03) for the Supervisor Stack Pointer value and location (04-07) for the Program Counter value. These eight bytes should be permanent values. Therefore, external circuitry must be designed to supply these addresses after a reset or they may be held in ROM. The initialization routine which is then executed can initialize the remaining values in the other vector locations and perform other necessary processing. In MC68332-based computers, the vector table may be relocated in memory.

Table 10.8 CPU32 Exception Vector Table

Vector Number	Vector Offset Dec	Vector Offset Hex	Assignment
0	0	000	Reset: Initial SSP
1	4	004	Reset: Initial PC
2	8	008	Bus Error
3	12	00C	Address Error
4	16	010	Illegal instruction
5	20	014	Zero divide
6	24	018	CHK, CHK2 instructions
7	28	01C	TRAPcc, TRAP instructions
8	32	020	Privilege violation
9	36	024	Trace
10	40	028	Line 1010 emulator
11	44	02C	Line 1111 emulator
12	48	030	Hardware breakpoint
13	52	034	(Reserved)
14	56	038	Format error
15	60	03C	Uninitialized interrupt
16–23	64	040	(Reserved)
	92	05C	
24	96	060	Spurious interrupt
25	100	064	Level 1 autovector
26	104	068	Level 2 autovector
27	108	06C	Level 3 autovector
28	112	070	Level 4 autovector
29	116	074	Level 5 autovector
30	120	078	Level 6 autovector
31	124	07C	Level 7 autovector
32–47	128	080	TRAP instruction
	188	0BC	vectors, 0-15
48–63	192	0C0	Unassigned or reserved
	252	0FC	
64–255	256	100	User defined vectors
	1020	3FC	(192)

Note:
Reserved vectors may be used on some Motorola products.

Upon initialization, the Vector Base Register (VBR) contains the beginning address of the vector table and its initial value is $00000000. A particular vector address is thus located by the CPU as

$$\text{vector address} = (\text{VBR}) + <\text{OFFSET}>$$

where OFFSET is the offset value given in Table 10.8. If a supervisor program changes the contents of the VBR using the MOVEC instruction described in Section 10.2, the vector table begins at the new address. In a product with ROM-based programs, the vector table will reside in a fixed area of memory which is not changed during product operation.

Initialization procedure. Table 10.9 outlines, in simplified form, the possible action of an initialization program. First, the base address for the module registers and the system protection features are selected. It is necessary to initialize the System Integration Module (SIM) before any of the other modules or any peripheral devices. Chapter 14 is devoted to the SIM operation and initialization procedure.

Table 10.9 Typical Product Initialization Procedure

Operation of Initialization Program	Comments
After reset, begin initialization program	Begin execution at location of initial PC
Set module registers base address, and enable system protection in the SIM	Initialize submodules of the System Integration Module
Enable on-chip RAM	Select base address of RAM
Initialize contents of any memory locations needed by the supervisor program	As needed
Initialize QSM, TPU as required	To allow control of modules by applications programs
Initialize any peripherals	As needed for Input/Output devices
Pass Control to Applications Program	
Initialize USP	(USP) ← User stack address
Push format word	((SSP)) ← Format word
Push starting address	((SSP)) ← Start of program
Push status	((SSP)) ← User (SR)
Transfer control to program in user mode	RTE

The program then enables the on-chip RAM and sets its base address. If the RAM is used as the supervisor stack, the (SSP) would be set to the word location just above the highest address of the RAM since this stack grows down in memory. The on-chip RAM of the MC68332 is typically used as the supervisor stack since access to it is faster than to external memory.[8] Alternatively, external RAM could be used for the system stack to reserve the on-chip RAM for special purposes. The other initialization steps for the MC68332 set up initial values in memory, and initialize the modules and any peripheral units that require initialization at this time. Chapter 12 describes the initialization of the QSM. Chapter 13 covers the TPU.

[8] As described in Chapter 14. the on-chip RAM can be accessed in two clock cycles whereas external memory accesses typically require at least three clock cycles. The RAM base address can be set to any boundary that is a multiple of 2^{11} (2Kbytes).

After the product is properly initialized, the User Stack Pointer, Status Register, and Program Counter contents are set to pass control to the applications program. The format word, user PC and SR are pushed on the stack so that the RTE instruction can be used to provide an orderly transition between the supervisor program and the application program. The RTE instruction and the stack contents were described in Subsection 10.2.4. In the sequence shown in Table 10.9, the applications programs are assumed to operate in the user mode . As shown in that table, the supervisor program controls all systems operations and the initial setting of the User Stack Pointer for the applications programs. Examples of actual initialization programs are given in the appropriate chapter where a module is described in detail.

Example 10.3

Assume that a supervisor program is to pass control to a user-mode program that starts at location $8000. Also, assume that the user stack is to begin at location $FC00. Following the sequence outlined in Table 10.9 to pass control to an application program, the instruction sequence could be as follows:

MOVE.L	#$FC00, USP	; USER STACK POINTER
MOVE.W	#$0000, −(SP)	; FORMAT WORD
MOVE.L	#$8000, −(SP)	; USER PC
MOVE.W	#$0000, −(SP)	; USER STATUS REG.
RTE		; TRANSFER CONTROL

The User Stack Pointer is initialized directly by loading the USP with the user stack address. The other MOVE instructions set up the stack frame for the RTE instruction as previously shown in Figure 10.5. The format word of $0000 indicates that a four-word stack is to be processed. After the RTE instruction executes, the CPU is in the user mode with all interrupts enabled since the new Status Register value is $0000. Execution of the user-mode program begins automatically at location $8000.

10.3.3 BCC System Example

The author's Business Card Computer (BCC) development system is a single-board computer with the 332BUG monitor. As previously described in Chapter 5, the BCC allows program and hardware development with a minimum of additional resources. Chapter 16 presents a more complete description of the BCC. However, a simplified block diagram and memory map of the author's system using the BCC is presented here to aid the reader in understanding many of the examples to follow in later chapters.

Figure 10.8 shows a simplified block diagram of the MC68332 on the BCC as it is connected to several external devices. The system shown is used for various applications as discussed in the chapters to follow. In the figure, 64Kbytes of RAM and the 332BUG EPROM is available via the external bus of the System Integration Module (SIM). The EPROM is a nonvolatile memory that can be reprogrammed electrically using circuits external to the BCC.

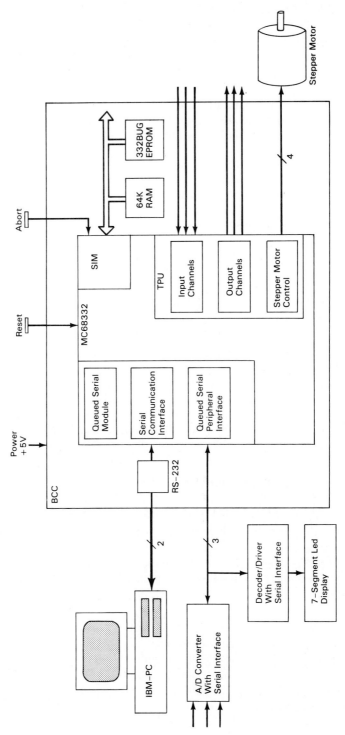

Figure 10.8 BCC system for applications.

Two pushbuttons are shown that allow an operator to reset the system or abort an executing program. The abort button causes a level 7 autovectored interrupt as explained in Section 11.7. When pushed by the operator, the reset button causes system initialization.[9]

Various devices for I/O and control applications are attached to the modules by their signal lines. The operator's console uses the Serial Communication Interface (SCI) for communication with 332BUG and the applications programs. An A/D converter inputs data using the Queued Serial Peripheral Interface (QSPI). The QSPI also outputs data to a display. Four of the Time Processor Unit (TPU) channels control a stepper motor. Various other TPU channels are used to monitor inputs or generate output waveforms. The signals to the external devices for grounds are not shown in Figure 10.8.

Table 10.10 BCC system memory map

Address	Item	Use
$0–$3FC	Vector table	Vectors for 332BUG and application
$400–$2FFF	RAM	332BUG RAM area
$3000–$FFFF	RAM	Routines for application and system stacks
$3000–$3FFF		Supervisor routines for application
$4000–$4FFF		SIM, QSM and TPU initialization routines
$5000–$6FFF		TRAP handler routines for application
$7000–$7FFF		Interrupt handler routines for application
$8000–$FFFF		Applications programs and system stacks
$60000–$7FFFFF	EPROM	332BUG ROM
$FFFF00–$FFF7FF	RAM	On-chip RAM
$FFF800–$FFFFFF	Registers	SIM, RAM control , QSM and TPU registers

Note:
The memory locations not given in the table are not used in the system. The Supervisor Stack Pointer is initialized to $10000 and the User Stack Pointer is initialized to $FC00.

Table 10.10 defines the important addresses in the memory map of the BCC system. The first 64Kbytes of memory are RAM. The vectors point to exception-handling routines that are a selection of routines from the 332BUG monitor such as the trace routine and those routines added for the specific application. Section 11.1 defines the specific vectors used in the system. For example, interrupt vector 65 ($40) is used to locate the SCI interrupt routine used in Example 12.6.

The 332BUG monitor uses the next RAM area up to location $2FFF. RAM locations $3000 to $FFFF contain programs and the system stacks. Since the stacks grow down in memory, care must be taken to assure that no conflicts arise with the programs. The area up to $60000 contains no memory in this system but additional memory can be added. The 332BUG monitor occupies 128Kbytes of EPROM on

---

[9] The circuitry and the buttons that control reset and abort are actually on the platform board of the Motorola Evaluation System (EVS). Section 16.2 describes the EVS.

the BCC card. It is possible to reprogram the EPROM to add a special-purpose supervisor program that replaces 332BUG. For example, the Evaluation System (EVS) described in Section 16.2 can be used to reprogram the EPROM. The on-chip RAM and the module registers occupy the highest locations in memory.

After a reset, 332BUG initializes the system for program loading and debugging by initializing the SIM and the CPU vector table. A reset passes control to the monitor in ROM as explained in Section 14.6. Once the system is initialized for debugging, 332BUG waits for an operator command as described previously in Section 5.1. The programs that are used in the application can then be loaded into memory and executed. The first program to be executed typically initializes the system for the application in a manner similar to that described in Table 10.9. For example, since the CPU vector table is held in RAM, the initialization includes writing the appropriate vector addresses into the vector table. This allows certain exceptions to pass control the exception-handling routines that have been added to the system software rather than passing control to 332BUG routines.

EXERCISES

10.3.1. The instruction sequence

> MOVE.W   #$0000, SR
>
> JMP   USER

could be used to transfer control to a program at location USER. Why is the approach in Example 10.3 using RTE better? Consider the case when the memory is segmented into supervisor program space and user program space so that a program in the user mode cannot access the supervisor's memory area.

10.3.2. Design an interrupt-handling routine to respond to a level 7 interrupt. The routine should simply display "Level 7 Interrupt" on the operator's display screen when the interrupt is recognized. The vector address is $07C in a standard MC68332-based computer system. If possible, test the routine on the system you are using. For example, the "abort" button on the BCC card causes a level 7 interrupt as explained previously in Subsection 10.3.3.

10.3.3. Define several reasons for having the Vector Base Register. Consider first the cases in which the VBR is used to relocate the exception vector table after system initialization. Next, consider systems in which more than one exception vector table is needed.

10.3.4. If the reader is using an MC68332-based computer system, print the exception vector table and label all the exceptions that are handled by the monitor program or the operating system. Refer to Table 10.8 for the names of the specific exceptions.

FURTHER READING

For a specific computer system, the *User's manuals* must be consulted for detailed information concerning system initialization and operation at the level discussed in this chapter. For example, when power is applied to the Business Card Computer (BCC), the 332BUG monitor initializes the system.

11

Exception-Handling Techniques

This chapter describes the exception-handling capability of the MC68332 CPU. Exceptions are provided to ensure an orderly transfer of control from an executing program to an exception-handling routine. CPU32 exceptions may be broadly divided into those caused by an instruction, including an unusual condition arising during its execution, and those caused by events external to the CPU. Exceptions in the first category are called *traps*. These traps represent exceptional conditions that are detected by the CPU during execution of a program.

System events and other conditions initiated by MC68332 modules other than the CPU or by external hardware represent the second category of exceptions. The *interrupt* and the *bus-error exception* are two such external events recognized by the processor. When any type of exception is detected, the CPU enters the exception state and program control of the CPU is passed to an exception-handling routine.

This chapter covers the CPU response to exceptions as well as the techniques to create exception-handling routines. Section 11.1 introduces all of the exceptions of the CPU32 and defines the exception vector allocation in the CPU vector table. Section 11.2 discusses system design considerations for exception handling. Sections 11.3 through 11.6 define specific exceptions and present examples of their use. Interrupt priorities and interrupt handling by the CPU32 are described in Section 11.7. Section 11.8 summarizes the form of the exception stack frames that are created by the various exceptions. Section 11.8 also presents the priority scheme defined for the CPU32 when multiple exceptions occur simultaneously.

11.1 CPU32 EXCEPTIONS AND EXCEPTION PROCESSING

Table 11.1 lists the CPU32 exceptions and their causes. The descriptions in Table 11.1 are a general summary of the cause or effect of each exception. This chapter presents the precise operation of most of these exceptions in later sections. The reset exception was discussed previously in Chapter 10. The types of exceptions in Table 11.1 that result from instruction execution can be divided into those generated by TRAP instructions, program checks, special exceptions, and instruction error conditions. The bus error and hardware breakpoints result from the action of circuitry external to the CPU. The MC68332 modules and external devices make interrupt requests.

11.1.1 Exception Processing and the CPU32 Vector Table

Figure 11.1 illustrates the processing sequence for most exceptions except the reset exception that was described in Chapter 10. Upon recognition of the exception as shown in the figure, the CPU saves a copy of the current contents of the Status Register (SR), enters the supervisor mode, suspends tracing, and determines the vector number of the exception. As defined in Section 10.1, the term *exception processing* refers to the automatic processing by the CPU. The term *exception handling* refers to execution of the exception-handling routine. The vector location in memory contains the starting address of the exception-handling routine.

Figure 11.2 shows the vector number and corresponding memory address for each CPU32 exception in the CPU vector table. The location in memory of the vector table is determined by the contents of the Vector Base Register (VBR) as previously discussed in Section 10.3. The VBR is assumed to be initialized to its reset address of $00000000 in this chapter. The vectors in Figure 11.2 labeled "reserved" may be used by Motorola processors other than the MC68332.[1] They would not normally be used in an MC68332-based product.

After recognizing an exception, the CPU begins exception processing. Section 10.1 described the exception state that the CPU enters upon recognition of an exception. Except for a reset exception, the CPU saves information concerning the particular exception by creating a *stack frame* on the supervisor stack during exception processing. The stack frame contains data that allows the CPU to return control to the interrupted program after the exception-handling routine completes. In the case of exceptions caused by errors in software or hardware, the stacked information can be examined to determine the source of the error. The information saved on the supervisor stack includes at least a format word and the previous values from the Program Counter and the Status Register. The format word defines the type of stack frame and the vector number for the exception.

The general format of the exception stack frame for the CPU32 is shown in Figure 11.3(a).[2] The minimum length of the stack frame is four 16-bit words if no

---

[1] For example, the MC68020 vector table contains a number of exception vectors in the reserved area between addresses $C0 and $FC.

[2] For certain exceptions (bus error), the stacking order from higher to lower memory locations may not be followed during exception processing. However, the order of information in the stack frame after stacking is as shown in Figure 11.3.

Table 11.1 CPU32 Exceptions

Type	Description
Reset:	Causes system initialization
Trap instruction:	
TRAP #<N>; N = 0, 1, ... , 15	Sixteen trap routines may be defined and used by a program
Program checks:	
DIVS, DIVSL, DIVU, DIVUL	Trap when divisor is zero
CHK, CHK2	Trap if register value is out of bounds
TRAPcc	Trap on one of 14 arithmetic conditions
TRAPV	Trap on overflow; i.e. if V = {1}
Special exceptions:	
Unimplemented instruction trap	Trap if op-code bits [15:12] are either {1010} or {1111} for an unimplemented instruction
Trace exceptions	Trace after single instruction or after change of control flow
Breakpoint (BKPT)	Causes a breakpoint acknowledgement cycle
Instruction error *conditions:*	
Privilege violation	Trap if user-mode program attempts to execute a privileged instruction
Illegal instruction	Trap if operation word of an instruction is not a valid bit pattern
Address error	Trap if processor attempts to access a word or longword or an instruction at an odd address
System errors and *conditions:*	
Bus error	Externally generated exception
Format error	Trap if error occurs during RTE
Hardware breakpoint	Externally generated breakpoint
Interrupt system:	
Autovector	Automatic vectoring for seven levels of priority
Vectored	192 possible interrupt vectors; priority determined by hardware design
Spurious interrupt, Uninitialized interrupt	Interrupt related errors

additional processor-state information is pushed on the stack when an exception is recognized. This stack is shown in Figure 11.3(b). Certain exceptions require additional information which will be described in this chapter when specific exceptions are discussed. Figure 11.3(c) shows a six-word stack frame as an example. The bits [15:12] of the format word associated with each stack frame is used by the CPU to determine the length of the stack frame. The vector offset in the format word is the offset from the start of the CPU vector table to the location of the vector for the exception-handling routine. Subsection 10.3.2 describes the calculation for a nonzero value in the Vector

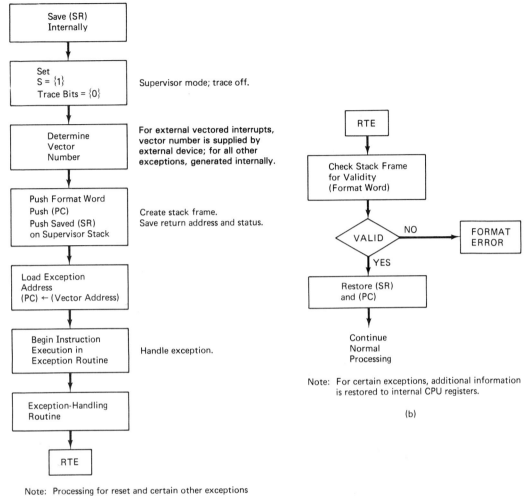

Figure 11.1 Exception processing.

Base Register. Section 11.8 describes the other entries in the exception stack frames in more detail.

Once this exception processing sequence is complete, the new PC value is read from the vector table and loaded into the Program Counter. Thus, program control of the CPU is passed to the exception-handling routine.

If control is to be returned to the program that was interrupted when exception processing began, the exception-handling routine completes by executing an RTE (Return from Exception) instruction as was described in Section 10.2. Using the data in the stack frame for the exception, the CPU passes control to the program that was executing when the exception occurred. The return sequence is also shown in Fig-

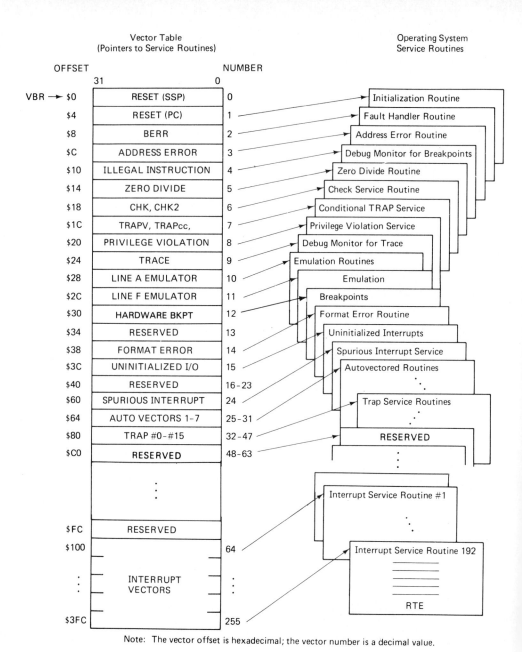

OFFSET   NUMBER

OFFSET	31	Vector	0	NUMBER	Service Routine
VBR → $0		RESET (SSP)		0	Initialization Routine
$4		RESET (PC)		1	Fault Handler Routine
$8		BERR		2	Address Error Routine
$C		ADDRESS ERROR		3	Debug Monitor for Breakpoints
$10		ILLEGAL INSTRUCTION		4	Zero Divide Routine
$14		ZERO DIVIDE		5	Check Service Routine
$18		CHK, CHK2		6	Conditional TRAP Service
$1C		TRAPV, TRAPcc,		7	Privilege Violation Service
$20		PRIVILEGE VIOLATION		8	Debug Monitor for Trace
$24		TRACE		9	Emulation Routines
$28		LINE A EMULATOR		10	Emulation
$2C		LINE F EMULATOR		11	Breakpoints
$30		HARDWARE BKPT		12	Format Error Routine
$34		RESERVED		13	Uninitialized Interrupts
$38		FORMAT ERROR		14	Spurious Interrupt Service
$3C		UNINITIALIZED I/O		15	Autovectored Routines
$40		RESERVED		16–23	
$60		SPURIOUS INTERRUPT		24	Trap Service Routines
$64		AUTO VECTORS 1–7		25–31	
$80		TRAP #0–#15		32–47	RESERVED
$C0		RESERVED		48–63	
		⋮			Interrupt Service Routine #1
$FC		RESERVED			
$100				64	Interrupt Service Routine 192
⋮		INTERRUPT VECTORS		⋮	
$3FC				255	RTE

Note: The vector offset is hexadecimal; the vector number is a decimal value.

Figure 11.2 Vector allocation.

ure 11.1. If the stack frame format is valid, the previous (PC) and (SR) are restored
and the stack pointer is set to the value it contained before the exception occurred.
Any other information on the stack is then loaded into internal registers of the CPU.
As discussed later, control may not always be returned to a program after exception

handling if an error in the program caused an exception. In other cases, the information on the stack may be modified by the supervisor program before control is returned.

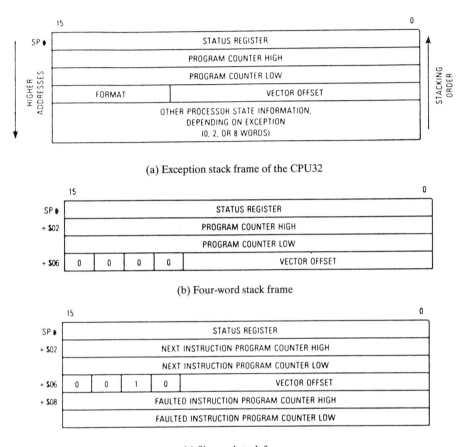

(a) Exception stack frame of the CPU32

(b) Four-word stack frame

(c) Six-word stack frame

Figure 11.3 Stack frames.

11.1.2 BCC System Example

The author's Business Card Computer (BCC) system was described previously in Subsection 10.3.3. The BCC controls a number of peripheral devices used to illustrate program and hardware design examples in this textbook. Some applications require exception-handling routines to control the peripheral devices and perform other services. To locate the exception handlers, the starting addresses of these routines must be written into the CPU vector table by the author's initialization program. The 332BUG monitor uses several of the vectors to point to monitor routines which aid debugging and perform I/O services for an applications program.

Table 11.2 lists the important vectors used in the author's BCC system. Those that are used by the 332BUG monitor point to routines in the 332BUG ROM. The breakpoint (illegal) and trace exceptions are typically used during program debugging as described in Section 11.4. The level 7 autovector interrupt occurs when the BCC Abort button is pushed as described in Section 10.3. The operator typically uses the Abort button to terminate program execution during debugging. The purpose is to return control to the monitor.

Table 11.2 BCC System Vectors

Vector Number and Offset (Hex)	Name	Exception address	Use
4 ($10)	Illegal instruction	– –	332BUG
5 ($14)	Zero divide	$5300	Zero divide trap
6 ($18)	CHK, CHK2	$5400	Check register bounds trap
9 ($24)	Trace	– –	332BUG
31 ($07C)	Level 7 Autovector	– –	332BUG Abort
32 ($80)	TRAP #0	$3600	Call EXEC
33 ($84)	TRAP #1	$6600	SCI I/O driver
47 ($BC)	TRAP #15	– –	332BUG I/O Call
64 ($100)	Interrupt	$7500	SCI interrupt service routine
65 ($104)	Interrupt	$7700	QSPI interrupt service routine
66 ($108)	Interrupt	$7800	PIT interrupt service routine
80 ($140)	Channel 0	$7A00	TPU channels interrupt service routines
.	. . .	. . .	. . .
.	. . .	. . .	
95 ($17C)	Channel 15	$7F00	

The TRAP #15 call to 332BUG was described previously in Section 7.6 where the call was used to initiate I/O with the operator's terminal. The TRAP #15 calls to 332BUG use the Serial Communication Interface (SCI) of the MC68332 to communicate. If an applications program uses the SCI, the 332BUG monitor cannot be used for program debugging. Chapter 12 presents examples showing the use of the SCI for I/O applications without using 332BUG. In this case, a TRAP #1 instruction with exception handler at location $6600 is used to request I/O with the SCI.

The interrupt service routines for the MC68332 modules are assigned the vectors listed in Table 11.2. For example, the interrupt service routine for the SCI starts at location $7500. Section 11.7 explains the interrupt system of the CPU32. The specific service routines are described in subsequent chapters. Other exceptions that are not listed in Table 11.2 return control to the 332BUG monitor when they occur. None of the exceptions that return control to 332BUG should occur once the programs for a particular application are operating correctly.

11.2 EXCEPTION HANDLING

A supervisor program for an MC68332-based product will typically have a number of exception-handling routines as part of the system software. The addition of the exception-handling routines to the system software is simple in principle. First, after the routines are designed and coded to meet the product requirements, the system memory map should define the memory location of each exception-handling routine. A memory map similar to that presented in Section 10.3 could be used to specify the locations. Before execution of any of the applications programs, the routines must be present in memory and the starting addresses of the routines must be present in the CPU exception vector table. The vector locations are defined in Figure 11.2 or Table 10.8.

If the CPU vector table and the routines are held in RAM, the vectors are initialized and the routines loaded into memory by an initialization routine as previously discussed in Section 10.3. If the CPU vector table is held in ROM, the ROM locations from $000000 to $0003FC must contain the reset vector (initial SSP and PC) and the appropriate addresses for the exception-handling routines.

Subsection 11.2.1 explains the general applications of various exceptions. Subsection 11.2.2 describes the techniques for initialization of the CPU vector table and the return to an interrupted program after an exception-handling routine completes execution. Subsection 11.2.3 discusses the addition of exception handling routines to a commercially available operating system for the MC68332.

11.2.1 Uses of Exception Handling Routines

The exceptions listed in Table 11.1 can be broadly classified according to their typical use in a product. These categories are as follows:
(a) request for supervisor services (TRAP);
(b) error detection;
(c) debugging;
(d) special purpose (Bus error);
(e) I/O and interrupt handling.

The TRAP instruction can be used to request specific supervisor services. For example, a specific service is requested by the

TRAP   #<N>

instruction in most MC68332-based systems. The constant N is used to define one of 16 possible requests to the operating system; $N = 0, 1, 2, \ldots, 15$. Several examples in Chapter 7 showed the use of the TRAP instruction to request supervisor services of the 332BUG monitor. In particular, Example 7.12 presented a program to request various I/O operations using the TRAP #15 instruction. Example 11.3 in Section 11.3 presents another use of the TRAP instruction to request various services associated with a real-time executive (supervisor). The requested services are called *supervisor services* because execution of the TRAP instruction causes execution of a routine in the supervisor mode of the CPU.

Various errors cause exceptions as listed in Table 11.1. Certain errors are associated with specific instructions such as the exception caused by a zero divisor when a division instruction is executed. The check (CHK) and trap on condition (TRAPcc) instructions are added to a program to cause exceptions if various conditions arise during program execution. Such exceptions are provided to prevent program errors from causing undesired results.

Other errors are detected by the CPU to prevent unpredictable or invalid operation of the system during program execution. The privilege violation, illegal instruction, address error, and format error exceptions are examples of exceptions designed to protect the system. Several error conditions are also associated with the interrupt exceptions as discussed in Section 11.7.

During product development and debugging, a number of the errors just discussed can be expected to occur. The exception-handling routines for these errors typically return control to the supervisor program. For a programming error, the programmer would correct the faulty program and execute the corrected version to continue debugging. Hardware errors would also be corrected.

In a finished product, none of the exceptions in Figure 11.2 caused by errors should occur. However, every exception vector in Figure 11.2 should be initialized to pass control to an exception-handling routine in case a hardware failure causes an unexpected exception. To avoid unpredictable operation of the finished product if an error occurs, the system is typically reset or reinitialized when an error is recognized. The techniques to handle such situations are discussed in Chapter 15.

During debugging, the trace exceptions and the breakpoint (illegal) exceptions are often used. The trace facility of the 332BUG monitor was described briefly in Section 5.1. Subsection 11.4.2 discusses the trace exception in detail. The 332BUG uses the illegal instruction exception to insert breakpoints in a program. The breakpoints and the illegal exception are introduced in Subsection 11.4.3 in this chapter and discussed further in Chapter 16.

The bus error exception is caused by a system event external to the CPU. Although the use of the bus error exception is determined by a particular application, it is often used to indicate a system condition such as an error that prevents continued operation of the product until the cause of the bus error is corrected. Section 11.6 describes the bus error in more detail.

The CPU interrupt exceptions are used to handle requests from external devices or other modules of the MC68332. For example, the Periodic Interrupt Timer (PIT) of the MC68332 can be programmed to interrupt the CPU program at fixed time intervals. Described in Section 14.3, this timer is part of the MC68332 System Integration Module. The PIT interrupt handling-routine might update the time being kept by a clock routine.

Another important use of interrupts is during I/O transfers that are controlled by interrupts. The interrupt-handling routine is typically one of the system routines that control the operation of a specific peripheral device. Chapter 12 presents examples of the use of interrupt routines for I/O transfers with the Queued Serial Module of the MC68332. Chapter 13 presents other uses of interrupt routines to control the operation of the Time Processor Unit (TPU). Chapter 14 describes the interrupt signal lines of the external bus.

11.2.2 Design of Exception Handlers

Many MC68332-based products will contain specific exception-handling routines to meet the product requirements. Figure 11.4 shows an example operation of the product when an exception is recognized. As shown in Figure 11.4, exception-handling routines may be included to service interrupt requests, to respond to TRAP instructions, or to handle special situations. These legitimate exceptions are handled by appropriate routines. If another type of exception occurs that is not expected during product operation, the product can be reinitialized as described in Section 10.3. Of course, many other possibilities exist. For example, if a reset is not desirable in case of an error, the appropriate exception-handling routine could attempt to recover from the error. Chapter 15 describes some of the possible responses to error conditions that arise during product operation.

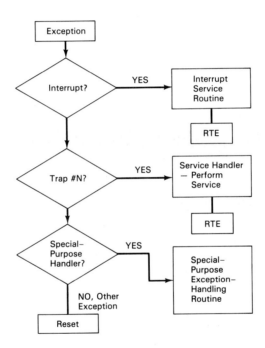

Figure 11.4 Example exception handling in an MC68332-based product.

As shown in Figure 11.4, control typically is returned to the applications program that was interrupted after an interrupt is serviced. A program executing a TRAP instruction continues execution after the trap-handling routine performs the requested service such as an I/O transfer. To return control, the Return from Exception (RTE) instruction is the last instruction in the interrupt and TRAP routines. Other exceptions may not allow control to be returned to the applications program. The exception-handling routine is designed in this case to pass control to a supervisor program which must take appropriate action. Subsection 11.1.2 described the specific exceptions used in the author's BCC system.

The considerations in the design and implementation of an exception-handling routine consist of the following:

(a) design and testing of the routine to perform a specified function;
(b) initialization of the CPU vector table;
(c) returning control to the interrupted program or the supervisor program after the exception-handling routine has serviced the exception.

Many of the examples in this chapter and succeeding chapters present exception-handling routines for various applications. The design and testing of the routine depends on the application. This subsection considers the initialization of the CPU vector table and the techniques for the exception-handling routine to return control to another program.

Example 11.1

A CPU vector table in RAM can be initialized in several ways. For example, assume the trap-handling routine for a TRAP #0 instruction is to be loaded starting at location $3600. This TRAP instruction uses the vector at location $80 in the CPU vector table as shown in Figure 11.2. The instruction

        MOVE.L   #$3600, $80   ; TRAP 0 VECTOR

initializes the TRAP #0 vector when the instruction executes. Another approach is to initialize the vector when the initialization program is loaded. For example, the instruction sequence

        ORG $80   ; TRAP 0 VECTOR
        DC.L $3600

causes $3600 to be written in location $80 after assembly and program loading.

Except for the bus error exception, a four word or six word stack frame will be created by an exception as shown in Figure 11.3. In the four word stack frame, the PC value points to the next instruction to be executed or to the instruction that caused the exception. After an interrupt for example, the PC value on the four word stack in Figure 11.3(b) points to the next instruction to be executed when control is returned to the interrupted program. The instruction

        RTE   ; RETURN

described in Section 10.2 returns control to the interrupted program by reloading the SR and PC with the stacked values. Figure 11.1(b) shows the return sequence.

However, if the instruction that caused the exception does not execute, the PC value on a four word stack frame will point to the faulted instruction not to the next instruction in sequence. For example, this is the case for an instruction that causes an illegal instruction or a privilege violation exception. The CPU will not execute the instruction or increment the saved PC value beyond the instruction address in memory. Obviously, executing the RTE instruction in the exception-handling routine after one of these error conditions would cause the same error repeatedly. The solution is to return control to a supervisor program rather than to the program causing the error. One way to transfer control to the supervisor is to have the exception-handling routine modify the values in the stack frame. The routine does this by writing the appropriate values of the Program Counter and Status Register to replace the stacked values. Then, the execution of RTE passes control to the proper program.

Example 10.3 showed how a stack frame can be created to pass control to a user program at a specified location. Example 11.2 describes how the stack contents may be modified if the return PC value on the stack must be altered. Example 11.3 presents a program example.

Example 11.2

When an exception-handling routine completes by executing the RTE instruction, control is passed to the instruction location indicated by the return PC value on the exception stack frame. For both a four-word and a six-word stack, the return PC value is held at location (SP)+2 as shown in Figure 11.3.

The initial return PC value in the stack frame is not correct to return control to the proper instruction for certain exceptions. For example, this is the case when the instruction causing the exception does not execute as previously discussed. The return PC value must also be modified when a TRAP instruction that is followed by a constant parameter causes the exception. The constant is one or more words to be passed to an exception-handling routine. Example 7.12 used this method to request supervisor services from the 332BUG monitor. As described in that example, the instruction sequence

```
TRAP          #15                    ; WRITE LINE
DC.W          $0024
```

requests that a line of text be written to the screen of the operator's terminal. The PC value on the four-word exception stack after the TRAP instruction executes points to the constant value ($0024) which is not an executable instruction. The constant defines the requested service for the monitor routine to output a line of text.

To return to the next executable instruction following the TRAP instruction after the requested service is performed, the exception-handling routine must modify the return PC value on the stack which initially points to the constant. After the PC value is modified, execution of an RTE instruction returns control to the correct location. The method to modify the PC value is similar to that presented in Section 9.4 in connection with in-line coding.

After the TRAP instruction executes, the stack location (SP)+2 holds the return PC value as shown in Figure 11.3(b). The exception-handling routine must retrieve the constant word from the instruction stream and increment the stored PC value by 2 to skip over the constant in the instruction stream of the program that executed the TRAP instruction. The exception instruction sequence could be

```
MOVEA.L       (2, SP), A0            ; GET PC VALUE
MOVE.W        (A0)+, D1             ; GET CONSTANT
MOVE.L        A0, (2, SP)           ; STORE RETURN PC
```

in which the constant is held in D1 for processing by the exception-handling routine. The MOVE.W instruction writes the constant into D1 and also adds 2 to the value in A0 which is now the correct PC value. After the new PC value is stored on the stack, the routine need only execute an RTE instruction to return control to the instruction following the TRAP instruction. Example 11.3 presents a program segment that modifies the return address on the stack after a TRAP #0 call to a supervisor routine.

11.2.3 Commercially-Available Operating Systems

A number of supervisor programs are available for the M68300 family of microcontrollers. Section 16.4 presents several real-time operating systems as examples. These operating systems typically provide I/O, file management and multitasking operations for the computer system. The operating system may contain routines to control standard peripheral devices. These peripheral control routines are frequently called *I/O drivers* or *device drivers* as discussed further in Chapter 12. Examples of such standard peripheral devices include disk-storage units and operator terminals. Exception-handling routines such as interrupt service routines are typically part of the I/O driver software.

In most applications, conditions occur during operation of a product that require specific exception-handling routines to meet the requirements of the application. These conditions cannot be anticipated by the company providing a general-purpose operating system. Therefore, some of the necessary exception-handling routines must be designed and tested based on the specific requirements of the applications. For example, an interrupt service routine for a special-purpose peripheral device such as an A/D converter might be required. These routines could be added to the operating system once they are completed. The supervisor program for the product thus becomes a modified operating system which includes both standard and special-purpose exception-handling routines.[3]

Since the commercially available operating systems for MC68332-based products are general-purpose, the product designer may decide that a new operating system should be designed and included in the product. The creation of exception-handling routines is part of the software design and implementation effort. However, even if no operating system is used in the product, routines for exception handling to service interrupts and perform other services must be part of the system software. The remainder of this chapter discusses the various types of exception handlers that could be included in the system software of a product.

EXERCISES

11.2.1. Consider the operation of a completed product. What are the possible actions to be taken when each of the exceptions in Table 11.1 is recognized? Be sure to distinguish between legitimate exceptions and program errors that might be intermittent.

---

[3] The technique to add a special-purpose routine to an operating system depends completely on the design of the operating system. Specific details are typically given in the *User's Manual* for the operating system being considered.

11.2.2. Select an operating system of interest and describe how the system software provides for input/output and interrupt handling. If the operating system is not for an MC68332-based computer, describe how the exceptions handled by the operating system might be implemented on a Motorola system that uses the MC68332.

11.3 EXCEPTIONS CAUSED BY TRAP INSTRUCTIONS AND PROGRAM CHECKS

Several CPU32 instructions which can cause exception processing are available to the programmer to control the operation of a program. These exceptions are generally referred to as *traps* to distinguish them from other exceptions such as interrupts. The instructions that may create trap exceptions as listed in Table 11.3 are caused by one of the following:

(a) TRAP instruction;
(b) instructions to check program conditions;
(c) trap on condition instructions (TRAPcc and TRAPV).

The vector offset in Table 11.3 refers to the offset from the starting location of the CPU vector table shown in Figure 11.2.

The TRAP instruction is inserted in a program to cause a trap exception when the instruction executes. A TRAP instruction is typically used to pass control to a specific supervisor routine when some type of supervisor service is required. Motorola's operating systems and monitor programs such as 332BUG use this technique to handle requests from executing programs as previously described in Section 7.6 and Example 11.2.

The instructions in Table 11.3 to check the operation of a program are used to test various arithmetic conditions or the numerical range of a value held in a register. These instructions will only cause a trap exception if the specified condition is detected when the instruction executes. The exception-handling routine can attempt to recover from the condition causing the trap and return control to the program causing the trap. However, in many cases when the cause of the trap is considered to be an error in an applications program, the offending program is not allowed to continue executing. The exact response depends completely on the design of the supervisor software and its exception-handling routines. Section 11.2 presented several examples showing the techniques to return from an exception-handling routine.

11.3.1 The TRAP Instruction

The TRAP instruction has the assembly-language format

    TRAP   #<vector>

in which the trap number (0,...,15) is indicated by the parameter <vector>. When the instruction is executed, a format word, the contents of the Program Counter and the Status Register are pushed on the supervisor stack. Then, the exception-handling

Table 11.3 Trap Instructions and Program Checks

Type of trap	Cause of trap	Vector offset	Comments
TRAP instruction	Instruction execution	$80-$BC	Typical method to call supervisor program
Program checks			
DIVS, DIVSL, DIVU, DIVUL	Divisor is zero	$14	Arithmetic check
CHK, CHK2	Value in a register is out of bounds	$18	Bounds check
TRAP<cc>	Logical condition <cc> was detected	$1C	One of 16 conditions can be selected
TRAPV	Execution with V = {1}	$1C	Trap on arithmetic overflow

routine begins execution at the address specified in the vector location. The value <vector> is an integer in the range 0-15 and is used by the CPU to calculate the location of the vector in the CPU vector table as follows:

$$\text{vector address} = (\text{VBR}) + 80_{16} + 4 * <\text{vector}>$$

where the offset 80_{16} indicates the first vector for the TRAP instructions as shown in Figure 11.2 or Table 11.3. The vector number is multiplied by 4 to keep the vector address on a long-word boundary since each vector address is 32 bits long. The Vector Base Register (VBR) was previously described in Section 10.3.

The exception-handling routine begins at the location loaded into the Program Counter as

$$(\text{PC}) \leftarrow (\text{vector address})$$

where the address is 32 bits in length. For convenience, the vector addresses for the TRAP instructions when (VBR) = 0 are listed in Table 11.4. These locations must be initialized with the vector addresses before a TRAP instruction is executed.

Applications of the TRAP instruction. The TRAP instruction has numerous uses. For a program operating in the user mode, execution of the TRAP instruction returns control to the supervisor program at the location of the designated trap routine. The 16 possible traps allow a user-mode program to call the supervisor for processing. For example, a call via the TRAP instruction might be used to input or output data using peripheral devices which are controlled by the supervisor. Example 11.2 described the operation of the 332BUG monitor after an I/O request using the TRAP #15 instruction. Example 12.6 in Chapter 12 shows the use of a TRAP #1 instruction to request I/O transfer by the Serial Communications Interface (SCI) of the Queued Serial Module. In that application, the TRAP #1 instruction is used to call the I/O driver for the SCI.

Table 11.4 Trap Vector Addresses

TRAP #<N> instruction	Vector address (hexadecimal)
TRAP #0	$80
TRAP #1	$84
TRAP #2	$88
TRAP #3	$8C
TRAP #4	$90
TRAP #5	$94
TRAP #6	$98
TRAP #7	$9C
TRAP #8	$A0
TRAP #9	$A4
TRAP #10	$A8
TRAP #11	$AC
TRAP #12	$B0
TRAP #13	$B4
TRAP #14	$B8
TRAP #15	$BC

Note:
The trap number N is decimal.

In effect, the trap is a software interrupt. For example, this mechanism could be used in debugging operations to simulate interrupts. The TRAP can also be used to emulate a special instruction that is not part of the CPU32 instruction set as described in Subsection 11.4.1. The TRAP instruction is also a means of returning control to the supervisor mode after an applications program has completed if the sequence of execution for individual programs is controlled by an operating system or monitor. Many program examples in this textbook terminate with a TRAP #15 instruction to return control to the 332BUG monitor in the author's development system. Other examples of the use of the TRAP instruction were given in Chapter 7.

Example 11.3

Figure 11.5(a) contains a program segment in a real-time executive (supervisor) which can be invoked by the calling program with the

TRAP   #0

instruction followed by a 16-bit constant to define the requested operation. Information is coded in the calling program in assembly-language by following the TRAP instruction with a Define Constant (DC.W) directive to define a 16-bit integer (function number). This integer selects the particular executive service being requested by the user. The allowed function numbers are 0, 1, 2, or 3. In this example, functions 1 and 2 are handled by the same routine SCHED. Figure 11.5(b) shows the segment of a program that executes the TRAP #0 call. The TRAP instruction is at location $8100 in the example and the constant is held at word address $8102.

As part of system initialization, the vector address $3600 (EXEC) which is the location of the TRAP #0 exception handler must be stored at location $080 before the

```
abs. rel.   LC   obj. code    source line
----  ----  ----  ---------    -----------
  1     1   0000                          TTL     'FIGURE 11.5(a)'
  2     2   3600                          ORG     $3600
  3     3         0000 0010    EEXEC       EQU     $10        ; ERROR CODE IN EXECUTIVE
  4     4         0000 3100    DIALL       EQU     $3100      ; ROUTINE TO DISABLE INTERRUPTS
  5     5         0000 3200    DISP        EQU     $3200      ; ROUTINE TO DISPATCH
  6     6         0000 3300    INTSCH      EQU     $3300      ; ROUTINE TO SAVE INTERRUPTED TASKS
  7     7         0000 3400    SCHED       EQU     $3400      ; ROUTINE TO PERFORM SCHEDULING
  8     8         0000 3500    RTERRX      EQU     $3500      ; ROUTINE FOR ERROR PROCESSING
  9     9   3600              *
 10    10   3600              *           THIS ROUTINE DETERMINES THE EXECUTIVE FUNCTION REQUESTED AND TRANSFERS
 11    11   3600              *           CONTROL TO IT.  EXEC PLACES 15 REGISTERS ON THE STACK AND USES A
 12    12   3600              *           JUMP TABLE TO PASS CONTROL TO THE APPROPRIATE FUNCTION.
 13    13   3600              *
 14    14   3600              *           EXEC EXECUTES IN THE SUPERVISOR MODE AND
 15    15   3600              *             IS INVOKED AS FOLLOWS IN THE CALLING PROGRAM:
 16    16   3600              *                   TRAP    #0
 17    17   3600              *                   DC.W    #FUNCTION (0=DISP,1=SCHED,
 18    18   3600              *                                      2=TMSCH,3=INTSCH)
 19    19   3600              *
 20    20   3600              *           EXEC INVOKES THE FOLLOWING ROUTINES:
 21    21   3600              *               DIALL  - DISABLE INTERRUPTS
 22    22   3600              *               DISP   - DISPATCHER
 23    23   3600              *               INTSCH - INTERRUPTED TASK SCHEDULER
 24    24   3600              *               RTERRX - ERROR EXIT
 25    25   3600              *               SCHED  - TASK SCHEDULER
 26    26   3600              *           EXEC USES THE FOLLOWING DATA:
 27    27   3600              *               EEXEC  - ERROR CODE IN EXEC (I.E. ILLEGAL)
 28    28   3600              *               ERRAD  - ERROR ADDRESS
 29    29   3600              *               ERRCD  - ERROR CODE
 30    30   3600              *               EXECTB - EXECUTIVE CONTROL JUMP TABLE
 31    31   3600              *               EXTBLN - EXECUTIVE CONTROL TABLE LENGTH
 32    32   3600              *
 33    33   3600 4EB8 3100    EXEC        JSR     DIALL            ;DISABLE INTERRUPTS
 34    34   3604 48E7 FFFE                MOVEM.L D0-D7/A0-A6,-(SP) ;SAVE REGISTERS
 35    35   3608 206F 003E                MOVE.L  (62,SP),A0       ;GET PC (POINTS TO DATA
 36    36   360C              *                                    ; FOLLOWING TRAP #0 CALL)
 37    37   360C 4281                     CLR.L   D1
 38    38   360E 3218                     MOVE.W  (A0)+,D1         ;GET FUNCTION NO. REQUESTED
 39    39   3610 0C41 0004                CMPI.W  #EXTBLN,D1       ;IS FUNCTION LEGAL?
 40    40   3614 6C0E                     BGE.S   EXEC10           ;IF NOT, PROCESS ERROR
 41    41   3616 43F9 0000                LEA     EXECTB,A1        ; ELSE, GET ADDR OF FUNCTION
 41        361A 363E
 42    42   361C E589                     LSL.L   #2,D1            ;  REQUESTED
 43    43   361E D3C1                     ADD.L   D1,A1            ; (FUNC. NO.*4+TABLE ADDRESS)
 44    44   3620 2F11                     MOVE.L  (A1),-(SP)       ; AND PLACE ON STACK
 45    45   3622 4E75                     RTS                      ;EXECUTE 'RETURN' TO FUNCTION
 46    46   3624              *                                    ; WHOSE ADDRESS WAS STACKED
 47    47   3624              *
 48    48   3624              *           ERROR DETECTION PROCESSING
 49    49   3624              *
 50    50   3624 4CDF 7FFF    EXEC10      MOVEM.L (SP)+,D0-D7/A0-A6 ;RESTORE REGISTERS
 51    51   3628 23EF 0002                MOVE.L  (2,SP),ERRAD     ;ADDRESS OF ERROR
 51        362C 0000 3652
 52    52   3630 23FC 0000                MOVE.L  #EEXEC,ERRCD     ;STORE ERROR CODE
 52        3634 0010 0000
 52        3638 364E
 53    53   363A 4EF8 3500                JMP     RTERRX           ;ERROR EXIT
 54    54   363E              *
 55    55   363E              *
 56    56   363E              *           EXECUTIVE CONTROL JUMP TABLE AND OTHER DATA
 57    57         0000 0004    EXTBLN      EQU     4         ; EXECUTIVE CONTROL TABLE LENGTH
 58    58   363E 0000 3200    EXECTB      DC.L    DISP      ; DISPATCHER
 59    59   3642 0000 3400                DC.L    SCHED     ; SCHEDULER
 60    60   3646 0000 3400                DC.L    SCHED     ; TIMED SCHEDULER
 61    61   364A 0000 3300                DC.L    INTSCH    ; INTERRUPTED TASK SCHEDULER
 62    62   364E              ERRCD       DS.L    1         ; ERROR CODE
 63    63   3652              ERRAD       DS.L    1         ; ERROR ADDRESS
 64    64   3656                          END
64 lines assembled
```

Figure 11.5(a) Program example of TRAP usage.

```
abs. rel.   LC   obj. code    source line
---- ----   ----  ---------   -----------
   1    1   0000                 |         TTL      'FIGURE 11.5(b)'
   2    2   0000                 |*
   3    3   0000                 |*        EXAMPLE TRAP #0 CALL TO 'EXEC' TO SCHEDULE A TASK.
   4    4   0000                 |*          CONTROL IS RETURNED BY ROUTINE 'RTNUSER'
   5    5   0000                 |*
   6    6   8100                 |         ORG      $8100
   7    7   0000                 |*
   8    8   8100                 |*        SET CODE FOR TRAP #0 CALL TO SCHEDULER
   9    9   8100                 |*
  10   10   8100  4E40           |T1       TRAP     #0       ;CALL SCHEDULER
  11   11   8102  0001           |         DC.W     $1
  12   12   8104  4E71           |         NOP               ;CONTINUE EXECUTION
  13   13   8106                 |*          .
  14   14   8106                 |*          .
  15   15   8106                 |*          .
  16   16   8106  4E4F           |         TRAP     #15      ;RETURN TO MONITOR
  17   17   8108  0063           |         DC.W     $0063
  18   18   810A                 |         END
  18 lines assembled
```

Figure 11.5(b)   Program example of a TRAP call.

programs execute. Example 11.1 in Section 11.2 presented several techniques to initialize the vector location. Also, the routines used by EXEC such as DIALL and the calling program must be in memory. Definition of the vector address and loading of any necessary routines held in RAM is part of the initialization sequence for the computer system as treated in Chapter 10.

After the TRAP #0 instruction is executed, the program segment starting at EXEC first disables all interrupts by calling subroutine DIALL (not shown) which would mask the interrupts using the instructions described in Section 10.2. Then, the program saves all 15 of the calling program's general-purpose registers on the stack using 60 ($3C) bytes. Section 6.1 describes the stack frame created by the MOVEM instruction. Next, the PC value from the calling program is retrieved from the stack. This address points to the location following the TRAP instruction which contains the 16-bit function number. Address register A0 contains the address of the function number following the TRAP #0 instruction that requested the executive function.

The function number is validated and a jump table is used to obtain the address of the selected executive routine if the function is legal. This address is pushed on the stack and a return (RTS) is executed to transfer control to the selected function. This simple transfer of control is possible since all the routines listed in Figure 11.5(a) execute in the supervisor mode of the CPU.

Error processing occurs when an illegal function number is detected. The routine RTERRX (not shown) processes the error. The register contents are first restored by the instruction at label EXEC10. The address of the function number following the TRAP instruction causing the error and the error code are then saved before control is transferred to the error processing routine.

Notice that the program shown in Figure 11.5(a) does not return control to the program that executed the TRAP instruction. The PC value on the stack caused by the TRAP instruction points to the constant at $8102 that defines the requested function. If control is eventually to be returned to the calling program, the PC value on the stack must be modified.

When the particular routine that performs the requested function completes, control can be returned to the requesting program by the instruction sequence shown in Figure 11.5(c). The program RTNUSER modifies the return PC on the stack at location

```
abs. rel.   LC   obj. code   source line
---- ----   ----  ---------   -----------
   1    1   0000               |        TTL      'FIGURE 11.5(c)'
   2    2   3700               |        ORG      $3700
   3    3   0000               |*
   4    4   3700               |*       ROUTINE TO RETURN CONTROL TO THE PROGRAM
   5    5   3700               |*          THAT EXECUTED A TRAP #0 CALL TO 'EXEC'.
   6    6   3700               |*
   7    7   3700 206F 003E     |RTNUSER MOVEA.L (62,SP),A0       ;GET STACKED PC
   8    8   3704 5488          |        ADDA.L  #2,A0            ;INCREMENT PAST FUNCTION NO.
   9    9   3706 2F48 003E     |        MOVE.L  A0,(62,SP)       ;STORE RETURN PC
  10   10   370A 4CDF 7FFF     |        MOVEM.L (SP)+,D0-D7/A0-A6 ;RESTORE REGISTERS
  11   11   370E 4E73          |        RTE
  12   12   3710               |        END
  12 lines assembled
```

Figure 11.5(c) Program example of stack modification.

(SP)+62 and returns control to the program that executed the TRAP instruction.

The program trace in Figure 11.5(d) shows register contents and the values on the stack at various times during program testing. The comments to the right of the displayed information were added after the trace was completed. The first register display shows the register set before the TRAP #0 call in Figure 11.5(b). The program is in the user mode since (SR)=$0000 and the Supervisor Stack Pointer points to location $10000. The general purpose registers contain arbitrary values to make their contents easy to locate on the stack. For example, D0 contains $DDDD0000.

A breakpoint is inserted at the RTS instruction that passed control to the routine to perform the function called in Figure 11.5(a). Another breakpoint is inserted after the TRAP instruction in Figure 11.5(b). After execution of the TRAP #0 instruction, the register set of the EXEC is shown at the first breakpoint in Figure 11.5(d). Here the stack pointer value is $FFB8.

The leftmost column in the stack display contains the beginning stack address for each row of 8 words of stack information. For example, the stack contains the address of the routine for function number 1 (SCHED at $3400) at longword location $FFB8. The stored contents of the data and address registers follow at higher memory addresses until stack location $FFF8 which holds the (SR) to be returned. Longword location $FFFA holds the return PC which points to the constant at $8102. The format word ($0080) indicates that a stack for a TRAP #0 exception was created.

Another breakpoint is inserted in routine RTNUSER of Figure 11.5(c) just before the register set is restored. After execution, the register set of RTNUSER and a portion of the stack contents are displayed. The four word stack frame starting at address $FFF8 now contains the modified PC value of $8104 since RTNUSER incremented the return PC value to point to the next executable instruction after the constant in Figure 11.5(b).

After RTNUSER restores the registers and executes an RTE instruction, execution continues in the program that originally executed the TRAP #0 instruction. The register display caused by the breakpoint shows that the PC now points to $8104 as it should with all of the register values restored.

11.3.2 Divide-By-Zero Exception

Certain arithmetic errors in an applications program can be detected and trapped by the CPU. In particular, execution of any of the division instructions described in Chapter 7 with a zero divisor automatically causes exception processing using vector address

```
332Bug>RD
PC  =00008100 SR  =0000=TR:OFF_._0_.....  VBR  =00000000  ;REGISTER DISPLAY
SFC =6=SP    DFC =6=SP    USP* =0000FC00 SSP  =00010000  ; BEFORE TRAP #0 CALL
D0  =DDDD0000 D1  =DDDD1111 D2  =00000000 D3   =00000000
D4  =00000000 D5  =00000000 D6  =00000000 D7   =DDDD7777
A0  =AAAA0000 A1  =AAAA1111 A2  =00000000 A3   =00000000
A4  =00000000 A5  =00000000 A6  =AAAA6666 A7   =0000FC00
00008100 4E40              TRAP      #$0
332Bug>BR 3622                                            ;BKPT BEFORE RTS
BREAKPOINTS                                               ; TO 'SCHED'
00003622                   00008104
332Bug>GO                                                 ;TRAP #0 CALL
Effective address: 00008100
At Breakpoint
PC  =00003622 SR  =2000=TR:OFF_S_0_.....  VBR  =00000000  ;'EXEC' REGISTER SET
SFC =6=SP    DFC =6=SP     USP =0000FC00 SSP* =0000FFB8
D0  =DDDD0000 D1  =00000004 D2  =00000000 D3   =00000000
D4  =00000000 D5  =00000000 D6  =00000000 D7   =DDDD7777
A0  =00008104 A1  =00003642 A2  =00000000 A3   =00000000
A4  =00000000 A5  =00000000 A6  =AAAA6666 A7   =0000FFB8
00003622 4E75              RTS
332Bug>MD FFB0
0000FFB0 0000  0000  0000  0000  0000  3400  DDDD  0000    ;STACK BEFORE RTS TO 'SCHED'.
0000FFC0 DDDD  1111  0000  0000  0000  0000  0000  0000    ; TRAP #0 RETURN ($FFFA) TO $8102
0000FFD0 0000  0000  0000  0000  DDDD  7777  AAAA  0000
0000FFE0 AAAA  1111  0000  0000  0000  0000  0000  0000
0000FFF0 0000  0000  AAAA  6666  0000  0000  8102  0080
332Bug>NOBR 3622
BREAKPOINTS
00008104
332Bug>BR 370A
BREAKPOINTS
0000370A                   00008104
332Bug>GO
Effective address: 00003622
At Breakpoint
PC  =0000370A SR  =2000=TR:OFF_S_0_.....  VBR  =00000000  ;'RTNUSER' REGISTER SET
SFC =6=SP    DFC =6=SP     USP =0000FC00 SSP* =0000FFBC
D0  =DDDD0004 D1  =00000004 D2  =00000000 D3   =00000000
D4  =00000000 D5  =00000000 D6  =00000000 D7   =DDDD7777
A0  =00008104 A1  =00003642 A2  =00000000 A3   =00000000
A4  =00000000 A5  =00000000 A6  =AAAA6666 A7   =0000FFBC
0000370A 4CDF7FFF          MOVEM.L   (A7)+,D0-D7/A0-A6
332Bug>MD FFF0                                            ;TRAP #0 RETURN STACK.
0000FFF0 0000  0000  AAAA  6666  0000  0000  8104  0080    ; RETURN ($FFFA) TO $8104
332Bug>GO
Effective address: 0000370A
At Breakpoint
PC  =00008104 SR  =0000=TR:OFF_._0_.....  VBR  =00000000  ;RESTORED REGISTER SET
SFC =6=SP    DFC =6=SP    USP* =0000FC00 SSP  =00010000
D0  =DDDD0000 D1  =DDDD1111 D2  =00000000 D3   =00000000
D4  =00000000 D5  =00000000 D6  =00000000 D7   =DDDD7777
A0  =AAAA0000 A1  =AAAA1111 A2  =00000000 A3   =00000000
A4  =00000000 A5  =00000000 A6  =AAAA6666 A7   =0000FC00
00008104 4E71              NOP
332Bug>GO                                                 ;RETURN TO MONITOR
Effective address: 00008104
332Bug>
```

Figure 11.5(d) Program trace of stack for TRAP handler routine.

$14 in the CPU vector table. The divide-by-zero trap creates a six-word stack frame shown in Figure 11.3(c) which includes the instruction address for the instruction that caused the trap above the format word on the stack frame. The "next instruction" PC value on the stack points to the next instruction to be executed if the RTE instruction in the trap-handling routine is executed to return control to the program that caused the trap.

During program development, most operating systems for development would terminate the program that caused this trap, since further arithmetic processing after division by zero is rarely desired by the programmer. Thus, the trap-handling routine in a general-purpose computer typically indicates the type of error on the operator's terminal and transfers control back to the operating system rather than to the "trapped" program. The operating system may then schedule another program for execution.

In a finished product, termination of the executing program may not be desirable. For example, the zero divisor may be derived from a temporarily malfunctioning sensor that is used to input data for processing. Example 11.4 shows how a trap-handling routine could allow an applications program to recover from a divide-by-zero trap.

Example 11.4

Figure 11.6 shows an example of processing a divide-by-zero trap. The first program at location $8000 stores the address of the trap handler routine in the trap vector location at $14. Then, the short program segment causes a divide-by-zero to occur to test the trap routine. Of course, the test program would not appear in the final system. However, the vector address could be initialized as shown.

The trap handler routine in Figure 11.6(b) begins at $5300. When a divide-by-zero trap occurs because of a zero divisor in D0, the routine sets the quotient in D1 to the maximum value based on the value of the dividend; either the most positive or most negative 16-bit quotient. Although the answer is not correct mathematically, setting the quotient to a known value allows the results of continued program execution using the quotient to be predicted. The RTE instruction returns control to the program that caused the trap after the quotient is given its value.

A more sophisticated handler routine could allow any of the data registers rather than just D0 and D1 to be used by the divide instruction. Such a routine is able to determine which registers held the zero divisor and the dividend by decoding the divide instruction that caused the exception. The address of the instruction is held on the system stack at location (SP)+8. Example 11.5 presents an example of instruction decoding using the stacked value of the PC.

11.3.3 CHK and CHK2 Instructions

The CPU32 has two instructions to allow a value in a register to be tested for a proper numerical range. The CHK instruction checks the value in a data register within a range from zero to a specified upper bound. A second instruction, CHK2, tests an address or data register value between two bounds. For either instruction, a trap occurs if the value in the tested register is out of bounds. The CHK2 instruction is analogous to the CMP2 instruction introduced in Chapter 9, but the CMP2 instruction does not cause a trap if the register value is outside the specified range.

CHK instruction. The Check Register Against Bounds instruction (CHK) has the symbolic form

CHK.$<l_1>$ $<EA>,<Dn>$

```
abs.   LC    obj. code    source line
----   ----  ----------   -----------
  1    0000                     TTL       'FIGURE 11.6a'
  2          0000 0063   .RETURN EQU       $0063
  3    8000                     ORG       $8000
  4    0000               *
  5    8000               *   SET THE ZERO DIVIDE TRAP VECTOR
  6    8000               *
  7    8000 21FC 0000             MOVE.L    #$5300,$14 ;ZERO-DIVIDE TRAP
       8004 5300 0014
  8    8008               *                          ; ROUTINE ADDR.
  9    8008               *
 10    8008               *
 11    8008               *
 12    8008               * EXECUTE A DIVIDE BY ZERO WITH
 13    8008               *   INPUTS :    (D0.W) = DIVISOR (SET TO 0 FOR TEST)
 14    8008               *               (D1.L) = DIVIDEND.
 15    8008               *   OUTPUT :    (D1.W) = LARGEST VALUE BASED ON SIGN
 16    8008               *                          OF DIVIDEND
 17    8008               *
 18    8008 4280                 CLR.L     D0         ;SET DIVISOR TO ZERO
 19    800A 83C0                 DIVS.W    D0,D1      ;DIVIDE D1[31:0] BY
 20    800C               *                          ;   D0[15:0]=0
 21    800C               *
 22    800C 4E4F                 TRAP      #15        ;RETURN TO MONITOR
 23    800E 0063                 DC.W      .RETURN
 24    8010               *
 25    8010                      END
```

(a) Program to cause a divide by zero

```
abs.   LC    obj. code    source line
----   ----  ----------   -----------
  1    0000                     TTL       'FIGURE 11.6b'
  2    0000               *
  3    0000               *   ZERO-DIVIDE TRAP HANDLER ROUTINE
  4    0000               *
  5    5300                     ORG       $5300
  6    5300 4A81         ZDIV    TST.L     D1
  7    5302 6B00 000C            BMI       ZDIV01     ;IF DIVIDEND IS POSITIVE,
  8    5306 223C 0000            MOVE.L    #$7FFF,D1  ; RETURN WITH
       530A 7FFF                                     ;
  9    530C 6000 0008            BRA       RTN        ; (D1).W=LARGEST POSITIVE
 10    5310               *                          ;   VALUE
 11    5310               *                          ;
 12    5310 223C 0000     ZDIV01  MOVE.L   #$8000,D1  ; ELSE RETURN LARGEST
       5314 8000                                     ;
 13    5316               *                          ;   NEGATIVE VALUE
 14    5316 4E73          RTN     RTE
 15    5318                      END
```

(b) Trap handling routine

Figure 11.6 Program for divide-by-zero trap.

where <EA> is designated by a data addressing mode. This allows all addressing modes except address register direct. The length $<l_1>$ is either word ($<l_1> = $ W) or longword ($<l_1> = $ L).

The CHK instruction determines if the contents of <Dn> is between 0 and the value contained in <EA> and causes a trap if the contents of <Dn> are not within this range. The upper bound held in (EA) is treated as a two's-complement integer.

The operation of CHK is as follows:

if $0 \leq (Dn)[l_1] \leq (EA)$ **then**
    continue
else *trap* and
    set N = {1} **if** $(Dn)[l_1] < 0$ or set N = {0} **if** $(Dn)[l_1] > (EA)$.

The exception routine begins at the address in location $18 if the trap is taken. The CHK instruction is typically placed in a program after the calculation of an offset or an index value to assure that the limits of the value are not exceeded. This facilitates testing whether an array address fits within the dimensions of the array when the address register indirect with indexing addressing mode is used to locate array elements. For example, the sequence

```
CHK.W        #99, D1
MOVE.B       (0, A1, D1.W), D2
```

would trap if (D1)[15:0] exceeded 99 decimal. If A1 held the base address of the array with 100 byte-length elements, the addressing range of the MOVE instruction is limited to values within this array. The addressing of arrays in FORTRAN is not always protected in this manner, but array boundary checking is typically provided in languages such as Pascal.[4]

Other uses of the CHK instruction include the testing of the space used by a stack or keeping a program from accessing data outside its designated space. For these applications, a value in an address register must be transferred to a data register in order to perform the bounds check.

CHK2 instruction. The CHK2 (Check Register Against Bounds) instruction has the assembly-language format

```
CHK2.<l>      <EA>, <Rn>
```

where <l> = B, W, or L and <EA> defines the address in memory of the bounds used to check against the value in register <Rn>. The register can be any address or data register. A value designated in an address register as byte or word length is sign-extended to 32 bits for comparison. The effective address <EA> must be defined by a control addressing mode, thus prohibiting register direct, predecrement or postincrement and immediate addressing.

In memory, at the location designated by <EA>, the lower bound occupies a byte, word, or longword according to the length specification <l>. The upper bound must follow in the next location of the appropriate length. The comparison is

$$(<EA>) \leq (Rn) \leq (<EA + k>)$$

where k = 1, 2, or 4 for byte, word, or longword operands, respectively. When the instruction executes, the condition codes are set as for the CMP2 instruction but a trap occurs if the register value is out of range. Except for the trap that occurs on an out-of-range condition, the CHK2 instruction operates identically to the CMP2 instruction described in Section 9.3. Example 9.9 showed the use of the CMP2 instruction to check the bounds of a value held in a register. The CHK2 instruction can be used in

---

[4] The compiler determines whether or not array boundary checking is provided for an executing program. Boundary checking is an optional feature of some compilers.

the same manner. However, an out-of-range condition causes a trap using the vector address at location $018. The exception-handling routine located by that vector must determine the appropriate action when the register value being tested is not in range.

Example 11.5

The CHK and CHK2 instructions both cause a trap using the vector at location $018 when the register value being checked is out of range. If the exception-handling routine must differentiate between a CHK exception and a CHK2 exception, the routine can determine which exception occurred only by examining the operation word for the instruction that caused the exception. The location of this instruction is placed in the exception stack frame when the exception is processed.

Figure 11.7(a) shows the six-word stack frame created when a CHK or CHK2 instruction causes an exception. In addition to the (SR), (PC), and format word, the stack contains the address of the instruction that caused the exception. The address is offset by +08 bytes from the location indicated by (SP) itself. Thus, the instruction is easily examined. The machine-language formats for the CHK and CHK2 instructions are shown in Figure 11.7(b) and Figure 11.7(c), respectively.

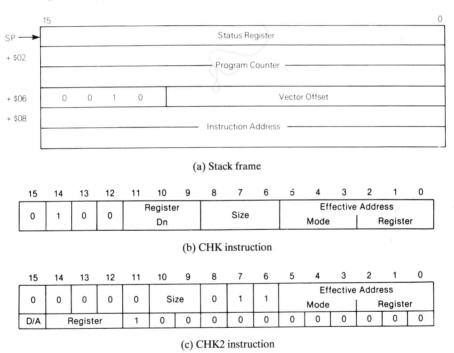

(a) Stack frame

(b) CHK instruction

(c) CHK2 instruction

Figure 11.7 Stack frame and instruction formats for CHK and CHK2.

The program of Figure 11.8 is an example exception-handling routine. It requires that the vector address for the CHK and CHK2 exception-handling routine is address CHKTRAP in location $018 before the routine executes. If a trap occurs, the op-code bits of the instruction that caused the exception are examined. The branch instructions then cause the appropriate code segment to execute. For a CHK2 exception, the segment defined at address CHK2SUB is executed. In the example, the processing consists of simply returning control to the monitor program via a TRAP #15 instruction. If a CHK exception occurs, the code segment at CHKSUB is executed.

```
abs.    LC    obj. code    source line
----    ----  ---------    -----------
   1    0000                           TTL      'FIGURE 11.8'
   2    0000                           LLEN     100
   3          0000 0063    .RETURN EQU  $0063        ;MONITOR
   4    5400                           ORG      $5400
   5    0000               *
   6    5400               *  DETERMINE THE CAUSE OF THE TRAP,
   7    5400               *  EXECUTE THE APPROPRIATE ROUTINE,
   8    5400               *  AND RETURN TO MONITOR.
   9    5400               *
  10    5400               *     IF CHK2 -EXECUTE CHK2SUB AND RETURN
  11    5400               *     IF CHK  -EXECUTE CHKSUB AND RETURN
  12    5400               *
  13    5400               *     (REGISTERS A0 AND D0 ARE USED BUT NOT RESTORED)
  14    5400               *
  15    5400 206F 0008     CHKTRAP MOVE.L  (8,SP),A0  ;INSTRUCTION ADDR.
  16    5404 3010                  MOVE.W  (A0),D0    ;EXAMINE OPCODE
  17    5406 0240 F000              ANDI    #$F000,D0
  18    540A               *
  19    540A 6700 0006              BEQ     CHK2SUB    ;BRANCH IF CHK2
  20    540E 6000 0008              BRA     CHKSUB
  21    5412               *
  22    5412               *     DUMMY ROUTINES
  23    5412               *
  24    5412 4E71          CHK2SUB NOP                ;PROCESS AS REQUIRED
  25    5414               *
  26    5414               *
  27    5414 4E4F                  TRAP    #15
  28    5416 0063                  DC.W    .RETURN
  29    5418               *
  30    5418 4E71          CHKSUB  NOP
  31    541A               *
  32    541A               *
  33    541A 4E4F                  TRAP    #15
  34    541C 0063                  DC.W    .RETURN
  35    541E               *
  36    541E                       END
```

Figure 11.8 Program example of CHK and CHK2 exception handling.

11.3.4 Trap on Condition Instructions (TRAPcc and TRAPV)

The trap on condition instructions are used in a program to control the program based on the results created by instructions that set the condition codes. These trap on condition instructions are the TRAPcc and TRAPV instructions. A TRAPcc instruction causes a trap on one of 14 arithmetic conditions when the condition <cc> is true as the instruction executes. The condition <cc> is defined by the appropriate mnemonic in an assembly-language statement as defined in Table 11.5.

For example, a trap on overflow condition (TRAPVS) instruction could be inserted in a program after each arithmetic instruction so that control is returned to the supervisor program when an overflow is detected in signed arithmetic. The purpose is to prevent the program being trapped from executing further with an erroneous arithmetic result. The reader is referred to Chapter 7 for a more detailed discussion of the use of the condition bits after arithmetic operations.

The TRAPV instruction is a separate instruction that traps only when the overflow condition code bit is set ($V = \{1\}$). The equivalent TRAPcc instruction is

TRAPVS. These two instructions (TRAPV and TRAPVS) perform the same function but they do not generate the same machine-language code as defined in Appendix IV.

When any trap on condition instruction causes an exception, CPU exception processing creates a six word stack. Then, control is passed to the exception-handling routine using vector 7 at location $1C in the CPU exception vector table shown in Figure 11.2. Also, exception vector 7 in the CPU vector table is shared by the TRAPcc, and TRAPV instructions.

Table 11.5 TRAPcc Instruction

Syntax	Operation
(a) Instruction syntax	
T<cc> or TRAP<cc>	Trap **if** <cc> = true **else** next instruction
TPcc.<l> #<data> or TRAPcc.<l> #<data>	Trap **if** <cc> = true **else** next instruction after <data>

Note: <l> = W or L. If <l> = W, <data> is a 16-bit value. If <l> = L, <data> is a 32-bit value.

(b) Conditions <cc>

CC	Carry clear	0100	$\overline{C}$	LS	Low or same	0011	$C+Z$
CS	Carry set	0101	C	LT	Less than	1101	$N \cdot \overline{V} + \overline{N} \cdot V$
EQ	Equal	0111	Z	MI	Minus	1011	N
F	Never true	0001	0	NE	Not equal	0110	$\overline{Z}$
GE	Greater or equal	1100	$N \cdot V + \overline{N} \cdot \overline{V}$	PL	Plus	1010	$\overline{N}$
GT	Greater than	1110	$N \cdot V \cdot \overline{Z} + \overline{N} \cdot \overline{V} \cdot \overline{Z}$	T	Always true	0000	1
HI	High	0010	$\overline{C} \cdot \overline{Z}$	VC	Overflow clear	1000	$\overline{V}$
LE	Less or equal	1111	$Z + N \cdot \overline{V} + \overline{N} \cdot V$	VS	Overflow set	1001	V

Note:
For some assemblers, <CS> = <LO> and <CC> = <HS>.

TRAPcc instruction. As defined in Table 11.5(a), the TRAPcc instruction has several assembly-language forms, which correspond to the allowed syntax for Motorola's CPU32 assembler. The mnemonics for the conditions <cc> are defined in Table 11.5(b). For example, the instructions

TEQ   ; Trap if Z = {1}

and

TRAPEQ

are identical for the Motorola assembler. Thus, either the mnemonic "T" or "TRAP" can be used to define the basic instruction.

When the TRAPcc instruction executes with the condition <cc> true, control is passed to the exception handling routine using vector 7 (address $1C) of the CPU exception vector table. As with the DBcc instruction described in Chapter 6, there are 16 logical conditions possible although the conditions true (T) and false (F) in Table 11.5(b) are rarely used since they do not test the condition code bits. Table 11.5(b) lists the mnemonic for a condition followed by the four condition bits coded in the machine-language instruction and the setting of the condition code bits that cause the condition to be true. For example, the Trap if Minus (TMI) instruction will cause exception processing if the N condition code bit is {1} when the TMI instruction executes. The instruction TPL traps if $\overline{N}$ is true, i.e. N={0}, when TPL executes.

If the trap occurs, the stack frame holds six words as shown in Figure 11.3(c). The address of the trap instruction is stored at location (SP)+8 so that the exception-handling routine can decode the instruction and determine the actual cause of the trap if necessary. The PC value on the stack frame at location (SP)+2 is the address of the next instruction in sequence after the TRAPcc instruction including its data. Execution continues at the next instruction if the exception-handling routine executes the RTE instruction to return control to the program causing the trap.

TRAPcc instruction with constant data. Another form of the TRAPcc instruction allows the programmer to define a constant value to follow the TRAPcc instruction in memory. The designation for the Motorola assembler is either TRAPcc or TPcc. This constant can be used to pass information from the program causing the trap to the exception-handling routine.

Example 11.6

The example instruction, Trap if Minus,

        TPMI.W   #$DE

causes a trap if N = {1} when it executes. In memory, following the TPMI instruction at the next word location is the constant $DE for this example. According to Table 11.5(a), the constant can be a word length or a longword value as needed. The exception-handling routine must retrieve the constant from memory using the trap instruction PC value on the stack at location (SP)+8. The constant is held is the next word location in memory.

If the instruction must be decoded, the trap instruction can be loaded into a data register by an instruction sequence such as

        MOVEA.L   (8, PC), A0   ; GET TRAP INST. ADDRESS
        MOVE.W   (A0)+, D0   ; GET TRAP INST.

The TRAPcc instruction in D0 can now be examined to determine the specific condition causing the exception by decoding the machine-language form as given in Appendix IV of this textbook. Bits [11:8] of the operand word hold the condition. These bits are also defined in Table 11.5(b). Example 11.5 shows the technique to decode the CHK instructions after the instruction is loaded into a CPU register. The conditional trap instruction can be decoded in a similar manner.

In the instruction sequence just shown, register A0 holds the address of the constant in the instruction stream because the postincrement addressing mode incremented the value in A0 to point two bytes beyond the TPMI instruction. The constant can be loaded into another register by the instruction

MOVE.W　　　(A0), D1　　　　　; GET CONSTANT

The exception-handling routine can now decode the instruction in D0 and take appropriate action based on the constant value in D1.

If control is to be returned to the program that caused the trap with an RTE instruction, no modification of the return PC value on the stack frame is necessary to point to the next instruction as was the case in the discussion in Example 11.2 since the PC value at (SP)+2 contains the address of the next instruction in line.

TRAPV instruction.　　The TRAPV instruction is included in the CPU32 instruction set to assure compatibility with programs written for the MC68000. The CPU32 equivalent, TRAPVS (Trap if V is Set), can be used in CPU32 programs where compatibility is not an issue. As the instruction TRAPcc does not exist in the MC68000 instruction set, such programs written for the MC68332 family of processors would not execute properly on 16-bit family members.

EXERCISES

11.3.1. If the instruction

TRAP　　　　#1

is located at location $9004 and executes when (SR) = $A000 and (SP) = $7FFE, show the contents of the system stack before and after the TRAP instruction executes. Initialize the TRAP #1 vector so that the trap routine starts at location $8000.

11.3.2. Draw the system stack for Example 11.3 as it changes during program execution. Assume that the system stack pointer is at location $10000 before the TRAP instruction executes. Write the program instructions to return control to the program that executed the TRAP instruction.

11.3.3. Write a program that pushes word-length values on the user stack beginning at location $5000. If the stack length is 10 words maximum, use the CHK instruction to return control to the supervisor program when the stack overflows.

11.3.4. Using the program in Example 9.8 as a model, write a routine to check register bounds using the CHK2 instruction. Design the exception-handling routine to return the condition codes in register D1 if a trap occurs and then return control to the monitor or operating system.

11.3.5. Modify the program of Example 11.5 to indicate the cause of a CHK trap as follows:
(a) register value below lower bound;
(b) register value above upper bound.
Set a flag in register D1 if the bounds are exceeded.

11.3.6. Write a routine to determine the cause of a vector 7 (TRAPcc or TRAPV) exception. The program should first differentiate between the two classes of instructions that use vector 7. Then for the TRAPcc instruction, decode the op-word and use the condition as the selector of addresses in a jump table. The addresses in the jump table should contain the starting address for the appropriate trap handling routine. Then, have the routine print the cause of the trap on screen of the operator's terminal.

11.4 UNIMPLEMENTED INSTRUCTION EXCEPTION, TRACE, AND BREAKPOINTS

The CPU32 has several special exceptions that are available to aid program development and debugging by a programmer. For hardware or software emulation, the unimplemented instruction trap may be useful.[5] The trace exception and the BKPT (Breakpoint) instruction are used to aid a programmer while testing and debugging programs. Program breakpoints may also be set using the ILLEGAL instruction of the CPU32. Each of these exceptions is discussed in this section.

11.4.1 Unimplemented Instruction Trap

The MC68332 CPU recognizes instructions whose most significant four bits [15:12] are {1010}($A) or {1111}($F) as special instructions. These are referred to as A-line and F-line instructions, respectively. Instructions with these bit patterns in bits [15:12] are also called *unimplemented instructions* if the machine-language code for an A-line or F-line instruction does not correspond to a legal CPU32 instruction. Since no CPU32 instructions have the A-line format, an A-line instruction encountered during program execution causes an unimplemented instruction exception using vector 10 in the CPU vector table shown in Figure 11.2. The CPU32 instruction set uses the F-line format for certain instructions. However, if an F-line instruction is encountered that is not part of the CPU instruction set, exception processing occurs using vector 11 of the CPU vector table to locate the exception-handling routine.

The *CPU32 Reference Manual* indicates that unimplemented instructions with the A-line or F-line formats are reserved and may be used by Motorola for enhancements on future processors. Motorola recommends the use of the ILLEGAL instruction or a TRAP #N instruction for instruction emulation and other special purposes as discussed in Subsection 11.4.3. However, the A-line bit pattern can be used as the high order bits of a programmer defined machine-language instruction if compatibility is not a consideration.

The A-line exception can be used to emulate a special instruction or even the hardware capability of another computer system. The remaining 12 bits [11:0] in the operation word of the A-line instruction can be used to select various options when

---

[5] *Emulation* as used here means executing the programs of a target computer and perhaps handling external events (input/output, interrupts, etc.) realistically. As defined in Chapter 1, a *simulator* program executes the programs of a target computer.

the exception-handling routine executes. This routine might perform string manipulation, implement a Fast Fourier Transform (FFT) algorithm, or provide any other capability according to the design of the routine. For an applications programmer, the newly created A-line instructions appear as additional "macroinstructions" added to the CPU32 instruction set.

When an unimplemented instruction is encountered in an instruction stream, a four word stack as shown in Figure 11.3(b) is created during exception processing. Since the instruction is not executed, the PC value on the exception stack frame points to the unimplemented instruction that caused the exception.

Example 11.7

In an assembly-language program, the statement

    DC.W $AXXX   ; DEFINE NEW INSTRUCTION

where "XXX" is an arbitrary three-digit hexadecimal value would cause a trap using vector 10 if the CPU attempted to execute this A-line instruction. When the exception occurs, a four-word stack frame is created which holds the contents of the Status Register, the address of the unimplemented A-line instruction, and a format word. As explained in Example 11.2, the address is obtained by an instruction of the form

    MOVEA.L   (2, SP), A1   ; GET INST. ADDRESS

which skips over the contents of the Status Register saved on the stack and loads A1 with the value saved for the PC. This value locates the unimplemented instruction and allows decoding of any other bits used to select options for the exception-handling routine.

To return control to the program with the unimplemented instruction, the PC value on the stack must be modified to point to the next instruction in line. The PC value must be incremented by the number of bytes that represent the length of the unimplemented instruction in a manner similar to that explained in Example 11.2. Once the PC value is modified to point to the next instruction after the unimplemented instruction, control is returned after the exception-handling routine executes the RTE instruction.

F-line instruction.   The use of an F-line instruction is similar to that for the A-line instruction if the F-line instruction is an unimplemented instruction. The routine handling the exception may perform any function according to its design. For example, the appropriate F-line instructions could be created to allow the CPU32 to perform software emulation of a floating-point coprocessor such as the MC68881. In other M68000-family processors, the F-line instructions may be used for special purposes.[6]

The CPU32 uses the F-line format for its table lookup and interpolation instructions. These instructions for interpolation are described in Section 7.7. A programmer creating any new F-line instructions must take care that the operation word of a new instruction does not match the machine code used by the interpolation instructions.

---

[6] The F-line instructions are used to control a coprocessor in MC68020-based systems, for example.

11.4.2 Trace Exceptions

While debugging and testing a program under development, it is frequently convenient for a programmer to cause the CPU to execute a single instruction or a short sequence of instructions followed by a display of information useful for debugging purposes. The CPU32 provides two trace exceptions which satisfy these requirements for program testing. The two trace exceptions are called *single-instruction* trace and trace on *change of flow*, respectively. Tracing can occur in either the supervisor mode or the user mode. However, the trace bits (T0,T1) in the CPU Status Register can be changed only by an instruction executed in the supervisor mode. Since only the Status Register contents are modified to enable tracing, the program in memory being traced is not modified in any way by tracing. Thus, tracing can occur for programs in RAM or ROM.

Example 11.8

An operating system or monitor program can enable the single-instruction trace with the instruction

    ORI   #\$8000, SR   ; set T1 = {1}

to set (SR)[15] to {1}. The trace on change of control flow could be enabled by the instruction

    ORI   #\$4000, SR   ; set T0 = {1}

to set (SR)[14] to {1}. These trace modes are disabled by setting T0 and T1 to {0}. The instructions to modify the contents of the Status Register were described previously in Section 10.2.

When either trace exception is recognized by the CPU after the instruction causing the trace is executed, the trace exception-handling routine is executed using vector 9 at address \$024 in the CPU vector table. Before passing control to the exception-handling routine, tracing is disabled by the CPU and a six-word stack frame is created as shown in Figure 11.3(c).

The stored value of the Status Register at location (SP) on the stack frame can be examined by the trace routine to determine the type of tracing. The PC value on the stack at address (SP)+2 is the address of the next instruction to be executed if the instruction being traced actually executes. When an executable instruction is being traced, the trace routine returns control to the program being traced by executing the RTE instruction. Unless the contents of the Status Register at address (SP) on the stack is modified by the trace routine to disable tracing, tracing is enabled again after the RTE executes. The stack frame also contains the address of the instruction that caused the trace exception at location (SP)+8 so that the trace routine can determine which instruction is being traced.

Trace on change of flow. The trace on change of flow (T0 = {1}) exception is taken when it is enabled under one of the following conditions:
(a) an instruction causes the Program Counter to be updated nonsequentially;

(b) an instruction modifies the Status Register.

The instructions and conditions that will cause a trace on change of flow include all branch instructions when the branch is taken, jump instructions, traps, and returns from either subroutines or exception-handling routines. Certain instructions that manipulate the Status Register contents also cause a trace on change of flow exception when this trace mode is enabled.

Example 11.9

The typical trace routine is designed to display the disassembled instruction being traced and the contents of CPU registers associated with execution of the program being traced. Examples of the trace facility of the 332BUG monitor were given in Chapter 5. For that monitor, described in Subsection 5.1.3, the trace modes are initiated by the command T (trace one instruction) or TC (trace on change of flow) as operator commands.

The 332BUG trace routine displays the contents of the registers of the CPU when a trace is requested. Then, control is returned to the monitor to accept the next operator command.

A special-purpose trace routine could be written to perform any desired function if the standard tracing provided by the monitor is not sufficient for an application.

Special considerations with trace.   When single instruction trace is used, the trace exception is taken whenever any instruction executes to completion. However, if the CPU encounters an illegal or unimplemented instruction or an instruction that causes a privilege violation, that instruction will not cause a trace since it is not executed. In most cases, the occurrence of an unexecutable instruction represents an error in the program so the appropriate exception should be taken.

In case the instruction being traced is a programmer defined unimplemented instruction as defined in Subsection 14.1.1, the instruction emulation routine must perform the tracing also. The emulation routine determines if tracing is enabled by examining the saved contents of the Status Register on the exception stack.

If an interrupt is pending, the trace exception is processed before the interrupt exception is processed. Thus, the stack frame for the trace is created first, followed by the interrupt stack frame. However, the interrupt exception-handling routine executes first. These priorities for exception processing are described further in Section 11.7.

If the STOP or LPSTOP instructions are encountered while tracing is enabled, the CPU will execute the trace routine but the processor will not enter the stopped condition. This is because execution will continue at the instruction following the STOP or LPSTOP instruction if the trace routine completes with an RTE instruction.

11.4.3 Breakpoints and the BKPT Instruction

The trace options for the CPU32 allow normal program execution to be suspended when certain events occur. Specifically, a trace exception is taken after the execution of a single instruction if $SR[15] = \{1\}$ or after an instruction causes a change in flow of control if $SR[14] = \{1\}$. In some cases during debugging, a programmer or a hardware designer wishes to suspend normal program execution when the CPU addresses a certain location in memory. As with the trace exceptions, control should be passed to a routine to aid debugging when the designated access occurs. If the location contains an instruction, the program is said to have reached a *program breakpoint*. At a breakpoint, an exception-handling routine typically executes to display register contents and other information of interest concerning the program being tested.

This section describes the instructions that are used to insert a breakpoint into a program. A program breakpoint is said to be placed in a program in memory when one of these instructions is deliberately written into a memory location containing an instruction of the program. The instructions cause an exception when encountered.

ILLEGAL instruction breakpoint. In MC68332 systems, there are several ways to define breakpoints in a program. One way is the use of the instruction

ILLEGAL

in the assembly-language program. Of course, the breakpoint then becomes a permanent part of the program when created in this way.

Another method is to define the breakpoint locations when the program is being debugged. A supervisor routine can do this by writing the code for the ILLEGAL instruction at the desired location before the program is executed. The machine-language operation word is $4AFC for the ILLEGAL instruction. When encountered during program execution, this instruction causes an illegal instruction exception using vector 4 at location $010.

The operating system or monitor program of computer systems used for program development contains debugging routines to place and remove breakpoints at selected locations in a program being tested. Typically, on command of the operator, the debugging program of the system software replaces an instruction at the designated location with an instruction that causes an exception. When the breakpoint is encountered, control is passed to an exception handling routine. This routine typically displays CPU registers and other information of interest as was the case for the trace handling routine described in Example 11.9. Example 5.2 shows the breakpoint capability of the 332BUG monitor.

After the exception-handling routine performs its function to aid in debugging the program, the routine must replace the instruction causing the breakpoint with the original instruction if program execution is to continue at the breakpointed location.

In MC68332-based systems either the ILLEGAL instruction or one of the TRAP instructions could be used to replace the instruction to be breakpointed. Thus, either of these instructions at the breakpoint address would cause an exception when the program executes. However, the exception-handling routine must distinguish between these exceptions used as breakpoints and their usual use in a program as described in Section 11.3 for the TRAP instruction and in Subsection 11.5.1 for the illegal instruction exception. In the case of an illegal instruction exception, this is done by decoding the instruction whose address is held on the exception stack at location (SP)+2.

Breakpoint (BKPT) instruction. Program breakpoints can be inserted in a program using the BKPT (Breakpoint) instruction. The assembly language syntax for the instruction is

BKPT   #<N>   ; BREAKPOINT

where $N = 0, 1, \ldots, 7$ is the breakpoint number. Thus, up to eight breakpoints can be inserted into a program with this instruction. A supervisor routine uses one of the machine language codes for BKPT ($4848–$484F) to insert a breakpoint into a program. The breakpoint number is coded into bits [2:0] of the instruction as shown in Appendix IV. Thus, the exception handling routine can decode the instruction and determine which BKPT instruction caused the breakpoint.

When the BKPT instruction is executed, it causes the execution of an external breakpoint cycle that requires a response from external circuits. These circuits either cause an illegal instruction exception or provide an operation word to the CPU for execution. If an instruction is provided, program execution continues without exception processing. However, a bus error response causes the illegal instruction exception as described in Subsection 11.6.1. Chapter 14 presents the hardware aspects of the breakpoint cycle . Chapter 16 discusses other uses of the BKPT instruction and other types of breakpoints for the MC68332.

After the BKPT instruction is encountered and an illegal instruction exception occurs, a four word stack is created as in Figure 11.3(b). The PC value points to the instruction causing the breakpoint which can be decoded by the breakpoint routine in a manner similar to that described in Example 11.7. Since the eight BKPT instructions have the operation words $4848 through $484F, the breakpoint routine can be written so that illegal instructions with other opcodes will not be processed as breakpoints.

EXERCISES

11.4.1. Using A-line instructions, emulate a "macroinstruction" that moves a string of characters of arbitrary length from one area of memory to another. Assume that D1 holds the length, A1 the starting address of the string, and A2 the destination location for the first character to be moved. Discuss other techniques to emulate the "Move String" instruction.

11.4.2. What is the disadvantage of a trace routine that only displays the values in every CPU register after the execution of each instruction?

11.4.3. Assume that the trace is enabled when the following conditions occur:
(a) STOP #$2000 is executed.
(b) An illegal instruction is encountered by the CPU in an instruction stream.
What is the operation of the CPU in these cases?

11.4.4. Define the features of a general-purpose debugging routine that are desirable to aid a programmer while testing and debugging a program.

11.4.5. Write a simple trace routine to print the contents of all the processor registers when a trace exception is taken. Test the tracing by writing a simple program in which each instruction is traced. (*Note:* The routine to print the values is provided by the operating system or monitor program in most systems. This use of the 332BUG monitor to convert values to ASCII and to display the results was discussed in Chapters 5 and 7.)

11.4.6. Write a breakpoint routine to respond to the BKPT #N instruction. The routine should display the information required in Exercise 11.4.5.

11.5 PROGRAM ERRORS CAUSING TRAPS

The CPU32 is designed to protect the computer system from errors that could cause unpredictable behavior. Table 11.6 lists the errors caused by instruction execution that are trapped by the CPU. The privilege violation, illegal instruction, and address error traps usually occur when a program is being debugged. An operating system or monitor program used for program development will typically terminate execution of the program that caused one of these error exception. In most cases, further execution of an offending program is not desirable when one of these exceptions occurs. The CPU creates a stack frame that allows an exception-handling routine to determine the cause of the exception. In certain cases, as when an illegal instruction exception is caused by a breakpoint in a program, the exception handler will return control to the program causing the error.

Table 11.6 Program Errors Causing Traps

Error	Cause	Comments
Privilege violation	In user mode, attempt to execute a privileged instruction	If S = {0}, attempt to execute: ANDI, MOVE, or ORI to SR; MOVE from SR; MOVE to USP; LPSTOP or STOP; MOVEC; MOVES; RESET; RTE.
Illegal instruction	Bit pattern of opcode [15:12] not recognized	PC value on stack is address of illegal instruction
Address error	Attempted fetch of instruction, word-length or longword operand at odd address	Bus error exception stack frame is created

Notes:
1. When these exceptions occur, the instruction causing the exception is not executed.
2. The illegal instruction exception can be used to implement a breakpoint feature as described in Section 11.4.

11.5.1 Privilege Violation

If a program operating in the user mode attempts to execute one of the privileged instructions listed in Table 11.6, an exception is caused using vector 8 at location $020 in the CPU vector table of Figure 11.2. The privilege exception causes a four-word stack frame to be created as shown in Figure 11.3(b). The PC value on the stack frame indicates the location of the instruction that caused the violation. Section 10.2 described the privileged instructions in detail.

11.5.2 Illegal Instruction

The *illegal instruction* exception, with vector at location $10, is used to protect the system from the effects of an incorrect machine code or localized memory failure. If the CPU does not recognize the bit pattern of an instruction as a valid instruction, an illegal instruction exception is taken.[7]

The exception causes a four word stack to be created in which the PC value at location (SP)+2 points to the illegal instruction. The exception can be taken deliberately if the ILLEGAL instruction or a BKPT instruction is included in a program. The use of these instructions to create breakpoints was described in Subsection 11.4.3.

If various processors of the M68000 family are used to execute the same program, the illegal instruction exception may not be taken for all family members when an illegal instruction is encountered by the CPU32. For example, the Bit Field instructions of the MC68020 have machine-language forms that are illegal for the CPU32. The LPSTOP instruction of the CPU32 would be illegal for any other family members except those in the M68300 family.

11.5.3 Address Error

If the processor attempts to access an instruction, a word-length operand or a long-word operand at an odd address, an address error exception is caused using the vector at location $0C. Thus, the exception occurs during instruction execution if the value in the PC is an odd address. The exception also occurs if the source or destination location is an odd address in an executing instruction that specifies word or longword operands.

The conditions for an address error can occur if a label used to reference an instruction or an operand in an assembly language program represents an odd address due to a misaligned instruction, word operand, or longword operand. The assembler normally will not treat such cases as an error. The address error exception will occur when the program executes. Also, the address error may be caused by a hardware failure or when a routine modifies the PC value incorrectly during program execution. The information saved on the stack can be used to diagnose the problem. The stack frame created is similar to that for a bus error exception, to be described in Section 11.8.

EXERCISES

11.5.1. Consider the use of the privilege violation exception when a new operating system is being developed. The new operating system should be able to execute privileged instructions. However, because of the design of the CPU32, the operating system under development must execute in the user mode. Also, the

---

[7] The illegal instruction exception is also taken if a MOVEC instruction is attempted without a proper register specification. The exception is taken also if the extension word for an indexed addressing mode is incorrect.

exceptions must be handled by the true operating system for the development computer (i.e., the operating system executing in the supervisor mode). Assume that the new operating system has its own vector table. Explain how the true operating system could allow the operating system under development to emulate privileged instructions.

11.5.2. Describe several ways an unexpected illegal instruction exception could occur when a program is executing. Consider both errors in hardware and software that could result in an illegal instruction being created.

11.5.3. Create an illegal instruction exception handler to be located at location $5500. The handler should pass control to a supervisor program at location $4000 after an illegal instruction is recognized in a user-mode program. Leave the faulted stack frame from the illegal instruction on the stack and create a new stack frame below it to pass control to location $4000.

Figure 11.3(b) shows the four-word stack frame for the illegal instruction. The format word on the illegal instruction stack frame does not have to be modified.

11.6 SYSTEM ERRORS AND CONDITIONS

The CPU recognizes a number of system errors and conditions that are used to control and protect a product. One of the most important in MC68332-based systems is the bus error exception. As described first in this section, the bus error is used for a variety of purposes, including error detection in a computer system. The format error exception and the halted state are also treated in this section.

11.6.1 Bus Error Exception

A bus error exception is caused when the bus error signal-line ($\overline{BERR}$) of the CPU32 is asserted. This signal can be asserted by special-purpose external circuitry or by the bus monitor of the System Integration Module. After the $\overline{BERR}$ signal is asserted, the bus error exception-handling routine determines the action to be taken. Table 11.7 lists typical situations that may occur to cause the bus error signal-line to be asserted in an MC68332-based product. Subsection 11.8.2 discusses the use of the bus error signal in systems with virtual memory.

Generally speaking, the bus error signal-line is asserted by circuitry external to the MC68332 when an error or special condition arises in the execution of a hardware bus cycle. The bus error signal indicates that an external device cannot complete the external bus cycle in progress. For example, when the CPU executes an instruction, it expects a response from a selected external device to indicate that the device acknowledges the instruction and can complete the processing as required.[8] If the device cannot respond correctly or if an error is detected in the bus cycle, the device should assert the bus error signal.

As listed in Table 11.7, memory circuits could assert the bus error signal if an

---

[8] The signal lines involved in the CPU bus cycles are defined in Chapter 14.

error is detected during a memory access. By causing a bus error, the external circuits protect the system and prevent the CPU from processing data that are in error due to a fault in the memory. Also, external memory management circuits could assert the bus error signal if a user mode program attempts to access an area of memory reserved for the supervisor program. Subsection 14.5.2 describes the circuitry that could provide such memory protection.

The System Integration Module (SIM) contains a bus monitor with a hardware watchdog timer. If a data transfer operation does not complete in the specified time, a bus error is generated from the watchdog time-out. For example, the memory may not respond because a nonexistent location in memory was accessed by a CPU instruction. The maximum allotted time is specified when the SIM is initialized as described in Chapter 14.

The SIM watchdog timer also monitors interrupt and breakpoint acknowledgement cycles. Notice in Table 11.7 that a time-out during an interrupt acknowledgement cycle causes a spurious interrupt exception. Subsection 11.7.2 describes the spurious interrupt exception. The breakpoint cycle after a BKPT instruction executes causes an illegal instruction exception in response to a bus error signal. This response can be used to process a program breakpoint as previously described in Subsection 11.4.3.

Table 11.7 Example Uses of Bus Error Signal

Situation	Cause of bus error	CPU action
Memory error	Error-detection circuitry	Bus error exception
No response of a memory location or peripheral device	Hardware watchdog timer (SIM)	Bus error exception
Interrupt acknowledgement cycle not acknowledged	Hardware watchdog timer (SIM)	Spurious interrupt exception
Breakpoint acknowledgement cycle with no hardware response	Hardware watchdog timer (SIM)	Illegal instruction exception when breakpoint is taken

Note:
The bus monitor of the System Integration Module (SIM) can be programmed to monitor all data transfers and the interrupt acknowledgement cycle.

When a bus error is detected, a 12 word stack is created. The exact data pushed on the stack depend on the type of CPU cycle that is taking place when the bus error occurs. Section 11.8 describes the bus error stack frame in more detail. The information on the stack can be used to determine the instruction address and access address of an operand that was being used by the CPU when the bus error occurs. The type of CPU bus cycle such as a read, write, breakpoint acknowledge, etc. can also be determined. However, the actual external cause of the bus error cannot be determined from the information on the stack if there are possible multiple causes of a bus error in a product. In most cases, recovery from a bus error by the exception-handling routine is not desirable unless the bus error is an expected part of system operation. This is the case in virtual memory systems discussed in Section 11.8.

11.6.2 Format Error

When the RTE instruction is executed, the format code on the stack frame at location (SP) + 6 is checked for validity. If the format code is not correct, a format error exception is taken. If the RTE is executed after a bus error exception is recognized, the other data for the processor stored on the stack are also checked for validity before the stacked information (12 words) is restored to internal CPU registers. If these values are not correct, a format error exception occurs. In any case, a four word stack frame is created in which the PC value at location (SP)+2 is the address of the RTE instruction that caused the format error. The format exception handler address is held in vector 14 of the CPU vector table in Figure 11.2.

The valid format codes in bits [15:12] of the format word in the stacks of Figure 11.3 are $0 or $2 for the four word and six word stack, respectively. The twelve word stack of the bus error exception has format code $C. Any other format code will cause a format exception when an RTE instruction executes. In a single processor system, a format error usually means that the contents of the format word on the exception stack or the stack pointer has been altered in an invalid manner between the time the exception was recognized and the RTE instruction executes.

However, another format error can arise in a multiprocessor system that mixes different M68000 family processors. The bus error exception stack frames of the different family processors such as the MC68010, MC68020 and MC68332 are not the same. Thus, for the bus error stack frame, the version number of the processor that processed the bus error is written on the stack at location (SP)+14. The RTE instruction compares the version number on the stack with that of the processor that is executing the RTE and attempting to read the stack. If the version numbers do not match, a format error occurs to prevent one type of CPU from processing the exception stack of another type if such tasks are shared among the processors.

11.6.3 Halted State

As described in Chapter 10, unless the background mode is enabled, the CPU enters the halted state when the CPU determines that it can no longer continue exception processing. The reader is reminded that exception processing as defined in Section 10.1 refers to the storing of information on the supervisor stack when an exception is recognized or the reloading of registers by the RTE instruction. Execution of the exception-handling routine is not considered part of exception processing as the term is used here. The halted state is entered only when a catastrophic failure in the system is detected. Once in the halted state, the processor can only be restarted by a reset.

Without background mode enabled, the CPU enters the halted state if an address error or bus error occurs during the exception processing of an address error, bus error, or reset. Also, if either one of these exceptions occurs while the processor is loading internal registers from the stack during the execution of an RTE instruction, the processor enters the halted state. Any one of these conditions that halts the processor is called a *double bus fault*. Chapter 14 explains the hardware aspects of the double bus fault. Chapter 16 describes the CPU operation with the background mode enabled.

EXERCISES

11.6.1. Assume that an illegal (odd) address is stored in the address error vector location. What would be the result if the processor detects an address error during execution of a program?

11.6.2. Describe the cause of the possible errors or failures and the subsequent action of the bus-error handling routine when a bus error exception occurs in the following cases:
(a) during CPU access to external memory;
(b) during an interrupt acknowledgement cycle.

11.6.3. Since there can be a number of sources of a bus error in an MC68332-based product, what methods might be used by the exception handler to determine the exact source? Assume that the information to determine the source of the error is not included in the exception stack frame.

11.6.4. Assume that the SIM watchdog timer causes a bus error when nonexistent memory is accessed. Write a routine to determine the amount of RAM in the system. Start the test of memory above the known locations of RAM that holds the monitor and the programs being developed. The address that caused the bus error is held in the stack frame at location (SP)+8.

The bus error stack created has a form similar to that shown in Figure 11.12 in Section 11.8 except that (SP)+$C holds the data buffer (32-bits) for the data value read or written. Also, bits [15:14] of (SP)+$16 are {00} for a data fault.

11.7 INTERRUPT PROCESSING BY THE CPU32

The interrupt system of the CPU32 allows an external device or one of the MC68332 modules to interrupt the processor execution. The interrupt causes program control to be passed to an exception-handling routine designed to perform the operations required by the interrupt request. The exception handling routine is variously called the interrupt handling routine or more commonly the *interrupt service* routine. These terms are used interchangeably in this textbook. This section defines the interrupt processing sequence for the CPU32 and defines the various types of interrupts and errors associated with interrupts.

The examples of interrupt service routines and hardware aspects of interrupts are not presented in this chapter. Specific examples of interrupt service routines for the Queued Serial Module and the Time Processor Unit are presented in Chapter 12 and Chapter 13, respectively. The signal lines used for interrupt requests and acknowledgments are discussed in Chapter 14. Chapter 15 describes the control of the external interrupt requests by the System Integration Module.

11.7.1 Interrupt Priorities and Interrupt Mask for the CPU32

An interrupt request from an MC68332 module or an external device can occur at one of seven levels of CPU priority. The priority is that level 1 is the lowest and level 7 is the highest. These priorities allow a routine that is servicing a lower-level interrupt to be interrupted by a higher-level interrupt request. After the highest-level interrupt routine completes execution, control returns to the next-lower-level interrupt routine that is waiting to complete execution. Once all the interrupt requests are serviced, control finally returns to the program that was originally interrupted.

The priority of external interrupt requests is set by the connection of peripheral devices to the seven, external interrupt signal-lines of the MC68332. The priority level of the internal modules is programmable and is typically defined during system initialization. Section 15.2 discusses the system design considerations in setting interrupt priorities.

From the processor's point-of-view, an interrupt is an externally generated request for exception processing. The interrupt request may be considered active, pending, or disabled. An *active* request is processed immediately after the completion of any instruction currently executing provided that no higher-priority exceptions take precedence. The request is *pending* if the processor is currently processing a higher-priority exception. In normal operation, pending requests will be serviced when the higher-priority interrupt handling routine completes. If an interrupt level is disabled, an interrupt request at that level and all lower levels is ignored until the level is enabled by changing the interrupt mask in the Status Register, (SR)[10:8] shown in Figure 11.9.

The interrupt mask bits are shown in Figure 11.9, which includes the mask value for each level. For levels 1 through level 6, the interrupt request will not be accepted from the level that is masked (disabled) or from any lower priority interrupt. The level 7 request is an exception to this rule and will be processed regardless of the setting of the interrupt mask. If the mask is set to {000}, all interrupt levels are enabled.

In a computer system that uses volatile memory to store the vector table, the interrupt system must be initialized by a supervisor program during system initialization. This is accomplished by loading the starting addresses of each interrupt service routine into the appropriate location in the vector table and enabling interrupts. In other computer systems in which the vector table is held in nonvolatile memory such as ROM, the operating system does not need to initialize the vector table. However, any initialization required is usually performed with all interrupt levels disabled except level 7, which cannot be disabled. The interrupt levels are enabled just before control is passed from the supervisor program to the first application program to be executed. Section 14.3 contains initialization examples for the MC68332 that illustrate the technique.

The vector table for interrupts is shown in Table 11.8. The two classifications of interrupts are *autovector* and *vectored* interrupts. The type of interrupt is specified

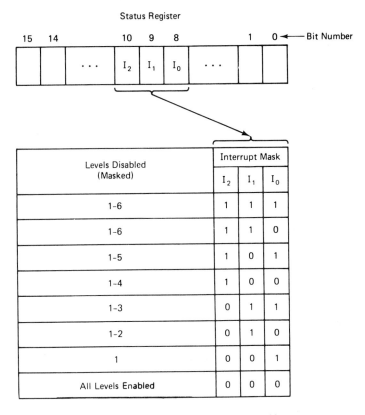

Figure 11.9 Interrupt mask for the CPU32.

by the requesting device during the CPU interrupt acknowledgement cycle. After an interrupt request from an external device, selection between these modes of operation for the interrupt system is determined entirely by external circuitry as defined in Subsection 14.5.3. As described in Section 14.6, the chip select signals of the System Integration Module can also request autovector or vectored interrupts. The difference in hardware operation has no effect on the design of interrupt routines.

During interrupt processing, the CPU recognizes certain types of errors. If the external device requesting the interrupt does not respond properly, a spurious interrupt or an uninitialized interrupt could occur. Subsection 11.7.3 discusses the causes of these errors.

11.7.2 Interrupt Processing by the CPU32

If the processor is executing instructions in the normal state as defined in Section 10.1, an interrupt request that is acknowledged initiates a sequence of events designed to pass control to a designated interrupt routine. This routine performs the interrupt service as required, and then returns control to the interrupted program. This sequence of events is shown in Figure 11.10.

Table 11.8 Vector Table for Interrupt Routines

Vector number (decimal)	Memory location (hexadecimal)	Name
15	$003C	Uninitialized interrupt vector
24	$0060	Spurious interrupt vector
25	$0064	Level 1 autovector
26	$0068	Level 2 autovector
27	$006C	Level 3 autovector
28	$0070	Level 4 autovector
29	$0074	Level 5 autovector
30	$0078	Level 6 autovector
31	$007C	Level 7 autovector
.	.	
.	.	
.	.	
64	$0100	Interrupt vector 1
65	$0104	Interrupt vector 2
.	.	
.	.	
.	.	
255	$03FC	Interrupt vector 192

Notes:
1. Vector 15 should be provided by an uninitialized external device if the CPU requests a vector number.
2. A spurious interrupt or an uninitialized interrupt occurs when the CPU detects an error during interrupt processing.

After the CPU determines that an interrupt request is from an enabled level, an interrupt acknowledgement cycle is executed to determine the vector number associated with the interrupt. The expected response is an interrupt vector number on the data signal lines or an autovector request. This represents the normal interrupt sequence in a correctly operating product. However, if an error occurs as indicated by a bus error response, a spurious interrupt exception is taken. Another possibility is that the module or external device requesting the interrupt responds with an uninitialized interrupt vector ($15). These error responses are described later in this section.

Once the vector number is determined, the interrupt vector address in the CPU vector table is calculated as 4 times the vector number to determine the offset into the table. Thus, the address in the table is calculated as

$$\text{vector address} = 4 \times \text{vector number} + (\text{VBR})$$

where the Vector Base Register (VBR) is assumed to be initialized to $00000000 and is not included in the calculation in Figure 11.10. Section 10.3 describes the VBR for relocating the CPU vector table. The recommended interrupt vector addresses are shown in Table 11.8. However, the CPU will respond to any vectored interrupt request from vector number 0 through 255. Ordinarily, only the vectors in Table 11.8 would be used for interrupts in a product to avoid conflict with the other vector addresses shown in Figure 11.2.

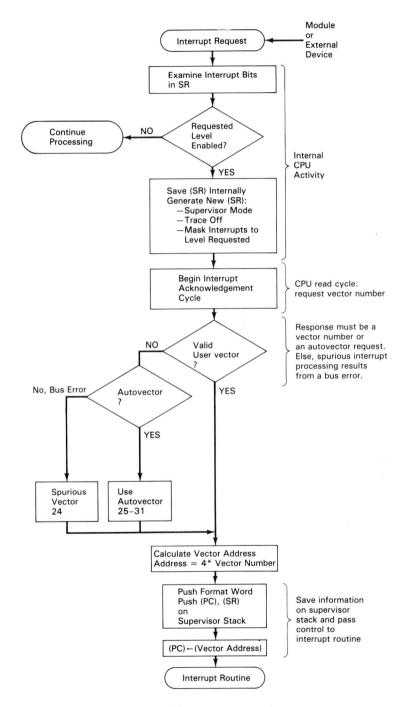

Figure 11.10 Interrupt processing.

The operations in Figure 11.10 are performed automatically by the CPU until control is passed to the interrupt routine. The processing required in the interrupt routine is entirely dependent on the application. For example, use of interrupts for I/O programming is considered in Chapter 12 and Chapter 14.

Example 11.10

The processing of an interrupt consists of saving the format word, (PC), and (SR) on the supervisor stack. As an example, shown in Figure 11.11, assume that an interrupt occurs when the initial contents of selected registers have the values

$$(SR) = \$2008$$
$$(PC) = \$0000164A$$
$$(SSP) = \$0000 \text{ FFFE}$$

which indicates that a supervisor-mode program was about to execute the instruction at location $164A when the interrupt was recognized. The processing causes the format word with format code $0 and vector offset $74 to be pushed at location $FFFC, followed by (PC) at longword location $FFF8 and (SR) at location $FFF6.

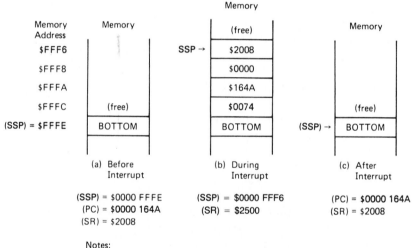

Figure 11.11 System stack during interrupt processing.

The interrupt routine may use the supervisor stack as required as long as (SSP) is restored to the value $0000FFF6 before the routine executes an RTE instruction to return control to the interrupted program. An exception-handling routine for the level 5 autovectored interrupt is located by the address (vector 29) stored in location $0074.

The interrupt-handling routine begins execution with

$$(PC) = (\$0074)$$
$$(SR) = \$2500$$

which allows execution at the vectored location with interrupts at level 5 and below disabled. When the RTE instruction in the interrupt-handling routine is executed, control is returned to the interrupted program at location $0000164A.

11.7.3 Vectored Interrupts, Autovector interrupts, Spurious Interrupts, and Uninitialized interrupts

The source of an interrupt to the CPU may be one of the MC68332 modules or an external device. Each module of the MC68332 except the on-chip memory can have one or more interrupt vectors associated with it. These interrupts are termed *vectored* interrupts to distinguish them from autovectored interrupts. Table 11.8 defines the vector locations using vector numbers 64 through 255. The priority level (1–7) and the vector number is selected by the initialization program for the modules as discussed in the chapter where a particular module is introduced.

External devices can request either a vectored interrupt or an autovector interrupt. In the first case, a correctly operating external device supplies a vector number as part of the CPU interrupt acknowledgement cycle depicted in Figure 11.10. If the external device is not designed to supply a vector number, it should be designed to request an autovector level. The bus activity during the interrupt acknowledgement cycle is controlled and monitored by the System Integration Module (SIM). The hardware design of interrupt interfaces for both types of interrupts is presented in Chapter 14.

As part of the interrupt acknowledgement cycle, the SIM monitors the internal bus if the interrupt request was initiated by one of the MCU modules. Otherwise, the SIM monitors the external bus activity when the interrupt request comes from an external device. In either case, if the requesting module or external device does not respond correctly by providing a vector number, a bus error signal is generated by the SIM to the CPU. The bus error response will cause a spurious interrupt exception.

Spurious interrupt.   The spurious interrupt monitor of the SIM causes a *spurious* interrupt exception using vector 24 if a vector number or an autovector request is not provided by the requesting device during the interrupt acknowledgement cycle. The cause of this error may be due to a hardware failure or to an unexpected electrical disturbance that caused an interrupt request. The action to be taken after the spurious interrupt is processed depends only on the spurious interrupt exception-handling routine.

Uninitialized interrupt.   The MC68332 modules that can interrupt the CPU and certain peripheral chips in the M68000 family of support chips allow the interrupt vector number to be selected by a program. Examples of such support chips were given in Section 1.2. The vector number for the module or chip is chosen by the initialization program. If the vector number is programmable, it is Motorola's convention that the programmable vector numbers are set to $0F (15) after a reset of the MCU or a peripheral chip.

An uninitialized interrupt occurs if the initialization program does not change the vector number from 15 and the module or peripheral chip makes an interrupt request. When this condition arises, it indicates that the initialization program has not specified all of the vector numbers correctly. Examples in Chapter 12, Chapter 13 and Chapter 14 show how the programmable interrupt vector is defined for the various MC68332 modules that can interrupt the CPU.

Example 11.11

External signal lines determine whether an external interrupt request is an *autovector* or a *vectored interrupt*. When the autovector mode is requested by an external device, the CPU automatically provides the vector number. Otherwise, in the vectored mode, the external device must provide the vector number. This number is multiplied internally by 4 to give the address of the exception vector as previously explained. The signal lines involved when the vector number is supplied to the CPU from the external device is discussed in Chapter 14.

In either case, the product designer must specify the following information to define the interrupts and the interrupt routines:

(a) the type of interrupt as autovectored or vectored;

(b) the priority level to be assigned by the hardware design of the system for external devices and the priority to be initialized for the MC68332 modules;

(c) the vector number in the CPU vector table that holds the starting address of the interrupt service routine;

(d) the starting address of the routine;

(e) details of the functional operation of the interrupt routine as determined by the hardware requirements.

The priority level and the type as vectored or autovectored for each interrupt is determined by the product requirements, primarily the timing constraints of external devices as discussed in detail in Chapter 15. For example, an interrupt indicating an event that must be serviced quickly or that is critical to the system operation would be given a high priority so that the service would not be delayed by the servicing of lower priority interrupts. The priority selected for each interrupt source will in turn define the hardware design for external interrupt sources and the initialization required to define interrupts from the MC68332 modules.

The location of the interrupt routine is typically decided during the software design phase for a product. Selection of the location depends on factors such as the size of the interrupt service routine and the memory layout chosen for the product as previously discussed in Section 10.3.

The programmer who creates the interrupt service routine must obviously understand the required operation of the routine in terms of the application involved. The interrupt priority is important to the programmer only if the interrupt routine manipulates the interrupt mask to mask higher level interrupts. The masking occurs when the Status Register bits (SR)[10:8] are changed as previously described. In most applications, the interrupt mask would not be changed by the interrupt service routine since the CPU automatically masks and unmasks interrupts. However, there are occasions when interrupts should be masked by a program to prevent additional interrupt requests from being received. Section 15.3 describes an example where a critical section of code is protected by masking interrupts.

EXERCISES

11.7.1. What are some system applications for the level 7, nonmaskable interrupt?

11.7.2. How many vectored plus autovectored interrupt vectors are available according to the exception vector table? The vector number is an 8-bit integer allowing 256 entries to address the exception vector table, but not all entries can be associated with interrupts according to the table. Or can they? In other words, is a designer forbidden from using vectors 0 through 23 or vectors 32 through 47 as interrupt vectors?

11.7.3. Describe the exception-handling routines required in the following operating systems:
(a) software development system;
(b) real-time operating system in a finished product.

11.7.4. What are some possible actions to be taken by the exception-handling routines when the CPU recognizes the following:
(a) a spurious interrupt;
(b) an uninitialized interrupt.

11.8 STACK FRAMES AND EXCEPTION PRIORITIES

In this section we summarize a number of details concerning exception processing. The format of the stack frames for each exception is presented first. Then, Section 11.8.2 treats the bus error and virtual memory support. Next, the priority of exceptions is defined to determine which exception is processed first when two exceptions occur simultaneously.

11.8.1 Stack Frames

The stack frame which is created when an exception is recognized can contain as few as four words or as many as 12 words. Most exceptions create either four-word or six-word stack frames. A bus error exception creates a 12-word stack frame.

Four-word stack frame. Figure 11.3(b) showed the basic four-word stack frame created by exception processing. This stack frame is for interrupts, format errors, TRAP instructions, illegal instructions, A-line and F-line emulator traps, and privilege violations.

Six-word stack frame. The six-word stack frame of Figure 11.3(c) contains the address of the instruction that caused the exception as well as the format word, the (PC), and the (SR). If an RTE instruction is executed that uses this stack frame, the (PC) indicates the next instruction to be executed. This stack frame is created by CHK, CHK2, TRAPcc, TRAPV, hardware breakpoint, trace, and zero divide exceptions. The instruction address is used to determine the exact cause of the trap when several traps share the same vector location. An example was given in Subsection 11.3.3 for the CHK and CHK2 instructions.

Bus-cycle-fault stack frame. If a bus error occurs, a 12-word stack frame is created. An example is shown in Figure 11.12. In some cases, the exception-handling routine could determine and correct the problem causing the bus error as discussed in the next subsection. The information on the stack is restored to various CPU registers if the RTE instruction is executed after the exception-handling routine corrects the situation that caused the exception. Other 12-word stack frames are created under special circumstances when a bus error is detected. The reader is referred to the *CPU32 Reference Manual* for a complete discussion.

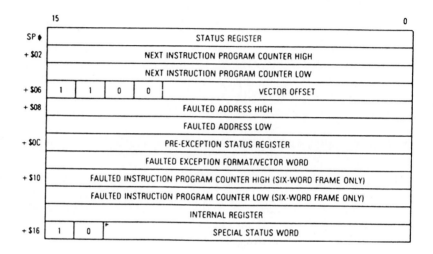

Figure 11.12 Bus error stack frame.

11.8.2 Bus Error Recovery and Virtual Memory Support

During hardware and software development, testing a product may reveal situations that cause bus errors. These can be due to hardware or software errors or a combination of both. The solution at this stage is to correct the problem and retest the product. In a completed product, no unexpected bus error should ever occur. If it does, the normal procedure is either to reset and reinitialize the product or stop its operation completely. Reset of the MCU could correct a random and temporary error so that the product will operate normally after the reset. Replacement or repair of one or more of the product's components is usually necessary when a reset does not eliminate unwanted bus error exceptions.

In certain applications, it may be necessary for the bus-error handling routine to determine the cause of the bus error and correct the situation so that program execution may continue. This would be the case, for example, with a computer using an operating system that allows virtual memory management.

416 Exception-Handling Techniques Chap. 11

Virtual memory. A *virtual memory* system has the advantage that a computer with a relatively small physical memory space can allow programs of any size to be executed, up to the maximum addressing range of the CPU. Basically, the operating system allows a program to reference any address in the "virtual" addressing space which typically represents areas for programs and data held on a disk unit. All or only part of a program may be in physical memory as it executes. The addresses generated by the program are called *logical* addresses and they refer to the virtual space. These are translated by memory-management circuits into the appropriate *physical* addresses in memory. If the complete program is in physical memory, no problems arise during program execution.

When the program addresses a location in the virtual space that is not also held in physical memory, a "fault" is said to occur. This is indicated to the CPU in M68000-family systems by a bus-error signal. The exception handler must fetch the appropriate program or data from disk storage and load it into memory. Then, the instruction that caused the fault must either be restarted or continued.[9] This is done automatically when the RTE instruction is executed after the exception-handling routine has corrected the fault. The reader is referred to the Motorola *CPU32 Reference Manual* for more information about recovery from faults that cause bus-error exceptions.

11.8.3 Exception Priorities

Exceptions can be categorized according to their priorities. These priorities are fixed by the design of the CPU32 and cannot be changed. To define the priority, the *CPU32 Reference Manual* divides exceptions into five groups, as shown in Table 11.9. The highest priority exception is the reset exception in group 0, which causes system initialization as described in Chapter 10. If this exception occurs, any other processing is immediately terminated. All the other exceptions are processed according to priority if two or more occur simultaneously.

The group 1 exceptions take precedence over all the other exceptions except reset. Even the exception processing for a lower-priority exception to save information on the stack is suspended when an address error or bus error is recognized. Thus, group 1 exceptions will be processed and handled before processing or handling of lower-priority exceptions.

As an instruction in group 2 causes an exception, the processing takes place as part of the instruction execution. The execution of these instructions will always be completed unless a group 1 or reset exception occurs. If the program and system are operating properly, only a reset exception would cause the processing and handling of these exceptions to be aborted.

In group 3, any instruction causing an exception is not executed. However, exception processing occurs and execution continues in the exception-handling routine if no higher-priority exception is detected during exception processing.

---

[9] Various techniques are used to support a virtual memory. The MC68020, for example, allows instruction continuation after the fault is corrected. In contrast, the CPU32 allows instruction restart except for faults that occur while the MOVEM instruction is executing.

Table 11.9 Exception Priority

Group/ Priority	Exception and relative priority	Characteristics
0	0.0 Reset	Aborts all processing for instruction or exception and does not save old context
1	1.1 Address error 1.2 Bus error	Suspends processing for instruction or exception and saves internal context
2	BKPT, CHK, CHK2, divide-by-zero, RTE, TRAP, TRAPcc, TRAPV	Exception processing is part of instruction execution
3	Illegal instruction, Line-A, Line-F, privilege violation	Exception processing begins before instruction is executed
4	4.1 Trace 4.2 Hardware breakpoint 4.3 Interrupt	Exception processing begins when current instruction or previous exception processing is completed

Note:
Priority 0.0 is the highest priority, 4.3 is the lowest.

Exceptions in group 4 cannot occur until instruction execution and exception processing for any instruction causing an exception is complete. However, if an interrupt is recognized when a trace exception is pending, exception processing for the trace occurs first, followed by exception processing for the interrupt. This is the significance of the subpriorities for group 4 exceptions shown in Table 11.9. However, when normal processing continues after the stacking of the trace and interrupt information, execution continues in the interrupt handler. When the interrupt routine completes, control passes to the trace-handling routine.

EXERCISES

11.8.1. Describe how the bus error exception-handling routine might work after a fault occurs in a system with virtual memory.

11.8.2. Describe the activity that occurs because of each of the following conditions:
(a) the trap, trace, and interrupt exceptions are pending simultaneously;
(b) a bus error occurs during exception processing for a trace;
(c) an illegal instruction is recognized while a single-instruction trace is enabled.

FURTHER READING

The exceptions that are recognized by the Motorola 32-bit processors are described in detail in the *User's manuals* for those processors. The reader is referred to these manuals for exact details concerning the various exceptions.

12

The Queued Serial Module

This chapter describes the Queued Serial communications Module (QSM) as it is used for serial communications and general Input/Output (I/O) transfers. The module and the programming procedure are introduced in Section 12.1. First, the module is described in terms of its functional operation. Then, its programmable register set is defined. This description format will be followed for the Time Processor Unit in Chapter 13 and the System Integration Module in Chapter 14.

Section 12.2 presents a brief introduction to data transfer techniques. The discussion explains unconditional, conditional, and interrupt-controlled I/O between the CPU and the QSM. Descriptions of asynchronous and synchronous serial communication are also included in Section 12.2. Both methods of communication can be used between the QSM and external devices.

The Queued Serial Module has two communications interfaces that are referred to as serial I/O ports. Section 12.3 treats the Serial Communication Interface (SCI) which is a UART I/O port. The UART is a Universal Asynchronous Receiver Transmitter for asynchronous, serial data transfer. Section 12.4 describes the Queued Serial Peripheral Interface (QSPI). This I/O port is used for synchronous, serial data transfer. Both of these interfaces allow communication between peripheral devices or peripheral chips and the microcontroller. Thus, they provide I/O capability for a computer system or product with devices that use serial data transfer.

If some of the QSM signal lines are not used for serial communication, these signal lines are available for general-purpose I/O. Section 12.5 describes the QSM as it is used to perform general purpose I/O.

12.1 QSM OPERATION

The Queued Serial Module (QSM) provides the MC68332 MCU with two serial communication interfaces. This module consists of two independent submodules with the features listed in Table 12.1. The Serial Communication Interface (SCI) is a Universal Asynchronous Receiver Transmitter (UART) interface. As described in Table 12.1, the SCI is used for serial communication in a product. In many applications, the SCI transfers ASCII characters between the MC68332 and one or more external devices that have a UART interface. For example, the SCI is often employed for communication with an operator's terminal.

The Queued Serial Peripheral Interface (QSPI) provides synchronous, serial transfer of data for communication and I/O expansion. The QSPI can act as a master or slave device in a network of devices with compatible serial interfaces. As master, the QSPI controls the data format and timing of transfers between the QSPI and slave devices. This submodule contains a queue which allows up to 16 independent transfers without CPU intervention. As master, the QSPI chip select signal lines select the specific peripheral device involved in each transfer.

As described in Section 12.5, the signal lines of the QSM can be used for general-purpose I/O if they are not used for their primary communications function. However, the present section defines the signal lines of the QSM for serial communication. The register set and the techniques of QSM initialization are also presented.

Table 12.1 Features of the QSM

Function or Submodule	Feature	Example Uses
Serial Communications Interface (SCI)	Asynchronous serial transfer (UART)	Communication with an operator's terminal or similar unit
Queued Serial Peripheral Interface (QSPI)	Synchronous serial transfer	Communication with peripheral devices that have a synchronous interface
Queue	16 element queue	Allows up to 16 transfers without CPU intervention
Peripheral Chip Select Signals	4 independent signal lines	Selection of peripheral devices by QSPI as master
General Purpose I/O	Discrete or parallel I/O	Provides an 8-bit I/O port

12.1.1 QSM Signal Lines

The nine signal lines of the QSM are shown in Figure 12.1 and defined for I/O communication in Table 12.2. Only two of its signal lines are needed by the SCI to achieve serial communication. The connection to another UART device requires only three conductors: TxD for transmission, RxD for reception and one for ground.

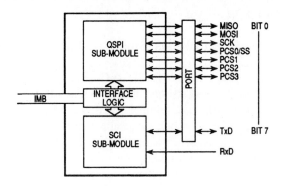

Figure 12.1 Signal Lines of the QSM.

Table 12.2 Definition of the Signal Lines of the QSM

Signal Mnemonic	Signal Name	Function
SCI:		
RxD	Receive Data	Serial data to SCI
TxD	Transmit Data	Serial data from SCI
QSPI:		
MISO	Master In/Slave Out	Serial data to QSPI (master)/ Serial data from QSPI (slave)
MOSI	Master Out/Slave In	Serial data from QSPI (master)/ Serial data to QSPI (slave)
SCK	Serial clock	Clock output (master)/ Clock input (slave)
PCS1-PCS3	Peripheral chip select signals	Output to select peripheral
PCS0/SS	Peripheral chip select/ Slave select	Select peripheral (master)/ Select QSPI (slave)

Notes:

1. All of the signal lines except RxD can be used for general-purpose I/O if they are not used for their primary SCI or QSPI purpose.

2. TxD is an output signal when the SCI is used for serial communication. When used for general-purpose I/O, the direction of signal line TxD is programmable.

Since the QSPI can act in a master or slave mode, its signals for data and the clock are bidirectional. When acting as a master in a network consisting of devices with compatible interfaces, three signals (SCK, MOSI, MISO) plus a ground are used for communication. The peripheral select signals (PCS3–PCS0) can be used by the QSPI as output signals to select a particular device for communication. Subsection 12.4.3 describes the chip select signals in detail.

The QSM signal lines can also form an 8-bit port (PORT D) if the signals are not used for serial communications. Figure 12.1 shows the I/O port bits 0–7. Section 12.5 describes the I/O port of the QSM.

12.1.2 QSM Memory Map and Register Set

Figure 12.2 shows the memory map of the QSM registers in the CPU memory space. The registers start at address $YFFC00 where Y = $F or Y = $7 according to the initial address selected after a reset of the MC68332 as described in Chapter 14. Several of the registers are available only to a supervisor-mode program. These are the "global" registers of the module used to initialize the QSM. The other registers can be restricted to supervisor-mode access only or they can be assigned for unrestricted access by programs in either supervisor or user mode.

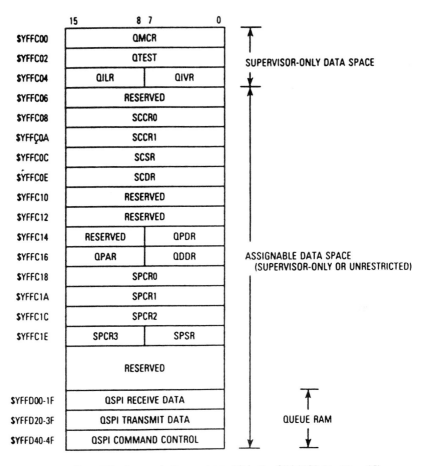

Y = m111 where m is the modmap bit in the SIM MCR (Y = $7 or $F).

Figure 12.2 Memory Map of the QSM Registers.

For convenience, the entire register set of the QSM is shown in Figure 12.3. In that figure, each bit is labeled according to the definitions in Table 12.3. The reset value of {0} or {1} is shown in Figure 12.3 below the label for each bit. Specific

Register / Address	15	14	13	12	11	10	9	8	7	6	5	4	3	2	1	0
QMCR $YFFC00	STOP	FRZ1	FRZ0	0	0	0	0	0	SUPV	0	0	0	IARB			
	0	0						0	1				0	0	0	0
QTEST $YFFC02	0	0	0	0	0	0	0	0	0	0	0	0	TSBD	SYNC	TQSM	TMMO
QILR–QIVR $YFFC04	0	0	ILQSPI			ILSCI			INTV — Interrupt Vector							
	0	0	0	0	0	0	0	0	0	0	0	0	1	1	1	1
Reserved $YFFC06	Reserved															
SCCR0 $YFFC08	0	0	0	BR												
	0	0	0	0	0	0	0	0	0	0	0	0	0	1	0	0
SCCR1 $YFFC0A	0	LOOPS	WOMS	ILT	PT	PE	M	WAKE	TIE	TCIE	RIE	ILIE	TE	RE	RWU	SBK
	0	0	0	0	0	0	0	0	0	0	0	0	0	0	0	0
SCSR $YFFC0C	0	0	0	0	0	0	0	TDRE	TC	RDRF	RAF	IDLE	OR	NF	FE	PF
								1	1	0	0	0	0	0	0	0
SCDR $YFFC0E	0	0	0	0	0	0	0	R8/T8	R7/T7	R6/T6	R5/T5	R4/T4	R3/T3	R2/T2	R1/T1	R0/T0
								U	U	U	U	U	U	U	U	U
Reserved $YFFC10	Reserved															
Reserved $YFFC12	Reserved															
QPDR $YFFC14	0	0	0	0	0	0	0	0	TXD	PCS3	PCS2	PCS1	PCS0¹	SCK	MOSI	MISO
									0	0	0	0	0	0	0	0
QPAR–QDDR $YFFC16	0	PCS3	PCS2	PCS1	PCS0¹	0	MOSI	MISO	TXD	PCS3	PCS2	PCS1	PCS0¹	SCK	MOSI	MISO
		0	0	0	0		0	0	0	0	0	0	0	0	0	0
SPCR0 $YFFC18	MSTR	WOMQ	BITS				CPOL	CPHA	BAUD							
	0	0	0	0	0	0	0	1	0	0	0	0	0	1	0	0
SPCR1 $YFFC1A	SPE	DSCKL							DTL							
	0	0	0	0	0	0	1	.0	0	0	0	0	0	1	0	0
SPCR2 $YFFC1C	SPIFIE	WREN	WRTO	0	ENDQP				0	0	0	0	NEWQP			
	0	0	0		0	0	0	0					0	0	0	0
SPCR3–SPSR $YFFC1E	0	0	0	0	0	LOOPQ	HMIE	HALT	SPIF	MODF	HALTA	0	CPTQP			
						0	0	0	0	0	0		0	0	0	0
Reserved $YFFC20–$YFFCFF	Reserved															
REC.RAM $YFFD00–$YFFD1F	QSPI Receive Data (16 Words)															
TRAN.RAM $YFFD20–$YFFD3F	QSPI Transmit Data (16 Words)															
COMD.RAM $YFFD40–$YFFD4F	CONT	BITSE	DT	DSCK	PCS3	PCS2	PCS1	PCS0¹	CONT	BITSE	DT	DSCK	PCS3	PCS2	PCS1	PCS0¹

Y   m111, where m is the modmap bit in the module configuration register of the SIM (Y = $7 or $F).

NOTE:

1. The PCSØ bit listed above represents the dual-functon bit PCS0/SS.

Figure 12.3 QSM Register Set.

Table 12.3 QSM Register Bits

Bit/Field Mnemonic	Function	Register	Register Location
BAUD	Serial Clock Baud Rate	SPCR0	QSPI
BITS	Bits Per Transfer	SPCR0	QSPI
BITSE	Bits Per Transfer Enable	QSPI RAM	QSPI
BR	Baud Rate	SCCR0	SCI
CONT	Continue	QSPI RAM	QSPI
CPHA	Clock Phase	SPCR0	QSPI
CPOL	Clock Polarity	SPCR0	QSPI
CPTQP	Completed Queue Pointer	SPSR	QSPI
DSCK	Peripheral Select Chip (PSC) to Serial Clock (SCK) Delay	QSPI RAM	QSPI
DSCKL	Delay before Serial Clock (SCK)	SPCR1	QSPI
DT	Delay after Transfer	QSPI RAM	QSPI
DTL	Length of Delay after Transfer	SPCR1	QSPI
ENDQP	Ending Queue Pointer	SPCR2	QSPI
FE	Framing Error Flag	SCSR	SCI
FRZØ	Freeze / bits	QMCR	QSM
HALT	Halt	SPCR3	QSPI
HALTA	Halt Acknowledge Flag	SPSR	QSPI
HMIE	Halt Acknowledge Flag (HALTA) and Mode Fault Flag (MODF) Interrupt Enable	SPCR3	QSPI
IARB	Interrupt Arbitration	QMCR	QSM
IDLE	Idle Line Detected Flag	SCSR	SCI
ILIE	Idle Line Interrupt Enable	SCCR1	SCI
ILQSPI	Interrupt Level for QSPI	QILR	QSM
ILSCI	Interrupt Level of SCI	QILR	QSM
ILT	Idle Line Detect Type	SCCR1	SCI
INTV	Interrupt Vector	QIVR	QSM
LOOPS	SCI Loop Mode	SCCR1	SCI
LOOPQ	QSPI Loop Mode	SPCR3	QSPI
M	Mode Select (8/9 Bit)	SCCR1	SCI
MISO	Master In Slave Out	QPAR/QDDR/QPDR	QSM
MODF	Mode Fault Flag	SPSR	QSPI
MOSI	Master Out Slave In	QPAR/QDDR/QPDR	QSM
MSTR	Master/Slave Mode Select	SPCR0	QSPI

Table 12.3 QSM Register Bits (Cont.)

Bit/Field Mnemonic	Function	Register	Register Location
NEWQP	New Queue Pointer Value	SPCR2	QSPI
NF	Noise Error Flag	SCSR	SCI
OR	Overrun Error Flag	SCSR	SCI
PCS0/SS	Peripheral Chip Select/Slave Select	QPAR/QDDR/QPDR	QSM
PCS3–PCS1	Peripheral Chip Selects	QPAR/QDDR/QPDR	QSM
PE	Parity Enable	SCCR1	SCI
PF	Parity Error Flag	SCSR	SCI
PT	Parity Type	SCCR1	SCI
R8–R0	Receive 8–0	SCDR	SCI
RAF	Receiver Active Flag	SCSR	SCI
RDRF	Receive Data Register Full Flag	SCSR	SCI
RE	Receiver Enable	SCCR1	SCI
RIE	Receiver Interrupt Enable	SCCR1	SCI
RWU	Receiver Wakeup	SCCR1	SCI
SBK	Send Break	SCCR1	SCI
SCK	Serial Clock	QDDR/QPDR	QSM
SPE	QSPI Enable	SPCR1	QSPI
SPIF	QSPI Finished Flag	SPSR	QSPI
SPIFIE	SPI Finished Interrupt Enable	SPCR2	QSPI
STOP	Stop	QMCR	QSM
SUPV	Supervisor/Unrestricted	QMCR	QSM
T8–T0	Transmit 8–0	SCDR	SCI
TC	Transmit Complete Flag	SCSR	SCI
TCIE	Transmit Complete Interrupt Enable	SCCR1	SCI
TDRE	Transmit Data Register Empty Flag	SCSR	SCI
TE	Transmit Enable	SCCR1	SCI
TIE	Transmit Interrupt Enable	SCCR1	SCI
TXD	Transmit Data	QDDR/QPDR	QSM
WAKE	Wakeup Type	SCCR1	SCI
WOMQ	Wired-OR Mode for QSPI Pins	SPCR0	QSPI
WOMS	Wired-OR Mode for SCI Pins	SCCR1	SCI
WREN	Wrap Enable	SPCR2	QSPI
WRTO	Wrap To Select	SPCR2	QSPI

registers will be discussed in this chapter as various applications of the QSM are introduced.

12.1.3 QSM Initialization after Reset

As previously discussed in Section 10.3, all of the modules of the MC68332 MCU should be initialized after a reset . The System Integration Module must be initialized first as described in Chapter 14. Then, the QSM and other modules of the MC68332 can be initialized according to the requirements of a particular application.

Table 12.4 defines the general steps for a supervisor-mode program to initialize the registers of the QSM. Initialization of the global registers consists of first defining the interrupt arbitration between modules of the MCU and specifying the allowed program access to the other registers of the QSM. These selections are made by the initialization program when it writes the appropriate bit pattern into the QSM Configuration Register (QMCR). Example 12.1 presents a program to perform QSM global initialization.

The CPU interrupt levels and the corresponding vector numbers for the QSM must also be defined initially. There is a separate interrupt level for the SCI and the QSPI. These levels determine the priority level at which the CPU is interrupted when an SCI or a QSPI interrupt is recognized.[1]

Table 12.4 QSM Initialization Sequence

Operation	Purpose	Registers
Initialization of global registers	(1) Set interrupt arbitration and access to QSM registers	Configuration register (QMCR)
	(2) Set interrupt level and vector for SCI and QSPI	Interrupt registers (QILR–QIVR)
Initialization of SCI	Select baud rate and other characteristics of SCI; enable SCI	SCI control registers (SCCR0, SCCR1)
Initialization of QSPI	(1) Assign pins to QSPI or general purpose I/O	Pin control registers (QPAR, QDDR, QPDR)
	(2) Select master or slave operation, baud rate, and other QSPI characteristics; define queue entries; enable QSPI	QSPI control registers (SPCR0–SPCR3); QSPI RAM; SPCR1

The global registers are in the supervisor data space of the memory. They contain parameters used by both submodules. Thus, the global registers must be initialized first before either submodule is used. If the SUPV bit of the QSM configuration register, (QMCR)[7] in Figure 12.3, is set to {1}, only a supervisor-mode program may

---

[1] Section 11.7 describes the CPU32 interrupt priorities and the CPU vector table. Chapter 14 describes the interrupt arbitration levels and interrupt arbitration by the SIM. The interrupt arbitration levels and CPU priority levels for the system are defined during product design as discussed in Chapter 15.

initialize the SCI and QSPI submodules. This would be the case when the product contains an operating system which controls the QSM. A user-mode program would request I/O operations using a TRAP instruction, for example, but the applications program could not directly program the QSM registers. This approach to I/O is similar to the use of the TRAP #15 instruction for I/O requests to the 332BUG monitor discussed in Chapter 7. If the supervisor access bit SUPV = {0}, an applications program operating in the user mode could perform the initialization of the SCI and the QSPI.

The interrupt arbitration field IARB (QMCR[3:0]) in Figure 12.3 is $0 at reset to disable interrupt arbitration for QSM interrupts. The arbitration level can be set from the lowest level ($1) to the highest ($F) to enable arbitration. The arbitration level determines the priority of the QSM when several interrupts occur simultaneously. The IARB value in this field does not affect the CPU interrupt level as defined previously in Section 11.7.

The CPU interrupt vector numbers for the SCI and the QSPI are defined in the QSM Interrupt Vector Register INTV field (QIVR[7:0]). This field is $0F after a reset to cause an uninitialized interrupt to the CPU if the SCI or QSPI interrupts before the proper vector number is defined in the INTV field. The interrupt number in the INTV field should be in the range $40–$FE using an even numbered vector. The vector number in INTV actually selects only the SCI vector. The QSPI vector is the next odd numbered vector in the CPU vector table. Thus, if QIVR[7:0]=$40, the SCI uses vector $40 and the QSPI uses vector $41 for interrupts. The two fields ILQSPI and ILSCI in register QILR define the CPU interrupt level for the QSPI and the interrupt level for the SCI, respectively. The CPU levels are independent and each has the range from $0 (disabled) to $7 (highest priority).

Table 12.4 also defines the specific selections and the registers involved when the submodules are initialized. The submodule initialization defines the serial communications parameters used by either submodule. Section 12.3 gives specific examples of SCI initialization. Section 12.4 describes initialization of the QSPI.

Example 12.1

Figure 12.4 lists a short sequence of instructions to initialize the QSM global registers. In an actual product, the initialization instructions would be part of a complete initialization routine. For convenience, the QSM global initialization program is treated separately here. The program segment starts at location QSMINIT. It is assumed that the module base address for the register set is location $FFF000 in the system memory. The register address in the program added to the offset REGBASE gives the address of the register. Notice that if REGBASE is defined to be $0 and the program is reassembled, the initialization program could be used if the QSM registers were located beginning at address $7FFC00.

The first MOVE instruction initializes the QSM configuration register (QMCR) to select both supervisor and user mode access to the other QSM registers since SUPV={0}. The instruction also initializes the interrupt arbitration (IARB) field to assign arbitration level 1 for the QSM. This selection gives the QSM the lowest priority if two or more modules simultaneously request an interrupt at the same CPU priority level. The MC68332 modules arbitrate the simultaneous interrupt request as explained in Section 15.2.

The interrupt levels and vector number of the QSM are initialized next. The vector number for the SCI is selected as $40 (QIVR[7:0] = $40). The value $40 (64) selects the

```
abs. rel.   LC    obj. code    source line
---- ----   ----  ---------    -----------
   1    1   0000                         TTL      'FIGURE 12.4'
   2    2   0000               *
   3    3   0000               *     INITIALIZATION OF GLOBAL REGISTERS OF QSM
   4    4   0000               *
   5    5   4200                         ORG      $4200          ;GLOBAL QSM INITIALIZATION
   6    6   0000               *
   7    7        0080 0000     REGBASE   EQU      $800000                 ;MODULE REGS AT $FFF000
   8    8   4200               *
   9    9        00FF FC00     QMCR      EQU      $7FFC00+REGBASE         ;CONFIGURATION REGISTER
  10   10        00FF FC04     QILR      EQU      $7FFC04+REGBASE         ;QILR-QIVR
  11   11   4200               *
  12   12   4200               *     INITIALIZE QMCR, QILR-QIVR
  13   13   4200               *     SUPV={0}, IARB=1
  14   14   4200               *     QSPI LEVEL=3, SCI LEVEL=2, VECTOR=$40
  15   15   4200               *
  16   16   4200 33FC 0001     QSMINIT   MOVE.W   #$0001,QMCR    ;USER/SUPV ACCESS;IARB=1
  16        4204 00FF FC00
  17   17   4208 33FC 1A40               MOVE.W   #$1A40,QILR    ;QILR QSPI=LEVEL3; SCI=LEVEL2
  17        420C 00FF FC04
  18   18   4210               *                                ;QIVR VECTOR $40;
  19   19   4210               *
  20   20   4210 4E75                    RTS                     ;RETURN
  21   21   4212                         END
```

Figure 12.4 Program example of QSM global initialization.

vector at offset location $100 in the CPU vector table shown in Figure 11.2 or Table 11.8. The QSPI vector number is $41 because the QSPI vector always follows the SCI vector in the CPU vector table. The reader is referred to Section 11.7 for a discussion of the interrupt vectors.

The same instruction selects the vector and the CPU interrupt levels as level 3 for the QSPI and level 2 for the SCI. This is all accomplished by one MOVE.W instruction since the registers QILR-QIVR form a 16-bit register at location $FFFC04 in this example. Vector $40 at offset address $100 and vector $41 at location $104 in the CPU vector table must contain the starting addresses of the interrupt handling routines before the QSM interrupts are enabled.

EXERCISES

12.1.1. With reference to Figure 12.3 and Table 12.3, determine the state of the QSM after a reset.

12.1.2. Determine the register and the bits to be programmed to initialize the following:
   (a) set QSM interrupt arbitration to level 5;
   (b) allow user access to QSM registers;
   (c) define the interrupt level of QSPI as level 4;
   (d) select vector $51 for the QSPI interrupt to the CPU.

12.2 DATA TRANSFER TECHNIQUES AND SERIAL COMMUNICATION

This section introduces the Queued Serial Module (QSM) as it is used for serial data transfer. The QSM acts under control of a CPU program to transfer data between an external device and the module's internal storage area. However, before any transfer can occur between the QSM and an external device, the QSM submodule involved must be initialized. Once the transfer is completed, the SCI or the QSPI indicates this for the CPU program in a status register or by causing an interrupt. Programming and data transfer techniques for the QSM are presented in Subsection 12.2.1.

Subsection 12.2.2 defines the techniques and terms pertaining to serial I/O transfer between the QSM submodules and external devices. These definitions are presented to help the reader understand the operation of the SCI and the QSPI as described in Section 12.3 and Section 12.4 respectively.

12.2.1 The QSM and Data Transfer Techniques

A CPU program writes commands, reads status and transfers data to and from the QSM via the intermodule bus (IMB) of the MC68332. Figure 12.5 shows a simplified diagram of the functional connection between the CPU and the QSM. The data signal lines of the IMB are used to transfer commands, data, and status. The diagram of Figure 12.5 shows that the CPU communicates only with the QSM and not directly with the external device. This is typically the case when the MC68332 performs serial communication. The external device is connected to one of the submodules of the QSM by a serial communication channel. This channel consists of circuit conductors usually in the form of a cable which connects the QSM signal lines to the serial communications signals of the external device. The reader is referred to Section 12.1 for the definitions of the QSM signal lines.

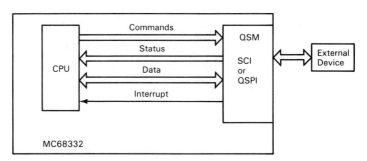

SCI   Serial Communications Interface
QSPI Queued Serial Peripheral Interface

Figure 12.5 Simplified diagram of the connection between the CPU, QSM, and an external device.

Once the global registers of the QSM are initialized, the SCI or the QSPI can perform I/O transfers. Each transfer by the SCI typically involves one ASCII character which represents the transfer of a seven or eight bit character plus several control bits over the serial channel. The QSPI can also be programmed to transfer a series of bits, whose meaning is determined entirely by the application. For output, either submodule converts the bits in a CPU register to serial form and transmits the bits when the external device is ready. For an input transfer, the bits from the external device are converted to parallel form so that the CPU program can store the input data in one of its registers or in memory. The sequence and timing of the external transfer is controlled automatically by the SCI or the QSPI as described later in this chapter.

Program controlled transfer of commands, status information, and data values between the CPU program and the QSM can occur one of several ways. The types of transfers are categorized as unconditional, conditional or interrupt-controlled.[2] Table 12.5 summarizes these transfers and describes their typical use.

Table 12.5 Data Transfer Techniques for the QSM

Type	CPU Operation	Typical Use
Unconditional	Transfer data, read status or write command	CPU write to a QSM command register for initialization or CPU read of status or CPU controlled transfer of data between QSM and CPU
Conditional	Test status of module and wait until ready; then transfer	Data transfer without interrupt control
Interrupt-controlled	(1) Transfer data or write new command when interrupt occurs (2) Clear interrupt request after transfer is complete	Data transfer between module and CPU when module is ready

Unconditional transfer.   An *unconditional* transfer is said to occur when the CPU program executes an instruction that reads or writes the contents of one of the module's registers. For example, this type of transfer results when the CPU executes a MOVE instruction using an address within the addressing space of a module. Such operations force the module to transfer data when the CPU instruction is executed.

Unconditional transfer is typically used to initialize a module's control registers after a reset or to read the value in its status register. The program of Example 12.1 shows the use of unconditional transfers to initialize the QSM global registers.

Conditional transfer.   *Conditional transfer* is similar to unconditional transfer because the CPU program controls the operation. However, conditional transfer

---
[2] These I/O transfer techniques also apply to transfers between the CPU program and external devices via the external bus of the MC68332. Chapter 14 discusses such transfers.

differs from unconditional transfer in that the module is not requested to transfer data until its status indicates that the module is ready; i.e., the module has completed its previous operation and it is ready for another operation. Correct procedure requires that the CPU program for I/O transfer test a module's status before a transfer is requested.

The CPU program first reads the contents of the module's status register to determine when the module is ready to receive a new command or to transfer the next value. When the module is ready, the CPU executes the specific instructions to cause the operation. If the CPU program continually checks status in a so-called "busy-wait" loop until the module is ready, a considerable amount of CPU execution time could be wasted since the QSM submodules transfer a value to an external device very slowly compared to the rate at which the CPU can execute instructions for I/O transfer. To avoid the delay caused by conditional I/O, interrupt-controlled transfer is preferred in many applications.

Interrupt-controlled transfers. *Interrupt-controlled transfer* as illustrated in Figure 12.6 can be used for transfers between the CPU and the SCI or QSPI. For input transfers, the data received from an external device are transferred from the submodule involved to the CPU by instructions in the interrupt handling routine. During output, the data written by the interrupt routine to the submodule could be data to be transmitted to an external device or the values could be commands to the submodule.

As shown in the Figure 12.6, the submodule first must be initialized to allow interrupt-controlled transfers. When the SCI or QSPI finishes its current operation, an interrupt occurs and control is passed to an interrupt-handling routine. The routine typically transfers data, and then resets (clears) the interrupt request. If an error is detected, the routine takes the appropriate action according to its design. After the interrupt handling routine completes execution, control is returned to the program that was interrupted. While a submodule actually transfers data to or from an external device, the CPU is free to execute another program. This allows the CPU and the submodule to operate independently except when the interrupt handling routine is executing. The increased time that the CPU is available to execute other programs as compared to that for conditional transfer is the principal advantage of interrupt-controlled transfer.

In the case of the QSM, the SCI and the QSPI would have separate interrupt routines since these submodules operate independently of each other. Section 12.3 and Section 12.4 explore these considerations in more detail.

12.2.2 Serial Data Transfer

Serial data transfer refers to a communication method which transmits one data bit at a time via a single conductor. The stream of bits transmitted is encoded electrically according to the particular method used. A serial shift register connected to the signal conductor holds the data bits to be sent and those received. These data bits are stored in a CPU register or in memory in parallel form.

Figure 12.7 shows a simplified block diagram of the MC68332 circuitry needed for serial communication. For output, circuits convert data from the parallel form

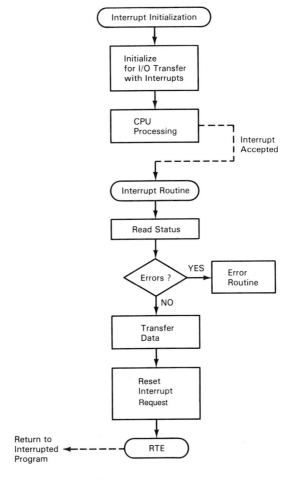

Figure 12.6 Interrupt-controlled transfer.

stored in memory to serial data for transmission. Bits received in serial fashion are accumulated and stored in parallel form. The series of bits is sent to or received from an external device not shown in the figure. The precise characteristics of the serial bit stream being transferred depends on the particular serial communications scheme employed. The scheme is defined by the protocol used, the signaling characteristics, and the physical characteristics of the interfaces involved.

In serial transmission, the receiver must sample the signal at precise time intervals to determine whether a data bit is a {1} or a {0}. To do so, the receiver must know exactly when a transmission starts and stops. These and other issues are specified by a precisely defined set of rules for data transmission that are often called *protocols*. Standard protocols have been defined for both asynchronous and synchronous methods of transfer.

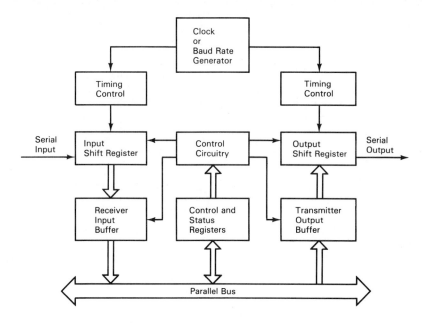

Figure 12.7 Serial data communication circuitry.

Asynchronous and synchronous communication.   In *asynchronous communication*, information is transmitted as individual data items bracketed by a start bit and either one or two stop bits. A typical example is shown in Figure 12.8(a) for the transmission of 8 data bits bracketed by one start bit and one stop bit. This format could be used to transmit an ASCII character plus a parity bit.[3] The complete sequence of bits is called a *frame*.

Some interfaces, such as the SCI of the Queued Serial Module, allow a ninth bit to be added to the data frame. The format for each frame with the added bit is shown in Figure 12.8(b). The extra bit is used for communication between master and slave devices as will be described in Section 12.3.

The time between frames is called the *idle time* and it may vary from frame to frame. Figure 12.8(a) shows three idle bits after the nth frame. No idle bits between frames are shown in Figure 12.8(b). A frame is detected by the receiving device when the signal voltage drops from HIGH (logic {1}) to LOW (logic {0}) as the start bit is recognized. This synchronizes the frame between receiver and transmitter. However, the transmission method is called *asynchronous* because the receiver and transmitter have separate clocks which are not synchronized in time. As described in Example 12.2 and Example 12.3, the clocks determine the bit transmission rate (baud rate).

After the start bit is recognized, the receiver must determine the location of each bit boundary and sample the value. The receiver does this by measuring the voltage of the input signal a fixed number of times during the period of each bit. The bit is stored as a {0} or a {1} according to the results of the measurement. Subsection 12.3.1

---

[3] Section 8.3 presented a program example to add a parity bit to an ASCII character.

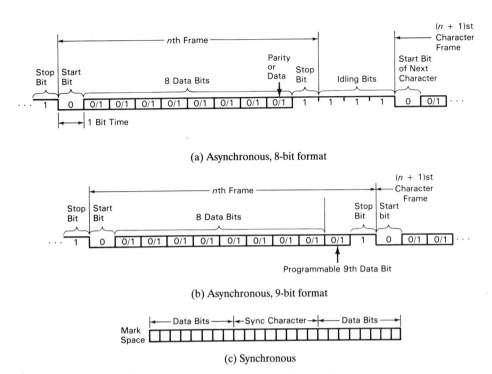

(a) Asynchronous, 8-bit format

(b) Asynchronous, 9-bit format

(c) Synchronous

Figure 12.8 Asynchronous and synchronous frame formats.

explains the relationship between the receiver clock frequency and the baud rate for the SCI.

The asynchronous method is often used for data transmission between a computer and a low-speed peripheral device such as an operator's terminal or printer. Since start and stop bits are needed in every frame, the method is not generally as efficient for the transfer of information as synchronous transfers.

In *synchronous communication* information is transmitted in blocks. A possible format is shown in Figure 12.8(c). The receiver and transmitter clocks are synchronized in time because a clock signal is transmitted along with the data. The clock signal can be sent on a separate conductor or it may be encoded with the data in a self-clocking scheme. In either case, the start and stop bits of asynchronous transfer are eliminated. There is no idle time between blocks, but when no data are being sent a "sync" (synchronizing) character is transmitted. The receiver's clock is thus always synchronized with the transmitter's clock. Very high transmission rates can be achieved reliably as compared to asynchronous transfer.

Signaling Characteristics. Once the type of format for serial data transmissions is selected, the signaling characteristics must be defined.[4] Two important

---

[4] Encoding techniques and other characteristics of the signal are discussed in several of the references cited in the Further Reading section of this chapter. One common encoding technique for asynchronous communication is termed non-return-to-zero (NRZ).

parameters are the bit rate measured in bits per second and the digital encoding technique.

Since the bit is the smallest unit of information for serial communications, the signaling speed is defined in terms of bits per second transmitted. This is frequently called the *baud rate* when only two-level signaling is used.[5] The baud rate is the reciprocal of the length (in seconds) of the shortest element in the signaling code. If more than two voltage levels are used in transmission, the bit rate is higher than the baud rate.

Example 12.2

The baud rate for two-level signaling is the reciprocal of the time duration of a bit. The frequency of the transmitter and receiver clocks determine the baud rate for an asynchronous communications channel. The clocks must not differ in frequency by more than several percent or transmission errors may result. At 9600 baud for example, each bit has a duration of 1/9600 seconds or about 0.104 milliseconds. A frame of 10 bits thus requires about a millisecond to be received or transmitted. This rate would allow the transmission of 1000 ASCII characters per second.

In applications using the SCI for interrupt controlled transfers, the CPU would be interrupted after each character is received. The interrupt handling routine would read the character from the SCI receiver's input register and store it in memory. For transmission, the CPU is interrupted each time the transmitter is ready for a new character. The interrupt handling routine must transfer each character from one of the CPU registers or memory to the transmitter's output register for transmission.

Since the parallel registers of the SCI hold only one character, the CPU is involved in each transfer. However, at the transfer rates typically used by the SCI, only a small percentage of the CPU's time is spent servicing the interrupts. The QSPI can provide even more efficient operation since it has a buffer area in the form of a queue that stores up to 16 data values for transmission and reception. It is straightforward to calculate the percentage of time used by the CPU for transfers when the transfer rate and the duration of the interrupt handling routine is known. Several of the exercises at the end of Section 12.2 require this calculation.

The baud rate for the SCI and QSPI is derived from the system clock. The rate is programmable for the SCI between 64 baud and 524,000 baud with a 16.78MHz system clock. A signaling rate of between 33kHz and 4.19MHz is possible for the QSPI. The baud rate of the SCI and the signaling rate of the QSPI correspond to the number of bits per second that are transmitted or received.

QSM electrical characteristics. The input and output pins of the SCI and QSPI operate with a logic HIGH of +5 volts and a logic LOW of 0 volts when the power supply voltage is +5 volts. These voltage levels are appropriate for data transmission between microcontrollers. Signal lines from one SCI serial port, for example, can be connected directly to another SCI port without any intervening circuitry. The connection is described in Section 12.3.

When the MC68332 SCI is used as a UART (Universal Asynchronous Receiver Transmitter) port, the voltage levels from the SCI must be translated to those of the

---

[5] Baud is a contraction of the surname of J.M.F. Baudot according to the *Encyclopedia of Computer Science*, Van Nostrand Reinhold Company, 1976. Baudot invented a French telegraph code adopted in 1877.

peripheral interface if the interface requires different voltage levels. Also, the physical connection must be considered if a cable is used to connect the peripheral device to a microcontroller-based product. A widely employed standard for such communication is the EIA RS-232C (Electronic Industries Association recommended standard 232C). This standard defines the voltage levels for signaling and the physical connection required to meet the standard. The author's BCC system described in Section 10.3 contains an RS-232 interface chip to connect the BCC to an operator's terminal.

The QSPI is typically used for communication between the MC68332 and peripheral chips or other microcontrollers with QSPI compatible interfaces. When used in this manner, no additional interfacing circuitry is required. Section 12.4 discusses connections between the QSPI and compatible devices.

EXERCISES

12.2.1. Compare interrupt-controlled and conditional transfer of data with respect to each of the following:
(a) system speed of operation;
(b) programming complexity;

12.2.2. Describe the program and system operation for a conditional I/O transfer routine when a string of characters is to be transferred. If a character is ready from an external unit every 0.1 second, compute the time required to input 10 characters if the CPU processing time is 10^{-5} seconds per character. What is the percentage of time the CPU is idle waiting for a character? This timing is typical for an operator's terminal transferring data at 110 baud.

12.2.3. Suppose an asynchronous transfer requires 11 bits per frame to transmit a seven bit ASCII character. If the transfer rate is 1200 baud, calculate the following:
(a) the overhead in percent used by the control bits for each character;
(b) the actual transmission rate in characters per second.

12.2.4. Consider an asynchronous transmission in the full-duplex mode (simultaneous transmission in both directions) at 1200 baud. The format is seven bits plus parity per character with one start and one stop bit. If interrupt-controlled transfer is used, calculate the following:
(a) the number of characters per second that are transmitted and received;
(b) the time the CPU has to respond to an interrupt indicating that the receiver buffer is full;
(c) the percentage of CPU time taken servicing the interrupts if each interrupt routine requires 10 microseconds to execute.

12.2.5. Answer the questions in Exercise 12.2.4 if the baud rate is 500,000 baud for the system.

12.3 THE SERIAL COMMUNICATION INTERFACE

This section describes the Universal Asynchronous Receiver Transmitter (UART) of the Serial Communications Interface (SCI). The interface can be used to connect an operator's terminal to an MC68332-based product. In other applications, the interface allows several computers or a network of microcontroller units (MCUs) to be connected to form a serial communications network. Units in such a network can be widely distributed which is the advantage of a UART type of interface.[6] For short connections, the other serial interface of the MC68332 designated as the QSPI is used for synchronous serial communication. Section 12.4 describes the QSPI in detail.

Subsection 12.3.1 describes the SCI register set and initialization techniques to set the baud rate and other parameters for serial communication. Next, Subsection 12.3.2 discusses the use of the SCI as a UART device. Subsection 12.3.3 explains the use of the SCI for serial I/O expansion of the MC68332. The last subsection also describes the capability of several MCUs or other devices to communicate with the SCI.

12.3.1 SCI Operation

The serial communications interface (SCI) is one of the two submodules that form the Queued Serial Module. The QSM was described in Section 12.1. In particular, the initialization procedure for the global registers of the QSM was treated there. Once initialized, the SCI and QSPI submodules are available for serial communications applications. The present subsection describes the programming techniques needed for the SCI and gives examples of its use.

The SCI is a full-duplex, UART type of asynchronous serial interface. Thus, transmission and reception can occur simultaneously. Although the transmitter and receiver section are effectively independent for data transmission, they must employ the same baud rate and data format. The format for this protocol allows one start bit, eight or nine data bits and one or two stop bits in a frame. The allowed frames have a total of either 10 or 11 bits.

The basic features of the SCI are listed in Table 12.6. This subsection describes each of the major features. For those readers familiar with Motorola's 8-bit MCUs, the SCI of the MC68332 is an enhanced version of the serial communication interface of the MCUs in the M68HC11 and M68HC05 families.

SCI register set.   Figure 12.9 and Figure 12.10 show a simplified block diagram of the SCI indicating the registers involved in serial communication. For convenience, the complete register set of the QSM was shown in Figure 12.3 with a definition of each bit given in Table 12.3 of Section 12.1. The discussion here concerns the control, status and data registers of the SCI.

---

[6] The UART was developed to allow reliable serial data transmission between a computer and its peripheral devices. In general usage, the term UART means a single-chip integrated circuit to implement serial communication. The Motorola MC6850 Asynchronous Communications Interface Adapter (ACIA) is a typical example.

Table 12.6 Features of the SCI

Feature	Use
General:	
Standard SCI	Assures compatibility with other MCUs
Full-duplex operation	Allows simultaneous transmission in both directions
Programmable baud rate	Selection from 64 baud to over 500,000 baud
Programmable data word length	Allows selection of data format
Separate transmitter and receiver enable bits	Allows independent use of transmitter and receiver
Separate transmitter and receiver interrupt enable	Allows interrupt-controlled data transfers
Optional parity bit generation and detection	Enhances reliability
Double-buffered operation	Prevents overrun errors
Receiver:	
Extensive error detection capability	Allows various errors to be detected during transmission
Idle-line detection and receiver active flag	Adds efficiency and reliability to network communication
Transmitter:	
Transmit complete bit	Enables the program to determine when the transmitter is not busy with external transmission
Programmable idle frame or break frames	Allows notification of idle state or a break to external device

The diagrams of Figure 12.9 and Figure 12.10 indicate that the receiver and transmitter are independent with respect to the data registers, the status bits and the interrupts. Figure 12.11 presents the registers of the SCI involved in data transfer. The baud rate for both receiver and transmitter is defined by writing a value into Control Register 0 (SCCR0) shown in Figure 12.11. Control Register 1 (SCCR1) is used to select the data format and other features of the SCI. The Status Register (SCSR) is read to determine the status after a value is sent or received.

The data registers are at the address of SCDR ($YFFC0E) for both transmitter and receiver. The Receiver Data Register (RDR) is a read-only register to hold a value received over the serial channel. A value to be transmitted is first written to the write-only Transmitter Data Register (TDR). The transmitter then sends the bits out in a serial form, adding any additional bits needed to complete a frame. The status flags in SCSR are used by a CPU program to determine when the receiver and transmitter have completed an operation and are ready for the next operation.

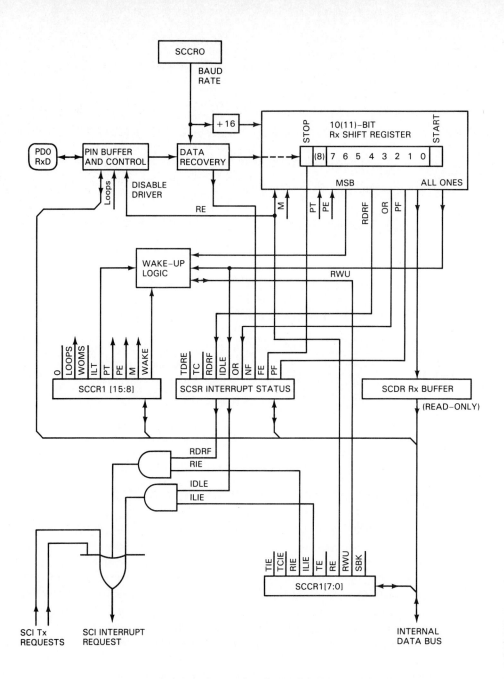

Figure 12.9 SCI Receiver Block Diagram.

SCI baud rate. Since the SCI receiver operates asynchronously, the SCI requires an internal clock to synchronize itself to the incoming data bit stream. As shown in Figure 12.12, the baud rate generator is derived from the system clock to yield a

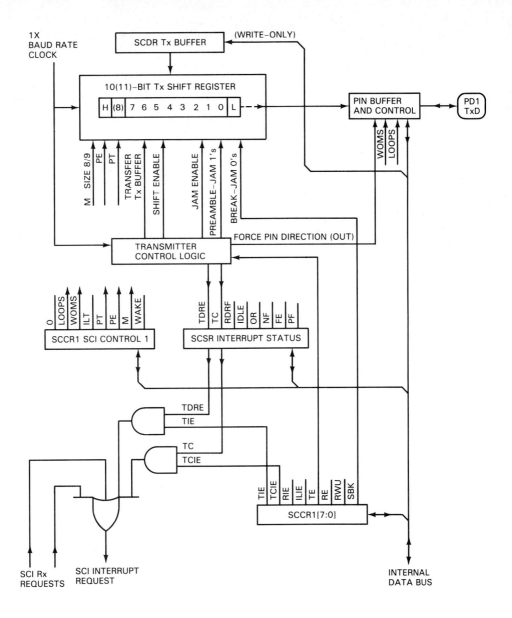

Figure 12.10 SCI Transmitter Block Diagram.

sampling rate corresponding to sixteen times that of the baud rate selected.

For example, if the receiver clock is set to measure the value on the input line 16 times during the time each bit is present, the receiver can count 24 clock periods after the starting edge of the start bit to find the center of the first bit. This scheme allows the receiver to capture the value close to the middle of the data bit. After this, the receiver samples and captures each bit value until the stop bit occurs. The main requirement

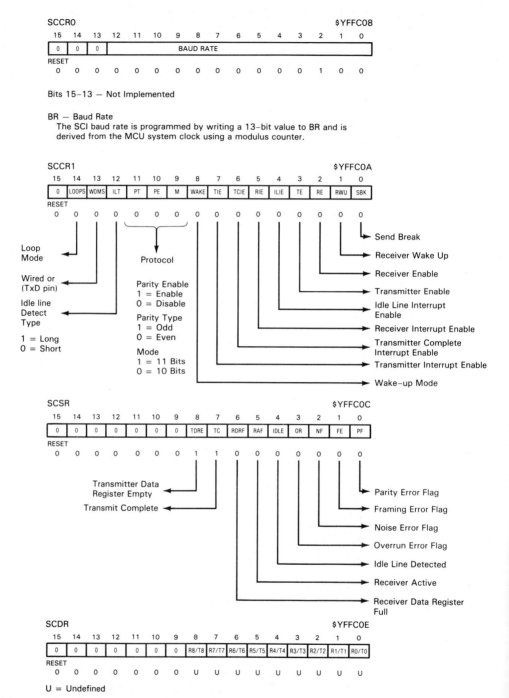

Figure 12.11 SCI register bits.

for success of this scheme is that the receiver's clock frequency (number of pulses per second) is close to that of the transmitter's clock. A small difference error of 1% or 2% can be tolerated in most systems. The SCI actually uses a more sophisticated method to sample the bit value to reduce the possibility of error in transmission. The reader is referred to the *MC68332 User's Manuals* for further information about the sampling scheme used by the SCI.

The baud rate for the SCI is set by writing SCCR0[12:0] with the appropriate value as defined in Table 12.7. The table assumes that the clock frequency is 16.7772MHz; i.e., 2^{24} Hertz.

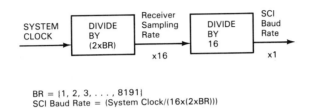

BR = {1, 2, 3, . . . , 8191}
SCI Baud Rate = (System Clock/(16x(2xBR)))

Figure 12.12 Baud rate generation of SCI.

Table 12.7 Baud Rates of SCI

Nominal Baud Rate	Actual Baud Rate	Percent Error	Decimal Value Of BR	Hexadecimal Value of BR
500,000	524,288	+4.86	1	$1
38,400	37,449.14	−2.48	14	$E
32,768	32,768.00	00.00	16	$10
19,200	19,418.07	+1.14	27	$1B
9,600	9,532.51	−0.70	55	$37
4,800	4,809.98	+0.21	109	$6D
2,400	2,404.99	+0.21	218	$DA
1,200	1,199.74	−0.02	437	$1B5
600	599.87	−0.02	874	$33A
300	299.94	−0.02	1748	$694
110	110.01	+0.01	4766	$129E
64	64.00	+0.01	8191	$1FFF

Notes:
1. The system clock frequency is 2^{24} Hz.
2. BR is the value to be used in SCCR0[12:0].

Example 12.3

The baud rate of the SCI is calculated as

$$\text{SCI baud} = \text{clock frequency}/(32 \times \text{BR}) \qquad (12.1)$$

where the clock frequency is in Hertz and BR is the appropriate divisor. The nearest integer to that calculated in Equation 12.1 would be used to set the baud rate in SCCR0[12:0].

The integer range of BR is $[1, 2, 3, \ldots, 8191]$. Values in Table 12.7 were calculated with a system clock frequency of 2^{24} Hertz.

The maximum baud rate is

$$\text{SCI baud} = 2^{24}/(32)(1) = 524,288 \quad \text{baud.}$$

Corresponding to this rate is the standard (nominal) baud rate of 500,000 baud. The SCI baud rate is slightly high. The percentage error is

$$\frac{(524,288 - 500,000)}{500,000} \times 100 = 4.86\%.$$

SCI data Format. The SCI is capable of transmitting and receiving either ten or eleven bits per frame according to the selection made in SCCR1. Figure 12.8 shows the general frame formats for 8-bit and 9-bit data. The selection is controlled by the Mode select (M) bit, SCCR1[9], and the Parity Enable (PE) bit SCCR1[10]. Possible choices are summarized in Table 12.8. The frames with M = {0} have a total of 10 bits. If PE = {1}, parity is enabled. The Parity Type bit PT, SCCR1[11], selects even or odd parity. Transmission of ASCII characters with parity, for example, would use a start bit, seven data bits, a parity bit and one stop bit.

Table 12.8 Data Formats of the SCI

Bits in SCCR1 M	PE	Format
0	0	start bit, seven data bits, two stop bits; start bit, seven data bits, address bit, stop bit; start bit, eight data bits, stop bit
0	1	start bit, seven data bits, parity bit, stop bit
1	0	start bit, seven data bits, address bit, two stop bits; start bit, eight data bits, two stop bits; start bit, eight data bits, address bit, stop bit
1	1	start bit, eight data bits, parity bit, stop bit

Note:
If parity is enabled (PE = {1}), then PT = {1} selects odd parity and PT = {0} selects even parity in bit SCCR1[11].

If parity is disabled, either seven-bit or eight-bit coding could be used for each character. The standard ASCII character set as defined in Appendix I can be coded in seven bits. Two stop bits can be programmed in a frame by setting the last data bit to {1} for every frame. Program examples will be given in Subsection 12.3.2. Subsection 12.3.3 describes the use of the address bit.

SCI status register SCSR. The SCI status register in Figure 12.11 holds status flags that indicate the status of the receiver and transmitter. The bits held in SCSR[6:0] define the receiver status. Any bit set to {1} indicates the status defined in Figure 12.11. For example, the receiver is in use when the RAF bit is {1}. The Receiver Active Flag (RAF) is set when the receiver is monitoring the serial input line. The Receiver Data Register Full flag (RDRF) is set when the received data value in the input serial shifter is transferred to the Receiver Data Register RDR. The CPU program controlling the SCI can read the received value after RDRF={1} and then clear RDRF. An overrun error occurs if the RDRF flag is not clear when a new data value is received from an external device. The meaning of the receiver status bits is discussed in more detail when the receiver operation is explained later in the chapter.

The status bits for the transmitter are held in SCSR[8:7]. The Transmitter Data Register Empty flag (TDRE) is set to {1} after the data value in the Transmitter Data Register (TDR) is transferred to the output serial shifter. A new value can be written to the TDR after the CPU program reads the SCSR. The Transmit Complete flag (TC) is set to {1} by the SCI when the transmitter finishes shifting out all the bits for a transmission. Even though the transmitter may be disabled before the last valid character is completely transmitted, the SCI is designed to finish the transmission successfully. These bits are discussed in more detail when the transmitter operation is described later.

To clear any receiver status flags that are set to {1}, the SCSR must first be read by a CPU instruction. Then, the RDR must be read to clear the receiver status bits. To allow TDRE or TC to be cleared by the SCI transmitter as it operates, SCSR must be read first. A subsequent write to the TDR causes TDRE and TC to be set to {0} until the data value is transferred to the output shifter and the transmission is complete, respectively. This is the normal sequence of accessing the receiver data or transmitting a value by a CPU program. Thus, in most cases no extra instructions in the program are necessary to clear the receiver status flags that are set or to allow the SCI to clear the transmitter flags while the transmitter is operating.

SCI receiver operation. Once the baud rate is programmed in SCCR0, the receiver is activated by writing the appropriate bits in SCCR1. The bits that can be set in SCCR1 as shown in Figure 12.11 determine the following:
(a) data format and parity (SCCR1[11:9]);
(b) interrupts to be enabled (SCCR1[5:4]);
(c) special operation (wakeup or loop mode);
(d) receiver enable (SCCR1[2]).

When RE = {1} in SCCR1, the receiver will receive a frame of data when it is transmitted to the SCI. The SCI also can detect the presence of an idle line, indicated by a frame of continuous {1} bits. An interrupt can be caused after a frame is received if RIE = {1} in SCCR1. If ILIE = {1}, an interrupt is caused after an idle line is detected. A typical procedure for a routine to handle a receiver interrupt is shown in Figure 12.13.

The interrupt handling routine must first read the status register SCSR to determine the cause of the interrupt. Either the Receiver Data Register is full or an idle line was detected. Idle-line processing is discussed in Subsection 12.3.3. The interrupt

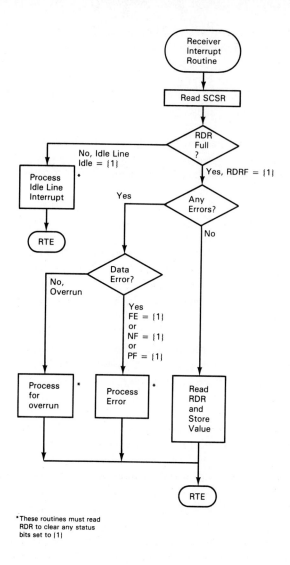

Figure 12.13 Processing by a typical receiver-interrupt routine.

caused by the Receiver Data Register Full flag (RDRF) indicates that the register contains a data value. However, as the value is received various error conditions can arise. These errors may be caused by a mismatch between the baud rate set for the receiver and a remote transmitter or by electrical noise pick-up on the communications channel. In any case, the errors that can be detected are a framing error, noise error, parity error or an overrun.

A *framing* error, indicated by FE = {1} in the SCSR, means that there was an error in the bit pattern of a received frame. This flag is set whenever the receiver detected a {0} where a stop bit should have occurred. Possible causes are a mismatch in baud rate between the transmitter and receiver or electrical noise on the signal lines. A break signal, consisting of 10 or 11 continuous {0} bits, will also cause a framing error.

When the logic level changes during the 16 samples of an input bit, a *noise* error results. The SCI samples each bit it is receiving sixteen times. If three selected samples are not at the same logic level, the noise flag is set in the status register after the entire frame is received.

The *parity* error indicates that the parity bit received is not correct for the selected parity type. This can be caused by electrical noise during transmission that changes a bit's logic level. Alternatively, it can be caused by an incorrect choice of parity type at the transmitter.

A framing error, noise error, or parity error indicates a problem with data received. In contrast, an *overrun* error occurs when a received value is ready to be transferred to the Receiver Data Register but the RDR is already full. This means that the CPU program did not read the Receiver Data Register before the next received frame was completed.

When errors occur, the error processing shown in Figure 12.13 may consist of any operations as required by a specific application. As examples, the data value could be ignored or the receiving CPU could request a retransmission of data. However, whether errors occur or not, any flag bits set in SCSR are *not* cleared until the Receiver Data Register is read by the interrupt routine. Thus, status bits cannot be inadvertently cleared by a CPU read of the SCSR. When the SCSR and RDR are read in order, the SCI is ready to receive the next frame. As previously defined, the RDR is actually the read-only register of the SCDR.

SCI transmitter operation. In normal operation, the transmitter sends 8-bit or 9-bit data values after each value is written into its Transmitter Data Register (TDR). The TDR is the write-only register at the address of the SCDR. The transmitter is enabled by setting SCCR1[3] = {1}. For interrupt-controlled transfer, the CPU program must set the Transmitter Interrupt Enable bit TIE (SCCR1[7]) to {1}. Then, the CPU program must read the SCI status register to assure that TDRE is {1} before a value is written into the TDR. The bits from TDR are then transferred to the transmitter serial shift register for output and TDRE is {0} during the transfer. The transmitter registers are double buffered so that a character can be written to the TDR while another character is being shifted out during transmission.

To indicate that the TDR is ready for the next value, the Transmitter Data Register Empty Flag (TDRE), SCSR[8], is automatically set to {1} after the value is transferred from the TDR to the serial shift register.

No errors in transmission are indicated in the status register. The start and stop bits are automatically added to the frame before it is transmitted according to the data format selected in SCCR1.

The SCI sets the Transmit Complete (TC) flag in SCSR to indicate the end of transmission. Before an external device is disabled by a CPU program, this flag should be {1}. The TDRE flag only indicates that the transmitter register TDR is ready for another character. Thus, a transmission may be in progress while TDRE={1} but TC={0}.

In addition to transmitting data, the transmitter can be programmed to output a "break" signal or an idle signal. The break is controlled by the Send Break (SBK) bit, SCCR1[0]. An idle frame called a *preamble* consisting of 10 or 11 contiguous {1} bits is automatically transmitted when the Transmitter Enable (TE) bit is changed from {0} to {1}. The use of this special signal is discussed in Subsection 12.3.3.

SCI loop mode for testing.   For test purposes, the transmitter's output can be connected to the receiver's serial shift register without changing the voltage levels on the TxD or RxD pin. This "loop" mode is entered when the LOOPS bit, SCCR1[14], is set to {1}. Data transfer programs written for the SCI can be tested without connecting external devices in this mode.

12.3.2 UART Communication

Asynchronous serial communication using the UART protocol is widely used because of the relatively simple programming and interfacing requirements. A typical connection is shown in Figure 12.14 in which the SCI is used to communicate between an MC68332-based system or product and a keyboard for input and a display unit for output. The display unit and keyboard in the figure are assumed to be completely independent to emphasize the fact that input and output data transfers are not necessarily related. For certain products, the keyboard and display could be part of an operator's terminal that is connected by an RS-232 interface. This terminal might be used only for diagnostic purposes and not be an integral part of the product.

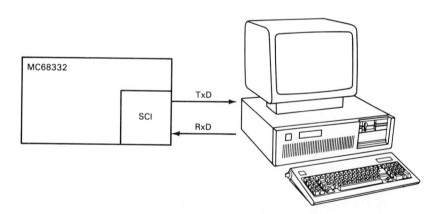

Figure 12.14 SCI connection for input and display.

The display unit could be a built-in CRT or other type of unit that is used to display computed results. In fact, it could be any type of unit that accepts the UART protocol. Line printers, motor controllers and a variety of other units are available with UART and RS-232 interfaces for connection to a computer.

Input devices that use the UART interface to transmit information to the computer include digitizers, mice, trackballs and joy sticks as well as standard keyboards.

Many of these units also are available with parallel interfaces if high speed of operation is required. Various input and output devices suitable for connection to the SCI are discussed in references listed in the Further Reading section of this chapter.

The software that is part of the product to control communications using the SCI can be conveniently divided into two categories. Routines in the first category control the operation of the SCI as it transmits and receives data. These routines include initialization routines and routines to cause specific I/O operations. Collectively, these routines are sometimes called the *I/O driver* for a specific input or output unit. The purpose of an I/O driver is to control the data transfer between an external unit and the SCI. If the product contains an operating system, the I/O drivers are typically part of the operating system software.

Programs in the second category, further removed from the hardware, are used to cause the product to perform its intended purpose. These *applications programs* cause data transfers and similar operations by calling I/O drivers. The applications programmer is freed from understanding all of the details of the hardware since the I/O driver usually performs high-level functions. For example, an I/O driver for the SCI might allow an applications program to call for the output of an entire string of characters to a CRT unit. The I/O driver instructions cause the output of each character in sequence until the string is transmitted. If the transfer is controlled by interrupts, the interrupt handler would be considered part of the I/O driver software.

Of course, the manner in which the communication function is divided between application's programs and I/O routines that are part of an I/O driver depend completely on the software design for the product. In this subsection, routines to control the operations of the SCI are presented and explained.

As previously discussed in Section 12.2, data transfers between the CPU and the SCI registers can occur via conditional transfer or interrupt-controlled transfer. The simplest type of conditional transfer would be completely controlled by the CPU as shown in Figure 12.15(a). In that figure, the CPU is shown to be idle (i.e. waiting for the I/O operation) until the SCI is ready for transfer. For transfers at 9600 baud for example, the time between transfers would be about one millisecond. This type of transfer is used only if the CPU has no other processing to do until the I/O operation is completed.

Interrupt-controlled transfers allow *concurrent* operation. The timing is shown in Figure 12.15(b). There, the I/O operations are said to occur concurrently with other computation carried out in the time between reading or transmitting a frame of data. In a single-processor system, concurrency is achieved by means of interrupts that allow other CPU processing to be suspended temporarily while the I/O operations are performed.[7] Various approaches to concurrent operation are discussed in Chapter 15.

SCI conditional I/O transfer. Conditional I/O transfer requires that both the SCI and the external device be ready for the transfer. The I/O driver routines to

---

[7] To utilize the CPU during the idle time of conditional I/O transfers, a routine could test the status of the SCI periodically to see if a transfer has completed. This method could use interrupts from a real-time clock or timer to determine when to check the status. This improves the utilization of the CPU over that of conditional transfer but is less efficient than interrupt-controlled I/O.

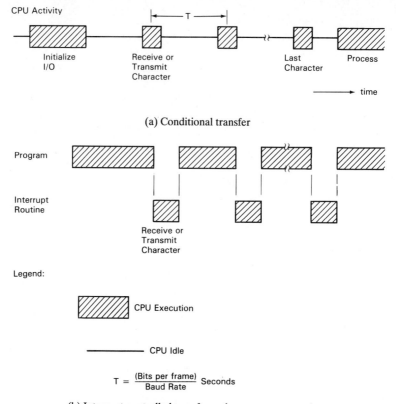

(a) Conditional transfer

Legend:

CPU Execution

CPU Idle

$$T = \frac{\text{(Bits per frame)}}{\text{Baud Rate}} \text{ Seconds}$$

(b) Interrupt-controlled transfer and concurrent operation

Figure 12.15 I/O transfer timing.

control the SCI for typical transfers must perform the operations to initialize the SCI and transfer data as follows:

(a) initialize the SCI baud rate in SCCR0[12:0];

(b) define the data format in SCCR1[11:9] and enable the SCI with options as necessary in SCCR1[9:0];

(c) test status and read the value in the receiver data register (RDR) when it is full;

(d) test status and write a value to the transmitter data register (TDR) when it is empty.

These operations might be carried out as shown in Figure 12.16 for initialization and to read or transmit data. The data items might be ASCII characters or they could be coded in another manner.

The initialization sequence in Figure 12.16 first defines the baud rate and data format for both the transmitter and receiver. An optional self test could be performed using the loop mode of the SCI by setting SCCR1[14] to {1}. If an error is detected the SCI itself is not operating properly. Once the self test is successfully completed, the SCI is ready for data transfers with a peripheral device. After initialization, any data frame sent by an external device will be received. The data bits of the frame

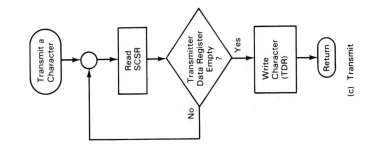

(c) Transmit

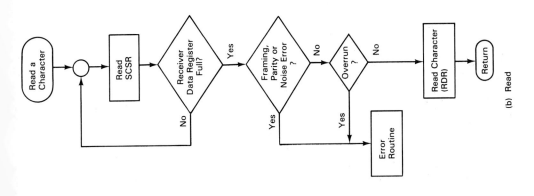

(b) Read

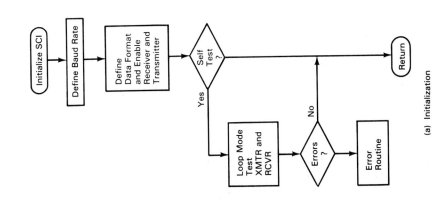

(a) Initialization

Figure 12.16 SCI operations for conditional I/O.

representing the character received will be put in the RDR of the SCI. The transmitter will transmit any character written to the TDR.

As shown in Figure 12.16(b), a routine to read and store a character must wait until the Receiver Data Register Full (RDRF) bit in the status register (SCSR[6]) is {1}. This routine should also test the error bits in SCSR[3:0]. Figure 12.16(b) shows the data error test separately from the overrun error test. Of course, a CPU program reads all of the status bits simultaneously. If a framing error, parity error, or noise error occurs, the character is invalid. The overrun error indicates that the last data value is lost. An error handling routine must determine the next procedure if one of these errors is detected. For example, the routine might request retransmission of the character if the external unit is capable of this. For peripheral units that are not computer controlled this is normally not possible and the character should be ignored. The applications program that requested the I/O operation must decide how to cope with the situation.

After a character is received, the CPU program must read the character from the RDR and store it for processing. If the status register has been read previously with RDRF set to {1}, the read from the RDR also clears the RDRF bit to allow the next character to be received.

The conditional I/O routine of Figure 12.16 for the receiver is almost identical to that for interrupt controlled I/O shown in Figure 12.13. The absence of the busy-wait loop in the interrupt handler is the major difference.

A character is transmitted as shown in Figure 12.16 when the I/O routine writes a value to the transmitter's TDR when the Transmitter Data Register Empty (TDRE) bit in SCSR is {1}. There is no indication that the transmission was successful. If the external unit has a status register, another routine not shown in Figure 12.16 must assure that the unit is ready to receive before the SCI transmits the character. As an example, the status register of a printer should be read before transmission. The printer might not be ready because it is out of paper, off-line or turned off. An I/O driver for a line printer would typically test the printer's status and display a message to the operator if the printer is not ready.

Example 12.4

Figure 12.17 shows the sequence of operations and program modules for accepting operator commands from an input unit, processing, and displaying the results. This could be used in a measuring instrument that is controlled by a human operator. When the instrument is ready for the first command, the CPU program controlling the instrument uses the SCI to display a heading message to prompt the operator. The input routine is now ready to accept a command.

Each character of the command would be transmitted to the RDR of the SCI from a keyboard or keypad and stored in memory by the input routine until the command is completed. Then, the input string of characters is compared to the valid set of commands for the instrument. If an invalid command is entered, the operator is prompted to enter another command. When a valid command is received, the instrument begins measurement and processing as required. The results would be converted to appropriate engineering units and displayed. Then, the system is ready for the next command. When the operator has completed the measurements, control is returned to the supervisor program by a method not shown in Figure 12.17. For example, the operator could push a button that causes an interrupt to exit the measurement and display loop.

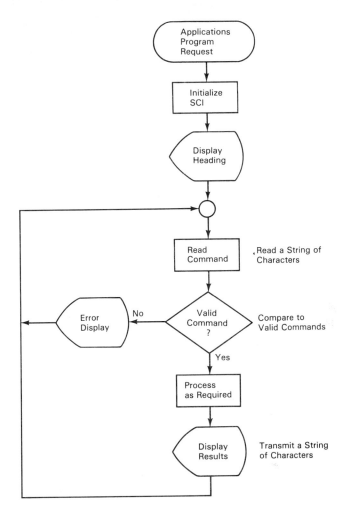

Figure 12.17 Program structure for operator-controlled processing.

In this example, conditional I/O transfer between the SCI and the input and output units is appropriate because the instrument, controlled by its MCU, cannot begin measuring and processing data until the operator's command is received. It is also assumed that display of the results cannot begin until the CPU processing of data is completed. Notice that the program modules to validate the commands, process, and display the results are executed sequentially in time. Transfer of control occurs only after a program unit has completed its task. Interrupt-controlled transfer allows a more complicated interaction between the program units as described in other examples in this textbook.

Example 12.5

Figure 12.18 shows a routine (SCIINIT) to initialize the SCI for 8-bit conditional I/O transfers at 9600 baud. Two other routines are included to read the receiver data register

```
abs. rel.   LC    obj. code    source line
---- ----   ----  ---------    -----------
   1    1    0000                     |         TTL      'FIGURE 12.18'
   2    2    0000                     |*
   3    3    0000                     |*        INITIALIZE SCI FOR CONDITIONAL I/O
   4    4    0000                     |*
   5    5    4250                     |         ORG      $4250
   6    6    0000                     |*
   7    7          0080 0000          |REGBASE  EQU      $800000           ;REGS. AT $FFFF000
   8    8          00FF FC08          |SCCR0    EQU      $007FFC08+REGBASE
   9    9          00FF FC0A          |SCCR1    EQU      $007FFC0A+REGBASE
  10   10          00FF FC0C          |SCSR     EQU      $007FFC0C+REGBASE
  11   11          00FF FC0E          |SCDR     EQU      $007FFC0E+REGBASE
  12   12          00FF FC0F          |RDR      EQU      SCDR+1
  13   13          00FF FC0F          |TDR      EQU      RDR
  14   14    4250                     |*
  15   15    4250                     |*
  16   16    4250  2F00               |SCIINIT  MOVE.L   D0,-(SP)          ;SAVE D0
  17   17    4252  33FC 0000          |         MOVE.W   #$0000,SCCR1      ;DISABLE TxD, RxD
  17        4256  00FF FC0A          |
  18   18    425A  3039 00FF          |         MOVE.W   SCSR,D0           ;CLEAR RxD FLAGS
  18        425E  FC0C               |
  19   19    4260  3039 00FF          |         MOVE.W   SCDR,D0           ; READ SCSR, THEN SCDR
  19        4264  FC0E               |
  20   20    4266                     |*
  21   21    4266                     |*        SET BAUD RATE AND ENABLE RxD AND TxD
  22   22    4266                     |*
  23   23    4266  33FC 0037          |         MOVE.W   #$0037,SCCR0      ;9600 BAUD
  23        426A  00FF FC08          |
  24   24    426E  0079 000C          |         ORI.W    #$000C,SCCR1      ;ENABLE; NO PARITY
  24        4272  00FF FC0A          |
  25   25    4276                     |*                                  ; OR INTERRUPTS
  26   26    4276  201F               |         MOVE.L   (SP)+,D0
  27   27    4278  4E75               |         RTS
  28   28    427A                     |*
  29   29    427A                     |*        READ AN 8-BIT CHARACTER AND RETURN STATUS
  30   30    427A                     |*
  31   31    427A                     |*        OUTPUTS : (D0)[3:0] =  0 : NO ERROR
  32   32    427A                     |*                            =  ERROR FLAGS
  33   33    427A                     |*                  (D1.B)    =  CHARACTER RECEIVED
  34   34    427A                     |*
  35   35    427A  3039 00FF          |INCHR    MOVE.W   SCSR,D0           ;READ SCI STATUS
  35        427E  FC0C               |
  36   36    4280  0800 0006          |         BTST.L   #6,D0             ;RDR FULL?
  37   37    4284  67F4               |         BEQ.S    INCHR             ; IF NOT, WAIT UNTIL
  38   38    4286                     |*                                  ;CHARACTER RECEIVED
  39   39    4286  0240 000F          |         ANDI.W   #$000F,D0         ; ERROR FLAGS IN (D0)[3:0]
  40   40    428A  1239 00FF          |         MOVE.B   RDR,D1            ;SAVE CHARACTER AND
  40        428E  FC0F               |
  41   41    4290  4E75               |         RTS                       ;CLEAR RDRF
  42   42    4292                     |*
  43   43    4292                     |*        TRANSMIT A CHARACTER
  44   44    4292                     |*
  45   45    4292                     |*        INPUT : (D1.B) = CHARACTER TO TRANSMIT
  46   46    4292                     |*
  47   47    4292  0839 0000          |OUTCHR   BTST.B   #0,SCSR           ;TDR EMPTY?
  47        4296  00FF FC0C          |
  48   48    429A  67F6               |         BEQ.S    OUTCHR            ; IF NOT, WAIT
  49   49    429C  13C1 00FF          |         MOVE.B   D1,TDR            ; YES, OUTPUT
  49        42A0  FC0F               |
  50   50    42A2  4E75               |         RTS
  51   51    42A4                     |         END
```

Figure 12.18 Program for SCI conditional I/O.

(INCHR) and transmit a character (OUTCHR). The routines in Figure 12.18 control the basic operation of the SCI using the registers defined in Figure 12.11.

The routine SCIINIT initializes the SCI after first disabling it and clearing the control register bits in SCCR1. Next, the routine clears any receiver status flags left set from a previous transmission. After a reset, these actions are not strictly necessary since the

SCI is disabled with receiver status flags cleared. However, it is good practice to have the initialization routine load all the registers of the MC68332 with the initial values required by an application.

To clear any receiver status bits in SCSR, the status register (SCSR) must be read first and then the data register SCDR must be read. In the program, the receiver flags are cleared using two MOVE.W instructions which read the registers in turn. Figure 12.11 or Figure 12.3 shows that the status register SCSR and the data register SCDR share the same long word location at $YFFC0C. Thus, the instruction

MOVE.L   SCSR, D0   ; READ AND CLEAR SCSR

would accomplish the same thing since two 16-bit read cycles are used by the MOVE.L instruction.

Writing a value of $37 (55) in SCCR0[12:0] then sets the Baud rate to 9600 as defined in Table 12.7. Finally, the receiver and transmitter are enabled by setting the TE and RE bits of SCCR1[3:2] to {1} with an ORI instructions. The other bits in SCCR1 are {0} including SCCR1[11:9] which selects a 10-bit frame with no parity bit. The 10-bit frame for an ASCII character would consist of a start bit, and 8-bit character and one stop bit according to Table 12.8.

The routine INCHR tests the RDRF flag (SCSR[6]) and loops until the flag is set to {1}. The contents of the status register are left in D0 each time the BTST instruction executes. Once a character is received, the routine masks bits D0[15:4] to leave the error status flags in D0[3:0] for the calling program.

The received character is then loaded into D1[7:0]. This operation also clears the Receiver Data Register Full (RDRF) flag in SCSR since the BTST instruction in the loop serves to read the status register as required to allow any bits that are {1} to be cleared. Thus, no error is indicated to the calling program if D0[15:0] is $0000.

In case of an error, the program calling INCHR must process the error indicated by a nonzero value in D0[3:0] and determine the appropriate action. If an error is detected, the received character is stored in (D1)[7:0] for analysis by calling program.

A character is output by OUTCHR when the Transmitter Data Register is empty indicated by TDRE={1} in SCSR. The BTST.B instruction reads the upper byte of SCSR and tests bit 0. After the routine moves the character in (D1)[7:0] to the TDR, the TDRE flag is cleared before the character is transferred to the transmitter's serial shifter for output to the external device. Then, TDRE is reset to {1} when the TDR is ready for another character.

To input or output a string of characters, the routines would be repeatedly called until the string is completed. The initialization routine SCIINIT would only be called once since the SCI is ready for the next operation after each data transfer using routine INCHR or OUTCHR.

SCI interrupt-controlled I/O transfer. The CPU32 interrupt capability provides an efficient and convenient means to accomplish interrupt-controlled I/O transfer with the SCI. As shown in Figure 12.15(b), the CPU is free to execute another program during the I/O transfer of a string of characters except when the service routine for the interrupt is executing. The interrupt routine for I/O is designed to be as short and efficient as possible. Thus, an output or input routine for the SCI would be designed to handle one character at a time after an interrupt occurs. However, the applications program that requests the I/O transfer is normally designed to input or output a string of characters to minimize the interaction between the applications program and the interrupt handling routine. If an I/O driver for the SCI is part of the supervisor program of a product, the applications program would call the SCI I/O driver to transfer the string.

A typical I/O driver for the SCI using interrupts would perform the following actions in the sequence:
(a) initialization including enabling SCI interrupts;
(b) transfer the first character;
(c) transfer the rest of the string using interrupt-controlled I/O;
(d) disable the SCI interrupts when the transmission is complete.

The I/O driver is called by an applications program which must define the operation as input or output and provide the starting address of the input or output buffer in memory. The buffer could be a reserved memory area to hold one string or it could be a more complicated data structure such as a queue to hold several strings.

If the applications program executes in the user mode, the I/O driver can be called using a TRAP instruction. A possible calling sequence would be

```
LEA.L       BUFFER, A0        ; ADDRESS OF STRING

TRAP        #1                ; REQUEST TRANSFER
```

where BUFFER is the starting address of a string for output or of the input buffer for input. Another approach would be to define one or more constants in-line after the TRAP instructions. This technique was described in Example 11.2. The constants following the TRAP instruction could define the request as input or output and define the starting address if it is fixed. The advantage of using the LEA instruction to load the starting address before the call is that the trap handling routine is less complicated since it does not have to find and decode the in-line constants.

Using the TRAP instruction for an I/O transfer request allows the I/O driver to be divided into separate program segments. The trap handler initializes the SCI and begins the transfer. The interrupt handler transfers the characters and disables SCI interrupts when the transfer is complete. Such a design simplifies the software structure and allows independent testing of the trap handler and the interrupt handling routine. However, several issues must be resolved if the design is to be successful.

One consideration is how the string is to be terminated so that the interrupt handling routine can determine when the last character has been transferred. Typically, an ASCII string for output is terminated by a non-printing ASCII character such as the NUL character ($00). An input string can be terminated by any convenient ASCII character. An input string from an operator's terminal, for example, is usually terminated by a carriage return ($0D) typed by the operator. The interrupt routine must test each character and stop the transfer sequence when the termination character is reached.

Another important design issue concerns the overall operation of the system. The interrupts allow I/O operations to be overlapped with computation in the sense that the CPU main program and the I/O driver operate *concurrently*. As the MC68332 is a single processor microcontroller, concurrency is achieved by allowing the main program to be suspended temporarily while the interrupt handling routine executes. This concurrency improves the execution speed for the overall system or product but introduces possible timing conflicts between the programs and routines executing concurrently.

In the simplest case of concurrency, it is assumed that the I/O driver is not shared among calling programs. Once the I/O driver is called to perform an I/O operation, the trap handling routine and the interrupt handler are considered "busy" until the entire string has been transferred. This is necessary because a calling program can easily overrun the I/O driver with I/O requests. Since the programmer who creates the calling program is not normally expected to delay requests based on the timing of the I/O driver during transfers, the I/O driver must provide an indication that it is in use. Only after an entire string is transferred, will it accept another request. The availability of the I/O driver for transfers can be indicated by a variable called a *busy flag* which is set and cleared by the I/O driver.

Example 12.6

The programs of Figure 12.19 represent part of an I/O driver that outputs a string of characters to an operator's display unit. A main program (MAIN) calls the TRAP #1 handler to output the string at address MSG1. The address is passed in register A0. This message is to prompt the operator to input a command. The call and the trap and interrupt handlers for operator input are not shown in the figure. The flag OUTBUSY is used by the trap handling routine to indicate the availability of the I/O driver routines for output.

Before the main program executes the TRAP #1 instruction, an initialization program or the program that previously called the I/O driver must clear the OUTBUSY flag. Also, the SCI global registers must be initialized as described in Example 12.1. The baud rate and other options must be specified as explained in Subsection 12.3.1. Of course, the interrupt mask in the Status Register (SR) of the CPU must be set to the appropriate level to allow the SCI to interrupt the CPU. However, the transmitter and the interrupts are enabled by the trap handling routine not by these initializing routines.

The trap handling routine (TRAP1) uses the TAS instruction described in Section 8.3 to test OUTBUSY. If the flag is clear ($00), the TAS instruction sets it to $80 and causes the first character to be transferred. The pointer STROUT contains the starting address of the output string from A0. The string begins at address MSG1 in program MAIN.

One character is output after the trap handling routine transfers the character to the Transmitter Data Register (TDR) and enables the transmitter and interrupts by setting TE={1} and TIE={1} in SCCR1. The trap routine then returns control to the calling program. In this example, the "dummy" loop at label LOOP in the main program is used to simulate processing that could occur while the string is being output.

If the I/O driver, consisting of the trap and interrupt handling routines, is busy with a transfer when called, control is not returned to the calling program. The trap handler waits in the loop at TRAP1 until the interrupt handling routine clears the OUTBUSY flag. This prevents the calling program from requesting another output operation until the entire string has been transmitted. To improve the efficiency of the system, a queue of I/O requests could be used. After each request is entered in the queue, control would be returned to the calling program until the queue is full.

As each interrupt occurs when the transmitter's data register is empty, the interrupt handler in Figure 12.19(b) tests the next character to see if it is a NUL. If not, the

```
abs. rel.   LC   obj. code     source line
---- ----   ----  ----------   -----------
   1    1   0000                        TTL     'FIGURE 12.19(a)'
   2    2   8000                        ORG     $8000
   3    3   0000              *
   4    4   8000              *          EXAMPLE MAIN PROGRAM TO OUTPUT A MESSAGE
   5    5   8000              *
   6    6        0000 000D    CR         EQU     $0D              ;CARRIAGE RETURN
   7    7        0000 000A    LF         EQU     $0A              ;LINE FEED
   8    8        0000 0000    NUL        EQU     $00              ;END OF STRING
   9    9        0000 662C    OUTBUSY    EQU     $662C            ;BUSY FLAG
  10   10   8000              *
  11   11   8000 41F9 0000    MAIN       LEA     MSG1,A0          ;REQUEST OUTPUT OF
  11        8004 8012
  12   12   8006 4E41                    TRAP    #1               ;MESSAGE 1
  13   13   8008              *
  14   14   8008 4A38 662C    LOOP       TST.B   OUTBUSY          ;DUMMY LOOP TO SIMULATE
  15   15   800C 66FA                    BNE     LOOP             ; PROCESSING
  16   16   800E              *
  17   17   800E 4E4F                    TRAP    #15              ;RETURN TO SUPERVISOR
  18   18   8010 0063                    DC.W    $0063
  19   19   8012              *
  20   20   8012 494E 5055    MSG1       DC.B    'INPUT A COMMAND: '  ;PROMPT TO OPERATOR
  20   20   8016 5420 4120
  20   20   801A 434F 4D4D
  20   20   801E 414E 443A
  20   20   8022 20
  21   21   8023 0D0A 00                 DC.B    CR,LF,NUL
  22   22   8026                         END
------------------------------------------------------------------------------
   1    1   0000              |
   2    2   6600                         ORG     $6600
   3    3   0000              *
   4    4   6600              *          TRAP #1 HANDLER;  VECTOR AT $084
   5    5   6600              *
   6    6        0080 0000    REGBASE    EQU     $800000
   7    7        00FF FC0A    SCCR1      EQU     $007FFC0A+REGBASE
   8    8        00FF FC0E    SCDR       EQU     $007FFC0E+REGBASE
   9    9        00FF FC0C    SCSR       EQU     $007FFC0C+REGBASE
  10   10        00FF FC0F    TDR        EQU     SCDR+1
  11   11   6600              *
  12   12   6600 4AF9 0000    TRAP1      TAS     OUTBUSY          ;IF BUSY, WAIT
  12        6604 662C
  13   13   6606 66F8                    BNE     TRAP1
  14   14   6608 23C8 0000               MOVE.L  A0,STROUT        ;STRING ADDRESS
  14        660C 6628
  15   15   660E 0839 0000    OUT1ST     BTST.B  #0,SCSR          ;TDR EMPTY?
  15        6612 00FF FC0C
  16   16   6616 67F6                    BEQ.S   OUT1ST           ;IF NOT, WAIT
  17   17   6618 13D0 00FF               MOVE.B  (A0),TDR         ;FIRST CHARACTER
  17        661C FC0F
  18   18   661E 0079 0088               ORI.W   #$0088,SCCR1     ;ENABLE INTERRUPT AND TxD
  18        6622 00FF FC0A
  19   19   6626 4E73                    RTE
  20   20   6628              STROUT     DS.L    1                ;STRING ADDRESS
  21   21   662C              OUTBUSY    DS.B    1                ;BUSY FLAG
  22   22   662E                         END
```

Figure 12.19(a) Program for interrupt-controlled SCI output.

character is transmitted. When a NUL character is encountered, the transmitter inter-rupts are disabled and the OUTBUSY flag is cleared. The I/O driver is ready to accept the next output request once the OUTBUSY flag is cleared.

I/O transfer with queues.   Since the SCI receiver and transmitter are char-acter oriented rather than string oriented, it is often useful to employ *buffered* I/O. This technique compensates for the mismatch in speed of operation between a CPU

```
abs. rel.   LC    obj. code    source line
---- ----   ----  ----------   -----------
   1    1   0000                          TTL       'FIGURE 1219(b)'
   2    2   7500                          ORG       $7500
   3    3   0000               *
   4    4   7500               *          SCI INTERRUPT HANDLER- OUTPUT A STRING
   5    5   7500               *              VECTOR AT $100
   6    6   7500               *
   7    7        0080 0000     REGBASE EQU  $800000
   8    8        00FF FC0C     SCSR    EQU  $007FFC0C+REGBASE
   9    9        00FF FC0E     SCDR    EQU  $007FFC0E+REGBASE
  10   10        00FF FC0F     TDR     EQU  SCDR+1
  11   11        00FF FC0A     SCCR1   EQU  $007FFC0A+REGBASE
  12   12        0000 6628     STROUT  EQU  $6628         ;ADDRESS OF STRING TO OUTPUT
  13   13        0000 662C     OUTBUSY EQU  $662C         ;BUSY FLAG IN TRAP HANDLER
  14   14   7500               *
  15   15   7500 48E7 8080              MOVEM.L A0/D0,-(SP)    ;SAVE REGISTERS
  16   16   7504 2078 6628              MOVEA.L STROUT,A0      ;STRING ADDRESS
  17   17   7508 5288                   ADDQ.L  #1,A0          ;NEXT CHARACTER
  18   18   750A 21C8 6628              MOVE.L  A0,STROUT
  19   19   750E 4A10                   TST.B   (A0)           ;IF $00, QUIT
  20   20   7510 6700 0012              BEQ     OUTDONE
  21   21   7514 3039 00FF              MOVE.W  SCSR,D0        ;ELSE, CLEAR INTERRUPT FLAG
  21        7518 FC0C
  22   22   751A 13D0 00FF              MOVE.B  (A0),TDR       ; AND TRANSMIT CHARACTER
  22        751E FC0F
  23   23   7520 6000 0010              BRA     RETURN
  24   24   7524 0279 FF3F     OUTDONE ANDI.W  #$FF3F,SCCR1   ;DISABLE TX INTERRUPTS
  24        7528 00FF FC0A
  25   25   752C 11FC 0000              MOVE.B  #0,OUTBUSY     ; AND CLEAR BUSY FLAG
  25        7530 662C
  26   26   7532 4CDF 0101     RETURN  MOVEM.L (SP)+,A0/D0
  27   27   7536 4E73                   RTE
  28   28   7538                         END
```

Figure 12.19(b) SCI interrupt handler.

program and an I/O unit. For example, the CPU program can request that strings of characters be displayed or printed much faster than the SCI can output the strings even when the SCI is operating at its maximum baud rate. To avoid having the CPU program wait until each string transfer is complete as in Example 12.6, a buffer area for output data could be used. On input, characters can be buffered until one or more strings have been received.

In one approach to buffered I/O, input data values are placed in a buffer which is maintained as a circular queue by the receiver interrupt-handling routine. For output, the main program places data in an output queue whose characters are transmitted when the transmitter interrupt handling routine executes.[8] Since there is only one interrupt level for the SCI, the I/O driver must perform at least the following:

(a) determine the source of interrupt;
(b) test the input and output queues to avoid overruns;
(c) test the output queue for an empty queue;
(d) input or output a character if possible.

The operation of routines to manipulate input and output queues are discussed more fully in Section 12.4. The QSPI submodule contains a queue and program examples in Section 12.4 illustrate its use. Many of the principles discussed for the QSPI queue would apply to queues used by an I/O driver for the SCI.

---

[8] The queues could contain pointers to character strings rather than the characters themselves.

12.3.3 SCI Wakeup Feature and I/O Expansion

The SCI has a receiver "wakeup" feature that can be used when several systems having SCI interfaces are connected together. A possible network is shown in Figure 12.20. The connection allows multiple microcontrollers to communicate using only the serial communications signals of the UART interface. In this master-slave arrangement, the MC68332 addresses the desired slave processor and communicates with it. After the selection, the other slave processors ignore the data being transferred until the master terminates the exchange and selects another slave processor. The MC68332 has two different means to select the desired slave unit.

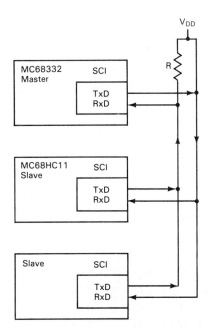

Figure 12.20 Multiple microcontroller connection using the SCI.

To begin communication, the master transmits a message to every receiver by sending an address frame at the beginning of a message. This interrupts the slave CPUs and allows their interrupt routines to determine which slave SCI is being addressed. The one being addressed receives the additional characters in the message. All of the receivers that are not addressed ignore the data frames that follow. The purpose is to have only the addressed slave CPU respond to the message from the master. The other processors are not interrupted during the transfer.

Each receiver in the network must determine if the message is addressed to it. This is accomplished by selecting the receiver wakeup feature in the appropriate control register. The registers of the SCI involved are shown in Figure 12.11. For example, the SCI of an MC68332 can be put in the wakeup mode when the Receiver Wake-Up (RWU) bit of SCCR1 is set to {1}. This would be used in a network when an MC68332 is one of the slave units. The members of the Motorola M68HC11 and MC68HC05 families of microcontrollers also have an SCI with the wakeup feature. The reader is referred to the *User's Manual* for a particular microcontroller for the specific details. The SCI of the MC68HC11 and MC68HC05 microcontrollers do not allow all the options available with the MC68332 SCI.

If the receiver wakeup feature is used in a network, the designer can select one of two possible methods as defined in Table 12.9. Motorola microcontrollers with the SCI use either the *address mark* or *idle-line* technique to wakeup a slave receiver. The selection of one or the other of the schemes depends on the type and frequency of the messages. The transmitter of the master and slave microprocessor operates in the same manner as for any transfer as far as the interrupt handling routine is concerned.

Table 12.9 Receiver Wakeup Methods

Selection	Operation
Address-mark	Receiver wakes up if the most significant bit is a {1}; the frame should contain the address of the receiver selected. If not selected, the receiver sets RWU={1} and waits for the next address mark.
Idle-line	Receiver detects 10 or 11 ones to wakeup; the next frame contains the address of the receiver selected. If not selected, the receiver sets RWU={1} and waits for the next idle-line.

Address-mark wakeup. The address-mark wakeup scheme uses the most significant bit in a transmission (eighth or ninth bit) to alert slave receivers that the frame contains an address. Thus, in Figure 12.8, the 8th or 9th bit is set to {1} by the transmitter routine. Each slave receiver set to wakeup would receive the address frame and interrupt its CPU to decode the address. This would be programmed for an MC68332 SCI by setting WAKE = {1} (SCCR1[8]), RIE = {1} (SCCR1[5]) and RE = {1} (SCCR1[2]) to enable the receiver and interrupts, and RWU = {1} (SCCR1[1]).

When the address mark bit is set in a data frame, the RWU bit is automatically cleared and the receiver interrupt handling routine determines if it was selected by decoding the address that is contained in the data bits. The selected receiver now acts as an SCI to receive characters from the master unit. If a particular receiver is not selected, its interrupt routine must set the wakeup bit RWU = {1}. This inhibits any change in the receiver status bits. Thus, the receivers not selected are effectively disabled until the next address mark frame is sent by the master transmitter. Obviously, as the master transmits characters to the selected slave unit, each data frame must have the address mark bit as a {0}. The selected slave should only transmit characters to the master's receiver upon command of the master so that no contention occurs on the shared signal lines of Figure 12.20.

Idle line detect wakeup. If the wakeup bit of the SCI control register is cleared (WAKE = {0}) and RWU = {1} to select wakeup, each slave receiver will wakeup when an idle frame is detected. The idle line consists of ten or eleven contiguous ones as selected by the mode select bit (SCCR1[9]). The idle-line interrupt enable bit (SCCR1[4]) should also be set to cause an interrupt when an idle frame is received. The master transmitter sends an idle frame when the Transmit Enable (TE) flag in SCCR1 is cleared and then set to {1} by the routine controlling the transmitter. A receiver interrupt routine for the idle-line detect wakeup scheme operates in the same general manner as that previously described for the address mark wakeup technique.

SCI wired-OR mode. The open-drain output should be selected for the slave TxD signals when they are wired together as in Figure 12.20 to avoid conflicts on the signal line. If the MC68332 is a slave, the open-drain state is selected when the Wired-OR mode bit, SCCR1[13], is {1}.

EXERCISES

12.3.1. Calculate the value of BR and the percent error from Equation 12.1 if the nominal rate is 9600 Baud. The clock frequency is 16.7772MHz.

12.3.2. If the system clock frequency is 8MHz, calculate the value for BR in Equation 12.1 to achieve 9600 Baud. What is the percent error made by rounding BR to the nearest integer?

12.3.3. What is the maximum error in percent allowed between the receiver and transmitter clocks for an 8-bit data frame with one start bit and one stop bit? The sampling clock frequency is 16 times the baud-rate frequency.

12.3.4. Complete the I/O driver of Example 12.6. Use TRAP #2 call to request an input string from the operator's terminal. The I/O driver should also handle several special cases as follows:
(**a**) set a flag if an error is recognized;
(**b**) echo the characters on the terminal;
(**c**) terminate the input when a carriage return is received and send a carriage return followed by a line feed;
(**d**) delete the previous character if a "backspace" character is received;
(**e**) terminate the input if a "break" is received.

12.3.5. Describe the difference between the address-mark and idle-line detect mode for receiver wakeup. Consider the type and frequency of messages that are best suited to each method.

12.4 THE QUEUED SERIAL PERIPHERAL INTERFACE (QSPI)

The Queued Serial Peripheral Interface (QSPI) is one of the two submodules of the Queued Serial Module. The QSPI of the QSM is used for synchronous, serial communication between the MC68332 and external devices. These devices could include analog-to-digital (A/D) converters, memories, and display drivers as well as other microcontrollers with an SPI type of interface. The queue of the QSPI is an 80 byte RAM area used for Input/Output transfers. The number of bits and other characteristics of the transfer are programmable.

The basic features of the QSPI are listed in Table 12.10. Synchronous transmission can be full-duplex using three signal conductors or half-duplex requiring only two signal conductors. The transfer rate and number of bits per transfer are selectable. In the continuous mode, up to 256 bits can be transferred in 16-bit frames using the queue. Interrupt-controlled transfer for one to sixteen transfers can be selected by the controlling program.

Table 12.10 Features of the QSPI

Feature	Use
General:	
Full-duplex or half duplex operation	Two or three conductor connection
Programmable baud rate	Transfers from 33kHz to 4.19MHz
Programmable data frame length	From 8 to 16 bits per frame
End-of-transmission interrupt bit	Allows interrupt-controlled transfers
Queue:	
80 byte RAM	For received data, transmitted data and commands
Programmable queue pointers	Up to 16 transfers without CPU intervention
Wraparound mode	Automatic, continuous transfers to and from queue
Programmable transfer length	From 8 bits to 256 bits per transfer
and continuous transfer mode	
Chip selects and transfer timing:	
Chip selects	Four chip select signal-lines (Master)
Programmable transfer delay	Selectable delay between data frames (Master)
Programmable clock phase	To interface to devices with
and polarity	different electrical characteristics
Compatibility:	
Enhanced SPI	Compatibility with M68HC11 and M68HC05 families of microcontrollers

Each queue entry contains 16 bits for received data, 16 bits for data to be transmitted and a command and control byte that will be called the *command* byte in this chapter. The command byte determines various characteristics of the data transfer when the QSPI is the master in a network. Up to 16 queue commands can be programmed with an interrupt to the CPU after all transfers are complete. In the automatic mode, called "wraparound," the queue commands will be executed again after the previous transfers are completed.

As master, the QSPI controls four chip select signal lines that select a specific peripheral device during a transfer. The four chip select signal lines can be programmed to select different external devices for each transfer. A time delay can be selected for devices that require delays between data transfers. The clock phase and polarity are programmable so that the electrical and timing characteristics of an external device can be matched. The QSPI is also compatible with the SPI (Serial Peripheral Interface) of the 8-bit microcontrollers from Motorola.

Because of its flexibility and high-speed of operation, the QSPI is ideally suited to allow I/O expansion of the system via a synchronous, serial interface. This interface is completely independent of the SCI previously discussed in Section 12.3.

Subsection 12.4.1 describes the QSPI control registers and initialization procedure. The queue and the QSPI status register are covered in Subsection 12.4.2. The final Subsection 12.4.3 explains the use of the QSPI for serial I/O expansion of the MC68332. Several program examples using the QSPI are presented in this section.

12.4.1 QSPI Registers and Initialization

Initialization of the QSM global registers as described in Section 12.1 sets the interrupt level and vector for the QSPI. The present subsection describes QSPI initialization for applications. Subsection 12.4.2 treats the queue of the QSPI and gives examples of its use.

Figure 12.21 shows a simplified block diagram of the QSPI. The interface can be programmed for master or slave operation according to the signal definitions in Table 12.2 of Section 12.1. For example, in the master mode, Master Out/Slave In (MOSI), Serial Clock (SCK) and the chip selects (PCS3–PCS0) would be programmed as outputs. Master In/Slave Out (MISO) would be used for input data. Any signal lines not used by the QSPI could be programmed for general-purpose I/O as explained in Section 12.5.

The QSPI is controlled by the register set shown in Figure 12.22. The figure also defines the byte or word address of the registers where $Y is $7 or $F as previously explained. After global initialization as described in Section 12.1, the QSPI is available for applications when the appropriate registers in Figure 12.22 are initialized. Table 12.11 lists the general steps to initialize the QSPI for an application. The order of initialization of the control registers SPCR0, SPCR2 and the queue entries in the QSPI RAM is not important. However, the QSPI should not be enabled by setting SPCR1[15] to {1} until all of the other selections have been made by the initialization program.

QSPI registers QPAR, QPDR, QDDR.   The registers QPAR (QSM Pin Assignment Register), QPDR (QSM Port Data Register) and QDDR (QSM Data Direction Register) are used to assign QSM pins (signal lines) to the QSM, define the initial states of the chip select signals, and determine the direction of each signal line, respectively. Any bit in QPAR that is {1} assigns the corresponding signal line to the QSM. A {0} assigns the pin for general-purpose I/O.

QPDR is used to assign the initial value of the QSPI signal lines that are used for output. A value of {1} in any bit of QPDR causes a HIGH as an output on the

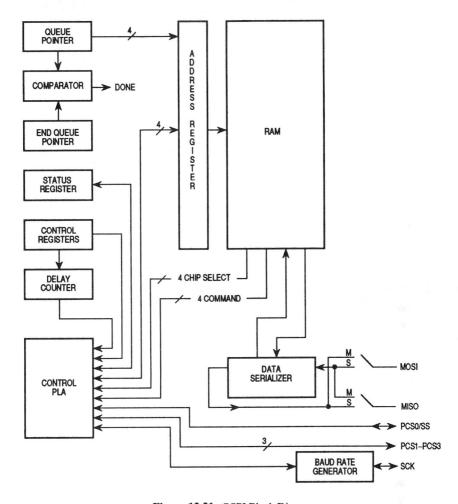

Figure 12.21 QSPI Block Diagram.

corresponding output signal line when the QSPI is enabled. A value of {0} causes a LOW output.

QDDR determines whether a signal line is an input or an output line. A {1} in any bit defines the corresponding line to be an output. A {0} defines the line as an input.

Example 12.7

Referring to Figure 12.22, the register bits of QPAR, QPDR, and QDDR must be initialized after a reset if the appropriate QSM signals are to be assigned to the QSPI. As shown in Figure 12.22, the reset assignment in QPAR assigns the pins to general-purpose I/O since all of the bits are {0} after reset. The address of QPAR is the byte address $YFFC16 where $Y is $7 or $F as determined by the SIM initialization. In examples in this chapter, the QSM register set begins at address $FFFC00. The entire QSM memory map is shown in Figure 12.2 of Section 12.1.

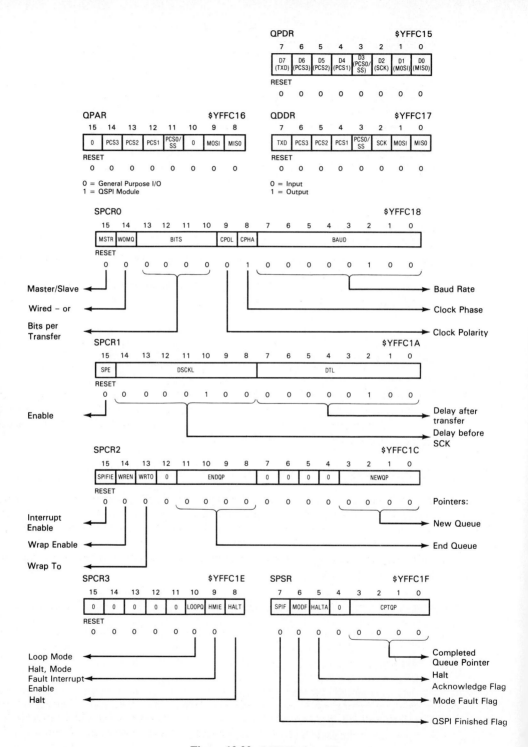

Figure 12.22 QSPI Register Bits.

Table 12.11 QSPI Initialization

Selection	Register
Assign pins to QSPI	QPAR; {1} = QSPI pin, {0} = general-purpose I/O
Define initial states of chip select signals	QPDR; {1} = HIGH, {0} = LOW
Select direction of signal lines	QDDR; {1} = Output, {0} = Input
Select master/slave , wired-or, bits per transfer, clock polarity and phase, and baud rate	SPCR0[1]
Enable interrupts if used and select queue characteristics	SPCR2, SPCR3[2]
Initialize queue with commands and data to be transmitted	QSPI queue (RAM)[3]
Enable QSPI and select transfer delays	SPCR1

Notes:
1. When the QSPI is a master, the transfer length is determined in SPCR0 only if BITSE={1} in the command byte of the queue RAM.
2. SPCR3 is used to enable interrupts for HALT and MODF (mode fault) and to select LOOP mode.
3. The command byte is used only when the QSPI is master.

The instruction

    MOVE.B   #$7B, QPAR   ; PIN ASSIGNMENT

assigns the chip select signals and MOSI and MISO to the QSPI. The serial clock signal (SCK) does not have to be assigned since SCK is used by the QSPI whenever it is enabled.
    The assignment of the initial state of the chip select lines HIGH and the serial clock (SCK) signal LOW can be accomplished with the instruction

    MOVE.B   #$7B, QPDR   ; INITIAL DATA

which does not affect the SCI TxD signal bit in QPDR. A specific initial state for the signals is defined to avoid enabling (selecting) peripheral devices as soon as the QSPI is enabled but before transfers should begin. In this case, it is assumed that peripheral devices are enabled by a LOW value on the chip select lines and that SCK is active HIGH to transfer individual bits. Thus, the opposite state is defined for the initial signal states.
    The instruction

    MOVE.B   #$7E, QDDR   ; PIN DIRECTION

assigns the chip selects, SCK and MOSI as outputs for the QSPI as master of the serial network. MISO is assigned as input. These initial values are used in program examples in this section.

QSPI control register SPCR0. As shown in Figure 12.22, the value in control register SPCR0 defines the QSPI as a master or slave device, determines certain electrical characteristics of the QSPI pins and defines the baud rate for communication. The master bit [15] must be set to {1} after a reset to define the QSPI as the master device on the serial communications channel. A {0} in SPCR0[15] assigns the QSPI as a slave device. Subsection 12.4.3 defines the electrical characteristics of the signal lines and defines the meaning of the WOMQ, CPOL, and CPHA bits in SPCR0. The value BITS is discussed later in connection with the data format for transfer.

Baud rate. The frequency of the baud rate clock is programmable in a range from 33kHz to 4.19MHz using a system clock frequency of 2^{24} Hz (16.7772MHz). The baud rate is set by writing the register field BAUD (SPCR0[7:0]) with an integer in the range [2,3,4, ... ,255]. The value determines the corresponding signal frequency that is present on the SCK signal line when the QSPI is a master device. A BAUD value of $00 or $01 disables the QSPI baud rate generator.

Example 12.8

The baud rate of the QSPI is calculated as

$$\text{SCK baud rate} = (f_{(system)})/(2 \times \text{BAUD}) \tag{12.2}$$

where the system clock frequency is defined as $f_{(system)}$. The value BAUD in Equation 12.2 is the value to be written into SPCR0[7:0] to define the baud rate. The SCK baud rate in Hertz corresponds to the frequency of the signal on the SCK signal line. This is the number of bits per second that can be transmitted and received. Table 12.12 shows the baud rate for several example values of BAUD with $f_{(system)} = 2^{24}$ Hz (16.78Mhz).
For example, the instruction

> MOVE.W   #$8054, SPCR0   ; ASSIGN MASTER AND BAUD

assigns the QSPI as master and sets the SCK frequency (baud rate) to approximately 100kHz if the system clock frequency is 16.78MHz. The SPCR0[7:0] reset value of $04 in Figure 12.22 initializes the SCK frequency to approximately 2.1MHz.

Table 12.12 Examples of QSPI Baud Rates

BAUD (Hex)	Division Ratio	Baud rate (Hz)
2 ($02)	4	4.19MHz
4 ($04)	8	2.10MHz
8 ($8)	16	1.05MHz
17 ($11)	34	493kHz
84 ($54)	168	99.9kHz
255 ($FF)	510	32.9kHz

Notes:
1. BAUD has the range [2, 3, . . ., 255]. A value of 0 or 1 disables the baud rate clock.
2. The clock frequency for the system is assumed to be 2^{24} Hz. The frequency of the SCK signal is equal to the baud rate in Hertz.

Data Format. An initialization program can define the number of bits transferred in each data frame. The selection is from 8 to 16 bits. When the QSPI is a slave device, the number of bits is specified in the field BITS of SPCR0[13:10]. The possible values of BITS are $0, $8, $9, \ldots,$ or $F corresponding to 16-bit, 8-bit, 9-bit, 10-bit, ..., or 15-bit transfers, respectively.

When the QSPI is the master, the number of bits transferred per frame can be selected in two mutually exclusive ways. As a master device, the value BITS will only be used if the bit BITSE = {1} in the command byte of the queue. In this case, the value of BITS determines the number of bits per transfer as for the QSPI as slave. However, if BITSE = {0}, the transfer size for a queue entry will be 8 bits regardless of the value of BITS. Subsection 12.4.2 describes the command byte of the queue in detail.

QSPI control registers SPCR1 and SPCR2. SPCR1 is used to enable the QSPI to begin data transfers. Setting the QSPI enable bit SPE (SPCR1[15]) to {1} causes the QSPI to begin serial transfers when the QSPI is the master. If the QSPI is a slave device, the QSPI begins monitoring the PCS0/SS signal to respond to a data transfer. In either case, the QSPI should not be enabled until a program defines all of the other register values for the QSPI.

Subsection 12.4.3 describes the time delay fields (DSCKL, DTL) in SPCR1. These values determine the timing aspects of the data transfer when the QSPI is a master.

SPCR2[15] is the QSPI Finished Interrupt Enable (SPIFIE) bit. This bit is set to {1} to allow the QSPI to interrupt after data transfers are complete. Subsection 12.4.2 describes the sources of interrupts for the QSPI. SPCR2 is also used to define characteristics of the QSPI queue as described in Subsection 12.4.2.

QSPI control register SPCR3. The bits in SPCR3 control the loop mode, halt and mode fault interrupts, and enable a halt for the QSPI. The loop mode is used to test the operation of the QSPI. The halt and mode fault conditions are described later in the text.

LOOP mode. If the LOOPQ bit in SPCR3 is set to {1}, the QSPI operates in the *loop mode* for testing. In this mode, bits output from the QSPI are transferred directly into the data serializer in Figure 12.21 rather than being treated as received data. LOOPQ = {0} for normal operation of the QSPI.

12.4.2 The QSPI Queue, Interrupts and Status Register

The QSPI contains an 80-byte area of dual access RAM that can be accessed by the QSPI and the CPU. When programming the QSPI for data transfers, this RAM area is treated as a queue with up to 16 entries, each with three distinct items per entry. Any bytes not used for the QSPI queue may be used as RAM by a CPU program. For addressing purposes when used as a queue, the RAM is divided into three segments: receive data, transmit data, and command control. Figure 12.23 shows the RAM organization and the addresses of each item. The queue structure is shown differently in Figure 12.24 to emphasize the relationship between the 16 entries in the queue.

Each queue entry contains a 16-bit receiver and transmitter word and a command byte. Thus, each queue entry should be thought of as consisting of these three parts since transmission and reception occurs simultaneously. The command byte determines the particular characteristics of a transfer when the QSPI is the master in a network of devices using serial transfer. This subsection describes the operation of the queue during data transfers, the QSPI interrupts, and the QSPI status register SPSR. Example 12.9 describes the programming aspects to initialize and use the QSPI queue. Connection of the QSPI and its use in a serial network is described in Subsection 12.4.3.

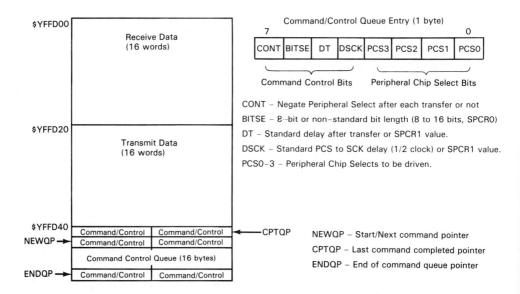

Figure 12.23 Organization of the QSPI RAM.

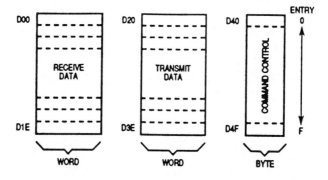

Figure 12.24 QSPI queue structure.

Operation of the queue. Before the QSPI is enabled, the CPU program initializing the QSPI must write commands into the command bytes if the QSPI is master, and also write the corresponding data to be transmitted in the transmitter queue entries. The queue pointers that define the starting and ending queue locations must also be initialized. Once a program enables the QSPI by writing {1} to SPCR1[15], the QSPI executes the commands in the queue in sequence and transmits each frame. Simultaneously, the received data frame is placed in the corresponding QSPI receiver queue entry.

During transfers, the QSPI operates on the queue using three pointers. The value in a queue pointer indicates the location of a queue entry as an offset from the start of the queue as shown in Figure 12.24. Thus, the pointers for the 16 entry queue are four bits and have values from \$0 to \$F. The pointers are defined as follows:

(a) NEWQP (SPCR2[3:0]) points to the first queue entry in the queue;
(b) CPTQP (SPSR[3:0]) points to the last queue entry used in a transfer;
(c) ENDQP (SPCR2[11:8]) points to the last queue entry in the queue.

A program must initialize NEWQP and ENDQP to define the length of the queue for each series of transfers. The QSPI updates CPTQP as it operates. When the QSPI is master and the QSPI is enabled, the commands between NEWQP and ENDQP are executed in sequence. Values are transmitted and received in each corresponding transmitter and receiver queue location, respectively. In the slave mode, received bits are stored in the appropriate receiver queue location.

At any time, the CPU program can determine which transfer has occurred by reading the Completed Queue Pointer (CPTQP) that is held in the status register (SPSR[3:0]). When CPTQP is equal to ENDQP, the QSPI stops unless wraparound mode is enabled. The wraparound mode is explained later in this subsection.

Since the queue is a circular data structure, NEWQP and ENDQP can be set to any value in the range \$0 to \$F. If NEWQP is less than ENDQP, the queue locations between the two pointers are used for data transfers. If ENDQP points to a location higher in the queue than NEWQP, the QSPI transfers data for each queue entry in sequence until the location at \$F and then continues execution at \$0 until CPTQP equals ENDQP. The reader is referred to the discussion in Section 9.3 for a more complete explanation of queues.

NEWQP and ENDQP may be written at any time to change the flow of execution of the queue commands and the length of the queue, respectively. In fact, by changing NEWQP appropriately while the QSPI is operating, the CPU program can use multiple queues in the QSPI RAM. If the reset values of NEWQP and ENDQP are left as \$0 as shown in Figure 12.22, a single transfer occurs using queue location \$0 when the QSPI is enabled.

When the QSPI reaches the end of the queue of commands, the QSPI indicates the completion in the QSPI Status Register (SPSR) shown in Figure 12.22. When all the queue entries of data have been transmitted and received, the QSPI sets the Finished flag SPIF (SPSR[7]) to {1} in the status register. An interrupt is generated if interrupts were enabled (SPCR1[15] = {1}). The QSPI clears the QSPI enable bit SPE (SPCR1[15]) and stops operation unless the wraparound mode is enabled. The programming aspects involved in clearing the status flags and interrupt request are described later.

QSPI interrupts and halt. The QSPI interrupt is enabled by setting

$$SPCR2[15] \ (SPIFIE) = \{1\}$$

in the initialization of SPCR2. The QSPI has three possible sources of interrupts but only one CPU interrupt vector. Thus, the CPU interrupt service routine must determine the source of the interrupt by reading the status bits in status register SPSR. For example, the QSPI requests an interrupt whenever the QSPI Finished Flag (SPIF) in the status register becomes $\{1\}$ when the QSPI interrupt is enabled. If the Halt acknowledge and Mode fault interrupts are enabled by setting

$$HMIE = \{1\}$$

in SPCR3, an interrupt occurs if either the Mode Fault Flag (MODF) or the Halt Acknowledge Flag (HALTA) becomes $\{1\}$ in the status register (SPSR).

In normal operation, the interrupt occurs when the QSPI finishes all the transfers in the queue. The interrupt routine should clear the source of the interrupt by reading SPSR followed by a write of $\{0\}$ to the flag in SPSR that caused the interrupt. Future interrupts are disabled by writing a $\{0\}$ to SPIFIE in SPCR2[15].

Although the QSPI registers can be written by a CPU program at any time, changing a value while the QSPI is enabled may disrupt operation. Therefore, a CPU program should write a $\{1\}$ to the HALT bit in SPCR3 to halt the QSPI on a queue boundary. The QSPI finishes the current transfer after the HALT bit is asserted and sets HALTA to $\{1\}$ (SPSR[5]). This also causes an interrupt if the halt acknowledge interrupt is enabled (HMIE=$\{1\}$) in SPCR3. If the last queue transfer has not been completed, execution continues when the CPU program clears the HALT flag. If the HALT bit is asserted during the last queue transfer, the QSPI sets HALTA and SPIF to $\{1\}$ after the transfer and disables itself by setting SPE in SPCR1 to $\{0\}$.

QSPI status register SPSR. A CPU program reads the QSPI Status Register (SPSR) to determine the status of the QSPI and the position of CPTQP in the queue. Once any one of the SPIF, MODF or HALTA status flags are set to $\{1\}$, the CPU program can only clear a flag by reading the status register value and then writing a $\{0\}$ to the bit position. The CPTQP value in SPSR is not changed by a write to the status register.

The read of SPSR required before clearing a bit can be caused by any CPU instruction that transfers the contents of SPSR to the CPU. Example instructions are BTST or a MOVE instruction with SPSR as the source operand. Also, all CPU reads of the QSPI registers transfer 16 bits to the intermodule bus even if the CPU instruction only designates the upper or lower byte of a word location. For example, Figure 12.3 shows that SPCR3 and SPSR share the same word location in the QSPI register set. Even a byte read of register SPCR3 by a CPU instruction will access the contents of SPSR and allow subsequent clearing of any status flag that is $\{1\}$ in SPSR without reading SPSR again.

For example, the Finished flag SPIF is set to $\{1\}$ by the QSPI when the QSPI finishes executing the last command in the queue. An interrupt is generated if QSPI interrupts are enabled. The bit can be cleared by the instruction sequence

```
    MOVE.B       SPSR, D0          ; READ STATUS
    ANDI.B       #$7F, SPSR        ; CLEAR SPIF
```

where SPSR has been defined previously in the program as the address of the status register. The instruction

```
    MOVE.B       #$00, SPSR        ; CLEAR SPSR[7:5]
```

will clear all of the status flags after the status register value has been read.

Example 12.9

Figure 12.25 shows programs to initialize the QSPI for master operation and perform sixteen transfers of 8-bit characters. The program MAIN in Figure 12.25(a) generates the data to be transmitted in buffer TDATA and calls the initialization routines for the QSPI. Figure 12.25(b) shows the initialization routines. When the QSPI is finished, the MAIN program stores the received data in buffer RDATA.

The data buffers TDATA and RDATA following the program MAIN are for data to be transmitted and data received, respectively. The word location SPIBUSY after the buffers holds a 16-bit flag that indicates the availability of the QSPI to other programs. The word length flag SPIBUSY is set to $FFFF ($-1$) when the program MAIN executes. Another program such as an interrupt routine should not attempt to use the QSPI while the SPIBUSY flag indicates that the QSPI is busy. The flag is cleared when the transmission is complete. QSPI interrupts are not enabled for this example.

The program MAIN stores data to be transmitted in buffer TDATA and passes the address of TDATA to the QSPI routines in A0. In this example, sixteen integers are loaded in buffer TDATA to test the programs. The JSR call to SPIINIT causes the routine SPIINIT in Figure 12.25(b) to execute and initialize the QSPI for data transfer.

QSPI initialization. Routine SPIINIT disables the QSPI in SPCR1 and clears the QSPI status flags in SPSR by first reading SPSR and then writing {0} to the status flags with an ANDI instruction. Next, QPDR is initialized to force all the chip select signals HIGH initially and SCK is LOW. During transfers, the QSPI drives PCS0 LOW to enable the peripheral device and data bits are clocked with SCK HIGH. Then, the value moved into QPAR assigns the QSM signal lines to the QSPI and the direction of the signals is defined in QDDR. Example 12.7 described the choices being made for the QSPI signal lines. Figure 12.26 in the next subsection shows a typical connection between the QSPI and several peripheral devices.

In SPCR0, the QSPI is selected as master and other characteristics of the transfer and the baud rate are defined. The QSPI is the master with a baud rate of 2.1MHz since SPCR0 is initialized with

$$SPCR0[15] = \{1\} \quad \text{and} \quad SPCR0[7:0] = \$04$$

as previously explained in Example 12.8 to select the baud rate. Since the value BITS (SPCR0[13:0]) is $0, the default transfer size would be 16 bits according to the discussion of the data format given in Subsection 12.4.1. However, the parameter BITSE in the queue command byte will determine the transfer size as described later.

In SPCR2, interrupts and the wraparound mode are disabled and the queue pointers are initialized as

$$NEWQP (SPCR2[3:0]) = \$0 \quad \text{and} \quad ENDQP (SPCR2[11:8]) = \$F$$

```
abs. rel.   LC   obj. code   source line
----  ----  ----  ----------  -----------
   1    1   0000                      |          TTL      'FIGURE 12.25(a)'
   2    2   8000                      |          ORG      $8000
   3    3   0000                      |*
   4    4   8000                      |*        TRANSFER 16 CHARACTERS WITH THE QSPI
   5    5   8000                      |*
   6    6   8000                      |*        INPUT  : RECRAM  16 CHARACTERS RECEIVED FROM QSPI
   7    7   8000                      |*        OUTPUTS: SPIBUSY= 0  NOT BUSY
   8    8   8000                      |*                       = -1 BUSY
   9    9   8000                      |*                  (A0)  = ADDRESS OF TDATA
  10   10   8000                      |*
  11   11        0080 0000  REGBASE EQU      $800000
  12   12        00FF FC1F  SPSR     EQU      $7FFC1F+REGBASE      ;STATUS REGISTER
  13   13        00FF FD00  RECRAM   EQU      $7FFD00+REGBASE      ;RECEIVER DATA
  14   14        0000 4300  SPIINIT  EQU      $4300                ;INITIALIZE SPI
  15   15        0000 4348  ENABLE   EQU      $4348                ;ENABLE SPI AND
  16   16   8000                      |*                                ; SEND CHARACTERS
  17   17   8000 48E7 C0F8  MAIN      MOVEM.L  A0-A4/D0-D1,-(SP)   ;SAVE REGS.
  18   18   8004 33FC FFFF            MOVE.W   #$FFFF,SPIBUSY      ;SET BUSY WORD
  18        8008 0000 808C
  19   19   800C 303C 000F            MOVE.W   #15,D0              ;LOAD TDATA BUFFER
  20   20   8010 4201               CLR.B    D1                  ;TEMP. DATA BUFFER
  21   21   8012 207C 0000            MOVEA.L  #TDATA,A0           ;ADDRESS OF DATA
  21        8016 806C
  22   22   8018 10C1      LDTDATA MOVE.B   D1,(A0)+            ;STORE TEST DATA IN TDATA
  23   23   801A 5241               ADD.W    #1,D1
  24   24   801C 51C8 FFFA            DBRA     D0,LDTDATA
  25   25   8020                      |*                                ;CALL QSPI:
  26   26   8020 207C 0000            MOVEA.L  #TDATA,A0           ;ADDRESS OF DATA TO TRANSMIT
  26        8024 806C
  27   27   8026 4EB8 4300            JSR      SPIINIT             ;INITIALIZE SPI
  28   28   802A 4EB8 4348            JSR      ENABLE              ;TRANSMIT AND RECEIVE DATA
  29   29   802E                      |*
  30   30   802E 0839 0007  WAIT      BTST.B   #7,SPSR             ;IF QSPI BUSY, WAIT
  30        8032 00FF FC1F
  31   31   8036 67F6                 BEQ      WAIT
  32   32   8038 267C 00FF  STORE     MOVEA.L  #RECRAM,A3          ; ELSE: STORE RECEIVED DATA
  32        803C FD00
  33   33   803E 287C 0000            MOVEA.L  #RDATA,A4           ;   AND CLEAR SPIF AND SPIBUSY FLAG
  33        8042 807C
  34   34   8044 303C 000F            MOVE.W   #15,D0              ;COUNTER FOR 16 TRANSFERS
  35   35   8048 4241                 CLR.W    D1                  ;TEMP. DATA BUFFER
  36   36   804A 321B      LDRDATA MOVE.W   (A3)+,D1            ;STORE 8-BIT DATA IN RDATA
  37   37   804C 18C1                 MOVE.B   D1,(A4)+
  38   38   804E 51C8 FFFA            DBRA     D0,LDRDATA
  39   39   8052                      |*
  40   40   8052 0239 007F            ANDI.B   #$7F,SPSR           ;CLEAR SPI FINISHED FLAG-SPIF
  40        8056 00FF FC1F
  41   41   805A 33FC 0000            MOVE.W   #$0000,SPIBUSY      ;CLEAR SPIBUSY WORD
  41        805E 0000 808C
  42   42   8062                      |*
  43   43   8062 4E71      PROCESS NOP                          ;PROCESS DATA
  44   44   8064                      |*
  45   45   8064 4CDF 1F03            MOVEM.L  (SP)+,A0-A4/D0-D1
  46   46   8068 4E4F                 TRAP     #15                 ;RETURN TO SUPERVISOR
  47   47   806A 0063                 DC.W     $0063
  48   48   806C                      |*
  49   49   806C           TDATA    DS.B     16                  ;DATA TO BE TRANSMITTED
  50   50   807C           RDATA    DS.B     16                  ;DATA RECEIVED
  51   51   808C           SPIBUSY DS.W     1                   ;BUSY FLAG
  52   52   808E                      |          END
```

Figure 12.25(a) Program example using the QSPI.

to indicate 16 transfers starting with queue location $0. After this initialization, control is returned to program MAIN. The main program then calls routine ENABLE to load the QSPI transmitter and command byte values.

In routine ENABLE in Figure 12.25(b), the first code segment defines the address pointers to the QSPI RAM and writes the data to be transmitted from the data buffer

```
abs. rel.   LC    obj. code   source line
---- ----   ----  ---------   -----------
  1    1   0000                        TTL    'FIGURE 12.25(b)'
  2    2   4300                        ORG    $4300
  3    3   0000               *
  4    4   4300               *        INITIALIZE AND ENABLE THE QSPI FOR 16 TRANSFERS
  5    5   4300               *
  6    6   4300               *        INPUT  : (A0)   ADDRESS OF OUTPUT BUFFER
  7    7   4300               *        RESULTS: RECRAM  16 CHARACTERS RECEIVED
  8    8   4300               *
  9    9         0080 0000    REGBASE EQU    $800000
 10   10         00FF FC15    QPDR    EQU    $7FFC15+REGBASE    ;PORT DATA
 11   11         00FF FC16    QPAR    EQU    $7FFC16+REGBASE    ;PIN ASSIGNMENT
 12   12         00FF FC17    QDDR    EQU    $7FFC17+REGBASE    ;DATA DIRECTION
 13   13         00FF FC18    SPCR0   EQU    $7FFC18+REGBASE    ;CONTROL REG. 0
 14   14         00FF FC1A    SPCR1   EQU    $7FFC1A+REGBASE    ;CONTROL REG. 1
 15   15         00FF FC1C    SPCR2   EQU    $7FFC1C+REGBASE    ;CONTROL REG. 2
 16   16         00FF FC1E    SPCR3   EQU    $7FFC1E+REGBASE    ;CONTROL REG. 3
 17   17         00FF FC1F    SPSR    EQU    $7FFC1F+REGBASE    ;STATUS REGISTER
 18   18         00FF FD00    RECRAM  EQU    $7FFD00+REGBASE    ;RECEIVER DATA
 19   19         00FF FD20    TXDRAM  EQU    $7FFD20+REGBASE    ;TRANSMITTER DATA
 20   20         00FF FD40    CMDRAM  EQU    $7FFD40+REGBASE    ;COMMAND DATA
 21   21   4300               *
 22   22   4300  48E7 8000    SPIINIT MOVEM.L D0,-(SP)          ;SAVE REGS.
 23   23   4304  0279 007F            ANDI.W  #$7F,SPCR1        ;DISABLE QSPI AND
 23        4308  00FF FC1A
 24   24   430C  1039 00FF            MOVE.B  SPSR,D0           ; CLEAR FLAGS
 24        4310  FC1F
 25   25   4312  0239 0000            ANDI.B  #$00,SPSR
 25        4316  00FF FC1F
 26   26   431A               *
 27   27   431A  13FC 007B            MOVE.B  #$7B,QPDR         ;INITIAL STATE PCS0-PCS3 HIGH
 27        431E  00FF FC15
 28   28   4322               *                                ;  SCK LOW
 29   29   4322  13FC 007B            MOVE.B  #$7B,QPAR         ;ASSIGN PINS TO QSPI
 29        4326  00FF FC16
 30   30   432A  13FC 007E            MOVE.B  #$7E,QDDR         ;PCS0-PCS3, SCK, MOSI OUTPUT
 30        432E  00FF FC17
 31   31   4332               *                                ;  MISO INPUT
 32   32   4332  33FC 8004            MOVE.W  #$8004,SPCR0      ;MASTER, 2.1MHz
 32        4336  00FF FC18
 33   33   433A  33FC 0F00            MOVE.W  #$0F00,SPCR2      ;NO INTERRUPTS OR WRAP
 33        433E  00FF FC1C
 34   34   4342               *                                ; ENDQP=$F, NEWQP=$0
 35   35   4342  4CDF 0001            MOVEM.L (SP)+,D0
 36   36   4346  4E75                 RTS                       ;RETURN FROM SPIINIT
 37   37   4348               *
 38   38   4348  48E7 00E0    ENABLE  MOVEM.L A0-A2,-(SP)       ;SAVE REGS.
 39   39   434C  303C 000F            MOVE.W  #15,D0            ;COUNTER FOR RAM
 40   40   4350  4281                 CLR.L   D1                ;TEMP. DATA BUFFER
 41   41   4352  227C 00FF            MOVEA.L #TXDRAM,A1        ;TRANSMITTER RAM
 41        4356  FD20
 42   42   4358  247C 00FF            MOVEA.L #CMDRAM,A2        ;COMMAND RAM
 42        435C  FD40
 43   43   435E  1218         LDRAM   MOVE.B  (A0)+,D1          ;TXDRAM: STORE 8 BIT DATA
 44   44   4360  32C1                 MOVE.W  D1,(A1)+          ; RIGHT JUSTIFIED
 45   45   4362  14FC 000E            MOVE.B  #$0E,(A2)+        ;CMDRAM: STD. DELAYS, 8-BITS;
 46   46   4366  51C8 FFF6            DBRA    D0,LDRAM          ; PSC0 LOW TO SELECT
 47   47   436A               *
 48   48   436A  13FC 0000            MOVE.B  #$00,SPCR3        ;NO LOOP
 48        436E  00FF FC1E
 49   49   4372  33FC 8000            MOVE.W  #$8000,SPCR1      ;ENABLE
 49        4376  00FF FC1A
 50   50   437A  4CDF 0700            MOVEM.L (SP)+,A0-A2
 51   51   437E  4E75                 RTS                       ;RETURN FROM ENABLE
 52   52   4380                       END
```

Figure 12.25(b)   QSPI initialization program.

located by (A0) to the transmitter queue entries beginning at address TXDRAM. The 8-bit characters must be right justified in TXDRAM. The received data will be right justified in the receiver queue locations.

The code segment at ENABLE also initializes the command bytes with $0E to indicate that 8-bit values are to be transmitted. Since the QSPI is the master, the number of bits to be transferred is determined by the setting of the BITSE bit in the command byte shown in Figure 12.23. Eight bits are transmitted and received for each queue entry since

$$BITSE = \{0\}$$

for each transfer as defined in the command byte bit [6]. The value BITS (SPCR0[13:10]) is not used in this example.

The selection $0E for each command byte also specifies standard delay times during transfers and that PCS0 is to be driven LOW before each transfer begins. The exact meaning of the command byte for the chip selects and the transfer timing will be discussed in Subsection 12.4.3. Once the transmitter and command queue entries are loaded, the QSPI can be enabled for transfers.

SPCR3 is initialized to $00 to disable the loop mode, the interrupts for halt acknowledge and mode fault, and the halt condition. To test the routines without connecting the QSPI to an external device, the LOOPQ bit in SPCR3[10] would be set to {1} to enable the loop mode. The received data would then be an echo of the transmitted data when the QSPI is enabled.

The QSPI is enabled by setting SPCR1[15] to {1}. After being enabled, the QSPI starts operation and control is returned to the MAIN program at label WAIT.

MAIN program. Since interrupts are not enabled in this example, the program MAIN should wait until the QSPI has finished all 16 transfers before reading the received data. The loop at label WAIT simulates the processing that could take place while the QSPI transfers data. Before the MAIN program accesses the received data in the QSPI receiver RAM, the status of the QSPI should be tested to be sure that the transfers are complete. The program loops at label WAIT until completion of the queue commands is indicated when the QSPI Finished Flag (SPIF) becomes {1}. The BTST instruction in the wait loop tests SPSR[7] by reading SPSR and setting the CPU condition codes according to the state of the bit. Once the SPIF bit is set, SPIF can be cleared by writing {0} to SPSR[7] without an additional read of SPSR.

When the QSPI is finished, the received data are in the receiver RAM and the QSPI automatically disables itself with SPIF set to {1}. The main program at label STORE transfers the received data to the buffer area at address RDATA for further processing. The main program then clears the QSPI Finished Flag in the QSPI status register SPSR by writing {0} to SPIF with an ANDI instruction. Finally, the flag SPIBUSY is cleared and control returns to the supervisor program.

QSPI wraparound mode. The *wraparound* mode of the QSPI is enabled when Wrap Enable (WREN) in SPCR2[14] is set to {1}. The QSPI begins transfers when enabled by the SPE bit in SPCR1 and continues transferring data until the queue entry indicated by ENDQP is encountered. This causes the QSPI Finished flag SPIF in SPSR to be set to {1} and an interrupt is generated if interrupts are enabled. However, the QSPI does not stop transfers but begins a new cycle of transfers. The bit WRTO (Wrap To) determines the new starting location. If WRTO (SPCR2[13]) is {0}, the transfers begin at queue location $0. If Wrap To (WRTO) is {1}, transfers begin at the queue location indicated by NEWQP.

If the CPU program does not change the transmitter queue entries or the commands, the same information is transmitted on each cycle through the queue. However, the received data represent the latest values input. For example, if a number of A/D converters are supplying values to the queue entries, the CPU program can read the latest values at any time. In effect, the peripheral devices with serial interfaces connected to the QSPI appear to transfer parallel data to the CPU program. The CPU program simply reads the appropriate queue entry to acquire a data value. No conflict will occur between serial data acquisition and the CPU reads because of the dual-access capability of the receiver RAM.

12.4.3 I/O Expansion with the QSPI and Chip Selects

In many applications, the most limited resource of a microcontroller is the number of I/O signal-lines available. One approach to I/O expansion is to use serial transfers rather than parallel I/O ports. The QSPI, with very few additional circuit chips, can control up to sixteen external devices using synchronous, serial transfers. A block diagram of a possible system is shown in Figure 12.26. The signal lines MOSI and MISO are used for data transfers. Selection of a specific peripheral unit and the timing of the transfers is controlled by the peripheral chip select and the serial clock SCK signal.

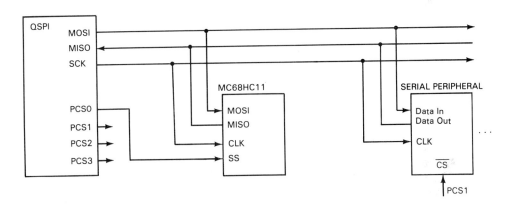

Figure 12.26 Block diagram of a serial interface system.

As drawn, the system of Figure 12.26 would allow up to four peripheral units to be attached to the QSPI. Sixteen peripherals could be attached by decoding the 4 peripheral chip select signals properly. In the figure, the MC68HC11 attaches directly to the QSPI since it has a compatible interface. Other peripheral units with serial interfaces including another MC68332 could be connected to the system. The electrical and timing requirements of the peripheral unit can be accommodated without additional circuitry in most cases since the QSPI signal characteristics can be selected by programming. In Figure 12.26, the Slave Select signal ($\overline{SS}$) of the MC68HC11 is connected to a peripheral select signal to enable the MC68HC11.

Table 12.13 lists a few of the Motorola devices that are directly compatible with the QSPI. Although many of these and similar devices also have parallel interfaces, the economy of I/O signals for serial transfers allows a product designer great flexibility using the devices. Many other peripheral devices and chips produced by Motorola and other manufacturers are suitable for connection to the QSPI.

Table 12.13 Peripheral Devices for the QSPI

Type	Part Number
Microcontrollers	MC68332, MC68HC11, M68HC05
Analog-to-Digital converters	MC145040, MC145050
Digital-to-Analog converters	MC14410
Display drivers (LCD, LED)	MC14543, MC14499
Phase-Locked Loops	MC145155
Shift registers	MC74HC589, MC74HC595
EEPROM	MCM2814

Chip select signals and the queue command byte.   In the master mode, the QSPI can use a chip select signal to enable a particular device for transfers. Program initialization of the chip select signals is necessary as follows:
(a) select the initial states in QPDR;
(b) assign pins to QSPI in QPAR;
(c) define the pins as output in QDDR.
To avoid briefly driving the signal lines to incorrect states, the initial states should be defined in QPDR before the pins are assigned as outputs in QDDR. Example 12.7 explained the initialization procedure. Table 12.14 summarizes the command byte of a queue entry and the use of the chip select bits.

After initialization, the Peripheral Chip Select signal lines (PCS3-PCS0) are controlled by the command and control byte for each queue entry as shown in Figure 12.23. When the QSPI is enabled, the chip select signals are driven to the states defined in the command byte (Bits[3:0]) as each transfer in the queue occurs. Between transfers, the chip select signals are changed according to the values in the QSM Port Data Register (QPDR) unless the Continue (CONT) bit of the command byte is set to {1}.

In programming, the state of the signals for each transfer must be carefully selected since the chip select signals are independent and more than one may be activated at a time. In fact, activation of several chip select signals at once is appropriate when an external circuit is used to decode the signals to select one of sixteen devices.

Timing and clock characteristics.   The timing characteristics of a specific transfer are controlled by the QSPI in the master mode. Overall timing for a complete transfer is determined for each transfer by the baud rate selected in SPCR0. The initialization program can select the time relationship between the assertion of a chip select signal and SCK as well as the time delay between each complete transfer. The timing required is determined by the characteristics of the peripheral device.

Table 12.14 The Queue Command Byte

Bits	Value	Use
PCS3-PCS0[3:0]	{0}	PCSx is driven LOW
	{1}	PCSx is driven HIGH
DSCK[4]	{0}	SCK transition 1/2 SCK cycle after chip select
(Enable Lead time)	{1}	DSCKL field in SPCR1 determines delay from chip select valid to SCK transition
DT[5]	{0}	Delay is 17 system clock cycles
(Transfer Delay)	{1}	DTL field in SPCR1 determines delay between transfers
BITSE[6]	{0}	Transfer length is 8 bits
	{1}	BITS field in SPCR0 defines transfer length
CONT[7]	{0}	Chip select signals are determined by values in QPDR between transfers
	{1}	Chip select signals are continuously asserted

The length of the time delays during transfer are selected by the DSCK and DT bits in the queue command byte for each transfer. Either standard delays can be selected or the timing fields in SPCR1 can determine the delays. The command byte also determines the state of the chip select signals between transfers as defined by the value of the CONT (Continue) bit. To begin each transfer, the peripheral chip select signals assume the logical values determined by bits [3:0] in the command byte.

Figure 12.27 shows a transfer timing diagram. The operating frequency for the SCK signal is determined by the value BAUD in SPCR0 as explained in Example 12.8. The period for each SCK pulse ranges from a minimum of four system clock cycles (BAUD = 2) to a maximum of 510 system clock cycles when BAUD = 255. The time per SCK cycle is

$$t_{SCK} = 1/(\text{SCK baud rate}) \quad \text{seconds}$$

where the SCK baud rate is calculated by Equation 12.2. For a 16.78MHz system clock, the range of t_{SCK} is from approximately 238ns to a maximum of 0.03ms.

DSCKL delay before SCK. Once the chip select signals are valid, the serial clock SCK transitions begin after the *Enable Lead Time* shown in Figure 12.27. The time delay defined by DSCKL allows a setup time for the peripheral device after the device is selected. The time delay is controlled by the DSCK bit in the queue command byte. When DSCK = {1} in the command byte for a specific transfer, the delay time between the chip select for that transfer and the first SCK transition is specified by the DSCKL field in SPCR1[14:8]. The Enable Lead time is seconds in this case is

$$\text{PCSx to SCK delay} = \frac{\text{DSCKL}}{f_{(\text{system})}} \quad (2 \leq \text{DSCKL} \leq 127) \qquad (12.3)$$

where PCSx is PCS0, PCS1, PCS2, or PCS3 for a specific chip select signal line. The possible values for DSCKL are [0,1,2,...,127]. However, a value of $00 for DSCKL specifies a delay of 128 system clock cycles. A value of $01 causes a 2 cycle delay.

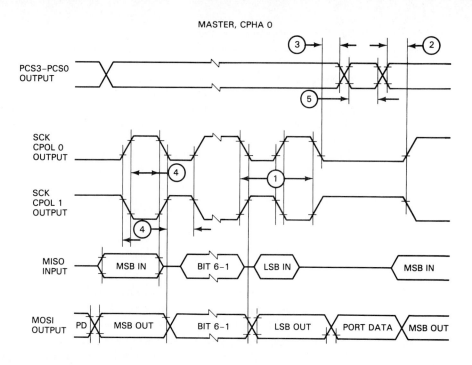

MASTER, CPHA 0

Num	Function	Min	Max	Unit
	Operating Frequency			
	Master–SCK	DC	1/4	System Clock Frequency
	Slave	DC	1/4	System Clock Frequency
1	Cycle Time			
	Master–SCK	4	510	System Clocks
2	Enable Lead Time			
	Master–DSCKL	2	128	System Clocks
	Slave			
3	Enable Lag Time			
	Master	1/2	1/2	SCK
	Slave	—	—	
4	Clock (SCK) High or Low Time			
	Master	2	255	System Clocks
	Slave	2	—	System Clocks
5	Transfer Delay			
	Master–DTL	17	8192	System Clocks
	Slave (Does Not Require Deselect)	13	—	System Clocks

Figure 12.27 QSPI timing as a master (CPHA={0}).

The minimum delay PCSx to SCK is two system clock periods or 0.12μs using a 16.78MHz system clock. A value of $00 for DSCKL causes a delay of 128 system clock periods or 7.6 μs.

As listed in Table 12.14, a selection of

$$\text{Command byte[4] (DSCK)} = \{0\}$$

in the queue command byte causes a delay between the chip select and SCK transition of 1/2 of the SCK period. The DSCKL field in SPCR1 is not used when DSCK is {0}.

DTL delay between transfers. If the DT bit in the queue command byte is {1}, a program specified delay occurs between transfers of each frame of data. This Transfer Delay time in Figure 12.27 allows an external device to complete its current operation before the next transfer.

The Transfer Delay time specified by the DTL field (SPCR1[7:0]) when the command byte bit DT = {1} is

$$t_{(\text{DTL})} = (32 \times \text{DTL})/f_{(\text{system})} \quad \text{seconds} \tag{12.4}$$

where DTL equals one of the values [1, 2, 3, ..., 255] or $00. The range of delay is from 1 to $489\mu s$ with a 16.78MHz system clock. Maximum Transfer Delay of 8192 (32×256) system clock periods is selected when DTL = $00.

Table 12.14 shows that when

$$\text{Command byte[5] (DT)} = \{0\}$$

the DTL field in SPCR1 is ignored and a standard delay of 17 system clock periods for the QSPI as master is selected. The delay is approximately one $1\mu s$ with a 16.78MHz system clock. The minimum transfer delay time for a slave device is slightly less since the command byte of the QSPI does not have to be read when the QSPI is a slave.

Clock polarity and phase. The polarity and phase of the clock signal are determined by values selected in SPCR0 as shown in Figure 12.22. The two possible polarities are shown in Figure 12.27. If CPOL (SPCR0[9]) is {0}, a HIGH state of the clock signal is the active state as shown by CPOL 0 in the figure. If CPOL is {1}, the active state is LOW. This selection allows the product designer to select the correct polarity of the clock to accommodate peripheral devices. The designer can also select the edge of SCK which causes the transitions of data bits. The clock phase bit (CPHA) is SPCR0[8].

Figure 12.27 shows the
$$\text{CPHA} = \{0\}$$
selection in which a data bit is captured on the leading edge of SCK and changes on the following edge. A selection of CPHA = {1} causes data to be changed on the leading edge and be captured on the following edge. The selection of clock phase is determined by the timing requirements of the external unit. For example, for serial input to a device that requires the serial data to be latched on the rising edges of the clock, the choice
$$\text{CPOL} = \{0\} \quad \text{and} \quad \text{CPHA} = \{0\}$$
could be used to hold a data bit for one-half a SCK clock cycle before latching. The SCK signal is considered active HIGH in this case.

QSPI data transfers and chip selects. In the master mode, the QSPI begins execution of queue commands as soon as the QSPI is enabled. The chip select signal for a particular transfer is asserted and enables the receiving device. The SCK signal begins after the Enable Lead Time in Figure 12.27 elapses. Then, the transfer of the data bits begins on the MOSI line from the QSPI and on the MISO line to the QSPI. The external device reads the data bits on the selected edge of the SCK signal. When all the bits are transferred and received, the chip select signal is negated unless the Continue (CONT) bit is set in the command byte. The remaining commands in the queue are then executed in turn in a similar manner.

The continue (CONT) bit of the queue command byte determines the use of the peripheral chip select signals between transfers. If CONT = {1}, the peripheral select signals do not change between transfers. Thus, an external device could be continuously selected for several transfers. If CONT is set to {0}, the state of the peripheral chip select signals is determined by the value in QPDR. This register should be initialized with an appropriate value before the QSPI is enabled if the continuous mode for the peripheral chip select signals is not chosen.

The reader is referred to the *MC68332 User's Manuals* for a complete description of the electrical characteristics of the QSPI signal lines. The exact timing, drive capability, voltage range and other details are defined in the manuals. The *User's Manuals* for the M68HC11 family of 8-bit microcontrollers also contain detailed descriptions of the compatible Serial Peripheral Interface (SPI) for various applications.

A/D converter example. The Motorola MC145050 A/D converter is a serial output device that is used here to illustrate the selection of the parameters just discussed. The CPU program controlling the A/D converter must follow the timing constraints and protocol published in the A/D converter data sheet. Figure 12.28 defines the circuit connections between the QSPI and the A/D converter used in the examples to follow. The necessary power and grounding connections are not shown in the figure.

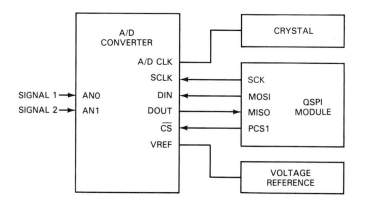

Figure 12.28 A/D converter to QSPI connection.

The MC145050 is a 10-bit A/D converter with eleven analog input channels and three internal calibration channels. Figure 12.28 shows only the two channels used in examples in this section. The serial input (DIN) and output (DOUT) pins in Figure 12.28 allow simultaneous transfers between the QSPI and the A/D converter. When the A/D converter is selected by the QSPI, a setup time delay must occur before a particular A/D channel is addressed. A converted value is obtained by sending the address of the *next* channel to be converted while simultaneously reading the value converted on the previously addressed channel. However, the QSPI must not request a new conversion until the previous conversion is completed.

The A/D channels are addressed by the four *most significant* bits of the serial input to the A/D converter signal line DIN. The fourteen channels are thus addressed as

$$\$0XXX, \$1XXX, \ldots, \$DXXX$$

where the hexadecimal digits indicated as X are ignored. Each transfer can be from 10 bits to 16 bits. However, the A/D converter ignores the bits after the 10th. The conversion for a channel begins after the 10th bit is received.

Channels 0 through 10 can be connected to analog input signals. Three internal channels are available to calibrate the system. Reading channel 11 ($B) results in a half-scale 10-bit value of $200. Channel 12 yields a zero value. Channel 13 outputs the full-scale value of $3FF. The full-scale value corresponds to a voltage input equal to V_{REF} shown in Figure 12.28. The resulting reading is right justified in the QSPI receiver queue entry if 10 bit transfers are used. If 16 bit transfers are used, the result is left justified in the RAM.

Using 16-bit transfers, the received values for half-scale and full-scale would be $8000 and $FFC0, respectively. In this case, the result read into the QSPI receiver queue should be shifted right by 6-bit positions if the purpose is to measure the voltage range from $0000 to $03FF since each transfer is 16 bits but the A/D converter has only 10 bit precision. The corresponding true analog voltage is defined by the voltage reference in Figure 12.28.

Figure 12.28 also shows a separate A/D clock oscillator that is crystal controlled. The maximum A/D clock (A/DCLK) frequency is 2.1MHz. The maximum independent serial clock (SCK) frequency is also 2.1MHz.

Example 12.10

This example first shows how to calculate the minimum A/D converter setup time. Then, the necessary delay time between transfers is calculated. The example assumes 16 bit transfers between the A/D converter and the QSPI.

For this particular example, the following clock frequencies are used:

(a) 864kHz crystal oscillator for A/DCLK;
(b) 1.05MHz SCK selected in QSPI register SPCR0;
(c) 16.78MHz system clock ($f_{(system)}$).

The periods for the clocks are thus

$$t_{SCK} = 1/(1.05 \times 10^6) = 0.95 \mu s$$

and

$$t_{(A/DCLK)} = 1/(864 \times 10^3) = 1.16 \mu s.$$

The A/D *setup time* T_{SU} is defined in the A/D converter specifications as the minimum delay between the assertion of chip select ($\overline{CS}$) and the first rising edge of SCK. This is the *Enable Lead Time* in Figure 12.27 which is defined by DSCKL in SPCR1[14:8] when the DSCK bit is {1} in the command byte of a queue entry. The published setup time is

$$T_{SU} \geq 2 \times t_{(A/DCLK)} + 0.425\mu s.$$

The 864kHz A/DCLK with a $1.16\mu s$ period yields a minimum setup time of approximately $2.74\mu s$. Equation 12.3 is used to determine the minimum DSCKL value as

$$DSCKL = T_{SU} \times f_{(system)}$$

where the setup time T_{SU} was substituted for the PCSx to SCK delay time. For this example, the result for the minimum value of DSCKL is

$$DSCKL = 2.74 \times 10^{-6} sec \times (16.78 \times 10^{6} Hz) = 46 \ (\$2E).$$

which is the value to be written in SPCR1[14:8].

Next, the *Transfer Delay* in Figure 12.27 is calculated. The conversion time for this A/D converter is 44 A/DCLK cycles after the 10th bit is received. Thus, the delay time between conversion commands to select the channel to be read must be at least

$$T_{(A/D \ delay)} = \frac{44}{864 \times 10^{3} Hz} = 50.9\mu s.$$

$T_{(A/D \ delay)}$ will determine the value of the DTL parameter in SPCR1[7:0]. However, the Transfer Delay time in Figure 12.27 is not necessarily the same as $T_{(A/D \ delay)}$ since the A/D converter begins conversion after the 10th bit is received.

If the transfer length between the QSPI and the A/D converter is longer than 10 bits, the transfer time of the bits $11, 12, \ldots, N$ can be counted as part of the necessary Transfer Delay time. In this example, the QSPI is programmed to transfer 16 bits with an SCK frequency of 1.05MHz. Since the time required to transmit each bit is $t_{SCK} = 0.95\mu s$, the transmission of the first 10 bits takes $9.5\mu s$. The last 6 bits which are ignored by the A/D converter require $6 \times .95\mu s = 5.7\mu s$ to transmit. Thus, the required Transfer Delay time is calculated as the difference between the A/D converter conversion time and the time taken to transmit the last 6 bits. This time is

$$t_{DTL} = T_{(A/D \ delay)} - 5.7\mu s = 50.9\mu s - 5.7\mu s = 45.2\mu s$$

with the clock frequencies selected for this example. Using Equation 12.4, DTL is selected as

$$DTL = \frac{16.78 \times 10^{6} Hz}{32} \times (45.2 \times 10^{-6} \ seconds) = 23.7$$

assuming a system clock frequency of 16.78MHz. As an integer, DTL is chosen to be 24 (\$18) in SPCR1[7:0]. Using the value \$18, the actual delay is then $45.8\mu s$. Exercise 12.4.7 considers cases in which other values are necessary for the time delay between transfers.

The MC145050 data sheet indicates that the A/D channel address is clocked in on the first four rising edges of SCK. Thus, the parameters

$$CPOL = \{0\} \ and \ CPHA = \{0\}$$

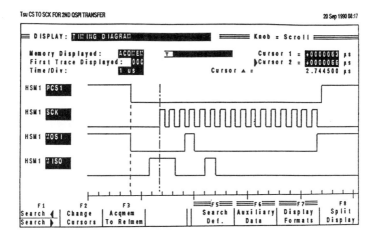

(a) PCS1 to SCK for transfer

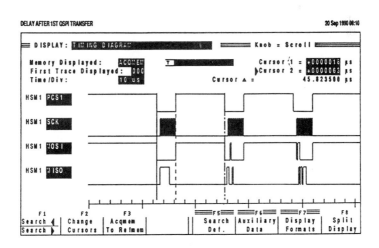

(b) A/D conversion timing

Figure 12.29 Timing diagram for Example 12.10 and Example 12.11.

are chosen for the clock polarity and phase in SPCR0.

Timing diagram. Figure 12.29 presents a logic analyzer trace of the timing involved in transfers between the QSPI and the MC145050. Example 12.11 explains the program that controls these transfers. The present purpose is to relate the timing diagrams of Figure 12.29 with the timing parameters just selected in this example and the timing definitions in Figure 12.27.

Figure 12.29(a) shows a transfer with a $1\mu s$ per division time scale. The signal PCS1 goes LOW at an arbitrary time on the display. The SCK signal starts after the Enable Lead Time of $2.74\mu s$ selected by DSCKL in QSPI register SPCR1. This is the time between the vertical cursors in Figure 12.29(a). The SCK period is $0.95\mu s$. The SCK goes HIGH 16 times during the transfer to transmit and receive data. The output on signal line MOSI is $1000 in this case with the most significant bit sent first to address A/D converter channel 1. The A/D converter responds on signal line MISO with the value from the previous conversion. After 16 bits have been transferred, SCK stays LOW and PCS1 goes HIGH 1/2 SCK cycle later. This is the Enable Lag Time in Figure 12.27.

Figure 12.29(b) shows three transfers with a time scale of $10\mu s$ per division. The QSPI is addressing channels $0, $1, and $B (11) in that order. The Transfer Delay Time of $45.8\mu s$ between the vertical cursors occurs because of the DTL parameter in QSPI register SPCR1.

Example 12.11

Figure 12.30 presents programs to control a Motorola MC145050 A/D converter. This example assumes that QSM global registers and interrupts are initialized as shown in Example 12.1. The program MAIN in Figure 12.30(a) calls the A/D converter initialization routine SPIAD and then causes conversions for two analog channels and a calibration channel with a call to routine ADREAD. Figure 12.30(b) shows these routines. Before conversion, the flag ADBUSY is set to -1 to indicate that the A/D converter is busy. Since interrupts are initialized as in Example 12.1, the QSPI interrupts the CPU at level 3 using vector $41 at location $104 in the CPU vector table when the conversions are completed. The interrupt routine in Figure 12.30(a) clears the SPIF flag in SPSR and the busy flag ADBUSY. The program MAIN ignores the first three readings of the A/D converter as explained later.

During conversions, the program MAIN can perform other processing. In the program as shown, the MAIN program waits until the conversions are complete before exiting the loop at label WAIT. Then, MAIN calls the routine CONVERT to read the values on the three A/D converter channels and waits at label WAIT1. After conversion, the main program stores the three converted values in buffer RDATA for further processing. Figure 12.29 of Example 12.10 presented the timing trace for the QSPI signal lines while the program executed.

QSPI initialization. In the routine SPIAD, the QSPI is first disabled and any status flags set in SPSR are cleared. Then, the routine initializes various QSPI registers. Before the QSPI is enabled, the QSM pins must be assigned and their initial states defined to allow synchronous serial transfers as described in Subsection 12.4.1. Initially, the chip selects should be HIGH assuming that a LOW level on PCSx (x=0, 1, 2, 3) selects a peripheral device. The falling edge of PCS1 selects the A/D converter in this example. The serial clock SCK is initially to be LOW. The selection of initial levels on the pins is made in the QSM Port Data Register QPDR. The bits in the QSM Pin Assignment Register QPAR are written with a {1} to assign each chip select, MOSI, and MISO to the QSPI. The QSM Data Direction Register bits are written with a {1} to define PCS3–0,

```
abs. rel.   LC   obj. code    source line
---- ----   ----  ---------   -----------
   1    1   0000                     |       TTL     'FIGURE 12.30(a)'
   2    2   8000                     |       ORG     $8000
   3    3   0000                     |*
   4    4   8000                     |*      SETUP QSPI TO READ A/D CHANNELS
   5    5   8000                     |*
   6    6   8000                     |*      INPUT  : QSPI GLOBAL REGISTERS ARE
   7    7   8000                     |*                 ASSUMED TO BE INITIALIZED
   8    8   8000                     |*
   9    9   8000                     |*      OUTPUTS: CONVERTED VALUES IN RECEIVER QUEUE
  10   10   8000                     |*                 AFTER CALL TO ADREAD
  11   11   8000                     |*
  12   12        0080 0000   REGBASE EQU     $800000
  13   13        00FF FD00   RECRAM  EQU     $7FFD00+REGBASE   ;RECEIVER DATA
  14   14        0000 4400   SPIAD   EQU     $4400             ;INITIALIZATION ROUTINE
  15   15        0000 4450   ADREAD  EQU     $4450             ;A/D ENABLE ROUTINE
  16   16        0000 447C   CONVERT EQU     $447C             ;A/D CONVERT ROUTINE
  17   17        0000 448E   ADBUSY  EQU     $448E             ;A/D BUSY FLAG
  18   18   8000                     |*
  19   19   8000 48E7 8018   MAIN    MOVEM.L D0/A3-A4,-(SP)    ;SAVE REGISTERS
  20   20   8004                     |*
  21   21   8004 4EB8 4400           JSR     SPIAD             ;INITIALIZE QSPI
  22   22   8008                     |*
  23   23   8008 4EB8 4450           JSR     ADREAD            ;READ A/D CHANNELS
  24   24   800C                     |*
  25   25   800C 4A78 448E   WAIT    TST.W   ADBUSY            ;WAIT FOR A/D TO FINISH
  26   26   8010 66FA                BNE     WAIT              ; 1ST TIME
  27   27   8012                     |*
  28   28   8012 4E71                NOP                       ;OTHER PROCESSING
  29   29   8014                     |*
  30   30   8014 4EB8 447C           JSR     CONVERT           ;REQUEST CONVERSION
  31   31   8018 4A78 448E   WAIT1   TST.W   ADBUSY            ;WAIT FOR A/D TO FINISH
  32   32   801C 66FA                BNE     WAIT1             ;
  33   33   801E 267C 00FF           MOVEA.L #RECRAM,A3        ;STORE RECEIVED DATA
  33        8022 FD00
  34   34   8024 287C 0000           MOVEA.L #RDATA,A4
  34        8028 803C
  35   35   802A 303C 0002           MOVE.W  #2,D0
  36   36   802E 38DB        LDRDATA MOVE.W  (A3)+,(A4)+
  37   37   8030 51C8 FFFC           DBRA    D0,LDRDATA
  38   38   8034                     |*
  39   39   8034 4CDF 1801           MOVEM.L (SP)+,D0/A3-A4    ;RESTORE REGISTERS
  40   40   8038 4E4F                TRAP    #15               ;RETURN
  41   41   803A 0063                DC.W    #$0063
  42   42   803C                RDATA DS.W   16                ;RECEIVED DATA
  43   43   805C                     END
```

```
abs. rel.   LC   obj. code    source line
---- ----   ----  ---------   -----------
   1    1   0000                     |*
   2    2   0000                     |*
   3    3   0000                     |*      INTERRUPT HANDLER FOR QSPI
   4    4   0000                     |*         CLEARS ADBUSY FLAG
   5    5   0000                     |*
   6    6   7700                     |       ORG     $7700             ;QSPI INTERRUPT HANDLER FOR A/D
   7    7   0000                     |*
   8    8        0080 0000   REGBASE EQU     $800000           ;MODULE REGS AT $FFF000
   9    9        00FF FC1F   SPSR    EQU     $7FFC1F+REGBASE   ;STATUS REGISTER
  10   10        0000 448E   ADBUSY  EQU     $448E
  11   11   7700                     |*
  12   12   7700 48E7 8000   SPIIRQ  MOVEM.L D0,-(SP)          ;SAVE REG.
  13   13   7704 1039 00FF           MOVE.B  SPSR,D0           ;READ STATUS
  13        7708 FC1F
  14   14   770A 0239 007F           ANDI.B  #$7F,SPSR         ;CLEAR SPIF
  14        770E 00FF FC1F
  15   15   7712 4278 448E           CLR.W   ADBUSY            ;CLEAR ADBUSY FLAG
  16   16   7716 4CDF 0001           MOVEM.L (SP)+,D0
  17   17   771A 4E73                RTE
  18   18   771C                     END
```

Figure 12.30(a) Program example of QSPI control of the MC145050.

```
abs. rel.   LC   obj. code    source line
---- ----   ----  ----------   -----------
  1    1   0000                   TTL     'FIGURE 12.30(b)'
  2    2   4400                   ORG     $4400
  3    3   0000           |  *
  4    4   4400           |  *        SETUP QSPI TO READ A/D CHANNELS
  5    5   4400           |  *        OUTPUTS: CONVERTED VALUES IN RECEIVER QUEUE
  6    6   4400           |  *                 AFTER CALL TO ADREAD
  7    7   4400           |  *
  8    8   0080 0000      | REGBASE EQU     $800000
  9    9   00FF FC15      | QPDR    EQU     $7FFC15+REGBASE     ;PORT DATA
 10   10   00FF FC16      | QPAR    EQU     $7FFC16+REGBASE     ;PIN ASSIGNMENT
 11   11   00FF FC17      | QDDR    EQU     $7FFC17+REGBASE     ;DATA DIRECTION
 12   12   00FF FC18      | SPCR0   EQU     $7FFC18+REGBASE     ;CONTROL REG. 0
 13   13   00FF FC1A      | SPCR1   EQU     $7FFC1A+REGBASE     ;CONTROL REG. 1
 14   14   00FF FC1C      | SPCR2   EQU     $7FFC1C+REGBASE     ;CONTROL REG. 2
 15   15   00FF FC1E      | SPCR3   EQU     $7FFC1E+REGBASE     ;CONTROL REG. 3
 16   16   00FF FC1F      | SPSR    EQU     $7FFC1F+REGBASE     ;STATUS REGISTER
 17   17   00FF FD00      | RECRAM  EQU     $7FFD00+REGBASE     ;RECEIVER DATA
 18   18   00FF FD20      | TXDRAM  EQU     $7FFD20+REGBASE     ;TRANSMITTER DATA
 19   19   00FF FD40      | COMDRAM EQU     $7FFD40+REGBASE     ;COMMAND DATA
 20   20   4400           |  *
 21   21   4400 48E7 8000 | SPIAD   MOVEM.L D0,-(SP)            ;SAVE REG.
 22   22   4404 0279 007F |         ANDI.W  #$7F,SPCR1          ;DISABLE QSPI AND
 22        4408 00FF FC1A |
 23   23   440C 1039 00FF |         MOVE.B  SPSR,D0             ; CLEAR FLAGS
 23        4410 FC1F      |
 24   24   4412 0239 0000 |         ANDI.B  #$00,SPSR
 24        4416 00FF FC1F |
 25   25   441A           |  *
 26   26   441A 13FC 007B | SPIINIT MOVE.B  #$7B,QPDR           ;INITIAL STATE PCS0-PCS3 HIGH
 26        441E 00FF FC15 |
 27   27   4422           |  *                                 ;  SCK LOW
 28   28   4422 13FC 007B |         MOVE.B  #$7B,QPAR           ;ASSIGN PINS TO QSPI
 28        4426 00FF FC16 |
 29   29   442A 13FC 007E |         MOVE.B  #$7E,QDDR           ;PCS0-PCS3, MOSI OUTPUT
 29        442E 00FF FC17 |
 30   30   4432           |  *                                 ; MISO INPUT
 31   31   4432 33FC 8008 |         MOVE.W  #$8008,SPCR0        ;MASTER, 16 BITS, 1.05MHz
 31        4436 00FF FC18 |
 32   32   443A 33FC 8200 |         MOVE.W  #$8200,SPCR2        ;INTERRUPT, NO WRAP
 32        443E 00FF FC1C |
 33   33   4442           |  *                                 ; ENDQP=$2, NEWQP=$0
 34   34   4442 13FC 0000 |         MOVE.B  #$00,SPCR3          ;NO LOOP
 34        4446 00FF FC1E |
 35   35   444A 4CDF 0001 |         MOVEM.L (SP)+,D0
 36   36   444E 4E75      |         RTS
 37   37   4450           |  *
 38   38   4450           |  *        CONVERT CHANNELS 0,1 AND 11 OF A/D CONVERTER
 39   39   4450           |  *
 40   40   4450 48E7 00C0 | ADREAD  MOVEM.L A0-A1,-(SP)
 41   41   4454 207C 00FF |         MOVEA.L #TXDRAM,A0          ;TRANSMITTER RAM
 41        4458 FD20      |
 42   42   445A 227C 00FF |         MOVEA.L #COMDRAM,A1         ;COMMAND RAM
 42        445E FD40      |
 43   43   4460           |  *
 44   44   4460 30FC 0000 |         MOVE.W  #$0000,(A0)+        ;CHANNEL 0
 45   45   4464 30FC 1000 |         MOVE.W  #$1000,(A0)+        ;CHANNEL 1
 46   46   4468 30FC B000 |         MOVE.W  #$B000,(A0)+        ;CHANNEL 11
 47   47   446C 12FC 007D |         MOVE.B  #$7D,(A1)+          ;CONT=0, SPCR0[13:10]=LENGTH
 48   48   4470 12FC 007D |         MOVE.B  #$7D,(A1)+          ;DELAY AFTER TRANSFER=DTL,
 49   49   4474 12FC 007D |         MOVE.B  #$7D,(A1)+          ;DSCKL DELAY AFTER PSC1 LOW
 50   50   4478           |  *                                 ; TO SCK
 51   51   4478 4CDF 0300 |         MOVEM.L (SP)+,A0-A1         ;RESTORE REGISTERS
 52   52   447C 33FC FFFF | CONVERT MOVE.W  #$FFFF,ADBUSY       ;SET A/D BUSY FLAG
 52        4480 0000 448E |
 53   53   4484 33FC AE18 |         MOVE.W  #$AE18,SPCR1        ;ENABLE QSPI; SET DSCLK AND DTL
 53        4488 00FF FC1A |
 54   54   448C 4E75      |         RTS
 55   55   448E           | ADBUSY  DS.W    1                   ;A/D BUSY FLAG
 56   56   4490           |         END
```

Figure 12.30(b)   QSPI initialization and A/D converter control.

SCK and MOSI as outputs. MISO is defined as an input by writing {0} to QDDR[0]. The values initialized by routine SPIAD are as follows:

(a) QPDR = $7B;

(b) QPAR = $7B;

(c) QDDR = $7E.

The QSPI control register SPCR0 is programmed to contain the SCK frequency and the transfer length. Control register SPCR2 is used to define the characteristics of the queue and also to enable QSPI interrupts. SPCR3 is written as $00 in this example since the loop mode and the halt mode are not used. The command byte and the transmitter data register are initialized as described later.

The value $8008 written in SPCR0 selects the QSPI as master and BAUD=$8 to select a 1.05MHz baud rate as listed in Table 12.12. The QSPI is programmed for 16-bit transfers in SPCR0 since SPSR0[13:10]={0} and BITSE={1} in the command bytes.

In the example of Figure 12.30, A/D channels 0, 1 and 11 are read when the QSPI is enabled. Channel 0 and channel 1 are monitoring two analog input channels. Channel 11 should yield a half-scale value of $8000 in the corresponding receiver queue location. This value is $200 when shifted right by 6-bit positions. Since only three channels are read, the queue pointers have the following values:

(a) NEWQP = $0 (SPCR2[11:8]);

(b) ENDQP = $2 (SPCR2[3:0]).

QSPI interrupts are enabled by writing {1} to SPCR2[15]. These values are written to the appropriate fields of SPCR2 before the QSPI is enabled. SPCR1 should be written last since SPCR1[15] enables the QSPI when this SPE bit is {1}.

In summary, the control register values to be written are as follows:

(a) SPCR0[15:0] = $8008 – Master, 16 bit transfers, 1.05MHz;

(b) SPCR1[15:0] = $AE18 – Enable, DSCKL=$2E (2.74μs), DTL=$18 (45.8$\mu$s);

(c) SPCR2[15:0] = $8200 – Enable interrupt, ENDQP=$2, NEWQP=$0;

(d) SPCR3[7:0] = $00 – No loop.

In the routine SPIAD of Figure 12.30(b), the registers SPCR0, SPCR2 and SPCR3 are initialized before control is returned to the main program.

QSPI queue. The subroutine ADREAD is called by MAIN to initialize the transmitter and command byte queue entries. The routine also sets the ADBUSY flag to -1 and enables the QSPI by writing $AE18 into SPCR1.

The first three transmitter RAM locations hold the channel addresses. The command byte for the three queue locations used should define PCS1 as LOW when the A/D is selected. Figure 12.23 and Table 12.14 define the RAM command bits. The bits DSCK, DT and BITSE are set to {1} to specify a DSCKL delay after chip select, a DTL delay between transfer and a 16-bit transfer defined in SPCR0, respectively. The continuous mode bit CONT is set to {0} in this example so that PCS1 goes high between transfers. Thus, each command byte of the queue is initialized with the value $7D.

As the QSPI addresses channel 0, channel 1 and channel 11 in turn, the A/D converter returns the value converted on the previous channel. The first time the ADREAD subroutine is called, the receiver queue will contain the following data after the conversions are complete:

$$(\$FFFD00) = \text{channel x}$$

$$(\$FFFD02) = \text{channel 0}$$

$$(\$FFFD04) = \text{channel 1}$$

where the channel x value is returned when the QSPI addresses channel 0 the first time. This value should be ignored by the program controlling the A/D converter. Program

MAIN calls routine ADREAD to initialize the transmitter and command queue RAM and cause the conversions. However, the main program ignores the data received from the A/D converter as a result of the first request for conversion of the three channels.

On the second and subsequent requests for conversions, a call to the subroutine CONVERT sets the ADBUSY flag and causes the A/D channels to be converted and read. The receiver queue locations will contain the converted values:

$$(\$FFFD00) = \text{channel 11 value}$$
$$(\$FFFD02) = \text{channel 0 value}$$
$$(\$FFFD04) = \text{channel 1 value}$$

as desired. A program using the A/D converter should take into account the order of the channel data in the receiver queue after subsequent conversions.

Interrupt routine. If the QSPI interrupt is enabled as in this example, an interrupt request is generated and QSPI disables itself after the three conversions. The interrupt routine in Figure 12.30(a) clears the QSPI Finished Flag (SPIF) in the QSPI Status Register SPSR[7] and the ADBUSY flag. The SPIF flag is cleared after the routine reads the value in SPSR and then writes to SPCR to clear SPIF to {0}.

MAIN program. After program MAIN calls CONVERT, the program loops at label WAIT1 in this example until the interrupt routine clears the ADBUSY flag. Of course, the program could do other processing until the interrupt is received. After the flag ADBUSY is cleared, the program stores the converted values into buffer RDATA. Program MAIN or any other program can request conversion of the channels at any time by calling routine CONVERT. As long as none of the QSPI initialization parameters need to be changed, no additional initialization of the QSPI is necessary.

QSPI slave mode and mode fault.   The slave mode is selected by setting

$$SPCR0[15] = \{0\},$$

so that the QSPI is unable to initiate serial transfers. However, the QSPI receives and transmits data from the queue. The MOSI, SCK and PCS0/$\overline{SS}$ signals must be initialized as input signals and the MISO signal is for serial output. An external master must select the QSPI by driving slave select ($\overline{SS}$) LOW. The queue command byte is not used in the slave mode. All the other registers of the QSPI must be initialized appropriately to allow transfers to take place.

The Mode Fault flag MODF in SPSR is set to {1} if the QSPI is the master and the Slave Select line is pulled LOW. This is only possible if the PCS0/$\overline{SS}$ signal line is defined as an input in QDDR. An interrupt occurs when MODF is set if the mode fault interrupt is enabled by the HMIE bit in SPCR3.

EXERCISES

12.4.1. Show the QSPI register values and queue entries to select the following operations:

(a) master, 8-bit transfers, 100kHz SCK;

(b) enable interrupts, set ENDQP for 4 transfers;

(c) select a peripheral with PCS0 LOW, add a DTL delay of 96 system clock cycles and enable the QSPI.

Assume that the system clock frequency is 16.78MHz.

12.4.2. Modify the program of Example 12.9 to use interrupts and the wraparound mode for the queue.

12.4.3. By consulting appropriate data catalogs, list a number of devices or peripheral chips that are suitable for connection to the QSPI. Explain the use of each item in I/O expansion of a product.

12.4.4. Describe the uses of a phase-locked loop chip connected to the QSPI. Explain several specific applications for such a chip in areas such as automotive product design.

12.4.5. Show the external circuits required to allow up to 16 peripheral devices to be connected to the QSPI. Use a block diagram and an electrical circuit diagram to explain the connections.

12.4.6. Design the circuit and the program to use the QSPI to program an EEPROM (Electrical Erasable Programmable ROM). Information about specific types of EEPROMs is found in the appropriate data sheets or Data Catalogs from manufacturers. For example, Motorola's *Memory Data Handbook* discusses serial transfers with the Motorola MCM2814 EEPROM.

12.4.7. Consider the A/D converter timing described in Example 12.10. Determine the minimum delay between transfers and the value of the parameter DTL for the following cases:

(a) 16-bit transfers with SCK frequency of 100kHz;

(b) 10-bit transfers with SCK frequency of 2.1MHz;

(c) 10-bit transfers with SCK frequency of 1.05MHz.

12.4.8. Write the program to control 8 channels of the MC145050 A/D converter connected to the QSPI. Assume the input channels are multiplexed and that the first four bits of the transfers to the A/D converter contain the channel number whose input is to be converted. The delay between conversions must be at least 30 microseconds. The QSPI queue entries controlling the A/D convertor are to be used in the wraparound mode without interrupts. Once the first set of conversions complete, the CPU program should be able to read the converted values in the QSPI receiver RAM at any time. (The Motorola MC145040 and MC145050 A/D converters are examples of A/D chips that can be directly connected to the QSPI. Further information can be found in Motorola's Data sheets for these chips.)

12.4.9. Consider the software design factors involved in a network of several microcontrollers each using the QSPI. In particular, assume that an MC68332 is the master with an MC68HC11 as a slave. Assuming that the I/O drivers for both MCUs are interrupt controlled, design the software for each microcontroller.

12.5   GENERAL-PURPOSE I/O WITH THE QSM

Eight of the signal lines of the QSM depicted in Figure 12.1 can be assigned to general-purpose I/O if they are not used for their primary communications purpose. Only the RxD signal cannot be programmed for general use. To select one or more signal lines for general-purpose I/O, the CPU program must initialize the QSM port and pin registers as follows:

(a) select the specific signal lines in the QSM Pin Assignment Register (QPAR);

(b) write the first bits to be output to the QSM Port Data Register (QPDR);

(c) select the direction in the QSM Data Direction Register (QDDR).

Each signal line can be assigned on a pin-by-pin basis to general-purpose I/O. The reset value in QPAR assigns all of the QSM signal lines except RxD to this function. For an output, the value of {1} or {0} should be written to the appropriate bit of QPDR before QDDR is initialized. This assures that the initial output is correct when the output direction for a signal line is chosen in the Data Direction Register (QDDR).

If the SCI transmitter is enabled in the SCI control register (SCCR1[3]), the TxD pin is controlled by the SCI and cannot be used for general-purpose I/O . The QSPI cannot use any of the signal lines unless they are assigned to it in QPAR.

EXERCISES

12.5.1. Write the instruction sequence to assign the QSPI pins to general-purpose I/O. Let MISO, MOSI, SCK and PCS0 be used for output and the remaining signals for input.

FURTHER READING

The Serial Communications Interface (SCI) and the Serial Peripheral Interface (SPI) are treated in most textbooks and references that discuss the Motorola M68HC11 family of microcontrollers. In particular, Lipovski's textbook and Peatman's textbook referenced in Chapter 1 cover the SCI and SPI in detail. Although the SCI and the QSPI of the MC68332 have more capability than the serial interfaces of the 8-bit microcontrollers, many of the 8-bit applications can be used to guide the design of MC68332-based products.

Motorola provides various *Applications Notes* for its microcontroller products. Contact a Motorola representative to obtain the *Applications Notes* pertaining to serial communication.

13

The Time Processor Unit

13.0 INTRODUCTION

This chapter describes the Time Processor Unit (TPU) of the MC68332. The TPU is a powerful programmable timer with 16 channels. The module provides a number of timing functions that can be used for a variety of timing and control applications. Many of these applications are discussed in this chapter which includes numerous programming examples.

For measurement and control applications, the *programmable timer* unit of a microcontroller is the most important and flexible module on the chip. For example, the programmable timer can create pulse trains with precise periods or pulses with exact pulse widths. The signals may be used to control motors, solenoids and similar devices. The input channels can be used for event counting, period measurement, pulse-width measurement or measurement of frequency.

The timing functions of a programmable timer are controlled by one or more counter registers. These registers are often called timer/counter registers because the application is counting time intervals. One important advantage of the programmable timer is that the timing of the module is independent of the CPU instruction timing once a CPU program initializes the programmable timer.

Section 13.1 introduces the TPU module and describes its functional operation. First, the module's functions, signal lines and programmable register set are defined. Then, the initialization procedure for the TPU and its 16 channels is presented.

Section 13.2 describes the Input Capture or Input Transition Counter function of the TPU. This function is used to capture the time reference associated with signal transitions on an input channel. Section 13.3 presents the Period or Pulse Width Accumulator function. Measurements of time intervals, pulse widths and pulse accumulation techniques are described. Section 13.4 explains the Output Compare capability of the TPU to generate output pulses at precise time intervals. Pulses with programmed widths and exact time relationships between the pulses can be output. Section 13.5 describes the TPU capability to generate Pulse Width Modulated output waveforms.

The TPU can generate the pulse sequences to accelerate, rotate and decelerate a stepper motor as the motor seeks a specific shaft position. Section 13.6 explains this capability of the TPU. The TPU channels can also be used for discrete I/O as described in Section 13.7.

The complete description of the MC68332 TPU is contained in the *M68300 Family TPU (Time Processor Unit) Reference Manual*. In this chapter, this manual is referred to as the *TPU Reference Manual*. The reader is encouraged to refer to the manual for more detailed information about the various time functions discussed in this chapter.

13.1 TIME PROCESSOR UNIT (TPU) OPERATION

Figure 13.1 shows the block diagram of the TPU. There are 16 channels for connection of external devices. Each channel is independent of the others and each may be used for either input or output depending on the application. A channel consists of the signal pin and a number of registers and a data area to program its operation. Each channel also contains a compare/match register which is used to determine the time at which an event is to occur. The timing of input or output events is measured relative to the values in two Timer/Counter Registers, TCR1 and TCR2. These are 16-bit counters that may be assigned as timers on any of the TPU channels. Timer TCR1 is a free-running counter clocked by the system clock. Timer TCR2 may be clocked from the system clock or by an external signal.

In a typical timer chip, a CPU program controlling the timer responds to timer interrupt requests and reprograms the timer to create the complex interaction between input captures and output matches needed in some applications. As shown in Figure 13.1, the CPU program of the MC68332 does not directly program the TPU timer channels. The channels are instead controlled by microcode within the TPU.

The TPU is actually a microcontroller dedicated to timing control. The operation of each channel is controlled by a microcode sequence held in the control store (memory) of the TPU. The CPU interacts with the TPU via the Intermodule Bus (IMB) and the host interface. This host interface consists of registers and data areas which are initialized by the CPU program to define the operation of the TPU. The microcoded sequences to perform specific operations such as stepper-motor control are called *TPU functions*.

Subsection 13.1.1 describes the time functions implemented in the control store.

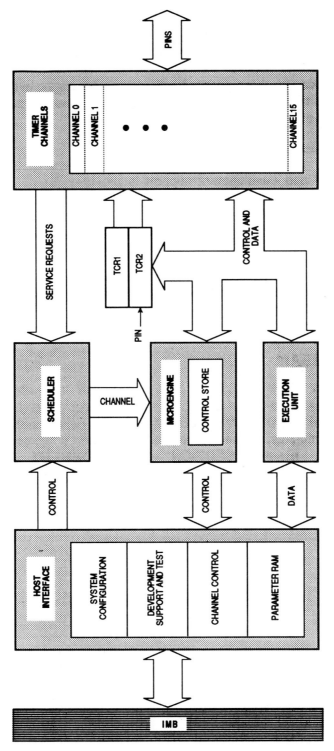

Figure 13.1 Simplified Block Diagram of the TPU.

A CPU program communicates with the TPU via the host interface shown in Figure 13.1. This interface is described in detail in Subsection 13.1.2.

A CPU program must first initialize the TPU system configuration registers in the host interface. These are global registers for the TPU that define the time resolution of the TPU timers and the interrupt parameters for the TPU as explained in Subsection 13.1.3. After global initialization using the system configuration registers, each channel to be used in an application must be initialized using the channel control registers and the parameter RAM shown in Figure 13.1. Subsection 13.1.4 describes TPU channel initialization for the various time functions that are available.

13.1.1 TPU Time Functions

Table 13.1 lists the TPU time functions implemented by Motorola for the MC68332.[1] The sections in this chapter listed in Table 13.1 explain the functions for Input Capture, Period or Pulse Width Accumulation, Output Compare, Pulse Width Modulation, Stepper Motor control and Discrete I/O.

Table 13.1 TPU Time Functions for the MC68332

Timer Function	Description	Section
Input Capture or Input Transition Counter	Detect the occurrence of an input transition or count the number of input transitions	Section 13.2
Period or Pulse Width Accumulator	Accumulate the period or pulse width of a programmable number of input pulses	Section 13.3
Output Compare	Cause an output transition or generate a pulse train at specified time	Section 13.4
Pulse Width Modulation	Output a pulse-width modulated waveform with programmable period and duty cycle	Section 13.5
Synchronized Pulse Width Modulation	Output pulse-width modulated waveforms which are synchronized in time between channels	–
Stepper Motor Control	Control the acceleration, positioning and deceleration of a stepper motor	Section 13.6
Discrete I/O	Determine the state of an input signal or cause a specific state for output	Section 13.7
Period Measurement with Additional Transition Detect	Determine the period of a periodic pulse train separated by an extra transition	–
Period Measurement with Missing Transition Detect	Determine the period of a periodic pulse train with a missing transition	–
Position-synchronized Pulse generator	Output a pulse based on the timing of events on another channel	–

[1] Since the functions are microcoded, different versions of the TPU can be easily created with other functions. In fact, the internal RAM of the MC68332 can be used as a writable control store for custom function microcode. The reader is referred to the *TPU Reference Manual* for more details.

Input Capture or Input Transition Counter. The fundamental operation on an input channel would be to store or "capture" the value in one of the free-running TPU timer/counter registers when a change in the input signal occurs. This is called an *Input Capture*. After the input signal transition occurs, the TPU channel can interrupt the CPU and cause a link to up to eight other channels if this is needed in an application. For example, linking to other channels can be used to synchronize in time the input transition with the generation of output waveforms.

In another mode, the Input Transition Counter function is used to count a specified number of input signal transitions before the CPU is interrupted. After the programmed number of transitions are counted, the channel can generate a link to other channels.

Period or Pulse Width Accumulation. The Period or Pulse Width Accumulator (PPWA) function is used to accumulate the period or the pulse width of an input signal measured in counts of the channel's timer. From one to 255 periods or pulse widths can be measured. For period measurement, the result is the counter value that accumulated from the first falling edge of the input signal until the specified number of periods is counted. The pulse width measurement accumulates the number of counts corresponding to the time the input signal was HIGH until the specified number of pulses is counted. If no linking to other channels is desired, the resulting count can be a 24-bit result.

The PPWA function can also be used to generate links to other channels. For example, output waveforms can be created by the linked channels that have a period that is proportional to the period or the pulse width of an input signal. Thus, one or more output signals can be generated with frequencies that are multiples or a division of the input signal frequency.

Output Compare. The *Output Compare* is a fundamental operation on an output channel. The function is designed to create an output match at a predetermined time. An *output match* is said to occur when the free-running counter value for an output channel matches a preset value in the channel's compare/match register. At this time, a signal transition would occur on the channel's pin. The Output Compare function can also be used to output a square wave with a programmable period when the output channel receives a link request from an input channel.

Pulse Width Modulation. The Pulse Width Modulation (PWM) function can generate a pulse-width modulated output waveform with a programmable duty cycle from 0% to 100%. A CPU program can change the duty cycle at any time while the waveform is being output. The Synchronized Pulse Width Modulation function is used to synchronize the PWM waveforms between up to eight output channels.

Stepper Motor control. The Stepper Motor function creates the output signals in the proper phase and sequence to control a stepper motor. From two to eight channels can be used for control of one motor. The algorithm to rotate the motor provides for linear acceleration and deceleration of the stepper motor with up to fourteen step rates.

Discrete I/O. The Discrete I/O function allows any TPU channel to output a logic {0} (LOW) or {1} (HIGH) under control of a CPU program. The function can also be used to monitor and store the logic level on an input channel at periodic time intervals.

Other functions. Several other special functions were incorporated for automobile engine control. For example, the Period Measurement with Additional transition and Missing transition detection functions are used to detect missing or additional special teeth on the flywheel to identify reference points in the engine's rotation. The Position Synchronized Pulses are designed to fire spark plugs and supply fuel via a fuel injector at precise angles of rotation of the engine. Figure 2.11 in Section 2.2 shows such an application. The *TPU Reference Manual* discusses these special functions in detail.

13.1.2 TPU Programming Model

Figure 13.1 shows the host interface of the TPU. The TPU communicates with the "host" via the MC68332 Intermodule Bus. Although any bus master can act as host, in this chapter the term host refers exclusively to the CPU32 processor of the MC68332. A CPU program must initialize the TPU system configuration registers to initialize the entire TPU. This initialization process is called *global initialization*. After global initialization, the individual channels can be initialized by writing appropriate values to the channel's control registers. Several of these registers also indicate the status of a channel activity after the channel is initialized. The parameter RAM in Figure 13.1 contains channel parameters that are initialized by the CPU program to define attributes of the time function being used. Also, the TPU channel stores results such as accumulated counts in the parameter RAM area.

The CPU program initialization process for the TPU and a specific channel can be summarized as follows:
(a) initialize the TPU global registers;
(b) initialize selected channel control registers for a particular time function;
(c) initialize the parameter RAM for the specific channel;
(d) assign the channel priority to enable the channel.
Every register and RAM location should be read or written with a CPU instruction using a word or longword access except the TPU Channel Interrupt Status Register which allows byte accesses.

Once a channel is initialized, the CPU program can monitor the status held in the Host Service Request register to determine when a time function has completed operation. Alternatively, interrupts can be enabled for the channel so that the CPU program is interrupted upon completion of the time function.

TPU registers and memory map. Figure 13.2(a) shows the memory map of the TPU registers in the CPU memory space. The registers start at address $YFFE00 where Y = $F or Y = $7 according to the initial address selected in the SIM Module Configuration Register after a reset as described in Chapter 14. The registers are assigned beginning address $FFFE00 in the examples in this chapter. Most of the registers are available only to a supervisor-mode program. The other registers and the parameter RAM area in Figure 13.2(b) beginning at $YFFF00 can be restricted to supervisor-mode access only or they can be assigned for unrestricted access by programs in either supervisor or user mode.

	ADDRESS	<--------------------- WORD ---------------------> 15 BYTE n 8 | 7 BYTE n+1 0
S	$YFFE00	MODULE CONFIGURATION REGISTER
S	$YFFE02	TEST CONFIGURATION REGISTER
S	$YFFE04	DEVELOPMENT SUPPORT CONTROL REGISTER
S	$YFFE06	DEVELOPMENT SUPPORT STATUS REGISTER
S	$YFFE08	INTERRUPT CONFIGURATION REGISTER
S	$YFFE0A	INTERRUPT ENABLE REGISTER
S	$YFFE0C	CHANNEL FUNCTION SELECT REGISTER 0
S	$YFFE0E	CHANNEL FUNCTION SELECT REGISTER 1
S	$YFFE10	CHANNEL FUNCTION SELECT REGISTER 2
S	$YFFE12	CHANNEL FUNCTION SELECT REGISTER 3
X	$YFFE14	HOST SEQUENCE REGISTER 0
X	$YFFE16	HOST SEQUENCE REGISTER 1
X	$YFFE18	HOST SERVICE REQUEST REGISTER 0
X	$YFFE1A	HOST SERVICE REQUEST REGISTER 1
S	$YFFE1C	CHANNEL PRIORITY REGISTER 0
S	$YFFE1E	CHANNEL PRIORITY REGISTER 1
S	$YFFE20	INTERRUPT STATUS REGISTER
S	$YFFE22	LINK REGISTER
S	$YFFE24	SERVICE GRANT LATCH REGISTER
S	$YFFE26	DECODED CHANNEL NUMBER REGISTER
	$YFFE28	RESERVED
	$YFFEFF	

S = Supervisor accessable only.
X = Assignable as supervisor accessable only (if SUPV = 1) or unrestricted (if SUPV = 0). Unrestricted allows both user and supervisor access.
Y = m111, where m is the modmap signal state on the IMB, which reflects the state of the modmap in the module configuration register of the system integration module (Y = $7 or $F).

Figure 13.2(a) Memory map of the TPU registers.

For convenience, Figure 13.3 summarizes all the bits in the TPU programmable register set. In that figure, each bit is labeled according to the definitions in Table 13.2

Channel	\multicolumn{8}{c}{Parameter}

Channel	0	1	2	3	4	5	6	7
0	X $YFFF00	02	04	06	08	0A	—	—
1	X $YFFF10	12	14	16	18	1A	—	—
2	X $YFFF20	22	24	26	28	2A	—	—
3	X $YFFF30	32	34	36	38	3A	—	—
4	X $YFFF40	42	44	46	48	4A	—	—
5	X $YFFF50	52	54	56	58	5A	—	—
6	X $YFFF60	62	64	66	68	6A	—	—
7	X $YFFF70	72	74	76	78	7A	—	—
8	X $YFFF80	82	84	86	88	8A	—	—
9	X $YFFF90	92	94	96	98	9A	—	—
10	X $YFFFA0	A2	A4	A6	A8	AA	—	—
11	X $YFFFB0	B2	B4	B6	B8	BA	—	—
12	X $YFFFC0	C2	C4	C6	C8	CA	—	—
13	X $YFFFD0	D2	D4	D6	D8	DA	—	—
14	X $YFFFE0	E2	E4	E6	E8	EA	EC	EE
15	X $YFFFF0	F2	F4	F6	F8	FA	FC	FE

— Not implemented

X = Assignable as Supervisor accessable only (if SUPV = 1) or unrestriced (if SUPV = 0). Unrestriced allows both user and Supervisor access.

Y — m111, where m is the modmap signal state on the IMB, which reflects the state of the modmap in the module configuration register of the system integration module (Y = $7 or $F).

Figure 13.2(b) Parameter RAM locations of the TPU.

Register	15	14	13	12	11	10	9	8	7	6	5	4	3	2	1	0
TMCR $YFFE00	STOP	TCR1P PRESCALER		TCR2P PRESCALER		EMU	T2CG	STF	SUPV	PSCK	0	0	INTERRUPT ARBITRATION ID			
	0	0	0	0	0	0	0	0	1	0			0	0	0	0
TTCR $YFFE02	0	0	0	INCAD	TCR1C	ACUTR1-0		0	0	TSOSEL2-0			TSISEL2-0			TMM
				0	0	0	0			0	0	0	0	0	0	0
DSCR $YFFE04	HOT4	0	0	0	0	BLC	CLKS	FRZ1-0		CCL	BP	BC	BH	BL	BM	BT
	0					0	0	0	0	0	0	0	0	0	0	0
DSSR $YFFE06	0	0	0	0	0	0	0	0	BKPT	PCBK	CHBK	SRBK	TPUF	0	0	0
	0	0	0	0	0	0	0	0	0	0	0	0	0	0	0	0
TICR $YFFE08	0	0	0	0	0	CHANNEL INTERRUPT REQUEST LEVEL			CHANNEL BASE VECTOR				0	0	0	0
						0	0	0	0	0	0	0				
CIER $YFFE0A	CHAN 15	CHAN 14	CHAN 13	CHAN 12	CHAN 11	CHAN 10	CHAN 9	CHAN 8	CHAN 7	CHAN 6	CHAN 5	CHAN 4	CHAN 3	CHAN 2	CHAN 1	CHAN 0
	0	0	0	0	0	0	0	0	0	0	0	0	0	0	0	0
CFS R0 $YFFE0C	CHANNEL 15				CHANNEL 14				CHANNEL 13				CHANNEL 12			
	0	0	0	0	0	0	0	0	0	0	0	0	0	0	0	0
CFS R1 $YFFE0E	CHANNEL 11				CHANNEL 10				CHANNEL 9				CHANNEL 8			
	0	0	0	0	0	0	0	0	0	0	0	0	0	0	0	0
CFS R2 $YFFE10	CHANNEL 7				CHANNEL 6				CHANNEL 5				CHANNEL 4			
	0	0	0	0	0	0	0	0	0	0	0	0	0	0	0	0
CFS R3 $YFFE12	CHANNEL 3				CHANNEL 2				CHANNEL 1				CHANNEL 0			
	0	0	0	0	0	0	0	0	0	0	0	0	0	0	0	0
HSQR0 $YFFE14	CHANNEL 15		CHANNEL 14		CHANNEL 13		CHANNEL 12		CHANNEL 11		CHANNEL 10		CHANNEL 9		CHANNEL 8	
	0	0	0	0	0	0	0	0	0	0	0	0	0	0	0	0
HSQR1 $YFFE16	CHANNEL 7		CHANNEL 6		CHANNEL 5		CHANNEL 4		CHANNEL 3		CHANNEL 2		CHANNEL 1		CHANNEL 0	
	0	0	0	0	0	0	0	0	0	0	0	0	0	0	0	0
HSRR0 $YFFE18	CHANNEL 15		CHANNEL 14		CHANNEL 13		CHANNEL 12		CHANNEL 11		CHANNEL 10		CHANNEL 9		CHANNEL 8	
	0	0	0	0	0	0	0	0	0	0	0	0	0	0	0	0
HSRR1 $YFFE1A	CHANNEL 7		CHANNEL 6		CHANNEL 5		CHANNEL 4		CHANNEL 3		CHANNEL 2		CHANNEL 1		CHANNEL 0	
	0	0	0	0	0	0	0	0	0	0	0	0	0	0	0	0
CPR0 $YFFE1C	CHANNEL 15		CHANNEL 14		CHANNEL 13		CHANNEL 12		CHANNEL 11		CHANNEL 10		CHANNEL 9		CHANNEL 8	
	0	0	0	0	0	0	0	0	0	0	0	0	0	0	0	0
CPR1 $YFFE1E	CHANNEL 7		CHANNEL 6		CHANNEL 5		CHANNEL 4		CHANNEL 3		CHANNEL 2		CHANNEL 1		CHANNEL 0	
	0	0	0	0	0	0	0	0	0	0	0	0	0	0	0	0
CISR $YFFE20	CHAN 15	CHAN 14	CHAN 13	CHAN 12	CHAN 11	CHAN 10	CHAN 9	CHAN 8	CHAN 7	CHAN 6	CHAN 5	CHAN 4	CHAN 3	CHAN 2	CHAN 1	CHAN 0
	0	0	0	0	0	0	0	0	0	0	0	0	0	0	0	0

Y = m111, where m is the state of the modmap bit in the module configuration register of the system integration module (Y = $7 or $F). (For information on the system integration module, refer to the MC68332 user's manual (formerly *MC68332 SIM User's Manual*), document number MC68332UM/AD).

Figure 13.3 TPU Register Set.

for the TPU global registers. The register names in Figure 13.3 correspond to the designations in the *TPU Reference Manual*. In this chapter, each TPU register will have the prefix "T" before its designation. Figure 13.3 also defines the reset value of {0} or {1} below the label for each bit. Specific registers will be discussed in this chapter as various applications of the TPU are introduced.

Table 13.2 TPU Register Bits

Bit/Field Mnemonic	Function	Register Name	Address	Bits
ACUTR1–0	TPU Response to ACUT Line	Test Configuration	$FFE02	10–9
BC	Channel Register Match	Dev. Support Control	$FFE04	4
BH	Host Service Latch	Dev. Support Control	$FFE04	3
BKPT	Breakpoint Asserted	Dev. Support Status	$FFE06	7
BL	Link Service Latch	Dev. Support Control	$FFE04	2
BLC	Branch Latch Control	Dev. Support Control	$FFE04	10
BM	Match Recognition Latch	Dev. Support Control	$FFE04	1
BP	μPC Match	Dev. Support Control	$FFE04	5
BT	Transition Detect Latch	Dev. Support Control	$FFE04	0
CCL	Channel Conditions Latch	Dev. Support Control	$FFE04	6
TINTV	Most Significant Nibble of Vector	Interrupt Configuration	$FFE08	7–4
TINTL	Channel Interrupt Request Level	Interrupt Configuration	$FFE08	10–8
CHBK	Channel Register Breakpoint Flag	Dev. Support Status	$FFE06	5
CLKS	Stop TCRs During Halt	Dev. Support Control	$FFE04	9
EMU	Emulation Control	Module Configuration	$FFE00	10
FRZ1–0	IMB Freeze Response Select	Dev. Support Control	$FFE04	8–7
HOT4	Halt on Next T4 State	Dev. Support Control	$FFE04	15
INCAD	Increment μPC Counter	Test Configuration	$FFE02	12
IARB	Interrupt Arbitration ID	Module Configuration	$FFE00	3–0
PAC	Pin Action Control	Channel Parameters		4–2
PCBK	μPC Match Breakpoint Flag	Dev. Support Status	$FFE06	6
PSC	Pin State Control	Channel Parameters		1–0
PSCK	Prescaler Clock (TCR1)	Module Configuration	$FFE00	6
TSISEL2–0	Scan In Data Selector	Test Configuration	$FFE02	3–1
TSOSEL2–0	Scan Out Data Selector	Test Configuration	$FFE02	6–4
SRBK	Service Request Breakpoint Flag	Dev. Support Status	$FFE06	4
STF	Stop Status Flag	Module Configuration	$FFE00	8
STOP	Stop Internal Clocks	Module Configuration	$FFE00	15
SUPV	Supervisor Data Space	Module Configuration	$FFE00	7
T2CG	TCR2 Clock/Gate Control	Module Configuration	$FFE00	9
TBS	Time Base/Directionality Control	Channel Parameters		8–5
TCR1 P	TCR1 Prescale Controls	Module Configuration	$FFE00	14–13
TCR1C	TCR Clock Source	Test Configuration	$FFE02	11
TCR2 P	TCR2 Prescale Controls	Module Configuration	$FFE00	12–11
TMM	Test Memory Map	Test Configuration	$FFE02	0
TPUF	TPU in Freeze Flag	Dev. Support Status	$FFE06	3

13.1.3 TPU Global Initialization

As previously discussed in Section 10.3, all of the modules of the MC68332 MCU should be initialized after a reset. The System Integration Module must be initialized first as described in Chapter 14. Then, the TPU and other modules of the MC68332 can be initialized according to the requirements of a particular application.

Figure 13.4 shows the registers involved in the global initialization of the TPU. Figure 13.5 defines the various bit fields in the global registers that must be initialized. The registers for testing and development support are not discussed in this chapter. The interested reader should consult the *TPU Reference Manual* for details concerning these registers.

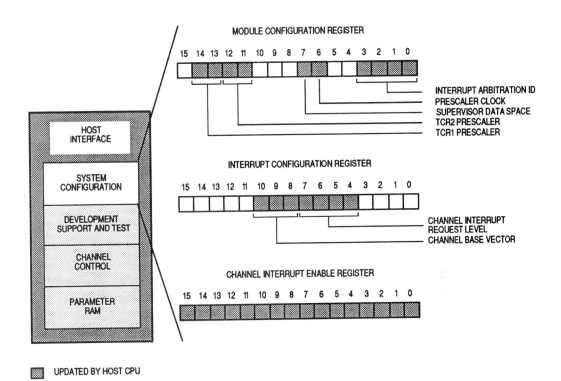

Figure 13.4 TPU registers for global initialization.

The TPU Module Configuration Register (TMCR) is initialized first to define the resolution of the TPU timers TCR1 and TCR2, program access to other TPU registers and the interrupt arbitration level. The meaning of the bits that control the timers is discussed later. If the SUPV bit of the TMCR, (TMCR)[7]) in Figure 13.5, is set to {1}, only a supervisor-mode program may initialize the TPU. If the supervisor access bit SUPV is set to {0}, an application program operating in the user mode could control the TPU channels once they are initialized.

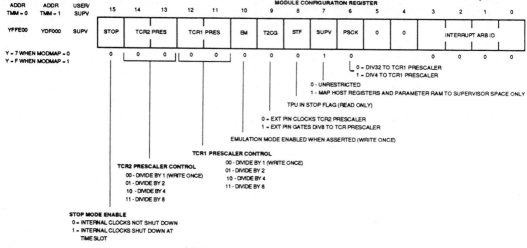

(a) TPU Module Configuration Register (TMCR)

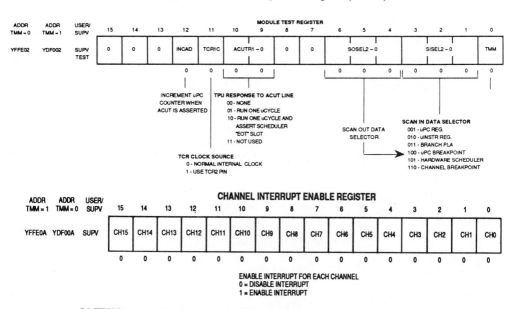

(b) TPU Interrupt Configuration (TICR) and Channel Interrupt Enable (TCIER) register

Figure 13.5 TPU global registers.

The interrupt arbitration level field, TMCR[3:0], must be specified as nonzero if the TPU is to interrupt the CPU. This is the arbitration level for the TPU module with respect to other modules such as the QSM and SIM of the MC68332.

The CPU interrupt level and vector addresses for the TPU channels must also be defined initially in the TPU Interrupt Configuration Register (TICR). These values determine the level at which the CPU is interrupted after a TPU interrupt is recognized.[2] Initialization of the channel interrupt level is explained after the timers are discussed. The other bits in the TMCR (STOP, EMU and STF) should be {0} for normal operation.

TPU timers TCR1 and TCR2. The timing of signal transitions on each channel can be synchronized to either of the two 16-bit, timer/counter registers of the TPU. These are designated as TCR1 and TCR2. Timer TCR1 is a *free-running* counter that is incremented by one count on every clock pulse to the timer. Timer TCR2 can be a free-running timer using the system clock or TCR2 can be clocked by an external signal at a periodic or nonperiodic rate.

When the count reaches $FFFF, the timer/counter is reset to $0000 and counting continues. Thus, the timing of input or output events on a TPU channel signal line is always relative to the current value of the timer selected for the channel. The actual length of time between increments of the timer/counter register is defined as the time *resolution* of the timer. The time in seconds corresponding to each count is determined by the frequency of the clock signal that increments the timer and the settings of the timer control fields in the TPU Module Configuration Register. Since TCR1 and TCR2 are independent, the two timers can be initialized with different time resolutions.

The maximum amount of time that can be measured before the timer completes a cycle of counting is 2^{16} times the time resolution for the 16-bit timers. This parameter is the timing *range* for the timer. The maximum range T_{Ri} is

$$T_{Ri} = T_{ci} \times 2^{16} \quad \text{seconds}$$

where T_{ci} is the resolution in seconds and $i = 1$ or 2 for timer TCR1 or TCR2, respectively. Thus, a tradeoff must be made between resolution and range. For example, a nominal $2\mu s$ second resolution allows a timing range of

$$T_R = 2^{16} \times 2\mu s = 131 \text{ms}.$$

In many applications, the programmed timing of signal transitions on the TPU channel pins is defined as an interval in seconds. The time between events should not exceed the timing range. On the other hand, events that occur with durations shorter than the resolution may not be recognized. For example, a very short pulse may be missed entirely on an input channel. During product design, a timing diagram showing the TPU channel requirements could be used to assure that the resolution and timing range of the timers is adequate for the application.

The prescale values in the TMCR shown in Figure 13.5(a) define a power of 2 as the divisor of the source clock frequency. The prescale fields allow a designer to select various timer clock periods as multiples of the input clock signal period; i.e., the source clock frequency is divided by the power of 2 selected by the prescale values to determine the timer clock frequency. The prescale values for dividing the source clock frequency for TCR1 are defined in TMCR[14:13]. Those for TCR2 are in TMCR[12:11].

---

[2] The selection of interrupt levels and arbitration is discussed in Chapter 15.

These prescale values can only be written once after a reset. They are set to {00} after each reset to yield a divisor of 1 (2^0) if they are not changed by an initialization routine.

Timer TCR1. The clock source for incrementing TCR1 is derived from the system clock of the MC68332. The range of possible system clock frequencies is discussed in detail in Chapter 14. The maximum frequency is 2^{24}Hz (16.78MHz). The maximum timer clock frequency for TCR1 is the system clock frequency divided by four.

The system clock frequency can be further divided to increase the timing range for TCR1 and correspondingly decrease the resolution. The divisor is determined by the TCR1 prescaler field (TMCR[14:13]) and a TCR1 prescaler clock bit (TMCR[6]). The specific bit fields involved are shown in Figure 13.5(a). The bit PSCK (TMCR[6]) defines the first division of the system clock frequency as either 4 (PSCK = {1}) or 32 (PSCK = {0}). The TCR1 Prescaler field TMCR[14:13] provides a further division by 2^n, where n is the prescale value 0, 1, 2 or 3.

Table 13.3 defines the possible clock frequencies, resolutions and timing range for TCR1 using a 16.78MHz system clock. The TMCR column in Table 13.3 shows the bit settings and the resulting division of the system clock frequency. The resolution is the period of the clock signal clocking TCR1. Example 13.1 shows the calculations that resulted in the values in Table 13.1.

Table 13.3 TCR1 Frequencies, Resolutions and Range

PSCK	TMCR[14:13]	Frequency	Resolution	Range
PSCK = 1	{00}/4	4.19MHz	238.4ns	15.6ms
	{01}/8	2.097MHz	476.8ns	31.25ms
	{10} /16	1.049MHz	953.7ns	62.5ms
	{11} /32	0.524MHz	$1.91\mu s$	125ms
PSCK = 0	{00}/32	524.3kHz	$1.91\mu s$	125ms
	{01}/64	262.1kHz	$3.81\mu s$	0.25 sec
	{10} /128	131.1kHz	$7.63\mu s$	0.5 sec
	{11} /256	65.53kHz	$15.3\mu s$	1.0 sec

Note:
The values were calculated using a 2^{24}Hz (16.78MHz) system clock.

Example 13.1

The clock for timer TCR1 is derived by a minimum division of the system clock frequency as follows:
(a) if PSCK (TMCR[6]) = {0}, the minimum divisor is 32;
(b) if PSCK (TMCR[6]) = {1}, the minimum divisor is 4.
The TCR1 clock frequency is further divided by the value in the TCR1 prescaler bits as a power of 2. The selection for TMCR[14:13] is one of the values [0, 1, 2 or 3], representing an additional division of 1, 2, 4 or 8, respectively. Thus, timer TCR1 is clocked from the system clock frequency divided by one of the values [4, 8, 16, 32, 64, 128, 256] to determine the timer's clock frequency.

The timer clock frequency is selected as one of the following:

$$\text{TCR1 frequency} = \frac{f_{(system)}}{(4 \times 2^n)} \quad ; \text{PSCK} = 1$$

where the divisor 4×2^n is either $[4, 8, 16, \text{ or } 32]$, or alternatively

$$\text{TCR1 frequency} = \frac{f_{(system)}}{(32 \times 2^n)} \quad ; \text{PSCK} = 0$$

where the divisor is either $[32, 64, 128, \text{ or } 256]$. In both cases, n is the decimal value in the TCR1 prescaler field (TMCR[14:13]).

The maximum timer clock frequency is selected when

$$\text{PSCK} = \{1\} \quad \text{and} \quad \text{TMCR}[14:13] = \{00\}$$

which yields a timer clock frequency of

$$\text{TCR1 frequency} = \frac{16.78\text{MHz}}{(4 \times 1)} = 4.19\text{MHz}$$

assuming a 16.78MHz (2^{24}Hz) system clock frequency. The resolution of the timer is thus

$$T_{c1} = \frac{1}{\text{TCR1 frequency}}.$$

This equation yields a 238.4ns period for T_{c1} calculated as the reciprocal of the maximum timer clock frequency. Thus, 238.4ns is the minimum resolution for TCR1. Other possible selections are shown in Table 13.3.

Timer/counter TCR2. TCR2 differs from TCR1 in that TCR2 can use either an external clock source input on TPU pin T2CLK or the system clock. The TPU signal lines are shown in Figure 14.1 of Chapter 14. The clock source for TCR2 is defined by the TCR2 Clock Gate control bit T2CG (TMCR[9]). The choices are as follows:
(a) T2CG = {0}, clock source is signal at T2CLK pin;
(b) T2CG = {1}, T2CLK HIGH – clock source is the system clock;
(c) T2CG = {1}, T2CLK LOW – no clocking of TCR2.

If T2CG is {0}, the clock gate for TCR2 uses the signal on TPU signal-line T2CLK as the clock source frequency divided by 2^n where n is the decimal value in the field TMCR[12:11]. The divisors are [1 ,2 ,4, or 8] in this case. The minimum resolution time of TCR2 is nominally 500ns.

If the count in timer TCR2 is incremented by an external signal, the value in TCR2 can represent any physical variable desired. For example, the value could represent mechanical position of an external device provided by a position encoder rather than time.

When bit T2CG (TMCR[9]) is {1} and the input signal at pin T2CLK is HIGH, timer TCR2 is clocked from the system clock. The maximum TCR2 clock frequency is the system clock frequency divided by 8 which is obtained when the TCR2 prescaler field (TMCR[12:11]) is {00}. With a 2^{24}Hz system clock, the maximum frequency of the TCR2 clock is thus approximately 2.1MHz yielding a minimum resolution of 477ns. The possible prescale divisors for TCR2 are 8, 16, 32, or 64 as selected by the value in the TCR2 prescaler field TMCR[12:11] as {00}, {01}, {10} or {11}, respectively.

If TCR2 is being clocked by the system clock and the input signal at pin T2CLK is LOW, timer TCR2 is not incremented.

Time measurements. Since the timers are 16-bit counters, the maximum timing range is calculated by multiplying the timer resolution by the number of bits. For either counter, the maximum timing range is

$$T_{Ri} = T_{ci} \times 2^{16} \text{ seconds}$$

where T_{ci} is the resolution of the timer T_{c1} or T_{c2} as defined previously in Example 13.1.

The elapsed time between an arbitrary number of counts is given by

$$T_{(\text{elapsed})} = T_{ci} \times (\text{number of counts}) \tag{13.1}$$

where $i = 1$ for TCR1 or $i = 2$ for TCR2. T_{ci} is the resolution in time for the counter selected in the TPU Module Control Register (TMCR) as explained in Example 13.1. For TCR1, the nominal values of T_{c1} are from 250ns to 16μseconds. Table 13.3 lists the exact resolution and the timing range for TCR1 using a 16.78MHz system clock. For example, the exact minimum resolution in time of TCR1 is 238.4ns.

The resolution for T_{c2} is nominally from 0.5μs to 4μs when the 16.78MHz system clock is chosen for the time base. If an external clock is selected for TCR2, the resolution is

$$T_{c2} = 2^{n} \times (\text{period of external clock})$$

where n is 0, 1, 2 or 3 as selected in the TCR2 prescaler field TMCR[12:11]. The minimum nominal resolution for TCR2 in any case is 500ns.

The reader should refer to the timing specifications for the particular version of the MC68332 being used since Motorola reserves the right to modify the MC68332 as newer versions are released. The specifications are published in the product description literature available from Motorola. A change in the timing specifications might affect the calculations presented in this chapter.

Register TICR, interrupt levels and vectors. The TPU Interrupt Configuration Register (TICR) at address $YFFE08 in Figure 13.3 contains two bit fields that must be initialized to allow interrupt requests to the CPU. Figure 13.5(b) defines the TICR bits in detail. The one CPU interrupt level for the TPU is selected in TICR[10:8] from level 0 (disabled) to level 7 (highest priority). For example, if TICR[10:8] is set to {100}, a level 4 CPU interrupt will be requested when one of the TPU channels causes an interrupt. The source of the interrupt can be any one of the 16 channels after the individual channel interrupts are enabled.

Each channel has a separate interrupt vector in the CPU vector table but the vectors are contiguous. The interrupt vector number is determined by concatenating the base vector number (TICR[7:4]) and the channel number. For example, a value of {101} in TICR[7:4] assigns vector $50 to channel 0, vector $51 to channel 1 and so on though vector $5F to channel 15. The vector addresses are calculated as 4 times the vector number so that vector $50 (80) occupies location $140 in the CPU vector table. If more than one channel requests an interrupt at the same time, the TPU recognizes the *lowest* numbered channel making a request.

Register TCIER, interrupt enable.   Before a channel can cause an interrupt, its interrupt must be enabled in the TPU Channel Interrupt Enable Register (TCIER) at address $YFFE0A. Figure 13.5(b) defines the TCIER bits. Any bit set to {1} in the TCIER allows interrupts on the specified channel. If a bit is {0}, no interrupt can be caused by the corresponding channel. Setting any of these bits will not cause an interrupt to occur until the channel is enabled as described in Subsection 13.1.4.

Example 13.2

Figure 13.6 is a routine to initialize the TPU global registers. The addresses of the registers involved are defined with Equate (EQU) directives. The executable initialization segment of the program begins at label TPUINIT. First, all channels are disabled and all interrupt requests are cleared. The instructions to disable the TPU and clear interrupt requests would not be necessary after an MC68332 reset.

The TPU Module Configuration Register (TMCR) is initialized to select a $7.63\mu s$ period (T_{c1}) for timer TCR1 assuming a 16.78MHz system clock frequency. Since T2CG (TMCR[9]) is {0}, the clock signal for timer TCR2 must be derived from an external source.

User mode programs may access the channel registers and the channel parameter RAM since SUPV (TMCR[7]) is set to {0}. Level 2 is selected for the interrupt arbitration level for the TPU. The modules arbitrate the interrupt requests if simultaneous interrupt requests occur as explained in Chapter 15.

The program next initializes the CPU interrupt level and base vector number in the TPU Interrupt Configuration Register (TICR). The choice here is CPU level 4 and base vector $50 for channel 0. The vector address for any channel in the CPU vector table will be

$$4 \times (\$50 + \text{channel number})$$

where the channel number $0 to $F is given in hexadecimal. The reader is referred to Section 11.7 for a discussion of the CPU interrupt vectors. Before any channel is enabled so that it can cause an interrupt, the starting address of the interrupt handling routine must be stored in the vector location and the CPU interrupts must be enabled to the appropriate level, at least level 4 in this case. Thus, the interrupt mask value in the CPU Status Register SR[10:8] must be 3 ({011}) or less as described in Subsection 11.7.1.

Finally, the routine writes $FFFF in the TPU Channel Interrupt Enable Register (TCIER) to allow every channel to interrupt if the channel is enabled. Interrupt requests are not cleared by writing {0} to the TCIER but simply disabled. The TPU channel Interrupt Status Register (TCISR) is used to clear individual interrupt requests after the interrupt is serviced as described in Subsection 13.1.4.

```
abs.   LC    obj. code   source line

  1   0000                          TTL      'FIGURE 13.6'
  2   0000              |*
  3   0000              |*          INITIALIZE THE TPU
  4   0000              |*           TCR1-SYSTEM CLOCK/128
  5   0000              |*           TCR2-EXTERNAL CLOCK
  6   4500                          ORG      $4500
  7   0000              |*
  8         0080 0000   |REGBASE  EQU      $800000              ;REGS AT $FFF000
  9         00FF FE00   |TMCR     EQU      $007FFE00+REGBASE    ;CONFIGURATION
 10         00FF FE08   |TICR     EQU      $007FFE08+REGBASE    ;CPU INTERRUPT LEVEL
 11         00FF FE0A   |TCIER    EQU      $007FFE0A+REGBASE    ;TPU CHANNEL INTERRUPTS
 12         00FF FE1C   |TCPR0    EQU      $007FFE1C+REGBASE    ;CHANNEL PRIORITY
 13         00FF FE1E   |TCPR1    EQU      TCPR0+2
 14         00FF FE20   |TCISR    EQU      $007FFE20+REGBASE    ;TPU INTERRUPT STATUS
 15   4500              |*
 16   4500 3F00         |TPUINIT  MOVE.W   D0,-(SP)             ;SAVE REGISTER
 17   4502 33FC 0000    |         MOVE.W   #$0000,TCPR0         ;DISABLE ALL CHANNELS
      4506 00FF FE1C    |
 18   450A 33FC 0000    |         MOVE.W   #$0000,TCPR1
      450E 00FF FE1E    |
 19   4512 3039 00FF    |         MOVE.W   TCISR,D0             ;CLEAR ALL TPU INTERRUPTS
      4516 FE20         |
 20   4518 33FC 0000    |         MOVE.W   #$0000,TCISR         ;  REQUESTS
      451C 00FF FE20    |
 21   4520 33FC 4002    |         MOVE.W   #$4002,TMCR          ;TCR1-DIVIDE BY 32x4
      4524 00FF FE00    |
 22   4528              |*                                     ;USER ACCESS;IARB=2
 23   4528 33FC 0450    |         MOVE.W   #$0450,TICR          ;CPU LEVEL 4;VECTOR=$50
      452C 00FF FE08    |
 24   4530 33FC FFFF    |         MOVE.W   #$FFFF,TCIER         ;ENABLE ALL TPU INTERRUPTS
      4534 00FF FE0A    |
 25   4538              |*
 26   4538 301F         |         MOVE.W   (SP)+,D0             ;RESTORE REGISTER
 27   453A 4E75         |         RTS
 28   453C              |         END
```

Figure 13.6 Program example of TPU global initialization.

13.1.4 TPU Channel Initialization

After the TPU is initialized to select the time base, interrupt level and other variables, each TPU channel used in an application must be initialized. Although the values are different for each time function, Figure 13.7 shows the channel variables that can be selected. Table 13.4 defines the variables and the registers involved. A CPU program would typically initiate a TPU channel function by initializing the channel variables in the order shown in Table 13.4. The interrupt enable field is initialized as described previously in Subsection 13.1.3. Appropriate sections of this chapter describe the six channel parameters for each particular function as each time function is introduced.

Registers TCFSR0–3, THSRR0–1, THSQR0–1. Table 13.5 defines all of the choices for initialization of the TPU Channel Function Select Registers (TCFSR0–3), the Host Service Request Registers (THSRR0–1) and the Host Sequence Registers designated THSQR0–1. Figure 13.3 defines the addresses of the registers and shows the bit fields used for each channel. For example, channel 0 is controlled by register fields TCFSR3[3:0], THSRR1[1:0], and THSQR1[1:0]. The four-bit function code selects the time function for the channel. The two-bit Host Service request defines the specific action to be taken.

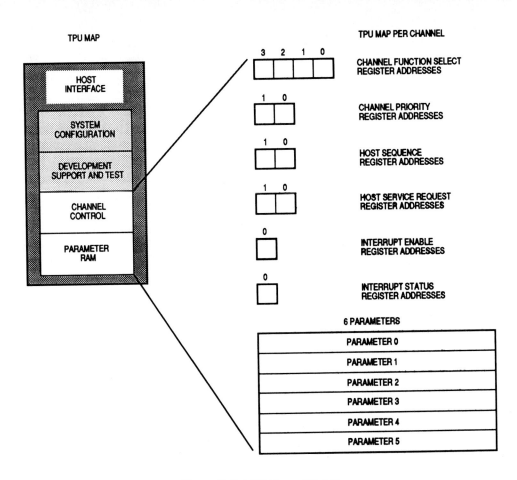

Figure 13.7 TPU Channel Variables.

Table 13.4 TPU Channel Registers and RAM Variables

Register	Address	Purpose
Selections:		
TCFSR0–3	$YFFE0C–12	Select Channel Function Code
TPRAM0–15	$YFFF00–FA	Define Channel RAM Parameters
THSQR0–1	$YFFE14–16	Select Host Sequence
THSRR0–1	$YFFE18–1A	Select Host Service Request
TCPR0–1	$YFFE1C–1E	Define Channel Priority and enable channel
Status:		
TCISR	$YFFE20	Interrupt status
THSRR0–1	$YFFE18–1A	Status of Host Service Request

For example, the stepper motor function is selected with the function code $D.

Table 13.5 TPU Time Functions and Options

Function Name	Function Code	Host Service Request Code	Host Sequence Code*
DIO Discrete Input/Output	$8	0 = None 1 = Force Output High 2 = Force Output Low 3 = Initialization, Input Specified 3 = Initialization, Periodic Input 3 = Update Pin Status Parameter	0 0 = Trans Mode - Record Pin on Transition 0 = Trans Mode - Record Pin on Transition 0= Trans Mode - Record Pin on Transition 1 = Match Mode - Record Pin at MATCH_RATE 2 = Record Pin State on HSR <u>11</u>
ITC Input Capture/ Input Transition Counter	$A	0 = None 1 = Initialization 2 = (Not Implemented) 3 = (Not Implemented)	0 = No Link, Single Mode 1 = No Link, Continuous Mode 2 = Link, Single Mode 3 = Link, Continuous Mode
OC Output Compare	$E	0 = None 1 = Host-Initiated Pulse Mode 2 = (Not Implemented) 3 = Continuous Pulse Mode	0 = Execute All Functions 1 = Execute All Functions 2 = Only Update TCRn Parameters 3 = Only Update TCRn Parameters
PWM Pulse-Width Modulation	$9	0 = None 1 = Immediate Update Request 2 = Initialization 3 = (Not Implemented)	(None Implemented)
SPWM Synchronized Pulse- Width Modulation	$7	0 = None 1 = (Not Implemented) 2 = Initialization 3 = Immediate Update Request	0 = Mode 0 1 = Mode 1 2 = Mode 2 3 =(Not Implemented)
PMA/PMM Period Measurement with Additional/Missing Transition Detect	$B	0 = None 1 = Initialization 2 = (Not Implemented) 3 = (Not Implemented)	0 = PMA Bank Mode 1 = PMA Count Mode 2 = PMM Bank Mode 3 = PMM Count Mode
PSP Position-Synchronized Pulse Generator	$C	0 = None 1 = Immediate Update Request 2 = Initialization 3 = Force Change	0 = Pulse Width Set by Angle 1 = Pulse Width Set by Time 2 = Pulse Width Set by Angle 3 = Pulse Width Set by Time
SM Stepper Motor	$D	0 = None 1 = None 2 = Initialization 3 = Step Request	(None Implemented)
PPWA Period/Pulse-Width Accumulator	$F	0 = None 1 = (Not Implemented) 2 = Initialization 3 = (Not Implemented)	0 = 24-Bit Period 1 = 16-Bit Period + Link 2 = 24-Bit Pulse Width 3 = 16-Bit Pulse Width + Link

*Host Sequence Code interpretation is determined by the function; some HSQ codes apply to all HSR codes, some only one, such as <u>Init</u>. See detailed function description for full information.

The CPU program writes a Host Service request of {10} (2) to initialize the channels involved. After the stepper motor function is initialized, a Host Service request of {11} (3) would be made to cause the motor shaft to change position. Certain functions such as the Input Capture/Input Transition Counter and the Period or Pulse Width Accumulation function only require one Host Service request to execute. The two-bit Host Sequence field in registers THSQR0–1 defines additional characteristics of a channel. In normal operation of the TPU, the "host" is always the MC68332 CPU.

To define the selections for a particular channel, the CPU program can define the Channel Function, Host Sequence, and Channel Priority values with ANDI or ORI instructions that change only the bits associated with one channel. However, the Host Service Request registers are written by the TPU with the channel status after initialization as explained later. Therefore, the Host Service Request register should be written with a MOVE instruction. Otherwise, the TPU could clear the Host Service bits on another channel during the read, modify and write cycle of an AND or OR instruction. Writing zero values to a channel's Host Service Request bits with a MOVE instruction has no effect since only the TPU can clear the bits.

Parameter RAM. Each channel has an associated number of parameters held in the TPU RAM area shown in Figure 13.2(b). The parameter area is used by a CPU program to define the characteristics of a channel for a particular time function. The TPU writes information into the RAM area that can be read by the CPU program as a channel operates or after a channel has completed a time function. Each parameter is described in detail in this chapter when specific time functions are discussed.

As shown in Figure 13.2(b), the address of TPU RAM area for a specific channel is defined as $YFFFW0 where W is the channel number in hexadecimal. For example, the RAM area for channel 0 begins at $YFFF00. As explained in Chapter 14, $Y is $7 or $F as defined in the SIM Module Configuration Register. The starting address is $FFFF00 in the author's system. Each channel has a maximum of six parameters. These parameters can be addressed with a word or longword access by a CPU instruction.

The parameters at offset locations $EC through $FE are used by certain time functions to pass results to a CPU program. For example, the Output Compare function writes the captured values in timers TCR1 and TCR2 to offset locations $EC and $EE, respectively.

Channel control options. A channel control parameter is used in each TPU function. The first location in the parameter RAM for a channel holds this parameter. The parameter CHANNEL_CONTROL shown in Figure 13.8 defines the characteristics of the channel signal line and selects the timer for the channel. The channel control parameter for each channel has the address

$$CHANNEL\_CONTROL = (\$YFFFW0)$$

where W is the channel number in hexadecimal.

There are three fields in the channel control parameter. The two bits in the Pin State Control (PSC) field define the initial signal level for output channels. The value in the Pin Action Control (PAC) field determines the channel's response as an input or output channel. For example, the PAC field specifies the type of signal transition to be detected for an input channel. For an output channel, the PAC field defines the signal transition when a match occurs. The match is indicated by the Match Recognition Latch (MRL) of the TPU channel. The Time Base Selection Control (TBS) field defines the channel as input or output and selects the timers for the channel to be matched and captured.

Various examples in this chapter illustrate the use of the channel control parameter for a particular TPU function. The other parameters held in the channel's RAM area are not common to all of the TPU functions. These other parameters are discussed as each function is introduced in this chapter.

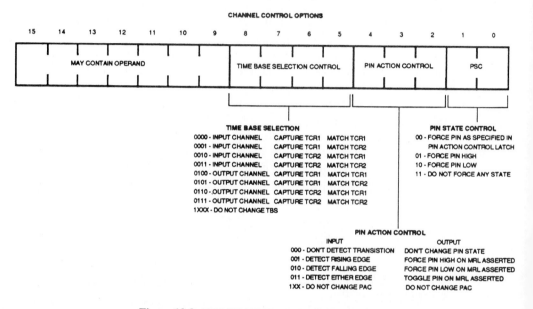

Figure 13.8 TPU CHANNEL_CONTROL parameter.

Registers TCPR0–1, channel priority. Once a CPU program defines the operation of a channel, including the channel parameters in RAM, the channel priority must be defined in register TCPR0 or TCPR1. Figure 13.3 shows that each channel has a 2-bit field to define priority. Channel 0 through channel 7 use TCPR1 at location $YFFE1E. Channel 8 through channel 15 use TCPR0 at location $YFFE1C. This is the priority assigned by the scheduler of the TPU in Figure 13.1. The priority is a two-bit field with the possible choices of {00} (disabled), {01} (low), {10} (middle), or {11} (high). When a nonzero priority for a channel is written in the appropriate bits of a TPU channel priority register, the channel is enabled and begins the operation defined by the Channel Function code and the Host Service request. Therefore, the priority should be assigned last after all other values have been initialized for a channel.

The priority assigned to a channel determines its priority in being serviced by the TPU microcode. This priority is assigned during the system design based on the maximum latency time desired for each channel. The interested reader is referred to the *TPU Reference Manual* for more information about channel priority and the method to calculate the latency time for a channel.

Registers TCISR and THSRR0–1, channel status. The TPU Channel Interrupt Status Register (TCISR) contains one interrupt status flag per channel. When a flag becomes {1} and the interrupt for the channel is enabled on an active channel, a CPU interrupt is generated. To clear the flag, it is necessary for the interrupt handling routine to first read the flag bit by reading either the byte containing the set flag or the whole word of TCISR and then writing a {0} to the flag bit location. The assertion of a flag bit by the TPU generally means that a particular TPU function has been completed.

The completion of a particular host service is indicated in a TPU Host Service Request Register (THSRR0 or THSRR1). After the TPU completes the requested host service, the Host Service request field is cleared to {00} by the TPU. At this time, a CPU program can request another host service for a particular time function.

EXERCISES

13.1.1. With reference to Figure 13.3 and Table 13.2, determine the state of the TPU and timers TCR1 and TCR2 after a reset.

13.1.2. The prescaler fields for TCR1 and TCR2 in TMCR can only be written once after a reset. What protection does this provide in a product using the TPU?

13.1.3. Define the register contents to initialize the TPU as follows:
(a) supervisor access, interrupt arbitration level 6;
(b) CPU interrupt level 5, base vector at $60 for channel 0;
(c) enable interrupts on channels 0, 3–7, and 14–15.

13.1.4. Write the program instruction to initialize TCR1 and TCR2 to have a nominal period of $4\mu s$ ($3.81\mu s$). Assume a system clock frequency of 16.78MHz.

13.1.5. Write the program instructions to initialize the register fields for channel 0 for the following operation:
(a) interrupts enabled;
(b) discrete I/O with output HIGH;
(c) middle channel priority.
Assume that the parameter RAM for the channel has been initialized.

13.2 INPUT CAPTURE OR INPUT TRANSITION COUNTER (IC/ITC)

This section describes the Input Capture or Input Transition Counter (IC/ITC) time function of the TPU. Input Capture (IC) and Input Transition Counting (ITC) are two basic operations for input events on a channel. An *Input Capture* refers to the capture of a specified Timer/Counter register (TCR) value when a single input event occurs. The event is a change in signal level on the input pin for the channel selected.

The *Input Transition Counter* mode allows a programmable number of input transitions to be counted. The particular mode as IC or ITC is selected by the count value programmed for the RAM parameter MAX_COUNT as explained later. The action taken when an input transition is detected depends upon the options selected for the TPU channel.

Figure 13.9 shows the register selections and RAM parameters of each channel configured for Input Capture or Input Transition Count. The Channel Function selection is $A. There are four options for Input Capture or Input Transition Counter as indicated by the selections in the channel's Host Sequence field. In the "single shot" mode, an interrupt request occurs when the count of input events is completed. Further transitions on the input pin are ignored. If the continual mode is selected, the TPU channel counts transitions until the selected number are detected and then generates an interrupt request. The transition count is then cleared to zero and the sequence begins again.

In either the single shot or continual mode, the channel can generate a link to a sequential block of up to eight channels after the programmed number of transitions are counted.

IC/ITC parameter RAM. Figure 13.9 specifies the RAM parameters for Input Capture or Input Transition Counter. The CHANNEL_CONTROL parameter consists of three fields. Figure 13.8 in Section 13.1 summarizes these fields. The selections for Input Capture or Input Transition Counter are the following:

(a) Pin State Control (PSC), bits[1:0] = {11};

(b) Pin Action Control (PAC), bits [4:2], select transition;

(c) Time Base Selection (TBS), bits [8:5], select timer.

The bits [15:9] are not used. The Pin State Control bits are {11} for inputs. The Pin Action Control field defines the response of the TPU channel to a change in the input signal as defined in Table 13.6 for IC or Table 13.7 for ITC. A rising edge, falling edge or either edge can be selected to cause an input capture or input transition count. The Time Base Selection field selects the channel's timer as either TCR1 or TCR2.

If the application requires linking to other channels, the linking parameters define the first channel to link and the number of consecutive channels to be linked. The bank address field contains the offset address in the parameter RAM of a 16-bit word that is to be incremented each time an input event occurs. This increment is only used by certain time functions. If the increment is not used, the address of an unused parameter such as number 06 ($0C) or 07 ($0E) shown in Figure 13.2 could be specified.

MAX_COUNT specifies the number of transitions to be counted by the channel. For a single Input Capture, MAX_COUNT is set to $0000 or $0001. The Input Transition Counter range is

$$0 < \text{MAX\_COUNT} \le \$FFFF.$$

When the number of transitions equals (or exceeds) the value specified in the channel parameter MAX_COUNT, an interrupt request is generated. This is indicated in the TPU Channel Interrupt Status Register (TCISR) by flag bit for the channel. An

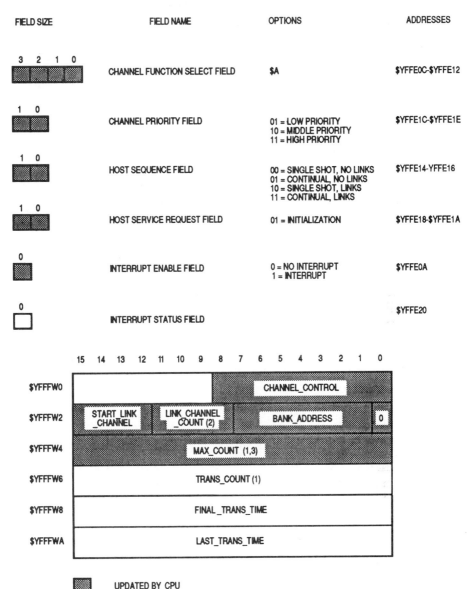

FIELD SIZE	FIELD NAME	OPTIONS	ADDRESSES
3 2 1 0	CHANNEL FUNCTION SELECT FIELD	$A	$YFFE0C-$YFFE12
1 0	CHANNEL PRIORITY FIELD	01 = LOW PRIORITY 10 = MIDDLE PRIORITY 11 = HIGH PRIORITY	$YFFE1C-$YFFE1E
1 0	HOST SEQUENCE FIELD	00 = SINGLE SHOT, NO LINKS 01 = CONTINUAL, NO LINKS 10 = SINGLE SHOT, LINKS 11 = CONTINUAL, LINKS	$YFFE14-YFFE16
1 0	HOST SERVICE REQUEST FIELD	01 = INITIALIZATION	$YFFE18-$YFFE1A
0	INTERRUPT ENABLE FIELD	0 = NO INTERRUPT 1 = INTERRUPT	$YFFE0A
0	INTERRUPT STATUS FIELD		$YFFE20

15 14 13 12 11 10 9 8 7 6 5 4 3 2 1 0

$YFFFW0	CHANNEL_CONTROL
$YFFFW2	START_LINK_CHANNEL / LINK_CHANNEL_COUNT (2) / BANK_ADDRESS / 0
$YFFFW4	MAX_COUNT (1,3)
$YFFFW6	TRANS_COUNT (1)
$YFFFW8	FINAL_TRANS_TIME
$YFFFWA	LAST_TRANS_TIME

█ UPDATED BY CPU

W = CHANNEL NUMBER

NOTES:
1. MAX_COUNT and TRANS_COUNT should be accessed coherently and reside on a double-word boundary.
2. The TPU does not perform checks on LINK_CHANNEL_COUNT value. If LINK_CHANNEL_COUNT is greater than eight or equal to zero, results are unpredictable.
3. MAX_COUNT should be between zero and $FFFF. If MAX_COUNT equals zero, the TPU counts one transition.

Figure 13.9 Input Capture/Input Transition Counter register selections and parameters.

Sec. 13.2   Input Capture or Input Transition Counter (IC/ITC)   **517** interrupt request is present when the bit corresponding to a specific channel is {1} in TCISR. If the channel's interrupts are enabled, a CPU interrupt request is generated. To allow future interrupts to occur, the CPU program must clear the request by reading TCISR and writing a zero to the bit that was set to {1}.

Subsection 13.2.1 and Subsection 13.2.2 describe the Input Capture or Input Transition Counter function of the TPU, respectively. The IC mode causes a TPU channel to recognize one signal transition and capture the channel timer value. ITC is used to count the number of transitions that occur until a specified count is reached.

One option allows an input event on one channel to cause an output event on one or more other channels by *linking* an input channel to one or more output channels. For example, linking is used to synchronize the timing of input and output events of channels. Both of the TPU functions considered in this section can employ linking between channels as described in Subsection 13.2.3.

13.2.1 Input Capture

Table 13.6 defines the channel parameters shown in Figure 13.9 that must be specified in the parameter RAM for the Input Capture function. The PSC field in parameter CHANNEL_CONTROL is set to define an input channel ({11}) and the type of input transition to be detected is defined in the PAC field. The TBS field selects the timer for the channel.

Table 13.6 Input Capture Parameters

Parameter	Value	Meaning
Inputs:		
CHANNEL_CONTROL		
PSC[1:0]	{11}	Input channel
PAC[4:2]	{000}	Do not detect transition
	{001}	Detect rising edge
	{010}	Detect falling edge
	{011}	Detect either edge
TBS[8:5]	{00xx}	Input channel
	{000x}	Capture TCR1
	{001x}	Capture TCR2
MAX_COUNT	$0001	Capture timer count for a single transition
BANK_ADDRESS	$00–$FE	(Optional)
Link Parameters		(Optional)
Output:		
FINAL_TRANS_TIME	$0000–$FFFF	Timer value when a transition occurs

Notes:
1. {x} is a Don't Care bit value.
2. BANK_ADDRESS should be assigned to an unused TPU RAM address unless a linked channel requires the parameter.

For a single Input Capture, MAX_COUNT is set to $0000 or $0001. When the transition occurs, the location defined by BANK_ADDRESS is incremented if a valid RAM address of another channel is selected for the bank address. For example, the increment of the bank address location is used by the Period Measurement with Additional Transition Detect (PMA) time function. A link is generated to other channels after the capture event if the linking parameters are specified.

The primary output parameter for a single Input Capture is the final transition time (FINAL_TRANS_TIME) parameter. This value is the timer value corresponding to the time when the transition occurred. This value can be used by another channel as its initial time reference if the Input Capture channel is linked to another channel. The other output parameters in Figure 13.9 are TRANS_COUNT and LAST_TRANS_TIME. These parameters are not used for the Input Capture function but for Input Transition Counter as explained later.

The simple Input Capture of one transition with no linking can be used for a variety of applications. Essentially, in this mode an input signal transition causes the TPU channel to request a CPU interrupt if channel interrupts are enabled. For single-shot operation, the Host Sequence field for the channel is set to {00} and only one signal transition will be recognized. In the continual mode of Input Capture, selected by {01} in the Host Sequence field, each input event will cause an interrupt request. The interrupt routine must clear the request in status register TCISR after each interrupt request is generated.

Example 13.3

The initialization program of Figure 13.10(a) selects a single Input Capture when the input signal level transitions from HIGH to LOW on Channel 14. The interrupt for the channel is enabled to cause a level 4 CPU interrupt when the input transition occurs. Example 13.1 presented an initialization program to initialize the TPU global registers and enable the channel interrupts. When the event occurs, the interrupt handling routine in Figure 13.10(b) saves the interrupt status and the TCR value in locations INPUTF and INPUTTM, respectively.

If vector $50 is selected as the base vector for the TPU as in Example 13.1, location $178 in the CPU vector table holds the starting address of the channel 14 interrupt routine. CPU interrupts must be enabled for level 4 and higher. The flag INPUTF that indicates an interrupt has been received should also be cleared by the initialization routine before the channel is initialized for Input Capture.

The TPU registers for the channel are initialized following the procedure described in Subsection 13.1.4. The program instructions beginning at label ICINIT disable channel 14 and select the Input Capture or Input Transition Counter function in the Channel Function register TCFSR0.

In the parameter RAM for channel 14, the CHANNEL_CONTROL parameter defines the channel as input to detect a falling edge on the input pin using TCR1 as the channel timer. No links are specified and the BANK_ADDRESS is set to an unused location ($DE) in the TPU RAM area since the increment is not used in this example. The parameter MAX_COUNT is defined as 1 to specify Input Capture of one transition.

The Host Sequence selection specifies single shot operation with no links. The Host Service request {01} specifies initialization of the channel. The value written to TCPR0[13:12] assigns high priority to channel 14.

```
abs. rel.   LC    obj. code    source line
---- ----   ----  ---------    -----------
   1    1   0000                          |          TTL 'FIGURE 13.10(a)'
   2    2   0000                          |*
   3    3   0000                          |*       TPU INPUT CAPTURE-CHANNEL 14
   4    4   0000                          |*
   5    5   0000                          |*       INITIAL VALUES:
   6    6   0000                          |*          HOST FUNCTION   = $A
   7    7   0000                          |*          HOST SEQUENCE   = {00};SINGLE CAPTURE
   8    8   0000                          |*          HOST SERVICE    = {01};INITIALIZATION
   9    9   0000                          |*          CHANNEL_CONTROL- DETECT FALLING EDGE;CAPTURE TCR1
  10   10   0000                          |*          MAX_COUNT       = 1 SINGLE CAPTURE
  11   11   0000                          |*          PRIORITY        = {11};HIGH PRIORITY
  12   12   0000                          |*       OUTPUT PARAMETERS IN CHANNEL RAM:
  13   13   0000                          |*          FINAL_TRANS_TIME = TCR1 VALUE AT CAPTURE
  14   14   0000                          |*                             IN LOCATION TPRAM14+8
  15   15   0000                          |*
  16   16   4600                          |          ORG     $4600
  17   17          0080 0000              |REGBASE EQU     $800000
  18   18          00FF FE0C              |TCFSR0  EQU     $007FFE0C+REGBASE ;FUNCTION
  19   19          00FF FE14              |THSQR0  EQU     $007FFE14+REGBASE ;SEQUENCE
  20   20          00FF FE18              |THSRR0  EQU     $007FFE18+REGBASE ;SERVICE
  21   21          00FF FE1C              |TCPR0   EQU     $007FFE1C+REGBASE ;PRIORITY
  22   22          00FF FFE0              |TPRAM14 EQU     $007FFFE0+REGBASE ;RAM
  23   23   4600                          |*
  24   24   4600   0279 CFFF              |ICINIT  ANDI.W  #$CFFF,TCPR0      ;DISABLE CHANNEL 14
  24        4604   00FF FE1C              |
  25   25   4608   0279 F0FF              |        ANDI.W  #$F0FF,TCFSR0     ;CLEAR CHANNEL FUNCTION REQUEST
  25        460C   00FF FE0C              |
  26   26   4610   0079 0A00              |        ORI.W   #$0A00,TCFSR0     ; AND SELECT INPUT CAPTURE
  26        4614   00FF FE0C              |
  27   27   4618                          |*
  28   28   4618                          |*       RAM PARAMETERS
  29   29   4618                          |*
  30   30   4618   33FC 000B              |        MOVE.W  #$000B,TPRAM14    ;CAPTURE TCR1 ON INPUT
  30        461C   00FF FFE0              |
  31   31   4620   33FC 00DE              |        MOVE.W  #$00DE,TPRAM14+2  ;BANK_ADDRESS ($DE)
  31        4624   00FF FFE2              |
  32   32   4628   33FC 0001              |        MOVE.W  #$0001,TPRAM14+4  ;MAX_COUNT=1
  32        462C   00FF FFE4              |
  33   33   4630                          |*
  34   34   4630   0279 CFFF              |        ANDI.W  #$CFFF,THSQR0     ;HOST SEQUENCE SINGLE SHOT, NO LINKS (00)
  34        4634   00FF FE14              |
  35   35   4638   33FC 1000              |        MOVE.W  #$1000,THSRR0     ;INITIALIZATION HOST SERVICE (01)
  35        463C   00FF FE18              |
  36   36   4640   0079 3000              |        ORI.W   #$3000,TCPR0      ;START CHANNEL
  36        4644   00FF FE1C              |
  37   37   4648   4E75                   |        RTS
  38   38   464A                          |        END
```

Figure 13.10(a) Program example of Input Capture.

Interrupt routine. Figure 13.10(b) shows the interrupt handling routine for the channel. When the signal on the input channel transitions from HIGH to LOW, a CPU interrupt is requested if interrupts are enabled. The routine first disables interrupts from the channel and stores the contents of TCISR in INPUTF. A nonzero value in INPUTF indicates to a CPU program that the interrupt request has been recognized. Then, the routine clears the interrupt request for channel 14.

The value from the RAM parameter FINAL_TRANS_TIME is stored in location INPUTTM. This value is the TCR1 count when the input signal transitioned from HIGH to LOW. A CPU program can use this value to schedule events that must be delayed with respect to the Input Capture on the channel. Since the single shot (non-continuous) mode is selected, the channel ignores all further transitions until initialized again by a CPU program.

```
abs. rel.   LC    obj. code    source line
----  ----  ----  ---------    -----------
  1    1    0000                          TTL      'FIGURE 13.10(b)'
  2    2    0000               |*
  3    3    0000               |*    OUTPUTS : (INPUTF)  = TCISR VALUE
  4    4    0000               |*                (INPUTTM) = FINAL_TRANS_TIME
  5    5    0000               |
  6    6    7E00                          ORG      $7E00                 ;INTERRUPT ROUTINE
  7    7    0000               |*                                       ; CHANNEL 14
  8    8          0080 0000    |REGBASE EQU    $800000
  9    9          00FF FE0A    |TCIER   EQU    $007FFE0A+REGBASE         ;INTERRUPT ENABLE
 10   10          00FF FE20    |TCISR   EQU    $007FFE20+REGBASE         ;INTERRUPT STATUS
 11   11          00FF FFE0    |TPRAM14 EQU    $007FFFE0+REGBASE         ;CHANNEL 14 PARAMETERS
 12   12    7E00               |*
 13   13    7E00 0279 BFFF               ANDI.W  #$BFFF,TCIER            ;DISABLE INTERRUPT
 13         7E04 00FF FE0A
 14   14    7E08 33F9 00FF               MOVE.W  TCISR,INPUTF            ;READ AND CLEAR INTERRUPT
 14         7E0C FE20 0000
 14         7E10 7E26
 15   15    7E12 0279 BFFF               ANDI.W  #$BFFF,TCISR            ; REQUEST CHANNEL 14
 15         7E16 00FF FE20
 16   16    7E1A 33F9 00FF               MOVE.W  TPRAM14+8,INPUTTM       ;SAVE FINAL_TRANS_TIME
 16         7E1E FFE8 0000
 16         7E22 7E28
 17   17    7E24 4E73                    RTE
 18   18    7E26               |INPUTF   DS.W    1
 19   19    7E28               |INPUTTM  DS.W    1
 20   20    7E2A               |                 END
```

Figure 13.10(b)   Interrupt handling routine for Input Capture.

13.2.2 Input Transition Counter

Any channel of the TPU can count the number of input capture events caused by input transitions. The initialization is similar to that of Input Capture but the parameter maximum count (MAX_COUNT) in Figure 13.9 must contain the number of transitions N to count. Table 13.7 defines the RAM parameters to be specified and the resulting output parameters.

For Input Transition Counter (ITC) mode , the CHANNEL_CONTROL parameter defines a channel as input in the PSC field and specifies the type of transitions to count in the PAC field. The timer value to be captured after N transitions is defined in the TBS field. For example, the selections

(a) PSC = {11},
(b) PAC = {011} and
(c) MAX_COUNT = N,

would specify that N input signal transitions be counted. This PAC field specifies the detection of either a rising or falling edge transition. If PAC is {001} only rising edge transitions are counted and the value {010} specifies falling edges.

Once the designated number of transitions are counted, the TPU channel requests an interrupt by setting the interrupt request bit in the TPU Channel Interrupt Status Register. If the interrupt is enabled, a CPU interrupt occurs. After the specified number of input events are counted, the channel can cause a link with up to 8 other channels if the link option is selected in the Host Sequence register. The next action depends on the choice in the Host Sequence field in Figure 13.9. The channel would terminate activity in the single-shot mode or clear TRANS_COUNT to zero and begin counting again in the continual mode.

Table 13.7 Input Transition Counter Parameters

Parameter	Value	Meaning
Inputs:		
CHANNEL_CONTROL		
PSC[1:0]	{11}	Input channel
PAC[4:2]	{000}	Do not detect transition
	{001}	Detect rising edge
	{010}	Detect falling edge
	{011}	Detect either edge
	{1xx}	Do not change PAC
TBS[8:5]	{00xx}	Input channel
	{000x}	Capture TCR1
	{001x}	Capture TCR2
MAX_COUNT	N $(0 < N \leq \$FFFF)$	Number of events to count
BANK_ADDRESS	$00–$FE	(Optional)
Link Parameters		(Optional)
Outputs:		
TRANS_COUNT	$0000–$FFFF	Number of transitions counted
FINAL_TRANS_TIME	$0000–$FFFF	Timer value when final transition occurs
LAST_TRANS_TIME	$0000–$FFFF	Timer value at previous transition

Notes:
1. {x} is a Don't Care bit value.
2. BANK_ADDRESS should be initialized to an unused TPU RAM address unless a linked channel requires the parameter.

Example 13.4

The routine of Figure 13.11 initializes TPU channel 13 for the Input Transition Counter function (ITC) for each falling edge of the input signal. The number of transitions to count must be supplied in D1[15:0] and the TPU global registers must be initialized before the routine ITCINIT is called.

The routine ITCINIT first disables channel 13 and selects the ITC function in the TPU Channel Function Select Register (TCFSR0). After the channel RAM parameters are defined, the Host Sequence value is written in register THSQR0 to specify continual operation with no links to other channels. Then, the Host Service register THSRR0 is written to initialize the channel. The value written to register TCPR0 defines high priority for the channel.

In the parameter RAM, the CHANNEL_CONTROL parameter specifies that the timer TCR1 is the time base and that the counter value is to be captured on each falling edge of the input signal. No links are specified and the BANK_ADDRESS parameter is defined to be an unused RAM location. The value in register D1 is written into parameter MAX_COUNT. The channel is enabled by the Host Service request for initialization and the assignment of high priority to the channel.

A CPU program can read any of the output parameters while the channel operates. When the last transition occurs, the TPU writes the TCR1 count value into FINAL_TRANS_TIME and requests a CPU interrupt for the channel if the channel in-

```
abs. rel.   LC    obj. code   source line
---- ----   ----  ---------   -----------
   1    1   0000                           TTL 'FIGURE 13.11'
   2    2   0000              |*
   3    3   0000              |*        TPU INPUT TRANSITION COUNT-CHANNEL 13
   4    4   0000              |*
   5    5   0000              |*        INPUT           : D1[15:0] = MAX_COUNT
   6    6   0000              |*        INITIAL VALUES  :
   7    7   0000              |*          HOST FUNCTION    = $A  ;ITC
   8    8   0000              |*          HOST SEQUENCE    = {01};CONTINUOUS CAPTURE
   9    9   0000              |*          HOST SERVICE     = {01};INITIALIZATION
  10   10   0000              |*          CHANNEL_CONTROL = DETECT FALLING EDGE;CAPTURE TCR1
  11   11   0000              |*          PRIORITY         = {11};HIGH PRIORITY
  12   12   0000              |*        OUTPUT PARAMETERS IN CHANNEL RAM:
  13   13   0000              |*          TRANS_COUNT      - RUNNING COUNT OF TRANSITIONS
  14   14   0000              |*          FINAL_TRANS_TIME- TCR1 VALUE AT COMPLETION
  15   15   0000              |*          LAST_TRANS_TIME - TCR1 VALUE AT EACH TRANSITION
  16   16   0000              |*
  17   17   4700                           ORG     $4700
  18   18         0080 0000   REGBASE EQU   $800000
  19   19         00FF FE0C   TCFSR0  EQU   $007FFE0C+REGBASE  ;FUNCTION
  20   20         00FF FE14   THSQR0  EQU   $007FFE14+REGBASE  ;SEQUENCE
  21   21         00FF FE18   THSRR0  EQU   $007FFE18+REGBASE  ;SERVICE
  22   22         00FF FE1C   TCPR0   EQU   $007FFE1C+REGBASE  ;PRIORITY
  23   23         00FF FFD0   TPRAM13 EQU   $007FFFD0+REGBASE  ;RAM
  24   24   4700              |*
  25   25   4700 0279 F3FF    ITCINIT ANDI.W #$F3FF,TCPR0      ;DISABLE CHANNEL 13
  25        4704 00FF FE1C
  26   26   4708 0279 FF0F            ANDI.W #$FF0F,TCFSR0     ;CLEAR FUNCTION REQUEST
  26        470C 00FF FE0C
  27   27   4710 0079 00A0            ORI.W  #$00A0,TCFSR0     ; AND SELECT ITC
  27        4714 00FF FE0C
  28   28   4718              |*
  29   29   4718              |*        RAM PARAMETERS
  30   30   4718              |*
  31   31   4718 33FC 000B            MOVE.W #$000B,TPRAM13    ;CAPTURE TCR1 ON FALLING EDGE
  31        471C 00FF FFD0
  32   32   4720 33FC 00DE            MOVE.W #$00DE,TPRAM13+2  ;BANK_ADDRESS-PRAM 7
  32        4724 00FF FFD2
  33   33   4728 33C1 00FF            MOVE.W D1,TPRAM13+4      ;MAX_COUNT=N
  33        472C FFD4
  34   34   472E              |*
  35   35   472E 0279 F3FF            ANDI.W #$F3FF,THSQR0     ;CONTINUOUS, NO LINKS
  35        4732 00FF FE14
  36   36   4736 0079 0400            ORI.W  #$0400,THSQR0
  36        473A 00FF FE14
  37   37   473E 33FC 0400            MOVE.W #$0400,THSRR0     ;INITIALIZATION
  37        4742 00FF FE18
  38   38   4746 0079 0C00            ORI.W  #$0C00,TCPR0      ;START CHANNEL
  38        474A 00FF FE1C
  39   39   474E 4E75                 RTS
  40   40   4750                       END
```

Figure 13.11 Program example of Input Transition Counting.

terrupt is enabled. The value of TCR1 in FINAL_TRANS_TIME would not be used if the application simply requires an interrupt request after N transitions. The interrupt routine must clear the TPU Channel Interrupt Status Register bit (TCISR[13]) so that the channel can interrupt again after the next series of transitions is counted. The bit is cleared by writing a {0} to TCIER[13] after the status register is read.

13.2.3 Channel Linking

The Input Capture or Input Transition Counter function can cause an output on one or more other channels if the link parameters in Figure 13.9 are specified. For example, the Output Compare function can be used with the input functions to create pulses or pulse trains that occur at a precise time relative to the time of the input event. The important parameter from the input channel is the value in

FINAL_TRANS_TIME

which would be used as the time reference by the channels that are linked. Subsection 13.4.3 presents examples of channel linking.

EXERCISES

13.2.1. Define the register contents and the parameter RAM contents to perform Input Capture using channel 15. The channel should detect either edge of the input signal. Use TCR2 as the channel timer, enable interrupts and assign high priority to the channel.

13.2.2. The TPU writes the final transition time into the parameter RAM when the Input Capture or Input Transition Counter function completes. What is the significance of this parameter?

13.2.3. Describe various applications for the following TPU IC/ITC functions:
  (a) Input Capture (IC);
  (b) Input Transition Counter (ITC);
  (c) ITC with TCR2 as the channel timer clocked by an external signal.

13.3   PERIOD OR PULSE WIDTH MEASUREMENT (PPWA)

The Period or Pulse Width Accumulation (PPWA) function is used to determine the period or the pulse width of an input signal. Figure 13.12 shows the register options and RAM parameters for this function. The channel function is specified as $F in the TPU Channel Function Select register. There are four basic options as indicated by the TPU Host Sequence Field in the figure. The options without links allow a 24-bit count to be accumulated to measure the period or pulse width of a signal with up to 255 periods or pulses. The linking feature allows an Output Compare on another channel to generate a signal proportional to the input on the PPWA channel.

Table 13.8 lists the parameters for the PPWA function. The selection of period accumulate or pulse width accumulate is made in the PAC field of the channel control parameter. The TBS field is used to select the capture and match timers for a channel.

The periods or the pulse widths of the input signal can be accumulated from 1 to 255 periods as set in parameter MAX_CNT. A value of 0 or 1 indicates the measurement of one period or the width of one pulse.

The parameter ACCUM_RATE determines the frequency at which the count in ACCUM is updated. The fastest rate is 1 which represents the frequency of the counter selected. The slowest is 255 ($FF). This determines the accuracy of the current, uncompleted, accumulation in ACCUM. The time between accumulations is determined as follows:

$$\text{Time of update of ACCUM} = \text{ACCUM\_RATE} \times T_{ci}$$

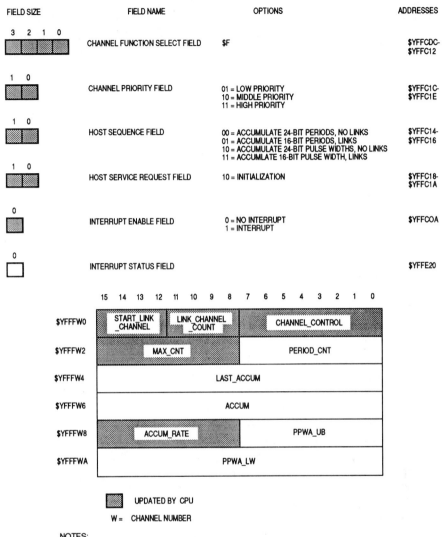

FIELD SIZE	FIELD NAME	OPTIONS	ADDRESSES

3 2 1 0
CHANNEL FUNCTION SELECT FIELD — $F — $YFFCDC- $YFFC12

1 0
CHANNEL PRIORITY FIELD — 01 = LOW PRIORITY / 10 = MIDDLE PRIORITY / 11 = HIGH PRIORITY — $YFFC1C- $YFFC1E

1 0
HOST SEQUENCE FIELD — 00 = ACCUMULATE 24-BIT PERIODS, NO LINKS / 01 = ACCUMULATE 16-BIT PERIODS, LINKS / 10 = ACCUMULATE 24-BIT PULSE WIDTHS, NO LINKS / 11 = ACCUMLATE 16-BIT PULSE WIDTH, LINKS — $YFFC14- $YFFC16

1 0
HOST SERVICE REQUEST FIELD — 10 = INITIALIZATION — $YFFC18- $YFFC1A

0
INTERRUPT ENABLE FIELD — 0 = NO INTERRUPT / 1 = INTERRUPT — $YFFCOA

0
INTERRUPT STATUS FIELD — — $YFFE20

```
       15  14  13  12  11  10   9   8   7   6   5   4   3   2   1   0
$YFFFW0   START_LINK      LINK_CHANNEL          CHANNEL_CONTROL
          _CHANNEL          _COUNT
$YFFFW2        MAX_CNT                              PERIOD_CNT
$YFFFW4                          LAST_ACCUM
$YFFFW6                            ACCUM
$YFFFW8        ACCUM_RATE                            PPWA_UB
$YFFFWA                           PPWA_LW
```

▨ UPDATED BY CPU

W = CHANNEL NUMBER

NOTES:

1. The TPU does not check the value of LNK CHN CNT. If this parameter is not > 0 and ≤ 8, the results are unpredictable.

2. MAX_CNT may be written at any time by the host CPU, but if the value written is ≤ PERIOD_CNT, a period or pulse-width accumulation is terminated. if this happens, the number of periods over which the accumulation is done will not correspond to MAX_CNT.

Figure 13.12 Period or Pulse Width Accumulation parameters.

where T_{ci} is the resolution of the match timer selected in the TBS field of the channel control parameter.

The parameter ACCUM_RATE is important when a CPU program reads the running accumulation ACCUM while the channel operates. However, the accuracy

Table 13.8 Period or Pulse Width Accumulation Parameters

Parameter	Value	Meaning
Inputs:		
CHANNEL_CONTROL		
PSC[1:0]	{11}	Input
PAC[4:2]	{001}	Pulse width accumulation
	{010}	Period accumulation
TBS[8:5]	{0000}	Capture TCR1
	{0011}	Capture TCR2
MAX_CNT	$00–$FF	Number of periods to count
	(1–255)	
ACCUM_RATE	$01–$FF	Rate of update of ACCUM
Link parameters		(optional)
Outputs:		
PERIOD_CNT	$00–$FF	Number of periods in current accumulation
LAST_ACCUM	$0000–$FFFF	Timer value for last transition
ACCUM	$0000–$FFFF	Current accumulated count
PPWA_UB	$00–$FF	Upper 8 bits of last accumulation (24-bit mode)
PPWA_LW	$0000–$FFFF	Lower 16-bits of last accumulation

Note:
PPWA_UB should be initialized to zero by the CPU program if a 24-bit count is used.

of the final accumulation parameter (PPWA) depends only on the resolution of the timer not on the accumulation rate. The *TPU Reference Manual* recommends that the rate be set to the slowest rate ($FF) if the running accumulation is not read by a CPU program. The reader is referred to the manual for more information about the accumulation rate.

Once initialized, the PPWA channel accumulates periods or pulse widths continuously until the channel is disabled. A CPU program can read the output parameters PERIOD_CNT, ACCUM and LAST_ACCUM at any time the channel is operating. The parameter PERIOD_CNT indicates the current number of periods or pulse widths that have been accumulated. Parameter LAST_ACCUM is the timer value that was captured at the most recent update of ACCUM.

An accumulation is complete when

$$PERIOD\_CNT \geq MAX\_CNT$$

at which time the TPU updates the accumulation. With no linking, the accumulation is a 24-bit count in PPWA_UB and PPWA_LW from ACCUM. Then, the TPU initializes ACCUM and PERIOD_CNT to zero for the next accumulation. An interrupt request is then asserted for the channel which causes a CPU interrupt if the channel's interrupt is enabled as described previously in Section 13.1. The operation with links to other channels allows only a 16-bit accumulation.

To create a continuous running accumulator, a CPU program could set the parameter MAX_CNT to its maximum value ($FF) initially and then periodically read ACCUM while resetting PERIOD_CNT to zero. This operation prevents the current period or pulse width count from becoming equal the maximum count in MAX_CNT so the channel does not cease operation when the specified number of periods or pulse widths are counted.

Applications of Period or Pulse Width Accumulation. The PPWA function is used to determine the time duration of an input event or a sequence of input events. Typical measurements are the following:
(a) determine the duration of a pulse train;
(b) determine the frequency of the input signal;
(c) determine the cumulative HIGH time of an input signal;
(d) determine the duration of an event indicated by a HIGH input.
The items (a) and (b) use period measurement and items (c) and (d) are derived from pulse width accumulation measurements.

In many applications, the value of a physical quantity such as position, voltage or temperature is converted to a pulse train with a precise number of pulses. The number of pulses could be proportional to the value of the quantity being measured. For example, analog sensing devices such as tachometers and pressure sensors may use a voltage-to-frequency converter to output a series of pulses to define the analog value of the variable being measured. Once the pulses are counted, a program would convert the pulse count to appropriate units such as RPM, or pressure units. Thus, the number of pulses over a specific period of time is counted and then converted to useful physical units to measure the value of a continuous variable. The pulse counting method can be also used to determine the value of a discrete variable that does not represent a physical quantity varying continuously in time.

Accumulated time. When the Host Sequence field is {00} or {10}, a 24-bit accumulation with no links is specified. The timing range of the parameter PPWA in the parameter RAM is calculated as

$$T_{Ri} = T_{ci} \times 2^k \quad \text{seconds}$$

where k is 24 and T_{ci} is the resolution for the channel timer. The possible timer resolutions T_{ci} were defined previously in Subsection 13.1.3.

For example, a 24-bit count using TCR1 with a resolution of $T_{c1} = 15.3\mu s$ could be as long as

$$T_{R1} = 15.3\mu s \times 2^{24} \quad \text{seconds}$$

yielding a range of 256 seconds.

The exact time range for an accumulation using TCR1 as the channel timer with a 2^{24}Hz (16.78MHz) system clock can be calculated in terms of the TCR1 prescaler value set in TMCR as described in Section 13.1. For example, when TMCR[6] (PSCK) is {0} to indicate a divide by 32 of the system clock frequency, the timing range is

$$T_{R1} = \frac{(2^n \times 32)}{2^{24}\text{Hz}} \times 2^{24} \text{ seconds}; \quad \text{PSCK}=0$$

where n is the prescale value in TMCR[14:13] of 0, 1, 2 or 3 as defined in Section 13.1. The equation is easily simplified to

$$T_{R1} = 2^{n+5} \text{ seconds (24-bit accumulation)}$$

where $n = 0, 1, 2$ or 3. Thus, the longest range can be 32, 64, 128 or 256 seconds for a 24-bit count using TCR1 as the timer with a 2^{24}Hz system clock frequency. If the PSCK bit in TMCR is {1}, the system clock frequency is divided by 4 instead of 32 before the TCR1 prescaler field selects a further division in frequency.

Using TCR2 clocked by the system clock, the minimum frequency division of the system clock frequency is 8. For a 24-bit accumulation the maximum timing range is 8, 16, 32 or 64 seconds depending on the selection in the prescaler field TMCR[12:11] for TCR2. However, if an external clock is used to clock TCR2, the maximum accumulation period is determined by the period of the external clock.

If links are specified, the accumulation value in PPWA_LW allows only a 16-bit accumulation. Using TCR1 as the time base would allow a maximum accumulation time of 1 second if T_{c1} is 15.3μs as previously explained in Section 13.1.

Maximum frequency. Each TPU time function has a specified latency time for initialization and a maximum frequency of operation for detecting input transitions or causing output transitions. The timing calculations are described in the *TPU Reference Manual*. However, the reader should consult the timing specifications for the particular version of the MC68332 chip being used since the timings are subject to change with new revisions of the chip.

As an example, the author's *TPU Reference Manual* specifies a minimum latency of 16 system clock cycles for the setup time of the PPWA function. For a 2^{24}Hz system clock, the cycle time (period) is 59.6ns. The latency during initialization is thus 954ns.

The minimum time to recognize a HIGH to LOW transition and begin to accumulate the LOW time is 70 clock cycles. Thus, the input pulse should not have a LOW time of less than 70×59.6ns or 4.17μs. Assuming a periodic input, the minimum period is 8.34μs corresponding to a maximum frequency of approximately 110kHz. The results of accumulations may be in error if signals of higher frequency are input for the PPWA function.

Section outline. Subsection 13.3.1 describes the period accumulation mode of the PPWA function. This mode is used to determine the period of an input signal. Subsection 13.3.2 treats the pulse width accumulation mode of the PPWA function used to determine the pulse width of an input pulse or the HIGH time of a pulse train. Subsection 13.3.3 explains the linking option for the PPWA function.

13.3.1 Period Accumulation

Figure 13.13(a) shows the operation of the period accumulation option. After initialization, the channel accumulates the count associated with each period beginning with the first HIGH to LOW transition of the input signal. The function accumulates the sum of the counts for each period for 1 to 255 periods. The total count would be the sum:

$$N_p = N_{p1} + N_{p2} + \cdots + N_{pN} \qquad (13.2(a))$$

where N_{pi} is the count for the ith period. This value is accumulated in the RAM parameter PPWA. The accumulated count can be converted to time in seconds by multiplying by the time resolution of the timer (TCR1 or TCR2) selected for the channel. Thus, the length of the pulse train in seconds is

$$T_p = N_p \times T_{ci} \qquad (13.2(b))$$

where T_{ci} is the time resolution of either TCR1 or TCR2 as described in Section 13.1. Example 13.5 presents a numerical example.

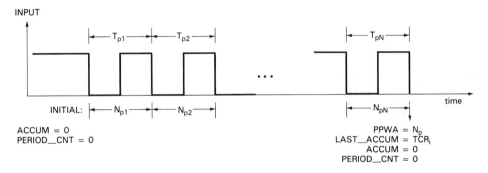

(a) Period accumulation

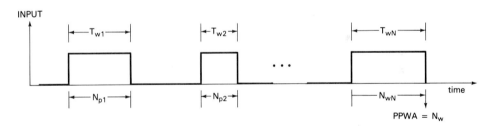

(b) Pulse Width accumulation

Figure 13.13 Period or Pulse Width Accumulation waveforms.

Example 13.5

Assume that a transducer converts a physical quantity to a voltage which in turn is converted to a pulse train by a device such as a voltage-to-frequency converter. For a constant input voltage, the voltage to frequency conversion results in a pulse train as shown in Figure 13.13(a) with equal periods for each pulse. If the period of each pulse is T, the frequency in Hertz is calculated as

$$f_p = 1/T \qquad \text{Hertz}$$

where T is measured in seconds.[3] When the measured variable varies with time, the frequency of the pulse train is not constant. Dividing the total pulse train duration given in Equation 13.2(b) by the number of pulses would yield an average frequency and hence the average value of the variable over the time interval.

```
abs. rel.   LC    obj. code   source line
---- ----   ----  ----------  -----------
   1    1   0000                |         TTL 'FIGURE 13.14(a)'
   2    2   0000                |*
   3    3   0000                |*        TPU PERIOD MEASUREMENT-CHANNEL 12
   4    4   0000                |*
   5    5   0000                |*        INPUT          : D1[7:0] = MAX_COUNT
   6    6   0000                |*        INITIAL VALUES :
   7    7   0000                |*           HOST FUNCTION  = $F
   8    8   0000                |*           HOST SEQUENCE  = {00};ACCUMULATE PERIODS
   9    9   0000                |*           HOST SERVICE   = {10};INITIALIZATION
  10   10   0000                |*           CHANNEL_CONTROL= DETECT FALLING EDGE;CAPTURE TCR1
  11   11   0000                |*           ACCUM_RATE     = $14 UPDATE RATE OF ACCUM
  12   12   0000                |*           PRIORITY       = {11};HIGH PRIORITY
  13   13   0000                |*        OUTPUT PARAMETERS IN CHANNEL RAM:
  14   14   0000                |*           PERIOD_COUNT  - RUNNING COUNT OF PERIODS
  15   15   0000                |*           LAST_ACCUM    - TCR1 VALUE AT LAST UPDATE OF ACCUM
  16   16   0000                |*           ACCUM         - RUNNING TCR1 VALUE
  17   17   0000                |*           PPWA_UB       - UPPER 8 BITS OF ACCUMULATION
  18   18   0000                |*           PPWA_LW       - LOWER 16 BITS OF ACCUMULATION
  19   19   0000                |*
  20   20   4800                |         ORG    $4800
  21   21         0080 0000     |REGBASE EQU   $800000
  22   22         00FF FE0C     |TCFSR0  EQU   $007FFE0C+REGBASE ;FUNCTION
  23   23         00FF FE14     |THSQR0  EQU   $007FFE14+REGBASE ;SEQUENCE
  24   24         00FF FE18     |THSRR0  EQU   $007FFE18+REGBASE ;SERVICE
  25   25         00FF FE1C     |TCPR0   EQU   $007FFE1C+REGBASE ;PRIORITY
  26   26         00FF FFC0     |TPRAM12 EQU   $007FFFC0+REGBASE ;RAM
  27   27   4800                |*
  28   28   4800 0279 FCFF      |PMINIT  ANDI.W #$FCFF,TCPR0    ;DISABLE CHANNEL 12
  28        4804 00FF FE1C      |
  29   29   4808 0279 FFF0      |         ANDI.W #$FFF0,TCFSR0  ;CLEAR FUNCTION REQUEST
  29        480C 00FF FE0C      |
  30   30   4810 0079 000F      |         ORI.W  #$000F,TCFSR0  ; AND SELECT PPWA
  30        4814 00FF FE0C      |
  31   31   4818                |*
  32   32   4818                |*        RAM PARAMETERS
  33   33   4818                |*
  34   34   4818 33FC 000B      |         MOVE.W #$000B,TPRAM12    ;CAPTURE TCR1 ON FALLING EDGE
  34        481C 00FF FFC0      |
  35   35   4820 E149           |         LSL.W  #8,D1            ;SHIFT N TO UPPER BYTE
  36   36   4822 33C1 00FF      |         MOVE.W D1,TPRAM12+2     ;MAX_COUNT=N
  36        4826 FFC2           |
  37   37   4828 33FC 1400      |         MOVE.W #$1400,TPRAM12+8  ;ACCUM_RATE=$14;
  37        482C 00FF FFC8      |
  38   38   4830                |*                                ; AND CLEAR PPWA_UB
  39   39   4830 33FC 0000      |         MOVE.W #$0000,TPRAM12+$A ;CLEAR PPWA_LW
  39        4834 00FF FFCA      |
  40   40   4838                |*
  41   41   4838 0279 FCFF      |         ANDI.W #$FCFF,THSQR0    ;24-BIT ACCUMULATION, NO LINKS
  41        483C 00FF FE14      |
  42   42   4840 33FC 0200      |         MOVE.W #$0200,THSRR0    ;INITIALIZATION
  42        4844 00FF FE18      |
  43   43   4848 0079 0300      |         ORI.W  #$0300,TCPR0     ;HIGH PRIORITY; START CHANNEL
  43        484C 00FF FE1C      |
  44   44   4850 4E75           |         RTS
  45   45   4852                |         END
```

Figure 13.14(a) Program for frequency measurement.

---

[3] The frequency of operation in Hertz is considered the reciprocal of the cycle time. More precisely, it refers to the frequency of the fundamental sinusoidal wave in a Fourier series analysis of the input pulse train.

```
abs. rel.   LC    obj. code   source line
---- ----   ----  ---------   -----------
   1    1   0000                            TTL      'FIGURE 13.14(b)'
   2    2   0000               |*
   3    3   0000               |*       OUTPUTS : (PMFLAG) = TCISR VALUE
   4    4   0000               |*                 (PERIOD) = PPWA RESULTS
   5    5   0000               |
   6    6   7C00               |         ORG      $7C00                    ;INTERRUPT ROUTINE
   7    7   0000               |*                                         ; CHANNEL 12
   8    8         0080 0000    |REGBASE  EQU      $800000
   9    9         00FF FE20    |TCISR    EQU      $007FFE20+REGBASE        ;INTERRUPT STATUS
  10   10         00FF FFC0    |TPRAM12  EQU      $007FFFC0+REGBASE        ;CHANNEL 12 PARAMETERS
  11   11   7C00               |*
  12   12   7C00 2F00          |CH12IRQ  MOVE.L   D0,-(SP)                 ;SAVE REGISTER
  13   13   7C02 4280          |         CLR.L    D0
  14   14   7C04 2039 00FF     |         MOVE.L   TPRAM12+8,D0             ;SAVE PPWA_UB AND PPWA_LW
  14       7C08 FFC8           |
  15   15   7C0A 0279 FF00     |         ANDI.W   #$FF00,TPRAM12+8         ; AND CLEAR PPWA_LB
  15       7C0E 00FF FFC8      |
  16   16   7C12 0280 00FF     |         ANDI.L   #$00FFFFFF,D0            ;MASK D0[31:24]
  16       7C16 FFFF           |
  17   17   7C18 23C0 0000     |         MOVE.L   D0,PERIOD                ;STORE ACCUMULATED COUNT
  17       7C1C 7C36           |
  18   18   7C1E 33F9 00FF     |         MOVE.W   TCISR,PMFLAG             ;READ AND CLEAR INTERRUPT
  18       7C22 FE20 0000      |
  18       7C26 7C34           |
  19   19   7C28 0279 EFFF     |         ANDI.W   #$EFFF,TCISR             ; REQUEST CHANNEL 12
  19       7C2C 00FF FE20      |
  20   20   7C30 201F          |         MOVE.L   (SP)+,D0                 ;RESTORE REGISTER
  21   21   7C32 4E73          |         RTE
  22   22   7C34               |PMFLAG   DS.W     1
  23   23   7C36               |PERIOD   DS.L     1
  24   24   7C3A               |         END
```

Figure 13.14(b)   Interrupt routine for frequency measurement.

The routine of Figure 13.14(a) initializes TPU channel 12 to measure the accumulated period of a pulse train. It is assumed that the TPU is initialized globally as in Example 13.2 before the routine PMINIT is called. Thus, timer TCR1 resolution is $7.63\mu s$ and the channel interrupt is enabled. Register D1[7:0] must contain the number of periods to count before the routine is called. Also, the interrupt flag PMFLAG in Figure 13.14(b) should be cleared before channel initialization.

The count value is shifted left to the upper byte of D1[16:0] before this value is written to the parameter MAX_COUNT since only word-length transfers are allowed for the RAM parameters. The accumulation rate of 20 ($14) selects an update rate for ACCUM of

$$\text{time of update of ACCUM} = 20 \times 7.63\mu s$$

or $152\mu s$ with a TCR1 resolution of

$$T_{c1} = 7.63\mu s$$

as selected as in Example 13.2. The instruction that writes the accumulation rate also clears PPWA_UB. The maximum time of accumulation before a counter overflow occurs is $7.63\mu s \times 2^{24}$Hz or 128 seconds.

Then, the 16-bit accumulator value PPWA_LW is cleared. Clearing PPWA_LW is not strictly necessary since the TPU updates this parameter with the value in ACCUM when the accumulation is complete. Finally, the channel priority is defined to start the channel's operation.

After the specified number of periods are accumulated, the channel requests an interrupt if interrupts are enabled and begins another accumulation unless the channel is disabled.

Interrupt routine. The interrupt routine of Figure 13.14(b) transfers the accumulated period values from the parameter RAM to the location at label PERIOD. The count of a 24-bit accumulation is calculated as

$$N_p = 2^8 \times (\text{PPWA\_UB}) + \text{PPWA\_LW}$$

in terms of the accumulation count in the parameter RAM if PPWA_UB and PPWA_LW are read separately. The longword accumulation result is transferred to D0 in the interrupt routine and the upper 8 bits of D0 are masked to form the correct longword result in location PERIOD.

The interrupt routine sets the flag PMFLAG to a nonzero value by storing the contents of TCISR in the flag location. The flag would be used to determine that a new period measurement had occurred by a program (not shown) that reads the PERIOD value . The flag should be cleared after PERIOD is read by the program so that the next interrupt will change the flag to a nonzero value.

Test case. The results of a particular accumulation of 128 periods using the author's development system were as follows:
(a) PERIOD_CNT = $00
(b) LAST_ACCUM = $F091;
(c) ACCUM = $0000
(d) PERIOD = $272DF (160479)
where the values were read from the parameter RAM and the location PERIOD defined in the interrupt routine. As expected, the TPU set PERIOD_CNT and ACCUM parameters to zero after accumulating the total period of 128 periods. The last accumulation value is the TCR1 count when the last accumulation is completed. The value is not used in this example.

The total time for the pulse train is

$$T_p = 160479 \times 7.63\mu s = 1.22 \text{ seconds}$$

using $N_p = 160479$ in Equation 13.2(b). For a signal that is almost periodic, the average period of each cycle is

$$T_{pi} = \frac{N_p \times T_{c1}}{(\text{MAX\_CNT})} = 1.22/128 \quad \text{seconds}$$

or 9.56ms. The corresponding wavetrain frequency is the reciprocal

$$f_{pi} = \frac{(\text{MAX\_CNT})}{N_p \times T_{c1}} = 104.5\text{Hz}.$$

The test signal was a square wave with a frequency of approximately 100Hz.

13.3.2 Pulse Width Accumulation.

Figure 13.13(b) shows that the accumulated count in the pulse width measurement mode is proportional to the HIGH time of the signal. The count accumulated in RAM parameter PPWA by the TPU channel is

$$N_w = N_{w1} + N_{w2} + \cdots + N_{wN} \tag{13.3(a)}$$

where N_{wi} is the count for the ith pulse. The HIGH time for 1 to 255 pulses is the sum:

$$T_w = T_{w1} + T_{w2} + \cdots + T_{wN} \tag{13.3(b)}$$

where T_{wi} is the HIGH time (pulse-width) of the ith pulse. The total HIGH time of the pulse train in seconds is

$$T_w = N_w \times T_{ci} \tag{13.3(c)}$$

where T_{ci} is the resolution in time for the channel's timer.

The time duration for which an input signal is in a particular state is often used to determine the duration of external events. For example, the input could be driven HIGH when an event begins and then reset to LOW upon termination of the activity. The Pulse Width Accumulation function of the TPU can measure the HIGH time for N such events as shown in Equation 13.3. The result could represent the actual time elapsed or another quantity such as total power consumed by an external device. Once the total accumulated time is stored, the value can be converted to the appropriate units.

Example 13.6

The routine of Figure 13.15 initializes the TPU to accumulate the pulse widths represented by the HIGH time of a pulse train on channel 15. Before the routine is called, the TPU must be initialized in a manner similar to that shown in Example 13.2. However, TCR1 resolution was selected as 15.3μs in TMCR[14:13] for this example. The interrupt vector address was written into location $17C for channel 15. When an accumulation is complete, the TPU channel will request a level 4 CPU interrupt if interrupts are enabled. Register D1[7:0] must contain the number of pulses to count.

The routine first disables the channel and selects the PPWA function in the TPU Channel Function Select register. The CHANNEL_CONTROL parameter for pulse-width accumulation in this example selects TCR1 as the time base in the TBS field. The PAC field is initialized to select rising edge detection to begin accumulation. The parameter MAX_CNT is written from the low order byte of register D1 shifted up to the high-order byte of the wordlength parameter. The accumulation rate parameter (AC-CUM) is set to $14. Thus, the time between updates of the ACCUM parameter is

$$T_{(ACCUM)} = 15.3\mu s \times 20$$

or every 0.3ms.

The upper byte of the 24-bit count parameter (PPWA_UB) is cleared before the channel is enabled. The maximum time of accumulation for the pulses for a 24-bit count is

$$T_{(pmax)} = 2^{24} \times 2^{-16} = 256 \text{ seconds}$$

since the resolution of TCR1, T_{c1}, is 15.3μs (2^{-16} seconds). Once the count is complete, the total elapsed HIGH time can be calculated by Equation 13.3(c).

After the parameter RAM is initialized, the Host Sequence field is defined to select the continuous pulse width accumulation mode. Initialization of the channel function is next requested in THSRR0. The accumulation begins when the signal on channel 15 goes HIGH after the channel priority is selected in TCPR0[15:14].

A CPU interrupt is requested when the input signal goes LOW after the last pulse. The interrupt routine (not shown) should store the accumulated count and clear the accumulation parameters. Then, the routine clears the channel's interrupt request. An

```
abs. rel.   LC    obj. code    source line
---- ----   ----  ---------    -----------
   1    1   0000                        TTL 'FIGURE 13.15'
   2    2   0000               *
   3    3   0000               *    TPU PULSE WIDTH MEASUREMENT-CHANNEL 15
   4    4   0000               *
   5    5   0000               *    INPUT            : D1[7:0] = MAX_COUNT
   6    6   0000               *    INITAL VALUES    :
   7    7   0000               *       HOST FUNCTION  = $F
   8    8   0000               *       HOST SEQUENCE  = {10};ACCUMULATE PULSE-WIDTHS
   9    9   0000               *       HOST SERVICE   = {10};INITIALIZATION
  10   10   0000               *       CHANNEL_CONTROL= DETECT RISING EDGE;CAPTURE TCR1
  11   11   0000               *       ACCUM_RATE     = UPDATE RATE OF ACCUM
  12   12   0000               *       PRIORITY       = {11};HIGH PRIORITY
  13   13   0000               *    OUTPUT PARAMETERS IN CHANNEL RAM:
  14   14   0000               *       PERIOD_COUNT   = RUNNING COUNT OF PULSE WIDTH
  15   15   0000               *       LAST_ACCUM     = TCR1 VALUE AT LAST UPDATE OF ACCUM
  16   16   0000               *       ACCUM          = RUNNING TCR1 VALUE
  17   17   0000               *       PPWA_UB        = UPPER 8 BITS OF ACCUMULATION
  18   18   0000               *       PPWA_LW        = LOWER 16 BITS OF ACCUMULATION
  19   19   0000               *
  20   20   4900                        ORG      $4900
  21   21         0080 0000    REGBASE EQU   $800000
  22   22         00FF FE0C    TCFSR0  EQU   $007FFE0C+REGBASE ;FUNCTION
  23   23         00FF FE14    THSQR0  EQU   $007FFE14+REGBASE ;SEQUENCE
  24   24         00FF FE18    THSRR0  EQU   $007FFE18+REGBASE ;SERVICE
  25   25         00FF FE1C    TCPR0   EQU   $007FFE1C+REGBASE ;PRIORITY
  26   26         00FF FFF0    TPRAM15 EQU   $007FFFF0+REGBASE ;RAM
  27   27   4900               *
  28   28   4900  0279 3FFF    PPWINIT ANDI.W  #$3FFF,TCPR0     ;DISABLE CHANNEL 15
  28        4904  00FF FE1C
  29   29   4908  0079 F000            ORI.W   #$F000,TCFSR0    ;SELECT PPWA
  29        490C  00FF FE0C
  30   30   4910               *
  31   31   4910               *    RAM PARAMETERS
  32   32   4910               *
  33   33   4910  33FC 0007            MOVE.W  #$0007,TPRAM15   ;CAPTURE TCR1 ON RISING EDGE
  33        4914  00FF FFF0
  34   34   4918  E149                 LSL.W   #8,D1            ;SHIFT N TO UPPER BYTE
  35   35   491A  33C1 00FF            MOVE.W  D1,TPRAM15+2     ;MAX_COUNT=N
  35        491E  FFF2
  36   36   4920  33FC 1400            MOVE.W  #$1400,TPRAM15+8 ;ACCUM_RATE=$14;
  36        4924  00FF FFF8
  37   37   4928               *                               ; CLEAR PPWA_UB
  38   38   4928  33FC 0000            MOVE.W  #$0000,TPRAM15+$A ;CLEAR PPWA_LW
  38        492C  00FF FFFA
  39   39   4930  0279 3FFF            ANDI.W  #$3FFF,THSQR0    ;24-BIT ACCUMULATION, NO LINKS
  39        4934  00FF FE14
  40   40   4938  0079 8000            ORI.W   #$8000,THSQR0
  40        493C  00FF FE14
  41   41   4940  33FC 8000            MOVE.W  #$8000,THSRR0    ;INITIALIZATION
  41        4944  00FF FE18
  42   42   4948  0079 C000            ORI.W   #$C000,TCPR0     ;START CHANNEL
  42        494C  00FF FE1C
  43   43   4950  4E75                 RTS
  44   44   4952                       END
```

Figure 13.15 Program example of pulse width accumulation.

applications program can now retrieve the stored count and convert the value to any convenient units for display or further processing.

   Test case. The test signal was a pulse train with periodic pulses of period approximately 1ms and a duty cycle of 25%. MAX_CNT was initialized to 100. The result was ACCUM = $0681 (1665). Thus, the total HIGH time becomes

$$T_w = 1665 \times 15.3\mu s = 25.4 ms$$

and the average HIGH time per pulse is 25.4ms/100 or 0.254ms as expected for the input test signal.

13.3.3 Channel Linking

The PPWA function can cause a link with up to eight channels. The number of the first channel ($0–$F) and the number of channeis to link (1–8) are specified in the first RAM parameter for the input channel as shown in Figure 13.12. The results for PPWA with linking are as follows:

(a) LAST_ACCUM = the timer value when the last accumulation occurred;

(b) PPWA_LW = the accumulation value of periods or pulse widths.

These values can be used by the channels being linked to synchronize operation with the PPWA channel.

A link occurs under one of two conditions. First, a link occurs when the accumulation for the specified number of periods or pulse widths is complete. Secondly, a link occurs if the 16-bit count in PPWA_LW overflows. In this case, PPWA_LW is set to zero. This condition can occur if the input pulses stop and the input signal is held HIGH or LOW since accumulation of time continues even with no input pulses. In any case, an interrupt request is generated by the channel after the link occurs. Subsection 13.4.3 presents an example of channel linking.

EXERCISES

13.3.1. Determine the resolutions in time and the total accumulation times that are possible using TCR2 as the channel timer for the Period or Pulse Width Accumulation function. Assume a 16.78MHz (2^{24}Hz) system clock frequency is used to clock TCR2 .

13.3.2. Determine the conversions necessary to change the measured frequency to physical units for the following:

(a) thermocouple to frequency converter, 0 to $60°C$ represents 0 to 600Hz;

(b) humidity to frequency converter, 0 to 100% relative humidity represents 0 to 1000Hz;

(c) a position sensor produces 10 pulses per second per revolution of a flywheel to be converted to RPM;

(d) voltage to frequency converter, the range -10 volts to 10 volts represents 0 to 1000Hz.

13.3.3. Determine the accuracy in frequency if a 3000Hz signal is sampled for the following time periods:

(a) 1 second;

(b) 0.1 second;

(c) 10ms.

Assume that the pulse count can be in error by 1 count.

13.3.4. Write a program to count an arbitrary number of pulses on channel 15 during the time that the input is HIGH on channel 14.

13.4 OUTPUT COMPARE

The Output Compare function generates a specific level, a pulse, or a pulse train on an output channel of the TPU. The time at which a specific level (HIGH or LOW) or a change in level occurs is determined by parameters defined for the channel. Figure 13.16 shows these parameters and the possible register selections. The reference address parameters in Figure 13.16 are 8-bit values that refer to the relative addresses in the parameter RAM area.

There are two major modes of operation as selected in the TPU Host Service Request Register field of the channel as follows:

(a) *Host-initiated pulse* mode, or

(b) *Continuous pulse* mode.

Host (CPU) initiated pulses occur due to the parameters selected by the CPU program that initializes the TPU channel. A CPU program also initializes the continuous pulse mode but the output is initiated by a link from another channel.

Subsection 13.4.1 describes the host-initiated pulse mode. This mode causes output match events to occur at predetermined times after the channel is initialized. Subsection 13.4.2 explains the continuous pulse mode that creates a pulse train output with a programmed period for the pulses. Subsection 13.4.3 defines the method to link an input channel and one or more Output Compare channels. The linking capability allows an input event to initiate output events with a precise time relationship between input and output channel transitions.

13.4.1 Host-Initiated Output Match

The host-initiated pulse mode of the Output Compare function requires a CPU program to initiate the match event on the output channel. The mode can be used to force the output signal to a specified level (HIGH or LOW) or to toggle the level. The change in level occurs after a specified delay time defined in RAM parameter OFFSET. As shown in Figure 13.16, the Channel Function Select value is $E and the Host Service Request is {01}. There are two choices for the TPU Host Sequence Register field to determine the action that results from a match to the match timer for the channel. The options are explained subsequently after the channel parameters are described.

The specific RAM parameters associated with the host-initiated pulse mode are defined in Table 13.9. The CHANNEL_CONTROL parameter defines the output characteristics and timers for the channel. Every option for this parameter was defined by Figure 13.8 in Subsection 13.1.4. For Output Compare, the PSC field defines the output level when the function is initialized. The PAC field specifies the action when the match event occurs. The TBS field defines the timers for capture and match.

When the channel is initialized, the timer values in TCR1 and TCR2 are written into RAM locations at offset $EC and $EE respectively. If the CPU program specified the Host Sequence request {10}, the TPU only writes the timer values into the specified RAM locations and requests an interrupt for the channel. In this case, no output match event is scheduled.

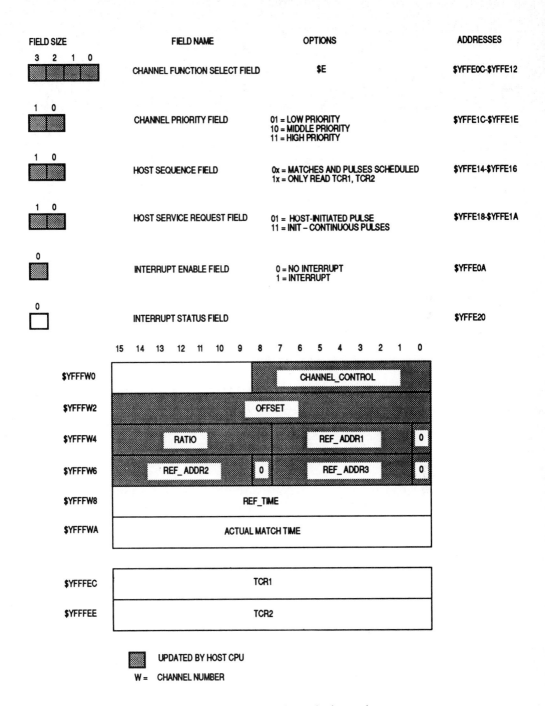

Figure 13.16 Output Compare register selections and parameters.

Table 13.9 Output Compare Parameters for Host-Initiated Pulses

Parameter	Value	Meaning
Inputs:		
CHANNEL_CONTROL		
PSC[1:0]	{00}	Use PAC field
	{01}	Force pin HIGH
	{01}	Force pin LOW
	{11}	Do not force any state
PAC[4:2]	{000}	Do not change pin state
	{001}	HIGH on match
	{010}	LOW on match
	{011}	Toggle on match
	{1xx}	Do not change PAC
TBS[8:5]	{01xx}	Output channel
	{0100}	Capture TCR1, match TCR1
	{0101}	Capture TCR1, match TCR2
	{0110}	Capture TCR2, match TCR1
	{0111}	Capture TCR2, match TCR2
	{1xxx}	Do not change TBS
OFFSET	$0000–$8000	Count value for offset to next match
REF_ADD1	$00–$FE	Pointer to reference value in RAM used as the time reference
Outputs:		
REF_TIME	$0000–$FFFF	Timer/Counter value for next match or most recent match
ACTUAL_MATCH_TIME	$0000–$FFFF	Timer value captured for last match
TCR1 and TCR2	$0000–$FFFF	Most recent timer/counter values written to RAM locations $EC and $EE

Note:
{x} is a don't care bit value.

If the Host Sequence request is {00}, the channel is initialized, the timer values are written into RAM and a match event is scheduled. The output match occurs when the match timer count for the channel is equal to a reference time count plus the offset. The reference value is held in the RAM location pointed to by parameter REF_ADDR1. Thus, the reference time for the output match is calculated by the TPU channel and written into parameter REF_TIME as

$$REF\_TIME = (REF\_ADDR1) + OFFSET.$$

The actual match time is therefore delayed from the reference time pointed to by REF_ADDR1 by

$$T_{(\text{delay})} = OFFSET \times T_{ci} \quad \text{seconds}$$

where T_{ci} is the resolution of the match timer TCR1 or TCR2.

The pointer REF_TIME can point to the timer count TCR1 ($EC) or TCR2 ($EE) or to another RAM location. For example, the pointer could designate the channel's REF_TIME parameter as the reference in location $YFFFW8 where $W is the channel number. Initially, this value represents the time of the last match event for the channel. The pointer value would be initialized as $W8 in this case.

Figure 13.17 shows two possible uses of this mode. In each case, assume the output level is LOW before initialization of the channel. In Figure 13.17(a), the output goes HIGH after the delay specified by the RAM parameter OFFSET. The TPU calculates the delay from the reference time in the RAM location pointed to by parameter REF_ADDR1.

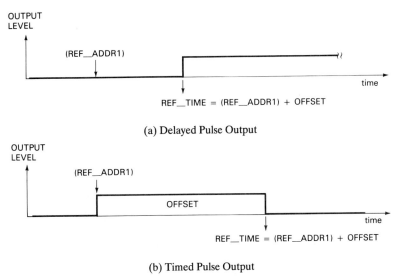

(a) Delayed Pulse Output

(b) Timed Pulse Output

Figure 13.17 Examples of Output Match Pulses.

Figure 13.17(b) illustrates the generation of a pulse which begins at the reference time that is stored in REF_TIME and continues for a specified time determined by OFFSET.

Thus, a CPU program can create a variety of HIGH or LOW states with specified timing by setting the channel control parameters properly and specifying OFFSET. The allowed values of OFFSET to delay a match are $0 to $8000 as measured from the reference time pointed to by REF_ADDR1. An offset greater than $8000 causes a greater than (>) compare in the channel's comparator register resulting in an immediate match when the channel is initialized. When a match occurs, the TPU updates the reference time in REF_TIME and stores the value in the capture timer corresponding to the actual match time in parameter ACTUAL_MATCH_TIME. After the match occurs, the channel generates an interrupt request.

The host-initiated pulse mode can be used to generate a pulse of arbitrary duration on an output channel. Figure 13.17(b) shows a pulse in which the output signal is driven HIGH for the time period specified by OFFSET. The reference address is initialized to point to either the most recent value of TCR1 or TCR2, the value of the last transition time in REF_TIME, or a similar parameter associated with another channel. To create a series of pulses with arbitrary timing, a CPU program must reinitialize the TPU channel after each match event. The TPU writes the counter value corresponding to the time of the match into ACTUAL_MATCH_TIME. The timer TCR1 or TCR2 whose value is captured is determined by the Time Base Select (TBS) field of the channel control parameter.

Example 13.7

Figure 13.18 shows a routine to toggle the output signal after a programmed delay referenced to timer TCR1 used as the match timer. The resulting output is similar to that of Figure 13.17(b) except that the output toggles the level at the match time. The capture timer is TCR2 which is clocked by an external signal. Thus, the time in TCR1 and the count in TCR2 will be stored when the match occurs. The input to the program in D0[15:0] is the parameter OFFSET which should be in the range $0000 to $8000.

The TPU must be initialized as described in Subsection 13.1.3 before the routine is called. Interrupts are not used in the example. If the TCR1 resolution T_{c1} is $7.63\mu s$, then the time delay specified is

$$T_{(\text{delay})} = 7.63\mu s \times \text{OFFSET} \quad \text{seconds.}$$

Subsection 13.1.3 explained the timing characteristics of the timers and the selections for global initialization of the TPU.

In this example, the routine initializes channel 4 for the Output Compare function in TCFSR2[3:0]. The channel control parameters are set as follows:
(a) do not force state (PSC[1:0] = {11});
(b) toggle on match (PAC[4:2] = {011});
(c) use TCR1 to match but capture TCR2 (TBS[8:5] = {0110}).
These parameters are in location $YFFF40 (CHANNEL_CONTROL) for channel 4.

The OFFSET is written to location $FFFF42 from D0 when the routine executes. The reference address points to the value of TCR1 since the routine defines

$$\text{REF\_ADDR1} = \text{\$EC.}$$

Wordlength operands are always used to initialize the RAM locations. The parameter RATIO is also set to $00 by the MOVE instruction that initializes the reference address. However, the ratio parameter is not used in the host-initiated pulse mode.

When the host-initiated pulse mode is initialized in the author's system, the most recent value of TCR1 will be written into the RAM location $FFFFEC. This causes the OFFSET delay to be referenced to the current count when the channel is initialized. The TCR2 value is written into location $FFFFEE.

The register selections define output match in THSQR1[9:8], and host-initiated pulse mode in THSRR1[9:8]. Once initialized by setting the priority in TCPR1[9:8], the channel will delay by the specified number of counts and then toggle the output state. The match is indicated to a CPU program when TCISR[4] becomes {1} in the TPU Channel Interrupt Status Register.

Test case. The OFFSET selection for the test case was $8000 corresponding to a delay before match of

$$7.63\mu s \times \$8000 = 0.25 \text{ seconds.}$$

When the routine in Figure 13.18 completes execution, the output level toggles after the delay time. The input signal at the T2CLK pin was a series of manually generated pulses to simulate event counting by an external device. These pulses incremented TCR2.

```
abs. rel.   LC    obj. code    source line
---- ----   ----  ---------    -----------
  1    1    0000                        TTL 'FIGURE 13.18'
  2    2    0000               *
  3    3    0000               *        TPU OUTPUT MATCH-CHANNEL 4
  4    4    0000               *
  5    5    0000               *        INPUT          : D0[15:0] = OFFSET ($0-$8000)
  6    6    0000               *        INITIAL VALUES  :
  7    7    0000               *           HOST FUNCTION  = $E
  8    8    0000               *           HOST SEQUENCE  = {00}  ;MATCH
  9    9    0000               *           HOST SERVICE   = {01}  ;HOST INITIATED INITIALIZATION
 10   10    0000               *           CHANNEL_CONTROL= TOGGLE ON MATCH; CAPTURE TCR2
 11   11    0000               *           REF_ADDR1      = $EC (TCR1)
 12   12    0000               *           PRIORITY       = {11}  ;HIGH PRIORITY
 13   13    0000               *        OUTPUT PARAMETERS IN CHANNEL RAM:
 14   14    0000               *           REF_TIME          = TIMER VALUE TO MATCH
 15   15    0000               *           ACTUAL_MATCH_TIME = TIMER VALUE AT MATCH
 16   16    0000               *           TCR1 COUNT        = ($EC)
 17   17    0000               *
 18   18    4A00                        ORG      $4A00
 19   19          0080 0000    REGBASE  EQU      $800000
 20   20          00FF FE10    TCFSR2   EQU      $007FFE10+REGBASE ;FUNCTION
 21   21          00FF FE16    THSQR1   EQU      $007FFE16+REGBASE ;SEQUENCE
 22   22          00FF FE1A    THSRR1   EQU      $007FFE1A+REGBASE ;SERVICE
 23   23          00FF FE1E    TCPR1    EQU      $007FFE1E+REGBASE ;PRIORITY
 24   24          00FF FF40    TPRAM4   EQU      $007FFF40+REGBASE ;RAM
 25   25    4A00               *
 26   26    4A00 0279 FCFF     OCINIT   ANDI.W   #$FCFF,TCPR1      ;DISABLE CHANNEL 4
 26         4A04 00FF FE1E
 27   27    4A08 0279 FFF0              ANDI.W   #$FFF0,TCFSR2     ;SELECT OC ON
 27         4A0C 00FF FE10
 28   28    4A10 0079 000E              ORI.W    #$000E,TCFSR2     ; CHANNEL 4
 28         4A14 00FF FE10
 29   29    4A18               *
 30   30    4A18               *        RAM PARAMETERS
 31   31    4A18               *
 32   32    4A18 33FC 00CF              MOVE.W   #$00CF,TPRAM4     ;TOGGLE ON MATCH TCR1; CAPTURE TCR2
 32         4A1C 00FF FF40
 33   33    4A20 33C0 00FF              MOVE.W   D0,TPRAM4+2       ;OFFSET-INPUT IN D0[W]
 33         4A24 FF42
 34   34    4A26 33FC 00EC              MOVE.W   #$00EC,TPRAM4+4   ;REF_ADDR1 (TCR1)
 34         4A2A 00FF FF44
 35   35    4A2E               *
 36   36    4A2E 0279 FCFF              ANDI.W   #$FCFF,THSQR1     ;MATCH AND TOGGLE OUTPUT
 36         4A32 00FF FE16
 37   37    4A36 33FC 0100              MOVE.W   #$0100,THSRR1     ;HOST-INITIATED PULSES
 37         4A3A 00FF FE1A
 38   38    4A3E 0079 0300              ORI.W    #$0300,TCPR1      ;START CHANNEL
 38         4A42 00FF FE1E
 39   39    4A46 4E75                   RTS
 40   40    4A48                        END
```

Figure 13.18 Program example of output match.

Once the output signal toggled after the match time, a CPU program can read the parameters as follows:

(a) REF_TIME = TCR1 value when match occurred;

(b) ACTUAL_MATCH_TIME = count in capture timer TCR2 after match;

(c) ($EE) = count in TCR2 initially.

Thus, the CPU program can determine the number of counts in TCR2 that occurred during the 0.25 second interval by subtracting the value in location $EE from the value in parameter ACTUAL_MATCH_TIME value. This count must not exceed 2^{16} since no indication of TCR2 overflow is given.

13.4.2 Continuous Pulse Mode After a Link

The continuous pulse mode of the Output Compare function is used to generate a 50% duty-cycle (square wave) output after a link from another channel. Figure 13.16 defined the register selections and the RAM parameters for the function. Table 13.10 defines in detail the RAM parameters that must be specified for the continuous pulse mode.

The channel control parameters for Pin State Control (PAC) and Time Base Selection (TBS) have the same meaning as those for the host-initiated Output Match function previously defined in Table 13.9. The parameter RATIO and the reference addresses have the meanings defined in Table 13.10 for the continuous pulse mode.

Table 13.10 Parameters for Output Compare with Links

Parameter	Value	Meaning
Inputs:		
CHANNEL_CONTROL		
PSC[1:0]	{00}	Use PAC field
	{01}	Force pin HIGH
	{01}	Force pin LOW
	{11}	Do not force any state
PAC[4:2]	{000}	Do not change pin state
	{001}	HIGH on match
	{010}	LOW on match
	{011}	Toggle on match
	{1xx}	Do not change PAC
TBS[8:5]	{01xx}	Output channel
	{0100}	Capture TCR1, match TCR1
	{0101}	Capture TCR1, match TCR2
	{0110}	Capture TCR2, match TCR1
	{0111}	Capture TCR2, match TCR2
	{1xxx}	Do not change TBS
RATIO	$00–$FF	Fraction to calculate OFFSET as OFFSET = (REF_ADDR2)×RATIO/256
REF_ADDR1	$00–$FE	Pointer: value pointed to updates REF_TIME on second and subsequent links
REF_ADDR2	$00–$FE	Pointer: value pointed to used to calculate OFFSET
REF_ADDR3	$00–$FE	Pointer: value pointed to used only on the first link after initialization; the value is written to REF_TIME when the first link occurs.
Outputs:		
REF_TIME	$0000–$FFFF	Timer/Counter value for next match or most recent match
TCR1 and TCR2	$0000–$FFFF	Most recent timer/counter values

Note:
The register selections for this function are defined in Figure 13.16.

Figure 13.19 shows an example of a pulse train and the parameters involved after the first link to the Output Compare channel from another channel. Figure 13.19 shows that at the first link a match event is set up to occur based on the value pointed to by REF_ADDR3. REF_ADDR3 points to a value used to synchronize events between the input and output channels. This reference time is written into parameter REF_TIME when the 1st match occurs. OFFSET is then used to calculate the time of the next output match.

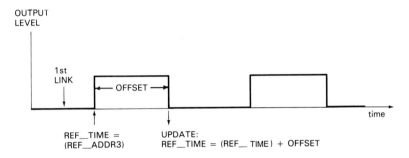

Figure 13.19 Continuous pulse output.

The second match occurs when the reference timer count reaches the value:

$$REF\_TIME + OFFSET.$$

The OFFSET parameter is a calculated value that determines the HIGH time of the output pulses. Since the output is a square wave, the period is twice the value in OFFSET.

The width of the pulse in counts of TCR1 or TCR2 is the value

$$OFFSET = (REF\_ADDR2) \times \frac{RATIO}{256}$$

where OFFSET is a 16-bit integer and RATIO/256 ($0 < RATIO \leq 255$ ($FF)) is treated as an 8-bit fractional value that scales the count contained in parameter REF_ADDR2. If OFFSET becomes a fractional value, the OFFSET is zero and the channel is reinitialized as explained later. The period of each pulse is

$$2 \times OFFSET \times T_{ci} \quad (seconds)$$

where T_{ci} is the resolution of the timer for the channel.

In many applications, REF_ADDR2 is initialized to point to the accumulated value of a period or pulse width accumulation on the input channel. The frequency of the output waveform is

$$f_{out} = 1/2 \times \frac{1}{OFFSET \times T_{ci}}.$$

Thus, if the reference count in REF_ADDR2 represents the period of the input signal, RATIO has the effect of multiplying the frequency of the input signal by the value 128/RATIO. Example 13.8 presents a program for frequency multiplication.

Continuous output occurs with the period of the waveform determined by OFFSET until another link is recognized. On the 2nd and subsequent links from the input channel, REF_ADDR1 points to the reference time used for subsequent pulses to determine the output match time.

For example, if the output channel parameter

$$(REF\_ADDR1) = REF\_TIME$$

the OFFSET is added to the time of the most recent match for the output channel. Alternatively, the reference could point to a time value of the channel causing the links. If channel interrupts are enabled, each match event causes an interrupt request to the CPU.

13.4.3 Linking Input and Output Channels

Both the Input Capture/Input Transition Counter and Period or Pulse Width Accumulation functions can link with up to eight output channels to produce an output waveform that is synchronized in time with events on the input channel. The channel parameters for the *input channel* that causes the links are as follows:
(a) START_LINK_CHANNEL — the number of the first channel to be linked;
(b) LINK_CHANNEL_COUNT — the number of channels to link (1–8).
Section 13.2 described these parameters for the input functions.

The Output Compare channel parameters for the time synchronization defined in Figure 13.16 are the following:
(a) REF_ADDR3 — points to a synchronization reference value used only once when the first link occurs;
(b) REF_ADDR1 — points to a reference value to which OFFSET is added to form a new match value on the 2nd and subsequent links.
The parameters RATIO and REF_ADDR2 determine the period of the output waveform as previously discussed.

Frequency multiplication and division. Figure 13.20 shows the relationship between Period Accumulation (PPWA) on an input channel and the 50% duty cycle (square wave) output. In this example, a link occurs to the output channel after each accumulation. For frequency multiplication, the parameter MAX_CNT shown in Figure 13.12 for the PPWA function is set to 1 to specify accumulation over one period.

The parameter PPWA_LW on the input channel defines the period of each input pulse. REF_ADDR2 points to this accumulated value. REF_ADDR3 points to the last accumulation time of the PPWA input channel to synchronize the input and output at the time of the first link. If REF_ADDR1 points to REF_TIME of the output channel, the output is a periodic pulse train that starts at the time pointed to by REF_ADDR3 and continues until the next link from the input channel.

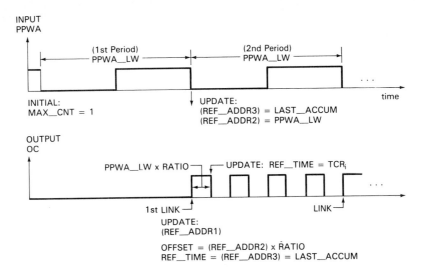

Figure 13.20 Period Accumulation with Links.

If the period of the ith input pulse is designated as T_{Ii}, the period of the corresponding output pulse T_{Oi} is

$$T_{Oi} = 2 \times T_{Ii} \times \frac{\text{RATIO}}{256} \quad \text{seconds}$$

where T_{Ii} is the accumulation value in the parameter PPWA_LW multiplied by the resolution of the timer for the input channel. The factor 2 in the equation arises because, as shown in Figure 13.20, RATIO scales the HIGH time of the output not the period. The value of RATIO should be $0 < \text{RATIO} \leq \$80$ for frequency multiplication as shown in Figure 13.20 since a link is received for each input pulse. The value $\$80$ (128) yields an output period equal to the input period.

This parameter RATIO can be used to perform frequency multiplication or division. If the maximum count is set to a value larger than 1, frequency division is possible since N input pulses would accumulate before linking occurs. If the input pulses stop, the value OFFSET would become zero. This causes the OC function to be reinitialized each time a link occurs from the input channel. As explained in Subsection 13.3.3 linking can occur even if there is no input signal since an overflow of the 16-bit accumulator for the PPWA causes a link.

The pulse-width accumulation mode of the PPWA function could be used also. In this case, the period of the output pulses would be proportional to the HIGH time of the input pulses as accumulated in parameter PPWA_LW of the PPWA channel.

Example 13.8

The routine of Figure 13.21 initializes channel 11 for Period Accumulation with a link to output channel 5. The RATIO parameter must be supplied in register D0[7:0] before the routine is called. Channel 11 is initialized for continuous operation to accumulate one period each time since MAX_CNT specifies 1 period. After each accumulation, a link is generated to channel 5.

The parameters for the output channel are the following:
(a) REF_ADDR1 = REF_TIME ($58) of output channel 5;
(b) REF_ADDR2 = PPWA_LW ($BA) of PPWA channel 11;
(c) REF_ADDR3 = LAST_ACCUM ($B4) of PPWA channel 11.

These selections cause the period of the output pulse to be multiplied by the selected ratio. If the input wave is periodic and $0 < \text{RATIO} \leq \$80$, the output waveform then has an equal or higher frequency since

$$0 < \frac{\text{RATIO}}{256} \leq 1/2.$$

Test case. The timer resolution for the OC channel was $7.63\mu s$. A 1kHz square wave as the input signal causes an accumulation of approximately 131 ($83) counts in PPWA_LW. A RATIO of $80 caused a 1kHz output as expected. A RATIO of $04 yielded a 64kHz square wave output. However, a RATIO of $01 to create a 128kHz square wave would not work because the OFFSET value becomes

$$\text{OFFSET} = 131 \times \frac{1}{256} < 1$$

which results in an integer value of OFFSET equal to zero.

EXERCISES

13.4.1. Write a routine to initialize a TPU output channel and create a pulse of fixed time duration T_p. Specify the range of T_p for the timer resolution selected.

13.4.2. Write a routine that causes the TPU to multiply or divide the frequency of an input wave train by a specified amount by linking the input channel to an output channel.

13.4.3. Write a routine that initializes a TPU channel to recognize an input event and then causes outputs with different delays on each of several output channels.

13.5 PULSE WIDTH MODULATION

Any TPU channel can generate a pulse-width modulated (PWM) output. Figure 13.22 shows the register options and channel parameters for the PWM function. These parameters are defined in Table 13.11. The channel control parameter, the HIGH time and the period of the pulse must be defined before the channel is enabled.

```
abs. rel.   LC    obj. code    source line
---- ----   ----  ---------    -----------
  1    1   0000                        TTL 'FIGURE 13.21'
  2    2   0000             |**  FREQUENCY MULTIPLY- CH11 (PPWA) IN/CH5 (OC) OUT
  3    3   4B00             |          ORG      $4B00
  4    4         0080 0000  |REGBASE  EQU      $800000
  5    5         00FF FE10  |TCFSR2   EQU      $007FFE10+REGBASE ;FUNCTION CH5 [7:4]
  6    6         00FF FE16  |THSQR1   EQU      $007FFE16+REGBASE ;SEQUENCE [11:10]
  7    7         00FF FE1A  |THSRR1   EQU      $007FFE1A+REGBASE ;SERVICE [11:10]
  8    8         00FF FE1E  |TCPR1    EQU      $007FFE1E+REGBASE ;PRIORITY [11:10]
  9    9         00FF FF50  |TPRAM5   EQU      $007FFF50+REGBASE ;RAM CHANNEL 5
 10   10         00FF FE0E  |TCFSR1   EQU      $007FFE0E+REGBASE ;FUNCTION CH11 [15:12]
 11   11         00FF FE14  |THSQR0   EQU      $007FFE14+REGBASE ;SEQUENCE [7:6]
 12   12         00FF FE18  |THSRR0   EQU      $007FFE18+REGBASE ;SERVICE [7:6]
 13   13         00FF FE1C  |TCPR0    EQU      $007FFE1C+REGBASE ;PRIORITY [7:6]
 14   14         00FF FFB0  |TPRAM11  EQU      $007FFFB0+REGBASE ;RAM CHANNEL 11
 15   15   4B00             |*
 16   16   4B00             |*   INPUT PARAMETERS CH11:  PERIOD MEASUREMENT ON CH11 AND LINK CH5
 17   17   4B00             |*     FUNCTION=$F, SEQUENCE={01}, SERVICE={10}, PRIORITY={11}
 18   18   4B00             |*     LINK CH5, DETECT FALLING EDGE;CAPTURE TCR1, MAX_COUNT=1
 19   19   4B00             |*   OUTPUT PARAMETERS CH11: LAST_ACCUM, PPWA_LW
 20   20   4B00             |*   INPUT PARAMETERS CH5:
 21   21   4B00             |*     D0[7:0]        = RATIO ($0-$FF)
 22   22   4B00             |*     HOST FUNCTION  = $E, SEQUENCE={00}, SERVICE={11}, PRIORITY={11}
 23   23   4B00             |*     CHANNEL_CONTROL = TOGGLE ON MATCH; CAPTURE TCR1
 24   24   4B00             |*     REF_ADDR1      = $58 (CH5 REF_TIME)
 25   25   4B00             |*     REF_ADDR2      = $BA (CH11 PPWA_LW)
 26   26   4B00             |*     REF_ADDR3      = $B4 (CH11 LAST_ACCUM FOR 1ST LINK)
 27   27   4B00             |*   OUTPUT PARAMETERS CH5: REF_TIME, ACTUAL_MATCH_TIME
 28   28   4B00             |*
 29   29   4B00 0279 F3FF   |FMINIT  ANDI.W  #$F3FF,TCPR1     ;DISABLE CHANNEL 5
 29        4B04 00FF FE1E   |
 30   30   4B08 0279 FF3F   |        ANDI.W  #$FF3F,TCPR0     ;DISABLE CHANNEL 11
 30        4B0C 00FF FE1C   |
 31   31   4B10 33FC 008F   |        MOVE.W  #$008F,TPRAM5    ;RAM CH5: TOGGLE ON MATCH; CAPTURE TCR1
 31        4B14 00FF FF50   |
 32   32   4B18 33FC 0000   |        MOVE.W  #$0000,TPRAM5+2  ;OFFSET-CALCULATED BY TPU
 32        4B1C 00FF FF52   |
 33   33   4B20 E148        |        LSL.W   #8,D0            ;RATIO INPUT IN D0[B];SHIFT TO UPPER BYTE
 34   34   4B22 0640 0058   |        ADDI.W  #$0058,D0        ;REF_ADDR1= CH5 REF_TIME
 35   35   4B26 33C0 00FF   |        MOVE.W  D0,TPRAM5+4      ;
 35        4B2A FF54        |
 36   36   4B2C 33FC BAB4   |        MOVE.W  #$BAB4,TPRAM5+6  ;REF_ADDR2=PPWA, REF_ADDR3=LASTACCUM (CH11)
 36        4B30 00FF FF56   |
 37   37   4B34 33FC 510B   |        MOVE.W  #$510B,TPRAM11   ;RAM CH11: LINK CH5, CAPTURE TCR1
 37        4B38 00FF FFB0   |
 38   38   4B3C 33FC 0100   |        MOVE.W  #$0100,TPRAM11+2 ;MAX_COUNT=1
 38        4B40 00FF FFB2   |
 39   39   4B44 33FC FF00   |        MOVE.W  #$FF00,TPRAM11+8 ;ACCUM_RATE=$FF;
 39        4B48 00FF FFB8   |
 40   40   4B4C 0279 FF0F   |        ANDI.W  #$FF0F,TCFSR2    ;REGISTERS: SELECT OC CH5
 40        4B50 00FF FE10   |
 41   41   4B54 0079 00E0   |        ORI.W   #$00E0,TCFSR2    ;
 41        4B58 00FF FE10   |
 42   42   4B5C 0279 F3FF   |        ANDI.W  #$F3FF,THSQR1    ;MATCH
 42        4B60 00FF FE16   |
 43   43   4B64 0079 F000   |        ORI.W   #$F000,TCFSR1    ;SELECT PPWA CH11
 43        4B68 00FF FE0E   |
 44   44   4B6C 0279 FF3F   |        ANDI.W  #$FF3F,THSQR0    ;16-BIT, LINK
 44        4B70 00FF FE14   |
 45   45   4B74 0079 0040   |        ORI.W   #$0040,THSQR0
 45        4B78 00FF FE14   |
 46   46   4B7C 33FC 0080   |        MOVE.W  #$0080,THSRR0    ;INITIALIZATION CH11
 46        4B80 00FF FE18   |
 47   47   4B84 0079 00C0   |        ORI.W   #$00C0,TCPR0     ;PRIORITY CHANNEL 11
 47        4B88 00FF FE1C   |
 48   48   4B8C 33FC 0C00   |        MOVE.W  #$0C00,THSRR1    ;INITIALIZATION CH5
 48        4B90 00FF FE1A   |
 49   49   4B94 0079 0C00   |        ORI.W   #$0C00,TCPR1     ;PRIORITY CHANNEL 5
 49        4B98 00FF FE1E   |
 50   50   4B9C 4E75        |        RTS
```

Figure 13.21 Program example of frequency multiplication.

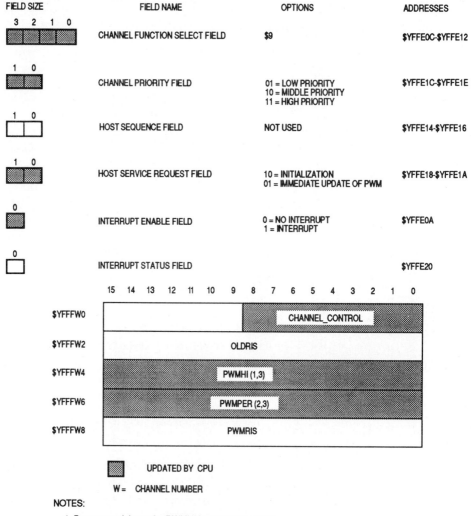

FIELD SIZE	FIELD NAME	OPTIONS	ADDRESSES

Figure 13.22 Pulse Width Modulation Parameters.

Figure 13.23 shows the relationship between the RAM parameters and a PWM output wave train. The duty cycle of the pulse is computed as

$$\text{Duty cycle} = \frac{\text{PWMHI}}{\text{PWMPER}}.$$

At initialization, the timer count at the first LOW to HIGH transition replaces the count in the OLDRIS parameter and the match count values for the next transitions

Table 13.11 Pulse Width Modulation Parameters

Parameter	Value	Meaning
Inputs:		
CHANNEL_CONTROL		
PSC[1:0]	{01}	Force pin HIGH (Normal Operation)
	{10}	Force pin LOW (0% duty cycle)
PAC[4:2]	{1xx}	Do not change PAC
TBS[8:5]	{0100}	Use TCR1 as channel timer
	{0111}	Use TCR2 as channel timer
PWMHI	$0–$8000	Count value defining the HIGH time
PWMPER	$0–$FFFF	Count value defining the Period
Outputs:		
OLDRIS	$0000–$FFFF	Timer value at previous HIGH-to-LOW transition
PWMRIS	$0000–$FFFF	Calculated match time to next rise time (LOW to HIGH)

Note:
Minimum times are specified in the *TPU Reference Manual* for the period and high time.

are calculated by the TPU. The parameter PWMRIS determines the match time for the next rising edge (LOW to HIGH transition) as

$$PWMRIS = OLDRIS + PWMPER.$$

If the CPU program changes PWMPER and PWMHI after a pulse begins, the TPU channel will generate the next pulse using the new values as shown in Figure 13.23.

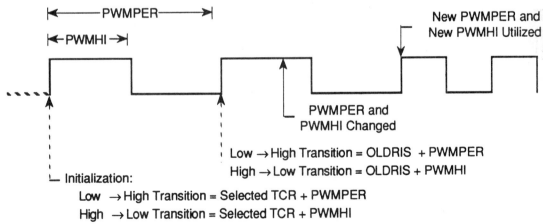

Figure 13.23 Example PWM waveform and TPU parameters.

The actual period in seconds is calculated from the period in timer counts held in PWMPER as

$$T_p = PWMPER \times T_{ci}$$

where T_{ci} is the resolution in seconds of the timer TCR1 or TCR2 of the channel.

The high time (PWMHI) is a 16-bit parameter with the specifications:

(a) PWMHI < PWMPER in normal operation;

(b) PWMHI ≥ PWMPER for 100% duty cycle (HIGH output);

(c) PWMHI = 0 for 0% duty cycle (LOW output).

The channel's Channel Function Select register field should contain $9 before the channel is initialized. For normal operation, the channel control PSC field should be set to force the pin HIGH after initialization. The PSC field should be set to force the output LOW only if a 0% duty cycle is desired. A Host Service request of {10} initializes the PWM channel. An interrupt request is generated when initialization is complete.

A CPU program can force an immediate change in the PWM output by a Host Service Request of {01} for the channel. Alternatively, the CPU program can write a new period and high time in the parameter RAM that will take effect after the next LOW to HIGH transition.

The *TPU Reference Manual* specifies that the parameters PWMHI and PWM-PER must be written coherently, i.e. with a long-word operand in a MOVE instruction that updates these values. Also, the difference between the period and the high time in counts should not exceed $8000.

Minimum values. The *TPU Reference Manual* defines the minimum number of system clock cycles for the period and the high time. In the author's laboratory tests using a 16.78MHz system clock, the minimum high time achievable was $2.38\mu s$ (40 system clock cycles) and the minimum period was $3.43\mu s$ corresponding to 58 system clock cycles. The timer resolution was 238ns for the channel.

EXERCISES

13.5.1. The Pulse Width Modulation output signal has a number of important applications including:

(a) DC motor control;

(b) control of a heater coil;

(c) simple D/A converter when the output is filtered.

For each of these applications, describe the possible application and the interfacing circuitry (if any) needed to allow a TPU channel to generate the required signal. Reference to other literature other than this textbook may be necessary to answer this question.

13.5.2. Write a routine that initializes a TPU channel for PWM output. The period and the high time in units of timer counts should be specified as variables in the CPU program to be supplied in CPU registers when the PWM routine is called.

13.6 STEPPER MOTOR CONTROL

The stepper motor is a device that converts input voltage pulses into analog rotary motion for mechanical positioning.[4] The frequency and relative phase of the input signals determine the position and velocity of the stepper motor. Subsection 13.6.1 describes the general characteristics of stepper motors that are suitable for control by the TPU. Subsection 13.6.2 defines the parameters and programming techniques for the TPU channels to control a stepper motor.

13.6.1 Stepper Motor Characteristics

Figure 13.24 shows a much simplified diagram of a stepper motor with two phase windings (Bipolar). The bridge circuits control the direction of current flow through the windings. Switching current on and off to the two phases creates a rotating electromagnetic field. The sequence of switching controls the direction of motor shaft rotation. The frequency of the switching controls the velocity of the motor shaft. The transistors of the bridge circuit designated Q_i ($1 \leq i \leq 8$) in Figure 13.24 accomplish the switching of the motor current. These transistors can be turned on and off by the output signals of a microcontroller directly or through driver circuits to cause the motor to rotate. If the control signals retain the same phase to maintain a constant current in the motor windings, the rotor does not move.

In many applications, the microcontroller cannot drive the switching transistors directly due to the current required. The design of the driver circuits is considered in several of the references in the Further Reading section of this chapter.

In the discussion in this section, four TPU channels are used to control a stepper motor in a scheme called full-step control. This requires a four-step switching sequence. Many other possibilities exist for stepper motor control. For example, the *TPU Reference Manual* describes full-step and half-step control of a bipolar motor using two and four TPU channels, respectively. Stepper motors with unipolar windings (Bifilar) can be controlled by simpler driver circuits requiring only four transistors.

Since the actual connection depends on the control scheme and the characteristics of the motor itself, the reader is referred to the motor manufacturer's literature and references in the Further Reading section of this chapter for more information about the actual circuit connections needed for stepper motor control.

Stepping sequence and stepping rate. Figure 13.25 shows the output of four TPU channels versus time that would cause rotation of the motor shaft. In the author's system, this corresponds to counter-clockwise (CCW) of the motor as seen from the motor shaft. The sequence is explained in more detail in Example 13.9. If the motor permits 200 steps per complete revolution, each step represents 360°/200 or 1.8° of rotation. A half-stepping sequence (not shown) yields a resolution of 1/2 of the full-step resolution in an eight-step sequence. It appears from Figure 13.25 that

---

[4] The stepper motor falls into a broad class of devices often called *actuators*. These devices convert electrical energy into a physical quantity such as position. The motion of a stepping actuator may be rotary or linear as described in several of the references in the Further Reading section of this chapter.

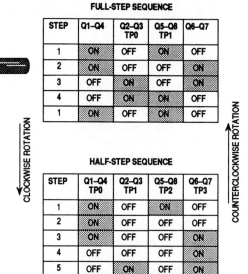

FULL-STEP SEQUENCE

STEP	Q1–Q4 TP0	Q2–Q3 TP1	Q5–Q8	Q6–Q7
1	ON	OFF	ON	OFF
2	ON	OFF	OFF	ON
3	OFF	ON	OFF	ON
4	OFF	ON	ON	OFF
1	ON	OFF	ON	OFF

HALF-STEP SEQUENCE

STEP	Q1–Q4 TP0	Q2–Q3 TP1	Q5–Q8 TP2	Q6–Q7 TP3
1	ON	OFF	ON	OFF
2	ON	OFF	OFF	OFF
3	ON	OFF	OFF	ON
4	OFF	OFF	OFF	ON
5	OFF	ON	OFF	ON
6	OFF	ON	OFF	OFF
7	OFF	ON	ON	OFF
8	OFF	OFF	ON	OFF
1	ON	OFF	ON	OFF

CLOCKWISE ROTATION

COUNTERCLOCKWISE ROTATION

Figure 13.24 Simplified Stepper Motor Diagram.

the full-step sequence requires four TPU channels. However, two channels are sufficient if external inverters are added to the system since the output levels on channels TP1 and TP3 are the logical inverse of those on channels TP0 and TP2, respectively. The examples in this section use four-channel control to avoid additional inverters to control the motor.

The channels labeled TP0, TP1, TP2, and TP3 are four consecutive TPU channels. However, TP0 does not necessarily correspond to TPU channel 0 since any four consecutive TPU channels can be used for four channel control. Each TPU channel would control two transistors in series in Figure 13.24. As opposite pairs of transistors are turned on and off, current flows through a winding in opposite directions. The 90° (electrical) phase difference between the two windings due to the sequence in Figure 13.25 causes rotation.

The time duration of each step is constant in Figure 13.25. This would cause the motor to rotate at a constant speed. The speed of the motor is defined as the number of steps per second called the *stepping rate*. The maximum stepping rate for different general-purpose stepping motors ranges from several hundred steps per second to many thousands of steps per second. The stepping rate is varied for a specific motor by varying the time between changes in the signals that cause stepping.

For the purpose of programming the TPU, the important characteristics of a stepper motor are the following:
(a) number of steps per revolution;

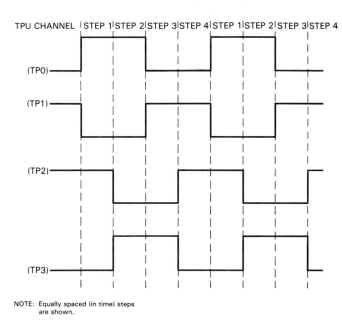

TPU CHANNEL STEP 1 STEP 2 STEP 3 STEP 4 STEP 1 STEP 2 STEP 3 STEP 4

(TP0)

(TP1)

(TP2)

(TP3)

NOTE: Equally spaced (in time) steps are shown.

Figure 13.25 Stepping sequence.

(b) maximum number of steps per second.

The number of steps per revolution determines the change in position measured in degrees when the motor is rotated a given number of steps. The maximum number of steps per second is typically specified by the manufacturer for a given load on the motor shaft. As the load increases, the speed (steps/second) versus torque curve determines the maximum rate of rotation without error. For example, the maximum may be 400 steps per second at no load and reduce to 100 steps per second at a load requiring 0.8 oz-in of torque for a small stepper motor. If the motor is accelerated to beyond the maximum stepping rate, the error in the actual final position with respect to the desired position will increase.

13.6.2 TPU Control of Stepper Motors

Figure 13.26 shows the register options and the parameters for the stepper motor function. From two to eight channels are used to generate the control signals. The first channel is designated as the master or primary channel and the others are called secondary channels. The primary channel must be the lowest numbered TPU channel in the group of channels that control the motor. The parameter RAM locations for the primary channel and the first secondary channel hold the parameters that determine the position and stepping rate of the motor.

Table 13.12 defines the RAM parameters for stepper motor control. The parameters in Table 13.12 must be defined before the TPU channels are initialized by a Host Service Request. The priority of the channels is defined last in the TPU Channel Priority Register.

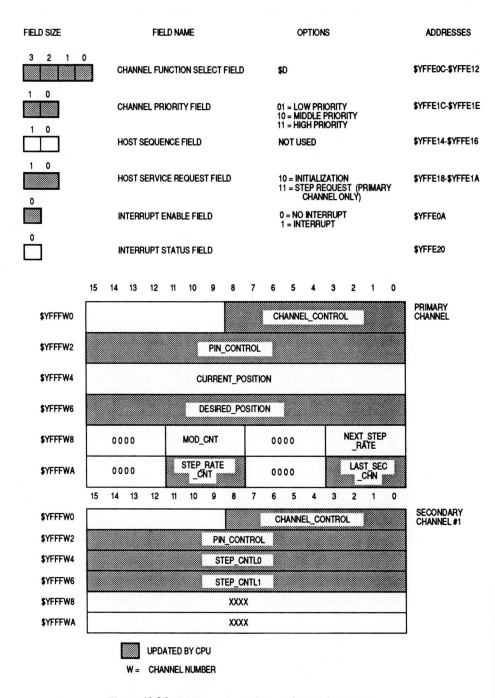

Figure 13.26 Stepper motor register options and parameters.

The Function Code is $D for each channel involved. The TPU channels use the parameter CHANNEL_CONTROL to define the initial state of the output signals. For initialization of each channel, the CPU program writes a Host Service Request of {10} into the appropriate TPU Host Service Request Register (THSR0 or THSR1) and defines the channel priority. Initialization is complete when the TPU clears the Host Service Request field to {00} for all channels. An interrupt occurs if interrupts are enabled.

After initialization is complete, a CPU program steps the motor shaft by writing the desired position into the DESIRED_POSITION parameter of the primary channel and writing a Host Service Request of {11} in the Host Service Field for the channel. The desired position is measured relative to the current position. If the absolute position of the motor shaft is needed in an application, the zero position of the motor shaft must be determined by an external sensor. A CPU interrupt occurs when stepping is complete if interrupts are enabled.

Table 13.12 Input Parameters for Stepper Motor Control

Input Parameter	Value	Meaning
Primary Channel:		
CHANNEL_CONTROL		
PSC[1:0]	{01}	Force pin HIGH
	{10}	Force pin LOW
TBS[8:5]	{0100}	Use TCR1
PIN_CONTROL	$0–$FFFF	Sequence of pin transitions on primary channel
CURRENT_POSITION	$0–$FFFF	Initial position of motor shaft
DESIRED_POSITION	$0–$FFFF	Desired position for stepping
MOD_CNT	$0	Modulo 16 count of rotations of CHANNEL_CONTROL bits (updated by TPU)
NEXT_STEP_RATE	$1	Initial value
STEP_RATE_CNT	$1–$E	Number of step rates in acceleration/deceleration profile
LAST_SEC_CHN	$0–$F	Channel number of last secondary channel
First secondary Channel:		
CHANNEL_CONTROL	{01}	Force pin HIGH
	{10}	Force pin LOW
PIN_CONTROL	$0–$FFFF	Sequence of pin transitions on first secondary channel
STEP_CNTL0 STEP_CNTL1	$0–$FFFF	Parameters to define linear acceleration rate
Other Secondary Channels:		
CHANNEL_CONTROL	{01}	Force pin HIGH
	{10}	Force pin LOW
PIN_CONTROL	$0–$FFFF	Sequence of pin transitions on secondary channels

Table 13.13 defines the output parameters written by the TPU. A CPU program can read these parameters at any time to determine the position and the next step rate for the motor. The parameter MOD_CNT is used by the TPU to determine the shift count for the output sequence of pulses as described later.

Table 13.13 Output Parameters for Stepper Motor Control

Output Parameter	Value	Meaning
CURRENT_POSITION	$0–$FFFF	Current step position of motor
MOD_CNT	$0–$F	Number of shifts (modulo 16)
NEXT_STEP_RATE	$0–$F	Calculated value of step rate for next step

Note:
When MOD_CNT = 0, the output sequence starts again.

CHANNEL_CONTROL and PIN_CONTROL parameters. The two-bit Pin State Control field of the channel control parameter determines the initial state of the TPU channels controlling the motor. The PIN_CONTROL parameter defines the sequence of 16 pin transitions as HIGH or LOW as the motor is rotated. The requirement is that the initial state of each channel (HIGH or LOW) be set equal to the logical value of the most significant bit (bit 15) of PIN_CONTROL. This is because the TPU shifts the bit pattern in PIN_CONTROL to set the pin states to rotate the motor.

During initialization, the bit pattern in the pin control parameter is transferred to parameter CHANNEL_CONTROL for shifting. When stepping is requested and the desired position is greater than the current position, the bit pattern from parameter PIN_CONTROL defines the output levels starting from the Least Significant Bit (LSB) and continuing to the Most Significant Bit (MSB). If the desired position is less than the current position, the bit pattern is output at the programmed step rate from the MSB to LSB. After shifting through 16 bit positions right or left, CHANNEL_CONTROL is again updated with PIN_CONTROL. At this time, the parameter MOD_CNT is reset to zero and the sequence begins again.

Example 13.9

Table 13.14 shows the values of the parameter PIN_CONTROL and the PSC field of CHANNEL_CONTROL for 4-channel, full stepping control of a stepper motor. The initial state is set equal to a level that corresponds to the most significant bit of the PIN_CONTROL parameter. The output sequence for the channels from MSB to LSB would be as follows:

(a) Step 1: HIGH, LOW, HIGH, LOW;
(b) Step 2: HIGH, LOW, LOW, HIGH;
(c) Step 3: LOW, HIGH, LOW, HIGH;
(d) Step 4: LOW, HIGH, HIGH, LOW.

For subsequent steps, the sequence repeats. Figure 13.25 shows the signal output for this sequence to rotate the motor shaft counterclockwise. The sequence is output in the reverse order to reverse the direction of rotation.

Table 13.14 Example Four Channel Stepper Motor Control

Channel	PIN_CONTROL		CHANNEL_CONTROL[1:0]
	Hex	MSD (binary)	Binary value and level
Primary	CCCC	{1100}	{01} (HIGH)
Secondary	3333	{0011}	{10} (LOW)
Secondary	9999	{1001}	{01} (HIGH)
Secondary	6666	{0110}	{10} (LOW)

Note:
MSD is the most significant hexadecimal digit of PIN_CONTROL.

Position and step rate.   One of the important characteristics of a stepper motor is that the angular position and velocity (stepping rate) can be controlled very accurately without feedback. However, the position of the shaft is measured relative to an arbitrary starting point with such open-loop control. If the initial shaft position is set externally, the RAM parameter value

$$CURRENT\_POSITION = \$7FFF$$

allows rotation in both directions from this arbitrary middle position. The number of steps taken N_s is defined by the parameter DESIRED_POSITION as

$$N_s = DESIRED\_POSITION - CURRENT\_POSITION$$

where the direction of rotation depends on the sign of N_s. The actual number of degrees rotated by the motor shaft is determined by the number of steps per revolution of the motor. An applications program must relate the number of steps N_s to the physical rotation of the motor shaft. From the zero value in CURRENT_POSITION, N_s can be as large as $2^{16} - 1$ ($FFFF).

The TPU has a microcoded algorithm to rotate a stepper motor at varying stepping rates depending on the current position and the desired position as defined in the parameter RAM for the primary channel. For each step request, the TPU calculates the distance in steps between the desired position and the current position as stored in the RAM parameters. If the distance is sufficient, the TPU will output signals to accelerate the motor at a linearly increasing stepping rate until the maximum rate as determined by RAM parameters is reached. Then, the motor is rotated toward the desired position at a constant stepping rate until the TPU begins decelerating the motor when the current position approaches the desired position. During deceleration, the output signals cause the motor to step at a decreasing rate for each step until the desired position is reached. The function that describes the stepping rate versus time is sometimes called the *acceleration profile*. The TPU controls the stepping rate by varying the duration (period) of its output signals at each step when a variable stepping rate is used.

The TPU RAM parameters for stepper motor control include values to specify the period between steps in units of timer counts. There can be from 1 to 14 stepping rates during acceleration and deceleration. The number of different rates is specified in the RAM parameter STEP_RATE_CNT. Figure 13.27(a) shows a typical acceleration profile for acceleration, running and deceleration. For example, Figure 13.27(b) shows the time between steps versus the output signals on TPU channels TP0 and TP2 using the parameters in Table 13.14. The figure shows the selection

$$STEP\_RATE\_CNT = 5$$

yielding 5 step rates for acceleration and deceleration. TPU channels TP1 and TP3 have inverted signals from TP0 and TP2, respectively. Two TPU channels (TP0, TP1) could be used for full-stepping control if external inverters are used on these channels to create the other two signals that are needed.

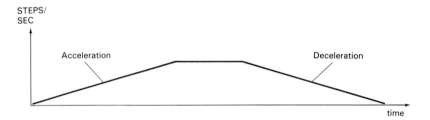

(a) Average acceleration profile

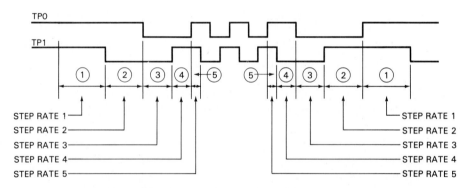

(b) Example stepping sequence with STEP_RATE_CNT = 5

Figure 13.27   Stepper motor control for two-channel, full-step control.

The relative period in counts between steps is defined mathematically as

$$P(r) = K_1 - (K_2 \times r) \tag{13.5}$$

where r is 1 for the first step and increases by 1 until $r_{(max)}$ steps are made during acceleration. The value $r_{(max)}$ is defined as

$$r_{(max)} = STEP\_RATE\_CNT$$

and ranges from 1 to 14. At each step, the next step rate is calculated by the TPU.

The actual time between steps is

$$P_r(t) = P(r) \times T_{c1} \qquad (13.6)$$

where T_{c1} is the resolution of timer TCR1 and $1 \leq r \leq r_{(max)}$. The reciprocal of $P_r(t)$ represents the number of steps per second when the motor is turning at a constant speed.

As the motor steps during acceleration, the time between steps decreases from

$$P(1) = (K_1 - K_2) \times T_{c1}$$

to a minimum value

$$P(r_{(max)}) = (K_1 - K_2 \times r_{(max)}) \times T_{c1}$$

where $r_{(max)} \leq 14$. Thus, K_2 represents the decrease in period for each step as the motor is accelerated. During deceleration, the TPU slows the motor by increasing the time between steps by the factor K_2. Thus, the variable r in Equation 13.5 is decremented from $r_{(max)}$ to 1 as the motor is decelerated.

The time $P(1)$ represents the delay that expires before a new stepping sequence begins. This delay assures that the final step of the motor, due to a previous request, is not disturbed before a time $P(1)$ elapses. During deceleration, P(1) is the last step rate. If the number of steps is less than $r_{(max)}$, the motor steps to the new position using $P(1)$ as the step period. If the motor direction is reversed while the motor is rotating, the TPU decelerates the motor and delays by the period $P(1)$ before causing the motor to change direction.

The variables K_1 and K_2 in Equation 13.5 are not directly defined in the TPU parameter RAM. Instead, the TPU calculates the period between steps as

$$P(r) = \text{STEP\_CNTL1} - \text{STEP\_CNTL0} \times (1 + r) \qquad (13.7(a))$$

where r varies as

$$1 \leq r \leq \text{STEP\_RATE\_CNT}. \qquad (13.7(b))$$

Table 13.15 defines the RAM parameters for the primary channel and the first secondary channel used in Equation 13.7 in terms of the variables K_1 and K_2 in Equation 13.5.

Table 13.15 Step Rate Parameters

RAM Parameters	Variable
STEP_CNTL0	K_2
STEP_CNTL1	$K_1 + \text{STEP\_CNTL0}$
STEP_RATE_CNT (1–14)	$r_{(max)}$

Example 13.10

Assume that the TPU is controlling a stepper motor with the following limitations:
(a) maximum step rate of 250 steps/second;
(b) starting and stopping stepping rate of 100 steps/second.
The maximum step rate can be used after the motor is accelerated to its running speed. The minimum step rate is necessary to prevent errors in position when the motor starts or is being stopped.

Assume the timer TCR1 resolution T_{c1} is $7.63\mu s$ and 11 step rates are selected. The starting period is 1/100 or 10.0ms. The minimum period between steps is 1/250 or 4.0ms. Thus, the stepping delay for starting and the last stepping rate for stopping the motor is

$$P(1) = (K_1 - K_2) \times T_{c1} = 10\text{ms}.$$

The running stepping period is

$$P(11) = (K_1 - 11K_2) \times T_{c1} = 4\text{ms}$$

where T_{c1} is $7.63\mu s$ in this example. Solving for K_1 and K_2 yields

$$K_1 = 1389 \quad \text{and} \quad K_2 = 79.$$

In terms of the RAM parameters defined in Table 13.15, the values are

$$\text{STEP\_CNTL0} = K_2 = 79$$
$$\text{STEP\_CNTL1} = K_1 + \text{STEP\_CNTL0} = 1468$$
$$\text{STEP\_RATE\_CNT} = 11$$

Thus, Equation 13.7 becomes

$$P(r) = 1468 - 79 \times (1 + r)$$

where $1 \leq r \leq 11$. Equation 13.6 yields the actual time between steps as

$$P_r(t) = 11.2 - 0.6 \times (1 + r) \text{ ms}$$

when T_{c1} is $7.63\mu s$.

It is easily verified that the time between steps decreases by 0.6ms for each step until step 11 during acceleration. During deceleration, the stepping period increases from 4ms by 0.6ms in each of 11 steps until the motor stops.

Example 13.11

The program of Figure 13.28(a) is an applications program to control a stepper motor. A global initialization routine (not shown) similar to that of Example 13.2 must initialize the TPU. The resolution of TCR1 is assumed to be $7.63\mu s$ and the TPU interrupts the CPU at level 4.

The main program begins by initializing two word-length variables as follows:
(a) SMINITF = $FF indicating that channel initialization has not been performed;
(b) SMSTEPF = $FF indicating the TPU is not available for stepping the motor.

```
abs. rel.   LC    obj. code   source line
----  ----   ----  ---------   -----------
  1    1    0000                    TTL     'FIGURE 13.28(a)'
  2    2    0000               *
  3    3          0000 7A38    SMINITF  EQU  $7A38           ;INITIALIZATION FLAG
  4    4          0000 7A3A    SMSTEPF  EQU  $7A3A           ;STEP FLAG
  5    5          0000 4C00    SMINIT   EQU  $4C00           ;STEPPER MOTOR INITIALIZATION ROUTINE
  6    6          0000 4C92    SMSTEP   EQU  $4C92           ;STEPPING ROUTINE
  7    7          0000 0063    .RETURN  EQU  $0063
  8    8    0000               *
  9    9    8000                       ORG   $8000
 10   10    8000 31FC 00FF             MOVE.W #$00FF,SMINITF  ;SET INITIALIZATION FLAG
 10         8004 7A38
 11   11    8006 31FC 00FF             MOVE.W #$00FF,SMSTEPF  ;SET STEP FLAG
 11         800A 7A3A
 12   12    800C 4EB8 4C00             JSR   SMINIT          ;STEPPER MOTOR INITIALIZE
 13   13    8010 4A78 7A38   WAITIN    TST.W SMINITF         ;WAIT FOR INITIALIZATION
 14   14    8014 66FA                  BNE   WAITIN
 15   15    8016               *
 16   16    8016 4E71                  NOP                   ;OTHER PROCESSING
 17   17    8018               *
 18  ,18    8018 303C 80C7             MOVE.W #$80C7,D0       ;EXAMPLE DESIRED POSITION
 19   19    801C 4EB8 4C92             JSR   SMSTEP
 20   20    8020               *
 21   21    8020 4E71                  NOP                   ;OTHER PROCESSING
 22   22    8022               *
 23   23    8022 4A78 7A3A   WAITST    TST.W SMSTEPF         ;WAIT FOR STEPPER MOTOR TO REACH
 24   24    8026 66FA                  BNE   WAITST          ; DESIRED POSITION
 25   25    8028               *
 26   26    8028 4E4F                  TRAP  #15
 27   27    802A 0063                  DC.W  .RETURN
 28   28    802C                       END
```

Figure 13.28(a) Program for stepper motor control.

The location of these variables are defined in the interrupt routine of Figure 13.28(c) since the interrupt routine clears these locations after initialization and after each stepping sequence is complete. SMINITF being set to $FF prevents a step request before initialization is complete. SMSTEPF is set to $FF when a step request is made and cleared when the motor has completed stepping. An applications program should not make a step request if either of these flags is set.

After setting the flags, the main program then calls routine SMINIT to initialize the stepper motor channels. When the interrupt routine clears the flag SMINITF, the program can request stepping. The example shown causes the motor to rotate 200 ($C8) steps from the initial position of $7FFF. The CPU program continues to execute while the motor turns. After the SMSTEPF is cleared by the interrupt routine, the program could request stepping again. In the program shown, control returns to the monitor after the motor rotation is complete.

Initialization. The routine in Figure 13.28(b) beginning at label SMINIT selects the stepper motor function ($D) for channels 0–3 and initializes the channel control and pin control RAM variables with the values of Example 13.9. This specifies full-step, four channel control. The current position and desired position parameters are arbitrarily initialized to $7FFF.

Eleven step rates are selected to accelerate or decelerate the motor. The first step period is 10ms and the final step period is 4ms as described in Example 13.10. The values to control the acceleration are
(a) STEP_CNTL0 = $4F (79);
(b) STEP_CNTL1 = $5BC (1468).
These values were calculated using $T_{c1} = 7.63\mu s$.

```
abs. rel.   LC    obj. code   source line
----  ----  ----  ---------   -----------
  1    1    0000                        TTL      'FIGURE 13.28(b)'
  2    2    0000              *
  3    3          0080 0000   REGBASE    EQU      $800000
  4    4          00FF FE0A   TCIER      EQU      $007FFE0A+REGBASE   ;INTERRUPT ENABLE
  5    5          00FF FE12   TCFSR3     EQU      $007FFE12+REGBASE   ;FUNCT SELECT_3 (3,2,1,0)
  6    6          00FF FE1A   THSRR1     EQU      $007FFE1A+REGBASE   ;HOST SERVICE (CHNS 7-0)
  7    7          00FF FE1E   TCPR1      EQU      $007FFE1E+REGBASE   ;PRIORITY (CHNS 7-0)
  8    8          00FF FF00   TPRAM0     EQU      $007FFF00+REGBASE   ;TPU PARAMETER RAM
  9    9          00FF FF10   TPRAM1     EQU      $007FFF10+REGBASE
 10   10          00FF FF20   TPRAM2     EQU      $007FFF20+REGBASE
 11   11          00FF FF30   TPRAM3     EQU      $007FFF30+REGBASE
 12   12          0000 7A3A   SMSTEPF    EQU      $7A3A
 13   13    0000              *
 14   14    0000              ****************************************************************
 15   15    0000              *     STEPPER MOTOR INITIALIZATION SUBROUTINE  CH0-3
 16   16    0000              *     CHANNEL 0 IS PRIMARY CHN, PSC=01 PIN HIGH, TBS=100(TCR1)
 17   17    0000              ****************************************************************
 18   18    4C00                        ORG      $4C00
 19   19    4C00 33FC DDDD   SMINIT     MOVE.W   #$DDDD,TCFSR3   ;STEPPER MOTOR =$D(13)
 19         4C04 00FF FE12
 20   20    4C08 33FC 0081              MOVE.W   #$0081,TPRAM0   ;CH0 - CHN CONTROL PIN HIGH
 20         4C0C 00FF FF00
 21   21    4C10 33FC 0082              MOVE.W   #$0082,TPRAM1   ;CH1 - CHN CONTROL PIN LOW
 21         4C14 00FF FF10
 22   22    4C18 33FC 0081              MOVE.W   #$0081,TPRAM2   ;CH2 - CHN CONTROL PIN HIGH
 22         4C1C 00FF FF20
 23   23    4C20 33FC 0082              MOVE.W   #$0082,TPRAM3   ;CH3 - CHN CONTROL PIN LOW
 23         4C24 00FF FF30
 24   24    4C28 33FC CCCC              MOVE.W   #$CCCC,TPRAM0+2 ;CH0 - PIN CONTROL
 24         4C2C 00FF FF02
 25   25    4C30 33FC 3333              MOVE.W   #$3333,TPRAM1+2 ;CH1 - PIN CONTROL
 25         4C34 00FF FF12
 26   26    4C38 33FC 9999              MOVE.W   #$9999,TPRAM2+2 ;CH2 - PIN CONTROL
 26         4C3C 00FF FF22
 27   27    4C40 33FC 6666              MOVE.W   #$6666,TPRAM3+2 ;CH3 - PIN CONTROL
 27         4C44 00FF FF32
 28   28    4C48 33FC 7FFF              MOVE.W   #$7FFF,TPRAM0+4 ;CH0 - CURRENT POSITION
 28         4C4C 00FF FF04
 29   29    4C50 33FC 7FFF              MOVE.W   #$7FFF,TPRAM0+6 ;CH0 - DESIRED POSITION
 29         4C54 00FF FF06
 30   30    4C58 33FC 0001              MOVE.W   #$0001,TPRAM0+8 ;CH0 - MOD_CNT=0, NEXT_STEP_RATE=1
 30         4C5C 00FF FF08
 31   31    4C60 33FC 0B03              MOVE.W   #$0B03,TPRAM0+$A ;CH0 - STEP_RATE_CNT=11, LAST CHN=3
 31         4C64 00FF FF0A
 32   32    4C68 33FC 004F              MOVE.W   #$004F,TPRAM1+4 ;CH1 P2 - STEP CONTROL 0
 32         4C6C 00FF FF14
 33   33    4C70 33FC 05BC              MOVE.W   #$05BC,TPRAM1+6 ;CH1 P3 - STEP CONTROL 1
 33         4C74 00FF FF16
 34   34    4C78 0079 000F              ORI.W    #$000F,TCIER    ;ENABLE INTERRUPTS CH0-CH3
 34         4C7C 00FF FE0A
 35   35    4C80 33FC 00AA              MOVE.W   #$00AA,THSRR1   ;REQUEST INITIALIZATION
 35         4C84 00FF FE1A
 36   36    4C88 0079 00FF              ORI.W    #$00FF,TCPR1    ;SET PRIORITY HIGH CH0-CH3
 36         4C8C 00FF FE1E
 37   37    4C90 4E75                   RTS                      ;EXIT SMINIT
 38   38    4C92              ****************************************************************
 39   39    4C92              *    ROUTINE TO ROTATE MOTOR AFTER INITIALIZATION
 40   40    4C92              *    (D0).W CONTAINS THE DESIRED POSITION
 41   41    4C92              ****************************************************************
 42   42    4C92 50F8 7A3A   SMSTEP     ST       SMSTEPF         ;SET STEP FLAG
 43   43    4C96 33C0 00FF              MOVE.W   D0,TPRAM0+6     ;DESIRED POSITION
 43         4C9A FF06
 44   44    4C9C 33FC 0003              MOVE.W   #$0003,THSRR1   ;ROTATE
 44         4CA0 00FF FE1A
 45   45    4CA4 4E75                   RTS
 46   46    4CA6                        END
```

Figure 13.28(b) Initialization and stepping routine for stepper motor control.

The SMINIT routine finally enables TPU interrupts for the channels and specifies a Host Service Request of {10} to initialize the channels. The channel priority is set to high priority. The TPU indicates that channel initialization is complete by setting the Host Service Request fields to {00} and requesting an interrupt. In the present example, it is assumed that CPU interrupts are enabled.

```
abs. rel.   LC   obj. code   source line
---- ----   ----  ---------   -----------
   1    1   0000                        TTL     'FIGURE 13.28(c)'
   2    2   0000             *
   3    3   0000             *    CLEAR INTERRUPTS CHNS 0-3 AND CLEAR FLAGS
   4    4   0000             *      IF SMINITF=0, INITIALIZATION IS COMPLETE
   5    5   0000             *
   6    6        0080 0000   REGBASE EQU   $800000
   7    7        00FF FE20   TCISR   EQU   $007FFE20+REGBASE  ;INTERRUPT STATUS REGISTER
   8    8        00FF FF00   TPRAM0  EQU   $007FFF00+REGBASE
   9    9   7A00                      ORG   $7A00
  10   10   7A00 2F00        SMIRQ   MOVE.L  D0,-(A7)         ;SAVE REGISTER
  11   11   7A02 3039 00FF           MOVE.W  TCISR,D0         ;READ INTERRUPT STATUS AND
  11        7A06 FE20
  12   12   7A08 0279 FFF0           ANDI.W  #$FFF0,TCISR     ;CLEAR REQUESTS 0-3
  12        7A0C 00FF FE20  *
  13   13   7A10            *
  14   14   7A10            *    CLEAR INITIALIZATION FLAG THE FIRST TIME
  15   15   7A10            *
  16   16   7A10 4A79 0000           TST.W   SMINITF          ;IF SMINITF = $00, GO TO INTR
  16        7A14 7A38
  17   17   7A16 6700 000C           BEQ     INTR             ; ELSE CLEAR SMINITF FIRST TIME
  18   18   7A1A 4279 0000           CLR.W   SMINITF
  18        7A1E 7A38
  19   19   7A20 6000 0008           BRA     DONE
  20   20   7A24            *
  21   21   7A24            *    CLEAR STEP FLAG, READ CURRENT POSITION AND STORE IT
  22   22   7A24            *
  23   23   7A24 4279 0000  INTR    CLR.W   SMSTEPF          ;CLEAR STEP FLAG
  23        7A28 7A3A
  24   24   7A2A 33F9 00FF  DONE    MOVE.W  TPRAM0+4,CURR_POS ;CURRENT POSITION
  24        7A2E FF04 0000
  24        7A32 7A3C
  25   25   7A34 201F               MOVE.L  (A7)+,D0         ;RESTORE REGISTER
  26   26   7A36 4E73               RTE
  27   27   7A38            *
  28   28   7A38            SMINITF DS.W   1                ;INITIALIZATION FLAG
  29   29   7A3A            SMSTEPF DS.W   1                ;STEP FLAG
  30   30   7A3C            CURR_POS DS.W  1                ;CURRENT POSITION
  31   31   7A3E                    END
```

Figure 13.28(c)   Interrupt routine for stepper motor control.

Interrupt routine. The interrupt routine SMIRQ in Figure 13.28(c) executes after initialization or stepping is complete. If the global selections of Example 13.2 are used, the vector $50 at location $140 must contain the address SMIRQ and CPU interrupts must be enabled at least for level 4 and above. The interrupt routine stores the value of the current position (CURRENT_POSITION) and clears the flag SMINITF in response to the first interrupt request. Then, the interrupt requests are cleared before control is returned to the CPU program that was interrupted.

After initialization, subsequent interrupts due to stepping requests cause the routine to clear the flag SMSTEPF and store the current position. Although the program enables the interrupts on all the channels for stepper motor control, only the primary channel makes interrupt requests.

Stepping routine. The stepping routine at label SMSTEP in Figure 13.28(b) is particularly simple. When the routine is called, the flag SMSTEPF is set to $FF to indicate that a step request is being serviced. The desired position in register D0[15:0] is written to the parameter RAM. Then, a Host Service Request of {11} is made on the primary channel. An interrupt request occurs when the stepping is complete.

Test case. The author's BCC system described in Chapter 10 controls a Superior Electric M091-FD06 stepper motor. The specifications recommend a typical time between steps of 3.9ms corresponding to 256 steps/second. The maximum step rate was chosen to be 250 steps per second for testing. There are 200 steps per revolution for full-step control. The program of Figure 13.28(a) causes a complete revolution when executed.

EXERCISES

13.6.1. The stepper motor control scheme uses the relative position of the motor shaft for positioning. Describe various ways to obtain the absolute position of the motor shaft.

13.6.2. Draw the acceleration profile for the motor of Example 13.10 if 100 steps are taken. How long does it take the motor shaft to rotate 100 steps?

13.6.3. Compute the step control parameters to control a motor for the following case: timer resolution is $1.91\mu s$ for the channels; the starting period between steps is 4.0ms and the running period is 2.0ms; the number of step rates is 5.

13.7 DISCRETE I/O

Figure 13.29 presents the channel variables for the Discrete I/O function. For an input channel the function is used for one of the following operations:
(a) detect an input transition;
(b) sample the input level upon a CPU request in the *transition* mode;
(c) sample the input level at a specified time interval in the *match* mode.
Table 13.16 lists the RAM parameters and register settings for the input operations. As an output channel, the Host Service Request field determines whether the output is set Low or High. Table 13.16 also defines the proper values for outputs.

In each case, the TPU updates the parameter PIN_LEVEL to record the 16 previous levels as either {0} (LOW) or {1} (HIGH). Bit 15 contains the most recent value. When updated, the 16 values are shifted right by one bit and the most recent logical level is placed in bit 15. After each update, an interrupt request is generated by the channel. The CPU program is interrupted if the channel interrupt is enabled.

EXERCISES

13.7.1. Write a routine to accept an application's program request to set the level of channel 4 to HIGH or LOW. The routine should first determine the level on the channel and then change the level or do nothing if the level is already the one requested.

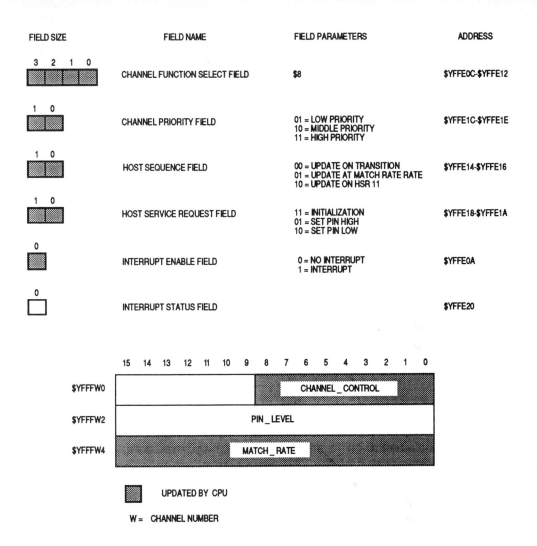

FIELD SIZE	FIELD NAME	FIELD PARAMETERS	ADDRESS
3 2 1 0	CHANNEL FUNCTION SELECT FIELD	$8	$YFFE0C-$YFFE12
1 0	CHANNEL PRIORITY FIELD	01 = LOW PRIORITY 10 = MIDDLE PRIORITY 11 = HIGH PRIORITY	$YFFE1C-$YFFE1E
1 0	HOST SEQUENCE FIELD	00 = UPDATE ON TRANSITION 01 = UPDATE AT MATCH RATE RATE 10 = UPDATE ON HSR 11	$YFFE14-$YFFE16
1 0	HOST SERVICE REQUEST FIELD	11 = INITIALIZATION 01 = SET PIN HIGH 10 = SET PIN LOW	$YFFE18-$YFFE1A
0	INTERRUPT ENABLE FIELD	0 = NO INTERRUPT 1 = INTERRUPT	$YFFE0A
0	INTERRUPT STATUS FIELD		$YFFE20

```
          15  14  13  12  11  10  9   8   7   6   5   4   3   2   1   0
$YFFFW0  |                          |        CHANNEL _ CONTROL          |
$YFFFW2  |                    PIN _ LEVEL                               |
$YFFFW4  |                    MATCH _ RATE                              |
```

▨ = UPDATED BY CPU

W = CHANNEL NUMBER

Figure 13.29 Discrete I/O register selections and parameters.

13.7.2. Write a routine to initialize channel 14 to detect a transition on the input pin and cause an interrupt. Once a transition is detected, a routine should sample the input level every 2ms for 20ms. If the level is constant for four consecutive samples, the level as {1} or {0} should be stored for use by an application's program. Assume that TCR1 resolution is 15.3μs. This in effect "debounces" the input signal and eliminates the error that could be caused by too rapid a signal transition on the signal line.

Table 13.16 Discrete I/O Variables

Variable	Value	Meaning
Input functions:		
(1) Transition		Update PIN_LEVEL on input transition
CHANNEL_CONTROL	$0F	Input
Host Sequence Request	{00}	Update on transition
Host Service Request	{11}	Initialize
(2) Host request		Update PIN_LEVEL on request
CHANNEL_CONTROL	$0F	Input
Host Sequence Request	{10}	Update on request
Host Service Request	{11}	Initialize
(3) Match		Update PIN_LEVEL periodically
CHANNEL_CONTROL	$03	Use TCR1 counter
MATCH_RATE	$0–$FFFF	Number of counts between updates
Host Sequence Request	{01}	Update on each MATCH_RATE counts
Host Sequence Request	{11}	Initialize
Output function:		
CHANNEL_CONTROL	$8F	Output
Host Service Request	{10}	set level LOW
	{01}	Set level HIGH

FURTHER READING

The article by Dunn and Harwood describes the TPU operation and presents program examples. Georgopoulos describes a variety of microprocessor and microcontroller applications. A number of the control systems cited in his textbook could be designed using the MC68332 with its modules. Peatman's textbook presents designs using 8-bit microcontrollers. The TPU of the MC68332 is well suited to a number of the applications.

Bannies' article compares stepper motors and DC motors and concludes that the DC motor is superior in many positioning applications. The textbook by Sinha has an extensive chapter dealing with stepper motor control and DC motor control.

The MC68332 TPU

DUNN, JOHN, and ANN HARWOOD, "Programming the 68332," *Embedded Systems Programming*, **2**, No. 10 (November 1989), 38–47.

Applications of timers and counters

GEORGOPOULOS, CHRIS J., *Interface Fundamentals in Microprocessor-Controlled Systems* (Dordrecht, Holland:) D Reidel Publishing Company, 1985

PEATMAN, JOHN B., *Design with Microcontrollers*. New York, N.Y.: McGraw-Hill, 1988.

Motor Control

BANNIES, HANS E., "DC motors bring advantages to positioning," *Laser Focus World*, **25**, No. 9 (September 1989), 140–142.

SINHA, P. K., *Microprocessors for Engineers.* New York, N.Y.: John Wiley & Sons (Ellis Horwood Limited), 1987.

14

The System Integration Module

The System Integration Module (SIM) determines the state of the MC68332 micro-controller after a reset and during initialization. The SIM is composed of several submodules that control system operation. After a reset, programmable registers that control the submodules of the SIM must be initialized to define various aspects of the hardware and software configuration for the MC68332. In particular, an initialization program can specify the system clock frequency as well as select various protection options such as the software watchdog timer. The initialization program can also assign the function of many of the signal lines on the external bus. In addition to the submodules for system configuration and protection and external bus control, the SIM contains a test submodule to allow diagnostic tests of the MC68332.

Section 14.1 introduces the SIM and contains a description of each of its major features. A block diagram of the MC68332 and the SIM register set presented in Section 14.1 explains the overall operation of the SIM. Section 14.2 describes the reset state of the SIM and the system. Section 14.3 presents the necessary programming steps for initialization of the SIM. Initialization defines the system configuration and the function of the external bus. The protection provided for systems and applications programs is also defined during initialization. Section 14.3 also presents the programming techniques necessary to initialize the internal RAM module of the MC68332.

Other sections of this chapter describe hardware design aspects of the MC68332. Interface design techniques are presented in Section 14.4. Section 14.5 treats the signal lines of the external bus from the interface designer's point of view. These signal lines are used for data transfer, interrupt requests, bus control, and the detection of hardware errors. Section 14.6 describes program and hardware design using the chip select signals. The chip select signals simplify interface design in many applications.

568

The SIM test submodule can be used during the product development cycle. Chapter 16 describes the features of the SIM for system testing.

14.1 INTRODUCTION TO THE SYSTEM INTEGRATION MODULE (SIM)

The System Integration Module (SIM) consists of various submodules that control the reset state and initial operation of the MC68332 microcontroller unit (MCU). After a reset, a number of default states and certain external signal lines define the reset configuration for the MCU. An initialization program writes values into the programmable registers of the SIM to define specific characteristics that must be changed from the default states at reset.

Table 14.1 lists the major features of the SIM and describes their use and the selections that are possible by an initialization program. A detailed description of each of these features except the test mode is presented in the appropriate sections in this chapter. Chapter 16 includes a description of the test submodule.

Table 14.1 Features of the SIM

Feature	Use	Initialization
Configuration:		
Module configuration	Select overall configuration	Mode of operation, register access, module mapping, and interrupt arbitration
Protection:		
Bus monitor	Hardware watchdog	Timeout period
Halt monitor	Responds to CPU halt	Enable or disable
Software watchdog timer	Program protection	Timeout period
Spurious interrupt monitor	Monitors interrupt acknowledgement	—
Reset status	Defines cause of reset	—
Timing:		
Clock synthesizer	System clock	Clock frequency
Periodic interrupt timer	Periodic interrupts	Period between interrupts
External bus control:		
External bus interface	External data transfers	Pin assignment
Chip selects	Bootstrap program and enable peripheral chips	Base address, block size, and other options
System test:		
Test Module	Debugging	Enable or disable

Figure 14.1 presents a block diagram of the MC68332 to show its external signal lines and the various modules. The SIM submodules in Figure 14.1 that affect external signals are the chip select, External Bus Interface (EBI), clock and test submodules. The system configuration and protection submodule that communicates with the Intermodule Bus (IMB) is not shown in the figure.

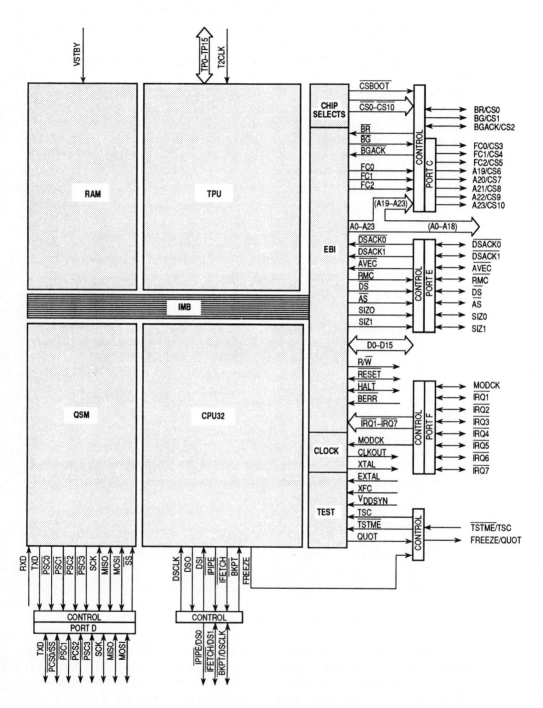

Figure 14.1 MC68332 block diagram.

Figure 14.2 shows the protection and timing circuits of the SIM with their primary control signals and control registers. Table 14.2 defines the registers and their use. Table 14.3 describes each bit. The bus monitor always monitors the internal IMB. A CPU bus-error exception occurs if the response time for a module is excessive. Internal to external data transfers are monitored if the external bus monitor is enabled by setting the Bus Monitor Enable (BME) bit in the System Protection Control Register (SYPCR) during initialization. The spurious interrupt monitor causes a CPU spurious-interrupt exception if any internal module or an external device does not respond in time during an interrupt acknowledgement cycle. The spurious interrupt monitor asserts a bus error signal when an error is detected which in turn causes a spurious interrupt exception as previously explained in Section 11.6.

The halt monitor can cause a reset in response to a CPU halt signal. As described in Section 11.6, a halt occurs when the CPU detects a bus error or an address error during exception processing for another bus error or address error or a reset. The halt monitor is enabled or disabled by the System Protection Control Register. If enabled, the halt monitor causes a reset when a halt occurs. Section 14.5 of this chapter treats hardware aspects of the signal-lines monitored by the bus monitor submodule.

Once enabled, the software watchdog requires a special service sequence of two writes to its Software Service Register (SSR) during each timeout period. If the periodic servicing does not occur, the software watchdog timer asserts a reset request when it times out. Subsection 14.3.1 describes the software watchdog in detail.

The Periodic Interrupt Timer (PIT) is an 8-bit counter that requests an interrupt at periodic time intervals after it is enabled. A count in the Periodic Interrupt Timing Register (PITR) determines the periodic interval. The CPU interrupt level and vector for the periodic interrupt timer are specified in the Periodic Interrupt Control Register (PICR). Subsection 14.3.4 explains this timer.

A programmable clock synthesizer generates the system clock signal. At reset, the frequency is 8.39MHz when an external crystal of 32.768kHz is used as a reference. The frequency is programmable in the clock Synthesizer Control Register (SYNCR) as described in Section 14.3. If enabled, a Loss of Clock (LOC) reset occurs if the external frequency reference is lost.

The SIM Reset Status Register (RSR) indicates the cause of the latest reset. Section 14.2 describes the RSR.

14.1.1 Register Set of the SIM

Figure 14.3 presents the complete register set of the SIM. Figure 14.3(a) shows the control registers for the SIM submodules other than the chip select registers. Figure 14.3(b) shows the registers that control the chip select signals. The starting address for the registers is $YFFA00 where $Y is either $7 or $F as set in the SIM Module Configuration Register (SMCR) after a reset. The default beginning address at reset is $FFFA00.

In Figure 14.3, those registers with a Function Code (FC) of {101} can only be accessed by a supervisor mode program. Those with Function Code {x01} can be accessed by a program in either the supervisor or user mode if the supervisor bit

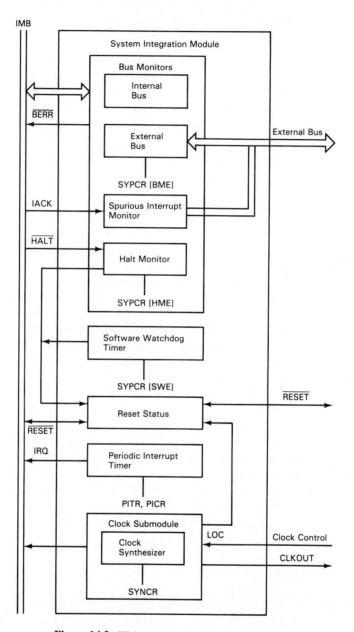

Figure 14.2 SIM protection and clock submodules.

(SUPV) in the SIM Module Configuration Register is set to {0} during initialization. Section 14.5 explains the meaning of the Function Codes on the external bus.

Table 14.2 defines the registers of the SIM used in normal operation and describes their use. The SIM registers are functionally grouped as follows:

(a) global initialization registers;
(b) registers to control the Periodic Interrupt Timer;
(c) the Software Service Register;
(d) registers for port control;
(e) registers for chip selects;
(f) registers for the test mode.

The registers for the test mode are not included in Table 14.2.

FC	ADDRESS	15 8	7 0	
101	YFFA00	MODULE CONFIGURATION (MCR)		
101	YFFA02	MODULE TEST (SIMTR)		
101	YFFA04	CLOCK SYNTHESIZER CONTROL (SYNCR)		CLOCK
101	YFFA06	UNUSED	RESET STATUS REGISTER (RSR)	
101	YFFA08	MODULE TEST E (SIMTRE)		EBI
101	YFFA0A	UNUSED	UNUSED	
101	YFFA0C	UNUSED	UNUSED	
101	YFFA0E	UNUSED	UNUSED	
X01	YFFA10	UNUSED	PORT E DATA (PORTE)	
X01	YFFA12	UNUSED	PORT E DATA (PORTE)	
X01	YFFA14	UNUSED	PORT E DATA DIRECTION (DDRE)	
101	YFFA16	UNUSED	PORT E PIN ASSIGNMENT (PEPAR)	
X01	YFFA18	UNUSED	PORT F DATA (PORTF)	
X01	YFFA1A	UNUSED	PORT F DATA (PORTF)	
X01	YFFA1C	UNUSED	PORT F DATA DIRECTION (DDRF)	
101	YFFA1E	UNUSED	PORT F PIN ASSIGNMENT (PFPAR)	—
101	YFFA20	UNUSED	SYSTEM PROTECTION CONTROL (SYPCR)	SYSTEM PROTECTION
101	YYFA22	PERIODIC INTERRUPT CONTROL (PICR)		
101	YFFA24	PERIODIC INTERRUPT TIMING (PITR)		
101	YFFA26	UNUSED	SOFTWARE SERVICE (SWSR)	
101	YFFA28	UNUSED	UNUSED	—
101	YFFA30	TEST MODULE MASTER SHIFT A (TSTMSRA)		TEST
101	YFFA32	TEST MODULE MASTER SHIFT B (TSTMSRB)		
101	YFFA34	TEST MODULE SHIFT COUNT (TSTSC)		
101	YFFA36	TEST MODULE REPETITION COUNTER (TSTRC)		
101	YFFA38	TEST MODULE CONTROL (CREG)		
X01	YFFA3A	TEST MODULE DISTRIBUTED REGISTER (DREG)		
		UNUSED	UNUSED	—
X01	YFFA40	UNUSED	PORT C DATA (PORTC)	CHIP SELECT
X01	YFFA42	UNUSED	UNUSED	

Figure 14.3(a) SIM control registers.

The specific programming details for most of the SIM registers are presented in appropriate sections of this chapter. Chapter 16 discusses the test mode of the SIM. All of the registers in Table 14.2 must be initialized after a reset unless the default settings are correct for an application.

101	YFFA44	CHIP-SELECT PIN ASSIGNMENT (CSPAR0)
101	YFFA46	CHIP-SELECT PIN ASSIGNMENT (CSPAR1)
101	YFFA48	CHIP-SELECT BASE BOOT (CSBARBT)
101	YFFA4A	CHIP-SELECT OPTION BOOT (CSORBT)
101	YFFA4C	CHIP-SELECT BASE 0 (CSBAR0)
101	YFFA4E	CHIP-SELECT OPTION 0 (CSOR0)
101	YFFA50	CHIP-SELECT BASE 1 (CSBAR1)
101	YFFA52	CHIP-SELECT OPTION 1 (CSOR1)
101	YFFA54	CHIP-SELECT BASE 2 (CSBAR2)
101	YFFA56	CHIP-SELECT OPTION 2 (CSOR2)
101	YFFA58	CHIP-SELECT BASE 3 (CSBAR3)
101	YFFA5A	CHIP-SELECT OPTION 3 (CSOR3)
101	YFFA5C	CHIP-SELECT BASE 4 (CSBAR4)
101	YFFA5E	CHIP-SELECT OPTION 4 (CSOR4)
101	YFFA60	CHIP-SELECT BASE 5 (CSBAR5)
101	YFFA62	CHIP-SELECT OPTION 5 (CSOR5)
101	YFFA64	CHIP-SELECT BASE 6 (CSBAR6)
101	YFFA66	CHIP-SELECT OPTION 6 (CSOR6)
101	YFFA68	CHIP-SELECT BASE 7 (CSBAR7)
101	YFFA6A	CHIP-SELECT OPTION 7 (CSOR7)
101	YFFA6C	CHIP-SELECT BASE 8 (CSBAR8)
101	YFFA6E	CHIP-SELECT OPTION 8 (CSOR8)
101	YFFA70	CHIP-SELECT BASE 9 (CSBAR9)
101	YFFA72	CHIP-SELECT OPTION 9 (CSOR9)
101	YYFA74	CHIP-SELECT BASE 10 (CSBAR10)
101	YFFA76	CHIP SELECT OPTION 10 (CSOR10)

X = Depends on state of SUPV bit in SIM MCR.
Y = m111 where m is the modmap bit in the SIM MCR (Y = $7or $F).

Figure 14.3(b) SIM chip select registers.

14.1.2 The SIM Global Registers and System Operation

Figure 14.4 summarizes the bits and the reset states of the SIM global registers. Table 14.3 defines the bits that can be changed during initialization. The SIM Module Control Register (SMCR) defines the mode of operation of the MC68332 and the interrupt arbitration level for SIM interrupts. The System Protection Control Register (SYPCR) is used to enable the system monitors and define the timing for the software watchdog timer and the bus monitor. The clock Synthesizer Control Register (SYNCR) defines the system clock frequency and the mode of operation of the clock synthesizer. These register values are typically written first when the SIM is initialized after a reset.

After a reset, the bits in the SIM Module Control Register (SMCR[7:0]) define the interrupt arbitration level, the module memory map and the access to certain SIM registers. Section 14.3 presents a complete discussion of the options available during program initialization. The high-order bits (SMCR[15:8]) are used to define the op-

Table 14.2 SIM Registers

Register Name	Address	Use
Global:		
SMCR: Module Configuration Register[2]	$YFFA00[1]	Set interrupt arbitration, module memory map, show cycles, slave mode, freeze, and external CLKOUT signal
SYNCR: Clock Synthesizer Control Register	$YFFA04	System clock frequency selection; define Loss of Clock source, reset, and stop mode operation
RSR: Reset Status Register	$YFFA07	Indicates cause of reset (read only)
SYPCR: System Protection Control Register	$YFFA21	Enable software watchdog, bus monitor and halt monitor; select timeout periods
Periodic Interrupt:		
PICR - Periodic Interrupt Control	$YFFA22	Define interrupt vector and level for Periodic Interrupt Timer (PIT)
PITR: Periodic Interrupt Timing	$YFFA24	Select period of timer
Software service:		
SWSR: Software Service Register	$YFFA27	Reset register for software watchdog timer
Port control:		
PEPAR, PFPAR: Port assignment	$YFFA17 – $YFFA1F	Assign Port E and Port F as bus control pins or I/O ports
Port E control	$YFFA11 – $YFFA15	Data direction and data for Port E
Port F control	$YFFA18 – $YFFA1D	Data direction and data for Port F
PORTC: Port C data register	$YFFA41	Port C data
Chip selects:		
Chip select registers	$YFFA44 – $YFFA76	Enable chip selects, select base address, block size and options

Notes:
1. $Y = $7 or $F as set in SMCR[6].
2. The SIM Module Configuration is designated as SMCR in this chapter to differentiate it from the QSM and TPU configuration registers QMCR and TMCR.

eration of the SIM and the MC68332 during software and hardware debugging. For example, the FRZSW and FRZBM bits determine the protection available after the CPU asserts the FREEZE signal line. This signal is asserted when the CPU enters the background mode as described in Chapter 16. The slave mode option allows an external bus master to control the Intermodule Bus and gain access to the registers of the MC68332 modules. Chapter 16 presents a discussion of all the debugging options and these options are not discussed further in this chapter.

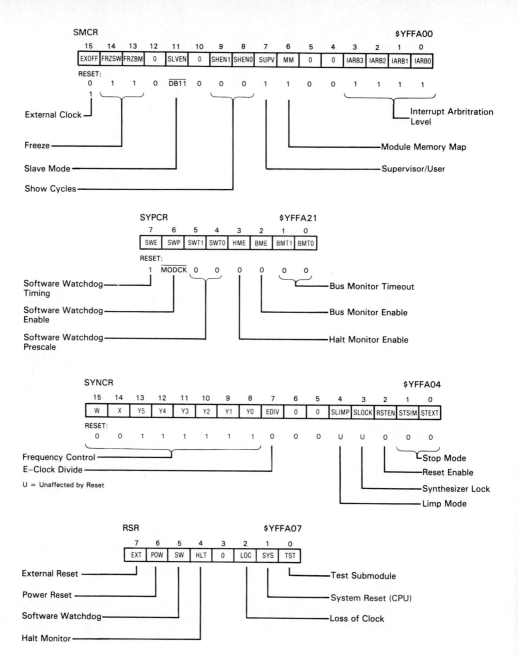

Figure 14.4 SIM global registers and reset status register.

Table 14.3 SIM Global Register Bits

Register bit	Value	Meaning
SMCR:		Module Configuration Register:
IARB3–0[3:0]	$0-$F	Interrupt arbitration level
MM[6]	{1}	Modules at $FFF000–$FFFFFF
	{0}	Modules at $7FF000–$7FFFFF
SUPV[7]	{1}	Supervisor access to SIM registers
	{0}	Supervisor or user access
SHEN1–0[9:8]	{00}	Show cycles disabled
	{01}	Show cycles enabled without external arbitration
	{10}	Show cycles enabled with
	{11}	external arbitration
SLVEN [11]	$\overline{DB11}$	Slave mode if DB11 is LOW at reset
FRZBM[13]	{0}	If FREEZE, bus monitor disabled
	{1}	If FREEZE, bus monitor enabled
FRZSW[14]	{0}	If FREEZE, disable software watchdog and Periodic Interrupt Timer
	{1}	If FREEZE, enable timers
EXOFF[15]	{0}	CLKOUT pin is driven
	{1}	CLKOUT pin in high-impedance state
SYPCR:		System Protection Control Register:
BMT1–0[1:0]	{00}–{11}	Bus monitor timeout period in clock cycles (8-64)
BME[2]	{0}	Disable bus monitor for internal to external bus cycle
	{1}	Enable
HME[3]	{0}	Disable halt monitor
	{1}	Enable
SWT1–0[5:4],	{00}–{11}	Software watchdog timing
SWP[6]	$\overline{MODCK}$	Software watchdog prescale
SWE[7]	{0}	Disable software watchdog
	{1}	Enable
SYNCR:		Clock Synthesizer Control Register:
STEXT[0],	{00}–{11}	Clock control after
STSIM[1]		LPSTOP instruction
RSTEN[2]	{0}	Disable Loss of Clock source reset
	{1}	Enable
SLOCK[3]	{0}	Status: VCO is not locked
	{1}	VCO is locked or clock is driven externally
SLIMP[4]	{0}	External clock source is VCO reference
	{1}	Loss of Clock source; limp mode
EDIV[7]	{0}	E-clock: divide system clock by 16
	{1}	E-clock: divide system clock by 8
SYNCR[15:8]	$00–$CF	System clock frequency

Notes:
1. DB11 is the level of bit 11 of the data bus and MODCK is an input signal at reset.
2. FREEZE and show cycles are used in debugging modes.
3. The E-clock is a synchronization signal for MC6800 (8-bit) peripheral chips.

The halt and external bus monitors are disabled at reset as indicated by the reset state of the System Protection Control Register (SYPCR) in Figure 14.4. However, the software watchdog timer is enabled. The software watchdog must be either disabled or serviced during initialization as described in Section 14.3. The state of the Clock Mode Select (MODCK) signal line at reset determines the system clock source and the period for the software watchdog timer when the timer is enabled. The SYPCR is a *write once* register after a reset unless the MC68332 is in the test mode.

The clock synthesizer submodule is controlled by the clock Synthesizer Control Register (SYNCR). The reset frequency for the system clock is 2^{23}Hz (8.39MHz) when a 32.768kHz crystal is used as the reference frequency. The initial clock frequency is one-half the maximum system clock frequency of 16.78MHz. The low-order bits (SYNCR[7:0]) control operation of the frequency synthesizer and Voltage Controlled Oscillator (VCO) under various conditions as explained in Section 14.3.

The SIM Reset Status Register (RSR) is a read-only register that indicates the cause of the most recent reset. The RSR is discussed in detail in Section 14.2.

EXERCISES

14.1.1. Hardware design: determine the number and type of external chips necessary to replace the functions of the SIM as defined in Table 14.1.

14.2 RESET STATE

Section 10.3 introduced the reset state for the CPU32 and the initialization procedure for the entire MC68332 MCU. Figure 14.5 summarizes the CPU operation after a reset. The reset vector contains the initial value of the System Stack Pointer (SSP) and Program Counter (PC). Program execution begins at the PC location in the reset vector. This vector and the initialization program for the CPU and SIM must reside in non-volatile memory, typically a "bootstrap" ROM in the system. The MC68332 is designed to select the bootstrap ROM upon reset using the signal $\overline{\text{CSBOOT}}$ as described in Section 14.6.

In a correctly functioning system or product, the reset would be caused by a reset signal or by applying power to the unit. However, the MC68332 has a number of other sources of a reset that are caused by serious error conditions. Table 14.4 summarizes the sources of a reset. The SIM Reset Status Register shown in Figure 14.4 indicates the source of the reset for the initialization program. For example, the system reset bit RSR[1] (SYS) is set to {1} when the CPU executes a RESET instruction. The RESET instruction is used to initialize external devices as described in Section 14.4 but the instruction does not cause a reset of the CPU or SIM.

In applications, different program actions may be taken according to the source of the reset. The external sources of reset ($\overline{\text{RESET}}$ and powerup V_{DD}) cannot be disabled. When the external reset signal is held LOW or the applied voltage rises to the threshold value after power is applied, a reset will occur. The protection circuits

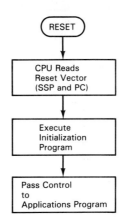

Figure 14.5 CPU32 reset sequence.

that cause a reset are typically disabled during debugging but should be enabled in a working product. However, a reset from these sources usually indicates that the product or system is not able to continue normal operation.

Table 14.4 Reset Sources

Type	Source	Cause
External	$\overline{\text{RESET}}$	External signal
Powerup	External Bus Interface	V_{DD}[1]
Software	Software Watchdog Timer	Time out [2]
Halt	SIM halt monitor	CPU issues halt[2]
Loss of Clock	SIM clock submodule	Loss of frequency reference[2]
System	CPU	RESET instruction
Test	SIM test submodule	Test mode

Notes:
1. V_{DD} is the supply voltage for the MC68332.
2. These sources of reset can be disabled.

Figure 14.6 summarizes the signal lines and submodules of the SIM that are active at reset. Those signals that are indicated as inputs are used by the SIM during reset to specify the reset hardware configuration and the clock frequency. Subsection 14.2.1 defines the reset software state as determined by the default values in SIM registers. Section 14.2.2 presents the hardware configuration after a reset. The CPU break point ($\overline{\text{BKPT}}$) input signal enables the background mode of the CPU. Chapter 16 discusses the background mode.

Sec. 14.2   Reset State

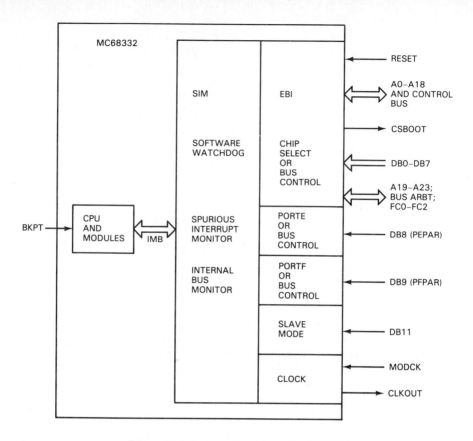

Figure 14.6 Reset configuration of the MC68332.

14.2.1 Reset Software Configuration

When a reset is recognized, the SIM uses the reset bit values in its registers to define the initial state of the MC68332. Figure 14.4 in Section 14.1 summarizes these reset register values. Table 14.5 defines each bit in the SIM registers that affect the software configuration of the SIM. The reset values in the registers must be changed by an initialization program if the default values are not appropriate for the application. Section 14.3 describes program initialization of the SIM.

After a reset, SIM interrupts are enabled.[1] The module registers are addressed at the highest addresses in memory beginning at $FFF000. In the bus monitor submodule, only the internal bus monitor and the spurious interrupt monitors are enabled. The software watchdog timer is enabled. The software timeout period is initially determined by the frequency of the clock reference signal and the software watchdog timer scaling bits (SYPCR[5:4]). Section 14.3 presents the full range of software watchdog timeout periods.

---

[1] Early versions of the MC68332 were initialized with the interrupt arbitration disabled. Thus, bits SMCR[3:0] = $0 after a reset in some versions of the MC68332.

In most applications, the system clock reference source will be an oscillator whose frequency is controlled by a crystal. However, the external reference can be a crystal-controlled oscillator or an external clock source. The clock synthesizer for the system clock provides an 8.39MHz (2^{23} Hz) signal after reset if a 32.768kHz crystal is the external reference. If the MODCK signal line is LOW during reset, an external high-frequency clock source should be provided as discussed further in Subsection 14.4.2. At reset, the Periodic Interrupt Timer is disabled.

Table 14.5 Software Reset Configuration Summary

Register bits	Value	Meaning
SMCR:		Module configuration register:
SMCR[3:0]	{1111}	SIM interrupts enabled
SMCR[6]	{1}	Module registers at $FFF000
SMCR[7]	{1}	Supervisor access only
SMCR[9:8]	{00}	Show cycles disabled
SMCR[11]	$\overline{\text{DB11}}$	Slave mode enabled if DB11 is LOW
SMCR[14:13]	{11}	If FREEZE, disable software watchdog timer and external bus monitor[1]
SMCR[15]	{0}	CLKOUT signal enabled
SYPCR:		System Protection Control Register:
SYPCR[1:0]	{00}	Bus monitor time out: 64 clock cycles
SYPCR[2]	{0}	Disable internal to external bus monitor
SYPCR[3]	{0}	Disable halt monitor
SYPCR[5:4]	{00}	Software watchdog timeout:minimum
SYPCR[6]	$\overline{\text{MODCK}}$:	Select timer prescaler[2]
	{0}	- No prescale
	{1}	- Prescale by 2^9
SYPCR[7]	{1}	Software watchdog enabled
SYNCR:		Clock Synthesizer Control Register:
SYNCR[1:0]	{00}	If LPSTOP, disable system clock
SYNCR[2]	{0}	If loss of clock source, limp mode
SYNCR[7]	{0}	E-clock frequency[3] : divide by 8
SYNCR[15-8]	$3F	System clock frequency[4]: $f_{(\text{source})} \times 2^8$
PICR:		Periodic Interrupt Control Register:
PICR[3:0]	$F	Uninitialized interrupt
PICR[7:4]	$0	Vector 0
PICR[10:8]	{000}	Disabled

Notes:
1. FREEZE is signal asserted by CPU when in background mode.
2. $\overline{\text{MODCK}}$ is the complement of the logic level on the MODCK signal line.
3. The E-clock is a synchronization signal for MC6800 (8-bit) peripheral chips.
4. Assuming MODCK is HIGH during reset. Otherwise, an external clock source is used.

14.2.2 Reset Hardware Configuration

As shown in Figure 14.6, a number of external signals determine the hardware reset configuration. The state of the signals at reset defines the system clock source and the function of various signals on the external bus as well as other characteristics of the SIM. Table 14.6 summarizes the hardware conditions at reset and the register bits or external signals that define the configuration.

Table 14.6 Hardware Reset Configuration Summary

Condition	Register bits	Control Signal	Meaning
CLKOUT	SMCR[15] = {0}	—	CLKOUT Pin driven
Slave mode	SMCR[11]	DB11	If DB11=LOW, enable slave mode If DB11=HIGH, disable slave mode
Bus monitor	SYPCR[2]={0}	—	Bus monitor disabled for internal to external transfers
	SYPCR[1:0]={00}	—	Timeout period is 64 system clock cycles for internal cycles
Halt Monitor	SYPCR[3]={0}	—	Disabled
Clocks:	—	MODCK	Determines source and scaling
MODCK=HIGH	—	HIGH	Internal clock source
	SYPCR[6]={0}	HIGH	No prescale for software watchdog
	PITR[8]={0}	HIGH	No prescale for periodic interrupt timer
MODCK=LOW	—	LOW	External clock source
	SYPCR[6] ={1}	LOW	Prescale software watchdog
	PITR[8]={1}	LOW	Prescale Periodic Interrupt Timer
Chip selects:	CSPAR0–CSPAR1	DB0–DB7	Bus signals
CSBOOT	CSPAR0	DB0	Enabled
CS0–CS10	CSPAR0–CSPAR1	DB1–DB7	Chip selects disabled
PORT E control	PEPAR	DB8	If DB8=LOW, select PORT E If DB8=HIGH, select bus control
PORT F control	PFPAR	DB9	If DB9=LOW, select PORT F If DB9=HIGH, select bus control

Data signal line 11 (DB11) enables the slave mode if the signal is LOW at reset. An external bus master has access to the module registers if slave mode is enabled. If DB11 is HIGH, slave mode is disabled. If input signal MODCK is HIGH during reset, an internal Voltage-Controlled Oscillator (VCO) generates the system clock signal. If MODCK is LOW, an external clock signal at the EXTAL pin furnishes the system clock signal. The maximum frequency for the external clock is 16.78MHz.

Those options that are selected automatically at reset can be changed during initialization. For example, the disabled external bus monitor and halt monitor are typically enabled by an initialization program. The initialization procedure is described in Section 14.3. The other selections for the clock source and the chip selects imply a specific hardware configuration for the entire system at reset. Normally, the bits set or cleared by the external signals should not be changed during initialization. However, any chip select signals other than $\overline{\text{CSBOOT}}$ to be used during normal operation must be defined and enabled by an initialization program. Section 14.6 describes the initialization for the chip selects and the I/O ports.

EXERCISES

14.2.1. By reference to various figures and tables in this section, explain the SIM parameters that should be defined during reset and initialization.

14.3 PROGRAM INITIALIZATION OF THE SIM

After a reset, an initialization program must execute to initialize SIM register values. The program is typically held in the bootstrap ROM of the system or product. The program defines the system protection and the software and hardware configuration for the MC68332 MCU. This initialization also defines the time periods for the system clock, software watchdog timer and the periodic interrupt timer if the timers are enabled. The subsections to follow here describe each aspect of SIM initialization. Subsection 14.3.5 summarizes the initialization procedure and presents a complete initialization example for the SIM.

SIM initialization is part of the complete initialization procedure described previously in Section 10.3 for the MC68332 and its modules. The various test and debugging modes for the SIM and the MC68332 are not treated in this chapter. Chapter 16 presents the details for these modes used during product development.

14.3.1 System Configuration, Protection and Software Watchdog Timer

The SIM Module Configuration Register, System Protection Control Register, and clock Synthesizer Control Register are the SIM registers initialized first after a reset. This subsection describes the configuration and system protection options. Subsection 14.3.2 presents the initialization procedure to set the frequency of the system clock.

Figure 14.7 shows the registers that control system configuration and protection. The SMCR and SYPCR are repeated from Figure 14.4 for convenience. These global registers can only be accessed by a supervisor-mode program. With the reset default values shown in Figure 14.7, several of the SIM protection submodules are disabled after a reset. However, the software watchdog timer begins its time out sequence immediately. The software watchdog timer must either be disabled or values must be written to the Software Service Register (SSR) shortly after a reset. Figure 14.7(c) shows the Software Service Register. The use of the SSR is described later.

SIM Module Configuration Register (SMCR). The low-order byte of the SIM Module Configuration Register (SMCR) shown in Figure 14.7(a) determines the SIM interrupt arbitration level, module memory map and supervisor or user access

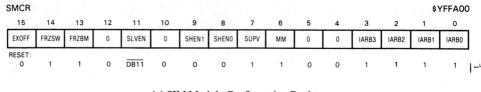

(a) SIM Module Configuration Register

(b) System Protection Control Register

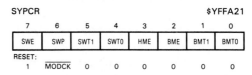

(c) Software Service Register

Figure 14.7 SIM configuration and protection registers.

Table 14.7 SIM Module Configuration Register Initialization

Register bits	Value	Reset	Meaning
SMCR[3:0] (IARB)	$0–$F	IARB=$F	Interrupt arbitration level
SMCR[6] (MM)	{1} {0}	MM={1} —	Module registers at $FFF000 Module registers at $7FF000
SMCR[7] (SUPV)	{1} {0}	SUPV = {1} —	Supervisor access Supervisor/user access

Note:
The bits SMCR[15:8] are used for testing and debugging modes.

to various registers of the SIM. Table 14.7 summarizes the reset state and initialization options for the low-order byte of the SMCR. The reset value of the IARB field (SMCR[3:0]) is $F indicating that SIM interrupts are enabled. The IARB field should be initialized with a value from $1 (lowest priority) to $F (highest priority). This arbitration level applies between modules of the MC68332 and does not determine the CPU interrupt level requested by an external interrupt, the TPU, the QSPI, or the Periodic Interrupt Timer of the SIM. The CPU interrupt level is selected in a control register for each module or submodule that can request an interrupt. Chapter 15 discusses the significance of interrupt arbitration and priority levels.

At reset, the module registers begin at address $FFF000. This is the beginning address for CPU program access to the module registers on the internal bus. All twenty-four address lines are used for addressing if the Module Map bit MM

(SMCR[6]) is left {1}. Setting the MM bit to {0} changes the starting address of the module registers to $7FF000. The MM bit of the SMCR can only be written once after reset. Figure 10.6 in Section 10.3 presents a typical memory layout after initialization.

If the Supervisor bit SUPV is {1} after initialization, only a supervisor program can access the SIM registers. If SUPV = {0}, a user mode program can also access the SIM registers that determine the direction and data values for the I/O ports. Figure 14.3 in Section 14.1 shows the complete SIM register set and those registers affected by the SUPV bit. The registers that may allow supervisor or user program access are indicated by a Function Code (FC) of {x01} in Figure 14.3.

During normal operation, the bit values in the upper byte (SMCR[15:8]) of the Module Configuration Register in Figure 14.7(a) has no effect on system or product operation. These bits are important in the test or debugging modes as described in Chapter 16.

Example 14.1

Typical initial settings for the SMCR bits selected by an initialization program are as follows:
(a) IARB = $F (highest priority interrupt arbitration);
(b) MM = {1} (Module memory map at $FFF000);
(c) SUPV = {1} (Supervisor access only).
The instruction

       MOVE.W   #$00CF, $FFFA00   ; INITIALIZE SMCR

sets these initial values. The SIM has the highest arbitration level among the MC68332 modules. The highest arbitration level gives precedence in the system to SIM interrupts which includes external interrupt requests. The module registers are addressed at the highest memory locations and only supervisor-mode program access is allowed to SIM registers.

Notice that the settings in this example are the reset values. Thus, program initialization of the low-order byte of SMCR is not strictly necessary. However, it is the author's practice to initialize every control register with desired values regardless of the default settings.

System Protection Register (SYPCR). Figure 14.7(b) shows the bits and reset values for the System Protection Control Register (SYPCR). Table 14.8 defines the bit settings that determine the system protection features and set the bus timeout period. The software watchdog timeout period will be discussed separately later in this subsection. Unless the SIM is in the test mode, the System Protection Control Register may be written only once following a reset.

The Bus Monitor Enable bit BME (SYPCR[2]) enables the external bus monitor. When enabled, the external bus monitor monitors the response time for an internal to external data transfer. If an external peripheral does not respond within the time period set in SYPCR[1:0], a $\overline{BERR}$ signal is asserted to the CPU causing a bus error exception. The timeout period $T_{(bus)}$ is defined as

$$T_{(bus)} = \frac{T_{(system)} \times 64}{2^n} \tag{14.1}$$

Table 14.8 System Protection Control Register

Register bits	Value	Reset	Meaning
Bus Monitor:			Bus monitor timeout:
SYPCR[1:0]	{00}	{00}	64 clock periods
(BMT1–0)	{01}	—	32 clock periods
	{10}	—	16 clock periods
	{11}	—	8 clock periods
SYPCR[2]	{0}	{0}	Disable external bus monitor
(BME)	{1}	—	Enable
SYPCR[3]	{0}	{0}	Disable Halt Monitor
(HME)	{1}	—	Enable
Software Watchdog:			
SYPCR[7]	{1}	{1}	Enable software watchdog
(SWE)	{0}	—	Disable

Note:
SYPCR[6:4] determines the timeout period of the software watchdog timer.

where $n = 0, 1, 2$ or 3 is the value in SYPCR[1:0] (BMT1–0). The periods in seconds based on a 16.78MHz system clock frequency are as follows:

(a) BMT1–0 = {00}, 3.81μs;

(b) BMT1–0 = {01}, 1.91μs;

(c) BMT1–0 = {10}, 0.954μs;

(d) BMT1–0 = {11}, 0.477μs.

If the halt monitor is enabled by setting the Halt Enable bit HME (SYPCR[3]) to {1}, a CPU halt signal causes a reset. A CPU halt is caused by a double bus fault as described in Chapter 11. This condition typically indicates a catastrophic system failure from which program recovery is not possible.

The software watchdog timer is enabled at reset. This watchdog timer is disabled by setting the Software Watchdog Enable bit SWE (SYPCR[7]) to {0} during initialization. During software debugging, the software watchdog timer is typically disabled. The watchdog timer would be enabled during normal operation of a product. Once the bit is set or cleared after a reset, the selection cannot be changed until the next reset unless the MC68332 is in the test mode.

The spurious interrupt monitor and the internal bus monitor cannot be disabled. Thus, the bits of the SYPCR have no effect on the operation of these monitors.

Software watchdog timer. The software watchdog timer is typically used in a product whose programs execute repeatedly during product operation. Figure 14.8 shows an example of a software design built around a loop of routines or tasks. After initialization, the individual routines or tasks execute until the last one has completed. Then, the software watchdog timer must be reset by writing the bit pattern $55 followed by $AA into the Software Service Register shown in Figure 14.7(c). The two-step process to reset the software watchdog is intended to prevent a runaway program from accidentally executing the reset sequence and thus defeating the purpose of the watchdog. The overall timing around the loop in Figure 14.8 must take into account the added time for any interrupt service routines or exception handling routines in addition to the time allotted to each task or routine in the loop.

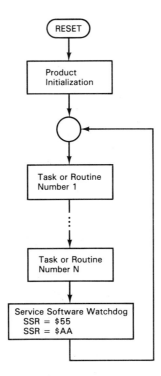

Figure 14.8 Software watchdog flowchart.

The service program to reset the software watchdog timer must execute in the supervisor mode of the CPU. The applications programs that are being timed can operate in either supervisor or user mode. If a CPU program does not execute the watchdog reset sequence within the timeout period, a reset occurs. The typical cause of the error is that a branch was taken to an incorrect location or a program loop has taken excessive time to complete. The program action to be taken in case of a reset is determined entirely by the requirements of an application. For example, after an unexpected reset in a control system, it may be necessary to bring the elements being controlled to a safe state and then shut down the system. In other applications, the MC68332 can be initialized again after the reset to allow the product to continue operation. Chapter 15 discusses the effects on system operation caused by an unexpected reset.

The timeout period for the software watchdog timer is determined by the selections in the System Protection Control Register shown in Figure 14.7(b). The reference source can be an external crystal-controlled oscillator or an external clock supplied at the EXTAL input pin of the MCU. Assuming that the frequency of the reference source is $f_{(source)}$, the software watchdog period $T_{(SWW)}$ is

$$T_{(SWW)} = \frac{2^9 \times 2^{2n} \times 2^{SWP \times 9}}{f_{(source)}} \qquad (14.2)$$

where the frequency of the reference source $f_{(source)}$ is determined by an external circuit. A crystal-controlled oscillator frequency will be designated as $f_{(crystal)}$. If an external clock is the reference source, the frequency will be designated as $f_{(external)}$.

In Equation 14.2, $n = 0, 1, 2$ or 3 as defined in SYPCR[5:4]. The software watchdog prescale bit SWP (SYPCR[6]) has a reset value determined by the input signal line MODCK. If MODCK is HIGH at reset, SWP is {0} in Equation 14.2 and the shortest software watchdog period is 2^9 times the period of the reference source. If MODCK is LOW at reset, the minimum period is 2^{18} times the period of the external clock source since SWP is {1} in Equation 14.2.

Example 14.2

Table 14.9 summarizes the periods of the software watchdog timer when a 32.768kHz (2^{15}Hz) crystal oscillator is the reference source as calculated from Equation 14.2. The MODCK signal should be HIGH at reset. The period of the source is the reciprocal of the frequency which yields

$$T_{(crystal)} = 2^{-15} \text{ seconds or } 30.5\mu s.$$

The minimum timeout period occurs if SYPCR[6:4] is {000}. The minimum period is 2^9 times $T_{(crystal)}$ or 15.6ms. The longest time out period occurs when SYPCR[6:4] is {011}. The maximum period is thus 2^{15} times $T_{(crystal)}$ or 1 second.

The reader can easily show that the same timeout periods are obtained if $f_{(external)}$ is 16.78MHz and MODCK is LOW at reset. In this case, SWP = 1 in Equation 14.2.

Table 14.9 Software Watchdog Timeout Periods

{SWP, SWT1, SWT0}	Multiplier	Period
{000}	2^9	15.6ms
{001}	2^{11}	62.5ms
{010}	2^{13}	250ms
{011}	2^{15}	1 second

Note:
The reference source frequency is 32.768kHz.

14.3.2 System Clock Frequency and Register SYNCR

The Clock Synthesizer Control Register (SYNCR) shown in Figure 14.9 controls the frequency of the system clock and other aspects of the SIM clock submodule. Table 14.10 defines the bits and shows the default values at reset. The reference source for the system clock can be an external crystal oscillator or an external clock signal.

The crystal or external clock connection to the MC68332 is discussed in Chapter 15. In this subsection, it is assumed that a 32.768kHz crystal oscillator serves as the clock reference source. The clock circuitry consists of a phased-locked loop with a Voltage Controlled Oscillator (VCO) to create the clock signal.[2] The clock signal generated internally is used as the system clock. The clock waveform is available for external devices on the CLKOUT pin of the MC68332. This subsection explains the register bit settings to select the system clock frequency. Section 15.2 describes the clock synthesizer in more detail.

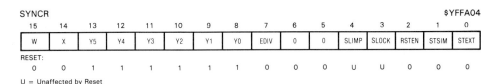

Figure 14.9 Clock Synthesizer Control Register (SYNCR).

Table 14.10 Clock Synthesizer Control Register Bits

Register bits	Value	Reset	Meaning
SYNCR[0]	{0}	{0}	If LPSTOP, stop external clock
(STEXT)	{1}	—	If LPSTOP, drive CLKOUT
SYNCR[1]	{0}	{0}	If LPSTOP, stop VCO
(STSIM)	{1}	—	If LPSTOP, use VCO
SYNCR[2]	{0}	{0}	Loss of clock source causes limp mode
(RSTEN)	{1}	—	Loss of clock source causes reset
SYNCR[7]	{0}	{0}	E-clock divide by 8
(EDIV)	{1}	—	E-clock divide by 16
SYNCR[15:8]	$00 – $CF	$3F	System clock frequency
(W, X, Y5–Y0)			(8.39MHz default)
Status:			
SYNCR[3]	{0}	—	VCO not locked
(SLOCK)	{1}	—	VCO locked or external clock
SYNCR[4]	{0}	—	External clock reference is used
(SLIMP)	{1}	—	Loss of clock source

Table 14.10 summarizes the bit selections in the SYNCR. The system clock frequency is calculated from a crystal-controlled oscillator frequency by the equation

$$f_{(\text{system})} = f_{(\text{crystal})}[4(Y + 1) \times 2^{2W+X}] \tag{14.3}$$

where Y has one of the values from 0 to 63. The Y value is specified in SYNCR[13:8]. Setting the X bit (SYNCR[14]) doubles the system clock frequency. Setting the W

---

[2] The reader is referred to the *MC68332 User's Manuals* for a complete discussion of the clock circuits. Chapter 15 of this textbook describes the VCO of the clock generator in more detail and provides references for additional study.

bit (SYNCR[15]) multiplies the frequency by a factor of 4. However, the frequency limits of the clock circuitry must be observed. Using a 32.768kHz reference source, the frequency range in Equation 14.3 is limited from 131kHz to 16.78MHz for the 16.78MHz version of the MC68332.

Example 14.3

Table 14.11 lists selected system clock frequencies using a reference of

$$f_{(crystal)} = 32.768\text{kHz}$$

in Equation 14.3. The frequency control bit W (SYNCR[15]) is {0} in the cases listed. After a reset, the clock frequency is 8.389MHz since both the X bit and the W bit are {0}. Setting X = {1} doubles the clock frequency to 16.78MHz. In some applications, it is desirable to initialize the clock frequency to a lower value to reduce power consumption. The values for Y in Table 14.11 are given in hexadecimal and decimal.

Table 14.11 System Clock Frequencies

Y (SYNCR[13:8])	X = 0	X = 1
$0 (0)	131kHz	262kHz
$F (15)	2.097MHz	4.194MHz
$1F (31)	4.194MHz	8.39MHz
$30 (48)	6.423MHz	12.85MHz
$3F (63)	8.389MHz	16.78MHz

Notes:
1. Reference Frequency is 32.768kHz.
2. X bit is SYNCR[14]; W (SYNCR[15]) = {0}.

Other clock (SYNCR) options. During initialization, several options can be selected for the SIM clock submodule. The bits STEXT and STSIM determine the state of the clocks if the LPSTOP (Low Power Stop) instruction is executed by a CPU program. If these bits are left in their reset state of {00} as defined in Table 14.10, the clock module assumes its minimum power consumption configuration after LPSTOP. The output clock signal (CLKOUT) is held LOW and the voltage controlled oscillator of the clock submodule is stopped. The external clock source continues to supply the reference signal. If STEXT is {1} when LPSTOP is executed, CLKOUT is driven by the SIM clock submodule. If STSIM is {1}, the LPSTOP instruction does not affect the system clock operation.

The SIM clock submodule can operate even without an external clock source but the Voltage Controlled Oscillator (VCO) operates at approximately half of maximum frequency. This mode of operation is called the *limp* mode. If a loss of clock reference on the EXTAL input pin is detected, the clock submodule will cause either a reset if RSTEN (SYNCR[2]) is {1} or begin the limp mode if RSTEN is {0}. Limp mode is indicated by the status bit SLIMP (SYNCR[4]).

The status bit SLOCK (SYNCR[3]) indicates the state of the VCO when the VCO generates the system clock frequency. Each change in the control bits W or Y requires the VCO to relock onto the desired frequency. When the oscillator is stable, SLOCK = {1}. The SLOCK bit value {1} can also mean that an external clock is being used to generate the system clock.

The EDIV (SYNCR[7]) bit determines the frequency of the E-clock signal when this signal is used to synchronize MC6800 (8-bit) family peripheral chips. Section 14.4 discusses the E-clock signal with 8-bit peripheral devices. Section 14.6 explains the E-clock signal relationship to chip select signals.

14.3.3 Chip selects and I/O ports

Once the system configuration and protection submodule and the clock submodule are initialized, the chip select submodule should be initialized. Initialization of the chip select submodule defines the function of a number of the signal lines on the external bus that have multiple uses. Figure 14.1 in Section 14.1 shows these signals. In particular, the signals associated with the chip select submodule can function as bus control signals or chip select signals. The chip select signals designated CS3–CS10 can also serve as output Port C signals if they are not used as chip select signals or bus control signals. The signals of PORT E and PORT F can function as either bidirectional I/O port signal lines or as bus control signals. The choice at reset depends on the level (HIGH or LOW) of the data-bus signal lines DB0–DB9.

After the reset, an initialization program can change the selections if necessary. The initialization program must enable any signal lines defined as chip select signals except for $\overline{\text{CSBOOT}}$ which cannot be disabled. The CPU initialization program enables one or more chip select signals by writing appropriate values to the option registers (CS0R0–10) for the signals. Section 14.6 describes these registers in detail.

Since the reset state for the external bus is determined by the system hardware configuration, a discussion of the initialization procedure for the chip select signals is deferred until the hardware aspects of the signal lines have been presented. Section 14.6 describes the initialization of the chip select signals and the I/O ports.

14.3.4 Periodic Interrupt Timer

The Periodic Interrupt Timer (PIT) of the SIM can be used to provide a precise time base for the software modules of a product. The PIT is often called a *real-time clock* when applied in this way. An interrupt request is generated by the PIT each time the programmed time interval is reached. This will cause a CPU interrupt if both the SIM interrupts and the CPU interrupts are enabled at the appropriate level. Chapter 15 discusses real-time considerations in product design. The present subsection defines the PIT control registers and initialization technique.

Figure 14.10 shows the registers that control the Periodic Interrupt Timer. The Periodic Interrupt Control Register (PICR) is used to define the vector number and CPU interrupt level for the PIT. The reset values indicate that the PIT interrupt is disabled since PICR[10:8] = {000}. The periodic interrupt vector number (PICR[7:0]) is $F at reset to indicate an uninitialized interrupt.

The vector number written in PICR[7:0] in Figure 14.10(a) should be between $40 (64) and $FF (256) to select a vectored interrupt in the CPU interrupt vector table.

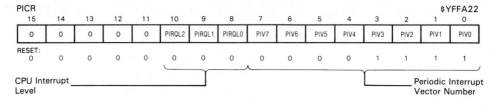

(a) Periodic Interrupt Control Register

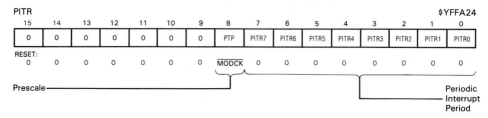

(b) Periodic Interrupt Timing Register

Figure 14.10 Periodic Interrupt Timer registers.

Section 11.7 described the CPU interrupt processing and the vector table in detail. The address in memory of the vector is 4 times the vector number. An interrupt level from {001} (level 1) to {111} (level 7) must be written to PICR[10:8] to enable the PIT interrupt requests. For example, the instruction

> MOVE.W   #$0642, $FFFA22   ; INITIALIZE PIT IRQ

selects interrupt level 6 and vector $42. The starting address of the interrupt handling routine must be stored in location $108 (4 × $42) before the first interrupt occurs.

The Periodic Interrupt Timing Register (PITR) controls the periodic time interval. If the timer period control bits (PITR[7:0]) are $00, the PIT is disabled regardless of the setting of any other bits. This is the case at reset as shown in Figure 14.10(b). The state of the MODCK signal at reset or the Periodic Timer Prescaler Control bit (PTP) during initialization determines the scale factor for the clock reference of the Periodic Interrupt Timer. The prescale values are as follows:
(a) PTP = {0}, scale by 1;
(b) PTP = {1}, scale by 2^9.
The minimum period in either case is 4 times the clock period determined by the prescaler value. The periodic interrupt time $T_{(PIT)}$ is thus

$$T_{(PIT)} = \frac{4 \times P \times 2^{PTP \times 9}}{f_{(source)}} \tag{14.4}$$

where P is the value in PITR[7:0] that ranges from $1 to $FF when the PIT is enabled.

Example 14.4

Table 14.12 lists a few of the timing intervals using a 32.768kHz reference source in Equation 14.4. MODCK should be HIGH at reset if the external reference source is a low-frequency oscillator. The PTP bit, $\overline{\text{MODCK}}$, is {0}. When PTP is {0}, the period ranges from 122μs to 31.1ms.

If PTP is changed to {1}, the periodic timing interval ranges from 62.5ms to 15.9 seconds. For example, the value

$$PITR[15:0] = \$0110$$

yields a periodic interrupt interval of 1 second.

Table 14.12 PIT Timing Intervals

PITR[7:0]	PTP = {0}	PTP = {1}
$00	Disabled	Disabled
$01	122μs	62.5ms
$02	244μs	125ms
$04	488μs	250ms
$08	977μs	500ms
$10	1.95ms	1.0 seconds
$20	3.9ms	2.0 seconds
$40	7.8ms	4.0 seconds
$A0	19.5ms	10.0 seconds
$FF	31.1ms	15.9 seconds

Note:
A 32.768kHz reference is assumed.

Example 14.5

Figure 14.11 is a short routine to initialize the Periodic Interrupt Timer to cause interrupts at 1 second intervals. This routine should only be called during an initialization after the other registers of the SIM have been initialized. CPU interrupts must be enabled to at least level 6 for the periodic interrupts to occur. The CPU vector at memory location $108 (vector $42) must contain the starting address of the interrupt handling routine (not shown).

14.3.5 Initialization Program for SIM and Internal RAM

After a reset, each global register of an MC68332 module should be initialized to contain a known value. Table 14.13 lists a typical sequence for initialization after an external or power up reset that occurs as part of the normal operation of a product or system. The initialization sequence does not consider the previous state of the system before the reset.[3] Thus, the only assumption is that the CPU reset vector and the initialization program itself reside in non-volatile memory. The signal line CSBOOT is designed to address the reset vector locations ($0000-$0004) after a reset. Subsection 14.6.2 describes this chip select signal.

---

[3] In certain applications, operating information may be saved periodically in non-volatile memory such as the RAM module with battery backup. If a reset occurs because of a temporary power failure or a watchdog timer timeout or loss of clock reference, the initialization program could use the stored information to determine the appropriate action.

```
abs. rel.   LC   obj. code   source line
----  ----  ----  ----------   -----------
  1    1   0000                          TTL  'FIGURE 14.11'
  2    2   0000              |*
  3    3   0000              |*
  4    4   0000              |*   INITIALIZE PIT FOR 1 SECOND INTERRUPTS WITH 16.78MHz
  5    5   0000              |*       SYSTEM CLOCK
  6    6   0000              |*   LEVEL 6 INTERRUPT; VECTOR 66($42) (LOCATION $108)
  7    7   0000              |*
  8    8        0000 4100    |PITINIT   EQU   $4100                    ;INITIALIZE
  9    9   0000              |*
 10   10        0080 0000    |REGBASE   EQU   $800000
 11   11   0000              |*
 12   12   0000              |*
 13   13        00FF FA22    |PICR      EQU   $007FFA22+REGBASE        ;PIT INTERRUPT CONTROL
 14   14        00FF FA24    |PITR      EQU   $007FFA24+REGBASE        ;PIT TIMING CONTROL
 15   15   0000              |*
 16   16   0000              |*   INITIALIZE PIT
 17   17   0000              |*
 18   18   4100              |          ORG   #PITINIT
 19   19   4100 33FC 0642    |          MOVE.W #$0642,PICR             ;LEVEL 6
 19        4104 00FF FA22    |
 20   20   4108              |*                                       ;VECTOR 66 ($108)
 21   21   4108              |*
 22   22   4108 33FC 0110    |          MOVE.W #$0110,PITR             ;PRESCALE BY 512
 22        410C 00FF FA24    |
 23   23   4110              |*                                       ;1 SEC AT 16.78MHz
 24   24   4110 4E75         |          RTS
 25   25   4112              |*
 26   26   4112              |          END
```

Figure 14.11 Program to initialize Periodic Interrupt Timer.

The global registers of the SIM, internal RAM, Queued Serial Module (QSM) and Timer Processor Unit (TPU) should be initialized to define the system configuration and protection and the interrupt levels and vectors for the modules. After the modules are initialized including the Periodic Interrupt Timer if it is used, the CPU interrupts must be enabled at the proper level. Then, the CPU passes control to the first program to be executed. This program could load other programs into external RAM for example. If all the programs for a product are in ROM, the first program to execute would typically initialize the QSM and TPU for the specific application. The QSM and the TPU are described in Chapter 12 and Chapter 13, respectively.

Internal RAM.   Figure 14.12 shows the registers that enable and control the internal RAM. Table 14.14 defines the bits that must be initialized for normal operation of the RAM. The reader is referred to the *MC68332 User's Manuals* for a complete discussion of the test modes and other uses of the RAM. Chapter 15 discusses the standby operation of the RAM when a standby power supply is used in a product.

The RAM is disabled after a reset. An initialization program should define the address space of the RAM as either supervisor only by setting RAMMCR[8] = {1} or available to either supervisor or user mode programs by setting RAMMCR[8] to {0}. The RAM is enabled and the base address is defined in register RAMBAR. The base address can be any 2K byte boundary in the system but it should not overlap the address space of the module registers. These registers are at locations $YFFA00 to $YFFFFF where $Y = $7 or $F as defined in the SIM Module Configuration Register.

Table 14.13 Example Initialization Sequence

Initialization	Register	Selection
Reset:		
CPU reset configuration	—	Reset vector (SSP, PC) at location $0000, addressed by $\overline{\text{CSBOOT}}$
CPU status	(SR) = $2700	Supervisor; interrupts masked
SIM:		
System configuration	SMCR	Debugging or normal state; supervisor or user; module memory map; interrupt arbitration
System clock	SYNCR	System clock frequency
System protection	SYPCR	Bus monitor; halt monitor; software watchdog timeout
Chip selects	CSPAR0, CSPAR1, CSBAR0–10, CSOR0–10	Chip select base address and options
I/O Ports	PEPAR, PFPAR	Port E and Port F Pin assignments
RAM:		
Internal RAM	RAMMCR RAMBAR	Supervisor/user space; Base address
Modules:		
QSPI	QMCR QILR, QIVR	Supervisor/user, interrupt arbitration Interrupt level and vector
TPU	TMCR TICR	Time base, supervisor/user; interrupt arbitration Interrupt level and vector
Periodic Timer:		
PIT	PICR PITR	Interrupt level and vector Periodic time period
CPU:		
Enable CPU interrupts	SR	Set mask SR[10:8]
Pass control to applications program	USP, SR, PC	Define User Stack Pointer address, status, and initial PC

Table 14.14 RAM Control Registers

Register Bits	Value	Reset	Meaning
RAMMCR:			RAM Module Configuration Register:
RAMMCR[8]	{1}	{1}	RAM is in supervisor space
(RASP)	{0}	—	RAM access is unrestricted
RAMMCR[15]	{0}	{0}	Normal operation
(STOP)	{1}	—	Low-power stop mode
RAMBAR:			RAM Base Address register:
RAMBAR[0]	{1}	{1}	RAM is disabled
(RAMDS)	{0}	—	RAM is enabled
RAMBAR [15:3]	A23–A11	0	RAM base address

RAMMCR $YFFB00

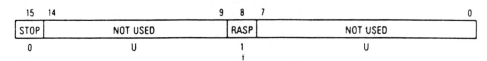

(a) RAM Module Configuration Register

RAMBAR $YFFB04

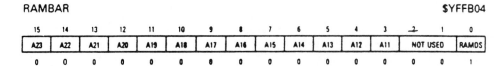

(b) RAM Base Address Register

Figure 14.12 RAM control registers.

Initialization program example. Initialization of the MC68332 MCU after
a reset defines the software and hardware configuration that is controlled by MCU
registers. The external circuitry for the system or product as described in Section 14.3
through Section 14.6 determines in part the selections made during initialization. In
particular, the initialization of the SIM chip select signals and I/O ports cannot be
made properly without knowledge of the overall system design. Section 14.6 describes
the initialization procedure for these hardware dependent signals. The present section presents an initialization program for the SIM and RAM control registers without presenting the necessary program instructions to initialize the SIM chip select
submodule.

Example 14.6

Figure 14.13 shows an initialization program to initialize the SIM global registers, the
internal RAM and the Periodic Interrupt Timer. The CPU vector table must contain the
appropriate vectors as described previously in Section 10.3. The reset vector Program
Counter (PC) at location $0004 should contain the address SIMINIT. The SIM global
register values select the following options:

(a) interrupt arbitration $F, module map at $FFFF00, and supervisor or user access to
SIM I/O port registers;
(b) all bus monitors enabled;
(c) bus monitor timeout 64 cycles and software watchdog timeout 250ms;
(d) 16.78MHz system clock assuming a 32.786kHz oscillator reference.

The internal RAM base address is $FFFF00 after reset and initialization. The
RAM is thus addressable from $FFFF00 to $FFF7FF. The Periodic Interrupt Timer (PIT)
interrupts at CPU level 6. Vector $42 at location $108 must contain the starting address
of the PIT interrupt handling routine. A one second period is selected for the PIT.

The program in Figure 14.13 does not show the complete details of an initialization
program. For example, initialization routines for the QSM and TPU must also be executed as explained in Chapter 12 for the QSM and Chapter 13 for the TPU. Section 10.3
describes the technique to pass control to an applications program using the RTE instruction.

```
abs.   LC   obj. code    source line
----   ----  ---------   -----------
  1   0000                  TTL      'FIGURE 14.13'
  2   0000               |*
  3   0000               |*
  4   0000               |*     INITIALIZE SIM FOR 16.78MHz SYSTEM CLOCK
  5   0000               |*
  6   0000               |*     1 SECOND PERIODIC INTERRUPTS
  7   0000               |*        LEVEL 6 INTERRUPT; VECTOR 66($42) (LOCATION $108)
  8   0000               |*
  9   0000 4000          |SIMINIT  EQU      $4000                  ;INITIALIZE
 10   0000
 11   0000               |*
 12   0080 0000          |REGBASE  EQU      $800000
 13   0000               |*
 14   0000               |*
 15        00FF FA00     |SMCR     EQU      $007FFA00+REGBASE      ;SIM MODULE CONFIG REG.
 16        00FF FA04     |SYNCR    EQU      $007FFA04+REGBASE      ;SYSTEM CLOCK CONTROL REG.
 17        00FF FA21     |SYPCR    EQU      $007FFA21+REGBASE      ;SYSTEM PROTECTION CONTROL REG.
 18        00FF FA22     |PICR     EQU      $007FFA22+REGBASE      ;PIT INTERRUPT CONTROL
 19        00FF FA24     |PITR     EQU      $007FFA24+REGBASE      ;PIT TIMING CONTROL
 20        00FF FB00     |RAMMCR   EQU      $007FFB00+REGBASE      ;RAM MODULE CONFIG REG.
 21        00FF FB04     |RAMBAR   EQU      $007FFB04+REGBASE      ;RAM BASE ADDRESS
 22   0000               |*
 23   0000               |*     INITIALIZE CPU AND SIM
 24   0000               |*
 25   4000               |         ORG      #SIMINIT
 26   4000 46FC 2700     |         MOVE.W   #$2700,SR             ;SUPERVISOR, MASK INTERRUPTS
 27   4004 33FC 004F     |         MOVE.W   #$004F,SMCR           ;MM=1, IARB=F
      4008 00FF FA00     |
 28   400C 13FC 00AC     |         MOVE.B   #$AC,SYPCR            ;SWWD 250MS., HME, BME
      4010 00FF FA21     |
 29   4014               |*                                      ; 64 CLOCK CYCLES
 30   4014 33FC 7F00     |         MOVE.W   #$7F00,SYNCR          ;16.78MHz
      4018 00FF FA04     |
 31   401C               |*
 32   401C               |*     INITIALIZE CHIP SELECTS AS NEEDED
 33   401C               |*
 34   401C               |*
 35   401C               |*     INITIALIZE INTERNAL RAM
 36   401C               |*
 37   401C 33FC 0100     |         MOVE.W   #$0100,RAMMCR         ;SUPERVISOR ACCESS
      4020 00FF FB00     |
 38   4024 33FC FFF0     |         MOVE.W   #$FFF0,RAMBAR         ;BASE ADDR $FFF000
      4028 00FF FB04     |
 39   402C               |*
 40   402C               |*     INITIALIZE QSPI AND TPU GLOBAL REGISTERS
 41   402C               |*        AS NEEDED
 42   402C               |*
 43   402C               |*     INITIALIZE PIT
 44   402C               |*
 45   402C 33FC 0642     |         MOVE.W   #$0642,PICR           ;LEVEL 6
      4030 00FF FA22     |
 46   4034               |*                                      ;VECTOR 66 ($108)
 47   4034 33FC 0110     |         MOVE.W   #$0110,PITR           ;PRESCALE BY 512
      4038 00FF FA24     |
 48   403C               |*                                      ;1 SEC AT 16.78MHz
 49   403C 46FC 2000     |         MOVE.W   #$2000,SR             ;ENABLE CPU INTERRUPTS
 50   4040               |*
 51   4040               |*     GO TO SUPERVISOR ROUTINES AND PASS CONTROL
 52   4040               |*        TO APPLICATIONS PROGRAMS
 53   4040               |*
 54   4040 4E4F          |         TRAP     #15
 55   4042 0063          |         DC.W     $0063
 56   4044               |         END
```

Figure 14.13 Initialization program.

EXERCISES

14.3.1. Write the program instructions to accomplish the following:
(**a**) set the SIM interrupt arbitration level to $A with other SMCR bits unchanged;
(**b**) select external bus monitor timeout period of 8 clock cycles, enable the halt monitor and set software watchdog timeout period to 15.6ms.

14.3.2. Determine the allowed values in SYNCR[15:8] to yield a 16.78MHz system clock if the reference frequency is 32.768kHz.

14.3.3. If W(SYNCR[15]) is {1}, determine the allowable values for SYNCR[14:0] to limit the maximum clock frequency to 16.78MHz.

14.3.4. For each source of reset, define the possible hardware or software causes of the condition and the action to be taken by an initialization program that executes after a reset.

14.3.5. Determine the value in the Periodic Timing Register PITR to yield a 4ms period if the reference is 32.768kHz crystal oscillator. What is the error in the closest value obtainable?

14.3.6. Write a program to create a time-of-day clock. A routine should initialize the Periodic Interrupt Timer to interrupt every second. The interrupt routine should update a software clock that determines the time of day in hours, minutes and seconds.

14.4 INTERFACE DESIGN AND SUPPORT CHIPS

This section introduces the external bus of the MC68332 MCU and interfacing techniques. Figure 14.14 shows a simplified block diagram of an MC68332-based system and the interfaces for ROM, RAM, peripheral chips and custom devices. The signal lines of the MCU are used for data transfer, interrupt requests, bus control and the detection of hardware errors. The peripheral devices of the Queued Serial Module (QSM) and Time Processor Unit (TPU) are shown separately.

The external bus in Figure 14.14 is controlled by the System Integration Module (SIM). The bus connects the MCU to other devices of the system that require bus control signals. Each peripheral chip register and memory location on the external bus has a unique address. As the CPU executes instructions to access external memory or devices, the external bus selects a particular address with the address bus and a chip select signal line. The MCU then reads or writes data using the common, bidirectional, data bus. Since all of the devices are in parallel electrically on the external bus, only one device can be selected at a time. The devices that are not being addressed on a particular bus cycle must be kept electrically isolated from the bus by their interfaces.

In Figure 14.14, a device is selected when the chip select input for the device is asserted. This input pin is typically designated as Chip Select ($\overline{CS}$). The notation $\overline{CS}$ indicates that the chip select signal for a device is asserted when the signal is held LOW. The signals $\overline{CS}$ for all the other devices that are not selected must be held HIGH. The actual way the MC68332 accomplishes device selection is described in Section 14.6.

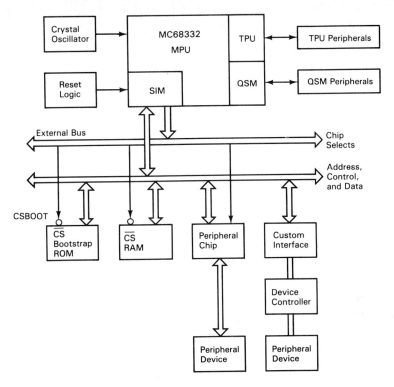

Figure 14.14 Typical microcontroller system organization.

The present section concentrates on the functional design of custom interfaces and the use of standard peripheral chips to control I/O devices in a system.

14.4.1 Functional Design of Interfaces

Figure 14.14 shows the organization of a typical microcontroller system, emphasizing the role played by the interfacing circuitry. The interface electrically connects the external bus with the device controller and resolves differences in timing or formats between the CPU and the external device. The MCU, through its logical circuitry and I/O routines, controls the operation of the system. The I/O routines prepare the interface for data transfers with the peripheral device, which itself is controlled by the device controller.

When the device is initialized and ready for transfer, it can perform its function, such as transmitting a character to the MCU or memory. Transfers to the MCU usually involve an interrupt request. High-speed transfers of blocks of characters are accomplished with Direct Memory Access (DMA) requests. If the device uses a DMA technique, the transfer request passes through the interface to the bus control circuits and the memory.

The design of an interface depends entirely on its application. For standard operations such as serial transfer of data to CRT terminals or parallel transfer to tape drives and disk units, the interface and perhaps part of the device controller are typically packaged together as a peripheral chip. When the interface is used to connect special-purpose devices, a custom interface may be required.

Table 14.15 lists some of the items to be specified when describing the functional operation of a custom interface. This functional description is normally prepared by the hardware designer. The design specifications should also include details of the programming required to control the interface.

Table 14.15 Functional Design of Interfaces

Item	Specification
General Description	Purpose of the interface Modes of operation: —Initialization —Data transfers or other operations
Hardware	Timing Electrical characteristics Physical characteristics
I/O Routines	Programming: transfer of data and commands
Testing	Test procedure

The functional description begins with a discussion of the purpose of the interface. This is governed by the requirements of the system design, particularly the type of peripheral device involved. Operational modes are described by defining the operation of the circuitry needed to perform initialization and data transfers. Timing considerations and similar hardware aspects of the interface must also be described.

Electrical and physical characteristics of the interface are also included in the functional description. The electrical details are dictated by the system bus and the electrical requirements of the device controller. Such details include specification of the voltage levels, maximum rate of change of signals (rise times), and the like. The physical considerations include environmental requirements and space limitations on the circuit boards involved. The temperature and humidity range for the environment determine the type of chip and the packaging required for integrated circuit chips. The size of the circuit boards influences the number of chips and their placement on a board.

The interface programming requirements can be defined once the modes of operation have been specified. An interface is controlled by sequences of logical variables or binary values written to the interfacing circuitry by an I/O routine. A sequence must be defined for each mode of operation. For example, the programming procedure to reset the interface and initialize it to some known state must be described. Programming a data transfer includes determining if the interface is ready for the transfer, performing the transfer, and checking for errors.

Finally, a test procedure for the interface must be defined. This usually includes a hardware procedure to verify that the interface is functional as well as the steps for testing of the interface under program control. The peripheral chips available as part of the Motorola family of products serve to simplify the design and programming of interfaces.

14.4.2 Peripheral Chips as Interfaces

Most standard peripheral devices are connected to a system using commercially available peripheral chips to act as the interfaces. Therefore, it is important to understand the general principle of operation of these chips, which function as programmable interfaces. Such interfaces require initialization and act under the control of an I/O routine. The use of these peripheral chips and the associated routines require cooperation between the hardware designer and the programmer since the addresses of the chip registers are defined by the connection on the external bus.

The M68000 family includes a number of peripheral chips for interfacing. These integrated circuits provide the interface to particular peripheral devices and eliminate a great deal of the hardware design associated with interfacing. These chips are designed to connect to a M68000 system bus directly or with a minimal amount of additional circuitry.

Peripheral chips are programmed by writing binary values into registers internal to the chips. The addresses of these registers are in the I/O space of the system. For MC68332-based systems, these addresses appear to be memory locations because of the memory-mapped I/O scheme of the MC68332.

Figure 14.15 shows the structure of a typical peripheral chip. The signals to the peripheral device typically include control and data signal lines to transfer data between the peripheral chip and the peripheral device. The CPU program controls the operation of the peripheral chip. Once the chip is selected, the signal lines between the MC68332 MCU and the peripheral chip transfer information between the CPU and internal registers of the chip.

In the M68000 family peripheral chips, each internal register has an I/O address. The base address for the chip is defined during the system design. The internal register address is read from the address lines of the MCU. After the peripheral chip acknowledges a read or write request from the MCU, the I/O transfer logic circuitry transfers commands, data and status information between the MCU data bus and the peripheral chip.

The control register receives a command from the CPU to control the chip's operation. For example, the CPU32 instruction

    MOVE.B   #<d8>, CREG   ; CONTROL REGISTER

could be used to transfer 8 bits to a control register at address CREG. Various bits in the command byte <d8> typically determine whether a transfer operation is input or output and whether interrupts from the chip are enabled or not.

A status register on the chip contains information about the transfer or about the chip. Bits in this register might indicate whether the chip is ready for data transfer, as well as the interrupt status and error conditions. An 8-bit status could be read with the instruction

    MOVE.B   SREG, D1   ; READ STATUS

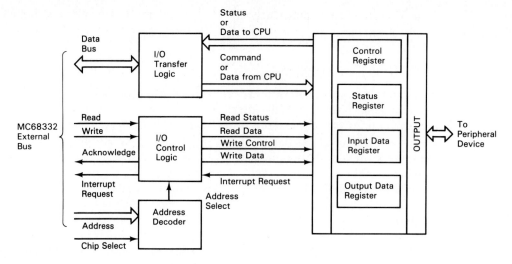

Figure 14.15 Typical peripheral chip.

if SREG is the address of the status register on the chip.

Two data registers are shown on the chip in Figure 14.15. One receives data from the peripheral device and the other stores data to be transmitted to it. The input data register is read in a manner similar to that used to read the status register. The CPU writes to the output data register as it does to the control register.

14.4.3 Programming Peripheral Chips, MOVEP, and RESET

The use of memory-mapped I/O in MC68332-based systems provides great flexibility to the programmer creating routines to control peripheral chips. Any instruction that references memory can be used to control or transfer data to and from a peripheral interface. The powerful instruction set and the various addressing modes of the CPU32 can be applied to such programming. In addition, two special instructions are available to control and access peripheral chips.

The RESET instruction listed in Table 14.16 asserts an MCU signal line which is used to cause interfaces to assume their initial hardware state. This instruction can be executed only in the supervisor mode and does not affect the processor state. Execution of the RESET instruction only resets the external devices and not the CPU or internal MC68332 modules.

Table 14.16 also lists a data movement instruction typically used for transfers to peripheral chips with 8-bit registers. The MOVEP (Move Peripheral Data) instruction transfers a word or longword value between a data register and alternate bytes of memory. This instruction is used to access peripheral chips whose register addresses are successive even or odd byte addresses in memory. For example, the instruction

    MOVEP.L   D1, (0, A1)   ; 8-BIT PERIPHERAL

Table 14.16 RESET and MOVEP Instructions

Syntax		Operation
RESET		RESET signal line asserted
MOVEP.<l>	<Dn>, (<d_{16}>, An)	Transfer to (EA), (EA + 2), ...
MOVEP.<l>	(<d_{16}>, An), <Dn>	Transfer from (EA), (EA+2), ...

Notes:
1. RESET is a privileged instruction.
2. For MOVEP, the effective address (EA) is specified by the address register indirect plus 16-bit displacement addressing mode where <d_{16}> is the displacement.
3. <l> is W or L for the MOVEP instruction.

transfers four bytes from D1 to every other byte beginning at the first byte addressed by (A1). The high-upper byte, (D1)[31:24], is transferred to location (A1); the middle-upper byte, (D1)[23:16], to byte address (A1) + 2; and so on. This method to access interface registers is used for the 8-bit M6800 family of peripheral chips and for some 16-bit chips from Motorola.

14.4.4 I/O Transfer Techniques

I/O transfers are divided into those initiated by the MCU and those initiated by the peripheral device and its controller. Table 14.17 lists transfer techniques in these categories and defines the required initialization and program operation. Before transfers begin, an I/O routine executed by the MCU performs the initialization for the interface.

Table 14.17 I/O Transfer Techniques

Type of transfer	Initialization by program	Program operation
CPU-initiated transfer:		
Unconditional	None	Transfer data
Conditional	Initialize device for direction of transfer	Test status of device and wait until ready; then transfer
Device-initiated transfer:		
Interrupt transfer	1. Initialize device for I/O transfer with interrupt 2. Enable interrupts	1. Transfer data when interrupt occurs 2. Clear interrupt request after transfer
DMA	1. Initialize device for I/O transfer 2. Load DMA registers (a) Count (b) Address 3. Issue command to begin	Process end-of-block interrupt

Notes:
Conditional I/O is sometimes called programmed I/O or polled I/O.

The *unconditional* transfer requires that the peripheral device be ready for transfers at all times. A common example of this type of transfer is found in systems where the "device" is a unit to display numbers or characters. The I/O routine simply transfers the data with a MOVE instruction to the proper address. Circuitry of the display unit is used to convert the binary word from the MCU to the proper display format. Another use of this method is to read a group of switches whose settings are coded into a binary sequence.

Conditional transfers are sometimes called *programmed I/O* or *polled I/O*. The operation of these transfers is illustrated in Figure 14.16. Once the interface is initialized, the I/O routine repeatedly checks the status register of the chip until the status indicates the device is ready. The routine then transfers the data to the peripheral chip. Since the MCU is in a wait loop until the device is ready, the usefulness of this transfer is limited. For example, a conditional transfer could be used to write into a control register during initialization of the interface.

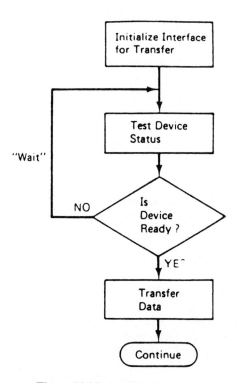

Figure 14.16 Conditional transfer.

For devices that transmit or receive data slowly compared to the execution times of the I/O routines, interrupt-controlled transfer is preferred. Figure 14.17 shows this transfer method. The interface is first initialized to transfer data. Then, the MCU executes other programs until an interrupt occurs. When control is passed to the interrupt routine, the peripheral chip status is tested for errors. If an error is detected, the appropriate action is taken. Otherwise, the transfer occurs. Afterward, the interrupt request from the interface must be reset (cleared) before the next transfer can occur.

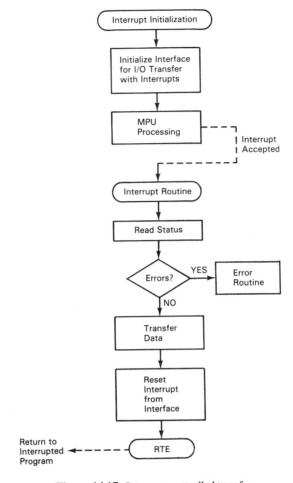

Figure 14.17 Interrupt-controlled transfer.

When a device is capable of transferring blocks of data at high speeds, the direct memory access (DMA) method of transfer is frequently used. A DMA interface typically contains two programmable registers. A counter register contains the number of values to transfer and an address register contains the starting address of the block. The initialization program loads these registers and sends a command to initiate the transfer. The CPU is then free to execute other programs. The transfer of data between the interface and memory is entirely controlled by DMA circuitry without the intervention of the CPU.

For each DMA transfer of a data value, the DMA circuitry requests use of the external bus. The MCU relinquishes the bus for the time of transfer, which is usually one bus cycle to read or write a value. During the transfer, the DMA interface controls the memory just as the MCU normally does. Subsection 14.5.4 describes the bus arbitration capability of the MC68332.

Typically, less than one bus cycle out of five is used for DMA transfers. This "cycle stealing" has little effect on system performance in most cases. For comparison, the MC68332 requires one bus cycle to fetch a 16-bit instruction. Upon completion of the transfer of an entire block of data, the DMA circuitry causes an interrupt. The MCU may now process the input data or initiate the next DMA transfer.

14.4.5 Motorola System Support Chips

Section 1.2 introduced the concept of the Motorola families of chips. A partial list of the chips in the 16-bit and 32-bit Motorola family of products is shown in Table 14.18. Each of these support chips fulfills a specific interfacing function and is programmed according to its unique requirements. Of course, a typical system would contain only a restricted selection from the range of chips that are available. The reader is referred to Motorola literature for details concerning a particular peripheral chip listed in Table 14.18.

Table 14.18 Motorola M68000 Family of Support Chips

Product	Device number	Description
Math processors:	MC68881	Floating-point coprocessor (FPCP)
	MC68882	Floating-point coprocessor
Bus controllers:	MC68452	Bus arbitration module (BAM)
	MC68153	Bus interrupter module (BIM)
DMA controllers:	MC68440	DMA controller (two-channel) (DDMA)
	MC68450	DMA controller (four-channel) (DMAC)
General-purpose I/O:	MC68230	Parallel interface timer (PI/T)
	MC68901	Multifunction peripheral (MFP)
Peripheral controller:	MC68120	Intelligent peripheral controller (IPC)
Data communications:	MC68561	Multiprotocol communications controller II (MPCCII)
	MC68562	Dual universal serial communications controllers
	MC68564	Serial input/output (SIO)
	MC68652	Multiprotocol communications controller (MPCC)
	MC68653	Polynomial generator checker (PGC)
	MC68661	Enhanced programmable communications interface (EPCI)
	MC68681	Dual universal asynchronous receiver/transmitter (DUART)
Disk controllers:	MC68454	Intelligent multiple-disk controller (IMDC)
	MC68465	Floppy disk controller (FDC)

Note:
Not all of the peripheral chips from Motorola are listed.

8-bit peripheral chips. The peripheral chips listed in Table 14.18 generally have a 16- or 32-bit data bus. The 16-bit devices are fully compatible with the MC68332 external bus. In some applications, it is economical to use peripheral chips designed for the 8-bit M6800 family of processors. For example, the MC6821 Peripheral Interface Adaptor (PIA) provides two 8-bit I/O ports. Many of these 8-bit peripheral chips require a clock signal called the E-clock (Enable). This is provided by the MC68332 as an option described in Section 14.6. The reader is referred to Motorola literature for more information about the peripheral chips that are available. The *Motorola Semiconductor Master Selection Guide*, for example, describes most of the peripheral support chips available from Motorola.

EXERCISES

14.4.1. MC68332-based systems use memory-mapped I/O for data transfer. Another scheme is called isolated I/O. With this technique, separate instructions for I/O are part of the CPU instruction set. Typically, there are several I/O instructions (IN or OUT) and a limited number of possible I/O locations or ports. These ports are accessed by separate signal lines which are not part of the system address bus. Describe the advantages and disadvantages of each scheme in terms of the system flexibility and the hardware requirements for interfacing.

14.4.2. Describe the steps in the program and the hardware sequence needed to initialize an interface to receive a byte of data from an external device. Define the operation of the interface and the use of its registers after the byte is received. What sequence is required of the processor itself to read the byte?

14.4.3. Refer to Motorola literature to describe the purpose and operation of the peripheral chips available for MC68332-based systems.

14.4.4. Compare interrupt, DMA, and conditional transfer with respect to each of the following:
(a) system speed of operation;
(b) programming complexity;
(c) interface complexity.

14.4.5. Assume that MPU processing takes 10 microseconds per byte of data transferred. Considering the data transfer techniques discussed in Table 14.17, which method of data transfer would be best for the following devices with the data transfer rates given in bytes per second?
(a) 1000 (communications link);
(b) 10,000 (tape unit);
(c) 1,000,000 (disk unit).

14.4.6. Draw the flowchart for a conditional I/O transfer routine when a string of characters is to be transferred. If a character is ready every 0.1 second, compute the time required to input 10 characters if the CPU processing time is 10^{-5} second per character. This timing is typical of a slow terminal. What advantage is to be gained by using the SCI submodule of the MC68332 if the transfer is an asynchronous, serial transfer. Consider both software and hardware design aspects. Chapter 12 describes the SCI in detail.

14.4.7. Write a routine using the CPU32 MOVEP instruction to transfer a table of values from one area of memory to either another area of memory or to a peripheral device. The table of values has M bytes located in consecutive even addresses which are to be deposited at consecutive odd addresses. Move four bytes at a time and assume that M is divisible by 4.

14.5 MC68332 EXTERNAL BUS SIGNALS

Figure 14.14 showed the electrical connection between devices in an MC68332 system via the external system bus. The bus contains address signal lines, data signal lines, and control signal lines. A few miscellaneous signal lines such as clock signals and power and ground reference are also included. All of the peripheral devices and the microcontroller are connected in parallel to the bus signals. In most applications, the MC68332 MCU acts as the system controller and determines the use of the bus for transfer of data with its control signals.

Figure 14.18 shows the MC68332 signal lines according to their function as bus signals on the external bus. Table 14.19 defines all of the signal lines of the MC68332 including those for the QSM and TPU. The signal lines of these modules are independent of the external bus signals. Figure 14.1 in Section 14.1 showed the complete signal set. This section only considers the bus control signals shown in Figure 14.18 that are used for data transfer, interrupt control, function codes, and bus control. Section 14.6 describes the alternate use of several of these signals for chip selects and I/O ports. Chapter 15 discusses the power and clock control signals in more detail. Chapter 16 describes the use of external bus signals for debugging.

The signal lines are defined by function, mnemonic, and characteristics in Table 14.19. The signal lines that are described as "three-state" in the table are put in a high-impedance (hi-Z) state when the processor relinquishes the use of the bus to other devices. In effect, these signal lines are disconnected electrically from the bus when in the high impedance state.

An understanding of the use of the MC68332 signal lines for fundamental operations is necessary in order to design interfaces. This section describes data transfer operations and the use of the function code lines during processor accesses to memory. The function code information is particularly important to the system designer when a memory management scheme is used to protect and segment various areas of memory. The function codes also indicate the occurrence of an interrupt acknowledgement cycle or other special bus cycle. The interrupt acknowledgement sequence, bus arbitration and various special signals are also described in this section.

It should be emphasized that the information in this section describes the functional operation of the MC68332 signal lines. The precise timing diagrams needed by an interface designer are not presented. The source of these diagrams is Motorola's data sheets for the MC68332 that contain the electrical specifications for the MCU. The electrical data included in the *MC68332 User's Manuals* also define the minimum and maximum times for signal changes and those times between changes on different signal lines to determine allowable timing margins.

Before discussing various hardware operations, the conventions used to specify the signal lines will be presented. Several references in the Further Reading section

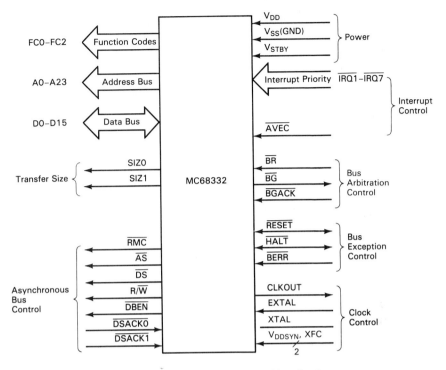

Figure 14.18 MC68332 external bus signals.

at the end of this chapter discuss hardware design in further detail.

Designation of signal lines. The electrical signals generated or received by the MC68332 may be specified in terms of their electrical characteristics and also by their functional or logical use. These electrical characteristics include the voltage level, current requirements, and speed of switching. A hardware designer must also consider other characteristics of the signal generated by the processor or by an external device and propagated along the signal lines of the external bus.

The processor and external devices respond to the signals according to the state of the signal. A signal line with two states is designated as active/inactive, HIGH/LOW, true/false, or {1}/{0}. These four designations are considered equivalent when the electrical characteristics are TTL (Transistor-Transistor Logic) compatible using the positive-true logic definition.

All the signal lines of the MC68332 are TTL compatible, so the processor can be electrically connected to any TTL chip as long as the specified loading conditions are not exceeded. Since the TTL family is the most popular logic type employed today for interfacing circuitry, the MC68332 processor is easily connected to a wide variety of TTL circuits which are available to implement various logical functions. The TTL signal line is considered to be in the LOW state when its steady-state voltage is a nominal 0 volts with respect to the ground reference. The TTL HIGH state is indicated

Table 14.19 MC68332 Bus Signals and States

Signal Name	Mnemonic	Input/Output	Active State	Three-State
Address Bus	A23–A0	Output	High	Yes
Data Bus	D15–D0	Input/Output	High	Yes
Function Codes	FC2–FC0	Output	High	Yes
Boot Chip Select	$\overline{\text{CSBOOT}}$	Output	Low	No
Chip Selects	$\overline{\text{CS10}}$–$\overline{\text{CS0}}$	Output	Low	No
Bus Request	$\overline{\text{BR}}$	Input	Low	No
Bus Grant	$\overline{\text{BG}}$	Output	Low	No
Bus Grant Acknowledge	$\overline{\text{BGACK}}$	Input	Low	—
Data and Size Acknowledge	$\overline{\text{DSACK1}}$/ $\overline{\text{DSACK0}}$	Input	Low	—
Autovector	$\overline{\text{AVEC}}$	Input	Low	—
Read-Modify-Write Cycle	$\overline{\text{RMC}}$	Output	Low	Yes
Address Strobe	$\overline{\text{AS}}$	Output	Low	Yes
Data Strobe	$\overline{\text{DS}}$	Output	Low	Yes
Size	SIZ1/SIZ0	Output	High	Yes
Read/Write	R/$\overline{\text{W}}$	Output	High/Low	Yes
Interrupt Request Level	$\overline{\text{IRQ7}}$–$\overline{\text{IRQ1}}$	Input	Low	—
Reset	$\overline{\text{RESET}}$	Input/Output	Low	No
Halt	$\overline{\text{HALT}}$	Input/Output	Low	—
Bus Error	$\overline{\text{BERR}}$	Input	Low	—
System Clockout	CLKOUT	Input	—	—
Crystal Oscillator	EXTAL, XTAL	Input	—	—
External Filter Capacitor	XFC	Input	—	—
Clock Mode Select	MODCK	Input	High	—
Instruction Fetch	$\overline{\text{IFETCH}}$	Output	Low	—
Instruction Pipe	$\overline{\text{IPIPE}}$	Output	Low	—
Breakpoint	$\overline{\text{BKPT}}$	Input	Low	—
Freeze	FREEZE	Output	High	—
Quotient Out	QUOT	Output	High	—
Test Mode Enable	$\overline{\text{TSTME}}$	Input	Low	—
Three-State Control	TSC	Input	High	—
Development Serial In, Out, Clock	DSI,DSO,DSCLK	Input/Output	—	—
TPU Channels	TP15–TP0	Input/Output	High	—
TPU Clock In	T2CLK	Input	—	—
SCI Receive Data	RXD	Input	High	—
SCI Transmit Data	TXD	Output	High	—
Peripheral Chip Select	$\overline{\text{PCS3}}$–$\overline{\text{PCS0}}$	Input/Output	Low	—
Slave Select	$\overline{\text{SS}}$	Input/Output	Low	—
QSPI Serial Clock	SCK	Input/Output	—	—
Master-In Slave-Out	MISO	Input/Output	High	—
Master-Out Slave-In	MOSI	Input/Output	High	—
Standby RAM	V_{STBY}	Input	High	—
Synchronizer Power	V_{DDSYN}	Input	—	—
System Power Supply and Return	V_{DD}, V_{SS}	Input	—	—

by a voltage level with respect to a ground of 5 volts. The power-supply voltage for a TTL system, designated V_{CC}, is typically 5.0 volts. The CMOS equivalent voltage is designated V_{DD}.

Any signal line designated by its functional name (usually a mnemonic) is considered to be active or true or indicate a logical {1} when the voltage level is HIGH. Similarly, the line is inactive or false or indicates a {0} when the voltage level is LOW. Any signal, designated as the logical NOT of its function, represents the opposite conditions. In this case, a LOW voltage represents an active or true or {1} state and these signals will be designated with a bar (logical NOT symbol) above them.

Thus, the data lines of the MC68332 are designated D0, D1,..., D7 with a HIGH on any line representing {1} and a LOW representing a {0}. On the other hand, the signal line $\overline{AS}$ (Address Strobe) in a HIGH state indicates that the address strobe is not asserted (not active or not true). When the voltage is LOW on the $\overline{AS}$ line, the address strobe line is asserted (active or true). This use of an active-LOW signal is quite common with TTL logic and provides better immunity to electrical noise under certain conditions. Such a line is often referred to as an "active-low" signal line and is spoken of as "Address Strobe NOT". In print, such a distinction is not necessary since the form $\overline{AS}$ indicates the logical operation of the signal line.

14.5.1 Data Transfer Operations

This subsection describes the read and write operations of the MC68332 CPU that occur on the external bus. A *read* operation requires that data to be read by the CPU from an external device or memory be placed on the bus in response to a read request from the MC68332. During a *write* operation, the processor presents data on the bus to be written in memory or output to an external device. The MCU controls the bus to initiate data transfer operations in either direction, but waits for the selected device to acknowledge the transfer request. Such data transfer operations are termed *asynchronous* because the timing of the memory or peripheral device determines the timing of the transfer rather than the MCU timing.[4] The peripheral devices are typically slower to transfer data than the processor.

Figure 14.19 shows the timing of longword and word read cycles followed by longword and word write bus cycles. A bus cycle consists of as many system clock cycles as necessary to complete an operation such as read a 16-bit operand. Each clock cycle is approximately 59.6ns with a 16.78MHz system clock. The clock cycles are further divided into two states. The normal 16-bit read or write cycle takes three clock cycles and the normal longword transfers require six clock cycles.[5]

Each transfer operation is initiated by a CPU program instruction. The direction of transfer is defined by the R/$\overline{W}$ signal. The read cycles have R/$\overline{W}$ held HIGH. A write cycle is indicated by R/$\overline{W}$ LOW. The primary timing signal is Address Strobe ($\overline{AS}$). When $\overline{AS}$ is true (LOW), the address bus signals A23–A0 and the other control

---

[4] Synchronous operation based on the MPU clock is possible if appropriate external circuitry is added to the system. The *MC68332 User's Manuals* describe synchronous transfers.

[5] A two-cycle external bus transfer is possible for devices with fast access times. This "fast termination" uses a chip select signal as described in Section 14.6. If wait states are inserted in the cycle, more than three clock cycles are required.

signals shown in Figure 14.19 are valid. Address Strobe is asserted one-half clock cycle after the beginning of a read or write bus cycle. The bytes of an operand on each bus cycle are defined in Figure 14.20. For example, on the first cycle of a longword read, bytes designated OP0 and OP1 are transferred. The second cycle transfers OP2 and OP3.

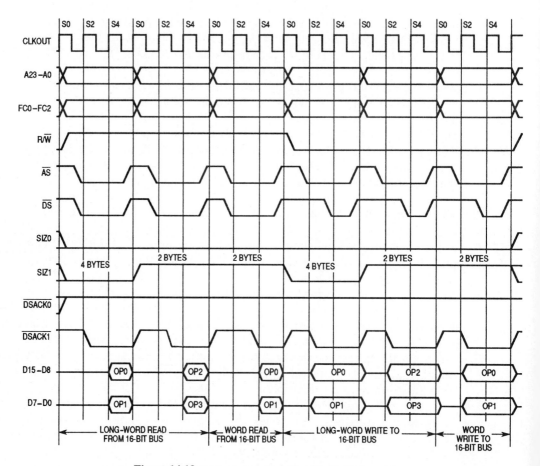

Figure 14.19 Longword and word read and write bus cycles.

Figure 14.20 also defines the control signals in Figure 14.19 that determine both the transfer size and the port size. The *port* size indicates the number of data signal lines connected to the 16-bit MCU data bus. The possible sizes are either 8 or 16 bits. The port size is indicated to the MPU by the Data Transfer and Size Acknowledge signals $\overline{\text{DSACK0}}$ and $\overline{\text{DSACK1}}$. These signals are referred to collectively as the $\overline{\text{DSACK}}$ signals if the individual levels are not important in a discussion. The output signals SIZ0 and SIZ1 indicate the length of the operand to be transferred as 8, 16 or 32 bits. For word transfers, the operand must be addressed at an even memory address. Long words must reside at addresses that are multiples of four. Word and longword operands located at the proper addressing boundaries are termed *aligned* operands. Misaligned words or longword transfers do not follow these addressing conventions. Such misaligned transfers are not allowed for the MC68332 but are allowed on other M68000 family processors such as the MC68020.

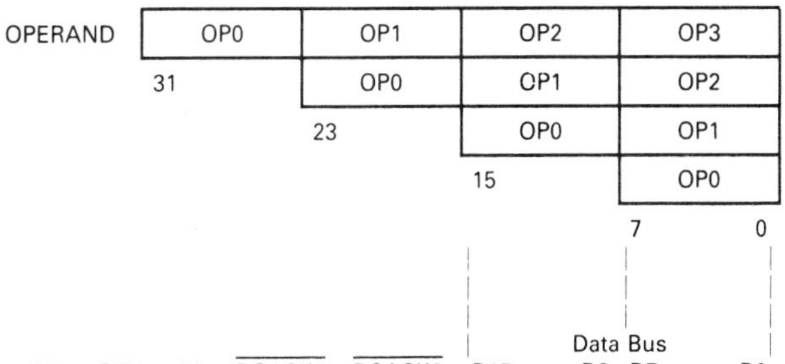

OPERAND	OP0	OP1	OP2	OP3
31		OP0	OP1	OP2
	23		OP0	OP1
		15		OP0
			7	0

							Data Bus	
Case	Transfer Case	SIZ1	SIZ0	A0	$\overline{DSACK1}$	$\overline{DSACK0}$	D15 ... D8	D7 ... D0
a)	Byte to Byte	0	1	X	1	0	OP0	(OP0)
b)	Byte to Word (Even)	0	1	0	0	X	OP0	(OP0)
c)	Byte to Word (Odd)	0	1	1	0	X	(OP0)	OP0
d)	Word to Byte (Aligned)	1	0	0	1	0	OP0	(OP1)
e)	Word to Byte (Misaligned)*	1	0	1	1	0	OP0	(OP0)
f)	Word to Word (Aligned)	1	0	0	0	X	OP0	OP1
g)	Word to Word (Misaligned)*	1	0	1	0	X	(OP0)	OP0
h)	3 Byte to Byte (Aligned)*†	1	1	0	1	0	OP0	(OP1)
i)	3 Byte to Byte (Misaligned)†	1	1	1	1	0	OP0	(OP0)
j)	3 Byte to Word (Aligned)*†	1	1	0	0	X	OP0	OP1
k)	3 Byte to Word (Misaligned)*†	1	1	1	0	X	(OP0)	OP0
l)	Long Word to Byte (Aligned)	0	0	0	1	0	OP0	(OP1)
m)	Long Word to Byte (Misaligned)*	0	0	1	1	0	OP0	(OP0)
n)	Long Word to Word (Aligned)	0	0	0	0	X	OP0	OP1
o)	Long Word to Word (Misaligned)*	0	0	1	0	X	(OP0)	OP0

NOTES:
Operands in parentheses are ignored by the MC68332 during read cycles.
Misaligned transfer cases, identified by an asterisk (*), are not supported by the MC68332.
†3-byte transfer cases only occur as a result of a long word to byte transfer.

Figure 14.20 Transfer size control signals.

Example 14.7

An instruction of the form

```
MOVE.L        MEMORY, D1        ; READ CYCLE
```

causes two 16-bit read cycles. The location specified by the label MEMORY could be a RAM or ROM location or a register of a peripheral chip. Assuming that the memory is a 16-bit port, the first transfer cycle in Figure 14.19 shows the bus signals. Figure 14.20 defines the states of the size and data transfer signals.

The first 16-bit read begins with the following signals from the MPU:

(a) $\overline{AS}$ = LOW;

(b) R/$\overline{W}$ = HIGH (Read);

(c) (SIZ1,SIZ0) = (LOW,LOW) to indicate a 32-bit transfer.

The memory control circuits must present the high-order 16 bits on the data lines after Address Strobe and Data Strobe ($\overline{DS}$) are true (LOW). When the data signals are valid, the memory control circuits must assert the $\overline{DSACK1}$–$\overline{DSACK0}$ signals. For a 16-bit port, the values are

$$(\overline{DSACK1}, \overline{DSACK0}) = (LOW, X)$$

where X indicates a Don't care state. This is the case "n" in Figure 14.20.

The MPU acquires the first 16 bits internally and indicates this by negating $\overline{AS}$ and $\overline{DS}$ (HIGH). The first read cycle is terminated after clock state four (S4) if the memory negates its $\overline{DSACK}$ signals. Then, the second read cycle begins with

$$(SIZ1,SIZ0) = (HIGH,LOW)$$

to indicate that there are 16-bits left to transfer. The external device must place bytes OP2 and OP3 on the data signal lines as shown in Figure 14.19. The control signals are indicated by case "f" in Figure 14.20 but OP0 and OP1 are replaced by the low-order word of the longword operand on the data bus. If the memory causes no delays, the entire 32-bit transfer takes six clock cycles.

If the memory circuits cannot respond to the read request by the end of state two (S2), the MCU generates a "wait" state one clock cycle in length. The MCU will continue to generate wait states until the memory responds. A "watchdog" timer must be present in the system to terminate the bus cycle if the memory cannot respond at all. The watchdog function can be provided by the bus monitor of the SIM as explained in Section 14.3. After the allotted time, the timer causes a bus error to indicate that the memory is defective or is not present at the address issued by the MCU. The bus error response is discussed in Subsection 14.5.5.

Write cycle. A CPU write cycle is similar to the read cycle in both sequence and timing. Figure 14.19 shows both a longword write and a word write cycle to a 16-bit port. The R/$\overline{W}$ signal line is held LOW to indicate a write operation. The processor does not remove valid data from the data signal lines until an external device or memory responds with $\overline{DSACK0}$ and $\overline{DSACK1}$. The signal $\overline{DS}$ when LOW indicates that valid data is on the data bus. This signal is asserted one clock cycle later than $\overline{AS}$ in a write cycle. Three clock cycles is the minimum time required for a normal 16-bit write cycle.

Peripheral port size. The data signal lines of the MC68332 can be used to transfer data between the CPU and an external device even if the external device cannot utilize all 16 bits of the CPU data bus. The port size of the device is defined as the number of bits of data it can transfer at once. MC68332-based systems allow port sizes of 8 or 16 bits. Devices of various sizes must be connected to the data bus as shown in Figure 14.20. A 16-bit port is connected to data signal lines D15–D0.

However, note that 8-bit ports must be connected to the upper portion of the 16-bit data bus. For a CPU read, the external 8-bit device places data on signal lines D15–D8. If the hardware connection is correct, a programmer need not be concerned with the hardware configuration.

The MC68332 allows byte, word, and longword operands to be transferred to or from 8-, or 16-bit ports. The instruction being executed determines the size of the operand, independent of the port size. However, the Data Transfer and Size Acknowledge signal lines are used to specify the port size for each read or write cycle. This capability of the MC68332 to transfer data between ports of different sizes is called *dynamic bus sizing*. It allows a flexible hardware design. Furthermore, the programmer can transfer operands of any size without concern for the details of the interface for data transfers.

As an example, the transfer

> MOVE.L   D1, BYTEREG   ; 32 BITS TO BYTE PORT

would cause four bytes in four write cycles to be transferred to the location BYTEREG if the device at that address has an 8-bit port. The $\overline{\text{DSACK1}}$ and $\overline{\text{DSACK0}}$ signal lines are used by the device to indicate its port size. For an 8-bit port, the values are (HIGH, LOW) as indicated in Figure 14.20.

14.5.2 Function Code Lines and Memory Usage

The signal lines FC0, FC1, and FC2 present a *function code* to external devices or memory indicating the type of activity occurring on the address or data signal lines. Table 14.20 lists the logical level of the function code signal lines of the MC68332 for each type of reference. The states not specified are not defined. The function code indicates the processor mode (supervisor or user) and the type of access (data or program) each time the processor initiates a read or write operation. The CPU space code indicates when an interrupt is being acknowledged or a special cycle is in progress. The decoding of CPU space cycles is not shown in Figure 14.21.

Table 14.20 Function Code References

FC2	FC1	FC0	Cycle type
0	0	0	(Undefined)
0	0	1	User data space
0	1	0	User program space
0	1	1	(Undefined)
1	0	0	(Undefined)
1	0	1	Supervisor data space
1	1	0	Supervisor program space
1	1	1	CPU space

Function codes for memory access. The processor mode is always determined by the setting of the supervisor status bit in the Status Register, (SR)[13]. The distinction between data and program references is determined by the addressing mode and the instruction being executed. Table 14.21 lists the addressing modes which cause the selection of various function code states during normal execution. Chapter 5 defines these addressing modes for CPU32 instructions.

Table 14.21 Addressing Modes and Function Codes

Function code reference	Addressing modes
Data	All indirect modes, unless used with JMP or JSR instructions
	Absolute modes, unless used with JMP or JSR instructions
Program	Relative modes
	Indirect and absolute modes with JMP or JSR instructions

Using the function code lines to select memory areas, the system memory can be segmented into supervisor and user space. These spaces, in turn, can be segmented into program and data areas. A simplified scheme to accomplish this is shown in Figure 14.21. Each distinct function code allows a selected memory area to be accessed using a decoder and selection circuitry. The address, control and data signal lines of the external bus are connected to each memory area. Thus, there are a maximum of 2^{24} bytes in each segment when all 24 address signal lines of the MC68332 are used to address memory. If the system hardware is operating properly, no errors should occur during memory accesses since the outputs on the function code signal lines are defined automatically by the CPU during read and write cycles.

The chip select signals can also be programmed to respond to the type of CPU access indicated by the function code signal lines. Section 14.6 discusses the chip select signals.

The DFC and SFC registers and the MOVES instruction. The Destination Function Code register (DFC) and the Source Function Code register (SFC) were introduced in Section 10.1. In that section, these special registers, accessible only by a supervisor-mode program, were defined as part of the supervisor programming model. Each register is 32-bits, although the upper 29 bits are read as zeros and ignored when written. The MOVEC (Move Control Register) instruction, described in Section 10.2, is used to read the register value or write a new value into the DFC or SFC.

The alternate function code registers (DFC and SFC) contain the address space values placed on FC0-FC2 during the operand read or write of a MOVES (Move Address Space) instruction. Thus, these registers are used by a supervisor-mode program to change the function code values temporarily while the MOVES instruction executes. Typically, the supervisor-mode program causes the appropriate function code

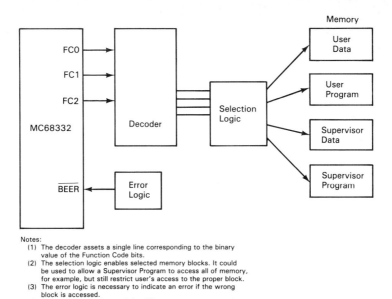

Notes:
 (1) The decoder assets a single line corresponding to the binary
     value of the Function Code bits.
 (2) The selection logic enables selected memory blocks. It could
     be used to allow a Supervisor Program to access all of memory,
     for example, but still restrict user's access to the proper block.
 (3) The error logic is necessary to indicate an error if the wrong
     block is accessed.
 (4) Address, data, and control signal lines to memory are not shown.

Figure 14.21 Memory protection.

for user space to be output if the memory is protected according to supervisor and user modes. In a protected system, the supervisor program can access all of the memory using the MOVES instruction. In systems without memory protection hardware that restricts supervisor access to user address space, such manipulation of the function code values is not necessary. The MOVES can also be used to write to program space if memory is protected by program and data access.

Example 14.8

The subroutine MTVUSER of Figure 14.22 transfers an array of 16-bit values from the supervisor area of memory to user space. Before the subroutine is called, register A0 must contain the starting address of the array in supervisor space. The destination address must be contained in register A1. The length of the array is specified in register D0.

In the loop to transfer values, the MOVEC instruction sets the Destination Function Code (DFC) register to indicate user space in memory when the MOVES instruction executes. Except for the transfers by the MOVES, all other memory references are to supervisor space. Therefore, the subroutine must be executed in the supervisor mode of the CPU. When the data values have been transferred, the saved register values are restored from the system stack and control is returned to the calling program.

CPU space. Normal processor bus cycles reference program areas or data areas in memory as defined by the function code values of Table 14.20. A third category of references is to the *CPU space* of a MC68332-based system. The CPU space is

```
abs.    LC    obj. code    source line
----    ----  ----------   -----------
   1    0000                              TTL      'FIGURE 14.22
   2    7600                              ORG      $7600
   3    0000               *
   4    7600               *  TRANSFER AN ARRAY OF WORDS FROM SUPERVISOR
   5    7600               *  SPACE TO USER DATA SPACE
   6    7600               *
   7    7600               *         INPUTS :  (A0.L) = ADDRESS OF SOURCE ARRAY
   8    7600               *                   (A1.L) = ADDRESS OF DESTINATION
   9    7600               *                            ARRAY
  10    7600               *                   (D0.L) = NUMBER OF WORDS IN ARRAY
  11    7600               *
  12    7600               *         OUTPUT    ARRAY IN USER DATA SPACE
  13    7600               *
  14         0000 0001     USERDAT  EQU      $0001                 ;USER DATA SPACE
  15    7600 48E7 F0C0     MVTUSER  MOVEM.L  A0-A1/D0-D3,-(A7)
  16    7604 7201                   MOVE.L   #USERDAT,D1
  17    7606 4283                   CLR.L    D3                    ;ZERO INDEX REG.
  18    7608 4E7B 1001     LOOP     MOVEC    D1,DFC                ;CHANGE TO USER
  19    760C 3418                   MOVE.W   (A0)+,D2
  20    760E 0E59 2800              MOVES.W  D2,(A1)+              ;TRANSFER
  21    7612 5283                   ADDI.L   #1,D3                 ;INCREMENT INDEX
  22    7614 B083                   CMP.L    D3,D0                 ;IF (D3) .LT. (D0)
  23    7616 62F0         BHI       LOOP                          ;  TRANSFER
  24    7618               *                                      ;ELSE RETURN
  25    7618 4CDF 030F              MOVEM.L  (A7)+,A0-A1/D0-D3
  26    761C 4E75                   RTS
  27    761E
```

Figure 14.22 Program example of MOVES instruction.

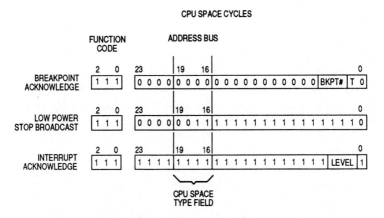

Figure 14.23 CPU Space Addressing.

distinguished by the function code values {111} as shown in Figure 14.23. This function code indicates that a special bus cycle is in progress and that the address bus value does not represent a memory address.

Address bus bits A16–A19 distinguish three types of CPU space activity. A breakpoint acknowledge cycle occurs when the BKPT (Breakpoint) instruction executes. The LPSTOP (Low Power Stop) broadcast cycle is generated by the CPU executing the LPSTOP instruction. An interrupt acknowledgement cycle is another CPU space cycle. The special cycles can be monitored by the interfaces of external devices to determine the appropriate response.

14.5.3 Interrupt Processing

Section 11.7 described programming considerations for interrupt-handling routines. In that section, the interrupt mask of the CPU Status Register (SR[10:8]) and the vector locations for interrupt routines were explained. The MC68332 interrupt circuitry allows seven levels of interrupt priorities, numbered from 1 to 7. All levels but level 7, the highest-priority interrupt, can be masked or disabled using the interrupt mask of the Status Register. The present discussion describes the external signal lines involved in interrupt processing.

An interrupt request can be made by one of the MPU modules or by an external device. The System Integration Module (SIM) receives external interrupts via its seven interrupt request signal lines $\overline{\text{IRQ7}}$–$\overline{\text{IRQ1}}$.

For an interrupt request to be recognized, an incoming interrupt request of level 1 through 6 must be higher than the mask level set in the Status Register. Level 7 is a nonmaskable interrupt level and cannot be disabled.

The CPU responds to an interrupt upon the completion of the current instruction cycle if no high-priority exceptions are pending. If the interrupt is valid, the CPU asserts the CPU space interrupt acknowledgement cycle to indicate that the MC68332 is servicing an interrupt request. The CPU must next determine the starting location of the interrupt service routine for the interrupt level requested. The requesting device can indicate its vector number in one of two ways. In the *vectored* mode, the external device supplies its vector number in response to the CPU interrupt acknowledge cycle. The CPU also allows an *autovectored* mode in which the CPU selects the proper autovectored location in the vector table based on the interrupt level requested. Each mode is discussed here followed by a discussion of the spurious interrupt response of the CPU.

Vectored interrupts. The diagram in Figure 14.24 describes the sequence of operations when an interrupt is accepted by the CPU. Figure 14.25 represents the corresponding timing diagram. The timing sequence begins when the interrupt request is accepted after the current instruction has completed. The CPU access is to CPU space, with address signal lines A19-A16 indicating an interrupt acknowledge cycle. Address signal lines A1-A3 indicate the interrupt level. The size and R/$\overline{\text{W}}$ lines indicate that the CPU is requesting an 8-bit data value, representing the vector number of the interrupting device. This occurs in the first clock cycle of the interrupt acknowledge cycle in Figure 14.25.

A requesting device employing the vectored mode of operation places its vector number on the least significant byte of its data signal lines. Thus, a device with an 8-bit port uses D15–D8, whereas a device with a 16-bit port places its vector number on D0–D7 according to the previous discussion of peripheral port size in Subsection 14.5.1. The vector number should specify one of the 192 user interrupt vectors in the exception vector table (locations $0100 through $03FC) as described in Section 11.7. The vector number from a module of the MC68332 is placed on the data signal lines of

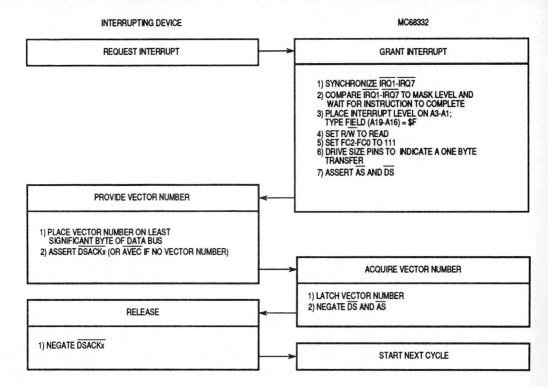

INTERRUPTING DEVICE   MC68332

REQUEST INTERRUPT

GRANT INTERRUPT

1) SYNCHRONIZE $\overline{\text{IRQ1}}$-$\overline{\text{IRQ7}}$
2) COMPARE $\overline{\text{IRQ1}}$-$\overline{\text{IRQ7}}$ TO MASK LEVEL AND WAIT FOR INSTRUCTION TO COMPLETE
3) PLACE INTERRUPT LEVEL ON A3-A1; TYPE FIELD (A19-A16) = $F
4) SET R/W TO READ
5) SET FC2-FC0 TO 111
6) DRIVE SIZE PINS TO INDICATE A ONE BYTE TRANSFER
7) ASSERT $\overline{\text{AS}}$ AND $\overline{\text{DS}}$

PROVIDE VECTOR NUMBER

1) PLACE VECTOR NUMBER ON LEAST SIGNIFICANT BYTE OF DATA BUS
2) ASSERT DSACKx (OR AVEC IF NO VECTOR NUMBER)

ACQUIRE VECTOR NUMBER

1) LATCH VECTOR NUMBER
2) NEGATE $\overline{\text{DS}}$ AND $\overline{\text{AS}}$

RELEASE

1) NEGATE $\overline{\text{DSACKx}}$

START NEXT CYCLE

Figure 14.24 Interrupt acknowledgement cycle.

the Intermodule Bus. An external device places the vector number on the data signal lines of the external bus.

The 192 possible vectors are distributed over the seven priority levels for interrupts. Any subpriorities for each of the seven CPU levels must be determined by circuits external to the CPU. After the CPU receives the vector number, interrupt processing begins and appropriate information is saved on the stack. Then, the interrupt-handling routine begins execution at the address found in the vector table.

Autovectored interrupts. An alternative mode of interrupt operation is *autovector* mode. The autovector requires less complicated circuitry since the requesting device need not supply a vector number. An external device requests autovectoring by asserting the external signal line $\overline{\text{AVEC}}$ LOW during the interrupt acknowledge cycle. The seven autovectored interrupts have vectors at fixed locations in the exception vector table at locations $064 through $07C as previously defined in Section 11.7. The autovector request level (1-7) corresponds to the CPU interrupt priority level. As described in Section 14.6, chip select signals can also provide an autovector request. This chip select option simplifies the external interfacing circuitry.

620   The System Integration Module   Chap. 14

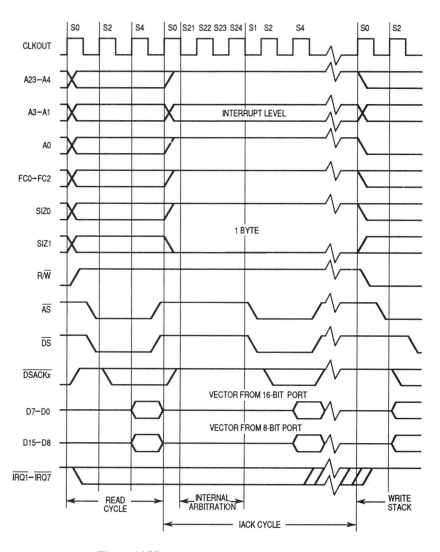

Figure 14.25 Interrupt acknowledgement cycle timing.

Spurious interrupt. During a CPU interrupt acknowledge cycle, a module or an external device must respond with a vector number for a vectored interrupt or $\overline{\text{AVEC}}$ for autovectoring if the cycle is to complete successfully. If no device responds, the spurious interrupt monitor of the System Integration Module asserts the Bus Error signal $\overline{\text{BERR}}$. In response to $\overline{\text{BERR}}$ during an interrupt acknowledgement cycle, the CPU processes a spurious interrupt exception rather than a bus error exception as explained in Section 11.6.

14.5.4 Bus Arbitration, RMC, BUS Error, Halt and Reset

Two special bus cycles discussed here control the operation of the CPU and the external bus in various ways. A *bus arbitration* cycle is used when an external device or another CPU must take control of the external bus. In multiprocessor systems, a Read-Modify-Write Cycle (RMC) is used to assure the validity of a shared flag or semaphore that can be modified by several processors. This subsection discusses these special bus cycles.

When a problem occurs during a bus cycle of the CPU, the bus error request signal line ($\overline{\text{BERR}}$) is used by an external device or the SIM to indicate an unusual condition. If two serious errors occur during certain CPU bus cycles, a *halt* condition causes the CPU to terminate all processing. This condition is called a double bus fault. The reset ($\overline{\text{RESET}}$) signal line and other special bus signals and cycles are also discussed in this subsection.

Bus arbitration. In most single-processor systems, the MC68332 CPU controls the external bus via the SIM as the CPU fetches and executes instructions. The CPU determines the activity on the bus by presenting control signals and addresses on the address signal lines. All other devices on the system bus respond to the CPU control signals to perform I/O transfers and other operations. However, there are many computer systems in which another device must take control of the external bus to perform some operation independent of the CPU that usually controls the bus. In these systems, the CPU that normally controls the system bus must relinquish use of the bus when another device requests its use. This is accomplished electrically when the MC68332 places its external address, data, and control signal lines in the high-impedance state in response to a bus request signal from another device. The technique to determine which device controls the bus during any given bus cycle is called *bus arbitration*.

The most common example of the need for bus arbitration occurs in systems that include devices with Direct Memory Access (DMA) capability. These devices take control of the system bus to perform high-speed I/O transfers between memory and a peripheral device. Multiprocessor systems also need bus arbitration. In such systems, two or more processors share the external bus.

The processor or DMA device that controls the external bus at any given time is termed the *bus master*. When only one MPU and one DMA device share the bus, the bus arbitration signal lines of the MC68332 are sufficient to perform bus arbitration. If several devices that can be bus masters share the bus with the MC68332, special circuitry to perform bus arbitration is required. The circuitry determines the priority of the requests if several requests to use the bus occur simultaneously.

Figure 14.26 shows the sequence of events when an external device with DMA capability requests the use of a system bus being controlled by the MC68332. The device first asserts the Bus Request ($\overline{\text{BR}}$) signal line LOW to request the bus. The CPU is forced to respond with a Bus Grant ($\overline{\text{BG}}$) signal at the beginning of the next bus cycle. In response to $\overline{\text{BG}}$ being LOW, the device asserts the Bus Grant Acknowledge ($\overline{\text{BGACK}}$) signal. As long as the $\overline{\text{BGACK}}$ signal line is held LOW, the requesting device acts as the temporary bus master. When the device completes its operation, the device negates the $\overline{\text{BGACK}}$ signal line and the MC68332 resumes control as bus master.

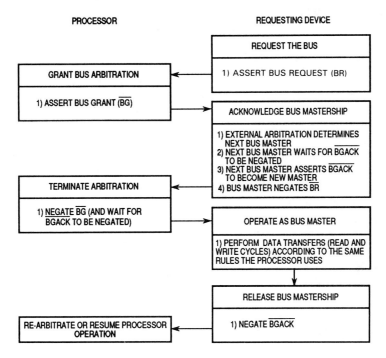

Figure 14.26 Bus arbitration flowchart.

In the diagram represented in Figure 14.26, the interface for the DMA device must contain the circuitry to request the bus and take control of the address, data, and control signal lines. If more that one device can request the bus at the same time, external circuitry must recognize the several requests and determine which device will be the next bus master. For example, the Motorola MC68452 bus arbitration module is an integrated-circuit chip designed to arbitrate among eight devices that can act as bus masters. The reader is referred to the references in the Further Reading section of this chapter for more details about bus arbitration.

Read-Modify-Write cycle. A read-modify-write cycle (RMC) occurs when the CPU32 executes a Test and Set (TAS) instruction. When executed, the instruction causes the MC68332 to assert the Read-Modify-Write ($\overline{\text{RMC}}$) signal line LOW for the entire operation of reading a value in a location, modifying the value if required, and writing the value back to the same address.

When an instruction causing a read-modify-write cycle executes, the CPU that is bus master while executing the instruction will not issue a Bus Grant ($\overline{\text{BG}}$) signal in response to a Bus Request ($\overline{\text{BR}}$) signal. Thus, the CPU executing a TAS instruction will not relinquish the system bus until the instruction has completed.

Bus error.   The CPU begins processing a bus error exception when the Bus Error ($\overline{\text{BERR}}$) signal line is held LOW to indicate that a bus cycle in progress cannot be completed. The bus error signal can be caused by the SIM bus monitor when an external device fails to respond during data transfer operation. During a transfer, if the device cannot assert its Data Transfer and Size Acknowledge ($\overline{\text{DSACK0}}$, $\overline{\text{DSACK1}}$) signal lines in response to a CPU read or write cycle, the bus monitor asserts the $\overline{\text{BERR}}$ signal to cause a bus error exception. A spurious interrupt also causes a Bus Error signal to the CPU but results in a spurious interrupt exception as previously explained.

Processor halt condition and double bus fault.   If an address error or bus error occurs during the exception processing for an address error, bus error, or reset exception, a *double bus fault* is said to have occurred. The CPU recognizes this condition and asserts the Halt ($\overline{\text{HALT}}$) signal line LOW to indicate that it cannot continue processing. Only a reset of the MC68332 can cause the processor to begin executing instructions again. As explained in Section 16.3, a double bus fault will cause entry into the background mode if this mode is enabled.

$\overline{\text{RESET}}$ signal-line.   The Reset ($\overline{\text{RESET}}$) signal line is a bidirectional signal line used during system initialization. When asserted by external circuitry as input to the MC68332, the CPU begins exception processing for the reset exception. As an output signal, $\overline{\text{RESET}}$ is asserted LOW by the CPU when the RESET instruction is executed. This instruction is used to cause external devices to reset or initialize their interface circuitry. The reset exception for the CPU was described in Chapter 10. The RESET instruction was discussed in Section 10.2 and Section 14.4. Chapter 15 describes system design considerations for resets and reset circuitry.

Special bus cycles.   Table 14.22 lists a number of special bus cycles. Chapter 15 describes the Low Power Stop operation. The breakpoint, halt and testing cycles are used during product development and testing as discussed in Chapter 16. The retry operation is requested by an external device to cause the SIM to rerun a bus cycle. Further information for these special bus cycles can be found in the *MC68332 User's Manuals*.

Table 14.22 Special Bus Cycles

Type of Cycle	Meaning
LPSTOP	CPU LPSTOP instruction
Breakpoint	Software or hardware breakpoint
$\overline{\text{HALT}}$ Input	Single step request
Testing	Slave mode and show cycles
Retry	Rerun bus cycle

EXERCISES

14.5.1. The instruction

      MOVE.B   D1, $2001

is executed. Define the value or condition for the address lines, data lines, and other signal lines as the operand is transferred to memory.

14.5.2. Determine the type of memory reference that occurs and the values of the function code lines for each of the following instructions:
(a) MOVE.W   D1, (A1) ; USER MODE
(b) JSR   (A1) ; USER MODE
(c) MOVE.W   D1, DISP(PC) ; SUPERVISOR MODE
(d) CLR.L $2000 ; SUPERVISOR MODE

14.5.3. What vector address in the exception vector table is being requested by a device that supplied vector number 64 in response to an interrupt? Could an interface supply vector numbers between 2 and 47? If so, what problems might arise in the system?

14.5.4. Draw the timing diagram for a longword transfer to an 8-bit port.

14.6 CHIP SELECT SIGNALS AND I/O PORTS

The function of a number of MC68332 signal lines can be assigned during reset or initialization. Those signals with multiple functions are shown in Figure 14.1 connected to the chip select submodule and External Bus Interface (EBI) of the SIM. The selection is between signals used either as bus control signals, chip select signals, or I/O ports. Section 14.5 described the bus control signals.

Subsection 14.6.1 describes the selection between bus control signals, chip selects and output Port C. Subsection 14.6.2 treats the chip select signals and applications. Subsection 14.6.3 describes the registers used to control the I/O ports.

14.6.1 Chip Select Pin Assignments

The exact use of the MC68332 signal lines that can function as chip select signals is controlled by two Chip Select Pin Assignment Registers (CSPAR0-1). Figure 14.27 shows the registers and the two-bit encoding that selects the function of a particular signal line. Table 14.23 summarizes the three possible uses of specific signal lines.[6]

The two-bit fields of CSPAR0 and CSPAR1 have reset values determined by the level on certain external data bus signals. When a reset occurs, the CPU reads the appropriate data values. For example, bits CSPAR0[7,5,3] all assume the logical value of data bus signal DB1. The data signal lines are pulled high internally so that

---

[6] In this section, the data bus signal lines are designated DB0, DB1, . . ., DB15 so that no confusion arises with Port C Discrete Output signals DO0, DO1, . . ., DO6. Elsewhere when no ambiguity is possible, the data bus signal lines are usually designated as D0, D1, . . ., D15.

the default values of DB0–DB7 are HIGH or {1}. According to Figure 14.27, the default HIGH values assign the chip selects $\overline{\text{CSBOOT}}$, $\overline{\text{CS10}}$–$\overline{\text{CS0}}$ as chip selects for 16-bit ports.

If any of the data signals DB0–DB7 are held LOW during reset, certain signal lines are selected to perform their bus control function. These hardware controlled selections would not normally be changed by an initialization program after a reset. However, an initialization program must write {00} to a selection field in CSPAR0 or CSPAR1 to select the discrete output (DO0–6) option shown in Table 14.23.

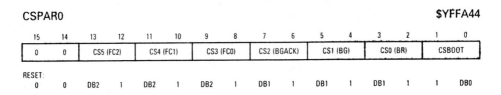

BIT 15–14 — Not Used
These bits always read zero; write has no effect.

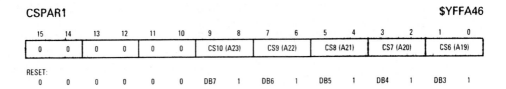

BIT 15–10 — Not Used
These bits always read zero; write has no effect.

Register Bit Encoding

Bits	Description
00	Discrete Output (E Clock on A23)*
01	Default Function
10	Chip Select (8-Bit Port)
11	Chip Select (16-Bit Port)

*Except for $\overline{\text{BR}}$, $\overline{\text{BG}}$, and $\overline{\text{BGACK}}$

Figure 14.27 Chip select pin assignment registers.

Reset configuration. Table 14.24 summarizes the selections immediately after a reset according to the reset level on DB0-DB7. $\overline{\text{CSBOOT}}$ selects either a 16-bit port (DB0 HIGH) or an 8-bit port (DB0 LOW). If DB1 or DB2 is LOW at reset, the

Table 14.23 Pin Assignment Options

Bus Control	Chip Select	Discrete Output Pin
$\overline{BR}$	$\overline{CS0}$	– – –
$\overline{BG}$	$\overline{CS1}$	– – –
$\overline{BGACK}$	$\overline{CS2}$	– – –
FC0	$\overline{CS3}$	DO0
FC1	$\overline{CS4}$	DO1
FC2	$\overline{CS5}$	DO2
A19	$\overline{CS6}$	DO3
A20	$\overline{CS7}$	DO4
A21	$\overline{CS8}$	DO5
A22	$\overline{CS9}$	DO6
A23	$\overline{CS10}$	E-Clock

Notes:
1. The selection of the use of a pin is made in registers CSPAR0 and CSPAR1.
2. Register CSPDR determines DO0-DO6 output levels for Port C discrete outputs.

whole group of signals controlled by the data signal line is assigned to the bus control function. Thus, if DB1 is LOW, $\overline{BR}$, $\overline{BG}$, and $\overline{BGACK}$ are assigned to their bus control functions. Otherwise, the group is assigned to chip selects. DB1 being HIGH at reset assigns chip selects $\overline{CS0}$, $\overline{CS1}$, and $\overline{CS2}$.

In the case of DB3 through DB7, if a signal is LOW, its associated address signal and all less significant address signals lines listed in Table 14.24 function as address lines. However, more significant address lines are assigned as chip selects if the higher-order data bits are left HIGH.

Table 14.24 Pin Assignment During Reset

Data Bus	HIGH	Pulled LOW
DB0	$\overline{CSBOOT}$ (16-bit)	$\overline{CSBOOT}$ (8- bit)
DB1	$\overline{CS0}$	$\overline{BR}$
	$\overline{CS1}$	$\overline{BG}$
	$\overline{CS2}$	$\overline{BGACK}$
DB2	$\overline{CS3}$	FC0
	$\overline{CS4}$	FC1
	$\overline{CS5}$	FC2
DB3	$\overline{CS6}$	A19
DB4	$\overline{CS7} - \overline{CS6}$	A20–A19
DB5	$\overline{CS8} - \overline{CS6}$	A21–A19
DB6	$\overline{CS9} - \overline{CS6}$	A22–A19
DB7	$\overline{CS10} - \overline{CS6}$	A23–A19

Example 14.9

Assume that data signal lines DB7–DB0 have the following levels at reset

$$\{1, 1, 0, 1, 1, 1, 1, 1\}$$

indicating that only DB5 is LOW. Here $\overline{\text{CSBOOT}}$ selects a 16-bit port because DB0 is HIGH. Signals $\overline{\text{CS5}} - \overline{\text{CS0}}$ are selected as chip selects since DB1 and DB2 are HIGH. DB5 being LOW assigns signals A19, A20 and A21 as address lines. Since DB6 and DB7 are HIGH, address lines A22 and A23 are assigned as chip selects $\overline{\text{CS9}}$ and $\overline{\text{CS10}}$, respectively.

14.6.2 Chip Select Options and Applications

Figure 14.28 shows a simplified block diagram of the chip select circuitry. On each external CPU access, the chip select circuitry compares the address and control signal lines to the values programmed for each chip select that is enabled. If a match occurs, the chip select is asserted LOW to select the external chip being addressed by the CPU. For convenience in the present discussion, the type of CPU access is categorized as either a read or write data cycle or an interrupt acknowledgement cycle. The data cycles will be considered first in this subsection. The unique signal $\overline{\text{CSBOOT}}$ will also be discussed separately.

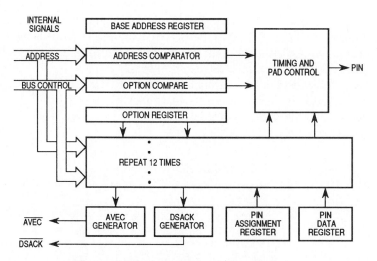

Figure 14.28 Block diagram of chip select logic.

Chip select address selection.   The basic purpose of the chip select logic is to decode the CPU bus signal lines and generate a chip select signal on a match to select a memory block or a specific peripheral chip. For each CPU access to external memory or a peripheral chip, the address bits are chosen for comparison according to the value written into the base address register for the chip select signals.

Figure 14.29 shows the single Chip Select Base Address Register for $\overline{\text{CSBOOT}}$, designated CSBARBT. Each of the 11 chip selects $\overline{\text{CS0}}$–$\overline{\text{CS10}}$ has a corresponding base address register designated CSBAR0, CSBAR1, . . ., CSBAR10, respectively.

The range of addresses decoded by a specific chip select signal is determined by the value in its Chip Select Base Address Register. Each register is divided into a base address field in bits [15:3] and a block size field in bits [2:0]. The only restriction is that the value of the base address should be a multiple of the block size for a unique decoding.

In effect, the chip select logic divides the address space up into blocks. The base address is the starting address for the block enabled by a given chip select. Each address bit that is set to {1} in the base address field is compared to the corresponding CPU address bits before a memory access. Those address bits that correspond to a {0} in the register are not compared. Then, the block size determines the range of addresses that are valid in the address space above the base address. The table accompanying Figure 14.29 shows the possible choices of block sizes from 2KB to 1MByte.

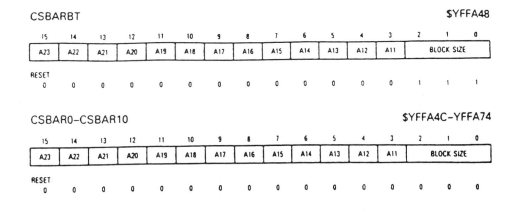

Block Size Encoding

Block Size Field	Block Size	Address Lines Compared
000	2K	A23–A11
001	8K	A23–A13
010	16K	A23–A14
011	64K	A23–A16
100	128K	A23–A17
101	256K	A23–A18
110	512K	A23–A19
111	1M	A23–A20

Figure 14.29 Chip select base address registers.

Example 14.10

To select the upper 64Kbytes of memory using $\overline{CS0}$, the following value would be used

$$CSBAR0[15:0] = \$FF03$$

to choose A23–A16 for comparison as determined by bits [15:3]. The block size selected is 64Kbytes in bits [2:0]. The addresses \$FF0000 through \$FFFFFF would be selected by $\overline{CS0}$ if the access is compared by address alone. Other options can be used to further define the type of access such as read or write that is to cause a match.

Chip select options.   Figure 14.30 shows the Chip Select Option Registers and the possible selections for the various fields. These selections allow a chip select signal to be generated when the type of CPU access and other parameters match the conditions set in the option registers.

After a reset, all of the option registers except CSORBT which controls the $\overline{CSBOOT}$ signal are disabled since the BYTE fields, CSOR0–10[14:13], are {00}. An initialization program must write the proper value into each chip select option register that controls a chip select signal used in the system. The interrupt selections, bits [3:0], are discussed later in this section. For read/write data cycles, the interrupt field bits are set to \$0.

For a match to occur and cause a chip select signal to be asserted (LOW), each field in the chip select option register must be matched by the CPU signal lines during an external access. The address signal lines must also match the value in the base address register for a chip select signal as previously discussed.

The SPACE field in the option registers, bits [5:4], is compared to the Function Codes of the CPU. For example, the choice for data transfer cycles is either user space ({01}), or supervisor space ({10}), or both ({11}). If the SPACE field is {00}, only CPU space cycles are matched. Subsection 14.5.2 explained the function codes and the CPU space cycles.

The Data Transfer and Size Acknowledge signals described in Subsection 14.5.1 can be generated by the external device or by the chip select logic. The value in the DSACK field other than \$E or \$F indicates the number of wait states before the chip select logic generates the acknowledgement. Each wait states begin after the second clock cycle of a read or write bus cycle shown in Figure 14.19 of Section 14.5. The total length in time of a normal bus cycle is three clock cycles plus the number of wait clock cycles. Two special options are also provided for the DSACK field as follows:
(a) DSACK = \$F (external DSACK);
(b) DSACK = \$E (fast termination).
The selection DSACK = \$F indicates that the external device will terminate the bus cycles with DSACK signals. If the DSACK field is \$E, a fast termination after two clock cycles is possible. The reader is referred to the *MC68332 User's Manuals* for more information about the fast termination cycle.

The value in the Strobe (STRB) field chooses whether the chip select is asserted simultaneously with a Data Strobe ({1}) or an Address Strobe ({0}). Figure 14.19 shows that $\overline{DS}$ and $\overline{AS}$ are asserted simultaneously during a read cycle. During a write cycle, $\overline{DS}$ is asserted one clock cycle later than $\overline{AS}$.

The R/$\overline{W}$ field specifies whether the chip select should be asserted on a read cycle ({01}), a write cycle ({10}) or on either type of access ({11}). The reserved (Rsvd) value of {00} should not be used. For a read-only device as an example, the chip select signal could serve to enable the device's output data lines when an address

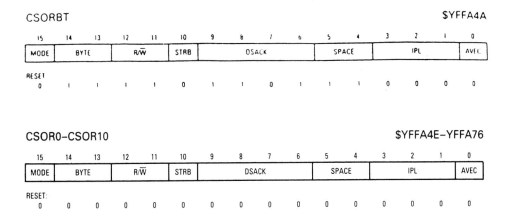

CSORBT $YFFA4A

15	14	13	12	11	10	9	8	7	6	5	4	3	2	1	0
MODE	BYTE		R/W̄		STRB		DSACK				SPACE		IPL		AVEC

RESET
| 0 | 1 | 1 | 1 | 1 | 0 | 1 | 1 | 0 | 1 | 1 | 1 | 0 | 0 | 0 | 0 |

CSOR0–CSOR10 $YFFA4E–YFFA76

15	14	13	12	11	10	9	8	7	6	5	4	3	2	1	0
MODE	BYTE		R/W̄		STRB		DSACK				SPACE		IPL		AVEC

RESET:
| 0 | 0 | 0 | 0 | 0 | 0 | 0 | 0 | 0 | 0 | 0 | 0 | 0 | 0 | 0 | 0 |

Mode	Byte	R/W̄	STRB	DSACK	Space	IPL	AVEC
0 = ASYNC	00 = Off	00 = Rsvd	0 = A̅S̅	0000 = 0 WAIT	00 = CPU SP	000 = All	0 = Off
1 = SYNC	01 = Lower	01 = Read	1 = D̅S̅	0001 = 1 WAIT	01 = User SP	001 = Level 1	1 = On
	10 = Upper	10 = Write		0010 = 2 WAIT	10 = Supv SP	010 = Level 2	
	11 = Both	11 = Both		0011 = 3 WAIT	11 = S/U SP	011 = Level 3	
				0100 = 4 WAIT		100 = Level 4	
				0101 = 5 WAIT		101 = Level 5	
				0110 = 6 WAIT		110 = Level 6	
				0111 = 7 WAIT		111 = Level 7	
				1000 = 8 WAIT			
				1001 = 9 WAIT			
				1010 = 10 WAIT			
				1011 = 11 WAIT			
				1100 = 12 WAIT			
				1101 = 13 WAIT			
				1110 = F term			
				1111 = External			

Figure 14.30 Chip select option registers.

match was detected. If the selection {01} is made in the read/write field, the device
could never be enabled on a write cycle. For a read/write device, the chip select signal
and the external bus R/W̄ signal would be used to enable the device to output data
or read the external data bus. The selection in the read/write field would be {11} for
read/write devices.

The BYTE field must be nonzero to enable the chip select signal. The field is
used only when a 16-bit port is connected to the external data lines. The selections in

Figure 14.30 define the signal lines to be used if a byte is transferred to the 16-bit port.

The MODE field specifies either 16-bit asynchronous mode for transfers ({0}) or synchronous 8-bit type of transfers ({1}). The synchronous mode causes the chip select timing to be synchronous with that of the E-clock used for M6800 family peripheral chips described in Subsection 14.4.5.

Example 14.11

Figure 14.31 shows a simplified diagram of the possible connection of RAM and ROM to the MC68332. The two RAM chips are 32K by 8-bit static RAMs. An example is the Motorola MCM6206 RAM chip. The RAM enabled by $\overline{CS0}$ is connected to the upper byte of the 16-bit data bus. Chip select $\overline{CS1}$ controls the RAM connected to the lower byte of the data bus. The ROM is enabled by the $\overline{CSBOOT}$ signal. Example 14.12 considers ROM control.

The values initialized for the RAM Chip Select Base Address Registers are as follows:
(a) CSBAR0 = $0003;
(b) CSBAR1 = $0003.
From Figure 14.29, these values define a base address of $0000 with a block size of 64KB. The option registers are initialized as follows:
(a) CSOR0 = $5830;
(b) CSOR1 = $3830.
Figure 14.30 shows the register fields.

The options chosen for the RAM chips allows supervisor or user mode program access since the SPACE field is {11}. No wait states are inserted during an access since the DSACK field is $0. The chip select signals are asserted with Address Strobe (STRB = {0}). Both read and write accesses are allowed. The control signal $R/\overline{W}$ defines the type of access to the RAM chips. When a RAM chip is selected on a read cycle, the RAM's output drivers are enabled to allow the CPU to read data. If $R/\overline{W}$ is LOW, the RAM reads data from the bus.

The RAM chip controlled by $\overline{CS0}$ accesses the upper (even) byte since the BYTE field (CSOR1[14:13]) is {10}. The BYTE field CSOR1[14:13] specifies access to the lower byte controlled by signal $\overline{CS1}$. On a word or longword access, both chip selects are enabled and 16-bits are read simultaneously for each bus cycle.

CSBOOT. The CSBARBT and CSORBT registers shown in Figure 14.29 and Figure 14.30 respectively control the bootstrap chip select signal $\overline{CSBOOT}$. This chip select is enabled at reset. The reset value in CSBARBT specifies a 1MB block starting at address $000000. The reset CSORBT value enables $\overline{CSBOOT}$ for read or write access with 13 wait states. The bootstrap device which is usually a ROM is defined as a 16-bit port unless DB0 is held LOW during reset to change the default value of the CSBOOT field in CSPAR0 shown in Figure 14.27.

With the reset values in CSBARBT and CSORBT, every CPU access in the addressing range $000000 to $100000 enables the bootstrap device. This is convenient when the initialization program is held in ROM but may not be appropriate after initialization. The initialization program can either disable $\overline{CSBOOT}$ or reprogram CSBARBT and CSORBT so that the bootstrap ROM appears at some fixed address in memory. At reset, the bootstrap device appears at address $000000 as it must provide the CPU reset vector at this location.

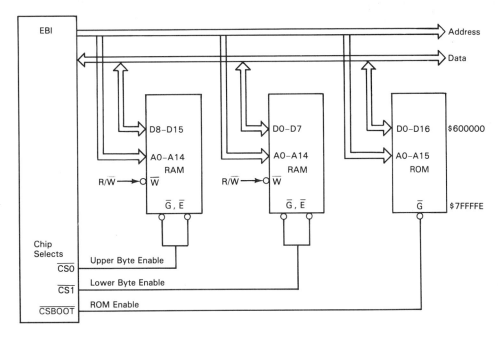

EBI

Address

Data

D8–D15
A0–A14
RAM
R/W — W
G̅, E̅

D0–D7
A0–A14
RAM
R/W — W
G̅, E̅

D0–D16 $600000
A0–A15
ROM
G̅ $7FFFFE

Chip
Selects
C̅S̅0̅   Upper Byte Enable
C̅S̅1̅   Lower Byte Enable
C̅S̅B̅O̅O̅T̅ ROM Enable

Figure 14.31 Chip select control of RAM and ROM.

Example 14.12

Figure 14.31 shows a 128KByte ROM connected to the MC68332. At reset, the ROM should appear at address $000000. The first two longword locations contain the initial supervisor stack pointer (SSP) and the initial Program Counter (PC) of the CPU reset vector. The initialization program in the ROM initializes the System Integration Module, chip selects and internal RAM as previously defined in Section 14.3. The ROM can then be "moved" in the address space of the system to its intended address. This is accomplished by programming CSBARBT and CSORBT with the proper values.

Since the ROM has 16 address signal lines and each addresses a word location, external bus signal lines A16–A1 address all of ROM. After a reset with a 1MB block size, the ROM is addressed beginning with address $00000, $20000, $40000, $60000, etc.

To place the ROM at location $60000 for example, the initialization program specifies the following values:

(a) CSBARBT = $0604;
(b) CSORBT = $68B0.

According to Figure 14.29, the CSBARBT value defines a 128K block of memory selected with address signal lines A18–A17. Thus, the ROM has address $60000 through $7FFFE. Address signals A16–A1 access a particular word location in ROM when the ROM is enabled by C̅S̅B̅O̅O̅T̅. From Figure 14.30, the value in CSORBT defines the ROM as read only (R/W̅ = {01}) requiring 2 wait states (DSACK = $2).

Assuming that the RAM chip selects are initialized as in Example 14.11 and the ROM chip select is initialized as just described, the system in Figure 14.31 contains RAM between addresses $000000 and $00FFFFF and ROM between addresses $60000 and $7FFFF. If a reset occurs, the ROM chip enable C̅S̅B̅O̅O̅T̅ will have its reset value and the RAM chip select will be disabled.

Interrupt acknowledgement.   Each chip select can be programmed to respond to an interrupt acknowledgement cycle with an $\overline{\text{AVEC}}$ signal to the CPU. This eliminates the external circuitry that would be necessary for the interrupting device to respond to the CPU interrupt acknowledgement. For autovector response with chip select, the chip select logic must match on a CPU space cycle at the proper level. The CPU space cycle was discussed in Subsection 14.5.2. As shown in Figure 14.23, each address signal line A23–A4 is {1} during the acknowledgement cycle.

Thus, the Chip Select Base Address Register must be programmed with a base address field of all $FFF8 and a block size of 64K or less to allow the address comparator to check address signals A23–A16. The option register must be initialized with the following values in the fields:

(a) AVEC = {1} (enabled);
(b) IPL   = level 1–7 or any level;
(c) SPACE = {00} (CPU space);
(d) R/$\overline{\text{W}}$ = {01} (Read).

Example 14.13

Assume that an external device pulls interrupt request signal $\overline{\text{IRQ7}}$ LOW to interrupt the MC68332. This request will cause a level 7 autovector interrupt if one of the chip selects is programmed to cause $\overline{\text{AVEC}}$. For example, the values

$$\text{CSBAR8} = \$FFF8 \quad \text{and} \quad \text{CSOR8} = \$680F$$

assign chip select 8.

14.6.3 I/O Ports of the SIM

Figure 14.32 shows the registers that control the SIM I/O ports when the signal lines are not used for bus control or chip selects. Port C is a 7-bit output port when any or all of DO6-DO0 in Figure 14.32(a) are selected in CSPAR0 and CSPAR1 as previously discussed in Subsection 14.6.1. When any pin of Port C is assigned as a discrete output, the value written into register CSPDR appears on the output signal line. The Port C signals replace bus control signals or chip select signals when Port C signals are used for discrete output. At reset, Port C is disabled for discrete output.

Port E signals used for general-purpose I/O replace the bus control signals shown in the Port E Pin Assignment Register (PEPAR) in Figure 14.32(b) when any bit in PEPAR is set to {0}. At reset, the level of data bus signal DB8 determines the use of the Port E signals. If DB8 is HIGH at reset, the signals are used for bus control. If DB8 is LOW at reset, the Port E signals are defined for I/O. When the signals are used for I/O, the direction is determined by the bits in the Port E Data Direction Register (DDRE). A {1} in any bit defines the signal as an output. A {0} in any bit of DDRE configures the corresponding signal as an input. The Port E Data Register (PORTE) is written with the bit value to be output for any Port E signal defined as output. A CPU read of register PORTE returns the value input on the corresponding signal line

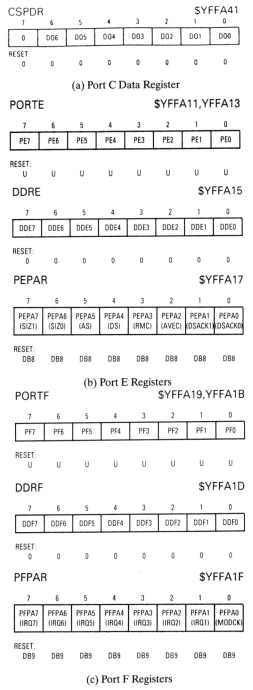

CSPDR $YFFA41

7	6	5	4	3	2	1	0
0	DO6	DO5	DO4	DO3	DO2	DO1	DO0

RESET:
0   0   0   0   0   0   0   0

(a) Port C Data Register

PORTE $YFFA11,YFFA13

7	6	5	4	3	2	1	0
PE7	PE6	PE5	PE4	PE3	PE2	PE1	PE0

RESET:
U   U   U   U   U   U   U   U

DDRE $YFFA15

7	6	5	4	3	2	1	0
DDE7	DDE6	DDE5	DDE4	DDE3	DDE2	DDE1	DDE0

RESET:
0   0   0   0   0   0   0   0

PEPAR $YFFA17

7	6	5	4	3	2	1	0
PEPA7 (SIZ1)	PEPA6 (SIZ0)	PEPA5 (AS)	PEPA4 (DS)	PEPA3 (RMC)	PEPA2 (AVEC)	PEPA1 (DSACK1)	PEPA0 (DSACK0)

RESET:
DB8   DB8   DB8   DB8   DB8   DB8   DB8   DB8

(b) Port E Registers

PORTF $YFFA19,YFFA1B

7	6	5	4	3	2	1	0
PF7	PF6	PF5	PF4	PF3	PF2	PF1	PF0

RESET:
U   U   U   U   U   U   U   U

DDRF $YFFA1D

7	6	5	4	3	2	1	0
DDF7	DDF6	DDF5	DDF4	DDF3	DDF2	DDF1	DDF0

RESET:
0   0   0   0   0   0   0   0

PFPAR $YFFA1F

7	6	5	4	3	2	1	0
PFPA7 (IRQ7)	PFPA6 (IRQ6)	PFPA5 (IRQ5)	PFPA4 (IRQ4)	PFPA3 (IRQ3)	PFPA2 (IRQ2)	PFPA1 (IRQ1)	PFPA0 (MODCK)

RESET:
DB9   DB9   DB9   DB9   DB9   DB9   DB9   DB9

(c) Port F Registers

Figure 14.32 SIM I/O Port registers.

for each signal line defined as input. PORTE is a single register but it can be accessed at two locations shown in Figure 14.32(b).

The Port F registers shown in Figure 14.32(c) function in the same general manner as the Port E registers. However, data signal line DB9 determines the use of Port F signals after a reset.

EXERCISES

14.6.1. Define the reset levels for DB0–DB7 to specify the following signal lines after a reset:
(a) $\overline{\text{CSBOOT}}$ selects a 16-bit port;
(b) $\overline{\text{CS0}}$ and $\overline{\text{CS1}}$ as chip selects;
(c) function code signals are enabled;
(d) A21–A19 as address lines and $\overline{\text{CS9}}$ and $\overline{\text{CS10}}$ as chip selects;
(e) bus control signals for the remaining signals.

14.6.2. Assume that the value

$$\text{CSBAR0} = \$FF03$$

is defined during initialization and $\overline{\text{CS0}}$ is enabled for read/write cycles. What addresses are enabled by this chip select signal?

14.6.3. Define the values in the chip select control registers to enable a 64KB RAM area occupied by two 32KB $\times$ 8 chips beginning at location $80000:
(a) $\overline{\text{CS8}}$, read both bytes with 1 wait state;
(b) $\overline{\text{CS10}}$, write upper byte with 0 wait states.
In each case access can be either by a user or supervisor mode program.

14.6.4. Define the register values to allow chip select 4 to return an autovector response to a level 4 interrupt request.

14.6.5. Hardware design: draw the circuit connections for a system that uses EPROM for the first 32KB of memory and then RAM in 32KB increments for a total of 128KB of memory. Design the circuits in two ways as follows:
(a) using the chip select signals of the MC68332;
(b) using an external address decoder such as the 74LS138.
Use the $\overline{\text{DS}}$ signal and R/$\overline{\text{W}}$ to enable the memory outputs for a read and the write strobe for the RAMs.

FURTHER READING

A brief description of each peripheral chip available from Motorola for the MC68000 family is given in the *Motorola Semiconductor Master Selection Guide*. For more details regarding a particular chip, the *User's Manual* or the data sheet for the chip should be consulted. These documents are available from the manufacturer. For example, the MC68452 Bus Arbitration Module is described in the product information brochure listed here from Motorola. The author's previous textbooks describe I/O programming techniques for several of the peripheral chips of the MC68000 family.

The textbook by Slater considers many aspects of hardware circuit design. The text discusses design with several of chips in the 16-bit M68000 family.

HARMAN, THOMAS L. and BARBARA LAWSON, *The Motorola MC68000 Microprocessor Family*. Englewood Cliffs, N.J.: Prentice Hall, 1985.

HARMAN, THOMAS L., *The Motorola MC68020 and MC68030 Microprocessors*. Englewood Cliffs, N.J.: Prentice Hall, 1989.

MC68452 Bus Arbitration Module, Product Information ADI-696. Motorola, Inc.

SLATER, MICHAEL, *Microprocessor-Based Design*. Mountain View, Calif.: Mayfield Publishing Company, 1987.

15

Product Design
and Real-time Considerations

This chapter presents a number of topics that must be considered during the design of an MC68332-based product. The product design criteria discussed in this chapter partially specify the hardware configuration, software, and the timing selections necessary to meet the requirements of an application. Section 15.1 outlines the general specifications that are required to define the operation of an MC68332-based product. The discussion follows from the general aspects of product design introduced in Section 1.3.

Section 15.2 describes specific specifications for a product and the operation of the MC68332 itself. Section 15.3 summarizes many of the timing considerations involved in the specification of a product's performance. The specifications described in this chapter are typically used in the detailed hardware and software design for the product. Chapter 16 continues the discussion of product design and development. In particular, Chapter 16 covers product development and testing for a prototype product.

15.1 PRODUCT SPECIFICATIONS

During product design, the designer defines all the important specifications that allow the product to meet the requirements of an application. A number of specific aspects of product design were introduced in Section 2.3 as they apply to MC68332-based products. Table 15.1 lists selected specifications that affect the hardware and software design of a product. The specifications in Table 15.1 were chosen because they lead directly to specific design decisions. These decisions in turn determine the software and hardware configuration during initialization and operation of the product. Other considerations such as cost, safety, reliability, maintainability, etc. are not considered in this textbook. References in the Further Reading section of this chapter describe such aspects of product design and specification in general terms.

Table 15.1 Product Analysis and Specification

Specification	Criteria	Selection
Product configuration	Function, performance, processing and protection required	Number and type of peripheral units; memory size and layout
Product timing considerations	Bus transfer rate, number of interrupts per second, processing rate	Speed of operation of the MCU, memory and peripheral devices
Interrupt arbitration and priority	Frequency and criticality of interrupts	Priority for modules and external interrupts
Start-up, reset, bus error, LPSTOP and shutdown operation	Initial operation, error response and system protection required	Hardware and software sequence in special modes of operation; timing and power requirements
Environmental considerations	Temperature range and electrical noise	Packaging and power requirements

Product analysis and specification.   The product configuration listed in Table 15.1 is typically represented by a block diagram for the hardware and a memory map showing the addresses for software and registers of peripheral units. Requirements for input, display and control determine the number and type of peripheral units and chips used to construct the product. For the MC68332, the required peripheral units determine the use of the external bus and chip select signals. These signals have been described previously in Chapter 14. Memory size is determined by the length of the programs and the size of data areas.

Timing.   The overall product timing requirement can be estimated for an application if the timing is defined precisely in terms of data rates, number of interrupts per second and the execution speed of various programs. Depending on the application, timing estimates may be fairly easy to make or practically impossible to determine. In any case, some estimate must be made to determine the required I/O transfer rate, the instruction processing rate and the interrupt response time.[1] These values, in turn, define the minimum number of operations per second required for the external bus, the on-chip modules, the CPU and the memory modules. An exact specification of the memory storage requirements and product timing may be difficult,

---

[1] Benchmark programs are often used for this purpose. References in the Further Reading section of this chapter discuss the benchmarking approach to help a designer estimate product performance.

but an estimate can be made, perhaps based on the designer's experience with similar products.

In many applications, the necessary response time of the product and the program algorithms are determined by the electronic or mechanical devices controlled by the product. For example, a program for motor control must respond to inputs, execute the control algorithm, and generate control signals quickly enough to control the physical motion of the motor. In an MC68332-based product, the motor control function could constrain the timing requirements for the CPU and memory as well as one of the modules such as the Time Processor Unit (TPU).

Interrupts. A product that must respond to external interrupts immediately is frequently called a *real-time* or interrupt-driven product. Such products used in control applications generally have a relatively large number of I/O channels and must respond rapidly to multiple interrupt requests. The *vectored priority interrupt* structure of the MC68332 allows a product designer great flexibility in defining the interrupt configuration of the product. The frequency of an interrupt, its criticality for successful product operation and the length of the interrupt handling routine represent the factors that must be considered to assign priority to one interrupt source over another.

Special modes of operation. Various special modes of operation must be considered during product design. The sequence of hardware and software operations during start-up and shutdown of a product require careful attention, particularly when the product serves to control equipment that could be hazardous to life or property if improperly controlled. For example, the response to an unexpected reset must be defined in detail. A reset can be caused by one of the watchdog monitors of the System Integration Module (SIM) when a timeout occurs due to a software or hardware error. A bus error could be another type of unexpected event that is encountered during operation. The bus error typically occurs when a peripheral device does not respond properly during normal operation of a product and external circuitry or the SIM recognizes the error.

Certain products use the Low-Power Stop mode of the MCU to conserve power when the product is idle or after a main power failure if battery backup power is available. A correct design would define the sequence to enter and leave the Low-Power Stop mode and specify the power required if this power conserving mode is used.

Environment. The physical and electrical environment of the product may constrain the design specifications. Temperature and voltage limits for the MC68332 and other chips in the product must be observed for reliable operation. The operating temperature range for the MC68332 version designated MC68332CFC is $-40°C$ to $+85°C$. The chip has a greater operating range than many semiconductor devices because the MC68332 is intended to operate in environments such as automobiles where the temperature variations are not easily controlled.

The power supply and clock oscillator may require careful design to minimize electrical noise in the system. Good product design and construction techniques are necessary at the operating frequencies of modern microcontrollers.

EXERCISES

15.1.1. List the types of programs and data structures to be included in an estimate of the required memory for a product.

15.1.2. Consider a four channel A/D converter module connected to the external bus of the MC68332. If each channel is sampled at the rate of 40,000, 16-bit samples per second for 1024 samples per channel, what is the system specification for the following:
(a) data transfer to memory in megabytes per second;
(b) the buffer size required in bytes;
(c) the total sampling time to sample all the channels and fill the buffer area.

15.2 MC68332 CHARACTERISTICS FOR PRODUCT DESIGN

Figure 15.1 shows a simplified diagram of the hardware configuration for a typical product using the MC68332. The diagram illustrates other components that can be connected to the MC68332 chip to form a complete product.

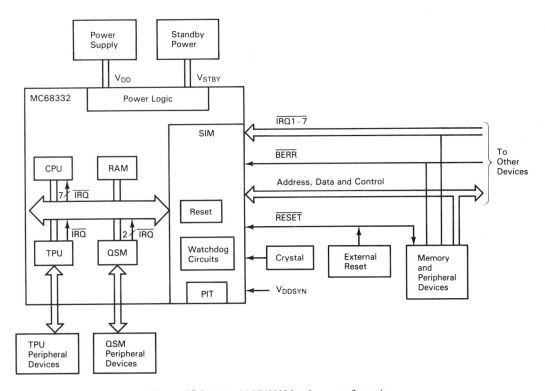

Figure 15.1 Typical MC68332 hardware configuration.

This section presents various topics that must be considered in the design of a product using the MC68332 as the MCU. The major items include the system clock reference source, interrupts and priority, system protection, and power requirements. Each of these topics is discussed in the subsections to follow.

Either a crystal-controlled oscillator or an external clock signal can supply the frequency reference for the system clock. A separate power supply can supply the voltage for the clock circuits to provide stability and noise immunity. Subsection 15.2.1 describes the requirements for the oscillator and the clock power supply.

Subsection 15.2.2 describes interrupt arbitration and priorities. There are seven external interrupt signals with separate levels of CPU interrupt priority. The Queued Serial Module (QSM) can interrupt the CPU on two priority levels. The Time Processor Unit (TPU) has one CPU interrupt request level. When two interrupt requests occur at the same level, the modules arbitrate for priority as described in Subsection 15.2.2.

A reset of the MC68332 MCU can be caused by one of the watchdog timers of the SIM or by the $\overline{\text{RESET}}$ signal line. Subsection 15.2.3 describes the hardware and software aspects of a reset.

Subsection 15.2.4 explains the power requirements of the MC68332. That subsection also considers the design and use of a standby power source. The reader is reminded that different versions of the MC68332 may have different maximum frequencies of operation and power consumption. During the design, the manufacturer's specifications for the specific version employed should be consulted.

15.2.1 System Clock Source

The system clock waveform for the MC68332 can be generated by the on-chip clock synthesizer or by an external clock signal.[2] Figure 15.2 shows a simplified diagram of the clock synthesizer of the MC68332 System Integration Module (SIM). The frequency source for the clock synthesizer can be an external crystal-controlled oscillator or an external clock source. If the input signal MODCK is HIGH during reset, the internal clock synthesizer generates the system clock signal at a frequency multiple of the crystal-controlled oscillator frequency as previously explained in Chapter 14.

The operating frequency of the MC68332 is from 0Hz (DC) to 16.78MHz. As long as power is applied, the internal registers of the MC68332 retain their values even at 0Hz. An external clock source can operate up to 16.78MHz.

The system clock frequency generated by the phase-locked loop and voltage controlled oscillator (VCO) of the clock synthesizer is thus

$$f_{(\text{system})} = K \times f_{(\text{crystal})}$$

as previously described in Section 14.3. The value K is determined by the value in the clock Synthesizer Control Register (SYNCR) of the SIM. The minimum synthesizer

---

[2] The selection between clock sources has been described previously in Section 14.2. If the input signal MODCK is LOW during reset, an external clock source appearing at the EXTAL pin furnishes the system clock signal.

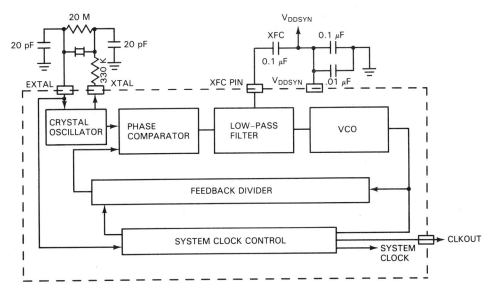

Figure 15.2 Clock synthesizer of the MC68332.

frequency is 4 times the reference oscillator frequency. For example, a 32.768kHz crystal reference yields an allowable frequency range for $f_{(system)}$ of

$$131\text{kHz} \leq f_{(system)} \leq 16.78\text{MHz}.$$

The allowed oscillator frequency is in the range

$$25\text{kHz} \leq f_{(crystal)} \leq 50\text{kHz}.$$

yielding a minimum system clock frequency of 4 times the oscillator frequency to a maximum of 16.78MHz.

The design of crystal oscillator circuits is covered in Exercise 15.2.2 and in references listed in the Further Reading section of this chapter. Data sheets from Motorola and the crystal manufacturer should be consulted to determine recommended values for the components in the crystal oscillator circuit.

A separate power pin shown in Figure 15.1, (V_{DDSYN}), can be used to supply power to the clock circuit. This separate power supply provides increased immunity from electrical noise for the clock circuits. The separate supply could also power the clock circuits when the rest of the product is powered down.

15.2.2 Interrupt Priority and Arbitration

The MC68332 CPU allows seven priority levels for interrupts as discussed previously in Section 11.7. CPU interrupts at level 1 through level 6 are enabled or disabled by the interrupt mask bits in the Status Register of the CPU. The Queued Serial Module (QSM), the System Integration Module (SIM) and the Time Processor Unit (TPU)

Table 15.2 Interrupt Sources and Enabling Conditions

Source	Enabled by (Register)
SIM:	SIM arbitration level nonzero (SMCR)
External	SIM arbitration level nonzero
PIT	Selection of nonzero CPU level (PICR)
QSM:	QSM arbitration level nonzero (QMCR)
SCI	Selection of nonzero CPU level (QILR)
	and enable specific interrupts (SCCR1)
QSPI	Selection of nonzero CPU level (QILR)
	and enable specific interrupts (SPCR2, SPCR3)
TPU:	TPU arbitration level nonzero (TMCR)
	and selection of nonzero CPU level (TICR)
Channel X	Enable specific channel (TCIER)
	and select channel priority (TCPR0-1)

Notes:

1. External interrupts and the Periodic Interrupt Timer (PIT) have the SIM arbitration level. The periodic time period must be defined before the PIT can interrupt.
2. Channel X is any one of the 15 channels of the TPU.

can request an interrupt at any one of the CPU levels. In addition, each MCU module that can interrupt has an interrupt arbitration level. This level must be written as a nonzero value during initialization for the module to interrupt the CPU as indicated in Table 15.2.

Table 15.2 summarizes the interrupt sources for the MC68332 and defines the method to enable the interrupt from a specific source. The registers involved are also listed. For more detailed information, the reader is referred to the chapters in this textbook that describe the modules. A product designer must first define the arbitration level which determines the priority of the modules in requesting interrupts. Then, the CPU interrupt level for each source of interrupt must be defined. Table 15.3 summarizes the interrupt level, vectors and registers involved to select a CPU interrupt level and vector number in the CPU vector table.

The System Integration Module (SIM) receives all external interrupt requests. If the SIM arbitration level is nonzero, external interrupts will be accepted. For a vectored interrupt, the vector number must be supplied by the requesting device during the interrupt acknowledgement cycle as described in Section 14.5. The CPU level requested is determined by the hardware design. An autovector request requires no vector number from the external device.

The Periodic Interrupt Timer (PIT) is enabled when the SIM arbitration level is nonzero and the CPU level and vector number are selected in the appropriate registers of the SIM as defined in Table 15.3. The PIT begins generating interrupt requests at the periodic rate after the periodic time period has been selected in the Periodic Interrupt Timing Register (PITR) as described in Section 14.3.

The Serial Communications Interface (SCI) and the Queued Serial Peripheral Interface (QSPI) of the QSM can have separate CPU interrupts levels. After the QSM arbitration level and the CPU levels and vectors for the submodules are specified, the

Table 15.3 Interrupt Levels and Vectors

Module	Level and Register[1]	Vector Number
SIM:		
External	(1) CPU level 1-7	Vector supplied by peripheral device
	(2) CPU level 1-7, autovector	Vector supplied by CPU
PIT	CPU level 1-7, in PICR[10:8]	PICR[7:0] holds the vector number
QSM:		
SCI	CPU level 1-7 in QILR[10:8]	QIVR[7:0] holds the vector number; the two QSM vectors are contiguous[2]
QSPI	CPU level 1-7 in QILR[13:11]	
TPU:	CPU level 1-7 in TICR[10:8]	TICR[7:4] holds the base vector number; the 16 TPU vectors are contiguous[3]

Notes:
1. A specification of level 0 disables interrupts for an interrupt source.
2. If both the QSPI and SCI have the same CPU level of interrupt, the QSPI has priority. Specific interrupt sources for the SCI and QSPI must be enabled in control registers of the QSM.
3. The TPU interrupts for each channel must be enabled in the TPU Channel Interrupt Enable Register (TCIER).

SCI or QSPI can request an interrupt if the specific interrupt sources are enabled. Chapter 12 describes each interrupt source of the QSM.

Each of the sixteen channels of the TPU can request an interrupt. An initialization program must specify the TPU arbitration level, CPU level and vectors in the appropriate TPU registers. To allow interrupts from a specific TPU channel, the interrupt must be enabled in the TPU Channel Interrupt Enable Register (TCIER) and the channel priority must be defined as nonzero. The lowest numbered channel's interrupt request is recognized first if two channels interrupt simultaneously. The channel priority field in the TPU Channel Priority Register (TCPR0 or TCPR1) does not determine interrupt priority for a channel. This value defines the priority as LOW, MIDDLE, or HIGH when the channel is being serviced by the TPU microcode. The reader is referred to Chapter 13 for more details.

Selection of the priority of interrupts is an important part of the product design. Section 15.3 discusses the subject of interrupts and interrupt latency in more detail.

Interrupt arbitration between modules. The interrupt arbitration level for each module, including the SIM itself, is set in the module's configuration register during initialization and has one of the values $0, $1, ..., $F. Arbitration level $0 disables the module's interrupts. The arbitration level $F represents the highest priority. If two modules simultaneously request the same CPU interrupt level, the module with the highest arbitration level will have priority. Thus, no two modules can have the same arbitration level. External interrupts have the arbitration priority of the SIM.

15.2.3 Reset and System Protection

The reset circuitry of the MC68332 starts (or restarts) the MCU from a known state when a reset occurs. Section 14.2 described the reset state of the MC68332 in detail. This present subsection considers the causes of a reset and the system protection features afforded by various reset sources. Table 15.4 summarizes the type and possible causes of resets for the MC68332 used in a typical application. In some products, the external resets may not be necessary at all. A powerup reset occurs automatically after power is turned on. The watchdog circuits can be enabled or disabled during program initialization of the MCU.

Table 15.4 Resets and Typical Causes

Type of Reset	Typical Cause
External:	Manual reset or
	low-voltage circuit
Powerup:	V_{DD} reaches specified minimum value
Watchdog circuits:	
Software watchdog	Improper software sequence
Halt monitor	CPU halt (catastrophic failure)
Loss of Clock	Loss of frequency reference

Notes:
1. The external sources use the $\overline{\text{RESET}}$ signal line.
2. The software watchdog timer and halt monitor can be disabled.
3. The Loss of Clock reset can be disabled.

External reset. An external reset occurs when the MCU recognizes that the signal line $\overline{\text{RESET}}$ is held LOW. When the external circuit causes the signal line to go HIGH, the internal reset control logic asserts the bidirectional $\overline{\text{RESET}}$ signal line LOW as an output for 512 clock cycles to allow external devices to reset. Then, reset processing occurs as previously described in Section 10.3.

Any external circuit capable of pulling the $\overline{\text{RESET}}$ signal LOW and subsequently releasing it to a HIGH state can serve as the reset source. The purpose and type of circuitry depend entirely on the application.

Example 15.1

Figure 15.3 shows a typical reset circuit that allows either manual reset or low-voltage reset. The push button switch with debouncing circuitry is used for manual resets. A manual reset is useful in a development system or a prototype product to reset the MCU after an error is encountered. The manual reset circuit may not be needed in the final product.

The Motorola MC34064P in Figure 15.3 is an under-voltage sensing circuit designed as a reset source for a microcontroller. When the supply voltage V_{DD} drops below a specified minimum (typically 4.6 volts), the reset output pulls the MCU $\overline{\text{RESET}}$ signal line LOW. This prevents the CPU from executing instructions if the supply voltage

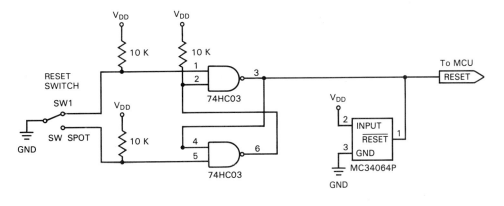

Figure 15.3 External reset circuit.

is below the required minimum. If the supply voltage returns to its specified value, the under-voltage circuit allows $\overline{\text{RESET}}$ to become HIGH and reset processing begins.

Powerup reset.   The internal powerup reset circuitry holds the MCU in the reset state until the supply voltage reaches its operating voltage. This prevents unpredictable operation of the processor when power is first applied to operate a product. However, if precise control of the operating voltage and time duration of the reset state is required for other components in the product, external powerup and under voltage circuits should be added.

Watchdog resets.   As described previously in Section 14.3, various protection options can be selected during initialization in the SIM Protection Control Register (SYPCR). The software watchdog timer is enabled after a reset but can be disabled. The halt monitor is disabled after a reset and must be enabled by the initialization program if a reset is to occur upon detection of a CPU halt. The clock synthesizer of the SIM contains a loss-of-clock detection circuit. The circuit detects the loss of an external frequency reference signal for the system clock. The operation after a loss of clock is determined by the program selections in the Synthesizer Control Register (SYNCR). One option causes a reset if a loss of clock reference is detected.

Software considerations after reset.   In normal circumstances if a product is operating properly, a reset should only occur when power is applied to a product to begin its operation. This reset causes an initialization program to execute and initialize the system. Unless an error or unusual condition occurs during normal operation, the protection circuits of the MC68332 will not cause another reset. If an unexpected reset occurs, software or external circuits must take appropriate action if the MCU is restarted by a reset caused by an error or failure. The source of the reset can be determined by reading the Reset Status Register of the SIM.

The possible actions to be taken after a watchdog reset occurs during normal operation include one or more of the following:

(a) restart and attempt to continue operation;

(b) alarm;

(c) shutdown.

In many products, an alarm is given to a human operator after an unexpected reset occurs in conjunction with either a restart or shutdown sequence. In a control system, an attempted restart sequence must take into account the state of the entire system when the reset occurred. Thus, data that define the state must be stored as the product operates. For applications that are not critical, the product state could be restored to some reasonable condition that allows the control function to continue.

15.2.4 Power Requirements and the LPSTOP Instruction

Microcontrollers such as the MC68332 are designed to use the minimum power possible as they operate. One reason is to limit power dissipation of the chip to prevent unacceptable temperatures inside the chip and subsequent failure. Another reason is to allow a product designer to utilize the smallest power supply for a given application. This subsection defines the power consumption of the MC68332 in normal operation and in the low-power stop mode. Battery backup circuits are also discussed.

Power consumption. The MC68332 is fabricated using high density Complementary Metal-Oxide Semiconductor (CMOS) technology. The electrical power consumption of the MCU depends primarily on the supply voltage V_{DD} and the frequency of operation. The power is consumed in switching, i.e. charging and discharging capacitances internal to the chip as well as external load capacitances driven by output signal lines. As the frequency of operation is reduced to 0Hz, the power consumption is determined by the very small dc leakage current of the chip. The instruction LPSTOP discussed later takes advantage of this to reduce power consumption way below the normal operating power needed by the chip.

Example 15.2

If the supply voltage is V_{DD} and the current is I_{DD}, the power consumed is

$$P_D = V_{DD} \times I_{DD} \text{ watts.}$$

The MC68332 supply voltage can range from -0.3 volts to $+7.0$ volts. At 16.78MHz, the input current is specified as 125mA maximum. The expected power dissipation with V_{DD} at 5.0 volts is thus

$$P_D = 5.0 \text{ volts} \times 125\text{mA}$$

or 625 milliwatts.

For one version of the MC68332, the maximum power is specified as 690mW. Thus, the 625mW estimate based on input voltage and current is reasonable and within approximately 10% of the manufacturer's specification. The reader should consult the data sheet for a specific MCU version to determine the exact maximum power consumption.

LPSTOP.   In many products, particularly portable battery-operated units, minimizing average power consumption is an important design goal. The power consuming components in the product include the MCU, external memory and other devices such as displays. These power consuming components of a product collectively may draw hundreds of milliamperes of current from the power supply during normal operation. It would be convenient to reduce the power consumption dramatically at times when the product is idle. An instrument is idle, for example, when the CPU is not processing instructions but simply waiting for operator input to direct the operation of the instrument. Some products may automatically be placed in the low-power consumption mode if an operator input does not occur within a specified time period. As soon as the input is received, perhaps via a keyboard, the product must continue normal operation immediately.

The MC68332 CPU instruction set includes a Low-Power Stop (LPSTOP) instruction. When executed, LPSTOP causes the CPU to stop fetching and executing instructions. The system clock signal is also stopped in the low-power stop mode. The instruction format is

> LPSTOP   #<data>   ; LOW POWER MODE

where <data> is a 16-bit constant that is loaded into the CPU Status Register. Bits [10:8] contain the CPU interrupt mask as previously described in Section 10.2.

The LPSTOP instruction is a privileged instruction and must be executed by a supervisor-mode program. The low-power stop mode is exited when a trace, interrupt or reset exception occurs. Chapter 11 describes these exceptions in detail. A trace exception will occur if the trace option is enabled when LPSTOP executes. The trace option is selected in the CPU Status Register (SR[15:14]) for debugging. An external reset via the $\overline{\text{RESET}}$ signal-line always initiates reset processing. In a typical application, an external interrupt would cause the MCU to exit the low-power stop mode and begin processing.

If an interrupt request is asserted with a higher CPU priority than the current priority level set in SR by the operand <data> in the LPSTOP instruction, the interrupt request is processed. Otherwise, the interrupt request is ignored. The interrupt request that removes the MCU from the low-power stop mode can be generated externally or by the Periodic Interrupt Timer of the SIM.

Table 15.5 defines the effect of LPSTOP on the MCU modules and submodules. After LPSTOP, the CPU is in the stopped condition as described in Section 10.1. This condition should not be confused with the halted state which can only be exited by a reset. The watchdog monitors of the System Integration Module (SIM) are stopped but the SIM will respond to an interrupt request or a reset. The Periodic Interrupt Timer (PIT) is not disabled by LPSTOP. Thus, the PIT can bring the MCU out of the low-power stop mode when it interrupts. The PIT clock source is the external clock or crystal-controlled oscillator that provides the frequency reference for the SIM clock submodule so the PIT timing period is not changed by the LPSTOP instruction.

The Voltage Controlled Oscillator (VCO) of the clock synthesizer will be turned off by LPSTOP if the STSIM bit of the SIM clock Synthesizer Register (SYNCR [1]) is {0}. If STSIM is {1}, the VCO will continue operation. Turning off the VCO

Table 15.5 Effects of LPSTOP

Module	Effect
CPU:	Instruction fetching and execution stopped
SIM:	System clock stopped
Software watchdog timer	Stopped
Bus monitor	Stopped
Halt monitor	Stopped
Spurious interrupt monitor	Stopped
Interrupt and reset detection	Enabled
Periodic Interrupt Timer	Operating if enabled
System clock submodule	VCO controlled by bit SYNCR[1]
External clock (CLKOUT)	Controlled by bit SYNCR[0]
RAM: (on-chip)	Controlled by bit RAMMCR[15]
QSM:	Controlled by bit QMCR[15]
TPU:	Controlled by bit TMCR[15]

saves additional power but causes a delay after the low-power mode is exited until the phased-locked loop in the clock submodule stabilizes. The delay time could be several milliseconds.

After LPSTOP, the output clock signal (CLKOUT) will be driven from an internal SIM clock if the Stop Mode External Clock (STEXT) bit, SYNCR[0], is {1}. If STEXT is {0}, the CLKOUT signal is held LOW to conserve power while the MCU is in the low-power stop mode.

Stopping the modules. To assure an orderly transition from normal operation to the low-power stop mode, the other MC68332 modules should be stopped before the LPSTOP instruction is executed. The on-chip RAM is placed in the stop mode by writing {1} to the STOP bit in the RAM Module Configuration Register (RAMMCR[15]). In this mode, the RAM retains its contents, but cannot be read or written by the CPU.

The Queued Serial Module (QSM) is stopped by writing {1} to the QSM Configuration Register STOP bit (QMCR[15]). However, the program initiating the low-power stop mode should disable the SCI receiver and transmitter before stopping the QSM. Also, the program should stop the QSPI by asserting the HALT bit in QSPI Control Register 3 (SPCR3). The QSM can be stopped after the Halt Acknowledge bit is set to {1} by the QSPI in the QSPI Status Register (SPSR[5]).

When the STOP bit in the TPU Module Configuration Register (TMCR[15]) is set to {1}, the TPU stops its internal clocks that control the TPU timers. The timers retain their previous values during the low-power stopped mode.

The CPU program that initiates the low-power stop mode for the MCU must stop each module in an orderly manner before the LPSTOP instruction is executed. Conversely, the RAM, QSM and TPU must be taken out of the stop mode before the MCU can resume normal operation. The register values for the CPU and the other modules as well as the on-chip RAM contents will be retained during the low-power stop mode. Thus, initialization of the modules is not necessary except to enable any functions such as the SCI receiver and transmitter that were disabled during low-power operation.

Example 15.3

According to the manufacturer's specifications, the MC68332 requires a maximum of $500\mu A$ during the low-power stop mode with the clock synthesizer VCO off. With a 5 volt supply, the power consumption is 2500 microwatts. This is a factor of 276 less than the 690mW power consumption during normal operation.

When the LPSTOP instruction is executed, the CPU causes an LPSTOP "broadcast" cycle that is presented on the external bus. The function code and address signal lines indicate an LPSTOP broadcast cycle as discussed in Section 14.5. The interrupt mask bits of the CPU Status Register are presented on the data bus so that external devices can determine the CPU interrupt levels that are enabled during the low-power stop mode.

Battery backup. When a product is battery powered, the battery is connected between the V_{DD} pin and ground. An analysis of the power consumption of the product should determine the size and type of battery that is appropriate. The power available from a battery is determined by its *ampere-hour* (Ah) capacity. For example, a 10Ah battery can supply 1 ampere for 10 hours, or 100 milliamperes for 100 hours.[3] If the battery supply to the product is turned off, all the data in MCU registers and volatile memory are lost. This information is also lost if a product is powered by an ac supply that is turned off or suffers a power outage.

In certain applications, it is desirable to retain some information even when the product is turned off or the power to the product is interrupted. One solution is to store critical data during normal operation in a non-volatile memory such as an Electrical Erasable Programmable Read Only Memory (EEPROM). The information stored will be available to the CPU when power is returned to the product. Another approach is to provide *battery backup* for all or a selected portion of the volatile RAM in the product.[4]

The MC68332 on-chip RAM is normally powered by the voltage V_{DD}. However, the V_{STBY} pin of the MCU shown in Figure 15.1 allows another supply to provide power to the RAM in the *standby mode* of the MCU. The standby voltage can be as low as 3.0 volts. The RAM standby current is a maximum of $50\mu A$. Circuitry within the RAM module automatically switches between V_{DD} and V_{STBY}, whichever is higher, with no loss of data. Thus, no external circuitry is necessary to switch between power sources in a product if the on-chip RAM provides enough storage capacity for critical information.

---

[3] A designer should consult the battery manufacturer's literature before attempting to design the power supply. Many factors determine the actual capacity of a battery when used in a product.

[4] Complete battery backup for the product can be provided in case of interruption of the main ac supply voltage. This requires a switchover circuit that allows V_{DD} to be supplied by the ac powered supply during normal operation and then switchover to the battery supply when ac power is lost.

EXERCISES

15.2.1. The MC68332 system clock can be derived from the frequency synthesizer on the chip or from an external clock signal. The recommended frequency source for the frequency synthesizer is a crystal-controlled oscillator circuit. By reference to other textbooks and literature if necessary, discuss the advantages and disadvantages of using a crystal-controlled oscillator source versus a clock generator circuit for the frequency reference.

15.2.2. Designing a crystal oscillator circuit for an MCU is not a trivial task. The resonant circuit consists of the crystal itself, the MCU impedance at the crystal connection pins, and the external circuit components (capacitors and resistors) added to cause the crystal circuit to start oscillating and continue oscillating at the proper frequency. One MCU *User's manual* states: "Exact values for the external (circuit) components are a function of wafer processing parameters, package capacitance and inductance, socket capacitance, operating voltage, crystal technology, and frequency."
By reference to literature from the MCU manufacturer or a crystal manufacturer, show a typical circuit for a 32.768kHz crystal oscillator. For example, Seiko Instruments (Torrance, California) and Statek (Orange, California) manufacture crystals suitable for microcontroller oscillator circuits.

15.2.3. Consider an MC68332-based controller that is controlling the temperature and heating-cycle time for an oven. Suppose an unexpected reset due to a watchdog circuit occurs and it is desirable to attempt to restart the control system after such a reset. Design the software and hardware that would be involved in restarting the system. Also, define the data that should be stored during normal operation to allow a successful restart.

15.2.4. Assume that the power dissipation of a CMOS device is given as

$$P_D = K \times V_{DD}^2 \times f_{(system)}$$

where $f_{(system)}$ is the system clock frequency. This equation ignores a slight leakage current component. Calculate the following:
(a) show that the power dissipation P_D associated with capacitor charging and discharging is of the form shown;
(b) if the power dissipation of a device is 690mW with a clock frequency of 16.78MHz and a supply voltage of 5.0 volts, what is the power dissipation at 1MHz? What is the power dissipation if V_{DD} is 3.0 volts and $f_{(system)}$ is 1MHz?

15.2.5. Discuss the advantages of operating an MCU at the lowest possible clock frequency to satisfy the requirements of an application. Consider such items as reliability, size and cost of the product, and battery operation. (*Hint:* The failure rate of semiconductor devices generally increases rapidly with an increase in operating temperature.)

15.2.6. Describe the differences between the low-power stop mode and the standby mode of the MC68332.

15.2.7. Suppose an MC68332-based product must sample input values every T seconds and process them. Assume that the CPU instructions for processing require N system clock cycles. After the inputs are sampled and processed, the MCU can be put in the low-power stop mode to minimize the average power consumption during each interval T. Let $P_{(stop)}$ be the power consumption in the low-power stop mode. P_{op} is the power consumption during normal operation defined as

$$P_{op} = K \times V_{DD}^2 \times f_{(system)}$$

where $f_{(system)}$ is the system clock frequency. Answer the following questions:
(a) determine the time, T_{op}, the MCU must operate in the normal mode to meet the product timing requirements as a function of the system clock frequency;
(b) write an equation for the average power consumed in each period T if the MCU is put in the low-power stop mode after CPU processing is complete;
(c) if the clock frequency $f_{(system)}$ is fixed, determine the average power consumption if

$$P_{op} = 690\text{mW},$$
$$P_{(stop)} = 2.5\text{mW and}$$
$$T_{op} = 1/4T;$$

(d) if the clock frequency can be chosen to minimize the energy consumption over the interval T, show that the optimum value is

$$f_{(system)} = N/T.$$

Thus, the low-power stop mode is not needed in this case.

15.2.8. Suppose the MCU is to be put in the low-power stop mode until a periodic interrupt occurs. Write the routine to enter the low-power stop mode and the routine to exit the mode when the interrupt is received.

15.3 REAL-TIME PROGRAMMING CONSIDERATIONS

This section covers a number of issues that effect the timing specification for a product. Subsection 15.3.1 describes the MCU system clock waveform and presents the factors that influence instruction execution time. Subsection 15.3.2 summarizes the clock and timer specifications that must be defined during initialization of the MCU. The techniques to include a time-of-day clock in a product are also presented. Subsection 15.3.3 discusses interrupts, interrupt latency and other factors that effect product design.

15.3.1 MC68332 Clock Waveform and Instruction Timing

The MC68332 CPU timing is controlled by the system clock. This clock is a circuit that generates a periodic sequence of pulses to synchronize all changes in the processor's signal lines. The length of time of every CPU operation is determined by the number of clock pulses required for the operation. If the number of pulses per second (called the clock rate) is increased, the speed of operation of the processor is increased. Similarly, if the rate is decreased, the CPU operates more slowly. During normal operation of a product, the MCU modules and external devices such as memory use the system clock for timing. The reader is referred to Section 14.5 for a complete discussion of timing for memory accesses.

System clock waveform. Figure 15.4 shows the clock signal for a typical clock. Table 15.6 lists the frequency of operation in megahertz (MHz) and other timing specifications for the clock signal. The frequency of operation is sometimes called the *speed of operation* for the processor.[5] The MC68332 version designated MC68332CFC operates normally between 131kHz and 16.78MHz with a 32.768kHz (2^{15}Hz) oscillator as the reference source for the system clock. Although the MCU registers will retain data even at 0Hz, the operating frequency range for normal operation is determined by the clock synthesizer on the chip as discussed previously in Section 14.3. The cycle time is the reciprocal of the frequency and represents the *period* of one clock pulse. The period will be designated as t_{CYC} in this chapter. The minimum cycle time for the 16.78MHz version of the MC68332 is 59.6 nanoseconds (ns). At the minimum frequency of 131kHz, the cycle time becomes 7.6μs.

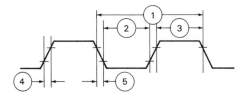

Note: Table 15.6 defines the timing parameters

Figure 15.4 Typical clock waveform.

Instruction timing. The time required by an instruction, T_{INST}, can be calculated in terms of the cycle time of the clock t_{CYC} as

$$T_{INST} = \text{number of clock cycles} \times t_{CYC}$$

in seconds. For each instruction, the number of clock cycles required is published in the *MC68332 User's Manuals*. However, due to the complexity of the MC68332 CPU,

---

[5] The frequency of operation in hertz is considered the reciprocal of the cycle time. More precisely, it refers to the frequency of the fundamental sinusoidal wave in a Fourier series analysis of the clock waveform.

654   Product Design and Real-time Considerations   Chap. 15

Table 15.6 Clock Timing Specifications

Number	Characteristic	Symbol	Min	Max	Unit
—	Frequency of operation	$f_{(system)}$	0.131	16.78	MHz
1	Clock period	t_{CYC}	59.6	7.6×10^3	ns
2, 3	Clock pulse width	t_{CW}	28	—	ns
4, 5	Clock rise and fall time	t_{CRF}	—	5	ns

Note:
The number in the left-most column refers to the number on the clock waveform in Figure 15.4. The clock reference source is a 32.768kHz oscillator.

adding up the instruction times based on the published number of clock cycles per instruction will rarely be accurate when one attempts to determine the execution time of a series of instructions in a program.

Section 4.1 described the pipeline and prefetch capability of the CPU. For many instruction sequences, the overall processing time is less than the sum of the individual execution times of the instructions because of the overlap in execution due to the pipeline. Without overlap, the basic time for instruction execution is determined by the sum of the number of clock cycles required for the following:

(a) instruction fetch;
(b) effective address calculation;
(c) operand read or write.

The total execution time is reduced by the number of cycles that can be over-lapped in an instruction stream. Other factors that modify the instruction execution timing include the cycle time of memory and the length of the operands involved. The minimum memory bus cycle (read or write time) is two system clock cycles for a 16-bit operand. Two clock cycle reads or writes can be achieved by using the on-chip RAM of the MCU or by the fast termination cycle to external memory. The fast termination cycle was described previously in Section 14.5. The minimum read or write time to external memory without fast termination is three clock cycles. If wait states are required by slower memory, the wait cycles must be added to the time of each external access. If longword operands are involved, two bus cycles per transfer are required.

As an example, the instruction

ADD.W   D1, D2

requires one fetch cycle for the instruction but no extra time to compute the operand addresses and calculate the sum. In a typical product, the instruction requires three system clock cycles to fetch the instruction. With instruction prefetch and overlap, the actual effective execution time might be 0 cycles. Effective instruction cycle times can vary from 0 cycles to a maximum of 518 cycles for the RESET instruction. The reader is referred to the *CPU32 Reference Manual* for a more complete discussion of instruction timing.

15.3.2 MC68332 Clocks and Timers

Specification of the clock rates and timer intervals is an important aspect of product design. For a MC68332-based product, a number of timing parameters must be specified during initialization of the product. Table 15.7 summarizes the selections and the registers that are used to define the timing of the MCU, periodic interrupts, watchdog circuits and the QSM and TPU. The table also lists the parameters affected by the clocks or timers. The system clock frequency, the periodic interrupt interval, the software watchdog timeout period and the bus monitor timeout period are determined by settings in the registers of the System Integration Module. Chapter 14 of this textbook describes the specific SIM registers and settings.

The two submodules of the Queued Serial Module (QSM) must be initialized to provide the proper baud rate for serial transfers. The Queued Serial Peripheral Interface (QSPI) allows selection of the baud rate as well as the precise timing characteristics for transfers between the QSPI and an external device. The baud rate for the Serial Communications Interface (SCI) must be specified for asynchronous serial transfers. Chapter 12 is devoted to the QSM and its submodules.

The time interval for the Time Processor Unit (TPU) timers must also be defined during initialization of the MC68332. The time interval represents the resolution of a TPU channel for input and output transitions. Chapter 13 describes the TPU and the timing selections in detail.

Table 15.7 Clock and Timer Selections

Clock or Timer	Register	Parameter defined
System Clock	SYNCR	Instruction execution and memory access time
Periodic Interrupt Timer	PITR	Periodic interrupt period
Software Watchdog Timer	SYPCR	Software timeout period
Bus monitor	SYPCR	Hardware timeout period
QSPI baud rate	SPCR0	Baud rate for synchronous transfer
QSPI delay before SCK	SPCR1	Delay for device setup using QSPI queue[1]
QSPI delay after transfer	SPCR1	Delay between transfers using QSPI queue[1]
SCI baud rate	SCCR0	Baud rate for asynchronous transfer
TPU timers	TMCR	TCR1 and TCR2 time resolution[2]

Notes:
1. The QSPI delays are also controlled by the command byte of each queue entry.
2. TPU timer TCR2 can be clocked by an external signal.

Real-time clock. The clocks and timers of the MC68332 provide precise time intervals for clocking software and hardware events during the operation of a product. For example, the Periodic Interrupt Timer (PIT) may be programmed to interrupt the CPU at precise intervals of time. If the periodic interrupts are used to schedule events such as periodic task execution, the periodic interrupt is often defined as a *real-time clock*, although the designation interval timer might be more descriptive. However, no information is available about the actual time of day at which a periodic interrupt occurred unless the system contains a time-of-day clock.

Time-of-Day clock.   A module that keeps the actual time of day for the system is called herein a *time-of-day* clock.[6] The clock module records the time of day in hours, minutes, seconds, etc. For example, the time-of-day clock allows the product to begin control actions based on a preset time of day. Environmental control systems and energy management systems often use the time of day as the basis for their control actions. In products with a time-of-day clock, the precision and reliability of the clock is critical to proper operation of the product.

The time-of-day clock can be implemented in software or hardware. In either case, the time must be updated periodically. For example, to obtain a 0.01 second resolution, the update rate must be at least 100 times a second.

A straightforward software solution could utilize the Periodic Interrupt Timer to interrupt at a time interval that is less than the desired resolution of the clock. The interrupt routine would update counters that hold the time increments such as seconds, minutes and hours. When 60 seconds elapse, the minute counter is incremented and the second count begins again. In turn, the minute counter would be used to increment the hour counter until 24 hours have elapsed. Software could be included to record the day, month and year if a calendar is required. The program must provide for operator input to initialize the current time and date. Unless battery backup is provided for the product, the time of day will be lost if the system power fails.

One important design consideration is the effect of the periodic interrupt on the interrupt response time of the product. If the clock interrupt is given high priority, lower priority interrupts will be delayed by the time it takes the clock update routine to execute. When the clock interrupt is given low priority to minimize the delay (latency) for other interrupt sources, the designer must be sure that the execution time of all of the higher priority interrupt routines does not exceed the clock interrupt period. If this occurs, the result is a loss of the correct time. Subsection 15.3.3 considers interrupt latency in more detail.

Adding a clock chip to the product is another approach to implementing a time-of-day clock. A typical chip is Motorola's MC146818A "Real-Time Clock Plus RAM" chip. The chip has a time-of-day clock and a 100-year calendar. Such a chip relieves the software from the timekeeping function. The date and time are stored in the MC146818A RAM in binary or BCD. The chip can be programmed to interrupt periodically. A separate crystal-controlled oscillator and battery backup circuit can be connected to the chip to allow it to operate independently of the MCU clock and power supply. A small lithium battery, for example, can power the clock chip for several years. The MC146818A appears to the MCU as a 64 byte RAM in the memory-mapped address space of the MCU. A Motorola *Applications Note*, AN894A, listed in the Further Reading section of this chapter describes the MC146818 in detail. The MC146818A is an enhanced version of the MC146818 that is described in Motorola data sheets for the device.

---

[6] The term *real-time* clock is sometimes used to describe a periodic timer in a system that also computes the time of day. In this section, the terms real-time clock and time-of-day clock are not used interchangeably in order to distinguish the two functions.

15.3.3 Interrupts and Latency

In this textbook, the designation *real-time* system refers to a system or product that must respond and generate some timely action in response to external events. Typically, a real-time system performs data acquisition and control under strict timing constraints. One of the primary parameters defining a real-time system is the time-related performance. The *performance* with respect to time is determined by the system response time to external events and other factors such as its data transfer rate. In this subsection, one key parameter that affects the system response time is taken to be the *interrupt latency*. The interrupt latency time is the time lag necessary to respond to an interrupt and pass control to the interrupt handling routine. The total interrupt response time for the product to recognize and service an interrupt is another parameter that determines system performance.[7]

Interrupt latency. The minimum interrupt *latency time* for the CPU32 is calculated by adding the times of the following contributions:
(a) completion of current instruction;
(b) acknowledgement and vector acquisition;
(c) stacking of format word, PC and SR;
(d) read of vector address from CPU vector table;
(e) fetch of first instruction and prefetch of next instruction.
This list of contributions to the latency follows from the discussion of interrupt handling in Section 11.7. Items (b) through (e) represent the interrupt *processing* by the CPU as the term is defined in Section 11.7. The entire interrupt cycle including interrupt processing, executing the interrupt routine, and restoring control to the interrupted program is usually called interrupt *handling* or interrupt *servicing*. Figure 15.5 shows the complete interrupt cycle and defines the various parameters of interest.

For a single interrupt source, the total execution time of the interrupt routine is the sum of the time for interrupt acknowledgement, the time for context switching, the time of execution of the instructions in the interrupt routine, and the time to restore the original context and return to the interrupted program. The *context switching* time can be defined as the time for interrupt processing by the CPU. In MC68332-based products, the interrupt processing includes the stacking of the format word, Program Counter and Status Register values and the time to fetch the interrupt vector address and pass control to the interrupt handling routine. The first instructions of the interrupt routine typically save register values and other data that must be restored after the interrupt routine completes.[8] After executing the instructions that perform the

---

[7] A number of other factors determine the overall response time of the system or product. The operating speed of the CPU and access time to external memory are two items that affect the response. Also, other characteristics than response time may be important in determining the system performance. Reliability, fault tolerance and similar factors are critical specifications for certain real-time systems. Such factors are not considered in this textbook.

[8] The *context switching* time is sometimes defined to include both the time for interrupt processing and the time taken to save registers and other data. In M68000 family processors, the saving of the contents of general-purpose registers is not automatic. Thus, instructions such as Move Multiple Registers (MOVEM) are required in the interrupt routine to save (and restore) general-purpose register contents.

658   Product Design and Real-time Considerations   Chap. 15

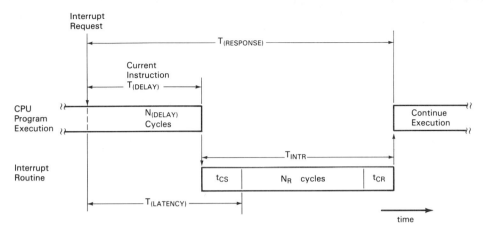

Figure 15.5 Interrupt timing parameters.

required action to service the interrupt, general-purpose register contents must be restored by program instructions. The context switch back to the interrupted program is accomplished with the Return From Exception (RTE) instruction described in detail in Section 10.2.

The parameters in Figure 15.5 are defined as follows:

$$
\begin{aligned}
T_{(\text{DELAY})} &: \text{time between interrupt request and processing} \\
t_{\text{CS}} &: \text{time for interrupt processing (context switch)} \\
T_{(\text{LATENCY})} &: \text{time between interrupt request and} \\
&: \text{execution of the interrupt routine} \\
T_{\text{INTR}} &: \text{time for interrupt handling and context switching} \\
t_{\text{CR}} &: \text{time to restore context} \\
T_{(\text{RESPONSE})} &: \text{total time for interrupt servicing.}
\end{aligned}
$$

The time for interrupt servicing, T_{INTR}, includes both the context switch time (t_{CS}) and the time t_{CR} to return control to the CPU program.

Neglecting instruction overlap and special instructions such as RESET and RTE, the CPU instructions take from 2 to 64 clock cycles (DIVS.L) to execute. To this time must be added the number of cycles to compute the effective addresses of any operands. Depending on the number of clock cycles to read and write memory, the interrupt processing may be delayed from 2 clock cycles to more than 70 cycles plus any wait states (1 clock cycle each) added because of slow memory. The additional delay before the interrupt routine executes depends on the memory access time as the CPU performs stacking, fetching of the vector address from the CPU vector table and fetching of the first instruction. Section 14.5 defines the number of system clock cycles for various types of CPU memory accesses. CPU accesses to the on-chip RAM or external accesses using fast termination take two clock cycles. Most external memories require at least three clock cycles for a CPU read or write cycle if no wait states are necessary.

Example 15.4

Figure 15.5 shows the complete interrupt cycle. Assume that the present instruction takes $N_{(DELAY)}$ clock cycles to complete before interrupt processing begins. The latency time until the first instruction of the interrupt routine begins execution is

$$T_{(LATENCY)} = T_{(DELAY)} + t_{CS} \qquad (15.1).$$

For a system clock frequency of $f_{(system)}$ Hertz, the clock cycle time is

$$t_{CYC} = 1/f_{(system)} \text{ seconds.}$$

Since $T_{(DELAY)} = N \times t_{CYC}$ for the current instruction to complete, the latency time from Equation 15.1 is thus

$$T_{(LATENCY)} = N_{(DELAY)} \times t_{CYC} + t_{CS} \qquad (15.2).$$

For the MC68332, timing estimates for the interrupt latency can be obtained from the instruction timings given in the *MC68332 User's Manuals*. For this example, 70 cycles will be assumed as the worst case delay for the current instruction to complete. The interrupt processing time t_{CS} includes 4 memory read cycles for interrupt acknowledgement (1 cycle), reading the vector address from the CPU vector table (2 cycles) and fetching the first instruction from memory. This requires 39 clock cycles if each memory access requires 3 clock cycles. Substituting these example number of cycles in Equation 15.2 for a clock period of 59.6ns (16.78 MHz) yields the result

$$T_{(LATENCY)} = (70 + 39) \times 59.6\text{ns}$$

or 6.5μs.

According to Motorola's data for instruction timing, the RTE instruction takes 30 clock cycles to restore control to the interrupted program. Thus, the time the CPU program is interrupted would be

$$T_{INTR} = (39 + N_R + 30) \times t_{CYC} \text{ seconds}$$

where N_R is the number of clock cycles required by the interrupt routine. The calculation of the number of cycles required by the RTE instruction is based on the four read cycles required to restore the 4 words of information placed on the stack during context switching and two additional read cycles to fetch the first two words from the interrupted program. It is assumed here that each read cycle requires 3 clock cycles. The other clock cycles taken by the RTE are for internal processing.

Interrupt priorities. When multiple interrupt sources are present, interrupt priority must be established. The purpose is to assure that the most important interrupts are serviced within a predefined time regardless of other events including lower priority interrupt requests. In many products, interrupt servicing for one interrupt may be interrupted by another, higher priority interrupt. To determine whether the product's timing specifications can be met, the product designer must estimate the latency and the execution time of the interrupt handler for each interrupt source.

Several factors can delay the execution of an interrupt routine. For example, the interrupt at the requested CPU level could be disabled when the interrupt request occurs. Lower level interrupt requests are disabled when a higher priority interrupt routine is executing. The lower priority interrupt must wait to be recognized until interrupts are enabled at its priority level. An interrupt request can also be delayed if the interrupt levels are deliberately disabled by a CPU program. The CPU program may disable all interrupts (except level 7 which is not maskable in M68000 family processors) to protect a critical region of code as discussed later. Another possibility is that a higher priority exception such as a bus error is being processed when the interrupt request occurs. Section 11.8 explains exception priorities. An interrupt is simply one of the many possible exceptions recognized by the MC68332 CPU.

Example 15.5

Figure 15.6 summarizes the timing involved for an interrupt request and execution of the interrupt service routine. The worst-case total response time as seen by an external device is defined as $T_{(RESPONSE)}$. This response time is the important parameter to use in determining the overall timing for the system or product. The response time is the sum of the delay time before interrupt processing begins and the total time required for the interrupt handling routine. This worst case estimate of response time is used because the action that actually services the interrupt request may occur anywhere in the interrupt routine, including during the execution of the last instruction.

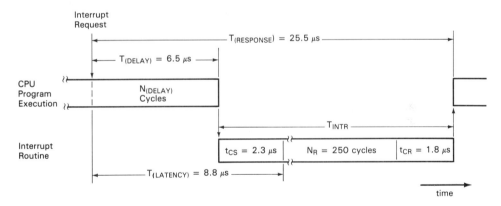

Figure 15.6 Interrupt timing.

In Figure 15.6, the latency time $T_{(LATENCY)}$ discussed in Example 15.4 includes the delay time $T_{(DELAY)}$ until the interrupt is recognized and the context switching time t_{CS}. If no higher priority interrupt routines are executing, the delay is the time required for the current instruction to complete execution as described in Example 15.4.

When interrupts are disabled at the requested level by a higher priority interrupt routine or for any other reason, $T_{(DELAY)}$ represents the time between the interrupt request and the time that interrupts are reenabled at the requested level. The total time from the interrupt request until control is returned to the interrupted program is

$$T_{(RESPONSE)} = T_{(DELAY)} + T_{INTR}. \tag{15.3}$$

This time includes the time to restore the context, t_{CR}.

As an example, assume the following values have been determined:

$$T_{(DELAY)} = 6.5\mu s$$
$$t_{CS} = 2.3\mu s$$
$$t_{CR} = 1.8\mu s.$$

If the interrupt routine executes 50 instructions that average 5 clock cycles each, the total number of cycles is $N_R = 250$. The clock frequency, $f_{(system)}$ is assumed to be 16.78MHz. The latency until the interrupt routine begins execution is

$$T_{(LATENCY)} = T_{(DELAY)} \ (6.5\mu s) + t_{CS} \ (2.3\mu s)$$

or $8.8\mu s$ in this example.

The response time is therefore

$$T_{(RESPONSE)} = T_{(DELAY)} + t_{CS} + N_R \times t_{CYC} + t_{CR}$$
$$= 6.5\mu s + 2.3\mu s + 250 \times 59.5ns + 1.8\mu s$$
$$= 25.5\mu s$$

using where t_{CYC} is the period of the 16.78MHz system clock.

Considering the overall system timing, a CPU program would be interrupted for T_{INTR} seconds or $19.\mu s$ in this example. The action to be taken by the interrupt routine to respond to the interrupt request would not occur until after the interrupt routine begins executing at least $t_{(LATENCY)}$ seconds after the request. A worse case estimate of the response time would be $t_{(LATENCY)}$ plus the total time of the interrupt routine or $25.5\mu s$ in our example.

Interrupt frequency and density. During normal operation of a product, some interrupt sources may interrupt randomly in time and other sources may request interrupts periodically. For example, an interrupt request from the TPU in response to an input capture might occur at a random time. On the other hand, the SCI may periodically interrupt when data are being transferred as discussed in Subsection 12.3.2. For interrupt-controlled input at 9600 Baud, for example, the CPU must respond to each SCI interrupt and read a character from the SCI receiver register approximately every millisecond.

The product designer must assure that every interrupt that can occur within a given time interval is serviced and that no interrupt service is delayed beyond the maximum allowable response time for the interrupt. Thus, during the specification of interrupt timing, the following conditions must be considered:
(a) the worst case interrupt density;
(b) the worst case delay time for any interrupt.

The *interrupt density* determines the percentage of CPU time taken up by interrupt service routines. The value is the ratio of the sum of the interrupt routine times divided by an arbitrary time period associated with the product's operation. For example, if a control system performs data acquisition, processing and control actions periodically, the cycle time, $T_{(CYCLE)}$, for the complete sequence could be taken as the periodic reference time for the product. If the ith interrupt routine requires $T_{\text{INTR}i}$ seconds to switch context and complete execution, the interrupt density is calculated as

$$\frac{T_{\text{INTR}1} + T_{\text{INTR}2} + \cdots + T_{\text{INTR}n}}{T_{(\text{CYCLE})}} < 1.0. \qquad (15.4)$$

When the inequality of Equation 15.4 is satisfied, a product designer can be sure that the interrupt routines do not consume all of the CPU execution time during $T_{(\text{CYCLE})}$. The time left in the cycle for normal CPU processing is obviously $T_{(\text{CYCLE})}$ minus the sum of the times taken by the interrupt routines.

Example 15.6

Another calculation based on Equation 15.4 will determine whether the periodic interrupt with the minimum time period can be serviced. Assume that a low priority interrupt at level 3 interrupts every 500 μs. The time $T_{(\text{CYCLE})}$ in Equation 15.4 becomes 500μs. Further assume that level 4 and level 5 interrupts occur during the time $T_{(\text{CYCLE})}$ and that the total times taken by the routines are as follows:

$$T_{\text{INTR}3} = 20\mu s$$
$$T_{\text{INTR}4} = 20\mu s$$
$$T_{\text{INTR}5} = 20\mu s.$$

According to Equation 15.4, the interrupt density is

$$\frac{20\mu s + 20\mu s + 20\mu s}{500\mu s} = .12$$

or 12%. Thus, 86% of the time between the fastest interrupt requests is available for CPU execution of other programs.

Once assured that all interrupts can be serviced and the CPU can execute its main program, the designer must calculate the maximum delay time associated with any interrupt. If an interrupt at level i, $(1 \leq i \leq 7)$, must be serviced within a time T_{Pi}, the maximum delay time for this interrupt must satisfy the equality

$$T_{(\text{DELAY})} < T_{Pi} - T_{\text{INTR}i} \qquad (15.5)$$

when the term $T_{\text{INTR}i}$ represents the total time to service the interrupt. As in Example 15.4, $T_{\text{INTR}i}$ includes the context switch time, the execution time for the interrupt routine and the time to restore context and return to the interrupted program. As expected, the equation states that the maximum allowable delay time is equal to the minimum time between interrupt requests for this interrupt source minus the time for the interrupt routine. Even if the interrupt routines are very short and the interrupt density is low, a low-priority interrupt that interrupts frequently might not be serviced in time if the delay is excessive.

Critical regions of code. The concept of critical regions of code is another aspect of interrupt-driven systems that must be considered by a product designer. A *critical region* of code is defined for the present purposes as a sequence of instructions that should not be interrupted while the instructions execute. The critical region of code can arise in several circumstances.[9] The primary example occurs when a CPU program and an interrupt routine use the same variable in memory or in a register to synchronize their operation. If both the CPU program and the interrupt routine can each read and modify a variable, an error could result if the CPU program reads a value but was interrupted before the value was updated. Assuming that the interrupt routine also reads the value and updates it, the value would be in error if the updated value depended on the previous value that should have been written by the CPU program.

When a problem could arise from the interruption of several instructions in sequence, these instructions form the critical region of code. The solution to assure reliable operation of the product is to disable interrupts at the appropriate level. The interrupt should be disabled only during the critical region of code so that no interrupts are missed or delayed beyond their maximum allowed delay time.

EXERCISES

15.3.1. For the instruction,

MOVE.L   X, Dn   ; MEMORY TO REGISTER

tabulate the number of read bus cycles required to fetch the instruction and the operand addressed by X for each of the addressing modes of the MC68332 CPU defined in Section 5.3. The complete instruction execution time must include the fetch cycles as well as the time for the CPU to calculate the effective address of the operands. The time to calculate the effective addresses for the various addressing modes are published in the *CPU32 reference Manual*.

15.3.2. Define the conditions for which a product will execute instructions twice as fast if the system clock frequency is doubled. Consider all the causes of delay for instruction execution not just the CPU internal execution time.

15.3.3. Assume that an instruction takes N clock cycles plus M memory access cycles to execute. If memory is slow, the MPU adds wait states to each memory access as explained in Section 14.5. Write an equation for the instruction execution time if W wait states (one clock cycle each) are added to each memory access cycle. The relationship should include the parameters N, M, W, and the clock frequency $f_{(system)}$.

15.3.4. Suppose that the frequency of the oscillator controlling a time-of-day clock drifts and results in a 1.2Hz increase over its normal operating frequency of 32.768kHz. What is the error in seconds per 30-day month?

---

[9] Critical regions frequently occur in multiprocessor systems that communicate through a shared memory. Section 8.3 discusses the synchronization problem for multiprocessing systems and describes the Test and Set (TAS) instruction used to avoid conflicts. The discussion in the present section concentrates on critical regions made necessary because of priority interrupts.

15.3.5. In certain critical applications, interrupts are not used in the system and all external devices must be polled to determine if they need service. What are the advantages and disadvantages of the polling approaches versus interrupt-driven operation? How does the lack of interrupts simplify system design?

15.3.6. Considering the MC68332 with its modules, how many possible sources of interrupts are available? Reference to Chapter 12, Chapter 13 and Chapter 14 of this textbook may be necessary to answer this question.

15.3.7. A product receives an average number of 1000 interrupts a second. Each interrupt routine requires $20\mu s$ total time. What percent of CPU time is spent servicing interrupts?

15.3.8. Assume that the MCU accepts interrupts from five priority levels. Each interrupt handler requires $15\mu s$ to execute. The context switch time, t_{CS}, for each level is estimated to be $3\mu s$. In addition, the CPU program may encounter a critical region during which all these interrupts are disabled. Calculate the interrupt density and the latency time for each interrupt if the minimum time between interrupts at any level is $100\mu s$. Calculate the values for the following cases:
(a) the critical region code requires $10\mu s$ to execute;
(b) the critical region code requires the maximum time possible to execute.
In part (b), what is the maximum possible delay due to the critical region code?

15.3.9. Suppose that during the operation of a product, an interrupt designated I_1 occurs as often as every $70\mu s$. This interrupt requires $25\mu s$ to recognize and service. A second interrupt source I_2 has a minimum time between interrupts of $100\mu s$. This second interrupt requires $40\mu s$. A critical region of code of length $13\mu s$ is possible. Answer the following:
(a) if I_1 has the highest priority, will I_1 and I_2 be serviced properly?
(b) if I_2 is given the highest priority will both interrupts be serviced?
Calculate the maximum delay allowed for each interrupt considering the critical region and the time required by the higher priority interrupt for both cases.

FURTHER READING

The textbook by Savitzky describes the design approach for real-time systems. Savitzky explains the complete design process including hardware and software aspects.

The Article Reprint (AR254) from Motorola covers the design of phase-locked loops. Protopapas explores the design of crystal-controlled oscillator circuits for microprocessors and presents other timing information useful to the hardware designer.

Breneman's article presents applications of watchdog timers. The Motorola Application Note (AN894A) analyzes the MC146818 clock chip, emphasizing the hardware aspects.

Peatman analyzes interrupt response times and the factors that contribute to latency. Although his textbook covers 8-bit microcontrollers, the discussion of interrupts has a much wider application.

Real-time Systems

SAVITZKY, STEPHEN R., *Real-Time Microprocessor Systems*. New York, N.Y.: Van-Nostrand Reinhold, 1985.

Crystals Oscillators and Phase-Locked Loops

Phase-Locked Loop Design Articles, Motorola Article Reprint AR254, 1987.

PROTOPAPAS, D. A., *Microcomputer Hardware Design*, Englewood Cliffs, N.J.: Prentice Hall, 1988.

Watchdog Timers and Clocks

BRENEMAN, BRIAN H., "Watchdog timers keep computer failures from having catastrophic results," *Personal Engineering & Instrumentation News*, **6**, No. 9 (September 1989), 53–56.

SVATEK, PATRICK, "User Considerations for MC146818 Real Time Clock Applications," Motorola Application Note AN894A, 1985.

Interrupts

PEATMAN, JOHN B., *Design with Microcontrollers*, New York, N.Y.: McGraw-Hill, 1988.

16

Product Development and Testing

This chapter discusses product development and testing for MC68332-based products. The purpose is to describe the type of development aids that are available to the programmer and the hardware designer. Product development begins after the product design is complete. The design defines the characteristics and performance of the product. In addition, the complete design includes the detailed hardware and software design. The development phase considered in this chapter consists of hardware and software development as well as hardware/software integration for the prototype product. Testing and debugging during product development assures that the product performs as it should before the overall design is finalized and the product is put into production.

Section 16.1 discusses the various techniques and support items that programmers and hardware designers use to create a prototype product. As examples of support, Section 16.2 presents various Motorola products to assist development. Section 16.3 describes the features and modes of the MC68332 that are included in the MCU to aid hardware and software debugging. Section 16.4 presents a summary of development support products that are commercially available from Motorola and other manufacturers.

Once an MC68332-based product is successfully created, testing during production or even during operation may be necessary to assure the level of reliability required. Section 16.5 describes the test modes of the MC68332.

Other references.   Other sections of this textbook have discussed aspects of product design and development. Section 1.3 described the complete product design and development cycle. Section 1.2 presented the integrated-circuit chips, software and other products in the M68000 family that are available to aid product development. Section 5.1 described the software development cycle as applied to assembly-language programming. Section 14.4 discussed interface design and implementation.

The references in the Further Reading section at the end of the chapter cover many of the topics presented in this chapter. In particular, the references discuss development systems, logic analyzers, and in-circuit emulation. Additional information about these development aids may be obtained by contacting the manufacturers of microcontroller development support products.

16.1   SUPPORT FOR PRODUCT DEVELOPMENT

Table 16.1 summarizes the items usually employed or created during design and development of a product. The design phase produces the documents that define the product's feasibility, operation, specifications and detailed design. Since microcontroller-based products are made up of hardware and software, the design documents should specify the detailed hardware and software configuration for the product. The development phase involves the creation (implementation) and testing of the necessary hardware and software for the product.

16.1.1   Hardware Development

The hardware development phase results in the creation of the prototype hardware from the circuit diagrams produced during the design phase. The logic of the hardware system and specific timing must be tested to assure that the hardware meets the hardware specifications. The general-purpose testing tools are oscilloscopes, logic analyzers, voltmeters and similar instruments. Such instruments typically display the voltage (analog) or logic level (digital) on a signal line versus time as the hardware operates. However, these instruments that are sufficient to test and debug ordinary circuits are usually not sufficient for a microprocessor-based product. This is because general-purpose test instruments do not relate the signals being monitored to the CPU's instruction execution.

A number of specialized instruments are available to aid hardware development for products that are controlled by a microcontroller. The implication of a microcontroller-based product is that some software must be available to be executed during testing of the hardware even if the test programs are not those to be included in the final product. At least part of the hardware testing involves monitoring the microcontroller external bus and other signal lines that are controlled by an executing program.

The *bus state analyzer* and *in-circuit emulator* are two debugging aids that are commonly used for hardware development. These instruments for testing and analysis differ from the general-purpose logic analyzer because the bus-state analyzer and in-circuit emulator are designed to operate with a particular microcontroller. The results are presented in terms of the CPU instructions being executed and the specific bus signals of the microcontroller being used. The bus state analyzer and in-circuit em-

Table 16.1 Support for Product Design and Development

Activity	Item	Purpose or Result
Product Design: Documents	Feasibility study	Describes the technical and commercial objectives
	General specifications	Describes the operation and capabilities of the product
	Detailed requirements and Functional specifications Detailed hardware and Software design	Describes the performance and method of implementation Circuit diagrams, flow charts, timing diagrams, etc.
Hardware Development: Implementation	Prototype	Preliminary product hardware for testing
Testing	Logic analyzer, oscilloscope, bus state analyzer and in-circuit emulator	To verify the hardware operation
Software Development: Code generation	Editor, assembler or compiler, linker and loader	Preliminary product software for testing
Testing	Debugger	To verify the software operation
Hardware and Software Integration: Integration	Development system with hardware and software testing support	To verify the correct operation of the product

ulator are often combined in a *microcontroller development system* as described later in this section.

16.1.2 Software Development

Table 16.1 lists a number of programming aids that are available for software development. The programs for code generation execute on a host computer that is used as a software development system. If the host CPU is different from the target microcontroller in the product under development, the language programs to aid development are termed *cross-assemblers* or *cross-compilers* as previously discussed in Section 1.2. The debugging program may be a monitor program that executes on the target product or a more sophisticated debugger executing on the host computer.

Section 5.1 describes one approach to software development. The examples in Chapter 5 were generated using a cross-assembler and tested with the EPROM-based monitor (332BUG) on the Motorola BCC (Business Card Computer) single-board computer. Figure 16.1 shows the connection between the host computer and the BCC. Section 16.2 describes the BCC in more detail.

In response to programmer commands, the monitor loads a program from the host computer into the RAM memory of the BCC and allows execution and debugging of the program. Example 5.2 illustrated a typical debugging session using the monitor. During a debugging session, the addresses for execution, breakpoints, memory dumps, etc. must be defined by the programmer as absolute addresses.

To determine the absolute address in memory that corresponds to a particular symbol (label) in an assembly-language program, the programmer may have to refer to the linker listing and symbol table as well as the assembler listing. Debugging by using absolute addresses can be tedious and even somewhat unproductive for complicated programs. Fortunately, the 332BUG monitor provides offset registers to define the starting and ending addresses of programs being debugged. The displayed addresses can be relative to the starting address so they will correspond to the relative addresses in the assembly-language listing.

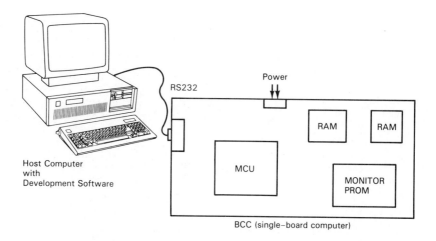

Figure 16.1 Software development using the Motorola BCC.

A *symbolic* debugger allows debugging to be performed using symbols in the program instead of absolute addresses. The symbolic debugger keeps its own symbol table with the name of each symbol in the program and its absolute address. The labels assigned in an assembly-language program are the symbols when the source program is created in assembly language.

When a high-level language such as C is used, a *source level* debugger is a useful debugging aid. In the debugging session, the programmer causes execution of source language statements rather than single assembly-language statements as well as complete functions (in C) before the results are displayed.

The debugging software controls the execution of a program by the target CPU in the product under development.[1] Control is achieved by the debugging program

---

[1] A simulator program that simulates the instruction execution of the MCU could be used to test the program under development instead of using the MCU chip itself. However, a simulator does not replicate the exact timing of the MCU.

when software breakpoints are inserted in the program. In an MC68332-based system, a TRAP instruction, the ILLEGAL instruction, or the BKPT (Breakpoint) instruction could be used to cause a breakpoint as previously described in Section 11.4. Obviously, the insertion of a breakpoint in a program by a debugging program modifies the program. This precludes debugging of ROM-based programs using software breakpoints.

By combining the software debugging function with hardware emulation, the integration and debugging of both the hardware and software of a product may be carried out in a systematic way. When debugging and emulation features are combined in a microcontroller development system, ROM-based programs can be executed and monitored. Also, a development system allows real-time tracing without interrupting the program under test with software breakpoints.

16.1.3 Microprocessor Development Systems

As the independent development of software and hardware for a product proceeds, there is an increasing need to integrate the two parts into a working prototype. Although the integration process ideally should have been going on from the beginning of the development effort, the integration phase will be treated here separately for clarity. The purpose of the integration phase is to assure that the software and hardware work together correctly to meet the product requirements. The main emphasis during integration is testing of the combined software and hardware in as realistic a manner as possible. Ideally, the prototype product should be tested as if it were the completed product ready for production. To accomplish realistic testing, the test equipment should affect the prototype's operation as little as possible. The modern microprocessor development system is designed with this purpose in mind.

The *microprocessor development system* combines the testing and debugging aids discussed previously for both hardware and software development. In fact, the microprocessor development system is suited for all of the aspects of product development including:
(a) hardware development;
(b) software development;
(c) integration of software and hardware.
The development system is therefore a useful aid to the programmer and hardware designer working either separately or together.

The development systems available for the MC68332 from different manufacturers certainly differ in appearance and in the features offered. However, a complete development system typically consists of the following elements:
(a) host computer with development software;
(b) debugger for software debugging and control of emulation;
(c) emulator with RAM, bus state analyzer and in-circuit emulator connection.

Figure 16.2 shows the elements of a complete microcontroller development system. The hardware items are the host computer, the emulator system with an in-circuit emulator cable and MCU and the target prototype being tested. The development path is also shown in Figure 16.2. Software implementation begins with the creation of the source program.

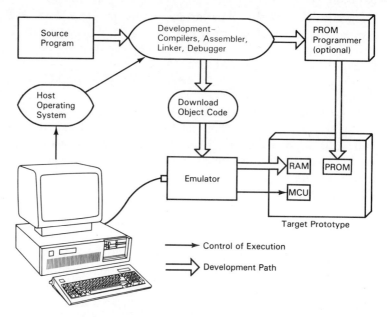

Figure 16.2 Microcontroller development path.

The programmer creates the source program using an editor or word processor program that executes on the host computer. The host computer could be a general-purpose computer such as the IBM- PC (personal computer) or a work station. The development software allows the programmer to create a program in object code form (binary) for execution. In many products, part or all of the executable code is held in a ROM. During development, an EPROM may be substituted in the prototype product since this memory may be erased and reprogrammed if the program must be changed. The EPROM programmer is a circuit that connects to the host computer for the purpose of storing a program in an EPROM.

The *emulator* shown in Figure 16.2 is designed to execute the program under development exactly as the MCU would in a product. For example, this is accomplished for the MC68332 by including an MC68332 MCU in the emulator. In addition to emulation of MCU execution, the emulator provides the capability to aid software and hardware development and integration.

Figure 16.3 shows a block diagram of a typical microcontroller development system that emphasizes the role of the emulator. The emulator is controlled during debugging by the debugging program executing on the host computer. The emulator also contains its own RAM memory. The emulator memory allows the emulator to operate in several modes. For convenience, the three modes of operations will be designated as:

(a) software development mode;
(b) in-circuit emulation mode using emulator RAM;
(c) complete prototype test mode.

In the *software development* mode, the host computer is used to download the

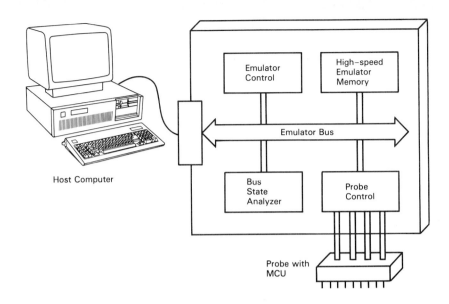

Figure 16.3 Microcontroller development system.

object code into the emulator RAM. Execution and debugging takes place using the emulator only. Thus, this mode does not use any prototype hardware. All hardware related activities such as I/O must be simulated using the host's peripheral units. For example, keyboard entry and display routines could be tested with the host computer's keyboard and operator's display unit. One advantage of performing software development with an emulator is that the software can be tested and debugged using the MCU even before the prototype hardware is complete.

Figure 16.4 shows the development system as it is connected to perform in-circuit emulation. *In-circuit emulation* consists of replacing the target MCU in the prototype product with the MCU on the emulator probe and then executing a program under control of the debugging software of the host computer. The in-circuit emulator MCU will act functionally and electrically identical to the target MCU.[2]

With in-circuit emulation, the program under test can be stored either in emulation RAM or in the memory of the prototype. In-circuit emulation using the emulator RAM tests most of the prototype hardware including I/O devices. However, the emulator MCU fetches instructions from the emulator RAM rather than the program

---

[2] The presence of the emulator probe changes the electrical characteristics and timing slightly. This usually has little effect as long as the emulator MCU can operate at the intended clock frequency of the product. In the emulators discussed in this chapter, the emulator's MCU is placed at the prototype end of the connecting cable to minimize skews and propagation delays. Another approach to testing would be to clip the emulator cable over the target MCU in the prototype product. For most MCUs, it would be necessary to break certain connections between the microcontroller and the prototype circuitry to perform the emulator control functions. The MC68332 features a background mode of operation that can be used for emulator control without breaking connections. Section 16.3 describes the background mode of the MC68332.

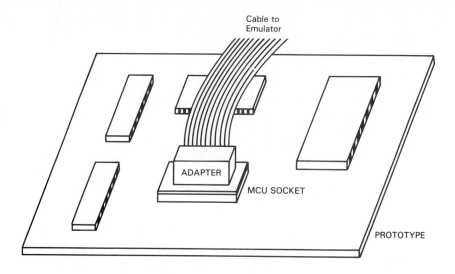

Cable to
Emulator

ADAPTER

MCU SOCKET

PROTOTYPE

Figure 16.4 In-circuit emulation.

memory of the prototype. This mode of operation is also convenient when the prototype hardware is not complete but simple test routines must be executed to control part of the existing hardware for the product.

For complete prototype testing, the development system is used to download programs into the prototype RAM for execution. If the programs are to reside eventually in ROM, that portion of the RAM memory space of the prototype can be declared read-only for the purposes of testing.

The *bus state analyzer* in Figure 16.3 is a critical part of the emulator. Under control of the debugging program, the analyzer acquires address, data and control signal-line information during each MCU bus cycle of interest. Once each clock pulse, the signal lines are sampled in parallel and the logic levels of {0} or {1} are stored in the analyzer's memory for eventual display. The combination of debugging software and emulator with bus state analyzer allows almost complete debugging and testing of a prototype product.[3]

16.1.4 Hardware and Software Integration

Although the features and capabilities of different microcontroller development systems are not standardized, Table 16.2 lists the major features common to most development systems that include both in-circuit emulation and software development support. The emulator itself as previously described is the "interface" between the development system software and the prototype product. The operator (programmer

---

[3] Analog signals require an oscilloscope or similar instrument for analysis. Also, certain types of digital signals may be difficult to analyze with a bus state analyzer that captures data only on each MCU clock cycle. For example, a very fast noise spike (glitch) on a signal line may be missed entirely. To find such short pulses, a logic analyzer with a clock frequency much higher than the MCU clock frequency is needed.

or hardware designer) uses the development system to control program execution and display certain results of interest.

An important capability of a microcontroller development system is that events can be recognized and results displayed based on MCU bus cycles. In contrast, a software debugger depends essentially on instruction execution to control and analyze the program under test. The software breakpoint capability listed in Table 16.2 is used mainly for program debugging and is based on instruction replacement as in a software development system.

Table 16.2 Features of Microprocessor Development Systems

Feature	Use
Triggers and Breakpoints:	
Software breakpoints	Set instruction breakpoints in RAM
Hardware breakpoints	Trigger breakpoints at instructions or memory references in RAM or ROM
Conditional triggers	Trigger breakpoint on specific bus activities
Logic analysis:	
Post-triggering	Capture bus cycle up to a breakpoint
Analysis of specific types of bus cycles	Capture a certain class of bus cycles
Analysis of specific combinations of bus cycles	Capture bus cycles after a certain sequence of cycles occurs
Instruction trace and Memory control:	
Single stepping	Display instruction and register contents after instruction execution
Memory access	Examine or modify memory locations
Memory characteristics	Specify type of memory (RAM or ROM)

The bus state analyzer of a development system allows the operator to select various "triggers" which cause the capture and display of important data. The *trigger* is defined to be some combination of the microcontroller's address, data and control signals used to identify a particular event in the prototype program. The flow chart of Figure 16.5 shows a typical sequence during debugging. After the operator selects the trigger condition and display format, the command is given to start execution. The prototype program runs until the bus state analyzer recognizes the trigger condition. When the trigger condition occurs, the emulator creates a hardware breakpoint.[4] Then, control is returned to the host computer where the results are displayed in the selected format.

Table 16.2 lists example trigger conditions that can be used to create breakpoints during program execution. The simplest trigger condition is a comparison of the MCU address signal lines with a preset address. When the address appears during program execution, control is transferred to the development system to display information such as the contents of MCU registers. The preset address can be an instruction address or an operand or I/O access address.

[4] Section 16.3 defines the difference between hardware and software breakpoints for the MC68332.

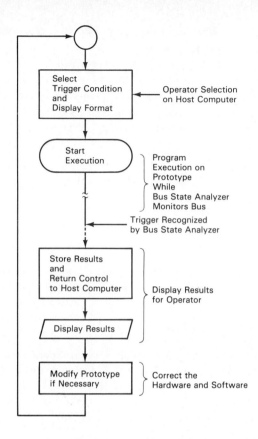

Figure 16.5 Debugging session.

A conditional trigger can be set to monitor specific bus activities or combinations of activities. When the control signal lines of the MCU are monitored to recognize the trigger condition, for example, any memory read or memory write can be selected to return control to the development system. Most development systems allow trigger conditions to be set according to the state of the MCU address, data and control signal lines. For example, an invalid write cycle to a specific memory location declared as read-only could be detected.

The triggers that cause hardware breakpoints usually result in the display of the current instruction and register contents when the trigger was recognized. Logic analysis is also possible which relates instruction execution to bus activity. Table 16.2 lists several possibilities. The bus analyzer continually stores the bit patterns on the bus each cycle for logic analysis. Because analyzer memory is limited, only data for the last N cycles are retained. For example, a specified number of bus cycles that occurred before the trigger event can be saved and displayed using a method called post-triggering. In post-triggering, the operator specifies the number of cycles to be collected after the trigger event. By varying this count from 0 to N, the operator can cause the analyzer to capture data before and after the triggering event.

The features listed in Table 16.2 for instruction trace and memory control are similar to those found on software development systems. Instruction execution may be traced and memory locations examined or changed as needed. Sections of memory can be defined with specific conditions such as read-only. Even though the operation of these commands is similar to those of a software development system, the microcontroller development system allows instruction tracing and other debugging features *without* using any memory of the prototype product for execution of the debugging program. This is in contrast to the intrusive nature of the 332BUG monitor of the BCC single-board computer previously discussed in Chapter 5. The 332BUG monitor takes the first 16k bytes of the system memory for its RAM area as well as 64Kbytes required by the monitor itself in EPROM.

EXERCISES

16.1.1. Outline the information that would be contained in the design documents for an MC68332-based machine tool controller. The motion of the machine is monitored and controlled by the product. There is a keypad for operator inputs, an LED display for outputs and a connection for a printer. The memory is to consist of EPROM and RAM.

After making design decisions about the use of the MCU and its modules, draw the block diagram for the hardware and software components. Refer to Chapter 15 for some of the design criteria that must be specified.

16.1.2. For the product of Exercise 16.1.1, describe the most appropriate and convenient development and testing aids for each phase of the development.

16.2 MOTOROLA DEVELOPMENT SUPPORT

Motorola produces a number of products that support software and hardware development for the M68300 family of microcontrollers. Table 16.3 lists some of these products that are available from Motorola.[5] The products include cross-assemblers and cross-compilers, evaluation modules and a microcontroller development system for the MC68332 MCU.

16.2.1 Software Development

The cross-assembler and cross-compiler listed in Table 16.3 execute under an MS/DOS operating system on an IBM-PC (Personal Computer) or equivalent as the host computer. The assembler translates source statements written in M68000 family assembly language into relocatable or absolute object code. Conditional assembly and macro-assembly are possible as discussed previously in Chapter 5. Structured assembly statements are provided using flow control structures (**for**, **repeat**, **while**) or conditional

[5] Motorola continually augments and enhances its product line to support a family of processors. The interested reader should contact a Motorola representative for the latest information concerning support products.

Table 16.3 Motorola Support Products

Support	Specific Product	Use
Software Development:		
Structured cross-assembler	M68MASM	Produces a relocatable object module
C cross-compiler	MC68332 C	Produces an object module suitable for linking
Utilities	—	Link object modules; convert to S-records; dump COFF files, etc.
Evaluation Modules:		
Single-board computer	BCC	Software development and evaluation
Evaluation system	M68332 EVS	Software and hardware development
Development Systems:		
Emulator	CDS32	Emulator and bus analyzer for MC68332 development projects

branches (**if–then**, **if–then–else**). When these structured statements are included in an assembly language program, the MASM assembler generates the appropriate assembly language instruction for their implementation. The C language cross-compiler produces program modules suitable for assembly and linking to create an object module.

The output file of the assembler or linker is produced in a format known as the Common Object File Format (COFF). A COFF file contains information that is used by utility programs to create an executable object module. For example, the utility program HEX converts a COFF file to Motorola S-records. The S-record file that results is suitable for loading on any computer system that includes a program to convert the S-records to executable code in binary. The specific S-record format was presented previously in Section 5.1.

16.2.2 Evaluation Modules

Motorola produces several evaluation systems suitable for initial testing of software for MC68332-based products. Figure 16.6 shows the Business Card Computer (BCC). This is a single-board computer, so named because of its small size of 2.25 × 3.5in (5.7 × 8.9cm). As shown in Figure 16.6, the BCC only requires a power supply and an RS-232 compatible connection to a terminal or host computer.

The features of the BCC include:
(a) MC68332 CPU;
(b) 128Kbyte EPROM for 332BUG monitor;
(c) 64Kbyte RAM;
(d) RS-232 I/O port;
(e) complete pin-outs of MC68332 signal lines.

The BCC is typically used as an inexpensive single-board computer for program testing. This application has been described in Section 5.1 where the 332BUG monitor is explained. Section 10.3 describes the author's BCC used in a control system. Figure 16.7 shows another application in which the BCC is connected into a prototype

Figure 16.6 Business Card Computer.

product. The prototype can be tested without an emulator using the serial communication port of the BCC.

Figure 16.8 shows the M68332EVS (Evaluation System) which includes the BCC and another single-board computer mounted on the larger platform board. The other BCC-sized module is the Business Card Computer Development Interface (BCCDI). The BCCDI is controlled by its own monitor program that is used to direct the operation of the BCC without disturbing the execution of programs by the BCC. A hardware breakpoint chip on the BCCDI invokes the background mode of the MC68332 for debugging. The background mode is explained in Section 16.3.

The platform board (PFB) of the EVS provides the base for both the BCC and the BCCDI. There are sockets for RAM or EPROM and a socket for a Motorola floating-point coprocessor. The pin connectors on the board allow connection of a logic analyzer or a prototype product.

16.2.3 Microcomputer Development Systems

The CDS32 emulator listed in Table 16.3 is a complete emulator for bus state analysis and in-circuit emulation. Physically, the CDS32 is practically identical to the emulator shown in Figure 1.2. The CDS32 uses two MC68332 chips. One controls the emulator

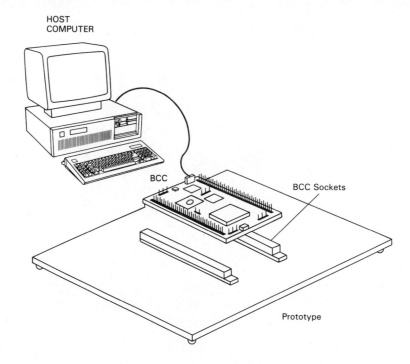

HOST
COMPUTER

BCC

BCC Sockets

Prototype

Figure 16.7 Testing a prototype with the BCC.

itself and the other is part of the probe for in-circuit emulation. Figure 16.9 shows the connections between the Host computer, the CDS32 and the target system under test. The features of the CDS32 for product development are those previously described in Section 16.1.

16.3 DEVELOPMENT SUPPORT BY THE MC68332

In addition to its other capabilities, the MC68332 was specifically designed to facilitate hardware and software development. Table 16.4 lists the major features of the MC68332 for development support. The features such as trace, unimplemented instruction exception and software breakpoints are primarily to aid a programmer during software debugging. The other features listed in Table 16.4 simplify the task of designing emulators and debugging software that is part of a microcontroller development system.

16.3.1 Trace and Unimplemented Instruction Exceptions

The trace and the unimplemented instruction exceptions were discussed previously in Section 11.4. Trace is enabled by setting the appropriate bits in the CPU status register. Single-instruction trace causes an exception after each instruction executes. Trace on change of flow is typically used to trace program branches and jumps. The trace

Figure 16.8 MC68332EVS.

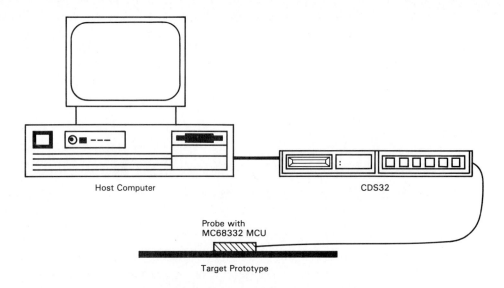

Figure 16.9 CDS32 emulator and development system.

Table 16.4 Development Support by the MC68332

Feature	Entry or Control	Use
Trace and Unimplemented Instruction Exceptions:		
Trace single instruction	SR[15] = {1}	Debug instruction execution
Trace on change of flow	SR[14] = {1}	Debug loops or subroutines
Unimplemented instruction exception	Op-Code $A or $F	Emulate unimplemented instructions
Breakpoints:		
Software	BKPT instruction	Debug software modules or subroutines
Hardware	$\overline{\text{BKPT}}$ signal	Externally generated breakpoint
Background Mode:		
Enable	$\overline{\text{BKPT}}$ signal at reset	Microcode debugger
Operation	$\overline{\text{BKPT}}$ signal, double bus fault or BGND instruction	Emulation support
Show Cycles:		
Bus cycles	SMCR[9:8]	Monitor internal bus cycles
Opcode Tracking:		
Pipeline	$\overline{\text{IFETCH}}$, $\overline{\text{IPIPE}}$	Track CPU execution

exception-handling routine usually perform functions such as displaying the contents of CPU registers when the trace exception occurs.

An unimplemented instruction exception occurs when the high-order four bits

[15:12] of an instruction are either $A or $F. The exception-handler is often used to emulate in software the execution of a function that is not implemented as part of the CPU instruction set. For example, the F-line exception ($F) is frequently used to emulate floating-point operations when a floating-point coprocessor is not present in the system.

16.3.2 Breakpoints

The CPU recognizes various types of software breakpoints as described previously in Section 11.4. The recommended method of creating an instruction breakpoint in a program, particularly when an emulator is monitoring the CPU bus, is to insert a Breakpoint (BKPT) instruction in the instruction stream. Execution of the instruction

```
BKPT            #N                    ; BREAKPOINT
```

causes a CPU breakpoint acknowledgement cycle as described in Section 14.5. During acknowledgement, the MCU signal lines indicate that a breakpoint was encountered for breakpoint N, where $N = 0, 1, \ldots, 7$. A CPU read cycle is part of the acknowledgement. External circuits are expected to respond with either
(a) data that represents an instruction, or
(b) a bus error request ($\overline{\text{BERR}}$).

If no emulator is present, a watchdog timeout circuit should cause the bus error response. During the breakpoint acknowledgement cycle, a circuit asserting $\overline{\text{BERR}}$ LOW causes an illegal instruction trap. An emulator can use the breakpoint acknowledge cycle to either cause an illegal instruction trap (by asserting $\overline{\text{BERR}}$) or place the instruction word to be executed on the data bus. In the latter case, the emulator can cause the breakpoint to be ignored for one or more loops through the breakpoint. When the breakpoint is to be activated, the emulator asserts the bus error signal.

Hardware breakpoints. A hardware breakpoint occurs when an emulator asserts the $\overline{\text{BKPT}}$ signal LOW to the MCU if the background mode of the CPU is not enabled. The emulator can assert $\overline{\text{BKPT}}$ in response to any of the trigger conditions discussed in Section 16.1. Thus, breakpoints can be requested when the MCU accesses a specific memory address or other conditions occur that are independent of an instruction fetch cycle. In contrast, a software breakpoint can only occur on instruction boundaries for RAM-based programs if the software breakpoint must be inserted in the program during debugging.

Exception processing for the hardware breakpoint begins after $\overline{\text{BERR}}$ is asserted LOW in response to a hardware breakpoint acknowledgement cycle. The exception vector is held in the CPU vector table at offset $030. Section 11.1 presents the complete CPU vector table.

16.3.3 Background Mode

The *background debug mode* (BDM) of the MC68332 CPU is a special operating mode in which normal instruction execution is suspended while microcoded routines in the

CPU perform the functions of a debugger. Once entered, the background mode allows a debugging program to control the operation of the CPU. Figure 16.10 shows the connection between the development system and the MCU in the background mode. The communication method is serial, synchronous, full-duplex transfer via three signal lines. Thus, the development system controls the CPU without using the external bus of the MCU for background mode commands.

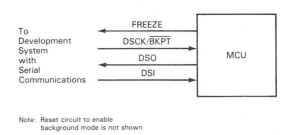

Note: Reset circuit to enable background mode is not shown

Figure 16.10 Background mode connection.

Each command in the background mode is one or more 17-bit sequences that are clocked into the CPU from the Serial Input Data (DSI) signal line by the serial clock signal (DSCLK). Data from the CPU is simultaneous transmitted to the development system on the Serial Output Data (DSO) signal line.[6] Figure 16.11 summarizes the background mode command set. The development system software must code each command in the proper binary format. For more information, the reader is referred to the *CPU32 Reference Manual*.

The background mode must be enabled during reset via the breakpoint ($\overline{\text{BKPT}}$) signal line. The $\overline{\text{BKPT}}$ signal must be held LOW while the $\overline{\text{RESET}}$ is LOW to enable the background mode. Once enabled, the background mode is entered by any one of the following:

(a) $\overline{\text{BKPT}}$ signal LOW;
(b) double bus fault;
(c) BGND instruction.

Table 16.5 summarizes the sources that cause a transition into background mode when it is enabled. When disabled, the sources cause their usual operations as listed in the table. Whenever the $\overline{\text{BKPT}}$ signal is acknowledged with background mode enabled, the CPU enters background mode. First, the FREEZE signal is asserted HIGH by the MCU. Then, the development system can transmit a command after the $\overline{\text{BKPT}}$ signal goes HIGH. As shown in Figure 16.10, the development system sends its clock signal (DSCLK) on the same signal line that it uses to initiate background mode ($\overline{\text{BKPT}}$).

A double bus fault, discussed in Section 11.6 and Section 14.5, causes entry into the enabled background mode. Program execution of the Background (BGND) instruction also causes the CPU to enter the enabled background mode. The hardware operation in the background mode is the same regardless of the source of entry.

---

[6] These signals serve a dual purpose as defined in Chapter 14 and in Subsection 16.3.5.

Command	Mnemonic	Description
Read A/D Register	RAREG/RDREG	Read the selected address or data register and return the results via the serial interface.
Write A/D Register	WAREG/WDREG	The data operand is written to the specified address or data register.
Read System Register	RSREG	The specified system control register is read. All registers that can be read in supervisor mode can be read in BDM.
Write System Register	WSREG	The operand data is written into the specified system control register.
Read Memory Location	READ	Read the sized data at the memory location specified by the long-word address. The source function code register (SFC) determines the address space accessed.
Write Memory Location	WRITE	Write the operand data to the memory location specified by the long-word address. The destination function code register (DFC) determines the address space accessed.
Dump Memory Block	DUMP	Used in conjunction with the READ command to dump large blocks of memory. An initial READ is executed to set up the starting address of the block and to retrieve the first result. Subsequent operands are retrieved with the DUMP command.
Fill Memory Block	FILL	Used in conjunction with the WRITE command to fill large blocks of memory. An initial WRITE is executed to set up the starting address of the block and to supply the first operand. Subsequent operands are written with the FILL command.
Resume Execution	GO	The pipeline is flushed and refilled before resuming instruction execution at the current PC.
Call User Code	CALL	Current PC is stacked at the location of the current SP. Instruction execution begins at user patch code.
Reset Peripherals	RST	Asserts RESET for 512 clock cycles. The CPU is **not** reset by this command. Synonymous with the CPU RESET instruction.
No Operation	NOP	NOP performs no operation and may be used as a null command.

Figure 16.11 Background mode command set.

However, an internal register holds a code which indicates the source. The register is read by the development system debugger with the RSREG command listed in Figure 16.11.

Table 16.5 Background Mode Sources and Actions

Source	Background enabled	Background disabled
BKPT	Background	Hardware breakpoint
Double bus fault	Background	CPU HALT
BGND instruction	Background	Illegal instruction exception

16.3.4 Show Cycles

In normal operation, the CPU performs internal data transfers with other modules of the MCU without using the external bus. For debugging purposes, it is possible to have the internal address and data information appear on the external bus. The term *show cycles* is used to describe internal bus accesses that appear on the external bus. The show cycles are disabled at reset and must be enabled by an initialization program writing to the SIM Module Configuration Register (SMCR[9:8]). Chapter 14 describes the initialization of the SMCR in detail.[7]

Table 16.6 lists the results of different settings of the show cycle bits SHEN1 (SMCR[9]) and SHEN0 (SMCR[8]). When show cycles are enabled, the signal $\overline{AS}$ is not asserted during the show cycle so that external peripheral devices do not respond to the address and data values. When the bus control signal Data Strobe ($\overline{DS}$) is LOW, the address signal lines have a valid address during the show cycle.

Arbitration of the external bus can be enabled or disabled during show cycles. Section 14.5 describes the bus arbitration cycle that allows an external device to request and take control of the external bus. In normal operation, internal bus cycles continue to occur when the external bus has been granted away. Setting both SHEN bits to {1} causes internal bus activity to halt when the external bus is being used by an external device.

Table 16.6 Show Cycle Control Bits

SHEN1	SHEN0	Action
{0}	{0}	Show cycles disabled
{0}	{1}	Show cycles enabled, external arbitration disabled
{1}	{0}	Show cycles enabled, external arbitration enabled
{1}	{1}	Show cycles enabled, external arbitration enabled; internal activity halted by a bus grant

Using the show cycle bits, a development system can control the type of bus cycles being monitored. Only external cycles or both internal and external cycles can be captured and the logic levels displayed for debugging.

---

[7] The SIM Module Configuration Register (SMCR) is referred to as the MCR in the *MC68332 User's Manuals*. The designation SMCR is used in this textbook to differentiate the SMCR from the module configuration registers of the QSM and TPU, designated QMCR and TMCR, respectively.

16.3.5 Opcode Tracking

The MC68332 provides two external signals, $\overline{\text{IFETCH}}$ and $\overline{\text{IPIPE}}$, that define the operation of the internal CPU pipeline described in Chapter 4. The signal $\overline{\text{IFETCH}}$ is pulse-width modulated to indicate whether an instruction is being fetched or the pipeline is being flushed because of a change in program control flow. The signal $\overline{\text{IPIPE}}$ is also pulse-width modulated to give an external indication of the conditions in the three-stage pipeline of the CPU. Either signal can be held LOW for one to three clock cycles depending on the condition being defined.

These signals serve a dual purpose. As defined in Chapter 14, they are designated $\overline{\text{IFETCH}}$/DSO and $\overline{\text{IPIPE}}$/DSI. In the background mode of the CPU, the signals serve for serial data transfer as described in Subsection 16.3.3.

Table 16.7 Development Support Products for the MC68332

Support	Company
Software:	
Assemblers, C compilers and	Motorola (Austin, TX)
source level debuggers	Intermetrics (Cambridge, MA)
	Introl (Milwaukee, WI)
Real-time Operating Systems	Eyring (Provo, Utah)
	Ready Systems (Sunnyvale, CA)
	Software Components Group (San Jose, CA)
Hardware:	
Logic analyzers	Hewlett Packard (Colorado Springs, CO)
	Tektronix (Beaverton, OR)
Integration and Test:	
Emulators	Hewlett Packard (Cupertino, CA)
	Motorola (Austin, TX)
	Tektronix (Beaverton, OR)

16.4 DEVELOPMENT SUPPORT FOR THE MC68332

A number of manufacturers other than Motorola provide development support products for the M68300 family of microcontrollers. Table 16.7 lists a sampling of the products that are available. The companies listed are representative and do not include all the sources of support products. For a more complete list, the reader is encouraged to contact a Motorola representative.

16.5 TEST MODES OF THE MC68332

In some circumstances, it becomes necessary to test the MC68332 itself to determine if it is operating correctly. This is obviously of concern during factory tests by Motorola. In fact, every MCU must have some capability to allow tests of its internal circuits before it is sold by the manufacturer. However, such MCU testing by the user is not possible for every MCU. Circuit testing of the MC68332 is possible because of the slave mode and the test submodule included in the System Integration Module (SIM).

Table 16.8 lists two testing modes for the MC68332. The *slave mode* is enabled if data signal line $\overline{\text{DB11}}$ is driven LOW during reset. An external bus master can request and be granted the use of both the external bus and the internal bus in the slave mode. This allows testing of the MCU modules at the machine-language level since the external bus master has gained access to all of the registers of the modules.

The *test mode* of the MCU allows very sophisticated testing of various circuit paths within the MCU. The techniques of signature analysis and scan-based testing are possible in the test mode. The test mode is entered when the signal line $\overline{\text{TSTME}}$ is held LOW.[8] Various registers in the test submodule and other modules determine the circuit paths to be tested and the test patterns. The reader is referred to the *MC68332 User's Manuals* for more information about the test mode. A reference in the Further Reading section of this chapter reviews various procedures for testing VLSI circuits.

Table 16.8 Testing Modes of the MC68332

Mode	Enabled by	Use
Slave mode	$\overline{\text{DB11}}$	An external master can replace the CPU and test the MCU modules
Test mode	$\overline{\text{TSTME}}$	Scan-base testing of MCU modules
RAM test	RAMTST	Open-circuit and array-current
QSM test	QTEST	Test QSM
TPU test	TMTR	Test TPU

Note:
The registers RAMTST, QTEST and TMTR are contained in the address space of the module register set.

EXERCISES

16.5.1. Describe an application in which it may be desirable to test the MCU during operation of a product. Testing would be done while the MCU is idle and waiting for an external event to trigger its operation.

FURTHER READING

The articles concerning development support describe various approaches to development of microcontroller-based products. The article about VLSI testing discusses testing techniques that are applied to complex logical circuits.

---

[8] If the $\overline{\text{TSTME}}$ signal is driven to $1.6 \times V_{DD}$, the MCU places its output drivers in a high-impedance state to isolate the MCU from the remainder of the system.

Development Support

HARDING, BILL, "Logic analyzers and emulators evolve with the times," *Computer Design*, **28**, No. 11, (June 1, 1989), 67–76.

HARDING, BILL, "Development tools stay in step with 32-bit designs," *Computer Design*, **28**, No. 17, (September 1, 1989), 61–70.

MERRIAM, RUDYARD, "68000 C Cross Compilers," *Embedded Systems Programming*, **3**, No. 11, (November 1990), 61–69.

MERRIAM, RUDYARD, "68000 C Cross Compilers, Part II," *Embedded Systems Programming*, **3**, No. 12, (December 1990), 65–71.

MITTAG, LARRY, "Logic Analyzers for Programmers," *Embedded Systems Programming*, **2**, No. 10, (November 1989), 67–73.

MULLIN, MIKE, "High-level languages, source-level debuggers ease microcontroller integration," *Personal Engineering & Instrumentation News*, **6**, No. 11, (November 1989), 32–40.

WILLIAMS, TOM, "Cross-development tools expand their horizons," *Computer Design*, **29**, No. 3, (February 1, 1990), 63–70.

VLSI Testing

WILLIAMS, THOMAS W., and KENNETH P. PARKER, "Design for Testability–A Survey," *IEEE Transactions on Computers*, **C-31**, No. 1, (January 1982), 2–15.

Answers to Selected Exercises

Chapter 2

2.2.4. (a) 12 bits (2^{12})
(b) 16 bits (2^{16})
(c) 24 bits (2^{24})

2.2.5. (a) 65,536 (2^{16})
(b) 1,048,576 (2^{20})
(c) 16,777,216 (2^{24})
(d) 4,294,967,296 (2^{32})

2.2.6. Twenty signal lines address the range \$00000–\$FFFFF. This is $\log_2(2^{20}) = 20$.

2.3.6. The highest priority interrupt R3 will be recognized and handled in $20 + 2.6 = 22.6$ microseconds.

      R2 will be recognized and handled in 32.6 microseconds unless R3 is in progress. The maximum time for R2 is $22.6 + 32.6 = 55.2$ microseconds.

      Interrupt R1 could be handled in as little as 22.6 microseconds. If R2 and R3 are in progress the total time could be $22.6 + 32.6 + 22.6 = 77.8$ microseconds.

2.3.7. A trap is caused by some condition occurring in the program and it is synchronous with the execution of the program. After a trap occurs, control is passed to the operating system for processing. The CPU32 divide instruction causes a trap if the divisor is zero as an example.

      Interrupts are caused by external devices. The time of occurrence is determined by the external device not the executing program. Interrupts to cause I/O transfers are common in computer systems with a number of peripheral units.

Chapter 3

3.1.1.1. The binary number $(0100.0110)_2$ has the decimal value

$$1 \times 4 + 1 \times (.25) + 1 \times (.125) = 4.375$$

3.1.1.2. The binary number $(1111\ 1111.1111\ 1111\ 1111\ 1111)_2$ has the decimal value

$$(2^8 - 1) + (1 - 2^{-16}) = 255.999984$$

3.1.1.3. (a) $130_9 = 1 \times 81 + 3 \times 9 = 108$
(b) $120_5 = 1 \times 25 + 2 \times 5 = 35$
(c) 0.97509766
(d) 61450

3.1.1.4. If $111_x = 31$, then $x^2 + x + 1 = 31$; $x = 5$

3.1.1.5. 4,294,967,295

3.1.2.1. (a) $1111\ 1001\ 1011\ 1001_2$
(b) $1111\ 1111\ 1111\ 0101_2$
(c) 11010.010_2

3.1.2.2. The complement of the most negative number is the same number. This is an out-of-range condition in the two's complement system.

3.1.2.3. (a) To sign-extend a positive number, repeat the leading zero to the left for m additional bits.
(b) To sign-extend a negative number, repeat the leading 1 to the left for m additional bits.

3.1.2.4. (a) 346.27
(b) 8223_{16}
(c) 1.1001111_2

3.1.2.5. (a) -127 to $+127$; -127 to $+127$; -128 to $+127$.
(b) -32767 to 32767; -32767 to 32767; -32768 to 32767
(c) $-2,147,483,647$ to $+2,147,483,647$;
$-2,147,483,647$ to $+2,147,483,647$;
$-2,147,483,648$ to $+2,147,483,647$.

3.1.2.6. The positive numbers have the range 0000 to 0999. The negative numbers have the range -1 to -1000 written as 9999, 9998,...9001, 9000.

3.1.3.1. (a) Dividing 1024 repeatedly by 2 and using the remainder results in the binary value $0100\ 0000\ 0000_2$.
(b) Dividing 53000 by 16 repeatedly and using the remainder yields the hexadecimal value $CF08_{16}$.
(c) The hexadecimal value $FFFFFFFF_{16}$ is $16^8 - 1 = 4,294,967,295$.
(d) Dividing 35 by 5 repeatedly and using the remainders yields the base 5 number 120_5.

3.1.3.2. 0.42857143

3.1.3.4. -0.0078125

3.1.3.5. 10.00, 10.01 ... 11.11, 00.00, 00.01, ... 01.11.

3.2.1.1. (a) $0000\ 0111_2$
(b) $0001\ 0011_2$

(c) $1001\ 1001_2$

3.2.1.2. **(a)** $1 \times (1000) + 9 \times (100) + 7 \times (10) = 1970$

(b) This is an invalid BCD value.

3.2.1.3. **(a)** 99

(b) 9999

(c) 99,999,999

3.2.1.4. Test the range of the sum or difference to be less than or equal to 10^L. There is an error if there is a carry in addition or a borrow in subtraction in the Lth decimal place.

3.2.2.1. 128 (BCD)

3.2.2.2. $1\ 1111\ 1101_2$

3.2.2.3. To perform BCD multiplication, multiply the Lth digit by the multiplier and then by 10^L. Then, convert the partial result to BCD format and sum into the result.

3.2.3.1. **(a)** $0000\ 0001\ 0010\ 0100_2$

(b) $1001\ 1001\ 1001\ 1001_2$

(c) $1001\ 0000\ 0000\ 0000_2$

(d) 5024 is not a valid number for 4-digit signed BCD values.

3.2.3.2. **(a)** -10 to $+9$

(b) -1000 to 999

(c) $-10,000,000$ to 9,999,999

3.3.1.2. $0\ 0111\ 1100\ 0000...{}_2$

3.3.1.3. **(a)** $4160\ 0000_{16} = (.100)_2 \times 2^5$

(b) $BFA0\ 0000_{16}$ obtained by writing $+1$ in floating-point notation and taking the two's complement.

3.3.2.1. **(a)** $3F00\ 0000_{16} = 1.0 \times 2^{-1}$

(b) $BF00\ 0000_{16} = -1.0 \times 2^{-1}$

(c) $0080\ 0000_{16} = 1.0 \times 2^{-126}$

3.3.2.2. 2×10^{38} (approximately)

3.3.2.3. **(a)** $401C\ 0000...00_{16} = (1.11)_2 \times 2^2$

(b) $C03E\ 0000...00_{16} = (1.111)_2 \times 2^4$

3.4.1. A text of 100,000 words requires 500,000 bytes of storage. The percentage of memory is 2.98%.

3.4.2. The text "THE MOTOROLA MC68332" has the ASCII equivalent:

54 48 45 20   THE

4D 4F 54 4F 52 4F 4C 41 20   MOTOROLA

4D 43 36 38 33 33 32   MC68332

3.4.3. **(a)** $1111\ 1111_2$

(b) 02 55

(c) 32 35 35 (hexadecimal)

3.4.5. No, the Morse code is ternary (dot, dash, space).

Chapter 4

4.2.1. **(a)** User mode; interrupts level 4 and below masked

(b) Supervisor mode

(c) Condition code Z={1}

(d) Trace in the supervisor mode

4.2.2. After a level 4 interrupt, (SR)= $2400.

4.2.3. A supervisor mode program requires use of SR, PC and SSP. A user mode program uses CCR, PC and USP.

4.3.1. The bytes at addresses 1000, 1001, 1002, and 1003 contain zero.

4.3.2. (a) (D2)[15:0] = $0801
(b) (1000) = $1901
(c) (1000) = $0000
(d) (D2)[15:0] = $0806

4.4.1. (a) ($7D0)[W] = ($3E8)
(b) (D1)[W] = ($1000)
(c) (D1)[B] = ($3E8)
(d) ($FFFFFC) = 00000000

4.4.2. (a) (D1)[W] = $3E8 (1000)
(b) (D1)[W] = $FFE0
(c) (D1)[W] = $FFE0
(d) (D1)[W] = $03E8

4.4.3. (a) (D1)[W] = $4142
(b) (D1)[W] = $00C1
(c) (D1)[W] = $03E8 (1000)

4.5.2. (a) ($1000) = 00
(b) ($1000, $1001) = 0000
(c) ($1000) = $1000
(d) (D1)[15:0] = $0010
(e) (D1)[15:0] = $1000

4.5.3. (a) CLR.W D1
(b) MOVE.L A3,D0
(c) MOVE.B #$2E,D0

4.5.4. (a) $4240
(b) $2008

4.5.5. Since the op-word is 16-bits, 65536 unique possibilities are available. The MOVE instruction itself takes many thousands of these possible instruction combinations.

The ADD instruction combines the operand length and an operand location into six bits in the operation word. This saves two bits in the instruction but reduces the number of possible addressing modes for the operands.

4.5.7. In some cases, the source code for a program may not be available or the disk space is not great enough to allow storage of the source program. In such cases, the object code must be used.

Source code compatibility between computers is necessary if a program must be modified after it is transferred to another system. This occurs frequently with programs written in a high-level language.

4.6.1. There are 24 addressing lines. Therefore, the addressing range is as follows:
(a) 16,777,216 bytes;
(b) 8,338,608 words;
(c) 4,194,304 long words.

4.6.2. (a) ($1000) = 1020 (BCD); ($1002) = 3040 (BCD)
(b) ($1000) = $0200; ($1002) = $00FC

4.6.3. ($1002) = $0002
($1004) = $FFF0

Chapter 5

5.1.1. The purpose of single-step instruction trace is to cause the CPU to trace the execution of one instruction. After execution, register contents of interest and other values are displayed for debugging. Since each instruction is traced, the single-step trace may be inconvenient when only portions of a program are to be debugged.

Program breakpoints are set at selected locations in a program to cause display of register contents after the program has reached the breakpoint location. Thus, only selected portions of a program are traced. This feature is also useful when testing the hardware. Breakpoints can be set in the program at locations that only cause tracing of instructions that affect the circuitry external to the CPU.

5.2.3. (a) 4E 20 49 53 (Hexadecimal)
(b) $14
(c) HERE = (location counter)
(d) Reserve 4 bytes
(e) location of "LABEL" +2

5.2.4. (a) $FFFE
(b) $10000
(c) $8000
(d) $5555

5.3.2. A program can clear an address register with the instruction: MOVEA.L #0,\<An\>

5.3.3. Absolute addresses are defined during assembly and cannot be changed without reassembly. Indirect and relative addresses can be changed as the program executes since the effective address is calculated when an instruction using one of these modes executes.

5.3.4. The short addressing mode requires only one extension word in an instruction, thus saving memory space. However, the range is limited to 65,536 locations as a two's-complement value.

5.3.5. (a) The operand address is $1000 − 1 = $0FFF
(b) The operand address is $1000
(c) The operand address is $1000 − 2 = $0FFE

5.3.6. (a) ((A0)) = ((A0+4))
(b) (D1)[W] = ($FFFF9000) since the value is sign-extended.
(c) (D1)[B] = ((A0)+(D1))

5.3.7. The value $8000 is sign-extended to $FFFF8000.

5.4.1. Example instruction: ADD.W ($1F00, A1, D1.L*2),D2. Thus, (D2)[W] = ($31F00).

Chapter 6

6.1.1. After the MOVE instruction executes, the V and C condition codes are cleared to allow a test for zero or negative.

6.1.4. Use of a MOVEM instruction results in more concise code. Also, the instruction is only fetched once from memory when saving several register values. This results in faster execution time for the program.

6.1.5. The SWAP instruction allows word-length operations on the most significant word of a longword after the exchange. Each byte in a longword may be accessed by byte-length operations if the operand is rotated so that the byte of interest is placed in the least significant position of the longword.

6.2.1. Assuming that a ROM contains routines with different starting addresses in different computers, the operating system could create a jump table in RAM to allow access to the ROM-based routines in a particular computer. The starting address of the ROM in a particular computer is determined by hardware design.

6.2.2. (a) The jump address is indicated by (A2); thus, (PC) = ((A2)).
(b) The operand address is held in A2; thus, (A1) = ((A2)).
(c) The operand address is held in D1; thus, (D2)[W] = ((D1))[W].

6.2.3. Since the CMP instruction calculates $J - I$, the correct tests are:
(a) BEQ ZERO
(b) BPL LESS
(c) BLT MORE

6.3.1. The offset between (PC) = $3014 and $3022 is $000E. The machine-language code is $610E.

6.3.2. The stack extends from $7FBC to $7FFD holding 66 bytes.

6.3.3. As subroutines are called, the return addresses and register values are pushed onto the stack. The number of nested subroutines allowed is determined by the designated length of the stack.

Chapter 7

7.1.1. The arithmetic instructions of the CPU32 change the N, Z, V, and C condition codes according to the result of the operation. The CMP instruction also affects the same condition codes. The MOVE and TST instructions only affect the N and Z condition codes.

7.1.2. If V ={1}, BGE branches on N = {1} but BPL branches on N = {0}. Thus, the instructions test the opposite results if the overflow bit is set.

7.1.3. The result -16384; V = {1} to indicate an error.

7.1.4. $N_1 + (r^m - N_2) = r^m + (N_1 - N_2)$. This is $(N_1 - N_2)$ in modulo r^m arithmetic when the result is valid.

7.2.1. (a) ADDI.B #1,D1 ; (D1)[W]=$FF00, C={1}, Z={1}
(c) SUBQ.B #1,D1 ; (D1)[W]=$FFFE, N={1}
(e) SUB.L D1,D1 ; (D1)=$00000000, Z={1}

7.3.1. (a) Q = $0002; R = $0000
(c) Q = $FFFE (-2); R = $0000
(d) Q = $FFFE (-2); R = $FFFF (-1)

7.3.5. (a) Overflow
(b) (D1) = FFFFFFFC (-4); N = {1}

7.3.6. (a) Q = $00000000
(b) Q = $00000004
(c) Q = $FFFFFFFF

7.4.1. The 64-bit unsigned integer range is approximately 0 to 1.8×10^{19}. The fractional range is 0 to 5.4×10^{-20}. The signed integer range is -9.2×10^{18} to 9.2×10^{18}.

7.4.3. The result is (D0) = $00000001; (D1) = $FFFFFFFC

7.4.4. (a) Since the quotient is larger than 32 bits, V = {1}.
(b) Q = $FFFFFFFF; R = $00000000

7.5.1. (a) $0037
(b) 9963

7.5.2. (a) 0435

(b) 2845, X = {1}. If only unsigned integers are allowed, the result is an overflow as indicated by X = {1}.

7.5.3. Using BCD notation, the addition of 127 and 299 yields the result $3C0 using binary addition. The correct result using decimal adjustment is 426.

7.7.1. $0.707 - 0.683 = 0.024$ (3.39% error)

7.7.2. 0.416

Chapter 8

8.2.1. Six bits are used to specify the shift count in the machine language instructions for shifting.

8.2.3. The value {11100101} represents -27 in two's complement notation. The result after three left shifts is {00101000} representing $+40$. The error is indicated by V={1}.

8.3.1. (a) bit 0 = {0}

(b) bit $(m - 1)$ = {1}

8.3.2. (a) BCLR #15,D2

(b) BSET #15,D2

Chapter 9

9.1.1. (a) $3000

(b) $0000A000

9.1.3. $FFFFA000

9.3.7. The range being checked is $ - 10 to $40. The value being checked is $FFFC or -4. Since this falls within the range, Z={0} and C={0} as a result.

9.4.2. An in-line parameter must be a fixed value since it is defined during assembly. This method cannot be used if the value must be changed during execution of a program. The advantage is that the address of the parameter is held on the system stack after a subroutine call so that the address need not be passed to the subroutine before the subroutine call.

9.4.5. The instruction sequence shown using LEA instructions accomplishes the same thing as the LINK instruction.

Chapter 10

10.1.3. The STOP instruction can be used to help debug I/O routines that use interrupt controlled data transfers. Once stopped, the CPU will only begin interrupt processing after receiving an interrupt request of higher priority than that specified in the interrupt mask bits of the Status Register.

10.1.4. The LPSTOP instruction is issued by a supervisor-mode program to reduce the power consumption of the MC68332. The instruction could be issued after the recognition of a power failure of the primary power source to minimize the drain on a back-up battery supply. Also, the LPSTOP instruction would be used when the product is to enter the stand-by mode. In the latter case for a portable instrument, the on-chip RAM is used to store information that allows the product to resume operation upon operator command. The values to be saved might include the previous display values and the setup data input by the operator before the low-power mode was entered.

10.2.1. (a) Trace off; user mode; disable level 4 and lower-level interrupts; clear condition codes.

(b) Change to user mode; clear V bit.

(c) Trace off; supervisor mode (unchanged); mask interrupts; clear CCR.

(d) Change to user mode.

10.2.2. (a) Set N, Z to {1}; clear X, V and C.

(b) C unchanged; clear X, N, Z and V.

(c) Privilege violation (trap).

10.3.1. The instruction MOVE.W #$0000,SR causes the CPU to enter the user mode. The next instruction is fetched from user program space. However, the CPU must remain in the supervisor mode if the memory is separated into supervisor and user areas to allow the program counter to be changed to point to user program space. Using the RTE instruction as described in Section 10.3 accomplishes the transition from supervisor to user mode in the correct manner.

Chapter 11

11.2.1. In a correctly working product, it is assumed that the software and hardware has been tested as thoroughly as possible. Therefore, only exceptions defined by the product designer or programmer should occur. The legitimate exceptions for a typical product might include the reset, TRAP #N calls and interrupts. The action to be taken after one of these exceptions is recognized depends on the software and hardware design.

11.4.2. The disadvantage of the single-instruction trace is that too much information may be presented if program segments rather than individual instructions are being debugged.

11.4.4. Debugging programs vary greatly in their capability to aid a programmer. The minimum requirement is that the debugging program allow a programmer to examine and modify both memory and register contents as well as execute selected segments of a program being debugged. More sophisticated debugging programs allow debugging using symbolic names rather than absolute addresses. These symbolic names are assembler labels and the other names defined in the source program.

11.6.1. When an address error occurs, information is stored on the system stack during the exception processing sequence. A double fault occurs and causes the CPU to halt if another error is detected before the execution of the first instruction of the address error handling-routine. If the vector contains an odd address, another address error exception occurs before the previous exception processing is completed and the CPU halts.

11.6.3. Since the bus error is caused by specific circuitry external to the CPU, the bus error handling routine must poll the possible sources to determine the cause of the bus error signal. Typically, each source of a bus error would have a status register bit to define when a bus error request had been made by that source.

11.7.2. There are 192 vectors for vectored interrupts and seven priority interrupt vectors (autovectors) for a total of 199 vectors. Other vectors in the vector table could be used for vectored interrupts since there is no distinction between vectors as far as the CPU is concerned when a vectored interrupt is recognized. In principal, any vector other than the reset vector could be used as an interrupt vector. However, use of another vector other than one of the assigned interrupt vectors could lead to conflicts when other exceptions occur.

Chapter 12

12.1.1. The QSPI and SCI are disabled after a reset.

12.2.2. **(a)** QMCR[3:0] = $5
(c) QILR[13:11] = {100}
(d) QIVR[7:0] = $50

12.2.2. The transfer of 10 characters takes approximately 1 second. For each character, the CPU is idle for 0.1s out of $0.1 + 10^{-5}$ seconds or about 99.99% of the time.

12.2.3. **(a)** There are 4 control bits out of 11; the overhead is 7/11 = 36%.
(b) The transmission rate is (1200 bits/sec)/11 = 109 characters per second.

12.3.1. BR = $16.77772 \times 10^6/(32)(9600) = 54.6$. Thus, choose the nearest integer BR = 55. The actual baud rate is 9532.5 baud. The error is −0.70%.

12.3.2. Choosing BR = 26, the baud rate is 9615.38. The error is 0.16%.

12.4.1. **(a)** SPCR0[15:0] = $A054
(b) SPCR2[15:0] = $8300
(c) SPCR1[15:0] = $8003

Chapter 13

13.1.1. After a reset, the TPU channels are disabled since the priority fields contain the value zero (TCPR0–1[15:0] = $0000).

13.1.2. The prescaler fields are write once fields after a reset to prevent a program error from changing the time resolution of the timers.

13.1.3. **(a)** TMCR[15:0] = $0086
(b) TICR[15:0] = $0560
(c) TCIER[15:0] = $C0F9

13.3.1. The system clock frequency can be divided by 8, 16, 32, or 64 to generate the TCR2 resolution. The times range from 478.8ns to $3.815\mu s$ with a 16.78MHz system clock.

13.3.3. **(a)** .03%
(b) .33%
(c) 3.33%

Chapter 14

14.3.2. SYNCR[15:8] determines the system clock frequency. Several settings result in a frequency of 16.78MHz. The possibilities are $CF, $9F, and $7F.

14.3.3. With a 32.768Hz source frequency, the maximum values of SYNCR[14:8] are $1F if the bit X = {1} and $4F if X = {0} to limit the system clock frequency to 16.78MHz.

14.3.5. The minimum resolution of the PIT is $122\mu s$. A value of 33 ($21) in PITR[7:0] yields a periodic interval of 4.0283ms. The error is about 0.7%

Appendix I

ASCII Character Set and Powers of 2 and 16

Appendix I contains the American Standard Code for Information Interchange (ASCII) and a table of powers of two and sixteen. The hexadecimal ASCII values are used in memory to represent letters, numbers and other special characters. Powers of 2^n and 16^k are given in the table of powers for $n = 0, 2, \ldots 32$ and $k = 0, 1, \ldots 8$.

TABLE I.1 ASCII CHARACTER SET

Character	Comments	Hex value
NUL	Null or tape feed	00
SOH	Start of heading	01
STX	Start of Text	02
ETX	End of Text	03
EOT	End of Transmission	04
ENQ	Enquire (who are you, WRU)	05
ACK	Acknowledge	06
BEL	Bell	07
BS	Backspace	08
HT	Horizontal Tab	09
LF	Line Feed	0A
VT	Vertical Tab	0B
FF	Form Feed	0C
RETURN	Carriage Return	0D
SO	Shift Out (to red ribbon)	0E
SI	Shift In (to black ribbon)	0F
DLE	Data Link Escape	10
DC1	Device Control 1	11
DC2	Device Control 2	12
DC3	Device Control 3	13
DC4	Device Control 4	14
NAK	Negative Acknowledge	15
SYN	Synchronous Idle	16
ETB	End of Transmission Block	17
CAN	Cancel	18
EM	End of Medium	19
SUB	Substitute	1A
ESC	Escape, prefix	1B
FS	File Separator	1C
GS	Group Separator	1D
RS	Record Separator	1E
US	Unit Separator	1F
SP	Space or Blank	20

TABLE I.1 (continued)

Character	Comments	Hex value
!	Exclamation point	21
"	Quotation marks (dieresis)	22
#	Number sign	23
$	Dollar sign	24
%	Percent sign	25
&	Ampersand	26
'	Apostrophe (acute accent, closing single quote)	27
(	Opening parenthesis	28
)	Closing parenthesis	29
*	Asterisk	2A
+	Plus sign	2B
,	Comma (cedilla)	2C
-	Hyphen (minus)	2D
.	Period (decimal point)	2E
/	Slant	2F
0	Digit 0	30
1	Digit 1	31
2	Digit 2	32
3	Digit 3	33
4	Digit 4	34
5	Digit 5	35
6	Digit 6	36
7	Digit 7	37
8	Digit 8	38
9	Digit 9	39
:	Colon	3A
;	Semicolon	3B
<	Less than	3C
=	Equals	3D
>	Greater than	3E
?	Question mark	3F
@	Commercial at	40

TABLE I.1 (continued)

Character	Comments	Hex value
A	Upper-case letter A	41
B	Upper-case letter B	42
C	Upper-case letter C	43
D	Upper-case letter D	44
E	Upper-case letter E	45
F	Upper-case letter F	46
G	Upper-case letter G	47
H	Upper-case letter H	48
I	Upper-case letter I	49
J	Upper-case letter J	4A
K	Upper-case letter K	4B
L	Upper-case letter L	4C
M	Upper-case letter M	4D
N	Upper-case letter N	4E
O	Upper-case letter O	4F
P	Upper-case letter P	50
Q	Upper-case letter Q	51
R	Upper-case letter R	52
S	Upper-case letter S	53
T	Upper-case letter T	54
U	Upper-case letter U	55
V	Upper-case letter V	56
W	Upper-case letter W	57
X	Upper-case letter X	58
Y	Upper-case letter Y	59
Z	Upper-case letter Z	5A
[	Opening bracket	5B
\	Reverse slant	5C
]	Closing bracket	5D
^	Circumflex	5E
_	Underline	5F

TABLE I.1 (continued)

Character	Comments	Hex value
'	Quotation mark	60
a	Lower-case letter a	61
b	Lower-case letter b	62
c	Lower-case letter c	63
d	Lower-case letter d	64
e	Lower-case letter e	65
f	Lower-case letter f	66
g	Lower-case letter g	67
h	Lower-case letter h	68
i	Lower-case letter i	69
j	Lower-case letter j	6A
k	Lower-case letter k	6B
l	Lower-case letter l	6C
m	Lower-case letter m	6D
n	Lower-case letter n	6E
o	Lower-case letter o	6F
p	Lower-case letter p	70
q	Lower-case letter q	71
r	Lower-case letter r	72
s	Lower-case letter s	73
t	Lower-case letter t	74
u	Lower-case letter u	75
v	Lower-case letter v	76
w	Lower-case letter w	77
x	Lower-case letter x	78
y	Lower-case letter y	79
z	Lower-case letter z	7A
{	Opening brace	7B
|	Vertical line	7C
}	Closing brace	7D
~	Equivalent	7E
	Delete	7F

TABLE I.2 POWERS OF TWO AND SIXTEEN

16^k 2^n	n	k	2^{-n}
1	0	0	1.0
2	1		0.5
4	2		0.25
8	3		0.125
16	4	1	0.062 5
32	5		0.031 25
64	6		0.015 625
128	7		0.007 812 5
256	8	2	0.003 906 25
512	9		0.001 953 125
1 024	10		0.000 976 562 5
2 048	11		0.000 488 281 25
4 096	12	3	0.000 244 140 625
8 192	13		0.000 122 070 312 5
16 384	14		0.000 061 035 156 25
32 768	15		0.000 030 517 578 125
65 536	16	4	0.000 015 258 789 062 5
131 072	17		0.000 007 629 394 531 25
262 144	18		0.000 003 814 697 265 625
524 288	19		0.000 001 907 348 632 812 5
1 048 576	20	5	0.000 000 953 674 316 406 25
2 097 152	21		0.000 000 476 837 158 203 125
4 194 304	22		0.000 000 238 418 579 101 562 5
8 388 608	23		0.000 000 119 209 289 550 781 25
16 777 216	24	6	0.000 000 059 604 664 775 390 625
33 554 432	25		0.000 000 029 802 322 387 695 312 5
67 108 864	26		0.000 000 014 901 161 193 847 656 25
134 217 728	27		0.000 000 007 450 580 596 923 828 125
268 435 456	28	7	0.000 000 003 725 290 298 461 914 062 5
536 870 912	29		0.000 000 001 862 645 149 230 957 031 25
1 073 741 824	30		0.000 000 000 931 322 574 615 478 515 625
2 147 483 648	31		0.000 000 000 465 661 287 307 739 257 812 5
4 294 967 296	32	8	0.000 000 000 232 830 643 653 869 628 906 25

ASCII Character Set and Powers

Appendix II

Comparison of M68000 Family Members

The summary of Appendix II represents a comparison of the MC68000, MC68008, MC68010, MC68020 and MC68030 processors. Important features of the processors are listed to indicate the differences between the central processor units of the Motorola M68000 family. These processors were introduced in Chapter 1 of this textbook.

Appendix II summarizes the characteristics of the microprocessors in the M68000 Family. M68000 UM/AD, *M68000 User's Manual* Sixth Edition includes more detailed information about the MC68000 and MC68010 differences.

	MC68000	MC68010	CPU32	MC68020
Data Bus Size (Bits)	16	16	8, 16	8, 16, 32
Address Bus Size (Bits)	24	24	24	32
Instruction Cache (In Words)		3*	3*	128

*Three-word cache for the loop mode.

Virtual Memory/Machine
MC68000	None
MC68010	Bus Error Detection, Instruction Continuation
CPU32	Bus Error Detection, Instruction Restart
MC68020	Bus Error Detection, Instruction Continuation

Coprocessor Interface
MC68000	Emulated in Software
MC68010	Emulated in Software
CPU32	Emulated in Software
MC68020	In Microcode

Word/Long-Word Data Alignment
MC68000	Word/Long-Word Data, Instructions, and Stack Must Be Word Aligned
MC68010	Word/Long-Word Data, Instructions, and Stack Must Be Word Aligned
CPU32	Word/Long-Word Data, Instructions, and Stack Must Be Word Aligned
MC68020	Only Instructions Must Be Word Aligned (Data Alignment Improves Performance)

Comparison

Control Registers
    MC68000   None
    MC68010   SFC, DFC, VBR
    CPU32   SFC, DFC, VBR
    MC68020   SFC, DFC, VBR, CACR, CAAR

Stack Pointers
    MC68000   USP, SSP
    MC68010   USP, SSP
    CPU32   USP, SSP
    MC68020   USP, SSP (MSP, ISP)

Status Register Bits
    MC68000   T, S, I0/I1/I2, X/N/Z/V/C
    MC68010   T, S, I0/I1/I2, X/N/Z/V/C
    CPU32   T1/T0, S, I0/I1/I2, X/N/Z/V/C
    MC68020   T1/T0, S, M, I0/I1/I2, X/N/Z/V/C

Function Code/Address Space
    MC68000   FC0–FC2 = 7 is Interrupt Acknowledge Only
    MC68010   FC0–FC2 = 7 is CPU Space
    CPU32   FC0–FC2 = 7 is CPU Space
    MC68020   FC0–FC2 = 7 is CPU Space

Indivisible Bus Cycles
    MC68000   Use $\overline{\text{AS}}$ Signal
    MC68010   Use $\overline{\text{AS}}$ Signal
    CPU32   Use $\overline{\text{RMC}}$ Signal
    MC68020   Use $\overline{\text{RMC}}$ Signal

Stack Frames
    MC68000   Supports Original Set
    MC68010   Supports Formats $0, $8
    CPU32   Supports Formats $0, $2, $C
    MC68020   Supports Formats $0, $1, $2, $9, $A, $B

M68000 Instruction Set Extensions

Mnemonic	Description	CPU32	M68020
Bcc	Supports 32-Bit Displacements	✔	✔
BFxxxx	Bit Field Instructions (BFCHG, BFCLR, BFEXTS, BFEXTU, BFFFO, BFINS, BFSET, BFTST)		✔
BGND	Background Operation	✔	
BKPT	New Instruction Functionality	✔	✔
BRA	Supports 32-Bit Displacements	✔	✔
BSR	Supports 32-Bit Displacements	✔	✔
CALLM	New Instruction		✔
CAS, CAS2	New Instructions		✔
CHK	Supports 32-Bit Operands	✔	✔
CHK2	New Instruction	✔	✔
CMPI	Supports Program Counter Relative Addressing	✔	✔
CMP2	New Instruction	✔	✔
cp	Coprocessor Instructions		✔
DIVS/DIVU	Supports 32-Bit and 64-Bit Operations	✔	✔
EXTB	Supports 8-Bit Extend to 32 Bits	✔	✔
LINK	Supports 32-Bit Displacements	✔	✔
LPSTOP	New Instruction	✔	
MOVEC	Supports New Control Registers	✔	✔
MULS/MULU	Supports 32-Bit Operands, 64-Bit Results	✔	✔
PACK	New Instruction		✔
RTM	New Instruction		✔
TABLE	New Instruction	✔	
TST	Supports Program Counter Relative, Immediate, and an Addressing	✔	✔
TRAPcc	New Instruction	✔	✔
UNPK	New Instruction		✔

M68000 Addressing Modes

Mode	Mnemonic	MC68010/ MC68000	CPU32	MC68020
Register Direct	Rn	✔	✔	✔
Address Register Indirect	(An)	✔	✔	✔
Address Register Indirect with Postincrement	(An) +	✔	✔	✔
Address Register Indirect with Predecrement	– (An)	✔	✔	✔
Address Register Indirect with Displacement	(d_{16},An)	✔	✔	✔
Address Register Indirect with Index (8-Bit Displacement)	(d_8,An,Xn)	✔	✔	✔
Address Register Indirect with Index (Base Displacement)	(bd,An,Xn*SCALE)		✔	✔
Memory Indirect with Postincrement	([bd,An],Xn,od)			✔
Memory Indirect with Predecrement	([bd,An,Xn],od)			✔
Absolute Short	(xxx).W	✔	✔	✔
Absolute Long	(xxx).L	✔	✔	✔
Program Counter Indirect with Displacement	(d_{16},PC)	✔	✔	✔
Program Counter Indirect with Index (8-Bit) Displacement	(d_8,PC,Xn)	✔	✔	✔
Program Counter Indirect with Index (Base Displacement)	(bd,PC,Xn*SCALE)		✔	✔
Immediate	#(data)	✔	✔	✔
Program Counter Memory Indirect with Postincrement	([bd,PC],Xn,od)			✔
Program Counter Memory Indirect with Predecrement	([bd,PC,Xn],od)			✔

Appendix III

The MC68331 and MC68340

MC68340

Technical Summary

INTEGRATED PROCESSOR UNIT

The MC68340 is a 32-bit integrated processor unit, combining high-performance data manipulation with powerful peripheral subsystems. The MC68340 is a member of the M68300 Family of modular devices featuring fully static, high-speed complementary metal-oxide semiconductor (HCMOS) technology. Based on the powerful MC68000, the CPU32 central processing module provides enhanced system performance and uses the extensive software base of the M68000 Family.

The main features of the MC68340 are as follows:

- Integrated System Functions in a Single Chip
- 32-Bit M68000 Family Central Processor (CPU32)
  - Upward Object-Code Compatible with the MC68000 and MC68010
  - New Instructions for Controller Applications
  - Higher Performance Execution
- Two-Channel DMA Capability for Low-Latency Memory Accesses
- Two Serial I/O Channels
- Two Multiple-Mode 16-Bit Timers
- Four Programmable Chip-Select Signals
- System Failure Protection:
  - Software Watchdog Timer
  - Periodic Interrupt Timer
  - Spurious Interrupt, Double Bus Fault, and Bus Timeout Monitors
  - Automatic Programmable Bus Termination
- Up to 16 Discrete I/O Pins
- Low-Power Operation
  - HCMOS Technology Reduces Power in Normal Operation
  - LPSTOP Mode Provides Static State for Lower Standby Drain
- Frequency: 16.78-MHz Maximum Frequency at 5-V Supply, Software Programmable
- Packages: 144-Pin Ceramic Quad Flat Pack (CQFP)
             145-Pin Plastic Pin Grid Array (PGA)

This document contains information on a new product. Specifications and information herein are subject to change without notice.

MC68331

Technical Summary
32-Bit Microcontroller

The MC68331 is one member of the M68300 Family of modular microcontroller units (MCUs). This family includes a series of modules from which numerous MCUs are being assembled. The MC68331 contains four modules: a central processing unit (CPU32), a general-purpose timer (GPT) module, a queued serial module (QSM), and a system integration module (SIM). These modules are connected on-chip via the intermodule bus (IMB).

Features

- Modular Architecture
- 32-Bit MC68000 Family CPU (CPU32):
  - Upward Object Code Compatible
  - New Instructions for Controller Applications
  - Virtual Memory Implementation
  - Loop Mode of Instruction Execution
  - Improved Exception Handling for Controller Applications
  - Trace on Change of Flow
  - Table Lookup and Interpolate Instruction
  - Hardware Breakpoint Signal, Background Mode
  - Fully Static Implementation
- General-Purpose Timer (GPT) Module:
  - Two 16-Bit Free-Running Counters with One Nine-Stage Prescaler
  - Three Input Capture Channels
  - Four Output Compare Channels
  - One Input Capture/Output Compare Channel
  - One Pulse Accumulator/Event Counter Input
  - Two Pulse-Width Modulation Outputs
  - Optional External Clock Input
- Two Serial Input/Output (I/O) Subsystems (QSM):
  - Enhanced Serial Communications Interface (SCI), Universal Asynchronous Receiver Transmitter (UART): Modulus Baud Rate, Parity
  - Queued Serial Peripheral Interface (SPI): 80-Byte RAM, Up to 16 Automatic Transfers,
  - Continuous Cycling, 8–16 Bits per Transfer
  - Dual Function I/O Ports
- System Integration Module (SIM):
  - External Bus Support
  - Twelve Programmable Chip Select Outputs
  - System Protection Logic
  - System Clock Based on 32.768-kHz Crystal for Low Power Operation
  - Watchdog Timer, Clock Monitor, and Bus Monitor
  - Test/Debug Submodule for Factory/User Test and Development

This document contains information on a new product. Specifications and information herein are subject to change without notice.

Appendix IV

CPU32 Instruction Set

ABCD   ABCD

Add Decimal with Extend

Operation: Source$_{10}$ + Destination$_{10}$ + X $\spadesuit$ Destination

Assembler
Syntax:
ABCD Dy,Dx
ABCD – (Ay), – (Ax)

Attributes: Size = (Byte)

Description: Adds the source operand to the destination operand along with the extend bit, and stores the result in the destination location. The addition is performed using binary coded decimal arithmetic. The operands, which are packed BCD numbers, can be addressed in two different ways:

1. Data register to data register: The operands are contained in the data registers specified in the instruction.

2. Memory to memory: The operands are addressed with the predecrement addressing mode using the address registers specified in the instruction.

This operation is a byte operation only.

Condition Codes:

X	N	Z	V	C
*	U	*	U	*

X   Set the same as the carry bit.
N   Undefined.
Z   Cleared if the result is nonzero. Unchanged otherwise.
V   Undefined.
C   Set if a decimal carry was generated. Cleared otherwise.

NOTE

Normally the Z condition code bit is set via programming before the start of an operation. This allows successful tests for zero results upon completion of multiple-precision operations.

Instruction Format:

15	14	13	12	11	10	9	8	7	6	5	4	3	2	1	0
1	1	0	0	REGISTER Rx			1	0	0	0	0	R/M	REGISTER Ry		

R/M Field: 0 = Data Register to Data Register   1 = Memory to Memory

If R/M = 0, Rx and Ry are Data Registers
If R/M = 1, Rx and Ry are Address Registers for the Predecrement Addressing Mode

---

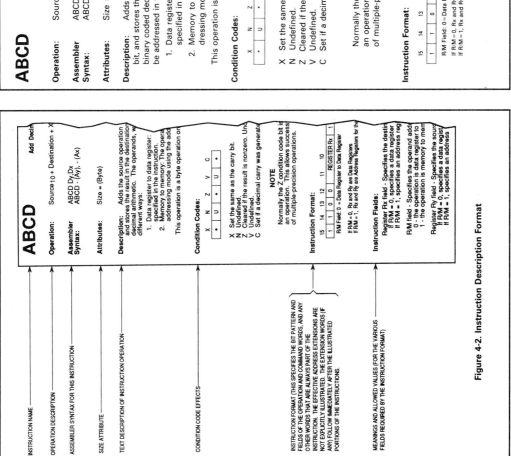

INSTRUCTION NAME

OPERATION DESCRIPTION

ASSEMBLER SYNTAX FOR THIS INSTRUCTION

SIZE ATTRIBUTE

TEXT DESCRIPTION OF INSTRUCTION OPERATION

CONDITION CODE EFFECTS

INSTRUCTION FORMAT (THIS SPECIFIES THE BIT PATTERN AND FIELDS OF THE OPERATION AND COMMAND WORDS, AND ANY OTHER WORDS THAT ARE ALWAYS PART OF THE INSTRUCTION. THE EFFECTIVE ADDRESS EXTENSIONS ARE NOT EXPLICITLY ILLUSTRATED. THE EXTENSION WORDS (IF ANY) FOLLOW IMMEDIATELY AFTER THE ILLUSTRATED PORTIONS OF THE INSTRUCTIONS.

MEANINGS AND ALLOWED VALUES (FOR THE VARIOUS FIELDS REQUIRED BY THE INSTRUCTION FORMAT)

Figure 4-2. Instruction Description Format

ABCD — Add Decimal with Extend

Instruction Fields:

Register Rx field — Specifies the destination register:
If R/M = 0, specifies a data register
If R/M = 1, specifies an address register for the predecrement addressing mode

R/M field — Specifies the operand addressing mode:
0 — the operation is data register to data register
1 — the operation is memory to memory

Register Ry field — Specifies the source register:
If R/M = 0, specifies a data register
If R/M = 1, specifies an address register for the predecrement addressing mode

---

ADD — Add

Operation: Source + Destination → Destination

Assembler Syntax:
ADD (ea),Dn
ADD Dn, (ea)

Attributes: Size = (Byte, Word, Long)

Description: Adds the source operand to the destination operand using binary addition, and stores the result in the destination location. The size of the operation may be specified as byte, word, or long. The mode of the instruction indicates which operand is the source and which is the destination as well as the operand size.

Condition Codes:

X	N	Z	V	C
*	*	*	*	*

X Set the same as the carry bit.
N Set if the result is negative. Cleared otherwise.
Z Set if the result is zero. Cleared otherwise.
V Set if an overflow is generated. Cleared otherwise.
C Set if a carry is generated. Cleared otherwise.

Instruction Format:

15	14	13	12	11	10	9	8	7	6	5	4	3	2	1	0
1	1	0	1	REGISTER			OPMODE			EFFECTIVE ADDRESS					
										MODE			REGISTER		

Instruction Fields:

Register field — Specifies any of the eight data registers.

Opmode field:

	Byte	Word	Long	Operation
	000	001	010	(ea) + (Dn) → (n)
	100	101	110	(Dn) + (ea) → (ea)

Add Address

Operation: Source + Destination → Destination

Assembler Syntax: ADDA (ea), An

Attributes: Size = (Word, Long)

Description: Adds the source operand to the destination address register, and stores the result in the address register. The size of the operation may be specified as word or long. The entire destination address register is used regardless of the operation size.

Condition Codes: Not affected.

Instruction Format:

15	14	13	12	11	10	9	8	7	6	5	4	3	2	1	0
1	1	0	1	REGISTER			OPMODE			EFFECTIVE ADDRESS					
										MODE			REGISTER		

Instruction Fields:

Register field — Specifies any of the eight address registers. This is always the destination.

Opmode field — Specifies the size of the operation:
011 — Word operation. The source operand is sign-extended to a long operand and the operation is performed on the address register using all 32 bits.
111 — Long operation.

Effective Address field — Specifies the source operand. All addressing modes are allowed as shown:

Addressing Mode	Mode	Register	Addressing Mode	Mode	Register
Dn	000	reg. number:Dn	$(xxx).W$	111	000
An	001	reg. number:An	$(xxx).L$	111	001
(An)	010	reg. number:An	#(data)	111	100
(An)+	011	reg. number:An			
-(An)	100	reg. number:An			
(d_{16},An)	101	reg. number:An	(d_{16},PC)	111	010
(d_8,An,Xn)	110	reg. number:An	(d_8,PC,Xn)	111	011
(bd,An,Xn)	110	reg. number:An	(bd,PC,Xn)	111	011

Effective Address Field — Determines addressing mode:

a. If the location specified is a source operand, all addressing modes are allowed as shown:

Addressing Mode	Mode	Register	Addressing Mode	Mode	Register
Dn	000	reg. number:Dn	$(xxx).W$	111	000
An*	001	reg. number:An	$(xxx).L$	111	001
(An)	010	reg. number:An	#(data)	111	100
(An)+	011	reg. number:An			
-(An)	100	reg. number:An			
(d_{16},An)	101	reg. number:An	(d_{16},PC)	111	010
(d_8,An,Xn)	110	reg. number:An	(d_8,PC,Xn)	111	011
(bd,An,Xn)	110	reg. number:An	(bd,PC,Xn)	111	011

*Word and Long Only

b. If the location specified is a destination operand, only memory alterable addressing modes are allowed as shown:

Addressing Mode	Mode	Register	Addressing Mode	Mode	Register
Dn	—	—	$(xxx).W$	111	000
An	—	—	$(xxx).L$	111	001
(An)	010	reg. number:An	#(data)	—	—
(An)+	011	reg. number:An			
-(An)	100	reg. number:An			
(d_{16},An)	101	reg. number:An	(d_{16},PC)	—	—
(d_8,An,Xn)	110	reg. number:An	(d_8,PC,Xn)	—	—
(bd,An,Xn)	110	reg. number:An	(bd,PC,Xn)	—	—

NOTES:
1. The Dn mode is used when the destination is a data register; the destination (ea) mode is invalid for a data register.
2. ADDA is used when the destination is an address register. ADDI and ADDQ are used when the source is immediate data. Most assemblers automatically make this distinction.

Effective Address field — Specifies the destination operand.
Only data alterable addressing modes are allowed as shown:

Addressing Mode	Mode	Register	Addressing Mode	Mode	Register
Dn	000	reg. number:Dn	(xxx).W	111	000
An	—	—	(xxx).L	111	001
(An)	010	reg. number:An	#(data)	—	—
(An)+	011	reg. number:An			
-(An)	100	reg. number:An			
(d16,An)	101	reg. number:An	(d16,PC)	—	—
(d8,An,Xn)	110	reg. number:An	(d8,PC,Xn)	—	—
(bd,An,Xn)	110	reg. number:An	(bd,PC,Xn)	—	—

Immediate field — (Data immediately following the instruction):
If size = 00, the data is the low-order byte of the immediate word.
If size = 01, the data is the entire immediate word.
If size = 10, the data is the next two immediate words.

Add Immediate

Operation: Immediate Data + Destination ◆ Destination

**Assembler
Syntax:** ADDI #(data),(ea)

Attributes: Size = (Byte, Word, Long)

Description: Adds the immediate data to the destination operand, and stores the result in the destination location. The size of the operation may be specified as byte, word, or long. The size of the immediate data matches the operation size.

Condition Codes:

X	N	Z	V	C
*	*	*	*	*

X   Set the same as the carry bit.
N   Set if the result is negative. Cleared otherwise.
Z   Set if the result is zero. Cleared otherwise.
V   Set if an overflow is generated. Cleared otherwise.
C   Set if a carry is generated. Cleared otherwise.

Instruction Format:

15	14	13	12	11	10	9	8	7	6	5	4	3	2	1	0
0	0	0	0	0	1	1	0	SIZE			EFFECTIVE ADDRESS				
											MODE		REGISTER		
WORD DATA (16 BITS)								BYTE DATA (8 BITS)							
LONG DATA (32 BITS)															

Instruction Fields:
Size field — Specifies the size of the operation:
00 — Byte operation
01 — Word operation
10 — Long operation

ADDQ   Add Quick   ADDQ

Operation: Immediate Data + Destination ➧ Destination

**Assembler
Syntax:**   ADDQ #⟨data⟩,⟨ea⟩

Attributes: Size = (Byte, Word, Long)

Description: Adds an immediate value of one to eight to the operand at the destination location. The size of the operation may be specified as byte, word, or long. Word and long operations are also allowed on the address registers. When adding to address registers, the condition codes are not altered, and the entire destination address register is used regardless of the operation size.

Condition Codes:

X	N	Z	V	C
*	*	*	*	*

X — Set the same as the carry bit.
N — Set if the result is negative. Cleared otherwise.
Z — Set if the result is zero. Cleared otherwise.
V — Set if an overflow occurs. Cleared otherwise.
C — Set if a carry occurs. Cleared otherwise.

The condition codes are not affected when the destination is an address register.

Instruction Format:

15	14	13	12	11	10	9	8	7	6	5	4	3	2	1	0
0	1	0	1		DATA		0		SIZE		EFFECTIVE ADDRESS				
											MODE			REGISTER	

Instruction Fields:

Data field — Three bits of immediate data, 7–0 (with the immediate value 0 representing a value of 8).
Size field — Specifies the size of the operation:
00 — Byte operation
01 — Word operation
10 — Long operation

ADDQ   Add Quick   ADDQ

Effective Address field — Specifies the destination location.
Only alterable addressing modes are allowed as shown:

Addressing Mode	Mode	Register	Addressing Mode	Mode	Register
Dn	000	reg. number:Dn	(xxx).W	111	000
An*	001	reg. number:An	(xxx).L	111	001
(An)	010	reg. number:An	#⟨data⟩	—	—
(An)+	011	reg. number:An			
–(An)	100	reg. number:An			
(d16,An)	101	reg. number:An	(d16,PC)	—	—
(d8,An,Xn)	110	reg. number:An	(d8,PC,Xn)	—	—
(bd,An,Xn)	110	reg. number:An	(bd,PC,Xn)	—	—

*Word and Long Only

CPU 32 Instruction Set   719

ADDX   ADDX

Add Extended

Operation: Source + Destination + X ⯈ Destination

Assembler
Syntax: ADDX Dy,Dx
ADDX −(Ay),−(Ax)

Attributes: Size = (Byte, Word, Long)

Description: Adds the source operand to the destination operand along with the extend bit and stores the result in the destination location. The operands can be addressed in two different ways:

1. Data register to data register: The data registers specified in the instruction contain the operands.
2. Memory to memory: The address registers specified in the instruction address the operands using the predecrement addressing mode.

The size of the operation can be specified as byte, word, or long.

Condition Codes:

X	N	Z	V	C
*	*	*	*	*

X Set the same as the carry bit.
N Set if the result is negative. Cleared otherwise.
Z Cleared if the result is nonzero. Unchanged otherwise.
V Set if an overflow occurs. Cleared otherwise.
C Set if a carry is generated. Cleared otherwise.

NOTE

Normally the Z condition code bit is set via programming before the start of an operation. This allows successful tests for zero results upon completion of multiple-precision operations.

Instruction Format:

15	14	13	12	11	10	9	8	7	6	5	4	3	2	1	0
1	1	0	1		REGISTER Rx		1		SIZE	0	0	R/M		REGISTER Ry	

ADDX   ADDX

Add Extended

Instruction Fields:

Register Rx field — Specifies the destination register:
If R/M = 0, specifies a data register.
If R/M = 1, specifies an address register for the predecrement addressing mode.

Size field — Specifies the size of the operation:
00 — Byte operation
01 — Word operation
10 — Long operation

R/M field — Specifies the operand address mode:
0 — The operation is data register to data register.
1 — The operation is memory to memory.

Register Ry field — Specifies the source register:
If R/M = 0, specifies a data register.
If R/M = 1, specifies an address register for the predecrement addressing mode.

AND Logical

Operation: Source·∧Destination → Destination

Assembler Syntax: AND (ea),Dn
AND Dn,(ea)

Attributes: Size = (Byte, Word, Long)

Description: Performs an AND operation of the source operand with the destination operand and stores the result in the destination location. The size of the operation can be specified as byte, word, or long. The contents of an address register may not be used as an operand.

Condition Codes:

X	N	Z	V	C
—	*	*	0	0

X Not affected.
N Set if the most significant bit of the result is set. Cleared otherwise.
Z Set if the result is zero. Cleared otherwise.
V Always cleared.
C Always cleared.

Instruction Format:

15	14	13	12	11	10	9	8	7	6	5	4	3	2	1	0
1	0	0	1		REGISTER			OPMODE			EFFECTIVE ADDRESS				
											MODE			REGISTER	

Instruction Fields:

Register field — Specifies any of the eight data registers.

Opmode field:

Byte	Word	Long	Operation
000	001	010	((ea))∧((Dn)) → Dn
100	101	110	((Dn))∧((ea)) → ea

AND Logical

Effective Address field — Determines addressing mode:
If the location specified is a source operand only data addressing modes are allowed as shown:

Addressing Mode	Mode	Register		Addressing Mode	Mode	Register
Dn	000	reg. number:Dn		(xxx).W	111	000
An	—	—		(xxx).L	111	001
(An)	010	reg. number:An		#(data)	111	100
(An)+	011	reg. number:An				
-(An)	100	reg. number:An				
(d16,An)	101	reg. number:An		(d16,PC)	111	010
(d8,An,Xn)	110	reg. number:An		(d8,PC,Xn)	111	011
(bd,An,Xn)	110	reg. number:An		(bd,PC,Xn)	111	011

If the location specified is a destination operand only memory alterable addressing modes are allowed as shown:

Addressing Mode	Mode	Register		Addressing Mode	Mode	Register
Dn	—	—		(xxx).W	111	000
An	—	—		(xxx).L	111	001
(An)	010	reg. number:An		#(data)	—	—
(An)+	011	reg. number:An				
-(An)	100	reg. number:An				
(d16,An)	101	reg. number:An		(d16,PC)	—	—
(d8,An,Xn)	110	reg. number:An		(d8,PC,Xn)	—	—
(bd,An,Xn)	110	reg. number:An		(bd,PC,Xn)	—	—

NOTES:
1. The Dn mode is used when the destination is a data register; the destination (ea) mode is invalid for a data register.
2. Most assemblers use ANDI when the source is immediate data.

ANDI AND Immediate ANDI

Operation: Immediate Data∧Destination ➡ Destination

Assembler Syntax: ANDI #(data),(ea)

Attributes: Size = (Byte, Word, Long)

Description: Performs an AND operation of the immediate data with the destination operand and stores the result in the destination location. The size of the operation can be specified as byte, word, or long. The size of the immediate data matches the operation size.

Condition Codes:

X	N	Z	V	C
—	*	*	0	0

X Not affected.
N Set if the most significant bit of the result is set. Cleared otherwise.
Z Set if the result is zero. Cleared otherwise.
V Always cleared.
C Always cleared.

Instruction Format:

15	14	13	12	11	10	9	8	7	6	5	4	3	2	1	0
0	0	0	0	0	0	1	0	SIZE		EFFECTIVE ADDRESS MODE			REGISTER		
WORD DATA (16 BITS)															
LONG DATA (32 BITS)															
BYTE DATA (8 BITS)															

Instruction Fields:
Size field — Specifies the size of the operation:
00 — Byte operation
01 — Word operation
10 — Long operation

ANDI AND Immediate ANDI

Effective Address field — Specifies the destination operand.
Only data alterable addressing modes are allowed as shown:

Addressing Mode	Mode	Register	Addressing Mode	Mode	Register
Dn	000	reg. number:Dn	(xxx).W	111	000
An	—	—	(xxx).L	111	001
(An)	010	reg. number:An	#(data)	—	—
(An)+	011	reg. number:An			
-(An)	100	reg. number:An			
(d16,An)	101	reg. number:An	(d16,PC)	—	—
(d8,An,Xn)	110	reg. number:An	(d8,PC,Xn)	—	—
(bd,An,Xn)	110	reg. number:An	(bd,PC,Xn)	—	—

Immediate field — (Data immediately following the instruction):
If size = 00, the data is the low-order byte of the immediate word.
If size = 01, the data is the entire immediate word.
If size = 10, the data is the next two immediate words.

Appendix IV

ANDI to SR

AND Immediate to the Status Register
(Privileged Instruction)

Operation: If supervisor state
then Source∧SR ⬦ SR
else TRAP

**Assembler
Syntax:** ANDI #⟨data⟩,SR

Attributes: Size = (Word)

Description: Performs an AND operation of the immediate operand with the contents of the status register and stores the result in the status register. All implemented bits of the status register are affected.

Condition Codes:

X	N	Z	V	C
*	*	*	*	*

X — Cleared if bit 4 of immediate operand is zero. Unchanged otherwise.
N — Cleared if bit 3 of immediate operand is zero. Unchanged otherwise.
Z — Cleared if bit 2 of immediate operand is zero. Unchanged otherwise.
V — Cleared if bit 1 of immediate operand is zero. Unchanged otherwise.
C — Cleared if bit 0 of immediate operand is zero. Unchanged otherwise.

Instruction Format:

15	14	13	12	11	10	9	8	7	6	5	4	3	2	1	0
0	0	0	0	0	0	1	0	0	1	1	1	1	1	0	0
							WORD DATA (16 BITS)								

ANDI to CCR

AND Immediate to Condition Codes

Operation: Source∧CCR ⬦ CCR

**Assembler
Syntax:** ANDI #⟨data⟩,CCR

Attributes: Size = (Byte)

Description: Performs an AND operation of the immediate operand with the condition codes and stores the result in the low-order byte of the status register.

Condition Codes:

X	N	Z	V	C
*	*	*	*	*

X — Cleared if bit 4 of immediate operand is zero. Unchanged otherwise.
N — Cleared if bit 3 of immediate operand is zero. Unchanged otherwise.
Z — Cleared if bit 2 of immediate operand is zero. Unchanged otherwise.
V — Cleared if bit 1 of immediate operand is zero. Unchanged otherwise.
C — Cleared if bit 0 of immediate operand is zero. Unchanged otherwise.

Instruction Format:

15	14	13	12	11	10	9	8	7	6	5	4	3	2	1	0
0	0	0	0	0	0	0	0	0	0	1	1	1	1	0	0
							BYTE DATA (8 BITS)								

ASL, ASR — Arithmetic Shift

Operation: Destination Shifted by ⟨count⟩ → Destination

Assembler Syntax:
ASd Dx,Dy
ASd #⟨data⟩,Dy
ASd ⟨ea⟩
where d is direction, L or R

Attributes: Size = (Byte, Word, Long)

Description: Arithmetically shifts the bits of the operand in the direction (L or R) specified. The carry bit receives the last bit shifted out of the operand. The shift count for the shifting of a register may be specified in two different ways:
1. Immediate — The shift count is specified in the instruction (shift range, 8–1).
2. Register — The shift count is the value in the data register specified in instruction modulo 64.

The size of the operation can be specified as byte, word, or long. An operand in memory can be shifted one bit only, and the operand size is restricted to a word.

For ASL, the operand is shifted left; the number of positions shifted is the shift count. Bits shifted out of the high-order bit go to both the carry and the extend bits; zeros are shifted into the low-order bit. The overflow bit indicates if any sign changes occur during the shift.

ASL:

For ASR, the operand is shifted right; the number of positions shifted is the shift count. Bits shifted out of the low-order bit go to both the carry and the extend bits; the sign-bit (MSB) is shifted into the high-order bit.

ASR:

ASL, ASR — Arithmetic Shift

Condition Codes:

X	N	Z	V	C
*	*	*	*	*

X Set according to the last bit shifted out of the operand. Unaffected for a shift count of zero.
N Set if the most significant bit of the result is set. Cleared otherwise.
Z Set if the result is zero. Cleared otherwise.
V Set if the most significant bit is changed at any time during the shift operation. Cleared otherwise.
C Set according to the last bit shifted out of the operand. Cleared for a shift count of zero.

Instruction Format (Register Shifts):

15	14	13	12	11	10	9	8	7	6	5	4	3	2	1	0
1	1	1	0	COUNT/REGISTER			dr	SIZE		i/r	0	0	REGISTER		

Instruction Fields (Register Shifts):

Count/Register field — Specifies shift count or register that contains the shift count:
If i/r = 0, this field contains the shift count. The values one to seven represent counts of one to seven; value of zero represents a count of eight.
If i/r = 1, this field specifies the data register that contains the shift count (modulo 64).

dr field — Specifies the direction of the shift:
0 — Shift right
1 — Shift left

Size field — Specifies the size of the operation:
00 — Byte operation
01 — Word operation
10 — Long operation

i/r field:
If i/r = 0, specifies immediate shift count.
If i/r = 1, specifies register shift count.

Register field — Specifies a data register to be shifted.

ASL, ASR   Arithmetic Shift   ASL, ASR

Instruction Format (Memory Shifts):

15	14	13	12	11	10	9	8	7	6	5	4	3	2	1	0
											EFFECTIVE ADDRESS				
											MODE			REGISTER	
1	1	0	0	0	0	0	dr	1	1						

Instruction Fields (Memory Shifts):

dr field — Specifies the direction of the shift:
0 — Shift right
1 — Shift left

Effective Address field — Specifies the operand to be shifted.
Only memory alterable addressing modes are allowed as shown:

Addressing Mode	Mode	Register	Addressing Mode	Mode	Register
Dn	—	—	(xxx).W	111	000
An	—	—	(xxx).L	111	001
(An)	010	reg. number:An	#(data)	—	—
(An)+	011	reg. number:An			
–(An)	100	reg. number:An	(d₁₆,PC)	—	—
(d₁₆,An)	101	reg. number:An	(d₈,PC,Xn)	—	—
(d₈,An,Xn)	110	reg. number:An	(bd,PC,Xn)	—	—
(bd,An,Xn)	110	reg. number:An			

Bcc   Branch Conditionally   Bcc

Operation: If (condition true) then PC + d ♦ PC

Assembler
Syntax: Bcc (label)

Attributes: Size = (Byte, Word, Long)

Description: If the specified condition is true, program execution continues at location (PC) + displacement. The PC contains the address of the instruction word of the Bcc instruction plus two. The displacement is a twos complement integer that represents the relative distance in bytes from the current PC to the destination PC. If the 8-bit displacement field in the instruction word is zero, a 16-bit displacement (the word immediately following the instruction) is used. If the 8-bit displacement field in the instruction word is all ones ($FF), the 32-bit displacement (long word immediately following the instruction) is used. Condition code cc specifies one of the following conditions:

CC	carry clear	0100	$\overline{C}$	LS	low or same	0011	$C + Z$
CS	carry set	0101	C	LT	less than	1101	$N \cdot \overline{V} + \overline{N} \cdot V$
EQ	equal	0111	Z	MI	minus	1011	N
GE	greater or equal	1100	$N \cdot V + \overline{N} \cdot \overline{V}$	NE	not equal	0110	$\overline{Z}$
GT	greater than	1110	$N \cdot V \cdot \overline{Z} + \overline{N} \cdot \overline{V} \cdot \overline{Z}$	PL	plus	1010	$\overline{N}$
HI	high	0010	$\overline{C} \cdot \overline{Z}$	VC	overflow clear	1000	$\overline{V}$
LE	less or equal	1111	$Z + N \cdot \overline{V} + \overline{N} \cdot V$	VS	overflow set	1001	V

Condition Codes:
Not affected.

Instruction Format:

15	14	13	12	11	10	9	8	7	6	5	4	3	2	1	0
0	1	1	0		CONDITION						8-BIT DISPLACEMENT				

16-BIT DISPLACEMENT IF 8-BIT DISPLACEMENT = $00
32-BIT DISPLACEMENT IF 8-BIT DISPLACEMENT = $FF

BCHG
BCHG   Test a Bit and Change   BCHG

Operation: ~((number) of Destination) → Z;
             ~((number) of Destination) → (bit number) of Destination

Assembler   BCHG Dn,(ea)
Syntax: BCHG #(data),(ea)

Attributes: Size = (Byte, Long)

Description: Tests a bit in the destination operand and sets the Z condition code appropriately, then inverts the specified bit in the destination. When the destination is a data register, any of the 32 bits can be specified by the modulo 32-bit number. When the destination is a memory location, the operation is a byte operation, and the bit number is modulo 8. In all cases, bit zero refers to the least significant bit. The bit number for this operation may be specified in either of two ways:

   1. Immediate — The bit number is specified in a second word of the instruction.
   2. Register — The specified data register contains the bit number.

Condition Codes:

X	N	Z	V	C
–	–	*	–	–

X   Not affected.
N   Not affected.
Z   Set if the bit tested is zero. Cleared otherwise.
V   Not affected.
C   Not affected.

Instruction Format (Bit Number Dynamic, specified in a register):

15	14	13	12	11	10	9	8	7	6	5	4	3	2	1	0
0	0	0	0		REGISTER		1	0	1		MODE			REGISTER	
												EFFECTIVE ADDRESS			

Bcc
Bcc   Branch Conditionally   Bcc

Instruction Fields:

Condition field — The binary code for one of the conditions listed in the table.

8-Bit Displacement field — Twos complement integer specifying the number of bytes between the branch instruction and the next instruction to be executed if the condition is met.

16-Bit Displacement field — Used for the displacement when the 8-bit displacement field contains $00.

32-Bit Displacement field — Used for the displacement when the 8-bit displacement field contains $FF.

NOTE

A branch to the immediately following instruction automatically uses the 16-bit displacement format because the 8-bit displacement field contains $00 (zero offset).

Test a Bit and Clear

Operation: ~((bit number) of Destination) → Z;
0 → (bit number) of Destination

**Assembler
Syntax:** BCLR Dn,(ea)
BCLR #(data),(ea)

Attributes: Size = (Byte, Long)

Description: Tests a bit in the destination operand and sets the Z condition code appropriately, then clears the specified bit in the destination. When a data register is the destination, any of the 32 bits can be specified by a modulo 32-bit number. When a memory location is the destination, the operation is a byte operation, and the bit number is modulo 8. In all cases, bit zero refers to the least significant bit. The bit number for this operation can be specified in either of two ways:

1. Immediate — The bit number is specified in a second word of the instruction.
2. Register — The specified data register contains the bit number.

Condition Codes:

X	N	Z	V	C
—	—	*	—	—

X Not affected.
N Not affected.
Z Set if the bit tested is zero. Cleared otherwise.
V Not affected.
C Not affected.

Instruction Format (Bit Number Dynamic, specified in a register):

15	14	13	12	11	10	9	8	7	6	5	4	3	2	1	0
0	0	0	0		REGISTER		1	1	0		EFFECTIVE ADDRESS			REGISTER	
											MODE				

Test a Bit and Change

Instruction Fields (Bit Number Dynamic):
Register field — Specifies the data register that contains the bit number.
Effective Address field — Specifies the destination location. Only data alterable addressing modes are allowed as shown:

Addressing Mode	Mode	Register		Addressing Mode	Mode	Register
Dn*	000	reg. number:Dn		(xxx).W	111	000
An	—	—		(xxx).L	111	001
(An)	010	reg. number:An		#(data)	—	—
(An)+	011	reg. number:An				
−(An)	100	reg. number:An		(d16,PC)	—	—
(d16,An)	101	reg. number:An		(d8,PC,Xn)	—	—
(d8,An,Xn)	110	reg. number:An		(bd,PC,Xn)	—	—
(bd,An,Xn)	110	reg. number:An				

*Long only; all others are byte only.

Instruction Format (Bit Number Static, specified as immediate data):

15	14	13	12	11	10	9	8	7	6	5	4	3	2	1	0
0	0	0	0	1	0	0	0	0	0	1		EFFECTIVE ADDRESS			REGISTER
											MODE				
0	0	0	0	0	0	0	0				BIT NUMBER				

Instruction Fields (Bit Number Static):
Effective Address field — Specifies the destination location. Only data alterable addressing modes are allowed as shown:

Addressing Mode	Mode	Register		Addressing Mode	Mode	Register
Dn*	000	reg. number:Dn		(xxx).W	111	000
An	—	—		(xxx).L	111	001
(An)	010	reg. number:An		#(data)	—	—
(An)+	011	reg. number:An				
−(An)	100	reg. number:An		(d16,PC)	—	—
(d16,An)	101	reg. number:An		(d8,PC,Xn)	—	—
(d8,An,Xn)	110	reg. number:An		(bd,PC,Xn)	—	—
(bd,An,Xn)	110	reg. number:An				

*Long only; all others are byte only.

Bit Number field — Specifies the bit number.

BGND

Enter Background Mode

BGND

Operation:
IF (background mode enabled) THEN
    Enter Background Mode
ELSE
    Format/Vector offset ♦ – (SSP)
    PC ♦ – (SSP)
    SR ♦ – (SSP)
    (Vector) ♦ PC

Assembler Syntax: BGND

Attributes: Size = (Unsized)

Description: The processor suspends instruction execution and enters background mode (if enabled). The freeze output is asserted to acknowledge entrance into background mode. Upon exiting background mode, instruction execution continues with the instruction pointed to by the current program counter.

If background mode is not enabled, the processor initiates illegal instruction exception processing. The vector number is generated to reference the illegal instruction exception vector. Background mode is covered in **SECTION 7 DEVELOPMENT SUPPORT**.

Condition Codes:

X	N	Z	V	C
–	–	–	–	–

X Not affected
N Not affected
Z Not affected
V Not affected
C Not affected

Instruction Format:

15	14	13	12	11	10	9	8	7	6	5	4	3	2	1	0
0	1	0	0	1	0	1	0	1	1	1	1	1	0	1	0

BCLR

Test a Bit and Clear

BCLR

Instruction Fields (Bit Number Dynamic):
Register field — Specifies the data register that contains the bit number.
Effective Address field — Specifies the destination location.
Only data alterable addressing modes are allowed as shown:

Addressing Mode	Mode	Register	Addressing Mode	Mode	Register
Dn*	000	reg. number:Dn	(xxx).W	111	000
An	–	–	(xxx).L	111	001
(An)	010	reg. number:An	#(data)	–	–
(An)+	011	reg. number:An			
–(An)	100	reg. number:An			
(d16,An)	101	reg. number:An	(d16,PC)	–	–
(d8,An,Xn)	110	reg. number:An	(d8,PC,Xn)	–	–
(bd,An,Xn)	110	reg. number:An	(bd,PC,Xn)	–	–

*Long only; all others are byte only.

Instruction Format (Bit Number Static, specified as immediate data):

15	14	13	12	11	10	9	8	7	6	5	4	3	2	1	0
0	0	0	0	1	0	0	0	1	0	MODE			REGISTER		
0	0	0	0	0	0	0	0					BIT NUMBER			

(EFFECTIVE ADDRESS: MODE | REGISTER)

Instruction Fields (Bit Number Static):
Effective Address field — Specifies the destination location.
Only data alterable addressing modes are allowed as shown:

Addressing Mode	Mode	Register	Addressing Mode	Mode	Register
Dn*	000	reg. number:Dn	(xxx).W	111	000
An	–	–	(xxx).L	111	001
(An)	010	reg. number:An	#(data)	–	–
(An)+	011	reg. number:An			
–(An)	100	reg. number:An			
(d16,An)	101	reg. number:An	(d16,PC)	–	–
(d8,An,Xn)	110	reg. number:An	(d8,PC,Xn)	–	–
(bd,An,Xn)	110	reg. number:An	(bd,PC,Xn)	–	–

*Long only; all others are byte only.

Bit Number field — Specifies the bit number.

BRA

BRA — Branch Always

Operation: PC + d ♦ PC

Assembler Syntax: BRA ⟨label⟩

Attributes: Size = (Byte, Word, Long)

Description: Program execution continues at location (PC) + displacement. The PC contains the address of the instruction word of the BRA instruction plus two. The displacement is a twos complement integer that represents the relative distance in bytes from the current PC to the destination PC. If the 8-bit displacement field in the instruction word is zero, a 16-bit displacement (the word immediately following the instruction) is used. If the 8-bit displacement field in the instruction word is all ones ($FF), the 32-bit displacement (long word immediately following the instruction) is used.

Condition Codes:
Not affected.

Instruction Format:

15	14	13	12	11	10	9	8	7	6	5	4	3	2	1	0
0	1	1	0	0	0	0	0				8-BIT DISPLACEMENT				

16-BIT DISPLACEMENT IF 8-BIT DISPLACEMENT = $00

32-BIT DISPLACEMENT IF 8-BIT DISPLACEMENT = $FF

Instruction Fields:

8-Bit Displacement field — Twos complement integer specifying the number of bytes between the branch instruction and the next instruction to be executed.

16-Bit Displacement field — Used for a larger displacement when the 8-bit displacement is equal to $00.

32-Bit Displacement field — Used for a larger displacement when the 8-bit displacement is equal to $FF.

NOTE

A branch to the immediately following instruction automatically uses the 16-bit displacement format because the 8-bit displacement field contains $00 (zero offset).

BKPT

BKPT — Breakpoint

Operation: Run breakpoint acknowledge cycle
If acknowledged
then execute returned operation word
else TRAP as illegal instruction

Assembler Syntax: BKPT #⟨data⟩

Attributes: Unsized

Description: Executes a breakpoint acknowledge bus cycle with the immediate data (value 0–7) on bits 2–4 of the address bus and zeros on bits 0 and 1 of the address bus.

The breakpoint acknowledge cycle accesses the CPU space, addressing type 0, and provides the breakpoint number specified by the instruction on address lines A4–A2. If the external hardware terminates the cycle with DSACKxs the data on the bus (an instruction word) is inserted into the instruction pipe and is executed after the breakpoint instruction. The breakpoint instruction requires a word to be transferred so if the first bus cycle accesses an 8-bit port, a second cycle is required. If the external logic terminates the breakpoint acknowledge cycle with BERR (i.e., no instruction word available) the processor takes an illegal instruction exception. Refer to **7.2.5 Software Breakpoints** for details of breakpoint operation.

This instruction supports breakpoints for debug monitors and real-time hardware emulators. The exact operation performed by the instruction is implementation-dependent. Typically, this instruction replaces an instruction in a program; that instruction is returned by the breakpoint acknowledge cycle.

Condition Codes:
Not affected.

Instruction Format:

15	14	13	12	11	10	9	8	7	6	5	4	3	2	1	0
0	1	0	0	1	0	0	0	0	1	0	0	1		VECTOR	

Instruction Fields:
Vector field — Contains the immediate data, a value in the range of 0–7. This is the breakpoint number.

Instruction Fields (Bit Number Dynamic):

Register field — Specifies the data register that contains the bit number.

Effective Address field — Specifies the destination location. Only data alterable addressing modes are allowed as shown:

Addressing Mode	Mode	Register
Dn*	000	reg. number:Dn
An	—	—
(An)	010	reg. number:An
(An)+	011	reg. number:An
−(An)	100	reg. number:An
(d$_{16}$,An)	101	reg. number:An
(d$_8$,An,Xn)	110	reg. number:An
(bd,An,Xn)	110	reg. number:An

Addressing Mode	Mode	Register
(xxx).W	111	000
(xxx).L	111	001
#(data)	—	—
(d$_{16}$,PC)	—	—
(d$_8$,PC,Xn)	—	—
(bd,PC,Xn)	—	—

*Long only; all others are byte only.

Instruction Format (Bit Number Static, specified as immediate data):

15	14	13	12	11	10	9	8	7	6	5	4	3	2	1	0
0	0	0	0	1	0	0	0	1	1	\multicolumn{3}{}{MODE}			\multicolumn{3}{}{REGISTER}		
0	0	0	0	0	0	0	0					BIT NUMBER			

(EFFECTIVE ADDRESS = MODE | REGISTER)

Instruction Fields (Bit Number Static):

Effective Address field — Specifies the destination location. Only data alterable addressing modes are allowed as shown:

Addressing Mode	Mode	Register
Dn*	000	reg. number:Dn
An	—	—
(An)	010	reg. number:An
(An)+	011	reg. number:An
−(An)	100	reg. number:An
(d$_{16}$,An)	101	reg. number:An
(d$_8$,An,Xn)	110	reg. number:An
(bd,An,Xn)	110	reg. number:An

Addressing Mode	Mode	Register
(xxx).W	111	000
(xxx).L	111	001
#(data)	—	—
(d$_{16}$,PC)	—	—
(d$_8$,PC,Xn)	—	—
(bd,PC,Xn)	—	—

*Long only; all others are byte only.

Bit Number field — Specifies the bit number.

BSET

Test a Bit and Set

Operation: ~((bit number) of Destination) → Z;
1 → (bit number) of Destination

Assembler Syntax: BSET Dn,(ea)
BSET #(data),(ea)

Attributes: Size = (Byte, Long)

Description: Tests a bit in the destination operand and sets the Z condition code appropriately. Then sets the specified bit in the destination operand. When a data register is the destination, any of the 32 bits can be specified by a modulo 32-bit number. When a memory location is the destination, the operation is a byte operation, and the bit number is modulo 8. In all cases, bit zero refers to the least significant bit. The bit number for this operation can be specified in either of two ways:
1. Immediate — The bit number is specified in the second word of the instruction.
2. Register — The specified data register contains the bit number.

Condition Codes:

X	N	Z	V	C
—	—	*	—	—

X Not affected.
N Not affected.
Z Set if the bit tested is zero. Cleared otherwise.
V Not affected.
C Not affected.

Instruction Format (Bit Number Dynamic, specified in a register):

15	14	13	12	11	10	9	8	7	6	5	4	3	2	1	0
0	0	0	0	\multicolumn{3}{}{REGISTER}			1	1	1	\multicolumn{3}{}{MODE}			\multicolumn{3}{}{REGISTER}		

(EFFECTIVE ADDRESS = MODE | REGISTER)

BTST   Test a Bit   BTST

Operation: −((bit number) of Destination) → Z;

Assembler Syntax:
BTST Dn,(ea)
BTST #(data),(ea)

Attributes: Size = (Byte, Long)

Description: Tests a bit in the destination operand and sets the Z condition code appropriately. When a data register is the destination, any of the 32 bits can be specified by a modulo 32 bit number. When a memory location is the destination, the operation is a byte operation, and the bit number is modulo 8. In all cases, bit zero refers to the least significant bit. The bit number for this operation can be specified in either of two ways:
1. Immediate — The bit number is specified in a second word of the instruction.
2. Register — The specified data register contains the bit number.

Condition Codes:

X	N	Z	V	C
–	–	*	–	–

X Not affected.
N Not affected.
Z Set if the bit tested is zero. Cleared otherwise.
V Not affected.
C Not affected.

Instruction Format (Bit Number Dynamic, specified in a register):

15	14	13	12	11	10	9	8	7	6	5	4	3	2	1	0
0	0	0	0	REGISTER			1	0	0	EFFECTIVE ADDRESS					

EFFECTIVE ADDRESS: MODE | REGISTER

BSR   Branch to Subroutine   BSR

Operation: SP − 4 → SP; PC → (SP); PC + d → PC

Assembler Syntax: BSR (label)

Attributes: Size = (Byte, Word, Long)

Description: Pushes the long word address of the instruction immediately following the BSR instruction onto the system stack. The PC contains the address of the instruction word plus two. Program execution then continues at location (PC) + displacement. The displacement is a twos complement integer that represents the relative distance in bytes from the current PC to the destination PC. If the 8-bit displacement field in the instruction word is zero, a 16-bit displacement (the word immediately following the instruction) is used. If the 8-bit displacement field in the instruction word is all ones ($FF), the 32-bit displacement (long word immediately following the instruction) is used.

Condition Codes:
Not affected.

Instruction Format:

15	14	13	12	11	10	9	8	7	6	5	4	3	2	1	0
0	1	1	0	0	0	0	1	8-BIT DISPLACEMENT							

16-BIT DISPLACEMENT IF 8-BIT DISPLACEMENT = $00

32-BIT DISPLACEMENT IF 8-BIT DISPLACEMENT = $FF

Instruction Fields:

8-Bit Displacement field — Twos complement integer specifying the number of bytes between the branch instruction and the next instruction to be executed.

16-Bit Displacement field — Used for a larger displacement when the 8-bit displacement is equal to $00.

32-Bit Displacement field — Used for a larger displacement when the 8-bit displacement is equal to $FF.

NOTE

A branch to the immediately following instruction automatically uses the 16-bit displacement format because the 8-bit displacement field contains $00 (zero offset).

BTST

Test a Bit

BTST

Instruction Fields (Bit Number Dynamic):

Register field — Specifies the data register that contains the bit number.
Effective Address field — Specifies the destination location. Only data addressing modes are allowed as shown:

Addressing Mode	Mode	Register
Dn*	000	reg. number:Dn
An	–	–
(An)	010	reg. number:An
(An)+	011	reg. number:An
–(An)	100	reg. number:An
(d16,An)	101	reg. number:An
(d8,An,Xn)	110	reg. number:An
(bd,An,Xn)	110	reg. number:An

Addressing Mode	Mode	Register
(xxx).W	111	000
(xxx).L	111	001
#(data)	111	100
(d16,PC)	111	010
(d8,PC,Xn)	111	011
(bd,PC,Xn)	111	011

*Long only; all others are byte only.

Instruction Format (Bit Number Static, specified as immediate data):

15	14	13	12	11	10	9	8	7	6	5	4	3	2	1	0
0	0	0	0	1	0	0	0	0	0		EFFECTIVE ADDRESS			MODE	REGISTER
0	0	0	0	0	0	0	0					BIT NUMBER			

Instruction Fields (Bit Number Static):

Effective Address field — Specifies the destination location. Only data addressing modes are allowed as shown:

Addressing Mode	Mode	Register
Dn	000	reg. number:Dn
An	–	–
(An)	010	reg. number:An
(An)+	011	reg. number:An
–(An)	100	reg. number:An
(d16,An)	101	reg. number:An
(d8,An,Xn)	110	reg. number:An
(bd,An,Xn)	110	reg. number:An

Addressing Mode	Mode	Register
(xxx).W	111	000
(xxx).L	111	001
#(data)	–	–
(d16,PC)	111	010
(d8,PC,Xn)	111	011
(bd,PC,Xn)	111	011

Bit Number field — Specifies the bit number.

CHK

Check Register Against Bounds

CHK

Operation: If Dn < 0 or Dn > Source then TRAP

**Assembler
Syntax:** CHK (ea),Dn

Attributes: Size = (Word, Long)

Description: Compares the value in the data register specified in the instruction to zero and to the upper bound (effective address operand). The upper bound is a twos complement integer. If the register value is less than zero or greater than the upper bound, a CHK instruction exception, vector number 6, occurs.

Condition Codes:

X	N	Z	V	C
–	*	U	U	U

X Not affected.
N Set if Dn < 0; cleared if Dn > effective address operand. Undefined otherwise.
Z Undefined.
V Undefined.
C Undefined.

Instruction Format:

15	14	13	12	11	10	9	8	7	6	5	4	3	2	1	0
0	1	0	0		REGISTER			SIZE		0	0		EFFECTIVE ADDRESS		
													MODE		REGISTER

Instruction Fields:

Register field — Specifies the data register that contains the value to be checked.
Size field — Specifies the size of the operation.
  11 — Word operation.
  10 — Long operation.

CHK2

Check Register Against Bounds CHK2

Operation: If Rn < lower bound or
Rn > upper bound
then TRAP

Assembler
Syntax: CHK2 (ea),Rn

Attributes: Size = (Byte, Word, Long)

Description: Compares the value in Rn to each bound. The effective address contains the bounds pair: the lower bound followed by the upper bound. For signed comparisons, the arithmetically smaller value should be used as the lower bound. For unsigned comparisons, the logically smaller value should be the lower bound.

The size of the data and the bounds can be specified as byte, word, or long. If Rn is a data register and the operation size is byte or word, only the appropriate low-order part of Rn is checked. If Rn is an address register and the operation size is byte or word, the bounds operands are sign-extended to 32 bits and the resultant operands are compared to the full 32 bits of An.

If the upper bound equals the lower bound, the valid range is a single value. If the register value is less than the lower bound or greater than the upper bound, a CHK instruction exception, vector number 6, occurs.

Condition Codes:

X	N	Z	V	C
—	U	*	U	*

X Not affected.
N Undefined.
Z Set if Rn is equal to either bound. Cleared otherwise.
V Undefined.
C Set if Rn is out of bounds. Cleared otherwise.

CHK

Check Register Against Bounds CHK

Effective Address field — Specifies the upper bound operand. Only data addressing modes are allowed as shown:

Addressing Mode	Mode	Register	Addressing Mode	Mode	Register
Dn	000	reg. number:Dn	(xxx).W	111	000
An	—	—	(xxx).L	111	001
(An)	010	reg. number:An	#⟨data⟩	111	100
(An)+	011	reg. number:An			
−(An)	100	reg. number:An			
(d16,An)	101	reg. number:An	(d16,PC)	111	010
(d8,An,Xn)	110	reg. number:An	(d8,PC,Xn)	111	011
(bd,An,Xn)	110	reg. number:An	(bd,PC,Xn)	111	011

CLR

Clear an Operand

CLR

Operation: 0 → Destination

Assembler Syntax: CLR ⟨ea⟩

Attributes: Size = (Byte, Word, Long)

Description: Clears the destination operand to zero. The size of the operation may be specified as byte, word, or long.

Condition Codes:

X	N	Z	V	C
—	0	1	0	0

X Not affected.
N Always cleared.
Z Always set.
V Always cleared.
C Always cleared.

Instruction Format:

15	14	13	12	11	10	9	8	7	6	5	4	3	2	1	0
								SIZE		EFFECTIVE ADDRESS					
0	1	0	0	0	0	1	0			MODE			REGISTER		

Instruction Fields:

Size field — Specifies the size of the operation.
00 — Byte operation
01 — Word operation
10 — Long operation

CHK2

Check Register Against Bounds

CHK2

Instruction Format:

15	14	13	12	11	10	9	8	7	6	5	4	3	2	1	0
					SIZE					EFFECTIVE ADDRESS					
0	0	0	0	0	0	0	0	1	1	MODE			REGISTER		
D/A	REGISTER			1	0	0	0	0	0	0	0	0	0	0	0

Instruction Fields:

Size field — Specifies the size of the operation.
00 — Byte operation
01 — Word operation
10 — Long operation

Effective Address field — Specifies the location of the bounds operands. Only control addressing modes are allowed as shown:

Addressing Mode	Mode	Register
Dn	—	—
An	—	—
(An)	010	reg. number:An
(An)+	—	—
-(An)	—	—
(d$_{16}$,An)	101	reg. number:An
(d$_8$,An,Xn)	110	reg. number:An
(bd,An,Xn)	110	reg. number:An

Addressing Mode	Mode	Register
(xxx).W	111	000
(xxx).L	111	001
#⟨data⟩	—	—
(d$_{16}$,PC)	111	010
(d$_8$,PC,Xn)	111	011
(bd,PC,Xn)	111	011

D/A field — Specifies whether an address register or data register is to be checked.
0 — Data register.
1 — Address register.
Register field — Specifies the address or data register that contains the value to be checked.

CMP

Compare

Operation: Destination — Source ▶ cc

**Assembler
Syntax:** CMP ⟨ea⟩, Dn

Attributes: Size = (Byte, Word, Long)

Description: Subtracts the source operand from the destination data register and sets the condition codes according to the result; the data register is not changed. The size of the operation can be byte, word, or long.

Condition Codes:

X	N	Z	V	C
—	*	*	*	*

X Not affected.
N Set if the result is negative. Cleared otherwise.
Z Set if the result is zero. Cleared otherwise.
V Set if an overflow occurs. Cleared otherwise.
C Set if a borrow occurs. Cleared otherwise.

Instruction Format:

15	14	13	12	11	10	9	8	7	6	5	4	3	2	1	0
1	0	1	1	REGISTER			OPMODE			EFFECTIVE ADDRESS					
										MODE			REGISTER		

Instruction Fields:
Register field — Specifies the destination data register.
Opmode field:

Byte	Word	Long	Operation
000	001	010	((Dn)) − ((ea))

CLR

Clear an Operand

Effective Address field — Specifies the destination location. Only data alterable addressing modes are allowed as shown:

Addressing Mode	Mode	Register
Dn	000	reg. number:Dn
An	—	—
(An)	010	reg. number:An
(An)+	011	reg. number:An
−(An)	100	reg. number:An
(d_{16},An)	101	reg. number:An
(d_8,An,Xn)	110	reg. number:An
(bd,An,Xn)	110	reg. number:An

Addressing Mode	Mode	Register
(xxx).W	111	000
(xxx).L	111	001
#⟨data⟩	—	—
(d_{16},PC)	—	—
(d_8,PC,Xn)	—	—
(bd,PC,Xn)	—	—

CMPA   Compare Address   CMPA

Operation: Destination − Source

Assembler Syntax: CMPA (ea), An

Attributes: Size = (Word, Long)

Description: Subtracts the source operand from the destination address register and sets the condition codes according to the result; the address register is not changed. The size of the operation can be specified as word or long. Word length source operands are sign extended to 32-bits for comparison.

Condition Codes:

X	N	Z	V	C
−	•	•	•	•

X Not affected.
N Set if the result is negative. Cleared otherwise.
Z Set if the result is zero. Cleared otherwise.
V Set if an overflow is generated. Cleared otherwise.
C Set if a borrow is generated. Cleared otherwise.

Instruction Format:

15	14	13	12	11	10	9	8	7	6	5	4	3	2	1	0
1	0	1	1	REGISTER			OPMODE			EFFECTIVE ADDRESS					
										MODE			REGISTER		

Instruction Fields:
Register field — Specifies the destination address register.
Opmode field — Specifies the size of the operation:
011 — Word operation. The source operand is sign-extended to a long operand and the operation is performed on the address register using all 32 bits.
111 — Long operation.

CMP   Compare   CMP

Effective Address field — Specifies the source operand. All addressing modes are allowed as shown:

Addressing Mode	Mode	Register
Dn	000	reg. number:Dn
An*	001	reg. number:An
(An)	010	reg. number:An
(An)+	011	reg. number:An
−(An)	100	reg. number:An
(d$_{16}$,An)	101	reg. number:An
(d$_8$,An,Xn)	110	reg. number:An
(bd,An,Xn)	110	reg. number:An

Addressing Mode	Mode	Register
(xxx).W	111	000
(xxx).L	111	001
#(data)	111	100
(d$_{16}$,PC)	111	010
(d$_8$,PC,Xn)	111	011
(bd,PC,Xn)	111	011

*Word and Long only.

NOTE

CMPA is used when the destination is an address register. CMPI is used when the source is immediate data. CMPM is used for memory-to-memory compares. Most assemblers automatically make the distinction.

CMPI

Compare Immediate

CMPI

Operation: Destination − Immediate Data

Assembler Syntax: CMPI #⟨data⟩,⟨ea⟩

Attributes: Size = (Byte, Word, Long)

Description: Subtracts the immediate data from the destination operand and sets the condition codes according to the result; the destination location is not changed. The size of the operation may be specified as byte, word, or long. The size of the immediate data matches the operation size.

Condition Codes:

X	N	Z	V	C
—	*	*	*	*

X Not affected.
N Set if the result is negative. Cleared otherwise.
Z Set if the result is zero. Cleared otherwise.
V Set if an overflow occurs. Cleared otherwise.
C Set if a borrow occurs. Cleared otherwise.

Instruction Format:

15	14	13	12	11	10	9	8	7	6	5	4	3	2	1	0
0	0	0	0	1	1	0	0	SIZE		EFFECTIVE ADDRESS					
										MODE			REGISTER		
WORD DATA (16 BITS)								BYTE DATA (8 BITS)							
LONG DATA (32 BITS)															

Instruction Fields:

Size field — Specifies the size of the operation:
00 — Byte operation
01 — Word operation
10 — Long operation

CMPA

Compare Address

CMPA

Effective Address field — Specifies the source operand. All addressing modes are allowed as shown:

Addressing Mode	Mode	Register	Addressing Mode	Mode	Register
Dn	000	reg. number:Dn	(xxx).W	111	000
An	001	reg. number:An	(xxx).L	111	001
(An)	010	reg. number:An	#⟨data⟩	111	100
(An)+	011	reg. number:An			
−(An)	100	reg. number:An			
(d16,An)	101	reg. number:An	(d16,PC)	111	010
(d8,An,Xn)	110	reg. number:An	(d8,PC,Xn)	111	011
(bd,An,Xn)	110	reg. number:An	(bd,PC,Xn)	111	011

Compare Memory

Operation: Destination — Source ♦ cc

Assembler Syntax: CMPM (Ay)+,(Ax)+

Attributes: Size = (Byte, Word, Long)

Description: Subtracts the source operand from the destination operand and sets the condition codes according to the results; the destination location is not changed. The operands are always addressed with the postincrement addressing mode, using the address registers specified in the instruction. The size of the operation may be specified as byte, word, or long.

Condition Codes:

X	N	Z	V	C
—	*	*	*	*

X Not affected.
N Set if the result is negative. Cleared otherwise.
Z Set if the result is zero. Cleared otherwise.
V Set if an overflow is generated. Cleared otherwise.
C Set if a borrow is generated. Cleared otherwise.

Instruction Format:

15	14	13	12	11	10	9	8	7	6	5	4	3	2	1	0
1	0	1	1	REGISTER Ax			1	SIZE		0	0	1	REGISTER Ay		

Instruction Fields:

Register Ax field — (always the destination). Specifies an address register in the postincrement addressing mode.
Size field — Specifies the size of the operation:
00 — Byte operation
01 — Word operation
10 — Long operation
Register Ay field — (always the source). Specifies an address register in the postincrement addressing mode.

Compare Immediate

Effective Address field — Specifies the destination operand. Only data addressing modes, except immediate are allowed as shown:

Addressing Mode	Mode	Register	Addressing Mode	Mode	Register
Dn	000	reg. number:Dn	(xxx).W	111	000
An	—	—	(xxx).L	111	001
(An)	010	reg. number:An	#⟨data⟩	—	—
(An)+	011	reg. number:An			
-(An)	100	reg. number:An			
(d$_{16}$,An)	101	reg. number:An	(d$_{16}$,PC)	111	010
(d$_8$,An,Xn)	110	reg. number:An	(d$_8$,PC,Xn)	111	011
(bd,An,Xn)	110	reg. number:An	(bd,PC,Xn)	111	011

Immediate field — (Data immediately following the instruction):
If size = 00, the data is the low-order byte of the immediate word.
If size = 01, the data is the entire immediate word.
If size = 10, the data is the next two immediate words.

CMP2   Compare Register Against Bounds   CMP2

Operation: Compare Rn < lower-bound or
Rn > upper-bound
and Set Condition Codes

Assembler
Syntax: CMP2 ⟨ea⟩,Rn

Attributes: Size = (Byte, Word, Long)

Description: Compares the value in Rn to each bound. The effective address contains the bounds pair: the lower bound followed by the upper bound. For signed comparisons, the arithmetically smaller value should be used as the lower bound. For unsigned comparisons, the logically smaller value should be the lower bound.

The size of the data and the bounds can be specified as byte, word, or long. If Rn is a data register and the operation size is byte or word, only the appropriate low-order part of Rn is checked. If Rn is an address register and the operation size is byte or word, the bounds operands are sign-extended to 32 bits and the resultant operands are compared to the full 32 bits of An.

If the upper bound equals the lower bound, the valid range is a single value.

NOTE

This instruction is identical to CHK2 except that it sets condition codes rather than taking an exception when the value in Rn is out of bounds.

Condition Codes:

X	N	Z	V	C
–	U	*	U	*

X Not affected.
N Undefined.
Z Set if Rn is equal to either bound. Cleared otherwise.
V Undefined.
C Set if Rn is out of bounds. Cleared otherwise.

CMP2   Compare Register Against Bounds   CMP2

Instruction Fields:

Size field — Specifies the size of the operation.
00 — Byte operation
01 — Word operation
10 — Long operation

Effective Address field — Specifies the location of the bounds pair. Only control addressing modes are allowed as shown:

Addressing Mode	Mode	Register
Dn	–	–
An	–	–
(An)	010	reg. number:An
(An)+	–	–
–(An)	–	–
(d$_{16}$,An)	101	reg. number:An
(d$_8$,An,Xn)	110	reg. number:An
(bd,An,Xn)	110	reg. number:An

Addressing Mode	Mode	Register
(xxx).W	111	000
(xxx).L	111	001
#⟨data⟩	–	–
(d$_{16}$,PC)	111	010
(d$_8$,PC,Xn)	111	011
(bd,PC,Xn)	111	011

D/A field — Specifies whether an address register or data register is compared.
0 — Data register.
1 — Address register.
Register field — Specifies the address or data register that contains the value to be checked.

DBcc Test Condition, Decrement, and Branch DBcc

Operation: If condition false then (Dn − 1 → Dn;
If Dn ≠ −1 then PC + d → PC)

**Assembler
Syntax:** DBcc Dn,⟨label⟩

Attributes: Size = (Word)

Description: Controls a loop of instructions. The parameters are: a condition code, a data register (counter), and a displacement value. The instruction first tests the condition (for termination); if it is true, no operation is performed. If the termination condition is not true, the low-order 16 bits of the counter data register are decremented by one. If the result is −1, execution continues with the next instruction. If the result is not equal to −1, execution continues at the location indicated by the current value of the PC plus the sign-extended 16-bit displacement. The value in the PC is the address of the instruction word of the DBcc instruction plus two. The displacement is a twos complement integer that represents the relative distance in bytes from the current PC to the destination PC.

Condition code cc specifies one of the following conditions:

CC	carry clear	0100	$\overline{C}$	LS	low or same	0011	$C+Z$
CS	carry set	0101	C	LT	less than	1101	$N\cdot\overline{V}+\overline{N}\cdot V$
EQ	equal	0111	Z	MI	minus	1011	N
F	never equal	0001	0	NE	not equal	0110	$\overline{Z}$
GE	greater or equal	1100	$N\cdot V+\overline{N}\cdot\overline{V}$	PL	plus	1010	$\overline{N}$
GT	greater than	1110	$N\cdot V\cdot\overline{Z}+\overline{N}\cdot\overline{V}\cdot\overline{Z}$	T	always true	0000	1
HI	high	0010	$\overline{C}\cdot\overline{Z}$	VC	overflow clear	1000	$\overline{V}$
LE	less or equal	1111	$Z+N\cdot\overline{V}+\overline{N}\cdot V$	VS	overflow set	1001	V

Condition Codes:
Not affected.

Instruction Format:

15	14	13	12	11	10	9	8	7	6	5	4	3	2	1	0
0	1	0	1			CONDITION			1	1	0	0	1		REGISTER
							DISPLACEMENT (16 BITS)								

DBcc Test Condition, Decrement, and Branch DBcc

Instruction Fields:
Condition field — The binary code for one of the conditions listed in the table.
Register field — Specifies the data register used as the counter.
Displacement field — Specifies the number of bytes to branch.

NOTES:
1. The terminating condition is similar to the UNTIL loop clauses of high-level languages. For example: DBMI can be stated as "decrement and branch until minus".
2. Most assemblers accept DBRA for DBF for use when only a count terminates the loop (no condition is tested).
3. A program can enter a loop at the beginning or by branching to the trailing DBcc instruction. Entering the loop at the beginning is useful for indexed addressing modes and dynamically specified bit operations. In this case, the control index count must be one less than the desired number of loop executions. However, when entering a loop by branching directly to the trailing DBcc instruction, the control count should equal the loop execution count. In this case, if a zero count occurs, the DBcc instruction does not branch, and the main loop is not executed.

DIVS
DIVSL

Signed Divide

Operation: Destination/Source ♦ Destination

Assembler Syntax:

DIVS.W (ea),Dn	32/16 ♦ 16r:16q
DIVS.L (ea),Dq	32/32 ♦ 32q
DIVS.L (ea),Dr:Dq	64/32 ♦ 32r:32q
DIVSL.L (ea),Dr:Dq	32/32 ♦ 32r:32q

Attributes: Size = (Word, Long)

Description: Divides the signed destination operand by the signed source operand and stores the signed result in the destination. The instruction uses one of four forms. The word form of the instruction divides a long word by a word. The result is a quotient in the lower word (least significant 16 bits) and the remainder is in the upper word (most significant 16 bits) of the result. The sign of the remainder is the same as the sign of the dividend.

The first long form divides a long word by a long word. The result is a long quotient; the remainder is discarded.

The second long form divides a quad word (in any two data registers) by a long word. The result is a long word quotient and a long word remainder.

The third long form divides a long word by a long word. The result is a long word quotient and a long word remainder.

Two special conditions may arise during the operation:
1. Division by zero causes a trap.
2. Overflow may be detected and set before the instruction completes. If the instruction detects an overflow, it sets the overflow condition code, and the operands are unaffected.

DIVS
DIVSL

Signed Divide

Condition Codes:

X	N	Z	V	C
—	*	*	*	0

X Not affected.
N Set if the quotient is negative. Cleared otherwise. Undefined if overflow or divide by zero occurs.
Z Set if the quotient is zero. Cleared otherwise. Undefined if overflow or divide by zero occurs.
V Set if division overflow occurs; undefined if divide by zero occurs. Cleared otherwise.
C Always cleared.

Instruction Format (word form):

15	14	13	12	11	10	9	8	7	6	5	4	3	2	1	0
1	0	0	0		REGISTER		1	1	1			EFFECTIVE ADDRESS			
											MODE			REGISTER	

Instruction Fields:

Register field — Specifies any of the eight data registers. This field always specifies the destination operand.

Effective Address field — Specifies the source operand. Only data addressing modes are allowed as shown:

Addressing Mode	Mode	Register
Dn	000	reg. number:Dn
An	—	—
(An)	010	reg. number:An
(An)+	011	reg. number:An
-(An)	100	reg. number:An
(d16,An)	101	reg. number:An
(d8,An,Xn)	110	reg. number:An
(bd,An,Xn)	110	reg. number:An

Addressing Mode	Mode	Register
(xxx).W	111	000
(xxx).L	111	001
#(data)	111	100
(d16,PC)	111	010
(d8,PC,Xn)	111	011
(bd,PC,Xn)	111	011

NOTE

Overflow occurs if the quotient is larger than a 16-bit signed integer.

DIVU
DIVUL

Unsigned Divide

Operation:	Destination/Source → Destination

Assembler
Syntax:

DIVU.W (ea),Dn	32/16 → 16r:16q
DIVU.L (ea),Dq	32/32 → 32q
DIVU.L (ea),Dr:Dq	64/32 → 32r:32q
DIVUL.L (ea),Dr:Dq	32/32 → 32r:32q

Attributes: Size = (Word, Long)

Description: Divides the unsigned destination operand by the unsigned source operand and stores the unsigned result in the destination. The instruction uses one of four forms. The word form of the instruction divides a long word by a word. The result is a quotient in the lower word (least significant 16 bits) and the remainder is in the upper word (most significant 16 bits) of the result.

The first long form divides a long word by a long word. The result is a long quotient; the remainder is discarded.

The second long form divides a quad word (in any two data registers) by a long word. The result is a long word quotient and a long word remainder.

The third long form divides a long word by a long word. The result is a long word quotient and a long word remainder.

Two special conditions may arise during the operation:
1. Division by zero causes a trap.
2. Overflow may be detected and set before the instruction completes. If the instruction detects an overflow, it sets the overflow condition code, and the operands are unaffected.

Condition Codes:

X	N	Z	V	C
—	*	*	*	0

X Not affected.
N Set if the quotient is negative. Cleared otherwise. Undefined if overflow or divide by zero occurs.
Z Set if the quotient is zero. Cleared otherwise. Undefined if overflow or divide by zero occurs.
V Set if division overflow occurs; undefined if divide by zero occurs. Cleared otherwise.
C Always cleared.

DIVS
DIVSL

Signed Divide

Instruction Format (long form):

15	14	13	12	11	10	9	8	7	6	5	4	3	2	1	0
0	1	0	0	1	1	0	0	0	1	MODE			REGISTER		
0	REGISTER Dq			1	SIZE	0	0	0	0	0	0	0	REGISTER Dr		

(Top word: EFFECTIVE ADDRESS — MODE (bits 5–3), REGISTER (bits 2–0))

Instruction Fields:

Effective Address field — Specifies the source operand. Only data addressing modes are allowed as shown:

Addressing Mode	Mode	Register
Dn	000	reg. number:Dn
An	—	—
(An)	010	reg. number:An
(An)+	011	reg. number:An
–(An)	100	reg. number:An
(d16,An)	101	reg. number:An
(d8,An,Xn)	110	reg. number:An
(bd,An,Xn)	110	reg. number:An

Addressing Mode	Mode	Register
(xxx).W	111	000
(xxx).L	111	001
#(data)	111	100
(d16,PC)	111	010
(d8,PC,Xn)	111	011
(bd,PC,Xn)	111	011

Register Dq field — Specifies a data register for the destination operand. The low-order 32 bits of the dividend comes from this register, and the 32-bit quotient is loaded into this register.

Size field — Selects a 32 or 64 bit division operation.
0 — 32-bit dividend is in Register Dq.
1 — 64-bit dividend is in Dr:Dq.

Register Dr field — After the division, this register contains the 32-bit remainder. If Dr and Dq are the same register, only the quotient is returned. If Size is 1, this field also specifies the data register that contains the high-order 32 bits of the dividend.

NOTE

Overflow occurs if the quotient is larger than a 32-bit signed integer.

DIVU
DIVUL

Unsigned Divide

DIVU
DIVUL

Unsigned Divide

Instruction Format (word form):

15	14	13	12	11	10	9	8	7	6	5	4	3	2	1	0
										EFFECTIVE ADDRESS					
										MODE			REGISTER		
1	0	0	0	REGISTER			0	1	1						

Instruction Fields:

Register field — Specifies any of the eight data registers. This field always specifies the destination operand.

Effective Address field — Specifies the source operand. Only data addressing modes are allowed as shown:

Addressing Mode	Mode	Register	Addressing Mode	Mode	Register
Dn	000	reg. number:Dn	(xxx).W	111	000
An	–		(xxx).L	111	001
(An)	010	reg. number:An	#(data)	111	100
(An)+	011	reg. number:An			
–(An)	100	reg. number:An			
(d16,An)	101	reg. number:An	(d16,PC)	111	010
(d8,An,Xn)	110	reg. number:An	(d8,PC,Xn)	111	011
(bd,An,Xn)	110	reg. number:An	(bd,PC,Xn)	111	011

NOTE

Overflow occurs if the quotient is larger than a 16-bit signed integer.

DIVU
DIVUL

Unsigned Divide

Instruction Format (long form):

15	14	13	12	11	10	9	8	7	6	5	4	3	2	1	0
										EFFECTIVE ADDRESS					
										MODE			REGISTER Dr		
0	1	0	0	REGISTER Dq			0	SIZE	0	0	0	0			

Instruction Fields:

Effective Address field — Specifies the source operand. Only data addressing modes are allowed as shown:

Addressing Mode	Mode	Register	Addressing Mode	Mode	Register
Dn	000	reg. number:Dn	(xxx).W	111	000
An	–		(xxx).L	111	001
(An)	010	reg. number:An	#(data)	111	100
(An)+	011	reg. number:An			
–(An)	100	reg. number:An			
(d16,An)	101	reg. number:An	(d16,PC)	111	010
(d8,An,Xn)	110	reg. number:An	(d8,PC,Xn)	111	011
(bd,An,Xn)	110	reg. number:An	(bd,PC,Xn)	111	011

Register Dq field — Specifies a data register for the destination operand. The low-order 32 bits of the dividend comes from this register, and the 32-bit quotient is loaded into this register.

Size field — Selects a 32- or 64-bit division operation.

0 — 32-bit dividend is in Register Dq.

1 — 64-bit dividend is in Dr:Dq.

Register Dr field — After the division, this register contains the 32-bit remainder. If Dr and Dq are the same register, only the quotient is returned. If Size is 1, this field also specifies the data register that contains the high-order 32 bits of the dividend.

NOTE

Overflow occurs if the quotient is larger than a 32-bit unsigned integer.

Exclusive OR Logical

Operation: Source $\oplus$ Destination $\rightarrow$ Destination

**Assembler
Syntax:** EOR Dn,⟨ea⟩

Attributes: Size = (Byte, Word, Long)

Description: Performs an exclusive OR operation on the destination operand using the source operand and stores the result in the destination location. The size of the operation may be specified to be byte, word, or long. The source operand must be a data register. The destination operand is specified in the effective address field.

Condition Codes:

X	N	Z	V	C
–	*	*	0	0

X   Not affected.
N   Set if the most significant bit of the result is set. Cleared otherwise.
Z   Set if the result is zero. Cleared otherwise.
V   Always cleared.
C   Always cleared.

Instruction Format (word form):

15	14	13	12	11	10	9	8	7	6	5	4	3	2	1	0
1	0	1	1	REGISTER			OPMODE			EFFECTIVE ADDRESS					
										MODE			REGISTER		

Instruction Fields:
Register field — Specifies any of the eight data registers.
Opmode field:

Byte	Word	Long	Operation
100	101	110	(⟨ea⟩) $\oplus$ ((Dn)) $\rightarrow$ ⟨ea⟩

Exclusive OR Logical

Effective Address field — Specifies the destination operand. Only data alterable addressing modes are allowed as shown:

Addressing Mode	Mode	Register
Dn	000	reg. number:Dn
An	–	–
(An)	010	reg. number:An
(An)+	011	reg. number:An
–(An)	100	reg. number:An
(d16,An)	101	reg. number:An
(d8,An,Xn)	110	reg. number:An
(bd,An,Xn)	110	reg. number:An

Addressing Mode	Mode	Register
(xxx).W	111	000
(xxx).L	111	001
#⟨data⟩	–	–
(d16,PC)	–	–
(d8,PC,Xn)	–	–
(bd,PC,Xn)	–	–

NOTE

Memory to data register operations are not allowed. Most assemblers use EORI when the source is immediate data.

EORI

Exclusive OR Immediate

EORI

Operation: Immediate Data $\oplus$ Destination $\rightarrow$ Destination

Assembler Syntax: EORI #$\langle$data$\rangle$,$\langle$ea$\rangle$

Attributes: Size = (Byte, Word, Long)

Description: Performs an exclusive OR operation on the destination operand using the immediate data and the destination operand and stores the result in the destination location. The size of the operation may be specified as byte, word, or long. The size of the immediate data matches the operation size.

Condition Codes:

X	N	Z	V	C
—	*	*	0	0

X Not affected.
N Set if the most significant bit of the result is set. Cleared otherwise.
Z Set if the result is zero. Cleared otherwise.
V Always cleared.
C Always cleared.

Instruction Format:

15	14	13	12	11	10	9	8	7	6	5	4	3	2	1	0
0	0	0	0	1	0	1	0	SIZE		EFFECTIVE ADDRESS					
										MODE			REGISTER		
WORD DATA (16 BITS)										BYTE DATA (8 BITS)					
LONG DATA (32 BITS)															

Instruction Fields:

Size field — Specifies the size of the operation:
00 — Byte operation
01 — Word operation
10 — Long operation

EORI

Exclusive OR Immediate

EORI

Effective Address field — Specifies the destination operand. Only data alterable addressing modes are allowed as shown:

Addressing Mode	Mode	Register
Dn	000	reg. number:Dn
An	—	—
(An)	010	reg. number:An
(An)+	011	reg. number:An
−(An)	100	reg. number:An
(d$_{16}$,An)	101	reg. number:An
(d$_8$,An,Xn)	110	reg. number:An
(bd,An,Xn)	110	reg. number:An

Addressing Mode	Mode	Register
(xxx).W	111	000
(xxx).L	111	001
#$\langle$data$\rangle$	—	—
(d$_{16}$,PC)	—	—
(d$_8$,PC,Xn)	—	—
(bd,PC,Xn)	—	—

Immediate field — (Data immediately following the instruction):
If size = 00, the data is the low-order byte of the immediate word.
If size = 01, the data is the entire immediate word.
If size = 10, the data is next two immediate words.

EORI to SR

EORI to SR

Exclusive OR Immediate to the Status Register
(Privileged Instruction)

Operation: If supervisor state
then Source $\oplus$ SR ► SR
else TRAP

Assembler
Syntax: EORI #(data),SR

Attributes: Size = (Word)

Description: Performs an exclusive OR operation on the contents of the status register using the immediate operand and stores the result in the status register. All implemented bits of the status register are affected.

Condition Codes:

X	N	Z	V	C
*	*	*	*	*

X Changed if bit 4 of immediate operand is one. Unchanged otherwise.
N Changed if bit 3 of immediate operand is one. Unchanged otherwise.
Z Changed if bit 2 of immediate operand is one. Unchanged otherwise.
V Changed if bit 1 of immediate operand is one. Unchanged otherwise.
C Changed if bit 0 of immediate operand is one. Unchanged otherwise.

Instruction Format:

15	14	13	12	11	10	9	8	7	6	5	4	3	2	1	0
0	0	0	0	1	0	1	0	0	1	1	1	1	1	0	0

						WORD DATA (16 BITS)									

EORI to CCR

EORI to CCR

Exclusive OR Immediate to Condition Code

Operation: Source $\oplus$ CCR ► CCR

Assembler
Syntax: EORI #(data),CCR

Attributes: Size = (Byte)

Description: Performs an exclusive OR operation on the condition code register using the immediate operand and stores the result in the condition code register (low-order byte of the status register). All implemented bits of the condition code register are affected.

Condition Codes:

X	N	Z	V	C
*	*	*	*	*

X Changed if bit 4 of immediate operand is one. Unchanged otherwise.
N Changed if bit 3 of immediate operand is one. Unchanged otherwise.
Z Changed if bit 2 of immediate operand is one. Unchanged otherwise.
V Changed if bit 1 of immediate operand is one. Unchanged otherwise.
C Changed if bit 0 of immediate operand is one. Unchanged otherwise.

Instruction Format:

15	14	13	12	11	10	9	8	7	6	5	4	3	2	1	0
0	0	0	0	1	0	1	0	0	0	1	1	1	1	0	0

								BYTE DATA (8 BITS)							

EXT
EXTB

Sign Extend

Operation: Destination Sign-extended → Destination

Assembler Syntax:
EXT.W Dn   extend byte to word
EXT.L Dn   extend word to long word
EXTB.L Dn   extend byte to long word

Attributes: Size = (Word, Long)

Description: Extends a byte in a data register to a word or a long word, or a word in a data register to a long word, by replicating the sign bit to the left. If the operation extends a byte to a word, bit [7] of the designated data register is copied to bits [15:8] of that data register. If the operation extends a word to a long word, bit [15] of the designated data register is copied to bits [31:16] of the data register. The EXTB form copies bit [7] of the designated register to bits [31:8] of the data register.

Condition Codes:

X	N	Z	V	C
–	*	*	0	0

X Not affected.
N Set if the result is negative. Cleared otherwise.
Z Set if the result is zero. Cleared otherwise.
V Always cleared.
C Always cleared.

Instruction Format:

15	14	13	12	11	10	9	8	7	6	5	4	3	2	1	0
0	1	0	0	1	0	0	0	OPMODE			0	0	0	REGISTER	

Instruction Fields:
Opmode field — Specifies the size of the sign-extension operation:
010 — Sign-extend low-order byte of data register to word.
011 — Sign-extend low-order word of data register to long.
111 — Sign-extend low-order byte of data register to long.
Register field — Specifies the data register to be sign-extended.

EXG

Exchange Registers

Operation: Rx  Ry

Assembler Syntax:
EXG Dx,Dy
EXG Ax,Ay
EXG Dx,Ay
EXG Ay, Dx

Attributes: Size = (Long)

Description: Exchanges the contents of two 32-bit registers. The instruction performs three types of exchanges:
1. Exchange data registers.
2. Exchange address registers.
3. Exchange a data register and an address register.

Condition Codes:
Not affected.

Instruction Format:

15	14	13	12	11	10	9	8	7	6	5	4	3	2	1	0
1	1	0	0	REGISTER Rx			1	OPMODE					REGISTER Ry		

Instruction Fields:
Register Rx field — Specifies either a data register or an address register depending on the mode. If the exchange is between data and address registers, this field always specifies the data register.
Opmode field — Specifies the type of exchange:
01000 — Data registers.
01001 — Address registers.
10001 — Data register and address register.
Register Ry field — Specifies either a data register or an address register depending on the mode. If the exchange is between data and address registers, this field always specifies the address register.

JMP

JMP   Jump

Operation: Destination Address ▸ PC

Assembler Syntax: JMP (ea)

Attributes: Unsized

Description: Program execution continues at the effective address specified by the instruction. The addressing mode for the effective address must be a control addressing mode.

Condition Codes:
Not affected.

Instruction Format:

15	14	13	12	11	10	9	8	7	6	5	4	3	2	1	0
0	1	0	0	1	1	1	0	1	1	MODE			REGISTER		

EFFECTIVE ADDRESS: MODE (bits 5-3), REGISTER (bits 2-0)

Instruction Fields:

Effective Address field — Specifies the address of the next instruction. Only control addressing modes are allowed as shown:

Addressing Mode	Mode	Register		Addressing Mode	Mode	Register
Dn	—	—		(xxx).W	111	000
An	—	—		(xxx).L	111	001
(An)	010	reg. number:An		#(data)	—	—
(An)+	—	—				
-(An)	—	—				
(d16,An)	101	reg. number:An		(d16,PC)	111	010
(d8,An,Xn)	110	reg. number:An		(d8,PC,Xn)	111	011
(bd,An,Xn)	110	reg. number:An		(bd,PC,Xn)	111	011

ILLEGAL

ILLEGAL   Take Illegal Instruction Trap   **ILLEGAL**

Operation:
SSP − 2 ▸ SSP; Vector Offset ▸ (SSP);
SSP − 4 ▸ SSP; PC ▸ (SSP);
SSP − 2 ▸ SSP; SR ▸ (SSP);
Illegal Instruction Vector Address ▸ PC

Assembler Syntax: ILLEGAL

Attributes: Unsized

Description: Forces an illegal instruction exception, vector number 4. All other illegal instruction bit patterns are reserved for future extension of the instruction set and should not be used to force an exception.

Condition Codes:
Not affected

Instruction Format:

15	14	13	12	11	10	9	8	7	6	5	4	3	2	1	0
0	1	0	0	1	0	1	0	1	1	1	1	1	1	0	0

LEA

Load Effective Address

Operation: ⟨ea⟩ ➡ An

Assembler Syntax: LEA ⟨ea⟩,An

Attributes: Size = (Long)

Description: Loads the effective address into the specified address register. All 32 bits of the address register are affected by this instruction.

Condition Codes:
Not affected.

Instruction Format:

15	14	13	12	11	10	9	8	7	6	5	4	3	2	1	0
0	1	0	0		REGISTER		1	1	1		EFFECTIVE ADDRESS MODE			REGISTER	

Instruction Fields:
Register field — Specifies the address register to be updated with the effective address.
Effective Address field — Specifies the address to be loaded into the address register. Only control addressing modes are allowed as shown:

Addressing Mode	Mode	Register	Addressing Mode	Mode	Register
Dn	–	–	(xxx).W	111	000
An	–	–	(xxx).L	111	001
(An)	010	reg. number:An	#⟨data⟩	–	–
(An)+	–	–			
-(An)	–	–			
(d16,An)	101	reg. number:An	(d16,PC)	111	010
(d8,An,Xn)	110	reg. number:An	(d8,PC,Xn)	111	011
(bd,An,Xn)	110	reg. number:An	(bd,PC,Xn)	111	011

JSR

Jump to Subroutine

Operation: SP – 4 ➡ Sp; PC ➡ (SP)
Destination Address ➡ PC

Assembler Syntax: JSR ⟨ea⟩

Attributes: Unsized

Description: Pushes the long word address of the instruction immediately following the JSR instruction onto the system stack. Program execution then continues at the address specified in the instruction.

Condition Codes:
Not affected.

Instruction Format:

15	14	13	12	11	10	9	8	7	6	5	4	3	2	1	0
0	1	0	0	1	1	1	0	1	0		EFFECTIVE ADDRESS MODE			REGISTER	

Instruction Fields:
Effective Address field — Specifies the address of the next instruction. Only control addressing modes are allowed as shown:

Addressing Mode	Mode	Register	Addressing Mode	Mode	Register
Dn	–	–	(xxx).W	111	000
An	–	–	(xxx).L	111	001
(An)	010	reg. number:An	#⟨data⟩	–	–
(An)+	–	–			
-(An)	–	–			
(d16,An)	101	reg. number:An	(d16,PC)	111	010
(d8,An,Xn)	110	reg. number:An	(d8,PC,Xn)	111	011
(bd,An,Xn)	110	reg. number:An	(bd,PC,Xn)	111	011

LPSTOP

Low Power Stop

LPSTOP

Operation:
If supervisor state
  Immediate Data ⬥ SR
  Interrupt Mask ⬥ External Bus Interface (EBI)
  STOP
else TRAP

Assembler
Syntax: LPSTOP #<data>

Attributes: Size =(Word) Privileged

Description: The immediate operand is moved into the entire status register, the Program Counter is advanced to point to the next instruction, and the processor stops fetching and executing instructions. A CPU LPSTOP broadcast cycle is executed to CPU space $3 to copy the updated interrupt mask to the external bus interface (EBI). The internal clocks are stopped.

Execution of instructions resumes when a trace, interrupt, or reset exception occurs. A trace exception will occur if the trace state is on when the LPSTOP instruction is executed. If an interrupt request is asserted with a higher priority that the current priority level set by the new status register value, an interrupt exception occurs; otherwise the interrupt request is ignored. If the bit of the immediate data corresponding to the S bit is off, execution of the instruction will cause a privilege violation. An external reset always initiates reset exception processing.

Condition Codes:
Set according to the immediate operand.

Instruction Format:

15	14	13	12	11	10	9	8	7	6	5	4	3	2	1	0
1	1	1	1	1	0	0	0	0	0	1	0	0	0	0	0
0	0	0	0	0	0	0	1	1	1	0	0	0	0	0	0

IMMEDIATE DATA

Instruction Fields:

Immediate field:
  Specifies the data to be loaded into the status register.

LINK

Link and Allocate

LINK

Operation:
Sp − 4 ⬥ Sp; An ⬥ (SP);
SP ⬥ An; SP+d ⬥ SP

Assembler
Syntax: LINK An, #<displacement>

Attributes: Size = (Word, Long)

Description: Pushes the contents of the specified address register onto the stack. Then loads the updated stack pointer into the address register. Finally, adds the displacement value to the stack pointer. For word size operation, the displacement is the sign-extended word following the operation word. For long size operation, the displacement is the long word following the operation word. The address register occupies one long word on the stack. The user should specify a negative displacement in order to allocate stack area.

Condition Codes:
Not affected.

Instruction Format:

15	14	13	12	11	10	9	8	7	6	5	4	3	2	1	0
0	1	0	0	1	1	1	0	0	1	0	1	0	1	| REGISTER |		

WORD DISPLACEMENT

15	14	13	12	11	10	9	8	7	6	5	4	3	2	1	0
0	1	0	0	1	0	0	0	0	0	0	0	0	1	| REGISTER |		

HIGH-ORDER DISPLACEMENT

LOW-ORDER DISPLACEMENT

Instruction Fields:

Register field — Specifies the address register for the link.
Displacement field — Specifies the twos complement integer to be added to the stack pointer.

NOTE

LINK and UNLK can be used to maintain a linked list of local data and parameter areas on the stack for nested subroutine calls.

Operation: Destination Shifted by ⟨count⟩ ♦ Destination

Assembler Syntax:
LSd Dx,Dy
LSd #⟨data⟩,Dy
LSd ⟨ea⟩
where d is direction, L or R

Attributes: Size = (Byte, Word, Long)

Description: Shifts the bits of the operand in the direction specified (L or R). The carry bit receives the last bit shifted out of the operand. The shift count for the shifting of a register is specified in two different ways:

1. Immediate — The shift count (1-8) is specified in the instruction.
2. Register — The shift count is the value in the data register specified in the instruction modulo 64.

The size of the operation for register destinations may be specified as byte, word, or long. The contents of memory, ⟨ea⟩, can be shifted one bit only, and the operand size is restricted to a word.

The LSL instruction shifts the operand to the left the number of positions specified as the shift count. Bits shifted out of the high-order bit go to both the carry and the extend bits; zeros are shifted into the low-order bit.

LSL:

The LSR instruction shifts the operand to the right the number of positions specified as the shift count. Bits shifted out of the low-order bit go to both the carry and the extend bits; zeros are shifted into the high-order bit.

LSR:

Condition Codes:

X	N	Z	V	C
*	*	*	0	*

X Set according to the last bit shifted out of the operand. Unaffected for a shift count of zero.
N Set if the result is negative. Cleared otherwise.
Z Set if the result is zero. Cleared otherwise.
V Always cleared.
C Set according to the last bit shifted out of the operand. Cleared for a shift count of zero.

Instruction Format (Register Shifts):

15	14	13	12	11	10	9	8	7	6	5	4	3	2	1	0
1	1	1	0	COUNT/REGISTER			dr	SIZE		i/r	0	1	REGISTER		

Instruction Field (Register Shifts):

Count/Register field:
If i/r = 0, this field contains the shift count. The values 1-7 represent shifts of 1-7; value of 0 specifies a shift count of 8.
If i/r = 1, the data register specified in this field contains the shift count (modulo 64).

dr field — Specifies the direction of the shift:
0 — Shift right
1 — Shift left

Size field — Specifies the size of the operation:
00 — Byte operation
01 — Word operation
10 — Long operation

i/r field:
If i/r = 0, specifies immediate shift count.
If i/r = 1, specifies register shift count.

Register field — Specifies a data register to be shifted.

Instruction Format (Memory Shifts):

15	14	13	12	11	10	9	8	7	6	5	4	3	2	1	0
1	1	1	0	0	0	1	dr	1	1			EFFECTIVE ADDRESS			
												MODE		REGISTER	

Instruction Fields (Memory Shifts):

dr field — Specifies the direction of the shift:
0 — Shift right
1 — Shift left

Effective Address field — Specifies the operand to be shifted. Only memory alterable addressing modes are allowed as shown:

Addressing Mode	Mode	Register
Dn	—	—
An	—	—
(An)	010	reg. number:An
(An)+	011	reg. number:An
-(An)	100	reg. number:An
(d$_{16}$,An)	101	reg. number:An
(d$_8$,An,Xn)	110	reg. number:An
(bd,An,Xn)	110	reg. number:An
([bd,An,Xn],od)	110	reg. number:An

Addressing Mode	Mode	Register
(xxx).W	111	000
(xxx).L	111	001
#⟨data⟩	—	—
(d$_{16}$,PC)	—	—
(d$_8$,PC,Xn)	—	—
(bd,PC,Xn)	—	—
([bd,PC,Xn],od)	—	—

MOVE   Move Data from Source to Destination   MOVE

Operation: Source ♦ Destination

Assembler Syntax: MOVE ⟨ea⟩,⟨ea⟩

Attributes: Size = (Byte, Word, Long)

Description: Moves the data at the source to the destination location, and sets the condition codes according to the data. The size of the operation may be specified as byte, word, or long.

Condition Codes:

X	N	Z	V	C
—	*	*	0	0

X Not affected.
N Set if the result is negative. Cleared otherwise.
Z Set if the result is zero. Cleared otherwise.
V Always cleared.
C Always cleared.

Instruction Format:

15	14	13	12	11	10	9	8	7	6	5	4	3	2	1	0
0	0	SIZE		DESTINATION			DESTINATION			SOURCE			SOURCE		
				REGISTER			MODE			MODE			REGISTER		

Instruction Fields:

Size field — Specifies the size of the operand to be moved:
01 — Byte operation
11 — Word operation
10 — Long operation

MOVEA — Move Address — MOVEA

Operation: Source → Destination

Assembler Syntax: MOVEA (ea),An

Attributes: Size = (Word, Long)

Description: Moves the contents of the source to the destination address register. The size of the operation is specified as word or long. Word-size source operands are sign-extended to 32-bit quantities.

Condition Codes: Not affected.

Instruction Format:

15	14	13	12	11	10	9	8	7	6	5	4	3	2	1	0
0	0	SIZE		DESTINATION REGISTER			0	0	1	MODE			REGISTER		
										SOURCE					

Instruction Fields:

Size field — Specifies the size of the operand to be moved:

11 — Word operation. The source operand is sign-extended to a long operand and all 32 bits are loaded into the address register.

10 — Long operation.

Destination Register field — Specifies the destination address register.

Effective Address field — Specifies the location of the source operand. All addressing modes are allowed as shown:

Addressing Mode	Mode	Register
Dn	000	reg. number:Dn
An	001	reg. number:An
(An)	010	reg. number:An
(An)+	011	reg. number:An
-(An)	100	reg. number:An
(d16,An)	101	reg. number:An
(d8,An,Xn)	110	reg. number:An
(bd,An,Xn)	110	reg. number:An

Addressing Mode	Mode	Register
(xxx).W	111	000
(xxx).L	111	001
#(data)	111	100
(d16,PC)	111	010
(d8,PC,Xn)	111	011
(bd,PC,Xn)	111	011

MOVE — Move Data from Source to Destination — MOVE

Destination Effective Address field — Specifies the destination location. Only data alterable addressing modes are allowed as shown:

Addressing Mode	Mode	Register
Dn	000	reg. number:Dn
An	—	—
(An)	010	reg. number:An
(An)+	011	reg. number:An
-(An)	100	reg. number:An
(d16,An)	101	reg. number:An
(d8,An,Xn)	110	reg. number:An
(bd,An,Xn)	110	reg. number:An

Addressing Mode	Mode	Register
(xxx).W	111	000
(xxx).L	111	001
#(data)	—	—
(d16,PC)	—	—
(d8,PC,Xn)	—	—
(bd,PC,Xn)	—	—

Source Effective Address field — Specifies the source operand. All addressing modes are allowed as shown:

Addressing Mode	Mode	Register
Dn	000	reg. number:Dn
An*	001	reg. number:An
(An)	010	reg. number:An
(An)+	011	reg. number:An
-(An)	100	reg. number:An
(d16,An)	101	reg. number:An
(d8,An,Xn)	110	reg. number:An
(bd,An,Xn)	110	reg. number:An

Addressing Mode	Mode	Register
(xxx).W	111	000
(xxx).L	111	001
#(data)	111	100
(d16,PC)	111	010
(d8,PC,Xn)	111	011
(bd,PC,Xn)	111	011

*For byte size operation, address register direct is not allowed.

NOTES:
1. Most assemblers use MOVEA when the destination is an address register.
2. MOVEQ can be used to move an immediate 8-bit value to a data register.

MOVE to CCR

MOVE to CCR — Move to Condition Codes

Operation: Source → CCR

Assembler Syntax: MOVE (ea),CCR

Attributes: Size = (Word)

Description: Moves the low-order byte of the source operand to the condition code register. The upper byte of the source operand is ignored; the upper byte of the status register is not altered.

Condition Codes:

X	N	Z	V	C
*	*	*	*	*

X — Set to the value of bit 4 of the source operand.
N — Set to the value of bit 3 of the source operand.
Z — Set to the value of bit 2 of the source operand.
V — Set to the value of bit 1 of the source operand.
C — Set to the value of bit 0 of the source operand.

Instruction Format:

15	14	13	12	11	10	9	8	7	6	5	4	3	2	1	0
0	1	0	0	0	1	0	0	1	1		EFFECTIVE ADDRESS MODE			REGISTER	

MOVE from CCR

MOVE from CCR — Move from the Condition Code Register

Operation: CCR → Destination

Assembler Syntax: MOVE CCR,(ea)

Attributes: Size = (Word)

Description: Moves the condition code bits (zero extended to word size) to the destination location. The operand size is a word. Unimplemented bits are read as zeros.

Condition Codes:
Not affected.

Instruction Format:

15	14	13	12	11	10	9	8	7	6	5	4	3	2	1	0
0	1	0	0	0	0	1	0	1	1		EFFECTIVE ADDRESS MODE			REGISTER	

Instruction Fields:

Effective Address field — Specifies the destination location. Only data alterable addressing modes are allowed as shown:

Addressing Mode	Mode	Register
Dn	000	reg. number:Dn
An	—	—
(An)	010	reg. number:An
(An)+	011	reg. number:An
−(An)	100	reg. number:An
(d$_{16}$,An)	101	reg. number:An
(d$_8$,An,Xn)	110	reg. number:An
(bd,An,Xn)	110	reg. number:An

Addressing Mode	Mode	Register
(xxx).W	111	000
(xxx).L	111	001
#(data)	—	—
(d$_{16}$,PC)	—	—
(d$_8$,PC,Xn)	—	—
(bd,PC,Xn)	—	—

NOTE

MOVE from CCR is a word operation. ANDI, ORI, and EORI to CCR are byte operations.

MOVE from SR

MOVE from SR

Move from the Status Register
(Privileged Instruction)

Operation: If supervisor state
then SR ◆ Destination
else TRAP

Assembler
Syntax: MOVE SR,(ea)

Attributes: Size = (Word)

Description: Moves the data in the status register to the destination location. The destination is word length. Unimplemented bits are read as zeros.

Condition Codes:
Not affected.

Instruction Format:

15	14	13	12	11	10	9	8	7	6	5	4	3	2	1	0
0	1	0	0	0	0	0	0	1	1	1	\	EFFECTIVE ADDRESS			
											MODE			REGISTER	

Instruction Fields:
Effective Address field — Specifies the destination location. Only data alterable addressing modes are allowed as shown:

Addressing Mode	Mode	Register	Addressing Mode	Mode	Register
Dn	000	reg. number:Dn	(xxx).W	111	000
An	—	—	(xxx).L	111	001
(An)	010	reg. number:An	#(data)	—	—
(An)+	011	reg. number:An			
−(An)	100	reg. number:An			
(d16,An)	101	reg. number:An	(d16,PC)	—	—
(d8,An,Xn)	110	reg. number:An	(d8,PC,Xn)	—	—
(bd,An,Xn)	110	reg. number:An	(bd,PC,Xn)	—	—

NOTE

Use the MOVE from CCR instruction to access only the condition codes.

MOVE to CCR

MOVE to CCR

Move to Condition Codes

Instruction Fields:
Effective Address field — Specifies the location of the source operand. Only data addressing modes are allowed as shown:

Addressing Mode	Mode	Register	Addressing Mode	Mode	Register
Dn	000	reg. number:Dn	(xxx).W	111	000
An	—	—	(xxx).L	111	001
(An)	010	reg. number:An	#(data)	111	100
(An)+	011	reg. number:An			
−(An)	100	reg. number:An			
(d16,An)	101	reg. number:An	(d16,PC)	111	010
(d8,An,Xn)	110	reg. number:An	(d8,PC,Xn)	111	011
(bd,An,Xn)	110	reg. number:An	(bd,PC,Xn)	111	011

NOTE

MOVE to CCR is a word operation. ANDI, ORI, and EORI to CCR are byte operations.

MOVE USP

Move User Stack Pointer
(Privileged Instruction)

Operation: If supervisor state
then USP → An or An → USP
else TRAP

Assembler
Syntax: MOVE USP,An
MOVE An,USP

Attributes: Size = (Long)

Description: Moves the contents of the user stack pointer to or from the specified address register.

Condition Codes: Not affected.

Instruction Format:

15	14	13	12	11	10	9	8	7	6	5	4	3	2	1	0
0	1	0	0	1	1	1	0	0	1	1	0	dr	REGISTER		

Instruction Fields:
dr field — Specifies the direction of transfer:
0 — Transfer the address register to the USP.
1 — Transfer the USP to the address register.
Register field — Specifies the address register for the operation.

MOVE to SR

Move to the Status Register
(Priviledged Instruction)

Operation: If supervisor state
then Source → SR
else TRAP

Assembler
Syntax: MOVE <ea>,SR

Attributes: Size = (Word)

Description: Moves the data in the source operand to the status register. The source operand is a word and all implemented bits of the status register are affected.

Condition Codes: Set according to the source operand.

Instruction Format:

15	14	13	12	11	10	9	8	7	6	5	4	3	2	1	0
0	1	0	0	0	1	1	0	1	1		EFFECTIVE ADDRESS				
											MODE			REGISTER	

Instruction Fields:
Effective Address field — Specifies the location of the source operand. Only data addressing modes are allowed as shown:

Addressing Mode	Mode	Register
Dn	000	reg. number:Dn
An	—	—
(An)	010	reg. number:An
(An)+	011	reg. number:An
-(An)	100	reg. number:An
(d16,An)	101	reg. number:An
(d8,An,Xn)	110	reg. number:An
(bd,An,Xn)	110	reg. number:An

Addressing Mode	Mode	Register
(xxx).W	111	000
(xxx).L	111	001
#(data)	111	100
(d16,PC)	111	010
(d8,PC,Xn)	111	011
(bd,PC,Xn)	111	011

MOVEM

Move Multiple Registers

Operation: Registers → Destination
Source → Registers

Assembler MOVEM register list,(ea)
Syntax: MOVEM (ea),register list

Attributes: Size = (Word, Long)

Description: Moves the contents of selected registers to or from consecutive memory locations starting at the location specified by the effective address. A register is selected if the bit in the mask field corresponding to that register is set. The instruction size determines whether 16 or 32 bits of each register are transferred. In the case of a word transfer to either address or data registers, each word is sign-extended to 32 bits, and the resulting long word is loaded into the associated register.

Selecting the addressing mode also selects the mode of operation of the MOVEM instruction, and only the control modes, the predecrement mode, and the postincrement mode are valid. If the effective address is specified by one of the control modes, the registers are transferred starting at the specified address, and the address is incremented by the operand length (2 or 4) following each transfer. The order of the registers is from data register 0 to data register 7, then from address register 0 to address register 7.

If the effective address is specified by the predecrement mode, only a register-to-memory operation is allowed. The registers are stored starting at the specified address minus the operand length (2 or 4), and the address is decremented by the operand length following each transfer. The order of storing is from address register 7 to address register 0, then from data register 7 to data register 0. When the instruction has completed, the decremented address register contains the address of the last operand stored. In the CPU 32, if the addressing register is also moved to memory, the value written is the decremented value.

If the effective address is specified by the postincrement mode, only a memory-to-register operation is allowed. The registers are loaded starting at the specified address; the address is incremented by the operand length (2 or 4) following each transfer. The order of loading is the same as that of control mode addressing. When the instruction has completed, the incremented address register contains the address of the last operand loaded plus the operand length. In the CPU32, if the addressing register is also loaded from memory, the value loaded is the value fetched plus the operand length.

MOVEC

Move Control Register
(Privileged Instruction)

Operation: If supervisor state
then Rc → Rn or Rn → Rc
else TRAP

Assembler MOVEC Rc,Rn
Syntax: MOVEC Rn,Rc

Attributes: Size = (Long)

Description: Moves the contents of the specified control register (Rc) to the specified general register (Rn) or copies the contents of the specified general register to the specified control register. This is always a 32-bit transfer even though the control register may be implemented with fewer bits. Unimplemented bits are read as zeros.

Condition Codes:
Not affected.

Instruction Format:

15	14	13	12	11	10	9	8	7	6	5	4	3	2	1	0
0	1	0	0	1	1	1	0	0	1	1	1	1	0	1	dr
A/D	REGISTER			CONTROL REGISTER											

Instruction Fields:

dr field — Specifies the direction of the transfer:
 0 — Control register to general register.
 1 — General register to control register.
A/D field — Specifies the type of general register:
 0 — Data register.
 1 — Address register.
Register field — Specifies the register number.
Control Register field — Specifies the control register.

Hex	Control Register
000	Source Function Code (SFC)
001	Destination Function Code (DFC)
800	User Stack Pointer (USP)
801	Vector Base Register (VBR)

Any other code causes an illegal instruction exception.

MOVEM

Move Multiple Registers

Condition Codes:
Not affected.

Instruction Format:

15	14	13	12	11	10	9	8	7	6	5	4	3	2	1	0
											EFFECTIVE ADDRESS				
0	1	0	0	1	dr	0	0	1	SIZE		MODE			REGISTER	
REGISTER LIST MASK															

Instruction Field:

dr field — Specifies the direction of the transfer:
0 — Register to memory
1 — Memory to register

Size field — Specifies the size of the registers being transferred:
0 — Word transfer
1 — Long transfer

Effective Address field — Specifies the memory address for the operation. For register-to-memory transfers, only control alterable addressing modes or the predecrement addressing mode are allowed as shown:

Addressing Mode	Mode	Register
Dn	–	–
An	–	–
(An)	010	reg. number:An
(An)+	–	–
-(An)	100	reg. number:An
(d16,An)	101	reg. number:An
(d8,An,Xn)	110	reg. number:An
(bd,An,Xn)	110	reg. number:An

Addressing Mode	Mode	Register
(xxx).W	111	000
(xxx).L	111	001
#(data)	–	–
(d16,PC)	–	–
(d8,PC,Xn)	–	–
(bd,PC,Xn)	–	–

MOVEM

Move Multiple Registers

For memory-to-register transfers, only control addressing modes or the postincrement addressing mode are allowed as shown:

Addressing Mode	Mode	Register
Dn	–	–
An	–	–
(An)	010	reg. number:An
(An)+	011	reg. number:An
-(An)	–	–
(d16,An)	101	reg. number:An
(d8,An,Xn)	110	reg. number:An
(bd,An,Xn)	110	reg. number:An

Addressing Mode	Mode	Register
(xxx).W	111	000
(xxx).L	111	001
#(data)	–	–
(d16,PC)	111	010
(d8,PC,Xn)	111	011
(bd,PC,Xn)	111	011

Register List Mask field — Specifies the registers to be transferred. The low-order bit corresponds to the first register to be transferred; the high-order bit corresponds to the last register to be transferred. Thus, both for control modes and for the postincrement mode addresses, the mask correspondence is:

15	14	13	12	11	10	9	8	7	6	5	4	3	2	1	0
A7	A6	A5	A4	A3	A2	A1	A0	D7	D6	D5	D4	D3	D2	D1	D0

For the predecrement mode addresses, the mask correspondence is reversed:

15	14	13	12	11	10	9	8	7	6	5	4	3	2	1	0
D0	D1	D2	D3	D4	D5	D6	D7	A0	A1	A2	A3	A4	A5	A6	A7

NOTE

An extra read bus cycle occurs for memory operands. This accesses an operand at one address higher than the last register image required.

MOVEP Move Peripheral Data MOVEP

Operation: Source ⟶ Destination

Assembler Syntax: MOVEP Dx,(d,Ay)
MOVEP (d,Ay),Dx

Attributes: Size = (Word, Long)

Description: Moves data between a data register and alternate bytes within the address space (typically assigned to a peripheral), starting at the location specified and incrementing by two. This instruction is designed for 8-bit peripherals on a 16-bit data bus. The high-order byte of the data register is transferred first and the low-order byte is transferred last. The memory address is specified in the address register indirect plus 16-bit displacement addressing mode. If the address is even, all the transfers are to or from the high-order half of the data bus; if the address is odd, all the transfers are to or from the low-order half of the data bus. The instruction also accesses alternate bytes on an 8- or 32-bit bus.

Example: Long transfer to/from an even address.

Byte Organization in Register

31		24	23		16	15		8	7		0
HI-ORDER			MID-UPPER			MID-LOWER			LOW-ORDER		

Byte Organization in Memory (Low Address at Top)

15	8	7	0
HI-ORDER			
MID-UPPER			
MID-LOWER			
LOW-ORDER			

MOVEP Move Peripheral Data MOVEP

Example: Word transfer to/from an odd address

Byte Organization in Register

31		24	23		16	15		8	7		0
						HI-ORDER			LOW-ORDER		

Byte Organization in Memory (Low Address at Top)

15	8	7	0
HI-ORDER			
LOW-ORDER			

Condition Codes:
Not affected.

Instruction Format:

15	14	13	12	11	10	9	8	7	6	5	4	3	2	1	0
0	0	0	0	DATA REGISTER			OPMODE			0	0	1	ADDRESS REGISTER		
DISPLACEMENT (16 BITS)															

Instruction Fields:
Data Register field — Specifies the data register for the instruction.
Opmode field — Specifies the direction and size of the operation:
100 — Transfer word from memory to register.
101 — Transfer long from memory to register.
110 — Transfer word from register to memory.
111 — Transfer long from register to memory.
Address Register field — Specifies the address register which is used in the address register indirect plus displacement addressing mode.
Displacement field — Specifies the displacement used in the operand address.

MOVES

Move Address Space
(Privileged Instruction)

MOVES

Operation: If supervisor state
then Rn ⬥ Destination [DFC] or Source [SFC] ⬥ Rn
else TRAP

**Assembler
Syntax:** MOVES Rn,(ea)
MOVES (ea),Rn

Attributes: Size = (Byte, Word, Long)

Description: Moves the byte, word, or long operand from the specified general register to a location within the address space specified by the destination function code (DFC) register; or, moves the byte, word, or long operand from a location within the address space specified by the source function code (SFC) register to the specified general register.

If the destination is a data register, the source operand replaces the corresponding low-order bits of that data register, depending on the size of the operation. If the destination is an address register, the source operand is sign-extended to 32 bits and then loaded into that address register.

Condition Codes:
Not affected.

Instruction Format:

15	14	13	12	11	10	9	8	7	6	5	4	3	2	1	0
0	0	0	0	1	1	1	0		SIZE			EFFECTIVE ADDRESS			
													MODE		REGISTER
A/D		REGISTER		dr	0	0	0	0	0	0	0	0	0	0	0

Instruction Fields:
Size field — Specifies the size of the operation:
00 — Byte operation
01 — Word operation
10 — Long operation

MOVEQ

Move Quick

MOVEQ

Operation: Immediate Data ⬥ Destination

**Assembler
Syntax:** MOVEQ #(data),Dn

Attributes: Size = (Long)

Description: Moves a byte of immediate data to a 32-bit data register. The data in an 8-bit field within the operation word is sign-extended to a long operand in the data register as it is transferred.

Condition Codes:

X	N	Z	V	C
—	*	*	0	0

X Not affected.
N Set if the result is negative. Cleared otherwise.
Z Set if the result is zero. Cleared otherwise.
V Always cleared.
C Always cleared.

Instruction Format:

15	14	13	12	11	10	9	8	7	6	5	4	3	2	1	0
0	1	1	1		REGISTER		0					DATA			

Instruction Fields:
Register field — Specifies the data register to be loaded.
Data field — Eight bits of data, which are sign-extended to a long operand.

MULS

Signed Multiply

MULS

Operation: Source * Destination → Destination

Assembler Syntax:
MULS.W (ea),Dn   16x16 → 32
MULS.L (ea),Dl   32x32 → 32
MULS.L (ea),Dh:Dl   32 x 32 → 64

Attributes: Size = (Word, Long)

Description: Multiplies two signed operands yielding a signed result. This instruction has a word operand form and a long word operand form.

In the word form, the multiplier and multiplicand are both word operands, and the result is a long word operand. A register operand is the low-order word; the upper word of the register is ignored. All 32 bits of the product are saved in the destination data register.

In the long form, the multiplier and multiplicand are both long word operands, and the result is either a long word or a quad word. The long word result is the low-order 32 bits of the quad word result; the high-order 32 bits of the product are discarded.

Condition Codes:

X	N	Z	V	C
—	*	*	*	0

X Not affected.
N Set if the result is negative. Cleared otherwise.
Z Set if the result is zero. Cleared otherwise.
V Set if overflow. Cleared otherwise.
C Always cleared.

NOTE

Overflow (V = 1) can occur only when multiplying 32-bit operands to yield a 32-bit result. Overflow occurs if the high-order 32 bits of the quad word product are not the sign extension of the low-order 32 bits.

Instruction Format (word form):

15	14	13	12	11	10	9	8	7	6	5	4	3	2	1	0
1	1	0	0	REGISTER			1	1	1	EFFECTIVE ADDRESS					
										MODE			REGISTER		

MOVES

Move Address Space
(Privileged Instruction)

MOVES

Effective Address field — Specifies the source or destination location within the alternate address space. Only memory alterable addressing modes are allowed as shown:

Addressing Mode	Mode	Register
Dn	—	—
An	—	—
(An)	010	reg. number:An
(An)+	011	reg. number:An
-(An)	100	reg. number:An
(d₁₆,An)	101	reg. number:An
(d₈,An,Xn)	110	reg. number:An
(bd,An,Xn)	110	reg. number:An

Addressing Mode	Mode	Register
(xxx).W	111	000
(xxx).L	111	001
#⟨data⟩	—	—
(d₁₆,PC)	—	—
(d₈,PC,Xn)	—	—
(bd,PC,Xn)	—	—

A/D field — Specifies the type of general register:
0 — Data register
1 — Address register

Register field — Specifies the register number.

dr field — Specifies the direction of the transfer:
0 — From ⟨ea⟩ to general register
1 — From general register to ⟨ea⟩

NOTE

For either of the two following examples with the same address register as both source and destination
MOVES.x An,(An)+
MOVES.x An, −(An)
the value stored is undefined. The current implementations of the MC68010, CPU32, and MC68020 store the incremented or decremented value of An.

MULS   Signed Multiply   **MULS**

Register Dl field — Specifies a data register for the destination operand. The 32-bit multiplicand comes from this register, and the low-order 32 bits of the product are loaded into this register.

Size field — Selects a 32- or 64-bit product.

  0 — 32-bit product to be returned to Register Dl.
  1 — 64-bit product to be returned to Dh:Dl.

Register Dh field — If Size is 1, specifies the data register into which the high-order 32 bits of the product are loaded. If Dh = Dl and Size is 1, the results of the operation are undefined. Otherwise, this field is unused.

MULS   Signed Multiply   **MULS**

Instruction Fields:

Register field — Specifies a data register as the destination.

Effective Address field — Specifies the source operand. Only data addressing modes are allowed as shown:

Addressing Mode	Mode	Register		Addressing Mode	Mode	Register
Dn	000	reg. number:Dn		(xxx).W	111	000
An	—	—		(xxx).L	111	001
(An)	010	reg. number:An		#(data)	111	100
(An)+	011	reg. number:An				
-(An)	100	reg. number:An		(d16,PC)	111	010
(d16,An)	101	reg. number:An		(d8,PC,Xn)	111	011
(d8,An,Xn)	110	reg. number:An		(bd,PC,Xn)	111	011
(bd,An,Xn)	110	reg. number:An				

Instruction Format (long form):

15	14	13	12	11	10	9	8	7	6	5	4	3	2	1	0
												EFFECTIVE ADDRESS			
													MODE		REGISTER
0	1	0	0	1	1	0	0	0	0	0	0	0			REGISTER Dr
0	REGISTER Dq			1	SIZE	0	0	0	0	0	0	0			REGISTER Dr

Instruction Fields:

Effective Address field — Specifies the source operand. Only data addressing modes are allowed as shown:

Addressing Mode	Mode	Register		Addressing Mode	Mode	Register
Dn	000	reg. number:Dn		(xxx).W	111	000
An	—	—		(xxx).L	111	001
(An)	010	reg. number:An		#(data)	111	100
(An)+	011	reg. number:An				
-(An)	100	reg. number:An		(d16,PC)	111	010
(d16,An)	101	reg. number:An		(d8,PC,Xn)	111	011
(d8,An,Xn)	110	reg. number:An		(bd,PC,Xn)	111	011
(bd,An,Xn)	110	reg. number:An				

MULU   Unsigned Multiply   MULU

Operation: Source * Destination ♦ Destination

Assembler   MULU.W ⟨ea⟩,Dn   16x16 ♦ 32
Syntax: MULU.L ⟨ea⟩,Dl   32x32 ♦ 32
                MULU.L ⟨ea⟩,Dh:Dl   32x32 ♦64

Attributes: Size = (Word, Long)

Description: Multiplies two unsigned operands yielding an unsigned result. This instruction has a word operand form and a long word operand form.

In the word form, the multiplier and multiplicand are both word operands, and the result is a long word operand. A register operand is the low-order word; the upper word of the register is ignored. All 32 bits of the product are saved in the destination data register.

In the long form, the multiplier and multiplicand are both long word operands, and the result is either a long word or a quad word. The long word result is the low-order 32 bits of the quad word result; the high-order 32 bits of the product are discarded.

Condition Codes:

X	N	Z	V	C
–	*	*	*	0

X   Not affected.
N   Set if the result is negative. Cleared otherwise.
Z   Set if the result is zero. Cleared otherwise.
V   Set if overflow. Cleared otherwise.
C   Always cleared.

NOTE

Overflow (V = 1) can occur only when multiplying 32-bit operands to yield a 32-bit result. Overflow occurs if any of the high-order 32 bits of the quad word product are not equal to zero.

MULU   Unsigned Multiply   MULU

Instruction Format (word form):

15	14	13	12	11	10	9	8	7	6	5	4	3	2	1	0
1	1	0	0		REGISTER			0	1	1		EFFECTIVE ADDRESS			
												MODE			REGISTER

Instruction Fields:

Register field — Specifies a data register as the destination.
Effective Address field — Specifies the source operand. Only data addressing modes are allowed as shown:

Addressing Mode	Mode	Register
Dn	000	reg. number:Dn
An	–	–
(An)	010	reg. number:An
(An)+	011	reg. number:An
–(An)	100	reg. number:An
(d16,An)	101	reg. number:An
(d8,An,Xn)	110	reg. number:An
(bd,An,Xn)	110	reg. number:An

Addressing Mode	Mode	Register
(xxx).W	111	000
(xxx).L	111	001
#⟨data⟩	111	100
(d16,PC)	111	010
(d8,PC,Xn)	111	011
(bd,PC,Xn)	111	011

Instruction Format (long form):

15	14	13	12	11	10	9	8	7	6	5	4	3	2	1	0
0	1	0	0	1	1	0	0	0	0		EFFECTIVE ADDRESS				
												MODE			REGISTER
0	REGISTER Dl			0	1	SIZE	0	0	0	0	0	0			REGISTER Dh

NBCD

NBCD   Negate Decimal with Extend   **NBCD**

Operation: $0 - (\text{Destination}_{10}) - X \blacklozenge$ Destination

**Assembler
Syntax:**   NBCD (ea)

Attributes: Size = (Byte)

Description: Subtracts the destination operand and the extend bit from zero. The operation is performed using binary coded decimal arithmetic. The packed BCD result is saved in the destination location. This instruction produces the tens complement of the destination if the extend bit is zero, or the nines complement if the extend bit is one. This is a byte operation only.

Condition Codes:

X	N	Z	V	C
*	U	*	U	*

X   Set the same as the carry bit.
N   Undefined.
Z   Cleared if the result is non-zero. Unchanged otherwise.
V   Undefined.
C   Set if a decimal borrow occurs. Cleared otherwise.

NOTE

Normally the Z condition code bit is set via programming before the start of the operation. This allows successful tests for zero results upon completion of multiple precision operations.

Instruction Format:

15	14	13	12	11	10	9	8	7	6	5	4	3	2	1	0
0	1	0	0	1	0	0	0	0	0	\multicolumn{3}{c	}{MODE}	\multicolumn{3}{c	}{REGISTER}

(EFFECTIVE ADDRESS: MODE, REGISTER)

MULU

MULU   Unsigned Multiply   **MULU**

Instruction Fields:

Effective Address field — Specifies the source operand. Only data addressing modes are allowed as shown:

Addressing Mode	Mode	Register		Addressing Mode	Mode	Register
Dn	000	reg. number:Dn		(xxx).W	111	000
An	—	—		(xxx).L	111	001
(An)	010	reg. number:An		#(data)	111	100
(An)+	011	reg. number:An				
-(An)	100	reg. number:An				
(d$_{16}$,An)	101	reg. number:An		(d$_{16}$,PC)	111	010
(d$_8$,An,Xn)	110	reg. number:An		(d$_8$,PC,Xn)	111	011
(bd,An,Xn)	110	reg. number:An		(bd,PC,Xn)	111	011

Register Dl field — Specifies a data register for the destination operand. The 32-bit multiplicand comes from this register, and the low-order 32 bits of the product are loaded into this register.

Size field — Selects a 32- or 64-bit product.
   0 — 32-bit product to be returned to Register Dl.
   1 — 64-bit product to be returned to Dh:Dl.

Register Dh field — If Size is 1, specifies the data register into which the high-order 32 bits of the product are loaded. If Dh = Dl and Size is 1, the results of the operation are undefined. Otherwise, this field is unused.

NEG

Negate

Operation: 0 – (Destination) ▶ Destination

Assembler
Syntax: NEG (ea)

Attributes: Size = (Byte, Word, Long)

Description: Subtracts the destination operand from zero and stores the result in the destination location. The size of the operation is specified as byte, word, or long.

Condition Codes:

X	N	Z	V	C
*	*	*	*	*

X Set the same as the carry bit.
N Set if the result is negative. Cleared otherwise.
Z Set if the result is zero. Cleared otherwise.
V Set if an overflow occurs. Cleared otherwise.
C Cleared if the result is zero. Set otherwise.

Instruction Format:

15	14	13	12	11	10	9	8	7	6	5	4	3	2	1	0
0	1	0	0	0	1	0	0	SIZE		EFFECTIVE ADDRESS					
										MODE			REGISTER		

Instruction Fields:
Size field — Specifies the size of the operation.
00 — Byte operation
01 — Word operation
10 — Long operation

NBCD

Negate Decimal with Extend

Instruction Fields:
Effective Address field — Specifies the destination operand. Only data alterable addressing modes are allowed as shown:

Addressing Mode	Mode	Register	Addressing Mode	Mode	Register
Dn	000	reg. number:Dn	(xxx).W	111	000
An	–	–	(xxx).L	111	001
(An)	010	reg. number:An	#(data)	–	–
(An)+	011	reg. number:An			
-(An)	100	reg. number:An			
(d$_{16}$,An)	101	reg. number:An	(d$_{16}$,PC)	–	–
(d$_8$,An,Xn)	110	reg. number:An	(d$_8$,PC,Xn)	–	–
(bd,An,Xn)	110	reg. number:An	(bd,PC,Xn)	–	–

NEGX Negate with Extend NEGX

Operation: 0 – (Destination) – X ▶ Destination

Assembler
Syntax: NEGX (ea)

Attributes: Size = (Byte, Word, Long)

Description: Subtracts the destination operand and the extend bit from zero. Stores the result in the destination location. The size of the operation is specified as byte, word, or long.

Condition Codes:

X	N	Z	V	C
*	*	*	*	*

X Set the same as the carry bit.
N Set if the result is negative. Cleared otherwise.
Z Cleared if the result is nonzero. Unchanged otherwise.
V Set if an overflow occurs. Cleared otherwise.
C Set if a borrow occurs. Cleared otherwise.

NOTE

Normally the Z condition code bit is set via programming before the start of the operation. This allows successful tests for zero results upon completion of multiple precision operations.

Instruction Format:

15	14	13	12	11	10	9	8	7	6	5	4	3	2	1	0
0	1	0	0	0	0	0	0	SIZE			EFFECTIVE ADDRESS				
											MODE			REGISTER	

Instruction Fields:
Size field — Specifies the size of the operation.
00 — Byte operation
01 — Word operation
10 — Long operation

NEG Negate NEG

Effective Address field — Specifies the destination operand. Only data alterable addressing modes are allowed as shown:

Addressing Mode	Mode	Register
Dn	000	reg. number:Dn
An	—	—
(An)	010	reg. number:An
(An)+	011	reg. number:An
-(An)	100	reg. number:An
(d16,An)	101	reg. number:An
(d8,An,Xn)	110	reg. number:An
(bd,An,Xn)	110	reg. number:An

Addressing Mode	Mode	Register
(xxx).W	111	000
(xxx).L	111	001
#(data)	—	—
(d16,PC)	—	—
(d8,PC,Xn)	—	—
(bd,PC,Xn)	—	—

NOP

Operation: None

Assembler Syntax: NOP

Attributes: Unsized

Description: Performs no operation. The processor state, other than the program counter, is unaffected. Execution continues with the instruction following the NOP instruction. The NOP instruction does not begin execution until all pending bus cycles are completed. This synchronizes the pipeline, and prevents instruction overlap.

Condition Codes: Not affected.

Instruction Format:

15	14	13	12	11	10	9	8	7	6	5	4	3	2	1	0
0	1	0	0	1	1	1	0	0	1	1	1	0	0	0	1

NEGX

Negate with Extend

Effective Address field — Specifies the destination operand. Only data alterable addressing modes are allowed as shown:

Addressing Mode	Mode	Register	Addressing Mode	Mode	Register
Dn	000	reg. number:Dn	(xxx).W	111	000
An	—	—	(xxx).L	111	001
(An)	010	reg. number:An	#(data)	—	—
(An)+	011	reg. number:An			
-(An)	100	reg. number:An	(d16,PC)	—	—
(d16,An)	101	reg. number:An	(d8,PC,Xn)	—	—
(d8,An,Xn)	110	reg. number:An	(bd,PC,Xn)	—	—
(bd,An,Xn)	110	reg. number:An			

Logical Complement

Operation: ~ Destination → Destination

**Assembler
Syntax:** NOT (ea)

Attributes: Size = (Byte, Word, Long)

Description: Calculates the ones complement of the destination operand and stores the result in the destination location. The size of the operation is specified as byte, word, or long.

Condition Codes:

X	N	Z	V	C
—	*	*	0	0

X Not affected.
N Set if the result is negative. Cleared otherwise.
Z Set if the result is zero. Cleared otherwise.
V Always cleared.
C Always cleared.

Instruction Format:

15	14	13	12	11	10	9	8	7	6	5	4	3	2	1	0
0	1	0	0	0	1	1	0	SIZE		EFFECTIVE ADDRESS					
										MODE			REGISTER		

Instruction Fields:
Size field — Specifies the size of the operation.
00 — Byte operation
01 — Word operation
10 — Long operation

Logical Complement

Effective Address field — Specifies the destination operand. Only data alterable addressing modes are allowed as shown:

Addressing Mode	Mode	Register	Addressing Mode	Mode	Register
Dn	000	reg. number:Dn	(xxx).W	111	000
An	—	—	(xxx).L	111	001
(An)	010	reg. number:An	#(data)	—	—
(An)+	011	reg. number:An			
−(An)	100	reg. number:An			
(d$_{16}$,An)	101	reg. number:An	(d$_{16}$,PC)	—	—
(d$_8$,An,Xn)	110	reg. number:An	(d$_8$,PC,Xn)	—	—
(bd,An,Xn)	110	reg. number:An	(bd,PC,Xn)	—	—

OR
Inclusive OR Logical
OR

Operation: Source V Destination → Destination

Assembler Syntax:
OR (ea),Dn
OR Dn,(ea)

Attributes: Size = (Byte, Word, Long)

Description: Performs an inclusive OR operation on the source operand and the destination operand and stores the result in the destination location. The size of the operation is specified as byte, word, or long. The contents of an address register may not be used as an operand.

Condition Codes:

X	N	Z	V	C
—	*	*	0	0

X Not affected.
N Set if the most significant bit of the result is set. Cleared otherwise.
Z Set if the result is zero. Cleared otherwise.
V Always cleared.
C Always cleared.

Instruction Format:

15	14	13	12	11 10 9	8 7 6	5 4 3	2 1 0
						EFFECTIVE ADDRESS	
1	0	0	0	REGISTER	OPMODE	MODE	REGISTER

Instruction Fields:

Register field — Specifies any of the eight data registers.

Opmode field:

Byte	Word	Long	Operation
000	001	010	((ea)) V ((Dn)) → (Dn)
100	101	110	((Dn)) V ((ea)) → (ea)

OR
Inclusive OR Logical
OR

Effective Address field — If the location specified is a source operand, only data addressing modes are allowed as shown:

Addressing Mode	Mode	Register	Addressing Mode	Mode	Register
Dn	000	reg. number:Dn	(xxx).W	111	000
An	—	—	(xxx).L	111	001
(An)	010	reg. number:An	#(data)	111	100
(An)+	011	reg. number:An			
-(An)	100	reg. number:An			
(d16,An)	101	reg. number:An	(d16,PC)	111	010
(d8,An,Xn)	110	reg. number:An	(d8,PC,Xn)	111	011
(bd,An,Xn)	110	reg. number:An	(bd,PC,Xn)	111	011

If the location specified is a destination operand, only memory alterable addressing modes are allowed as shown:

Addressing Mode	Mode	Register	Addressing Mode	Mode	Register
Dn	—	—	(xxx).W	111	000
An	—	—	(xxx).L	111	001
(An)	010	reg. number:An	#(data)	—	—
(An)+	011	reg. number:An			
-(An)	100	reg. number:An			
(d16,An)	101	reg. number:An	(d16,PC)	—	—
(d8,An,Xn)	110	reg. number:An	(d8,PC,Xn)	—	—
(bd,An,Xn)	110	reg. number:An	(bd,PC,Xn)	—	—

NOTES:
1. If the destination is a data register, it must be specified using the destination Dn mode, not the destination (ea) mode.
2. Most assemblers use ORI when the source is immediate data.

Inclusive OR

Operation: Immediate Data V Destination ♦ Destination

Assembler
Syntax: ORI #(data),(ea)

Attributes: Size = (Byte, Word, Long)

Description: Performs an inclusive OR operation on the immediate data and the destination operand and stores the result in the destination location. The size of the operation is specified as byte, word, or long. The size of the immediate data matches the operation size.

Condition Codes:

X	N	Z	V	C
—	*	*	0	0

X Not affected.
N Set if the most significant bit of the result is set. Cleared otherwise.
Z Set if the result is zero. Cleared otherwise.
V Always cleared.
C Always cleared.

Instruction Format:

15	14	13	12	11	10	9	8	7	6	5	4	3	2	1	0
											EFFECTIVE ADDRESS				
0	0	0	0	0	0	0	0	SIZE		MODE			REGISTER		
WORD DATA (16 BITS)								BYTE DATA (8 BITS)							
LONG DATA (32 BITS)															

Instruction Fields:
Size field — Specifies the size of the operation.
00 — Byte operation
01 — Word operation
10 — Long operation

Inclusive OR

Effective Address field — Specifies the destination operand. Only data alterable addressing modes are allowed as shown:

Addressing Mode	Mode	Register	Addressing Mode	Mode	Register
Dn	000	reg. number:Dn	(xxx).W	111	000
An	—	—	(xxx).L	111	001
(An)	010	reg. number:An	#(data)	—	—
(An)+	011	reg. number:An			
-(An)	100	reg. number:An			
(d16,An)	101	reg. number:An	(d16,PC)	—	—
(d8,An,Xn)	110	reg. number:An	(d8,PC,Xn)	—	—
(bd,An,Xn)	110	reg. number:An	(bd,PC,Xn)	—	—

Immediate field — (Data immediately following the instruction):
If size = 00, the data is the low-order byte of the immediate word.
If size = 01, the data is the entire immediate word.
If size = 10, the data is the next two immediate words.

ORI
to SR

Inclusive OR Immediate to the Status Register
(Privileged Instruction)

Operation: If supervisor state
then Source V SR ♦ SR
else TRAP

Assembler
Syntax: ORI #⟨data⟩,SR

Attributes: Size = (Word)

Description: Performs an inclusive OR operation of the immediate operand and the contents of the status register and stores the result in the status register. All implemented bits of the status register are affected.

Condition Codes:

X	N	Z	V	C
*	*	*	*	*

X Set if bit 4 of immediate operand is one. Unchanged otherwise.
N Set if bit 3 of immediate operand is one. Unchanged otherwise.
Z Set if bit 2 of immediate operand is one. Unchanged otherwise.
V Set if bit 1 of immediate operand is one. Unchanged otherwise.
C Set if bit 0 of immediate operand is one. Unchanged otherwise.

Instruction Format:

15	14	13	12	11	10	9	8	7	6	5	4	3	2	1	0
0	0	0	0	0	0	0	0	0	1	1	1	1	1	0	0
						WORD DATA (16 BITS)									

ORI
to CCR

Inclusive OR Immediate
to Condition Codes

Operation: Source V CCR ♦ CCR

Assembler
Syntax: ORI #⟨data⟩,CCR

Attributes: Size = (Byte)

Description: Performs an inclusive OR operation on the immediate operand and the condition codes and stores the result in the condition code register (low-order byte of the status register). All implemented bits of the condition code register are affected.

Condition Codes:

X	N	Z	V	C
*	*	*	*	*

X Set if bit 4 of immediate operand is one. Unchanged otherwise.
N Set if bit 3 of immediate operand is one. Unchanged otherwise.
Z Set if bit 2 of immediate operand is one. Unchanged otherwise.
V Set if bit 1 of immediate operand is one. Unchanged otherwise.
C Set if bit 0 of immediate operand is one. Unchanged otherwise.

Instruction Format:

15	14	13	12	11	10	9	8	7	6	5	4	3	2	1	0
0	0	0	0	0	0	0	0	0	0	1	1	1	1	0	0
								BYTE DATA (8 BITS)							

RESET

Reset External Devices
(Privileged Instruction)

RESET

Operation: If supervisor state
then Assert RESET Line
else TRAP

Assembler Syntax: RESET

Attributes: Unsized

Description: Asserts the RESET signal for 512 clock periods, resetting all external devices. The processor state, other than the program counter, is unaffected and execution continues with the next instruction.

Condition Codes:
Not affected.

Instruction Format:

15	14	13	12	11	10	9	8	7	6	5	4	3	2	1	0
0	1	0	0	1	1	1	0	0	1	1	1	0	0	0	0

PEA

Push Effective Address

PEA

Operation: Sp − 4 ♦ SP; (ea) ♦ (SP)

Assembler Syntax: PEA (ea)

Attributes: Size = (Long)

Description: Computes the effective address and pushes it onto the stack. The effective address is a long word address.

Condition Codes:
Not affected.

Instruction Format:

15	14	13	12	11	10	9	8	7	6	5	4	3	2	1	0
0	1	0	0	1	0	0	0	0	1		EFFECTIVE ADDRESS				
											MODE			REGISTER	

Instruction Fields:

Effective Address field — Specifies the address to be pushed onto the stack. Only control addressing modes are allowed as shown:

Addressing Mode	Mode	Register		Addressing Mode	Mode	Register
Dn	—	—		(xxx).W	111	000
An	—	—		(xxx).L	111	001
(An)	010	reg. number:An		#(data)	—	—
(An)+	—	—				
−(An)	—	—				
(d$_{16}$,An)	101	reg. number:An		(d$_{16}$,PC)	111	010
(d$_8$,An,Xn)	110	reg. number:An		(d$_8$,PC,Xn)	111	011
(bd,An,Xn)	110	reg. number:An		(bd,PC,Xn)	111	011

Operation: Destination Rotated by ⟨count⟩ ♦ Destination

Assembler
Syntax:
 ROd Dx,Dy
 ROd #⟨data⟩,Dy
 ROd ⟨ea⟩
 where d is direction, L or R

Attributes: Size = (Byte, Word, Long)

Description: Rotates the bits of the operand in the direction specified (L or R). The extend bit is not included in the rotation. The rotate count for the rotation of a register is specified in either of two ways:

1. Immediate — The rotate count (1-8) is specified in the instruction.
2. Register — The rotate count is the value in the data register specified in the instruction, modulo 64.

The size of the operation for register destinations is specified as byte, word, or long. The contents of memory ⟨ea⟩ can be rotated one bit only, and operand size is restricted to a word.

The ROL instruction rotates the bits of the operand to the left; the rotate count determines the number of bit positions rotated. Bits rotated out of the high-order bit go to the carry bit and also back into the low-order bit.

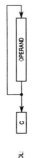

ROL:

The ROR instruction rotates the bits of the operand to the right; the rotate count determines the number of bit positions rotated. Bits rotated out of the low-order bit go to the carry bit and also back into the high-order bit.

ROR:

Condition Codes:

X	N	Z	V	C
—	*	*	0	*

X Not affected.
N Set if the most significant bit of the result is set. Cleared otherwise.
Z Set if the result is zero. Cleared otherwise.
V Always cleared.
C Set according to the last bit rotated out of the operand. Cleared when the rotate count is zero.

Instruction Format (Register Rotate):

15	14	13	12	11	10	9	8	7	6	5	4	3	2	1	0
1	1	1	0	COUNT/ REGISTER			dr	SIZE		i/r	1	1	REGISTER		

Instruction Fields (Register Rotate):

Count/Register field:
If i/r = 0, this field contains the rotate count. The values 1-7 represent counts of 1-7, and 0 specifies a count of 8.
If i/r = 1, this field specifies a data register that contains the rotate count (modulo 64).

dr field — Specifies the direction of the rotate:
 0 — Rotate right
 1 — Rotate left

Size field — Specifies the size of the operation:
 00 — Byte operation
 01 — Word operation
 10 — Long operation

i/r field — Specifies the rotate count location:
 If i/r = 0, immediate rotate count.
 If i/r = 1, register rotate count.

Register field — Specifies a data register to be rotated.

ROXL, ROXR   Rotate with Extend   ROXL, ROXR

Operation: Destination Rotated with X by (count) ♦ Destination

Assembler Syntax:
ROXd Dx,Dy
ROXd #(data),Dy
ROXd (ea)
where d is direction, L or R

Attributes: Size = (Byte, Word, Long)

Description: Rotates the bits of the operand in the direction specified (L or R). The extend bit is included in the rotation. The rotate count for the rotation of a register is specified in either of two ways:

1. Immediate — The rotate count (1-8) is specified in the instruction.
2. Register — The rotate count is the value in the data register specified in the instruction, modulo 64.

The size of the operation for register destinations is specified as byte, word, or long. The contents of memory, (ea), can be rotated one bit only, and operand size is restricted to a word.

The ROXL instruction rotates the bits of the operand to the left; the rotate count determines the number of bit positions rotated. Bits rotated out of the high-order bit go to the carry bit and the extend bit; the previous value of the extend bit rotates into the low-order bit.

The ROXR instruction rotates the bits of the operand to the right; the rotate count determines the number of bit positions rotated. Bits rotated out of the low-order bit go to the carry bit and the extend bit; the previous value of the extend bit rotates into the high-order bit.

ROL, ROR   Rotate (Without Extend)   ROL, ROR

Instruction Format (Memory Rotate):

15	14	13	12	11	10	9	8	7	6	5	4	3	2	1	0
1	1	0	1	0	1	1	dr	1	1	EFFECTIVE ADDRESS MODE			REGISTER		

Instruction Fields (Memory Rotate):

dr field — Specifies the direction of the rotate:
0 — Rotate right
1 — Rotate left

Effective Address field — Specifies the operand to be rotated. Only memory alterable addressing modes are allowed as shown:

Addressing Mode	Mode	Register
Dn	—	—
An	—	—
(An)	010	reg. number:An
(An)+	011	reg. number:An
-(An)	100	reg. number:An
(d16,An)	101	reg. number:An
(d8,An,Xn)	110	reg. number:An
(bd,An,Xn)	110	reg. number:An

Addressing Mode	Mode	Register
(xxx).W	111	000
(xxx).L	111	001
#(data)	—	—
(d16,PC)	—	—
(d8,PC,Xn)	—	—
(bd,PC,Xn)	—	—

ROXL, ROXR   Rotate with Extend   ROXL, ROXR

Instruction Format (Memory Rotate):

15	14	13	12	11	10	9	8	7	6	5	4	3	2	1	0
1	1	1	0	0	1	0	dr	1	1		MODE		EFFECTIVE ADDRESS		REGISTER

Instruction Fields (Memory Rotate):

dr field — Specifies the direction of the rotate:
0 — Rotate right
1 — Rotate left

Effective Address field — Specifies the operand to be rotated. Only memory alterable addressing modes are allowed as shown:

Addressing Mode	Mode	Register
Dn	—	—
An	—	—
(An)	010	reg. number:An
(An)+	011	reg. number:An
-(An)	100	reg. number:An
(d₁₆,An)	101	reg. number:An
(d₈,An,Xn)	110	reg. number:An
(bd,An,Xn)	110	reg. number:An

Addressing Mode	Mode	Register
(xxx).W	111	000
(xxx).L	111	001
#(data)	—	—
(d₁₆,PC)	—	—
(d₈,PC,Xn)	—	—
(bd,PC,Xn)	—	—

ROXL, ROXR   Rotate with Extend   ROXL, ROXR

Condition Codes:

X	N	Z	V	C
*	*	*	0	*

X Set to the value of the last bit rotated out of the operand. Unaffected when the rotate count is zero.
N Set if the most significant bit of the result is set. Cleared otherwise.
Z Set if the result is zero. Cleared otherwise.
V Always cleared.
C Set according to the last bit rotated out of the operand. When the rotate count is zero, set to the value of the extend bit.

Instruction Format (Register Rotate):

15	14	13	12	11	10	9	8	7	6	5	4	3	2	1	0
1	1	1	0		COUNT/ REGISTER		dr		SIZE		i/r	1	0		REGISTER

Instruction Fields (Register Rotate):

Count/Register field:
If i/r = 0, this field contains the rotate count. The values 1-7 represent counts of 1-7, and 0 specifies a count of 8.
If i/r = 1, this field specifies a data register that contains the rotate count (modulo 64).

dr field — Specifies the direction of the rotate:
0 — Rotate right
1 — Rotate left

Size field — Specifies the size of the operation:
00 — Byte operation
01 — Word operation
10 — Long operation

i/r field — Specifies the rotate count location:
If i/r = 0, immediate rotate count.
If i/r = 1, register rotate count.

Register field — Specifies a data register to be rotated.

RTE

Return from Exception
(Privileged Instruction)

Operation:
If supervisor state
then (SP) ♦ SR; SP + 2 ♦ SP; (SP) ♦ PC;
SP + 4 ♦ SP;
restore state and deallocate stack according to (SP)
else TRAP

Assembler Syntax: RTE

Attributes: Unsized

Description: Loads the processor state information stored in the exception stack frame located at the top of the stack into the processor. The instruction examines the stack format field in the format/offset word to determine how much information must be restored.

Condition Codes: Set according to the condition code bits in the status register value restored from the stack.

Instruction Format:

15	14	13	12	11	10	9	8	7	6	5	4	3	2	1	0
0	1	0	0	1	1	1	0	0	1	1	1	0	0	1	1

Format/Offset word (in stack frame):

15	14	13	12	11	10	9	8	7	6	5	4	3	2	1	0
FORMAT				0	0	VECTOR OFFSET									

RTD

Return and Deallocate

Operation: (SP) ♦ PC; SP + 4 + d ♦ SP

Assembler Syntax: RTD #(displacement)

Attributes: Unsized

Description: Pulls the program counter value from the stack and adds the sign-extended 16-bit displacement value to the stack pointer. The previous program counter value is lost.

Condition Codes: Not affected.

Instruction Format:

15	14	13	12	11	10	9	8	7	6	5	4	3	2	1	0
0	1	0	0	1	1	1	0	0	1	1	1	0	1	0	0
DISPLACEMENT (16 BITS)															

Instruction Field:
Displacement field — Specifies the twos complement integer to be sign extended and added to the stack pointer.

RTR

Return and Restore Condition Codes

RTR

Operation: (SP) ♦ CCR; SP + 2 ♦ SP;
(SP) ♦ PC; SP + 4 ♦ SP

**Assembler
Syntax:** RTR

Attributes: Unsized

Description: Pulls the condition code and program counter values from the stack. The previous condition codes and program counter values are lost. The supervisor portion of the status register is unaffected.

Condition Codes:

Set to the condition codes from the stack.

Instruction Format:

15	14	13	12	11	10	9	8	7	6	5	4	3	2	1	0
0	1	0	0	1	1	1	0	0	1	1	1	0	1	1	1

RTE

**Return from Exception
(Privileged Instruction)**

RTE

Format Field of Format/Offset Word:
Contains the format code, which implies the stack frame size (including the format/offset word).

0000 — Short Format, removes four words. Loads the status register and the program counter from the stack frame.

0001 — Throwaway Format, removes four words. Loads the status register from the stack frame and switches to the active system stack. Continues the instruction using the active system stack.

0010 — Instruction Error Format, removes six words. Loads the status register and the program counter from the stack frame and discards the other words.

1000 — MC68010 Long Format. The MC68020 takes a format error exception.

1001 — Coprocessor Mid-Instruction Format, removes 10 words. Resumes execution of coprocessor instruction.

1010 — MC68020 Short Format, removes 16 words and resumes instruction execution.

1011 — MC68020 Long Format, removes 46 words and resumes instruction execution.

Any other value in this field causes the processor to take a format error exception.

SBCD

Subtract Decimal with Extend

Operation: Destination10 – Source10 – X ♦ Destination

Assembler Syntax: SBCD Dx,Dy
SBCD – (Ax), – (Ay)

Attributes: Size = (Byte)

Description: Subtracts the source operand and the extend bit from the destination operand and stores the result in the destination location. The subtraction is performed using binary coded decimal arithmetic; the operands are packed BCD numbers. The instruction has two modes:

1. Data register to data register: The data registers specified in the instruction contain the operands.
2. Memory to memory: The address registers specified in the instruction access the operands from memory using the predecrement addressing mode.

This operation is a byte operation only.

Condition Codes:

X	N	Z	V	C
*	U	*	U	*

X Set the same as the carry bit.
N Undefined.
Z Cleared if the result is nonzero. Unchanged otherwise.
V Undefined.
C Set if a borrow (decimal) is generated. Cleared otherwise.

NOTE

Normally the Z condition code bit is set via programming before the start of an operation. This allows successful tests for zero results upon completion of multiple-precision operations.

RTS

Return from Subroutine

Operation: (SP) ♦ PC; SP + 4 ♦ SP

Assembler Syntax: RTS

Attributes: Unsized

Description: Pulls the program counter value from the stack. The previous program counter value is lost.

Condition Codes: Not affected.

Instruction Format:

15	14	13	12	11	10	9	8	7	6	5	4	3	2	1	0
0	1	0	0	1	1	1	0	0	1	1	1	0	1	0	1

Scc

Set According to Condition

Scc

Operation: If Condition True
then 1s → Destination
else 0s → Destination

Assembler
Syntax: Scc ⟨ea⟩

Attributes: Size = (Byte)

Description: Tests the specified condition code; if the condition is true, sets the byte specified by the effective address to TRUE (all ones). Otherwise, sets that byte to FALSE (all zeros). Condition code cc specifies one of the following conditions:

CC	carry clear	0100	C̄		LS	low or same	0011	C + Z
CS	carry set	0101	C		LT	less than	1101	N·V̄ + N̄·V
EQ	equal	0111	Z		MI	minus	1011	N
F	never true	0001	0		NE	not equal	0110	Z̄
GE	greater or equal	1100	N·V + N̄·V̄		PL	plus	1010	N̄
GT	greater than	1110	N·V·Z̄ + N̄·V̄·Z̄		T	always true	0000	1
HI	high	0010	C̄·Z̄		VC	overflow clear	1000	V̄
LE	less or equal	1111	Z + N·V̄ + N̄·V		VS	overflow set	1001	V

Condition Codes:
Not affected.

Instruction Format:

15	14	13	12	11	10	9	8	7	6	5	4	3	2	1	0
0	1	0	1		CONDITION			1	1		MODE			REGISTER	
											EFFECTIVE ADDRESS				

SBCD

Subtract Decimal with Extend

SBCD

Instruction Format:

15	14	13	12	11	10	9	8	7	6	5	4	3	2	1	0
1	0	0	0		REGISTER Ry		1	0	0	0	0	R/M		REGISTER Rx	

Instruction Fields:

Register Dy/Ay field — Specifies the destination register.
  If R/M = 0, specifies a data register.
  If R/M = 1, specifies an address register for the predecrement addressing mode.

R/M field — Specifies the operand addressing mode:
  0 — The operation is data register to data register.
  1 — The operation is memory to memory.

Register Dx/Ax field — Specifies the source register:
  If R/M = 0, specifies a data register.
  If R/M = 1, specifies an address register for the predecrement addressing mode.

STOP

Load Status Register and Stop
(Privileged Instruction)

STOP

Operation: If supervisor state
then Immediate Data ♦ SR; STOP
else TRAP

Assembler
Syntax: STOP #⟨data⟩

Attributes: Unsized

Description: Moves the immediate operand into the status register (both user and supervisor portions), advances the program counter to point to the next instruction, and stops the fetching and executing of instructions. A trace, interrupt, or reset exception causes the processor to resume instruction execution. A trace exception occurs if instruction tracing is enabled (T0=1, T1=0) when the STOP instruction begins execution. If an interrupt request is asserted with a priority higher than the priority level set by the new status register value, an interrupt exception occurs; otherwise, the interrupt request is ignored. External reset always initiates reset exception processing.

Condition Codes:
Set according to the immediate operand.

Instruction Format:

15	14	13	12	11	10	9	8	7	6	5	4	3	2	1	0
0	1	0	0	1	1	1	0	0	1	1	1	0	0	1	0

IMMEDIATE DATA

Instruction Fields:
Immediate field — Specifies the data to be loaded into the status register.

Scc

Set According to Condition

Scc

Instruction Fields:
Condition field — The binary code for one of the conditions listed in the table.
Effective Address field — Specifies the location in which the true/false byte is to be stored. Only data alterable addressing modes are allowed as shown:

Addressing Mode	Mode	Register	Addressing Mode	Mode	Register
Dn	000	reg. number:Dn	(xxx).W	111	000
An	—	—	(xxx).L	111	001
(An)	010	reg. number:An	#⟨data⟩	—	—
(An)+	011	reg. number:An			
−(An)	100	reg. number:An			
(d16,An)	101	reg. number:An	(d16,PC)	—	—
(d8,An,Xn)	110	reg. number:An	(d8,PC,Xn)	—	—
(bd,An,Xn)	110	reg. number:An	(bd,PC,Xn)	—	—

NOTE:
A subsequent NEG.B instruction with the same effective address can be used to change the Scc result from TRUE or FALSE to the equivalent arithmetic value (TRUE=1, FALSE=0).

780

Appendix IV

Operation: Destination − Source → Destination

Assembler
Syntax: SUB <ea>,Dn
SUB Dn,<ea>

Attributes: Size = (Byte, Word, Long)

Description: Subtracts the source operand from the destination operand and stores the result in the destination. The size of the operation is specified as byte, word, or long. The mode of the instruction indicates which operand is the source, which is the destination, and which is the operand size.

Condition Codes:

X	N	Z	V	C
*	*	*	*	*

X Set to the value of the carry bit.
N Set if the result is negative. Cleared otherwise.
Z Set if the result is zero. Cleared otherwise.
V Set if an overflow is generated. Cleared otherwise.
C Set if a borrow is generated. Cleared otherwise.

Instruction Format:

15	14	13	12	11	10	9	8	7	6	5	4	3	2	1	0
1	0	0	1		REGISTER			OPMODE			EFFECTIVE ADDRESS				
											MODE			REGISTER	

Instruction Fields:
Register field — Specifies any of the eight data registers.
Opmode field:

Byte	Word	Long	Operation
000	001	010	((Dn)) − ((ea)) → (Dn)
100	101	110	((ea)) − ((Dn)) → (ea)

Effective Address field — Determines the addressing mode. If the location specified is a source operand, all addressing modes are allowed as shown:

Addressing Mode	Mode	Register	Addressing Mode	Mode	Register
Dn	000	reg. number:Dn	(xxx).W	111	000
An*	001	reg. number:An	(xxx).L	111	001
(An)	010	reg. number:An	#<data>	111	100
(An)+	011	reg. number:An			
−(An)	100	reg. number:An			
(d16,An)	101	reg. number:An	(d16,PC)	111	010
(d8,An,Xn)	110	reg. number:An	(d8,PC,Xn)	111	011
(bd,An,Xn)	110	reg. number:An	(bd,PC,Xn)	111	011

*For byte size operation, address register direct is not allowed.

If the location specified is a destination operand, only memory alterable addressing modes are allowed as shown:

Addressing Mode	Mode	Register	Addressing Mode	Mode	Register
Dn	—	—	(xxx).W	111	000
An	—	—	(xxx).L	111	001
(An)	010	reg. number:An	#<data>	—	—
(An)+	011	reg. number:An			
−(An)	100	reg. number:An			
(d16,An)	101	reg. number:An	(d16,PC)	—	—
(d8,An,Xn)	110	reg. number:An	(d8,PC,Xn)	—	—
(bd,An,Xn)	110	reg. number:An	(bd,PC,Xn)	—	—

NOTES:
1. If the destination is a data register, it must be specified as a destination Dn address, not as a destination <ea> address.
2. Most assemblers use SUBA when the destination is an address register, and SUBI or SUBQ when the source is immediate data.

SUBA

Subtract Address

SUBA

Operation: Destination − Source ♦ Destination

Assembler Syntax: SUBA (ea),An

Attributes: Size = (Word, Long)

Description: Subtracts the source operand from the destination address register and stores the result in the address register. The size of the operation is specified as word or long. Word size source operands are sign extended to 32-bit quantities prior to the subtraction.

Condition Codes:
Not affected.

Instruction Format:

15	14	13	12	11	10	9	8	7	6	5	4	3	2	1	0
1	0	0	1	REGISTER			OPMODE			EFFECTIVE ADDRESS					
										MODE			REGISTER		

Opmode Field:

		Operation
Word	Long	
011	111	((An))−((ea)) ♦ (An)

Instruction Fields:

Register field — Specifies the destination, any of the eight address registers.
Opmode field — Specifies the size of the operation:
011 — Word operation. The source operand is sign extended to a long operand and the operation is performed on the address register using all 32 bits.
111 — Long operation.

SUBA

Subtract Address

SUBA

Effective Address field — Specifies the source operand. All addressing modes are allowed as shown:

Addressing Mode	Mode	Register
Dn	000	reg. number:Dn
An	001	reg. number:An
(An)	010	reg. number:An
(An) +	011	reg. number:An
− (An)	100	reg. number:An
(d16,An)	101	reg. number:An
(d8,An,Xn)	110	reg. number:An
(bd,An,Xn)	110	reg. number:An

Addressing Mode	Mode	Register
(xxx).W	111	000
(xxx).L	111	001
#(data)	111	100
(d16,PC)	111	010
(d8,PC,Xn)	111	011
(bd,PC,Xn)	111	011

Subtract Immediate SUBI

Operation: Destination − Immediate Data → Destination

Assembler Syntax: SUBI #⟨data⟩,⟨ea⟩

Attributes: Size = (Byte, Word, Long)

Description: Subtracts the immediate data from the destination operand and stores the result in the destination location. The size of the operation is specified as byte, word, or long. The size of the immediate data matches the operation size.

Condition Codes:

X	N	Z	V	C
*	*	*	*	*

X Set to the value of the carry bit.
N Set if the result is negative. Cleared otherwise.
Z Set if the result is zero. Cleared otherwise.
V Set if an overflow occurs. Cleared otherwise.
C Set if a borrow occurs. Cleared otherwise.

Instruction Format:

15	14	13	12	11	10	9	8	7	6	5	4	3	2	1	0
0	0	0	0	0	1	0	0		SIZE			EFFECTIVE ADDRESS		MODE	REGISTER
		WORD DATA (16 BITS)										BYTE DATA (8 BITS)			
						LONG DATA (32 BITS)									

Subtract Immediate SUBI

Instruction Fields:

Size field — Specifies the size of the operation.
00 — Byte operation
01 — Word operation
10 — Long operation

Effective Address field — Specifies the destination operand. Only data alterable addressing modes are allowed as shown:

Addressing Mode	Mode	Register
Dn	000	reg. number:Dn
An	—	—
(An)	010	reg. number:An
(An)+	011	reg. number:An
-(An)	100	reg. number:An
(d16,An)	101	reg. number:An
(d8,An,Xn)	110	reg. number:An
(bd,An,Xn)	110	reg. number:An

Addressing Mode	Mode	Register
(xxx).W	111	000
(xxx).L	111	001
#⟨data⟩	—	—
(d16,PC)	—	—
(d8,PC,Xn)	—	—
(bd,PC,Xn)	—	—

Immediate field — (Data immediately following the instruction)
If size = 00, the data is the low-order byte of the immediate word.
If size = 01, the data is the entire immediate word.
If size = 10, the data is the next two immediate words.

SUBQ   Subtract Quick   SUBQ

Operation: Destination − Immediate Data ▶ Destination

Assembler Syntax: SUBQ #⟨data⟩,⟨ea⟩

Attributes: Size = (Byte, Word, Long)

Description: Subtracts the immediate data (1-8) from the destination operand. The size of the operation is specified as byte, word, or long. Only word and long operations are allowed with address registers, and the condition codes are not affected. When subtracting from address registers, the entire destination address register is used, regardless of the operation size.

Condition Codes:

X	N	Z	V	C
*	*	*	*	*

X   Set to the value of the carry bit.
N   Set if the result is negative. Cleared otherwise.
Z   Set if the result is zero. Cleared otherwise.
V   Set if an overflow occurs. Cleared otherwise.
C   Set if a borrow occurs. Cleared otherwise.

Instruction Format:

15	14	13	12	11	10	9	8	7	6	5	4	3	2	1	0
0	1	0	1		DATA		1		SIZE		EFFECTIVE ADDRESS MODE			REGISTER	

Instruction Fields:

Data field — Three bits of immediate data; 1-7 represent immediate values of 1-7, and 0 represents 8.

Size field — Specifies the size of the operation:
00 — Byte operation
01 — Word operation
10 — Long operation

SUBQ   Subtract Quick   SUBQ

Effective Address field — Specifies the destination location. Only alterable addressing modes are allowed as shown:

Addressing Mode	Mode	Register	Addressing Mode	Mode	Register
Dn	000	reg. number:Dn	(xxx).W	111	000
An*	001	reg. number:An	(xxx).L	111	001
(An)	010	reg. number:An	#⟨data⟩	—	—
(An)+	011	reg. number:An			
-(An)	100	reg. number:An			
(d16,An)	101	reg. number:An	(d16,PC)	—	—
(d8,An,Xn)	110	reg. number:An	(d8,PC,Xn)	—	—
(bd,An,Xn)	110	reg. number:An	(bd,PC,Xn)	—	—

*Word and Long Only

SUBX

Subtract with Extend

Operation: Destination − Source − X ♦ Destination

Assembler SUBX Dx,Dy
Syntax: SUBX −(Ax), −(Ay)

Attributes: Size = (Byte, Word, Long)

Description: Subtracts the source operand and the extend bit from the destination operand and stores the result in the destination location. The instruction has two modes:

1. Data register to data register: The data registers specified in the instruction contain the operands.
2. Memory to memory: The address registers specified in the instruction access the operands from memory using the predecrement addressing mode.

The size of the operand is specified as byte, word, or long.

Condition Codes:

X	N	Z	V	C
*	*	*	*	*

X Set to the value of the carry bit.
N Set if the result is negative. Cleared otherwise.
Z Cleared if the result is nonzero. Unchanged otherwise.
V Set if an overflow occurs. Cleared otherwise.
C Set if a carry occurs. Cleared otherwise.

NOTE

Normally the Z condition code bit is set via programming before the start of an operation. This allows successful tests for zero results upon completion of multiple-precision operations.

Instruction Format:

15	14	13	12	11	10	9	8	7	6	5	4	3	2	1	0
1	0	0	1	REGISTER Ry			1	SIZE		0	0	R/M	REGISTER Rx		

SUBX

Subtract with Extend

Instruction Fields:

Register Dy/Ay field — Specifies the destination register:
If R/M = 0, specifies a data register.
If R/M = 1, specifies an address register for the predecrement addressing mode.

Size field — Specifies the size of the operation:
00 — Byte operation
01 — Word operation
10 — Long operation

R/M field — Specifies the operand addressing mode:
0 — The operation is data register to data register.
1 — The operation is memory to memory.

Register Dx/Ax field — Specifies the source register:
If R/M = 0, specifies a data register.
If R/M = 1, specifies an address register for the predecrement addressing mode.

CPU 32 Instruction Set

TBLS
TBLSN

Table Lookup and Interpolate (Signed)

Operation:

Rounded:

ENTRY(n) + [(ENTRY(n+1) − ENTRY(n))*Dx[7:0])/256 ♦ Dx

Unrounded:

ENTRY(n)*256 + ((ENTRY(n+1) − ENTRY(n))*Dx[7:0]) ♦ Dx

Where ENTRY(n) and ENTRY(n+1) are either:

1. Consecutive entries in the table pointed to by the <ea> and indexed by Dx[15:8]*size or,
2. The registers Dym, Dyn respectively

Assembler Syntax:

TBLS.<size>	<ea>,Dx	*Result rounded
TBLSN.<size>	<ea>,Dx	*Result not rounded
TBLS.<size>	Dym:Dyn, Dx	*Result rounded
TBLSN.<size>	Dym:Dyn, Dx	*Result not rounded

Attributes: Size = (Byte, Word, Long)

Description: The signed table lookup and interpolate instruction, TBLS, allows the efficient use of piecewise linear, compressed data tables to model complex functions. The TBLS instruction has two modes of operation: table lookup and interpolate mode and data register interpolate mode.

For table lookup and interpolate mode, data register Dx[15:0] contains the independent variable X. The effective address points to the start of a signed byte, word, or long-word table containing a linearized representation of the dependent variable, Y, as a function of X. In general, the independent variable, located in the low-order word of Dx, consists of an 8-bit integer part and an 8-bit fractional part. An assumed radix point is located between bits 7 and 8. The integer part, Dx[15:8], is scaled by the operand size and is used as an offset into the table. The selected entry in the table is subtracted from the next consecutive entry. A fractional portion of this difference is taken by multiplying by the interpolation fraction, Dx[7:0]. The adjusted difference is then added to the selected table entry. The result is returned in the destination data register, Dx.

For register interpolate mode, the interpolation occurs using the Dym and Dyn registers in place of the two table entries. For this mode, only the fractional portion, Dx[7:0], is used in the interpolation, and the integer portion, Dx[15:8], is ignored. The register interpolation mode may be used with several table lookup and interpolations to model multidimensional functions.

SWAP

Swap Register Halves

Operation: Register [31:16] ♦♦ Register [15:0]

Assembler Syntax: SWAP Dn

Attributes: Size = (Word)

Description: Exchange the 16-bit words (halves) of a data register.

Condition Codes:

X	N	Z	V	C
–	*	*	0	0

X Not affected.
N Set if the most significant bit of the 32-bit result is set. Cleared otherwise.
Z Set if the 32-bit result is zero. Cleared otherwise.
V Always cleared.
C Always cleared.

Instruction Format:

15	14	13	12	11	10	9	8	7	6	5	4	3	2	1	0
0	1	0	0	1	0	0	0	0	1	0	0	0		REGISTER	

Instruction Fields:

Register field — Specifies the data register to swap.

TBLS / TBLSN — Table Lookup and Interpolate (Signed)

Signed table entries range from -2^{n-1} to $2^{n-1}-1$; whereas, unsigned table entries range from 0 to 2^n-1 where n is 8, 16, or 32 for byte, word, and long-word tables, respectively.

Rounding of the result is optionally selected via the "R" instruction field. If R = 0 (TABLE), the fractional portion is rounded according to the round-to-nearest algorithm. The rounding procedure can be summarized by the following table.

Adjusted Difference Fraction	Rounding Adjustment
$\leq -1/2$	-1
$> -1/2$ and $< 1/2$	$+0$
$\geq 1/2$	$+1$

The adjusted difference is then added to the selected table entry. The rounded result is retuned in the destination data register, Dx. Only the portion of the register corresponding to the selected size is affected.

	31	24 23	16 15	8 7	0
Byte	Unaffected	Unaffected	Unaffected	Result	
Word	Unaffected	Unaffected	Result	Result	
Long	Result	Result	Result	Result	

If R = 1 (TABLENR), the result is returned in register Dx without rounding. If the size is byte, the integer portion of the result is returned in Dx(15:8); the integer portion of a word result is stored in Dx(23:8); the least significant 24 bits of a long result are stored in Dx(31:8). Byte and word results are sign extended to fill the entire 32-bit register.

	31	24 23	16 15	8 7	0
Byte	Sign Extended	Sign Extended	Result	Fraction	
Word	Sign Extended	Result	Result	Fraction	
Long	Result	Result	Result	Fraction	

NOTE

The long-word result contains only the least significant 24 bits of integer precision.

TBLS / TBLSN — Table Lookup and Interpolate (Signed)

For all sizes, the 8-bit fractional portion of the result is returned in the low byte of the data register, Dx(7:0). User software can make use of the fractional data to reduce cumulative errors in lengthy calculations or implement rounding algorithms different from that provided by other forms of TBLS. The assumed radix point described previously places two restrictions on the programmer:

1) Tables are limited to 257 entries in length.

2) Interpolation resolution is limited to 1/256 the distance between consecutive table entries. The assumed radix point should not, however, be construed by the programmer as a requirement that the independent variable be calculated as a fractional number in the range $0 <= X <= 255$. On the contrary, X should be considered to be an integer in the range $0 <= X <= 65535$; realizing that the table is actually a compressed representation of a linearized function in which only every 256th value is actually stored in memory.

See **4.5 INSTRUCTION FORMAT SUMMARY** for examples on using the TBLS instruction.

Condition Codes:

X	N	Z	V	C
—	*	*	*	0

X Not affected.
N Set if the most significant bit of the result is set. Cleared otherwise.
Z Set if the result is zero. Cleared otherwise.
V Set if the integer portion of an unrounded long result is not in the range, $-(2^{23}) \leq Result \leq (2^{23})-1$. Cleared otherwise.
C Always cleared.

Instruction Format:

Table Lookup and Interpolate:

15	14	13	12	11	10	9	8	7	6	5	4	3	2	1	0
1	1	1	1	1	0	0	0	Size		EFFECTIVE ADDRESS MODE			REGISTER		
1	REGISTER Dx			1	R	1	0	0	0	0	0	0	0	0	0

TBLS
TBLSN

Table Lookup and Interpolate (Signed)

Data Register Interpolate:

15	14	13	12	11	10	9	8	7	6	5	4	3	2	1	0
1	1	1	REGISTER Dx			1	R	0	0	0	0	SIZE	0	0	0	REGISTER Dym
0																REGISTER Dyn

Instruction Fields:

Effective address field (table lookup and interpolate mode only):
Specifies the destination location. Only control addressing modes are allowed as shown:

Addressing Mode	Mode	Register
Dn	—	—
An	—	—
(An)	010	reg. number:An
(An)+	—	—
−(An)	—	—
(d$_{16}$,An)	101	reg. number:An
(d$_8$,An,Xn)	110	reg. number:An
(bd,An,Xn)	110	reg. number:An

Addressing Mode	Mode	Register
(xxx).W	111	000
(xxx).L	111	001
#<data>	—	—
(d$_{16}$,PC)	111	010
(d$_8$,PC,Xn)	111	011
(bd,PC,Xn)	111	011

Size field:
Specifies the size of operation.
00 — byte operation
01 — word operation
10 — long operation

Register field:
Specifies the destination data register, Dx. On entry, the register contains the interpolation fraction and entry number.

Dym, Dyn field:
If the effective address mode field is nonzero, this operand register is unused and should be zero. If the effective address mode field is zero, the surface interpolation variant of this instruction is implied, and Dyn specifies one of the two source operands.

Rounding mode field:
The 'R' bit controls the rounding of the final result. When R = 0, the result is rounded according to the round-to-nearest algorithm. When R = 1, the result is returned unrounded.

TBLU
TBLUN

Table Lookup and Interpolation (Unsigned)

Operation:
Rounded:
ENTRY(n) + ((ENTRY(n + 1) − ENTRY(n))*Dx[7:0])/256 ⟶ Dx
Unrounded:
ENTRY(n)*256 + ((ENTRY(n + 1) − ENTRY(n))*Dx[7:0]) ⟶ Dx

Where ENTRY(n) and ENTRY(n + 1) are either:
1. Consecutive entries in the table pointed to by the <ea> and indexed by Dx[15:8]*size or,
2. The registers Dym, Dyn respectively

Assembler Syntax:

TBLU.<size>	<ea>,Dx	* Result rounded
TBLUN.<size>	<ea>,Dx	* Result not rounded
TBLU.<size>	Dym:Dyn, Dx	* Result rounded
TBLUN.<size>	Dym:Dyn, Dx	* Result not rounded

Attributes: Size = (Byte, Word, Long)

Description: The unsigned table lookup and interpolate instruction, TBLS, allows the efficient use of piecewise linear, compressed data tables to model complex functions. The TBLU instruction has two modes of operation: table lookup and interpolate mode and data register interpolate mode.

For table lookup and interpolate mode, data register Dx[15:0] contains the independent variable X. The effective address points to the start of a unsigned byte, word, or long-word table containing a linearized representation of the dependent variable, Y, as a function of X. In general, the independent variable, located in the low-order word of Dx, consists of an 8-bit integer part and an 8-bit fractional part. An assumed radix point is located between bits 7 and 8. The integer part, Dx[15:8], is scaled by the operand size and is used as an offset into the table. The selected entry in the table is subtracted from the next consecutive entry. A fractional portion of this difference is taken by multiplying by the interpolation fraction, Dx[7:0]. The adjusted difference is then added to the selected table entry. The result is returned in the destination data register, Dx.

For register interpolate mode, the interpolation occurs using the Dym and Dyn registers in place of the two table entries. For this mode, only the fractional portion, Dx[7:0], is used in the interpolation, and the integer portion, Dx[15:8], is ignored. The register interpolation mode may be used with several table lookup and interpolations to model multidimensional functions.

TBLU
TBLUN

Table Lookup and Interpolation (Unsigned)

TBLU
TBLUN

For all sizes, the 8-bit fractional portion of the result is returned in the low byte of the data register, Dx(7:0). User software can make use of the fractional data to reduce cumulative errors in lengthy calculations or implement rounding algorithms different from that provided by other forms of TBLS. The assumed radix point described previously places two restrictions on the programmer:

1) Tables are limited to 257 entries in length.

2) Interpolation resolution is limited to 1/256 the distance between consecutive table entries. The assumed radix point should not, however, be construed by the programmer as a requirement that the independent variable be calculated as a fractional number in the range $0 \leq X \leq 255$. On the contrary, X should be considered to be an integer in the range $0 \leq X \leq 65535$; realizing that the table is actually a compressed representation of a linearized function in which only every 256th value is actually stored in memory.

See **4.5 INSTRUCTION FORMAT SUMMARY** for examples on using the TBLU instruction.

Condition Codes:

X	N	Z	V	C
—	*	*	*	0

X Not affected.
N Set if the most significant bit of the result is set. Cleared otherwise.
Z Set if the result is zero. Cleared otherwise.
V Set if the integer portion of an unrounded long result is not in the range, $-(2^{23}) \leq \text{Result} \leq (2^{23}) - 1$. Cleared otherwise.
C Always cleared.

Instruction Format:

Table Lookup and Interpolate:

15	14	13	12	11	10	9	8	7	6	5	4	3	2	1	0
1	1	1	1	1	0	0	0	0	0		EFFECTIVE ADDRESS				
											MODE			REGISTER	
0		REGISTER Dx		0	R	0	1	Size		0	0	0	0	0	0

TBLU
TBLUN

Table Lookup and Interpolation (Unsigned)

TBLU
TBLUN

Signed table entries range from -2^{n-1} to $2^{n-1}-1$; whereas, unsigned table entries range from 0 to $2^n - 1$ where n is 8, 16, or 32 for byte, word, and long-word tables, respectively. The unsigned and unrounded table results will be zero extended instead of sign extended.

Rounding of the result is optionally selected via the "R" instruction field. If R = 0 (TABLE), the fractional portion is rounded according to the round-to-nearest algorithm. The rounding procedure can be summarized by the following table.

Adjusted Difference Fraction	Rounding Adjustment
$\geq 1/2$	+1
$< 1/2$	+0

The adjusted difference is then added to the selected table entry. The rounded result is retuned in the destination data register, Dx. Only the portion of the register corresponding to the selected size is affected.

	31	24 23	16 15	8 7	0
Byte	Unaffected	Unaffected	Unaffected	Unaffected	Result
Word	Unaffected	Unaffected	Result	Result	Result
Long	Result	Result	Result	Result	Result

If R = 1 (TBLUN), the result is returned in register Dx without rounding. If the size is byte, the integer portion of the result is returned in Dx(15:8); the integer portion of a word result is stored in Dx(23:8); the least significant 24 bits of a long result are stored in Dx(31:8). Byte and word results are sign extended to fill the entire 32-bit register.

	31	24 23	16 15	8 7	0
Byte	Sign Extended	Sign Extended	Result	Result	Fraction
Word	Sign Extended	Sign Extended	Result	Result	Fraction
Long	Result	Result	Result	Result	Fraction

NOTE

The long-word result contains only the least significant 24 bits of integer precision.

TAS

Test and Set an Operand

Operation: Destination Tested ♦ Condition Codes; 1 ♦ bit 7 of Destination

Assembler Syntax: TAS (ea)

Attributes: Size = (Byte)

Description: Tests and sets the byte operand addressed by the effective address field. The instruction tests the current value of the operand and sets the N and Z condition bits appropriately. TAS also sets the high-order bit of the operand. The operation uses a read-modify-write memory cycle that completes the operation without interruption. This instruction supports use of a flag or semaphore to coordinate several processors.

Condition Codes:

X	N	Z	V	C
—	*	*	0	0

X Not affected.
N Set if the most significant bit of the operand is currently set. Cleared otherwise.
Z Set if the operand was zero. Cleared otherwise.
V Always cleared.
C Always cleared.

Instruction Format:

15	14	13	12	11	10	9	8	7	6	5	4	3	2	1	0
0	1	0	0	1	0	1	0	1	1			EFFECTIVE ADDRESS			
												MODE			REGISTER

Instruction Fields:

Effective Address field — Specifies the location of the tested operand. Only data alterable addressing modes are allowed as shown:

Addressing Mode	Mode	Register	Addressing Mode	Mode	Register
Dn	000	reg. number:Dn	(xxx).W	111	000
An	—	—	(xxx).L	111	001
(An)	010	reg. number:An	#(data)	—	—
(An)+	011	reg. number:An			
−(An)	100	reg. number:An	(d16,PC)	—	—
(d16,An)	101	reg. number:An	(d8,PC,Xn)	—	—
(d8,An,Xn)	110	reg. number:An	(bd,PC,Xn)	—	—
(bd,An,Xn)	110	reg. number:An			

TBLU
TBLUN

Table Lookup and Interpolation (Unsigned)

Data Register Interpolate:

15	14	13	12	11	10	9	8	7	6	5	4	3	2	1	0
1	1	1	1	0	R	0	0	0	0	0	0	0	0	REGISTER Dym	
0	REGISTER Dx		1	0		0	SIZE		0	0	0	0		REGISTER Dyn	

Instruction Fields:

Effective address field (table lookup and interpolate mode only): Specifies the destination location. Only control addressing modes are allowed as shown:

Addressing Mode	Mode	Register	Addressing Mode	Mode	Register
Dn	—	—	(xxx).W	111	000
An	—	—	(xxx).L	111	001
(An)	010	reg. number:An	#(data)	—	—
(An)+	—	—			
−(An)	—	—	(d16,PC)	111	010
(d16,An)	101	reg. number:An	(d8,PC,Xn)	111	011
(d8,An,Xn)	110	reg. number:An	(bd,PC,Xn)	111	011
(bd,An,Xn)	110	reg. number:An			

Size field:
Specifies the size of operation.
00 — byte operation
01 — word operation
10 — long operation

Register field:
Specifies the destination data register, Dx. On entry, the register contains the interpolation fraction and entry number.

Dym, Dyn field:
If the effective address mode field is nonzero, this operand register is unused and should be zero. If the effective address mode field is zero, the surface interpolation variant of this instruction is implied, and Dyn specifies one of the two source operands.

Rounding mode field:
The 'R' bit controls the rounding of the final result. When R = 0, the result is rounded according to the round-to-nearest algorithm. When R = 1, the result is returned unrounded.

TRAPcc — TRAPcc

Trap on Condition

Operation: If cc then TRAP

Assembler Syntax:
TRAPcc
TRAPcc.W #⟨data⟩
TRAPcc.L #⟨data⟩

Attributes: Unsized or Size = (Word, Long)

Description: If the specified condition is true, causes a TRAPcc exception. The vector number is 7. The processor pushes the address of the next instruction word (currently in the program counter) onto the stack. If the condition is not true, the processor performs no operation, and execution continues with the next instruction. The immediate data operand should be placed in the next word(s) following the operation word and is available to the trap handler. Condition code cc specifies one of the following conditions.

CC	carry clear	0100	$\overline{C}$	LS	low or same	0011	$C + Z$
CS	carry set	0101	C	LT	less than	1101	$N \cdot \overline{V} + \overline{N} \cdot V$
EQ	equal	0111	Z	MI	minus	1011	N
F	never true	0001	0	NE	not equal	0110	$\overline{Z}$
GE	greater or equal	1100	$N \cdot V + \overline{N} \cdot \overline{V}$	PL	plus	1010	$\overline{N}$
GT	greater than	1110	$N \cdot V \cdot \overline{Z} + \overline{N} \cdot \overline{V} \cdot \overline{Z}$	T	always true	0000	1
HI	high	0010	$\overline{C} \cdot \overline{Z}$	VC	overflow clear	1000	$\overline{V}$
LE	less or equal	1111	$Z + N \cdot \overline{V} + \overline{N} \cdot V$	VS	overflow set	1001	V

Condition Codes:
Not affected.

Instruction Format:

15	14	13	12	11	10	9	8	7	6	5	4	3	2	1	0
0	1	0	1			CONDITION			1	1	1	1		OPMODE	

OPTIONAL WORD

OR LONG WORD

Instruction Fields:
Condition field — The binary code for one of the conditions listed in the table.
Opmode field — Selects the instruction form.
010 — Instruction is followed by word-size operand.
011 — Instruction is followed by long-word-size operand.
100 — Instruction has no operand.

TRAP — TRAP

Trap

Operation:
SSP − 2 ➧ SSP; Format/Offset ➧ (SSP);
SSP − 4 ➧ SSP; PC ➧ (SSP); SSP − 2 ➧ SSP;
SR ➧ (SSP); Vector Address ➧ PC

Assembler Syntax: TRAP #⟨vector⟩

Attributes: Unsized

Description: Causes a TRAP #⟨vector⟩ exception. The instruction adds the immediate operand (vector) of the instruction to 32 to obtain the vector number. The range of vector values is 0-15, which provides 16 vectors.

Condition Codes:
Not affected.

Instruction Format:

15	14	13	12	11	10	9	8	7	6	5	4	3	2	1	0
0	1	0	0	1	1	1	0	0	1	0	0			VECTOR	

Instruction Fields:
Vector field — Specifies the trap vector to be taken.

TST

Test an Operand

TST

Operation: Destination Tested ♦ Condition Codes

**Assembler
Syntax:** TST (ea)

Attributes: Size = (Byte, Word, Long)

Description: Compares the operand with zero and sets the condition codes according to the results of the test. The size of the operation is specified as byte, word, or long.

Condition Codes:

X	N	Z	V	C
–	*	*	0	0

X Not affected.
N Set if the operand is negative. Cleared otherwise.
Z Set if the operand is zero. Cleared otherwise.
V Always cleared.
C Always cleared.

Instruction Format:

15	14	13	12	11	10	9	8	7	6	5	4	3	2	1	0
0	1	0	0	1	0	1	0		SIZE		MODE			REGISTER	
											EFFECTIVE ADDRESS				

Instruction Fields:

Size field — Specifies the size of the operation:
00 — Byte operation
01 — Word operation
10 — Long operation

TRAPV

Trap on Overflow

TRAPV

Operation: If V then TRAP

**Assembler
Syntax:** TRAPV

Attributes: Unsized

Description: If the overflow condition is set, causes a TRAPV exception (vector number 7). If the overflow condition is not set, the processor performs no operation and execution continues with the next instruction.

Condition Codes:
Not affected.

Instruction Format:

15	14	13	12	11	10	9	8	7	6	5	4	3	2	1	0
0	1	0	0	1	1	1	0	0	1	1	1	0	1	1	0

UNLK

Unlink UNLK

Operation: An ⤓ SP; (SP) ⤓ An; SP + 4 ⤓ SP

Assembler Syntax: UNLK An

Attributes: Unsized

Description: Loads the stack pointer from the specified address register then loads the address register with the long word pulled from the top of the stack.

Condition Codes: Not affected.

Instruction Format:

15	14	13	12	11	10	9	8	7	6	5	4	3	2	1	0
0	1	0	0	1	1	1	0	0	1	0	1	1	REGISTER		

Instruction Fields:
Register field — Specifies the address register for the instruction.

TST

Test an Operand TST

Effective Address field — Specifies the destination operand. All addressing modes are allowed as shown:

Addressing Mode	Mode	Register	Addressing Mode	Mode	Register
Dn	000	reg. number:Dn	(xxx).W	111	000
An*	001	reg. number:An	(xxx).L	111	001
(An)	010	reg. number:An	#⟨data⟩	111	100
(An)+	011	reg. number:An			
-(An)	100	reg. number:An			
(d$_{16}$,An)	101	reg. number:An	(d$_{16}$,PC)	111	010
(d$_8$,An,Xn)	110	reg. number:An	(d$_8$,PC,Xn)	111	011
(bd,An,Xn)	110	reg. number:An	(bd,PC,Xn)	111	011

*Word or long word operation only.

Instruction Index

General Index

One's Complement Representation
  59, 65–70, 73–74, 80
Operating system (*see* supervisor pro-
    gram or system software) 342
Organization (Architecture) 22, 24
Overflow 65

Packed BCD 77
Pascal 309, 390
Peripheral chips 601–603
PLCC (plastic leaded chip carrier)
    90–92
Position Independent Code 123, 300–
    307
Positional notation 59–60, 63–64, 72
Product
  design 18–20, 42–46, 49, 638–642
  development 667–671
Program control branch and jump
    189, 196–200, 202–207, 209–214
Programmable controller 5
Pulse Width Modulation (*see also* TPU)
    33, 40

QSM (Queued Serial Module)
    26, 31–32, 37, 54, 420–421, 423,
    427–432
  (*see also* submodules SCI and
    QSPI) 420
  electrical characteristics 436–437
  features 421
  initialization after reset 427–429
  memory map 423
  QSPI (*see* QSPI) 32
  register set 423–424, 427
  SCI (*see* SCI) 32
  signal lines 421–422
QSPI (Queued Serial Peripheral Inter-
    face)
    420–422, 427–432, 436–438, 459,
    463–465, 467–473, 476–478, 481–
    483, 486, 489–492
  baud rate 468
  chip selects 477–482

data format 469
I/O expansion 477–478
initialization 464–465, 467, 473–476
loop mode 469
mode fault 490
peripheral chips 478
queue 32, 469–471, 474–477, 479,
    491
register SPCR0 467–469
register SPCR1 469
register SPCR2 469
register SPCR3 469
registers QPAR, QPDR, QDDR
    464–465, 467
SCK signal 479–482
slave mode 490
status register SPSR 472–473
wraparound mode 476–477
Queues 322–324, 327

Radix
    59, 67, 71, 82
  complement 65–67, 69, 75
  point 61–63, 80
Real-time
  clock 37, 591, 656–657
  operating system 17, 46, 56, 380
  programming 51, 653
Relocation by linker program 143, 159
Resident assembler 151
RISC (reduced or reusable instruction
    set computer) 96
Robotics 5
ROM (*see* Memory) 24
RS-232 437, 448

S-record format 143, 145, 149
Scc instructions (CPU32) 283, 285–
    286
SCI (Serial Communications Inter-
    face)
    32, 420–422, 427–432, 434–436,
    438–440, 443–445, 447–450, 452–
    462, 464, 467, 492